Professional
VB 2005 with .NET 3.0

Professional
VB 2005 with .NET 3.0

Bill Evjen
Billy Hollis
Tim McCarthy
Kent Sharkey
Bill Sheldon

Wiley Publishing, Inc.

Professional VB 2005 with .NET 3.0

Published by
Wiley Publishing, Inc.
10475 Crosspoint Boulevard
Indianapolis, IN 46256
www.wiley.com

Published simultaneously in Canada

ISBN: 978-0-470-124-703

Manufactured in the United States of America

10 9 8 7 6 5 4 3 2 1

Library of Congress Cataloging-in-Publication Data is available from the publisher

Credits

Acquisitions Editor
Katie Mohr

Development Editor
William Bridges

Technical Editor
Andrew Parsons

Production Editor
William A. Barton

Copy Editor
Luann Rouff

Editorial Manager
Mary Beth Wakefield

Production Manager
Tim Tate

Vice President and Executive Group Publisher
Richard Swadley

Vice President and Executive Publisher
Joseph B. Wikert

Composition
Maureen Forys, Happenstance Type-O-Rama

Proofreading
Jen Larsen, Word One

Indexing
Johnna VanHoose Dinse

About the Authors

Bill Evjen is an active proponent of .NET technologies and community-based learning initiatives for .NET. He has been actively involved with .NET since the first bits were released in 2000. In the same year, Bill founded the St. Louis .NET User Group (www.stlnet.org), one of the world's first such groups. Bill is also the founder and former executive director of the International .NET Association (www.ineta.org), which represents more than 450,000 members worldwide.

Based in St. Louis, Missouri, Bill is an acclaimed author and speaker on ASP.NET and XML Web Services. He has written or co-written more than 13 titles, including *Professional ASP.NET Special Edition*, *Professional XML*, *Professional C# 2005 with .NET 3.0*, and more. In addition to writing, Bill is a speaker at numerous conferences, including DevConnections, VSLive, and TechEd.

Bill is the technical architect of Lipper (www.lipperweb.com), a wholly owned subsidiary of Reuters, the international news and financial services company. You can reach Bill at evjen@yahoo.com and he presently keeps his weblog at www.geekswithblogs.net/evjen.

This book, like most, took an entire team to get out the door. First and foremost, I would like to thank Katie Mohr for providing me with the opportunity to write this book. Big thanks go to Bill Bridges, the book's development editor, who kept the book together. Thanks to my family for putting up with this second job. I love you all greatly. My share of this work is dedicated to Tuija.

Billy Hollis is an author and software consultant based in Nashville, Tennessee. Billy was co-author of the first book ever published on Visual Basic .NET, as well as many other books on software development. He is a member of the Microsoft Regional Director program and a Microsoft MVP. In 2002, Billy was selected as one of the original .NET "Software Legends." He is heavily involved with consulting, training, and development on the .NET platform, focusing on architecture, smart-client development, commercial packages, and user-interface technologies. He regularly speaks on software development at major conferences all over the world, including Microsoft's PDC and TechEd events, DevConnections, VSLive, and architecture events such as the Patterns and Practices Architect Summit.

I owe tremendous thanks to my family, who have somehow learned to put up with marathon writing sessions, and to my business partner, Gary Bailey, for keeping our clients happy while I'm writing.

Tim McCarthy is a principal engineer at InterKnowlogy, where he architects and builds applications utilizing the latest Microsoft technologies. He is a Microsoft Certified Application Developer, Microsoft Certified Solution Developer, Microsoft Certified Trainer, and Microsoft Certified Database Administrator. Tim is also an IEEE Certified Software Development Professional.

Tim speaks regularly at several San Diego area user groups (including both .NET and SQL Server groups) and he has been a speaker at Microsoft Developer Days in San Diego for the last several years. He also presents MSDN webcasts, many of which are repeat requests from Microsoft.

He holds a BBA in marketing from the Illinois Institute of Technology as well as an MBA in marketing from National University. Before becoming an application developer, Tim was an officer in the United States Marine Corps. His passion for .NET is surpassed only by his passion for Notre Dame athletics.

I would like to thank my family for putting up with some of the long hours I had to put in to work on my various books, articles, and presentations. Jasmine, maybe someday you will be writing books. I also want to dedicate this book to my mom and dad, who recently celebrated their fiftieth wedding anniversary. Thank you for always giving me the self-confidence to do anything that I set my mind to do.

Kent Sharkey is an independent consultant who lives and codes in the midst of the wilds of Vancouver Island. Before going solo, Kent worked at Microsoft as a Technical Evangelist and Content Strategist, promoting the use of .NET technologies. When not coding or writing, he's hiking, biking, or canoeing (or exploring the wilds of Azeroth). He shares his house with his wife, Margaret, and two "children," Squirrel and Cica.

To Babi, for keeping me alive and putting up with me—hopefully, for a long time to come.

Bill Sheldon is a software architect and engineer, originally from Baltimore, Maryland. Holding a degree in computer science from the Illinois Institute of Technology (IIT), Bill has been actively employed as a software engineer since resigning his commission with the United States Navy. He is employed as a principal engineer with InterKnowlogy in Carlsbad, California, and works as an instructor for Visual Basic and Team System–related courses at the University of California San Diego Extension.

In addition to writing books, Bill has published dozens of articles, including the Developer Update Newsletter and occasional feature articles with *SQL Server* magazine and other Penton publications. He is an established online presenter for MSDN and speaks at live events such as Microsoft Developer Days and community events such as user groups and code camp. Bill is an avid cyclist and is active in the fight against diabetes.

To my wonderful wife, Tracie, who is forced to carry on while I isolate myself to concentrate on writing. And to all the children who have joined our extended Sheldon family over the past three years: Nikita, Elena, Ben, Billy V, and Abigail—each and every one of you is a valuable part of our lives.

Contents

Contents

Contents

Contents

Contents

Contents

Contents

Contents

Contents

Contents

Contents

Contents

Contents

Contents

Introduction

In 2002, Visual Basic took the biggest leap in innovation since it was released, with the introduction of Visual Basic .NET (as it was renamed). After more than a decade, Visual Basic was overdue for a major overhaul. Nevertheless, .NET goes beyond an overhaul. It changes almost every aspect of software development. From integrating Internet functionality to creating object-oriented frameworks, Visual Basic .NET challenged traditional VB developers to learn dramatic new concepts and techniques.

2005 brought forth an even more enhanced Visual Basic language (renamed again, but this time to Visual Basic 2005). New features have been added that cement this language's position as a true object-oriented language. Visual Basic 2005 is still going to be a challenge for traditional VB6 developers to learn, but it's an easy road for those with any familiarity with previous versions, and this book is here to help you on your way.

This .NET Framework 3.0 version of the book provides details on not only the latest version of Visual Basic — version 2005 — but also the new framework that gives Visual Basic developers the capability to build new application types using Windows Presentation Foundation (WPF) and applications and libraries based upon the Windows Communication Foundation (WCF), the Windows Workflow Foundation (WF), and Windows CardSpace.

These additions are what constitute the .NET Framework 3.0, as this version of the framework installs and works from the previous .NET Framework 2.0. This book includes numerous chapters that focus on the new technologies brought forth by the .NET Framework 3.0.

First, it is necessary to learn the differences between Visual Basic 2005 and the older versions of the language. In some cases, the same functionality is implemented in a different way. This was not done arbitrarily — there are good reasons for the changes. However, you must be prepared to unlearn old habits and form new ones.

Next, you must be open to the new concepts. Full object orientation, new component techniques, new visual tools for both local and Internet interfaces — all of these and more must become part of your skill set to effectively develop applications in Visual Basic.

This book covers Visual Basic from start to finish. We begin by looking at the .NET Framework and end by looking at the best practices for deploying .NET applications. In between, you will learn everything from database access to integration with other technologies such as XML, along with investigating the new features in detail. You will see that Visual Basic 2005 has emerged as a powerful yet easy-to-use language that enables you to target the Internet just as easily as the desktop. This book covers both .NET Framework 2.0 and the newly released .NET Framework 3.0. If you are coding using version 1.0, 1.1, or just 2.0, some sections of the book will not work for you. Items that are new to the .NET Framework 3.0 are specifically noted as such.

The Importance of Visual Basic

Early in the adoption cycle of .NET, Microsoft's new language, C#, got the lion's share of attention. However, as .NET adoption has increased, Visual Basic's continuing importance has also been apparent. Microsoft has publicly stated that it considers Visual Basic to be the language of choice for applications where developer productivity is one of the highest priorities.

Future development of Visual Basic is emphasizing capabilities that enable access to the whole expanse of the .NET Framework in the most productive way, while C# development is emphasizing the experience of writing code. That fits the traditional role of Visual Basic as the language developers use in the real world to create business applications as quickly as possible.

This difference is more than academic. One of the most important advantages of the .NET Framework is that it enables applications to be written with dramatically less code. In the world of business applications, the goal is to concentrate on writing business logic and to eliminate routine coding tasks as much as possible. In other words, of greatest value in this new world is writing robust, useful applications with as little code as possible, not churning out a lot of code.

Visual Basic is an excellent fit for this type of development, which makes up the bulk of software development in today's economy. Moreover, it will grow to be an even better fit as it is refined and evolves for exactly that purpose.

Who This Book IS For

This book is written to help experienced developers learn Visual Basic 2005. From those who are just starting the transition from earlier versions to those who have used Visual Basic for a while and need to gain a deeper understanding, this book provides information on the most common programming tasks and concepts you need.

Professional Visual Basic 2005 with .NET 3.0 offers a wide-ranging presentation of Visual Basic concepts, but the .NET Framework is so large and comprehensive that no single book can cover it all. The main area in which this book does not attempt to be complete is Web development. While chapters discussing the basics of browser-based programming in Visual Basic are included, professional Web developers should instead refer to *Professional ASP.NET 2.0 Special Edition* (Wrox Press).

What You Need to Use This Book

Although it is possible to create Visual Basic applications using the command-line tools contained in the .NET Framework SDK, you need Visual Studio 2005 (Professional or higher), which includes the .NET Framework SDK, to get the most out of this book. You may use Visual Studio .NET 2002 or Visual Studio 2003 instead, but in some cases the exercises won't work because functionalities and capabilities are not available in these older versions. In addition, note the following:

❑ You need .NET Framework 3.0 (which will install the .NET Framework 2.0 by default if it isn't already present on the machine).

❑ Some chapters make use of SQL Server 2005, but you can also run the example code using Microsoft's SQL Express, which ships with Visual Studio 2005.

❑ Several chapters make use of Internet Information Services (IIS). IIS ships with Windows 2003 Server, Windows 2000 Server, Windows 2000 Professional, and Windows XP, although it is not installed by default.

❑ Chapter 28 makes use of MSMQ to work with queued transactions. MSMQ ships with Windows 2003 Server, Windows 2000 Server, Windows 2000 Professional, and Windows XP, although it is not installed by default.

What This Book Covers

Chapter 1, "Understanding the .NET Framework Architecture" — This chapter explains the importance of .NET and how much it changes application development. You gain an understanding of why you need .NET by looking at what's wrong with the current development technologies, including COM and the DNA architectural model. It explains how .NET corrects the drawbacks by using the common language runtime (CLR). This chapter also reviews the details of the .NET Framework 2.0 and 3.0 and how to install these frameworks.

Chapter 2, "Visual Basic 2005 Core Basics" — This chapter introduces many of the types commonly used in Visual Basic 2005. Topics discussed in this chapter include type coverage, type conversion, reference types, arrays and other collections, parameter passing, and boxing. The full syntax basics of Visual Basic are provided in this chapter.

Chapter 3, "Object Syntax Introduction" — This is the first of three chapters that explore object-oriented programming in Visual Basic. This chapter defines objects, classes, instances, encapsulation, abstraction, polymorphism, and inheritance.

Chapter 4, "Object Oriented Programming" — This chapter examines inheritance and how it can be used within Visual Basic. You create simple and abstract base classes and learn how to create base classes from which other classes can be derived. This chapter puts the theory for much of what has been discussed thus far into practice. The four defining object-oriented concepts (abstraction, encapsulation, polymorphism, inheritance) are described, and we explain how these concepts can be applied in design and development to create effective object-oriented applications.

Chapter 5, "The Common Language Runtime" — This chapter examines the core of the .NET platform, the common language runtime (CLR). The CLR is responsible for managing the execution of code compiled for the .NET platform. We cover versioning and deployment, memory management, cross-language integration, metadata, and the IL Disassembler.

Chapter 6, "Localization" — Developers usually build applications in the English language. Then, as the audience for the application expands, they realize the need to globalize the application. Of course, the ideal is to build the application to handle an international audience right from the start — but in many cases this may not be possible because of the extra work it requires. The .NET Framework made a considerable effort to address the internationalization of the applications you build. You quickly realize that changes to the API, the addition of capabilities to the server controls, and even Visual Studio itself equip you to do the extra work required more easily to bring your application to an international audience. This chapter looks at some of the important items to consider when building your applications for the world. It looks closely at the `System.Globalization` namespace and everything it offers your applications.

Introduction

Chapter 7, "Generics" — This chapter focuses on one of the biggest enhancements to Visual Basic in this version — generics. Generics enables you to make a generic collection that is still strongly typed — providing fewer chances for errors, increasing performance, and giving you IntelliSense features when you are working with your collections.

Chapter 8, "Namespaces" — This chapter introduces namespaces and their hierarchical structure. An explanation of namespaces and some common ones are provided. In addition, you learn how to create new namespaces, and how to import and alias existing namespaces within projects. This chapter also looks at the new `My` namespace available in Visual Basic 2005.

Chapter 9, "Exception Handling and Debugging" — This chapter covers how error handling and debugging work in Visual Basic 2005 by discussing the CLR exception handler and the new `Try...Catch...Finally` structure. Also covered are error and trace logging, and how you can use these methods to obtain feedback about how your program is working.

Chapter 10, "Data Access with ADO.NET 2.0" — This chapter focuses on what you need to know about the ADO.NET object model in order to build flexible, fast, and scalable data access objects and applications. The evolution of ADO into ADO.NET is explored, and the main objects in ADO.NET that you need to understand in order to build data access into your .NET applications are explained.

Chapter 11, "Using XML in Visual Basic 2005" — This chapter presents the features of the .NET Framework that facilitate the generation and manipulation of XML. We describe the .NET Framework's XML-related namespaces, and a subset of the classes exposed by these namespaces is examined in detail. This chapter also touches on a set of technologies that utilize XML — specifically, ADO.NET and SQL Server.

Chapter 12, "Security in the .NET Framework 2.0" — This chapter examines additional tools and functionality with regard to the security provided by .NET. `Caspol.exe` and `Permview.exe`, which assist in establishing and maintaining security policies, are discussed. The `System.Security.Permissions` namespace is also covered, and we discuss how it relates to managing permissions. Finally, we examine the `System.Security.Cryptography` namespace and run through some code to demonstrate its capabilities.

Chapter 13, "Visual Studio 2005" — This chapter introduces the next generation of the major IDE for developing .NET applications: Visual Studio 2005. Previous releases of this IDE included Visual Studio .NET 2003 and Visual Studio .NET 2002. This chapter focuses on the Visual Studio 2005 release and how you can use it to build better applications more quickly.

Chapter 14, "Working with SQL Server" — This chapter describes how to work with the new SQL Server 2005 along with your .NET applications. SQL Server provides a strong connection to your applications, and this chapter explains how to effectively utilize this powerful database.

Chapter 15, "Windows Forms" — This chapter looks at Windows Forms, concentrating primarily on forms and built-in controls. What is new and what has been changed from previous versions of Visual Basic are discussed, along with the `System.Windows.Forms` namespace.

Chapter 16, "Windows Forms Advanced Features" — This chapter looks at some of the more advanced features that are available to you in building your Windows Forms applications.

Chapter 17, "Windows Presentation Foundation" — A new component of .NET 3.0, the Windows Presentation Foundation offers a new vehicle for building applications. This chapter includes the new way in which Microsoft is promoting the presentation of a GUI, and WPF provides a presentation layer that you should find rather fluid and enriching. This chapter describes the basics of WPF and how to build simple XAML-based applications.

Chapter 18, "Integrating WPF with Windows Forms" — Many organizations have made significant investments in Windows Forms, and they are not ready to fully switch their applications to this new technology. For this reason, Microsoft has provided significant means to integrate WPF into your Windows Forms applications as well as the capability to bring your Windows Forms components to a WPF application. This chapter focuses on these capabilities.

Chapter 19, "Working with ASP.NET 2.0" — This chapter explores the basics of ASP.NET 2.0 in detail, including the new capabilities to use inline coding with Visual Studio, and the new code-behind model. Including application and page frameworks, this chapter covers new features of ASP.NET

Chapter 20, "ASP.NET 2.0 Advanced Features" — This chapter looks at a lot of the new and advanced features that are available to you with the latest release of ASP.NET 2.0. Examples of items covered include cross-page posting, master pages, site navigation, personalization, and more.

Chapter 21, "Assemblies" — This chapter examines assemblies and their use within the CLR. The structure of an assembly, what it contains, and the information it contains are examined. In addition, the manifest of the assembly and its role in deployment is looked at.

Chapter 22, "Deployment" — This chapter takes a close look at the available deployment options for Windows Forms and Web Forms, including the new ClickOnce deployment feature as well as at creating .msi files.

Chapter 23, "Working with Classic COM and Interfaces" — This chapter discusses COM and .NET component interoperability, and what tools are provided to help link the two technologies.

Chapter 24, "Threading" — This chapter explores threading and explains how the various objects in the .NET Framework enable any of its consumers to develop multithreaded applications. You will learn how threads can be created, how they relate to processes, and the differences between multitasking and multithreading.

Chapter 25, "Windows Workflow Foundation" — This chapter takes a look at the new .NET 3.0 capability to easily integrate workflow into your applications.

Chapter 26, "XML Web Services" — This chapter looks at how to create and consume Web Services using VB 2005. The abstract classes provided by the CLR to set up and work with Web Services are discussed, as well as some of the technologies that support Web Services. Also examined are some of the disadvantages to using any distributed architecture, and the future of Web Services.

Chapter 27, "Remoting" — This chapter takes a detailed look at how to use remoting in classic three-tier application design. You examine the basic architecture of remoting and build a basic server and client that uses a singleton object for answering client requests in the business tier. You will also learn how to use serialization to return more complex objects from the server to the client, and how to use the call context for passing extra data from the client to the server along with each call, without having to change the object model.

Chapter 28, "Enterprise Services" — This chapter explores the .NET component services — in particular, transaction processing and queued components.

Chapter 29, "Network Programming" — This chapter takes a look at working with some of the networking protocols that are available to you in your development and how to incorporate a wider network into the functionality of your applications.

Chapter 30, "Windows Communication Foundation" — This chapter looks at the new way to build service-oriented components that allow for standards-based communications over a number of protocols. WCF is Microsoft's new answer for component communications within and outside of the enterprise.

Chapter 31, "Windows Services" — This chapter examines how Visual Basic is used in the production of Windows Services. The creation, installation, running, and debugging of Windows Services are covered.

Chapter 32, "Visual Basic and the Internet" — This chapter looks at how to download resources from the Web, how to design your own communication protocols, and how to reuse the Web browser control in your applications.

Appendix A, "The Visual Basic Compiler" — This appendix looks at the Visual Basic compiler vbc.exe and the functionality it provides.

Appendix B, "Visual Basic References" — This appendix provides a short list of VB resources available to you.

Conventions

We have used a number of different styles of text and layout in this book to help differentiate between the different kinds of information. Here are examples of the styles we use and an explanation of what they mean:

Bullets appear indented, with each new bullet marked as follows:

- ❑ *New and important words* are in italics.
- ❑ Words that appear on the screen in menus, such as File or Window, are in a similar font to the one that you see onscreen.
- ❑ If you see something like Object, you'll know that it's a filename, object name, or function name.

Code in a gray box is new, important, pertinent code:

```
Dim objMyClass as New MyClass("Hello World")
Debug.WriteLine(objMyClass.ToString)
```

Sometimes code appears in a mixture of styles, such as the following:

```
Dim objVar as Object
  objVar = Me
CType(objVar, Form).Text = "New Dialog Title Text"
```

Code with a white background is code we've already looked at and that we don't wish to examine further.

> **Important pieces of information appear in shaded boxes like this.**

Advice, hints, and background information appear in an italicized, indented paragraph like this.

Customer Support

We always value hearing from our readers, and we want to know what you think about this book: what you liked, what you didn't like, and what you think we can do better next time. You can send us your comments, either by returning the reply card in the back of the book or by e-mail to feedback@wrox.com. Please be sure to mention the book title in your message.

How to Download the Sample Code for the Book

When you visit the Wrox site, www.wrox.com, simply locate the title through our Search facility or by using one of the title lists. Click Download in the Code column or click Download Code on the book's detail page.

Files available for download from our site have been archived using WinZip. When you have saved the attachments to a folder on your hard drive, extract the files using a decompression program such as WinZip or PKUnzip. When you extract the files, the code is usually extracted into chapter folders. When you start the extraction process, ensure that your software (WinZip, PKUnzip, and so on) is set to use folder names.

Errata

We've made every effort to make sure that there are no errors in the text or in the code. However, no one is perfect and mistakes do occur. If you find an error in one of our books, such as a spelling mistake or a faulty piece of code, we would be very grateful for feedback. By sending in errata, you may save another reader hours of frustration, and of course you will be helping us provide even higher quality information. Simply e-mail the information to support@wrox.com; your information will be checked and if correct, posted to the errata page for that title, or used in subsequent editions of the book.

To find errata on the website, go to www.wrox.com and simply locate the title through our Advanced Search or title list. Click the Book Errata link, which is below the cover graphic on the book's detail page.

p2p.wrox.com

For author and peer discussion, join the P2P mailing lists. Our unique system provides programmer to programmer™ contact on mailing lists, forums, and newsgroups, all in addition to our one-to-one e-mail support system. If you post a query to P2P, you can be confident that the many Wrox authors and other industry experts who are present on our mailing lists are examining it. At p2p.wrox.com you will find a number of different lists that will help you, not only while you read this book, but also as you develop your own applications.

> **Particularly appropriate to this book are the vb_dotnet and pro_vb_dotnet lists.**

To subscribe to a mailing list, just follow these steps:

1. Go to http://p2p.wrox.com.
2. Choose the appropriate category from the left menu bar.
3. Click the mailing list you wish to join.
4. Follow the instructions to subscribe and fill in your e-mail address and password.
5. Reply to the confirmation e-mail you receive.
6. Use the subscription manager to join more lists and set your e-mail preferences.

You can read messages in the forums without joining P2P, but in order to post your own messages, you must join.

Once you join, you can post new messages and respond to messages other users post. You can read messages at any time on the Web. If you would like to have new messages from a particular forum e-mailed to you, click the Subscribe to this Forum icon by the forum name in the forum listing.

For more information about how to use the Wrox P2P, be sure to read the P2P FAQs for answers to questions about how the forum software works as well as many common questions specific to P2P and Wrox books. To read the FAQs, click the FAQ link on any P2P page.

Understanding the .NET
Framework Architecture

New technologies force change, nowhere more so than in computers and software. Occasionally, a new technology is so innovative that it forces us to challenge our most fundamental assumptions. In the computing industry, the latest such technology is the Internet. It has forced us to rethink how software should be created, deployed, and used.

However, that process takes time. Usually, when a powerful new technology comes along, it is first simply strapped onto existing platforms. So it has been for the Internet. Before the advent of Microsoft .NET, developers used older platforms with new Internet capabilities "strapped on." The resulting systems worked, but they were expensive and difficult to produce, hard to use, and difficult to maintain.

Realizing this several years ago, Microsoft decided it was time to design a new platform from the ground up specifically for the post-Internet world. The result is called .NET. It represents a turning point in the world of Windows software for Microsoft platforms. Microsoft has staked its future on .NET and has publicly stated that henceforth almost all its research and development will be done on this platform. It is expected that, eventually, almost all Microsoft products will be ported to the .NET platform.

Microsoft is now at version 3.0 of the Microsoft .NET Framework, and the development environment associated with this version is called Visual Studio 2005. The version of Visual Basic in this version is thus called Visual Basic 2005, and this book is about using Visual Basic 2005 with the .NET Framework 3.0.

What Is the .NET Framework?

The .NET Framework includes an execution platform in the form of a virtual machine. It also includes several programming languages that can produce programs for this virtual machine, and extensive class libraries, to provide rich built-in functionality for those languages.

This chapter looks at the .NET Framework from the viewpoint of a Visual Basic developer. Unless you are quite familiar with the framework already, you should consider this introduction an essential first step in assimilating the information about Visual Basic 2005 that is presented in the rest of this book.

Versions of the .NET Framework

The first released product based on the .NET Framework was Visual Studio .NET 2002, which was publicly launched in February 2002, and included version 1.0 of the .NET Framework. Visual Studio .NET 2003 was introduced a year later and included version 1.1 of the .NET Framework.

In late 2005, version 2.0 of the .NET Framework was introduced, and along with it a new version of Visual Studio was released. That version is named Visual Studio 2005. (Note that the ".NET" part of the name was dropped for this version.)

In early 2007, Microsoft's new version of Windows, called Vista, was released to the public. At the same time, a new version of the .NET Framework was introduced, called .NET Framework 3.0. This version of the .NET Framework is built into Windows Vista, and is available to be installed on Windows XP and Windows Server 2003.

Earlier versions of the .NET Framework also worked on several versions of Windows before XP, but the .NET Framework 3.0 does not. It is only compatible with Windows XP, Windows 2003 Server, and Windows Vista.

No new version of Visual Studio was released with the .NET Framework 3.0. Visual Studio 2005 is compatible with this version of the framework.

This book assumes that you are using Visual Studio 2005 and .NET Framework 3.0. Some of the examples will work transparently with other versions of the .NET Framework and Visual Studio, but you should not count on this. Many examples in this edition emphasize features of .NET Framework 2.0 over 1.0/1.1, and of course many new examples require .NET Framework 3.0.

What's New in .NET Framework 3.0?

Most of the classes in .NET Framework 2.0 are unchanged in 3.0. The differences for .NET Framework 3.0 are new libraries that offer completely new functionality. The new capabilities in .NET Framework 3.0 are almost entirely contained in three new technologies:

Windows Presentation Foundation (WPF) — A completely new UI technology, based on the DirectX engine, which allows creation of vector-based user interfaces instead of the traditional Windows bitmapped UI. WPF is the platform for the next generation of interactive user interfaces, with built-in capabilities for scaling, animation, media, styling, and three-dimensional visualization.

Windows Communication Foundation (WCF) — A unified framework for machine-to-machine and process-to-process communication. WCF brings together the capabilities of various messaging and communications technologies, including Web Services, enterprise services, remoting, and Microsoft Message Queue, into one integrated programming model. WCF is designed to be the principal Microsoft platform for systems with Service-Oriented Architecture (SOA).

Windows Workflow (WF) — An engine for creation of workflow applications. WF serves as the kernel of workflow, handling threading, persistence, and other plumbing tasks. WF brings a consistent, component-oriented philosophy to workflow, and is expected to be the core of a range of workflow solutions from Microsoft and various third parties.

Platform for a Post-Internet World

The .NET Framework began as a rich and complex platform, and as indicated earlier, it continues to include new and innovative capabilities. These new technologies fit well with the original philosophy of .NET, which is to serve as a platform for all kinds of software in an Internet-enabled world.

The vision of Microsoft .NET is globally distributed systems, using XML as the universal glue to enable functions running on different computers across an organization or across the world to come together in a single application. In this vision, systems from servers to wireless palmtops, with everything in between, will share the same general platform, with versions of .NET available for all of them, and with each of them able to integrate transparently with the others.

This does not leave out classic applications as you have always known them, though. The .NET Framework also makes traditional business applications much easier to develop and deploy. Some of the technologies of the .NET Framework, such as Windows Forms, demonstrate that Microsoft has not forgotten the traditional business developer. In fact, such developers will find it possible to Internet-enable their applications more easily than with any previous platform.

From the perspective of a Visual Basic developer, the .NET Framework enables Visual Basic to be used for anything from a simple utility program to a worldwide distributed n-tier system, and to create software on anything from huge servers to portable devices.

Overcoming the Limitations of COM

The pre-.NET technologies used for development on Microsoft platforms encompassed the COM (Component Object Model) standard for creation of components. COM had several major drawbacks. It wasn't designed for an Internet-enabled world or for highly distributed systems. In addition, deployment of COM-based applications was quite expensive.

Pre-.NET versions of Visual Basic also had significant limitations, and many of them resulted from the limitations of COM, upon which VB6 was based. For example, VB6's lack of full object orientation was due in part to the fact that COM itself was not object oriented. This meant that producing frameworks for complex systems in versions of Visual Basic through VB6 was not very practical.

Add to this a limited threading model and limited options for exposing Internet user interfaces, and Visual Basic needed a complete overhaul. That was done as part of the creation of the .NET Framework.

An Overview of the .NET Framework

The .NET Framework covers all the layers of software development above the operating system level. It provides the richest level of integration among presentation technologies, component technologies, and data technologies ever seen on a Microsoft, or perhaps any, platform. The entire architecture has been created to make it as easy to develop Internet applications as it is to develop desktop applications.

The .NET Framework actually "wraps" the operating system, insulating software developed with .NET from most operating system specifics such as file handling and memory allocation. This prepares for a possible future in which the software developed for .NET is portable to a wide variety of hardware and operating system foundations.

The major components of the .NET Framework 3.0 are shown in Figure 1-1.

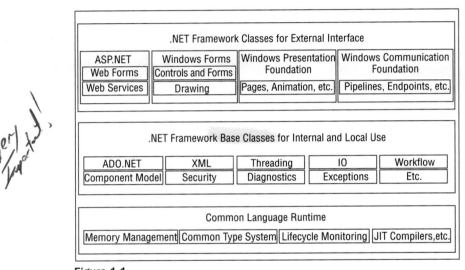

Figure 1-1

The framework starts all the way down at the memory management and component loading level and goes all the way up to multiple ways of rendering user and program interfaces. In between, there are layers that provide just about any system-level capability that a developer would need.

At the base is the common language runtime, often abbreviated to CLR. This is the heart of the .NET Framework — it is the engine that drives key functionality. It includes, for example, a common system of datatypes. These common types, plus a standard interface convention, make cross-language inheritance possible. In addition to allocation and management of memory, the CLR also does reference tracking for objects and handles garbage collection.

The middle layer includes the next generation of standard system services, such as classes that manage data and Extensible Markup Language (XML). These services are brought under control of the framework, making them universally available and making their usage consistent across languages.

The top layer includes user and program interfaces. There are four major ways of providing an interface from within .NET to entities outside .NET:

Technique	Description
ASP.NET	Provides browser-based user interfaces with Web Forms and system-to-system interface over the Web with Web Services
Windows Forms	Provides local forms-based interfaces, which can be Internet enabled with Web Services or Windows Communication Foundation (below). Based on the Windows Graphic Device Interface (GDI) kernel.
Windows Presentation Foundation	Provides vector-based user interfaces with a high degree of interaction. Based on DirectX technologies.
Windows Communication Foundation	Provides a highly flexible and configurable interface from system to system or process to process. Includes support for security, transactions, and other communication necessities.

All of these interfacing capabilities are available to any language based on the .NET platform, including, of course, Visual Basic 2005.

The Common Language Runtime

We are all familiar with runtimes — they go back further than DOS languages. However, the common language runtime (CLR) is as advanced over traditional runtimes as a machine gun is over a musket. Figure 1-2 shows a simple diagrammatic summary of the major pieces of the CLR.

Figure 1-2

Key Design Goals

The design of the CLR is based on the following primary goals:

- ❑ Simpler, faster development
- ❑ Automatic handling of system-level tasks such as memory management and process communication
- ❑ Excellent tool support
- ❑ Simpler, safer deployment
- ❑ Scalability

Many of these design goals directly address the limitations of COM. Let's look at some of these in detail.

Simpler, Faster Development

A broad, consistent framework enables developers to write less code, and to reuse code more. Using less code is possible because the system provides a rich set of underlying functionality. Programs in .NET access this functionality in a standard, consistent way, requiring less "hardwiring" and customization logic to interface with the functionality than was typically needed in earlier platforms. Programming is also simpler in .NET because of the standardization of datatypes and interface conventions.

The result is that programs written in VB 2005 that take proper advantage of the full capabilities of the .NET Framework typically have significantly less code than equivalent programs written in pre-.NET versions of Visual Basic. Less code means faster development, fewer bugs, and easier maintenance.

Excellent Tool Support

Although much of what the CLR does is similar to operating system functionality, it is very much designed to support development languages. It furnishes a rich set of object models that are useful to tools such as designers, wizards, debuggers, and profilers; and because the object models are at the runtime level, such tools can be designed to work across all languages that use the CLR. Many such tools are available from a variety of third-party vendors.

Simpler, Safer Deployment

Applications produced in the .NET Framework can be designed to install with a simple XCOPY. Just copy the files onto the disk and run the application (as long as the .NET Framework is already available on the machine). There are other more sophisticated deployment possibilities, but most rely on .NET's simple deployment model.

This model works because compilers in the .NET Framework embed identifiers (in the form of metadata, to be discussed later) into compiled modules, and the CLR manages those identifiers automatically. The identifiers provide all the information needed to load and run modules, and to locate related modules.

As a great by-product, the CLR can manage multiple versions of the same component (even a shared component) and have them run side by side. The identifiers tell the CLR which version is needed for a particular compiled module, because such information is captured at compile time. The runtime policy can be set in a module either to use the exact version of a component that was available at compile time, to use the latest compatible version, or to specify an exact version.

This has implications that might not be apparent at first. For example, .NET supports a program that can run directly from a CD or a shared network drive, without first running an installation program. This dramatically reduces the cost of deployment in many common scenarios.

Another significant deployment benefit in .NET is that applications only need to install their own core logic. An application produced in .NET does not need to install a runtime, for example, or modules for ADO or XML. Such base functionality is part of the .NET Framework, which is installed separately and only once for each system. As mentioned earlier, the .NET Framework 3.0 is included with the Windows Vista operating system, and can be installed on a one-time basis on Windows XP and Windows 2003 Server.

.NET programs can also be deployed across the Internet. Version 3.0 of the .NET Framework includes a technology specifically for that purpose called *ClickOnce*. This was a new capability in .NET 2.0, supplementing the "no touch deployment" of earlier versions. You can read about ClickOnce in Chapter 22.

Scalability

Since most of the system-level execution functions are concentrated in the CLR, they can be optimized and architected to allow a wide range of scalability for applications produced in the .NET Framework. As with most of the other advantages of the CLR, this one comes to all applications with little or no effort.

Memory and process management is one area where scalability can be built in. The memory management in the CLR is self-configuring and tunes itself automatically. Garbage collection (reclaiming memory that is no longer being actively used) is highly optimized, and the CLR supports many of the component management capabilities of COM+ (such as object pooling) in a portion of .NET called Enterprise Services. The result is that components can run faster and, thus, support more users.

This has some interesting side effects. For example, the performance and scalability differences among languages become smaller. All languages compile to a standard byte code called Microsoft Intermediate Language (MSIL), often referred to simply as IL. With all languages compiling down to similar byte code, it becomes unnecessary in most cases to look to other languages when performance is an issue. The difference in performance among .NET languages is minor — Visual Basic, for example, offers about the same performance as any of the other .NET languages.

Versions of the CLR are available on a wide range of devices. The vision is for .NET to be running at all levels, from smart mobile devices all the way up to Web farms. The same development tools work across the entire range. (The current version of .NET for mobile devices is still based on .NET Framework 2.0, but Visual Studio 2005 can still work with that version, which is known as the Compact Framework.)

Metadata

The .NET Framework needs a lot of information about an application to carry out several automatic functions. The design of .NET requires applications to carry that information within them. That is, applications are self-describing. The collected information that describes an application is called *metadata*.

The concept of metadata is not new. For example, COM components use a form of it called a *type library*, which contains metadata describing the classes exposed by the component and is used to facilitate OLE Automation. A component's type library, however, is stored in a separate file. In contrast, the metadata in .NET is stored in one place — inside the component it describes. Metadata in .NET also contains more information about the component and is better organized.

Chapter 5, "The Common Language Runtime," provides more information about metadata, and Chapter 21, "Assemblies," has additional detail. For now, the most important point for you to internalize is that metadata is key to the easy deployment in .NET. When a component is upgraded or moved, the necessary information about the component cannot be left behind. Metadata can never become out of sync with a .NET component because it is not in a separate file. Everything the CLR needs to know to run a component is supplied with the component.

Multiple-Language Integration and Support

The CLR is designed to support multiple languages and allow high levels of integration among those languages. By enforcing a common type system, and by having complete control over interface calls, the CLR enables languages to work together more transparently than ever before. The cross-language integration issues of COM simply don't exist in .NET.

 It is straightforward in the .NET Framework to use one language to subclass a class implemented in another. A class written in Visual Basic can inherit from a base class written in C#, or in a .NET version of COBOL for that matter. The VB program doesn't even need to know the language used for the base class. .NET offers full implementation inheritance with no problems that require recompilation when the base class changes.

A Common Type System

A key piece of functionality that enables multiple-language support is a common type system, in which all commonly used datatypes, even base types such as Long and Boolean, are actually implemented as objects. Coercion among types can now be done at a lower level for more consistency between languages. In addition, because all languages are using the same library of types, calling one language from another doesn't require type conversion or weird calling conventions.

This results in the need for some readjustment, particularly for developers who are only familiar with pre-.NET versions of VB. For example, what was called an Integer in VB6 and earlier is now known as a Short in VB 2005.

The "everything's an object" approach of .NET results in other potential surprises. For example, because String is a class in .NET instead of just a simple datatype, it has methods for string manipulation. Splitting a string into parts based on a delimiter is done with the String.Split method. VB6 developers might expect there to be a language keyword or a function in the library to do this, and wouldn't necessarily expect a method call right on the String object.

These adjustments are well worth the effort. The benefit is the ascension of Visual Basic to the status of a fully object-oriented language with no "glass ceiling" preventing it from being used for scenarios such as creating visual controls.

The CLR enforces the requirement that all datatypes satisfy the common type system. This has important implications, too. For example, it is not possible with the common type system to get the problem known in COM as a buffer overrun, which is the source of many security vulnerabilities. Programs written on .NET should have fewer such vulnerabilities because .NET is not dependent on the programmer to constantly check passed parameters for appropriate type and length. Such checking is done by default.

Chapter 2 goes into detail about the new type system in .NET.

Namespaces

One of the most important concepts in the .NET Framework is namespaces. Namespaces help organize object libraries and hierarchies, simplify object references, prevent ambiguity when referring to objects, and control the scope of object identifiers. The namespace for a class enables the CLR to unambiguously identify that class in the available .NET libraries that it can load.

Namespaces are discussed briefly in Chapter 2 and in more detail in Chapter 8. Understanding the concept of a namespace is essential for your progress in .NET, so do not skip those sections if you are unfamiliar with namespaces.

The Next Layer—The .NET Class Framework

The next layer up in the framework provides the services and object models for data, input/output, security, and so forth. It is called the .NET Class Framework, sometimes referred to as the .NET base classes.

The .NET Class Framework contains literally thousands of classes and interfaces. Here are just some of the functions of various libraries in the .NET Class Framework:

- ❑ Data access and manipulation

- ❑ Creation and management of threads of execution

- ❑ Interfaces from .NET to the outside world — Windows Forms, Web Forms, Web Services, and console applications

- ❑ Definition, management, and enforcement of application security

- ❑ Encryption, disk file I/O, network I/O, serialization of objects, and other system-level functions

- ❑ Application configuration

- ❑ Working with directory services, event logs, performance counters, message queues, and timers

- ❑ Sending and receiving data with a variety of network protocols

- ❑ Accessing metadata information stored in assemblies

Much of the functionality that a programmer might think of as being part of a language has been moved to the base classes. For example, the old VB6 keyword Sqr for extracting a square root is no longer available in .NET versions of Visual Basic. It has been replaced by the System.Math.Sqrt() method in the framework classes.

It's important to emphasize that all languages based on the .NET Framework have these framework classes available. That means that COBOL, for example, can use the same function mentioned above to get a square root. This makes such base functionality widely available and highly consistent across languages. All calls to Sqrt look essentially the same (allowing for syntactical differences among languages) and access the same underlying code. Here are examples in VB.NET and C#:

```
' Example using Sqrt in Visual Basic .NET
Dim dblNumber As Double = 200
```

```
Dim dblSquareRoot As Double
dblSquareRoot = System.Math.Sqrt(dblNumber)
Label1.Text = dblSquareRoot.ToString

' Same example in C#
Double dblNumber = 200;
Double dblSquareRoot = System.Math.Sqrt(dblNumber);
dblSquareRoot = System.Math.Sqrt(dblNumber);
label1.Text = dblSquareRoot.ToString;
```

Notice that the line using the Sqrt() function is exactly the same in both languages.

> *A programming shop can create its own classes for core functionality, such as globally available, already compiled functions. This custom functionality can then be referenced in code the same way as built-in .NET functionality.*

Much of the functionality in the base framework classes resides in a vast namespace called System. The System.Math.Sqrt() method was just mentioned. The System namespace contains dozens of such subcategories. The following table describes a few of the important ones, many of which you will be using in various parts of this book:

Namespace	What It Contains	Example Classes and Subnamespaces
System.Collections	Creation and management of various types of collections	Arraylist, Hashtable, SortedList
System.Data	Classes and types related to basic database management (see Chapter 10 for details)	DataSet, DataTable, DataColumn
System.Diagnostics	Classes to debug an application and to trace the execution of code	Debug, Trace
System.IO	Types that allow reading and writing to and from files and other data streams	File, FileStream, Path, StreamReader, StreamWriter
System.Math	Members to calculate common mathematical quantities, such as trigonometric and logarithmic functions	Sqrt (square root), Cos (cosine), Log (logarithm), Min (minimum)
System.Reflection	Capability to inspect metadata	Assembly, Module
System.Security	Types that enable security capabilities (see Chapter 12 for details)	Cryptography, Permissions, Policy

User and Program Interfaces in .NET

At the top layer, .NET provides four ways to render and manage user interfaces:

- ❏ Windows Forms
- ❏ Web Forms
- ❏ Windows Presentation Foundation
- ❏ Console applications (not shown in Figure 1-1)

.NET also provides several techniques for interprocess communication, either on the same machine or between different machines. These include Web Services, .NET Remoting, and the new Windows Communication Foundation.

Using .NET effectively requires understanding the strengths and intended uses of these technologies, and how to choose among them for specific circumstances. The following sections provide a brief overview, with references to additional chapters in the book that go into more depth.

Windows Forms

Windows Forms is a more advanced and integrated way to do standard Win32 screens. All languages that work on the .NET Framework can use the Windows Forms engine, which duplicates the functionality of the old VB forms engine. It provides a rich, unified set of controls and drawing functions. It effectively replaces the Windows graphical API, wrapping the Windows GDI kernel in such a way that developers normally have no need to go directly to the Windows API for any graphical or screen functions.

Chapter 15 describes Windows Forms in more detail and notes significant changes in Windows Forms versus older VB forms. Chapter 16 continues discussing advanced Windows Forms capabilities such as creation of Windows Forms visual controls.

Client Applications versus Browser-Based Applications

Before .NET, many internal corporate applications were browser-based simply because of the cost of installing and maintaining a client application on hundreds or thousands of workstations. Windows Forms and the .NET Framework change the economics of these decisions. A Windows Forms application is much easier to install and update than an equivalent VB6 desktop application. With a simple XCOPY deployment and no registration issues, installing and updating become much easier. Internet deployment via ClickOnce also makes applications more available across a wide geographic area, with automatic updating of changed modules on the client.

This means that "smart client" applications with a rich user interface are more practical under .NET, even for a large number of users. It may not be necessary to resort to browser-based applications just to save on installation and deployment costs.

As a consequence, don't dismiss Windows Forms applications as merely replacements for earlier VB6 desktop applications. Instead, examine applications in .NET and explicitly decide what kind of interface makes sense in a given scenario. In some cases, applications that you might have assumed should be browser-based simply because of a large number of users and wide geographic deployment instead can be smart-client-based, which can improve usability, security, and productivity.

In other cases, it might be appropriate for parts of your system to expose a Windows Forms interface, and other parts to expose a browser-based system. Because logic for data access and other system chores is compatible with both of those UI technologies, multiple forms of user interface could easily work with the same server-based functionality.

Web Forms

The part of .NET that handles communications over the Internet is called ASP.NET. It includes a forms engine, called Web Forms, which can be used to create browser-based user interfaces.

Divorcing layout from logic, Web Forms consist of two parts:

- ❏ A template, which contains HTML-based layout information for all user interface elements
- ❏ A component, which contains all logic to be hooked to the user interface

It is as if a standard Visual Basic form were split into two parts, one containing information on controls and their properties and layout, and the other containing the code. Just as in Visual Basic, the code operates "behind" the controls, with events in the controls activating event routines in the code.

As with Windows Forms, Web Forms are available to all .NET languages. This brings complete, flexible Web interface capability to a wide variety of languages. Chapters 19 and 20 go into detail about Web Forms and the controls that are used on them.

If you have only used ASP.NET in versions 1.0 or 1.1 of .NET, you should know that ASP.NET 2.0 has dramatic improvements. With even more built-in functionality for common browser tasks, applications can be written with far less code in ASP.NET 2.0 as compared to earlier versions. Capabilities such as user authentication can now be done with prebuilt ASP.NET components, so you no longer have to write such components yourself.

Windows Presentation Foundation

As mentioned at the beginning of this chapter, changing hardware technologies often force changes in our software platforms and development tools. Recent advances in display technologies provide an example. Video hardware has become more powerful. Display devices have become available in many different sizes, resolutions, and aspect ratios.

Developers are accustomed to making decisions about what resolution to support for their applications. Should it be 800×600? Or 1024×768? As such options multiply, decisions become much more complex, and it becomes desirable to find a more complete solution by supporting a wider variety of display devices.

Microsoft's answer is Windows Presentation Foundation (WPF). At its core, WPF is *vector-based*, rather than bit-mapped. This enables user interface objects such as controls and shapes to be scalable to any size or resolution. Users of vector-based drawing programs are familiar with this advance, but with WPF it becomes available for general programming use.

WPF also tightly integrates many other display-related technologies, such as animation, styling, and three-dimensional visualization. Media, such as video playback, can easily be placed on any user interface surface.

Microsoft's ambitions for WPF go beyond just supplementing Windows Forms for local interfaces. A version of WPF is planned for non-Windows systems. It is tentatively called WPF/e, sometimes referred to as WPF Everywhere. WPF/e will enable browser pages to incorporate many of WPF's sophisticated UI features, even if those pages are running on non-Windows systems such as the Apple Macintosh.

Chapter 17 provides an introduction to WPF, and Chapter 18 discusses integration and interoperability of WPF with Windows Forms.

Console Applications

Although Microsoft doesn't emphasize the .NET Framework's capability to write character-based applications, the framework does include an interface for such console applications. Batch processes, for example, can now have components integrated into them, and those components can write to a console interface.

As with Windows Forms and Web Forms, this console interface is available for applications written in any .NET language. Writing character-based applications in pre-.NET versions of Visual Basic, for example, was always a struggle, because those versions were completely oriented around a graphical user interface (GUI). Visual Basic 2005 is independent of user interface technology, and can be used for true console applications along with forms-based and browser-based user interfaces.

Web Services and Windows Communication Foundation

Application development is moving into the next stage of decentralization. The oldest idea of an application is a piece of software that accesses basic operating system services, such as the file system and graphics system. Then we moved to applications that used a lot of base functionality from other system-level applications, such as a database — this type of application added value by applying generic functionality to specific problems. The developer's job was to focus on adding business value, not building the foundation.

Web Services represented the next step in this direction. In Web Services, software functionality becomes exposed as a service that doesn't care what the consumer of the service is (unless there are security considerations). Web Services enable developers to build applications by combining local and remote resources for an overall integrated and distributed solution.

In .NET, Web Services are implemented as part of ASP.NET (refer to Figure 1-1), which handles all Web interfaces. It enables programs to talk to each other directly over the Web, using the SOAP standard. This has the potential to dramatically change the architecture of Web applications, allowing services running all over the Web to be integrated into a local application.

Chapter 26 contains a detailed discussion of Web Services.

Moving beyond Web services, the Windows Communication Foundation (WCF) provides the next generation of decentralization. WCF is new in .NET Framework 3.0. It subsumes most of the technologies used in earlier versions of .NET for interprocess communication. Web Services, for example, can be completely wrapped by WCF.

Other Microsoft technologies that are either wrapped or have their functionality replicated in WCF include Enterprise Services, Microsoft Message Queue (MSMQ), and .NET Remoting. All are exposed via a consistent API, so it is no longer necessary in .NET to learn a variety of APIs for cross-process or cross-machine interaction.

Microsoft's intent with WCF is to provide a platform for creating applications with a *Service-Oriented Architecture (SOA)*. Such an architecture does interprocess communication using messages, rather than function calls or their equivalent. The messages must satisfy a contract that specifies the format of the message and all the information in it. As long as each side of the communication understands how to use the contract, the way each side actually stores the data is irrelevant to the other side.

This type of architecture allows loose coupling between parts of the application. The parts don't have to know much about each other — they just need to understand the contract. That makes it much easier to replace a part of the application with similar functionality without significant modification to the rest of the application.

Chapter 30 covers the basics of WCF.

.NET Remoting is the remaining technology for interprocess communication. It is not intended for a Service-Oriented Architecture — instead, it allows actual object calls between different .NET processes. The advantage of .NET Remoting is speed on local area networks.

However, WCF has comparable performance capabilities on LANs, and is expected to be the basis for future innovation in interprocess communication. While .NET Remoting will continue to be supported in .NET indefinitely, it is no longer being enhanced. For new applications, WCF is usually preferred.

Chapter 27 covers .NET Remoting.

XML as the .NET Metalanguage

Much of the underlying integration of .NET is accomplished with XML. For example, Web Services depend completely on XML for interfacing with remote objects. Looking at metadata usually means looking at an XML version of it.

ADO.NET, the successor to ADO, is heavily dependent on XML for the remote representation of data. Essentially, when ADO.NET creates what it calls a *dataset* (a more complex successor to a recordset), the data is converted to XML for manipulation by ADO.NET. Then, changes to that XML are posted back to the datastore by ADO.NET when remote manipulation is finished.

.NET uses XML internally, too. The standard way of storing configuration information in .NET is XML-based.

With XML as an "entry point" into so many areas of .NET, integration opportunities are multiplied. Using XML to expose interfaces to .NET functions enables developers to tie components and functions together in new, unexpected ways. XML can be the glue that ties pieces together in ways that were never anticipated, both to Microsoft and non-Microsoft platforms.

Chapter 11 discusses XML in .NET in more detail.

The Role of COM

When the .NET Framework was introduced in 2002, some uninformed journalists interpreted it as the death of COM. That turned out to be completely incorrect. COM is not going anywhere for a while. In fact, Windows will not boot without COM.

.NET integrates very well with COM-based software. Any COM component can be treated as a .NET component by native .NET components. The .NET Framework wraps COM components and exposes an interface that .NET components can work with. That makes.NET interoperable with a tremendous amount of older COM-based software.

Going in the other direction, the .NET Framework can expose .NET components with a COM interface. This enables older COM components to use .NET-based components as if they were developed using COM.

Chapter 23 discusses COM interoperability in more detail.

No Internal Use of COM

Understand, however, that native .NET components do not interface using COM. The CLR implements a new way for components to interface, one that is not COM-based. Use of COM is only necessary when interfacing with COM components produced by non-.NET tools.

Over a long span of time, the fact that .NET does not use COM internally may lead to the decline of COM, but for any immediate purposes, COM is definitely important.

Major Differences in .NET 2.0

A list of major changes in the .NET Framework 3.0 was included early in this chapter. However, many developers who started with .NET Framework 1.0 or 1.1, and with the associated versions of Visual Basic, may not be familiar with differences between those versions and version 2.0 of the .NET Framework.

Here is a list of important additions and changes that first happened with .NET Framework 2.0/Visual Basic 2005, along with the chapter you should check for more information:

Feature	Description	Chapter(s)
Edit and Continue	Allows you to make changes to code while you are running it in the integrated development environment (IDE) and have the changes take effect immediately. (This feature was available in VB6 and earlier, but was not available in Visual Basic 2002 or 2003.)	13
Partial classes	Allows code for a class to be split over multiple code modules	3
Generics	Allows generic collections to handle specific types, declared when the collection is created	7
ClickOnce	New deployment technology for deploying across the Internet, with automatic updating	22
"My" classes	Provides quick access to commonly used classes in the .NET Framework	8
IsNot keyword	Simplifies `If` statements that check whether an object is `Nothing`	2
Using keyword	Automates disposing of objects created in a section of code	5
IDE improvements	Exception manager, code snippets with automatic fill-in, improved IntelliSense, and autocorrect are a few of the new capabilities of the IDE.	13

Summary

Visual Basic has left behind its roots in the COM-based, pre-Internet world. Visual Basic 2005 is built with completely different assumptions about the kind of software you need to develop, and it is built on a platform that is central to Microsoft's entire product strategy. This chapter discussed the overall structure of this platform, .NET, and summarized the purposes and capabilities of many of the major component pieces of it.

The .NET platform is now at version 3.0, and each version continues to add impressive new capabilities. Windows Presentation Foundation, Windows Communication Foundation, and Windows Workflow are the major new technologies for .NET Framework 3.0, and each looks poised to have a dramatic effect on the way we develop our software systems.

The next chapter takes a closer look at the core basics of VB 2005. It is a foundation for much of what follows. Following that, Chapters 3 and 4 discuss object orientation and syntax. Those three chapters provide the foundation for the rest of the book, as they go into detail about specific .NET technologies and Visual Basic features.

Visual Basic 2005 Core Elements

This chapter looks at the core elements that make up Visual Basic. Every software development language has unique elements of syntax and behavior. In Visual Basic 2005, many of these elements have evolved since the original Basic and the decade that's passed since it was introduced. Accordingly, Visual Basic has its origins in traditional procedural-based programming languages.

However, with the release of Visual Basic for .NET, Visual Basic completed a paradigm shift that began several releases earlier. With .NET, the Visual Basic language was truly extended to reference object-oriented development. The object paradigms extend what we'll call the *core elements* of the language. Therefore, while a very brief introduction to the existence of classes and objects within the language is presented in this chapter, the key concepts of object-oriented development are presented in detail in Chapters 3 and 4.

This chapter focuses on the core elements of the language and answers questions those not familiar with Visual Basic might ask, such as where semicolons should be placed. The areas of focus for this chapter include the following:

- ❏ Initial syntax and keywords to understand the basic language elements
- ❏ Value versus reference types
- ❏ Primitive types
- ❏ Value types (structures)
- ❏ Reference types (classes)
- ❏ Boxing
- ❏ Parameter passing `ByVal` and `ByRef`
- ❏ Datatype conversions
- ❏ Commands: `If Then Else`, `Select Case`, `For Each`, `For Next`, `Do While`

The main goal of this chapter is to familiarize you with Visual Basic. The chapter begins by looking at some of the keywords and language syntax you need. Experienced developers will probably gloss over this information, as this is just a basic introduction to working with Visual Basic. After this, the chapter discusses value types and reference types, explaining the underlying difference between how these objects are stored. This is important information for understanding concepts such as boxing and generics. The chapter then provides a clear definition of a logical grouping of objects called *primitive types*. Finally, it discusses details of value and reference objects and how they are used, moving on to some common command and control statements for Visual Basic.

Initial Keywords and Syntax

While it would be possible to just add a giant glossary of keywords, that isn't the focus of this chapter. Instead, a few basic elements of Visual Basic need to be spelled out, so that as you read you can understand the examples. Chapter 8, for instance, covers working with namespaces, but some examples and other code are introduced in this chapter.

Let's begin with namespace. When .NET was being created, the developers realized that attempting to organize all of these classes required a system. A namespace is an arbitrary system that the .NET developers used to group classes containing common functionality. A namespace can have multiple levels of grouping, each separated by a period (.). Thus, the System namespace is the basis for classes that are used throughout .NET, while the Microsoft.VisualBasic namespace is used for classes in the underlying .NET Framework but specific to Visual Basic. At its most basic level, a namespace does not imply or indicate anything regarding the relationships between the class implementations in that namespace; it is just a way of managing the complexity of the .NET Framework's thousands of classes. As noted earlier, namespaces are covered in detail in Chapter 8.

Next is the keyword Class. Chapters 3 and 4 provide details on object-oriented syntax and the related keywords for objects, but a basic definition of this keyword is needed here. The Class keyword designates a common set of data and behavior within your application. The class is the definition of an object, in the same way that your source code, when compiled, is the definition of an application. When someone runs your code, it is considered to be an instance of your application. Similarly, when your code creates or instantiates an object from your class definition, it is considered to be an instance of that class, or an instance of that object.

Creating an instance of an object has two parts. The first part is the New command, which tells the compiler to create an instance of that class. This command instructs code to call your object definition and instantiate it. In some cases you might need to run a method and get a return value, but in most cases you'll use the New command to assign that instance of an object to a variable.

To declare a variable in Visual Basic, you use the Dim statement. Dim is short for "Dimension" and comes from the ancient past of Basic as a language. The idea is that you are telling the system to allocate or dimension a section of memory to hold data. The Dim statement is used to declare a variable, to which the system can then assign a value. Each variable declaration uses a Dim statement similar to the example that follows, which declares a new variable, winForm:

```
Dim winForm As System.Windows.Forms.Form = New System.Windows.Forms.Form()
```

As a best practice, always set a variable equal to something when it is declared. In the preceding example, the code declares a new variable (winForm) of the type Form. This variable is then set to an instance of a Form object. It might also be assigned to an existing instance of a Form object or alternatively to Nothing. The Nothing keyword is a way of telling the system that the variable does not currently have any value, and as such is not actually using any memory on the heap. Later in this chapter, in the discussion of Value and Reference types, keep in mind that only reference types can be set to Nothing.

What do we mean when we refer to a class consisting of data and behavior? For "data" this means that the class specifies certain variables that are within its scope. Embedded in the class definition are one or more Dim statements that create variables used to store the properties of the class. When you create an instance of this class, you create these variables; and in most cases the class contains logic to populate them. The logic used for this and to carry out other actions is the *behavior*. This behavior is encapsulated in what, in the object-oriented world, are known as *methods*.

However, Visual Basic doesn't have a "method" keyword. Instead, it has two other keywords that are brought forward from VB's days as a procedural language. The first is Sub. Sub is short for "Subroutine," and it defines a block of code that carries out some action. When this block of code completes, it returns control to the code that called it. To declare a function, you write code similar to the following:

```
Private Sub Load(ByVal object As System.Object)

End Sub
```

The preceding example shows the start of a method called Load. For now you can ignore the word Private at the start of this declaration; this is related to the object and is further explained in the next chapter. This method is implemented as a Sub because it doesn't return a value and accepts one parameter when it is called. This parameter is declared as being of type System.Object, and the meaning of the ByVal qualifier is explained later in this chapter. The code that actually loads the object would be written between the line declaring this method and the End Sub line.

In Visual Basic, the only difference between a Sub and the second method type, a Function, is this return type. Note that the Function declaration shown in the following sample code specifies the return type of this function. A function works just like a Sub with the exception that a Function returns a value. This is an important distinction, because when you declare a function you expect it to include a Return statement. The Return statement is used to indicate that even though additional lines of code may remain within a function or sub, those lines of code should not be executed. Instead, the Function or Sub should end processing at the current line.

```
Public Function Add(ByVal ParamArray values() As Integer) As Long
    Dim result As Long = 0

    Return result
    'TODO: Implement this function
    'What if user passes in only 1 value, what about 3 or more...
    result = values(0) + values(1)
    Return result
End Function
```

In the preceding example, note that after the function initializes the second line of code, there is a Return statement. Since the implementation of this function isn't currently shown (it is shown later in this chapter in the discussion of parameters), the developer wanted the code to exist with a safe value until the code was completed. Notice that there are two `Return` statements in the code. However, as soon as the first `Return` statement is reached, none of the remaining code in this function is executed. The `Return` statement immediately halts execution of a method, even from within a loop. As shown in the preceding example, the function's return value is assigned to a local variable until returned as part of the `Return` statement. For a `Sub`, there would be no value on the line with the `Return` statement, as a `Sub` does not return a value when it completes. When returned, the return value is usually assigned to something else; this is shown in the next example line of code, which calls a function to retrieve the currently active control on the executing Windows Form:

```
Dim ctrl As System.Windows.Forms.Control = Me.GetContainerControl().ActiveControl()
```

The preceding example demonstrates a call to a function. The value returned by the function ActiveControl is of type Control, and the code assigns this to the variable ctrl. It also demonstrates another keyword that you should be aware of: Me. The Me keyword is the way, within an object, that you can reference the current instance of that object. For example, in the preceding example, the object being referenced is the current window.

You may have noticed that in all the sample code presented above each line is a complete command. If you're familiar with another programming language, then you may be used to seeing a specific character that indicates the end of a complete set of commands. Several popular languages use a semicolon to indicate the end of a command line. For those who are considering Visual Basic as their first programming language, consider the English language, whereby we end each complete thought with a period.

Visual Basic doesn't use visible punctuation to end each line. Instead, it views its source files more like a list, whereby each item on the list is placed on its own line. The result is that Visual Basic ends each command line with the carriage return linefeed. In some languages, a command such as X = Y can span several lines in the source file until a semicolon or other terminating character is reached. However, in Visual Basic that entire statement would be found on a single line unless the user explicitly indicated that it was to continue onto another line.

When a line ends with the underscore character, this tells Visual Basic that the code on that line does not constitute a completed set of commands. The compiler will then continue onto the next line to find the continuation of the command, and will end as soon as a carriage return linefeed is found without an accompanying underscore. In this way, Visual Basic enables you to use exceptionally long lines and indicate that the code has been spread across multiple lines to improve readability. The following line demonstrates the use of the underscore to extend a line of code:

```
MessageBox.Show("Hello World", "A First Look at VB.NET", _
                MessageBoxButtons.OK, MessageBoxIcon.Information)
```

It is also possible to place multiple different statements on a single line with Visual Basic, by separating the statements with colons. However, this is generally considered a poor coding practice because it reduces readability.

Console Applications

The simplest type of application is a *console application*. This application doesn't have much of a user interface; in fact, for those old enough to remember the MS-DOS operating system, a console application looks just like an MS-DOS application. It works in a command window with no support for graphics or graphical devices such as a mouse. A console application is a text-based user interface that reads and writes characters from the screen.

The easiest way to create a console application is to use Visual Studio. However, for our purposes let's just look at a sample source file for a console application, as shown in the following example. Notice that the console application contains a single method, a Sub called Main. However, this Sub isn't contained in a class. Instead, the Sub is contained in a Module:

```
Module Module1
    Sub Main()
        Dim myObject As Object = New Object()
        Console.WriteLine("Hello World")
    End Sub
End Module
```

A module is another item dating to the procedural days of Visual Basic. It isn't a class, but a block of code that can contain methods, which are then referenced by classes — or, as in this case, it can represent the execution start for a program. The module in the preceding example contains a single method called Main. The Main method indicates the start point for running this application. Once a local variable is declared, the only other action taken by this method is to output a line of text to the console.

Note that in this usage, the Console refers to the text-based window, which hosts a command prompt from which this program is run. The console window is best thought of as a window encapsulating the older nongraphical-style user interface whereby literally everything was driven from the command prompt. The Console class is automatically created when you start your application, and it supports a variety of Read and Write methods. In the preceding example, if you were to run the code from within Visual Studio's debugger, the console window would open and close immediately. To prevent that, you include a final line in the Main Sub, which executes a Read statement so that the program continues to run while waiting for user input.

Because so many keywords have been covered, a glossary might be of use. The following table briefly summarizes most of the keywords discussed in the preceding section, and provides a short description of their meaning in Visual Basic:

Keyword	Description
Namespace	A collection of classes that provide related capabilities. For example, the System.Drawing namespace contains classes associated with graphics.
Class	A definition of an object. Includes properties (variables) and methods, which can be subs or functions.
Instance	When a class is created, the resulting object is an instance of the class's definition. Not a keyword in Visual Basic.
Method	A generic name for a named set of commands. In Visual Basic, both subs and functions are types of methods. Not a keyword in Visual Basic.

Table continues on next page

Keyword	Description
Sub	A method that contains a set of commands, allows data to be transferred as parameters, and provides scope around local variables and commands.
Function	A method that contains a set of commands, returns a value, allows data to be transferred as parameters, and provides scope around local variables and commands.
Return	Ends the currently executing sub or function. Combined with a return value for functions.
Dim	Declares and defines a new variable
New	Creates an instance of an object
Nothing	Used to indicate that a variable has no value. Equivalent to null in other languages and databases
Me	A reference to the instance of the object within which a method is executing
Console	A type of application that relies on a command-line interface. Console applications are commonly used for simple test frames. Also refers to a command window to and from which applications can read and write text data.
Module	A code block that isn't a class but which can contain sub and function methods. Not frequently used for application development but is part of a console application.

Value and Reference Types

Experienced developers generally consider integers, characters, Booleans, and strings to be the basic building blocks of any language. In .NET, all objects share a logical inheritance from the base Object class. One of the advantages of this common heritage is the ability to rely on certain common methods of every variable. Another is that this allows all of .NET to build on a common type system. Visual Basic builds on the common type system shared across .NET languages.

Because all datatypes are based on the core Object class, every variable you dimension can be assured of having a set of common characteristics. However, this logical inheritance does not require a common physical implementation for all variables. This might seem like a conflicting set of statements, but .NET has a base type of Object and then allows simple structures to inherit from this base class. While everything in .NET is based on the Object class, under the covers .NET has two major variable types: value and reference.

For example, what most programmers see as some of the basic underlying types, such as Integer, Long, Character, and even Byte, are not implemented as classes. Thus, on the one hand, all types inherit from the Object class, and on the other hand, there are two core types. This is important, as you'll see when we discuss boxing and the cost of transitioning between value types and reference types.

The key is that every type, whether it is a built-in structure such as an integer or string, or a custom class such as `WroxEmployee`, does in fact inherit from the `Object` class. The difference between value and reference types is an underlying implementation difference:

❑   Value types represent simple data storage located on the stack. The stack is used for items of a known size, so items on the stack can be retrieved faster than those on the managed heap.

❑   Reference types are based on complex classes with implementation inheritance from their parent classes, and custom storage on the managed heap. The managed heap is optimized to support dynamic allocation of different size objects.

Notice that the two implementations are stored in different portions of memory. The result is that value and reference types are treated differently within assignment statements, and their memory management is handled differently. It is important to understand how these differences affect the software you will write in Visual Basic. Understanding the foundations of how data is manipulated in the .NET Framework will enable you to build more reliable and better-performing applications.

Consider the difference between the stack and the heap. The stack is a comparatively small memory area in which processes and threads store data of fixed size. An integer or decimal value needs the same number of bytes to store data, regardless of the actual value. This means that the location of such variables on the stack can be efficiently determined. (When a process needs to retrieve a variable, it has to search the stack. If the stack contained variables that had dynamic memory sizes, such a search could take a long time.)

Reference types do not have a fixed size — a string can vary in size from two bytes to nearly all the memory available on a system. The dynamic size of reference types means that the data they contain is stored on the heap, rather than the stack. However, the address of the reference type (that is, the location of the data on the heap) does have a fixed size, and thus can be (and in fact is) stored on the stack. By storing a reference only to a custom allocation on the stack, the program as a whole runs much more quickly, as the process can rapidly locate the data associated with a variable.

Storing the data contained in fixed and dynamically sized variables in different places results in differences in the way variables behave. Rather than limit this discussion to the most basic of types in .NET, this difference can be illustrated by comparing the behavior of the `System.Drawing.Point` structure (a value type) and the `System.Text.StringBuilder` class (a reference type).

The `Point` structure is used as part of the .NET graphics library, which is part of the `System.Drawing` namespace. The `StringBuilder` class is part of the `System.Text` namespace and is used to improve performance when you're editing strings.

First, here is an example of how the `System.Drawing.Point` structure is used:

```
Dim ptX As New System.Drawing.Point(10, 20)
Dim ptY As New System.Drawing.Point

ptY = ptX
ptX.X = 200

Console.WriteLine(ptY.ToString())
```

The output from this operation will be {*X* = 10, *Y* = 20}, which seems logical. When the code copies ptX into ptY, the data contained in ptX is copied into the location on the stack associated with ptY. Later, when the value of ptX changes, only the memory on the stack associated with ptY is altered. Altering the value of ptX had no effect on ptY. This is not the case with reference types. Consider the following code, which uses the System.Text.StringBuilder class:

```
Dim objX As New System.Text.StringBuilder("Hello World")
Dim objY As System.Text.StringBuilder

objY = objX
objX.Replace("World", "Test")

Console.WriteLine(objY.ToString())
```

The output from this operation will be "Hello Test," not "Hello World." The previous example using points demonstrated that when one value type is assigned to another, the data stored on the stack is copied. Similarly, this example demonstrates that when objY is assigned to objX, the data associated with objX on the stack is copied to the data associated with objY on the stack. However, what is copied in this case isn't the actual data, but rather the address on the managed heap where the data is actually located. This means that objY and objX now reference the same data. When the data on the heap is changed, the data associated with every variable that holds a reference to that memory is changed. This is the default behavior of reference types, and is known as a *shallow copy*. Later in this chapter, you'll see how this behavior has been overridden for strings (which perform a *deep copy*).

The differences between value types and reference types go beyond how they behave when copied, and later in this chapter you'll encounter some of the other features provided by objects. First, though, let's take a closer look at some of the most commonly used value types and learn how .NET works with them.

Primitive Types

Visual Basic, in common with other development languages, has a group of elements such as integers and strings that are termed *primitive types*. These primitive types are identified by keywords such as String, Long, and Integer, which are aliases for types defined by the .NET class library. This means that the line

```
Dim i As Long
```

is equivalent to the line

```
Dim i As System.Int64
```

The reason why these two different declarations are available has to do with long-term planning for your application. In most cases (as was the case when Visual Basic transitioned to .NET), you want to use the Short, Integer, and Long designations. When Visual Basic moved to .NET, the Integer type went from 16 bits to 32 bits. Code written with this Integer type would automatically use the larger value if you rewrote the code in .NET. Interestingly enough, however, the Visual Basic Migration Wizard actually recast Visual Basic 6 Integer values to Visual Basic .NET Short values.

This is the same reason why `Int16`, `Int32`, and `Int64` exist. These types specify a physical implementation; therefore, if your code is someday migrated to a version of .NET that maps the `Integer` value to `Int64`, then those values defined as `Integer` will reflect the new larger capacity, while those declared as `Int32` will not. This could be important if your code was manipulating part of an interface where changing the physical size of the value could break the interface.

The following table lists the primitive types that Visual Basic 2005 defines, and the structures or classes to which they map:

Primitive Type	.NET Class or Structure
Byte	System.Byte (structure)
Short	System.Int16 (structure)
Integer	System.Int32 (structure)
Long	System.Int64 (structure)
Single	System.Single (structure)
Double	System.Double (structure)
Decimal	System.Decimal (structure)
Boolean	System.Boolean (structure)
Date	System.DateTime (structure)
Char	System.Char (structure)
String	System.String (class)

The `String` primitive type stands out from the other primitives. Strings are implemented as a class, not a structure. More important, strings are the one primitive type that is a reference type.

You can perform certain operations on primitive types that you can't on other types. For example, you can assign a value to a primitive type using a literal:

```
Dim i As Integer = 32
Dim str As String = "Hello"
```

It's also possible to declare a primitive type as a constant using the `Const` keyword, as shown here:

```
Dim Const str As String = "Hello"
```

Chapter 2: Visual Basic 2005 Core Elements

The value of the variable `str` in the preceding line of code cannot be changed elsewhere in the application containing this code at runtime. These two simple examples illustrate the key properties of primitive types. As noted, most primitive types are, in fact, value types. The next step is to take a look at the specific behavior of some of the common value types in Visual Basic.

Value Types (Structures)

Value types aren't as versatile as reference types, but they can provide better performance in many circumstances. The core value types (which include the majority of primitive types) are `Boolean`, `Byte`, `Char`, `DateTime`, `Decimal`, `Double`, `Guid`, `Int16`, `Int32`, `Int64`, `SByte`, `Single`, and `TimeSpan`. These are not the only value types, but rather the subset with which most Visual Basic developers consistently work. As you've seen, value types by definition store data on the stack.

Value types can also be referred to by their proper name: structures. The underlying principles and syntax of creating custom structures mirrors that of creating classes, covered in the next chapter. This section focuses on some of the built-in types provided by the .NET Framework — in particular, those built-in types known as *primitives*.

Boolean

The .NET `Boolean` type has been implemented in such a way that when converted to an integer, false is 0; true, when converted to an integer, has one of two possible values. In contrast to most languages (in which Boolean `True` equates to `1` `'one'`), Visual Basic converts a value of `True` to `-1` `'negative one'`. This is one of the few (but not the only) legacy carryovers from older versions of Visual Basic. It was done to save developers who were migrating code that didn't follow best practices, and actually relied on the underlying numeric value of the Boolean instead of checking for true or false. This allowed the VB migration wizard and the human developer to not examine every Boolean expression to ensure valid return values.

Visual Basic works as part of a multi-language environment, with metadata-defining interfaces, so the external value of `True` is as important as its internal value. Fortunately, Microsoft implemented Visual Basic in such a way that, while `-1` is supported within Visual Basic, the .NET standard of `1` is exposed from Visual Basic methods to other languages.

Of course, this compromise involves making some decisions that add complexity to `True` or `False` evaluations. While a `True` value in a Boolean expression equates to `-1`, when converted to any other format, it equates to `1`. This is best illustrated by some sample Visual Basic code. Keep in mind, though, that this code follows poor programming practice because it references Boolean values as integers (and does so with implicit conversions):

```
Dim blnTrue As Boolean = True
Dim blnOne As Boolean = 1
Dim blnNegOne As Boolean = -1
Dim blnFalse As Boolean = False
```

The following condition, which is based on the implicit conversion of the `Boolean`, works even though the `blnOne` variable was originally assigned a value of `1`:

```
    If blnOne = -1 Then
        Console.WriteLine(blnTrue)
        Console.WriteLine(blnOne.ToString)
        Console.WriteLine(Convert.ToString(Convert.ToInt32(blnNegOne)))
    End If
```

Implicit conversions such as the one in the preceding example work differently from explicit conversions. If you add sample code to explicitly convert the value of a `Boolean` type to an `Integer` type, and then test the result, the integer will be a positive 1. The implicit and explicit conversion of Boolean values is not consistent in Visual Basic. Converting `blnNegOne` to an integer results in a positive value, regardless of what was originally assigned:

```
    If Convert.ToInt16(blnNegOne) = 1 Then
        Console.WriteLine(blnFalse)
        Console.WriteLine(Convert.ToString(Convert.ToInt32(blnFalse)))
    End If
```

The preceding code won't compile if you are using `Option Strict` (more on this later), but it is a good illustration of what you should expect when casting implicitly, rather than explicitly. The output from this code is shown in Figure 2-1.

Figure 2-1

This demonstrates the risk involved in relying on implicitly converted values. If at some point the default value associated with `True` were to change, this code would execute differently. The difference between an explicit and implicit conversion is subtle, and you should ensure the following in order to avoid difficulty:

Always use the `True` *and* `False` *constants when working with Boolean variables.*

The final area where this can be an issue is across languages. Here you need to consider the behavior of a referenced component within your Visual Basic code. You can look at a hypothetical class called `MyCSharpClass` that might have a single method `TestTrue()`. The method doesn't need any parameters; it simply returns a `Boolean`, which is always `True`.

From the Visual Basic example, you can create an instance of `MyCSharpClass` and make calls to the `TestTrue()` method:

```
Dim objMyClass as New MyCSharpClass.MyCSharpClass()

If objMyClass.TestTrue() = 1 Then
    Console.WriteLine("CSharp uses a 1 for true but does it" & _
                  " implicitly convert to a 1 in VB?")
Else
    Console.WriteLine("Even classes implemented in other .NET languages" & _
                  " are evaluated implicitly as -1 in Visual Basic")
End If

If objMyClass.TestTrue() = True Then
    Console.WriteLine("CSharp True always converts to Visual Basic True.")
End If
```

It's probably unclear whether the first conditional in this code will ever work; after all, C# uses a value of 1 to represent `True`. However, this code is running in Visual Basic, so the rules of Visual Basic apply. Even when you return a `Boolean` from a .NET language that uses 1, not -1, to represent `True`, the Visual Basic compiler ensures that the value of `True` is implicitly interpreted as −1. Figure 2-2 illustrates that the behavior of the second conditional is both clear and safe from future modifications of the VB language. If Visual Basic is modified at some future date to no longer use -1 to equate to `True`, then statements that instead compare to the Boolean `True` remain unaffected.

Figure 2-2

To create reusable code, it is always better to avoid implicit conversions. In the case of `Boolean`s, if the code needs to check for an integer value, then you should explicitly evaluate the `Boolean` and create an appropriate integer. The code will be far more maintainable and prone to fewer unexpected results.

The Integer Types

Now that `Boolean`s have been covered in depth, the next step is to examine the `Integer` types that are part of Visual Basic. Visual Basic 6.0 included two types of integer values: The `Integer` type was limited to a maximum value of 32767, and the `Long` type supported a maximum value of 2147483647. The .NET Framework adds a new integer type, the `Short`. The `Short` is the equivalent of the `Integer` value from Visual Basic 6.0; the `Integer` has been promoted to support the range previously supported by the `Long` type, and the `Long` type is bigger than ever. In addition, each of these types also has two alternative types. In all, Visual Basic supports nine `Integer` types:

Type	Allocated Memory	Minimum Value	Maximum Value
Short	2 bytes	−32768	32767
Int16	2 bytes	−32768	32767
UInt16	2 bytes	0	65535
Integer	4 bytes	−2147483648	2147483647
Int32	4 bytes	−2147483648	2147483647
UInt32	4 bytes	0	4294967295
Long	8 bytes	−9223372036854775808	9223372036854775807
Int64	8 bytes	−9223372036854775808	9223372036854775807
UInt64	8 bytes	0	18446744073709551615

Short

A Short value is limited to the maximum value that can be stored in two bytes. This means there are 16 bits and the value can range between −32768 and 32767. This limitation may or may not be based on the amount of memory physically associated with the value; it is a definition of what must occur in the .NET Framework. This is important, because there is no guarantee that the implementation will actually use less memory than when using an Integer value. It is possible that in order to optimize memory or processing, the operating system will allocate the same amount of physical memory used for an Integer type and then just limit the possible values.

The Short (or Int16) value type can be used to map SQL smallint values.

Integer

An Integer is defined as a value that can be safely stored and transported in four bytes (not as a four-byte implementation). This gives the Integer and Int32 value types a range from −2147483648 to 2147483647. This range is more than adequate to handle most tasks.

The main reason to use an Int32 in place of an integer value is to ensure future portability with interfaces. For example, the Integer value in Visual Basic 6.0 was limited to a two-byte value, but is now a four-byte value. In future 64-bit platforms, the Integer value might be an eight-byte value. Problems could occur if an interface used a 64-bit Integer with an interface that expected a 32-bit Integer value, or, conversely, if code using the Integer type is suddenly passed to a variable explicitly declared as Int32. The solution is to be consistent. Use Int32, which would remain a 32-bit value, even on a 64-bit platform, if that is what you need. In addition, as a best practice, use Integer so your code can be unconcerned with the underlying implementation.

The new Integer value type matches the size of an integer value in SQL Server, which means that you can easily align the column type of a table with the variable type in your programs.

Long

The Long type is aligned with the Int64 value. Longs have an eight-byte range, which means that their value can range from –9223372036854775808 to 9223372036854775807. This is a big range, but if you need to add or multiply Integer values, then you need a large value to contain the result. It's common while doing math operations on one type of integer to use a larger type to capture the result if there's a chance that the result could exceed the limit of the types being manipulated.

The Long value type matches the bigint type in SQL.

Unsigned Types

Another way to gain additional range on the positive side of an Integer type is to use one of the unsigned types. The unsigned types provide a useful buffer for holding a result that might exceed an operation by a small amount, but this isn't the main reason they exist. The UInt16 type happens to have the same characteristics as the Character type, while the UInt32 type has the same characteristics as a system memory pointer on a 32-byte system. However, never write code that attempts to leverage this relationship. Such code isn't portable, as on a 64-bit system the system memory pointer changes and uses the UInt64 type. However, when larger integers are needed and all values are known to be positive, these values are of use. As for the low-level uses of these types, certain low-level drivers use this type of knowledge to interface with software that expects these values and are the underlying implementation for other value types. This is why, when you move from a 32-bit to a 64-bit system, you need new drivers for your devices, and why applications shouldn't leverage this same type of logic.

The Decimal Types

Just as there are several types to store integer values, there are three implementations of value types to store real number values. The Single and Double types work the same way in Visual Basic as they did in Visual Basic 6.0. The difference is the Visual Basic 6.0 Currency type (which was a specialized version of a Double type), which is now obsolete; a new Decimal value type takes its place for very large real numbers.

Type	Allocated Memory	Negative Range	Positive Range
Single	4 bytes	– 3.402823E38 to –1.401298E-45	1.401298E-45 to 3.402823E38
Double	8 bytes	– 1.79769313486231E308 to – 4.94065645841247E-324	4.94065645841247E-324 to 1.79769313486232E308
Currency	Obsolete	—	—
Decimal	16 bytes	– 79228162514264337593543950335 to 0.0000000000000000000000000001	0.0000000000000000000000000001 to 79228162514264337593543950335

Single

The Single type contains four bytes of data, and its precision can range anywhere from 1.401298E-45 to 3.402823E38 for positive values and from –3.402823E38 to –1.401298E-45 for negative values.

It can seem strange that a value stored using four bytes (the same as the Integer type) can store a number that is larger than even the Long type. This is possible because of the way in which numbers are stored; a real number can be stored with different levels of precision. Note that there are six digits after the decimal point in the definition of the Single type. When a real number gets very large or very small, the stored value is limited by its significant places.

Because real values contain fewer significant places than their maximum value, when working near the extremes it is possible to lose precision. For example, while it is possible to represent a Long with the value of 9223372036854775805, the Single type rounds this value to 9.223372E18. This seems like a reasonable action to take, but it isn't a reversible action. The following code demonstrates how this loss of precision and data can result in errors:

```
Dim l As Long
Dim s As Single

l = Long.MaxValue
Console.WriteLine(l)

s = Convert.ToSingle(l)
s -= 1000000000000
l = Convert.ToInt64(s)

Console.WriteLine(l)
```

This code creates a Long that has the maximum value possible, and outputs this value. Then it stores the value in a Single, subtracts 1000000000000, stores the value of the Single in the Long, and outputs the results, as shown in Figure 2-3. Notice that the results aren't consistent with what you might expect.

Figure 2-3

As you can see, the result of what is stored in the single where the math operation actually occurs is not accurate in relation to what is computed using the long value. Therefore, both the Single and Double types have limitations, which are eventually addressed with the decimal type.

Double

The behavior of the previous example changes if you replace the value type of Single with Double. A Double uses eight bytes to store values, and as a result has greater precision and range. The range for a Double is from 4.94065645841247E-324 to 1.79769313486232E308 for positive values and from −1.79769313486231E308 to − 4.94065645841247E-324 for negative values. The precision has increased so that a number can contain 15 digits before the rounding begins. This greater level of precision makes the Double value type a much more reliable variable for use in math operations. It's possible to represent most operations with complete accuracy with this value.

Decimal

The Decimal type (new in Visual Basic) is a hybrid that consists of a 12-byte integer value combined with two additional 16-bit values that control the location of the decimal point and the sign of the overall value. A Decimal value consumes 16 bytes in total and can store a maximum value of 79228162514264337593543950335. This value can then be manipulated by adjusting where the decimal place is located. For example, the maximum value while accounting for four decimal places is 7922816251426433759354395.0335. This is because a Decimal isn't stored as a traditional number, but as a 12-byte integer value, with the location of the decimal in relation to the available 28 digits. This means that a Decimal does not inherently round numbers the way a Double does.

As a result of the way values are stored, the closest precision to zero that a Decimal supports is 0.0000000000000000000000000001. The location of the decimal point is stored separately, and the decimal type also stores a value that indicates whether its value is positive or negative separately from the actual value. This means that the positive and negative ranges are exactly the same, regardless of the number of decimal places.

Thus, the system makes a trade-off whereby the need to store a larger number of decimal places reduces the maximum value that can be kept at that level of precision. This trade-off makes a lot of sense. After all, it's not often that you need to store a number with 15 digits on both sides of the decimal point, and for those cases you can create a custom class that manages the logic and leverages one or more decimal values as its properties.

Char and Byte

The default character set under Visual Basic is Unicode. Therefore, when a variable is declared as type Char, Visual Basic creates a two-byte value, since, by default, all characters in the Unicode character set require two bytes. Visual Basic supports the declaration of a character value in three ways. Placing a c following a literal string informs the compiler that the value should be treated as a character, or the Chr and ChrW methods can be used. The following code snippet shows that all three of these options work similarly, with the difference between the Chr and ChrW methods being the range of valid input values that is available. The ChrW method allows for a broader range of values based on wide character input.

```
Dim chrLtr_a As Char = "a"c
Dim chrAsc_a As Char = Chr(97)
Dim chrAsc_b as Char = ChrW(98)
```

To convert characters into a string suitable for an ASCII interface, the runtime library needs to validate each character's value to ensure that it is within a valid range. This could have a performance impact for certain serial arrays. Fortunately, Visual Basic supports the Byte value type. This type contains a value between 0 and 255 that exactly matches the range of the ASCII character set. When interfacing with a system that uses ASCII, it is best to use a `Byte` array. The runtime knows there is no need to perform a Unicode-to-ASCII conversion for a `Byte` array, so the interface between the systems operates significantly faster.

In Visual Basic, the `Byte` value type expects a numeric value. Thus, to assign the letter "a" to a `Byte`, you must use the appropriate character code. One option to get the numeric value of a letter is to use the `Asc` method, as shown here:

```
Dim bytLtrA as Byte = Asc("a")
```

DateTime

The Visual Basic `Date` keyword has always supported a structure of both date and time. You can, in fact, declare date values using both the `DateTime` and `Date` types. Note that internally Visual Basic no longer stores a date value as a `Double`; however, it provides key methods for converting the current internal date representation to the legacy `Double` type. The `ToOADate` and `FromOADate` methods support backward compatibility during migration from previous versions of Visual Basic.

Visual Basic also provides a set of shared methods that provides some common dates. The concept of shared methods is described in more detail in the next chapter, which covers object syntax, but, in short, shared methods are available even when you don't create an instance of a class. For the `DateTime` structure, the `Now()` method returns a `Date` value with the local date and time. This method has not been changed from Visual Basic 6.0, but the `Today()` and `UtcNow()` methods have also been added. These methods can be used to initialize a `Date` object with the current local date, or the date and time based on Universal Coordinated Time (also known as Greenwich Mean Time), respectively. You can use these shared methods to initialize your classes, as shown in the following code sample:

```
Dim dteNow as Date = Now()
Dim dteToday as Date = Today()
Dim dteGMT as DateTime = DateTime.UtcNow()
```

Reference Types (Classes)

A lot of the power of Visual Basic is harnessed in objects. An object is defined by its class, which describes what data, methods, and other attributes an instance of that class supports. Thousands of classes are provided in the .NET Framework class library.

When code instantiates an object from a class, the object created is a reference type. Recall that the data contained in value and reference types is stored in different locations, but this is not the only difference between them. A class (which is the typical way to refer to a reference type) has additional capabilities, such as support for protected methods and properties, enhanced event-handling capabilities, constructors, and finalizers, and can be extended with a custom base class via inheritance. Classes can also be used to define how operators such as "=" and "+" work on an instance of the class.

The intention of this chapter is to introduce you to some commonly used classes, and to complement your knowledge of the common value types already covered. Chapters 3 and 4 contain a detailed look at object orientation in Visual Basic. This chapter examines the features of the `Object`, `String`, `DBNull`, and `Array` classes, as well as the `Collection` classes found in the `System.Collections` namespace.

The Object Class

The Object class is the base class for every type in .NET, both value and reference types. At its core, every variable is an object and can be treated as such. You can think of the Object class (in some ways) as the replacement for the Variant type found in COM and COM-based versions of Visual Basic, but take care. COM, a Variant type, represents a variant memory location; in Visual Basic, an Object type represents a reference to an instance of the Object class. In COM, a Variant is implemented to provide a reference to a memory area on the heap, but its definition doesn't define any specific ways of accessing this data area. As you'll see during this look at objects, an instance of an "object" includes all the information needed to define the actual type of that object.

Because the Object class is the basis of all types, you can assign any variable to an object. Reference types maintain their current reference and implementation but are generically handled, whereas value types are packaged into a box and placed into the memory location associated with the Object. For example, there are instance methods that are available on Object, such as ToString. This method, if implemented, returns a string representation of an instance value. Because the Object class defines it, it can be called on any object:

```
Dim objMyClass as New MyClass("Hello World")

Console.WriteLine(objMyClass.ToString)
```

This brings up the question of how the Object class knows how to convert custom classes to String objects. The answer is that it doesn't. For this method to actually return the data in an instance of a String, a class must override this method. Otherwise, when this code is run, the default version of this method defined at the Object level returns the name of the current class (MyClass) as its string representation. This section will be clearer after you read Chapter 3. The key point is that if you create an implementation of ToString() in your class definition, then even when an instance of your object is cast to the type Object, your custom method will still be called. The following snippet shows how to create a generic object under the Option Strict syntax:

```
Dim objVar as Object

objVar = Me

CType(objVar, Form).Text = "New Dialog Title Text"
```

That Object is then assigned a copy of the current instance of a Visual Basic form. In order to access the Text property of the original Form class, the Object must be cast from its declared type of Object to its actual type (Form), which supports the Text property. The CType command (covered later) accepts the object as its first parameter, and the class name (without quotes) as its second parameter. In this case, the current instance variable is of type Form, and by casting this variable, the code can reference the Text property of the current form.

The String Class

Another class that plays a large role in most development projects is the String class. Having Strings defined as a class is more powerful than the Visual Basic 6.0 datatype of String that you may be more familiar with. The String class is a special class within .NET, because it is the one primitive type that is not a value type. To make String objects compatible with some of the underlying behavior in .NET, they have some interesting characteristics.

These methods are shared, which means that the methods are not specific to any instance of a String. The String class also contains several other methods that are called based on an instance of a specific String object. The methods on the String class replace the functions that Visual Basic 6.0 had as part of the language for string manipulation, and they perform operations such as inserting strings, splitting strings, and searching strings.

String()

The String class has several different constructors for those situations in which you aren't simply assigning an existing value to a new string. The term *constructor* is expanded upon in Chapter 3. Constructors are methods that are used to construct an instance of a class. String() would be the default constructor for the String class, but the String class does not expose this constructor publicly. The following example shows the most common method of creating a String:

```
Dim strConstant as String = "ABC"
Dim strRepeat as New String("A"c, 20)
```

A variable is declared of type string and as a primitive is assigned the value 'ABC'. The second declaration uses one of the parameterized versions of the String constructor. This constructor accepts two parameters: The first is a character and the second is the number of times that character should be repeated in the string.

In addition to creating an instance of a string and then calling methods on your variable, the String class has several shared methods. A shared method refers to a method on a class that does not require an instance of that class. Shared methods are covered in more detail in relation to objects in Chapter 3; for the purpose of this chapter, the point is that you can reference the class string followed by a "." and see a list of shared methods for that class. For strings, this list includes the following:

Shared Methods	Description
Empty	This is actually a property. It can be used when an empty String is required. It can be used for comparison or initialization of a String.
Compare	Compares two objects of type String
CompareOrdinal	Compares two Strings, without considering the local national language or culture
Concat	Concatenates one or more Strings
Copy	Creates a new String with the same value as an instance provided
Equals	Determines whether two Strings have the same value
Equality operator (=)	An overloaded version of the equality operator that compares two String objects
Inequality operator (op_Inequality)	A method that accepts two String objects for comparison. The method returns True if the objects are not equal.
IsNullorEmpty	This static method is a very efficient way of determining whether a given variable has been set to the empty string or Nothing.

Not only have creation methods been encapsulated, but other string-specific methods, such as character and substring searching, and case changes, are now available from String objects instances.

The SubString Method

The .NET String class has a method called SubString. Thanks to overloading, covered in Chapter 3, there are two versions of this method: The first accepts a starting position and the number of characters to retrieve, while the second accepts simply the starting location. The following code shows examples of using both of these methods on an instance of a String:

```
Dim strMyString as String = "Hello World"

Console.WriteLine(strMystring.SubString(0,5))
Console.WriteLine(strMyString.SubString(6))
```

The PadLeft and PadRight Methods

These methods enable you to justify a String so that it is left- or right-justified. As with SubString, the PadLeft and PadRight methods are overloaded. The first version of these methods requires only a maximum length of the String, and then uses spaces to pad the String. The other version requires two parameters: the length of the returned String and the character that should be used to pad the original String. An example of working with the PadLeft method is as follows:

```
Dim strMyString as String = "Hello World"

Console.WriteLine(strMyString.PadLeft(30))
Console.WriteLine(strMyString.PadLeft(20,"."c))
```

The String Class Is Immutable

The Visual Basic String class isn't entirely different from the String type that VB programmers have used for years. The majority of string behaviors remain unchanged, and the majority of methods are now available as methods. However, to support the default behavior that people associate with the String primitive type, the String class isn't declared in the same way as several other classes. Strings in .NET do not allow editing of their data. When a portion of a string is changed or copied, the operating system allocates a new memory location and copies the resulting string to this new location. This ensures that when a string is copied to a second variable, the new variable references its own copy.

To support this behavior in .NET, the String class is defined as an *immutable class*. This means that each time a change is made to the data associated with a string, a new instance is created, and the original referenced memory is released for garbage collection. This is an expensive operation, but the result is that the String class behaves as people expect a primitive type to behave. Additionally, when a copy of a string is made, the String class forces a new version of the data into the referenced memory. This ensures that each instance of a string references only its own memory. Consider the following code:

```
Dim strMyString as String
Dim intLoop as Integer

For intLoop = 1 to 1000
    strMyString = strMyString & "A very long string "
Next
Console.WriteLine(strMyString)
```

This code does not perform well. For each assignment operation on the `strMyString` variable, the system allocates a new memory buffer based on the size of the new string, and copies both the current value of `strMyString` and the new text that is to be appended. The system then frees the previous memory that must be reclaimed by the garbage collector. As this loop continues, the new memory allocation requires a larger chunk of memory. The result is that operations such as this can take a long time. However, .NET offers an alternative in the `System.Text.StringBuilder` object, shown in the following sample code:

```
Dim objMyStrBldr as New System.Text.StringBuilder()
Dim intLoop as Integer

For intLoop = 1 to 1000
    ObjMyStrBldr.Append("A very long string ")
Next
Console.WriteLine(objMyStrBldr.ToString())
```

The preceding code works with strings but does not use the `String` class. The .NET class library contains a class called `System.Text.StringBuilder`, which performs better when strings will be edited repeatedly. This class does not store strings in the conventional manner; it stores them as individual characters, with code in place to manage the ordering of those characters. Thus, editing or appending more characters does not involve allocating new memory for the entire string. Because the preceding code snippet does not need to reallocate the memory used for the entire string, each time another set of characters is appended it performs significantly faster. Ultimately, an instance of the `String` class is never explicitly needed because the `StringBuilder` class implements the `ToString` method to roll up all of the characters into a string. While the concept of the `StringBuilder` class isn't new, the fact that it is now available as part of the Visual Basic implementation means developers no longer need to create their own string memory managers.

String Constants

If you ever have to produce output based on a string you'll quickly find yourself needing to embed certain constant values. For example, it's always useful to be able to add a carriage-return linefeed combination to trigger a new line in a message box. One way to do this is to learn the underlying ASCII codes and then embed these control characters directly into your string or string-builder object.

Visual Basic provides an easier solution for working with these: the Microsoft.VisualBasic.Constants class. The Constants class, which you can tell by its namespace is specific to Visual Basic, contains definitions for several standard string values that you might want to embed. The most common, of course, is Constants.VbCrLf, which represents the carriage return linefeed combination. Feel free to explore this class for additional constants that you might need to manipulate string output.

The DBNull Class and IsDBNull() Function

When working with a database, a value for a given column may not be defined. For a reference type this isn't a problem, as it is possible to set reference types to Nothing. However, for value types, it is necessary to determine whether a given column from the database or other source has an actual value. The first way to manage this task is to leverage the DBNull call and the IsDBNull function. The `IsDBNull` function accepts an object as its parameter and returns a `Boolean` that indicates whether the variable has been initialized.

In addition to this method, Visual Basic has access to the DBNull class. This class is part of the System namespace, and to use it you declare a local variable with the DBNull type. This variable is then used with an is comparison operator to determine whether a given variable has been initialized:

```
Dim sysNull As System.DBNull = System.DBNull.Value
Dim strMyString As String = Nothing

If strMyString Is sysNull Then
  strMyString = "Initialize my String"
End If
If Not IsDBNull(strMyString) Then
  Console.WriteLine(strMyString)
End If
```

In this code, the strMyString variable is declared and initialized to Nothing. The first conditional is evaluated to True, and as a result the string is initialized. The second conditional then ensures that the declared variable has been initialized. Because this was accomplished in the preceding code, this condition is also True. In both cases, the sysNull value is used not to verify the type of the object, but to verify that it has not yet been instantiated with a value.

Nullable Types

In addition to having the option to explicitly check for the DBNull value, with Visual Basic 2005 you can create a nullable value type. In the background, when this syntax is used, the system creates a reference type containing the same data that would be used by the value type. Your code can then check the value of the nullable type before attempting to set this into a value type variable. Nullable types are built using generics, discussed in Chapter 7.

For consistency, however, let's take a look at how nullable types work. The key, of course, is that value types can't be set to null. This is why nullable types aren't value types. The following statements shows how to declare a nullable integer:

```
Dim intValue as Nullable(Of Integer)
```

The intValue variable acts like an integer, but isn't actually an integer. As noted, the syntax is based on generics, which are covered in Chapter 7, but essentially you have just declared an object of type Nullable and declared that this object will in fact hold integer data. Thus, both of the following assignment statements are valid:

```
intValue = 123
intValue = Nothing
```

However, at some point you are going to need to pass intValue to a method as a parameter, or set some property on an object that is looking for an object of type Integer. Because intValue is actually of type Nullable, it has the properties of a nullable object. The nullable class has two properties of interest when you want to get the underlying value. The first is the property value. This represents the underlying value type associated with this object. In an ideal scenario you would just use the value property of the nullable object in order to assign to your actual value a type of integer and everything would work. If the intValue.value wasn't assigned, you would get the same value as if you had just declared a new Integer without assigning it a value.

Unfortunately, that's not how the nullable type works. If the `intValue.value` property contains `Nothing` and you attempt to assign it, then it throws an exception. To avoid getting this exception you always need to check the other property of the nullable type: `HasValue`. The HasValue property is a Boolean that indicates whether a value exists; if one does not, then you shouldn't reference the underlying value. The following code is an example of how to safely use a nullable type:

```
Dim int as Integer
If intValue.HasValue Then
  int = intValue.Value
End If
```

Of course, you could add an `Else` statement to the preceding and use either `Integer.MinValue` or `Integer.MaxValue` as an indicator that the original value was `Nothing`. The key point here is that nullable types enable you to easily work with nullable columns in your database, but you must still verify whether an actual value or null was returned.

Arrays

It is possible to declare any type as an array of that type. Because an array is a modifier of another type, the basic `Array` class is never explicitly declared for a variable's type. The `System.Array` class that serves as the base for all arrays is defined such that it cannot be created, but must be inherited. As a result, to create an `Integer` array, a set of parentheses is added to the declaration of the variable. These parentheses indicate that the system should create an array of the type specified. The parentheses used in the declaration may be empty or may contain the size of the array. An array can be defined as having a single dimension using a single number, or as having multiple dimensions.

All .NET arrays at an index of zero have a defined number of elements. However, the way an array is declared in Visual Basic varies slightly from other .NET languages such as C#. When the new .NET version of Visual Basic was announced, it was also announced that arrays would always begin at 0 and that they would be defined based on the number of elements in the array. In other words, Visual Basic would work the same way as the other initial .NET languages. However, in older versions of Visual Basic, it is possible to specify that an array should start at 1 instead of 0. This meant that a lot of existing code didn't define arrays based on their upper limit. To resolve this issue, the engineers at Microsoft decided on a compromise: All arrays in .NET begin at 0, but when an array is declared in Visual Basic, the definition is based on the upper limit of the array, not the number of elements.

The main result of this upper-limit declaration is that arrays defined in Visual Basic have one more entry by definition than those defined with other .NET languages. Note that it's still possible to declare an array in Visual Basic and reference it in C# or another .NET language. The following code illustrates some simple examples to demonstrate five different ways of creating arrays, using a simple integer array as the basis for the comparison:

```
Dim arrMyIntArray1(20) as Integer
Dim arrMyIntArray2() as Integer = {1, 2, 3, 4}
Dim arrMyIntArray3(4,2) as Integer
Dim arrMyIntArray4( , ) as Integer = _
    { {1, 2, 3},{4, 5, 6}, {7, 8, 9},{10, 11, 12},{13, 14 , 15} }
Dim arrMyIntArray5() as Integer
```

In the first case, the code defines an array of integers that spans from `arrMyIntArray1(0)` to `arrMyIntArray1(20)`. This is a 21-element array, because all arrays start at 0 and end with the value defined in the declaration as the upper bound. The second statement creates an array with four elements numbered 0 through 3, containing the values 1 to 4. The third statement creates a multidimensional array containing five elements at the first level, with each of those elements containing three child elements. The challenge is to remember that all subscripts go from 0 to the upper bound, meaning that each array contains one more element than its upper bound. The result is an array with 15 elements. The next line of code, the fourth, shows an alternative way of creating the same array, but in this case there are four elements, each containing four elements, with subscripts from 0 to 3 at each level. Finally, the last line demonstrates that it is possible to simply declare a variable and indicate that the variable is an array, without specifying the number of elements in that array.

Multidimensional Arrays

As shown earlier in the sample array declarations, the definition of `arrMyIntArray3` is a multidimensional array. This declaration creates an array with 15 elements (five in the first range, each containing three elements) ranging from `arrMyIntArray3(0,0)` through `arrMyIntArray3(2,1)` to `arrMyIntArray3(4,2)`. As with all elements of an array, when it is created without specific values, the value of each of these elements is created with the default value for that type. This case also demonstrates that the size of the different dimensions can vary. It is possible to nest deeper than two levels, but this should be done with care because such code is difficult to maintain.

The fourth declaration shown previously creates `arrMyIntArray4(, )` with predefined values. The values are mapped based on the outer set being the first dimension and the inner values being associated with the next inner dimension. For example, the value of `arrMyIntArray4(0,1)` is 2, while the value of `arrMyIntArray4(2,3)` is 12. The following code snippet illustrates this using a set of nested loops to traverse the array. Additionally, it provides an example of calling the `UBound` method with a second parameter to specify that you are interested in the upper bound for the second dimension of the array:

```
Dim intLoop1 as Integer
Dim intLoop2 as Integer
For intLoop1 = 0 to UBound(arrMyIntArray4)
  For intLoop2 = 0 to UBound(arrMyIntArray4, 2)
    Console.WriteLine arrMyIntArray4(intLoop1, intLoop2).ToString
  Next
Next
```

The UBound Function

Continuing to reference the arrays defined earlier, the declaration of `arrMyIntArray2` actually defined an array that spans from `arrMyIntArray2(0)` to `arrMyIntArray2(3)`. This is the case because when you declare an array by specifying the set of values, it still starts at 0. However, in this case you are not specifying the upper bound, but rather initializing the array with a set of values. If this set of values came from a database or other source, then it might not be clear what the upper limit on the array was. To verify the upper bound of an array, a call can be made to the `UBound` function:

```
Console.Writeline CStr(UBound(ArrMyIntArray2))
```

The preceding line of code retrieves the upper bound of the first dimension of the array. However, as noted in the preceding section, it is possible to specify an array with several different dimensions. Thus, this old-style method of retrieving the error carries the potential for an error of omission. The better way to retrieve the upper bound is to use the `GetUpperBound` method. In this case, you need to tell the array which upper-bound value you want, as shown here:

```
ArrMyIntArray2.GetUpperBound(0)
```

This is the preferred method of getting an array's upper bound because it explicitly indicates which upper bound is wanted when using multidimensional arrays.

The `UBound` function has a companion called `LBound`. The `LBound` function computes the lower bound for a given array. However, as all arrays and collections in Visual Basic are 0-based, it doesn't have much value anymore.

The ReDim Statement

The final declaration demonstrated previously is for `arrMyIntArray5()`. This is an example of an array that has not yet been instantiated. If an attempt were made to assign a value to this array, it would trigger an exception. The solution to this is to use the `ReDim` keyword. Although `ReDim` was part of Visual Basic 6.0, it has changed slightly. The first change is that code must first `Dim` an instance of the variable; it is not acceptable to declare an array using the `ReDim` statement. The second change is that code cannot change the number of dimensions in an array. For example, an array with three dimensions cannot grow to an array of four dimensions, nor can it be reduced to only two dimensions. To further extend the example code associated with arrays, consider the following, which manipulates some of the arrays previously declared. Note that the `arrMyIntArray5` declaration was repeated for this example because this variable isn't actually usable until after it is re-dimensioned in the following code:

```
Dim arrMyIntArray5() as Integer
' The commented statement below would compile but would cause a runtime exception.
'arrMyIntArray5(0) = 1

ReDim arrMyIntArray5(2)
ReDim arrMyIntArray3(5,4)
ReDim Preserve arrMyIntArray4(UBound(arrMyIntArray4),2)
```

The `ReDim` of `arrMyIntArray5` instantiates the elements of the array so that values can be assigned to each element. The second statement redimensions the `arrMyIntArray3` variable defined earlier. Note that it is changing the size of both the first and the second dimension. While it is not possible to change the number of dimensions in an array, it is possible to resize any of an array's dimensions. This capability is required if declarations such as `Dim arrMyIntArray6( , , )  As Integer` are to be legal.

By the way, while it is possible to repeatedly `ReDim` a variable, this is the type of action that should ideally be done only rarely, and never within a loop. If you intend to loop through a set of entries and add entries to an array, try to determine the number of entries you'll need before entering the loop, or at a minimum `ReDim` the size of your array in chunks to improve performance.

The Preserve Keyword

The last item in the code snippet in the preceding section illustrates an additional keyword associated with redimensioning. The `Preserve` keyword indicates that the data stored in the array prior to redimensioning should be transferred to the newly created array. If this keyword is not used, then the data stored in an array is lost. Additionally, in the preceding example, the `ReDim` statement actually reduces the second dimension of the array. While this is a perfectly legal statement, note that this means that even though you have asked to preserve the data, the data values 4, 8, 12, and 16 that were assigned in the original definition of this array will be discarded. These are lost because they were assigned in the highest index of the second array. Because `arrMyIntArray4(1,3)` is no longer valid, the value that resided at this location has been lost.

Arrays continue to be very powerful in Visual Basic, but the basic Array class is just that, basic. While it provides a powerful framework, it does not provide a lot of other features that would allow for more robust logic to be built into the array. To achieve more advanced features, such as sorting and dynamic allocation, the base `Array` class has been inherited by the classes that make up the `Collections` namespace.

Collections

The `Collections` namespace is part of the `System` namespace and provides a series of classes that implement advanced array features. While the capability to make an array of existing types is powerful, sometimes more power is needed in the array itself. The ability to inherently sort or dynamically add dissimilar objects in an array is provided by the classes of the `Collections` namespace. This namespace contains a specialized set of objects that can be instantiated for additional features when working with a collection of similar objects. The following table defines several of the objects that are available as part of the `System.Collections` namespace:

Class	Description
ArrayList	Implements an array whose size increases automatically as elements are added
BitArray	Manages an array of Booleans that are stored as bit values
Hashtable	Implements a collection of values organized by key. Sorting is done based on a hash of the key
Queue	Implements a first in, first out collection
SortedList	Implements a collection of values with associated keys. The values are sorted by key and are accessible by key or index.
Stack	Implements a last in, first out collection

Each of the objects listed is focused on storing a collection of objects. This means that in addition to the special capabilities each provides, it also provides one additional capability not available to objects created based on the `Array` class. In short, because every variable in .NET is based on the `Object` class, it is possible to have a collection defined, because one of these objects contains elements that are defined with different types. This is true because each of these collection types stores an array of objects, and since all classes are of type `Object`, a string could be stored alongside an integer value. The result is that it's possible within the collection classes for the actual objects being stored to be different. Consider the following example code:

```
Dim objMyArrList As New System.Collections.ArrayList()
Dim objItem As Object
Dim intLine As Integer = 1
Dim strHello As String = "Hello"
Dim objWorld As New System.Text.StringBuilder("World")

' Add an integer value to the array list.
objMyArrList.Add(intLine)

' Add an instance of a string object
objMyArrList.Add(strHello)

' Add a single character cast as a character.
objMyArrList.Add(" "c)

' Add an object that isn't a primitive type.
objMyArrList.Add(objWorld)

' To balance the string, insert a break between the line
' and the string "Hello", by inserting a string constant.
objMyArrList.Insert(1, ". ")

For Each objItem In objMyArrList
   ' Output the values...
   Console.Write(objItem.ToString())
Next
```

The preceding code is an example of implementing the new `ArrayList` collection class. The collection classes, as this example shows, are versatile. The preceding code creates a new instance of an ArrayList, along with some related variables to support the demonstration. The code then shows four different types of variables being inserted into the same ArrayList. Next, the code inserts another value into the middle of the list. At no time has the size of the array been declared, nor has a redefinition of the array size been required.

Part of the reason for this is that the `Add` and `Insert` methods on the `ArrayList` class are defined to accept a parameter of type `Object`. This means that the `ArrayList` object can literally accept any value in .NET. This comes at a slight performance cost for those variables that are value types because of boxing.

Specialized and Generic Collections

Visual Basic has additional classes available as part of the `System.Collections.Specialized` name-space. These classes tend to be oriented around a specific problem. For example, the `ListDictionary` class is designed to take advantage of the fact that while a hash table is very good at storing and retrieving a large number of items, it can be costly when there are only a few items. Similarly, the `StringCollection` and `StringDictionary` classes are defined so that when working with strings, the time spent interpreting the type of object is reduced and overall performance is improved. Each class defined in this namespace represents a specialized implementation that has been optimized for handling specific datatypes.

This specialization is different from the specialization provided by one of Visual Studio 2005's new features, generics. The `System.Collections.Generics` namespace contains versions of the collection classes that have been defined to support generics. The basic idea of generics is that because there are performance cost and reliability concerns associated with casting to and from the object type, collections should allow you to specify what specific type they will contain. Generics not only prevent you from paying the cost of boxing for value types but, more important, add to the capability to create type-safe code at compile time. Generics are a powerful extension to the .NET environment and are covered in detail in Chapter 7.

Boxing

Normally, when a conversion (implicit or explicit) occurs, the original value is read from its current memory location, and then the new value is assigned. For example, to convert a `Short` to a `Long`, the system reads the two bytes of `Short` data and writes them to the appropriate bytes for the `Long` variable. However, under Visual Basic, if a value type needs to be managed as an object, then the system performs an intermediate step. This intermediate step involves taking the value on the stack and copying it to the heap, a process referred to as *boxing*. As noted earlier, the `Object` class is implemented as a reference type, so the system needs to convert value types into reference types for them to be objects. This doesn't cause any problems or require any special programming, because boxing isn't something you declare or directly control, but it does affect performance.

If you're copying the data for a single value type, this is not a significant cost. However, if you're processing an array that contains thousands of values, the time spent moving between a value type and a temporary reference type can be significant.

Fortunately, there are ways to limit the amount of boxing that occurs. One method that works well is to create a class based on the value type you need to work with. This might seem counterintuitive at first because it costs more to create a class. The key is how often you reuse the data contained in the class. By repeatedly using the object to interact with other objects, you avoid the creation of a temporary boxed object.

Examples in two important areas will help illustrate boxing. The first involves the use of arrays. When an array is created, the portion of the class that tracks the element of the array is created as a reference object, but each element of the array is created directly. Thus, an array of integers consists of the array object and a set of integer value types. When you update one of these values with another integer value, no boxing is involved:

```
Dim arrInt(20) as Integer
Dim intMyValue as Integer = 1

arrInt(0) = 0
arrInt(1) = intMyValue
```

Neither of these assignments of an integer value into the integer array that was defined previously requires boxing. In each case, the array object identifies which value on the stack needs to be referenced, and the value is assigned to that value type. The point here is that just because you have referenced an object doesn't mean you are going to box a value. The boxing occurs only when the values being assigned are being transitioned from value to reference types:

```
Dim strBldr as New System.Text.StringBuilder()
Dim mySortedList as New System.Collections.SortedList()
Dim count as Integer
For count = 1 to 100
  strBldr.Append(count)
  mySortedList.Add(count, count)
Next
```

The preceding snippet illustrates two separate calls to object interfaces. One of these calls requires boxing of the value `intCount`, while the other does not. There is nothing in the code to indicate which call is which. The answer is that the `Append` method of `StringBuilder` has been overridden to include a version that accepts an integer, while the `Add` method of `SortedList` collection expects two objects. Although the integer values can be recognized by the system as objects, doing so requires the runtime library to box these values so that they can be added to the sorted list.

The key to boxing isn't that you are working with objects as part of an action, but that you are passing a value to a parameter that expects an object, or you are taking an object and converting it to a value type. However, boxing does not occur when you call a method on a value type. There is no conversion to an object, so if you need to assign an integer to a string using the `ToString` method, there is no boxing of the integer value as part of the creation of the string. Conversely, you are explicitly creating a new string object, so the cost is similar.

Parameter Passing

When an object's methods or an assembly's procedures and methods are called, it's often appropriate to provide input for the data to be operated on by the code. The values are referred to as *parameters*, and any object can be passed as a parameter to a Function or Sub.

When passing parameters, be aware of whether the parameter is being passed "by value" (ByVal) or "by reference" (ByRef). Passing a parameter by value means that if the value of that variable is changed, then when the Function/Sub returns, the system automatically restores that variable to the value it had before the call. Passing a parameter by reference means that if changes are made to the value of a variable, then these changes affect the actual variable and, therefore, are still present when the variable returns.

This is where it gets a little challenging for new Visual Basic developers. Under .NET, passing a parameter by value indicates only how the top-level reference (the portion of the variable on the stack) for that object is passed. Sometimes referred to as a *shallow copy operation*, the system copies only the top-level reference value for an object passed by value. This is important to remember because it means that referenced memory is not protected. When you pass an integer by value, if the program changes the value of the integer, then your original value is restored. However, if you pass a reference type, only the location of your referenced memory is protected, not the data located within that memory location. Thus, while the reference passed as part of the parameter remains unchanged for the calling method, the actual values stored in referenced objects can be updated even when an object is passed by value.

In addition to mandatory parameters, which must be passed with a call to a given function, it is possible to declare optional parameters. Optional parameters can be omitted by the calling code. This way, it is possible to call a method such as PadRight, passing either with a single parameter defining the length of the string and using a default of space for the padding character, or with two parameters, the first still defining the length of the string but the second now replacing the default of space with a dash.

```
Public Function PadRight(ByVal intSize as Integer, _
                         Optional ByVal chrPad as Char = " "c)
End Function
```

To use default parameters, it is necessary to make them the last parameters in the function declaration. Visual Basic also requires that every optional parameter have a default value. It is not acceptable just to declare a parameter and assign it the Optional keyword. In Visual Basic, the Optional keyword must be accompanied by a value that is assigned if the parameter is not passed in.

ParamArray

In addition to passing explicit parameters, it is also possible to tell .NET that you would like to allow a user to pass any number of parameters of the same type. This is called a *parameter array*, and it enables a user to pass as many instances of a given parameter as are appropriate. For example, the following code creates a function Add, which allows a user to pass an array of integers and get the sum of these integers:

```
Public Function Add(ByVal ParamArray values() As Integer) As Long
    Dim result As Long = 0
    For Each value As Integer In values
        result += value
    Next
    Return result
End Function
```

The preceding code illustrates a function (which was first shown at the start of this chapter without its implementation) that accepts an array of integers. Notice that the ParamArray qualifier is preceded by a ByVal qualifier for this parameter. The ParamArray requires that the associated parameters be passed by value and cannot be optional parameters.

You might think this looks like a standard parameter passed by value except that it's an array, but there is more to it than that. In fact, the power of the ParamArray is how it can be called, which also explains many of its limitations. The following code shows one way this method can be called:

```
Dim int1 as Integer = 2
Dim int2 as Integer = 3
Dim sum as Long = Add(1, int1, int2)
```

Notice that the preceding line, which calls this Add function, doesn't pass an array of integers; instead, it passes three distinct integer values. The ParamArray keyword tells Visual Basic to automatically join these three distinct values into an array for use within this method. However, notice that the following lines also represent an acceptable way to call this method, by passing an actual array of values:

```
Dim myIntArray() as Integer = {1, 2, 3, 4}
Dim sum as Long = Add(myIntArray)
```

Finally, note one last limitation on the ParamArray keyword — it can only be used on the last parameter defined for a given method. Because Visual Basic is grabbing an unlimited number of input values to create the array, there is no way to indicate the end of this array, so it must be the final parameter.

Variable Scope

The concept of variable scope encapsulates two key elements. In all the discussion so far of variables, we have not focused on the allocation and deallocation of those variables from memory. The first allocation challenge is related to what happens when you declare two variables with the same name but at different locations in the code. For example, suppose a class declares a variable called myObj that holds a property for that class. Then, within one of that class's methods, you declare a different variable also named myObj. What will happen in that method? Scope defines the lifetime and precedence of every variable you declare, and it handles this question.

Similarly, there is question of the removal of variables that you are no longer using, so you can free up memory. Chapter 5 deals with the collection of variables and memory once it is no longer needed by an application, so this discussion focuses on priority, with the understanding that when a variable is no longer "in scope," it is available to the garbage collector for cleanup.

.NET essentially defines four levels of variables scope. The outermost scope is *global*. Essentially, just as your source code defines classes, it can also declare variables that exist the entire time that your application runs. These variables have the longest lifetime because they exist as long as your application is executing. Conversely, these variables have the lowest precedence. Thus, if within a class or method you declare another variable with the same name, then the variable with the smaller, more local scope is used before the global version.

After global scope, the next scope is at the *class* or *module* level. When you add properties to a class, you are creating variables that will be created with each instance of that class. The methods of that class will then reference those member variables from the class, before looking for any global variables. Note that because these variables are defined within a class, they are only visible to methods within that class. The scope and lifetime of these variables is limited by the lifetime of that class, and when the class is removed from the system so are those variables. More important, those variables declared in one instance of a class are not visible in other classes or in other instances of the same class (unless you actively expose them, in which case the object instance is used to fully qualify a reference to them.) This concept is explored further in Chapter 3.

The next shorter lifetime and smaller scope is that of method variables. When you declare a new variable within a method, such variables as well as those declared as parameters are only visible to code that exists within that module. Thus, the method Add wouldn't see or use variables declared in the method Subtract in the same class.

Finally, within a given method are various commands that can encapsulate a block of code (discussed later in this chapter). Commands such as If Then and For Each create blocks of code within a method, and it is possible within this block of code to declare new variables. These variables then have a scope of only that block of code. Thus, variables declared within an If Then block or a For loop only exist within the constraints of the If block or execution of the loop. Creating variables in a For loop is a known performance mistake and should be avoided.

Datatype Conversions

So far, this chapter has focused primarily on individual variables. However, when developing software, it is often necessary to take a numeric value and convert it to a string to display in a text box. Similarly, it is often necessary to accept input from a text box and convert this input to a numeric value. These conversions, unlike some, can be done in one of two fashions: implicitly or explicitly.

Implicit conversions are those that rely on the system taking the data at runtime and adjusting it to the new type without any guidance. Often, Visual Basic's default settings allow developers to write code containing many implicit conversions that the developer may not even notice.

Explicit conversions, conversely, are those for which the developer recognizes the need to change a variable's type and assign it to a different variable. Unlike implicit conversions, explicit conversions are easily recognizable within the code. Some languages such as C# require that essentially all conversions that might be type unsafe be done through an explicit conversion; otherwise, an error is thrown.

It is therefore important to understand what a type-safe implicit conversion is. In short, it's a conversion that by nature of the data involved cannot fail. For example, if you assign the value of a smaller type, Short, into a larger type, Long, then there is no way this conversion can fail. As both values are integer-style numbers, and the maximum and minimum values of a Short variable are well within the range of a Long, this conversion will always succeed and can safely be handled as an implicit conversion:

```
Dim shortNumber As Short = 32767
Dim longNumber As Long = shortNumber
```

However, the reverse of this is not a type-safe conversion. In a system that demands explicit conversions, the assignment of a Long value to a Short variable results in a compilation error, as the compiler doesn't have any safe way of handling the assignment when the larger value is outside the range of the smaller value. It is still possible to explicitly cast a value from a larger type to a smaller type, but this is an explicit conversion. By default, Visual Basic supports certain unsafe implicit conversions. Thus, adding the following line will not, by default, cause an error under Visual Basic:

```
shortNumber = longNumber
```

This is possible for two reasons. One is based on Visual Basic's legacy support. Previous versions of Visual Basic supported the capability to implicitly cast across types that don't fit the traditional implicit casting boundaries. It has been maintained in the language because one of the goals of Visual Basic is to support rapid prototyping. In a rapid prototyping model, a developer is writing code that "works" for demonstration purposes but may not be ready for deployment. This distinction is important because in the discussion of implicit conversions, you should always keep in mind that they are not a best practice for production software.

Implicit Conversions and Compiler Options

As noted in the introduction to this section, Visual Basic supports certain unsafe implicit conversions. This capability is on by default but can be disabled in two ways. The first method is specific to each source file and involves adding a line to the top of the source file to indicate to the compiler the status of Option Strict.

The following line will override whatever the default project setting for Option Strict is for your project. However, while this can be done on a per-source listing basis, this is not the recommended way to manage Option Strict. For starters, consistently adding this line to each of your source files isn't a good practice:

```
Option Strict On
```

The preferred method to manage the Option Strict setting is to change the setting for your entire project. Without going into details of the XML associated with your project file, the easiest way to accomplish this is to use Visual Studio 2005. Visual Studio 2005 and the various versions of this tool are discussed in more detail in Chapter 13; however, for completeness, the compilation settings are discussed in this context.

Visual Studio 2005 includes a tab on the Project Settings page to edit the compiler settings for an entire project. You can access this screen by right-clicking the project in the Solution Explorer and selecting Properties from the context menu. As noted in the preceding chapter, the Project Properties dialog has a Compile tab. When you select this tab, you should see a window similar to the one shown in Figure 2-4.

Figure 2-4

Aside from your default project file output directory, this page contains several compiler options. These options are covered here because the Option Explicit and Option Strict settings directly impact your variable usage:

- ❏ `Option Explicit` — This option has not changed from previous versions of Visual Basic. When enabled, it ensures that every variable is explicitly declared. Of course, if you are using `Option Strict`, then this setting doesn't matter because the compiler won't recognize the type of an undeclared variable. To my knowledge, there's no good reason to *ever* turn this option off.

- ❏ `Option Strict` — When this option is enabled, the compiler must be able to determine the type of each variable, and if an assignment between two variables requires a type conversion — for example, from `Integer` to `Boolean` — the conversion between the two types must be expressed explicitly. This setting can be edited by adding an `Option Strict` declaration to the top of your source code file. The statement within a source file applies to all of the code entered in that source file, but only to the code in that file.

- ❏ `Option Compare` — This option determines whether strings should be compared as binary strings or whether the array of characters should be compared as text. In most cases, leaving this as binary is appropriate. Doing a text comparison requires the system to convert the binary values that are stored internally prior to comparison. However, the advantage of a text-based comparison is that the character "A" is equal to "a" because the comparison is case insensitive. This enables you to perform comparisons that don't require an explicit case conversion of the compared strings. In most cases, however, this conversion still occurs, so it's better to use binary comparison and explicitly convert the case as required.

In addition to setting `Option Explicit`, `Option Strict`, and `Option Compare` to either `On` or `Off` for your project, Visual Studio 2005 allows you to customize specific compiler conditions that may occur in your source file. Thus, it is possible to leverage individual settings, such as requiring early binding as opposed to runtime binding, without limiting implicit conversions. These individual settings are part of the table of individual compiler settings listed below the `Option Strict` setting.

Notice that as you change your Option Strict setting, the notifications with the top few conditions are automatically updated to reflect the specific requirements of this new setting. In general, this table lists a set of conditions that relate to programming practices you might want to avoid or prevent, and should definitely be aware of. The use of warnings for the majority of these conditions is appropriate, as there are valid reasons why you might want to use or avoid each.

The basic idea is that these conditions represent possible runtime error conditions that the compiler can't truly detect, except to identify that an increased possibility for error exists. Selecting Warning for a setting bypasses that practice, as the compiler will warn you but allow the code to remain. On the other hand, setting a practice to `Error` prevents compilation.

An example of why these conditions are noteworthy is the warning on accessing shared member variables. If you are unfamiliar with shared member values, they are part of the discussion of classes in Chapter 3. At this point, it's just necessary to know that these values are shared across all instances of a class. Thus, if a specific instance of a class is updating a shared member value, it is appropriate to get a warning to that effect. The action is one that can lead to errors, as new developers sometimes fail to realize that a shared member value is common across all instances of a class, so if one instance updates the value, then the new value is seen by all other instances.

While many of these conditions are only addressed as individual settings, Visual Studio 2005 carries forward the Option Strict setting. Most experienced developers agree that using Option Strict and being forced to recognize when type conversions are occurring is a good thing. Certainly, when developing software that will be deployed in a production environment, anything that can be done to help prevent runtime errors is desirable. However, Option Strict can slow the development of a program because you are forced to explicitly define each conversion that needs to occur. If you are developing a prototype or demo component that has a limited life, you might find this option limiting.

If that were the end of the argument, then many developers would simply turn the option off the current default and forget about it, but Option Strict has a runtime benefit. When type conversions are explicitly identified, the system performs them faster. Implicit conversions require the runtime system to first identify the types involved in a conversion and then obtain the correct handler.

Another advantage of Option Strict is that during implementation developers are forced to consider every place a conversion might occur. Perhaps the development team didn't realize that some of the assignment operations resulted in a type conversion. Setting up projects that require explicit conversions means that the resulting code tends to have type consistency to avoid conversions, thus reducing the number of conversions in the final code. The result is not only conversions that run faster, but also, it is hoped, a smaller number of conversions as well.

Performing Explicit Conversions

So, if you aren't going to use implicit conversions, then what's necessary to implement explicit conversions? Keep in mind that even if you choose to allow implicit conversions, these are only allowed for a relatively small number of datatypes. At some point you'll need to carry out explicit conversions. The following code is an example of some typical conversions between different integer types when Option Strict is enabled:

```vb
Dim myShort As Short
Dim myUInt16 As UInt16
Dim myInt16 As Int16
Dim myInteger As Integer
Dim myUInt32 As UInt32
Dim myInt32 As Int32
Dim myLong As Long
Dim myInt64 As Int64

myShort = 0
myUInt16 = Convert.ToUInt16(myShort)
myInt16 = myShort
myInteger = myShort
myUInt32 = Convert.ToUInt32(myShort)
myInt32 = myShort
myInt64 = myShort

myLong = Long.MaxValue
If myLong < Short.MaxValue Then
   myShort = Convert.ToInt16(myLong)
End If
myInteger = CInt(myLong)
```

The preceding snippet provides some excellent examples of what might not be intuitive behavior. The first thing to note is that you can't implicitly cast from Short to UInt16, or any of the other unsigned types for that matter. That's because with Option Strict the compiler won't allow an implicit conversion that might result in a value out of range or loss of data. You may be thinking that an unsigned Short has a maximum that is twice the maximum of a signed Short, but in this case, if the variable myShort contained a -1, then the value wouldn't be in the allowable range for an unsigned type.

Just for clarity, even with the explicit conversion, if myShort were a negative number, the Convert .ToUInt32 method would throw a runtime exception. Managing failed conversions requires either an understanding of exceptions and exception handling, as covered in Chapter 9, or the use of a conversion utility such as TryParse, covered later in this section.

The second item illustrated in this code is the shared method MaxValue. All of the integer and decimal types have this property. As the name indicates, it returns the maximum value for the specified type. There is a matching MinValue method for getting the minimum value. As shared properties, the properties can be referenced from the class (Long.MaxValue) without requiring an instance.

Finally, although this code will compile, it won't always execute correctly. It illustrates a classic error, which in the real world is often intermittent. The error occurs because the final conversion statement does not check to ensure that the value being assigned to myInteger is within the maximum range for an integer type. On those occasions when myLong is larger than the maximum allowed, this code will throw an exception.

Visual Basic has many ways to convert values. Some of them are updated versions of techniques that are supported from previous versions of Visual Basic. Others, such as the ToString method, are an inherent part of every class (although the .NET specification does not guarantee how a ToString class is implemented for each type).

The following set of conversion methods is based on the conversions supported by Visual Basic. They coincide with the primitive datatypes described earlier; however, continued use of these methods is not considered a best practice. That bears repeating: While you may find the following methods in existing code, you should strive to avoid and replace these calls:

CBool()	CByte()	CChar()	CDate()
CDbl()	CDec()	CInt()	CLng()
CObj()	CShort()	CSng()	CStr()

Each of these methods has been designed to accept the input of the other primitive datatypes (as appropriate) and to convert such items to the type indicated by the method name. Thus, the CStr class is used to convert a primitive type to a String. The disadvantage of these methods is that they have been designed to support any object. This means that if a primitive type is used, then the method automatically boxes the parameter prior to getting the new value. This results in a loss of performance. Finally, although these are available as methods within the VB language, they are actually implemented in a class (as with everything in the .NET Framework). Because the class uses a series of type-specific overloaded methods, the conversions run faster when the members of the Convert class are called explicitly:

```
Dim intMyShort As Integer = 200
```

```
Convert.ToInt32(intMyShort)
Convert.ToDateTime("9/9/2001")
```

The classes that are part of `System.Convert` implement not only the conversion methods listed earlier, but also other common conversions. These additional methods include standard conversions for things such as unsigned integers and pointers.

All the preceding type conversions are great for value types and the limited number of classes to which they apply, but these implementations are oriented toward a limited set of known types. It is not possible to convert a custom class to an `Integer` using these classes. More importantly, there should be no reason to have such a conversion. Instead, a particular class should provide a method that returns the appropriate type. That way, no type conversion is required. However, when `Option Strict` is enabled, the compiler requires you to cast an object to an appropriate type before triggering an implicit conversion. Note, however, that the `Convert` method isn't the only way to indicate that a given variable can be treated as another type.

Parse and TryParse

Most value types, at least those which are part of the .NET Framework, provide a pair of shared methods called Parse and TryParse. These methods accept a value of your choosing and then attempt to convert this variable into the selected value type. Note that the Parse and TryParse methods are only available on value types. Reference types have related methods called DirectCast and Cast, which are optimized for reference variables.

The Parse method has a single parameter. This input parameter accepts a value that is the target for the object you are looking to create of a given type. This method then attempts to create a value based on the data passed in. However, be aware that if the data passed into the Parse method cannot be converted, then this method will throw an exception that your code needs to catch. The following line illustrates how the Parse function works:

```
result = Long.Parse("100")
```

Unfortunately, when you embed this call within a Try-Catch statement for exception handling, you create a more complex block of code. Because you always need to encapsulate such code within a Try-Catch block, the .NET development team decided that it would make more sense to provide a version of this method that encapsulated that exception handling logic.

This is the origin of the TryParse method. The TryParse method works similarly to the Parse method except that it has two parameters and returns a Boolean instead of a value. Instead of assigning the value of the TryParse method, you test it as part of an If-Then statement to determine whether the conversion of your data to the selected type was successful. If the conversion was successful, the new value is stored in the second parameter passed to this method, which you can then assign to the variable you want to hold that value:

```
Dim converted As Long
If Long.TryParse("100", converted) Then
    result = converted
End If
```

CType

The CType method accepts two parameters. The first parameter is the object that is having its type cast, and the second parameter is the name of the object to which it is being cast. This system enables you to cast objects from parent to child types or from child to parent types. There is a limitation to the second parameter in that it can't be a variable containing the name of the casting target. Casting is defined at compile time, and any form of dynamic name selection would occur at runtime. An example of casting is shown as part of the discussion of working with the Object class earlier in this chapter.

Support for a runtime determination of object types is based on treating variables as objects and using the object metadata and the TypeOf operator to verify that an object supports various method and property calls. The CType method accepts both value and reference types. More detailed information regarding its use is presented in Chapter 3.

DirectCast and TryCast

The DirectCast method works similarly to the CType method, with a couple of minor differences. First, unlike CType, the DirectCast method accepts only reference types. This is because the DirectCast method is tied much more closely to objects and the use of inheritance and interfaces. Additionally, in order to make it perform faster, DirectCast does not include any logic to actually check for and convert an object to the requested type. The DirectCast method is meant to allow your code to take an object that has been cast as its base type of object and recast it in its original form. Similar to CType, these methods are covered in more detail in Chapter 3.

Commands

Unlike many programming languages, Visual Basic has been designed to focus on readability and clarity. Many languages are willing to sacrifice these attributes in order to allow developers to type as little as possible. Visual Basic, conversely, is designed under the paradigm that the readability of code matters more than saving a few keystrokes, so commands in Visual Basic tend to spell out the exact context of what is being done.

Literally dozens of commands make up the Visual Basic language, so there isn't nearly enough space here to address all of them. Moreover, many of the more specialized commands are covered later in this book. However, if you are not familiar with Visual Basic or are relatively new to programming, a few would be helpful to look at here. These fall into two basic areas: *conditional statements* and *looping statements*. This section addresses two statements within each of these categories.

Each of these statements has the ability not only to call another method, the preferred way to manage blocks of code, but also to literally encapsulate a block of code. As noted in the rules on scoping, the blocks of encapsulated code within these commands can declare variables local to that block and can act in many ways like an unnamed method call.

If Then

The conditional is one of two primary programming constructs (the other being the loop) that is present in almost every programming language. After all, even in those rare cases where the computer is just repeatedly adding values or doing some other repetitive activity, at some point a decision will be needed and a condition evaluated, even if the question is only "is it time to stop?" Visual Basic supports the

If-Then statement as well as the Else statement; and unlike some languages, the concept of an ElseIf statement. The ElseIf and Else statements are totally optional, and it is not only acceptable but common to encounter conditionals that do not utilize either of these code blocks. The following example illustrates a simple pair of conditions that have been set up serially:

```
If result > 1 Then
    'Code A1
ElseIf result < 1 Then
    'Code B2
Else
    'Code C3
End If
```

If the first condition is true, then code placed at marker A1 is executed. The flow would then proceed to the End If and the program would not evaluate any of the other conditions. Note that for best performance, it makes the most sense to have your most common condition first in this structure, since if it is successful none of the other conditions need to be tested.

If the initial comparison in the preceding example code were false, then control moves to the first Else statement, which in this case happens to be an ElseIf statement. The code would therefore test the next conditional to determine whether the value of `result` were less than 1. If this were the case, then the code associated with block B2 would be executed.

However, if the second condition were also false, then the code would proceed to the Else statement, which isn't concerned with any remaining condition and just executes the code in block C3. Note that not only is the Else optional, but even if an ElseIf is used, the Else condition is still optional. It is acceptable for the Else and C3 block to be omitted from the preceding example.

Comparison Operators

There are several ways to discuss what is evaluated in an If statement. Essentially, the code between the If and Then portion of the statement must eventually evaluate out to a Boolean. At the most basic level, this means you can write If True Then, which results in a valid statement, although the code would always execute the associated block of code with that If statement. The idea, however, is that for a basic comparison, you take two values and place between them a comparison operator. Comparison operators include the following symbols: =, >, <, >=, <=.

Additionally, certain keywords can be used with a comparison operator. For example, the keyword Not can be used to indicate that the statement should consider the failure of a given comparison as a reason to execute the code encapsulated by its condition. An example of this is shown in the next example:

```
If Not result = 1 Then
    'Code A1
End If
```

It is therefore possible to compare two values and then take the resulting Boolean from this comparison and reevaluate the result. In this case, the result is only reversed, but the If statement supports more complex comparisons using statements such as And and Or. These statements enable you to create a complex condition based on several comparisons, as shown here:

```
If Not result = 1 Or result < 0 And value < 0 Then
```

```
      'Code A1
Else
      'Code B2
End If
```

The And and Or conditions are applied to determine whether the first comparison's results are true or false along with the second value's results. The And conditional means that both comparisons must evaluate to true in order for the If statement to execute the code in block A1, and the Or statement means that if the condition on either side is true, then the If statement can evaluate code block A1. However, in looking at this statement, your first reaction should be to pause and attempt to determine in exactly what order all of the associated comparisons will occur.

There is a precedence. First, any numeric style comparisons are applied, followed by any unary operators such as Not. Finally, proceeding from left to right, each Boolean comparison of And and Or is applied. However, a much better way of writing the preceding statement is to use parentheses to identify in what order you want these comparisons to occur. The first If statement in the following example illustrates the default order, while the second and third use parentheses to force a different priority on the evaluation of the conditions:

```
If ((Not result = 1) Or result < 0) And (value < 0) Then
If (Not result = 1) Or (result < 0 And value < 0) Then
If Not ((result = 1 Or result < 0) And value < 0) Then
```

All three of the preceding If statements are evaluating the same set of criteria, yet their results are potentially very different. It is always best practice to enclose complex conditionals within parentheses to illustrate the desired order of evaluation. Of course, these comparisons have been rather simple; you could replace the variable value in the preceding examples with a function call that might include a call to a database. In such a situation, if the desired behavior were to execute this expensive call only when necessary, then you might want to use one of the shortcut comparison operators.

Since you know that for an And statement both sides of the If statement must be true, there are times when knowing that the first condition is false could save processing time; you would not bother executing the second condition. Similarly, if the comparison involves an Or statement, then once the first part of the condition is true, there is no reason to evaluate the second condition because you know that the net result is success. In this case, the AndAlso and OrElse statements allow for performance optimization.

```
If ((Not result = 1) Or result < 0) AndAlso (MyMethod() = "Success") Then
If Not result = 1 OrElse (result < 0 And MyMethod() = "Success") Then
```

In each of the preceding cases, there are situations where the code associated with MyMethod won't be evaluated. This is potentially important, not only from a performance standpoint, but also in a scenario where given the first condition your code might throw an error. For example, it's not uncommon to first determine whether a variable has been assigned a value and then to test that value. This introduces yet another pair of conditional elements: the Is and IsNot conditionals.

Using Is enables you to determine whether a variable has been given a value, or to determine its type. In the past it was common to see nested If statements as a developer first determined whether the value was null, followed by a separate If statement to determine whether the value was valid. With .NET 2.0, the short circuit conditionals enable you to check for a value and then check whether that value meets the desired criteria. The short circuit operator prevents the check for a value from occurring and causing an error if the variable is undefined, so both checks can be done with a single If statement:

```
Dim mystring as string = Nothing
If mystring IsNot Nothing AndAlso mystring.Length > 100 Then
    'Code A1
ElseIf mystring.GetType Is GetType(Integer) Then
    'Code B2
End If
```

The code in the preceding example would fail on the first comparison because mystring has only been initialized to Nothing, meaning that by definition it doesn't have a length. Note also that the second condition will fail because we know that myString isn't of type Integer.

Select Case

The preceding section makes it clear that the If statement is the king of conditionals. However, there is a scenario in which you may have a simple condition that needs to be tested repeatedly. For example, let's say a user selects a value from a drop-down list and different code executes depending on that value. This is a relatively simple comparison, but if you have 20 values, then you would potentially need to string together 20 different If Then and ElseIf statements to account for all of the possibilities.

A cleaner way of evaluating such a condition is to leverage a Select Case statement. This statement was designed to test a condition, but instead of returning a Boolean value, it returns a value that is then used to determine which block of code, each defined by a case statement, should be executed:

```
Select Case myIntegerValue
    Case 1
        'Code A1
    Case 2
        'Code B2
    Case Else
        'Code C3
End Select
```

The preceding sample code shows how the Select portion of the statement determines the value represented by the variable myIntegerValue. Depending on the value of this variable, the case statement executes the appropriate code block. For a value of 1, the code in block A1 is executed; similarly, a 2 results in code block B2 executing. For any other value, because this case statement includes an Else block, the case statement will execute the code represented by C3. Finally, the next example illustrates that the cases do not need to be integer values, and can in fact even be strings:

```
Dim mystring As String = "Intro"
Select Case mystring
    Case "Intro"
        'Code A1
    Case "Exit"
        'Code A2
    Case Else
        'Code A3
End Select
```

For Each and For Next

The `For` structure in Visual Basic is the primary way of managing loops. It actually has two different formats. A standard For Next statement enables you to set a loop control variable that can be incremented by the `For` statement and custom exit criteria from your loop. Alternatively, if you are working with a known collection, then it is possible to use a `For Each` loop to automatically loop through all of the items in that collection:

```
For control As Integer = 1 To 10 Step 2
    MyGrid.Rows(control).Visible = False
Next
```

The For Next structure is most commonly set up to traverse an array or similar construct (for example, a dataset). The control variable `control` in the preceding example must be numeric. The value can be incremented from a starting value to an ending value, which are 1 and 10, respectively, in this example. Finally, it is possible to accept the default increment of 1; or, if desired, you can add a "Step" qualifier to your command and update the control value by a value other than 1. Best practices call for your control value to be an integer. Note that the preceding example hides every other line in the grid starting with the second line, since like all .NET collections, the collection starts at 0.

In addition, Visual Basic provides two additional commands that can be used within the For loop's block to enhance performance. The first is `Exit For`; and as you might expect, this statement causes the loop to end and not continue to the end of the processing. The other is `Continue`, which tells the loop that you are finished executing code with the current control value and to move to increment the value and reenter the loop for its next iteration:

```
For control As Integer = 1 To 10 Step 2
    If MyGrid.Rows.Count < control Then Exit For
    If control = 5 Then Continue For
    MyGrid.Rows(control).Visible = False
Next
```

Each of these keywords has been used in the preceding example. Note how each uses a format of the If Then structure that places the command on the same line as the If statement so that no End If statement is required. This loop exits if the control value is larger than the number of rows defined for the grid. Additionally, if the control indicates you are looking at the sixth row (index of five), then this row is not to be hidden, so the code does not process the next line to hide that row.

However, those examples demonstrate that in most cases, since your loop is going to process a known collection, Visual Basic provides a command that encapsulates the management of the loop control variable. The For Each structure automates the counting process and enables you to quickly assign the current item from the collection, so that you can act on it in your code. It is a common way to process all of the rows in a data set or most any other collection, and all of the loop control elements such as Continue and Exit are still available.

```
For Each Row As DataGridViewRow In MyGrid.Rows
    'Code A1
Next
```

While, Do While, and Do Until

In addition to the For loop, Visual Basic includes the While and Do loops, with two different versions of the Do loop. The first is the Do While loop. With a Do While loop, your code starts by checking for a condition; and as long as that condition is true, it executes the code contained in the Do loop. Optionally, instead of starting the loop by checking the While condition, the code can enter the loop and then check the condition at the end of the loop. The Do Until loop is similar to the Do While loop:

```
Do While MyGrid.Rows.Count > 0
    'Code A1
    System.Threading.Thread.Sleep(500)
Loop
```

The Do Until differs from the Do While only in that, by convention, the condition for a Do-Until is placed after the code block, thus requiring the code in the Do block to execute once before the condition is checked. It bears repeating, however, that a Do Until block can place the Until condition with the Do statement instead of with the Loop statement, and a Do While block can similarly have its condition at the end of the loop:

```
Do
    'Code A1
    System.Threading.Thread.Sleep(500)
Loop Until (MyGrid.Rows.Count = 0)
```

In both cases, instead of basing the loop around an array of items or a fixed number of iterations, the loop is instead instructed to continue perpetually until a condition is met. A good use for these loops involves tasks that need to repeat for as long as your application is running. Similar to the For loop, there are Exit Do and Continue commands that end the loop or move to the next iteration, respectively. Note that parentheses are allowed but are not required for both the While and the Until conditional expression.

The other format for creating a loop is to omit the Do statement and just create a While loop. The While loop works similarly to the Do While loop. The differences are as follows: First, the While loop's end point is an End While statement. Second, the condition must be at the start of the loop with the While statement. The final difference is that the While loop has an Exit While statement instead of Exit Do, although the behavior is the same. An example is shown here:

```
While MyGrid.Rows.Count > 0
    'Code A1
    System.Threading.Thread.Sleep(500)
End While
```

The best way to explain the use of these potentially endless loops is to illustrate how you might use one. For example, if you were writing an e-mail program, you might want to check the user's mailbox on the server every 20 seconds. You would create a Do While or Do Until loop that would contain the code to open a network connection and check the server for any new mail messages to download. You would continue this process until either the application was closed or you were unable to connect to the server. If unable to connect to the server, you would then alert the user and probably start a new loop that would look for network connectivity on a regular basis. One warning with this type of loop: If you are going to monitor a system's status, always include a call to Thread.Sleep() so that the loop only executes a single iteration within a given time frame, to avoid consuming too much processor time.

Summary

This chapter looked at many of the basic building blocks of Visual Basic that are used throughout project development. Understanding not only the basic components, but also how they work will help you to write more stable and better performing software. Note the following highlights of this chapter:

- ❏ Beware of array sizes; all arrays start at 0 and are defined not by size but by the highest index.
- ❏ Remember to use the `StringBuilder` class for string manipulation.
- ❏ Pay attention to variable scope, and rely on it for cleaning up variables you no longer need.
- ❏ Use `Option Strict`; it's not just about style, it's about performance.
- ❏ Try to avoid legacy methods for conversions.
- ❏ Attempt to leverage the TryParse and TryCast methods.
- ❏ Understand variable scope and when variables will go out of scope.
- ❏ Take advantage of the new collection classes, especially generics.

While this chapter covered many other items, including the new `Decimal` type and how boxing works, these highlight some of the more important items. Whether you are creating a new library of methods or a new user interface, these items consistently turn up in some form. You have seen that while .NET provides a tremendous amount of power, that power comes at a sometimes significant performance cost.

3

Object Syntax Introduction

Visual Basic supports the four major defining concepts required for a language to be fully object-oriented:

❑ **Abstraction** — Abstraction is merely the ability of a language to create "black box" code, to take a concept and create an abstract representation of that concept within a program. A `Customer` object, for instance, is an abstract representation of a real-world customer. A `DataTable` object is an abstract representation of a set of data.

❑ **Encapsulation** — This is the concept of a separation between interface and implementation. The idea is that you can create an interface (`Public` methods, properties, fields, and events in a class), and, as long as that interface remains consistent, the application can interact with your objects. This remains true even when you entirely rewrite the code within a given method — thus, the interface is independent of the implementation. Encapsulation enables you to hide the internal implementation details of a class. For example, the algorithm you use to compute pi might be proprietary. You can expose a simple API to the end user, but hide all the logic used by the algorithm by encapsulating it within your class.

❑ **Polymorphism** — Polymorphism is reflected in the ability to write one routine that can operate on objects from more than one class — treating different objects from different classes in exactly the same way. For instance, if both `Customer` and `Vendor` objects have a `Name` property, and you can write a routine that calls the `Name` property regardless of whether you're using a `Customer` or `Vendor` object, then you have polymorphism.

Visual Basic supports polymorphism in two ways — through late binding (much like Smalltalk, a classic example of a true object-oriented language) and through the implementation of multiple interfaces. This flexibility is very powerful and is preserved within Visual Basic.

❑ **Inheritance** — Inheritance is the idea that a class can gain the preexisting interface and behaviors of an existing class. This is done by inheriting these behaviors from the existing class through a process known as *subclassing*.

Then next chapter discusses these four concepts in detail; this chapter focuses on the syntax that enables you to utilize these concepts.

Visual Basic is also a component-based language. Component-based design is often viewed as a successor to object-oriented design, so component-based languages have some other capabilities. These are closely related to the traditional concepts of object orientation:

❑ **Multiple interfaces** — Each class in Visual Basic defines a *primary interface* (also called the *default* or *native interface*) through its `Public` methods, properties, and events. Classes can also implement other, secondary interfaces in addition to this primary interface. An object based on this class has multiple interfaces, and a client application can choose with which interface it will interact with the object.

❑ **Assembly (component) level scoping** — Not only can you define your classes and methods as `Public` (available to anyone), `Protected` (available through inheritance), and `Private` (available only locally), but you can also define them as `Friend` — meaning they are available only within the current assembly or component. This is not a traditional object-oriented concept, but is very powerful when designing component-based applications.

In this chapter, you'll explore the creation and use of classes and objects in Visual Basic. You won't get too deeply into code, but it is important that you spend a little time familiarizing yourself with basic object-oriented terms and concepts.

Object-Oriented Terminology

To begin, let's take a look at the word *object* itself, along with the related *class* and *instance* terms. Then we'll move on to discuss the four terms that define the major functionality in the object-oriented world: encapsulation, abstraction, polymorphism, and inheritance.

Objects, Classes, and Instances

An *object* is a code-based abstraction of a real-world entity or relationship. For instance, you might have a `Customer` object that represents a real-world customer, such as customer number 123, or you might have a `File` object that represents `C:\config.sys` on your computer's hard drive.

A closely related term is *class*. A class is the code that defines an object, and all objects are created based on a class. A class is an abstraction of a real-world concept, and it provides the basis from which you create instances of specific objects. For example, in order to have a `Customer` object representing customer number 123, you must first have a `Customer` class that contains all of the code (methods, properties, events, variables, and so on) necessary to create `Customer` objects. Based on that class, you can create any number of objects, each one an *instance* of the class. Each object is identical to the others, except that it may contain different data.

You can create many instances of `Customer` objects based on the same `Customer` class. All of the `Customer` objects are identical in terms of what they can do and the code they contain, but each one contains its own unique data. This means that each object represents a different physical customer.

Composition of an Object

You use an interface to get access to an object's data and behaviors. The object's data and behaviors are contained within the object, so a client application can treat the object like a black box, accessible only through its interface. This is a key object-oriented concept called *encapsulation*. The idea is that any program that makes use of this object won't have direct access to the behaviors or data; rather, those programs must make use of your object's interface.

Let's walk through each of the three elements in detail.

Interface

The interface is defined as a set of methods (Sub and Function routines), properties (Property routines), events, and fields (also known as variables) that are declared Public in scope.

You can also have Private methods and properties in your code. While these methods can be called by code within your object, they are not part of the interface and cannot be called by programs written to use your object. Another option is to use the Friend keyword, which defines the scope to be your current project, meaning that any code within your project can call the method, but no code outside your project (that is, from a different .NET assembly) can call the method. To complicate things a bit, you can also declare methods and properties as Protected, and these are available to classes that inherit from your class. You'll look at Protected in Chapter 4, along with inheritance.

For example, you might have the following code in a class:

```
Public Function CalculateValue() As Integer

End Function
```

Because this method is declared with the Public keyword, it is part of the interface and can be called by client applications that are using the object. You might also have a method such as this:

```
Private Sub DoSomething()

End Sub
```

This method is declared as being Private, so it is not part of the interface. This method can only be called by code within the class — not by any code outside the class, such as the code in a program that is using one of the objects.

On the other hand, you can do something like this:

```
Public Sub CalculateValue()
   DoSomething()
End Sub
```

In this case, you're calling the Private method from within a Public method. While code using your objects can't directly call a Private method, you will frequently use Private methods to help structure the code in a class to make it more maintainable and easier to read.

Finally, you can use the Friend keyword:

```
Friend Sub DoSomething()

End Sub
```

In this case, the `DoSomething` method can be called by code within the class, or from other classes or modules within the current Visual Basic project. Code from outside the project will not have access to the method.

The `Friend` scope is very similar to the `Public` scope in that it makes methods available for use by code outside the object itself. However, unlike `Public`, the `Friend` keyword restricts access to code within the current Visual Basic project, preventing code in other .NET assemblies from calling the method.

Implementation or Behavior

The code inside a method is called the *implementation*. Sometimes it is also called *behavior*, as it is this code that actually makes the object do useful work. For instance, you might have an `Age` property as part of the object's interface. Within that method, you might have some code:

```
Private _Age As Integer

Public ReadOnly Property Age() As Integer
  Get
     Return _Age
  End Get
End Sub
```

In this case, the code is returning a value directly out of a variable, rather than doing something better like calculate the value based on a birth date. However, this kind of code is often written in applications, and it seems to work fine for a while.

The key point here is to understand that client applications can use the object even if you change the implementation, as long as you don't change the interface. If the method name and its parameter list and return datatype remain unchanged, then you can change the implementation any way you want.

The code necessary to call the `Age` property would look something like this:

```
theAge = myObject.Age
```

The result of running this code is that you get the `Age` value returned for your use. While the client application will work fine, you'll soon discover that hard-coding the age into the application is a problem, so at some point you'll want to improve this code. Fortunately, you can change the implementation without changing the client code:

```
Private _BirthDate As Date

Public ReadOnly Property Age() As Integer
  Get
     Return CInt(DateDiff(DateInterval.Year, _BirthDate, Now))
  End Get
End Sub
```

You've changed the implementation behind the interface, effectively changing how it behaves, without changing the interface itself. Now, when you run the client application, the `Age` value returned is accurate over time, whereas in the previous implementation it was not.

Keep in mind that encapsulation is a *syntactic* tool — it enables the code to continue to run without change. However, it is not *semantic,* meaning that just because the code continues to run, that doesn't mean it continues to do what you actually want it to do.

In this example, the client code may have been written to overcome the initial limitations of the implementation in some way, and thus the client code might not only rely on being able to retrieve the `Age` value, but also be counting on the result of that call being a fixed value over time.

While the update to the implementation won't stop the client program from running, it may very well prevent the client program from running correctly.

Fields or Instance Variables

The third key part of an object is its data, or state. In fact, it might be argued that the only important part of an object is its data. After all, every instance of a class is absolutely identical in terms of its interface and its implementation; the only thing that can vary at all is the data contained within that particular object.

Fields are variables that are declared so that they are available to all code within the class. Typically, fields that are declared `Private` in scope are available only to the code in the class itself. They are also sometimes referred to as *instance variables* or as *member variables.*

Don't confuse fields with properties. In Visual Basic, a `Property` is a type of method geared to retrieving and setting values, whereas a field is a variable within the class that may hold the value exposed by a `Property`. For instance, you might have a class that has fields:

```
Public Class TheClass

    Private _Name As String
    Private _BirthDate As Date
End Class
```

Each instance of the class — each object — will have its own set of these fields in which to store data. Because these fields are declared with the `Private` keyword, they are only available to code within each specific object.

While fields can be declared as `Public` in scope, this makes them available to any code using the objects in a manner you can't control. Such a choice directly breaks the concept of encapsulation, as code outside your object can directly change data values without following any rules that might otherwise be set in the object's code.

If you want to make the value of a field available to code outside of the object, you should instead use a property:

```
Public Class TheClass
    Private _Name As String
    Private _BirthDate As Date
```

```
Public ReadOnly Property Name() As String
  Get
    Return _Name
  End Get
End Property
```

```
End Class
```

Because the `Name` property is a method, you are not directly exposing the internal variables to client code, so you preserve encapsulation of the data. At the same time, through this mechanism, you are able to safely provide access to your data as needed.

Fields can also be declared with the `Friend` scope, which means that they are available to all code in your project. Therefore, like declaring them as `Public`, this breaks encapsulation and is strongly discouraged.

Now that you have a grasp of some of the basic object-oriented terminology, you're ready to explore the creation of classes and objects. First you'll see how Visual Basic enables you to interact with objects, and then you'll dive into the actual process of authoring those objects.

Working with Objects

In the .NET environment, and within Visual Basic in particular, you use objects all the time without even thinking about it. Every control on a form — in fact, every form — is an object. When you open a file or interact with a database, you are using objects to do that work.

Object Declaration and Instantiation

Objects are created using the `New` keyword, indicating that you want a new instance of a particular class. There are numerous variations on how or where you can use the `New` keyword in your code. Each one provides different advantages in terms of code readability or flexibility.

The most obvious way to create an object is to declare an object variable and then create an instance of the object:

```
Dim obj As TheClass
obj = New TheClass()
```

The result of this code is that you have a new instance of `TheClass` ready for use. To interact with this new object, you use the `obj` variable that you declared. The `obj` variable contains a reference to the object, a concept explored later.

You can shorten the preceding code by combining the declaration of the variable with the creation of the instance, as illustrated here:

```
Dim obj As New TheClass()
```

In previous versions of Visual Basic, this substitution was a bad idea because it had negative performance and maintainability effects. However, in Visual Basic 2005, there is no difference between the first example and this one, other than that the latter code is shorter.

The preceding code both declares the variable `obj` as datatype `TheClass` and creates an instance of the class, immediately creating an object that you can use. Another variation on this theme is as follows:

```
Dim obj As TheClass = New TheClass()
```

Again, this both declares a variable of datatype `TheClass` and creates an instance of the class. It is up to you how you create these instances, as it really a matter of style.

This third syntax example provides a great deal of flexibility while remaining compact. Though it is a single line of code, it separates the declaration of the variable's datatype from the creation of the object.

Such flexibility is very useful when working with inheritance or multiple interfaces. You might declare the variable to be of one type — say, an interface — and instantiate the object based on a class that implements that interface. You'll revisit this syntax when interfaces are covered in detail in Chapter 4.

So far you've been declaring a variable for new objects, but sometimes you may simply need to pass an object as a parameter to a method, in which case you can create an instance of the object right in the call to that method:

```
DoSomething(New TheClass())
```

This calls the `DoSomething` method, passing a new instance of `TheClass` as a parameter. This can be even more complex. Perhaps, instead of needing an object reference, your method needs an `Integer`. You can provide that `Integer` value from a method on the object:

```
Public Class TheClass
  Public Function GetValue() As Integer
    Return 42
  End Function
End Class
```

You can then instantiate the object and call the method all in one shot, thus passing the value returned from the method as a parameter:

```
DoSomething(New TheClass().GetValue())
```

Obviously, you need to carefully weigh the readability of such code against its compactness. At some point, having more compact code can detract from readability, rather than enhance it.

Object References

Typically, when you work with an object, you are using a reference to that object. Conversely, when you are working with simple datatypes, such as `Integer`, you are working with the actual value, rather than a reference. Let's explore these concepts and see how they work and interact.

When you create a new object using the New keyword, you store a reference to that object in a variable, as shown here:

```
Dim obj As New TheClass()
```

This code creates a new instance of TheClass. You gain access to this new object via the obj variable. This variable holds a reference to the object. You might then do something like this:

```
Dim another As TheClass
another = obj
```

Now, you have a second variable, another, which also has a reference to the same object. You can use either variable interchangeably, as they both reference the exact same object. Remember that the variable you have is not the object itself but just a reference or pointer to the object.

Dereferencing Objects

When you are done working with an object, you can indicate that you're through with it by *dereferencing* the object. To dereference an object, simply set the object reference to Nothing:

```
Dim obj As TheClass

obj = New TheClass()
obj = Nothing
```

Once any or all variables that reference an object are set to Nothing, the .NET runtime can tell that you no longer need that object. At some point, the runtime will destroy the object and reclaim the memory and resources consumed by the object. You can find more information on the garbage collector in Chapter 5.

Between the time that you dereference the object and the time that the .NET Framework gets around to actually destroying it, the object simply sits in the memory, unaware that it has been dereferenced. Right before .NET destroys the object, the Framework calls the Finalize method on the object (if it has one). The Finalize method is discussed in Chapter 4.

Early Binding versus Late Binding

One of the strengths of Visual Basic has long been that it provides access to both early and late binding when interacting with objects.

Early binding means that code directly interacts with an object by directly calling its methods. Because the Visual Basic compiler knows the object's datatype ahead of time, it can directly compile code to invoke the methods on the object. Early binding also enables the IDE to use IntelliSense to aid development efforts by enabling the compiler to ensure that you are referencing methods that exist and are providing the proper parameter values.

Late binding means that your code interacts with an object dynamically at runtime. This provides a great deal of flexibility because the code doesn't care what type of object it is interacting with as long as the object supports the methods you want to call. Because the type of the object isn't known by the IDE or compiler, neither IntelliSense nor compile-time syntax checking is possible, but in exchange you get unprecedented flexibility.

If you enable strict type checking by using Option Strict On in the project properties dialog or at the top of the code modules, then the IDE and compiler enforce early binding behavior. By default, Option Strict is turned off, so you have easy access to the use of late binding within the code. Chapter 2 discusses Option Strict. You can change this default directly in Visual Studio 2005 by selecting Tools ⇨ Options from the VS menu. You are then presented with the Options dialog, shown in Figure 3-1. Expanding the Projects and Solutions node reveals the VB defaults. Feel free to change any of these default settings.

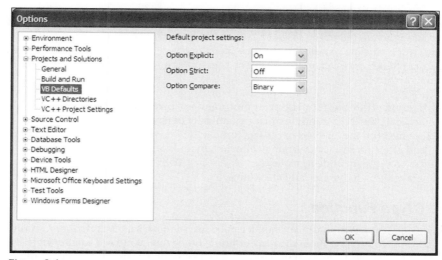

Figure 3-1

Implementing Late Binding

Late binding occurs when the compiler can't determine the type of object that you'll be calling. This level of ambiguity is achieved through the use of the Object datatype. A variable of datatype Object can hold virtually any value, including a reference to any type of object. Thus, code such as the following could be run against any object that implements a DoSomething method that accepts no parameters:

```
Option Strict Off

Module LateBind
  Public Sub DoWork(ByVal obj As Object)
    obj.DoSomething()
  End Sub
End Module
```

If the object passed into this routine does not have a DoSomething method that accepts no parameters, then an exception will be thrown. Thus, it is recommended that any code that uses late binding always provide exception handling:

```
Option Strict Off

Module LateBind
   Public Sub DoWork(ByVal obj As Object)
      Try
         obj.DoSomething()
      Catch ex As MissingMemberException
         ' do something appropriate given failure
         ' to call this method
      End Try
   End Sub
End Module
```

Here, the call to the DoSomething method has been put in a Try block. If it works, then the code in the Catch block is ignored; but in the case of a failure, the code in the Catch block is run. You need to write code in the Catch block to handle the case in which the object does not support the DoSomething method call. This Catch block only catches the MissingMemberException, which indicates that the method doesn't exist on the object.

While late binding is flexible, it can be error prone and is slower than early-bound code. To make a late-bound method call, the .NET runtime must dynamically determine whether the target object actually has a method that matches the one you're calling. It must then invoke that method on your behalf. This takes more time and effort than an early-bound call whereby the compiler knows ahead of time that the method exists and can compile the code to make the call directly. With a late-bound call, the compiler has to generate code to make the call dynamically at runtime.

Using the CType Function

Whether you are using late binding or not, it can be useful to pass object references around using the Object datatype, converting them to an appropriate type when you need to interact with them. This is particularly useful when working with objects that use inheritance or implement multiple interfaces, concepts discussed in Chapter 4.

If Option Strict is turned off, which is the default, then you can write code using a variable of type Object to make an early-bound method call:

```
Module LateBind
   Public Sub DoWork(obj As Object)

      Dim local As TheClass
      local = obj
      local.DoSomething()
   End Sub
End Module
```

This code uses a strongly typed variable, local, to reference what was a generic object value. Behind the scenes, Visual Basic converts the generic type to a specific type so that it can be assigned to the strongly typed variable. If the conversion can't be done, you get a trappable runtime error.

The same thing can be done using the CType function. If Option Strict is enabled, then the previous approach won't compile, and the CType function must be used. Here is the same code making use of CType:

```
Module LateBind
   Public Sub DoWork(obj As Object)

      Dim local As TheClass
      local = CType(obj, TheClass)
      local.DoSomething()
   End Sub
End Module
```

This code declares a variable of type TheClass, which is an early-bound datatype that you want to use. The parameter you're accepting, though, is of the generic Object datatype, so you use the CType() method to gain an early-bound reference to the object. If the object isn't of type TheClass, then the call to CType() fails with a trappable error.

Once you have a reference to the object, you can call methods by using the early bound variable, local. This code can be shortened to avoid the use of the intermediate variable. Instead, you can simply call methods directly from the datatype:

```
Module LateBind
   Public Sub DoWork(obj As Object)
      CType(obj, TheClass).DoSomething()
   End Sub
End Module
```

Even though the variable you're working with is of type Object and therefore any calls to it will be late bound, you use the CType method to temporarily convert the variable into a specific type — in this case, the type TheClass.

If the object passed as a parameter is not of type TheClass, you get a trappable error, so it is always wise to wrap this code in a Try...Catch block.

As Chapter 4 discusses, the CType function can also be very useful when working with objects that implement multiple interfaces. When an object has multiple interfaces, you can reference a single object variable through the appropriate interface as needed.

Using the DirectCast Function

Another function that is very similar to CType is DirectCast. DirectCast also converts values of one type into another type. It works in a more restrictive fashion than CType, but the trade-off is that it can be somewhat faster than CType:

```
Dim obj As TheClass

obj = New TheClass
DirectCast(obj, ITheInterface).DoSomething()
```

This is similar to the last example with CType, illustrating the parity between the two functions. There are differences, however. First, DirectCast works only with reference types, whereas CType accepts both reference and value types. For instance, CType can be used in the following code:

```
Dim int As Integer = CType(123.45, Integer)
```

Trying to do the same thing with `DirectCast` would result in a compiler error, as the value `123.45` is a value type, not a reference type.

Second, `DirectCast` is not as aggressive about converting types as `CType`. `CType` can be viewed as an intelligent combination of all the other conversion functions (such as `CInt`, `CStr`, and so on). `DirectCast`, on the other hand, assumes that the source data is directly convertible, and it won't take extra steps to convert the data.

As an example, consider the following code:

```
Dim obj As Object = 123.45

Dim int As Integer = DirectCast(obj, Integer)
```

If you were using `CType` this would work, as `CType` uses `CInt`-like behavior to convert the value to an `Integer`. `DirectCast`, however, will throw an exception because the value is not a directly convertible o `Integer`.

Using the TryCast Function

A function similar to `DirectCast` is `TryCast`. `TryCast` converts values of one type into another type, but unlike `DirectCast`, if it can't do the conversion, then `TryCast` doesn't throw an exception. Instead, `TryCast` simply returns `Nothing` if the cast can't be performed. `TryCast` only works with reference values; it cannot be used with value types such as `Integer` or `Boolean`.

Using `TryCast`, you can write code like this:

```
Module LateBind

  Public Sub DoWork(obj As Object)
    Dim temp As TheClass = TryCast(obj)
    If temp Is Nothing Then
      ' the cast couldn't be accomplished
      ' so do no work
    Else
      temp.DoSomething()
    End If
  End Sub

End Module
```

If you aren't sure whether a type conversion is possible, it is often best to use `TryCast`. This function avoids the overhead and complexity of catching possible exceptions from `CType` or `DirectCast` and still provides you with an easy way to convert an object to another type.

Creating Classes

Using objects is fairly straightforward and intuitive. It is the kind of thing that even the most novice programmers pick up and accept rapidly. Creating classes and objects is a bit more complex and interesting, and is covered throughout the rest of this chapter.

Basic Classes

As discussed earlier, objects are merely instances of a specific template (a class). The class contains the code that defines the behavior of its objects, as well as defining the instance variables that will contain the object's individual data.

Classes are created using the `Class` keyword, and include definitions (declaration) and implementations (code) for the variables, methods, properties, and events that make up the class. Each object created based on this class will have the same methods, properties, and events, and its own set of data defined by the fields in the class.

The Class Keyword

If you want to create a class that represents a person — a `Person` class — you could use the `Class` keyword:

```
Public Class Person

   ' Implementation code goes here

End Class
```

As you know, Visual Basic projects are composed of a set of files with the .vb extension. It's possible to have each file contain multiple classes, which means that within a single file you could have something like this:

```
Public Class Adult
   ' Implementation code goes here.
End Class

Public Class Senior
   ' Implementation code goes here.
End Class

Public Class Child
   ' Implementation code goes here.
End Class
```

The most common and preferred approach is to have a single class per file. This is because the Visual Studio 2005 Solution Explorer and the code-editing environment are tailored to make it easy to navigate from file to file to find code. For instance, if you create a single class file with all these classes, the Solution Explorer simply displays a single entry, as shown in Figure 3-2.

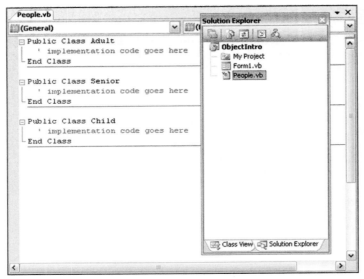

Figure 3-2

However, the Visual Studio IDE does provide the Class View window. If you do decide to put multiple classes in each physical .vb file, you can make use of the Class View window to quickly and efficiently navigate through the code, jumping from class to class without having to manually locate those classes in specific code files, as shown in Figure 3-3.

The Class View window is incredibly useful even if you stick with one class per file, as it still provides you with a class-based view of the entire application.

Figure 3-3

This chapter uses one class per file in its examples, as this is the most common approach. To begin, open the Visual Studio IDE and create a new Windows Application project named `ObjectIntro`. Choose the Project ⇨ Add Class menu option to add a new class module to the project. You'll be presented with the standard Add New Item dialog box. Change the name to `Person.vb` and click the Open button. The result will be the following code, which defines the `Person` class:

```
Public Class Person

End Class
```

With the `Person` class created, you're ready to start adding code to declare the interface, implement the behaviors, and declare the instance variables.

Fields

Fields are variables declared in the class that will be available to each individual object when the application is run. Each object gets its own set of data — basically, each object gets its own copy of the fields.

Earlier, you learned that a class is simply a template from which you create specific objects. Variables that you define within the class are also simply templates — and each object gets its own copy of those variables in which to store its data.

Declaring member variables is as easy as declaring variables within the `Class` block structure. Add the following code to the `Person` class:

```
Public Class Person

    Private mName As String
    Private mBirthDate As Date
End Class
```

You can control the scope of the fields by using the following keywords:

❑   `Private` — Available only to code within the class

❑   `Friend` — Available only to code within the project/component

❑   `Protected` — Available only to classes that inherit from the class (discussed in detail in Chapter 4)

❑   `Protected Friend` — Available to code within your project/component and classes that inherit from the class whether in the project or not (discussed in detail in Chapter 4)

❑   `Public` — Available to code outside the class and to any projects that reference the assembly

Typically, fields are declared using the `Private` keyword, making them available only to code within each instance of the class. Choosing any other option should be done with great care, because all the other options allow code outside the class to directly interact with the variable, meaning that the value could be changed and your code would never know that a change took place.

> *One common exception to making fields `Private` is the use of the `Protected` keyword, as discussed in Chapter 4.*

Methods

Objects typically need to provide services (or functions) that can be called when working with the object. Using their own data or data passed as parameters to the method, they manipulate information to yield a result or perform an action.

Methods declared as `Public`, `Friend`, or `Protected` in scope define the interface of the class. Methods that are `Private` in scope are available to the code only within the class itself and can be used to provide structure and organization to code. As discussed earlier, the actual code within each method is called an *implementation*, while the declaration of the method itself is what defines the interface.

Methods are simply routines that are coded within the class to implement the services you want to provide to the users of an object. Some methods return values or provide information to the calling code. These are called *interrogative methods*. Others, called *imperative methods*, just perform an action and return nothing to the calling code.

In Visual Basic, methods are implemented using `Sub` (for imperative methods) or `Function` (for interrogative methods) routines within the class module that defines the object. `Sub` routines may accept parameters, but they don't return any result value when they are complete. `Function` routines can also accept parameters, and they always generate a result value that can be used by the calling code.

A method declared with the `Sub` keyword is merely one that returns no value. Add the following code to the `Person` class:

```
Public Sub Walk()

  ' implementation code goes here

End Sub
```

The `Walk()` method presumably contains some code that performs some useful work when called but has no result value to return when it is complete. To make use of this method, you might write code such as this:

```
Dim myPerson As New Person()
myPerson.Walk()
```

Once you've created an instance of the `Person` class, you can simply invoke the `Walk()` method.

Methods That Return Values

If you have a method that does generate some value that should be returned, you need to use the `Function` keyword:

```
Public Function Age() As Integer
  Return CInt(DateDiff(DateInterval.Year, mBirthDate, Now()))
End Function
```

Notice that you must indicate the datatype of the return value when you declare a `Function`. This example returns the calculated age as a result of the method. You can return any value of the appropriate datatype by using the `Return` keyword.

You can also return the value without using the `Return` keyword, by setting the value of the function name itself:

```
Public Function Age() As Integer
    Age = CInt(DateDiff(DateInterval.Year, mBirthDate, Now()))
End Function
```

This is functionally equivalent to the previous code. Either way, you can use this method with code similar to the following:

```
Dim myPerson As New Person()
Dim age As Integer

age = myPerson.Age()
```

The `Age()` method returns an `Integer` data value that you can use in the program as required; in this case, you're just storing it in a variable.

Indicating Method Scope

Adding the appropriate keyword in front of the method declaration indicates the scope:

```
Public Sub Walk()
```

This indicates that `Walk()` is a `Public` method and thus is available to code outside the class and even outside the current project. Any application that references the assembly can use this method. Being `Public`, this method becomes part of the object's interface.

Alternately, you might choose to restrict access to the method somewhat:

```
Friend Sub Walk()
```

By declaring the method with the `Friend` keyword, you are indicating that it should be part of the object's interface only for code inside the project; any other applications or projects that make use of the assembly will not be able to call the `Walk()` method.

The `Private` keyword indicates that a method is only available to the code within your particular class:

```
Private Function Age() As Integer
```

`Private` methods are very useful to help organize complex code within each class. Sometimes the methods contain very lengthy and complex code. In order to make this code more understandable, you may choose to break it up into several smaller routines, having the main method call these routines in the proper order. Moreover, you can use these routines from several places within the class, so by making them separate methods, you enable reuse of the code. These subroutines should never be called by code outside the object, so you make them `Private`.

Method Parameters

You will often want to pass information into a method as you call it. This information is provided via parameters to the method. For instance, in the `Person` class, perhaps you want the `Walk()` method to track the distance the person walks over time. In such a case, the `Walk()` method would need to know how far the person is to walk each time the method is called. Add the following code to the `Person` class:

```
Public Class Person
   Private mName As String
   Private mBirthDate As Date
   Private mTotalDistance As Integer

   Public Sub Walk(ByVal distance As Integer)
      mTotalDistance += distance
   End Sub
   Public Function Age() As Integer
      Return CInt(DateDiff(DateInterval.Year, mBirthDate, Now()))
   End Function
End Class
```

With this implementation, a `Person` object will sum all of the distances walked over time. Each time the `Walk()` method is called, the calling code must pass an `Integer` value, indicating the distance to be walked. Your code to call this method would be similar to the following code:

```
Dim myPerson As New Person()
myPerson.Walk(12)
```

The parameter is accepted using the `ByVal` keyword. This indicates that the parameter value is a copy of the original value. This is the default way in which Visual Basic accepts all parameters. Typically, this is desirable because it means that you can work with the parameter inside the code, changing its value with no risk of accidentally changing the original value in the calling code.

If you do want to be able to change the value in the calling code, you can change the declaration to pass the parameter by reference by using the `ByRef` qualifier:

```
Public Sub Walk(ByRef distance As Integer)
```

In this case, you'll get a reference (or pointer) back to the original value, rather than receive a copy. This means that any change you make to the `distance` parameter is reflected back in the calling code, very similar to the way object references work, as discussed earlier in this chapter.

Using this technique can be dangerous, as it is not explicitly clear to the caller of the method that the value will change. Such unintended side effects can be hard to debug and should be avoided.

Properties

The .NET environment provides for a specialized type of method called a *property*. A property is a method specifically designed for setting and retrieving data values. For instance, you declared a variable in the `Person` class to contain a name, so the `Person` class may include code to allow that name to be set and retrieved. This can be done using regular methods:

```
Public Sub SetName(ByVal name As String)
   mName = name
End Sub
```

```
Public Function GetName() As String
   Return mName
End Function
```

Using methods like these, you write code to interact with the object:

```
Dim myPerson As New Person()

myPerson.SetName("Jones")
Messagebox.Show(myPerson.GetName())
```

While this is perfectly acceptable, it is not as nice as it could be with the use of a property. A `Property` style method consolidates the setting and retrieving of a value into a single structure, and makes the code within the class smoother overall. You can rewrite these two methods into a single property. Add the following code to the `Person` class:

```
Public Property Name() As String
   Get
      Return mName
   End Get
   Set(ByVal Value As String)
     mName = Value
   End Set
End Property
```

By using a property method instead, you can make the client code much more readable:

```
Dim myPerson As New Person()

myPerson.Name = "Jones"
Messagebox.Show(myPerson.Name)
```

The `Property` method is declared with both a scope and a datatype:

```
Public Property Name() As String
```

In this example, you've declared the property as `Public` in scope, but it can be declared using the same scope options as any other method — `Public`, `Friend`, `Private`, or `Protected`.

The return datatype of this property is `String`. A property can return virtually any datatype appropriate for the nature of the value. In this regard, a property is very similar to a method declared using the `Function` keyword.

Though a `Property` method is a single structure, it is divided into two parts: a getter and a setter. The getter is contained within a `Get...End Get` block and is responsible for returning the value of the property on demand:

```
Get
   Return mName
End Get
```

Though the code in this example is very simple, it could be more complex, perhaps calculating the value to be returned or applying other business logic to change the value as it is returned. Likewise, the code to change the value is contained within a `Set ... End Set` block:

```
Set(ByVal Value As String)
    mName = Value
End Set
```

The `Set` statement accepts a single parameter value that stores the new value. The code in the block can then use this value to set the property's value as appropriate. The datatype of this parameter must match the datatype of the property itself. Having the parameter declared in this manner enables you to change the name of the variable used for the parameter value if needed.

By default, the parameter is named `Value`, but you can change the parameter name to something else, as shown here:

```
Set(ByVal NewName As String)
    mName = NewName
End Set
```

In many cases, you can apply business rules or other logic within this routine to ensure that the new value is appropriate before you actually update the data within the object. It is also possible to restrict either the `Get` or `Set` block to be narrower in scope than the scope of the property itself. For instance, you may want to allow any code to retrieve the property value, but only allow other code in your project to alter the value. In this case, you can restrict the scope of the `Set` block to `Friend`, while the `Property` itself is scoped as `Public`:

```
Public Property Name() As String
  Get
     Return mName
  End Get
  Friend Set(ByVal Value As String)
     mName = Value
  End Set
End Property
```

The new scope must be more restrictive than the scope of the `Property` itself, and either the `Get` or `Set` block can be restricted, not both. The one you don't restrict uses the scope of the `Property` method.

Parameterized Properties

The `Name` property you created is an example of a single-value property. You can also create property arrays or parameterized properties. These properties reflect a range, or array, of values. For example, people often have several phone numbers. You might implement a `PhoneNumber` property as a parameterized property, storing not only phone numbers, but also a description of each number. To retrieve a specific phone number you'd write code such as the following:

```
Dim myPerson As New Person()
Dim homePhone As String

homePhone = myPerson.Phone("home")
```

Or, to add or change a specific phone number, you'd write the following code:

```
myPerson.Phone("work") = "555-9876"
```

Not only are you retrieving and updating a phone number property, but you're also updating a specific phone number. This implies a couple of things. First, you can no longer use a simple variable to hold the phone number, as you are now storing a list of numbers and their associated names. Second, you've effectively added a parameter to your property. You're actually passing the name of the phone number as a parameter on each property call.

To store the list of phone numbers, you can use the `Hashtable` class. The `Hashtable` is very similar to the standard VB `Collection` object, but it is more powerful — allowing you to test for the existence of a specific element. Add the following declaration to the `Person` class:

```
Public Class Person
   Private mName As String
   Private mBirthDate As Date
   Private mTotalDistance As Integer
   Private mPhones As New Hashtable
```

You can implement the `Phone` property by adding the following code to the `Person` class:

```
Public Property Phone(ByVal location As String) As String
  Get
    Return CStr(mPhones.Item(Location))
  End Get
  Set(ByVal Value As String)
    If mPhones.ContainsKey(location) Then
      mPhones.Item(location) = Value
    Else
      mPhones.Add(location, Value)
    End If
  End Set
End Property
```

The declaration of the `Property` method itself is a bit different from what you've seen:

```
Public Property Phone(ByVal location As String) As String
```

In particular, you've added a parameter, `location`, to the property itself. This parameter will act as the index into the list of phone numbers, and must be provided when either setting or retrieving phone number values.

Because the `location` parameter is declared at the `Property` level, it is available to all code within the property, including both the `Get` and `Set` blocks. Within your `Get` block, you use the `location` parameter to select the appropriate phone number to return from the `Hashtable`:

```
Get
  Return mPhones.Item(location)
End Get
```

With this code, if there is no value stored matching the `location`, then you get a trappable runtime error.

Similarly, in the `Set` block, you use the `location` to update or add the appropriate element in the `Hashtable`. In this case, you're using the `ContainsKey` method of `Hashtable` to determine whether the phone number already exists in the list. If it does, then you simply update the value in the list; otherwise, you add a new element to the list for the value:

```
Set(ByVal Value As String)
  If mPhones.ContainsKey(location) Then
    mPhones.Item(location) = Value
  Else
    mPhones.Add(location, Value)
  End If
End Set
```

In this way, you're able to add or update a specific phone number entry based on the parameter passed by the calling code.

Read-Only Properties

There are times when you may want a property to be read-only, so that it can't be changed. In the `Person` class, for instance, you may have a read-write property for `BirthDate`, but only a read-only property for `Age`. If so, the `BirthDate` property is a normal property, as follows:

```
Public Property BirthDate() As Date
  Get
    Return mBirthDate
  End Get
  Set(ByVal Value As Date)
   mBirthDate = Value
  End Set
End Property
```

The `Age` value, on the other hand, is a derived value based on `BirthDate`. This is not a value that should ever be directly altered, so it is a perfect candidate for read-only status.

You already have an `Age` method implemented as a `Function`. Remove that code from the `Person` class, because you'll be replacing it with a `Property` routine instead. The difference between a `Function` routine and a `ReadOnly Property` is quite subtle. Both return a value to the calling code, and either way the object is running a subroutine defined by the class module to return the value.

The difference is less a programmatic one than a design choice. You could create all your objects without any `Property` routines at all, just using methods for all interactions with the objects. However, `Property` routines are obviously attributes of an object, while a `Function` might be an attribute or a method. By carefully implementing all attributes as `ReadOnly Property` routines, and any interrogative methods as `Function` routines, you create more readable and understandable code.

To make a property read-only, use the `ReadOnly` keyword and only implement the `Get` block:

```
Public ReadOnly Property Age() As Integer
  Get
    Return CInt(DateDiff(DateInterval.Year, mdtBirthDate, Now()))
  End Get
End Property
```

Because the property is read-only, you'll get a syntax error if you attempt to implement a `Set` block.

Write-Only Properties

As with read-only properties, there are times when a property should be write-only, whereby the value can be changed but not retrieved.

Many people have allergies, so perhaps the `Person` object should have some understanding of the ambient allergens in the area. This is not a property that should be read from the `Person` object, as allergens come from the environment, rather than from the person, but it is data that the `Person` object needs in order to function properly. Add the following variable declaration to the class:

```
Public Class Person
  Private mstrName As String
  Private mdtBirthDate As Date
  Private mintTotalDistance As Integer
  Private colPhones As New Hashtable()
  Private mAllergens As Integer
```

You can implement an `AmbientAllergens` property as follows:

```
Public WriteOnly Property AmbientAllergens() As Integer
  Set(ByVal Value As Integer)
    mAllergens = Value
  End Set
End Property
```

To create a write-only property, use the `WriteOnly` keyword and only implement a `Set` block in the code. The property is write-only, so you'll get a syntax error if you attempt to implement a `Get` block.

The Default Property

Objects can implement a default property. A default property can be used to simplify the use of an object at times, by making it appear as if the object has a native value. A good example of this behavior is the `Collection` object, which has a default property called `Item` that returns the value of a specific item, allowing you to write the following:

```
Dim mData As New HashTable()

Return mData(index)
```

Default properties must be parameterized properties. A property without a parameter cannot be marked as the default. This is a change from previous versions of Visual Basic, where any property could be marked as the default.

Our `Person` class has a parameterized property — the `Phone` property you built earlier. You can make this the default property by using the `Default` keyword:

```
Default Public Property Phone(ByVal location As String) As String
  Get
    Return CStr(mPhones.Item(location))
  End Get
```

```
    Set(ByVal Value As String)
      If mPhones.ContainsKey(location) Then
        mPhones.Item(location) = Value
      Else
        mPhones.Add(location, Value)
      End If
    End Set
  End Property
```

Prior to this change, you would have needed code such as the following to use the Phone property:

```
Dim myPerson As New Person()

MyPerson.Phone("home") = "555-1234"
```

Now, with the property marked as Default, you can simplify the code:

```
myPerson("home") = "555-1234"
```

By picking appropriate default properties, you can potentially make the use of objects more intuitive.

Events

Both methods and properties enable you to write code that interacts with your objects by invoking specific functionality as needed. It is often useful for objects to provide notification as certain activities occur during processing. You see examples of this all the time with controls, where a button indicates that it was clicked via a Click event, or a text box indicates that its contents have been changed via the TextChanged event.

Objects can raise events of their own, providing a powerful and easily implemented mechanism by which objects can notify client code of important activities or events. In Visual Basic, events are provided using the standard .NET mechanism of *delegates*. Before discussing delegates, let's explore how to work with events in Visual Basic.

Handling Events

We are all used to seeing code in a form to handle the Click event of a button, such as the following code:

```
Private Sub Button1_Click(ByVal sender As System.Object, _
  ByVal e As System.EventArgs) Handles Button1.Click

End Sub
```

Typically, we write our code in this type of routine without paying a lot of attention to the code created by the Visual Studio IDE. However, let's take a second look at that code, as there are a couple of important things to note here.

First, notice the use of the Handles keyword. This keyword specifically indicates that this method will be handling the Click event from the Button1 control. Of course, a control is just an object, so what is indicated here is that this method will be handling the Click event from the Button1 object.

Second, notice that the method accepts two parameters. The `Button` control class defines these parameters. It turns out that any method that accepts two parameters with these datatypes can be used to handle the `Click` event. For instance, you could create a new method to handle the event:

```
Private Sub MyClickMethod(ByVal s As System.Object, _
    ByVal args As System.EventArgs) Handles Button1.Click

End Sub
```

Even though you've changed the method name and the names of the parameters, you are still accepting parameters of the same datatypes, and you still have the `Handles` clause to indicate that this method handles the event.

Handling Multiple Events

The `Handles` keyword offers even more flexibility. Not only can the method name be anything you choose, but a single method can handle multiple events if you desire. Again, the only requirement is that the method and all the events being raised must have the same parameter list.

> *This explains why all the standard events raised by the .NET system class library have exactly two parameters — the sender and an `EventArgs` object. Being so generic makes it possible to write very generic and powerful event handlers than can accept virtually any event raised by the class library.*

One common scenario where this is useful is when you have multiple instances of an object that raises events, such as two buttons on a form:

```
Private Sub MyClickMethod(ByVal sender As System.Object, _
    ByVal e As System.EventArgs) _
    Handles Button1.Click, Button2.Click

End Sub
```

Notice that the `Handles` clause has been modified so that it has a comma-separated list of events to handle. Either event will cause the method to run, providing a central location in which to handle these events.

The WithEvents Keyword

The `WithEvents` keyword tells Visual Basic that you want to handle any events raised by the object within the code:

```
Friend WithEvents Button1 As System.Windows.Forms.Button
```

The `WithEvents` keyword makes any events from an object available for use, while the `Handles` keyword is used to link specific events to the methods so that you can receive and handle them. This is true not only for controls on forms, but also for any objects that you create.

The `WithEvents` keyword cannot be used to declare a variable of a type that doesn't raise events. In other words, if the `Button` class didn't contain code to raise events, you'd get a syntax error when you attempted to declare the variable using the `WithEvents` keyword.

The compiler can tell which classes will and won't raise events by examining their interface. Any class that will be raising an event has that event declared as part of its interface. In Visual Basic, this means that you will have used the `Event` keyword to declare at least one event as part of the interface for the class.

Raising Events

Your objects can raise events just like a control, and the code using the object can receive these events by using the `WithEvents` and `Handles` keywords. Before you can raise an event from your object, however, you need to declare the event within the class by using the `Event` keyword.

In the `Person` class, for instance, you may want to raise an event anytime the `Walk` method is called. If you call this event `Walked`, you can add the following declaration to the `Person` class:

```
Public Class Person
    Private mstrName As String
    Private mdtBirthDate As Date
    Private mintTotalDistance As Integer
    Private colPhones As New Hashtable()
    Private mintAllergens As Integer
    Public Event Walked()
```

Events can also have parameters, values that are provided to the code receiving the event. A typical button's `Click` event receives two parameters, for instance. In the `Walked()` method, perhaps you want to also indicate the distance that was walked. You can do this by changing the event declaration:

```
    Public Event Walked(ByVal distance As Integer)
```

Now that the event is declared, you can raise that event within the code where appropriate. In this case, you'll raise it within the `Walk()` method, so anytime a `Person` object is instructed to walk, it fires an event indicating the distance walked. Make the following change to the `Walk()` method:

```
Public Sub Walk(ByVal distance As Integer)
    mTotalDistance += distance
    RaiseEvent Walked(distance)
End Sub
```

The `RaiseEvent` keyword is used to raise the actual event. Because the event requires a parameter, that value is passed within parentheses and is delivered to any recipient that handles the event.

In fact, the `RaiseEvent` statement causes the event to be delivered to all code that has the object declared using the `WithEvents` keyword with a `Handles` clause for this event, or any code that has used the `AddHandler` method. The `AddHandler` method is discussed shortly.

If more than one method will be receiving the event, the event is delivered to each recipient one at a time. By default, the order of delivery isn't defined — meaning you can't predict the order in which the recipients receive the event — but the event is delivered to all handlers. Note that this is a serial, synchronous process. The event is delivered to one handler at a time, and it is not delivered to the next handler until the current handler is complete. Once you call the `RaiseEvent` method, the event is delivered to all listeners one after another until it is complete; there is no way for you to intervene and stop the process in the middle.

Declaring and Raising Custom Events

As just noted, by default you have no control over how events are raised. You can overcome this limitation by using a more explicit form of declaration for the event itself. Rather than use the simple `Event` keyword, you can declare a custom event. This is for more advanced scenarios, as it requires that you provide the implementation for the event itself.

The concept of delegates is covered in detail later in this chapter, but it is necessary to look at them briefly here in order to declare a custom event. A delegate is a definition of a method signature. When you declare an event, Visual Basic defines a delegate for the event behind the scenes based on the signature of the event. The `Walked` event, for instance, has a delegate like the following:

```
Public Delegate Sub WalkedEventHandler(ByVal distance As Integer)
```

Notice how this code declares a "method" that accepts an `Integer` and has no return value. This is exactly what you defined for the event. Normally, you don't write this bit of code, because Visual Basic does it automatically. However, if you are to declare a custom event, then you need to manually declare the event delegate.

You also need to declare within the class a variable where you can keep track of any code that is listening for, or handling, the event. It turns out that you can tap into the prebuilt functionality of delegates for this purpose. By declaring the `WalkedEventHandler` delegate, you have defined a datatype that automatically tracks event handlers, so you can declare the variable like this:

```
Private mWalkedHandlers As WalkedEventHandler
```

Then you can use this variable to store and raise the event within the custom event declaration:

```
Public Custom Event Walked As WalkedEventHandler
  AddHandler(ByVal value As WalkedEventHandler)
    mWalkedHandlers = _
      CType([Delegate].Combine(mWalkedHandlers, value), WalkedEventHandler)
  End AddHandler

  RemoveHandler(ByVal value As WalkedEventHandler)
    mWalkedHandlers = _
      CType([Delegate].Remove(mWalkedHandlers, value), WalkedEventHandler)
  End RemoveHandler

  RaiseEvent(ByVal distance As Integer)
    If mWalkedHandlers IsNot Nothing Then
      mWalkedHandlers.Invoke(distance)
    End If
  End RaiseEvent
End Event
```

In this case, you've used the `Custom Event` key phrase, rather than just `Event` to declare the event. A `Custom Event` declaration is a block structure with three subblocks: `AddHandler`, `RemoveHandler`, and `RaiseEvent`.

The `AddHandler` block is called anytime a new handler wants to receive the event. The parameter passed to this block is a reference to the method that will be handling the event. It is up to you to store the reference to that method, which you can do however you choose. In this implementation, you're storing it within the delegate variable just like the default implementation provided by Visual Basic.

The `RemoveHandler` block is called anytime a handler wants to stop receiving your event. The parameter passed to this block is a reference to the method that was handling the event. It is up to you to remove the reference to the method, which you can do however you choose. In this implementation, you're replicating the default behavior by having the delegate variable remove the element.

Finally, the `RaiseEvent` block is called anytime the event is raised. Typically, it is invoked when code within the class uses the `RaiseEvent` statement. The parameters passed to this block must match the parameters declared by the delegate for the event. It is up to you to go through the list of methods that are handling the event and to call each of those methods. In the example shown here, you're allowing the delegate variable to do that for you, which is the same behavior you get by default with a normal event.

The value of this syntax is that you could opt to store the list of handler methods in a different type of data structure, such as a `Hashtable` or collection. You could then invoke them asynchronously, or in a specific order or based on some other behavior required by the application.

Receiving Events with WithEvents

Now that you've implemented an event within the `Person` class, you can write client code to declare an object using the `WithEvents` keyword. For instance, in the project's `Form1` code module, you can write the following code:

```
Public Class Form1
   Inherits System.Windows.Forms.Form
   Private WithEvents mPerson As Person
```

By declaring the variable `WithEvents`, you are indicating that you want to receive any events raised by this object. You can also choose to declare the variable without the `WithEvents` keyword, although in that case you would not receive events from the object as described here. Instead, you would use the `AddHandler` method, which is discussed after `WithEvents`.

You can then create an instance of the object, as the form is created, by adding the following code:

```
Private Sub Form1_Load(ByVal sender As System.Object, _
   ByVal e As System.EventArgs) Handles MyBase.Load

 mPerson = New Person()

End Sub
```

At this point, you've declared the object variable using `WithEvents` and have created an instance of the `Person` class, so you actually have an object with which to work. You can now proceed to write a method to handle the `Walked` event from the object by adding the following code to the form. You can name this method anything you like; it is the `Handles` clause that is important because it links the event from the object directly to this method, so it is invoked when the event is raised:

```
Private Sub OnWalk(ByVal distance As Integer) Handles mPerson.Walked
   MsgBox("Person walked " & distance)
End Sub
```

You're using the Handles keyword to indicate which event should be handled by this method. You're also receiving an Integer parameter. If the parameter list of the method doesn't match the list for the event, then you'll get a compiler error indicating the mismatch.

Finally, you need to call the Walk() method on the Person object. Add a button to the form and write the following code for its Click event:

```
Private Sub Button1_Click(ByVal sender As System.Object, _
    ByVal e As System.EventArgs) Handles button1.Click

  mPerson.Walk(42)

End Sub
```

When the button is clicked, you simply call the Walk method, passing an Integer value. This causes the code in your class to be run, including the RaiseEvent statement. The result is an event firing back into the form, because you declared the mPerson variable using the WithEvents keyword. The OnWalk() method will be run to handle the event, as it has the Handles clause linking it to the event.

The diagram in Figure 3-4 illustrates the flow of control, showing how the code in the button's Click event calls the Walk() method, causing it to add to the total distance walked and then to raise its event. The RaiseEvent causes the OnWalk() method in the form to be invoked; and once it is done, control returns to the Walk() method in the object. Because you have no code in the Walk method after you call RaiseEvent, the control returns to the Click event back in the form, and then you're done.

Many people have the misconception that events use multiple threads to do their work. This is not the case. Only one thread is involved in this process. Raising an event is much like making a method call, in that the existing thread is used to run the code in the event handler. This means that the application's processing is suspended until the event processing is complete.

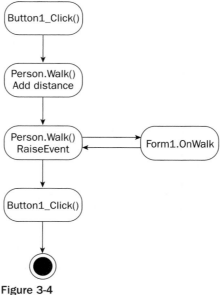

Figure 3-4

Receiving Events with AddHandler

Now that you've seen how to receive and handle events using the `WithEvents` and `Handles` keywords, let's take a look at an alternative approach. You can use the `AddHandler` method to dynamically add event handlers through your code, and `RemoveHandler` to dynamically remove them.

`WithEvents` and the `Handles` clause require that you declare both the object variable and event handler as you build the code, effectively creating a linkage that is compiled right into the code. `AddHandler`, on the other hand, creates this linkage at runtime, which can provide you with more flexibility. However, before getting too deeply into that, let's see how `AddHandler` works.

In `Form1`, you can change the way the code interacts with the `Person` object, first by eliminating the `WithEvents` keyword, as shown here:

```
Private mPerson As Person
```

And then by also eliminating the `Handles` clause:

```
Private Sub OnWalk(ByVal distance As Integer)
  MsgBox("Person walked " & distance)
End Sub
```

With these changes, you've eliminated all event handling for the object, and the form will no longer receive the event, even though the `Person` object raises it.

Now you can change the code to dynamically add an event handler at runtime by using the `AddHandler` method. This method simply links an object's event to a method that should be called to handle that event. Anytime after you've created the object, you can call `AddHandler` to set up the linkage:

```
Private Sub Form1_Load(ByVal sender As System.Object, _
    ByVal e As System.EventArgs) Handles MyBase.Load

  mPerson = New Person()
  AddHandler mPerson.Walked, AddressOf OnWalk
End Sub
```

This single line of code does the same thing as the earlier use of `WithEvents` and the `Handles` clause, causing the `OnWalk()` method to be invoked when the `Walked` event is raised from the `Person` object.

However, this linkage is performed at runtime, so you have more control over the process than you would have otherwise. For instance, you could have extra code to decide which event handler to link up. Suppose that you have another possible method to handle the event in the case that a message box is not desirable. Add this code to `Form1`:

```
Private Sub LogOnWalk(ByVal distance As Integer)
  System.Diagnostics.Debug.WriteLine("Person walked " & distance)
End Sub
```

Rather than pop up a message box, this version of the handler logs the event to the output window in the IDE.

Now you can enhance the `AddHandler` code to determine which handler should be used dynamically at runtime:

```
Private Sub Form1_Load(ByVal sender As System.Object, _
    ByVal e As System.EventArgs) Handles MyBase.Load

  mPerson = New Person()
  If Microsoft.VisualBasic.Command = "nodisplay" Then
    AddHandler mPerson.Walked, AddressOf LogOnWalk
  Else
    AddHandler mPerson.Walked, AddressOf OnWalk
  End If
End Sub
```

If the word `nodisplay` is on the command line when the application is run, then the new version of the event handler is used; otherwise, you continue to use the message box handler.

The counterpart to `AddHandler` is `RemoveHandler`. `RemoveHandler` is used to detach an event handler from an event. One example of when this is useful is if you ever want to set the `mPerson` variable to `Nothing` or to a new `Person` object. The existing `Person` object has its events attached to handlers, and before you get rid of the reference to the object, you must release those references:

```
  If Microsoft.VisualBasic.Command = "nodisplay" Then
    RemoveHandler mPerson.Walked, AddressOf LogOnWalk
  Else
    RemoveHandler mPerson.Walked, AddressOf OnWalk
  End If
  mPerson = New Person
```

If you don't detach the event handlers, the old `Person` object remains in memory because each event handler still maintains a reference to the object even after `mPerson` no longer points to the object.

This illustrates one key reason why the `WithEvents` keyword and `Handles` clause are preferable in most cases. `AddHandler` and `RemoveHandler` must be used in pairs, and failure to do so can cause memory leaks in the application, whereas the `WithEvents` keyword handles these details for you automatically.

Constructor Methods

In Visual Basic, classes can implement a special method that is always invoked as an object is being created. This method is called the *constructor,* and it is always named `New()`.

The constructor method is an ideal location for such initialization code, as it is always run before any other methods are ever invoked, and it is only run once for an object. Of course, you can create many objects based on a class, and the constructor method will be run for each object that is created.

You can implement a constructor in your classes as well, using it to initialize objects as needed. This is as easy as implementing a `Public` method named `New`. Add the following code to the `Person` class:

```
  Public Sub New()
    Phone("home") = "555-1234"
    Phone("work") = "555-5678"
  End Sub
```

In this example, you're simply using the constructor method to initialize the home and work phone numbers for any new Person object that is created.

Parameterized Constructors

You can also use constructors to allow parameters to be passed to the object as it is being created. This is done by simply adding parameters to the New() method. For example, you can change the Person class as follows:

```
Public Sub New(ByVal name As String, ByVal birthDate As Date)
   mName = name
   mBirthDate = birthDate
   Phone("home") = "555-1234"
   Phone("work") = "555-5678"
End Sub
```

With this change, anytime a Person object is created, you'll be provided with values for both the name and birth date. However, this changes how you can create a new Person object. Where you used to have code such as

```
Dim myPerson As New Person()
```

now you will have code such as

```
Dim myPerson As New Person("Peter", "1/1/1960")
```

In fact, because the constructor expects these values, they are mandatory — any code that needs to create an instance of the Person class must provide these values. Fortunately, there are alternatives in the form of optional parameters and method overloading (which enables you to create multiple versions of the same method, each accepting a different parameter list). These topics are discussed later in the chapter.

Termination and Cleanup

In the .NET environment, an object is destroyed and the memory and resources it consumes are reclaimed when there are no references remaining for the object. As discussed earlier in the chapter, when you are using objects, the variables actually hold a reference or pointer to the object itself. If you have code such as

```
Dim myPerson As New Person()
```

you know that the myPerson variable is just a reference to the Person object you created. If you also have code like

```
Dim anotherPerson As Person
anotherPerson = myPerson
```

you know that the anotherPerson variable is also a reference to the same object. This means that this specific Person object is being referenced by two variables.

When there are no variables left to reference an object, it can be terminated by the .NET runtime environment. In particular, it is terminated and reclaimed by a mechanism called *garbage collection,* or the *garbage collector,* covered in detail in Chapter 5.

Unlike COM (and thus VB6), the .NET runtime does not use reference counting to determine when an object should be terminated. Instead, it uses a scheme known as garbage collection to terminate objects. This means that, in Visual Basic, you do not have deterministic finalization, so it is not possible to predict exactly when an object will be destroyed.

Let's review how you can eliminate references to an object. You can explicitly remove a reference by setting the variable equal to Nothing, with the following code:

```
myPerson = Nothing
```

You can also remove a reference to an object by changing the variable to reference a different object. Because a variable can only point to one object at a time, it follows naturally that changing a variable to point at another object must cause it to no longer point to the first one. This means that you can have code such as the following:

```
myPerson = New Person()
```

This causes the variable to point to a brand-new object, thus releasing this reference to the prior object. These are examples of explicit dereferencing.

Visual Basic also provides facilities for implicit dereferencing of objects when a variable goes out of scope. For instance, if you have a variable declared within a method, then when that method completes, the variable is automatically destroyed, thus dereferencing any object to which it may have pointed. In fact, anytime a variable referencing an object goes out of scope, the reference to that object is automatically eliminated. This is illustrated by the following code:

```
Private Sub DoSomething()
  Dim myPerson As Person

  myPerson = New Person()
End Sub
```

Even though the preceding doesn't explicitly set the value of myPerson to Nothing, you know that the myPerson variable will be destroyed when the method is complete because it will fall out of scope. This process implicitly removes the reference to the Person object created within the routine.

Of course, another scenario in which objects become dereferenced is when the application itself completes and is terminated. At that point, all variables are destroyed, so, by definition, all object references go away as well.

Advanced Concepts

So far, you've learned how to work with objects, how to create classes with methods, properties, and events, and how to use constructors. You've also learned how objects are destroyed within the .NET environment and how you can hook into that process to do any cleanup required by the objects.

Now let's move on to discuss some more complex topics and variations on what has been discussed so far. First you'll look at some advanced variations of the methods you can implement in classes, including an exploration of the underlying technology behind events.

Overloading Methods

Methods often accept parameter values. The `Person` object's `Walk()` method, for instance, accepts an `Integer` parameter:

```
Public Sub Walk(ByVal distance As Integer)
  mTotalDistance += distance
  RaiseEvent Walked(distance)
End Sub
```

Sometimes there is no need for the parameter. To address this, you can use the `Optional` keyword to make the parameter optional:

```
Public Sub Walk(Optional ByVal distance As Integer = 0)
  mTotalDistance += distance
  RaiseEvent Walked(distance)
End Sub
```

This doesn't provide you with a lot of flexibility, however, as the optional parameter or parameters must always be the last ones in the list. In addition, all this allows you to do is choose to pass or not to pass the parameter. Suppose that you want to do something fancier, such as allow different datatypes, or even entirely different lists of parameters.

> Note that use of the `Optional` keyword makes the code harder to consume from C# or other .NET languages because they don't support optional parameters as VB does. If you are only working in Visual Basic, this may be a non-issue, but if you are working in a multilanguage environment, avoid using the `Optional` keyword. In addition, optional parameters require a default value.

Method overloading provides exactly those capabilities. By overloading methods, you can create several methods of the same name, with each one accepting a different set of parameters, or parameters of different datatypes.

As a simple example, instead of using the `Optional` keyword in the `Walk()` method, you could use overloading. You keep the original `Walk()` method, but you also add another `Walk()` method that accepts a different parameter list. Change the code in the `Person` class back to the following:

```
Public Sub Walk(ByVal distance As Integer)
  mTotalDistance += distance
  RaiseEvent Walked(distance)
End Sub
```

Then you can create another method with the same name, but with a different parameter list (in this case, no parameters). Add this code to the class, without removing or changing the existing `Walk()` method:

```
Public Sub Walk()
  RaiseEvent Walked(0)
End Sub
```

At this point, you have two `Walk()` methods. The only way to tell them apart is by the list of parameters each accepts: the first requiring a single `Integer` parameter, the second having no parameter.

There is an `Overloads` keyword as well. This keyword is not needed for simple overloading of methods as described here, but it is required when combining overloading and inheritance. This is discussed in Chapter 4.

You have the option of calling the `Walk` method in a couple of different ways. You can call it with a parameter:

```
objPerson.Walk(42)
```

Or without a parameter:

```
objPerson.Walk()
```

You can have any number of `Walk()` methods in the class as long as each individual `Walk()` method has a different method signature.

Method Signatures

All methods have a signature, which is defined by the method name and the datatypes of its parameters:

```
Public Function CalculateValue() As Integer

End Sub
```

In this example, the signature is $f()$. The letter f is often used to indicate a method or function. It is appropriate here because you don't care about the name of the function; only its parameter list is important.

If you add a parameter to the method, then the signature changes. For instance, you could change the method to accept a `Double`:

```
Public Function CalculateValue(ByVal value As Double) As Integer
```

In that case, the signature of the method is $f(\text{Double})$.

Notice that in Visual Basic the return value is not part of the signature. You can't overload a `Function` routine by just having its return value's datatype vary. It is the datatypes in the parameter list that must vary to utilize overloading.

Also note that the name of the parameter is totally immaterial; only the datatype is important. This means that the following methods have identical signatures:

```
Public Sub DoWork(ByVal x As Integer, ByVal y As Integer)

Public Sub DoWork(ByVal value1 As Integer, ByVal value2 As Integer)
```

In both cases, the signature is f(Integer, Integer).

The datatypes of the parameters define the method signature, but whether the parameters are passed ByVal or ByRef does not. Changing a parameter from ByVal to ByRef will not change the method signature.

Combining Overloading and Optional Parameters

Overloading is more flexible than using optional parameters, but optional parameters have the advantage that they can be used to provide default values, as well as making a parameter optional.

You can combine the two concepts: overloading a method and having one or more of those methods utilize optional parameters. Obviously, this sort of thing can become very confusing if overused, as you're employing two types of method "overloading" at the same time.

The Optional keyword causes a single method to effectively have two signatures. This means that a method declared as

```
Public Sub DoWork(ByVal x As Integer, Optional ByVal y As Integer = 0)
```

has two signatures at once: f(Integer, Integer) and f(Integer).

Because of this, when you use overloading along with optional parameters, the other overloaded methods cannot match either of these two signatures. However, as long as other methods don't match either signature, you can use overloading, as discussed earlier. For instance, you could implement methods with the following different signatures:

```
Public Sub DoWork(ByVal x As Integer, Optional ByVal y As Integer = 0)
```

and

```
Public Sub DoWork(ByVal data As String)
```

because there are no conflicting method signatures. In fact, with these two methods, you've really created three signatures:

- ❏ f(Integer, Integer)
- ❏ f(Integer)
- ❏ f(String)

The IntelliSense built into the Visual Studio IDE will indicate that you have two overloaded methods, one of which has an optional parameter. This is different from creating three different overloaded methods to match these three signatures, in which case the IntelliSense would list three variations on the method from which you could choose.

Overloading Constructor Methods

In many cases, you may want the constructor to accept parameter values for initializing new objects, but also want to have the capability to create objects without providing those values. This is possible through method overloading, which is discussed later, or through the use of optional parameters.

Optional parameters on a constructor method follow the same rules as optional parameters for any other Sub routine; they must be the last parameters in the parameter list, and you must provide default values for the optional parameters.

For instance, you can change the Person class as shown here:

```
Public Sub New(Optional ByVal name As String = "", _
    Optional ByVal birthDate As Date = #1/1/1900#)
  mName = name
  mBirthDate = birthDate

  Phone("home") = "555-1234"
  Phone("work") = "555-5678"
End Sub
```

Here, you've changed both the Name and BirthDate parameters to be optional, and you are providing default values for both of them. Now you have the option of creating a new Person object with or without the parameter values:

```
Dim myPerson As New Person("Peter", "1/1/1960")
```

or

```
Dim myPerson As New Person()
```

If you don't provide the parameter values, then the default values of an empty String and 1/1/1900 will be used and the code will work just fine.

Overloading the Constructor Method

You can combine the concept of a constructor method with method overloading to allow for different ways of creating instances of the class. This can be a very powerful combination, because it allows a great deal of flexibility in object creation.

You've already explored how to use optional parameters in the constructor. Now let's change the implementation in the Person class to make use of overloading instead. Change the existing New() method as follows:

```
Public Sub New(ByVal name As String, ByVal birthDate As Date)
  mName = name
  mBirthDate = birthDate
  Phone("home") = "555-1234"
  Phone("work") = "555-5678"
End Sub
```

With this change, you require the two parameter values to be supplied. Now add that second implementation, as shown here:

```
Public Sub New()
   Phone("home") = "555-1234"
   Phone("work") = "555-5678"
End Sub
```

This second implementation accepts no parameters, meaning that you can now create Person objects in two different ways — either with no parameters or by passing the name and birth date:

```
Dim myPerson As New Person()
```

or

```
Dim myPerson As New Person("Fred", "1/11/60")
```

This type of capability is very powerful, because it enables you to define the various ways in which applications can create objects. In fact, the Visual Studio IDE takes this into account, so when you are typing the code to create an object, the IntelliSense tooltip will display the overloaded variations on the method, providing a level of automatic documentation for the class.

Shared Methods, Variables, and Events

So far, all of the methods you've built or used have been instance methods, methods that require you to have an actual instance of the class before they can be called. These methods have used instance variables or member variables to do their work, which means that they have been working with a set of data that is unique to each individual object.

With Visual Basic you can create variables and methods that belong to the class, rather than to any specific object. In other words, these variables and methods belong to all objects of a given class and are shared across all the instances of the class.

You can use the Shared keyword to indicate which variables and methods belong to the class, rather than to specific objects. For instance, you may be interested in knowing the total number of Person objects created as the application is running — kind of a statistical counter.

Shared Variables

Because regular variables are unique to each individual Person object, they don't enable you to easily track the total number of Person objects ever created. However, if you had a variable that had a common value across all instances of the Person class, you could use that as a counter. Add the following variable declaration to the Person class:

```
Public Class Person
   Implements IDisposable
    Private Shared mCounter As Integer
```

By using the Shared keyword, you are indicating that this variable's value should be shared across all Person objects within your application. This means that if one Person object makes the value 42, then all other Person objects will see the value as 42: It is a shared piece of data.

You can now use this variable within the code. For instance, you can add code to the constructor method, New(), to increment the variable so that it acts as a counter — adding 1 each time a new Person object is created. Change the New() methods as shown here:

```
Public Sub New()
  Phone("home") = "555-1234"
  Phone("work") = "555-5678"
  mCounter += 1
End Sub
Public Sub New(ByVal name As String, ByVal birthDate As Date)
  mName = name
  mBirthDate = birthDate

  Phone("home") = "555-1234"
  Phone("work") = "555-5678"
  mCounter += 1
End Sub
```

The mCounter variable will now maintain a value indicating the total number of Person objects created during the life of the application. You may want to add a property routine to allow access to this value by writing the following code:

```
Public ReadOnly Property PersonCount() As Integer
  Get
    Return mCounter
  End Get
End Property
```

Notice that you're creating a regular property that returns the value of a shared variable. This is perfectly acceptable. As you'll see shortly, you could also choose to create a shared property to return the value.

Now you could write code to use the class as follows:

```
Dim myPerson As Person

myPerson = New Person()
myPerson = New Person()
myPerson = New Person()

Messagebox.Show(myPerson.PersonCount)
```

The resulting display would show 3, because you've created three instances of the Person class. You would also need to decrement the counter after the objects are destroyed.

Shared Methods

You can share not only variables across all instances of a class, but also methods. Whereas a regular method or property belongs to each specific object, a shared method or property is common across all instances of the class. There are a couple of ramifications to this approach.

First, because shared methods don't belong to any specific object, they can't access any instance variables from any objects. The only variables available for use within a shared method are shared variables, parameters passed into the method, or variables declared locally within the method itself. If you attempt to access an instance variable within a shared method, you'll get a compiler error.

In addition, because shared methods are actually part of the class rather than any object, you can write code to call them directly from the class without having to create an instance of the class first.

For instance, a regular instance method is invoked from an object:

```
Dim myPerson As New Person()

myPerson.Walk(42)
```

However, a shared method can be invoked directly from the class itself:

```
Person.SharedMethod()
```

This saves the effort of creating an object just to invoke a method, and can be very appropriate for methods that act on shared variables, or methods that act only on values passed in via parameters. You can also invoke a shared method from an object, just like a regular method. Shared methods are flexible in that they can be called with or without creating an instance of the class first.

To create a shared method, you again use the `Shared` keyword. For instance, the `PersonCount` property created earlier could easily be changed to become a shared method instead:

```
Public Shared ReadOnly Property PersonCount() As Integer
   Get
      Return mCounter
   End Get
End Property
```

Because this property returns the value of a shared variable, it is perfectly acceptable for it to be implemented as a shared method. With this change, you can now determine how many `Person` objects have ever been created without having to actually create a `Person` object first:

```
Messagebox.Show(CStr(Person.PersonCount))
```

As another example, in the `Person` class, you could create a method that compares the ages of two people. Add a shared method with the following code:

```
Public Shared Function CompareAge(ByVal person1 As Person, _
   ByVal person2 As Person) As Boolean
```

```
      Return person1.Age > person2.Age
   End Function
```

This method simply accepts two parameters — each a `Person` — and returns `True` if the first is older than the second. Use of the `Shared` keyword indicates that this method doesn't require a specific instance of the `Person` class in order for you to use it.

Within this code, you are invoking the `Age` property on two separate objects, the objects passed as parameters to the method. It is important to recognize that you're not directly using any instance variables within the method; rather, you are accepting two objects as parameters, and invoking methods on those objects. To use this method, you can call it directly from the class:

```
   If Person.CompareAge(myPerson1, myPerson2) Then
```

Alternately, you can also invoke it from any `Person` object:

```
   Dim myPerson As New Person()

   If myPerson.CompareAge(myPerson, myPerson2) Then
```

Either way, you're invoking the same shared method, and you'll get the same behavior, whether you call it from the class or a specific instance of the class.

Shared Properties

As with other types of methods, you can also have shared property methods. Properties follow the same rules as regular methods. They can interact with shared variables but not member variables. They can also invoke other shared methods or properties, but can't invoke instance methods without first creating an instance of the class. You can add a shared property to the `Person` class with the following code:

```
   Public Shared ReadOnly Property RetirementAge() As Integer
     Get
       Return 62
     End Get
   End Property
```

This simply adds a property to the class that indicates the global retirement age for all people. To use this value, you can simply access it directly from the class:

```
   Messagebox.Show(Person.RetirementAge)
```

Alternately, you can access it from any `Person` object:

```
   Dim myPerson As New Person()

   Messagebox.Show(myPerson.RetirementAge)
```

Either way, you're invoking the same shared property.

Shared Events

As with other interface elements, events can also be marked as Shared. For instance, you could declare a shared event in the Person class:

```
Public Shared Event NewPerson()
```

Shared events can be raised from both instance methods and shared methods. Regular events cannot be raised by shared methods. Because shared events can be raised by regular methods, you can raise this one from the constructors in the Person class:

```
Public Sub New()
  Phone("home") = "555-1234"
  Phone("work") = "555-5678"
  mCounter += 1
  RaiseEvent NewPerson()
End Sub
Public Sub New(ByVal name As String, ByVal birthDate As Date)
  mName = Name
  mBirthDate = BirthDate

  Phone("home") = "555-1234"
  Phone("work") = "555-5678"
  mCounter += 1
  RaiseEvent NewPerson()
End Sub
```

The interesting thing about receiving shared events is that you can get them from either an object, such as a normal event, or from the class itself. For instance, you can use the AddHandler method in the form's code to catch this event directly from the Person class.

First, let's add a method to the form to handle the event:

```
Private Sub OnNewPerson()
  Messagebox.Show("new person " & Person.PersonCount)
End Sub
```

Then, in the form's Load event, add a statement to link the event to this method:

```
Private Sub Form1_Load(ByVal sender As System.Object, _
    ByVal e As System.EventArgs) Handles MyBase.Load

    AddHandler Person.NewPerson, AddressOf OnNewPerson

    mPerson = New Person()
    If Microsoft.VisualBasic.Command = "nodisplay" Then
      AddHandler mPerson.Walked, AddressOf LogOnWalk
    Else
      AddHandler mPerson.Walked, AddressOf OnWalk
    End If
End Sub
```

Notice that you are using the class, rather than any specific object in the AddHandler statement. You could use an object as well, treating this like a normal event, but this illustrates how a class itself can raise an event. When you run the application now, anytime a Person object is created you'll see this event raised.

Shared Constructor

A class can also have a Shared constructor:

```
Shared Sub New()

End Sub
```

Normal constructors are called when an instance of the class is created. The Shared constructor is only called once during the lifetime of an application, immediately before any use of the class.

This means that the Shared constructor is called before any other Shared methods, and before any instances of the class are created. The first time any code attempts to interact with any method on the class, or attempts to create an instance of the class, the Shared constructor is invoked.

Because you never directly call the Shared constructor, it can't accept any parameters. Moreover, because it is a Shared method, it can only interact with Shared variables or other Shared methods in the class.

Typically, a Shared constructor is used to initialize Shared fields within an object. In the Person class for instance, you can use it to initialize the mCount variable:

```
Shared Sub New()
  mCount = 0
End Sub
```

Because this method is only called once during the lifetime of the application, it is safe to do one-time initializations of values in this constructor.

Operator Overloading

Many basic datatypes, such as Integer and String, support the use of operators including +, -, =, <>, and so forth. When you create a class, you are defining a new type, and sometimes it is appropriate for types to also support the use of operators.

In your class, you can write code to define how each of these operators works when applied to objects. What does it mean when two objects are added together? Or multiplied? Or compared? If you can define what these operations mean, you can write code to implement appropriate behaviors. This is called *operator overloading*, as you are overloading the meaning of specific operators.

Operator overloading is done by using the Operator keyword, much in the same way that you create a Sub, Function, or Property method.

Most objects at least provide for some type of comparison, and so will often overload the comparison operators (=, <>, and maybe <, >, <=, and >=). You can do this in the Person class, for example, by adding the following code:

```
Public Shared Operator =(ByVal person1 As Person, _
   ByVal person2 As Person) As Boolean

   Return person1.Name = person2.Name
End Operator

Public Shared Operator <>(ByVal person1 As Person, _
   ByVal person2 As Person) As Boolean

   Return person1.Name <> person2.Name
End Operator
```

Note that you overload both the = and <> operators. Many operators come in pairs, and this includes the equality operator. If you overload =, then you must overload <> or a compiler error will result. Now that you've overloaded these operators, you can write code in Form1 such as the following:

```
Dim p1 As New Person("Fred", #1/1/1960#)
Dim p2 As New Person("Mary", #1/1/1980#)
Dim p3 As Person = p1

Debug.WriteLine(CStr(p1 = p2))
Debug.WriteLine(CStr(p1 = p3))
```

Normally, it would be impossible to compare two objects using a simple comparison operator, but because you've overloaded the operator, this becomes valid code. The result will display False and True.

Both the = and <> operators accept two parameters, so these are called *binary operators*. There are also *unary operators* that accept a single parameter. For instance, you might define the ability to convert a String value into a Person object by overloading the CType operator:

```
Public Shared Narrowing Operator CType(ByVal name As String) As Person
   Dim obj As New Person
   obj.Name = name
   Return obj
End Operator
```

To convert a String value to a Person, you assume that the value should be the Name property. You create a new object, set the Name property, and return the result. Because String is a broader, or less-specific, type than Person, this is a Narrowing conversion. Were you to do the reverse, convert a Person to a String, that would be a Widening conversion:

```
Public Shared Widening Operator CType(ByVal person As Person) As String
   Return person.Name
End Operator
```

Few non-numeric objects will overload most operators. It is difficult to imagine the result of adding, subtracting, or dividing two Customer objects against each other. Likewise, it is difficult to imagine performing bitwise comparisons between two `Invoice` objects. The following chart lists the various operators that can be overloaded:

Operators	Meaning
=, <>	Equality and inequality. These are binary operators to support the `a = b` and `a <> b` syntax. If you implement one, then you must implement both.
>, <	Greater than and less than. These are binary operators to support the `a > b` and `a < b` syntax. If you implement one, then you must implement both.
>=, <=	Greater than or equal to and less than or equal to. These are binary operators to support the `a >= b` and `a <= b` syntax. If you implement one, then you must implement both.
IsFalse, IsTrue	Boolean conversion. These are unary operators to support the `AndAlso` and `OrElse` statements. The `IsFalse` operator accepts a single object and returns `False` if the object can be resolved to a `False` value. The `IsTrue` operator accepts a single value and returns `True` if the object can be resolved to a `True` value. If you implement one, then you must implement both.
CType	Type conversion. This is a unary operator to support the `CType(a)` statement. The `CType` operator accepts a single object of another type and converts that object to the type of your class. This operator must be marked as `Narrowing` to indicate that the type is more specific than the original type, or `Widening` to indicate that the type is broader than the original type.
+, -	Addition and subtraction. These operators can be unary or binary. The unary form exists to support the `a += b` and `a -= b` syntax, while the binary form exists to support `a + b` and `a - b`.
*, /, \, ^, Mod	Multiplication, division, exponent, and Mod. These are binary operators to support the `a * b`, `a / b`, `a \ b`, `a ^ b`, and `a Mod b` syntax.
&	Concatenation. This binary operator supports the `a & b` syntax. While this operator is typically associated with `String` manipulation, the `&` operator is not required to accept or return `String` values, so it can be used for any concatenation operation that is meaningful for your object type.
<<, >>	Bit shifting. These binary operators support the `a << b` and `a >> b` syntax. The second parameter of these operators must be a value of type `Integer`, which will be the integer value to be bit shifted based on your object value.
And, Or, Xor	Logical comparison or bitwise operation. These binary operators support the `a And b`, `a Or b`, and `a Xor b` syntax. If the operators return Boolean results, then they are performing logical comparisons. If they return results of other datatypes, then they are performing bitwise operations.
Like	Pattern comparison. This binary operator supports the `a Like b` syntax.

If an operator is meaningful for your datatype, then you are strongly encouraged to overload that operator.

Defining AndAlso and OrElse

Notice that neither the `AndAlso` nor the `OrElse` operators can be directly overloaded. This is because these operators use other operators behind the scenes to do their work. To overload `AndAlso` and `OrElse`, you need to overload a set of other operators, as shown here:

AndAlso	OrElse
Overload the `And` operator to accept two parameters of your object's type and to return a result of your object's type.	Overload the `Or` operator to accept two parameters of your object's type and to return a result of your object's type.
Overload `IsFalse` for your object's type (meaning that you can return `True` or `False` by evaluating a single instance of your object).	Overload `IsTrue` for your object's type (meaning that you can return `True` or `False` by evaluating a single instance of your object).

If these operators are overloaded in your class, then you can use `AndAlso` and `OrElse` to evaluate statements that involve instances of your class.

Delegates

There are times when it would be nice to be able to pass a procedure as a parameter to a method. The classic scenario is when building a generic sort routine, where you need to provide not only the data to be sorted, but also a comparison routine appropriate for the specific data.

It is easy enough to write a sort routine that sorts `Person` objects by name, or to write a sort routine that sorts `SalesOrder` objects by sales date. However, if you want to write a sort routine that can sort any type of object based on arbitrary sort criteria, that gets pretty difficult. At the same time, because some sort routines can get very complex, it would be nice to reuse that code without having to copy and paste it for each different sort scenario.

By using *delegates*, you can create such a generic routine for sorting; and in so doing, you can see how delegates work and can be used to create many other types of generic routines. The concept of a delegate formalizes the process of declaring a routine to be called and calling that routine.

> *The underlying mechanism used by the .NET environment for callback methods is the delegate. Visual Basic uses delegates behind the scenes as it implements the* `Event`, `RaiseEvent`, `WithEvents`, *and* `Handles` *keywords.*

Declaring a Delegate

In your code, you can declare what a delegate procedure must look like from an interface standpoint. This is done using the `Delegate` keyword. To see how this works, let's create a routine to sort any kind of data.

To do this, you'll declare a delegate that defines a method signature for a method that compares the value of two objects and returns a `Boolean` indicating whether the first object has a larger value than the second object. You'll then create a sort algorithm that uses this generic comparison method to sort data. Finally, you'll create an actual method that implements the comparison, and then you'll pass the address of that method to the sort routine.

Add a new module to the project by choosing the Project ➪ Add Module menu option. Name the module Sort.vb, and then add the following code:

```
Module Sort

    Public Delegate Function Compare(ByVal v1 As Object, ByVal v2 As Object) _
        As Boolean
End Module
```

This line of code does something interesting. It actually defines a method signature as a datatype. This new datatype is named Compare, and it can be used within the code to declare variables or parameters that are accepted by your methods. A variable or parameter declared using this datatype can actually hold the address of a method that matches the defined method signature, and you can then invoke that method by using the variable.

Any method with the signature

```
f(Object, Object)
```

can be viewed as being of type Compare.

Using the Delegate Datatype

You can write a routine that accepts this datatype as a parameter, meaning that anyone calling your routine must pass the address of a method that conforms to this interface. Add the following sort routine to the code module:

```
Public Sub DoSort(ByVal theData() As Object, ByVal greaterThan As Compare)
    Dim outer As Integer
    Dim inner As Integer
    Dim temp As Object

    For outer = 0 To UBound(theData)
    For inner = outer + 1 To UBound(theData)
        If greaterThan.Invoke(theData(outer), theData(inner)) Then
            temp = theData(outer)
            theData(outer) = theData(inner)
            theData(inner) = temp
        End If
    Next
    Next
End Sub
```

The GreaterThan parameter is a variable that holds the address of a method matching the method signature defined by the Compare delegate. The address of any method with a matching signature can be passed as a parameter to your Sort routine.

Note the use of the `Invoke` method, which is how a delegate is called from the code. Also note that the routine deals entirely with the generic `System.Object` datatype, rather than with any specific type of data. The specific comparison of one object to another is left to the delegate routine that is passed in as a parameter.

Implementing a Delegate Method

All that remains is to actually create the implementation of the delegate routine and call the sort method. On a very basic level, all you need to do is create a method that has a matching method signature. For instance, you could create a method such as the following:

```
Public Function PersonCompare(ByVal person1 As Object, _
  ByVal person2 As Object) As Boolean

End Function
```

The method signature of this method exactly matches what you defined by your delegate earlier:

```
Compare(Object, Object)
```

In both cases, you're defining two parameters of type `Object`.

Of course, there's more to it than simply creating the stub of a method. The method needs to return a value of `True` if its first parameter is greater than the second parameter. Otherwise, it should be written to deal with some specific type of data.

The `Delegate` statement defines a datatype based on a specific method interface. To call a routine that expects a parameter of this new datatype, it must pass the address of a method that conforms to the defined interface.

To conform to the interface, a method must have the same number of parameters with the same datatypes as defined in your `Delegate` statement. In addition, the method must provide the same return type as defined. The actual name of the method doesn't matter; it is the number, order, and datatype of the parameters and the return value that count.

To find the address of a specific method, you can use the `AddressOf` operator. This operator returns the address of any procedure or method, allowing you to pass that value as a parameter to any routine that expects a delegate as a parameter.

The `Person` class already has a shared method named `CompareAge` that generally does what you want. Unfortunately, it accepts parameters of type `Person`, rather than of type `Object` as required by the `Compare` delegate. You can use method overloading to solve this problem.

Create a second implementation of `CompareAge` that accepts parameters of type `Object` as required by the delegate, rather than of type `Person` as shown in the existing implementation:

```
Public Shared Function CompareAge(ByVal person1 As Object, _
    ByVal person2 As Object) As Boolean

  Return CType(person1, Person).Age > CType(person2, Person).Age

End Function
```

This method simply returns `True` if the first `Person` object's age is greater than the second's. The routine accepts two `Object` parameters, rather than specific `Person` type parameters, so you have to use the `CType()` method to access those objects as type `Person`. You accept the parameters as type `Object` because that is what is defined by the `Delegate` statement. You are matching its method signature:

```
f(Object, Object)
```

Because this method's parameter datatypes and return value match the delegate, you can use it when calling the `Sort` routine. Place a button on the form and write the following code behind that button:

```
Private Sub Button2_Click(ByVal sender As System.Object, _
    ByVal e As System.EventArgs) Handles button2.Click

  Dim myPeople(4) As Person

  myPeople(0) = New Person("Fred", #7/9/1960#)
  myPeople(1) = New Person("Mary", #1/21/1955#)
  myPeople(2) = New Person("Sarah", #2/1/1960#)
  myPeople(3) = New Person("George", #5/13/1970#)
  myPeople(4) = New Person("Andre", #10/1/1965#)

  DoSort(myPeople, AddressOf Person.CompareAge)
End Sub
```

This code creates an array of `Person` objects and populates them. It then calls the `DoSort` routine from the module, passing the array as the first parameter, and the address of the shared `CompareAge` method as the second parameter. To display the contents of the sorted array in the IDE's output window, you can add the following code:

```
Private Sub button2_Click(ByVal sender As System.Object, _
    ByVal e As System.EventArgs) Handles button2.Click

  Dim myPeople(4) As Person

  myPeople(0) = New Person("Fred", #7/9/1960#)
  myPeople(1) = New Person("Mary", #1/21/1955#)
  myPeople(2) = New Person("Sarah", #2/1/1960#)
  myPeople(3) = New Person("George", #5/13/1970#)
  myPeople(4) = New Person("Andre", #10/1/1965#)

  DoSort(myPeople, AddressOf Person.CompareAge)

  Dim myPerson As Person

  For Each myPerson In myPeople
    System.Diagnostics.Debug.WriteLine(myPerson.Name & " " & myPerson.Age)
  Next
End Sub
```

When you run the application and click the button, the output window displays a list of the people, sorted by age, as shown in Figure 3-5.

Figure 3-5

What makes this so very powerful is that you can change the comparison routine without changing the sort mechanism. Simply add another comparison routine to the `Person` class:

```
Public Shared Function CompareName(ByVal person1 As Object, _
    ByVal person2 As Object) As Boolean

  Return CType(person1, Person).Name > CType(person2, Person).Name

End Function
```

Then, change the code behind the button on the form to use that alternate comparison routine:

```
Private Sub Button2_Click(ByVal sender As System.Object, _
    ByVal e As System.EventArgs) Handles Button2.Click

  Dim myPeople(4) As Person

  myPeople(0) = New Person("Fred", #7/9/1960#)
  myPeople(1) = New Person("Mary", #1/21/1955#)
  myPeople(2) = New Person("Sarah", #2/1/1960#)
  myPeople(3) = New Person("George", #5/13/1970#)
  myPeople(4) = New Person("Andre", #10/1/1965#)

  DoSort(myPeople, AddressOf Person.CompareName)

  Dim myPerson As Person

  For Each myPerson In myPeople
    System.Diagnostics.Debug.WriteLine(myPerson.Name & " " & myPerson.Age)
  Next
End Sub
```

When you run this updated code, you'll find that the array contains a set of data sorted by name, rather than by age, as shown in Figure 3-6.

Simply by creating a new compare routine and passing it as a parameter, you can entirely change the way that the data is sorted. Better still, this sort routine can operate on any type of object, as long as you provide an appropriate delegate method that knows how to compare that type of object.

Figure 3-6

Classes versus Components

Visual Basic has another concept that is very similar to a class, the *component*. In fact, you can pretty much use a component and a class interchangeably, though there are some differences.

A component is really little more than a regular class, but it is one that supports a graphical designer within the Visual Studio IDE. This means that you can use drag-and-drop to provide the code in the component with access to items from the Server Explorer or from the toolbox.

To add a component to a project, select the Project ➪ Add Component menu option, give the component a name, and click Open in the Add New Item dialog box.

When you add a class to the project, you are presented with the Code window. When you add a component, you are presented with a graphical designer surface, much like what you'd see when adding a Web Form to the project.

If you switch to the code view (by right-clicking in the Designer view and choosing View Code), you will see the code that is created automatically, just as it is with a Windows Form, Web Form, or regular class:

```
Public Class Component1

End Class
```

This isn't a lot more code than you'd see with a regular class, though there are differences behind the scenes. A component uses the same partial class technology as Windows Forms or Web Forms. This means that the code here is only part of the total code in the class. The rest of the code is hidden behind the designer's surface and is automatically created and managed by Visual Studio.

In the designer code is an `Inherits` statement that makes every component inherit from `System` `.ComponentModel.Component`. Chapter 4 discusses the concept of inheritance, but note here that this `Inherits` line is what brings in all the support for the graphical designer in Visual Studio.

The designer also manages any controls or components that are dropped on the designer. Those controls or components are automatically made available to your code. For instance, if you drag and drop a Timer control from the Windows Forms tab of the toolbox onto the component, it will be displayed in the designer.

From here, you can set its properties using the standard Properties window in the IDE, just as you would for a control on a form. Using the Properties window, set the `Name` property to `theTimer`. You now automatically have access to a `Timer` object named `theTimer`, simply by dragging and dropping and setting some properties.

This means that you can write code within the component, just as you might in a class, to use this object:

```
Public Sub Start()
   theTimer.Enabled = True
End Sub

Public Sub Stop()
   theTimer.Enabled = False
End Sub

Private Sub theTimer_Tick(ByVal sender As System.Object, _
   ByVal e As System.EventArgs) Handles theTimer.Tick

   ' do work
End Sub
```

For the most part, you can use a component interchangeably with a basic class, but using a component also provides some of the designer benefits of working with Windows Forms or Web Forms.

Summary

Visual Basic offers a fully object-oriented language with all the capabilities you would expect. In this chapter, you explored the basic concepts around classes and objects, as well as the separation of interface from implementation and data.

You've learned how to use the `Class` keyword to create classes, and how those classes can be instantiated into specific objects, each one an instance of the class. These objects have methods and properties that can be invoked by the client code, and can act on data within the object stored in member or instance variables.

You also explored some more advanced concepts, including method overloading, shared or static variables and methods, and the use of delegates. Finally, the chapter wrapped up with a brief discussion of attributes and how they can be used to affect the interaction of classes or methods with the .NET environment.

The next chapter continues the discussion of object syntax as you explore the concept of inheritance and all the syntax that enables inheritance within Visual Basic. You will also walk through the creation, implementation, and use of multiple interfaces — a powerful concept that enables objects to be used in different ways, depending on the interface chosen by the client application.

Also covered in the next chapter is a discussion of objects and object-oriented programming, applying all of this syntax. It discusses the key object-oriented concepts of abstraction, encapsulation, polymorphism, and inheritance, and shows how they all tie together to provide a powerful way of designing and implementing applications.

Chapter 5 explores the .NET common language runtime (CLR). Because the .NET platform and runtime are object-oriented at their very core, this chapter examines how objects interact with the runtime environment, and covers topics such as using and disposing of objects, and memory management.

Object-Oriented Programming

Visual Basic is a fully object-oriented language. Chapter 3 covered the basics of creating classes and objects, including the creation of methods, properties, events, operators, and instance variables. You've seen the basic building blocks for abstraction, encapsulation, and polymorphism — concepts discussed in more detail at the end of this chapter. The final major techniques you need to understand are *inheritance* and the use of *multiple interfaces*.

Inheritance is the idea that you can create a class that reuses methods, properties, events, and variables from another class. You can create a class with some basic functionality, and then use that class as a base from which to create other, more detailed, classes. All these derived classes will have the same common functionality as that base class, along with new, enhanced, or even completely changed functionality.

This chapter covers the syntax that supports inheritance within Visual Basic. This includes creating the base classes from which other classes can be derived, as well as creating those derived classes.

Visual Basic also supports a related concept: multiple interfaces. As shown in Chapter 3, all objects have a native or default interface, which is defined by the public methods, properties, and events declared in the class. In the .NET environment, an object can have other interfaces in addition to this native interface — in other words, .NET objects can have multiple interfaces.

These secondary interfaces define alternative ways in which your object can be accessed by providing clearly defined sets of methods, properties, and events. Like the native interface, these secondary interfaces define how the client code can interact with your object, essentially providing a "contract" that enables the client to know exactly what methods, properties, and events the object will provide. When you write code to interact with an object, you can choose which of the interfaces you want to use; basically, you're choosing how you want to view or interact with that object.

This chapter uses relatively basic code examples so that you can focus on the technical and syntactic issues surrounding inheritance and multiple interfaces. The last part of this chapter revisits these concepts using a more sophisticated set of code as you continue to explore object-oriented programming and how to apply inheritance and multiple interfaces in a practical manner.

Keep in mind that just knowing the syntax and learning the tools is not enough to be successful. Successfully applying the object-oriented capabilities of Visual Basic to create applications requires an understanding of object-oriented programming. This chapter also applies Visual Basic's object-oriented syntax, showing how it enables you to build object-oriented applications. It further discusses the four major object-oriented concepts — abstraction, encapsulation, polymorphism, and inheritance. By the end of this chapter, you'll understand how these concepts can be applied in your design and development to create effective object-oriented applications.

Inheritance

Inheritance is the concept that a new class can be based on an existing class, inheriting its interface and functionality from the original class. In Chapter 3, you explored the relationship between a class and an object, where the class is essentially a template from which objects can be created.

While this is very powerful, it doesn't provide all the capabilities you might like. In particular, in many cases a class only partially describes what you need for your object. You may have a class called Person, for instance, which has all the properties and methods that apply to all types of people, things such as first name, last name, and birth date. While useful, this class probably doesn't have everything you need to describe a specific type of person, such as an employee or a customer. An employee would have a hire date and a salary, which are not included in Person, while a customer would have a credit rating, something neither the Person nor the Employee classes would need.

Without inheritance, you'd probably end up replicating the code from the Person class in both the Employee and Customer classes so that they'd have that same functionality as well as the ability to add new functionality of their own.

Inheritance makes it very easy to create classes for Employee, Customer, and so forth. You don't have to re-create that code for an employee to be a person; it automatically inherits any properties, methods, and events from the original Person class.

You can think of it this way: When you create an Employee class, which inherits from a Person class, you are effectively merging these two classes. If you then create an object based on the Employee class, it not only has the interface (properties, methods, and events) and implementation from the Employee class, but also those from the Person class.

While an Employee object represents the merger between the Employee and Person classes, it is important to realize that the variables and code contained in each of those classes remain independent. Two perspectives are involved.

From the outside, the client code that interacts with the Employee object sees a single, unified object that represents the merger of the Employee and Person classes.

From the inside, the code in the Employee class and the code in the Person class aren't totally intermixed. Variables and methods that are Private are only available within the class they were written. Variables and methods that are Public in one class can be called from the other class. Variables and methods that are declared as `Friend` are only available between classes if both classes are in the same Visual Basic project. As discussed later in the chapter, there is also a `Protected` scope that is designed to work with inheritance, but, again, this provides a controlled way for one class to interact with the variables and methods in the other class.

Visual Studio 2005 includes a Class Designer tool that enables you to easily create diagrams of your classes and their relationships. The Class Designer diagrams are a derivative of a standard notation called the *Unified Modeling Language (UML)* that is typically used to diagram the relationships between classes, objects, and other object-oriented concepts. The Class Designer diagrams more accurately and completely model .NET classes, so that is the notation used in this chapter. The relationship between the `Person`, `Employee`, and `Customer` classes is illustrated in Figure 4-1.

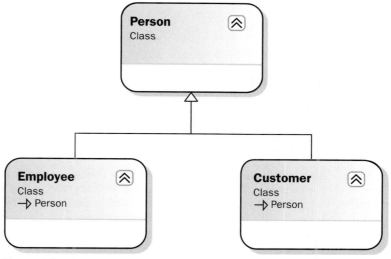

Figure 4-1

Each box in this diagram represents a class; in this case, you have `Person`, `Employee`, and `Customer` classes. The line from `Employee` back up to `Person`, terminating in a triangle, indicates that `Employee` is derived from, or inherits from, `Person`. The same is true for the `Customer` class.

Later in this chapter you will see in more detail when and how inheritance should be used in software design. The beginning part of this chapter covers the syntax and programming concepts necessary to implement inheritance. First, you'll create a base `Person` class. Then, you'll use that class to create both `Employee` and `Customer` classes that inherit behavior from `Person`.

Before getting into the implementation, however, it's necessary to understand some basic terms associated with inheritance — and there are a lot of terms, partly because there are often several ways to say the same thing. The various terms are all used quite frequently and interchangeably.

> *Though we attempt to use consistent terminology in this book, be aware that in other books and articles and online all these terms are used in various permutations.*

Inheritance, for instance, is also sometimes referred to as generalization because the class from which you are inheriting your behavior is virtually always a more general form of your new class. A person is more general than an employee, for instance.

The inheritance relationship is also referred to as an *is-a* relationship. When you create a `Customer` class that inherits from a `Person` class, that customer *is a* person. The employee is a person as well. Thus, you have this *is-a* relationship. As shown later in the chapter, multiple interfaces can be used to implement something similar to the *is-a* relationship, the *act-as* relationship.

When you create a class using inheritance, it inherits behaviors and data from an existing class. That existing class is called the *base class*. It is also often referred to as a *superclass* or a *parent class*.

The class you create using inheritance is based on the parent class. It is called a *subclass*. Sometimes, it is also called a *child class* or a *derived class*. In fact, the process of inheriting from a base class by a subclass is often referred to as *deriving*. You are deriving a new class from the base class. The process is also often called *subclassing*.

Implementing Inheritance

When you set out to implement a class using inheritance, you must first start with an existing class from which you will derive your new subclass. This existing class, or base class, may be part of the .NET system class library framework, it may be part of some other application or .NET assembly, or you may create it as part of your existing application.

Once you have a base class, you can then implement one or more subclasses based on that base class. Each of your subclasses automatically has all of the methods, properties, and events of that base class — including the implementation behind each method, property, and event. Your subclass can add new methods, properties, and events of its own, extending the original interface with new functionality. In addition, a subclass can replace the methods and properties of the base class with its own new implementation — effectively overriding the original behavior and replacing it with new behaviors.

Essentially, inheritance is a way of merging functionality from an existing class into your new subclass. Inheritance also defines rules for how these methods, properties, and events can be merged, including control over how they can be changed or replaced, and how the subclass can add new methods, properties, and events of its own. This is what you'll explore as you go forward — what these rules are and what syntax you use in Visual Basic to make it all work.

Creating a Base Class

Virtually any class you create can act as a base class from which other classes can be derived. In fact, unless you specifically indicate in the code that your class cannot be a base class, you can derive from it (you'll come back to this later).

Create a new Windows Application project in Visual Basic. Then add a class to the project using the Project ➪ Add Class menu option and name it `Person.vb`. Begin with the following code:

```
Public Class Person

End Class
```

At this point, you technically have a base class, as it is possible to inherit from this class even though it doesn't do or contain anything.

You can now add methods, properties, and events to this class as you normally would. All of those interface elements would be inherited by any class you might create based on `Person`. For instance, add the following code:

```
Public Class Person
   Private mName As String
   Private mBirthDate As Date

   Public Property Name() As String
     Get
        Return mName
     End Get
     Set(ByVal value As String)
        mName = value
     End Set
   End Property

   Public Property BirthDate() As Date
     Get
        Return mBirthDate
     End Get
     Set(ByVal value As Date)
        mBirthDate = value
     End Set
   End Property
End Class
```

This provides a simple method that can be used to illustrate how basic inheritance works. This class can be represented by the class diagram in Visual Studio, as shown in Figure 4-2.

Figure 4-2

In this representation of the class as it is presented from Visual Studio, the overall box represents the `Person` class. In the top section of this box, you have the name of the class and a specification that it is a class. The section below it contains a list of the instance variables, or fields, of the class, with their scope marked as `Private` (note the lock icon). The bottom section lists the properties exposed by the class, both marked as `Public`. If the class had methods or events, then they would be displayed in their own sections in the diagram.

Creating a Subclass

To implement inheritance, you need to add a new class to your project. Use the Project ⇨ Add Class menu option and add a new class named `Employee.vb`. Begin with the following code:

```
Public Class Employee
  Private mHireDate As Date
  Private mSalary As Double

  Public Property HireDate() As Date
    Get
      Return mHireDate
    End Get
    Set(ByVal value As Date)
      mHireDate = value
    End Set
  End Property

  Public Property Salary() As Double
    Get
      Return mSalary
    End Get
    Set(ByVal value As Double)
      mSalary = value
    End Set
  End Property
End Class
```

This is a regular standalone class with no explicit inheritance. It can be represented by the following class diagram (see Figure 4-3).

Figure 4-3

Again, you can see the class name, its list of instance variables, and the properties it includes as part of its interface. It turns out that, behind the scenes, this class inherits some capabilities from `System.Object`. In fact, every class in the entire .NET platform ultimately inherits from `System.Object` either implicitly or explicitly. This is why all .NET objects have a basic set of common functionality, including most notably the `GetType` method. This is discussed in detail later in the chapter.

While having an `Employee` object with a hire date and salary is useful, it should also have `Name` and `BirthDate` properties, just as you implemented in the `Person` class. Without inheritance, you'd probably just copy and paste the code from `Person` directly into the new `Employee` class, but with inheritance you can directly reuse the code from the `Person` class. Let's make the new class inherit from `Person`.

The Inherits Keyword

To make `Employee` a subclass of `Person`, add a single line of code:

```
Public Class Employee
    Inherits Person
```

The `Inherits` keyword indicates that a class should derive from an existing class, inheriting the interface and behavior from that class. You can inherit from almost any class in your project, or from the .NET system class library or from other assemblies. It is also possible to prevent inheritance, as covered later in the chapter. When using the `Inherits` keyword to inherit from classes outside the current project, you need to either specify the namespace that contains that class or have an `Imports` statement at the top of the class to import that namespace for your use.

The diagram in Figure 4-4 illustrates the fact that the `Employee` class is now a subclass of `Person`.

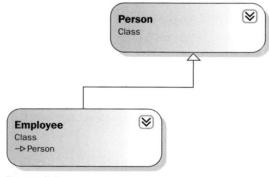

Figure 4-4

The line running from `Employee` back up to `Person` ends in an open triangle, which is the symbol for inheritance when using the Class Designer in Visual Studio. It is this line that indicates that the `Employee` class includes all the functionality, as well as the interface, of `Person`.

This means that an object created based on the `Employee` class has not only the methods `HireDate` and `Salary`, but also `Name` and `BirthDate`. To test this, bring up the designer for `Form1` (which is automatically part of your project, because you created a Windows Application project) and add the following TextBox controls along with a button to the form:

Control Type	Name	Text Value
TextBox	txtName	<blank>
TextBox	txtBirthDate	<blank>
TextBox	txtHireDate	<blank>
TextBox	txtSalary	<blank>
button	btnOK	OK

You can also add some labels to make the form more readable. The Form Designer should now look something like Figure 4-5.

Figure 4-5

Double-click the button to bring up the code window, and enter the following code:

```
Private Sub btnOK_Click(ByVal sender As System.Object, _
                    ByVal e As System.EventArgs) Handles btnOK.Click
    Dim emp As New Employee()

    With emp
      .Name = "Fred"
      .BirthDate = #1/1/1960#
      .HireDate = #1/1/1980#
      .Salary = 30000

      txtName.Text = .Name
      txtBirthDate.Text = Format(.BirthDate, "Short date")
      txtHireDate.Text = Format(.HireDate, "Short date")
      txtSalary.Text = Format(.Salary, "$0.00")
    End With
End Sub
```

The best Visual Basic practice is to use the `With` keyword, but be aware that this might cause issues with portability and converting code to other languages.

Even though `Employee` doesn't directly implement the `Name` or `BirthDate` methods, they are available for use through inheritance. When you run this application and click the button, your controls are populated with the values from the `Employee` object.

When the code in `Form1` invokes the `Name` property on the `Employee` object, the code from the `Person` class is executed, as the `Employee` class has no such method built in. However, when the `HireDate` property is invoked on the `Employee` object, the code from the `Employee` class is executed, as it does have that method as part of its code.

From the form's perspective, it doesn't matter whether a method is implemented in the `Employee` class or the `Person` class; they are all simply methods of the `Employee` object. In addition, because the code in these classes is merged to create the `Employee` object, there is no performance difference between calling a method implemented by the `Employee` class or calling a method implemented by the `Person` class.

Overloading Methods

Although your `Employee` class automatically gains the `Name` and `BirthDate` methods through inheritance, it also has methods of its own — `HireDate` and `Salary`. This shows how you've extended the base `Person` interface by adding methods and properties to the `Employee` subclass.

You can add new properties, methods, and events to the `Employee` class, and they will be part of any object created based on `Employee`. This has no impact on the `Person` class whatsoever, only on the `Employee` class and `Employee` objects.

You can even extend the functionality of the base class by adding methods to the subclass that have the same name as methods or properties in the base class, as long as those methods or properties have different parameter lists. You are effectively overloading the existing methods from the base class. It is essentially the same thing as overloading regular methods, as discussed in Chapter 3.

For example, your `Person` class is currently providing your implementation for the `Name` property. Employees may have other names you also want to store, perhaps an informal name and a very formal name in addition to their regular name. One way to accommodate this requirement is to change the `Person` class itself to include an overloaded `Name` property that supports this new functionality. However, you're really only trying to enhance the `Employee` class, not the more general `Person` class, so what you want is a way to add an overloaded method to the `Employee` class itself, even though you're overloading a method from its base class.

You can overload a method from a base class by using the `Overloads` keyword. The concept is the same as described in Chapter 3, but in this case an extra keyword is involved. To overload the `Name` property, for instance, you can add a new property to the `Employee` class. First, though, let's define an enumerated type using the `Enum` keyword. This `Enum` will list the different types of name you want to store. Add this `Enum` to the `Employee.vb` file, before the declaration of the class itself:

```
Public Enum NameTypes
   Informal = 1
   Formal = 2
End Enum
Public Class Employee
```

You can then add an overloaded `Name` property to the `Employee` class itself:

```
Public Class Employee
  Inherits Person

  Private mHireDate As Date
  Private mSalary As Double
  Private mNames As New Generic.Dictionary(Of NameTypes, String)

  Public Overloads Property Name(ByVal type As NameTypes) As String
    Get
      Return mNames(type)
    End Get
    Set(ByVal value As String)
      If mNames.ContainsKey(type) Then
        mNames.Item(type) = value
      Else
        mNames.Add(type, value)
      End If
    End Set
  End Property
End Property
```

This `Name` property is actually a property array, enabling you to store multiple values via the same property. In this case, you're storing the values in a `Generic.Dictionary(Of K, V)` object, which is indexed by using the `Enum` value you just defined. Chapter 7 discusses generics in detail. For now, you can view this generic `Dictionary` just like any collection object that stores key/value data.

> *If you omit the* `Overloads` *keyword here, your new implementation of the* `Name` *method will* shadow *the original implementation. Shadowing is very different from overloading, and is covered later in the chapter.*

Though this method has the same name as the method in the base class, the fact that it accepts a different parameter list enables you to use overloading to implement it here. The original `Name` property, as implemented in the `Person` class, remains intact and valid, but now you've added a new variation with this second `Name` property, as shown by Figure 4-6.

The diagram clearly indicates that the `Name` method in the `Person` class and the `Name` method in the `Employee` class both exist. If you hover over each `Name` property, you'll see a tooltip showing the method signatures, making it very clear that each one has a different signature.

You can now change `Form1` to make use of this new version of the `Name` property. First, add a couple of new text box controls and associated labels. The text box controls should be named `txtFormal` and `txt-Informal`, and the form should now look like the one shown in Figure 4-7. Double-click the button on the form to bring up the code window and add code to work with the overloaded version of the `Name` property:

```
Private Sub btnOK_Click(ByVal sender As System.Object, _
    ByVal e As System.EventArgs) Handles btnOK.Click

  Dim emp As New Employee()

  With emp
    .Name = "Fred"
    .Name(NameTypes.Formal) = "Mr. Frederick R. Jones, Sr."
    .Name(NameTypes.Informal) = "Freddy"
    .BirthDate = #1/1/1960#
```

```
        .HireDate = #1/1/1980#
        .Salary = 30000

        txtName.Text = .Name
        txtFormal.Text = .Name (NameTypes.Formal)
        txtInformal.Text = .Name (NameTypes.Informal)
        txtBirthDate.Text = Format(.BirthDate, "Short date")
        txtHireDate.Text = Format(.HireDate, "Short date")
        txtSalary.Text = Format(.Salary, "$0.00")
    End With
End Sub
```

Figure 4-6

Figure 4-7

As you can see, the code still interacts with the original `Name` property as implemented in the `Person` class, but you are now also invoking the overloaded version of the property implemented in the `Employee` class.

Overriding Methods

So far, you've seen how to implement a base class and then use it to create a subclass. You also extended the interface by adding methods, and you explored how to use overloading to add methods that have the same name as methods in the base class, but with different parameters.

However, sometimes you may want not only to extend the original functionality, but also to actually change or entirely replace the functionality from the base class. Instead of leaving the existing functionality and just adding new methods or overloaded versions of those methods, you might want to entirely override the existing functionality with your own.

You can do exactly that. If the base class allows it, you can substitute your own implementation of a method in the base class — meaning that your new implementation will be used instead of the original.

The Overridable Keyword

By default, you can't override the behavior of methods on a base class. The base class must be coded specifically to allow this to occur, by using the `Overridable` keyword. This is important, as you may not always want to allow a subclass to entirely change the behavior of the methods in your base class. However, if you do wish to allow the author of a subclass to replace your implementation, you can do so by adding the `Overridable` keyword to your method declaration.

Returning to the `Employee` example, you may not like the implementation of the `BirthDate` method as it stands in the `Person` class. Say, for instance, that you can't employ anyone younger than 16 years of age, so any birth date value more recent than 16 years ago is invalid for an employee.

To implement this business rule, you need to change the way the `BirthDate` property is implemented. While you could make this change directly in the `Person` class, that would not be ideal. It is perfectly acceptable to have a person under age 16, just not an employee.

Open the code window for the `Person` class and change the `BirthDate` property to include the `Overridable` keyword:

```
Public Overridable Property BirthDate() As Date
  Get
    Return mBirthDate
  End Get
  Set(ByVal value As Date)
    mBirthDate = value
  End Set
End Property
```

This change allows any class that inherits from `Person` to entirely replace the implementation of the `BirthDate` property with a new implementation.

By adding the `Overridable` keyword to your method declaration, you are indicating that you want to allow any subclass to override the behavior provided by this method. This means that you are giving permission for a subclass to totally ignore your prior implementation, or to extend your implementation by doing other work before or after your implementation is run.

If the subclass doesn't override this method, the method works just like a regular method and is automatically included as part of the subclass's interface. Putting the `Overridable` keyword on a method simply allows a subclass to override the method if you choose to have it do so.

The Overrides Keyword

In a subclass, you override a method by implementing a method of the same name, and with the same parameter list as the base class, and then you use the `Overrides` keyword to indicate that you are overriding that method.

This is different from overloading, because when you overload a method you're adding a new method with the same name but a different parameter list. When you override a method, you're actually replacing the original method with a new implementation.

Without the `Overrides` keyword, you'll receive a compilation error when you implement a method with the same name as one from the base class.

Open the code window for the `Employee` class and add a new `BirthDate` property:

```
Public Class Employee
  Inherits Person

  Private mHireDate As Date
  Private mSalary As Double
  Private mBirthDate As Date

  Private mNames As New Generic.Dictionary(Of NameTypes, String)

  Public Overrides Property BirthDate() As Date
    Get
      Return mBirthDate
    End Get
    Set(ByVal value As Date)
      If DateDiff(DateInterval.Year, Value, Now) >= 16 Then
        mBirthDate = value
      Else
        Throw New ArgumentException( _
          "An employee must be at least 16 years old.")
      End If
    End Set
  End Property
```

Because you're implementing your own version of the property, you have to declare a variable to store that value within the `Employee` class. This is not ideal, and there are a couple of ways around it, including the `MyBase` keyword and the `Protected` scope.

Notice also that you've enhanced the functionality in the Set block, so it now raises an error if the new birth date value would cause the employee to be less than 16 years of age. With this code, you've now entirely replaced the original BirthDate implementation with a new one that enforces your business rule (see Figure 4-8).

Figure 4-8

The diagram now includes a BirthDate method in the Employee class. While perhaps not entirely intuitive, this is how the class diagram indicates that you've overridden the method. If you hover the mouse over the property in the Employee class, the tooltip will show the method signature, including the Overrides keyword.

If you now run your application and click the button on the form, everything should work as it did before because the birth date you're supplying conforms to your new business rule. However, you can change the code in your form to use an invalid birth date:

```
With emp
  .Name = "Fred"
  .Name(NameTypes.Formal) = "Mr. Frederick R. Jones, Sr."
  .Name(NameTypes.Informal) = "Freddy"
  .BirthDate = #1/1/2000#
```

When you run the application (from within Visual Studio) and click the button, you'll receive an error indicating that the birth date is invalid. This proves that you are now using the implementation of the

`BirthDate` method from the `Employee` class, rather than the one from the `Person` class. Change the date value in the form back to a valid value so that your application runs properly.

The MyBase Keyword

You've just seen how you can entirely replace the functionality of a method in the base class by overriding it in your subclass. However, this can be somewhat extreme; sometimes it would be preferable to override methods so that you extend the base functionality, rather than replace the functionality.

To do this, you need to override the method using the `Overrides` keyword as you just did, but within your new implementation you can still invoke the original implementation of the method. This enables you to add your own code before or after the original implementation is invoked — meaning you can extend the behavior while still leveraging the code in the base class.

To invoke methods directly from the base class, you can use the `MyBase` keyword. This keyword is available within any class, and it exposes all the methods of the base class for your use.

> *Even a base class such as* `Person` *is an implicit subclass of* `System.Object`, *so it can use* `MyBase` *to interact with its base class as well.*

This means that within the `BirthDate` implementation in `Employee`, you can invoke the `BirthDate` implementation in the base `Person` class. This is ideal, as it means that you can leverage any existing functionality provided by `Person` while still enforcing your `Employee`-specific business rules.

To take advantage of this, you can enhance the code in the `Employee` implementation of `BirthDate`. First, remove the declaration of `mBirthDate` from the `Employee` class. You won't need this variable any longer because the `Person` implementation will keep track of the value on your behalf. Then, change the `BirthDate` implementation in the `Employee` class as follows:

```
Public Overrides Property BirthDate() As Date
  Get
    Return MyBase.BirthDate
  End Get

  Set(ByVal value As Date)
    If DateDiff(DateInterval.Year, Value, Now) >= 16 Then
      MyBase.BirthDate = value
    Else
      Throw New ArgumentException( _
        "An employee must be at least 16 years old.")
    End If
  End Set
End Property
```

Run your application and you'll see that it works just fine even though the `Employee` class no longer contains any code to actually keep track of the birth date value. You've effectively merged the `BirthDate` implementation from `Person` right into your enhanced implementation in `Employee`, creating a hybrid version of the property.

The `MyBase` keyword is covered in more detail later in the chapter. Here, you can see how it enables you to enhance or extend the functionality of the base class by adding your own code in the subclass but still invoking the base class method when appropriate.

Virtual Methods

The `BirthDate` method is an example of a *virtual method*. Virtual methods are those that can be overridden and replaced by subclasses.

Virtual methods are more complex to understand than regular nonvirtual methods. With a nonvirtual method, only one implementation matches any given method signature, so there's no ambiguity about which specific method implementation will be invoked. With virtual methods, however, there may be several implementations of the same method, with the same method signature, so you need to understand the rules that govern which specific implementation of that method will be called.

When working with virtual methods, keep in mind that the datatype of the object is used to determine the implementation of the method to call, rather than the type of the variable that refers to the object.

If you look at the code in your form, you can see that you're declaring an object variable of type `Employee`, and you are then creating an `Employee` object that you can reference via that object:

```
Dim emp As New Employee()
```

It is not surprising, then, that you are able to invoke any of the methods that are implemented as part of the `Employee` class, and through inheritance, any of the methods implemented as part of the `Person` class:

```
With emp
  .Name = "Fred"
  .Name(NameTypes.Formal) = "Mr. Frederick R. Jones, Sr."
  .Name(NameTypes.Informal) = "Freddy"
  .BirthDate = #1/1/1960#
  .HireDate = #1/1/1980#
  .Salary = 30000
```

When you call the `BirthDate` property, you know that you're invoking the implementation contained in the `Employee` class, which makes sense because you know that you're using a variable of type `Employee` to refer to an object of type `Employee`.

However, because your methods are virtual methods, you can experiment with some much more interesting scenarios. For instance, suppose that you change the code in your form to interact directly with an object of type `Person` instead of one of type `Employee`:

```
Private Sub btnOK_Click(ByVal sender As System.Object, _
    ByVal e As System.EventArgs) Handles btnOK.Click

  Dim person As New Person()

  With person
    .Name = "Fred"
    .BirthDate = #1/1/1960#

    txtName.Text = .Name
    txtBirthDate.Text = Format(.BirthDate, "Short date")
  End With

End Sub
```

You can no longer call the methods implemented by the `Employee` class, because they don't exist as part of a `Person` object, but only as part of an `Employee` object. However, you can see that both the `Name` and `BirthDate` properties continue to function as you'd expect. When you run the application now, it will work just fine. You can even change the birth date value to something that would be invalid for `Employee`:

```
.BirthDate = #1/1/2000#
```

The application will now accept it and work just fine, because the `BirthDate` method you're invoking is the original version from the `Person` class.

These are the two simple scenarios, when you have a variable and object of type `Employee` or a variable and object of type `Person`. However, because `Employee` is derived from `Person`, you can do something a bit more interesting. You can use a variable of type `Person` to hold a reference to an `Employee` object. For example, you can change the code in `Form1` as follows:

```
Private Sub btnOK_Click(ByVal sender As System.Object, _
    ByVal e As System.EventArgs) Handles btnOK.Click

  Dim person As Person
  person = New Employee()
  With person
    .Name = "Fred"
    .BirthDate = #1/1/2000#

    txtName.Text = .Name
    txtBirthDate.Text = Format(.BirthDate, "Short date")
  End With
End Sub
```

What you're doing now is declaring your variable to be of type `Person`, but the object itself is an instance of the `Employee` class. You've done something a bit complex here, as the datatype of the variable is not the same as the datatype of the object itself. Remember that a variable of a base class type can always hold a reference to an object of any subclass.

> This is the reason why a variable of type `System.Object` can hold a reference to literally anything in the .NET Framework, because all classes are ultimately derived from `System.Object`.

This technique is very useful when creating generic routines. It makes use of an object-oriented concept called *polymorphism,* which is discussed more thoroughly later in this chapter. This technique enables you to create a more general routine that populates your form for any object of type `Person`. Add the following code to the form:

```
Private Sub DisplayPerson(ByVal thePerson As Person)
  With thePerson
    txtName.Text = .Name
    txtBirthDate.Text = Format(.BirthDate, "Short date")
  End With
End Sub
```

Now you can change the code behind the button to make use of this generic routine:

```
Private Sub btnOK_Click(ByVal sender As System.Object, _
    ByVal e As System.EventArgs) Handles btnOK.Click

  Dim person As Person
  person = New Employee()

  With person
    .Name = "Fred"
    .BirthDate = #1/1/2000#
  End With

  DisplayPerson(person)
End Sub
```

The benefit here is that you can pass a `Person` object or an `Employee` object to `DisplayPerson` and the routine will work the same either way.

When you run the application now, things get interesting. You'll get an error when you attempt to set the `BirthDate` property because it breaks your 16-year-old business rule, which is implemented in the `Employee` class. How can this be when your `person` variable is of type `Person`?

This clearly demonstrates the concept of a virtual method. It is the datatype of the object, in this case `Employee`, that is important. The datatype of the variable is not the deciding factor when choosing which implementation of an overridden method is invoked.

The following table shows which method is actually invoked based on the variable and object datatypes when working with virtual methods:

Variable Type	Object Type	Method Invoked
Base	Base	Base
Base	Subclass	Subclass
Subclass	Subclass	Subclass

Virtual methods are very powerful and useful when you implement polymorphism using inheritance. A base class datatype can hold a reference to any subclass object, but it is the type of that specific object which determines the implementation of the method. Therefore, you can write generic routines that operate on many types of object as long as they derive from the same base class. You'll learn how to make use of polymorphism and virtual methods in more detail later in this chapter.

Overriding Overloaded Methods

Earlier, you wrote code in your `Employee` class to overload the `Name` method in the base `Person` class. This enabled you to keep the original `Name` functionality but also extend it by adding another `Name` method that accepted a different parameter list.

You've also overridden the `BirthDate` method. The implementation in the `Employee` class replaced the implementation in the `Person` class. Overriding is a related, but different concept from overloading. It is also possible to both overload and override a method at the same time.

In the earlier overloading example, you added a new `Name` property to the `Employee` class, while retaining the functionality present in the base `Person` class. You may decide that you not only want to have your second overloaded implementation of the `Name` method, but also want to replace the existing one by overriding the existing method provided by the `Person` class.

In particular, you may want to do this so that you can store the `Name` value in the `Hashtable` object along with your `Formal` and `Informal` names. Before you can override the `Name` method, you need to add the `Overridable` keyword to the base implementation in the `Person` class:

```
Public Overridable Property Name() As String
  Get
    Return mName
  End Get
  Set(ByVal value As String)
    mName = value
  End Set
End Property
```

With that done, the `Name` method can now be overridden by any derived classes. In the `Employee` class, you can now override the `Name` method, replacing the functionality provided by the `Person` class. First, add a `Normal` option to the `Enum` that controls the types of `Name` value you can store:

```
Public Enum NameTypes
  Informal = 1
  Formal = 2
  Normal = 3
End Enum
```

Now you can add code to the `Employee` class to implement a new `Name` property. This is in addition to the existing `Name` property already implemented in the `Employee` class:

```
Public Overloads Overrides Property Name() As String
  Get
    Return Name(NameTypes.Normal)
  End Get
  Set(ByVal value As String)
    Name(NameTypes.Normal) = value
  End Set
End Property
```

Notice that you're using both the `Overrides` keyword, to indicate that you're overriding the `Name` method from the base class, and the `Overloads` keyword, to indicate that you're overloading this method in the subclass.

This new `Name` property merely delegates the call to the existing version of the `Name` property that handles the parameter-based names. To complete the linkage between this implementation of the `Name` property and the parameter-based version, you need to make one more change to that original overloaded version:

```
Public Overloads Property Name(ByVal type As NameTypes) As String
  Get
    Return mNames(Type)
  End Get
  Set(ByVal value As String)
    If mNames.ContainsKey(type) Then
      mNames.Item(type) = value
    Else
      mNames.Add(type, value)
    End If

    If type = NameTypes.Normal Then
      MyBase.Name = value
    End If
  End Set
End Property
```

This way, if the client code sets the Name property by providing the Normal index, you are still updating the name in the base class as well as in the Dictionary object maintained by the Employee class.

Shadowing

Overloading allows you to add new versions of the existing methods as long as their parameter lists are different. *Overriding* allows your subclass to entirely replace the implementation of a base class method with a new method that has the same method signature. As you've just seen, you can even combine these concepts not only to replace the implementation of a method from the base class, but also to simultaneously overload that method with other implementations that have different method signatures.

However, anytime you override a method using the Overrides keyword, you are subject to the rules governing virtual methods — meaning that the base class must give you permission to override the method. If the base class doesn't use the Overridable keyword, then you can't override the method. Sometimes you may need to override a method that is not marked as Overridable, and shadowing enables you to do just that.

The Shadows keyword can also be used to entirely change the nature of a method or other interface element from the base class, although that is something which should be done with great care, as it can seriously reduce the maintainability of your code. Normally, when you create an Employee object, you expect that it can not only act as an Employee, but also as a Person because Employee is a subclass of Person. However, with the Shadows keyword, you can radically alter the behavior of an Employee class so that it doesn't act like a Person. This sort of radical deviation from what is normally expected invites bugs and makes code hard to understand and maintain.

Shadowing methods is very dangerous and should be used as a last resort. It is primarily useful in cases where you have a preexisting component such as a Windows Forms control that was not designed for inheritance. If you absolutely *must* inherit from such a component, you may need to use shadowing to "override" methods or properties. There are serious limits and dangers, but it may be your only option.

You'll explore this in more detail later. First, let's see how Shadows can be used to override nonvirtual methods.

Overriding Nonvirtual Methods

Earlier in the chapter, we discussed virtual methods and how they are automatically created in Visual Basic when the `Overrides` keyword is employed. You can also implement nonvirtual methods in Visual Basic. Nonvirtual methods are methods that cannot be overridden and replaced by subclasses, so most methods you implement are nonvirtual.

> If you don't use the `Overridable` keyword when declaring a method, then it is non-virtual.

In the typical case, nonvirtual methods are easy to understand. They can't be overridden and replaced, so you know that there's only one method by that name, with that method signature. Therefore, when you invoke it, there is no ambiguity about which specific implementation will be called. The reverse is true with virtual methods, where there may be more than one method of the same name, and with the same method signature, and you need to understand the rules governing which implementation will be invoked.

Of course, you knew it couldn't be that simple, and it turns out that you can override nonvirtual methods by using the `Shadows` keyword. In fact, you can use the `Shadows` keyword to override methods regardless of whether or not they have the `Overridable` keyword in the declaration.

> The `Shadows` keyword enables you to replace methods on the base class that the base class designer didn't intend to be replaced.

Obviously, this can be very dangerous. The designer of a base class must be careful when marking a method as `Overridable`, ensuring that the base class continues to operate properly even when that method is replaced by another code in a subclass. Designers of base classes typically just assume that if they don't mark a method as `Overridable` it will be called and not overridden. Thus, overriding a non-virtual method by using the `Shadows` keyword can have unexpected and potentially dangerous side effects, as you are doing something that the base class designer assumed would never happen.

If that isn't enough complexity, it turns out that shadowed methods follow different rules from virtual methods when they are invoked. That is, they don't act like regular overridden methods; instead, they follow a different set of rules to determine which specific implementation of the method will be invoked. In particular, when you call a nonvirtual method, the datatype of the variable refers to the object that indicates which implementation of the method is called, not the datatype of the object, as with virtual methods.

To override a nonvirtual method, you can use the `Shadows` keyword instead of the `Overrides` keyword. To see how this works, add a new property to the base `Person` class:

```
Public ReadOnly Property Age() As Integer
  Get
    Return CInt(DateDiff(DateInterval.Year, Now, BirthDate))
  End Get
End Property
```

Here you've added a new method, called Age, to the base class, and thus automatically to the subclass. This code has a bug, introduced on purpose for illustration. The DateDiff parameters are in the wrong order, so you'll get negative age values from this routine. We introduced a bug because sometimes you will find bugs in base classes that you didn't write (and which you can't fix because you don't have the source code).

The following example walks you through the use of the Shadows keyword to address a bug in your base class, acting under the assumption that for some reason you can't actually fix the code in the Person class.

Notice that you're not using the Overridable keyword on this method, so any subclass is prevented from overriding the method by using the Overrides keyword. The obvious intent and expectation of this code is that all subclasses will use this implementation and not override it with their own.

However, the base class cannot prevent a subclass from shadowing a method, so it doesn't matter whether you use Overridable or not; either way works fine for shadowing.

Before you shadow the method, let's see how it works as a regular nonvirtual method. First, you need to change your form to use this new value. Add a text box named txtAge and a related label to the form. Next, change the code behind the button to use the Age property. You'll include the code to display the data on the form right here to keep things simple and clear:

```
Private Sub btnOK_Click(ByVal sender As System.Object, _
    ByVal e As System.EventArgs) Handles btnOK.Click

  Dim person As Employee = New Employee()

  With person
    .Name = "Fred"
    .BirthDate = #1/1/1960#

    txtName.Text = .Name
    txtBirthDate.Text = Format(.BirthDate, "Short date")
    txtAge.Text = CStr(.Age)
  End With

End Sub
```

Don't forget to change the birth date value to something valid for an Employee.

At this point, you can run the application and the age field should appear in your display as expected, though with a negative value due to the bug we introduced. There's no magic or complexity here. This is basic programming with objects, and basic use of inheritance as discussed at the beginning of this chapter.

Of course, you don't want a bug in your code, but you don't have access to the Person class, and the Person class doesn't allow you to override the Age method, so what are you to do? The answer lies in the Shadows keyword, which allows you to override the method anyway.

Let's shadow the Age method within the Employee class, overriding and replacing the implementation in the Person class even though it is not marked as Overridable. Add the following code to the Employee class:

```
Public Shadows ReadOnly Property Age() As Integer
  Get
     Return CInt(DateDiff(DateInterval.Year, BirthDate, Now))
  End Get
End Property
```

In many ways, this looks very similar to what you've seen with the Overrides keyword, in that you're implementing a method in your subclass with the same name and parameter list as a method in the base class. In this case, however, you'll see some different behavior when you interact with the object in different ways.

Technically, the Shadows keyword is not required here. Shadowing is the default behavior when a subclass implements a method that matches the name and method signature of a method in the base class. However, if you omit the Shadows keyword, the compiler will give you a warning indicating that the method is being shadowed, so it is always better to include the keyword, both to avoid the warning and to make it perfectly clear that you knew what you were doing when you chose to shadow the method.

Remember that your code in the form is currently declaring a variable of type Employee and is creating an instance of an Employee object:

```
Dim person As Employee = New Employee()
```

This is a simple case, and, surprisingly, when you run the application now you'll see that the value of the age field is correct, indicating that you just ran the implementation of the Age property from the Employee class. At this point, you're seeing the same behavior that you saw when overriding with the Overrides keyword.

Let's take a look at the other simple case, where you're working with a variable and object that are both of datatype Person. Change the code in Form1 as follows:

```
Private Sub btnOK_Click(ByVal sender As System.Object, _
    ByVal e As System.EventArgs) Handles btnOK.Click

  Dim person As Person = New Person()

  With person
    .Name = "Fred"
    .BirthDate = #1/1/1960#

    txtName.Text = .Name
    txtBirthDate.Text = Format(.BirthDate, "Short date")
    txtAge.Text = CStr(.Age)
  End With
End Sub
```

Now you have a variable of type Person and an object of that same type. You would expect that the implementation in the Person class would be invoked in this case, and that is exactly what happens; the age field displays the original negative value, indicating that you're invoking the buggy implementation of the method directly from the Person class. Again, this is exactly the behavior you'd expect from a method overridden via the Overrides keyword.

This next example is where things get truly interesting. Change the code in Form1 as follows:

```
Private Sub btnOK_Click(ByVal sender As System.Object, _
    ByVal e As System.EventArgs) Handles btnOK.Click

    Dim person As Person = New Employee()
    With person
      .Name = "Fred"
      .BirthDate = #1/1/1960#

      txtName.Text = .Name
      txtBirthDate.Text = Format(.BirthDate, "Short date")
      txtAge.Text = CStr(.Age)
    End With
End Sub
```

Now you are declaring the variable to be of type Person, but you are creating an object that is of datatype Employee. You did this earlier in the chapter when exploring the Overrides keyword as well, and in that case you discovered that the version of the method that was invoked was based on the datatype of the object. The BirthDate implementation in the Employee class was invoked.

If you run the application now, you will find that the rules are different when the Shadows keyword is used. In this case, the implementation in the Person class is invoked, giving you the buggy negative value. When the implementation in the Employee class is ignored, you get the exact opposite behavior of what you got with Overrides.

The following table summarizes which method implementation is invoked based on the variable and object datatypes when using shadowing:

Variable Type	Object Type	Method Invoked
Base	Base	Base
Base	Subclass	Base
Subclass	Subclass	Subclass

In most cases, the behavior you will want for your methods is accomplished by the Overrides keyword and virtual methods. However, in cases where the base class designer doesn't allow you to override a method and you want to do it anyway, the Shadows keyword provides you with the needed functionality.

Shadowing Arbitrary Elements

The Shadows keyword can be used not only to override nonvirtual methods, but also to totally replace and change the nature of a base class interface element. When you override a method, you are providing a replacement implementation of that method with the same name and method signature. Using the Shadows keyword, you can do more extreme things, such as change a method into an instance variable or change a Property into a Function.

However, this can be very dangerous, as any code written to use your objects will naturally assume that you implement all the same interface elements and behaviors as your base class, because that is the nature of inheritance. Any documentation or knowledge of the original interface is effectively invalidated because the original implementation is arbitrarily replaced.

> **By totally changing the nature of an interface element, you can cause a great deal of confusion for programmers who might interact with your class in the future.**

To see how you can replace an interface element from the base class, let's entirely change the nature of the Age property. In fact, let's change it from a read-only property to a read-write property. You could get even more extreme — change it to a Function or a Sub.

Remove the Age property from the Employee class and add the following code:

```
Public Shadows Property Age() As Integer
  Get
    Return CInt(DateDiff(DateInterval.Year, BirthDate, Now))
  End Get
  Set(ByVal value As Integer)
    BirthDate = DateAdd(DateInterval.Year, -value, Now)
  End Set
End Property
```

With this change, the very nature of the Age method has changed. It is no longer a simple read-only property; now it is a read-write property that includes code to calculate an approximate birth date based on the age value supplied.

As it stands, your application will continue to run just fine because you're only using the read-only functionality of the property in your form. You can change the form to make use of the new read-write functionality:

```
Private Sub btnOK_Click(ByVal sender As System.Object, _
    ByVal e As System.EventArgs) Handles btnOK.Click

  Dim person As Person = New Employee()

  With person
    .Name = "Fred"
    .BirthDate = #1/1/1960#
    .Age = 20

    txtName.Text = .Name
    txtBirthDate.Text = Format(.BirthDate, "Short date")
```

```
        txtAge.Text = CStr(.Age)
    End With
End Sub
```

However, this will leave you with a syntax error. The variable you're working with, `person`, is of datatype `Person`, and that datatype does not provide a writeable version of the `Age` property. In order to use your enhanced functionality, you must use a variable and object of type `Employee`:

```
Dim person As Employee = New Employee()
```

If you now run the application and click the button, you'll see that the `Age` is displayed as 20, and the birth date is now a value calculated based on that age value, indicating that you are now running the shadowed version of the `Age` method as implemented in the `Employee` class.

As if that weren't odd enough, you can do some even stranger and more dangerous things. You can change `Age` into a variable, and you can even change its scope. For instance, you can comment out the `Age` property code in the `Employee` class and replace it with the following code:

```
Private Shadows Age As String
```

At this point, you've changed everything. `Age` is now a `String` instead of an `Integer`. It is a variable instead of a `Property` or `Function`. It has `Private` scope instead of `Public` scope. Your `Employee` object is now totally incompatible with the `Person` datatype, something that shouldn't occur normally when using inheritance.

This means that the code you wrote in `Form1` will no longer work. The `Age` property is no longer accessible and can no longer be used, so your project will no longer compile. This directly illustrates the danger in shadowing a base class element such that its very nature or scope is changed by the subclass.

Because this change prevents your application from compiling, remove the line in the `Employee` class that shadows `Age` as a `String` variable, and uncomment the shadowed `Property` routine:

```
Public Shadows Property Age() As Integer
  Get
    Return CInt(DateDiff(DateInterval.Year, BirthDate, Now))
  End Get
  Set(ByVal value As Integer)
    BirthDate = DateAdd(DateInterval.Year, -value, Now)
  End Set
End Property
```

This restores your application to a working state, and you can move on.

Levels of Inheritance

So far, you've created a single base class and a single subclass, thus demonstrating that you can implement inheritance that is a single level deep. However, you can create inheritance relationships that are several levels deep. These are sometimes referred to as *chains of inheritance*.

> *In reality, you've been creating a two-level inheritance hierarchy so far, because you know that your base class actually derived from* System.Object, *but for most purposes it is easiest to simply ignore that fact and treat only your classes as part of the inheritance hierarchy.*

Multiple Inheritance

Don't confuse multilevel inheritance with multiple inheritance, which is an entirely different concept that is not supported by either Visual Basic or the .NET platform itself. The idea behind multiple inheritance is that you can have a single subclass that inherits from two base classes at the same time.

For instance, you may have an application that has a class for Customer and another class for Vendor. It is quite possible that some customers are also vendors, so you might want to combine the functionality of these two classes into a CustomerVendor class. This new class would be a combination of both Customer and Vendor, so it would be nice to inherit from both of them at once.

While this is a useful concept, multiple inheritance is complex and somewhat dangerous. Numerous problems are associated with multiple inheritance, but the most obvious is the possibility of collisions of properties or methods from the base classes. Suppose that both Customer and Vendor have a Name property. CustomerVendor would need two Name properties, one for each base class. Yet it only makes sense to have one Name property on CustomerVendor, so to which base class does it link, and how will the system operate if it doesn't link to the other one?

These are complex issues with no easy answers. Within the object-oriented community there is continual debate as to whether the advantages of code reuse outweigh the complexity that comes along for the ride.

Multiple inheritance is not supported by the .NET Framework, so it is likewise not supported by Visual Basic. However, you can use multiple interfaces to achieve an effect similar to multiple inheritance, a topic discussed later in the chapter when we talk about implementing multiple interfaces.

Multilevel Inheritance

You've seen how a subclass derives from a base class with your Person and Employee classes. However, nothing prevents the Employee subclass from being the base class for yet another class, a sub-subclass so to speak. This is not at all uncommon. In the working example, you may find that you have different kinds of employees, some who work in the office and others who travel.

To accommodate this, you may want to have OfficeEmployee and TravelingEmployee classes. Of course, these are both examples of an employee and should share the functionality already present in the Employee class. The Employee class already reuses the functionality from the Person class. Figure 4-9 illustrates how these classes are interrelated.

The Employee is a subclass of Person, and your two new classes are both subclasses of Employee. While both OfficeEmployee and TravelingEmployee are employees, and thus also people, they are each unique. An OfficeEmployee almost certainly has a cube or office number, while a TravelingEmployee will keep track of the number of miles traveled.

Add a new class to your project and name it OfficeEmployee. To make this class inherit from your existing Employee class, add the following code to the class:

```
Public Class OfficeEmployee
   Inherits Employee

End Class
```

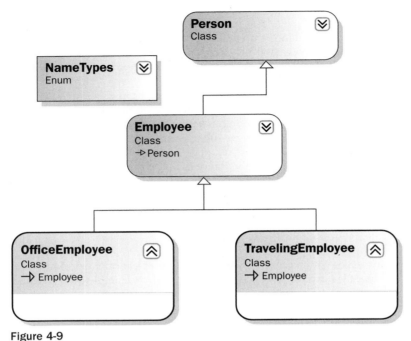

Figure 4-9

With this change, the new class now has Name, BirthDate, Age, HireDate, and Salary methods. Notice that methods from both Employee and Person are inherited. A subclass always gains all the methods, properties, and events of its base class.

You can now extend the interface and behavior of OfficeEmployee by adding a property to indicate which cube or office number the employee occupies:

```
Public Class OfficeEmployee
  Inherits Employee

  Private mOffice As String

  Public Property OfficeNumber() As String
    Get
      Return mOffice
    End Get
    Set(ByVal value As String)
      mOffice = value
    End Set
  End Property
End Class
```

To see how this works, let's enhance your form to display this value. Add a new TextBox control named txtOffice and an associated label so that your form looks like the one shown in Figure 4-10.

Figure 4-10

Now change the code behind the button to make use of the new property:

```
Private Sub btnOK_Click(ByVal sender As System.Object, _
    ByVal e As System.EventArgs) Handles btnOK.Click

    Dim person As OfficeEmployee = New OfficeEmployee()

    With person
        .Name = "Fred"
        .BirthDate = #1/1/1960#
        .Age = 20

        .OfficeNumber = "A42"

        txtName.Text = .Name
        txtBirthDate.Text = Format(.BirthDate, "Short date")
        txtAge.Text = CStr(.Age)

        txtOffice.Text = .OfficeNumber
    End With
End Sub
```

You've changed the routine to declare and create an object of type OfficeEmployee — thus enabling you to make use of the new property, as well as all existing properties and methods from Employee and Person, as they've been "merged" into the OfficeEmployee class via inheritance. If you now run the application, the name, birth date, age, and office values are displayed in the form.

Inheritance like this can go many levels deep, with each level extending and changing the behaviors of the previous levels. In fact, there is no specific technical limit to the number of levels of inheritance you can implement in Visual Basic, although very deep inheritance chains are typically not recommended and are often viewed as a design flaw, something discussed in more detail later in this chapter.

Interacting with the Base Class, Your Class, and Your Object

You've already seen how you can use the MyBase keyword to call methods on the base class from within a subclass. The MyBase keyword is one of three special keywords that enable you to interact with important object and class representations:

- ❏ Me
- ❏ MyBase
- ❏ MyClass

The Me Keyword

The Me keyword provides you with a reference to your current object instance. Typically, you don't need to use the Me keyword, as anytime you want to invoke a method within your current object you can just call that method directly.

To see clearly how this works, let's add a new method to the Person class that returns the data of the Person class in the form of a String. This is interesting in and of itself, as the base System.Object class defines the ToString method for this exact purpose. Remember that all classes in the .NET Framework ultimately derive from System.Object, even if you don't explicitly indicate it with an Inherits statement. This means that you can simply override the ToString() method from the Object class within your Person class by adding the following code:

```
Public Overrides Function ToString() As String
   Return Name
End Function
```

This implementation returns the person's Name property as a result when ToString() is called.

> By default, ToString() returns the class name of the class. Up to now, if you had called the ToString() method on a Person object, you would have gotten a result of InheritanceAndInterfaces.Person.

Notice that the ToString() method is calling another method within your same class — in this case, the Name method.

You could also write this routine using the Me keyword:

```
Public Overrides Function ToString() As String
   Return Me.Name
End Function
```

However, this is redundant because Me is the default for all method calls in a class. These two implementations are identical, so typically the Me keyword is simply omitted to avoid the extra typing.

To see how the ToString() method now works, you can change your code in Form1 to use this value instead of the Name property:

```
Private Sub btnOK_Click(ByVal sender As System.Object, _
    ByVal e As System.EventArgs) Handles btnOK.Click
```

```
        Dim objPerson As OfficeEmployee = New OfficeEmployee()

        With objPerson
          .Name = "Fred"
          .BirthDate = #1/1/1960#
          .Age = 20
          .OfficeNumber = "A42"

          txtName.Text = .ToString()
          txtBirthDate.Text = Format(.BirthDate, "Short date")
          txtAge.Text = CStr(.Age)
          txtOffice.Text = .OfficeNumber
        End With
    End Sub
```

When you run the application, you'll see that the person's name is displayed appropriately, which makes sense, as the `ToString()` method is simply returning the result from the `Name` property.

Earlier, we discussed virtual methods and how they work. Because either calling a method directly or calling it using the `Me` keyword invokes the method on the current object, the method calls conform to the same rules as an external method call. In other words, your `ToString()` method may not actually end up calling the `Name` method in the `Person` class if that method was overridden by a class farther down the inheritance chain, such as the `Employee` or `OfficeEmployee` classes.

For example, you could override the `Name` property in your `OfficeEmployee` class such that it always returns the informal version of the person's name, rather than the regular name. You can override the `Name` property by adding this method to the `OfficeEmployee` class:

```
Public Overloads Overrides Property Name() As String
  Get
    Return MyBase.Name(NameTypes.Informal)
  End Get
  Set(ByVal value As String)
    MyBase.Name = value
  End Set
End Property
```

This new version of the `Name` method relies on the base class to actually store the value, but instead of returning the regular name on request, now you are always returning the informal name:

```
Return MyBase.Name(NameTypes.Informal)
```

Before you can test this, you need to enhance the code in your form to actually provide a value for the informal name. Make the following change to the code:

```
Private Sub btnOK_Click(ByVal sender As System.Object,
    ByVal e As System.EventArgs) Handles btnOK.Click
  Dim objPerson As OfficeEmployee = New OfficeEmployee()

  With objPerson
    .Name = "Fred"
    .Name(NameTypes.Informal) = "Freddy"
```

```
      .BirthDate = #1/1/1960#
      .Age = 20
      .OfficeNumber = "A42"

      txtName.Text = .ToString()
      txtBirthDate.Text = Format(.BirthDate, "Short date")
      txtAge.Text = CStr(.Age)
      txtOffice.Text = .OfficeNumber
   End With
End Sub
```

When you run the application, you'll find that the name field displays the informal name. Even though the `ToString()` method is implemented in the `Person` class, it is invoking the implementation of `Name` from the `OfficeEmployee` class. This is because method calls within a class follow the same rules for calling virtual methods as code outside a class, such as your code in the form. You'll see this behavior with or without the `Me` keyword, as the default behavior for method calls is to implicitly call them via the current object.

While methods called from within a class follow the same rules for virtual methods, this is not the case for shadowed methods. Here, you'll find that the rules for calling a shadowed method from within your class are different from those outside your class.

To see how this works, make the `Name` property in `OfficeEmployee` a shadowed method instead of an overridden method:

```
Public Shadows Property Name() As String
   Get
      Return MyBase.Name(NameTypes.Informal)
   End Get
   Set(ByVal value As String)
      MyBase.Name = value
   End Set
End Property
```

Before you can run your application, you must adjust some code in the form. Because you've shadowed the `Name` property in `OfficeEmployee`, the version of `Name` from `Employee` that acts as a property array is now invalid.

> **Shadowing a method replaces all implementations from higher in the inheritance chain, regardless of their method signature.**

To make your application operate, you need to change the variable declaration and object creation to declare a variable of type `Employee` so that you can access the property array while still creating an instance of `OfficeEmployee`:

```
Dim person As Employee = New OfficeEmployee()
```

Because your variable is now of type `Employee`, you also need to comment out the lines that refer to the `OfficeNumber` property, as it is no longer available:

```
With person
  .Name = "Fred"
  .Name(NameTypes.Informal) = "Freddy"
  .BirthDate = #1/1/1960#
  .Age = 20

  '.OfficeNumber = "A42"

  txtName.Text = .ToString()
  txtBirthDate.Text = Format(.BirthDate, "Short date")
  txtAge.Text = CStr(.Age)

  'txtOffice.Text = .OfficeNumber
End With
```

When you run the application now, it displays the name `Fred`, rather than `Freddy`, meaning it is not calling the `Name` method from `OfficeEmployee`; instead, it is calling the implementation provided by the `Employee` class. Remember that the code to make this call still resides in the `Person` class, but it now ignores the shadowed version of the `Name` method.

Shadowed implementations in subclasses are ignored when calling the method from within a class higher in the inheritance chain.

You'll get this same behavior with or without the `Me` keyword. The `Me` keyword, or calling methods directly, follows the same rules for overridden methods as any other method call. For shadowed methods, however, any shadowed implementations in subclasses are ignored and the method is called from the current level in the inheritance chain.

Why, then, does the `Me` keyword exist? Primarily to enable you to pass a reference to the current object as a parameter to other objects or methods. As shown when you look at the `MyBase` and `MyClass` keywords, things can get very confusing, and there may be value in using the `Me` keyword when working with `MyBase` and `MyClass` to ensure that it is always clear which particular implementation of a method you intended to invoke.

The MyBase Keyword

While the `Me` keyword allows you to call methods on the current object instance, at times you might want to explicitly call into methods in your parent class. Earlier, you saw an example of this when you called back into the base class from an overridden method in the subclass.

The `MyBase` keyword references only the immediate parent class, and it works like an object reference. This means that you can call methods on `MyBase`, knowing that they are being called just as if you had a reference to an object of your parent class's datatype.

> There is no way to directly navigate up the inheritance chain beyond the immediate parent. This means that you can't directly access the implementation of a method in a base class if you are in a sub-subclass. Such behavior isn't a good idea anyway, which is why it isn't allowed.

The `MyBase` keyword can be used to invoke or use any `Public`, `Friend`, or `Protected` element from the parent class. This includes all elements directly on the base class, and any elements the base class inherited from other classes higher in the inheritance chain.

You've already used `MyBase` to call back into the base `Person` class as you implemented the overridden `Name` property in the `Employee` class.

> Any code within a subclass can call any method on the base class by using the `MyBase` keyword.

You can also use `MyBase` to call back into the base class implementation even if you've shadowed a method. Though it wasn't noted at the time, you've already done this in your shadowed implementation of the `Name` property in the `OfficeEmployee` class. The highlighted lines indicate where you're calling into the base class from within a shadowed method:

```
Public Shadows Property Name() As String
  Get
     Return MyBase.Name(NameTypes.Informal)
  End Get
  Set(ByVal value As String)
     MyBase.Name = value
  End Set
End Property
```

The `MyBase` keyword enables you to merge the functionality of the base class into your subclass code as you deem fit.

The MyClass Keyword

As you've seen, when you use the `Me` keyword or call a method directly, your method call follows the rules for calling both virtual and nonvirtual methods. In other words, as you discovered earlier with the `Name` property, a call to `Name` from your code in the `Person` class actually invoked the overridden version of `Name` located in the `OfficeEmployee` class.

While this behavior is often useful, sometimes you'll want to ensure that you really are running the specific implementation from your class; even if a subclass overrode your method, you still want to ensure you're calling the version of the method that is directly in your class.

Maybe you decide that your `ToString()` implementation in `Person` should always call the `Name` implementation that you write in the `Person` class, totally ignoring any overridden versions of `Name` in any subclasses.

This is where the `MyClass` keyword shines. This keyword is much like `MyBase`, in that it provides you with access to methods as though it were an object reference — in this case, a reference to an instance of the class that contains the code you're writing when using the `MyClass` keyword. This is true even when the instantiated object is an instance of a class derived from your class.

You've seen that a call to `ToString()` from within `Person` actually invokes the implementation in `Employee` or `OfficeEmployee` if your object is an instance of either of those types. Let's restore the `Name` property in `OfficeEmployee` so that it is an overridden method, rather than a shadowed method, to see how this works:

```
Public Overloads Overrides Property Name() As String
  Get
    Return MyBase.Name(NameTypes.Informal)
  End Get
  Set(ByVal value As String)
    MyBase.Name = value
  End Set
End Property
```

With this change, and based on your earlier testing, you know that the `ToString()` implementation in `Person` will automatically call this overridden version of the `Name` property, as the call to the `Name` method follows the normal rules for virtual methods. In fact, if you run the application now, the Name field on the form displays `Freddy`, the informal name of the person.

You can force the use of the implementation in the current class through the use of `MyClass`. Change the `ToString()` method in `Person` as follows:

```
Public Overrides Function ToString() As String
  Return MyClass.Name
End Function
```

You are now calling the `Name` method, but you're doing it using the `MyClass` keyword. When you run the application and click the button, the name field in the form displays `Fred` rather than `Freddy`, proving that the implementation from `Person` was invoked even though the datatype of the object itself is `OfficeEmployee`.

The `ToString()` method is invoked from `Person`, since neither `Employee` nor `OfficeEmployee` provide an overridden implementation. Then, because you're using the `MyClass` keyword, the `Name` method is invoked directly from `Person`, explicitly defeating the default behavior you'd normally expect.

Constructors

As discussed in Chapter 3, you can provide a special constructor method, named `New`, on a class and it will be the first code run when an object is instantiated. You can also receive parameters via the constructor method, allowing the code that creates your object to pass data into the object during the creation process.

Constructor methods are affected by inheritance differently than regular methods. A normal `Public` method, such as `BirthDate` on your `Person` class, is automatically inherited by any subclass. From there you can overload, override, or shadow that method, as discussed already.

Simple Constructors

Constructors don't quite follow the same rules. To explore the differences, let's implement a simple constructor method in the Person class:

```
Public Sub New()
   Debug.WriteLine("Person constructor")
End Sub
```

If you now run the application, you'll see the text displayed in the output window in the IDE. This occurs even though the code in your form is creating an object of type OfficeEmployee:

```
Dim person As Employee = New OfficeEmployee()
```

As you might expect, the New method from your base Person class is invoked as part of the construction process of the OfficeEmployee object, simple inheritance at work. However, interesting things occur if you implement a New method in the OfficeEmployee class itself:

```
Public Sub New()
   Debug.WriteLine("OfficeEmployee constructor")
End Sub
```

Notice that you are not using the Overrides keyword, nor did you mark the method in Person as Overridable. These keywords have no use in this context and, in fact, will cause syntax errors if you attempt to use them on constructor methods.

When you run the application now, you'd probably expect that only the implementation of New in OfficeEmployee would be invoked. Certainly, that is what would occur with a normal overridden method. Of course, New isn't overridden, so when you run the application, both implementations are run. Both strings are output to the output window in the IDE.

Note that the implementation in the Person class ran first, followed by the implementation in the OfficeEmployee class. This occurs because, as an object is created, all the constructors for the classes in the inheritance chain are invoked, starting with the base class and working out through all the subclasses one by one. In fact, if you implement a New method in the Employee class, you can see that it too is invoked:

```
Public Sub New()
   Debug.WriteLine("Employee constructor")
End Sub
```

When the application is run and the button clicked, you'll see all three strings in the output window. All three constructor methods were invoked, starting with the Person class and working down to the OfficeEmployee class.

Constructors in More Depth

The rules governing constructors without parameters are pretty straightforward, but things get a bit more interesting if you start requiring parameters on your constructors.

To understand what is going on, you need to consider how even your simple constructors are being invoked. While you see them as being invoked from the base class down through all subclasses to your final subclass, what is really happening is a bit different.

In particular, it is the subclass New method that is invoked first. However, Visual Basic is automatically inserting a line of code into your routine at compile time. For instance, in your OfficeEmployee class you have a constructor:

```
Public Sub New()
   Debug.WriteLine("OfficeEmployee constructor")
End Sub
```

Behind the scenes, Visual Basic inserts what is effectively a call to the constructor of your parent class on your behalf. You could do this manually by using the MyBase keyword with the following change:

```
Public Sub New()
   MyBase.New()
   Debug.WriteLine("OfficeEmployee constructor")
End Sub
```

This call must be the first line in your constructor. If you put any other code before this line, you'll get a syntax error indicating that your code is invalid. Because the call is always required, and because it always must be the first line in any constructor, Visual Basic simply inserts it for you automatically.

It is also worth noting that if you don't explicitly provide a constructor on a class by implementing a New method, Visual Basic creates one for you behind the scenes. The automatically created method simply has one line of code:

```
MyBase.New()
```

All classes have constructor methods, either created explicitly by you as you write a New method or created implicitly by Visual Basic as the class is compiled.

A constructor method is sometimes called a ctor, short for constructor. This term is often used by tools such as ILDASM or .NET Reflector.

By always calling MyBase.New() as the first line in every constructor, you are guaranteed that it is the implementation of New in your top-level base class that actually runs first. Every subclass invokes the parent class implementation all the way up the inheritance chain until only the base class remains. Then its code runs, followed by each individual subclass, as you've already seen.

Constructors with Parameters

This works great when your constructors don't require parameters, but if your constructor does require a parameter, then it becomes impossible for Visual Basic to automatically make that call on your behalf. After all, how would Visual Basic know what values you want to pass as parameters?

To see how this works, let's change the New method in the Person class to require a name parameter. You can use that parameter to initialize the object's Name property:

```
Public Sub New(ByVal name As String)
   Me.Name = name
   Debug.WriteLine("Person constructor")
End Sub
```

Now your constructor requires a String parameter and uses it to initialize the Name property.

You are using the Me keyword to make your code easier to read. Interestingly enough, the compiler will actually understand and correctly compile the following code:

```
Name = name
```

However, that is not at all clear to a developer reading the code. By prefixing the property name with the Me keyword, you've made it clear that you're invoking a property on the object and providing it with the parameter value.

At this point, your application won't compile because there is an error in the New method of the Employee class. In particular, Visual Basic's attempt to automatically invoke the constructor on the Person class fails because it has no idea what data value to pass for this new name parameter. There are three ways you can address this error:

❑ Make the name parameter Optional.

❑ Overload the New method with another implementation that requires no parameter.

❑ Manually provide the Name parameter value from within the Employee class.

If you make the Name parameter Optional, you're indicating that the New method can be called with or without a parameter. This means that one viable option is to call the method with no parameters, so Visual Basic's default of calling it with no parameters works just fine.

If you overload the New method, you can implement a second New method that doesn't accept any parameters, again allowing Visual Basic's default behavior to work as you've seen. Keep in mind that this solution only invokes the overloaded version of New with no parameter; the version that requires a parameter would not be invoked.

The final way you can fix the error is by simply providing a parameter value yourself from within the New method of the Employee class. To do this, change the Employee class:

```
Public Sub New()
    MyBase.New("George")
    Debug.WriteLine("Employee constructor")
End Sub
```

By explicitly calling the New method of the parent class, you are able to provide it with the required parameter value. At this point, your application will compile, but it won't run.

Constructors, Overloading, and Variable Initialization

What isn't clear from this code is that you've now introduced a very insidious bug. The constructor in the Person class is using the Name property to set the value:

```
Public Sub New(ByVal name As String)
    Me.Name = name
    Debug.WriteLine("Person constructor")
End Sub
```

However, the Name property is overridden by the Employee class, so it is that implementation that will be run. Unfortunately, that implementation makes use of a Dictionary object, which isn't available yet! It turns out that any member variables declared in a class with the New statement, such as the Dictionary object in Employee won't be initialized until after the constructor for that class has completed:

```
Private mNames As New Generic.Dictionary(Of NameTypes, String)
```

Because you are still in the constructor for Person, there's no way the constructor for Employee can be complete. To resolve this, you need to change the Employee class a bit so that it doesn't rely on the Dictionary being created in this manner. Instead, you'll add code to create it when needed.

First, change the declaration of the variable in the Employee class:

```
Private mNames As Generic.Dictionary(Of NameTypes, String)
```

Then, update the Name property so that it creates the Hashtable object if needed:

```
Public Overloads Property Name(ByVal type As NameTypes) As String
  Get
    If mNames Is Nothing Then mNames = New Generic.Dictionary(Of NameTypes, String)
    Return mNames(type)
  End Get
  Set(ByVal value As String)
    If mNames Is Nothing Then mNames = New Generic.Dictionary(Of NameTypes, String)
    If mNames.ContainsKey(type) Then
      mNames.Item(type) = value
    Else
      mNames.Add(type, value)
    End If
    If type = NameTypes.Normal Then
      MyBase.Name = value
    End If
  End Set
End Property
```

This ensures that a Dictionary object is created in the Employee class code even though its constructor hasn't yet completed.

More Constructors with Parameters

Obviously, you probably don't want to hard-code a value in a constructor as you did in the Employee class, so you may choose instead to change this constructor to also accept a name parameter. Change the Employee class constructor as shown:

```
Public Sub New(ByVal name As String)
  MyBase.New(name)
  Debug.WriteLine("Employee constructor")
End Sub
```

Of course, this just pushed the issue deeper, and now you'll find that the OfficeEmployee class has a compile error in its New method. Again, you can fix the problem by having that method accept a parameter so that it can provide it up the chain as required. Make the following change to OfficeEmployee:

```
Public Sub New(ByVal name As String)
  MyBase.New(name)
  Debug.WriteLine("OfficeEmployee constructor")
End Sub
```

Finally, the code in the form is no longer valid. You're attempting to create an instance of `OfficeEmployee` without passing a parameter value. Let's update that code and then you can run the application:

```
Private Sub btnOK_Click(ByVal sender As System.Object, _
    ByVal e As System.EventArgs) Handles btnOK.Click

    Dim person As Employee = New OfficeEmployee("Mary")
    With person
      '.Name = "Fred"
```

You're passing a `name` value to the constructor of `OfficeEmployee`. In addition, you've commented out the line of code that sets the `Name` property directly — meaning that the value passed in the constructor will be displayed in the form.

The Protected Scope

You've seen how a subclass automatically gains all the `Public` methods and properties that compose the interface of the base class. This is also true of `Friend` methods and properties; they are inherited as well and are available only to other code in the same project as the subclass.

`Private` methods and properties are not exposed as part of the interface of the subclass, meaning that the code in the subclass cannot call those methods, nor can any code using your objects. These methods are only available to the code within the base class itself. This can get confusing, as the implementations contained in the `Private` methods are inherited and are used by any code in the base class; it is just that they aren't available to be called by any other code, including code in the subclass.

There are times when you want to create methods in your base class that can be called by a subclass as well as the base class but not by code outside of those classes. Basically, you want a hybrid between `Public` and `Private` — methods that are private to the classes in the inheritance chain but are usable by any subclasses that might be created within the chain. This functionality is provided by the `Protected` scope.

`Protected` methods are very similar to `Private` methods in that they are not available to any code that calls your objects. Instead, these methods are available to code within the base class and to code within any subclass. The following table lists all the available scope options:

Scope	Description
Private	Available only to code within your class
Protected	Available only to classes that inherit from your class
Friend	Available only to code within your project/component
Protected Friend	Available to classes that inherit from your class (in any project) and to code within your project/component. This is a combination of `Protected` and `Friend`.
Public	Available to code outside your class

The `Protected` scope can be applied to `Sub`, `Function`, and `Property` methods. To see how the `Protected` scope works, let's add an `Identity` field to the `Person` class:

```
Public Class Person
    Private mName As String
    Private mBirthDate As String
    Private mID As String

    Protected Property Identity() As String
      Get
        Return mID
      End Get
      Set(ByVal value As String)
        mID = value
      End Set
    End Property
```

This data field represents some arbitrary identification number or value assigned to a person. This might be a social security number, an employee number, or whatever is appropriate.

The interesting thing about this value is that it is not currently accessible outside your inheritance chain. For instance, if you try to use it from your code in the form, you'll discover that there is no `Identity` property on your `Person`, `Employee`, or `OfficeEmployee` objects.

However, there is an `Identity` property now available inside your inheritance chain. The `Identity` property is available to the code in the `Person` class just like any other method. Interestingly, even though `Identity` is not available to the code in your form, it is available to the code in the `Employee` and `OfficeEmployee` classes, because they are both subclasses of `Person`. `Employee` is directly a subclass, and `OfficeEmployee` is indirectly a subclass of `Person` because it is a subclass of `Employee`.

Thus, you can enhance your `Employee` class to implement an `EmployeeNumber` property by using the `Identity` property. To do this, add the following code to the `Employee` class:

```
Public Property EmployeeNumber() As Integer
  Get
    Return CInt(Identity)
  End Get
  Set(ByVal value As Integer)
    Identity = CStr(value)
  End Set
End Property
```

This new property exposes a numeric identity value for the employee, but it uses the internal `Identity` property to manage that value. You can override and shadow `Protected` elements just as you do with elements of any other scope.

Protected Variables

Up to this point, we've focused on methods and properties and how they interact through inheritance. Inheritance, and, in particular, the `Protected` scope, also has an impact on instance variables and how you work with them.

Though it is not recommended, you can declare variables in a class using `Public` scope. This makes the variable directly available to code both within and outside of your class, allowing any code that interacts with your objects to directly read or alter the value of that variable.

Variables can also have `Friend` scope, which likewise allows any code in your class or anywhere within your project to read or alter the value directly. This is also generally not recommended because it breaks encapsulation.

> Rather than declare variables with `Public` or `Friend` scope, it is better to expose the value using a `Property` method so that you can apply any of your business rules to control how the value is altered as appropriate.

Of course, you know that variables can be of `Private` scope, and this is typically the case. This makes the variables accessible only to the code within your class, and it is the most restrictive scope.

As with methods, however, you can also use the `Protected` scope when declaring variables. This makes the variable accessible to the code in your class and to the code in any class that derives from your class — all the way down the hierarchy chain.

Sometimes this is useful, because it enables you to provide and accept data to and from subclasses, but to act on that data from code in the base class. At the same time, exposing variables to subclasses is typically not ideal, and you should use `Property` methods with `Protected` scope for this instead, as they allow your base class to enforce any business rules that are appropriate for the value, rather than just hope that the author of the subclass only provides good values.

Events and Inheritance

So far, we've discussed methods, properties, and variables in terms of inheritance — how they can be added, overridden, extended, and shadowed. In Visual Basic, events are also part of the interface of an object, and they are affected by inheritance as well.

Inheriting Events

Chapter 3 discusses how to declare, raise, and receive events from objects. You can add such an event to the `Person` class by declaring it at the top of the class:

```
Public Class Person
  Private mName As String
  Private mBirthDate As String
  Private mID As String

  Public Event NameChanged(ByVal newName As String)
```

Then, you can raise this event within the class anytime the person's name is changed:

```
Public Overridable Property Name() As String
  Get
    Return mName
  End Get
```

```
      Set(ByVal value As String)
        mName = value
        RaiseEvent NameChanged(mName)
      End Set
    End Property
```

At this point, you can receive and handle this event within your form anytime you're working with a `Person` object. The nice thing about this is that your events are inherited automatically by subclasses — meaning that your `Employee` and `OfficeEmployee` objects will also raise this event. Thus, you can change the code in your form to handle the event, even though you're working with an object of type `OfficeEmployee`.

First, you can add a method to handle the event to `Form1`:

```
    Private Sub OnNameChanged(ByVal newName As String)
      MsgBox("New name: " & newName)
    End Sub
```

Note that you're not using the `Handles` clause here. In this case, for simplicity, you use the `AddHandler` method to dynamically link the event to this method. However, you could have also chosen to use the `WithEvents` and `Handles` keywords, as described in Chapter 3 — either way works.

With the handler built, you can use the `AddHandler` method to link this method to the event on the object:

```
    Private Sub btnOK_Click(ByVal sender As System.Object, _
        ByVal e As System.EventArgs) Handles btnOK.Click

      Dim person As Employee = New OfficeEmployee("Mary")

      AddHandler person.NameChanged, AddressOf OnNameChanged

      With pPerson
        .Name = "Fred"
```

Also note that you're uncommenting the line that changes the `Name` property. With this change, you know that the event should fire when the name is changed.

When you run the application now, you'll see a message box, indicating that the name has changed and proving that the `NameChanged` event really is exposed and available even though your object is of type `OfficeEmployee`, rather than `Person`.

Raising Events from Subclasses

One caveat you need to keep in mind is that while a subclass exposes the events of its base class, the code in the subclass cannot raise the event. In other words, you cannot use the `RaiseEvent` method in `Employee` or `OfficeEmployee` to raise the `NameChanged` event. Only code directly in the `Person` class can raise the event.

To see this in action, let's add another event to the `Person` class, an event that can indicate the change of other arbitrary data values:

```
Public Class Person
  Private mName As String
  Private mBirthDate As String
  Private mID As String

  Public Event NameChanged(ByVal newName As String)
  Public Event DataChanged(ByVal field As String, ByVal newValue As Object)
```

You can then raise this event when the `BirthDate` is changed:

```
Public Overridable Property BirthDate() As Date
  Get
    Return mBirthDate
  End Get
  Set(ByVal value As Date)
    mBirthDate = value
    RaiseEvent DataChanged("BirthDate", value)
  End Set
End Property
```

It would also be nice to raise this event from the `Employee` class when the `Salary` value is changed. Unfortunately, you can't use the `RaiseEvent` method to raise the event from a base class, so the following code won't work (don't enter this code):

```
Public Property Salary() As Double
  Get
    Return mSalary
  End Get
  Set(ByVal value As Double)
    mSalary = value
    RaiseEvent DataChanged("Salary", value)
  End Set
End Property
```

Fortunately, there is a relatively easy way to get around this limitation. You can simply implement a `Protected` method in your base class that allows any derived class to raise the method. In the `Person` class, you can add such a method:

```
Protected Sub OnDataChanged(ByVal field As String, _
    ByVal newValue As Object)

  RaiseEvent DataChanged(field, newValue)
End Sub
```

You can use this method from within the `Employee` class to indicate that `Salary` has changed:

```
Public Property Salary() As Double
  Get
    Return mSalary
  End Get
  Set(ByVal value As Double)
    mSalary = value
    OnDataChanged("Salary", value)
```

```
      End Set
   End Property
```

Notice that the code in `Employee` is not raising the event, it is simply calling a `Protected` method in `Person`. It is the code in the `Person` class that actually raises the event, meaning everything will work as desired.

You can enhance the code in `Form1` to receive the event. First, create a method to handle the event:

```
Private Sub OnDataChanged(ByVal field As String, ByVal newValue As Object)
   MsgBox("New " & field & ": " & CStr(newValue))
End Sub
```

Then, link this handler to the event using the `AddHandler` method:

```
Private Sub btnOK_Click(ByVal sender As System.Object, _
      ByVal e As System.EventArgs) Handles btnOK.Click

   Dim person As Employee = New OfficeEmployee("Mary")
   AddHandler person.NameChanged, AddressOf OnNameChanged
   AddHandler person.DataChanged, AddressOf OnDataChanged
```

Finally, make sure you are changing and displaying the `Salary` property:

```
With person
   .Name = "Fred"
   .Name(NameTypes.Informal) = "Freddy"
   .BirthDate = #1/1/1960#
   .Age = 20
   .Salary = 30000

   txtName.Text = .ToString()
   txtBirthDate.Text = Format(.BirthDate, "Short date")
   txtAge.Text = CStr(.Age)
   txtSalary.Text = Format(.Salary, "0.00")
End With
```

When you run the application and click the button now, you'll get message boxes displaying the changes to the `Name` property, the `BirthDate` property (twice, once for the `BirthDate` property and once for the `Age` property, which changes the birth date), and the `Salary` property.

Shared Methods

Chapter 3 explored shared methods and how they work: providing a set of methods that can be invoked directly from the class, rather than requiring that you create an actual object.

Shared methods are inherited just like instance methods and so are automatically available as methods on subclasses, just as they are on the base class. If you implement a shared method in `BaseClass`, you can call that method using any class derived from `BaseClass`.

Like regular methods, shared methods can be overloaded and shadowed. They cannot, however, be overridden. If you attempt to use the `Overridable` keyword when declaring a `Shared` method, you will get a syntax error. For instance, you can implement a method in your `Person` class to compare two `Person` objects:

```
Public Shared Function Compare(ByVal person1 As Person, _
    ByVal person2 As Person) As Boolean

  Return (person1.Name = person2.Name)

End Function
```

To test this method, let's add another button to the form, name it `btnCompare`, and set its `Text` value to `Compare`. Double-click the button to bring up the code window and enter the following:

```
Private Sub btnCompare_Click(ByVal sender As System.Object, _
    ByVal e As System.EventArgs) Handles btnCompare.Click

  Dim emp1 As New Employee("Fred")
  Dim emp2 As New Employee("Mary")

  MsgBox(Employee.Compare(emp1, emp2))

End Sub
```

This code simply creates two `Employee` objects and compares them. Note, though, that the code uses the `Employee` class to invoke the `Compare()` method, displaying the result in a message box. This establishes that the `Compare()` method implemented in the `Person` class is inherited by the `Employee` class, as you'd expect.

Overloading Shared Methods

Shared methods can be overloaded using the `Overloads` keyword in the same manner as you overload an instance method. This means that your subclass can add new implementations of the shared method as long as the parameter list differs from the original implementation.

For example, you can add a new implementation of the `Compare` method to `Employee`:

```
Public Overloads Shared Function Compare(ByVal employee1 As Employee, _
    ByVal employee2 As Employee) As Boolean

  Return (employee1.EmployeeNumber = employee2.EmployeeNumber)

End Function
```

This new implementation compares two `Employee` objects, rather than two `Person` objects, and in fact compares them by employee number, rather than name.

You can enhance the code behind `btnCompare` in the form to set the `EmployeeNumber` properties:

```
Private Sub btnCompare_Click(ByVal sender As System.Object, _
    ByVal e As System.EventArgs) Handles btnCompare.Click

  Dim emp1 As New Employee("Fred")
```

```
    Dim emp2 As New Employee("Mary")

    emp1.EmployeeNumber = 1
    emp2.EmployeeNumber = 1

    MsgBox(Employee.Compare(emp1, emp2))
  End Sub
```

While it might make little sense for these two objects to have the same `EmployeeNumber` value, it will prove a point. When you run the application now, even though the `Name` values of the objects are different, your `Compare()` routine will return `True`, proving that you're invoking the overloaded version of the method that expects two `Employee` objects as parameters.

The overloaded implementation is available on the `Employee` class or any classes derived from `Employee`, such as `OfficeEmployee`. The overloaded implementation is not available if called directly from `Person`, as that class only contains the original implementation.

Shadowing Shared Methods

Shared methods can also be shadowed by a subclass. This allows you to do some very interesting things, including converting a shared method into an instance method or vice versa. You can even leave the method as shared but change the entire way it works and is declared. In short, just as with instance methods, you can use the `Shadows` keyword to entirely replace and change a shared method in a subclass.

To see how this works, use the `Shadows` keyword to change the nature of the `Compare()` method in `OfficeEmployee`:

```
  Public Shared Shadows Function Compare(ByVal person1 As Person, _
      ByVal person2 As Person) As Boolean

    Return (person1.Age = person2.Age)

  End Function
```

Notice that this method has the same signature as the original `Compare()` method you implemented in the `Person` class, but instead of comparing by name, here you're comparing by age. With a normal method you could have done this by overriding, but `Shared` methods can't be overridden, so the only thing you can do is shadow it.

Of course, the shadowed implementation is only available via the `OfficeEmployee` class. Neither the `Person` nor `Employee` classes, which are higher up the inheritance chain, are aware that this shadowed version of the method exists.

To use this from your `Form1` code, you can change the code for `btnCompare` as follows:

```
  Private Sub btnCompare_Click(ByVal sender As System.Object, _
      ByVal e As System.EventArgs) Handles btnCompare.Click

    Dim emp1 As New Employee("Fred")
    Dim emp2 As New Employee("Mary")
```

```
        emp1.Age = 20
        emp2.Age = 25

        MsgBox(OfficeEmployee.Compare(emp1, emp2))
    End Sub
```

Instead of setting the `EmployeeNumber` values, you're now setting the `Age` values on your objects. More important, notice that you're now calling the `Compare()` method via the `OfficeEmployee` class, rather than via `Employee` or `Person`. This causes the invocation of the new version of the method, and the ages of the objects are compared.

Shared Events

As discussed in Chapter 3, you can create shared events, events that can be raised by shared or instance methods in a class, whereas regular events can only be raised from within instance methods.

When you inherit from a class that defines a shared event, your new subclass automatically gains that event just as it does with regular events, as discussed earlier in this chapter.

As with instance events, a shared event cannot be raised by code within the subclass; it can only be raised using the `RaiseEvent` keyword from code in the class where the event is declared. If you want to be able to raise the event from methods in your subclass, you need to implement a `Protected` method on the base class that actually makes the call to `RaiseEvent`.

This is no different from what was discussed earlier in the chapter, other than that with a shared event you can use a method with `Protected` scope that is marked as shared to raise the event, rather than use an instance method.

Creating an Abstract Base Class

So far, you've seen how to inherit from a class, how to overload and override methods, and how virtual methods work. In all of the examples so far, the parent classes have been useful in their own right and could be instantiated and do some meaningful work. Sometimes, however, you want to create a class such that it can only be used as a base class for inheritance.

MustInherit Keyword

The current `Person` class is being used as a base class, but it can also be instantiated directly to create an object of type `Person`. Likewise, the `Employee` class is also being used as a base class for the `OfficeEmployee` class you created that derives from it.

If you want to make a class act only as a base class, you can use the `MustInherit` keyword, thereby preventing anyone from creating objects based directly on the class and requiring them instead to create a subclass and then create objects based on that subclass.

This can be very useful when you are creating object models of real-world concepts and entities. You'll look at ways to leverage this capability later in this chapter. You can change `Person` to use the `MustInherit` keyword:

```
    Public MustInherit Class Person
```

This has no effect on the code within `Person` or any of the classes that inherit from it, but it does mean that no code can instantiate objects directly from the `Person` class; instead, you can only create objects based on `Employee` or `OfficeEmployee`.

This doesn't prevent you from declaring variables of type `Person`, it merely prevents you from creating an object by using `New Person()`. You can also continue to make use of `Shared` methods from the `Person` class without any difficulty.

MustOverride Keyword

Another option you have is to create a method (`Sub`, `Function`, or `Property`) that must be overridden by a subclass. You might want to do this when you are creating a base class that provides some behaviors but relies on subclasses to also provide other behaviors in order to function properly. This is accomplished by using the `MustOverride` keyword on a method declaration.

If a class contains any methods marked with `MustOverride`, the class itself must also be declared with the `MustInherit` keyword or you'll get a syntax error:

```
Public MustInherit Class Person
```

This makes sense. If you're requiring that a method be overridden in a subclass, it only stands to reason that your class can't be directly instantiated; it must be subclassed to be useful.

Let's see how this works by adding a `LifeExpectancy` method in `Person` that has no implementation and must be overridden by a subclass:

```
Public MustOverride Function LifeExpectancy() As Integer
```

Notice that there is no `End Function` or any other code associated with the method. When using `MustOverride`, you cannot provide any implementation for the method in your class. Such a method is called an *abstract method* or *pure virtual function,* as it only defines the interface, and no implementation.

Methods declared in this manner must be overridden in any subclass that inherits from your base class. If you don't override one of these methods, you'll generate a syntax error in the subclass, and it won't compile. You need to alter the `Employee` class to provide an implementation for this method:

```
Public Overrides Function LifeExpectancy() As Integer
    Return 90
End Function
```

Your application will compile and run at this point because you are now overriding the `LifeExpectancy()` method in `Employee`, so the required condition is met.

Abstract Base Classes

You can combine these two concepts, using both `MustInherit` and `MustOverride`, to create something called an *abstract base class,* sometimes referred to as a *virtual class.* This is a class that provides no implementation, only the interface definitions from which a subclass can be created, as shown in the following example:

```
Public MustInherit Class AbstractBaseClass
  Public MustOverride Sub DoSomething()
  Public MustOverride Sub DoOtherStuff()
End Class
```

This technique can be very useful when creating frameworks or the high-level conceptual elements of a system. Any class that inherits `AbstractBaseClass` must implement both `DoSomething()` and `DoOtherStuff()` or a syntax error will result.

In some ways, an abstract base class is comparable to defining an interface using the `Interface` keyword. The `Interface` keyword is discussed in detail later in this chapter. You could define the same interface shown in this example with the following code:

```
Public Interface IAbstractBaseClass
  Sub DoSomething()
  Sub DoOtherStuff()
End Interface
```

Any class that implements the `IAbstractBaseClass` interface must implement both `DoSomething` and `DoOtherStuff` or a syntax error will result, and in that regard this technique is similar to an abstract base class.

Preventing Inheritance

If you want to prevent a class from being used as a base class, you can use the `NotInheritable` keyword. For instance, you can change your `OfficeEmployee` as follows:

```
Public NotInheritable Class OfficeEmployee
```

At this point, it is no longer possible to inherit from this class to create a new class. Your `OfficeEmployee` class is now sealed, meaning it cannot be used as a base from which to create other classes.

If you attempt to inherit from `OfficeEmployee`, you'll get a compile error indicating that it cannot be used as a base class. This has no effect on `Person` or `Employee`; you can continue to derive other classes from them.

Typically, you want to design your classes so that they can be subclassed, because that provides the greatest long-term flexibility in the overall design. Sometimes, however, you want to ensure that your class cannot be used as a base class, and the `NotInheritable` keyword addresses that issue.

Multiple Interfaces

In Visual Basic, objects can have one or more interfaces. All objects have a *primary*, or *native*, interface, which is composed of any methods, properties, events, or member variables declared using the `Public` keyword. You can also have objects implement secondary interfaces in addition to their native interface by using the `Implements` keyword.

Object Interfaces

The native interface on any class is composed of all the methods, properties, events, and even variables that are declared as anything other than `Private`. Though this is nothing new, let's quickly review what is included in the native interface to set the stage for discussing secondary interfaces. To include a method as part of your interface, you can simply declare a `Public` routine:

```
Public Sub AMethod()

End Sub
```

Notice that there is no code in this routine. Any code would be implementation and is not part of the interface. Only the declaration of the method is important when discussing interfaces. This can seem confusing at first, but it is an important distinction, as the separation of the interface from its implementation is at the very core of object-oriented programming and design.

Because this method is declared as `Public`, it is available to any code outside the class, including other applications that may make use of the assembly. If the method has a property, then you can declare it as part of the interface by using the `Property` keyword:

```
Public Property AProperty() As String

End Property
```

You can also declare events as part of the interface by using the `Event` keyword:

```
Public Event AnEvent()
```

Finally, you can include actual variables, or attributes, as part of the interface:

```
Public AnInteger As Integer
```

This is strongly discouraged, because it directly exposes the internal variables for use by code outside the class. Because the variable is directly accessible from other code, you give up any and all control over the way the value may be changed or code may be accessed.

Rather than make any variable `Public`, it is far preferable to make use of a `Property` method to expose the value. That way, you can implement code to ensure that your internal variable is only set to valid values and that only the appropriate code has access to the value based on your application's logic.

Using the Native Interface

Ultimately, the native (or primary) interface for any class is defined by looking at all the methods, properties, events, and variables that are declared as anything other than `Private` in scope. This includes any methods, properties, events, or variables that are inherited from a base class.

You're used to interacting with the default interface on most objects, so this should seem pretty straightforward. Consider this simple class:

```
Public Class TheClass
  Public Sub DoSomething()
```

```
    End Sub

    Public Sub DoSomethingElse()

    End Sub
  End Class
```

This defines a class and, by extension, defines the native interface that is exposed by any objects you instantiate based on this class. The native interface defines two methods, DoSomething() and DoSomethingElse(). To make use of these methods, you simply call them:

```
Dim myObject As New TheClass()

myObject.DoSomething()

myObject.DoSomethingElse()
```

This is the same thing you did in Chapter 3 and so far in this chapter. However, let's take a look at creating and using secondary interfaces, because they are a bit different.

Secondary Interfaces

Sometimes it's helpful for an object to have more than one interface, thus enabling you to interact with the object in different ways. Inheritance enables you to create subclasses that are specialized cases of the base class. For example, your Employee is a Person.

However, sometimes you have a group of objects that are not the same thing, but you want to be able to treat them as though they were the same. You want all these objects to act as the same thing, even though they are all different.

For instance, you may have a series of different objects in an application, product, customer, invoice, and so forth. Each of these would have default interfaces appropriate to each individual object — and each of them is a different class — so there's no natural inheritance relationship implied between these classes. At the same time, you may need to be able to generate a printed document for each type of object, so you'd like to make them all act as a printable object.

This chapter later discusses the is-a *and* act-as *relationships in more detail.*

To accomplish this, you can define a generic interface that enables generating such a printed document. You can call it IPrintableObject.

By convention, this type of interface is typically prefixed with a capital I to indicate that it is a formal interface.

Each of your application objects can choose to implement the IPrintableObject interface. Every object that implements this interface must include code to provide actual implementation of the interface, which is unlike inheritance, where the code from a base class is automatically reused.

By implementing this common interface, you are able to write a routine that accepts any object that implements the IPrintableObject interface and print it — while remaining totally oblivious to the "real" datatype of the object or the methods its native interface might expose.

Before you see how to use an interface in this manner, let's walk through the process of actually defining an interface.

Defining the Interface

You define a formal interface using the `Interface` keyword. This can be done in any code module in your project, but a good place to put this type of definition is in a standard module. An interface defines a set of methods (`Sub`, `Function`, or `Property`) and events that must be exposed by any class that chooses to implement the interface.

Add a module to the project using Project ➪ Add Module and name it `Interfaces.vb`. Then, add the following code to the module, outside the `Module` code block itself:

```
Public Interface IPrintableObject

End Interface

Module Interfaces

End Module
```

A code module can contain a number of interface definitions, and these definitions must exist outside of any other code block. Thus, they don't go within a `Class` or `Module` block; they are at a peer level to those constructs.

Interfaces must be declared using either `Public` or `Friend` scope. Declaring a `Private` or `Protected` interface results in a syntax error.

Within the `Interface` block of code, you can define the methods, properties, and events that make up your particular interface. Because the scope of the interface is defined by the `Interface` declaration itself, you can't specify scopes for individual methods and events; they are all scoped like the interface itself.

For instance, add the following code:

```
Public Interface IPrintableObject
    Function Label(ByVal index As Integer) As String
    Function Value(ByVal index As Integer) As String
    ReadOnly Property Count() As Integer
End Interface
```

This defines a new datatype, somewhat like creating a class or structure, which you can use when declaring variables. For instance, you can now declare a variable of type `IPrintableObject`:

```
Private printable As IPrintableObject
```

You can also have your classes implement this interface, which requires each class to provide implementation code for each of the three methods defined on the interface.

Before you implement the interface in a class, let's see how you can make use of the interface to write a generic routine that can print any object that implements `IPrintableObject`.

Using the Interface

Interfaces define the methods and events (including parameters and datatypes) that an object is required to implement if you choose to support the interface. This means that, given just the interface definition, you can easily write code that can interact with any object that implements the interface, even though you don't know what the native datatypes of those objects will be.

To see how you can write such code, let's create a simple routine in your form that can display data to the output window in the IDE from any object that implements `IPrintableObject`. Bring up the code window for your form and add the following routine:

```
Public Sub PrintObject(obj As IPrintableObject)
  Dim index As Integer

  For index = 0 To obj.Count
    Debug.Write(obj.Label(index) & ": ")
    Debug.WriteLine(obj.Value(index))
  Next
End Sub
```

Notice that you're accepting a parameter of type `IPrintableObject`. This is how secondary interfaces are used, by treating an object of one type as though it were actually of the interface type. As long as the object passed to this routine implements the `IPrintableObject` interface, your code will work fine.

Within the `PrintObject` routine, you're assuming that the object will implement three elements — `Count`, `Label`, and `Value` — as part of the `IPrintableObject` interface. Secondary interfaces can include methods, properties, and events, much like a default interface, but the interface itself is defined and implemented using some special syntax.

Now that you have a generic printing routine, you need a way to call it. Bring up the designer for `Form1`, add a button, and name it `btnPrint`. Double-click the button and put this code behind it:

```
Private Sub btnPrint_Click(ByVal sender As System.Object, _
    ByVal e As System.EventArgs) Handles btnPrint.Click

  Dim obj As New Employee("Andy")

  obj.EmployeeNumber = 123
  obj.BirthDate = #1/1/1980#
  obj.HireDate = #1/1/1996#

  PrintObject(obj)
End Sub
```

This code simply initializes an `Employee` object and calls the `PrintObject()` routine. Of course, this code produces runtime exceptions, because `PrintObject` is expecting a parameter that implements `IPrintableObject`, and `Employee` implements no such interface. Let's move on and implement that interface in `Employee` so that you can see how it works.

Implementing the Interface

Any class (other than an abstract base class) can implement an interface by using the `Implements` keyword. For instance, you can implement the `IPrintableObject` interface in `Employee` by adding the following line:

```
Public Class Employee
    Inherits Person
    Implements IPrintableObject
```

This causes the interface to be exposed by any object created as an instance of `Employee`. Adding this line of code and pressing the Enter key triggers the IDE to add skeleton methods for the interface to your class. All you need to do is provide implementations for the methods.

To implement an interface, you must implement all the methods and properties defined by that interface.

Before actually implementing the interface, however, let's create an array to contain the labels for the data fields so that you can return them via the `IPrintableObject` interface. Add the following code to the `Employee` class:

```
Public Class Employee
    Inherits Person
    Implements IPrintableObject

    Private mLabels() As String = {"ID", "Age", "HireDate"}
    Private mHireDate As Date
    Private mSalary As Double
```

To implement the interface, you need to create methods and properties with the same parameter and return datatypes as those defined in the interface. The actual name of each method or property doesn't matter because you are using the `Implements` keyword to link your internal method names to the external method names defined by the interface. As long as the method signatures match, you are all set.

This applies to scope as well. Although the interface and its methods and properties are publicly available, you don't have to declare your actual methods and properties as `Public`. In many cases, you can implement them as `Private`, so they don't become part of the native interface and are only exposed via the secondary interface.

However, if you do have a `Public` method with a method signature, you can use it to implement a method from the interface. This has the interesting side effect that this method provides implementation for both a method on the object's native interface and one on the secondary interface.

In this case, you'll use a `Private` method, so it is only providing implementation for the `IPrintableObject` interface. You can implement the `Label` method by adding the following code to `Employee`:

```
Private Function Label(ByVal index As Integer) As String _
        Implements IPrintableObject.Label

    Return mLabels(index)
End Function
```

This is just a regular `Private` method that returns a `String` value from the preinitialized array. The interesting part is the `Implements` clause on the method declaration:

```
Private Function Label(ByVal index As Integer) As String _
    Implements IPrintableObject.Label
```

By using the `Implements` keyword in this fashion, you're indicating that this particular method is the implementation for the `Label` method on the `IPrintableObject` interface. The actual name of the private method could be anything. It is the use of the `Implements` clause that makes this work. The only requirement is that the parameter datatypes and the return value datatype must match those defined by the `IPrintableObject` interface.

This is very similar to using the `Handles` clause to indicate which method should handle an event. In fact, like the `Handles` clause, the `Implements` clause allows you to have a comma-separated list of interface methods that should be implemented by this one function.

You can then move on to implement the other two elements defined by the `IPrintableObject` interface by adding this code to `Employee`:

```
Private Function Value(ByVal index As Integer) As String _
    Implements IPrintableObject.Value

  Select Case index
    Case 0
      Return CStr(EmployeeNumber)
    Case 1
      Return CStr(Age)
    Case Else
      Return Format(HireDate, "Short date")
  End Select
End Function

Private ReadOnly Property Count() As Integer _
    Implements IPrintableObject.Count
  Get
    Return UBound(mLabels)
  End Get
End Property
```

You can now run this application and click the button. The output window in the IDE will display your results, showing the ID, age, and hire date values as appropriate.

Any object could create a similar implementation behind the `IPrintableObject` interface, and the `PrintObject()` routine in your form would continue to work regardless of the native datatype of the object itself.

Reusing Common Implementation

Secondary interfaces provide a guarantee that all objects implementing a given interface have exactly the same methods and events, including the same parameters.

The `Implements` clause links your actual implementation to a specific method on an interface. For instance, your `Value` method is linked to `IPrintableObject.Value` using the following clause:

```
Private Function Value(ByVal index As Integer) As String _
    Implements IPrintableObject.Value
```

Sometimes, your method might be able to serve as the implementation for more than one method, either on the same interface or on different interfaces.

Add the following interface definition to `Interfaces.vb`:

```
Public Interface IValues
    Function GetValue(ByVal index As Integer) As String
End Interface
```

This interface defines just one method, `GetValue()`. Notice that it defines a single `Integer` parameter and a return type of `String`, the same as the `Value` method from `IPrintableObject`. Even though the method name and parameter variable name don't match, what counts here is that the parameter and return value datatypes do match.

Now bring up the code window for `Employee`. You'll have it implement this new interface in addition to the `IPrintableObject` interface:

```
Public Class Employee
    Inherits Person
    Implements IPrintableObject
    Implements IValues
```

You already have a method that returns values. Rather than reimplement that method, it would be nice to just link this new `GetValues()` method to your existing method. You can easily do this because the `Implements` clause allows you to provide a comma-separated list of method names:

```
Private Function Value(ByVal index As Integer) As String _
    Implements IPrintableObject.Value, IValues.GetValue

    Select Case Index
        Case 0
            Return CStr(EmployeeNumber)
        Case 1
            Return CStr(Age)
        Case Else
            Return Format(HireDate, "Short date")
    End Select

End Function
```

This is very similar to the use of the `Handles` keyword, covered in Chapter 3. A single method within the class, regardless of scope or name, can be used to implement any number of methods as defined by other interfaces as long as the datatypes of the parameters and return values all match.

Combining Interfaces and Inheritance

You can combine implementation of secondary interfaces and inheritance at the same time. When you inherit from a class that implements an interface, your new subclass automatically gains the interface and the implementation from the base class. If you specify that your base class methods are overridable, then the subclass can override those methods. This not only overrides the base class implementation for your native interface, but also overrides the implementation for the interface. For instance, you could declare the `Value()` method in the interface as follows:

```
Public Overridable Function Value(ByVal index As Integer) As String _
    Implements IPrintableObject.Value, IValues.GetValue
```

Now it is `Public`, so it is available on your native interface, and it is part of both the `IPrintableObject` and `IValues` interfaces. This means that you can access the property three ways in client code:

```
Dim emp As New Employee()
Dim printable As IPrintableObject = emp
Dim values As IValues = emp

Debug.WriteLine(emp.Value(0))
Debug.WriteLine(printable.Value(0))
Debug.WriteLine(values.GetValue(0))
```

Note that you're also now using the `Overrides` keyword in the declaration. This means that a subclass of `Employee`, such as `OfficeEmployee`, can override the `Value()` method. The overridden method will be the one invoked, regardless of whether you call the object directly or via an interface.

Combining the implementation of an interface in a base class along with overridable methods can provide a very flexible object design.

Abstraction

Abstraction is the process by which you can think about specific properties or behaviors without thinking about a particular object that has those properties or behaviors. Abstraction is merely the ability of a language to create "black box" code, to take a concept and create an abstract representation of that concept within a program.

A `Customer` object, for example, is an abstract representation of a real-world customer. A `DataSet` object is an abstract representation of a set of data.

Abstraction enables you to recognize how things are similar and to ignore differences, to think in general terms and not in specifics. A `TextBox` control is an abstraction because you can place it on a form and then tailor it to your needs by setting properties. Visual Basic enables you to define abstractions using classes.

Any language that enables a developer to create a class from which objects can be instantiated meets this criterion, and Visual Basic is no exception. You can easily create a class to represent a customer, essentially providing an abstraction. You can then create instances of that class, whereby each object can have its own attributes, representing a specific customer.

In Visual Basic, you implement abstraction by creating a class using the `Class` keyword. To see this in action, bring up Visual Studio and create a new Visual Basic Windows Application project named `OOExample`. Once the project is open, add a new class to the project using the Project ➪ Add Class menu option. Name the new class `Customer`, and add some code to make this class represent a real-world customer in an abstract sense:

```
Public Class Customer
    Private mID As Guid = Guid.NewGuid
    Private mName As String
    Private mPhone As String

    Public Property ID() As Guid
      Get
         Return mID
      End Get
      Set(ByVal value As Guid)
        mID = value
      End Set
    End Property

    Public Property Name() As String
      Get
         Return mName
      End Get
      Set(ByVal value As String)
        mName = value
      End Set
    End Property

    Public Property Phone() As String
      Get
         Return mPhone
      End Get
      Set(ByVal value As String)
        mPhone = value
      End Set
    End Property
End Class
```

You know that a real customer is a lot more complex than an ID, name, and phone number. Yet at the same time, you know that in an abstract sense, your customers really do have names and phone numbers, and that you assign them unique ID numbers to keep track of them. In this case, you're using a globally unique identifier (GUID) as a unique ID. Thus, given an ID, name, and phone number, you know which customer you're dealing with, and so you have a perfectly valid abstraction of a customer within your application.

You can then use this abstract representation of a customer from within your code. To do this, you use data binding to link the object to a form. Before proceeding, be sure to build the project. Now click the Data ➪ Show Data Sources menu option to open the Data Sources window. Then click the Add New Data Source link in the window to bring up the Data Source Configuration Wizard. Within the wizard, choose to add a new Object data source, click the Next button, and then select your `Customer` class, as shown in Figure 4-11.

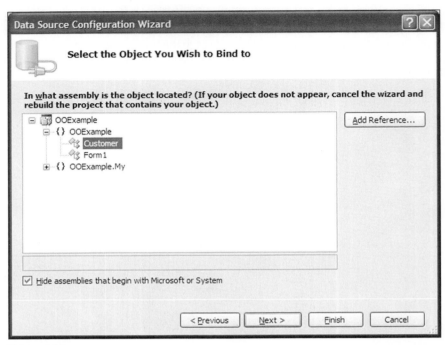

Figure 4-11

Finish the wizard, and the `Customer` class should be displayed as an available data source, as shown in Figure 4-12, if you are working in Design mode.

Figure 4-12

Click on `Customer` in the window. `Customer` should change its display to a combo box. Open the combo box and change the selection from DataGridView to Details. This way, you get a details view of the object on your form. Open the designer for `Form1` and drag the `Customer` class from the Data Sources window onto the form. The result should look something like the dialog shown in Figure 4-13.

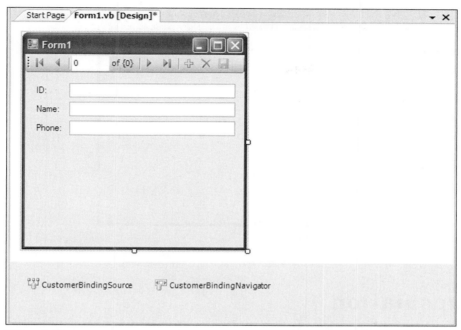

Figure 4-13

All you need to do now is add code to create an instance of the `Customer` class to act as a data source for the form. Double-click on the form to bring up its code window and add the following code:

```
Public Class Form1

    Private Sub Form1_Load(ByVal sender As System.Object, _
        ByVal e As System.EventArgs) Handles MyBase.Load

        Me.CustomerBindingSource.DataSource = New Customer

    End Sub

End Class
```

You're using the ability of Windows Forms to data bind to a property on an object. You'll learn more about data binding in Chapter 15. For now, it is enough to know that the controls on the form are automatically tied to the properties on your object.

Now you have a simple user interface (UI) that both displays and updates the data in your `Customer` object, with that object providing the UI developer with an abstract representation of the customer. When you run the application, you'll see a display like the one shown in Figure 4-14.

Here, you've displayed the pre-generated `ID` value, and have entered values for `Name` and `Phone` directly into the form.

Figure 4-14

Encapsulation

Perhaps the most important of the object-oriented concepts is that of *encapsulation*. Encapsulation is the concept that an object should totally separate its interface from its implementation. All the data and implementation code for an object should be entirely hidden behind its interface. Another way to put this is that an object should be a black box.

The idea is that you can create an interface (by creating public methods in a class) and, as long as that interface remains consistent, the application can interact with your objects. This remains true even if you entirely rewrite the code within a given method. The interface is independent of the implementation.

Encapsulation enables you to hide the internal implementation details of a class. For example, the algorithm you use to find prime numbers might be proprietary. You can expose a simple API to the end user, but you hide all of the logic used in your algorithm by encapsulating it within your class.

This means that an object should completely contain any data it requires and should contain all the code required to manipulate that data. Programs should interact with an object through an interface, using the properties and methods of the object. Client code should never work directly with the data owned by the object.

> Programs interact with objects by sending messages to the object that indicate which method or property they'd like to have invoked. These messages are generated by other objects or by external sources such as the user. The object reacts to these messages through methods or properties.

Visual Basic classes entirely hide their internal data and code, providing a well-established interface of properties and methods with the outside world.

Let's look at an example. Add the following class to your project; the code defines its native interface:

```
Public Class Encapsulation

  Public Function DistanceTo(ByVal x As Single, ByVal y As Single) As Single

  End Function

  Public Property CurrentX() As Single
    Get

    End Get
    Set(ByVal value As Single)

    End Set
  End Property

  Public Property CurrentY() As Single
    Get

    End Get
    Set(ByVal value As Single)

    End Set
  End Property

End Class
```

This creates an interface for the class. At this point, you can write client code to interact with the class, because from a client perspective all you care about is the interface. Bring up the designer for Form1 and add a button to the form, and then write the following code behind the button:

```
Private Sub btnEncapsulation_Click(ByVal sender As System.Object, _
  ByVal e As System.EventArgs) Handles btnEncapsulation.Click

  Dim obj As New Encapsulation
  MsgBox(obj.DistanceTo(10, 10))

End Sub
```

Even though you have no actual code in the Encapsulation class, you can still write code to use that class because the interface is defined.

This is a powerful idea. It means you can rapidly create class interfaces against which other developers can create the UI or other parts of the application while you are still creating the implementation behind the interface.

From here, you could do virtually anything you like in terms of implementing the class. For example, you could use the values to calculate a direct distance:

```
Imports System.Math

Public Class Encapsulation
```

```
    Private mX As Single
    Private mY As Single

    Public Function DistanceTo(ByVal x As Single, ByVal y As Single) As Single
      Return CSng(Sqrt((x - mX) ^ 2 + (y - mY) ^ 2))
    End Function

    Public Property CurrentX() As Single
    Get
        Return mX
    End Get
    Set(ByVal value As Single)
      mX = value
    End Set
  End Property

    Public Property CurrentY() As Single
    Get
        Return mY
    End Get
    Set(ByVal value As Single)
      mY = value
    End Set
  End Property
End Class
```

Now when you run the application and click the button, you get a meaningful value as a result. Even better, however, encapsulation enables you to change the implementation without changing the interface. For example, you can change the distance calculation to find the distance between the points (assuming that no diagonal travel is allowed):

```
Public Function DistanceTo(ByVal x As Single, ByVal y As Single) As Single
    Return Abs(x - mX) + Abs(y - mY)
End Function
```

This results in a different value being displayed when the program is run. You haven't changed the interface of the class, so your working client program has no idea that you have switched from one implementation to the other. You have achieved a total change of behavior without any change to the client code. This is the essence of encapsulation.

Of course, a user might have a problem if you make such a change to your object. If applications were developed expecting the first set of behaviors, and then you changed to the second, there could be some interesting side effects. However, the key point is that the client programs would continue to function, even if the results were quite different from when you began.

Polymorphism

Polymorphism is often considered to be directly tied to inheritance (which is discussed next). In reality, however, it's largely independent. Polymorphism means that you can have two classes with different implementations or code, but with a common set of methods, properties, or events. You can then write a program that operates upon that interface and doesn't care about which type of object it operates at runtime.

Method Signatures

To properly understand polymorphism, you need to explore the concept of a *method signature*, sometimes also called a *prototype*. All methods have a signature, which is defined by the method's name and the datatypes of its parameters. You might have code such as this:

```
Public Function CalculateValue() As Integer

End Sub
```

In this example, the signature is as follows:

```
f()
```

If you add a parameter to the method, the signature will change. For example, you could change the method to accept a `Double`:

```
Public Function CalculateValue(ByVal value As Double) As Integer
```

Then, the signature of the method is as follows:

```
f(Double)
```

Polymorphism merely says that you should be able to write client code that calls methods on an object, and as long as the object provides your methods with the method signatures you expect, it doesn't matter from which class the object was created. Let's look at some examples of polymorphism within Visual Basic.

Implementing Polymorphism

You can use several techniques to achieve polymorphic behavior:

❑ Late binding

❑ Multiple interfaces

❑ Reflection

❑ Inheritance

Late binding actually enables you to implement "pure" polymorphism, although at the cost of performance and ease of programming. Through multiple interfaces and inheritance, you can also achieve polymorphism with much better performance and ease of programming. Reflection enables you to use either late binding or multiple interfaces, but against objects created in a very dynamic way, even going so far as to dynamically load a DLL into your application at runtime so that you can use its classes.

You'll walk through each of these options to see how they are implemented and to explore their pros and cons.

Polymorphism through Late Binding

Typically, when you interact with objects in Visual Basic, you are interacting with them through strongly typed variables. For example, in `Form1` you interacted with the `Encapsulation` object with the following code:

```
Private Sub btnEncapsulation_Click(ByVal sender As System.Object, _
   ByVal e As System.EventArgs) Handles btnEncapsulation.Click

   Dim obj As New Encapsulation
   MsgBox(obj.DistanceTo(10, 10))

End Sub
```

The `obj` variable is declared using a specific type (`Encapsulation`) — meaning that it is strongly typed or early bound.

You can also interact with objects that are late bound. Late binding means that your object variable has no specific datatype, but rather is of type `Object`. To use late binding, you need to use the `Option Strict Off` directive at the top of your code file (or in the project's properties). This tells the Visual Basic compiler that you want to use late binding, so it will allow you to do this type of polymorphism. Add the following to the top of the `Form1` code:

```
Option Strict Off
```

With `Option Strict` turned off, Visual Basic treats the `Object` datatype in a special way, enabling you to attempt arbitrary method calls against the object even though the `Object` datatype doesn't implement those methods. For example, you could change the code in `Form1` to be late bound as follows:

```
Private Sub btnEncapsulation_Click(ByVal sender As System.Object, _
   ByVal e As System.EventArgs) Handles btnEncapsulation.Click

   Dim obj As Object = New Encapsulation
   MsgBox(obj.DistanceTo(10, 10))

End Sub
```

When this code is run, you get the same result as you did before, even though the `Object` datatype has no `DistanceTo` method as part of its interface. The late-binding mechanism, behind the scenes, dynamically determines the real type of your object and invokes the appropriate method.

When you work with objects through late binding, neither the Visual Basic IDE nor the compiler can tell whether you are calling a valid method. Here, there is no way for the compiler to know that the object referenced by your `obj` variable actually has a `DistanceTo()` method. It just assumes that you know what you're talking about and compiles the code.

At runtime, when the code is actually invoked, it attempts to dynamically call the `DistanceTo()` method. If that is a valid method, your code will work; if it is not, you'll get an error.

Obviously, there is a level of danger when using late binding, as a simple typo can introduce errors that can only be discovered when the application is actually run. However, it also offers a lot of flexibility, as code that makes use of late binding can talk to any object from any class as long as those objects implement the methods you require.

There is a substantial performance penalty for using late binding. The existence of each method is discovered dynamically at runtime, and that discovery takes time. Moreover, the mechanism used to invoke a method through late binding is not nearly as efficient as the mechanism used to call a method that is known at compile time.

To make this more obvious, you can change the code in Form1 by adding a generic routine that displays the distance:

```
Private Sub btnEncapsulation_Click(ByVal sender As System.Object, _
    ByVal e As System.EventArgs) Handles btnEncapsulation.Click

    Dim obj As New Encapsulation
    ShowDistance(obj)
End Sub

Private Sub ShowDistance(ByVal obj As Object)
    MsgBox(obj.DistanceTo(10, 10))
End Sub
```

Notice that the new ShowDistance routine accepts a parameter using the generic Object datatype — so you can pass it literally any value — String, Integer, or one of your own custom objects. It will throw an exception at runtime, however, unless the object you pass into the routine has a DistanceTo() method that matches the required method signature.

You know that your Encapsulation object has a method matching that signature, so your code works fine. However, let's add another simple class to demonstrate polymorphism. Add a new class to the project and name it Poly.vb:

```
Public Class Poly
    Public Function DistanceTo(ByVal x As Single, ByVal y As Single) As Single
        Return x + y
    End Function
End Class
```

This class is about as simple as you can get. It exposes a DistanceTo() method as part of its interface and provides a very basic implementation of that interface.

You can use this new class in place of the Encapsulation class without changing the ShowDistance() method by using polymorphism. Return to the code in Form1 and make the following change:

```
Private Sub btnEncapsulation_Click(ByVal sender As System.Object, _
    ByVal e As System.EventArgs) Handles btnEncapsulation.Click

    Dim obj As New Poly
    ShowDistance(obj)
End Sub
```

Even though you changed the class of object you're passing to ShowDistance() to one with a different overall interface and different implementation, the method called within ShowDistance() remains consistent, so your code will run.

Chapter 4: Object-Oriented Programming

Polymorphism with Multiple Interfaces

Late binding is flexible and easy, but it isn't ideal because it defeats the IDE and compiler type checking that enables you to fix bugs due to typos during the development process. It also has a negative impact on performance.

Another way to implement polymorphism is to use multiple interfaces. This approach avoids late binding, meaning that the IDE and compiler can check your code as you enter and compile it. Moreover, because the compiler has access to all the information about each method you call, your code will run much faster.

Remove the Option Strict directive from the code in Form1. This will cause some syntax errors to be highlighted in the code, but don't worry — you'll fix those soon enough.

Visual Basic not only supports polymorphism through late binding, but also implements a stricter form of polymorphism through its support of multiple interfaces. (Earlier you learned about multiple interfaces, including the use of the Implements keyword and how to define interfaces.)

With late binding, you've learned how to treat all objects as equals by making them all appear using the Object datatype. With multiple interfaces, you can treat all objects as equals by making them all implement a common datatype or interface.

This approach has the benefit that it is strongly typed, meaning the IDE and compiler can help you find errors due to typos because the names and datatypes of all methods and parameters are known at design time. It is also fast in terms of performance; because the compiler knows about the methods, it can use optimized mechanisms for calling them, especially compared to the dynamic mechanisms used in late binding.

Let's return to the project and implement polymorphism with multiple interfaces. First, add a module to the project using the Project ➪ Add Module menu option and name it Interfaces.vb. Replace the Module code block with an Interface declaration:

```
Public Interface IShared
    Function CalculateDistance(ByVal x As Single, ByVal y As Single) As Single
End Interface
```

Now you can make both the Encapsulation and Poly classes implement this interface. First, in the Encapsulation class add the following code:

```
Public Class Encapsulation
    Implements IShared

    Private mX As Single
    Private mY As Single

    Public Function DistanceTo(ByVal x As Single, ByVal y As Single) _
        As Single Implements IShared.CalculateDistance

    Return CSng(Sqrt((x - mX) ^ 2 + (y - mY) ^ 2))
    End Function
```

Here you're implementing the IShared interface, and because the CalculateDistance method's signature matches that of your existing DistanceTo method, you're simply indicating that it should act as the implementation for CalculateDistance().

You can make a similar change in the Poly class:

```
Public Class Poly
   Implements IShared

   Public Function DistanceTo(ByVal x As Single, ByVal y As Single) As Single _
       Implements IShared.CalculateDistance

        Return x + y
   End Function
End Class
```

Now this class also implements the IShared interface, and you're ready to see polymorphism implemented in your code. Bring up the code window for Form1 and change your ShowDistance() method as follows:

```
Private Sub ShowDistance(ByVal obj As IShared)
   MsgBox(obj.CalculateDistance(10, 10))
End Sub
```

Note that this eliminates the compiler error you saw after removing the Option Strict directive from Form1.

Instead of accepting the parameter using the generic Object datatype, you are now accepting an IShared parameter — a strong datatype known by both the IDE and the compiler. Within the code itself, you are now calling the CalculateDistance() method as defined by that interface.

This routine can now accept any object that implements IShared, regardless of what class that object was created from, or what other interfaces that object may implement. All you care about here is that the object implements IShared.

Polymorphism through Reflection

You've seen how to use late binding to invoke a method on any arbitrary object as long as that object has a method matching the method signature you're trying to call. You've also walked through the use of multiple interfaces, which enables you to achieve polymorphism through a faster, early-bound technique. The challenge with these techniques is that late binding can be slow and hard to debug, and multiple interfaces can be somewhat rigid and inflexible.

Enter *reflection*. Reflection is a technology built into the .NET Framework that enables you to write code that interrogates an assembly to dynamically determine the classes and datatypes it contains. Using reflection, you can load the assembly into your process, create instances of those classes, and invoke their methods.

When you use late binding, Visual Basic makes use of the System.Reflection namespace behind the scenes on your behalf. You can choose to manually use reflection as well. This gives you even more flexibility in how you interact with objects.

For example, suppose that the class you want to call is located in some other assembly on disk — an assembly you didn't specifically reference from within your project when you compiled it. How can you dynamically find, load, and invoke such an assembly? Reflection enables you to do this, assuming that the assembly is polymorphic. In other words, it has either an interface you expect or a set of methods you can invoke via late binding.

To see how reflection works with late binding, let's create a new class in a separate assembly (project) and use it from within your existing application. Choose File ⇨ Add ⇨ New Project to add a new class library project to your solution. Name it `Objects`. It begins with a single class module that you can use as a starting point. Change the code in that class to the following:

```
Public Class External
  Public Function DistanceTo(ByVal x As Single, ByVal y As Single) As Single
    Return x * y
  End Function
End Class
```

Now compile the assembly by choosing Build ⇨ Build Objects. Next, bring up the code window for `Form1`. Add an `Imports` statement at the top, and add back the `Option Strict Off` statement:

```
Option Strict Off

Imports System.Reflection
```

Remember that because you're using late binding, `Form1` also must use `Option Strict Off`. Without this, late binding is not available.

Then add a button with the following code:

```
Private Sub Button1_Click(ByVal sender As System.Object, _
    ByVal e As System.EventArgs) Handles button1.Click

  Dim obj As Object
  Dim dll As Assembly

  dll = Assembly.LoadFrom("..\..\Objects\bin\Objects.dll")

  obj = dll.CreateInstance("Objects.External")
  MsgBox(obj.DistanceTo(10, 10))
End Sub
```

There's a lot going on here, so let's walk through it. First, notice that you're reverting to late binding; your `obj` variable is declared as type `Object`. You'll look at using reflection and multiple interfaces in a moment, but for now you'll use late binding.

Next, you've declared a `dll` variable as type `Reflection.Assembly`. This variable will contain a reference to the `Objects` assembly that you'll be dynamically loading through your code. Note that you are not adding a reference to this assembly via Project ⇨ Add References. You'll dynamically get access to the assembly at runtime.

You then load the external assembly dynamically by using the `Assembly.LoadFrom` method:

```
dll = Assembly.LoadFrom("..\..\Objects\bin\Objects.dll")
```

This causes the reflection library to load your assembly from a file on disk at the location you specify. Once the assembly is loaded into your process, you can use the `myDll` variable to interact with it, including interrogating it to get a list of the classes it contains or to create instances of those classes.

> You can also use the `[Assembly].Load` method, which will scan the directory where your application's .exe file is located (and the global assembly cache) for any EXE or DLL containing the Objects assembly. When it finds the assembly, it loads it into memory, making it available for your use.

You can then use the `CreateInstance` method on the assembly itself to create objects based on any class in that assembly. In your case, you're creating an object based on the `External` class:

```
obj = dll.CreateInstance("Objects.External")
```

Now you have an actual object to work with, so you can use late binding to invoke its `DistanceTo()` method. At this point, your code is really no different from that in the earlier late-binding example, except that the assembly and object were created dynamically at runtime, rather than being referenced directly by your project.

At this point, you should be able to run the application and have it dynamically invoke the assembly at runtime.

Polymorphism via Reflection and Multiple Interfaces

You can also use both reflection and multiple interfaces together. You've seen how multiple interfaces enable you to have objects from different classes implement the same interface and thus be treated identically. You've also seen how reflection enables you to load an assembly and class dynamically at runtime.

You can combine these concepts by using an interface shared in common between your main application and your external assembly, and using reflection to load that external assembly dynamically at runtime.

First, create the interface that will be shared across both application and assembly. To do this, add a new Class Library project to your solution named `Interfaces`. Once it is created, drag and drop the `Interfaces.vb` module from your original application into the new project (hold down the Shift key as you move it). This makes the `IShared` interface part of that project and no longer part of your base application.

Of course, your base application still uses `IShared`, so you'll want to reference the `Interfaces` project from your application to gain access to the interface. Do this by right-clicking your `OOExample` project in the Solution Explorer window and selecting Add Reference. Then add the reference, as shown in Figure 4-15.

Figure 4-15

Because the `IShared` interface is now part of a separate assembly, add an `Imports` statement to `Form1`, `Encapsulation`, and `Poly` so that they are able to locate the `IShared` interface:

```
Imports Interfaces
```

Be sure to add this to the top of all three code modules.

You also need to have the `Objects` project reference `Interfaces`, so right-click `Objects` in Solution Explorer and choose Add Reference there as well. Add the reference to `Interfaces` and click OK. At this point, both the original application and the external assembly have access to the `IShared` interface. You can now enhance the code in `Objects` by changing the `External` class:

```
Imports Interfaces

Public Class External
   Implements IShared
   Public Function DistanceTo(ByVal x As Single, ByVal y As Single) _
      As Single Implements IShared.CalculateDistance

      Return x * y
   End Function
End Class
```

With both the main application and external assembly using the same datatype, you are now ready to implement the polymorphic behavior using reflection.

Remove the `Option Strict Off` code from `Form1`. In fact, you might also want to explicitly set `Option Script On`. This prohibits the use of late binding, thus ensuring that you must use a different technique for polymorphism.

Bring up the code window for `Form1` and change the code behind the button to take advantage of the `IShared` interface:

```
Private Sub btnReflection_Click(ByVal sender As System.Object, _
    ByVal e As System.EventArgs) Handles Button1.Click

    Dim obj As IShared
    Dim dll As Assembly

    dll = Assembly.LoadFrom("..\..\Objects\bin\Objects.dll")

    obj = CType(dll.CreateInstance("Objects.External"), IShared)
    ShowDistance(obj)
End Sub
```

All you've done here is change the code so that you can pass your dynamically created object to the `ShowDistance()` method, which you know requires a parameter of type `IShared`. Because your class implements the same `IShared` interface (from `Interfaces`) used by the main application, this will work perfectly. Rebuild and run the solution to see this in action.

This technique is very nice, as the code in `ShowDistance()` is strongly typed, providing all the performance and coding benefits, but both the DLL and the object itself are loaded dynamically, providing a great deal of flexibility to your application.

Polymorphism with Inheritance

Inheritance, discussed earlier in this chapter, can also be used to enable polymorphism. The idea here is very similar to that of multiple interfaces, as a subclass can always be treated as though it were the datatype of the parent class.

> Many people consider the concepts of inheritance and polymorphism to be tightly intertwined. As you've seen, however, it is perfectly possible to use polymorphism without inheritance.

At the moment, both your `Encapsulation` and `Poly` classes are implementing a common interface named `IShared`. You can use polymorphism to interact with objects of either class via that common interface. The same is true if these are child classes based on the same base class through inheritance. To see how this works, in the `OOExample` project, add a new class named `Parent` and insert the following code:

```
Public MustInherit Class Parent
  Public MustOverride Function DistanceTo(ByVal x As Single, _
      ByVal y As Single) As Single
End Class
```

As described earlier, this is an abstract base class, a class with no implementation of its own. The purpose of an abstract base class is to provide a common base from which other classes can be derived.

To implement polymorphism using inheritance, you do not need to use an abstract base class. Any base class that provides overridable methods (using either the `MustOverride` or `Overridable` keywords) will work fine, as all its subclasses are guaranteed to have that same set of methods as part of their interface and yet the subclasses can provide custom implementation for those methods.

185

Chapter 4: Object-Oriented Programming

In this example, you're simply defining the `DistanceTo()` method as being a method that must be overridden and implemented by any subclass of `Parent`. Now you can bring up the `Encapsulation` class and change it to be a subclass of `Parent`:

```
Public Class Encapsulation
   Inherits Parent
   Implements IShared
```

You don't need to stop implementing the `IShared` interface just because you're inheriting from `Parent`; inheritance and multiple interfaces coexist nicely. You do, however, have to override the `DistanceTo()` method from the `Parent` class.

The `Encapsulation` class already has a `DistanceTo()` method with the proper method signature, so you can simply add the `Overrides` keyword to indicate that this method will override the declaration in the `Parent` class:

```
Public Overrides Function DistanceTo( _
   ByVal x As Single, _ByVal y As Single) _
   As Single Implements IShared.CalculateDistance
```

At this point, the `Encapsulation` class not only implements the common `IShared` interface and its own native interface, but also can be treated as though it were of type `Parent`, as it is a subclass of `Parent`. You can do the same thing to the `Poly` class:

```
Public Class Poly
   Inherits Parent
   Implements IShared

   Public Overrides Function DistanceTo( _
       ByVal x As Single, ByVal y As Single) _
       As Single Implements IShared.CalculateDistance

     Return x + y
   End Function
End Class
```

Finally, you can see how polymorphism works by altering the code in `Form1` to take advantage of the fact that both classes can be treated as though they were of type `Parent`. First, you can change the `ShowDistance()` method to accept its parameter as type `Parent` and to call the `DistanceTo()` method:

```
Private Sub ShowDistance(ByVal obj As Parent)
   MsgBox(obj.DistanceTo(10, 10))
End Sub
```

Then, you can add a new button to create an object of either type `Encapsulation` or `Poly` and pass it as a parameter to the method:

```
Private Sub btnInheritance_Click(ByVal sender As System.Object, _
   ByVal e As System.EventArgs) Handles btnInheritance.Click

   ShowDistance(New Poly)
   ShowDistance(New Encapsulation)

End Sub
```

Polymorphism Summary

Polymorphism is a very important concept in object-oriented design and programming, and Visual Basic provides you with ample techniques through which it can be implemented.

The following table summarizes the different techniques and their pros and cons, and provides some high-level guidelines about when to use each:

Technique	Pros	Cons	Guidelines
Late binding	Flexible, "pure" polymorphism	Slow, hard to debug, no IntelliSense	Use to call arbitrary methods on literally any object, regardless of datatype or interfaces
			Useful when you can't control the interfaces that will be implemented by the authors of your classes
Multiple interfaces	Fast, easy to debug, full IntelliSense	Not totally dynamic or flexible, requires class author to implement formal interface	Use when you are creating code that interacts with clearly defined methods that can be grouped together into a formal interface
			Useful when you control the interfaces that will be implemented by the classes used by your application
Reflection and late binding	Flexible, "pure" polymorphism, dynamically loads arbitrary assemblies from disk	Slow, hard to debug, no IntelliSense	Use to call arbitrary methods on objects4 when you don't know at design time which assemblies you will be using
Reflection and multiple interfaces	Fast, easy to debug, full IntelliSense, dynamically loads arbitrary assemblies from disk	Not totally dynamic or flexible, requires class author to implement formal interface	Use when you are creating code that interacts with clearly defined methods that can be grouped together into a formal interface, but when you don't know at design time which assemblies you will be using
Inheritance	Fast, easy to debug, full IntelliSense, inherits behaviors from base class	Not totally dynamic or flexible, requires class author to inherit from common base class	Use when you are creating objects that have an *is-a* relationship, i.e., when you have subclasses that are naturally of the same datatype as a base class.
			Polymorphism through inheritance should occur because inheritance makes sense, not because you are attempting to merely achieve polymorphism.

Inheritance

Inheritance is the concept that a new class can be based on an existing class, inheriting its interface and functionality from the original class. The mechanics and syntax of inheritance are described earlier in this chapter, so we won't rehash them here. However, you haven't yet looked at inheritance from a practical perspective, and that is the focus of this section.

When to Use Inheritance

Inheritance is one of the most powerful object-oriented features a language can support. At the same time, inheritance is one of the most dangerous and misused object-oriented features.

Properly used, inheritance enables you to increase the maintainability, readability, and reusability of your application by offering you a clear and concise way to reuse code, via both interface and implementation. Improperly used, inheritance creates applications that are very fragile, whereby a change to a class can cause the entire application to break or require changes.

Inheritance enables you to implement an *is-a* relationship. In other words, it enables you to implement a new class that is a more specific type of its base class. Properly used, inheritance enables you to create child classes that are actually the same as the base class.

Perhaps a quick example is in order. You know that a duck is a bird. However, a duck can also be food, though that is not its primary identity. Proper use of inheritance enables you to create a `Bird` base class from which you can derive a `Duck` class. You would not create a `Food` class and subclass `Duck` from `Food`, as a duck isn't primarily food — it merely acts as food sometimes.

This is the challenge. Inheritance is not just a mechanism for code reuse, but a mechanism to create classes that flow naturally from another class. If you use it anywhere you want code reuse, you'll end up with a real mess on your hands. If you use it anywhere you just want a common interface but where the child class is not really the same as the base class, then you should use multiple interfaces — something we'll discuss shortly.

> The question you must ask when using inheritance is whether the child class is a more specific version of the base class.

For example, you might have different types of products in your organization. All of these products have some common data and behaviors; they'll all have a product number, description, and price. However, if you have an agricultural application, you might have chemical products, seed products, fertilizer products, and retail products. These are all different — each having its own data and behaviors — and yet there is no doubt that each one of them really is a product. You can use inheritance to create this set of products, as illustrated by the class diagram in Figure 4-16.

This diagram shows that you have an abstract base `Product` class, from which you derive the various types of product your system actually uses. This is an appropriate use of inheritance because each child class is obviously a more specific form of the general `Product` class.

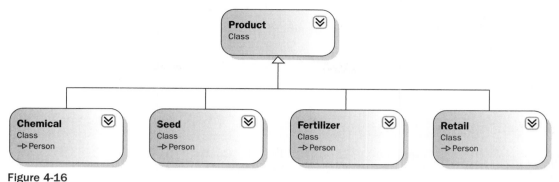

Figure 4-16

Alternately, you might try to use inheritance just as a code-sharing mechanism. For example, you may look at your application, which has Customer, Product, and SalesOrder classes, and decide that all of them need to be designed so that they can be printed to a printer. The code to handle the printing will all be somewhat similar, so to reuse that printing code, you create a base PrintableObject class. This would result in the diagram shown in Figure 4-17.

Figure 4-17

Intuitively, you know that this doesn't represent an *is-a* relationship. A Customer can be printed, and you are getting code reuse, but a customer isn't really a specific case of a printable object. Implementing a system following this design will result in a fragile design and application. This is a case where multiple interfaces are a far more appropriate technology, as you'll see later.

To illustrate this point, you might later discover that you have other entities in your organization that are similar to a customer but not quite the same. Upon further analysis, you may determine that Employee and Customer are related because they are specific cases of a Contact class. The Contact class provides commonality in terms of data and behavior across all these other classes (see Figure 4-18).

Figure 4-18

However, now your `Customer` is in trouble; you've said it is a `PrintableObject`, and you're now saying it is a `Contact`. You might be able to just derive `Contact` from `PrintableObject` (see Figure 4-19).

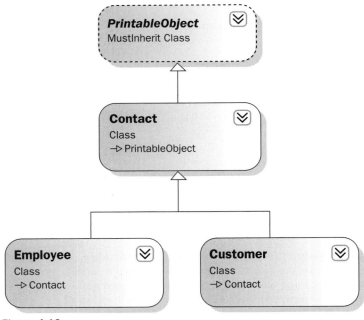

Figure 4-19

The problem with this is that now `Employee` is also of type `PrintableObject`, even if it shouldn't be, but you're stuck because unfortunately you decided early on to go against intuition and say that a `Customer` is a `PrintableObject`.

This problem could be solved by multiple inheritance, which would enable `Customer` to be a subclass of more than one base class — in this case, of both `Contact` and `PrintableObject`. However, the .NET platform and Visual Basic don't support multiple inheritance in this way. An alternative is to use inheritance for the *is-a* relationship with `Contact`, and use multiple interfaces to enable the `Customer` object to act as a `PrintableObject` by implementing an `IPrintableObject` interface.

Application versus Framework Inheritance

What you've just seen is how inheritance can accidentally cause reuse of code where no reuse was desired, but you can take a different view of this model by separating the concept of a framework from your actual application. The way you use inheritance in the design of a framework is somewhat different from how you use inheritance in the design of an actual application.

In this context, the word framework is being used to refer to a set of classes that provide base functionality that is not specific to an application, but rather may be used across a number of applications within the organization, or perhaps even beyond the organization. The .NET Framework base class library is an example of a very broad framework you use when building your applications.

The `PrintableObject` class discussed earlier, for example, may have little to do with your specific application, but may be the type of thing that is used across many applications. If so, it is a natural candidate for use as part of a framework, rather than being considered part of your actual application.

Framework classes exist at a lower level than application classes. For example, the .NET base class library is a framework on which all .NET applications are built. You can layer your own framework on top of the .NET Framework as well (see Figure 4-20).

Figure 4-20

If you take this view, then the `PrintableObject` class wouldn't be part of your application at all, but part of a framework on which your application is built. If so, then the fact that `Customer` is not a specific case of `PrintableObject` doesn't matter as much, as you're not saying that it is such a thing, but rather that it is leveraging that portion of the framework's functionality.

To make all this work requires a lot of planning and forethought in the design of the framework itself. To see the dangers you face, consider that you might want to not only print objects, but also store them in a file. In that case, you might have not only `PrintableObject`, but also `SavableObject` as a base class.

The question is, what do you do if Customer should be both printable and savable? If all printable objects are savable, you might have the result shown in Figure 4-21.

Figure 4-21

Or, if all savable objects are printable, you might have the result shown in Figure 4-22. However, neither of these truly provides a decent solution, as it is likely that the concept of being printable and the concept of being savable are different and not interrelated in either of these ways.

Figure 4-22

When faced with this sort of issue, it is best to avoid using inheritance and instead rely on multiple interfaces.

Inheritance and Multiple Interfaces

While inheritance is powerful, it is really geared around implementing the *is-a* relationship. Sometimes you will have objects that need a common interface, even though they aren't really a specific case of some base class that provides that interface. We've just explored that issue in the discussion of the PrintableObject, SavableObject, and Customer classes.

Sometimes multiple interfaces are a better alternative than inheritance. The syntax for creating and using secondary and multiple interfaces was discussed.

Multiple interfaces can be viewed as another way of implementing the *is-a* relationship, although it is often better to view inheritance as an *is-a* relationship and to view multiple interfaces as a way of implementing an *act-as* relationship.

To think about this further, we can say that the `PrintableObject` concept could perhaps be better expressed as an interface — `IPrintableObject`.

When the class implements a secondary interface such as `IPrintableObject`, you're not really saying that your class is a printable object, you're saying that it can act as a printable object. A `Customer` is a `Contact`, but at the same time it can act as a printable object. This is illustrated in Figure 4-23.

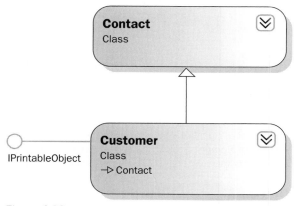

Figure 4-23

The drawback to this approach is that you have no inherited implementation when you implement `IPrintableObject`. Earlier you saw how to reuse common code as you implement an interface across multiple classes. While not as automatic or easy as inheritance, it is possible to reuse implementation code with a bit of extra work.

Applying Inheritance and Multiple Interfaces

Perhaps the best way to see how inheritance and multiple interfaces interact is to look at an example. Returning to the original `OOExample` project, the following example combines inheritance and multiple interfaces to create an object that has both an *is-a* and *act-as* relationship at the same time. As an additional benefit, you'll be using the .NET Framework's capability to print to a printer or Print Preview dialog.

Creating the Contact Base Class

You already have a simple `Customer` class in the project, so now let's add a `Contact` base class. Choose Project ➪ Add Class and add a class named `Contact`, adding the following code:

```
Public MustInherit Class Contact

  Private mID As Guid = Guid.NewGuid
  Private mName As String
```

```
    Public Property ID() As Guid
      Get
        Return mID
      End Get
      Set(ByVal value As Guid)
        mID = value
      End Set
    End Property

    Public Property Name() As String
      Get
        Return mName
      End Get
      Set(ByVal value As String)
        mName = value
      End Set
    End Property

End Class
```

Subclassing Contact

Now you can make the Customer class inherit from this base class because it is a Contact. In addition, because your base class now implements both the ID and Name properties, you can simplify the code in Customer by removing those properties and their related variables:

```
Public Class Customer
  Inherits Contact

  Private mPhone As String

  Public Property Phone() As String
    Get
      Return mPhone
    End Get
    Set(ByVal value As String)
      mPhone = value
    End Set
  End Property
End Class
```

This shows the benefit of subclassing Customer from Contact, as you're now sharing the ID and Name code across all other types of Contact as well.

Implementing IPrintableObject

You also know that a Customer should be able to act as a printable object. To do this in such a way that the implementation is reusable requires a bit of thought. First, though, you need to define the IPrintableObject interface.

You'll use the standard printing mechanism provided by .NET from the System.Drawing namespace. As shown in Figure 4-24, add a reference to System.Drawing.dll to the Interfaces project.

Figure 4-24

With that done, bring up the code window for `Interfaces.vb` in the `Interfaces` project and add the following code:

```
Imports System.Drawing

Public Interface IPrintableObject
  Sub Print()
  Sub PrintPreview()
  Sub RenderPage(ByVal sender As Object, _
      ByVal ev As System.Drawing.Printing.PrintPageEventArgs)
End Interface
```

This interface ensures that any object implementing `IPrintableObject` will have `Print` and `PrintPreview` methods, so you can invoke the appropriate type of printing. It also ensures that the object has a `RenderPage` method, which can be implemented by that object to render the object's data on the printed page.

At this point, you could simply implement all the code needed to handle printing directly within the `Customer` object. This isn't ideal, however, as some of the code will be common across any objects that want to implement `IPrintableObject`, and it would be nice to find a way to share that code.

To do this, you can create a new class, `ObjectPrinter`. This is a framework-style class, in that it has nothing to do with any particular application, but can be used across any application in which `IPrintableObject` will be used.

Add a new class named `ObjectPrinter` to the `OOExample` project. This class will contain all the code common to printing any object. It makes use of the built-in printing support provided by the .NET Framework class library. To use this, you need to import a couple of namespaces, so add the following code to the new class:

```
Imports System.Drawing
```

```
Imports System.Drawing.Printing
Imports Interfaces
```

You can then define a `PrintDocument` variable, which will hold the reference to your printer output. You'll also declare a variable to hold a reference to the actual object you'll be printing. Notice that you're using the `IPrintableObject` interface datatype for this variable:

```
Public Class ObjectPrinter
    Private WithEvents document As PrintDocument
    Private printObject As IPrintableObject
```

Now you can create a routine to kick off the printing process for any object implementing `IPrintableObject`. This code is totally generic; you'll write it here so it can be reused across any number of other classes:

```
Public Sub Print(ByVal obj As IPrintableObject)
  printObject = obj

  document = New PrintDocument()
  document.Print()
End Sub
```

Likewise, you can implement a method to show a print preview display of your object. This code is also totally generic, so add it here for reuse:

```
Public Sub PrintPreview(ByVal obj As IPrintableObject)
  Dim PPdlg As PrintPreviewDialog = New PrintPreviewDialog()

  printObject = obj

  document = New PrintDocument()
  PPdlg.Document = document
  PPdlg.ShowDialog()
End Sub
```

Finally, you need to catch the `PrintPage` event that is automatically raised by the .NET printing mechanism. This event is raised by the `PrintDocument` object whenever the document determines that it needs data rendered onto a page. Typically, it is in this routine that you would put the code to draw text or graphics onto the page surface. However, because this is a generic framework class, you won't do that here; instead, you'll delegate the call back into the actual application object that you want to print:

```
Private Sub PrintPage(ByVal sender As Object, _
    ByVal ev As System.Drawing.Printing.PrintPageEventArgs) _
    Handles document.PrintPage

  printObject.RenderPage(sender, ev)
End Sub

End Class
```

This allows the application object itself to determine how its data should be rendered onto the output page. Let's see how you can do that by implementing the IPrintableObject interface on the Customer class:

```
Imports Interfaces

Public Class Customer
   Inherits Contact
   Implements IPrintableObject
```

By adding this code, you require that your Customer class implement the Print(), PrintPreview(), and RenderPage() methods. To avoid wasting paper as you test the code, let's make both the Print() and PrintPreview() methods the same and have them just do a print preview display:

```
Public Sub Print() _
    Implements Interfaces.IPrintableObject.Print

    Dim printer As New ObjectPrinter()
    printer.PrintPreview(Me)

End Sub
```

Notice that you're using an ObjectPrinter object to handle the common details of doing a print preview. In fact, any class you ever create that implements IPrintableObject will have this exact same code to implement a print preview function, relying on your common ObjectPrinter to take care of the details.

You also need to implement the RenderPage() method, which is where you actually put your object's data onto the printed page:

```
Private Sub RenderPage(ByVal sender As Object, _
    ByVal ev As System.Drawing.Printing.PrintPageEventArgs) _
    Implements IPrintableObject.RenderPage

    Dim printFont As New Font("Arial", 10)
    Dim lineHeight As Single = printFont.GetHeight(ev.Graphics)
    Dim leftMargin As Single = ev.MarginBounds.Left
    Dim yPos As Single = ev.MarginBounds.Top

    ev.Graphics.DrawString("ID: " & ID.ToString, printFont, Brushes.Black, _
       leftMargin, yPos, New StringFormat())

    yPos += lineHeight
    ev.Graphics.DrawString("Name: " & Name, printFont, Brushes.Black, _
       leftMargin, yPos, New StringFormat())

    ev.HasMorePages = False

End Sub
```

All of this code is unique to your object, which makes sense because you're rendering your specific data to be printed. However, you don't need to worry about the details of whether you're printing to paper or print preview; that is handled by your `ObjectPrinter` class, which in turn uses the .NET Framework. This enables you to focus on generating the output to the page within your application class.

By generalizing the printing code in `ObjectPrinter`, you've achieved a level of reuse that you can tap into via the `IPrintableObject` interface. Anytime you want to print a `Customer` object's data, you can have it act as an `IPrintableObject` and call its `Print()` or `PrintPreview()` method. To see this work, add a new button control to `Form1` with the following code:

```
Private Sub btnPrint_Click(ByVal sender As System.Object, _
  ByVal e As System.EventArgs) Handles btnPrint.Click

  Dim obj As New Customer
  obj.Name = "Douglas Adams"
  CType(obj, IPrintableObject).PrintPreview()

End Sub
```

This code creates a new `Customer` object and sets its `Name` property. You then use the `CType()` method to access the object via its `IPrintableObject` interface to invoke the `PrintPreview` method.

When you run the application and click the button, you'll get a print preview display showing the object's data (see Figure 4-25).

Figure 4-25

How Deep to Go?

Most of the examples discussed so far have illustrated how you can create a child class based on a single parent class. That is called *single-level inheritance*. However, inheritance can be many levels deep. For example, you might have a deep hierarchy such as the one shown in Figure 4-26.

From the root of `System.Object` down to `NAFTACustomer` you have four levels of inheritance. This can be described as a four-level inheritance chain.

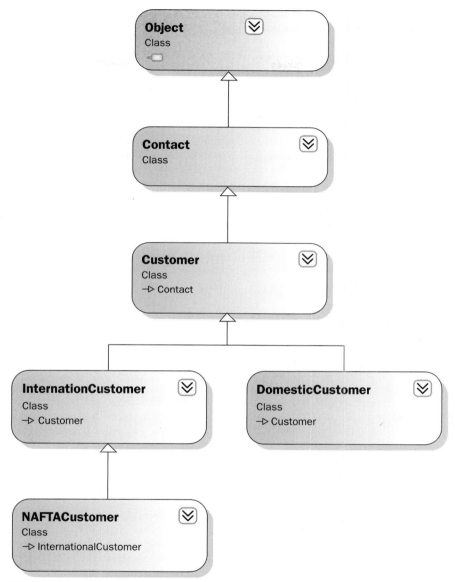

Object
Class

Contact
Class

Customer
Class
–▷ Contact

InternationCustomer
Class
–▷ Customer

DomesticCustomer
Class
–▷ Customer

NAFTACustomer
Class
–▷ InternationalCustomer

Figure 4-26

There is no hard-and-fast rule about how deep inheritance chains should go, but conventional wisdom and general experience with inheritance in other languages such as Smalltalk and C++ indicate that the deeper an inheritance chain becomes, the harder it is to maintain an application.

This happens for two reasons. First is the fragile base class or fragile superclass issue, which we'll discuss shortly. The second reason is that a deep inheritance hierarchy tends to seriously reduce the readability of your code by scattering the code for an object across many different classes, all of which are combined by the compiler to create your object.

One of the reasons for adopting object-oriented design and programming is to avoid so-called *spaghetti code,* whereby any bit of code you might look at does almost nothing useful but instead calls various other procedures and routines in parts of your application. To determine what is going on with spaghetti code, you must trace through many routines and mentally piece together what it all means.

Object-oriented programming can help you avoid this problem, but it is most definitely not a magic bullet. In fact, when you create deep inheritance hierarchies you are often creating spaghetti code because each level in the hierarchy not only extends the previous level's interface, but almost always also adds functionality. Thus, when you look at the final NAFTACustomer class it may have very little code. To figure out what it does or how it behaves, you have to trace through the code in the previous four levels of classes, and you might not even have the code for some of those classes, as they may come from other applications or class libraries you've purchased.

On the one hand, you have the benefit that you're reusing code, but on the other hand, you have the drawback that the code for one object is actually scattered through five different classes. Keep this in mind when designing systems with inheritance — use as few levels in the hierarchy as possible to provide the required functionality.

The Fragile Base Class Problem

You've explored where it is appropriate to use inheritance and where it is not. You've also explored how you can use inheritance and multiple interfaces in conjunction to implement both *is-a* and *act-as* relationships simultaneously within your classes.

Earlier, we noted that while inheritance is an incredibly powerful and useful concept, it can also be very dangerous if used improperly. You've seen some of this danger in the discussion of the misapplication of the *is-a* relationship, and how you can use multiple interfaces to avoid those issues.

One of the most classic and common problems with inheritance is the fragile base class problem. This problem is exacerbated when you have very deep inheritance hierarchies, but it exists even in a single-level inheritance chain.

The issue you face is that a change in the base class always affects all child classes derived from that base class. This is a double-edged sword. On the one hand, you get the benefit of being able to change code in one location and have that change automatically cascade through all derived classes. On the other hand, a change in behavior can have unintended or unexpected consequences farther down the inheritance chain, which can make your application very fragile and hard to change or maintain.

Interface Changes

There are obvious changes you might make, which require immediate attention. For example, you might change your Contact class to have FirstName and LastName instead of simply Name as a property. In the Contact class, replace the mName variable declaration with the following code:

```
Private mFirstName As String
Private mLastName As String
```

Now replace the `Name` property with the following code:

```
Public Property FirstName() As String
  Get
     Return mFirstName
  End Get
  Set(ByVal value As String)
     mFirstName = value
  End Set
End Property

Public Property LastName() As String
  Get
     Return mLastName
  End Get
  Set(ByVal value As String)
     mLastName = value
  End Set
End Property
```

At this point, the Error List window in the IDE will display a list of locations where you need to alter your code to compensate for the change. This is a graphic illustration of a base class change that causes cascading changes throughout your application. In this case, you've changed the base class interface, thus changing the interface of all subclasses in the inheritance chain.

To avoid having to fix code throughout your application, always strive to keep as much consistency in your base class interface as possible. In this case, you can implement a read-only `Name` property that returns the full name of the `Contact`:

```
Public ReadOnly Property Name() As String
  Get
     Return mFirstName & " " & mLastName
  End Get
End Property
```

This resolves most of the items in the Error List window. You can fix any remaining issues by using the `FirstName` and `LastName` properties. For example, in `Form1` you can change the code behind your button to the following:

```
Private Sub Button1_Click(ByVal sender As System.Object, _
    ByVal e As System.EventArgs) Handles button1.Click

  Dim obj As New Customer
  obj.FirstName = "Douglas"
  obj.LastName = "Adams"
  CType(obj, Interfaces.IPrintableObject).Print()
End Sub
```

Any change to a base class interface is likely to cause problems, so you must think carefully before making such a change.

Implementation Changes

Unfortunately, there's another, more subtle type of change that can wreak more havoc on your application: an implementation change. This is the core of the fragile base class problem.

Encapsulation provides you with separation of interface from implementation. However, keeping your interface consistent is merely a syntactic concept. If you change the implementation, you are making a semantic change, a change that doesn't alter any of your syntax but can have serious ramifications on the real behavior of the application.

In theory, you can change the implementation of a class, and as long as you don't change its interface, any client applications using objects based on that class will continue to operate without change. Of course, reality is never as nice as theory, and more often than not a change to implementation will have some consequences on the behavior of a client application.

For example, you might use a `SortedList` to sort and display some `Customer` objects. To do this, add a new button to `Form1` with the following code:

```
Private Sub btnSort_Click(ByVal sender As System.Object, _
  ByVal e As System.EventArgs) Handles btnSort.Click

    Dim col As New Generic.SortedDictionary(Of String, Customer)
    Dim obj As Customer

    obj = New Customer()
    obj.FirstName = "Douglas"
    obj.LastName = "Adams"
    col.Add(obj.Name, obj)

    obj = New Customer()
    obj.FirstName = "Andre"
    obj.LastName = "Norton"
    col.Add(obj.Name, obj)

    Dim item As Generic.KeyValuePair(Of String, Customer)
    Dim sb As New System.Text.StringBuilder

    For Each item In col
      sb.AppendLine(item.Value.Name)
    Next

    MsgBox(sb.ToString)
  End Sub
```

This code simply creates a couple of `Customer` objects, sets their `FirstName` and `LastName` properties, and inserts them into a generic `SortedDictionary` object from the `System.Collections.Generic` namespace.

Items in a `SortedDictionary` are sorted based on their key value, and you are using the `Name` property to provide that key, meaning that your entries will be sorted by name. Because your `Name` property is implemented to return first name first and last name second, your entries will be sorted by first name.

If you run the application, the dialog will display the following:

```
Andre Norton
Douglas Adams
```

However, you can change the implementation of your Contact class — not directly changing or affecting either the Customer class or your code in Form1 — to return last name first and first name second, as shown here:

```
Public ReadOnly Property Name() As String
  Get
    Return mLastName & ", " & mFirstName
  End Get
End Property
```

While no other code requires changing, and no syntax errors are flagged, the behavior of the application is changed. When you run it, the output will now be as follows:

```
Adams, Douglas
Norton, Andre
```

Maybe this change is inconsequential. Maybe it totally breaks the required behavior of your form. The developer making the change in the Contact class might not even know that someone was using that property for sort criteria.

This illustrates how dangerous inheritance can be. Changes to implementation in a base class can cascade to countless other classes in countless applications, having unforeseen side effects and consequences of which the base class developer is totally unaware.

Summary

This chapter demonstrated how Visual Basic enables you to create and work with classes and objects. Visual Basic provides the building blocks for abstraction, encapsulation, polymorphism, and inheritance.

You've learned how to create both simple base classes as well as abstract base classes. You've also explored how you can define formal interfaces, a concept quite similar to an abstract base class in many ways.

You also walked through the process of subclassing, creating a new class that derives both interface and implementation from a base class. The subclass can be extended by adding new methods or altering the behavior of existing methods on the base class.

By the end of this chapter, you've seen how object-oriented programming flows from the four basic concepts of abstraction, encapsulation, polymorphism, and inheritance. The chapter provided basic information about each concept and demonstrated how to implement them using Visual Basic.

By properly applying object-oriented design and programming, you can create very large and complex applications that remain maintainable and readable over time. Nonetheless, these technologies are not a magic bullet. Improperly applied, they can create the same hard-to-maintain code that you might create using procedural or modular design techniques.

It is not possible to fully cover all aspects of object-oriented programming in a single chapter. Before launching into a full-blown object-oriented project, we highly recommend looking at other books specifically geared toward object-oriented design and programming.

The Common Language Runtime

You've seen how to create simple applications and looked at how to create classes. Now it's time not only to start tying these elements together, but also to learn how to dispose of some of the classes that you have created. The architects of .NET realized that all procedural languages require certain base functionality. For example, many languages ship with their own runtime that provides features such as memory management, but what if, instead of each language shipping with its own runtime implementation, all languages used a common runtime? This would provide languages with a standard environment and access to all of the same features. This is exactly what the common language runtime (CLR) provides.

The CLR manages the execution of code on the .NET platform. .NET provided Visual Basic developers better support for many advanced features, including operator overloading, implementation inheritance, threading, and the ability to marshal objects. Building such features into a language is not trivial. The CLR enabled Microsoft to concentrate on building this plumbing one time and then reuse it across multiple different programming languages. Because the CLR supports these features and because Visual Basic is built on top of the CLR, Visual Basic can use these features. The result is that, going forward, Visual Basic is the equal of every other .NET language, with the CLR eliminating many of the shortcomings of the previous versions of Visual Basic.

Visual Basic developers can view the CLR as a better Visual Basic runtime. However, this runtime, unlike the old standalone Visual Basic runtime, is common across all of .NET regardless of the underlying operating system. Thus, the functionality exposed by the CLR is available to all .NET languages; more important, all of the features available to other .NET languages via the CLR are available to Visual Basic developers. Additionally, as long as you develop using managed code — code that runs in the CLR — you'll find that it doesn't matter whether your application is installed on a Windows XP client or Vista client; your application will just run. The CLR provides an abstraction layer away from the details of the operating system.

This chapter gets down into the belly of the application runtime environment, not to examine how .NET abstracts you away from the operating system, but instead to look at some specific features related to how you build applications that run against the CLR. This includes an introduction to several basic elements of working with applications that run in the CLR, including the following:

❑   Elements of a .NET application

❑   Versioning and deployment

❑   Integration across .NET languages

❑   Microsoft Intermediate Language (MSIL)

❑   Memory management and the Garbage Collector (GC)

Elements of a .NET Application

A .NET application is composed of four primary entities:

❑   **Classes** — The basic units that encapsulate data and behavior

❑   **Modules** — The individual files that contain the IL for an assembly

❑   **Assemblies** — The primary unit of deployment of a .NET application

❑   **Types** — The common unit of transmitting data between modules

Classes are covered in the preceding two chapters and are defined in the source files for your application or class library. Upon compilation of your source files, you produce a module. The code that makes up an assembly's modules may exist in a single executable (.exe) file or as a dynamic link library (.dll). A module is in fact a Microsoft Intermediate Language file, which is then used by the CLR when your application is run. However, compiling a .NET application doesn't produce only an MSIL file; it also produces a collection of files that make up a deployable application or assembly. Within an assembly, you will find several different types of files, including not only the actual executable files, but also configuration files, signature keys, and most important of all, the actual code modules.

Modules

A module contains Microsoft Intermediate Language (MSIL, often abbreviated to IL) code, associated metadata, and the assembly's manifest. By default, the Visual Basic compiler creates an assembly that is composed of a single module having both the assembly code and manifest.

IL is a platform-independent way of representing managed code within a module. Before IL can be executed, the CLR must compile it into the native machine code. The default method is for the CLR to use the JIT (Just-in-Time) compiler to compile the IL on a method-by-method basis. At runtime, as each method is called by an application for the first time, it is passed through the JIT compiler for compilation to machine code. Similarly, for an ASP.NET application, each page is passed through the JIT compiler the first time it is requested, to create an in-memory representation of the machine code that represents that page.

Additional information about the types declared in the IL is provided by the associated metadata. The metadata contained within the module is used extensively by the CLR. For example, if a client and an object reside within two different processes, then the CLR will use the type's metadata to marshal data between the client and the object. MSIL is important because every .NET language compiles down to IL. The CLR doesn't care or need to know what the implementation language was; it knows only what the IL contains. Thus, any differences in .NET languages exist at the level where the IL is generated; but once generated, all .NET languages have the same runtime characteristics. Similarly, because the CLR doesn't care in which language a given module was originally written, it can leverage modules implemented in entirely different .NET languages.

A question that continually arises when discussing the JIT compiler and the use of a runtime environment is: "Wouldn't it be faster to compile the IL language down to native code before the user asks to run it?" Although the answer is not always yes, Microsoft has provided a utility to handle this compilation: Ngen.exe. Ngen (short for native image generator) enables you to essentially run the JIT compiler on a specific assembly, and this assembly is then installed into the user's application cache in its native format. The obvious advantage is that now when the user asks to execute something in that assembly, the JIT compiler is not invoked, saving a small amount of time. However, unlike the JIT compiler, which only compiles those portions of an assembly that are actually referenced, Ngen.exe needs to compile the entire codebase, so the time required for compilation is not the same as what a user actually experiences.

Ngen.exe is executed from the command line. The utility was updated as part of .NET 2.0 and now automatically detects and includes most of the dependent assemblies as part of the image generation process. To use Ngen.exe, you simply reference this utility followed by an action; for example, install followed by your assembly reference. Several options are available as part of the generation process, but they go beyond the scope of this chapter, given that Ngen.exe itself is a topic that can generate heated debate regarding its use and value.

So where does the debate begin about when to use Ngen.exe? Keep in mind that in a server application, where the same assembly will be referenced by multiple users between machine restarts, the difference in performance on the first request is essentially lost. This means that compilation to native code is more valuable to client-side applications. Unfortunately, using Ngen.exe requires running it on each client machine, which can become cost-prohibitive in certain installation scenarios, particularly if you use any form of self-updating application logic. Another issue relates to using *reflection,* which enables you to reference other assemblies at runtime. Of course, if you don't know what assemblies you will reference until runtime, then the native image generator has a problem, as it won't know what to reference either. You may have occasion to use Ngen.exe for an application you've created, but you should fully investigate this utility and its advantages and disadvantages beforehand, keeping in mind that even native images execute within the CLR. Native image generation only changes the compilation model, not the runtime environment.

Assemblies

An assembly is the primary unit of deployment for .NET applications. It is either a dynamic link library (.dll) or an executable (.exe). An assembly is composed of a manifest, one or more modules, and (optionally) other files, such as .config, .ASPX, .ASMX, images, and so on.

The manifest of an assembly contains the following:

❑   Information about the identity of the assembly, including its textual name and version number

❑ If the assembly is public, then the manifest will contain the assembly's public key. The public key is used to help ensure that types exposed by the assembly reside within a unique namespace. It may also be used to uniquely identify the source of an assembly.

❑ A declarative security request that describes the assembly's security requirements (the assembly is responsible for declaring the security it requires). Requests for permissions fall into three categories: required, optional, and denied. The identity information may be used as evidence by the CLR in determining whether or not to approve security requests.

❑ A list of other assemblies that the assembly depends on. The CLR uses this information to locate an appropriate version of the required assemblies at runtime. The list of dependencies also includes the exact version number of each assembly at the time the assembly was created.

❑ A list of all types and resources exposed by the assembly. If any of the resources exposed by the assembly are localized, the manifest will also contain the default culture (language, currency, date/time format, and so on) that the application will target. The CLR uses this information to locate specific resources and types within the assembly.

The manifest can be stored in a separate file or in one of the modules, but by default for most applications, it is part of the .dll or .exe file, which is compiled by Visual Studio. For Web applications, you will find that although there is a collection of ASPX pages, the actual assembly information is located in a DLL referenced by those ASPX pages.

Types

The type system provides a template that is used to describe the encapsulation of data and an associated set of behaviors. It is this common template for describing data that provides the basis for the metadata that .NET uses when applications interoperate. There are two kinds of types: reference and value. The differences between these two types are discussed in Chapter 2.

Unlike COM, which is scoped at the machine level, types are scoped at either the global or the assembly level. All types are based on a common system that is used across all .NET languages. Similar to the MSIL code, which is interpreted by the CLR based upon the current runtime environment, the CLR uses a common metadata system to recognize the details of each type. The result is that all .NET languages are built around a common type system, unlike the different implementations of COM, which require special notation to allow translation of different datatypes between different .exe and .dll files.

A type has fields, properties, and methods:

❑ **Fields** — Variables that are scoped to the type. For example, a Pet class could declare a field called Name that holds the pet's name. In a well-engineered class, fields are often kept private and exposed only as properties or methods.

❑ **Properties** — These look like fields to clients of the type, but can have code behind them (which usually performs some sort of data validation). For example, a Dog datatype could expose a property to set its gender. Code could then be placed behind the property so that it could be set only to "male" or "female," and then this property could be saved internally to one of the fields in the dog class.

❑ **Methods** — Define behaviors exhibited by the type. For example, the Dog datatype could expose a method called Sleep, which would suspend the activity of the Dog.

The preceding elements make up each application. Note that this description mentions that some types are defined at the application level and others globally. Under COM, all components are registered globally, and certainly if you want to expose a .NET component to COM, you must register it globally. However, with .NET it is not only possible but often encouraged that the classes and types defined in your modules be only visible at the application level. The advantage of this is that you can run several different versions of an application side by side. Of course, once you have an application that can be versioned, the next challenge is knowing which version of that application you have.

Versioning and Deployment

Components and their clients are often installed at different times by different vendors. For example, a Visual Basic application might rely on a third-party grid control to display data. Runtime support for versioning is crucial in ensuring that an incompatible version of the grid control does not cause problems for the Visual Basic application.

In addition to this issue of compatibility, the deployment of applications written in previous versions of Visual Basic was problematic. Fortunately, .NET provides major improvements over the versioning and deployment offered by COM and the previous versions of Visual Basic.

Better Support for Versioning

Managing the version of components was challenging in previous versions of Visual Basic. The version number of the component could be set, but this version number was not used by the runtime. COM components are often referenced by their ProgID, but Visual Basic does not provide any support for appending the version number on the end of the ProgID.

For those of you who are unfamiliar with the term ProgID, it's enough to know that ProgIDs are developer-friendly strings used to identify a component. For example, Word.Application describes Microsoft Word. ProgIDs can be fully qualified with the targeted version of the component — for example Word.Application.10 — but this is a limited capability and relies on both the application and whether the person using it chooses this optional addendum. As you'll see in Chapter 8, a namespace is built on the basic elements of a ProgID, but provides a more robust naming system.

For many applications, .NET has removed the need to identify the version of each assembly in a central registry on a machine. However, some assemblies are installed once and used by multiple applications. .NET provides a Global Assembly Cache (GAC), which is used to store assemblies that are intended for use by multiple applications. The CLR provides versioning support for all components loaded in the GAC.

The CLR provides two features for assemblies installed within the GAC:

❑ **Side-by-side versioning** — Multiple versions of the same component can be simultaneously stored in the GAC.

❑ **Automatic Quick Fix Engineering (QFE), also known as hotfix support** — If a new version of a component, which is still compatible with the old version, is available in the GAC, the CLR will load the updated component. The version number, which is maintained by the developer who created the referenced assembly, drives this behavior.

The assembly's manifest contains the version numbers of referenced assemblies. The CLR uses the assembly's manifest at runtime to locate a compatible version of each referenced assembly. The version number of an assembly takes the following form:

```
Major.Minor.Build.Revision
```

Changes to the major and minor version numbers of the assembly indicate that the assembly is no longer compatible with the previous versions. The CLR will not use versions of the assembly that have a different major or minor number unless it is explicitly told to do so. For example, if an assembly was originally compiled against a referenced assembly with a version number of 3.4.1.9, then the CLR will not load an assembly stored in the GAC unless it has a major and minor number of 3 and 4.

Incrementing the revision and build numbers indicates that the new version is still compatible with the previous version. If a new assembly that has an incremented revision or build number is loaded into the GAC, the CLR can still load this assembly for applications that were compiled referencing a previous version. Versioning is discussed in greater detail in Chapter 21.

Better Deployment

Applications written using previous versions of Visual Basic and COM were often complicated to deploy. Components referenced by the application needed to be installed and registered; and for Visual Basic components, the correct version of the Visual Basic runtime needed to be available. The Component Deployment tool helped in the creation of complex installation packages, but applications could be easily broken if the dependent components were inadvertently replaced by incompatible versions on the client's computer during the installation of an unrelated product.

In .NET, most components do not need to be registered. When an external assembly is referenced, the application makes a decision between using a global copy (which must be in the GAC on the developer's system) or copying a component locally. For most references, the external assemblies are referenced locally, which means they are carried in the application's local directory structure. Using local copies of external assemblies enables the CLR to support the side-by-side execution of different versions of the same component. As noted earlier, to reference a globally registered assembly, that assembly must be located in the GAC. The GAC provides a versioning system that is robust enough to allow different versions of the same external assembly to exist side by side. For example, an application could use a newer version of ADO.NET without adversely affecting another application that relies on a previous version.

So long as the client has the .NET runtime installed (which only has to be done once), a .NET application can be distributed using a simple command like this:

```
xcopy \\server\appDirectory "C:\Program Files\appDirectory" /E /O /I
```

The preceding command would copy all of the files and subdirectories from `\\ server\appDirectory` to `C:\Program Files\appDirectory` and would transfer the file's access control lists (ACLs).

Besides the capability to XCopy applications, Visual Studio provides a built-in tool for constructing simple .msi installations. New with Visual Studio 2005 is the idea of a ClickOnce deployment project. These deployment settings can be customized for your project solution, enabling you to integrate the deployment project with your application output.

ClickOnce deployment provides an entirely new method of deployment, referred to as *smart client deployment*. In the smart-client model, your application is placed on a central server from which the clients access the application files. Smart-client deployment builds on the XML Web Services architecture about which you are learning. It has the advantages of central application maintenance combined with a richer client interface and fewer server communication requirements, all of which you have become familiar with in Windows Forms applications. ClickOnce deployment is discussed in greater detail in Chapter 22.

Cross-Language Integration

Prior to .NET, interoperating with the code written in other languages was challenging. There were pretty much two options for reusing functionality developed in other languages: COM interfaces or DLLs with exported C functions. As for exposing functionality written in Visual Basic, the only option was to create COM interfaces.

Because Visual Basic is now built on top of the CLR, it's able to interoperate with the code written in other .NET languages. It's even able to derive from a class written in another language. To support this type of functionality, the CLR relies on a common way of representing types, as well as rich metadata that can describe these types.

The Common Type System

Each programming language seems to bring its own island of datatypes with it. For example, previous versions of Visual Basic represent strings using the BSTR structure, C++ offers char and wchar datatypes, and MFC offers the CString class. Moreover, the fact that the C++ int datatype is a 32-bit value, whereas the Visual Basic 6 Integer datatype is a 16-bit value, makes it difficult to pass parameters between applications written using different languages.

To help resolve this problem, C has become the lowest common denominator for interfacing between programs written in multiple languages. An exported function written in C that exposes simple C datatypes can be consumed by Visual Basic, Java, Delphi, and a variety of other programming languages. In fact, the Windows API is exposed as a set of C functions.

Unfortunately, to access a C interface, you must explicitly map C datatypes to a language's native datatypes. For example, a Visual Basic 6 developer would use the following statement to map the GetUserNameA Win32 function (GetUserNameA is the ANSI version of the GetUserName function):

```
' Map GetUserName to the GetUserNameA exported function
' exported by advapi32.dll.
'    BOOL GetUserName(
'        LPTSTR lpBuffer, // name buffer
'        LPDWORD nSize // size of name buffer
' );
Public Declare Function GetUserName Lib "advapi32.dll" _
Alias "GetUserNameA" (ByVal strBuffer As String, nSize As Long) As Long
```

This code explicitly maps the lpBuffer C character array datatype to the Visual Basic 6 String parameter strBuffer. This is not only cumbersome, but also error prone. Accidentally mapping a variable declared as `Long` to `lpBuffer` wouldn't generate any compilation errors, but calling the function would more than likely result in a difficult-to-diagnose, intermittent-access violation at runtime.

COM provides a more refined method of interoperation between languages. Visual Basic 6 introduced a common type system (CTS) for all applications that supported COM — that is, variant-compatible datatypes. However, variant datatypes are as cumbersome to work with for non-Visual Basic 6 developers as the underlying C data structures that make up the variant datatypes (such as `BSTR` and `SAFEARRAY`) were for Visual Basic developers. The result is that interfacing between unmanaged languages is still more complicated than it needs to be.

The CTS provides a set of common datatypes for use across all programming languages. The CTS provides every language running on top of the .NET platform with a base set of types, as well as mechanisms for extending those types. These types may be implemented as classes or as structs, but in either case they are derived from a common `System.Object` class definition.

Since every type supported by the CTS is derived from `System.Object`, every type supports a common set of methods.

Method	Description
`Boolean Equals(Object)`	Used to test equality with another object. Reference types should return True if the Object parameter references the same object. Value types should return True if the Object parameter has the same value.
`Int32 GetHashCode()`	Generates a number corresponding to the value of an object. If two objects of the same type are equal, then they must return the same hash code.
`Type GetType()`	Gets a Type object that can be used to access metadata associated with the type. It also serves as a starting point for navigating the object hierarchy exposed by the Reflection API (discussed shortly).
`String ToString()`	The default implementation returns the fully qualified name of the object's class. This method is often overridden to output data that is more meaningful to the type. For example, all base types return their value as a string.

Metadata

Metadata is the information that enables components to be self-describing. Metadata is used to describe many aspects of a .NET component, including classes, methods, and fields, and the assembly itself. Metadata is used by the CLR to facilitate all sorts of things, such as validating an assembly before it is executed or performing garbage collection while managed code is being executed. Visual Basic developers have used metadata for years when developing and using components within their applications.

❑ Visual Basic developers use metadata to instruct the Visual Basic runtime how to behave. For example, you can set the Unattended Execution property to determine whether unhandled exceptions are shown on the screen in a message box or are written to the Event Log.

❑ COM components referenced within Visual Basic applications have accompanying type libraries that contain metadata about the components, their methods, and their properties. You can use the Object Browser to view this information. (The information contained within the type library is what is used to drive IntelliSense.)

❑ Additional metadata can be associated with a component by installing it within COM+. Metadata stored in COM+ is used to declare the support a component needs at runtime, including transactional support, serialization support, and object pooling.

Better Support for Metadata

Metadata associated with a Visual Basic 6 component was scattered in multiple locations and stored using multiple formats:

❑ Metadata instructing the Visual Basic runtime how to behave (such as the Unattended Execution property) is compiled into the Visual Basic–generated executable.

❑ Basic COM attributes (such as the required threading model) are stored in the registry.

❑ COM+ attributes (such as the transactional support required) are stored in the COM+ catalog.

.NET refines the use of metadata within applications in three significant ways:

❑ .NET consolidates the metadata associated with a component.

❑ Because a .NET component does not have to be registered, installing and upgrading the component is easier and less problematic.

❑ .NET makes a much clearer distinction between attributes that should only be set at compile time and those that can be modified at runtime.

All attributes associated with Visual Basic components are represented in a common format and consolidated within the files that make up the assembly.

Since much of a COM/COM+ component's metadata is stored separately from the executable, installing and upgrading components can be problematic. COM/COM+ components must be registered to update the registry/COM+ catalog before they can be used, and the COM/COM+ component executable can be upgraded without upgrading its associated metadata.

The process of installing and upgrading a .NET component is greatly simplified. Since all metadata associated with a .NET component must reside within the file that contains the component, no registration is required. Once a new component is copied into an application's directory, it can be used immediately. Since the component and its associated metadata cannot become out of sync, upgrading the component becomes much less of a problem.

Another problem with COM+ is that attributes that should only be set at compile time may be reconfigured at runtime. For example, COM+ can provide serialization support for neutral components. A component that does not require serialization must be designed to accommodate multiple requests from multiple clients simultaneously. You should know at compile time whether or not a component requires support for serialization from the runtime. However, under COM+, the attribute describing whether or not client requests should be serialized can be altered at runtime.

.NET makes a much better distinction between attributes that should be set at compile time and those that should be set at runtime. For example, whether a .NET component is serializable is determined at compile time. This setting cannot be overridden at runtime.

Attributes

Attributes are used to decorate entities such as assemblies, classes, methods, and properties with additional information. Attributes can be used for a variety of purposes. They can provide information, request a certain behavior at runtime, or even invoke a particular behavior from another application. An example of this can be shown by using the Demo class defined in the following code block:

```
Module Module1

  <Serializable()> Public Class Demo

    <Obsolete("Use Method2 instead.")> Public Sub Method1()
      ' Old implementation ...
    End Sub

    Public Sub Method2()
      ' New implementation ...
    End Sub

  End Class

  Public Sub Main()
    Dim d As Demo = New Demo()
    d.Method1()
  End Sub
End Module
```

Create a new Console application for Visual Basic and then add a new class into the sample file. Note that a best practice is to place each class in its own source file, but in order to simplify this demonstration, the class Demo has been defined within the main module.

The first attribute on the Demo class marks the class with the Serializable attribute. The base class library will provide serialization support for instances of the Demo type. For example, the ResourceWriter type can be used to stream an instance of the Demo type to disk. The second attribute is associated with Method1. Method1 has been marked as obsolete, but has not been made unavailable. When a method is marked as obsolete, there are two options, one being that Visual Studio should prevent applications from compiling. However, a better strategy for large applications is to first mark a method or class as obsolete and then prevent its use in the next release. The preceding code causes Visual Studio to display an IntelliSense warning if Method1 is referenced within the application, as shown in Figure 5-1. Not only does the line with Method1 have a visual hint of the issue, but a task has also been automatically added to the task window.

Figure 5-1

If the developer leaves this code unchanged and then compiles it, the application will compile correctly. As shown in Figure 5-2, the compilation is complete. However, the developer receives a warning with a meaningful message that the code should be changed to use the correct method.

There are also times when you might need to associate multiple attributes with an entity. The following code shows an example of using both of the attributes from the previous code at the class level. Note that in this case the `Obsolete` attribute has been modified to cause a compilation error by setting its second parameter to `True`:

```
<Serializable(), Obsolete("No longer used.", True)> Public Class Demo
    ' Implementation ...
End Class
```

Attributes play an important role in the development of .NET applications, particularly XML Web Services. As you'll see in Chapter 26, the declaration of a class as a Web Service and of particular methods as Web methods are all handled through the use of attributes.

Figure 5-2

The Reflection API

The .NET Framework provides the Reflection API for accessing metadata associated with managed code. You can use the Reflection API to examine the metadata associated with an assembly and its types, and even to examine the currently executing assembly.

The `Assembly` class in the `System.Reflection` namespace can be used to access the metadata in an assembly. The `LoadFrom` method can be used to load an assembly, and the `GetExecutingAssembly` method can be used to access the currently executing assembly. The `GetTypes` method can then be used to obtain the collection of types defined in the assembly.

It's also possible to access the metadata of a type directly from an instance of that type. Since every object derives from `System.Object`, every object supports the `GetType` method, which returns a `Type` object that can be used to access the metadata associated with the type.

The `Type` object exposes many methods and properties for obtaining the metadata associated with a type. For example, you can obtain a collection of properties, methods, fields, and events exposed by the type by calling the `GetMembers` method. The `Type` object for the object's base type can also be obtained by calling the `DeclaringType` property.

A good tool that demonstrates the power of reflection is Lutz Roeder's Reflector for .NET. Check out www.aisto.com/roeder/dotnet.

IL Disassembler

One of the many handy tools that ships with Visual Studio is the IL Disassembler (ildasm.exe). It can be used to navigate the metadata within a module, including the types the module exposes, as well as their properties and methods. The IL Disassembler can also be used to display the IL contained within a module.

The IL Disassembler can be found under your installation directory for Visual Studio 2005; the default path is C:\Program Files\Microsoft Visual Studio 8\SDK\v2.0\Bin\ILDasm.exe. Once the IL Disassembler has been started, select File ⇨ Open. Open mscorlib.dll, which is located in your system directory under the default path of C:\Windows\Microsoft.NET\Framework\V2.0.50727\mscorlib.dll. Once mscorlib.dll has been loaded, ILDasm will display a set of folders for each namespace in this assembly. Expand the System namespace, then the ValueType namespace, and finally double-click the Equals method. A window similar to the one shown in Figure 5-3 will be displayed.

```
System.ValueType::Equals : bool(object)
Find   Find Next

.method public hidebysig virtual instance bool
        Equals(object obj) cil managed
{
  // Code size       142 (0x8e)
  .maxstack  3
  .locals init (class System.RuntimeType V_0,
           class System.RuntimeType V_1,
           object V_2,
           object V_3,
           object V_4,
           class System.Reflection.FieldInfo[] V_5,
           int32 V_6)
  IL_0000:  ldarg.1
  IL_0001:  brtrue.s    IL_0005
  IL_0003:  ldc.i4.0
  IL_0004:  ret
  IL_0005:  ldarg.0
  IL_0006:  call        instance class System.Type System.Object::GetType()
  IL_000b:  castclass   System.RuntimeType
  IL_0010:  stloc.0
  IL_0011:  ldarg.1
  IL_0012:  callvirt    instance class System.Type System.Object::GetType()
  IL_0017:  castclass   System.RuntimeType
  IL_001c:  stloc.1
  IL_001d:  ldloc.1
```

Figure 5-3

Figure 5-3 shows the IL for the Equals method. Notice how the Reflection API is used to navigate through the instance of the value type's fields in order to determine whether the values of the two objects being compared are equal.

The IL Disassembler is a useful tool for learning how a particular module is implemented, but it could jeopardize your company's proprietary logic. After all, what's to prevent someone from using it to reverse engineer your code? Fortunately, Visual Studio 2005, like Visual Studio 2003, ships with a third-party tool called an *obfuscator*. The role of the obfuscator is to ensure that the IL Disassembler cannot build a meaningful representation of your application logic.

A complete discussion of the obfuscator that ships with Visual Studio 2005 is beyond the scope of this chapter, but to access this tool, select the Tools menu and choose Dotfuscator Community Edition. The obfuscator runs against your compiled application, taking your IL file and stripping out many of the items that are embedded by default during the compilation process.

Memory Management

This section looks at one of the larger underlying elements of managed code. One of the reasons why .NET applications are referred to as "managed" is that memory deallocation is handled automatically by the system. The CLR's memory management fixes the shortcomings of the COM's memory management. Developers are accustomed to worrying about memory management only in an abstract sense. The basic rule has been that every object created and every section of memory allocated needs to be released (destroyed). The CLR introduces a garbage collector (GC), which simplifies this paradigm. Gone are the days where a misbehaving component — for example, one that failed to properly dispose of its object references or allocated and never released memory — could crash a Web server.

However, the use of a GC introduces new questions about when and if objects need to be explicitly cleaned up. There are two elements in manually writing code to allocate and deallocate memory and system resources. The first is the release of any shared resources such as file handles and database connections. This type of activity needs to be managed explicitly and is discussed shortly. The second element of manual memory management involves letting the system know when memory is no longer in use by your application. Visual Basic COM developers, in particular, are accustomed to explicitly disposing of object references by setting variables to Nothing. While you can explicitly show your intent to destroy the object by setting it to Nothing manually, this doesn't actually free resources under .NET.

.NET uses a GC to automatically manage the cleanup of allocated memory, which means that you don't need to carry out memory management as an explicit action. Since the system is automatic, it's not up to you when resources are actually cleaned up; thus, a resource you previously used might sit in memory beyond the end of the method where you used it. Perhaps more important is the fact that the GC will at times reclaim objects in the middle of executing the code in a method. Fortunately, the system ensures that collection only happens as long as your code doesn't reference the object later in the method. As an example, you could actually end up extending the amount of time an object is kept in memory just by setting that object to Nothing. Thus, setting a variable to Nothing at the end of the method prevents the garbage collection mechanism from proactively reclaiming objects, and therefore is generally discouraged. After all, if the goal is simply to document a developer's intention, then a comment is more appropriate.

Given this change in paradigms, the next few sections take you through a comparison of the challenges of traditional memory management and a real look under the covers of how the garbage collector works, the basics of some of the challenges with COM-based memory management, and then a quick look at how the GC eliminates these challenges from your list of concerns. In particular, you should understand how you can interact with the garbage collector and why the Using command, for example, is recommended over a finalization method in .NET.

Traditional Garbage Collection

The Visual Basic 6 runtime environment provides limited memory management by automatically releasing objects when they are no longer referenced by any application. Once all the references are released on an object, the runtime automatically releases the object from memory. For example, consider the following Visual Basic 6 code that uses the `Scripting.FileSystem` object to write an entry to a log file:

```
' Requires a reference to Microsoft Scripting Runtime (scrrun.dll)
Sub WriteToLog(strLogEntry As String)
 Dim objFSO As Scripting.FileSystemObject
 Dim objTS As Scripting.TextStream

 objTS = objFSO.OpenTextFile("C:\temp\AppLog.log", ForAppending)
 Call objTS.WriteLine(Date & vbTab & strLogEntry)
End Sub
```

`WriteToLog` creates two objects, a `FileSystemObject` and a `TextStream`, which are used to create an entry in the log file. Because these are COM objects, they may live either within the current application process or in their own process. Once the routine exits, the Visual Basic runtime recognizes that they are no longer referenced by an active application and dereference the objects. This results in both objects being deactivated. However, there are situations in which objects that are no longer referenced by an application are not properly cleaned up by the Visual Basic 6 runtime. One cause of this is the *circular reference*.

Circular References

One of the most common situations in which the Visual Basic runtime is unable to ensure that objects are no longer referenced by the application is when these objects contain a circular reference. An example of a circular reference is when object *A* holds a reference to object *B* and object *B* holds a reference to object *A*.

Circular references are problematic because the Visual Basic runtime relies on the reference counting mechanism of COM to determine whether an object can be deactivated. Each COM object is responsible for maintaining its own reference count and for destroying itself once the reference count reaches zero. Clients of the object are responsible for updating the reference count appropriately, by calling the `AddRef` and `Release` methods on the object's `IUnknown` interface. However, in this scenario, object *A* continues to hold a reference to object *B*, and vice versa, and thus the internal cleanup logic of these components is not triggered.

In addition, problems can occur if the clients do not properly maintain the COM object's reference count. For example, an object will never be deactivated if a client forgets to call `Release` when the object is no longer referenced. To avoid this, the Visual Basic 6 runtime takes care of updating the reference count for you, but the object's reference count can be an invalid indicator of whether or not the object is still being used by the application. As an example, consider the references that objects *A* and *B* hold.

The application can invalidate its references to *A* and *B* by setting the associated variables equal to `Nothing`. However, even though objects *A* and *B* are no longer referenced by the application, the Visual Basic runtime cannot ensure that the objects are deactivated because *A* and *B* still reference each other. Consider the following (Visual Basic 6) code:

```
' Class:  CCircularRef

' Reference to another object.
```

```
Dim m_objRef As Object

Public Sub Initialize(objRef As Object)
  Set m_objRef = objRef
End Sub

Private Sub Class_Terminate()
  Call MsgBox("Terminating.")
  Set m_objRef = Nothing
End Sub
```

The CCircularRef class implements an Initialize method that accepts a reference to another object and saves it as a member variable. Notice that the class does not release any existing reference in the m_objRef variable before assigning a new value. The following code demonstrates how to use this CCircularRef class to create a circular reference:

```
Dim objA As New CCircularRef
Dim objB As New CCircularRef

Call objA.Initialize(objB)
Call objB.Initialize(objA)

Set objA = Nothing
Set objB = Nothing
```

After creating two instances (objA and objB) of CCircularRef, both of which have a reference count of one, the code then calls the Initialize method on each object by passing it a reference to the other. Now each of the object's reference counts is equal to two: one held by the application and one held by the other object. Next, explicitly setting objA and objB to Nothing decrements each object's reference count by one. However, since the reference count for both instances of CCircularRef is still greater than zero, the objects are not released from memory until the application is terminated. The CLR garbage collector solves the problem of circular references because it looks for a reference from the root application or thread to every class, and all classes that do not have such a reference are marked for deletion, regardless of what other references they might still maintain.

The CLR's Garbage Collector

The .NET garbage collection mechanism is complex, and the details of its inner workings are beyond the scope of this book. However, it is important to understand the principles behind its operation. The GC is responsible for collecting objects that are no longer referenced. It takes a completely different approach from that of the Visual Basic runtime to accomplish this. At certain times, and based on internal rules, a task will run through all the objects looking for those that no longer have any references from the root application thread or one of the worker threads. Those objects may then be terminated; thus, the garbage is collected.

As long as all references to an object are either implicitly or explicitly released by the application, the GC will take care of freeing the memory allocated to it. Unlike COM objects, managed objects in .NET are not responsible for maintaining their reference count, and they are not responsible for destroying themselves. Instead, the GC is responsible for cleaning up objects that are no longer referenced by the application. The GC periodically determines which objects need to be cleaned up by leveraging the information the CLR maintains about the running application. The GC obtains a list of objects that are directly referenced by the application. Then, the GC discovers all the objects that are referenced (both directly and indirectly) by the application's "root" objects. Once the GC has identified all the referenced objects, it is free to clean up any remaining objects.

The GC relies on references from an application to objects; thus, when it locates an object that is unreachable from any of the root objects, it can clean up that object. Any other references to that object will be from other objects that are also unreachable. Thus, the GC automatically cleans up objects that contain circular references.

In some environments, such as COM, objects are destroyed in a deterministic fashion. Once the reference count reaches zero, the object destroys itself, which means that you can tell exactly when the object will be terminated. However, with garbage collection, you can't tell exactly when an object will be destroyed. Just because you eliminate all references to an object doesn't mean that it will be terminated immediately. It just remains in memory until the garbage collection process gets around to locating and destroying it, a process called *nondeterministic finalization*.

This nondeterministic nature of CLR garbage collection provides a performance benefit. Rather than expend the effort to destroy objects as they are dereferenced, the destruction process can occur when the application is otherwise idle, often decreasing the impact on the user. Of course, if garbage collection must occur when the application is active, then the system may see a slight performance fluctuation as the collection is accomplished.

It is possible to explicitly invoke the GC by calling the `System.GC.Collect` method, but this process takes time, so it is not the sort of thing that should be done in a typical application. For example, you could call this method each time you set an object variable to `Nothing`, so that the object would be destroyed almost immediately. However, this forces the GC to scan all the objects in your application, a very expensive operation in terms of performance.

It's far better to design applications such that it is acceptable for unused objects to sit in the memory for some time before they are terminated. That way, the garbage collector, too, can run based on its optimal rules, collecting many dereferenced objects at the same time. This means you need to design objects that don't maintain expensive resources in instance variables. For example, database connections, open files on disk, and large chunks of memory (such as an image) are all examples of expensive resources. If you rely on the destruction of the object to release this type of resource, then the system might be keeping the resource tied up for a lot longer than you expect; in fact, on a lightly utilized Web server, it could literally be days.

The first principle is working with object patterns that incorporate cleaning up such pending references before the object is released. Examples of this include calling the `close` method on an open database connection or file handle. In most cases, it's possible for applications to create classes that do not risk keeping these handles open. However, certain requirements, even with the best object design, can create a risk that a key resource will not be cleaned up correctly. In such an event, there are two occasions when the object could attempt to perform this cleanup: when the final reference to the object is released and immediately before the GC destroys the object.

One option is to implement the `IDisposable` interface. When implemented, this interface is used to ensure that persistent resources are released. This is the preferred method for releasing resources. The second option is to add a method to your class that the system runs immediately before an object is destroyed. This option is not recommended for several reasons, including the fact that many developers fail to remember that the garbage collector is nondeterministic, meaning that you can't, for example, reference an SQLConnection object from your custom object's finalizer.

Finally, as part of .NET 2.0, Visual Basic introduced the Using command. The Using command is designed to change the way that you think about object cleanup. Instead of encapsulating your cleanup logic within your object, the Using command creates a window around the code that is referencing an instance of your object. When your application's execution reaches the end of this window, the system automatically calls the IDIsposable interface for your object to ensure that it is cleaned up correctly.

The Finalize Method

Conceptually, the GC calls an object's Finalize method immediately before it collects an object that is no longer referenced by the application. Classes can override the Finalize method to perform any necessary cleanup. The basic concept is to create a method that acts as what, in other object-oriented languages, is referred to as a *destructor*. Similarly, the Class_Terminate available in previous versions of Visual Basic does not have a functional equivalent in .NET. Instead, it is possible to create a Finalize method that is recognized by the GC and that prevents a class from being cleaned up until after the finalization method is completed, as shown in the following example:

```
Protected Overrides Sub Finalize()
  ' clean up code goes here
  MyBase.Finalize()
End Sub
```

This code uses both Protected scope and the Overrides keyword. Notice that not only does custom cleanup code go here (as indicated by the comment), but this method also calls MyBase.Finalize(), which causes any finalization logic in the base class to be executed as well. Any class implementing a custom Finalize method should always call the base finalization class.

Be careful, however, not to treat the Finalize method as if it were a destructor. A destructor is based on a deterministic system, whereby the method is called when the object's last reference is removed. In the GC system, there are key differences in how a finalizer works:

❑   Because the GC is optimized to clean up memory only when necessary, there is a delay between the time when the object is no longer referenced by the application and when the GC collects it. Therefore, the same expensive resources that are released in the Finalize method may stay open longer than they need to be.

❑   The GC doesn't actually run Finalize methods. When the GC finds a Finalize method, it queues the object up for the finalizer to execute the object's method. This means that an object is not cleaned up during the current GC pass. Because of how the GC is optimized, this can result in the object remaining in memory for a much longer period.

❑   The GC is usually triggered when available memory is running low. As a result, execution of the object's Finalize method is likely to incur performance penalties. Therefore, the code in the Finalize method should be as short and quick as possible.

❑   There's no guarantee that a service you require is still available. For example, if the system is closing and you have a file open, then .NET may have already unloaded the object required to close the file, and thus a Finalize method can't reference an instance of any other .NET object.

All cleanup activities should be placed in the `Finalize` method, but objects that require timely cleanup should implement a `Dispose` method that can then be called by the client application just before setting the reference to `Nothing`:

```
Class DemoDispose
  Private m_disposed As Boolean = False

  Public Sub Dispose()
    If (Not m_disposed) Then
      ' Call cleanup code in Finalize.
      Finalize()

      ' Record that object has been disposed.
      m_disposed = True

      ' Finalize does not need to be called.
      GC.SuppressFinalize(Me)
    End If
  End Sub

  Protected Overrides Sub Finalize()
    ' Perform cleanup here \dots
  End Sub
End Class
```

The `DemoDispose` class overrides the `Finalize` method and implements the code to perform any necessary cleanup. This class places the actual cleanup code within the `Finalize` method. To ensure that the `Dispose` method only calls `Finalize` once, the value of the `private m_disposed` field is checked. Once `Finalize` has been run, this value is set to `True`. The class then calls `GC.SuppressFinalize` to ensure that the GC does not call the `Finalize` method on this object when the object is collected. If you need to implement a `Finalize` method, this is the preferred implementation pattern.

This example implements all of the object's cleanup code in the `Finalize` method to ensure that the object is cleaned up properly before the GC collects it. The `Finalize` method still serves as a safety net in case the `Dispose` or `Close` methods were not called before the GC collects the object.

The IDisposable Interface

In some cases, the `Finalize` behavior is not acceptable. For an object that is using an expensive or limited resource, such as a database connection, a file handle, or a system lock, it is best to ensure that the resource is freed as soon as the object is no longer needed.

One way to accomplish this is to implement a method to be called by the client code to force the object to clean up and release its resources. This is not a perfect solution, but it is workable. This cleanup method must be called directly by the code using the object or via the use of the `Using` statement. The `Using` statement enables you to encapsulate an object's life span within a limited range, and automate the calling of the `IDisposable` interface.

The .NET Framework provides the `IDisposable` interface to formalize the declaration of cleanup logic. Be aware that implementing the `IDisposable` interface also implies that the object has overridden the `Finalize` method. Since there is no guarantee that the `Dispose` method will be called, it is critical that `Finalize` trigger your cleanup code if it was not already executed.

Having a custom finalizer ensures that, once released, the garbage collection mechanism will eventually find and terminate the object by running its `Finalize` method. However, when handled correctly, the `IDisposable` interface ensures that any cleanup is executed immediately, so resources are not consumed beyond the time they are needed.

Note that any class that derives from `System.ComponentModel.Component` automatically inherits the `IDisposable` interface. This includes all of the forms and controls used in a Windows Forms UI, as well as various other classes within the .NET Framework. Since this interface is inherited, let's review a custom implementation of the `IDisposable` interface based on the `Person` class defined in the preceding chapters. The first step involves adding a reference to the interface to the top of the class:

```
Public Class Person
    Implements IDisposable
```

This interface defines two methods, `Dispose` and `Finalize`, that need to be implemented in the class. Visual Studio automatically inserts both these methods into your code:

```
    Private disposed As Boolean = False

    ' IDisposable
    Private Overloads Sub Dispose(ByVal disposing As Boolean)
        If Not Me.disposed Then
            If disposing Then
                ' TODO: put code to dispose managed resources
            End If

            ' TODO: put code to free unmanaged resources here
        End If
        Me.disposed = True
    End Sub

#Region " IDisposable Support "
    ' This code added by Visual Basic to correctly implement the disposable pattern.
    Public Overloads Sub Dispose() Implements IDisposable.Dispose
        ' Do not change this code.
        ' Put cleanup code in Dispose(ByVal disposing As Boolean) above.
        Dispose(True)
        GC.SuppressFinalize(Me)
    End Sub

    Protected Overrides Sub Finalize()
        ' Do not change this code.
        ' Put cleanup code in Dispose(ByVal disposing As Boolean) above.
        Dispose(False)
        MyBase.Finalize()
    End Sub
#End Region
```

Notice the use of the Overloads and Overrides keywords. The automatically inserted code is following a best-practice design pattern for implementation of the IDisposable interface and the Finalize method. The idea is to centralize all cleanup code into a single method that is called by either the Dispose() method or the Finalize() method as appropriate.

Accordingly, you can add the cleanup code as noted by the TODO: comments in the inserted code. As mentioned in Chapter 13, the TODO: keyword is recognized by Visual Studio's text parser, which triggers an entry in the task list to remind you to complete this code before the project is complete. Because this code frees a managed object (the Hashtable), it appears as shown here:

```
Private Overloads Sub Dispose(ByVal disposing As Boolean)
   If Not Me.disposed Then
     If disposing Then
       ' TODO: put code to dispose managed resources
       mPhones = Nothing
     End If

     ' TODO: put code to free unmanaged resources here
   End If
   Me.disposed = True
End Sub
```

In this case, we're using this method to release a reference to the object that the mPhones variable points to. While not strictly necessary, this illustrates how code can release other objects when the Dispose method is called. Generally, it is up to our client code to call this method at the appropriate time to ensure that cleanup occurs. Typically, this should be done as soon as the code is done using the object.

This is not always as easy as it might sound. In particular, an object may be referenced by more than one variable, and just because code in one class is dereferencing the object from one variable doesn't mean that it has been dereferenced by all the other variables. If the Dispose method is called while other references remain, then the object may become unusable and cause errors when invoked via those other references. There is no easy solution to this problem, so careful design is required if you choose to use the IDisposable interface.

Using IDisposable

One way to work with the IDisposable interface is to manually insert the calls to the interface implementation everywhere you reference the class. For example, in an application's Form1 code, you can override the OnLoad event for the form. You can use the custom implementation of this method to create an instance of the Person object. Then you create a custom handler for the form's OnClosed event, and make sure to clean up by disposing of the Person object. To do this, add the following code to the form:

```
Private Sub Form1_Closed(ByVal sender As Object, _
    ByVal e As System.EventArgs) Handles MyBase.Closed

  CType(mPerson, IDisposable).Dispose()


End Sub
```

The `OnClosed` method runs as the form is being closed, so it is an appropriate place to do cleanup work. Note that because the `Dispose` method is part of a secondary interface, use of the `CType()` method to access that specific interface is needed in order to call the method.

This solution works fine for patterns where the object implementing `IDisposable` is used within a form. However, it is less useful for other patterns, such as when the object is used as part of a Web Service. In fact, even for forms, this pattern is somewhat limited in that it requires the form to define the object when the form is created, as opposed to either having the object created prior to the creation of the form or some other scenario that occurs only on other events within the form.

For these situations, Visual Basic 2005 introduces a new command keyword: `Using`. The `Using` keyword is a way to quickly encapsulate the lifecycle of an object that implements `IDisposable`, and ensure that the `Dispose` method is called correctly:

```
Dim mPerson as New Person()
Using (mPerson)
    'insert custom method calls
End Using
```

The preceding statements allocate a new instance of the `mPerson` object. The `Using` command then instructs the compiler to automatically clean up this object's instance when the `End Using` command is executed. The result is a much cleaner way to ensure that the `IDisposable` interface is called.

Faster Memory Allocation for Objects

The CLR introduces the concept of a *managed heap*. Objects are allocated on the managed heap, and the CLR is responsible for controlling access to these objects in a type-safe manner. One of the advantages of the managed heap is that memory allocations on it are very efficient. When unmanaged code (such as Visual Basic 6 or C++) allocates memory on the unmanaged heap, it typically scans through some sort of data structure in search of a free chunk of memory that is large enough to accommodate the allocation. The managed heap maintains a reference to the end of the most recent heap allocation. When a new object needs to be created on the heap, the CLR allocates memory on top of memory that has previously been allocated and then increments the reference to the end of heap allocations accordingly. Figure 5-4 is a simplification of what takes place in the managed heap for .NET.

- ❑ **State 1** — A compressed memory heap with a reference to the end point on the heap

- ❑ **State 2** — Object *B*, although no longer referenced, remains in its current memory location. The memory has not been freed and does not alter the allocation of memory or of other objects on the heap.

- ❑ **State 3** — Even though there is now a gap between the memory allocated for object *A* and object *C*, the memory allocation for *D* still occurs on the top of the heap. The unused fragment of memory on the managed heap is ignored at allocation time.

- ❑ **State 4** — After one or more allocations, before there is an allocation failure, the garbage collector runs. It reclaims the memory that was allocated to *B* and repositions the remaining valid objects. This compresses the active objects to the bottom of the heap, creating more space for additional object allocations, as shown in Figure 5-4.

This is where the power of the GC really shines. Before the CLR is unable to allocate memory on the managed heap, the GC is invoked. The GC not only collects objects that are no longer referenced by the application, but also has a second task: compacting the heap. This is important because if all the GC did was clean up objects, then the heap would become progressively more fragmented. When heap memory becomes fragmented, you can wind up with the common problem of having a memory allocation fail, not because there isn't enough free memory, but because there isn't enough free memory in a contiguous section of memory. Thus, not only does the GC reclaim the memory associated with objects that are no longer referenced, it also compacts the remaining objects. The GC effectively squeezes out all of the spaces between the remaining objects, freeing up a large section of managed heap for new object allocations.

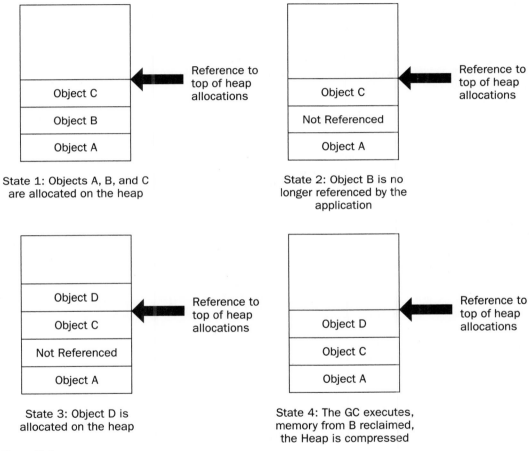

Figure 5-4

Garbage Collector Optimizations

The GC uses a concept known as *generations*, the primary purpose of which is to improve its performance. The theory behind generations is that objects that have been recently created tend to have a higher probability of being garbage-collected than objects that have existed on the system for a longer time.

To understand generations, consider the analogy of a mall parking lot where cars represent objects created by the CLR. People have different shopping patterns when they visit the mall. Some people spend a good portion of their day in the mall, and others stop only long enough to pick up an item or two. Applying the theory of generations to trying to find an empty parking space for a car yields a situation in which the highest probability of finding a parking space is a place where other cars have recently parked. In other words, a space that was occupied recently is more likely to be held by someone who just needed to quickly pick up an item or two. The longer a car has been parked, the higher the probability that its owner is an all-day shopper and the lower the probability that the parking space will be freed up anytime soon.

Generations provide a means for the GC to identify recently created objects versus long-lived objects. An object's generation is basically a counter that indicates how many times it has successfully avoided garbage collection. An object's generation counter starts at zero and can have a maximum value of two, after which the object's generation remains at this value regardless of how many times it is checked for collection.

You can put this to the test with a simple Visual Basic application. From the File menu, select either File ➪ New ➪ Project or, if you have an open solution, File ➪ Add ➪ New Project. This opens the Add New Project dialog box. Select a Console application, provide a name and directory for your new project, and click OK. After you create your new project, you will have a code module that looks similar to the code that follows. Within the Main module, add the highlighted code below. Right-click your second project, and select the Set as Startup Project option so that when you run your solution, your new project is automatically started.

```
Module Module1

  Sub Main()
    Dim myObject As Object = New Object()
    Dim i As Integer

    For i = 0 To 3
      Console.WriteLine(String.Format("Generation = {0}", _
                        GC.GetGeneration(myObject)))
      GC.Collect()
      GC.WaitForPendingFinalizers()
    Next i
  End Sub

End Module
```

Regardless of the project you use, this code sends its output to the .NET console. For a Windows application, this console defaults to the Visual Studio Output window. When you run this code, it creates an instance of an object and then iterates through a loop four times. For each loop, it displays the current generation count of myObject and then calls the GC. The GC.WaitForPendingFinalizers method blocks execution until the garbage collection has been completed.

As shown in Figure 5-5, each time the GC was run, the generation counter was incremented for myObject, up to a maximum of 2.

Figure 5-5

Each time the GC is run, the managed heap is compacted, and the reference to the end of the most recent memory allocation is updated. After compaction, objects of the same generation are grouped together. Generation-2 objects are grouped at the bottom of the managed heap, and generation-1 objects are grouped next. Since new generation-0 objects are placed on top of the existing allocations, they are grouped together as well.

This is significant because recently allocated objects have a higher probability of having shorter lives. Since objects on the managed heap are ordered according to generations, the GC can opt to collect newer objects. Running the GC over a limited portion of the heap is quicker than running it over the entire managed heap.

It's also possible to invoke the GC with an overloaded version of the Collect method that accepts a generation number. The GC will then collect all objects no longer referenced by the application that belong to the specified (or younger) generation. The version of the Collect method that accepts no parameters collects objects that belong to all generations.

Another hidden GC optimization is that a reference to an object may implicitly go out of scope; therefore, it can be collected by the GC. It is difficult to illustrate how the optimization occurs only if there are no additional references to the object and the object does not have a finalizer. However, if an object is declared and used at the top of a module and not referenced again in a method, then in the release mode, the metadata will indicate that the variable is not referenced in the later portion of the code. Once the last reference to the object is made, its logical scope ends, and if the garbage collector runs, the memory for that object, which will no longer be referenced, can be reclaimed before it has gone out of its physical scope.

Summary

This chapter introduced the CLR. It discussed the memory management features of the CLR, including how the CLR eliminates the circular reference problem that has plagued COM developers. Next, the chapter examined the Finalize method and explained why it should not be treated like the Class_Terminate method. Chapter highlights include the following:

❑   Whenever possible, do not implement the Finalize method in a class.

- ❑ If the `Finalize` method is implemented, then also implement the `IDisposable` interface that can be called by the client when the object is no longer needed.

- ❑ Code for the `Finalize` method should be as short and quick as possible.

- ❑ There is no way to accurately predict when the GC will collect an object that is no longer referenced by the application (unless the GC is invoked explicitly).

- ❑ The order in which the GC collects objects on the managed heap is nondeterministic. This means that the `Finalize` method cannot call methods on other objects referenced by the object being collected.

- ❑ Leverage the `Using` keyword to automatically trigger the execution of the `IDisposable` interface.

This chapter also examined the value of a common runtime and type system that can be targeted by multiple languages. You saw how the CLR offers better support for metadata. Metadata is used to make types self-describing and is used for language elements such as attributes. Included were examples of how metadata is used by the CLR and the .NET class library, and the chapter showed you how to extend metadata by creating your own attributes. Finally, the chapter presented a brief overview of the Reflection API and the IL Disassembler utility (`ildasm.exe`), which can display the IL contained within a module.

6

Localization

Developers usually build their applications in the English language. Then, as the audience for the application expands, they realize the need to globalize the application. Of course, the ideal is to build the application to handle an international audience right from the start — but in many cases this may not be possible because of the extra work it requires.

With the release of .NET Framework 2.0, a considerable effort has been made to address the internationalization of Web applications. Changes to the API, the addition of capabilities to the server controls, and even Visual Studio itself equip you to do the extra work required to bring your application to an international audience. This chapter takes a look at some of the important items to consider when building your applications for the world.

Cultures and Regions

The ASP.NET page that is pulled up in an end user's browser runs under a specific culture and region setting. When building an ASP.NET application or page, the defined culture in which it runs is dependent upon a culture and region setting specified either in the server in which the application is run or in a setting applied by the client (the end user). By default, ASP.NET runs under a culture setting defined by the server.

The world is made up of a multitude of cultures, each of which has a language and a set of defined ways in which it views and consumes numbers, uses currencies, sorts alphabetically, and so on. The .NET Framework defines cultures and regions using the Request for Comments 1766 standard definition (tags for identification of languages), which specifies a language and region using two-letter codes separated by a dash. The following table provides examples of some culture definitions:

Culture Code	Description
en-US	English language; United States
en-GB	English language; United Kingdom (Great Britain)
en-AU	English language; Australia
en-CA	English language; Canada

Looking at the examples in this table, you can see that four distinct cultures are defined. These four cultures have some similarities and some differences. All four cultures speak the same language (English), so the language code of en is used in each culture setting. After the language setting is the region setting. Even though these cultures speak the same language, it is important to distinguish them further by setting their region (such as US for the United States, GB for the United Kingdom, AU for Australia, and CA for Canada). As you are probably well aware, the English language in the United States is slightly different from the English language used in the United Kingdom, and so forth. Beyond language, differences exist in how dates and numerical values are represented. This is why a culture's language and region are presented together.

The differences don't break down by the country only. Many times, countries contain more than a single language, and each area has its own preference for notation of dates and other items. For example, en-CA specifies English speakers in Canada. Because Canada is not only an English-speaking country, it also includes the culture setting of fr-CA for French-speaking Canadians.

Understanding Culture Types

The culture definition just given is called a *specific culture* definition. This definition is as detailed as you can possibly get, defining both the language and the region. The other type of culture definition is a *neutral culture* definition. Each specific culture has a specified neutral culture with which it is associated. For instance, the English language cultures shown in the previous table are separate, but they also belong to one neutral culture EN (English). The diagram presented in Figure 6-1 displays how these culture types relate to one another.

From this diagram, you can see that many specific cultures belong to a neutral culture. Higher in the hierarchy than the neutral culture is an *invariant culture,* which is an agnostic culture setting that should be utilized when passing items (such as dates and numbers) around a network. When performing these kinds of operations, make your back-end data flows devoid of user-specific culture settings. Instead, apply these settings in the business and presentation layers of your applications.

In addition, pay attention to neutral culture when working with your applications. Invariably, you are going to build applications with views that are more dependent on a neutral culture than on a specific culture. For instance, if you have a Spanish version of your application, you'll probably make this version available to all Spanish speakers regardless of their regions. In many applications, it won't matter whether the Spanish speaker is from Spain, Mexico, or Argentina. In a case where it does make a difference, use the specific culture settings.

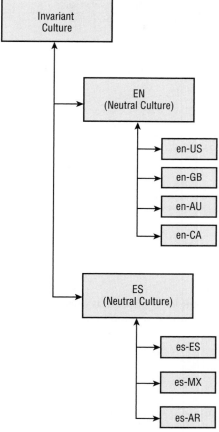

Figure 6-1

Looking at Your Thread

When the end user requests an ASP.NET page or runs a Windows Forms dialog, the item is executed on a thread from the thread pool. That thread has a culture associated with it. You can get information about the culture of the thread programmatically and then check for particular details about that culture.

To see an example of working with a thread and reading off the culture information of that thread, create a Windows Forms application that is laid out as shown in Figure 6-2.

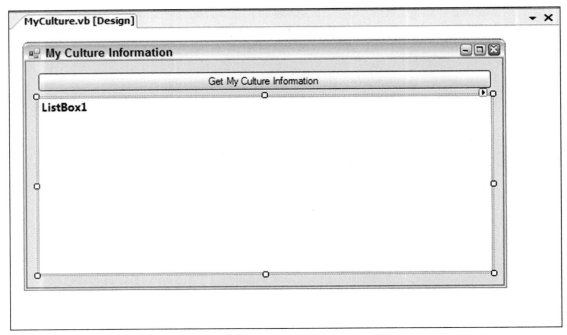

Figure 6-2

The idea here is that when the button on the form is pressed, the Button1_Click event is fired and the user's culture information is read and displayed in the ListBox control. The code for the form is presented here:

```
Imports System.Threading

Public Class MyCulture

    Private Sub Button1_Click(ByVal sender As System.Object, _
      ByVal e As System.EventArgs) Handles Button1.Click

        Dim ci As New _
          System.Globalization.CultureInfo( _
            Thread.CurrentThread.CurrentCulture.ToString())

        ListBox1.Items.Add("CURRENT CULTURE'S INFO")
        ListBox1.Items.Add("Culture's Name: " & ci.Name)
        ListBox1.Items.Add("Culture's Parent Name: " & ci.Parent.Name)
        ListBox1.Items.Add("Culture's Display Name: " & ci.DisplayName)
        ListBox1.Items.Add("Culture's English Name: " & ci.EnglishName)
        ListBox1.Items.Add("Culture's Native Name: " & ci.NativeName)
        ListBox1.Items.Add("Culture's Three Letter ISO Name: " & _
            ci.ThreeLetterISOLanguageName)
        ListBox1.Items.Add("Calendar Type: " & ci.Calendar.ToString())
    End Sub
End Class
```

Because this form is working with the Thread object, in order for this to work you need to make a reference to the System.Threading namespace at the top of the form, as is done with the Imports statement. Threading is covered in Chapter 24.

This simple form creates a CultureInfo object from the System.Globalization namespace and assigns the culture from the current thread that is running using the Thread.CurrentThread .CurrentCulture.ToString() call. Once the CultureInfo object is populated with the end user's culture, the details of that culture can be called using a number of available properties that the CultureInfo object offers. Example results of running the form are shown in Figure 6-3.

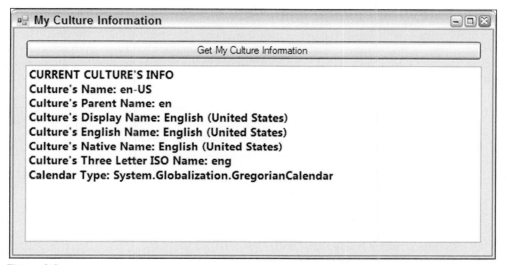

My Culture Information

Get My Culture Information

CURRENT CULTURE'S INFO
Culture's Name: en-US
Culture's Parent Name: en
Culture's Display Name: English (United States)
Culture's English Name: English (United States)
Culture's Native Name: English (United States)
Culture's Three Letter ISO Name: eng
Calendar Type: System.Globalization.GregorianCalendar

Figure 6-3

The CultureInfo object contains a number of properties that provide you with specific culture information. The items displayed are only a small sampling of what is available from the CultureInfo object. From this figure, you can see that the en-US culture is the default setting in which the thread (my thread at this time) executes. In addition to this, you can use the CultureInfo object to get at a lot of other descriptive information about the culture. You can always change a thread's culture on the overloads provided via a new instantiation of the CultureInfo object, as shown here:

```
Imports System.Globalization
Imports System.Threading

Public Class MyCulture

    Private Sub Button1_Click(ByVal sender As System.Object, _
      ByVal e As System.EventArgs) Handles Button1.Click

        Thread.CurrentThread.CurrentCulture = New CultureInfo("th-TH")
        Dim ci As CultureInfo = _
          System.Threading.Thread.CurrentThread.CurrentCulture
```

```
            ListBox1.Items.Add("CURRENT CULTURE'S INFO")
            ListBox1.Items.Add("Culture's Name: " & ci.Name)
            ListBox1.Items.Add("Culture's Parent Name: " & ci.Parent.Name)
            ListBox1.Items.Add("Culture's Display Name: " & ci.DisplayName)
            ListBox1.Items.Add("Culture's English Name: " & ci.EnglishName)
            ListBox1.Items.Add("Culture's Native Name: " & ci.NativeName)
            ListBox1.Items.Add("Culture's Three Letter ISO Name: " & _
                ci.ThreeLetterISOLanguageName)
            ListBox1.Items.Add("Calendar Type: " & ci.Calendar.ToString())
        End Sub
    End Class
```

In this example, only a couple of lines of code are changed to assign a new instance of the `CultureInfo` object to the `CurrentCulture` property of the thread being executed by the application. The culture setting enables the `CultureInfo` object to define the culture you want to utilize. In this case, the Thai language of Thailand is assigned, and the results produced in the `ListBox` control are illustrated in Figure 6-4.

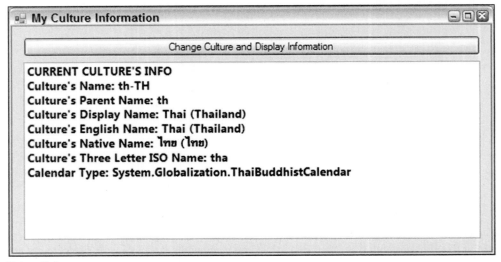

Figure 6-4

From this figure, you can see that the .NET Framework provides the native name of the language used even if it is not a Latin-based letter style. In this case, the results are presented for the Thai language in Thailand, including some of the properties associated with this culture (such as an entirely different calendar than the one used in Western Europe and the United States).

Declaring Culture Globally in ASP.NET

ASP.NET enables you to easily define the culture that is used either by your entire ASP.NET application or by a specific page within your Web application, using what are termed *server-side culture declarations*. You can specify the culture for any of your ASP.NET applications by means of the appropriate configuration files. In the default install of ASP.NET, no culture is specified, as is evident when you look at the global `web.config.comments` file found in the ASP.NET 2.0's `CONFIG` folder (`C:\WINDOWS\Microsoft.NET\Framework\v2.0.50727\CONFIG`). This file contains a `<globalization>` section of the configuration document, presented here:

```
<globalization requestEncoding="utf-8" responseEncoding="utf-8" fileEncoding=""
  culture="" uiCulture="" enableClientBasedCulture="false"
  responseHeaderEncoding="utf-8" resourceProviderFactoryType=""
  enableBestFitResponseEncoding="false" />
```

Note the two attributes represented in bold — `culture` and `uiCulture`. The `culture` attribute enables you to define the culture to use for processing incoming requests, whereas the `uiCulture` attribute enables you define the default culture needed to process any resource files in the application (use of these attributes is covered later in the chapter).

As you look at the configuration declaration in the preceding code block, you can see that nothing is specified for the culture settings. One option you have when specifying a culture on the server is to define this culture in the `web.config.comments` file. This causes every ASP.NET 2.0 application on this server to adopt this particular culture setting. The other option is to specify these settings in the `web.config` file of the application, as illustrated here:

```
<configuration>
   <system.web>

      <globalization culture="ru-RU" uiCulture="ru-RU" />

   </system.web>
</configuration>
```

In this case, the culture established for just this ASP.NET application is the Russian language in the country of Russia. In addition to setting the culture at either the server-wide or the application-wide level, another option is to set the culture at the page level. This is illustrated in the following example:

```
<%@ Page Language="VB" UICulture="ru-RU" Culture="ru-RU" %>
```

This example specifies that the Russian language and culture settings are used for everything on the page. You can see this in action by using this `@Page` directive and a simple calendar control on the page. Figure 6-5 shows the output.

≤	Август 2006 г.				≥	
Пн	**Вт**	**Ср**	**Чт**	**Пт**	**Сб**	**Вс**
31	1	2	3	4	5	6
7	8	9	10	11	12	13
14	15	16	17	18	19	20
21	22	23	24	25	26	27
28	29	30	31	1	2	3
4	5	6	7	8	9	10

Figure 6-5

Adopting Culture Settings in ASP.NET

In addition to using server-side settings to define the culture for your ASP.NET pages, you also have the option to define the culture with what the client has set as his or her preference in a browser instance.

When end users install Microsoft's Internet Explorer and some of the other browsers, they have the option to select their preferred cultures in a particular order (if they have selected more than a single culture preference). To see this in action in IE, select Tools ⇨ Internet Options from the IE menu. On the first tab provided (General) is a Languages button at the bottom of the dialog. Select this button and you are provided with the Language Preference dialog shown in Figure 6-6.

Language Preference

Some Web sites offer content in multiple languages. You can choose several languages below; they will be treated in order of priority.

Language:

Finnish [fi]
English (United States) [en-us]

Move Up
Move Down
Remove
Add...

Menus and dialog boxes are currently displayed in English (United States).

OK   Cancel

Figure 6-6

Two cultures are selected from the list of available cultures. To add any additional cultures to the list, click the Add button and select the appropriate culture from the list. After you have selected any cultures present in the list, you can select the order in which you prefer to use them. In the case of Figure 6-6, the Finnish culture is established as the most preferred culture, whereas the U.S. version of English is selected as the second preference. A user with this setting gets the Finnish language version of the application before anything else; if a Finnish version is not available, a U.S. English version is presented instead.

After you, as the end user, make this selection, you can use the new auto feature provided in ASP.NET 2.0. Instead of specifying a distinct culture in any of the configuration files or from the @Page directive, you can also state that ASP.NET should automatically select the culture provided by the end user requesting the page. This is done using the auto keyword, as illustrated here:

```
<%@ Page Language="VB" UICulture="auto" Culture="auto" %>
```

With this construction in your page, the dates, calendars, and numbers appear in the preferred culture of the requester. What happens if you have translated resources in resource files (shown later in the chapter) that depend on a culture specification? Or what if you have only specific translations and therefore can't handle every possible culture that might be returned to your ASP.NET page? In this case, you can specify the auto option with an additional fall-back option if ASP.NET cannot find the culture settings of the user (such as culture-specific resource files). This usage is illustrated in the following code:

```
<%@ Page Language="VB" UICulture="auto:en-US" Culture="auto:en-US" %>
```

In this case, the automatic detection is utilized, but if the culture the end user prefers is not present, then en-US is used.

Translating Values and Behaviors

In the process of globalizing your .NET application, you may notice a number of aspects that are done differently than building an application that is devoid of globalization, including how dates are represented and how currencies are shown. This section looks at some of these issues.

Understanding Differences in Dates

Different cultures specify dates and time very differently. For instance, take the following date as an example:

```
08/11/2007
```

What is this date exactly? Is it August 11, 2007 or is it November 8, 2007? Again, when storing values such as date/time stamps in a database or other type of back-end system, always use the same culture (or invariant culture) for these items so that you avoid any mistakes. It should be the job of the business logic layer or the presentation layer to convert these items for use by the end user.

Setting the culture at the server level in ASP.NET or within a Windows Forms application, as shown in the earlier samples, enables your .NET application to make these conversions for you. You can also simply assign a new culture to the thread in which the application is running. For instance, consider the following code:

```
Imports System.Globalization
Imports System.Threading

Public Class Differences

    Private Sub Button1_Click(ByVal sender As System.Object, _
      ByVal e As System.EventArgs) Handles Button1.Click

        Dim dt As DateTime = New DateTime(2007, 8, 11, 11, 12, 10, 10)

        Thread.CurrentThread.CurrentCulture = New CultureInfo("en-US")
        ListBox1.Items.Add( _
          Thread.CurrentThread.CurrentCulture.EnglishName & " : " & _
          dt.ToString())

        Thread.CurrentThread.CurrentCulture = New CultureInfo("ru-RU")
```

```
        ListBox1.Items.Add( _
            Thread.CurrentThread.CurrentCulture.EnglishName & " : " & _
            dt.ToString())

        Thread.CurrentThread.CurrentCulture = New CultureInfo("fi-FI")
        ListBox1.Items.Add( _
            Thread.CurrentThread.CurrentCulture.EnglishName & " : " & _
            dt.ToString())

        Thread.CurrentThread.CurrentCulture = New CultureInfo("th-TH")
        ListBox1.Items.Add( _
            Thread.CurrentThread.CurrentCulture.EnglishName & " : " & _
            dt.ToString())
    End Sub
End Class
```

In this case, a Windows Forms application is used again and four different cultures are utilized in the output. The date/time construction used by the defined culture is written to the ListBox control. The result from this code operation is presented in Figure 6-7.

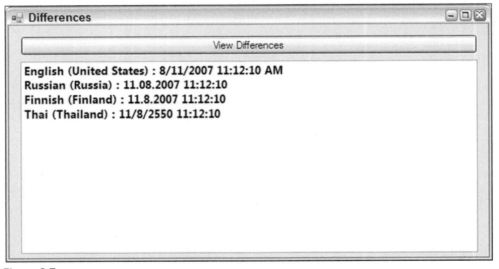

Figure 6-7

As you can see, the formats used to represent a date/time value are dramatically different from one another — and one of the cultures, the Thai culture (th-TH), even uses an entirely different calendar that labels 2007 as 2550.

Understanding Differences in Numbers and Currencies

In addition to date/time values, numbers are constructed quite differently from one culture to the next. How can a number be represented differently in different cultures? Well, it has less to do with the actual number (although certain cultures use different number symbols) and more to do with how the number separators are used for decimals or for showing amounts such as thousands, millions, and more. For instance, in the English culture of the United States (en-US), numbers are represented in the following fashion:

```
5,123,456.00
```

From this example, you can see that the en-US culture uses a comma as a separator for thousands and a period for signifying the start of any decimals that might appear after the number is presented. It is quite different when working with other cultures. The following code block shows an example of representing numbers in other cultures:

```
Imports System.Globalization
Imports System.Threading

Public Class Differences

    Private Sub Button1_Click(ByVal sender As System.Object, _
        ByVal e As System.EventArgs) Handles Button1.Click

        Dim myNumber As Double = 5123456.0

        Thread.CurrentThread.CurrentCulture = New CultureInfo("en-US")
        ListBox1.Items.Add(Thread.CurrentThread.CurrentCulture.EnglishName & _
            " : " & myNumber.ToString("n"))

        Thread.CurrentThread.CurrentCulture = New CultureInfo("vi-VN")
        ListBox1.Items.Add(Thread.CurrentThread.CurrentCulture.EnglishName & _
            " : " & myNumber.ToString("n"))

        Thread.CurrentThread.CurrentCulture = New CultureInfo("fi-FI")
        ListBox1.Items.Add(Thread.CurrentThread.CurrentCulture.EnglishName & _
            " : " & myNumber.ToString("n"))

        Thread.CurrentThread.CurrentCulture = New CultureInfo("fr-CH")
        ListBox1.Items.Add(Thread.CurrentThread.CurrentCulture.EnglishName & _
            " : " & myNumber.ToString("n"))
    End Sub
End Class
```

Running this short example produces the results presented in Figure 6-8.

Clearly, other cultures show numbers in quite a different format than that of the en-US culture. The second culture listed in the figure, vi-VN (Vietnamese in Vietnam), constructs a number exactly the opposite from the way it is constructed in en-US. The Vietnamese culture uses periods for the thousand separators and a comma for signifying decimals. Finnish uses spaces for the thousand separators and a comma for the decimal separator, whereas the French-speaking Swiss use a high comma for separating thousands and a period for the decimal separator. As you can see, it is important to "translate" numbers to the proper construction so that users of your application can properly understand the numbers represented.

Another scenario in which you represent numbers is when working with currencies. It is one thing to *convert* currencies so that end users understand the proper value of an item, but it is another to translate the construction of the currency just as you would a basic number.

Figure 6-8

Each culture has a distinct currency symbol used to signify that a number represented is an actual currency value. For instance, the en-US culture represents a currency in the following format:

```
$5,123,456.00
```

The en-US culture uses a U.S. dollar symbol ($), and the location of this symbol is just as important as the symbol itself. For en-US, the $ symbol directly precedes the currency value (with no space in between the symbol and the first character of the number). Other cultures use different symbols to represent currency and often place those currency symbols in different locations. Try changing the previous code block so that it now represents the number as a currency. The necessary changes are shown here:

```
Imports System.Globalization
Imports System.Threading

Public Class Differences

    Private Sub Button1_Click(ByVal sender As System.Object, _
      ByVal e As System.EventArgs) Handles Button1.Click

        Dim myNumber As Double = 5123456.0

        Thread.CurrentThread.CurrentCulture = New CultureInfo("en-US")
        ListBox1.Items.Add(Thread.CurrentThread.CurrentCulture.EnglishName & _
            " : " & myNumber.ToString("c"))

        Thread.CurrentThread.CurrentCulture = New CultureInfo("vi-VN")
        ListBox1.Items.Add(Thread.CurrentThread.CurrentCulture.EnglishName & _
            " : " & myNumber.ToString("c"))

        Thread.CurrentThread.CurrentCulture = New CultureInfo("fi-FI")
```

```
        ListBox1.Items.Add(Thread.CurrentThread.CurrentCulture.EnglishName & _
            " : " & myNumber.ToString("c"))

        Thread.CurrentThread.CurrentCulture = New CultureInfo("fr-CH")
        ListBox1.Items.Add(Thread.CurrentThread.CurrentCulture.EnglishName & _
            " : " & myNumber.ToString("c"))
    End Sub
End Class
```

Running this example shows how these cultures represent currency values (see Figure 6-9).

Differences

View Differences

English (United States) : $5,123,456.00
Vietnamese (Vietnam) : 5.123.456,00 đ
Finnish (Finland) : 5 123 456,00 €
French (Switzerland) : SFr. 5'123'456.00

Figure 6-9

Not only are the numbers constructed quite differently from one another, but the currency symbol and the location of the symbol in regard to the number are quite different as well.

When working with currencies, note that when you are using currencies on an ASP.NET page, you have provided an automatic culture setting for the page as a whole (such as setting the culture in the @Page directive). You must specify a specific culture for the currency that is the same in all cases *unless* you are actually doing a currency conversion. For instance, if you are specifying a U.S. dollar currency value on your ASP.NET page, you don't want to specify that the culture of the currency is something else (for example, the euro). An exception would be if you actually performed a currency conversion and showed the appropriate euro value along with the culture specification of the currency. Therefore, if you are using an automatic culture setting on your ASP.NET page and you are *not* converting the currency, you perform something similar to what is illustrated in the following code for currency values:

```
Dim myNumber As Double = 5123456.00
Dim usCurr As CultureInfo = New CultureInfo("en-US")
Response.Write(myNumber.ToString("c", usCurr))
```

Understanding Differences in Sorting Strings

You have learned to translate textual values and alter the construction of the numbers, date/time values, currencies, and more when you are globalizing an application. You should also take note when applying culture settings to some of the programmatic behaviors that you establish for values in your applications. One operation that can change based upon the culture setting applied is how .NET sorts strings. You might think that all cultures sort strings in the same way (and generally they do), but sometimes differences exist. To give you an example, the following example shows you a sorting operation occurring in the en-US culture:

```vb
Imports System.Globalization
Imports System.Threading

Public Class Differences

    Private Sub Button1_Click(ByVal sender As System.Object, _
        ByVal e As System.EventArgs) Handles Button1.Click

        Thread.CurrentThread.CurrentCulture = New CultureInfo("en-US")

        Dim myList As List(Of String) = New List(Of String)

        myList.Add("Washington D.C.")
        myList.Add("Helsinki")
        myList.Add("Moscow")
        myList.Add("Warsaw")
        myList.Add("Vienna")
        myList.Add("Tokyo")

        myList.Sort()

        For Each item As String In myList
            ListBox1.Items.Add(item.ToString())
        Next

    End Sub
End Class
```

For this example to work, you have to reference the `System.Collections` and the `System.Collections.Generic` namespaces because this example makes use of the `List(Of String)` object.

In this example, a generic list of capitals from various countries of the world is created in random order. Then the `Sort()` method of the generic `List(Of String)` object is invoked. This sorting operation sorts the strings based upon how sorting is done for the defined culture in which the application thread is running. The preceding code shows the sorting as it is done for the en-US culture. The result of this operation is presented in Figure 6-10.

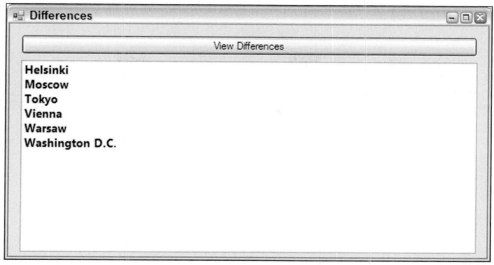

Figure 6-10

This is pretty much what you would expect. Now, however, change the previous example so that the culture is set to the Finnish culture:

```
Imports System.Globalization
Imports System.Threading

Public Class Differences

    Private Sub Button1_Click(ByVal sender As System.Object, _
        ByVal e As System.EventArgs) Handles Button1.Click

        Thread.CurrentThread.CurrentCulture = New CultureInfo("fi-FI")

        Dim myList As List(Of String) = New List(Of String)

        myList.Add("Washington D.C.")
        myList.Add("Helsinki")
        myList.Add("Moscow")
        myList.Add("Warsaw")
        myList.Add("Vienna")
        myList.Add("Tokyo")

        myList.Sort()

        For Each item As String In myList
            ListBox1.Items.Add(item.ToString())
        Next

    End Sub
End Class
```

If you run the same bit of code under the Finnish culture setting, you get the results presented in Figure 6-11.

Figure 6-11

If you examine the difference between the Finnish culture sorting done in Figure 6-11 and the U.S. English culture sorting done in Figure 6-10, you see that the city of Vienna is in a different place in the Finnish version. This is because, in the Finnish language, there is no difference between the letter V and the letter W. Because no difference exists, if you are sorting using the Finnish culture setting, then Vi comes after Wa, and thus Vienna comes last in the list of strings in the sorting operation.

Working with ASP.NET 2.0 Resource Files

When you work with ASP.NET 2.0, all resources are handled by a resource file. A resource file is an XML-based file that has a .resx extension. You can have Visual Studio 2005 help you construct this file. Resource files provide a set of items that are utilized by a specified culture. In your ASP.NET 2.0 applications, you store resource files as either local resources or global resources. The following sections describe how to use each type of resource.

Making Use of Local Resources

You would be surprised how easily you can build an ASP.NET page so that it can be *localized* into other languages. In fact, the only thing you need to do is build the ASP.NET page as you normally would and then use some built-in capabilities from Visual Studio 2005 to convert the page to a format that enables you to plug in other languages easily.

To see this in action, build a simple ASP.NET page as presented here (this is referred to later in the chapter as the "ASP.NET page code block"):

```
<%@ Page Language="VB" %>

<script runat="server">

</script>

<html xmlns="http://www.w3.org/1999/xhtml" >
<head runat="server">
    <title>Sample Page</title>
</head>
<body>
    <form id="form1" runat="server">
    <div>
        <asp:Label ID="Label1" runat="server"
         Text="What is your name?"></asp:Label><br />
        <br />
        <asp:TextBox ID="TextBox1" runat="server"></asp:TextBox> 
        <asp:Button ID="Button1" runat="server" Text="Submit Name" /><br />
        <br />
        <asp:Label ID="Label2" runat="server"></asp:Label>
    </div>
    </form>
</body>
</html>
```

As you can see, there isn't much to this page. It is composed of a couple of Label controls, as well as TextBox and Button controls. The end user enters her name into the text box, and then the Label2 server control is populated with the inputted name and a simple greeting.

The next step is what makes Visual Studio so great. To change the construction of this page so that it can be localized easily from resource files, open the page in Visual Studio and select Tools ⇨ Generate Local Resource from the Visual Studio menu. Note that you can select this tool only when you are in the design view of your page.

Selecting Generate Local Resource from the Tool menu causes Visual Studio to create an App_ LocalResources folder in your project if you already don't have one. A .resx file based upon this ASP.NET page is then placed in the folder. For instance, if you are working with the Default.aspx page, the resource file is named Default.aspx.resx. These changes are shown in Figure 6-12.

Figure 6-12

If you right-click on the `.resx` file and select View Code, notice that the `.resx` file is nothing more than an XML file with an associated schema at the beginning of the document. The resource file that is generated for you takes every possible property of every translatable control on the page and gives each item a key value that can be referenced in your ASP.NET page. Looking at the code of the page, notice that all the text values that you placed in the page have been retained, but they have also been placed inside the resource file. Visual Studio changed the code of the `Default.aspx` page as shown in the following code block:

```
<%@ Page Language="C#" Culture="auto" meta:resourcekey="PageResource1"
    UICulture="auto" %>

<script runat="server">

</script>

<html xmlns="http://www.w3.org/1999/xhtml" >
<head runat="server">
    <title>Sample Page</title>
</head>
<body>
    <form id="form1" runat="server">
    <div>
        <asp:Label ID="Label1" runat="server" Text="What is your name?"
         meta:resourcekey="Label1Resource1"></asp:Label><br />
        <br />
        <asp:TextBox ID="TextBox1" runat="server"
         meta:resourcekey="TextBox1Resource1"></asp:TextBox> 
        <asp:Button ID="Button1"
         runat="server" Text="Submit Name"
         meta:resourcekey="Button1Resource1" /><br />
        <br />
        <asp:Label ID="Label2" runat="server"
         meta:resourcekey="Label2Resource1"></asp:Label>
    </div>
    </form>
</body>
</html>
```

From this bit of code, you can see that the `Culture` and `UICulture` attributes have been added to the `@Page` directive with a value of `auto`, thus enabling this application to be localized. In addition, the attribute `meta:resourcekey` has been added to each of the controls, along with an associated value. This is the key from the `.resx` file that was created on your behalf. Double-clicking on the `Default.aspx.resx` file opens the resource file in the new Resource Editor, shown in Figure 6-13, built into Visual Studio.

Note that a few properties from each of the server controls have been defined in the resource file. For instance, the `Button` server control has its `Text` and `ToolTip` properties exposed in this resource file, and the Visual Studio localization tool has pulled the default `Text` property value from the control based on what you placed there. Looking more closely at the `Button` server control constructions in this file, you can see that both the `Text` and `ToolTip` properties have a defining `Button1Resource1` value preceding the property name. This is the key that is used in the `Button` server control shown earlier.

```
<asp:Button ID="Button1"
 runat="server" Text="Submit Name"
 meta:resourcekey="Button1Resource1" />
```

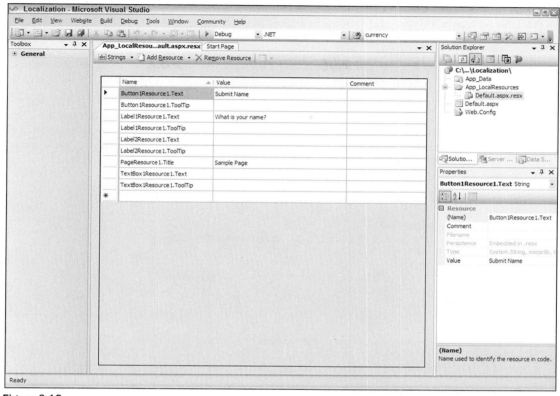

Figure 6-13

Here, a `meta:resourcekey` attribute has been added; and in this case it references `Button1Resource1`. All the properties using this key in the resource file (for example, the `Text` and `ToolTip` properties) are applied to this `Button` server control at runtime.

Adding Another Language Resource File

Now that the `Default.aspx.resx` file is in place, this is a file for an invariant culture. No culture is assigned to this resource file. If no culture can be determined, then this is the resource file that is utilized. To add another resource file for the `Default.aspx` page that handles another language altogether, copy and paste the `Default.aspx.resx` file into the same `App_LocalResources` folder and rename the newly copied file. If you use `Default.aspx.fi-FI.resx`, give the following keys the values shown to make a Finnish-language resource file:

```
Button1Resource1.Text    Lähetä Nimi
Label1Resource1.Text     Mikä sinun nimi on?
PageResource1.Title      Näytesivu
```

You want to create a custom resource in both resource files using the key `Label2Answer`. The `Default.aspx.resx` file should have the following new key:

```
Label2Answer             Hello
```

Now you can add the key `Label2Answer` to the `Default.aspx.fi-FI.resx` file as shown here:

Label2Answer	Hei

You now have resources for specific controls, and a resource that you can access later programmatically.

Finalizing the Building of the Default.aspx Page

Finalizing the `Default.aspx` page, you want to add a `Button1_Click` event so that when the end user enters a name into the text box and clicks the Submit button, the `Label2` server control provides a greeting pulled from the local resource files. When all is said and done, you should have a `Default.aspx` page that looks like the one here:

```
<%@ Page Language="VB" Culture="auto" meta:resourcekey="PageResource1"
    UICulture="auto" %>

<script runat="server">
    Protected Sub Button1_Click(ByVal sender As Object, _
      ByVal e As System.EventArgs)

        Label2.Text = GetLocalResourceObject("Label2Answer").ToString() & _
           " " & TextBox1.Text
    End Sub
</script>

<html xmlns="http://www.w3.org/1999/xhtml" >
<head runat="server">
    <title>Sample Page</title>
</head>
<body>
    <form id="form1" runat="server">
    <div>
        <asp:Label ID="Label1" runat="server" Text="What is your name?"
         meta:resourcekey="Label1Resource1"></asp:Label><br />
        <br />
        <asp:TextBox ID="TextBox1" runat="server"
         meta:resourcekey="TextBox1Resource1"></asp:TextBox> 
        <asp:Button ID="Button1"
         runat="server" Text="Submit Name"
         meta:resourcekey="Button1Resource1" OnClick="Button1_Click" /><br />
        <br />
        <asp:Label ID="Label2" runat="server"
         meta:resourcekey="Label2Resource1"></asp:Label>
    </div>
    </form>
</body>
</html>
```

In addition to pulling local resources using the `meta:resourcekey` attribute in the server controls on the page to get at the exposed attributes, you can also get at any property value contained in the local resource file by using the `GetLocalResourceObject`. When using `GetLocalResourceObject`, you simply use the name of the key as a parameter, as shown here:

```
GetLocalResourceObject("Label2Answer")
```

You could just as easily get at any of the controls' property values from the resource file programmatically using the same construct:

```
GetLocalResourceObject("Button1Resource1.Text")
```

With the code from the `Default.aspx` page in place and the resource files completed, you can run the page, entering a name in the text box and then clicking the button to get a response, as illustrated in Figure 6-14.

Figure 6-14

What happened behind the scenes that caused this page to be constructed in this manner? First, only two resource files — `Default.aspx.resx` and `Default.aspx.fi-FI.resx` — are available. The `Default.aspx.resx` resource file is the invariant culture resource file, whereas the `Default` `.aspx.fi-FI.resx` resource file is for a specific culture (fi-FI). Because I requested the `Default.aspx` page and my browser is set to en-US as my preferred culture, ASP.NET found the local resources for the `Default.aspx` page. From there, ASP.NET checked for an en-US specific version of the `Default.aspx` page. Because there isn't a specific page for the en-US culture, ASP.NET checked for an EN (neutral culture) specific page. Not finding a page for the EN neutral culture, ASP.NET was then forced to use the invariant culture resource file of `Default.aspx.resx`, producing the page shown in Figure 6-14.

Now, if you set your IE language preference as fi-FI and rerun the `Default.aspx` page, you see a Finnish version of the page (see Figure 6-15).

In this case, having set my IE language preference to fi-FI, I am presented with this culture's page instead of the invariant culture page that was presented earlier. ASP.NET found this specific culture through use of the `Default.aspx.fi-FI.resx` resource file.

You can see that all the control properties that were translated and placed within the resource file are utilized automatically by ASP.NET, including the page title presented in the title bar of IE.

Figure 6-15

Neutral Cultures Are Generally Preferred

When you are working with the resource files from this example, note that one of the resources is for a *specific culture*. The Default.aspx.fi-FI.resx file is for a specific culture — the Finnish language as spoken in Finland. Another option would be to make this file work not for a specific culture, but instead for a neutral culture. To do so, simply name the file Default.aspx.FI.resx. In this example, it really doesn't make that much difference because no other countries speak Finnish. It would make sense for languages such as German, Spanish, or French, which are spoken in multiple countries.

For instance, if you are going to have a Spanish version of the Default.aspx page, you could definitely build it for a specific culture such as Default.aspx.es-MX.resx. This construction is for the Spanish language as spoken in Mexico. With this in place, if someone requests the Default.aspx page with the language setting of es-MX, that user is provided with the contents of this resource file. What if the requester has a setting of es-ES? He won't get the Default.aspx.es-MX.resx resource file, but the invariant culture resource file of Default.aspx.resx. If you are going to make only a single translation for your site or any of your pages, construct the resource files to be for neutral cultures, rather than for specific cultures.

If you have the resource file Default.aspx.ES.resx, then it won't matter if the end user's preferred setting is set to es-MX, es-ES, or even es-AR — he gets the appropriate ES neutral culture version of the page.

Making Use of Global Resources

Besides using only local resources that specifically deal with a particular page in your ASP.NET application, you also have the option of creating *global* resources that can be used across multiple pages. To create a resource file that can be utilized across the entire application, right-click on the solution in the Solution Explorer of Visual Studio and select Add New Item. From the Add New Item dialog, select Resource file.

Selecting this option provides you with a Resource.resx file. Visual Studio places this file in a new folder called App_GlobalResources. Again, this first file is the invariant culture resource file. Add a single string resource, giving it the key of `PrivacyStatement` and a value of some kind (a long string).

After you have the invariant culture resource file completed, the next step is to add another resource file, but this time name it `Resource.fi-FI.resx`. Again, for this resource file, give a string key of `PrivacyStatement` and a different value altogether from the one you used in the other resource file.

The point of a global resource file is that you have access to these resources across your entire application. You can gain access to the values that you place in these files in several ways. One way is to work the value directly into any of your server control declarations. For instance, you can place this privacy statement in a `Label` server control as presented here:

```
<asp:Label ID="Label1" runat="server"
 Text='<%$ Resources: Resource, PrivacyStatement %>'></asp:Label>
```

With this construction in place, you can now grab the appropriate value of the `PrivacyStatement` global resource, depending on the language preference of the end user requesting the page. To make this work, you use the keyword `Resources` followed by a colon. Next, you specify the name of the resource file. In this case, the name of the resource file is `Resource` because this statement goes to the `Resource.resx` and `Resource.fi-FI.resx` files in order to find what it needs. After specifying the particular resource file to use, the next item in the statement is the key — in this case, `PrivacyStatement`.

Another way of achieving the same result is to use some built-in dialogs within Visual Studio. To accomplish this task, highlight the server control you want in Visual Studio from Design view so that the control appears within the Properties window. For my example, I highlighted a `Label` server control. From the Properties window, click the button within the Expressions property. This launches the Expressions dialog, where you can bind the `PrivacyStatement` value to the `Text` property of the control. This is illustrated in Figure 6-16.

To make this work, highlight the Text property in the Bindable properties list. Then select an expression type from the drop-down list on the right-hand side of the dialog. Your options include `AppSettings`, `ConnectionStrings`, and `Resources`. Select `Resources` and you are then asked for the `ClassKey` and `ResourceKey` property values. The `ClassKey` is the name of the file that should be utilized. In this example, the name of the file is `Resource.resx`. Therefore, use the `Resources` keyword as a value. You are provided with a drop-down list in the `ResourceKey` property section, with all the keys available in this file. Because only a single key exists at this point, only the `PrivacyStatement` key appears in this list. Make this selection and click OK. The `Label` server control changes and now appears as it was presented earlier in the two-line code block.

One nice feature is that the resources provided via global resources are available in a strongly typed manner. For instance, you can programmatically get at a global resource value by using the construction presented in the following example:

```
Label1.Text = Resources.Resource.PrivacyStatement.ToString()
```

Figure 6-17 shows that you can have full IntelliSense for these resource values.

Figure 6-16

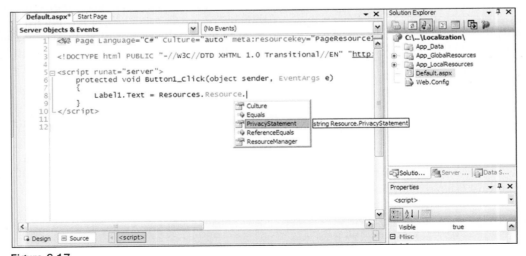

Figure 6-17

Resource Files in Windows Forms

Just as with ASP.NET, you can also work with resource files (.resx) right from Visual Studio. To see how to localize a Windows Forms application, create a new form in your Localization project called UsingResx.vb.

Like the ASP.NET form described earlier in this chapter (and identified as "ASP.NET page code block"), this Windows Form dialog contains a couple of Label controls, a Button, and a TextBox control. Ultimately, your form should look like the one shown in Figure 6-18.

Figure 6-18

Note that the controls were just laid out on the form and no text was added yet. Before you get started, let's turn on localization features for the form. You can also do this to a form that is already completed if you are later converting a form to deal with more than one language.

Highlighting the form in the designer, change the Localizable property to True. This will enable you to apply more than one language to a form and have the elements for a particular culture stored in a resource file. After you have set the Localizable property to True, you can then provide values to the Label and the Button controls on the form. The properties that you assign to the controls are done under the (Default) language setting. You will find this setting within the Language property of the form, as shown in Figure 6-19.

Setting the text values to the (Default) property setting means that if a culture is undetermined or a resource file isn't available for this culture, then the default one will be utilized.

From there, change the Language property of the form to Finnish. You can then change the values of three of the controls as follows:

```
Button1.Text    Lähetä Nimi
Label1.Text     Mikä sinun nimi on?
Label2.Text     Hei
```

Figure 6-19

Double-clicking on the form's button will allow you to create a `Button1_Click` event. The code for this page is as follows:

```
Imports System.Globalization
Imports System.Threading

Public Class UsingResx

    Sub New()

        Thread.CurrentThread.CurrentCulture = New CultureInfo("en-US")
        Thread.CurrentThread.CurrentUICulture = New CultureInfo("en-US")

        ' This call is required by the Windows Form Designer.
        InitializeComponent()

    End Sub

    Private Sub Button1_Click(ByVal sender As System.Object, _
      ByVal e As System.EventArgs) Handles Button1.Click

        Label2.Visible = True
        Label2.Text += TextBox1.Text
    End Sub
End Class
```

This assigns the `CurrentCulture` and the `CurrentUICulture` properties to `en-US`; the form it produces is shown in Figure 6-20.

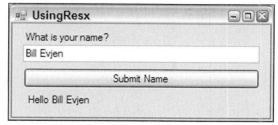

Figure 6-20

Now change the code so that it works with a Finnish culture setting:

```vb
Imports System.Globalization
Imports System.Threading

Public Class UsingResx

    Sub New()

        Thread.CurrentThread.CurrentCulture = New CultureInfo("fi-FI")
        Thread.CurrentThread.CurrentUICulture = New CultureInfo("fi-FI")

        ' This call is required by the Windows Form Designer.
        InitializeComponent()

    End Sub

    Private Sub Button1_Click(ByVal sender As System.Object, _
      ByVal e As System.EventArgs) Handles Button1.Click

        Label2.Visible = True
        Label2.Text += TextBox1.Text
    End Sub
End Class
```

Running the form with this change in place now produces the window shown in Figure 6-21.

Figure 6-21

So where are all the translations stored? Just like ASP.NET, they are stored in the resource file for this form. Looking in the Solution Explorer, you will now find a `UsingResx.resx` and a `UsingResx.fi.resx` file, as shown in Figure 6-22.

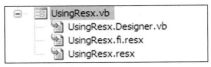

Figure 6-22

Opening the `UsingResx.resx` file will cause Visual Studio to open the file in a manner that allows you to directly edit the values it stores. The default resource file stores some type references as well as other properties of the controls on the form, as shown in Figure 6-23.

UsingResx.resx

abc Strings ▾   Add Resource ▾   ✕ Remove Resource

Name	Value	Comment
$this.Text	UsingResx	
>>$this.Name	UsingResx	
>>$this.Type	System.Windows.Forms.Form, System.Windows.Forms, Version=2.0.0.0,	
>>Button1.Name	Button1	
>>Button1.Parent	$this	
>>Button1.Type	System.Windows.Forms.Button, System.Windows.Forms, Version=2.0.0.0,	
>>Button1.ZOrder	1	
>>Label1.Name	Label1	
>>Label1.Parent	$this	
>>Label1.Type	System.Windows.Forms.Label, System.Windows.Forms, Version=2.0.0.0,	
>>Label1.ZOrder	3	
>>Label2.Name	Label2	
>>Label2.Parent	$this	
>>Label2.Type	System.Windows.Forms.Label, System.Windows.Forms, Version=2.0.0.0,	
>>Label2.ZOrder	0	
>>TextBox1.Name	TextBox1	
>>TextBox1.Parent	$this	
>>TextBox1.Type	System.Windows.Forms.TextBox, System.Windows.Forms, Version=2.0.0.0,	
>>TextBox1.ZOrder	2	
Button1.Text	Submit Name	
Label1.Text	What is your name?	
Label2.Text	Hello	

Figure 6-23

Opening the `UsingResx.fi.resx` file instead shows only the three different properties that you changed. The rest of the properties are read from the default resource file. The contents of the Finnish resource file are presented in Figure 6-24.

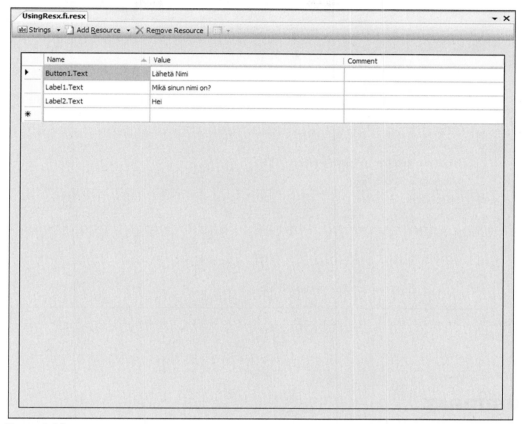

Figure 6-24

Working with the Resource Editor

Visual Studio 2005 provides a brand-new editor for working with resource files. You have already seen some of the views available from this new edition of the editor. Resources are now categorized visually according to the datatype of the resource. This chapter has covered only the handling of strings, but other categories exist (such as images, icons, audio files, miscellaneous files, and other items). These options are illustrated in Figure 6-25.

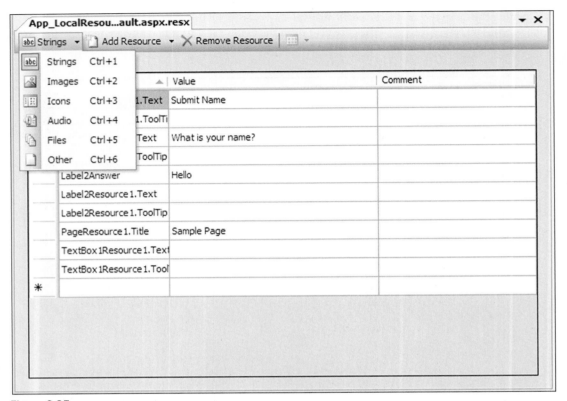

Figure 6-25

Summary

It is hoped that you see the value in localizing your .NET applications so that they can handle multiple cultures. This chapter described some of the issues you face when localizing your applications and looked at some of the built-in tools provided via both Visual Studio and the .NET Framework to make this process easier for you.

7

Generics

One of the things developers often need to do is create new types for their programs. Early attempts at type creation led to user-defined types, or the use of the VB `Structure` statement. Another approach is to use classes and objects to create new types. With the release of the .NET Framework 2.0, another approach is to use generics.

Generics refers to the technology built into the .NET Framework 2.0 that enables you to define a code template and then declare variables using that template. The template defines the operations that the new type can perform; and when you declare a variable based on the template, you are creating a new type. The benefit of generics over structures or objects is that a generic template makes it easier for your new types to be strongly typed. Generics also make it easier to reuse the template code in different scenarios.

The primary motivation for adding generics to .NET was to enable the creation of strongly typed collection types. Because generic collection types are strongly typed, they are significantly faster than the previous inheritance-based collection model. Anywhere you presently use collection classes in your code, you should consider revising that code to use generic collection types instead.

Visual Basic 2005 allows not only the use of preexisting generics, but also the creation of your own generic templates. Because the technology to support generics was created primarily to build collection classes, it naturally follows that you might create a generic collection anytime you would otherwise build a normal collection class. More specifically, anytime you find yourself using the `Object` datatype, you should instead consider using generics.

This chapter begins with a brief discussion of the use of generics, followed by a walkthrough of the syntax for defining your own generic templates.

Using Generics

There are many examples of generic templates in the .NET 2.0 Base Class Library (BCL). Many of them can be found in the `System.Collections.Generic` namespace, but others are scattered through the BCL as appropriate. Many of the examples focus on generic collection types, but this is only because it is here that the performance gains due to generics are most notable. In other cases, generics are used less for performance gains than for the strong typing benefits they provide. As noted earlier, anytime you use a collection datatype, you should consider using the generic equivalent instead.

A generic is often written as something like `List(Of T)`. The type (or class) name in this case is `List`. The letter `T` is a placeholder, much like a parameter. It indicates where you must provide a specific type value to customize the generic. For instance, you might declare a variable using the `List(Of T)` generic:

```
Dim data As New List(Of Date)
```

In this case, you're specifying that the type parameter, `T`, is a `Date`. By providing this type, you are specifying that the list will only contain values of type `Date`. To make this clearer, let's contrast the new `List(Of T)` collection with the older `ArrayList` type.

When you work with an `ArrayList`, you are working with a type of collection that can store many types of values at the same time:

```
Dim data As New ArrayList()
data.Add("Hello")
data.Add(5)
data.Add(New Customer())
```

This `ArrayList` is loosely typed, internally always storing the values as type `Object`. This is very flexible, but relatively slow because it is late bound. Of course, it offers the advantage of being able to store any datatype, with the disadvantage that you have no control over what's actually stored in the collection.

The `List(Of T)` generic collection is quite different. It isn't a type at all; it is just a template. A type isn't created until you declare a variable using the template:

```
Dim data As New Generic.List(Of Integer)
data.Add(5)
data.Add(New Customer()) ' throws an exception
data.Add("Hello") ' throws an exception
```

When you declare a variable using the generic, you must provide the type of value that the new collection will hold. The result is that a new type is created — in this case, a collection that can only hold `Integer` values.

The important thing here is that this new collection type is strongly typed for `Integer` values. Not only does its external interface (its `Item` and `Add` methods, for instance) require `Integer` values, but its internal storage mechanism only works with type `Integer`. This means that it is not late bound like `ArrayList`, but rather is early bound. The net result is much higher performance, along with all the type-safety benefits of being strongly typed.

Generics are useful because they typically offer a higher performance option compared to traditional classes. In some cases, they can also save you from writing code, as generic templates can provide code reuse where traditional classes cannot. Finally, generics can sometimes provide better type safety compared to traditional classes, as a generic adapts to the specific type you require, while classes often must resort to working with a more general type such as Object.

Note that generics come in two forms: generic types and generic methods. For instance, List(Of T) is a generic type in that it is a template that defines a complete type or class. In contrast, some otherwise normal classes have single methods that are just method templates and that assume a specific type when they are called. We'll look at both scenarios.

Generic Types

Now that you have a basic understanding of generics and how they compare to regular types, let's get into some more detail. To do this, you'll make use of some other generic types provided in the .NET Framework. A generic type is a template that defines a complete class, structure, or interface. When you want to use such a generic, you declare a variable using the generic type, providing the real type (or types) to be used in creating the actual type of your variable.

Basic Usage

To begin, create a new Windows Application project named Generics. On Form1 add a Button (named btnDictionary) and a TextBox control (named txtDisplay). Set the TextBox control's Multiline property to True and anchor it to take up most of the form. The result should look something like what is shown in Figure 7-1.

Figure 7-1

First, consider the Dictionary(Of K, T) generic. This is much like the List(Of T) discussed earlier, but this generic requires that you define the types of both the key data and the values to be stored. When you declare a variable as Dictionary(Of K, T), the new Dictionary type that is created only accepts keys of the one type and values of the other.

Add the following code in the `click` event handler for `btnDictionary`:

```
txtDisplay.Clear()

Dim data As New Generic.Dictionary(Of Integer, String)
data.Add(5, "Rocky")
data.Add(15, "Mary")

For Each item As KeyValuePair(Of Integer, String) In data
  txtDisplay.AppendText("Data: " & item.Key & ", " & item.Value)
  txtDisplay.AppendText(Environment.NewLine)
Next

txtDisplay.AppendText(Environment.NewLine)
```

As you type, watch the IntelliSense information on the `Add` method. Notice how the key and value parameters are strongly typed based on the specific types provided in the declaration of the `data` variable. In the same code, you can create another type of `Dictionary`:

```
txtDisplay.Clear()

Dim data As New Generic.Dictionary(Of Integer, String)

Dim info As New Generic.Dictionary(Of Guid, Date)
data.Add(5, "Rocky")
data.Add(15, "Mary")

For Each item As KeyValuePair(Of Integer, String) In data
  txtDisplay.AppendText("Data: " & item.Key & ", " & item.Value)
  txtDisplay.AppendText(Environment.NewLine)
Next

info.Add(Guid.NewGuid, Now)

For Each item As KeyValuePair(Of Guid, Date) In info
  txtDisplay.AppendText("Info: " & item.Key.ToString & ", " & item.Value)
  txtDisplay.AppendText(Environment.NewLine)
Next

txtDisplay.AppendText(Environment.NewLine)
```

This code contains two completely different types. Both have the behaviors of a `Dictionary`, but they are not interchangeable because they have been created as different types.

Generic types may also be used as parameters and return types. For instance, add the following method to `Form1`:

```
Private Function LoadData() As Generic.Dictionary(Of Integer, String)
  Dim data As New Generic.Dictionary(Of Integer, String)
  data.Add(5, "Rocky")
  data.Add(15, "Mary")

  Return data
End Function
```

To call this method from the `btnDictionary_Click` method, add this code:

```
Dim results As Generic.Dictionary(Of Integer, String)
results = LoadData()

For Each item As KeyValuePair(Of Integer, String) In results
  txtDisplay.AppendText("Results: " & item.Key & ", " & item.Value)
  txtDisplay.AppendText(Environment.NewLine)
Next

txtDisplay.AppendText(Environment.NewLine)
```

The results of running this code are shown in Figure 7-2.

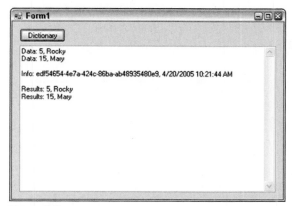

Figure 7-2

The reason why this works is because both the return type of the function and the type of the data variable are exactly the same. Not only are they both `Generic.Dictionary` derivatives, they have exactly the same types in the declaration.

The same is true for parameters:

```
Private Sub DoWork(ByVal values As Generic.Dictionary(Of Integer, String))
  ' do work here
End Sub
```

Again, the parameter type is not only defined by the generic type but also by the specific type values used to initialize the generic template.

Inheritance

It is possible to inherit from a generic type as you define a new class. For instance, the .NET BCL defines the `System.ComponentModel.BindingList(Of T)` generic type. This type is used to create collections that can support data binding. You can use this as a base class to create your own strongly typed, data-bindable collection. Add new classes named `Customer` and `CustomerList` to the project with the following code:

```
Public Class Customer
  Private mName As String

  Public Property Name() As String
    Get
      Return mName
    End Get
    Set(ByVal value As String)
      mName = value
    End Set
  End Property

End Class

Public Class CustomerList
  Inherits System.ComponentModel.BindingList(Of Customer)

  Private Sub CustomerList_AddingNew(ByVal sender As Object, _
    ByVal e As System.ComponentModel.AddingNewEventArgs) Handles Me.AddingNew

    Dim cust As New Customer
    cust.Name = "<new>"
    e.NewObject = cust

  End Sub
End Class
```

When you inherit from `BindingList(Of T)`, you must provide a specific type — in this case, `Customer`. This means that your new `CustomerList` class extends and can customize `BindingList(Of Customer)`. Here you're providing a default value for the `Name` property of any new `Customer` object added to the collection.

When you inherit from a generic type, you can employ all the normal concepts of inheritance, including overloading and overriding methods, extending the class by adding new methods, handling events, and so forth.

To see this in action, add a new `Button` named `btnCustomer` to `Form1` and add a new form named `CustomerForm` to the project. Add a `DataGridView` control to `CustomerForm` and dock it Fill.

Behind `btnCustomer`, add the following code:

```
CustomerForm.ShowDialog()
```

Then add the following code behind `CustomerForm`:

```
Dim list As New CustomerList

Private Sub CustomerForm_Load(ByVal sender As System.Object, _
```

```
    ByVal e As System.EventArgs) Handles MyBase.Load

    DataGridView1.DataSource = list

End Sub
```

This code creates an instance of `CustomerList` and makes it the `DataSource` for the grid control. When you run the program and click the button to open the `CustomerForm`, notice that the grid contains a newly added `Customer` object. As you interact with the grid, new `Customer` objects are automatically added, with a default name of `<new>`. An example is shown in Figure 7-3.

Figure 7-3

All this functionality of adding new objects and setting the default `Name` value occurs because `CustomerList` inherits from `BindingList(Of Customer)`.

Generic Methods

A generic method is a single method that is called not only with conventional parameters, but also with type information that defines the method. Generic methods are far less common than generic types. Due to the extra syntax required to call a generic method, they are also less readable than a normal method.

A generic method may exist in any class or module; it doesn't need to be contained within a generic type. The primary benefit of a generic method is avoiding the use of `CType` or `DirectCast` to convert parameters or return values between different types.

It is important to realize that the type conversion still occurs; generics merely provide an alternative mechanism to use instead of `CType` or `DirectCast`.

Without generics, code often uses the `Object` type. Add the following method to `Form1`:

```
Private Function AreEqual(ByVal a As Object, ByVal b As Object) As Boolean
    Return a.Equals(b)
End Function
```

The problem with this code is that a and b could be anything. There's no restriction here, nothing to ensure that they are even the same type. An alternative is to use generics. Add the following method to Form1:

```
Public Function AreEqual(Of T)(ByVal a As T, ByVal b As T) As Boolean
   Return a.Equals(b)
End Function
```

Now a and b are forced to be the same type, and that type is specified when the method is invoked.

Add a new Button named btnEqual to Form1 with the following code in its click event:

```
Dim result As Boolean

' use normal method
result = AreEqual(1, 2)
result = AreEqual("one", "two")
result = AreEqual(1, "two")

' use generic method
result = AreEqual(Of Integer)(1, 2)
result = AreEqual(Of String)("one", "two")
'result = AreEqual(Of Integer)(1, "two")
```

However, why not just declare the method as a Boolean? This code will probably cause some confusion.

The first three method calls are invoking the normal AreEqual() method. Notice that there's no problem asking the method to compare an Integer and a String.

The second set of calls looks very odd. At first glance, they look like nonsense to many people. This is because invoking a generic method means providing two sets of parameters to the method, rather than the normal one set of parameters.

The first set of parameters defines the type or types required to define the method. This is much like the list of types you must provide when declaring a variable using a generic class. In this case, you're specifying that the AreEqual() method will be operating on parameters of type Integer.

The second set of parameters are the conventional parameters that you'd normally supply to a method. What is special in this case is that the types of the parameters are being defined by the first set of parameters. In other words, in the first call, the type is specified to be Integer, so 1 and 2 are valid parameters. In the second call, the type is String, so "one" and "two" are valid. Notice that the third line is commented out. This is because 1 and "two" aren't the same type, so the compiler won't compile that line of code.

Creating Generics

Now that you have a good idea how to use preexisting generics in your code, let's take a look at how you can create generic templates. The primary reason to create a generic template instead of a class is to gain strong typing of your variables. Anytime you find yourself using the Object datatype, or a base class from which multiple types inherit, you may want to consider using generics. By using generics you can avoid the use of `CType` or `DirectCast`, which simplifies your code. If you are able to avoid using the `Object` datatype, you'll typically improve the performance of your code.

As discussed earlier, there are generic types and generic methods. A generic type is basically a class or structure that assumes specific type characteristics when a variable is declared using the generic. A generic method is a single method that assumes specific type characteristics, even though the method might be in an otherwise totally conventional class, structure, or module.

Generic Types

Recall that a generic type is a class, structure, or interface template. You can create such templates yourself to provide better performance, strong typing, and code reuse to the consumers of your types.

Classes

A generic class template is created in the same way that you create a normal class, with the exception that you require the consumer of your class to provide you with one or more types for use in your code. In other words, as the author of a generic template, you have access to the type parameters provided by the user of your generic.

For example, add a new class to the project named `SingleLinkedList`:

```
Public Class SingleLinkedList(Of T)

End Class
```

In the declaration of the type, you specify the type parameters that will be required:

```
Public Class SingleLinkedList(Of T)
```

In this case, you're requiring just one type parameter. The name, `T`, can be any valid variable name. In other words, you could declare the type like this:

```
Public Class SingleLinkedList(Of ValueType)
```

Make this change to the code in your project.

> *By convention (carried over from C++ templates), the variable names for type parameters are single uppercase letters. This is somewhat cryptic, and you may want to use a more descriptive convention for variable naming.*

Whether you use the cryptic standard convention or more readable parameter names, the parameter is defined on the class definition. Within the class itself, you then use the type parameter anywhere that you would normally use a type (such as `String` or `Integer`).

To create a linked list, you need to define a `Node` class. This will be a nested class (as discussed in Chapter 3):

```
Public Class SingleLinkedList(Of ValueType)
#Region " Node class "
```

```
Private Class Node
  Private mValue As ValueType
  Private mNext As Node

  Public ReadOnly Property Value() As ValueType
    Get
      Return mValue
    End Get
  End Property

  Public Property NextNode() As Node
    Get
      Return mNext
    End Get
    Set(ByVal value As Node)
      mNext = value
    End Set
  End Property

  Public Sub New(ByVal value As ValueType, ByVal nextNode As Node)
    mValue = value
    mNext = nextNode
  End Sub
End Class

#End Region
End Class
```

Notice how the `mValue` variable is declared as `ValueType`. This means that the actual type of `mValue` depends on the type supplied when an instance of `SingleLinkedList` is created.

Because `ValueType` is a type parameter on the class, you can use `ValueType` as a type anywhere in the code. As you write the class, you can't tell what type `ValueType` will be. That information is provided by the user of your generic class. Later, when someone declares a variable using your generic type, that person will specify the type, like this:

```
Dim list As New SingleLinkedList(Of Double)
```

At this point, a specific instance of your generic class is created, and all cases of `ValueType` within your code are replaced by the VB compiler with `Double`. Essentially, this means that for this specific instance of `SingleLinkedList`, the `mValue` declaration ends up as follows:

```
Private mValue As Double
```

Of course, you never get to see this code, as it is dynamically generated by the .NET Framework's JIT compiler at runtime based on your generic template code.

The same is true for methods within the template. Your example contains a constructor method, which accepts a parameter of type `ValueType`. Remember that `ValueType` will be replaced by a specific type when a variable is declared using your generic.

So, what type is ValueType when you're writing the template itself? Because it can conceivably be any type when the template is used, ValueType is treated like the Object type as you create the generic template. This severely restricts what you can do with variables or parameters of ValueType within your generic code.

The mValue variable is of ValueType, which means it is basically of type Object for the purposes of your template code. Therefore, you can do assignments (as you do in the constructor code), and you can call any methods that are on the System.Object type:

❑   Equals()

❑   GetHashValue()

❑   GetType()

❑   ToString()

No operations beyond these basics are available by default. Later in the chapter, you'll learn about the concept of *constraints*, which enables you to restrict the types that can be specified for a type parameter. Constraints have the added benefit that they expand the operations you can perform on variables or parameters defined based on the type parameter.

However, this capability is enough to complete the SingleLinkedList class. Add the following code to the class after the End Class from the Node class:

```
Private mHead As Node

Default Public ReadOnly Property Item(ByVal index As Integer) As ValueType
  Get
    Dim current As Node = mHead

    For index = 1 To index
      current = current.NextNode
      If current Is Nothing Then
        Throw New Exception("Item not found in list")
      End If
    Next

    Return current.Value
  End Get
End Property

Public Sub Add(ByVal value As ValueType)
  mHead = New Node(value, mHead)
End Sub

Public Sub Remove(ByVal value As ValueType)

  Dim current As Node = mHead
  Dim previous As Node = Nothing

  While current IsNot Nothing
    If current.Value.Equals(value) Then
```

```
          If previous Is Nothing Then
            ' this was the head of the list
            mHead = current.NextNode
          Else
            previous.NextNode = current.NextNode
          End If
          Exit Sub
        End If
        previous = current
        current = current.NextNode
      End While

      ' You got to the end without finding the item.
      Throw New Exception("Item not found in list")

    End Sub

    Public ReadOnly Property Count() As Integer
      Get
        Dim result As Integer = 0
        Dim current As Node = mHead

        While current IsNot Nothing
          result += 1
          current = current.NextNode
        End While

        Return result
      End Get
    End Property
```

Notice that the `Item` property and the `Add()` and `Remove()` methods all use `ValueType` either as return types or parameter types. More important, note the use of the `Equals` method in the `Remove()` method:

```
    If current.Value.Equals(value) Then
```

The reason why this compiles is because `Equals` is defined on `System.Object` and is therefore universally available. This code could not use the = operator, because that isn't universally available.

To try out the `SingleLinkedList` class, add a button to `Form1` named `btnList` and add the following code to `Form1`:

```
  Private Sub btnList_Click(ByVal sender As System.Object, _
    ByVal e As System.EventArgs) Handles btnList.Click

    Dim list As New SingleLinkedList(Of String)
    list.Add("Rocky")
    list.Add("Mary")
    list.Add("Erin")
    list.Add("Edward")
    list.Add("Juan")
    list.Remove("Erin")
```

```
      txtDisplay.Clear()
      txtDisplay.AppendText("Count: " & list.Count)
      txtDisplay.AppendText(Environment.NewLine)

      For index As Integer = 0 To list.Count - 1
        txtDisplay.AppendText("Item: " & list.Item(index))
        txtDisplay.AppendText(Environment.NewLine)
      Next

    End Sub
```

When you run the code, you'll see a display similar to Figure 7-4.

Figure 7-4

Other Generic Class Features

Earlier in the chapter, you used the `Dictionary` generic, which specifies multiple type parameters. To declare a class with multiple type parameters, you use syntax like the following:

```
Public Class MyCoolType(Of T, V)
  Private mValue As T
  Private mData As V

  Public Sub New(ByVal value As T, ByVal data As V)
    mValue = value
    mData = data
  End Sub
End Class
```

In addition, it is possible to use regular types in combination with type parameters, as shown here:

```
Public Class MyCoolType(Of T, V)
  Private mValue As T
  Private mData As V
  Private mActual As Double
```

```
      Public Sub New(ByVal value As T, ByVal data As V, ByVal actual As Double)
        mValue = value
        mData = data
        mActual = actual
      End Sub
    End Class
```

Other than the fact that variables or parameters of types T or V must be treated as type System.Object, you can write virtually any code you choose. The code in a generic class is really no different from the code you'd write in a normal class.

This includes all the object-oriented capabilities of classes, including inheritance, overloading, overriding, events, methods, properties, and so forth. However, there are some limitations on overloading. In particular, when overloading methods with a type parameter, the compiler doesn't know what that specific type might be at runtime. Thus, you can only overload methods in ways in which the type parameter (that could be any type) doesn't lead to ambiguity.

For instance, adding these two methods to MyCoolType will result in a compiler error:

```
    Public Sub DoWork(ByVal data As Integer)
      ' do work here
    End Sub

    Public Sub DoWork(ByVal data As V)
      ' do work here
    End Sub
```

This isn't legal because the compiler can't know whether V will be Integer at runtime. If V were to end up defined as Integer, then you'd have two identical method signatures in the same class. Likewise, the following is not legal:

```
    Public Sub DoWork(ByVal value As T)
      ' do work here
    End Sub

    Public Sub DoWork(ByVal data As V)
      ' do work here
    End Sub
```

Again, there's no way for the compiler to be sure that T and V will represent different types at runtime. However, you can declare overloaded methods like this:

```
    Public Sub DoWork(ByVal data As Integer)
      ' do work here
    End Sub

    Public Sub DoWork(ByVal value As T, ByVal data As V)
      ' do work here
    End Sub
```

This works because there's no possible ambiguity between the two method signatures. Regardless of what types T and V end up as, there's no way the two DoWork() methods can have the same signature.

Classes and Inheritance

Not only can you create basic generic class templates, you can also combine the concept with inheritance. This can be as basic as having a generic template inherit from an existing class:

```
Public Class MyControls(Of T)
   Inherits Control

End Class
```

In this case, the MyControls generic class inherits from the Windows Forms Control class, thus gaining all the behaviors and interface elements of a Control.

Alternately, a conventional class can inherit from a generic template. Suppose that you have a simple generic template:

```
Public Class GenericBase(Of T)

End Class
```

It is quite practical to inherit from this generic class as you create other classes:

```
Public Class Subclass
   Inherits GenericBase(Of Integer)

End Class
```

Notice how the Inherits statement not only references GenericBase, but also provides a specific type for the type parameter of the generic type. Anytime you use a generic type, you must provide values for the type parameters, and this is no exception. This means that your new Subclass actually inherits from a specific instance of GenericBase where T is of type Integer.

Finally, you can also have generic classes inherit from other generic classes. For instance, you can create a generic class that inherits from the GenericBase class:

```
Public Class GenericSubclass(Of T)
   Inherits GenericBase(Of Integer)

End Class
```

As with the previous example, this new class inherits from an instance of GenericBase where T is of type Integer.

Things can get far more interesting. It turns out that you can use type parameters to specify the types for other type parameters. For instance, you could alter GenericSubclass like this:

```
Public Class GenericSubclass(Of V)
   Inherits GenericBase(Of V)

End Class
```

Notice that you're specifying that the type parameter for `GenericBase` is `V` — which is the type provided by the caller when it declares a variable using `GenericSubclass`. Therefore, if a caller does

```
Dim obj As GenericSubclass(Of String)
```

then `V` is of type `String`, meaning that `GenericSubclass` is inheriting from an instance of `GenericBase` where its `T` parameter is also of type `String`. The type flows through from the subclass into the base class.

If that's not complex enough, consider the following class definition:

```
Public Class GenericSubclass(Of V)
  Inherits GenericBase(GenericSubclass(Of V))

End Class
```

In this case, the `GenericSubclass` is inheriting from `GenericBase`, where the `T` type in `GenericBase` is actually a specific instance of the `GenericSubclass` type. A caller can create such an instance as follows:

```
Dim obj As GenericSubclass(Of Date)
```

In this case, the `GenericSubclass` type has a `V` of type `Date`. It also inherits from `GenericBase`, which has a `T` of type `GenericSubclass(Of Date)`.

Such complex relationships are typically not useful, but it is important to recognize how types flow through generic templates, especially when inheritance is involved.

Structures

You can also define generic `Structure` types. Structures are discussed in Chapter 2. The basic rules and concepts are the same as for defining generic classes, as shown here:

```
Public Structure MyCoolStructure(Of T)
  Public Value As T
End Structure
```

As with generic classes, the type parameter or parameters represent real types that will be provided by the user of the structure in actual code. Thus, anywhere you see a `T` in the structure, it will be replaced by a real type such as `String` or `Integer`.

Code can use the structure in a manner similar to how a generic class is used:

```
Dim data As MyCoolStructure(Of Guid)
```

When the variable is declared, an instance of the `Structure` is created based on the type parameter provided. In this example, an instance of `MyCoolStructure` that holds `Guid` objects has been created.

Interfaces

Finally, you can define generic interface types. Generic interfaces are a bit different from generic classes or structures, because they are implemented by other types when they are used. You can create a generic interface using the same syntax used for classes and structures:

```
Public Interface ICoolInterface(Of T)
  Public Sub DoWork(ByVal data As T)
  Public Function GetAnswer() As T
End Interface
```

Then the interface can be used within another type. For instance, you might implement the interface in a class:

```
Public Class ARegularClass
  Implements ICoolInterface(Of String)

  Public Sub DoWork(ByVal data As String) _
   Implements ICoolInterface(Of String).DoWork

  End Sub

  Public Function GetAnswer() As String _
    Implements ICoolInterface(Of String).GetAnswer

  End Function

End Class
```

Notice that you provide a real type for the type parameter in the `Implements` statement and `Implements` clauses on each method. In each case, you're specifying a specific instance of the `ICoolInterface` interface — one that deals with the `String` datatype.

As with classes and structures, an interface can be declared with multiple type parameters. Those type parameter values can be used in place of any normal type (such as `String` or `Date`) in any `Sub`, `Function`, `Property`, or `Event` declaration.

Generic Methods

You've already seen examples of methods declared using type parameters such as `T` or `V`. While these are examples of generic methods, they've been contained within a broader generic type such as a class, structure, or interface.

It is also possible to create generic methods within otherwise normal classes, structures, interfaces, or modules. In this case, the type parameter isn't specified on the class, structure, or interface, but rather is specified directly on the method itself.

For instance, you can declare a generic method to compare equality like this:

```
Public Module Comparisons
```

```
     Public Function AreEqual(Of T)(ByVal a As T, ByVal b As T) As Boolean
       Return a.Equals(b)
     End Function

 End Module
```

In this case, the `AreEqual()` method is contained within a module, though it could just as easily be contained in a class or structure. Notice that the method accepts two sets of parameters. The first set of parameters is the type parameters, in this example just `T`. The second set of parameters consists of the normal parameters that a method would accept. In this example, the normal parameters have their types defined by the type parameter, `T`.

As with generic classes, it is important to remember that the type parameter is treated as a `System.Object` type as you write the code in your generic method. This severely restricts what you can do with parameters or variables declared using the type parameters. Specifically, you can perform assignment and call the four methods common to all `System.Object` variables.

In a moment you'll look at constraints, which enable you to restrict the types that can be assigned to the type parameters and expand the operations that can be performed on parameters and variables of those types.

As with generic types, a generic method can accept multiple type parameters:

```
 Public Class Comparisons

     Public Function AreEqual(Of T, R)(ByVal a As Integer, ByVal b As T) As R
       ' implement code here
     End Function

 End Class
```

In this example, the method is contained within a class, rather than a module. Notice that it accepts two type parameters, `T` and `R`. The return type is set to type `R`, whereas the second parameter is of type `T`. Also look at the first parameter, which is a conventional type. This illustrates how you can mix conventional types and generic type parameters in the method parameter list and return types, and by extension within the body of the method code.

Constraints

At this point, you've learned how to create and use generic types and methods, but there have been serious limitations on what you can do when creating generic type or method templates thus far. This is because the compiler treats any type parameters as the type `System.Object` within your template code. The result is that you can assign the values and call the four methods common to all `System.Object` instances, but you can do nothing else. In many cases, this is too restrictive to be useful.

Constraints offer a solution and at the same time provide a control mechanism. Constraints enable you to specify rules about the types that can be used at runtime to replace a type parameter. Using constraints, you can ensure that a type parameter is a `Class` or a `Structure`, or that it implements a certain interface or inherits from a certain base class.

Not only do constraints let you restrict the types available for use, but they also give the VB compiler valuable information. For example, if the compiler knows that a type parameter must always implement a given interface, then the compiler will allow you to call the methods on that interface within your template code.

Type Constraints

The most common type of constraint is a *type constraint*. A type constraint restricts a type parameter to be a subclass of a specific class or to implement a specific interface. This idea can be used to enhance the `SingleLinkedList` to sort items as they are added. First, change the declaration of the class itself to add the `IComparable` constraint:

```
Public Class SingleLinkedList(Of ValueType As IComparable)
```

With this change, `ValueType` is not only guaranteed to be equivalent to `System.Object`, it is also guaranteed to have all the methods defined on the `IComparable` interface.

This means that within the `Add()` method you can make use of any methods in the `IComparable` interface (as well as those from `System.Object`). The end result is that you can safely call the `CompareTo` method defined on the `IComparable` interface, because the compiler knows that any variable of type `ValueType` will implement `IComparable`:

```
Public Sub Add(ByVal value As ValueType)
  If mHead Is Nothing Then
    ' List was empty, just store the value.
    mHead = New Node(value, mHead)

  Else
    Dim current As Node = mHead
    Dim previous As Node = Nothing

    While current IsNot Nothing
      If current.Value.CompareTo(value) > 0 Then
        If previous Is Nothing Then
          ' this was the head of the list
          mHead = New Node(value, mHead)
        Else
          ' insert the node between previous and current
          previous.NextNode = New Node(value, current)
        End If
        Exit Sub
      End If
      previous = current
      current = current.NextNode
    End While

    ' you're at the end of the list, so add to end
    previous.NextNode = New Node(value, Nothing)
  End If
End Sub
```

Note the call to the `CompareTo()` method:

```
If current.Value.CompareTo(value) > 0 Then
```

This is possible because of the `IComparable` constraint on `ValueType`. If you run the code now, the items should be displayed in sorted order, as shown in Figure 7-5.

Figure 7-5

Not only can you constrain a type parameter to implement an interface, but you can also constrain it to be a specific type (class) or subclass of that type. For example, you could implement a generic method that works on any Windows Forms control:

```
Public Shared Sub ChangeControl(Of C As Control)(ByVal control As C)

    control.Anchor = AnchorStyles.Top Or AnchorStyles.Left

End Sub
```

The type parameter, `C`, is constrained to be of type `Control`. This restricts calling code to only specify this parameter as `Control` or a subclass of `Control` such as `TextBox`.

Then the parameter to the method is specified to be of type `C`, which means that this method will work against any `Control` or subclass of `Control`. Because of the constraint, the compiler now knows that the variable will always be some type of `Control` object, so it allows you to use any methods, properties, or events exposed by the `Control` class as you write your code.

Finally, it is possible to constrain a type parameter to be of a specific generic type:

```
Public Class ListClass(Of T, V As Generic.List(Of T))

End Class
```

The preceding code specifies that the V type must be a List(Of T), whatever type T might be. A caller can use your class like this:

```
Dim list As ListClass(Of Integer, Generic.List(Of Integer))
```

Earlier in the chapter, in the discussion of how inheritance and generics interact, you saw that things can get quite complex. The same is true when you constrain type parameters based on generic types.

Class and Structure Constraints

Another form of constraint enables you to be more general. Rather than enforce the requirement for a specific interface or class, you can specify that a type parameter must be either a reference type or a value type.

To specify that the type parameter must be a reference type, you use the Class constraint:

```
Public Class ReferenceOnly(Of T As Class)

End Class
```

This ensures that the type specified for T must be the type of an object. Any attempt to use a value type, such as Integer or Structure, results in a compiler error.

Likewise, you can specify that the type parameter must be a value type such as Integer or a Structure by using the Structure constraint:

```
Public Class ValueOnly(Of T As Structure)

End Class
```

In this case, the type specified for T must be a value type. Any attempt to use a reference type such as String, an interface, or a class results in a compiler error.

New Constraints

Sometimes you'll want to write generic code that creates instances of the type specified by a type parameter. In order to know that you can actually create instances of a type, you need to know that the type has a default public constructor. You can determine this using the New constraint:

```
Public Class Factories(Of T As New)

  Public Function CreateT() As T
    Return New T
  End Function

End Class
```

The type parameter, T, is constrained so that it must have a public default constructor. Any attempt to specify a type for T that doesn't have such a constructor will result in a compile error.

Because you know that T will have a default constructor, you are able to create instances of the type, as shown in the CreateT method.

Multiple Constraints

In many cases, you'll need to specify multiple constraints on the same type parameter. For instance, you might want to require that a type be a reference type and have a public default constructor.

Essentially, you're providing an array of constraints, so you use the same syntax you use to initialize elements of an array:

```
Public Class Factories(Of T As {New, Class})

   Public Function CreateT() As T
     Return New T
   End Function

End Class
```

The constraint list can include two or more constraints, letting you specify a great deal of information about the types allowed for this type parameter.

Within your generic template code, the compiler is aware of all the constraints applied to your type parameters, so it allows you to use any methods, properties, and events specified by any of the constraints applied to the type.

Generics and Late Binding

One of the primary limitations of generics is that variables and parameters declared based on a type parameter are treated as type System.Object inside your generic template code. While constraints offer a partial solution, expanding the type of those variables based on the constraints, you are still very restricted in what you can do with the variables.

One key example is the use of common operators. There's no constraint you can apply that tells the compiler that a type supports the + or – operators. This means that you can't write generic code like this:

```
Public Function Add(Of T)(ByVal val1 As T, ByVal val2 As T) As T
   Return val1 + val2
End Function
```

This will generate a compiler error because there's no way for the compiler to verify that variables of type T (whatever that is at runtime) support the + operator. Because there's no constraint that you can apply to T to ensure that the + operator will be valid, there's no direct way to use operators on variables of a generic type.

One alternative is to use Visual Basic's native support for late binding to overcome the limitations shown here. Recall that late binding incurs substantial performance penalties because a lot of work is done dynamically at runtime, rather than by the compiler when you build your project. It is also important to remember the risks that attend late binding — specifically, the fact that the code can fail at runtime in ways that early-bound code can't. Nonetheless, given those caveats, late binding can be used to solve your immediate problem.

To enable late binding, be sure to put Option Strict Off at the top of the code file containing your generic template (or set the project property to change Option Strict projectwide). Then you can rewrite the Add() function as follows:

```
Public Function Add(Of T)(ByVal val1 As T, ByVal val2 As T) As T
  Return CObj(value1) + CObj(value2)
End Function
```

By forcing the value1 and value2 variables to be explicitly treated as type Object, you're telling the compiler that it should use late binding semantics. Combined with the Option Strict Off setting, the compiler assumes that you know what you're doing and it allows the use of the + operator even though its validity can't be confirmed.

The compiled code uses dynamic late binding to invoke the + operator at runtime. If that operator does turn out to be valid for whatever type T is at runtime, then this code will work great. In contrast, if the operator is not valid, then a runtime exception will be thrown.

Summary

Generics enable you to create class, structure, interface, and method templates. These templates gain specific types based on how they are declared or called at runtime. Generics provide you with another code reuse mechanism, along with procedural and object-oriented concepts.

They also enable you to change code that uses parameters or variables of type Object (or other general types) to use specific datatypes. This often leads to much better performance and increases the readability of your code.

8

Namespaces

Even if you didn't realize it, you've been using namespaces since Chapter 2. For example, `System`, `System.Diagnostics`, and `System.Windows.Forms` are all namespaces contained within the .NET Framework. Namespaces are an easy concept to understand, but this chapter puts the ideas behind them on a firm footing — and clears up any misconceptions you might have about how they are used and organized.

If you're familiar with COM, you'll find that the concept of namespaces is the logical extension of programmatic identifier (`ProgID`) values. For example, the functionality of Visual Basic 6's `FileSystemObject` is now mostly encompassed in .NET's `System.IO` namespace, though this is not a one-to-one mapping. However, namespaces are about more than a change in name; they represent the logical extension of the COM naming structure, expanding its ease of use and extensibility.

In addition to the traditional `System` and `Microsoft` namespaces (for example, used in things such as Microsoft's Web Services Enhancements), .NET Framework 2.0 introduces a new way to get at some tough-to-find namespaces using the new `My` namespace. The `My` namespace is a powerful way of "speed-dialing" specific functionalities in the base.

This chapter covers the following:

- ❑ What namespaces are
- ❑ Which namespaces are used in Visual Studio 2005 projects by default
- ❑ Referencing namespaces and using the `Imports` statement
- ❑ How the compiler searches for class references
- ❑ How to alias namespaces
- ❑ Creating your own namespaces
- ❑ Using the new `My` namespace

What Is a Namespace?

Namespaces are a way of organizing the vast number of classes, structures, enumerations, delegates, and interfaces that the .NET Framework class library provides. Namespaces are a hierarchically structured index into a class library, which is available to all of the .NET languages, not only the Visual Basic 2005 language (with the exception of the new My namespace). The namespaces, or object references, are typically organized by function. For example, the System.IO namespace contains classes, structures, and interfaces for working with input/output streams and files. The classes in this namespace do not necessarily inherit from the same base classes (apart from Object, of course).

A namespace is a combination of a naming convention and an assembly, which organizes collections of objects and prevents ambiguity in object references. A namespace can be, and often is, implemented across several physical assemblies, but from the reference side it is the namespace that ties these assemblies together. A namespace consists of not only classes, but also other (child) namespaces. For example, IO is a child namespace of the System namespace.

Namespaces provide identification beyond the component name. With a namespace, it is possible to use a more meaningful title (for example, System) followed by a grouping (for example, Text) to group together a collection of classes that contain similar functions. For example, the System.Text namespace contains a powerful class called StringBuilder. To reference this class, you can use the fully qualified namespace reference of System.Text.StringBuilder, as shown here:

```
Dim sb As New System.Text.StringBuilder()
```

The structure of a namespace is not a reflection of the physical inheritance of classes that make up a namespace. For example, the System.Text namespace contains another child namespace called RegularExpressions. This namespace contains several classes, but they do not inherit or otherwise reference the classes that make up the System.Text namespace.

Figure 8-1 shows how the System namespace contains the Text child namespace, which also has a child namespace, called RegularExpressions. Both of these child namespaces, Text and Regular-Expressions, contain a number of objects in the inheritance model for these classes, as shown.

As you can see in Figure 8-1, while some of the classes in each namespace do inherit from each other, and while all of the classes eventually inherit from the generic Object, the classes in System.Text.RegularExpressions do not inherit from the classes in System.Text.

You may be wondering at this point what all the fuss is about. To emphasize the usefulness of namespaces, we can draw another good example from Figure 8-1. If you make a reference to System.Drawing.Imaging.Encoder in your application, then you are making a reference to a completely different Encoder class than the namespace shown in Figure 8-1 — System.Text.Encoder. Being able to clearly identify classes that have the same name though very different functions, and disambiguate them, is yet another advantage of namespaces.

If you are an experienced COM developer, you may note that unlike a ProgID, which is a one-level relationship between the project assembly and class, a single namespace can use child namespaces to extend the meaningful description of a class. The System namespace, imported by default as part of every project created with Visual Studio, contains not only the default Object class, but also many other classes that are used as the basis for every .NET language.

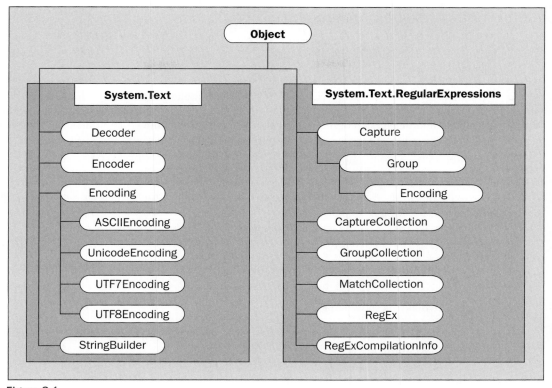

Figure 8-1

What if a class you need isn't available in your project? The problem may be with the references in your project. For example, by default, the System.DirectoryServices namespace, used for getting programmatic access to the Active Directory objects, isn't part of your project's assembly. Using it requires adding a reference to the project assembly. The concept of referencing a namespace is very similar to the ability to reference a COM object in VB6.

In fact, with all this talk about referencing, it's probably a good idea to look at an example of adding an additional namespace to a project. Before doing that, you need to know a little bit about how a namespace is actually implemented.

Namespaces are implemented within .NET assemblies. The System namespace is implemented in an assembly called System.dll provided with Visual Studio. By referencing this assembly, the project gains the ability to reference all of the child namespaces of System that happen to be implemented in this assembly. Using the preceding table, the project can import and use the System.Text namespace because its implementation is in the System.dll assembly. However, although it is listed, the project cannot import or use the System.Data namespace unless it references the assembly that implements this child of the System namespace, System.Data.dll.

Let's create a sample project so you can examine the role that namespaces play within it. Using Visual Studio 2005, create a new Visual Basic 2005 Windows Application project called Namespace_Sampler.

The `Microsoft.VisualBasic.Compatibility.VB6` library isn't part of Visual Basic 2005 projects by default. To gain access to the classes that this namespace provides, you need to add it to your project. You can do this by using the Add Reference dialog box (available by right-clicking the Project name node within the Visual Studio Solution Explorer). The Add Reference dialog box has five tabs, each containing elements that can be referenced from your project:

❑ The first tab, with the title of .NET, contains .NET assemblies that can be found in the GAC. In addition to providing you with the name of the assembly, you can also get the version of the assembly and the version of the framework to which the assembly is compiled. The final data point found in this tab is the location of the assembly on the machine.

❑ The second tab, COM, contains all the available COM components. This tab provides the name of the component, the TypeLib version, and the path of the component.

❑ The third tab, Projects, contains any custom .NET assemblies from any of the various projects contained within your solution.

❑ The fourth tab, Browse, enables you to look for any component files (`.dll`, `.tlb`, `.olb`, `.ocx`, `.exe`, or `.manifest`) that are on the network.

❑ The last and fifth tab, Recent, lists the most recently made references for quick referencing capabilities.

The Add Reference dialog is shown in Figure 8-2.

Figure 8-2

The available .NET namespaces are listed by *component name*. This is the same as the namespace name. Within the dialog you can see a few columns that supply the namespace of the component, the version number of the component, the version of the .NET Framework for which the particular component is targeted, and the path location of the file. You can select a single namespace to make a reference to by clicking your mouse on the component that you are interested in. Holding down the Ctrl key and pressing the mouse button enables you to select multiple namespaces to reference.

To select a range of namespaces, first click on either the first or last component in the dialog that is contained in the range, and then complete the range selection by holding down the Shift key and using the mouse to select the other component in the range. Once you have selected all the components that you are interested in referencing, press the OK button.

The example in Figure 8-2 is importing some namespaces from the `Microsoft.VisualBasic` namespace, even though only one selection has been made. This implementation, while a bit surprising at first, is very powerful. First, it shows the extensibility of namespaces. This is due to the fact that the single `Microsoft.VisualBasic.Compatibility.VB6` namespace is actually implemented in two separate assemblies. If you also make a reference to the `Microsoft.VisualBasic.Compatibility` namespace as well as the `Microsoft.VisualBasic.Compatibility.Data` namespace, you will see (through the Object Browser found in Visual Studio) that the `Microsoft.VisualBasic.Compatibility.VB6` namespace is really found in both locations. This is shown in Figure 8-3.

Figure 8-3

Second, this implementation is powerful in that it enables you to include only the classes that you need — in this case, those that are related to the VB6 (Visual Basic 6) environment or to database tools, or both types. Note some interesting points about the `Microsoft.VisualBasic` namespace. First, this namespace gives you access to all the functions that VB6 developers have had for years. Microsoft has implemented these in the .NET Framework and made them available for your use within your .NET projects. Because these functions have been implemented in the .NET Framework, there is absolutely no performance hit for using them, but you will most likely find the functionality that they provide available to you in newer .NET namespaces. Contrary to what the name of the namespace suggests, this namespace is available for use by all of the .NET languages, which means that even a C# developer could use the `Microsoft.VisualBasic` namespace if desired.

Namespaces and References

Highlighting their importance to every project, references (including namespaces) are no longer hidden from view — available only after opening a dialog box as they were in VB6. As shown in the Solution Explorer window in Figure 8-4, every new project comes with a set of referenced namespaces. (If you don't see the references listed in Solution Explorer, press the Show All Files button from the Solution Explorer menu.)

Figure 8-4

The list of default references varies based on the type of project. The example in Figure 8-4 shows the default references for a Windows Forms project in Visual Studio 2005. If the project type is an ASP.NET Web Application, the list of references changes appropriately — the reference to the `System.Windows.Forms` namespace assembly is replaced by a reference to `System.Web`. If the project type is an ASP.NET Web Service (not shown), then the `System.Windows.Forms` namespace is replaced by references to the `System.Web` and `System.Web.Services` namespaces.

In addition to making the namespaces available, references play a second important role in your project. One of the advantages of .NET is using services and components built on the common language runtime (CLR), which enables you to avoid DLL conflicts. The various problems that can occur related to DLL versioning, commonly referred to as DLL hell, involve two types of conflict.

The first situation occurs when you have a component that requires a minimum DLL version, and an older version of the same DLL causes your product to break. The alternative situation is when you require an older version of a DLL, and a new version is incompatible. In either case, the result is that a shared file, outside of your control, creates a systemwide dependency that impacts your software. As part of .NET, it is possible, but not required, to indicate that a DLL should be shipped as part of your project to avoid an external dependency.

To indicate that a referenced component should be included locally, you can select the reference in Solution Explorer and then examine the properties associated with that reference. One editable property is called `Copy Local`. You will see this property and its value in the Properties window within Visual Studio 2005. For those assemblies that are part of a Visual Studio 2005 installation, this value defaults to `False`. However, for custom references, this property defaults to `True` to indicate that the referenced DLL should be included as part of the assembly. Changing this property to `True` changes the path associated with the assembly. Instead of using the path to the referenced file's location on the system, the project creates a subdirectory based on the reference name and places the files required for the implementation of the reference in this subdirectory, as shown in Figure 8-5.

Figure 8-5

The benefit of this is that even when another version of the DLL is later placed on the system, your project's assembly will continue to function. However, this protection from a conflicting version comes at a price: Future updates to the namespace assembly to fix flaws will be in the system version but not in the private version that is part of your project's assembly.

To resolve this, Microsoft's solution is to place new versions in directories based on their version information. If you examine the path information for all of the Visual Studio 2005 references, you will see that it includes a version number. As new versions of these DLLs are released, they are installed in a separate directory. This method allows for an escape from DLL hell, by keeping new versions from stomping on old versions, and it enables old versions to be easily located for maintenance updates. For this reason, in many cases it is better to leave alone the default behavior of Visual Studio 2005, which is set to copy only locally custom components, until your organization implements a directory structure with version information similar to that of Microsoft.

The Visual Basic 2005 compiler will not allow you to add a reference to your assembly if the targeted implementation includes a reference that isn't also referenced in your assembly. The good news is that the compiler will help. If, after adding a reference, that reference doesn't appear in the IntelliSense list generated by Visual Studio 2005, go ahead and type the reference to a class from that reference. The compiler will flag it with one of its Microsoft Word–like spelling or grammar error underlines. Then, when you click the underlined text, the compiler will tell you which other assemblies need to be referenced in the project in order to use the class in question.

Common Namespaces

The generated list of references shown in Solution Explorer for the newly created `Namespace_Sampler` project includes most, but not all, of the namespaces that are part of your Windows Application project. For example, one namespace not displayed as a reference is `Microsoft.VisualBasic` and the accompanying `Microsoft.VisualBasic.dll`. Every Visual Basic 2005 project includes the namespace `Microsoft.VisualBasic`. This namespace is part of the Visual Studio project templates for Visual Basic 2005 and is, in short, what makes Visual Basic 2005 different from C# or any other .NET language. The implicit inclusion of this namespace is the reason why you can call `IsDBNull` and other methods of Visual Basic 2005 directly. The only difference in the default namespaces that are included with Visual Basic 2005 and C# Windows Application projects is that the former use `Microsoft.VisualBasic` and the latter use `Microsoft.CSharp`.

To see all of the namespaces that are imported automatically, such as the `Microsoft.VisualBasic` namespace, right-click the project name in Solution Explorer and select Properties from the context menu. This opens the project properties in the Visual Studio document window. Select the References tab from the left pane and you will see the reference `Microsoft.VisualBasic` at the top of the list (see Figure 8-6).

When looking at the project's global list of imports in the text area at the bottom of the page, you can see that in addition to the `Microsoft.VisualBasic` namespace, the `System.Collections` and `System.Diagnostics` namespaces are also imported into the project. This is signified by the check marks next to the namespace. Unlike the other namespaces in the list, these namespaces are not listed as references in the text area directly above this. That is because the implementation of the `System.Collections` and `System.Diagnostics` namespaces is part of the referenced `System.dll`. Similarly to `Microsoft.VisualBasic`, importing these namespaces allows references to the associated classes, such that a fully qualified path is not required. Because these namespaces contain commonly used classes, it is worthwhile to always include them at the project level.

The following list briefly summarizes some of the namespaces commonly used in Visual Basic 2005 projects:

- ❑ `System.Collections` — Contains the classes that support various feature-rich object collections. Included automatically, it has classes for arrays, lists, dictionaries, queues, hash tables, and so on. As of .NET 2.0, this namespace also includes the capability to work with the new generics — a way to build type-safe collections as well as provide generic methods and classes.

- ❑ `System.Data` — This namespace contains the classes to support the core features of ADO.NET.

- ❑ `System.Diagnostics` — Included in all Visual Basic 2005 projects, this namespace includes the debugging classes. The `Trace` and `Debug` classes provide the primary capabilities, but the namespace contains dozens of classes to support debugging.

- ❑ `System.Drawing` — This namespace contains simple drawing classes to support Windows Application projects.

Figure 8-6

- ❑ System.EnterpriseServices — Not included automatically, the System.EnterpriseServices implementation must be referenced to make it available. This namespace contains the classes that interface .NET assemblies with COM+.

- ❑ System.IO — This namespace contains important classes that enable you to read and write to files as well as data streams.

- ❑ System.Text — This commonly used namespace enables you to work with text in a number of different ways, usually in regard to string manipulation. One of the more popular objects that this namespace offers is the StringBuilder object.

- ❑ System.Threading — This namespace contains the objects to work with and manipulate threads within your application.

- ❑ System.Web — This is the namespace that deals with one of the more exciting features of the .NET Framework, ASP.NET. This namespace provides the objects that deal with browser-server communications. Two main objects include HttpRequest, which deals with the request from the client to the server, and HttpResponse, which deals with the response from the server to the client.

❑ `System.Web.Services` — This is the main namespace you use when you are creating XML Web Services, one of the more powerful capabilities provided with the .NET Framework. This namespace offers the classes that deal with SOAP messages and the manipulation of these messages.

❑ `System.Windows.Forms` — The namespace that provides classes to create Windows Forms in Windows Application projects. This namespace contains the form elements.

Of course, to really make use of the classes and other objects in this list, you need more detailed information. In addition to resources such as Visual Studio 2005's help files, the best source of information is the Object Browser. It is available directly in the Visual Studio 2005 IDE. You can find it by selecting View ➪ Object Browser if you are using Visual Studio 2005 or 2003, or View ➪ Other Windows ➪ Object Browser if you are using Visual Studio 2002. The Visual Studio 2005 Object Browser is shown in Figure 8-7.

The Object Browser displays each of the referenced assemblies and allows you to drill down into the various namespaces. Figure 8-7 illustrates how the `System.dll` implements a number of namespaces, including some that are part of the `System` namespace. By drilling down into a namespace, you can see some of the classes available. By further selecting a class, the browser shows not only the methods and properties associated with the selected class, but also a brief outline of what that class does.

Using the Object Browser is an excellent way to gain insight into which classes and interfaces are available via the different assemblies included in your project, and how they work. Clearly, the ability to actually see which classes are available and know how to use them is important in being able to work efficiently. Working effectively in the .NET CLR environment requires finding the right class for the task.

Figure 8-7

Importing and Aliasing Namespaces

Not all namespaces should be imported at the global level. Although you have looked at the namespaces that are included at this level, it is much better to import namespaces only in the module where they will be used. Importing a namespace at the module level does not change setting the reference, but it does mean that you don't add it into the list of imports on the project's property page. As with variables used in a project, it is possible to define a namespace at the module level. The advantage of this is similar to the use of local variables in that it helps to prevent different namespaces from interfering with each other. As this section shows, it is possible for two different namespaces to contain classes or even child namespaces with the same name.

Importing Namespaces

The development environment and compiler need a way to prioritize the order in which namespaces should be checked when a class is referenced. It is always possible to unequivocally specify a class by stating its complete namespace path. This is referred to as *fully qualifying* your declaration. The following example fully qualifies a `StringBuilder` object:

```
Dim sb As New System.Text.StringBuilder
```

However, if every reference to every class needed its full namespace declaration, that would make Visual Basic 2005 and every other .NET language very difficult to program in. After all, who wants to type `System.Collections.ArrayList` each time an instance of the `ArrayList` class is wanted? If you review the global references, you'll see the `System.Collections` namespace. Thus, you can just type `ArrayList` whenever you need an instance of this class, as the reference to the larger `System.Collections` namespace has already been made by the application.

In theory, another way to reference the `StringBuilder` class is to use `Text.StringBuilder`, but with all namespaces imported globally, there is a problem with this, caused by what is known as *namespace crowding*. Because there is a second namespace, `System.Drawing`, that has a child called `Text`, the compiler doesn't have a clear location for the `Text` namespace and, therefore, cannot resolve the `StringBuilder` class. The solution to this problem is to ensure that only a single version of the `Text` child namespace is found locally. That way, the compiler will use this namespace regardless of the global availability of the `System.Drawing.Text` namespace.

`Imports` statements specify to the compiler those namespaces that the code will use:

```
Imports Microsoft.Win32
Imports System
Imports SysDraw = System.Drawing
```

Once they are imported into the file, you are not required to fully qualify your object declarations in your code. For instance, if you imported the `System.Data.SqlClient` namespace into your file, you would then be able to create a `SqlConnection` object in the following manner:

```
Dim conn As New SqlConnection
```

Each of the preceding `Imports` statements illustrates a different facet of importing namespaces. The first namespace, `Imports Microsoft.Win32`, is not imported at the global level. Looking at the reference list, you may not see the Microsoft assembly referenced directly. However, opening the Object Browser reveals that this namespace is actually included as part of the `System.dll`.

As noted earlier, the `StringBuilder` references become ambiguous because both `System.Text` and `System.Drawing.Text` are valid namespaces at the global level. As a result, the compiler has no way to distinguish which `Text` child namespace is being referenced. Without any clear indication, the compiler flags `Text.StringBuilder` declarations in the command handler. However, using the `Imports System` declaration in the module tells the compiler that before checking namespaces imported at the global level, it should attempt to match incomplete references at the module level. Because the `System` namespace is declared at this level, if `System.Drawing` is not, then there is no ambiguity regarding which child namespace `Text.StringBuilder` belongs to.

This demonstrates how the compiler looks at each possible declaration:

❑ It first determines whether the item is a complete reference, such as `System.Text.StringBuilder`.

❑ If the declaration does not match a complete reference, then the compiler tries to determine whether the declaration is from a child namespace of one of the module-level imports.

❑ Finally, if a match has not been found, then the compiler looks at the global-level imports to determine whether the declaration can be associated with a namespace imported for the entire assembly.

While the preceding logical progression of moving from a full declaration through module- to global-level imports resolves the majority of issues, it does not handle all possibilities. Specifically, if you import `System.Drawing` at the module level, the namespace collision would return. This is where the third import statement becomes important — this import statement uses an alias.

Aliasing Namespaces

Aliasing has two benefits in .NET. First, aliasing allows a long namespace such as `System.EnterpriseServices` to be replaced with a shorthand name such as `COMPlus`. Second, it adds a way to prevent ambiguity among child namespaces at the module level.

As noted earlier, the `System` and `System.Drawing` namespaces both contain a child namespace of `Text`. Because you will be using a number of classes from the `System.Drawing` namespace, it follows that this namespace should be imported into the form's module. However, were this namespace imported along with the `System` namespace, the compiler would once again find references to the `Text` child namespace ambiguous. By aliasing the `System.Drawing` namespace to `SysDraw`, the compiler knows that it should only check the `System.Drawing` namespace when a declaration begins with that alias. The result is that although multiple namespaces with the same child namespace are now available at the module level, the compiler knows that one (or more) of them should only be checked at this level when they are explicitly referenced.

Aliasing as defined here is done in the following fashion:

```
Imports SysDraw = System.Drawing
```

Referencing Namespaces in ASP.NET

Making a reference to a namespace in ASP.NET is quite similar to working with Windows Forms, but you have to take some simple, additional steps. From your ASP.NET solution, first make a reference to the assemblies from the References folder, just as you do with Windows Forms. Once there, import these namespaces at the top of the page file in order to avoid having to fully qualify the reference every time on that particular page.

For example, instead of using System.Collections.Generic for each instance of use, use the `<%# Import %>` page directive at the top of the ASP.NET page (if the page is constructed using the inline coding style) or use the Imports keyword at the top of the ASP.NET page's code-behind file (just as you would with Windows Forms applications). The following shows how to perform this task when using inline coding for ASP.NET pages:

```
<%# Import Namespace="System.Collections.Generic" %>
```

Now that this reference is in place on the page, you can gain access to everything this namespace contains without the need to fully qualify the object you are accessing. Note that the Import keyword in the inline example is not missing an "s" at the end. When importing in this manner, it is Import (without the "s") instead of Imports — as it is in the ASP.NET code-behind model and in Windows Forms.

In ASP.NET 1.0/1.1, if you used a particular namespace on each page of your application, you would need the Import statement on each and every page where that namespace was needed. ASP.NET 2.0 introduces the capability to use the web.config file to make a global reference so that you don't need to make further references on the pages themselves, as shown in the following example:

```
<pages>
    <namespaces>
        <add namespace="System.Drawing" />
        <add namespace="Wrox.Books" />
    </namespaces>
</pages>
```

In this example, using the <namespaces> element in the web.config file, references are made to the System.Drawing namespace and the Wrox.Books namespace. Because these references are now contained within the web.config file, there is no need to again reference them on any of the ASP.NET pages contained within this solution.

Creating Your Own Namespaces

Every assembly created in .NET is part of some root namespace. By default, this logic actually mirrors COM, in that assemblies are assigned a namespace that matches the project name. However, unlike COM, in .NET it is possible to change this default behavior. In this way, just as Microsoft has packaged the system-level and CLR classes using well-defined names, it is possible for you to create your own namespaces. Of course, it's also possible to create projects that match existing namespaces and extend those namespaces, but that is very poor programming practice.

Creating an assembly in a custom namespace can be done at one of two levels. However, unless you want the same name for each assembly that will be used in a large namespace, you would normally reset the root namespace for the assembly. This is done through the assembly's project pages, reached by right-clicking the solution name in the Solution Explorer window and working off the first tab (Application) within the Properties page that opens in the Document window, as shown in Figure 8-8.

The next step is optional, but, depending on whether you want to create a class at the top level or at a child level, you can add a `Namespace` command to your code. There is a trick to being able to create top-level namespaces or multiple namespaces within the modules that make up an assembly. Instead of replacing the default namespace with another name, you can delete the default namespace and define the namespaces only in the modules, using the `Namespace` command.

The `Namespace` command is accompanied by an `End Namespace` command. This `End Namespace` command must be placed after the `End Class` tag for any classes that will be part of the namespace. The following code demonstrates the structure used to create a `MyMetaNamespace` namespace, which contains a single class:

```
Namespace MyMetaNamespace
    Class MyClass1
        ' Code
    End Class
End Namespace
```

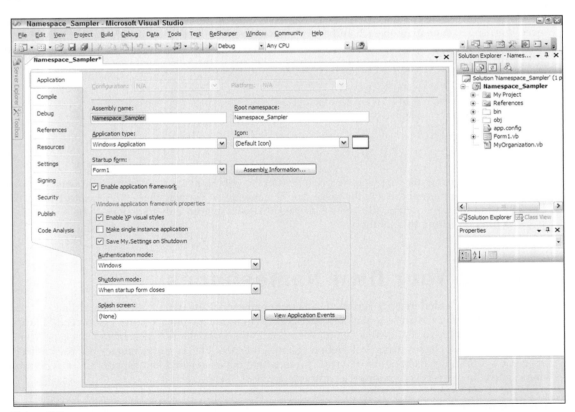

Figure 8-8

You can then utilize the `MyClass1` object simply by referencing its namespace, `MyMetaNamespace.MyClass1`. It is also possible to have multiple namespaces in a single file, as shown here:

```
Namespace MyMetaNamespace1
    Class MyClass1
       ' Code
    End Class
  End Namespace
Namespace MyMetaNamespace2
    Class MyClass2
       ' Code
    End Class
  End Namespace
```

Using this kind of structure, if you want to utilize `MyClass1`, then you get at it through the namespace `MyMetaNamespace.MyClass1`. This does not give you access to `MyMetaNamespace2` and the objects that it offers; instead, you have to make a separate reference to `MyMetaNamespace2.MyClass2`.

The `Namespace` command can also be nested. Using nested `Namespace` commands is how child namespaces are defined. The same rules apply — each `Namespace` must be paired with an `End Namespace` and must fully encompass all of the classes that are part of that namespace. In the following example, the `MyMetaNamespace` has a child namespace called `MyMetaNamespace.MyChildNamespace`:

```
Namespace MyMetaNamespace
    Class MyClass1
       ' Code
    End Class

    Namespace MyChildNamespace
       Class MyClass2
          ' Code
       End Class
    End Namespace
End Namespace
```

This is another point to be aware of when you make references to other namespaces within your own custom namespaces. Consider the following example:

```
Imports System
Imports System.Data
Imports System.Data.SqlClient
Namespace MyMetaNamespace1
    Class MyClass1
       ' Code
    End Class
End Namespace
Namespace MyMetaNamespace2
    Imports System.IO

    Class MyClass2
       ' Code
    End Class
End Namespace
```

In this example, a number of different namespaces are referenced in the file. The three namespaces referenced at the top of the code listing — the `System`, `System.Data`, and `System.Data.SqlClient` namespace references — are available to every namespace developed in the file. This is because these three references are sitting outside of any particular namespace declarations. However, the same is not true for the `System.IO` namespace reference. Because this reference is made within the `MyMetaNamespace2` namespace, it is unavailable to any other namespace in the file.

> **When you create your own namespaces, Microsoft recommends that you use a convention of** `CompanyName.TechnologyName` **— for example,** `Wrox.Books`. **This helps to ensure that all libraries are organized in a consistent way.**

Sometimes when you are working with custom namespaces, you might find that you have locked yourself out of accessing a particular branch of a namespace, purely due to naming conflicts. For this reason, Visual Basic has introduced the new `Global` keyword in this latest version, which can be used as the outermost root class available in the .NET Framework class library. Figure 8-9 shows a diagram of how the class structure looks with the new `Global` keyword.

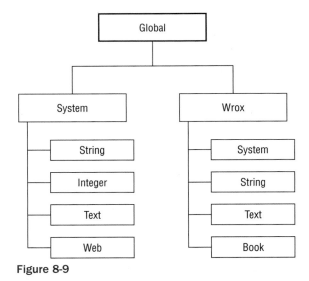

Figure 8-9

This means that you can make specifications such as

```
Global.System.String
```

or

```
Global.Wrox.System.Titles
```

The My Keyword

The My keyword is a novel concept introduced in the .NET Framework 2.0 to quickly give you access to your application, your users, your resources, the computer, or the network on which the application resides. The My keyword has been referred to as a way of speed-dialing common but complicated resources to which you need access. Using the My keyword, you can quickly access a wide variety of items, such as user details or specific settings of the requestor's browser.

Though not really considered a true namespace, the My object declarations that you make work the same as the .NET namespace structure you are used to working with. To give you an example, let's first look at how you get the user's machine name using the traditional namespace structure:

```
Environment.MachineName.ToString()
```

For this example, you simply need to use the Environment class and use this namespace to get at the MachineName property. Now let's look at how you would accomplish this same task using the new My keyword:

```
My.Computer.Info.MachineName.ToString()
```

Looking at this example, you may be wondering what the point is if the example, using My, is lengthier than the first example that just works off of the Environment namespace. Remember that the point isn't the length of what you type to get access to specific classes, but a logical way to find frequently accessed resources without spending a lot of time hunting them down. Would you have known to look in the Environment class to get the machine name of the user's computer? Maybe, but maybe not. Using My.Computer.Info.MachineName.ToString() is a tremendously more logical approach; and once compiled, this namespace declaration will be set to work with the same class as previously without a performance hit.

If you type the My keyword in your Windows Forms application, you will notice that IntelliSense provides you with seven items to work with — Application, Computer, Forms, Resources, Settings, User, and WebServices. Though this new keyword works best in the Windows Forms environment, there are still things that you can use in the Web Forms world. If you are working for a Web application, then you will have three items off of the My keyword — Application, Computer, and User. Each of these is broken down in the following sections.

My.Application

The My.Application namespace gives you quick access to specific settings and points that deal with your overall application. The following table details the properties and methods of the My.Application namespace:

Property/Method	Description
ApplicationContext	Returns contextual information about the thread of the Windows Forms application

Table continues on the next page

Property/Method	Description
ChangeCulture	A method that allows you to change the culture of the current application thread
ChangeUICulture	A method that allows you to change the culture that is being used by the Resource Manager
Culture	Returns the current culture being used by the current thread
Deployment	Returns an instance of the ApplicationDeployment object, which allows for programmatic access to the application's ClickOnce features
GetEnvironmentVariable	A method that allows you to get at the value of an environment variable
Info	Provides quick access to the assembly of the Windows Forms. You can get at assembly information such as version number, name, title, copyright information, and more.
IsNetworkDeployed	Returns a Boolean value that indicates whether the application was distributed via the network using the ClickOnce feature. If True, then the application was deployed using ClickOnce — otherwise False.
Log	This property allows you to write to your application's Event Log listeners.
MinimumSplashScreen DisplayTime	Allows you to set the time for the splash screen
OpenForms	Returns a FormCollection object, which allows access to the properties of the forms currently open
SplashScreen	Allows you to programmatically assign the splash screen for the application
UICulture	Returns the current culture being used by the Resource Manager

While much can be accomplished using the My.Application namespace, for an example of its use let's focus on the use of the Info property. This property provides access to the information stored in the application's AssemblyInfo.vb file, as well as other details about the class file. In one of your applications, you can create a message box that is displayed using the following code:

```
MessageBox.Show("Company Name: " & My.Application.Info.CompanyName & _
    vbCrLf & _
    "Description: " & My.Application.Info.Description & vbCrLf & _
    "Directory Path: " & My.Application.Info.DirectoryPath & vbCrLf & _
```

```
"Copyright: " & My.Application.Info.Copyright & vbCrLf & _
"Trademark: " & My.Application.Info.Trademark & vbCrLf & _
"Name: " & My.Application.Info.AssemblyName & vbCrLf & _
"Product Name: " & My.Application.Info.ProductName & vbCrLf & _
"Title: " & My.Application.Info.Title & vbCrLf & _
"Version: " & My.Application.Info.Version.ToString())
```

From this example, it is clear that you can get at quite a bit of information concerning the assembly of the running application. Running this code produces a message box similar to the one shown in Figure 8-10.

Figure 8-10

Another interesting property to look at from the `My.Application` namespace is the `Log` property. This property enables you to work with the log files for your application. For instance, you can easily write to the system's Application Event Log by first changing the application's `app.config` file to include the following:

```xml
<?xml version="1.0" encoding="utf-8" ?>
<configuration>
    <system.diagnostics>
        <sources>
            <source name="DefaultSource" switchName="DefaultSwitch">
                <listeners>
                    <add name="EventLog"/>
                </listeners>
            </source>
        </sources>
        <switches>
            <add name="DefaultSwitch" value="Information" />
        </switches>
        <sharedListeners>
            <add name="EventLog" type="System.Diagnostics.EventLogTraceListener"
                initializeData="EvjenEventWriter" />
        </sharedListeners>
    </system.diagnostics>
</configuration>
```

Once the configuration file is in place, you can record entries to the Application Event Log as shown in the following simple example:

```
Private Sub Form1_Load(ByVal sender As System.Object, _
    ByVal e As System.EventArgs) Handles MyBase.Load

    My.Application.Log.WriteEntry("Entered Form1_Load", _
        TraceEventType.Information, 1)

End Sub
```

You could also just as easily use the `WriteExceptionEntry` method in addition to the `WriteEntry` method. After running this application and looking in the Event Viewer, you will see the event shown in Figure 8-11.

Figure 8-11

The previous example showed how to write to the Application Event Log when working with the objects that write to the event logs. In addition to the Application Event Log, there is also a Security Event Log and a System Event Log. Note that when using these objects, it is impossible to write to the Security Event Log, and it is only possible to write to the System Event Log if the application does it under either the Local System or the Administrator accounts.

In addition to writing to the Application Event Log, you can just as easily write to a text file. As with writing to the Application Event Log, writing to a text file also means that you are going to need to make changes to the app.config file:

```xml
<?xml version="1.0" encoding="utf-8" ?>
<configuration>
    <system.diagnostics>
        <sources>
            <source name="DefaultSource" switchName="DefaultSwitch">
                <listeners>
                    <add name="EventLog"/>
                    <add name="FileLog" />
                </listeners>
            </source>
        </sources>
        <switches>
            <add name="DefaultSwitch" value="Information" />
        </switches>
        <sharedListeners>
            <add name="EventLog" type="System.Diagnostics.EventLogTraceListener"
             initializeData="EvjenEventWriter" />
            <add name="FileLog"
             type="Microsoft.VisualBasic.Logging.FileLogTraceListener,
             Microsoft.VisualBasic, Version=8.0.0.0, Culture=neutral,
             PublicKeyToken=b03f5f7f11d50a3a, processorArchitecture=MSIL"
             initializeData="FileLogWriter"/>
        </sharedListeners>
    </system.diagnostics>
</configuration>
```

Now with this app.config file in place, you simply need to run the same WriteEntry method as before. This time, however, in addition to writing the Application Event Log, the information is also written to a new text file. You can find the text file at C:\Documents and Settings\[username]\Application Data\[AssemblyCompany]\[AssemblyProduct]\[Version]. For instance, in my example, the log file was found at C:\Documents and Settings\Administrator\Application Data\Wrox\Log Writer\1.2.0.0\. In the .log file found, you will see a line such as the following:

```
DefaultSource     Information     1     Entered Form1_Load
```

By default it is separated by tabs, but you can change the delimiter yourself by adding a delimiter attribute to the FileLog section in the app.config file:

```xml
<add name="FileLog"
 type="Microsoft.VisualBasic.Logging.FileLogTraceListener,
 Microsoft.VisualBasic, Version=8.0.0.0, Culture=neutral,
 PublicKeyToken=b03f5f7f11d50a3a, processorArchitecture=MSIL"
 initializeData="FileLogWriter" delimiter=";" />
```

In addition to writing to Event Logs and text files, you can also write to XML files, console applications, and more.

My.Computer

The `My.Computer` namespace can be used to work with the parameters and details of the computer in which the application is running. The following table details the objects contained in this namespace:

Property	Description
Audio	This object enables you to work with audio files from your application. This includes starting, stopping, and looping audio files.
Clipboard	This object enables you to read and write to the clipboard.
Clock	This enables access to the system clock to get at GMT and the local time of the computer running the application. You can also get at the tick count, which is the number of milliseconds that has elapsed since the computer was started.
FileSystem	This object provides a large collection of properties and methods that enable programmatic access to drives, folders, and files. This includes the ability to read, write, and delete items in the file system.
Info	This provides access to the computer's details, such as amount of memory, the operating system type, which assemblies are loaded, and the name of the computer itself.
Keyboard	This object provides access to knowledge of which keyboard keys are pressed by the end user. Also included is a single method, SendKeys, which enables you to send the pressed keys to the active form.
Mouse	This provides a handful of properties that enable detection of the type of mouse installed, including details such as whether the left and right mouse buttons have been swapped, whether a mouse wheel exists, and how much to scroll when the user uses the wheel.
Name	This is a read-only property that provides access to the name of the computer.
Network	This object provides a single property and some methods that enable you to interact with the network to which the computer on which the application is running is connected. With this object, you can use the IsAvailable property to first verify that the computer is connected to a network. If so, then the Network object allows you to upload or download files, and ping the network.
Ports	This object can provide notification if there are available ports as well as allow access to the ports.
Registry	This object provides programmatic access to the registry and the registry settings. Using the Registry object, you can determine whether keys exist, determine values, change values, and delete keys.
Screen	This provides the ability to work with one or more screens that may be attached to the computer.

There is a lot to the `My.Computer` namespace, and it is impossible to cover all or even most of it. For an example that uses this namespace, let's take a look at the `FileSystem` property. The `FileSystem` property enables you to easily and logically access drives, directories, and files on the computer.

To illustrate the use of this property, first create a Windows Form with a `DataGridView` with a single column and a `Button` control. It should appear as shown in Figure 8-12.

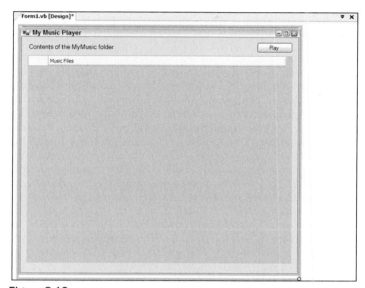

Figure 8-12

This little application will look in the user's My Music folder and list all of the .mp3 files found therein. Once listed, the user of the application will be able to select one of the listed files; and after pressing the Play button, the file will be launched and played inside Microsoft's Windows Media Player.

The first step after getting the controls on the form in place is to make a reference to the Windows Media Player DLL. You can find this on the COM tab, and the location of the DLL is C:\WINDOWS\System32\ wmp.dll. This gives you an object called `WMPLib` in the References folder of your solution.

You might be wondering why you would make a reference to a COM object in order to play a .wma file from your application, instead of using the `My.Computer.Audio` namespace that is provided to you. The `Audio` property only allows for the playing of .wav files, because to play .wma, .mp3, and similar files, users must have the proper codecs on their machine. These codecs are not part of the Windows OS, but are part of Windows Media Player.

Now that the reference to the wmp.dll is in place, let's put some code in the `Form1_Load` event:

```
Private Sub Form1_Load(ByVal sender As System.Object, _
    ByVal e As System.EventArgs) Handles MyBase.Load

        For Each MusicFile As String _
```

```
          In My.Computer.FileSystem.GetFiles _
             (My.Computer.FileSystem.SpecialDirectories.MyMusic, _
             FileIO.SearchOption.SearchAllSubDirectories, "*.wma*")
                Dim MusicFileInfo As System.IO.FileInfo = _
                   My.Computer.FileSystem.GetFileInfo(MusicFile.ToString())
                Me.DataGridView1.Rows.Add(MusicFileInfo.Directory.Parent.Name & _
                   "\" & MusicFileInfo.Directory.Name & "\" & MusicFileInfo.Name)
          Next

End Sub
```

In this example, the `My.Computer.FileSystem.GetFiles()` method points to the My Music folder through the use of the `SpecialDirectories` property. This property enables logical and easy access to folders such as Desktop, My Documents, My Pictures, Programs, and more. Though it is possible to use just this first parameter with the `GetFiles()` method, this example makes further definitions. The second parameter defines the `recurse` value — which specifies whether the subfolders should be perused as well. In this case, the `SearchOption` enumeration is set to `SearchAllSubDirectories`. The last parameter defines the wildcard that should be used in searching for elements. In this case, the value of the `wildcard` is `*.wma`, which instructs the `GetFile` method to get only the files that are of type `.wma`. You could just as easily set it to `*.mp3` or even just `*.*` to get at anything contained within the folders. Once retrieved with the `GetFile()` method, the retrieved file is then placed inside the `DataGridView` control, again using the `My.Computer.FileSystem` namespace to define the value of the item placed within the row.

Once the `Form1_Load` event is in place, the last event to construct is the `Button1_Click` event:

```
Private Sub Button1_Click(ByVal sender As System.Object, _
   ByVal e As System.EventArgs) Handles Button1.Click
      Dim MediaPlayer As New WMPLib.WindowsMediaPlayer
      MediaPlayer.openPlayer(My.Computer.FileSystem.SpecialDirectories.MyMusic & _
         "\" & DataGridView1.SelectedCells.Item(0).Value)
End Sub
```

From this example, you can see that it is pretty simple to play one of the provided .wma files. It is as simple as creating an instance of the `WMPLib.WindowsMediaPlayer` object and using the `openPlayer()` method, which takes as a parameter the location of the file to play. In this case, you are again using the `SpecialDirectories` property. The nice thing about using this property is that it could be more difficult to find the user's My Music folder due to the username changing the actual location of the files that the application is looking for, but using the `My` namespace enables it to figure out the exact location of the items. When built and run, the application provides a list of available music files, enabling you to easily select one for playing in the Media Player. This is illustrated in Figure 8-13.

Though it would be really cool if it were possible to play these types of files using the `Audio` property from the `My.Computer` namespace, it is still possible to use the `My.Computer.Audio` namespace for playing `.wav` files and system sounds.

To play a system sound, you use the following construct:

```
My.Computer.Audio.PlaySystemSound(SystemSounds.Beep)
```

Figure 8-13

The system sounds in the `SystemSounds` enumeration include `Asterisk`, `Beep`, `Exclamation`, `Hand`, and `Question`.

My.Forms Namespace

The `My.Forms` namespace provides a quick and logical way of getting at the properties and methods of the forms contained within your solution. For instance, to get at the first form in your solution (assuming that it's named `Form1`), use the following namespace construct:

```
My.Form.Form1
```

To get at other forms, you simply change the namespace so that the name of the form you are trying to access follows the `Form` keyword in the namespace construction.

My.Resources

The `My.Resources` namespace is a tremendously easy way to get at the resources stored in your application. If you open the `MyResources.resx` file from the My Projects folder in your solution, you can easily create as many resources as you wish. For example, you could create a single `String` resource titled `MyResourceString` and give it a value of `St. Louis Rams`.

To access the resources that you create, use the simple reference shown here:

```
My.Resources.MyResourceString.ToString()
```

Using IntelliSense, you will find all of your created resources listed after you type the period after the `My.Resources` string.

My.User

The `My.User` namespace enables you to work with the `IPrincipal` interface. You can use the `My.User` namespace to determine whether the user is authenticated or not, what the user's name is, and more. For instance, if you have a login form in your application, you could allow access to a particular form with code similar to the following:

```
If (Not My.User.IsInRole("Administrators")) Then
    ' Code here
End If
```

You can also just as easily get at the user's name with the following:

```
My.User.Name
```

In addition, you can check whether the user is authenticated:

```
If My.User.IsAuthenticated Then
    ' Code here
End If
```

My.WebServices

When not using the `My.WebServices` namespace, you access your Web Services references in a lengthier manner. The first step in either case is to make a Web reference to some remote XML Web Service in your solution. These references will then appear in the Web References folder in Solution Explorer in Visual Studio 2005. Before the introduction of the `My` namespace, you would have accessed the values that the Web reference exposed in the following manner:

```
Dim ws As New ReutersStocks.GetStockDetails
Label1.Text = ws.GetLatestPrice.ToString()
```

This works, but now with the `My` namespace, you can use the following construct:

```
Label1.Text = My.WebServices.GetStockDetails.GetLatestPrice.ToString()
```

Summary

The introduction of namespaces with the .NET Framework provides a powerful tool that helps to abstract logical capabilities from their physical implementation. While there are differences in the syntax of referencing objects from a namespace and referencing the same object from a COM-style component implementation, there are several similarities. After demonstrating the hierarchical structure of namespaces, this chapter covered the following:

❑   Why namespace hierarchies are not related to class hierarchies

❑   How to review and add references to a project

❑   How to import and alias namespaces at the module level

❑   How to create custom namespaces

❑   How to use the new My namespace

Namespaces play an important role in enterprise software development. Namespaces enable you to separate the implementation of related functional objects while retaining the ability to group these objects, which improves the overall maintainability of your code. Anyone who has ever worked on a large project has experienced situations in which a fix to a component was delayed because of the potential impact on other components in the same project. Regardless of the logical separation of components in the same project, developers who take part in the development process worry about testing. With totally separate implementations for related components, it is not only possible to alleviate this concern, but also easier than ever before for a team of developers to work on different parts of the same project.

9

Exception Handling and Debugging

All professional-grade programs need to handle unexpected conditions. In programming languages before Microsoft .NET, this was often called *error handling*. Unexpected conditions generated error codes, which were trapped by programming logic that took appropriate action.

The common language runtime in .NET does not generate error codes. When an unexpected condition occurs, the CLR creates a special object called an *exception*. This object contains properties and methods that describe the unexpected condition in detail and communicate various items of useful information about what went wrong.

Because .NET deals with exceptions instead of errors, the term "error handling" is seldom used in the .NET world. Instead, the term "exception handling" is preferred. This term refers to the techniques used in .NET to detect exceptions and take appropriate action.

This chapter covers how exception handling works in Visual Basic 2005. There are many improvements over pre-.NET versions of Visual Basic. This chapter discusses the common language runtime (CLR) exception handler in detail and the programming methods that are most efficient in catching errors. Specifically, this chapter covers the following:

- ❑ A brief review of error handling in Visual Basic 6 (VB6)
- ❑ The general principles behind exception handling
- ❑ The `Try...Catch...Finally` structure, the `Exit Try` statement, and nested `Try` structures
- ❑ The exception object's methods and properties
- ❑ Capabilities in Visual Studio .NET to work with exceptions
- ❑ Error and trace logging and how you can use these methods to obtain feedback on how your program is working

You'll begin with a quick review of error handling in previous versions of Visual Basic to use as a reference point. Then you will learn new ways to handle exceptions in .NET.

A Brief Review of Error Handling in VB6

For compatibility, Visual Basic 2005 and other .NET versions of Visual Basic still support the old-style syntax for error handling that was used in Visual Basic 6 and earlier versions. That means you can still use the syntax presented in this review. However, it is strongly recommended that you avoid using this old-style syntax in favor of the exception handling features that are native to .NET. Using the new `Try...Catch` syntax (presented after this review) will give you more flexibility and better code structure.

The old-style syntax in VB6 was handed down from DOS versions of BASIC. The `On Error` construct was created in an era when line labels and `GoTo` statements were commonly used. Such error handling is difficult to use and has limited functionality compared to more modern alternatives.

In VB6, a typical routine with error handling code looks like this:

```
Private Function OpenFile(sFileName As String) As Boolean

On Error GoTo ErrHandler:
Open sFileName For Random As #1
OpenFile = True
Exit Sub

ErrHandler:
Select Case Err.Number
    Case 53 ' File not found
        MessageBox.Show "File not found"
    Case Else
        MessageBox.Show "Other error"
End Select
OpenFile = False

End Function
```

The top of the routine points to a section of code called an *error handler,* which is usually placed at the bottom of the routine. The error handler takes control as soon as an error is detected in the routine, and it checks the error number to determine what action to take. The error number is available as a property of the `Err` object, which is a globally available object that holds error information in VB6.

There are several other error handling syntax options not included in the preceding error-handling code. If the error handler can take care of the error without breaking execution, then it can resume execution with the line of code that generated the error (`Resume`), the one after that (`Resume Next`), or at a particular location (`Resume {LineLabel}`).

Error handling code becomes more complex if the error handling needs to vary in the routine. Multiple `On Error GoTo` statements must be used to send errors to various error handlers, all of which are clustered at the bottom of the routine. With such a lack of organization of error handling code, it is easy to become confused about what should happen under various conditions. There is also very little information available about the error during the process, except for the error number. You can't tell, for example, the line number on which the error was generated without single-stepping through the code.

Such logic can rapidly become convoluted and unmanageable. There's a much better way to manage errors in VB 2005, called *structured exception handling*. The rest of this chapter discusses this new way to work with code errors, and uses the term structured exception handling throughout, except for the small sections that discuss compatibility with older error-handling techniques.

Exceptions in .NET

.NET implements a systemwide, comprehensive approach to exception handling. As noted in the chapter introduction, instead of an *error number*, there is an *exception object*. This object contains information relevant to the error, exposed as properties of the object. Later you'll see a summary of the properties and the information they expose in a table.

Such an object is an instance of a class that derives from a class named `System.Exception`. As shown later, a variety of subclasses of `System.Exception` are used for different circumstances.

Important Properties and Methods of an Exception

The `Exception` class has properties that contain useful information about the exception, as shown in the following table:

Property	Description
HelpLink	A string indicating the link to help for this exception
InnerException	Returns the `exception` object reference to an inner (nested) exception
Message	A string that contains a description of the error, suitable for displaying to users
Source	A string containing the name of an object that generated the error
StackTrace	A read-only property that holds the stack trace as a text string. The stack trace is a list of the pending method calls at the point at which the exception was detected. That is, if `MethodA` called `MethodB`, and an exception occurred in `MethodB`, the stack trace would contain both `MethodA` and `MethodB`.
TargetSite	A read-only string property that holds the method that threw the exception

The two most important methods of the Exception class are as follows:

Method	Description
GetBaseException	Returns the first exception in the chain
ToString	Returns the error string, which might include as much information as the error message, the inner exceptions, and the stack trace, depending on the error

You will see these properties and methods used in the code examples given later, once you have covered the syntax for detecting and handling exceptions.

How Exceptions Differ from the Err Object in VB6

Because an exception contains all of the information needed about an error, structured exception handling does not use error numbers and the Err object. The exception object contains all the relevant information about the error.

However, whereas there is only one global Err object in VB6, there are many types of exception objects in VB 2005. For example, if a divide by zero is done in code, then an OverflowException is generated. There are several dozen types of exception classes in VB 2005, and in addition to using the ones that are available in the .NET Framework, you can inherit from a class called ApplicationException and then create your own exception classes (see Chapter 4 for a discussion of inheritance).

In .NET, all exceptions inherit from System.Exception. Special-purpose exception classes can be found in many namespaces. The following table lists four representative examples of the classes that extend Exception:

Namespace	Class	Description
System	InvalidOperationException	Generated when a call to an object method is inappropriate because of the object's state
System	OutOfMemoryException	Results when there is not enough memory to carry out an operation
System.XML	XmlException	Often caused by an attempt to read invalid XML
System.Data	DataException	Represents errors in ADO.NET components

There are literally dozens of exception classes scattered throughout the .NET Framework namespaces. It is common for an exception class to reside in a namespace with the classes that typically generate the exception. For example, the DataException class is in System.Data, with the ADO.NET components that often generate a DataException instance.

Having many types of exceptions in VB 2005 enables different types of conditions to be trapped with different exception handlers. This is a major advance over VB6. The syntax to accomplish that is discussed next.

Structured-Exception-Handling Keywords

Structured exception handling depends on several new keywords in VB 2005:

❑   `Try` — Begins a section of code in which an exception might be generated from a code error. This section of code is often called a `Try` block. In some respects, this would be the equivalent of an `On Error` statement in VB6. However, unlike an `On Error` statement, a `Try` statement does not indicate where a trapped exception should be routed. Instead, the exception is automatically routed to a `Catch` statement (discussed next).

❑   `Catch` — Begins an exception handler for a type of exception. One or more `Catch` code blocks follow a `Try` block, with each `Catch` block catching a different type of exception. When an exception is encountered in the `Try` block, the first `Catch` block that matches that type of exception receives control. A `Catch` statement is analogous to the line label used in a VB6 `On Error` statement, but the ability to route different types of exceptions to different `Catch` statements is a radical improvement over VB6.

❑   `Finally` — Contains code that runs when the `Try` block finishes normally, or when a `Catch` block receives control and then finishes. That is, the code in the `Finally` block always runs, regardless of whether an exception was detected. Typically, the `Finally` block is used to close or dispose of any resources, such as database connections, that might have been left unresolved by the code that had a problem. There is no equivalent of a `Finally` in VB6.

❑   `Throw` — Generates an exception. This is similar to `Err.Raise` in VB6. It's usually done in a `Catch` block when the exception should be kicked back to a calling routine or in a routine that has itself detected an error such as a bad argument passed in.

The Try, Catch, and Finally Keywords

Here is an example showing some typical simple structured exception handling code in VB 2005. In this case, the most likely source of an error is the `iItems` argument. If it has a value of zero, then this would lead to dividing by zero, which would generate an exception.

First, create a Windows Application in Visual Basic 2005 and place a button on the default `Form1` created in the project. In the button's click event, place the following two lines of code:

```
Dim sngAvg As Single
sngAvg = GetAverage(0, 100)
```

Then put the following function in the form's code:

```
Private Function GetAverage(iItems As Integer, iTotal As Integer) as Single
    ' Code that might throw an exception is wrapped in a Try block
  Try
      Dim sngAverage As Single
```

```
                  ' This will cause an exception to be thrown if iItems = 0
                  sngAverage = CSng(iTotal \ iItems)

                  ' This only executes if the line above generated no error
                  MessageBox.Show("Calculation successful")
                  Return sngAverage

          Catch excGeneric As Exception
                  ' If the calculation failed, you get here
                  MessageBox.Show("Calculation unsuccessful - exception caught")
                  Return 0
          End Try

      End Function
```

This code traps all the exceptions with a single generic exception type, and you don't have any `Finally` logic. Run the program and press the button. You will be able to follow the sequence better if you place a breakpoint at the top of the `GetAverage` function and step through the lines.

Here is a more complex example that traps the divide-by-zero exception explicitly. This second version of the `GetAverage` function (notice that the name is `GetAverage2`) also includes a `Finally` block:

```
    Private Function GetAverage2(iItems As Integer, iTotal As Integer) as Single
         ' Code that might throw an exception is wrapped in a Try block
        Try
              Dim sngAverage As Single

              ' This will cause an exception to be thrown.
              sngAverage = CSng(iTotal \ iItems)

              ' This only executes if the line above generated no error.
              MessageBox.Show("Calculation successful")
              Return sngAverage
         Catch excDivideByZero As DivideByZeroException
                ' You'll get here with an DivideByZeroException in the Try block
                MessageBox.Show("Calculation generated DivideByZero Exception")
                Return 0
        Catch excGeneric As Exception
                ' You'll get here when any exception is thrown and not caught in
                ' a previous Catch block.
                MessageBox.Show("Calculation failed - generic exception caught")
                Return 0
        Finally
                ' Code in the Finally block will always run.
                 MessageBox.Show("You always get here, with or without an error")
        End Try
    End Function
```

This code contains two `Catch` blocks for different types of exceptions. If an exception is generated, then .NET will go down the `Catch` blocks looking for a matching exception type. That means the `Catch` blocks should be arranged with specific types first and more generic types after.

Place the code for `GetAverage2` in the form, and place another button on `Form1`. In the `Click` event for the second button, place the following code:

```
Dim sngAvg As Single
sngAvg = GetAverage2(0, 100)
```

Run the program again and press the second button. As before, it's easier to follow if you set a breakpoint early in the code and then step through the code line by line.

The Throw Keyword

Sometimes a `Catch` block is unable to handle an error. Some exceptions are so unexpected that they should be "sent back up the line" to the calling code, so that the problem can be promoted to code that can decide what to do with it. A `Throw` statement is used for that purpose.

A `Throw` statement, like an `Err.Raise`, ends execution of the exception handler — that is, no more code in the `Catch` block after the `Throw` statement is executed. However, `Throw` does not prevent code in the `Finally` block from running. That code still runs before the exception is kicked back to the calling routine.

You can see the `Throw` statement in action by changing the earlier code for `GetAverage2` to look like this:

```
Private Function GetAverage3(iItems As Integer, iTotal as Integer) as Single
    ' Code that might throw an exception is wrapped in a Try block
    Try
        Dim sngAverage As Single

        ' This will cause an exception to be thrown.
        sngAverage = CSng(iTotal \ iItems)

        ' This only executes if the line above generated no error.
        MessageBox.Show("Calculation successful")
        Return sngAverage

    Catch excDivideByZero As DivideByZeroException
        ' You'll get here with an DivideByZeroException in the Try block.
        MessageBox.Show("Calculation generated DivideByZero Exception")
        Throw excDivideByZero
        MessageBox.Show("More logic after the throw - never executed")

    Catch excGeneric As Exception
        ' You'll get here when any exception is thrown and not caught in
        ' a previous Catch block.
        MessageBox.Show("Calculation failed - generic exception caught")
        Throw excGeneric
    Finally
        ' Code in the Finally block will always run, even if
        ' an exception was thrown in a Catch block.
        MessageBox.Show("You always get here, with or without an error")
    End Try
End Function
```

Here is some code to call `GetAverage3`. You can place this code in another button's `click` event to test it out:

```
Try
    Dim sngAvg As Single
    sngAvg = GetAverage3(0, 100)
Catch exc As Exception
    MessageBox.Show("Back in the click event after an error")
Finally
    MessageBox.Show("Finally block in click event")
End Try
```

Throwing a New Exception

`Throw` can also be used with exceptions that are created on-the-fly. For example, you might want your earlier function to generate an `ArgumentException`, since you can consider a value of `iItems` of zero to be an invalid value for that argument.

In such a case, a new exception must be instantiated. The constructor allows you to place your own custom message into the exception. To show how this is done, let's change the aforementioned example to throw your own exception instead of the one caught in the `Catch` block:

```
Private Function GetAverage4(iItems As Integer, iTotal as Integer) as Single

    If iItems = 0 Then
        Dim excOurOwnException As New _
            ArgumentException("Number of items cannot be zero")

        Throw excOurOwnException
    End If

' Code that might throw an exception is wrapped in a Try block.
    Try
        Dim sngAverage As Single

        ' This will cause an exception to be thrown.
        sngAverage = CSng(iTotal \ iItems)

        ' This only executes if the line above generated no error.
        MessageBox.Show("Calculation successful")
        Return sngAverage

    Catch excDivideByZero As DivideByZeroException
        ' You'll get here with an DivideByZeroException in the Try block.
        MessageBox.Show("Calculation generated DivideByZero Exception")
        Throw excDivideByZero
        MessageBox.Show("More logic after the thrown - never executed")
    Catch excGeneric As Exception
        ' You'll get here when any exception is thrown and not caught in
        ' a previous Catch block.
        MessageBox.Show("Calculation failed - generic exception caught")
        Throw excGeneric
    Finally
        ' Code in the Finally block will always run, even if
```

320

```
                ' an exception was thrown in a Catch block.
                MessageBox.Show("You always get here, with or without an error")
            End Try
    End Function
```

This code can be called from a button with similar code for calling `GetAverage3`. Just change the name of the function called to `GetAverage4`.

This technique is particularly well suited to dealing with problems detected in property procedures. Property `Set` procedures often do checking to ensure that the property is about to be assigned a valid value. If not, throwing a new `ArgumentException` (instead of assigning the property value) is a good way to inform the calling code about the problem.

The Exit Try Statement

The `Exit Try` statement will, under a given circumstance, break out of the `Try` or `Catch` block and continue at the `Finally` block. In the following example, you are going to exit a `Catch` block if the value of `iItems` is 0, because you know that your error was caused by that problem:

```
Private Function GetAverage5(iItems As Integer, iTotal as Integer) As Single
    ' Code that might throw an exception is wrapped in a Try block.
    Try
        Dim sngAverage As Single

        ' This will cause an exception to be thrown.
        sngAverage = CSng(iTotal \ iItems)

        ' This only executes if the line above generated no error.
        MessageBox.Show("Calculation successful")
        Return sngAverage

    Catch excDivideByZero As DivideByZeroException
        ' You'll get here with an DivideByZeroException in the Try block.
        If iItems = 0 Then
            Return 0
            Exit Try
        Else
            MessageBox.Show("Error not caused by iItems")
        End If
        Throw excDivideByZero
        MessageBox.Show("More logic after the thrown - never executed")

    Catch excGeneric As Exception
        ' You'll get here when any exception is thrown and not caught in
        ' a previous Catch block.
        MessageBox.Show("Calculation failed - generic exception caught")
        Throw excGeneric
    Finally
        ' Code in the Finally block will always run, even if
        ' an exception was thrown in a Catch block.
        MessageBox.Show("You always get here, with or without an error")
    End Try
End Sub
```

In your first `Catch` block, you have inserted an `If` block so that you can exit the block given a certain condition (in this case, if the overflow exception was caused by the value of `intY` being 0). The `Exit Try` goes immediately to the `Finally` block and completes the processing there:

```
If iItems = 0 Then
  Return 0
  Exit Try
Else
  MessageBox.Show("Error not caused by iItems")
End If
```

Now, if the overflow exception is caused by something other than division by zero, then you'll get a message box displaying `Error not caused by iItems`.

Nested Try Structures

In some cases, particular lines in a `Try` block may need special exception processing. Moreover, errors can occur within the `Catch` portion of the `Try` structures and cause further exceptions to be thrown. For both of these scenarios, nested `Try` structures are available. You can alter the example under the section "The Throw Keyword" to demonstrate the following code:

```
Private Function GetAverage6(iItems As Integer, iTotal as Integer) As Single
    ' Code that might throw an exception is wrapped in a Try block.
    Try
        Dim sngAverage As Single

        ' Do something for performance testing....
        Try
            LogEvent("GetAverage")
        Catch exc As Exception
            MessageBox.Show("Logging function unavailable")
        End Try

        ' This will cause an exception to be thrown.
        sngAverage = CSng(iTotal \ iItems)

        ' This only executes if the line above generated no error.
        MessageBox.Show("Calculation successful")
        Return sngAverage

    Catch excDivideByZero As DivideByZeroException
        ' You'll get here with an DivideByZeroException in the Try block.
        MessageBox.Show("Error not divide by 0")
        Throw excDivideByZero
        MessageBox.Show("More logic after the thrown - never executed")
    Catch excGeneric As Exception
        ' You'll get here when any exception is thrown and not caught in
        ' a previous Catch block.
        MessageBox.Show("Calculation failed - generic exception caught")
        Throw excGeneric
    Finally
        ' Code in the Finally block will always run, even if
```

```
            ' an exception was thrown in a Catch block.
            MessageBox.Show("You always get here, with or without an error")
        End Try
End Function
```

In the preceding example, you are assuming that a function exists to log an event. This function would typically be in a common library, and might log the event in various ways. You will look at logging exceptions in detail later in the chapter, but a simple LogEvent function might look like this:

```
Public Function LogEvent(ByVal sEvent As String)
    FileOpen(1, "logfile.txt", OpenMode.Append)
    Print(1, DateTime.Now & "-" & sEvent & vbCrLf)
    FileClose(1)

End Function
```

In this case, you don't want a problem logging an event, such as a "disk full" error, to crash the routine. The code for the GetAverage function triggers a message box to indicate trouble with the logging function.

A Catch block can be empty. In that case, it has a similar effect as On Error Resume Next in VB6. The exception is ignored. However, execution does not pick up with the line after the line that generated the error, but instead picks up with either the Finally block or the line after the End Try if no Finally block exists.

Using Exception Properties

The previous examples have displayed hard-coded messages into message boxes, and this is obviously not a good technique for production applications. Instead, a message box or log entry describing an exception should provide as much information as possible concerning the problem. To do this, various properties of the exception can be used.

The most brutal way to get information about an exception is to use the ToString method of the exception. Suppose that you modify the earlier example of GetAverage2 to change the displayed information about the exception like this:

```
Private Function GetAverage2(ByVal iItems As Integer, ByVal iTotal As Integer) _
        As Single
    ' Code that might throw an exception is wrapped in a Try block.
    Try
        Dim sngAverage As Single

        ' This will cause an exception to be thrown.
        sngAverage = CSng(iTotal \ iItems)
        ' This only executes if the line above generated no error.
        MessageBox.Show("Calculation successful")
        Return sngAverage

    Catch excDivideByZero As DivideByZeroException
        ' You'll get here with an DivideByZeroException in the Try block.
        MessageBox.Show(excDivideByZero.ToString)
        Throw excDivideByZero
```

```
        MessageBox.Show("More logic after the thrown - never executed")

    Catch excGeneric As Exception
        ' You'll get here when any exception is thrown and not caught in
        ' a previous Catch block.
        MessageBox.Show("Calculation failed - generic exception caught")
        Throw excGeneric
    Finally
        ' Code in the Finally block will always run, even if
        ' an exception was thrown in a Catch block.
        MessageBox.Show("You always get here, with or without an error")
    End Try
End Function
```

When the function is accessed with iItems = 0, a message box similar to the one in Figure 9-1 will be displayed.

Figure 9-1

The Message Property

The message in the dialog shown in Figure 9-1 is helpful to a developer because it contains a lot of information, but it's not something you would typically want users to see. Instead, a user normally needs to see a short description of the problem, and that is supplied by the Message property.

If the previous code is changed so that the Message property is used instead of ToString, then the message box will provide something like what is shown in Figure 9-2.

Figure 9-2

The InnerException and TargetSite Properties

The InnerException property is used to store an exception trail. This comes in handy when multiple exceptions occur. It's quite common for an exception to occur that sets up circumstances whereby further exceptions are raised. As exceptions occur in a sequence, you can choose to stack your exceptions for later reference by use of the `InnerException` property of your `Exception` object. As each exception joins the stack, the previous `Exception` object becomes the inner exception in the stack.

For simplicity, you'll start a new code sample, with just a subroutine that generates its own exception. You'll include code to add a reference to an `InnerException` object to the exception you are generating with the `Throw` method.

This example also includes a message box to show what's stored in the exception's `TargetSite` property. As shown in the results, `TargetSite` will contain the name of the routine generating the exception — in this case, `HandlerExample`. Here's the code:

```
Sub HandlerExample()
 Dim intX As Integer
 Dim intY As Integer
 Dim intZ As Integer
 intY = 0
 intX = 5
 ' First Required Error Statement.
 Try
    ' Cause a "Divide by Zero"
    intZ = CType((intX \ intY), Integer)
 ' Catch the error.
 Catch objA As System.DivideByZeroException
    Try
       Throw (New Exception("0 as divisor", objA))
    Catch objB As Exception
      Dim sError As String
      sError = "My Message: " & objB.Message & vbCrLf & vbCrLf
      sError &= "Inner Exception Message: " & _
          objB.InnerException.Message & vbCrLf & vbCrLf
      sError &= "Method Error Occurred: " & objB.TargetSite.Name
      MessageBox.Show(sError)
    End Try
 Catch
    Messagebox.Show("Caught any other errors")
 Finally
    Messagebox.Show(Str(intZ))
 End Try
End Sub
```

As before, you catch the divide-by-zero error in the first `Catch` block, and the exception is stored in `objA` so that you can reference its properties later.

You throw a new exception with a more general message (`"0 as divisor"`) that is easier to interpret, and you build up your stack by appending `objA` as the `InnerException` object using an overloaded constructor for the `Exception` object:

```
Throw (New Exception("0 as divisor", objA))
```

You catch your newly thrown exception in another `Catch` statement. Note how it does not catch a specific type of error:

```
Catch objB As Exception
```

Then you construct an error message for the new exception and display it in a message box:

```
Dim sError As String
sError = "My Message: " & objB.Message & vbCrLf & vbCrLf
sError &= "Inner Exception Message: " & _
    objB.InnerException.Message & vbCrLf & vbCrLf
sError &= "Method Error Occurred: " & objB.TargetSite.Name
MessageBox.Show(sError)
```

The message box that is produced is shown in Figure 9-3.

My Message: 0 as divisor

Inner Exception Message: Attempted to divide by zero.

Method Error Occurred: HandlerExample

OK

Figure 9-3

First your own message is included, based on the new exception thrown by your own code. Then the InnerException gets the next exception in the stack, which is the divide-by-zero exception, and its message is included. Finally, the TargetSite property gives you the name of the method that threw the exception. TargetSite is particularly helpful in logs or error reports from users that are used by developers to track down unexpected problems.

After this message box, the Finally clause displays another message box that just displays the current value of intZ, which is zero because the divide failed. This second box also occurs in other examples that follow.

Source and StackTrace

The Source and StackTrace properties provide the user with information regarding where the error occurred. This supplemental information can be invaluable for the user to pass on to the troubleshooter in order to help resolve errors more quickly. The following example uses these two properties and shows the feedback when the error occurs:

```
Sub HandlerExample2()
  Dim intX As Integer
  Dim intY As Integer
  Dim intZ As Integer
  intY = 0
  intX = 5
  ' First Required Error Statement.
```

```
      Try
          ' Cause a "Divide by Zero"
          intZ = CType((intX \ intY), Integer)
      ' Catch the error.
      Catch objA As System.DivideByZeroException
            objA.Source = "HandlerExample2"
            Messagebox.Show("Error Occurred at :" & _
                objA.Source & objA.StackTrace)
      Finally
          Messagebox.Show(Str(intZ))
      End Try
  End Sub
```

The output from the `Messagebox` statement is very detailed, providing the entire path and line number where the error occurred, as shown in Figure 9-4.

Error Occurred at :HandlerExample2   at ProVBNETChap9.Form1.HandlerExample2() in
C:\Demonstration\ProVBNETChap9\Form1.vb:line 150

OK

Figure 9-4

Notice that this information is also included in the `ToString` method examined earlier (refer to Figure 9-1).

GetBaseException

The `GetBaseException` method comes in very handy when you are deep in a set of thrown exceptions. This method returns the originating exception, which makes debugging easier and helps keep the troubleshooting process on track by sorting through information that can be misleading:

```
Sub HandlerExample3()
   Dim intX As Integer
   Dim intY As Integer
   Dim intZ As Integer
   intY = 0
   intX = 5
   ' First Required Error Statement.
   Try
      ' Cause a "Divide by Zero"
     intZ = CType((intX \ intY), Integer)
   ' Catch the error.
   Catch objA As System.DivideByZeroException
        Try
          Throw (New Exception("0 as divisor", objA))
        Catch objB As Exception
          Try
            Throw (New Exception("New error", objB))
          Catch objC As Exception
            Messagebox.Show(objC.GetBaseException.Message)
```

```
            End Try
         End Try
      Finally
        Messagebox.Show(Str(intZ))
      End Try
   End Sub
```

The `InnerException` property provides the information that the `GetBaseException` method needs, so as your example executes the `Throw` statements, it sets up the `InnerException` property. The purpose of the `GetBaseException` method is to provide the properties of the initial exception in the chain that was produced. Hence, `objC.GetBaseException.Message` returns the `Message` property of the original `OverflowException` message even though you've thrown multiple errors since the original error occurred:

```
Messagebox.Show(objC.GetBaseException.Message)
```

To put it another way, the code traverses back to the exception caught as `objA` and displays the same message as the `objA.Message` property would, as shown in Figure 9-5.

Figure 9-5

HelpLink

The `HelpLink` property gets or sets the help link for a specific `Exception` object. It can be set to any string value, but is typically set to a URL. If you create your own exception in code, you might want to set `HelpLink` to some URL describing the error in more detail. Then the code that catches the exception can go to that link. You could create and throw your own custom application exception with code like the following:

```
Dim exc As New ApplicationException("A short description of the problem")
exc.HelpLink = "http://mysite.com/somehtmlfile.htm"
Throw exc
```

When trapping an exception, the `HelpLink` can be used to launch a viewer so the user can see the details about the problem. The following example shows this in action, using the built-in Explorer in Windows:

```
Sub HandlerExample4()
Try
    Dim exc As New ApplicationException("A short description of the problem")
    exc.HelpLink = "http://mysite.com/somehtmlfile.htm"
    Throw exc

    ' Catch the error.
Catch objA As System.Exception
```

```
            Shell("explorer.exe " & objA.HelpLink)

    End Try
End Sub
```

This results in launching Internet Explorer to show the page specified by the URL. Most exceptions thrown by the CLR or the .NET Framework's classes have a blank HelpLink property. You should only count on using HelpLink if you have previously set it to a URL (or some other type of link information) yourself.

Interoperability with VB6-Style Error Handling

Because VB 2005 still supports the older On Error statement, it is possible that you will use code that handles errors that way instead of with structured exception handling. You can use both techniques in a single program, but it is not possible to use both forms in a single routine. If you attempt to use both On Error and Try...Catch in a single routine, you will get a syntax error.

The VB compiler does allow the two techniques for handling errors to communicate with each other. For example, suppose you have a routine that uses On Error and then uses Err.Raise to promote the error to the calling code. Also suppose that the calling code makes the call in a Try...Catch block. In that case, the error created by Err.Raise becomes an exception in the calling code and is trapped by a Catch block just as a normal exception would be. Here's a code example to illustrate.

First, create a subroutine that creates an error with Err.Raise, like this:

```
    Private Sub RaiseErrorWithErrRaise()
        Err.Raise(53)    ' indicates File Not Found
    End Sub
```

Then call this routine from a button's click event, with the call inside a Try...Catch block:

```
    Private Sub Button2_Click(ByVal sender As System.Object, _
        ByVal e As System.EventArgs) Handles Button2.Click
        Try
            RaiseErrorWithErrRaise()
        Catch ex As Exception
            MessageBox.Show(ex.Message)
        End Try
    End Sub
```

When the button is clicked, it will display a message box with File Not Found. Even though the File Not Found error is raised by Err.Raise, it is translated to a .NET exception automatically.

Similarly, exceptions that are generated by a Throw statement in a called routine can be trapped by On Error in a calling routine. The exception is then translated into an Err object that works like the VB6 Err object.

Error Logging

Error logging is important in many applications for thorough troubleshooting. It is common for end users of an application to not remember what the error said exactly. Recording specific errors in a log enables you to get the specific error message without recreating the error.

While error logging is very important, you only want to use it to trap specific levels of errors because it carries overhead and can reduce the performance of your application. Specifically, log only errors that are critical to your application integrity — for instance, an error that would cause the data that the application is working with to become invalid.

There are three main approaches to error logging:

❑ Write error information in a text file or flat file located in a strategic location.

❑ Write error information to a central database.

❑ Write error information to the system Event Log, which is available on all the versions of Windows supported by the .NET Framework 3.0. The .NET Framework includes a component that can be used to write and read from the System, Application, and Security Logs on any given machine.

The type of logging you choose depends on the categories of errors you wish to trap and the types of machines on which you will run your application. If you choose to write to the Event Log, you need to categorize the errors and write them in the appropriate log file. Resource-, hardware-, and system-level errors fit best into the System Event Log. Data access errors fit best into the Application Event Log. Permission errors fit best into the Security Event Log.

The Event Log

Three Event Logs are available: the System, Application, and Security Logs. Events in these logs can be viewed using the Event Viewer, which is accessed from the Control Panel. Access Administrative Tools and then select the Event Viewer subsection to view events. Typically, your applications would use the Application Event Log.

Event logging is available in your program through an `EventLog` component, which can both read and write to all of the available logs on a machine. The `EventLog` component is part of the `System .Diagnostics` namespace. The component allows adding and removing custom Event Logs, reading and writing to and from the standard Windows Event Logs, and creating customized Event Log entries.

Event Logs can become full, as they have a limited amount of space, so you only want to write critical information to your Event Logs. You can customize each of your system Event Log's properties by changing the log size and specifying how the system will handle events that occur when the log is full. You can configure the log to overwrite data when it is full or overwrite all events older than a given number of days. Remember that the Event Log that is written to is based on where the code is running from, so if there are many tiers, then you must locate the proper Event Log information to research the error further.

There are five types of Event Log entries you can make. These five types are divided into event type entries and audit type entries.

Event type entries are as follows:

- ❑ **Information** — Added when events such as a service starting or stopping occurs
- ❑ **Warning** — Occurs when a noncritical event happens that might cause future problems, such as disk space getting low
- ❑ **Error** — Should be logged when something occurs that prevents normal processing, such as a startup service not being able to start

Audit type entries usually go into the Security Log and can be either of the following:

- ❑ **Success audit** — For example, a success audit might be a successful login through an application to an SQL Server.
- ❑ **Failure audit** — A failure audit might come in handy if a user doesn't have access to create an output file on a certain file system.

If you don't specify the type of Event Log entry, an information type entry is generated.

Each entry in an Event Log has a `Source` property. The `Source` property is required and is a programmer-defined string that is assigned to an event that helps categorize the events in a log. A new `Source` must be defined prior to being used in an entry in an Event Log. The `SourceExists` method is used to determine whether a particular source already exists on the given computer. We recommend that you use a string that is relevant to where the error originated, such as the component's name. Packaged software often uses the software name as the `Source` in the Application Log. This helps group errors that occur by specific software package.

The `EventLog` component is in the `System.Diagnostics` namespace. To use it conveniently, include an `Imports System.Diagnostics` statement in the declarations section of your code.

> **Certain security rights must be obtained in order to manipulate Event Logs. Ordinary programs can read all of the Event Logs and write to the Application Event Log. Special privileges, on the administrator level, are required to perform tasks such as clearing and deleting Event Logs. Your application should not normally need to do these tasks, or to write to any log besides the Application Event Log.**

The most common events, methods, and properties for the `EventLog` component are listed and described in the following tables.

Events, Methods, and Properties

The following table describes the relevant event:

Event	Description
EntryWritten	Generated when an event is written to a log

The following table describes the relevant methods:

Methods	Description
CreateEventSource	Creates an event source in the specified log
DeleteEventSource	Deletes an event source and associated entries
WriteEntry	Writes a string to a specified log
Exists	Can be used to determine whether a specific event log exists
SourceExists	Used to determine whether a specific source exists in a log
GetEventLogs	Retrieves a list of all Event Logs on a particular computer
Delete	Deletes an entire Event Log. Use this method with care.

The following table describes the relevant properties:

Properties	Description
Source	Specifies the source of the entry to be written
Log	Used to specify a log to write to. The three logs are System, Application, and Security. The System Log is the default if not specified.

The following example illustrates some of these methods and properties:

```
Sub LoggingExample1()
  Dim objLog As New EventLog()
  Dim objLogEntryType As EventLogEntryType
  Try
    Throw (New EntryPointNotFoundException())
  Catch objA As System.EntryPointNotFoundException
    If Not EventLog.SourceExists("Example") Then
      EventLog.CreateEventSource("Example", "System")
    End If
    objLog.Source = "Example"
    objLog.Log = "System"
    objLogEntryType = EventLogEntryType.Information
    objLog.WriteEntry("Error: " & objA.Message, objLogEntryType)
  End Try
End Sub
```

The preceding code declares two variables: one to instantiate your log and one to hold your entry's type information. Note that you need to check for the existence of a source prior to creating it. The following two lines of code accomplish that:

```
If Not EventLog.SourceExists("Example") Then
   EventLog.CreateEventSource("Example", "System")
```

Once you have verified or created your source, you can set the `Source` property of the `EventLog` object, the `Log` property to specify which log you want to write to, and `EventLogEntryType` to `Information` (other options are `Warning`, `Error`, `SuccessAudit`, and `FailureAudit`). If you attempt to write to a source that does not exist in a specific log, you get an error. After you have set these three properties of the `EventLog` object, you can then write your entry. In this example, you concatenated the word `Error` with the actual exception's `Message` property to form the string to write to the log:

```
objLog.Source = "Example"
objLog.Log = "System"
objLogEntryType = EventLogEntryType.Information
objLog.WriteEntry("Error: " & objA.Message, objLogEntryType)
```

Writing to Trace Files

As an alternative to the Event Log, you can write your debugging and error information to trace files. A *trace file* is a text-based file that you generate in your program to track detailed information about an error condition. Trace files are also a good way to supplement your event logging if you wish to track detailed information that would potentially fill the Event Log.

A more detailed explanation of the variety of trace tools and uses in debugging follows in the section "Analyzing Problems and Measuring Performance via the Trace Class," but this section covers some of the techniques for using the `StreamWriter` interface in your development of a trace file.

The concepts involved in writing to text files include setting up streamwriters and debug listeners. The `StreamWriter` interface is handled through the `System.IO` namespace. It enables you to interface with the files in the file system on a given machine. The `Debug` class interfaces with these output objects through listener objects. The job of any listener object is to collect, store, and send the stored output to text files, logs, and the Output window. In the example, you will use the `TextWriterTraceListener` interface.

As you will see, the `StreamWriter` object opens an output path to a text file, and by binding the `StreamWriter` object to a listener object you can direct debug output to a text file.

Trace listeners are output targets and can be a `TextWriter` or an `EventLog`, or can send output to the default Output window (which is `DefaultTraceListener`). The `TextWriterTraceListener` accommodates the `WriteLine` method of a `Debug` interface by providing an output object that stores information to be flushed to the output stream, which you set up by the `StreamWriter` interface.

The following table lists some of the commonly used methods from the `StreamWriter` object:

Method	Description
Close	Closes the `StreamWriter`
Flush	Flushes all content of the `StreamWriter` to the output file designated upon creation of the `StreamWriter`
Write	Writes byte output to the stream. Optional parameters allow designation of where in the stream (offset).
WriteLine	Writes characters followed by a line terminator to the current stream object

The following table lists some of the methods associated with the `Debug` object, which provides the output mechanism for your text file example to follow:

Method	Description
Assert	Checks a condition and displays a message if `False`
Close	Executes a flush on the output buffer and closes all listeners
Fail	Emits an error message in the form of an Abort/Retry/Ignore message box
Flush	Flushes the output buffer and writes it to the listeners
Write	Writes bytes to the output buffer
WriteLine	Writes characters followed by a line terminator to the output buffer
WriteIf	Writes bytes to the output buffer if a specific condition is `True`
WriteLineIF	Writes characters followed by a line terminator to the output buffer if a specific condition is `True`

The following example shows how you can open an existing file (called `mytext.txt`) for output and assign it to the `Listeners` object of the `Debug` object so that it can catch your `Debug.WriteLine` statements:

```
Sub LoggingExample2()
  Dim objWriter As New _
      IO.StreamWriter("C:\mytext.txt", True)
  Debug.Listeners.Add(New TextWriterTraceListener(objWriter))
  Try
    Throw (New EntryPointNotFoundException())
  Catch objA As System.EntryPointNotFoundException
    Debug.WriteLine(objA.Message)
```

```
            objWriter.Flush()
            objWriter.Close()
            objWriter = Nothing
      End Try
   End Sub
```

Looking in detail at this code, you first create a `StreamWriter` that is assigned to a file in your local file system:

```
Dim objWriter As New _
    IO.StreamWriter("C:\mytext.txt", True)
```

You then assign your `StreamWriter` to a debug listener by using the `Add` method:

```
Debug.Listeners.Add(New TextWriterTraceListener (objWriter))
```

This example forces an exception and catches it, writing the `Message` property of the `Exception` object (which is `Entry point was not found`) to the debug buffer through the `WriteLine` method:

```
Debug.WriteLine(objA.Message)
```

Finally, you flush the listener buffer to the output file and free your resources:

```
objWriter.Flush()
objWriter.Close()
objWriter = Nothing
```

Analyzing Problems and Measuring Performance via the Trace Class

The trace tools in the .NET Framework make use of the `Trace` class, which provides properties and methods that help you trace the execution of your code. By default, tracing is enabled in VB 2005, so not unlike your previous debug discussion, all you have to do is set up the output and utilize its capabilities.

You can specify the detail level you want to perform for your tracing output by configuring trace switches. You will see an example of setting a trace switch shortly, but it is important to understand what a trace switch can do and what the settings for trace switches mean.

Trace switches can be either `BooleanSwitch` or `TraceSwitch`. `BooleanSwitch` has a value of either 0 or 1 and is used to determine whether tracing is off or on, respectively, while `TraceSwitch` allows you to specify a level of tracing based on five enumerated values. You can manage a `BooleanSwitch` or `TraceSwitch` as an environment variable. Once a switch is established, you can create and initialize it in code and use it with either trace or debug.

A `TraceSwitch` can have five enumerated levels, which can be read as 0–4 or checked with four properties provided in the switch class interface. The four properties return a Boolean value based on whether the switch is set to a certain level or higher. The five enumerated levels for `TraceSwitch` are as follows:

Level	Description
0	None
1	Only error messages
2	Warning and error messages
3	Information, warning, and error messages
4	Verbose, information, warning, and error messages

The four properties are `TraceError`, `TraceWarning`, `TraceInfo`, and `TraceVerbose`. For example, if your switch were set at number 2 and you asked for the `TraceError` or `TraceWarning` properties, they would return `True`, while the `TraceInformation` and `TraceVerbose` properties would return `False`.

An environment variable managed either via the command line or under My computer ⇨ Properties ⇨ Advanced within the Environment Variables button.

Within the Environment Variables button, you add a new `User` variable, giving it the `SwitchName` and `Value` for that switch.

From the command line, type **Set _Switch_MySwitch = 0**

The value on the left of the = symbol is the name of the switch, and the value on its right is either 0 or 1 for a `BooleanSwitch` or 0–4 for a `TraceSwitch`. Note that there is a space between the word `Set` and the leading underscore of `_Switch`. Once you have typed this line, if you follow that by the plain `SET` command at the command line, it will show your new switch as an environment variable, as shown in Figure 9-6.

Figure 9-6

For the example that follows, you have the output directed to the default Output window:

```
Sub TraceExample1()
  Dim objTraceSwitch As TraceSwitch
  objTraceSwitch = New TraceSwitch("ExampleSwitch", "Test Trace Switch")
  objTraceSwitch.Level = TraceLevel.Error
  Try
    Throw (New EntryPointNotFoundException())
  Catch objA As System.EntryPointNotFoundException
    Trace.WriteLineIf(objTraceSwitch.TraceVerbose, _
        "First Trace " & objA.Source)
    Trace.WriteLineIf(objTraceSwitch.TraceError, _
        "Second Trace " & objA.Message)
  End Try
End Sub
```

You begin by assigning your switch to an existing registry entry and setting its level:

```
objTraceSwitch = New TraceSwitch("ExampleSwitch", "Test Trace Switch")
objTraceSwitch.Level = TraceLevel.Error
```

After you throw your exception, you first cause your trace output listener to catch the Source property of your Exception object based on whether the value of your switch is TraceVerbose or better:

```
Trace.WriteLineIf(objTraceSwitch.TraceVerbose, _
    "First Trace " & objA.Source)
```

Because the tracing level is set to Error, this line is skipped; and you continue by writing a trace to the Output window to include the message information if the level is set to Error:

```
Trace.WriteLineIf(objTraceSwitch.TraceError, _
    "Second Trace " & objA.Message)
```

As indicated in your Output window, you successfully wrote only the second trace line based on the level being Error on your trace switch (see Figure 9-7).

Figure 9-7

Tracing can also be helpful in determining the performance of your application. Overall, your application might appear to be working fine, but it is always good to be able to measure the performance of your application so that environment changes or degradation over time can be counteracted. The basic concept here is to use conditional compilation so that you can toggle your performance-measuring code on and off:

```
Sub TraceExample2()
  Dim connInfo As New Connection()
  Dim rstInfo As New Recordset()
  #Const bTrace = 1
  Dim objWriter As New _
    IO.StreamWriter(IO.File.Open("c:\mytext.txt", IO.FileMode.OpenOrCreate))
  connInfo.ConnectionString = "Provider = sqloledb.1" & _
    ";Persist Security Info = False;" & "Initial Catalog = Northwind;" & _
    "DataSource = LocalServer"
  connInfo.Open(connInfo.ConnectionString, "sa")
  Trace.Listeners.Add(New TextWriterTraceListener(objWriter))
  #If bTrace Then
    Trace.WriteLine("Begun db query at " & now())
  #End If
  rstInfo.Open("SELECT CompanyName, OrderID, " & _
    "OrderDate FROM Orders AS a LEFT JOIN Customers" & _
    " AS b ON a.CustomerID = b.CustomerID WHERE " & _
    "a.CustomerID = 'Chops'", connInfo, _
    CursorTypeEnum.adOpenForwardOnly, _
    LockTypeEnum.adLockBatchOptimistic)
  #If bTrace Then
    Trace.WriteLine("Ended db query at " & now())
  #End If
  Trace.Listeners.Clear()
  objWriter.Close()
  rstInfo.Close()
  connInfo.Close()
  rstInfo = Nothing
  connInfo = Nothing
End Sub
```

> **This subroutine uses ADO, so be sure to add a reference to an ADO library and an** `Imports ADODB` **statement in the declarations section of the module.**

In this simple example, you are trying to measure the performance of a database query using a conditional constant defined as `bTrace` by the following code:

```
#Const bTrace = 1
```

You establish your database connection strings, and then right before you execute your query you write to a log file based on whether you are in tracing mode or not:

```
#If bTrace Then
  Trace.WriteLine("Begun db query at " & now())
#End If
```

Again, after your query returns you write to your log only if you are in tracing mode:

```
#If bTrace Then
  Trace.WriteLine("Ended db query at" & now())
#End If
```

Always remember that tracing can potentially slow the application down, so use this functionality only when troubleshooting, not all the time.

Summary

As mentioned in Chapter 1, a major weakness of pre-.NET versions of Visual Basic was limited error-handling capabilities. As you've seen in this chapter, that problem has been thoroughly addressed. Errors and unexpected conditions are now packaged as exceptions, and these exception objects have special syntax to detect and manage them. The `Try...Catch...Finally...End Try` construct allows Visual Basic's error-handling capabilities to be on a par with other advanced languages.

This chapter reviewed the exception object and the syntax available to work with exceptions. You have looked at the various properties of exceptions and learned how to use the exposed information. You have also seen how to promote exceptions to consuming code using the `Throw` statement, and how structured exception handling interoperates with the old-style `On Error`. As discussed, any new code you write should use the new exception-handling capabilities of .NET. Avoid using the old-style `On Error` except for maintenance tasks in old code.

Also covered are other topics related to error handling:

❑   Error logging to Event Logs and trace files

❑   Instrumentation and measuring performance

❑   Tracing techniques

Using the full capabilities for error handling that are now available in VB 2005 can make your applications more reliable and help you diagnose problems faster when they do occur. Proper use of tracing and instrumentation can also help you tune your application for better performance.

10

Data Access with ADO.NET 2.0

ADO.NET 1.*x* was the successor to ActiveX Data Objects 2.6 (ADO). The main goal of ADO.NET 1.*x* was to enable developers to easily create distributed, data-sharing applications in the .NET Framework. The main goals of ADO.NET 2.0 are to improve the performance of existing features in ADO.NET 1.*x*, to provide easier use, and to add new features without breaking backward compatibility.

> *Throughout this chapter, when ADO.NET is mentioned without a version number after it (that is, 1.x or 2.0), this means that the statement applies to all versions of ADO.NET.*

ADO.NET 1.*x* was built upon industry standards such as XML, and it provided a data access interface to communicate with data sources such as SQL Server and Oracle. ADO.NET 2.0 builds upon these concepts, while increasing performance. Applications can use ADO.NET to connect to these data sources and retrieve, manipulate, and update data. ADO.NET 2.0 does not break any compatibility with ADO.NET 1.*x*; it only adds to the stack of functionality.

In solutions that require disconnected or remote access to data, ADO.NET 2.0 uses XML to exchange data between programs or with Web pages. Any component that can read XML can make use of ADO.NET components. A receiving component does not even have to be an ADO.NET component if a transmitting ADO.NET component packages and delivers a data set in an XML format. Transmitting information in XML-formatted data sets enables programmers to easily separate the data-processing and user interface components of a data-sharing application onto separate servers. This can greatly improve both the performance and maintainability of systems that support many users.

For distributed applications, ADO.NET 1.*x* proved that the use of XML data sets provided performance advantages relative to the COM marshaling used to transmit disconnected data sets in ADO. Since transmission of data sets occurred through XML streams in a simple text-based standard accepted throughout the industry, receiving components did not require any of the architectural restrictions required by COM. XML data sets used in ADO.NET 1.*x* also avoided the processing cost of converting values in the Fields collection of a `Recordset` to datatypes recognized by COM. Virtually any two components from different systems can share XML data sets provided that they both use the same XML schema for formatting the data set. This continues to be true in ADO.NET 2.0, but the story gets better. The XML integration in ADO.NET 2.0 is even stronger now, and extensive work was done to improve the performance of the `DataSet` object, particularly in the areas of serialization and memory usage.

ADO.NET also supports the scalability required by Web-based data-sharing applications. Web applications must often serve hundreds, or even thousands, of users. By default, ADO.NET does not retain lengthy database locks or active connections that monopolize limited resources. This allows the number of users to grow with only a small increase in the demands made on the resources of a system.

In this chapter, you will see that ADO.NET 2.0 is a very extensive and flexible API for accessing many types of data, and because ADO.NET 2.0 is an incremental change to ADO.NET 1.x, all previous ADO.NET knowledge already learned can be leveraged. In fact, to get the most out of this chapter you should be fairly familiar with ADO.NET 1.x and the entire .NET Framework 1.x.

This chapter demonstrates how to use the ADO.NET 2.0 object model in order to build flexible, fast, scalable data access objects and applications. Specifically, it covers the following:

- ❑ The ADO.NET 2.0 architecture
- ❑ Some of the new features offered in ADO.NET 2.0, specifically batch updates, `DataSet` performance improvements, and asynchronous processing
- ❑ Working with the Common Provider Model
- ❑ Building a data access component

ADO.NET 2.0 Architecture Enhancements

The main design goals of ADO.NET 2.0 are as follows:

- ❑ To add many new customer-driven features yet still remain backwardly compatible with ADO.NET 1.x
- ❑ Improve upon performance of ADO.NET 1.x
- ❑ Provide more power for power users
- ❑ Take advantage of new SQL Server 2005 features

In distributed applications, the concept of working with disconnected data is very common. In a disconnected model, once you have retrieved the data you need, the connection to the data source is dropped — you work with the data locally. This model is very popular because it frees up precious database server resources, which leads to highly scalable applications. The ADO.NET solution for disconnected data is the `DataSet` object.

ADO.NET Components

To better support the disconnected model, the ADO.NET components separate data access from data manipulation. This is accomplished via two main components, the DataSet and the .NET Data Provider. Figure 10-1 illustrates the concept of separating data access from data manipulation.

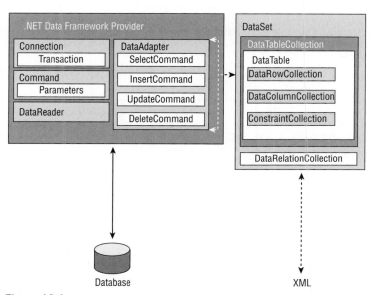

Figure 10-1

The DataSet is the core component of the disconnected architecture of ADO.NET. It is explicitly designed for data access independent of any data source. As a result, it can be used with multiple and differing data sources, with XML data, or even to manage data local to an application such as an in-memory data cache. The DataSet contains a collection of one or more DataTable objects made up of rows and columns of data, as well as primary key, foreign key, constraint, and relation information about the data in the DataTable objects. It is basically an in-memory database, but what sets it apart is that it doesn't care whether its data is obtained from a database, an XML file, a combination of the two, or somewhere else. You can apply inserts, updates, and deletes to the DataSet and then push the changes back to the data source, no matter where the data source lives! This chapter offers an in-depth look at the DataSet object family and its ADO.NET 2.0 enhancements.

The other core element of the ADO.NET architecture is the .NET Data Provider, whose components are designed for data manipulation (as opposed to data access with the DataSet). These components are listed in the following table.

The DataAdapter uses Command objects to execute SQL commands at the data source to both load the DataSet with data and to reconcile changes made to the data in the DataSet with the data source. You will take a closer look at this later in the detailed discussion of the DataAdapter object.

.NET Data Providers can be written for any data source, though this topic is beyond the scope of this chapter.

Object	Activity
Connection	Provides connectivity to a data source
Command	Enables access to database commands to return and modify data, run stored procedures, and send or retrieve parameter information
DataReader	Provides a high-performance, read-only stream of data from the data source
DataAdapter	Provides the bridge between the DataSet object and the data source

The .NET Framework 2.0 ships with three .NET Data Providers: the SQL Server .NET Data Provider, the Oracle .NET Data Provider, and the OLE DB .NET Data Provider.

> **Do not confuse the OLE DB .NET Data Provider with generic OLE DB providers.**

The rule of thumb when deciding which data provider to use is to first use a .NET Relational Database Management System (RDBMS)–specific Data Provider if it is available, and to use the .NET OLE DB Provider when connecting to any other data source. For example, if you were writing an application that uses SQL Server, then you would want to use the SQL Server .NET Data Provider. The .NET OLE DB Provider is used to access any data source exposed through OLE DB, such as Microsoft Access, Open DataBase Connectivity (ODBC), and so on. You will be taking a closer look at these later.

.NET Data Providers

.NET Data Providers are used for connecting to a RDBMS-specific database (such as SQL Server or Oracle), executing commands, and retrieving results. Those results are either processed directly (via a DataReader) or placed in an ADO.NET DataSet (via a DataAdapter) in order to be exposed to the user in an ad hoc manner, combined with data from multiple sources, or passed around between tiers. NET Data Providers are designed to be lightweight, to create a minimal layer between the data source and the .NET programmer's code, and to increase performance while not sacrificing any functionality. Currently, the .NET Framework supports three Data Providers: the SQL Server .NET Data Provider (for Microsoft SQL Server 7.0 or later), the Oracle .NET Data Provider, and the OLE DB .NET Data Provider. Most RDBMS vendors are now producing their own .NET Data Providers in order to encourage .NET developers to use their databases.

Connection Object

To connect to a specific data source, you use a data Connection object. To connect to Microsoft SQL Server 7.0 or later, you need to use the SqlConnection object of the SQL Server .NET Data Provider. You need to use the OleDbConnection object of the OLE DB .NET Data Provider to connect to an OLE

DB data source, or the OLE DB Provider for SQL Server (SQLOLEDB) to connect to versions of Microsoft SQL Server earlier than 7.0.

Connection String Format — OleDbConnection

For the OLE DB .NET Data Provider, the connection string format is the same as the connection string format used in ADO, with the following exceptions:

❑   The `Provider` keyword is required.

❑   The `URL`, `Remote Provider`, and `Remote Server` keywords are not supported.

Here is an example `OleDbConnection` connection string connecting to an Oracle database (note this is all one line):

```
Provider=msdaora;Data Source=MyOracleDB;User Id=myUsername;Password=myPassword;
```

Connection String Format — SqlConnection

The SQL Server .NET Data Provider supports a connection string format that is similar to the OLE DB (ADO) connection string format. The only thing that you need to omit, obviously, is the provider name-value pair, since you know you are using the SQL Server .NET Data Provider. Here is an example of a `SqlConnection` connection string:

```
data source=(local);initial catalog=pubs;Integrated Security=SSPI;
```

Command Object

After establishing a connection, you can execute commands and return results from a data source (such as SQL Server) using a `Command` object. A `Command` object can be created using the `Command` constructor, or by calling the `CreateCommand` method of the `Connection` object. When creating a `Command` object using the `Command` constructor, you need to specify a SQL statement to execute at the data source, and a `Connection` object. The `Command` object's SQL statement can be queried and modified using the `CommandText` property. The following code is an example of executing a `SELECT` command and returning a `DataReader` object:

```
' Build the SQL and Connection strings.
Dim sql As String = "SELECT * FROM authors"
Dim connectionString As String = "Initial Catalog=pubs;" _
 & "Data Source=(local);Integrated Security=SSPI;"
' Initialize the SqlCommand with the SQL
' and Connection strings.
Dim command As SqlCommand = New SqlCommand(sql, _
    New SqlConnection(connectionString))
' Open the connection.
command.Connection.Open()
' Execute the query, return a SqlDataReader object.
' CommandBehavior.CloseConnection flags the
' DataReader to automatically close the DB connection
' when it is closed.
Dim dataReader As SqlDataReader = _
    command.ExecuteReader(CommandBehavior.CloseConnection)
```

The `CommandText` property of the `Command` object executes all SQL statements in addition to the standard `SELECT`, `UPDATE`, `INSERT`, and `DELETE` statements. For example, you could create tables, foreign keys, primary keys, and so on, by executing the applicable SQL from the `Command` object.

The `Command` object exposes several `Execute` methods to perform the intended action. When returning results as a stream of data, `ExecuteReader` is used to return a `DataReader` object. `ExecuteScalar` is used to return a singleton value. In ADO.NET 2.0, the `ExecuteRow` method has been added, which returns a single row of data in the form of a `SqlRecord` object. `ExecuteNonQuery` is used to execute commands that do not return rows, which usually includes stored procedures that have output parameters and/or return values. (You'll learn about stored procedures in a later section.)

When using a `DataAdapter` with a `DataSet`, `Command` objects are used to return and modify data at the data source through the `DataAdapter` object's `SelectCommand`, `InsertCommand`, `UpdateCommand`, and `DeleteCommand` properties.

> Note that the `DataAdapter` object's `SelectCommand` property must be set before the `Fill` method is called.

The `InsertCommand`, `UpdateCommand`, and `DeleteCommand` properties must be set before the `Update` method is called. You will take a closer look at this when you look at the `DataAdapter` object.

Using Stored Procedures with Command Objects

This section offers a quick look at how to use stored procedures, before delving into a more complex example later in the chapter demonstrating how you can build a reusable data access component that also uses stored procedures. The motivation for using stored procedures is simple. Imagine you have the following code:

```
SELECT au_lname FROM authors WHERE au_id='172-32-1176'
```

If you pass that to SQL Server using `ExecuteReader` on `SqlCommand` (or any execute method, for that matter), SQL Server has to compile the code before it can run it, in much the same way that VB .NET applications have to be compiled before they can be executed. This compilation takes up SQL Server's time, so it's easy to deduce that if you can reduce the amount of compilation that SQL Server has to do, database performance should increase. (Compare the speed of execution of a compiled application against interpreted code.)

That's what stored procedures are all about: You create a procedure, store it in the database, and because the procedure is recognized and understood ahead of time, it can be compiled ahead of time and ready for use in your application.

Stored procedures are very easy to use, but the code to access them is sometimes a little verbose. The next section demonstrates some code that can make accessing stored procedures a bit more straightforward, but to make things clearer, let's start by building a simple application that demonstrates how to create and call a stored procedure.

Creating a Stored Procedure

To create a stored procedure, you can either use the tools in Visual Studio .NET or you can use the tools in SQL Server's Enterprise Manager if you are using SQL Server 2000 or in SQL Server Management Studio if you are using SQL Server 2005. (Technically, you can use a third-party tool or just create the stored procedure in a good old-fashioned SQL script.)

This example builds a stored procedure that returns all of the columns for a given author ID. The SQL to do this looks like this:

```
SELECT
    au_id, au_lname, au_fname, phone,
    address, city, state, zip, contract
FROM
    authors
WHERE
    au_id = whatever author ID you want
```

The "whatever author ID you want" part is important. When using stored procedures, you typically have to be able to provide parameters into the stored procedure and use them from within code. This isn't a book about SQL Server, so this example focuses only on the principle involved. You can find many resources on the Web about building stored procedures (they've been around a very long time, and they're most definitely not a .NET-specific feature).

Variables in SQL Server are prefixed by the @ symbol, so if you have a variable called au id, then your SQL will look like this:

```
SELECT
    au_id, au_lname, au_fname, phone,
    address, city, state, zip, contract
FROM
    authors
WHERE
    au_id = @au_id
```

In Visual Studio 2005, stored procedures can be accessed using the Server Explorer. Simply add a new data connection (or use an existing data connection), and then drill down into the Stored Procedures folder in the management tree. A number of stored procedures are already loaded. The byroyalty procedure is a stored procedure provided by the sample pubs database developers. Figure 10-2 illustrates the stored procedures of the pubs database in Visual Studio 2005.

To create a new stored procedure, just right-click the Stored Procedures folder in the Server Explorer and select Add New Stored Procedure to invoke the Editor window.

A stored procedure can be either a single SQL statement or a complex set of statements. T-SQL supports branches, loops, and other variable declarations, which can make for some pretty complex stored procedure code. However, your stored procedure is just a single line of SQL. You need to declare the parameter that you want to pass in (@au_id) and the name of the procedure: usp_authors_Get_By_ID. Here's code for the stored procedure:

```
CREATE PROCEDURE usp_authors_Get_By_ID
    @au_id varchar(11)
```

```
AS
SELECT
    au_id, au_lname, au_fname, phone,
    address, city, state, zip, contract
FROM
    authors
WHERE
    au_id = @au_id
```

Figure 10-2

Click OK to save the stored procedure in the database. You're now able to access this stored procedure from code.

Calling the Stored Procedure

Calling the stored procedure is just a matter of creating a `SqlConnection` object to connect to the database, and a `SqlCommand` object to run the stored procedure.

The sample code for this chapter demonstrates a solution called `Examples.sln`, which includes a project called `AdoNetFeaturesTest`.

> For all of the data access examples in this chapter, you need the pubs database, which can be downloaded from MSDN. In addition, be sure to run the `examples.sql` file — available with the code download for this chapter — in SQL Server 2005 Management Studio before running the code examples. This creates the necessary stored procedures and functions in the pubs database.

Now you have to decide what you want to return by calling the stored procedure. In this case, you return an instance of the SqlDataReader object. The TestForm.vb file contains a method called GetAuthorSqlReader that takes an author ID and returns an instance of a SqlDataReader. Here is the code for the method:

```
Private Function GetAuthorSqlReader(ByVal authorId As String) As SqlDataReader
    ' Build a SqlCommand
    Dim command As SqlCommand = New SqlCommand("usp_authors_Get_By_ID", _
        GetPubsConnection())
    ' Tell the command we are calling a stored procedure
    command.CommandType = CommandType.StoredProcedure
    ' Add the @au_id parameter information to the command
    command.Parameters.Add(New SqlParameter("@au_id", authorId))
    ' The reader requires an open connection
    command.Connection.Open()
    ' Execute the sql and return the reader
    Return command.ExecuteReader(CommandBehavior.CloseConnection)
End Function
```

Notice that in the SqlCommand's constructor call you have factored out creating a connection to the pubs database into a separate helper method. This is used later in other code examples in your form.

Here is the code for the GetPubsConnection helper method:

```
Private Function GetPubsConnection() As SqlConnection
    ' Build a SqlConnection based on the config value.
    Return New _
        SqlConnection(ConfigurationSettings.AppSettings("dbConnectionString"))
End Function
```

The most significant thing this code does is to grab a connection string to the database from the application's configuration file, the app.config file. Here is what the entry in the app.config file looks like:

```
<appSettings>
    <add key="dbConnectionString" value="data source=(local);initial
        catalog=pubs;Integrated Security=SSPI;" />
</appSettings>
```

Although the helper method doesn't do much, it is nice to place this code in a separate method. This way, if the code to get a connection to the databases needs to be changed, then the code only has to be changed in one place.

Accessing a stored procedure is more verbose (but not more difficult) than accessing a normal SQL statement through the methods discussed thus far. The approach is as follows:

- ❑ Create a SqlCommand object.
- ❑ Configure it to access a stored procedure by setting the CommandType property.
- ❑ Add parameters that exactly match those in the stored procedure itself.
- ❑ Execute the stored procedure using one of the SqlCommand object's Execute*** methods

There's no real need to build an impressive UI for this application, as we're about to add a button named `getAuthorByIdButton` that calls the `GetAuthorSqlRecord` helper method and displays the selected author's name. Here is the button's `Click` event handler:

```
Private Sub _getAuthorByIdButton_Click(ByVal sender As System.Object, _
    ByVal e As System.EventArgs) Handles _getAuthorByIdButton.Click
    Dim reader As SqlDataReader = Me. GetAuthorSqlReader ("409-56-7008")
    If reader.Read()
        MsgBox(reader("au_fname").ToString() & "  " _
            & reader("au_lname").ToString())
    End If

    reader.Close()
End Sub
```

This has hard-coded an author ID of 409-56-7008. Run the code now and you should see the result shown in Figure 10-3.

Figure 10-3

DataReader Object

You can use the `DataReader` to retrieve a read-only, forward-only stream of data from the database. Using the `DataReader` can increase application performance and reduce system overhead because only one buffered row at a time is ever in memory. With the `DataReader` object, you are getting as close to the raw data as possible in ADO.NET; you do not have to go through the overhead of populating a `DataSet` object, which sometimes may be expensive if the `DataSet` contains a lot of data. The disadvantage of using a `DataReader` object is that it requires an open database connection and increases network activity.

After creating an instance of the `Command` object, a `DataReader` is created by calling the `ExecuteReader` method of the `Command` object. Here is an example of creating a `DataReader` and iterating through it to print out its values to the screen:

```
Private Sub TraverseDataReader()

    ' Build the SQL and Connection strings.
    Dim sql As String = "SELECT * FROM authors"
    Dim connectionString As String = "Initial Catalog=pubs;" _
        & "Data Source=(local);Integrated Security=SSPI;"
```

```vb
        ' Initialize the SqlCommand with the SQL query and connection strings.
        Dim command As SqlCommand = New SqlCommand(sql, _
            New SqlConnection(connectionString))
        ' Open the connection.
        command.Connection.Open()
        ' Execute the query, return a SqlDataReader object.
        ' CommandBehavior.CloseConnection flags the
        ' DataReader to automatically close the DB connection
        ' when it is closed.
        Dim reader As SqlDataReader = _
            command.ExecuteReader(CommandBehavior.CloseConnection)
        ' Loop through the records and print the values.
        Do While reader.Read
            Console.WriteLine(reader.GetString(1) & " " & reader.GetString(2))
        Loop
        ' Close the DataReader (and its connection).
        reader.Close()

    End Sub
```

This code snippet uses the `SqlCommand` object to execute the query via the `ExecuteReader` method. This method returns a populated `SqlDataReader` object, which you loop through and print out the author names. The main difference between this code and looping through the rows of a `DataTable` is that you have to stay connected while you loop through the data in the `DataReader` object; this is because the `DataReader` reads in only a small stream of data at a time to conserve memory space.

> At this point, an obvious design question is whether to use the `DataReader` or the `DataSet`. The answer depends upon performance. If you want high performance, and you are only going to access the data you are retrieving once, then the `DataReader` is the way to go. If you need access to the same data multiple times, or if you need to model a complex relationship in memory, then the `DataSet` is the way to go. As always, test each option thoroughly before deciding which one is the best.

The `Read` method of the `DataReader` object is used to obtain a row from the results of the query. Each column of the returned row may be accessed by passing the name or ordinal reference of the column to the `DataReader`, or, for best performance, the `DataReader` provides a series of methods that enable you to access column values in their native datatypes (`GetDateTime`, `GetDouble`, `GetGuid`, `GetInt32`, and so on). Using the typed accessor methods when the underlying datatype is known reduces the amount of type conversion required (converting from type `Object`) when retrieving the column value.

The `DataReader` provides a nonbuffered stream of data that enables procedural logic to efficiently process results from a data source sequentially. The `DataReader` is a good choice when retrieving large amounts of data; only one row of data is cached in memory at a time. You should always call the `Close` method when you are through using the `DataReader` object, as well as close the `DataReader` object's database connection; otherwise, the connection won't be closed until the garbage collector gets around to collecting the object. Note how you use the `CommandBehavior.CloseConnection` enumeration value on the `SqlDataReader.ExecuteReader` method. This tells the `SqlCommand` object to automatically close the database connection when the `SqlDataReader.Close` method is called.

> If your command contains output parameters or return values, they will not be available until the `DataReader` is closed.

Executing Commands Asynchronously

In ADO.NET 2.0, additional support enables `Command` objects to execute their commands asynchronously, which can result in a huge perceived performance gain in many applications, especially in Windows Forms applications. This can come in very handy, especially if you ever have to execute a long-running SQL statement. This section examines how this new functionality enables you to add asynchronous processing to enhance the responsiveness of an application.

The `SqlCommand` object provides three different asynchronous call options: `BeginExecuteReader`, `BeginExecuteNonQuery`, and `BeginExecuteXmlReader`. Each of these methods has a corresponding "end" method — that is, `EndExecuteReader`, `EndExecutreNonQuery`, and `EndExecuteXmlReader`. As you have just finished covering the `DataReader` object, let's look at an example using the `BeginExecuteReader` method to execute a long-running query.

In the `AdoNetFeaturesTest` project, I have added a `Button` and an associated `Click` event handler to the form that will initiate the asynchronous call to get a `DataReader` instance:

```
Private Sub _testAsyncCallButton_Click(ByVal sender As System.Object, _
    ByVal e As System.EventArgs) Handles _testAsyncCallButton.Click

    ' Build a connection for the async call to the database.
    Dim connection As SqlConnection = GetPubsConnection()
    connection.ConnectionString &= "Asynchronous Processing=true;"

    ' Build a command to call the stored procedure.
    Dim command As New SqlCommand("usp_Long_Running_Procedure", connection)

    ' Set the command type to stored procedure.
    command.CommandType = CommandType.StoredProcedure

    ' The reader requires an open connection.
    connection.Open()

    ' Make the asynchronous call to the database.
    command.BeginExecuteReader(AddressOf Me.AsyncCallback, _
    command, CommandBehavior.CloseConnection)
End Sub
```

The first thing you do is reuse your helper method `GetPubsConnection` to get a connection to the pubs database. Next, and this is very important, you append the statement `Asynchronous Processing=true` to your `Connection` object's connection string. This must be set in order for ADO.NET 2.0 to make asynchronous calls to SQL Server.

After getting the connection set, you then build a `SqlCommand` object and initialize it to be able to execute the `usp_Long_Running_Procedure` stored procedure. This procedure uses the SQL Server 2005 `WAITFOR DELAY` statement to create a 20-second delay before it executes the `usp_Authors_Get_All` stored procedure. As you can probably guess, the usp_authors_Get_All stored procedure simply selects all of the authors from the authors table. The delay is added simply to demonstrate that while this stored procedure is executing, you can perform other tasks in your Windows Forms application. Here is the SQL code for the usp_Long_Running_Procedure stored procedure:

```
CREATE PROCEDURE usp_Long_Running_Procedure
AS
SET NOCOUNT ON

WAITFOR DELAY '00:00:20'
EXEC usp_authors_Get_All
```

The last line of code in the Button's Click event handler is the call to BeginExecuteReader. In this call, the first thing you are passing in is a delegate method (Me.AsyncCallback) for the System.AsyncCallback delegate type. This is how the .NET Framework calls you back once the method is finished running asynchronously. You then pass in your initialized SqlCommand object so that it can be executed, as well as the CommandBehavior value for the DataReader. In this case, you pass in the CommandBehavior.CloseConnection value so that the connection to the database will be closed once the DataReader has been closed. You will look at the DataReader in more detail in the next section.

Now that you have initiated the asynchronous call, and have defined a callback for your asynchronous call, let's look at the actual method that is being called back, the AsyncCallback method:

```
Private Sub AsyncCallback(ByVal ar As IAsyncResult)
    ' Get the command that was passed from the AsyncState of the IAsyncResult.
    Dim command As SqlCommand = CType(ar.AsyncState, SqlCommand)
    ' Get the reader from the IAsyncResult.
    Dim reader As SqlDataReader = command.EndExecuteReader(ar)
    ' Get a table from the reader.
    Dim table As DataTable = Me.GetTableFromReader(reader, "Authors")
    ' Call the BindGrid method on the Windows main thread, passing in the table.
    Me.Invoke(New BindGridDelegate(AddressOf Me.BindGrid), _
        New Object() {table})
End Sub
```

The first line of the code is simply retrieving the SqlCommand object from the AsyncState property of the IAsyncResult that was passed in. Remember that when you called BeginExecuteReader earlier, you passed in your SqlCommand object. You need it so that you can call the EndExecuteReader method on the next line. This method gives you your SqlDataReader. On the next line, you then transform the SqlDataReader into a DataTable (covered later when the DataSet is discussed).

The last line of this method is probably the most important. If you tried to just take your DataTable and bind it to the grid, it would not work, because right now you are executing on a thread other than the main Windows thread. The helper method named BindGrid can do the data binding, but it must be called only in the context of the Windows main thread. To bring the data back to the main Windows thread, it must be marshaled via the Invoke method of the Form object. Invoke takes two arguments: the delegate of the method you want to call and (optionally) any parameters for that method. In this case, you define a delegate for the BindGrid method, called BindGridDelegate. Here is the delegate declaration:

```
Private Delegate Sub BindGridDelegate(ByVal table As DataTable)
```

Notice how the signature is exactly the same as the `BindGrid` method shown here:

```
Private Sub BindGrid(ByVal table As DataTable)
    ' Clear the grid.
    Me._authorsGridView.DataSource = Nothing
    ' Bind the grid to the DataTable.
    Me._authorsGridView.DataSource = table
End Sub
```

Here is another look at the call to the form's `Invoke` method:

```
Me.Invoke(New BindGridDelegate(AddressOf Me.BindGrid), _
    New Object() {table})
```

You pass in a new instance of the `BindGridDelegate` delegate and initialize it with a pointer to the `BindGrid` method. As a result, the .NET worker thread that was executing your query can now safely join up with the main Windows thread.

DataAdapter Objects

Each .NET Data Provider included with the .NET Framework has a `DataAdapter` object. The OLE DB .NET Data Provider includes an `OleDbDataAdapter` object, and the SQL Server .NET Data Provider includes a `SqlDataAdapter` object. A `DataAdapter` is used to retrieve data from a data source and populate `DataTable` objects and constraints within a `DataSet`. The `DataAdapter` also resolves changes made to the `DataSet` back to the data source. The `DataAdapter` uses the `Connection` object of the .NET Data Provider to connect to a data source, and `Command` objects to retrieve data from, and resolve changes to, the data source from a `DataSet` object. This differs from the `DataReader`, in that the `DataReader` uses the `Connection` to access the data directly, without having to use a `DataAdapter`. The `DataAdapter` essentially decouples the `DataSet` object from the actual source of the data, whereas the `DataReader` is tightly bound to the data in a read-only fashion.

The `SelectCommand` property of the `DataAdapter` is a `Command` object that retrieves data from the data source. A nice, convenient way to set the `DataAdapter`'s `SelectCommand` property is to pass in a `Command` object in the `DataAdapter`'s constructor. The `InsertCommand`, `UpdateCommand`, and `DeleteCommand` properties of the `DataAdapter` are `Command` objects that manage updates to the data in the data source according to the modifications made to the data in the `DataSet`. The `Fill` method of the `DataAdapter` is used to populate a `DataSet` with the results of the `SelectCommand` of the `DataAdapter`. It also adds or refreshes rows in the `DataSet` to match those in the data source. The following example code demonstrates how to fill a `DataSet` object with information from the authors table in the pubs database:

```
Private Sub TraverseDataSet()
    ' Build the SQL and Connection strings.
    Dim sql As String = "SELECT * FROM authors"
    Dim connectionString As String = "Initial Catalog=pubs;" _
        & "Data Source=(local);Integrated Security=SSPI;"

    ' Initialize the SqlDataAdapter with the SQL
    ' and Connection strings, and then use the
    ' SqlDataAdapter to fill the DataSet with data.
    Dim adapter As New SqlDataAdapter(sql, connectionString)
    Dim authors As New DataSet
```

```
        adapter.Fill(authors)

        ' Iterate through the DataSet's table.
        For Each row As DataRow In authors.Tables(0).Rows
            Console.WriteLine(row("au_fname").ToString _
                & " " & row("au_lname").ToString)
        Next

        ' Print the DataSet's XML.
        Console.WriteLine(authors.GetXml())
        Console.ReadLine()

    End Sub
```

Note how you use the `SqlDataAdapter`'s constructor to pass in and set the `SelectCommand`, as well as pass in the connection string in lieu of a `SqlCommand` object that already has an initialized `Connection` property. You then just call the `SqlDataAdapter` object's `Fill` method and pass in an initialized `DataSet` object. If the `DataSet` object is not initialized, then the `Fill` method raises an exception (`System.ArgumentNullException`).

In ADO.NET 2.0, a significant performance improvement was made in the way that the `DataAdapter` updates the database. In ADO.NET 1.*x*, the `DataAdapter`'s `Update` method would loop through each row of every `DataTable` object in the `DataSet` and subsequently make a trip to the database for each row that was being updated. In ADO.NET 2.0, batch update support was added to the `DataAdapter`. This means that when the `Update` method is called, the `DataAdapter` batches all of the updates from the `DataSet` in one trip to the database.

Now let's take a look at a more advanced example in which you use a `DataAdapter` to insert, update, and delete data from a `DataTable` back to the pubs database:

```
Private Sub _batchUpdateButton_Click(ByVal sender As System.Object, _
        ByVal e As System.EventArgs) Handles _batchUpdateButton.Click

        ' Build insert, update, and delete commands.

        ' Build the parameter values.
        Dim insertUpdateParams() As String = {"@au_id", "@au_lname", "@au_fname", _
            "@phone", "@address", "@city", "@state", "@zip", "@contract"}
```

The preceding code begins by initializing a string array of parameter names to pass into the `BuildSqlCommand` helper method:

```
        ' Insert command.
        Dim insertCommand As SqlCommand = BuildSqlCommand("usp_authors_Insert", _
            insertUpdateParams)
```

Next, you pass the name of the stored procedure to execute and the parameters for the stored procedure to the `BuildSqlCommand` helper method. This method returns an initialized instance of the `SqlCommand` class. Here is the `BuildSqlCommand` helper method:

```
Private Function BuildSqlCommand(ByVal storedProcedureName As String, _
        ByVal parameterNames() As String) As SqlCommand
```

```
      ' Build a SqlCommand.
      Dim command As New SqlCommand(storedProcedureName, GetPubsConnection())
      ' Set the command type to stored procedure.
      command.CommandType = CommandType.StoredProcedure
      ' Build the parameters for the command.
      ' See if any parameter names were passed in.
      If Not parameterNames Is Nothing Then
          ' Iterate through the parameters.
          Dim parameter As SqlParameter = Nothing
          For Each parameterName As String In parameterNames
              ' Create a new SqlParameter.
              parameter = New SqlParameter()
              parameter.ParameterName = parameterName
              ' Map the parameter to a column name in the DataTable/DataSet.
              parameter.SourceColumn = parameterName.Substring(1)
              ' Add the parameter to the command.
              command.Parameters.Add(parameter)
          Next
      End If
      Return command
  End Function
```

This method first initializes a `SqlCommand` class and passes in the name of a stored procedure; it then uses the `GetPubsConnection` helper method to pass in a `SqlConnection` object to the `SqlCommand`. The next step is to set the command type of the `SqlCommand` to a stored procedure. This is important because ADO.NET uses this to optimize how the stored procedure is called on the database server. You then check whether any parameter names have been passed (via the `parameterNames` string array); if so, you iterate through them. While iterating through the parameter names, you build up `SqlParameter` objects and add them to the `SqlCommand`'s collection of parameters.

The most important step in building up the `SqlParameter` object is setting its `SourceColumn` property. This is what the `DataAdapter` later uses to map the name of the parameter to the name of the column in the `DataTable` when its `Update` method is called. An example of such a mapping is associating the `@au_id` parameter name with the `au_id` column name. As shown in the code, the mapping assumes that the stored procedure parameters all have exactly the same names as the columns, except for the mandatory @ character in front of the parameter. That's why when assigning the `SqlParameter`'s `SourceColumn` property value, you use the `Substring` method to strip off the @ character to make sure that it maps correctly.

You then call the `BuildSqlCommand` method two more times to build your update and delete `SqlCommand` objects:

```
      ' Update command.
      Dim updateCommand As SqlCommand = BuildSqlCommand("usp_authors_Update", _
          insertUpdateParams)

      ' Delete command.
      Dim deleteCommand As SqlCommand = BuildSqlCommand("usp_authors_Delete", _
          New String() {"@au_id"})
```

Now that the `SqlCommand` objects have been created, the next step is to create a `SqlDataAdapter` object. Once the `SqlDataAdapter` is created, you set its `InsertCommand`, `UpdateCommand`, and `DeleteCommand` properties with the respective `SqlCommand` objects that you just built:

```
' Create an adapter.
Dim adapter As New SqlDataAdapter()

' Associate the commands with the adapter.
adapter.InsertCommand = insertCommand
adapter.UpdateCommand = updateCommand
adapter.DeleteCommand = deleteCommand
```

The next step is to get a `DataTable` instance of the authors table from the pubs database. You do this by calling the `GetAuthorsSqlReader` helper method to first get a `DataReader` and then the `GetTableFromReader` helper method to load a `DataTable` from a `DataReader`:

```
' Get the authors reader.
Dim reader As SqlDataReader = GetAuthorsSqlReader()
' Load a DataTable from the reader.
Dim table As DataTable = GetTableFromReader(reader, "Authors")
```

Once you have your `DataTable` filled with data, you begin modifying it so you can test the new batch update capability of the `DataAdapter`. The first change to make is an insert in the `DataTable`. In order to add a row, you first call the `DataTable`'s `NewRow` method to give you a `DataRow` initialized with the same columns as your `DataTable`:

```
' Add a new author to the DataTable.
Dim row As DataRow = table.NewRow
```

Once that is done, you then go ahead and set the values of the columns of the `DataRow`:

```
row("au_id") = "335-22-0707"
row("au_fname") = "Tim"
row("au_lname") = "McCarthy"
row("phone") = "760-930-0075"
row("contract") = 0
```

Then you call the `Add` method of the `DataTable`'s `DataRowCollection` property and pass in the newly populated `DataRow` object:

```
table.Rows.Add(row)
```

Now that there is a new row in the `DataTable`, the next test is to update one of its rows:

```
' Change an author in the DataTable.
table.Rows(0)("au_fname") = "Updated Name!"
```

Finally, you delete a row from the `DataTable`. In this case, it is the second-to-last row in the `DataTable`:

```
' Delete the second to last author from the table
table.Rows(table.Rows.Count - 2).Delete()
```

Now that you have performed an insert, update, and delete action on your `DataTable`, it is time to send the changes back to the database. You do this by calling the `DataAdapter`'s `Update` method and passing in either a `DataSet` or a `DataTable`. Note that you are calling the `GetChanges` method of the `DataTable`; this is important, because you only want to send the changes to the `DataAdapter`:

```
' Send only the changes in the DataTable to the database for updating.
adapter.Update(table.GetChanges())
```

To prove that the update worked, you get back a new `DataTable` from the server using the same technique as before, and then bind it to the grid with your helper method to see the changes that were made:

```
' Get the new changes back from the server to show that the update worked.
reader = GetAuthorsSqlReader()
table = GetTableFromReader(reader, "Authors")
' Bind the grid to the new table data.
BindGrid(table)
End Sub
```

SQL Server .NET Data Provider

The SQL Server .NET Data Provider uses Tabular Data Stream (TDS) to communicate with the SQL Server. This offers a great performance increase, as TDS is SQL Server's native communication protocol. As an example of how much of an increase you can expect, when I ran some simple tests accessing the authors table of the pubs database, the SQL Server .NET Data Provider performed about 70 percent faster than the OLE DB .NET Data Provider.

The SQL Server .NET Data Provider is lightweight and performs very well, thanks to not having to go through the OLE DB or ODBC layer. What it actually does is establish a networking connection (usually sockets-based) and drags data from this directly into managed code and vice versa.

> This is very important, as going through the OLE DB or ODBC layers means that the CLR has to marshal (convert) all of the COM datatypes to .NET CLR datatypes each time data is accessed from a data source. When using the SQL Server .NET Data Provider, everything runs within the .NET CLR, and the TDS protocol is faster than the other network protocols previously used for SQL Server.

To use this provider, you need to include the `System.Data.SqlClient` namespace in your application. Note that it works only for SQL Server 7.0 and later. I highly recommend using SQL Server .NET Data Provider anytime you are connecting to a SQL Server 7.0 and later database server. The SQL Server .NET Data Provider requires the installation of MDAC 2.6 or later.

OLE DB .NET Data Provider

The OLE DB .NET Data Provider uses native OLE DB through COM Interop (see Chapter 20 for more details) to enable data access. The OLE DB .NET Data Provider supports both manual and automatic transactions. For automatic transactions, the OLE DB .NET Data Provider automatically enlists in a transaction and obtains transaction details from Windows 2000 Component Services. The OLE DB .NET

Data Provider does not support OLE DB 2.5 interfaces. OLE DB Providers that require support for OLE DB 2.5 interfaces will not function properly with the OLE DB .NET Data Provider. This includes the Microsoft OLE DB Provider for Exchange and the Microsoft OLE DB Provider for Internet Publishing. The OLE DB .NET Data Provider requires the installation of MDAC 2.6 or later. To use this provider, you need to include the `System.Data.OleDb` namespace in your application.

The DataSet Component

The `DataSet` object is central to supporting disconnected, distributed data scenarios with ADO.NET. The `DataSet` is a memory-resident representation of data that provides a consistent relational programming model regardless of the data source. The `DataSet` represents a complete set of data, including related tables, constraints, and relationships among the tables; basically, it's like having a small relational database residing in memory.

> *Because the `DataSet` contains a lot of metadata, you need to be careful about how much data you try to stuff into it, as it will be consuming memory.*

The methods and objects in a `DataSet` are consistent with those in the relational database model. The `DataSet` can also persist and reload its contents as XML, and its schema as XSD. It is completely disconnected from any database connections, so it is totally up to you to fill it with whatever data you need in memory.

ADO.NET 2.0 has added several new features to the `DataSet` and the `DataTable` classes, as well as enhancements to existing features. The new features covered in this section are as follows:

- ❑ The binary serialization format option
- ❑ Additions to make the `DataTable` more of a standalone object
- ❑ The capability to expose `DataSet` and `DataTable` data as a stream (`DataReader`), and loading stream data into a `DataSet` or `DataTable`

DataTableCollection

An ADO.NET `DataSet` contains a collection of zero or more tables represented by `DataTable` objects. The `DataTableCollection` contains all of the `DataTable` objects in a `DataSet`.

A `DataTable` is defined in the `System.Data` namespace and represents a single table of memory-resident data. It contains a collection of columns represented by the `DataColumnCollection`, which defines the schema and rows of the table. It also contains a collection of rows represented by the `DataRowCollection`, which contains the data in the table. Along with the current state, a `DataRow` retains its original state and tracks changes that occur to the data.

DataRelationCollection

A `DataSet` contains relationships in its `DataRelationCollection` object. A relationship (represented by the `DataRelation` object) associates rows in one `DataTable` with rows in another `DataTable`. The relationships in the `DataSet` can have constraints, which are represented by `UniqueConstraint` and

ForeignKeyConstraint objects. It is analogous to a JOIN path that might exist between the primary and foreign key columns in a relational database. A DataRelation identifies matching columns in two tables of a DataSet.

Relationships enable you to see what links information within one table to another. The essential elements of a DataRelation are the name of the relationship, the two tables being related, and the related columns in each table. Relationships can be built with more than one column per table, with an array of DataColumn objects for the key columns. When a relationship is added to the DataRelationCollection, it may optionally add ForeignKeyConstraints that disallow any changes that would invalidate the relationship.

ExtendedProperties

DataSet (as well as DataTable and DataColumn) has an ExtendedProperties property. ExtendedProperties is a PropertyCollection where a user can place customized information, such as the SELECT statement that was used to generate the result set, or a date/time stamp indicating when the data was generated. Because the ExtendedProperties contains customized information, this is a good place to store extra user-defined data about the DataSet (or DataTable or DataColumn), such as a time when the data should be refreshed. The ExtendedProperties collection is persisted with the schema information for the DataSet (as well as DataTable and DataColumn). The following code is an example of adding an expiration property to a DataSet:

```
Private Shared Sub DataSetExtended()

    ' Build the SQL and Connection strings.
    Dim sql As String = "SELECT * FROM authors"
    Dim connectionString As String = "Initial Catalog=pubs;" _
        & "Data Source=(local);Integrated Security=SSPI;"

    ' Initialize the SqlDataAdapter with the SQL
    ' and Connection strings, and then use the
    ' SqlDataAdapter to fill the DataSet with data.
    Dim adapter As SqlDataAdapter = _
        New SqlDataAdapter(sql, connectionString)
    Dim authors As New DataSet
    adapter.Fill(authors)

    ' Add an extended property called "expiration."
    ' Set its value to the current date/time + 1 hour.
    authors.ExtendedProperties.Add("expiration", _
        DateAdd(DateInterval.Hour, 1, Now))

    Console.Write(authors.ExtendedProperties("expiration").ToString)
    Console.ReadLine()

End Sub
```

This code begins by filling a DataSet with the authors table from the pubs database. It then adds a new extended property, called expiration, and sets its value to the current date and time plus one hour. You then simply read it back. As you can see, it is very easy to add extended properties to DataSet objects. The same pattern also applies to DataTable and DataColumn objects.

Creating and Using DataSet Objects

The ADO.NET DataSet is a memory-resident representation of the data that provides a consistent relational programming model, regardless of the source of the data it contains. A DataSet represents a complete set of data, including the tables that contain, order, and constrain the data, as well as the relationships between the tables. The advantage to using a DataSet is that the data it contains can come from multiple sources, and it is fairly easy to get the data from multiple sources into the DataSet. In addition, you can define your own constraints between the data tables in a DataSet.

There are several methods of working with a DataSet, which can be applied independently or in combination:

❑ Programmatically create DataTables, DataRelations, and Constraints within the DataSet and populate them with data.

❑ Populate the DataSet or a DataTable from an existing RDBMS using a DataAdapter.

❑ Load and persist a DataSet or DataTable using XML.

❑ Load a DataSet from an XSD schema file.

❑ Load a DataSet or a DataTable from a DataReader.

Here is a typical usage scenario for a DataSet object:

1. A client makes a request to a Web Service.

2. Based on this request, the Web Service populates a DataSet from a database using a DataAdapter and returns the DataSet to the client.

3. The client then views the data and makes modifications.

4. When finished viewing and modifying the data, the client passes the modified DataSet back to the Web Service, which again uses a DataAdapter to reconcile the changes in the returned DataSet with the original data in the database.

5. The Web Service may then return a DataSet that reflects the current values in the database.

6. Optionally, the client can then use the DataSet class's Merge method to merge the returned DataSet with the client's existing copy of the DataSet; the Merge method will accept successful changes and mark with an error any changes that failed.

The design of the ADO.NET DataSet makes this scenario fairly easy to implement. Because the DataSet is stateless, it can be safely passed between the server and the client without tying up server resources such as database connections. Although the DataSet is transmitted as XML, Web Services and ADO.NET automatically transform the XML representation of the data to and from a DataSet, creating a rich, yet simplified, programming model.

In addition, because the DataSet is transmitted as an XML stream, non-ADO.NET clients can consume the same Web Service consumed by ADO.NET clients. Similarly, ADO.NET clients can interact easily with non-ADO.NET Web Services by sending any client DataSet to a Web Service as XML and by consuming any XML returned as a DataSet from the Web Service. However, note the size of the data; if your DataSet contains a large number of rows, then it will eat up a lot of bandwidth.

Programmatically Creating DataSet Objects

You can programmatically create a DataSet object to use as a data structure in your programs. This could be quite useful if you have complex data that needs to be passed around to another object's method. For example, when creating a new customer, instead of passing 20 arguments about the new customer to a method, you could just pass the programmatically created DataSet object with all of the customer information to the object's method.

Here is the code for building an ADO.NET DataSet object that is comprised of related tables:

```
Private Sub BuildDataSet()

    Dim customerOrders As New Data.DataSet("CustomerOrders")
    Dim customers As Data.DataTable = customerOrders.Tables.Add("Customers")
    Dim orders As Data.DataTable = customerOrders.Tables.Add("Orders")
    Dim row As Data.DataRow

    With customers
        .Columns.Add("CustomerID", Type.GetType("System.Int32"))
        .Columns.Add("FirstName", Type.GetType("System.String"))
        .Columns.Add("LastName", Type.GetType("System.String"))
        .Columns.Add("Phone", Type.GetType("System.String"))
        .Columns.Add("Email", Type.GetType("System.String"))
    End With

    With orders
        .Columns.Add("CustomerID", Type.GetType("System.Int32"))
        .Columns.Add("OrderID", Type.GetType("System.Int32"))
        .Columns.Add("OrderAmount", Type.GetType("System.Double"))
        .Columns.Add("OrderDate", Type.GetType("System.DateTime"))
    End With

    customerOrders.Relations.Add("Customers_Orders", _
    customerOrders.Tables("Customers").Columns("CustomerID"), _
    customerOrders.Tables("Orders").Columns("CustomerID"))

    row = customers.NewRow()
    row("CustomerID") = 1
    row("FirstName") = "Miriam"
    row("LastName") = "McCarthy"
    row("Phone") = "555-1212"
    row("Email") = "tweety@hotmail.com"
    customers.Rows.Add(row)

    row = orders.NewRow()
    row("CustomerID") = 1
    row("OrderID") = 22
    row("OrderAmount") = 0
    row("OrderDate") = #11/10/1997#
    orders.Rows.Add(row)

    Console.WriteLine(customerOrders.GetXml())
    Console.ReadLine()

End Sub
```

Here is what the resulting XML of the `DataSet` looks like:

```
<CustomerOrders>
  <Customers>
    <CustomerID>1</CustomerID>
    <FirstName>Miriam</FirstName>
    <LastName>McCarthy</LastName>
    <Phone>555-1212</Phone>
    <Email>tweety@hotmail.com</Email>
  </Customers>
  <Orders>
    <CustomerID>1</CustomerID>
    <OrderID>22</OrderID>
    <OrderAmount>0</OrderAmount>
    <OrderDate>1997-11-10T00:00:00.0000</OrderDate>
  </Orders>
</CustomerOrders>
```

You begin by first defining a `DataSet` object (`CustomerOrders`) named `CustomerOrders`. You then create two tables: one for customers (`customers`) and one for orders (`orders`). Then you define the columns of the tables. Note that you call the `Add` method of the `DataSet`'s `Tables` collection. You then define the columns of each table and create a relation in the `DataSet` between the Customers table and the Orders table on the CustomerID column. Finally, you create instances of `Rows` for the tables, add the data, and then append the `Rows` to the `Rows` collection of the `DataTable` objects.

If you create a `DataSet` object with no name, then it is given the default name of `NewDataSet`.

ADO.NET DataTable Objects

A `DataSet` is made up of a collection of tables, relationships, and constraints. In ADO.NET, `DataTable` objects are used to represent the tables in a `DataSet`. A `DataTable` represents one table of in-memory relational data. The data is local to the .NET application in which it resides, but can be populated from a data source such as SQL Server using a `DataAdapter`.

The `DataTable` class is a member of the `System.Data` namespace within the .NET Framework class library. You can create and use a `DataTable` independently or as a member of a `DataSet`, and `DataTable` objects can be used by other the .NET Framework objects, including the `DataView`. You access the collection of tables in a `DataSet` through the `DataSet` object's `Tables` property.

The schema, or structure, of a table is represented by columns and constraints. You define the schema of a `DataTable` using `DataColumn` objects as well as `ForeignKeyConstraint` and `UniqueConstraint` objects. The columns in a table can map to columns in a data source, contain calculated values from expressions, automatically increment their values, or contain primary key values.

If you populate a `DataTable` from a database, it inherits the constraints from the database, so you don't have to do all of that work manually. A `DataTable` must also have rows in which to contain and order the data. The `DataRow` class represents the actual data contained in the table. You use the `DataRow` and its properties and methods to retrieve, evaluate, and manipulate the data in a table. As you access and change the data within a row, the `DataRow` object maintains both its current and original state.

You can create parent-child relationships between tables within a database, such as SQL Server, using one or more related columns in the tables. You create a relationship between `DataTable` objects using a `DataRelation`, which can then be used to return a row's related child or parent rows.

ADO.NET 2.0 Enhancements to DataSet and DataTable

One of the main complaints developers had in ADO.NET 1.*x* was related to the performance of the `DataSet` and its `DataTable` children — in particular, when they contained a large amount of data. The performance hit comes in two different ways. The first way is the time it takes to actually load a `DataSet` with a lot of data. As the number of rows in a `DataTable` increases, the time to load a new row increases almost proportionally to the number of rows. The second way is when the large `DataSet` is serialized and remoted. A key feature of the `DataSet` is the fact that it automatically knows how to serialize itself, especially when you want to pass it between application tiers. Unfortunately, the serialization is quite verbose and takes up a lot of memory and network bandwidth. Both of these performance problems are addressed in ADO.NET 2.0.

Indexing

The first improvement to the `DataSet` family was a complete rewrite of the indexing engine for the `DataTable`, which now scales much better for large datasets. The addition of the new indexing engine results in faster basic inserts, updates, and deletes, which also means faster `Fill` and `Merge` operations. Just as in relational database design, if you are dealing with large `DataSets`, then it pays big dividends now if you add unique keys and foreign keys to your `DataTable`. Best of all is that you do not have to change any of your code at all to take advantage of this new feature.

Serialization

The second improvement made to the `DataSet` family was adding new options to the way the `DataSet` and `DataTable` are serialized. The main complaint about retrieving `DataSet` objects from Web Services and remoting calls was that they were way too verbose and took up too much network bandwidth. In ADO.NET 1.*x*, the `DataSet` serializes as XML, even when using the binary formatter. In ADO.NET 2.0, in addition to this behavior, you can also specify true binary serialization, by setting the newly added `RemotingFormat` property to `SerializationFormat.Binary`, rather than (the default) `SerializationFormat.XML`. In the `AdoNetFeaturesTest` project of the Examples solution I have added a `Button` (`serializationButton`) to the form and its associated `Click` event handler that demonstrates how to serialize a `DataTable` in binary format:

```
Private Sub _serializationButton_Click(ByVal sender As System.Object, _
    ByVal e As System.EventArgs) Handles _serializationButton.Click
    ' Get the authors reader.
    Dim reader As SqlDataReader = GetAuthorsSqlReader()
    ' Load a DataTable from the reader
    Dim table As DataTable = GetTableFromReader(reader, "Authors")
```

This code begins by calling the helper methods `GetAuthorsSqlReader` and `GetTableFromReader` to get a `DataTable` of the authors from the pubs database. The next code block, shown here, is where you are actually serializing the `DataTable` out to a binary format:

```
Using fs As New FileStream("c:\authors.dat", FileMode.Create)
    table.RemotingFormat = SerializationFormat.Binary
```

```
        Dim format As New BinaryFormatter
        format.Serialize(fs, table)
    End Using

    ' Tell the user what happened.
    MsgBox("Successfully serialized the DataTable!")
End Sub
```

This code takes advantage of the newly added `Using` statement for VB.NET to wrap up creating and disposing of a `FileStream` instance that will hold your serialized `DataTable` data. The next step is to set the `DataTable`'s `RemotingFormat` property to the `SerializationFormat.Binary` enumeration value. Once that is done, you simply create a new `BinaryFormatter` instance, and then call its `Serialize` method to serialize your `DataTable` into the `FileStream` instance. You then finish by showing users a message box indicating that the data has been serialized.

DataReader Integration

Another nice feature of the `DataSet` and `DataTable` classes is the ability to both read from and write out to a stream of data in the form of a `DataReader`. You will first take a look at how you can load a `DataTable` from a `DataReader`. To demonstrate this, I have added a `Button` (`loadFromReaderButton`) and its associated `Click` event handler to `TestForm.vb` of the `AdoNetFeaturesTest` project in the Examples solution:

```
Private Sub _loadFromReaderButton_Click(ByVal sender As System.Object, _
    ByVal e As System.EventArgs) Handles _loadFromReaderButton.Click

    ' Get the authors reader.
    Dim reader As SqlDataReader = GetAuthorsSqlReader()

    ' Load a DataTable from the reader.
    Dim table As DataTable = GetTableFromReader(reader, "Authors")

    ' Bind the grid to the table.
    BindGrid(table)
End Sub
```

This method is a controller method, meaning that it only calls helper methods. It begins by first obtaining a `SqlDataReader` from the `GetAuthorsReader` helper method. It then calls the `GetTableFromReader` helper method to transform the `DataReader` into a `DataTable`. The `GetTableFromReader` method is where you actually get to see the `DataTable`'s new load functionality:

```
Private Function GetTableFromReader(ByVal reader As SqlDataReader, _
    ByVal tableName As String) As DataTable
    ' Create a new DataTable using the name passed in.
    Dim table As New DataTable(tableName)
    ' Load the DataTable from the reader.
    table.Load(reader)
    ' Close the reader.
    reader.Close()
    Return table
End Function
```

This method begins by first creating an instance of a `DataTable` and initializing it with the name passed in from the `tableName` argument. Once the new `DataTable` has been initialized, you call the new `Load` method and pass in the `SqlDataReader` that was passed into the method via the `reader` argument. This is where the `DataTable` takes the `DataReader` and populates the `DataTable` instance with the column names and data from the `DataReader`. The next step is to close the `DataReader`, as it is no longer needed; and finally, you return the newly populated `DataTable`.

DataTable Independence

One of the most convenient enhancements to ADO.NET 2.0 is the addition of several methods from the `DataSet` class to the `DataTable` class. The `DataTable` is now much more versatile and useful than it was in ADO.NET 1.x. The `DataTable` now supports all of the same read and write methods for XML as the `DataSet` — specifically, the `ReadXml`, `ReadXmlSchema`, `WriteXml`, and `WriteXmlSchema` methods.

The `Merge` method of the `DataSet` has now been added to the `DataTable` as well, and in addition to the existing functionality of the `DataSet` class, some of the new features of the `DataSet` class have been added to the `DataTable` class — namely, the `RemotingFormat` property, the `Load` method, and the `GetDataReader` method.

Working with the Common Provider Model

In ADO.NET 1.x, you could either code to the provider-specific classes, such as `SqlConnection`, or the generic interfaces, such as `IDbConnection`. If there were a possibility that the database you were programming against would change during your project, or if you were creating a commercial package intended to support customers with different databases, then you had to use the generic interfaces. You can't call a constructor on an interface, so most generic programs included code that accomplished the task of obtaining the original `IDbConnection` by means of their own factory method, such as a `GetConnection` method that would return a provider-specific instance of the `IDbConnection` interface.

ADO.NET 2.0 has a more elegant solution for getting the provider-specific connection. Each data provider registers a `ProviderFactory` class and a provider string in the .NET `machine.config`. A base `ProviderFactory` class (`DbProviderFactory`) and a `System.Data.Common.ProviderFactories` class can return a `DataTable` of information about different data providers registered in `machine.config`, and can return the correct `ProviderFactory` given the provider string (called `ProviderInvariantName`) or a `DataRow` from the `DataTable`. Instead of writing your own framework to build connections based on the name of the provider, ADO.NET 2.0 makes it much more straightforward, flexible, and easy to solve this problem.

Let's look at an example of using the common provider model to connect to the pubs database and display some rows from the authors table. In the `AdoNetFeaturesTest` project, on the `TestForm.vb` form, the `providerButton` Button's `Click` event handler shows this functionality. The code is broken down into six steps.

The first step is get the provider factory object based on a configuration value of the provider's invariant name:

```
Private Sub _providerButton_Click(ByVal sender As System.Object, _
  ByVal e As System.EventArgs) Handles _providerButton.Click
```

```
        ' 1. Factory
        ' Create the provider factory from config value.
        Dim factory As DbProviderFactory =
DbProviderFactories.GetFactory(ConfigurationSettings.AppSettings("providerInvariant
Name"))
```

You are able to get the factory via the `DbProviderFactories` object's `GetFactory` method and pass in the string name of the provider invariant that you are storing in the project's `app.config` file. Here is the entry in the `app.config` file:

```
<add key="providerInvariantName" value="System.Data.SqlClient" />
```

In this case, you are using the SQL Server Data Provider. Once you have the factory object, the next step is to use it to create a connection:

```
        ' 2. Connection
        ' Create the connection from the factory.
        Dim connection As DbConnection = factory.CreateConnection()
        ' Get the connection string from config.
        connection.ConnectionString =
ConfigurationSettings.AppSettings("dbConnectionString")
```

The connection is created by calling the `DbProviderFactory`'s `CreateConnection` method. In this case, the factory is returning a `SqlConnection`, because you chose to use the `System.Data.SqlClient` provider invariant. To keep your code generic, you will not be directly programming against any of the classes in the `System.Data.SqlClient` namespace. Note how the connection class you declare is a `DbConnection` class, which is part of the `System.Data` namespace.

The next step is to create a `Command` object, so you can retrieve the data from the authors table:

```
        ' 3. Command
        ' Create the command from the connection.
        Dim command As DbCommand = connection.CreateCommand()
        ' Set the type of the command to stored procedure.
        command.CommandType = CommandType.StoredProcedure
        ' Set the name of the stored procedure to execute.
        command.CommandText = "usp_authors_Get_All"
```

You begin by declaring a generic `DbCommand` class variable and then using the `DbConnection`'s `CreateCommand` method to create the `DbCommand` instance. Once you have done that, you set the command type to stored procedure and then set the stored procedure name.

This example uses a `DbDataAdapter` to fill a `DataTable` with the authors data. Here is how you create and initialize the `DbDataAdapter`:

```
        ' 4. Adapter
        ' Create the adapter from the factory.
        Dim adapter As DbDataAdapter = factory.CreateDataAdapter()
        ' Set the adapter's select command.
        adapter.SelectCommand = command
```

Just as you did when you created your `DbConnection` instance, you use the factory to create your `DbDataAdapter`. After creating it, you then set the `SelectCommand` property's value to the instance of the previously initialized `DbCommand` instance.

After finishing these steps, the next step is to create a `DataTable` and fill it using the `DataAdapter`:

```
' 5. DataTable
' Create a new DataTable.
Dim authors As New DataTable("Authors")
' Use the adapter to fill the DataTable.
adapter.Fill(authors)
```

The final step is to bind the table to the form's grid:

```
' 6.  Grid
' Populate the grid with the data.
BindGrid(authors)
```

You already looked at the `BindGrid` helper method in the asynchronous example earlier. In this example, you are simply reusing this generic method again:

```
Private Sub BindGrid(ByVal table As DataTable)
        ' Clear the grid.
        Me._authorsGridView.DataSource = Nothing
        ' Bind the grid to the DataTable.
        Me._authorsGridView.DataSource = table
    End Sub
```

The main point to take away from this example is that you were able to easily write database-agnostic code with just a few short lines of code. ADO.NET 1.*x* required a lot of lines of code to create this functionality; you had to write your own abstract factory classes and factory methods in order to create instances of the generic database interfaces, such as `IDbConnection`, `IDbCommand`, and so on.

Connection Pooling Enhancements in ADO.NET 2.0

Pooling connections can significantly enhance the performance and scalability of your application. Both the SQL Client .NET Data Provider and the OLE DB .NET Data Provider automatically pool connections using Windows Component Services and OLE DB Session Pooling, respectively. The only requirement is that you must use the exact same connection string each time if you want a pooled connection.

ADO.NET 2.0 enhances the connection pooling functionality offered in ADO.NET 1.*x* by enabling you to close all of the connections currently kept alive by the particular managed provider that you are using. You can clear a specific connection pool by using the shared `SqlConnection.ClearPool` method or clear all of the connection pools in an application domain by using the shared `SqlConnection.ClearPools` method. Both the SQL Server and Oracle managed providers implement this functionality.

Building a Data Access Component

To better demonstrate what you have learned so far about ADO.NET, in this section you are going to build a data access component. This component is designed to abstract the processing of stored procedures. The component you build is targeted at SQL Server, and it is assumed that all data access to the database will be through stored procedures. The idea of only using stored procedures to access data in a database has a number of advantages, such as scalability, performance, flexibility, and security. The only disadvantage is that you have to use stored procedures, and not SQL strings. Through the process of building this component, you will see how stored procedures are implemented in ADO.NET. You will also be building on the knowledge that you have gained from the previous chapters.

This component's main job is to abstract stored procedure calls to SQL Server, and one of the ways you do this is by passing in all of your stored procedure parameter metadata as XML (covered later in this section). The other job of the component is to demonstrate the use of some of the new objects in ADO.NET.

The code for this project is quite extensive and you will only examine the key parts of it in this chapter. The full source is available in the code download.

Let's start with the beginning of the component. The first thing you do is declare your class and the private members of the class:

```
Option Explicit On
Option Strict On

Imports System
Imports System.Data
Imports System.Data.SqlClient
Imports System.Xml
Imports System.Collections
Imports System.Diagnostics

''' <summary>
''' This class wraps stored procedure calls to SQL Server. It requires that all
''' stored procedures and their parameters be defined in an XML document before
''' calling any of its methods. The XML can be passed in as an XmlDocument
''' instance or as a string of XML.  The only exceptions to this rule are
''' stored procedures that do not have parameters. This class also caches
''' SqlCommand objects. Each time a stored procedure is executed, a SqlCommand
''' object is built and cached into memory so that the next time the stored
''' procedure is called the SqlCommand object can be retrieved from memory.
''' </summary>
Public NotInheritable Class StoredProcedureHelper

    Private _connectionString As String = ""
    Private _spParamXml As String = ""
    Private _spParamXmlDoc As XmlDocument = Nothing
    Private _spParamXmlNode As XmlNode = Nothing
    Private _commandParametersHashTable As New Hashtable()

    Private Const ExceptionMsg As String = "There was an error in the method.  " _
        & "Please see the Windows Event Viewer Application log for details"
```

You begin with your `Option` statements. Note that you are using the `Option Strict` statement. This helps prevent logic errors and data loss that can occur when you work between variables of different types. Next, you import the namespaces that you need for your component. In this case, most of your dependencies are on `System.Data.SqlClient`. You call your class `StoredProcedureHelper` to indicate that it wraps calling stored procedures to SQL Server. Next, you declare your private data members. You use the `ExceptionMsg` constant to indicate a generic error message for any exceptions that you throw.

Constructors

Now you get to declare your constructors for the `StoredProcedureHelper` class. This is where you can really take advantage of method overloading, and it gives you a way to pass data to your class upon instantiation. First, you declare a default constructor:

```
''' <summary>
''' Default constructor.
''' </summary>
Public Sub New()
End Sub
```

The default constructor is provided in case users want to pass data to your class through public properties instead of through constructor arguments.

The next constructor you create allows for a database connection string to be passed in. By abstracting the database connection string out of this component, you give users of your component more flexibility in how they decide to store and retrieve their database connection strings. Here is the code for the constructor:

```
''' <summary>
''' Overloaded constructor.
''' </summary>
''' <param name="connectionString">The connection string to the
''' SQL Server database.</param>
Public Sub New(ByVal connectionString As String)
    Me._connectionString = connectionString
End Sub
```

The only difference between this constructor and the default constructor is that you are passing in a database connection string.

In the next constructor, you pass in both a database connection string and a string of XML representing the stored procedure parameters for the stored procedures you want to call. Here is the code for the constructor:

```
''' <summary>
''' Overloaded constructor.
''' </summary>
''' <param name="connectionString">The connection string to the
''' SQL Server database.</param>
''' <param name="spParamXml">A valid XML string which conforms to
''' the correct schema for stored procedure(s) and their
```

```
    ''' associated parameter(s).</param>
    Public Sub New(ByVal connectionString As String, ByVal spParamXml As String)
        Me.New(connectionString)
        Me._spParamXml = spParamXml
        Me._spParamXmlDoc = New XmlDocument
        Try
            Me._spParamXmlDoc.LoadXml(spParamXml)
            Me._spParamXmlNode = Me._spParamXmlDoc.DocumentElement
        Catch e As XmlException
            LogError(e)
            Throw New Exception(ExceptionMsg, e)
        End Try
    End Sub
```

This constructor sets the database connection string by calling the first overloaded constructor. This handy technique enables you to avoid writing duplicate code in your constructors. The constructor then loads the stored procedure parameter configuration into a private XmlDocument instance variable as well as a private XmlNode instance variable.

The remaining constructors enable you to pass in combinations of database connection strings as well as either a valid XmlDocument instance representing the stored procedure parameters or a valid XmlNode instance that represents the stored procedure parameters.

Properties

Now let's look at the properties of your class. Your object contains the following properties: ConnectionString, SpParamXml, and SpParamXmlDoc. All of the properties are provided as a courtesy in case the user of your object did not want to supply them via a constructor call. The ConnectionString property provides the same functionality as the first overloaded constructor you looked at. The SpParamXml property enables the user of the object to pass in a valid XML string representing the stored procedures parameter metadata. All of the properties are read-write. The SpParamXmlDoc property enables the user to pass in an XmlDocument instance representing the stored procedures' parameter metadata.

Here is the code for the SpParamXml property:

```
    ''' <summary>
    ''' A valid XML string which conforms to the correct schema for
    ''' stored procedure(s) and their associated parameter(s).
    ''' </summary>
    Public Property SpParamXml() As String
        Get
            Return Me._spParamXml
        End Get
        Set(ByVal Value As String)
            Me._spParamXml = Value
            ' Set the XmlDocument instance to null, since
            ' an XML string is being passed in.
            Me._spParamXmlDoc = Nothing
            Try
                Me._spParamXmlDoc.LoadXml(Me._spParamXml)
```

```
            Me._spParamXmlNode = Me._spParamXmlDoc.DocumentElement
        Catch e As XmlException
            LogError(e)
            Throw New Exception(ExceptionMsg)
        End Try
    End Set
End Property
```

Note that this property resets the XmlDocument instance to Nothing before trying to load the document. This is done in case it was already set in one of the overloaded constructors, or from a previous call to this property. It also sets the XmlNode instance to the DocumentElement property of the XmlDocument instance, thus keeping them both in sync.

Stored Procedure XML Structure

In this case, rather than have the user of this class be responsible for populating the Parameters collection of a Command object, you will abstract it out into an XML structure. The structure is very simple; it basically enables you to store the metadata for one or more stored procedures at a time. This has a huge advantage because you can change all of the parameters on a stored procedure without having to recompile the project. The following is what the XML structure for the metadata looks like:

```
<StoredProcedures>
 <StoredProcedure name>
  <Parameters>
   <Parameter name size datatype direction isNullable sourceColumn />
  </Parameters>
 </StoredProcedure>
</StoredProcedures>
```

Here is what some sample data for the XML structure looks like:

```
<?xml version="1.0"?>
<StoredProcedures>
 <StoredProcedure name="usp_Get_Authors_By_States">
  <Parameters>
   <Parameter name="@states" size="100" datatype="VarChar"
    direction="Input" isNullable="True" />
   <Parameter name="@state_delimiter" size="1" datatype="Char"
    direction="Input" isNullable="True" />
  </Parameters>
 </StoredProcedure>
</StoredProcedures>
```

The valid values for the direction attribute are Input, Output, ReturnValue, and InputOutput. These values map directly to the System.Data.Parameter enumeration values. The valid values for the datatype attribute are BigInt, Binary, Bit, Char, DateTime, Decimal, Float, Image, Int, Money, NChar, NText, NVarChar, Real, SmallDateTime, SmallInt, SmallMoney, Text, Timestamp, TinyInt, UniqueIdentifier, VarBinary, VarChar, and Variant. These values map directly to the System.Data.SqlDbType enumeration values.

Methods

That completes our look at the stored procedure XML structure the class expects, as well as the public properties and public constructors for the class. Now let's turn our attention to the public methods of your class.

ExecSpReturnDataSet

This public function executes a stored procedure and returns a `DataSet` object. It takes a stored procedure name (`String`), an optional `DataSet` name (`String`), and an optional list of parameter names and values (`IDictionary`). Here is the code for `ExecSpReturnDataSet`:

```
''' <summary>
''' Executes a stored procedure with or without parameters and returns a
''' populated DataSet object.
''' </summary>
''' <param name="spName">The name of the stored procedure to execute.</param>
''' <param name="dataSetName">An optional name for the DataSet instance.</param>
''' <param name="paramValues">A name-value pair of stored procedure parameter
''' name(s) and value(s).</param>
''' <returns>A populated DataSet object.</returns>
Public Function ExecSpReturnDataSet(ByVal spName As String, _
              ByVal dataSetName As String, _
              ByVal paramValues As IDictionary) As DataSet
    Dim command As SqlCommand = Nothing
    Try
        ' Get the initialized SqlCommand instance.
        command = GetSqlCommand(spName)
        ' Set the parameter values for the SqlCommand.
        SetParameterValues(command, paramValues)
        ' Initialize the SqlDataAdapter with the SqlCommand object.
        Dim sqlDA As New SqlDataAdapter(command)

        ' Initialize the DataSet.
        Dim ds As New DataSet()

        If Not (dataSetName Is Nothing) Then
            If dataSetName.Length > 0 Then
                ds.DataSetName = dataSetName
            End If
        End If

        ' Fill the DataSet.
        sqlDA.Fill(ds)

        ' Return the DataSet.
        Return ds
    Catch e As Exception
        LogError(e)
        Throw New Exception(ExceptionMsg, e)
    Finally
        ' Close and release resources.
        DisposeCommand(command)
    End Try
End Function
```

This function uses three main objects to accomplish its mission: the `SqlCommand`, `SqlDataAdapter`, and the `DataSet` objects. You first wrap everything in a `Try-Catch-Finally` block to ensure that you trap any exceptions that are thrown and to properly close and release the `SqlCommand` and `SqlConnection` resources. You first call a helper method, `GetSqlCommand`, in order to get a fully initialized `SqlCommand` instance, to include any `SqlParameter` objects the `SqlCommand` may have based on your object's internal `XmlDocument`. Here is the code for `GetSqlCommand` and its overload:

```
''' <summary>
''' Initializes a SqlCommand object based on a stored procedure name
''' and a SqlTransaction instance. Verifies that the stored procedure
''' name is valid, and then tries to get the SqlCommand object from
''' cache. If it is not already in cache, then the SqlCommand object
''' is initialized and placed into cache.
''' </summary>
''' <param name="transaction">The transaction that the stored
''' procedure will be executed under.</param>
''' <param name="spName">The name of the stored procedure to execute.</param>
''' <returns>An initialized SqlCommand object.</returns>
Public Function GetSqlCommand(ByVal transaction As SqlTransaction, _
    ByVal spName As String) As SqlCommand

    Dim command As SqlCommand = Nothing

    ' Get the name of the stored procedure.
    If spName.Length < 1 Or spName.Length > 127 Then
        Throw New ArgumentOutOfRangeException("spName", _
            "Stored procedure name must be from 1 - 128 characters.")
    End If

    ' See if the command object is already in memory.
    Dim hashKey As String = Me._connectionString & ":" & spName
    command = CType(_commandParametersHashTable(hashKey), SqlCommand)
    If command Is Nothing Then
        ' It was not in memory.
        ' Initialize the SqlCommand.
        command = New SqlCommand(spName, GetSqlConnection(transaction))

        ' Tell the SqlCommand that you are using a stored procedure.
        command.CommandType = CommandType.StoredProcedure

        ' Build the parameters, if there are any.
        BuildParameters(command)

        ' Put the SqlCommand instance into memory.
        Me._commandParametersHashTable(hashKey) = command
    Else
        ' It was in memory, but you still need to set the
        ' connection property.
        command.Connection = GetSqlConnection(transaction)
    End If

    ' Return the initialized SqlCommand instance.
    Return command
End Function
```

```
''' <summary>
''' Overload. Initializes a SqlCommand object based on a stored
''' procedure name, with no SqlTransaction instance.
''' Verifies that the stored procedure name is valid, and then tries
''' to get the SqlCommand object from cache. If it is not already in
''' cache, then the SqlCommand object is initialized and placed into cache.
''' </summary>
''' <param name="spName">The name of the stored procedure to execute.</param>
''' <returns>An initialized SqlCommand object.</returns>
Public Function GetSqlCommand(ByVal spName As String) As SqlCommand
    ' Return the initialized SqlCommand instance.
    Return GetSqlCommand(Nothing, spName)
End Function
```

The difference between this method and its overload is that the first method takes in a `SqlTransaction` instance argument, and the overload does not require the `SqlTransaction` instance to be passed in. The overload simply calls the first method and passes in a value of `Nothing` for the `SqlTransaction` argument.

This method first performs a check to ensure that the stored procedure name is between 1 and 128 characters long, in accordance with SQL Server's object naming conventions. If it is not, then you throw an exception. The next step this method performs is to try to get an already initialized `SqlCommand` object from your object's private `Hashtable` variable, `commandParametersHashTable`, using your object's database connection string and the name of the stored procedure as the key. If the `SqlCommand` is not found, then you go ahead and build the `SqlCommand` object by calling its constructor and passing in the stored procedure name and a `SqlConnection` instance returned from the `GetSqlConnection` helper method. The code then sets the `SqlCommand`'s `CommandType` property. You ensure that you pass in the `CommandType.StoredProcedure` enumeration value, as you are executing a stored procedure.

Once the `SqlCommand` object is properly initialized, you pass it to the `BuildParameters` method. You will take a look at this method in more detail later. After this step, the `SqlCommand` is fully initialized, and you then place it into your object's internal cache (the `commandParametersHashTable Hashtable` variable). Finally, the `SqlCommand` is returned to the calling code.

Getting back to the `ExecSpReturnDataSet` method, now that the `SqlCommand` object has been properly initialized, you need to set the values of the parameters. This is done via another helper method called `SetParameterValues`. `SetParameterValues` takes two arguments: a reference to a `SqlCommand` object and an `IDictionary` interface. You are using an `IDictionary` interface instead of a class such as a `Hashtable` (which implements the `IDictionary` interface) in order to make your code more flexible. This is a good design practice and works quite well — for example, in the cases where the user of your class has built his or her own custom dictionary object that implements the `IDictionary` interface. It then loops through the `SqlCommand`'s `Parameters` collection and sets each `SqlParameter`'s value based on the corresponding name-value pair in the `IDictionary` object as long as the parameter's direction is not `Output`. Following is the code for the `SetParameterValues` method:

```
''' <summary>
''' Traverses the SqlCommand's SqlParameters collection and sets the values
''' for all of the SqlParameter(s) objects whose direction is not Output and
''' whose name matches the name in the dictValues IDictionary that was
''' passed in.
''' </summary>
```

```vb
''' <param name="command">An initialized SqlCommand object.</param>
''' <param name="dictValues">A name-value pair of stored procedure parameter
''' name(s) and value(s).</param>
Public Sub SetParameterValues(ByVal command As SqlCommand, _
    ByVal dictValues As IDictionary)
    If command Is Nothing Then
        Throw New ArgumentNullException("command", _
            "The command argument cannot be null.")
    End If
    ' Traverse the SqlCommand's SqlParameters collection.
    Dim parameter As SqlParameter
    For Each parameter In command.Parameters
        ' Do not set Output parameters.
        If parameter.Direction <> ParameterDirection.Output Then
            ' Set the initial value to DBNull.
            parameter.Value = TypeCode.DBNull
            ' If there is a match, then update the parameter value.
            If dictValues.Contains(parameter.ParameterName) Then
                parameter.Value = dictValues(parameter.ParameterName)
            Else
                ' There was not a match.
                ' If the parameter value cannot be null, throw an exception.
                If Not parameter.IsNullable Then
                    Throw New ArgumentNullException(parameter.ParameterName, _
                        "Error getting the value for the " _
                        & parameter.ParameterName & " parameter.")
                End If
            End If
        End If
    Next parameter
End Sub
```

When traversing the SqlCommand's Parameters collection, if a SqlParameter's value cannot be found in the IDictionary instance, then a check is made to see whether the SqlParameter's value is allowed to be null or not. If it is allowed, then the value is set to DBNull; otherwise, an exception is thrown.

After setting the values of the parameters, the next step is to pass the SqlCommand object to the SqlDataAdapter's constructor:

```vb
' Initialize the SqlDataAdapter with the SqlCommand object.
Dim sqlDA As New SqlDataAdapter(command)
```

Then try to set the name of the DataSet using the dataSetName method argument:

```vb
' Try to set the name of the DataSet.
If Not (dataSetName Is Nothing) Then
    If dataSetName.Length > 0 Then
        ds.DataSetName = dataSetName
    End If
End If
```

After doing this, you call the `Fill` method of the `SqlDataAdapter` to fill your `DataSet` object:

```
' Fill the DataSet.
sqlDA.Fill(ds)
```

You then return the `DataSet` object back to the caller:

```
' Return the DataSet.
Return ds
```

If an exception was caught, then you log the exception data to the Windows Application Log via the `LogError` private method, and then throw a new exception with your generic exception message. Nest the original exception inside of the new exception via the `innerException` constructor parameter:

```
Catch e As Exception
    LogError(e)
    Throw New Exception(ExceptionMsg, e)
```

In the `Finally` block, you close and release the `SqlCommand` object's resources via the `DisposeCommand` helper method:

```
Finally
    ' Close and release resources
    DisposeCommand(command)
```

The `DisposeCommand` helper function closes the `SqlCommand`'s `SqlConnection` property and disposes of the `SqlCommand` object:

```
''' <summary>
''' Disposes a SqlCommand and its underlying SqlConnection.
''' </summary>
''' <param name="command"></param>
Private Sub DisposeCommand(ByVal command As SqlCommand)
    If Not (command Is Nothing) Then
        If Not (command.Connection Is Nothing) Then
            command.Connection.Close()
            command.Connection.Dispose()
        End If
        command.Dispose()
    End If
End Sub
```

BuildParameters

This private method is the heart of this object and does the most work. It is responsible for parsing the stored procedure parameter XML and mapping all of the `SqlParameter` objects into the `Parameters` property of the `SqlCommand` object. Here is the signature of the method:

```
''' <summary>
''' Finds the parameter information for the stored procedure from the
''' stored procedures XML document and then uses that information to
''' build and append the parameter(s) for the SqlCommand's
```

```
''' SqlParameters collection.
''' </summary>
''' <param name="command">An initialized SqlCommand object.</param>
Private Sub BuildParameters(ByVal command As SqlCommand)
```

The first thing you do in this method is determine whether any XML is being passed in or not. Here is the code that checks for the XML:

```
' See if there is an XmlNode of parameter(s) for the stored procedure.
If Me._spParamXmlNode Is Nothing Then
    ' No parameters to add, so exit.
    Return
End If
```

The last bit of code simply checks whether there is an `XmlNode` instance of parameter information. If the `XmlNode` has not been initialized, then you exit the method. It is entirely possible that users of this object may have stored procedures with no parameters at all. You choose an `XmlNode` object to parse the XML because loading all of the stored procedure XML into memory will not hurt performance; it is a small amount of data. As an alternative, you could use an `XmlReader` object to load into memory only what you need at runtime.

The next step is to clear the `SqlCommand` object's `Parameters` collection:

```
' Clear the parameters collection for the SqlCommand
command.Parameters.Clear()
```

You then use the name of the stored procedure as the key in your XPath query of the XML, and execute the following XPath query to get the list of parameters for the stored procedure:

```
' Get the node list of <Parameter>'s for the stored procedure.
Dim xpathQuery As String = "//StoredProcedures/StoredProcedure[@name='" _
    & command.CommandText & "']/Parameters/Parameter"
Dim parameterNodes As XmlNodeList = Me._spParamXmlNode.SelectNodes(xpathQuery)
```

This query is executed off the `XmlDocument` object and returns an `XmlNodeList` object. You start the loop through the `Parameter` elements in the XML and retrieve all of the mandatory `Parameter` attributes:

```
Dim parameterNode As XmlElement
For Each parameterNode In parameterNodes
    ' Get the attribute values for the <Parameter> element.

    ' Get the attribute values for the <Parameter> element.
    ' name
    Dim parameterName As String = parameterNode.GetAttribute("name")
    If parameterName.Length = 0 Then
        Throw New ArgumentNullException("name", "Error getting the 'name' " _
            & "attribute for the <Parameter> element.")
    End If

    ' size
    Dim parameterSize As Integer = 0
```

```vbnet
            If parameterNode.GetAttribute("size").Length = 0 Then
                Throw New ArgumentNullException("size", "Error getting the 'size' " _
                    & "attribute for the <Parameter> element.")
            Else
                parameterSize = Convert.ToInt32(parameterNode.GetAttribute("size"))
            End If

            ' datatype
            Dim sqlDataType As SqlDbType
            If parameterNode.GetAttribute("datatype").Length = 0 Then
                Throw New ArgumentNullException("datatype", "Error getting the " _
                    & "'datatype' attribute for the <Parameter> element.")
            Else
                sqlDataType = CType([Enum].Parse(GetType(SqlDbType), _
                    parameterNode.GetAttribute("datatype"), True), SqlDbType)
            End If

            ' direction
            Dim parameterDirection As ParameterDirection = parameterDirection.Input
            If parameterNode.GetAttribute("direction").Length > 0 Then
                parameterDirection = CType([Enum].Parse(GetType(ParameterDirection), _
                    parameterNode.GetAttribute("direction"), True), ParameterDirection)
            End If
        End If
    End If
```

Because these attributes are mandatory, if any of them are missing, then you throw an exception. The interesting part of this code is using the `Enum.Parse` static method to convert the string value from the XML into the correct .NET enumeration datatype for the `sqlDataType` and `parameterDirection` variables. This is possible because the probable values in your XML for these attributes map directly to the names of their respective enumeration datatypes in .NET. Next, you get the optional attributes:

```vbnet
    ' Get the optional attribute values for the <Parameter> element.

    ' isNullable
    Dim isNullable As Boolean = False
    Try
        If parameterNode.GetAttribute("isNullable").Length > 0 Then
            isNullable = Boolean.Parse(parameterNode.GetAttribute("isNullable"))
        End If
    Catch
    End Try

    ' sourceColumn -- This must map to the name of a column in a DataSet.
    Dim sourceColumn As String = ""
    Try
        If parameterNode.GetAttribute("sourceColumn").Length > 0 Then
            sourceColumn = parameterNode.GetAttribute("sourceColumn")
        End If
    Catch
    End Try
```

These attributes are optional mainly because of their datatypes. Because `isNullable` is Boolean, you go ahead and convert it to `False` if it is missing; and if `sourceColumn` is missing, then you just ignore it entirely.

Now you are ready to create the `SqlParameter` object and set its `Direction` property:

```
' Create the parameter object.  Pass in the name, datatype,
' and size to the constructor.
Dim sqlParameter As SqlParameter = New SqlParameter(parameterName, _
    sqlDataType, parameterSize)

'Set the direction of the parameter.
sqlParameter.Direction = parameterDirection
```

You then set the optional property values of the `SqlParameter` object:

```
' If the optional attributes have values, then set them.
' IsNullable
If isNullable Then
    sqlParameter.IsNullable = isNullable
End If
' SourceColumn
sqlParameter.SourceColumn = sourceColumn
```

Finally, you add the `SqlParameter` object to the `SqlCommand` object's `Parameters` collection, complete your loop, and finish the method:

```
' Add the parameter to the SqlCommand's parameter collection.
        command.Parameters.Add(sqlParameter)
    Next parameterNode
End Sub
```

Now it's time to look at `ExecSpReturnDataReader`. This function is almost identical to `ExecSpReturnDataSet` except that it returns a `SqlDataReader` object instead of a `DataSet` object.

ExecSpReturnDataReader

This public function executes a stored procedure and returns a `SqlDataReader` object. Similar to the `ExecSpReturnDataSet` method, it takes a stored procedure name (`String`) and an optional list of parameter names and values (`IDictionary`). Here is the code for `ExecSpReturnDataReader`:

```
''' <summary>
''' Executes a stored procedure with or without parameters and returns a
''' SqlDataReader instance with a live connection to the database. It is
''' very important to call the Close method of the SqlDataReader as soon
''' as possible after using it.
''' </summary>
''' <param name="spName">The name of the stored procedure to execute.</param>
''' <param name="paramValues">A name-value pair of stored procedure parameter
''' name(s) and value(s).</param>
''' <returns>A SqlDataReader object.</returns>
Public Function ExecSpReturnDataReader(ByVal spName As String, _
    ByVal paramValues As IDictionary) As SqlDataReader
  Dim command As SqlCommand = Nothing
  Try
    ' Get the initialized SqlCommand instance.
    command = GetSqlCommand(spName)
```

```
    ' Set the parameter values for the SqlCommand.
    SetParameterValues(command, paramValues)
    ' Open the connection.
    command.Connection.Open()

    ' Execute the sp and return the SqlDataReader.
    Return command.ExecuteReader(CommandBehavior.CloseConnection)
Catch e As Exception
    LogError(e)
    Throw New Exception(ExceptionMsg, e)

End Try

End Function
```

This function uses two objects to accomplish its mission: the `SqlCommand` and `SqlDataReader` objects. The only part where this function differs from `ExecSpReturnDataSet` is right after you call the `SetParameterValues` private method. In this case, you have to make sure that the `SqlCommand` object's `SqlConnection` is opened because the `SqlDataReader` requires an open connection. You then call the `ExecuteReader` method of the `SqlCommand` object to get your `SqlDataReader` object, passing in the `CommandBehavior.CloseConnection` value for the method's behavior argument.

Because this method returns a `SqlDataReader` object, which requires an open database connection, you do not close the connection in this method. It is up to the caller to close the `SqlDataReader` and the connection when finished. Since you used the `CommandBehavior.CloseConnection` value for the behavior argument, the user of the method only has to remember to call the `SqlDataReader`'s `Close` method in order to close the underlying `SqlConnection` object.

The next function you are going to look at, `ExecSpReturnXmlReader`, is almost identical to the last two functions, except that it returns an `XmlReader` instead of a `DataSet` or a `SqlDataReader`.

ExecSpReturnXmlReader

This public function executes a stored procedure and returns an `XmlReader` instance. The function requires the stored procedure to contain a `FOR XML` clause in its SQL statement. Once again, it takes a stored procedure name (`String`) and an optional list of parameter names and values (`IDictionary`). Here is the code for `ExecSpReturnXmlReader`:

```
''' <summary>
''' Executes a stored procedure with or without parameters and returns an
''' XmlReader instance with a live connection to the database. It is
''' very important to call the Close method of the XmlReader as soon
''' as possible after using it. Only use this method when calling stored
''' procedures that return XML results (FOR XML ...).
''' </summary>
''' <param name="spName">The name of the stored procedure to execute.</param>
''' <param name="paramValues">A name-value pair of stored procedure parameter
''' name(s) and value(s).</param>
''' <returns>An XmlReader object.</returns>
Public Function ExecSpReturnXmlReader(ByVal spName As String, _
    ByVal paramValues As IDictionary) As XmlReader
    Dim command As SqlCommand = Nothing
```

```
      Try
          ' Get the initialized SqlCommand instance.
          command = GetSqlCommand(spName)
          ' Set the parameter values for the SqlCommand.
          SetParameterValues(command, paramValues)

          ' Open the connection.
          command.Connection.Open()
          ' Execute the sp and return the XmlReader.
          Return command.ExecuteXmlReader()
      Catch e As Exception
          LogError(e)
          Throw New Exception(ExceptionMsg, e)
      End Try
  End Function
```

The only difference between this method and `ExecSpReturnDataReader` is that you call the `ExecuteXmlReader` method of the `SqlCommand` object instead of the `ExecuteReader` method. Like the `ExecSpReturnDataReader` method, users of this method need to close the returned `XmlReader` after using it in order to properly release resources.

This method works only with SQL Server 2000 and later.

Next up is the `ExecSp` method, which needs only the `SqlCommand` object to get its work done. Its job is to execute stored procedures that do not return result sets.

ExecSp

This public method executes a stored procedure and does not return a value. It takes a stored procedure name (`String`) and an optional list of parameter names and values (`IDictionary`) for its arguments. Here is the code for `ExecSp`:

```
''' <summary>
''' Executes a stored procedure with or without parameters that
''' does not return output values or a resultset.
''' </summary>
''' <param name="transaction">The transaction that the stored procedure
''' will be executed under.</param>
''' <param name="spName">The name of the stored procedure to execute.</param>
''' <param name="paramValues">A name-value pair of stored procedure parameter
''' name(s) and value(s).</param>
Public Sub ExecSp(ByVal spName As String, ByVal paramValues As IDictionary)
    Dim command As SqlCommand = Nothing
    Try
        ' Get the initialized SqlCommand instance.
        command = GetSqlCommand(transaction, spName)
        ' Set the parameter values for the SqlCommand.
        SetParameterValues(command, paramValues)
        ' Run the stored procedure.
        RunSp(command)
    Catch e As Exception
        LogError(e)
```

```
            Throw New Exception(ExceptionMsg, e)
        Finally
            ' Close and release resources.
            DisposeCommand(command)
        End Try
    End Sub
```

It is almost identical to the other `Exec*` functions, except when it executes the stored procedure. The code inside of the private `RunSp` method opens the `SqlCommand`'s `SqlConnection` object and then calls the `SqlCommand` object's `ExecuteNonQuery` method. This ensures that the `SqlCommand` does not return any type of `DataReader` object to read the results. This method is used mostly to execute `INSERT`, `UPDATE`, and `DELETE` stored procedures that do not return any results. It also has an overload that does not include the `SqlTransaction` argument.

Following is the code for `RunSp`:

```
''' <summary>
''' Opens the SqlCommand object's underlying SqlConnection and calls
''' the SqlCommand's ExecuteNonQuery method.
''' </summary>
''' <param name="command">An initialized SqlCommand object.</param>
Private Sub RunSp(ByRef command As SqlCommand)
    ' Open the connection.
    command.Connection.Open()

    ' Execute the stored procedure.
    command.ExecuteNonQuery()
End Sub
```

Finally, the last public function you are going to create is `ExecSpOutputValues`.

ExecSpOutputValues

This last public function in your component executes a stored procedure and returns an `IDictionary` object that contains output parameter name-value pairs. It is not meant for stored procedures that return result sets. As with the previous examples, this function takes a stored procedure name (`String`) and an optional list of parameter names and values (`IDictionary`) for its arguments. Here is the code for `ExecSpOutputValues`:

```
''' <summary>
''' Executes a stored procedure with or without parameters and returns an
''' IDictionary instance with the stored procedure's output parameter
''' name(s) and value(s).
''' </summary>
''' <param name="transaction">The transaction that the stored procedure
''' will be executed under.</param>
''' <param name="spName">The name of the stored procedure to execute.</param>
''' <param name="paramValues">A name-value pair of stored procedure parameter
''' name(s) and value(s).</param>
''' <returns>An IDictionary object.</returns>
Public Function ExecSpOutputValues(ByVal transaction As SqlTransaction, _
```

```
                                    ByVal spName As String, _
                                    ByVal paramValues As IDictionary) As IDictionary
    Dim command As SqlCommand = Nothing
    Try
        ' Get the initialized SqlCommand instance.
        command = GetSqlCommand(transaction, spName)
        ' Set the parameter values for the SqlCommand.
        SetParameterValues(command, paramValues)

        ' Run the stored procedure.
        RunSp(command)
        ' Get the output values.
        Dim outputParams As New Hashtable()
        Dim param As SqlParameter
        For Each param In command.Parameters
            If param.Direction = ParameterDirection.Output _
                Or param.Direction = ParameterDirection.InputOutput Then
                outputParams.Add(param.ParameterName, param.Value)
            End If
        Next param
        Return outputParams
    Catch e As Exception
        LogError(e)
        Throw New Exception(ExceptionMsg, e)
    Finally
        ' Close and release resources.
        DisposeCommand(command)
    End Try
End Function
```

This function is almost identical to `ExecSp` except that after the `SqlCommand.ExecuteNonQuery` method is called you iterate through the `SqlCommand` object's `Parameters` collection and look for all of the parameters that are output parameters. Next, you take the values of the output parameters and add the name-value pair to the `IDictionary` instance that you return. This method also has an overload that does not include the `SqlTransaction` argument.

Using DataSet Objects to Bind to DataGrids

Now that you have built your data access component, it is time to test it. A nice way to do that is to call the `ExecSpReturnDataSet` method, take the `DataSet` object that was created, and then bind the `DataSet` to a `DataGrid`. (You can find more about data binding in Chapter 14.) You also get to see how easily the `DataSet` and the `DataGrid` control integrate together. This exercise uses a Windows Application project called `SqlServerWrapperTestHarness`, added to the Examples solution. It contains references to `System`, `System.Data`, `System.Drawing`, `System.Windows.Forms`, and `System.Xml`, as well as a project reference to the `SqlServerWrapper` project. Added to the project is a form named `TestForm.vb` with two buttons, one for testing the `ExecSpReturnDataSet` method and one for testing the `ExecSpReturnSqlRecord` method. In this example, you will be looking only at the code for testing the `ExecSpReturnDataSet` method. Figure 10-4 shows what the test form looks like.

Figure 10-4

Figure 10-5 shows what your references should look like.

Figure 10-5

Here is the code for the declarations and private members of the form:

```
Option Explicit On
Option Strict On

Imports SqlServerWrapper
Imports System.Data.SqlClient
Imports System.Xml
Imports System.Configuration
```

```
Public Class TestForm
    Inherits System.Windows.Forms.Form

    Private _helper As StoredProcedureHelper = Nothing
```

These declarations should look pretty familiar by now. Note that you are declaring a private variable (_helper) for the StoredProcedureHelper class that you are using so you can get to the class from other parts of the form instead of just a Button Click event handler.

Next, you initialize the _helper variable in the form's Load event handler:

```
Private Sub TestForm_Load(ByVal sender As System.Object, _
    ByVal e As System.EventArgs) Handles MyBase.Load
    ' Set the SQL connection string
    Dim connectionString As String =
ConfigurationSettings.AppSettings("dbConnectionString")

    ' Call the SqlServer wrapper constructor and
    ' pass the DB connection string and the stored procedures config.
    helper = New StoredProcedureHelper(connectionString, _
        CType(ConfigurationSettings.GetConfig("StoredProcedureSettings"), _
        XmlNode))
End Sub
```

As in the earlier examples, this code begins by retrieving a connection string to the pubs database from the app.config file. You then create a new instance of the StoredProcedureHelper and assign it to the _helper class variable. During the constructor call to the StoredProcedureHelper class, you first pass in your connection string, and then you pass in an XmlNode of the stored procedure metadata for the StoredProcedureHelper class to consume. Note that you are passing the stored procedure metadata in to your class via the GetConfig method of the ConfigurationSettings class. This is because you have created a section inside of your app.config file called StoredProcedureSettings, and you have configured a SectionHandler to let the .NET Framework application configuration functionality consume your XML and give it back to you as an XmlNode. Here is what this section looks like inside of the app.config file:

```
<configSections>
    <section name="StoredProcedureSettings"
type="SqlServerWrapper.StoredProcedureSectionHandler, SqlServerWrapper" />
  </configSections>
  <StoredProcedureSettings>
    <StoredProcedures>
      <StoredProcedure name="usp_Get_Authors_By_States">
        <Parameters>
          <Parameter name="@states" datatype="VarChar" direction="Input"
isNullable="false" size="100" />
          <Parameter name="@state_delimiter" datatype="Char" direction="Input"
isNullable="false" size="1" />
        </Parameters>
      </StoredProcedure>
      <StoredProcedure name="usp_Get_Author_By_ID">
        <Parameters>
```

```
        <Parameter name="@au_id" datatype="VarChar" direction="Input"
isNullable="false" size="11" />
      </Parameters>
    </StoredProcedure>
  </StoredProcedures>
</StoredProcedureSettings>
```

This is nice because you do not need to include a separate XML file for your project; you just integrate seamlessly into the `app.config` file. Note how you are defining what class in what assembly will handle consuming your `<StoredProcedureSettings>` section in the `<section>` element. The requirement for this to work is that the class defined must implement the `System.Configuration.IConfigurationSectionHandler` interface. Here is the code for your section handler:

```
Option Explicit On
Option Strict On

Imports System
Imports System.Configuration
Imports System.Xml
Imports System.Xml.Serialization
Imports System.Xml.XPath

Public Class StoredProcedureSectionHandler
    Implements IConfigurationSectionHandler

    Public Function Create(ByVal parent As Object, _
        ByVal configContext As Object, _
        ByVal section As System.Xml.XmlNode) As Object _
            Implements IConfigurationSectionHandler.Create
        Return section("StoredProcedures")
    End Function
End Class
```

This code is pretty simple; you just return the XML node named `StoredProcedures` to the caller of your handler.

Back to your `Button`'s `Click` event handler, once you have the `StoredProcedureHelper` class instance fully initialized, you then create the parameter values for the stored procedure you want to execute and pass these arguments to the `ExecSpReturnDataSet` method:

```
' Add the two parameter name-values.
Dim params As New Hashtable
params.Add("@states", "CA")
params.Add("@state_delimiter", "^")

' Execute the sp, and get the DataSet object back.
Dim ds As DataSet = _helper.ExecSpReturnDataSet("usp_Get_Authors_By_States", _
    "", params)
```

The last step is to actually bind the data to the form's grid:

```
' Bind the DataGrid to the DataSet object.
dgdAuthors.SetDataBinding(ds.Tables(0), Nothing)
```

The results should look like the dialog shown in Figure 10-6.

Figure 10-6

Summary

This chapter took a look at ADO.NET and the new features of ADO.NET 2.0. You have seen and used the main objects in ADO.NET that you need to quickly get up and running in order to build data access into your .NET applications. You took a fairly in-depth look at the `DataSet` and `DataTable` classes, as these are the core classes of ADO.NET.

You also looked at stored procedures, including how to create them in SQL Server and how to access them from your code. Finally, you built your own custom data access component, which makes it easy to call stored procedures and separate data access code from the rest of business logic code in a .NET application.

11

Using XML in Visual Basic 2005

This chapter describes how you can generate and manipulate *Extensible Markup Language (XML)* using Visual Basic 2005. However, using XML in Visual Basic is a vast area to cover (more than possibly could be covered in a chapter). The .NET Framework exposes five XML-specific namespaces that contain over a hundred different classes. In addition, dozens of other classes support and implement XML-related technologies, such as ADO.NET, SQL Server, and BizTalk. Consequently, this chapter focuses on the general concepts and the most important classes.

Visual Basic relies on the classes exposed in the following XML-related namespaces to transform, manipulate, and stream XML documents:

- ❑ `System.Xml` provides core support for a variety of XML standards (including DTD, namespace, DOM, XDR, XPath, XSLT, and SOAP).

- ❑ `System.Xml.Serialization` provides the objects used to transform objects to and from XML documents or streams using serialization.

- ❑ `System.Xml.Schema` provides a set of objects that enable schemas to be loaded, created, and streamed. This support is achieved using a suite of objects that support the in-memory manipulation of the entities that compose an XML schema.

- ❑ `System.Xml.XPath` provides a parser and evaluation engine for the XML Path Language (XPath).

- ❑ `System.Xml.Xsl` provides the objects necessary when working with Extensible Stylesheet Language (XSL) and XSL Transformations (XSLT).

The XML-related technologies utilized by Visual Basic include other technologies that generate XML documents and enable XML documents to be managed as a data source:

❑ **ADO** — The legacy COM objects provided by ADO have the ability to generate XML documents in stream or file form. ADO can also retrieve a previously persisted XML document and manipulate it. (Although ADO is not used in this chapter, ADO and other legacy COM APIs can be accessed seamlessly from Visual Basic.)

❑ **ADO.NET** — This uses XML as its underlying data representation: The in-memory data representation of the ADO.NET `DataSet` object is XML; the results of data queries are represented as XML documents; XML can be imported into a `DataSet` and exported from a `DataSet`. (ADO.NET is covered in Chapter 10.)

❑ **SQL Server 2000** — XML-specific features were added to SQL Server 2000 (`FOR XML` queries to retrieve XML documents and `OPENXML` to represent an XML document as a rowset). Visual Basic can use ADO.NET to access SQL Server's XML-specific features (the documents generated and consumed by SQL Server can then be manipulated programmatically). Recently, Microsoft also released SQLXML, which provides an SQL Server 2000 database with some excellent XML capabilities, such as querying a database using XQuery, getting back XML result sets from a database, working with data just as if it were XML, taking huge XML files and having SQLXML convert them to relational data, and much more. SQLXML enables you to perform these functions and more via a set of managed .NET classes. You can download SQLXML free from the Microsoft SQLXML website at `http://msdn.microsoft.com/sqlxml`.

❑ **SQL Server 2005** — SQL Server has now been modified with XML in mind. SQL Server 2005 can natively understand XML because it is now built into the underlying foundation of the database. The ability to query and understand XML documents is a valuable addition to this database server. SQL Server 2005 also comes in a lightweight (and free) version called SQL Server Express Edition.

This chapter makes sense of this range of technologies by introducing some basic XML concepts and demonstrating how Visual Basic, in conjunction with the .NET Framework, can make use of XML. Specifically, you will

❑ Learn the rationale behind XML.

❑ Look at the namespaces within the .NET Framework class library that deal with XML and XML-related technologies.

❑ Take a closer look at some of the classes contained within these namespaces.

❑ Gain an overview of some of the other Microsoft technologies that utilize XML, particularly SQL Server and ADO.NET.

At the end of this chapter, you will be able to generate, manipulate, and transform XML using Visual Basic.

An Introduction to XML

XML is a tagged markup language similar to HTML. In fact, XML and HTML are distant cousins and have their roots in the Standard Generalized Markup Language (SGML). This means that XML leverages one of the most useful features of HTML — readability. However, XML differs from HTML in that XML represents data, whereas HTML is a mechanism for displaying data. The tags in XML describe the data, as shown in the following example:

```
<?xml version="1.0" encoding="utf-8" ?>
<Movies>
  <FilmOrder name="Grease" filmId="1" quantity="21"></FilmOrder>
  <FilmOrder name="Lawrence of Arabia" filmId="2" quantity="10"></FilmOrder>
  <FilmOrder name="Star Wars" filmId="3" quantity="12"></FilmOrder>
  <FilmOrder name="Shrek" filmId="4" quantity="14"></FilmOrder>
</Movies>
```

This XML document represents a store order for a collection of movies. The standard used to represent an order of films would be useful to movie rental firms, collectors, and others. This information can be shared using XML for the following reasons:

❑   The data tags in XML are self-describing.

❑   XML is an open standard and supported on most platforms today.

XML supports the parsing of data by applications not familiar with the contents of the XML document. XML documents can also be associated with a description (a schema) that informs an application as to the structure of the data within the XML document.

At this stage, XML looks simple — it's just a human-readable way to exchange data in a universally accepted format. The essential points that you should understand about XML are as follows:

❑   XML data can be stored in a plain text file.

❑   A document is said to be well formed if it adheres to the XML standard.

❑   Tags are used to specify the contents of a document — for example, `<FilmOrder>`.

❑   XML elements (also called *nodes*) can be thought of as the objects within a document.

❑   Elements are the basic building blocks of the document. Each element contains a start tag and end tag. A tag can be both a start and an end tag in one — for example, `<FilmOrder />`. In this case, the tag specifies that there is no content (or inner text) to the element (there isn't a closing tag because none is required due to the lack of inner-text content). Such a tag is said to be *empty*.

❑   Data can be contained in the element (the element content) or within attributes contained in the element.

❑   XML is hierarchical. One document can contain multiple elements, which can themselves contain child elements, and so on. However, an XML document can only have one root element.

This last point means that the XML document hierarchy can be thought of as a tree containing nodes:

❑   The example document has a root node, `<Movies>`.

❑   The branches of the root node are elements of type `<FilmOrder>`.

❑   The leaves of the XML element, `<FilmOrder>`, are its attributes: `name`, `quantity`, and `filmId`.

Of course, we're interested in the practical use of XML by Visual Basic. A practical manipulation of the example XML is to display, for example, for the staff of a movie supplier, a particular movie order in an application so that the supplier can fill the order and then save the information to a database. This chapter explains how you can perform such tasks using the functionality provided by the .NET Framework class library.

XML Serialization

The simplest way to demonstrate Visual Basic's support for XML is not with a complicated technology, such as SQL Server or ADO.NET, but with a practical use of XML, serializing a class.

The serialization of an object means that it is written out to a stream, such as a file or a socket (this is also known as *dehydrating* an object). The reverse process can also be performed: An object can be deserialized (or rehydrated) by reading it from a stream.

> *The type of serialization described in this chapter is XML serialization, where XML is used to represent a class in serialized form.*

To help you understand XML serialization, let's examine a class named `FilmOrder` (which can be found in the code download from www.wrox.com). This class is implemented in Visual Basic and is used by the company for processing an order for movies. The class could be instantiated on a firm's PDA, laptop, or even mobile phone (as long as the .NET Framework were installed).

An instance of `FilmOrder` corresponding to each order could be serializing to XML and sending over a socket using the PDA's cellular modem. (If the person making the order had a PDA that did not have a cellular modem, the instance of `FilmOrder` could be serialized to a file.) The order could then be processed when the PDA was dropped into a docking cradle and synced. We are talking about data in a propriety form here, an instance of `FilmOrder` being converted into a generic form — XML — that can be universally understood.

The `System.Xml.Serialization` namespace contains classes and interfaces that support the serialization of objects to XML, and the deserialization of objects from XML. Objects are serialized to documents or streams using the `XmlSerializer` class. Let's look at how you can use `XmlSerializer`. First, you need to define an object that implements a default constructor, such as `FilmOrder`:

```
Public Class FilmOrder

  ' These are Public because we have yet to implement
  ' properties to provide program access.

  Public name As String
  Public filmId As Integer
  Public quantity As Integer

  Public Sub New()

  End Sub
```

```
    Public Sub New(ByVal name As String, _
                   ByVal filmId As Integer, _
                   ByVal quantity As Integer)
        Me.name = name
        Me.filmId = filmId
        Me.quantity = quantity
    End Sub
End Class
```

This class should be created in a console application. From there, we can move on to the module. Within the module's Sub Main, create an instance of XmlSerializer, specifying the object to serialize and its type in the constructor (you need to make a reference to System.Xml.Serialization for this to work):

```
Dim serialize As XmlSerializer = _
    New XmlSerializer(GetType(FilmOrder))
```

Create an instance of the same type passed as a parameter to the constructor of XmlSerializer:

```
Dim MyFilmOrder As FilmOrder = _
    New FilmOrder("Grease", 101, 10)
```

Call the Serialize() method of the XmlSerializer instance, and specify the stream to which the serialized object is written (parameter one, Console.Out) and the object to be serialized (parameter two, MyFilmOrder):

```
serialize.Serialize(Console.Out, MyFilmOrder)
Console.ReadLine()
```

To make reference to the XmlSerializer object, you need to make reference to the System.Xml.Serialization namespace:

```
Imports System.Xml
Imports System.Xml.Serialization
```

Running the module, the following output is generated by the preceding code:

```
<?xml version="1.0" encoding="IBM437"?>
<FilmOrder xmlns:xsd="http://www.w3.org/2001/XMLSchema"
                    xmlns:xsi="http://www.w3.org/2001/XMLSchema-instance">
    <name>Grease</name>
    <filmId>101</filmId>
    <quantity>10</quantity>
</FilmOrder>
```

This output demonstrates the default way in which the Serialize() method serializes an object:

❑   Each object serialized is represented as an element with the same name as the class — in this case, FilmOrder.

❑   The individual data members of the class serialized are contained in elements named for each data member — in this case, name, filmId, and quantity.

Also generated are the following:

❑   The specific version of XML generated — in this case, `1.0`

❑   The encoding used — in this case, `IBM437`

❑   The schemas used to describe the serialized object — in this case,
     `www.w3.org/2001/XMLSchema-instance` and `www.w3.org/2001/XMLSchema`

A schema can be associated with an XML document and describe the data it contains (name, type, scale, precision, length, and so on). Either the actual schema or a reference to where the schema resides can be contained in the XML document. In either case, an XML schema is a standard representation that can be used by all applications that consume XML. This means that applications can use the supplied schema to validate the contents of an XML document generated by the `Serialize()` method of the `XmlSerializer` object.

The code snippet that demonstrated the `Serialize()` method of `XmlSerializer` displayed the XML generated to `Console.Out`. Clearly, we do not expect an application to use `Console.Out` when it would like to access a `FilmOrder` object in XML form. The point was to show how serialization can be performed in just two lines of code (one call to a constructor and one call to method). The entire section of code responsible for serializing the instance of `FilmOrder` is presented here:

```
Try
    Dim serialize As XmlSerializer = _
                New XmlSerializer(GetType(FilmOrder))
    Dim MyMovieOrder As FilmOrder = _
            New FilmOrder("Grease", 101, 10)
    serialize.Serialize(Console.Out, MyMovieOrder)
    Console.Out.WriteLine()
    Console.Readline()
Catch ex As Exception
    Console.Error.WriteLine(ex.ToString())
End Try
```

The `Serialize()` method's first parameter is overridden so that it can serialize XML to a file (the filename is given as type `String`), a `Stream`, a `TextWriter`, or an `XmlWriter`. When serializing to `Stream`, `TextWriter`, or `XmlWriter`, adding a third parameter to the `Serialize()` method is permissible. This third parameter is of type `XmlSerializerNamespaces` and is used to specify a list of namespaces that qualify the names in the XML-generated document. The permissible overrides of the `Serialize()` method are as follows:

```
Public Sub Serialize(Stream, Object)
Public Sub Serialize(TextWriter, Object)
Public Sub Serialize(XmlWriter, Object)
Public Sub Serialize(Stream, Object, XmlSerializerNamespaces)
Public Sub Serialize(TextWriter, Object, XmlSerializerNamespaces)
Public Sub Serialize(XmlWriter, Object, XmlSerializerNamespaces)
Public Sub Serialize(XmlWriter, Object, XmlSerializerNamespaces, String)
Public Sub Serialize(XmlWriter, Object, XmlSerializerNamespaces, String, String)
```

An object is reconstituted using the `Deserialize()` method of `XmlSerializer`. This method is over-ridden and can deserialize XML presented as a `Stream`, a `TextReader`, or an `XmlReader`. The overloads for `Deserialize` are as follows:

```
Public Function Deserialize(Stream) As Object
Public Function Deserialize(TextReader) As Object
Public Function Deserialize(XmlReader) As Object
Public Function Deserialize(XmlReader, XmlDeserializationEvents) As Object
Public Function Deserialize(XmlReader, String) As Object
Public Function Deserialize(XmlReader, String, XmlDeserializationEvents) As Object
```

Before demonstrating the `Deserialize()` method, we will introduce a new class, `FilmOrder_Multiple`. This class contains an array of film orders (actually an array of `FilmOrder` objects). `FilmOrder_Multiple` is defined as follows:

```
Public Class FilmOrder_Multiple
    Public multiFilmOrders() As FilmOrder

    Public Sub New()

    End Sub

    Public Sub New(ByVal multiFilmOrders() As FilmOrder)
        Me.multiFilmOrders = multiFilmOrders
    End Sub
End Class
```

The `FilmOrder_Multiple` class contains a fairly complicated object, an array of `FilmOrder` objects. The underlying serialization and deserialization of this class is more complicated than that of a single instance of a class that contains several simple types, but the programming effort involved on your part is just as simple as before. This is one of the great ways in which the .NET Framework makes it easy for you to work with XML data, no matter how it is formed.

To work through an example of the deserialization process, first create a sample order stored as an XML file called `Filmorama.xml`:

```
<?xml version="1.0" encoding="utf-8" ?>
<FilmOrder_Multiple xmlns:xsi="http://www.w3.org/2001/XMLSchema-instance"
 xmlns:xsd="http://www.w3.org/2001/XMLSchema">
    <multiFilmOrders>
        <FilmOrder>
            <name>Grease</name>
            <filmId>101</filmId>
            <quantity>10</quantity>
        </FilmOrder>
        <FilmOrder>
            <name>Lawrence of Arabia</name>
            <filmId>102</filmId>
            <quantity>10</quantity>
        </FilmOrder>
        <FilmOrder>
            <name>Star Wars</name>
            <filmId>103</filmId>
```

```
            <quantity>10</quantity>
        </FilmOrder>
    </multiFilmOrders>
</FilmOrder_Multiple>
```

Once the XML file is in place, the next step is to change your console application so it will take this XML file and deserialize its contents. Once you have the XML file in place, it is important to ensure that your console application has made the proper namespace references:

```
Imports System.Xml
Imports System.Xml.Serialization
Imports System.IO
```

Then, the following code demonstrates an object of type `FilmOrder_Multiple` being deserialized (or rehydrated) from a file, `Filmorama.xml`. This object is deserialized using this file in conjunction with the `Deserialize()` method of `XmlSerializer`:

```
' Open file, ..\Filmorama.xml
Dim dehydrated As FileStream = _
    New FileStream("Filmorama.xml", FileMode.Open)

' Create an XmlSerializer instance to handle deserializing,
' FilmOrder_Multiple
Dim serialize As XmlSerializer = _
    New XmlSerializer(GetType(FilmOrder_Multiple))

' Create an object to contain the deserialized instance of the object.
Dim myFilmOrder As FilmOrder_Multiple = _
    New FilmOrder_Multiple

' Deserialize object
myFilmOrder = serialize.Deserialize(dehydrated)
```

Once deserialized, the array of film orders can be displayed:

```
Dim SingleFilmOrder As FilmOrder

For Each SingleFilmOrder In myFilmOrder.multiFilmOrders
    Console.Out.WriteLine("{0}, {1}, {2}", _
        SingleFilmOrder.name, _
        SingleFilmOrder.filmId, _
        SingleFilmOrder.quantity)
Next

Console.ReadLine()
```

This example is just code that serializes an instance of type `FilmOrder_Multiple`. The output generated by displaying the deserialized object containing an array of film orders is as follows:

```
Grease, 101, 10
Lawrence of Arabia, 102, 10
Star Wars, 103, 10
```

XmlSerializer also implements a CanDeserialize() method. The prototype for this method is as follows:

```
Public Overridable Function CanDeserialize(ByVal xmlReader As XmlReader) _
    As Boolean
```

If CanDeserialize() returns True, then the XML document specified by the xmlReader parameter can be deserialized. If the return value of this method is False, then the specified XML document cannot be deserialized.

The FromTypes() method of XmlSerializer facilitates the creation of arrays that contain XmlSerializer objects. This array of XmlSerializer objects can be used in turn to process arrays of the type to be serialized. The prototype for FromTypes() is shown here:

```
Public Shared Function FromTypes(ByVal types() As Type) As XmlSerializer()
```

Before exploring the System.Xml.Serialization namespace, take a moment to consider the various uses of the term "attribute."

Source Code Style Attributes

Thus far, you have seen attributes applied to a specific portion of an XML document. Visual Basic has its own flavor of attributes, as do C# and each of the other .NET languages. These attributes refer to annotations to the source code that specify information (or metadata) that can be used by other applications without the need for the original source code. We will call such attributes *Source Code Style attributes*.

In the context of the System.Xml.Serialization namespace, Source Code Style attributes can be used to change the names of the elements generated for the data members of a class or to generate XML attributes instead of XML elements for the data members of a class. To demonstrate this, we will use a class called ElokuvaTilaus, which contains data members named name, filmId, and quantity. It just so happens that the default XML generated when serializing this class is not in a form that can be readily consumed by an external application.

For example, assume that a Finnish development team has written this external application; hence, the XML element and attribute names are in Finnish (minus the umlauts), rather than English. To rename the XML generated for a data member, name, a Source Code Style attribute will be used. This Source Code Style attribute would specify that when ElokuvaTilaus is serialized, the name data member would be represented as an XML element, <Nimi>. The actual Source Code Style attribute that specifies this is as follows:

```
<XmlElementAttribute("Nimi")> Public name As String
```

ElokuvaTilaus, which means *MovieOrder* in Finnish, also contains other Source Code Style attributes:

❑ <XmlAttributeAttribute("ElokuvaId")> specifies that filmId is to be serialized as an XML attribute named ElokuvaId.

❑ <XmlAttributeAttribute("Maara")> specifies that quantity is to be serialized as an XML attribute named Maara.

`ElokuvaTilaus` is defined as follows:

```
Imports System.Xml.Serialization

Public Class ElokuvaTilaus

  ' These are Public because we have yet to implement
  ' properties to provide program access.

  <XmlElementAttribute("Nimi")> Public name As String
  <XmlAttributeAttribute("ElokuvaId")> Public filmId As Integer
  <XmlAttributeAttribute("Maara")> Public quantity As Integer

  Public Sub New()
  End Sub

  Public Sub New(ByVal name As String, _
              ByVal filmId As Integer, _
              ByVal quantity As Integer)
    Me.name = name
    Me.filmId = filmId
    Me.quantity = quantity
  End Sub

End Class
```

`ElokuvaTilaus` can be serialized as follows:

```
Dim serialize As XmlSerializer = _
    New XmlSerializer(GetType(ElokuvaTilaus))
Dim MyMovieOrder As ElokuvaTilaus = _
    New ElokuvaTilaus("Grease", 101, 10)

serialize.Serialize(Console.Out, MyMovieOrder)
Console.Readline()
```

The output generated by this code reflects the Source Code Style attributes associated with class `ElokuvaTilaus`:

```
<?xml version="1.0" encoding="IBM437"?>
<ElokuvaTilaus xmlns:xsi="http://www.w3.org/2001/XMLSchema-instance"
 xmlns:xsd="http://www.w3.org/2001/XMLSchema"
 ElokuvaId="101" Maara="10">
    <Nimi>Grease</Nimi>
</ElokuvaTilaus>
```

The value of `filmId` is contained in an XML attribute, `ElokuvaId`, and the value of `quantity` is contained in an XML attribute, `Maara`. The value of `name` is contained in an XML element, `Nimi`.

The example only demonstrates the Source Code Style attributes exposed by the `XmlAttributeAttribute` and `XmlElementAttribute` classes in the `System.Xml.Serialization` namespace. A variety of other Source Code Style attributes exist in this namespace that also control the form of XML generated by serialization. The classes associated with such Source Code Style attributes include `XmlTypeAttribute`, `XmlTextAttribute`, `XmlRootAttribute`, `XmlIncludeAttribute`, `XmlIgnoreAttribute`, and `XmlEnumAttribute`.

System.Xml Document Support

The `System.Xml` namespace implements a variety of objects that support standards-based XML processing. The XML-specific standards facilitated by this namespace include XML 1.0, Document Type Definition (DTD) support, XML namespaces, XML schemas, XPath, XQuery, XSLT, DOM Level 1 and DOM Level 2 (Core implementations), as well as SOAP 1.1, SOAP 1.2, SOAP Contract Language, and SOAP Discovery. The `System.Xml` namespace exposes over 30 separate classes in order to facilitate this level of the XML standard's compliance.

With respect to generating and navigating XML documents, there are two styles of access:

❑   **Stream-based** — `System.Xml` exposes a variety of classes that read XML from and write XML to a stream. This approach tends to be a fast way to consume or generate an XML document because it represents a set of serial reads or writes. The limitation of this approach is that it does not view the XML data as a document composed of tangible entities, such as nodes, elements, and attributes. An example of where a stream could be used is when receiving XML documents from a socket or a file.

❑   **Document Object Model (DOM)-based** — `System.Xml` exposes a set of objects that access XML documents as data. The data is accessed using entities from the XML document tree (nodes, elements, and attributes). This style of XML generation and navigation is flexible but may not yield the same performance as stream-based XML generation and navigation. DOM is an excellent technology for editing and manipulating documents. For example, the functionality exposed by DOM might make merging your checking, savings, and brokerage accounts simpler.

XML Stream-Style Parsers

When demonstrating XML serialization, XML stream-style parsers were mentioned. After all, when an instance of an object is serialized to XML, it has to be written to a stream, and when it is deserialized, it is read from a stream. When an XML document is parsed using a stream parser, the parser always points to the current node in the document. The basic architecture of stream parsers is shown in Figure 11-1.

Figure 11-1

The following classes that access a stream of XML (read XML) and generate a stream of XML (write XML) are contained in the `System.Xml` namespace:

❑ `XmlWriter` — This abstract class specifies a noncached, forward-only stream that writes an XML document (data and schema).

❑ `XmlReader` — This abstract class specifies a noncached, forward-only stream that reads an XML document (data and schema).

Your diagram of the classes associated with the XML stream-style parser referred to one other class, `XslTransform`. This class is found in the `System.Xml.Xsl` namespace and is not an XML stream-style parser. Rather, it is used in conjunction with `XmlWriter` and `XmlReader`. This class is covered in detail later.

The `System.Xml` namespace exposes a plethora of additional XML manipulation classes in addition to those shown in the architecture diagram. The classes shown in the diagram include the following:

❑ `XmlResolver` — This abstract class resolves an external XML resource using a Uniform Resource Identifier (URI). `XmlUrlResolver` is an implementation of an `XmlResolver`.

❑ `XmlNameTable` — This abstract class provides a fast means by which an XML parser can access element or attribute names.

Writing an XML Stream

An XML document can be created programmatically in .NET. One way to perform this task is by writing the individual components of an XML document (schema, attributes, elements, and so on) to an XML stream. Using a unidirectional write-stream means that each element and its attributes must be written in order — the idea is that data is always written at the head of the stream. To accomplish this, you use a writable XML stream class (a class derived from `XmlWriter`). Such a class ensures that the XML document you generate correctly implements the W3C Extensible Markup Language (XML) 1.0 specification and the Namespaces in XML specification.

Why is this necessary when you have XML serialization? You need to be very careful here to separate interface from implementation. XML serialization works for a specific class, such as the `ElokuvaTilaus` class. This class is a proprietary implementation and not the format in which data is exchanged. For this one specific case, the XML document generated when `ElokuvaTilaus` is serialized just so happens to be the XML format used when placing an order for some movies. `ElokuvaTilaus` was given a little help from Source Code Style attributes so that it would conform to a standard XML representation of a film order summary.

In a different application, if the software used to manage an entire movie distribution business wants to generate movie orders, then it will have to generate a document of the appropriate form. The movie distribution management software achieves this using the `XmlWriter` object.

Before reviewing the subtleties of `XmlWriter`, note that this class exposes over 40 methods and properties. The example in this section provides an overview that touches on a subset of these methods and properties. This subset allows an XML document that corresponds to a movie order to be generated.

This example builds a module that generates an XML document corresponding to a movie order. You will use an instance of `XmlWriter`, called `FilmOrdersWriter`, which is actually a file on disk. This means that the XML document generated is streamed to this file. Because the `FilmOrdersWriter` variable represents a file, you have to take a few actions against the file. For instance, you have to make sure the file is

- **Created** — The instance of `XmlWriter`, `FilmOrdersWriter`, is created using the `Create()` method as well as by assigning all the properties of this object with the `XmlWriterSettings` object.

- **Opened** — The file the XML is streamed to, `FilmOrdersProgrammatic.xml`, is opened by passing the filename to the constructor associated with `XmlWriter`.

- **Generated** — The process of generating the XML document is described in detail at the end of this section.

- **Closed** — The file (the XML stream) is closed using the `Close()` method of `XmlWriter` or by simply making use of the Using keyword, which ensures that the object is closed at the end of the Using statement.

Before you create the `XmlWriter` object, you first need to customize how the object operates by using the `XmlWriterSettings` object. This object, new to .NET 2.0, enables you to configure the behavior of the `XmlWriter` object before you instantiate it:

```
Dim myXmlSettings As New XmlWriterSettings
myXmlSettings.Indent = True
myXmlSettings.NewLineOnAttributes = True
```

You can specify a few settings for the `XmlWriterSettings` object that define how XML creation will be handled by the `XmlWriter` object. The following table details the properties of the `XmlWriterSettings` class:

Property	Initial Value	Description
CheckCharacters	True	This property, if set to `True`, performs a character check on the contents of the `XmlWriter` object. Legal characters can be found at www.w3.org/TR/REC-xml#charsets.
CloseOutput	False	Specifies whether the `XmlWriter` should also close the stream or the `System.IO.TextWriter` object
ConformanceLevel	Conformance Level.Document	Allows the XML to be checked to ensure that it follows certain specified rules. Possible conformance-level settings include `Document`, `Fragment`, and `Auto`.
Encoding	Encoding.UTF8	Defines the encoding of the XML generated

Table continues on the next page

Property	Initial Value	Description
Indent	True	Defines whether the XML generated should be indented or not. Setting this value to False will not indent child nodes from parent nodes.
IndentChars	Two spaces	Specifies the number of spaces by which child nodes will be indented from parent nodes. This setting only works when the Indent property is set to True. If you want, you can assign this any string value you choose.
NewLineChars	\r\n	Assigns the characters that are used to define line breaks
NewLineHandling	NewLineHandling.Replace	Defines whether to normalize line breaks in the output. Possible values include Replace, Entitize, and None.
NewLineOn Attributes	True	Defines whether a node's attributes should be written to a new line in the construction. This will occur if set to True.
OmitXml Declaration	False	Defines whether an XML declaration should be generated in the output. This omission only occurs if set to True.
OutputMethod	OutputMethod.Xml	Defines the method to serialize the output. Possible values include Xml, Html, Text, and AutoDetect.

Once the XmlWriterSettings object has been instantiated and assigned the values you deem necessary, the next steps are to invoke the XmlWriter object and make the association between the XmlWriterSettings object and the XmlWriter object.

The basic infrastructure for managing the file (the XML text stream) and applying the settings class is

```
Dim FilmOrdersWriter As XmlWriter = _
    XmlWriter.Create("..\FilmOrdersProgrammatic.xml", myXmlSettings)

FilmOrdersWriter.Close()
```

or the following, if you are utilizing the Using keyword, which is new to the .NET Framework 2.0 and highly recommended:

```
Using FilmOrdersWriter As XmlWriter = _
    XmlWriter.Create("..\FilmOrdersProgrammatic.xml", myXmlSettings)
End Using
```

With the preliminaries completed (file created and formatting configured), the process of writing the actual attributes and elements of your XML document can begin. The sequence of steps used to generate your XML document is as follows:

❑ Write an XML comment using the `WriteComment()` method. This comment describes from whence the concept for this XML document originated and generates the following code:

```
<!-- Same as generated by serializing, ElokuvaTilaus -->
```

❑ Begin writing the XML element, `<ElokuvaTilaus>`, by calling the `WriteStartElement()` method. You can only begin writing this element because its attributes and child elements must be written before the element can be ended with a corresponding `</ElokuvaTilaus>`. The XML generated by the `WriteStartElement()` method is as follows

```
<ElokuvaTilaus>
```

❑ Write the attributes associated with `<ElokuvaTilaus>` by calling the `WriteAttributeString()` method twice. The XML generated by calling the `WriteAttributeString()` method twice adds to the `<ElokuvaTilaus>` XML element that is currently being written to the following:

```
<ElokuvaTilaus ElokuvaId="101" Maara="10">
```

❑ Using the `WriteElementString()` method, write the child XML element `<Nimi>` contained in the XML element, `<ElokuvaTilaus>`. The XML generated by calling this method is as follows:

```
<Nimi>Grease</Nimi>
```

❑ Complete writing the `<ElokuvaTilaus>` parent XML element by calling the `WriteEndElement()` method. The XML generated by calling this method is as follows:

```
</ElokuvaTilaus>
```

Let's now put all this together in the `Module1.vb` file shown here:

```
Imports System.Xml
Imports System.Xml.Serialization
Imports System.IO

Module Module1

    Sub Main()

        Dim myXmlSettings As New XmlWriterSettings
        myXmlSettings.Indent = True
        myXmlSettings.NewLineOnAttributes = True

        Using FilmOrdersWriter As XmlWriter = _
            XmlWriter.Create("..\FilmOrdersProgrammatic.xml", myXmlSettings)

            FilmOrdersWriter.WriteComment(" Same as generated " & _
                "by serializing, ElokuvaTilaus ")
            FilmOrdersWriter.WriteStartElement("ElokuvaTilaus")
            FilmOrdersWriter.WriteAttributeString("ElokuvaId", "101")
```

```
                    FilmOrdersWriter.WriteAttributeString("Maara", "10")
                    FilmOrdersWriter.WriteElementString("Nimi", "Grease")
                    FilmOrdersWriter.WriteEndElement() ' End ElokuvaTilaus

            End Using

        End Sub

    End Module
```

Once this is run, you will find the XML file `FilmOrdersProgrammatic.xml` created in the same folder as the `Module1.vb` file or in the `bin/Debug` or `bin/Release` folders. The content of this file is as follows:

```xml
<?xml version="1.0" encoding="utf-8"?>
<!-- Same as generated by serializing, ElokuvaTilaus -->
<ElokuvaTilaus
  ElokuvaId="101"
  Maara="10">
  <Nimi>Grease</Nimi>
</ElokuvaTilaus>
```

The previous XML document is the same in form as the XML document generated by serializing the `ElokuvaTilaus` class. Notice that in the previous XML document the `<Nimi>` element is indented two characters and that each attribute is on a different line in the document. This was achieved using the `XmlWriterSettings` class.

The sample application covered only a small portion of the methods and properties exposed by the XML stream-writing class, `XmlWriter`. Other methods implemented by this class manipulate the underlying file, such as the `Flush()` method, and some methods allow XML text to be written directly to the stream, such as the `WriteRaw()` method.

The `XmlWriter` class also exposes a variety of methods that write a specific type of XML data to the stream. These methods include `WriteBinHex()`, `WriteCData()`, `WriteString()`, and `WriteWhiteSpace()`.

You can now generate the same XML document in two different ways. You have used two different applications that took two different approaches to generating a document that represents a standardized movie order. However, there are even more ways to generate XML, depending on the circumstances. Using the previous scenario, you could receive a movie order from a store, and this order would have to be transformed from the XML format used by the supplier to your own order format.

Reading an XML Stream

In .NET, XML documents can be read from a stream as well. Data is traversed in the stream in order (first XML element, second XML element, and so on). This traversal is very quick because the data is processed in one direction and features such as write and move backward in the traversal are not supported. At any given instance, only data at the current position in the stream can be accessed.

Before exploring how an XML stream can be read, you need to understand why it should be read in the first place. Let's return to our movie supplier example. Imagine that the application that manages the movie orders can generate a variety of XML documents corresponding to current orders, preorders, and returns. All the documents (current orders, preorders, and returns) can be extracted in stream form and processed by a report-generating application. This application prints the orders for a given day, the preorders that are going to be due, and the returns that are coming back to the supplier. The report-generating application processes the data by reading in and parsing a stream of XML.

One class that can be used to read and parse such an XML stream is XmlReader. Other classes in the .NET Framework are derived from XmlReader, such as XmlTextReader, which can read XML from a file (specified by a string corresponding to the file's name), a Stream, or an XmlReader. This example uses an XmlReader to read an XML document contained in a file. Reading XML from a file and writing it to a file is not the norm when it comes to XML processing, but a file is the simplest way to access XML data. This simplified access enables you to focus on XML-specific issues.

In creating a sample, the first step is to make the proper imports into the Module1.vb file:

```
Imports System.Xml
Imports System.Xml.Serialization
Imports System.IO
```

From there, the next step in accessing a stream of XML data is to create an instance of the object that will open the stream (the readMovieInfo variable of type XmlReader) and then open the stream itself. Your application performs this as follows (where MovieManage.xml is the name of the file containing the XML document):

```
Dim myXmlSettings As New XmlReaderSettings()
Using readMovieInfo As XmlReader = XmlReader.Create(fileName, myXmlSettings)
```

Note that because the XmlWriter has a settings class, the XmlReader also has a settings class. Though you can make assignments to the XmlReaderSettings object, in this case you do not. Later, this chapter covers the XmlReaderSettings object.

The basic mechanism for traversing each stream is to traverse from node to node using the Read() method. Node types in XML include Element and Whitespace. Numerous other node types are defined, but this example focuses on traversing XML elements and the white space that is used to make the elements more readable (carriage returns, linefeeds, and indentation spaces). Once the stream is positioned at a node, the MoveToNextAttribute() method can be called to read each attribute contained in an element. The MoveToNextAttribute() method only traverses attributes for nodes that contain attributes (nodes of type element). An example of an XmlReader traversing each node and then traversing the attributes of each node follows:

```
While readMovieInfo.Read()
    ' Process node here.
    While readMovieInfo.MoveToNextAttribute()
        ' Process attribute here.
    End While
End While
```

This code, which reads the contents of the XML stream, does not utilize any knowledge of the stream's contents. However, a great many applications know exactly how the stream they are going to traverse is structured. Such applications can use XmlReader in a more deliberate manner and not simply traverse the stream without foreknowledge.

Once the example stream has been read, it can be cleaned up using the `End Using` call:

```
End Using
```

This `ReadMovieXml` subroutine takes the filename containing the XML to read as a parameter. The code for the subroutine is as follows (and is basically the code just outlined):

```
Private Sub ReadMovieXml(ByVal fileName As String)
    Dim myXmlSettings As New XmlReaderSettings()
    Using readMovieInfo As XmlReader = XmlReader.Create(fileName, myXmlSettings)
        While readMovieInfo.Read()
            ShowXmlNode(readMovieInfo)
            While readMovieInfo.MoveToNextAttribute()
                ShowXmlNode(readMovieInfo)
            End While
        End While
    End Using
    Console.ReadLine()
End Sub
```

For each node encountered after a call to the `Read()` method, `ReadMovieXml()` calls the `ShowXmlNode()` subroutine. Similarly, for each attribute traversed, the `ShowXmlNode()` subroutine is called. This subroutine breaks down each node into its sub-entities:

❑ **Depth** — The `Depth` property of `XmlReader` determines the level at which a node resides in the XML document tree. To understand depth, consider the following XML document composed solely of elements: `<A><B></B><C><D></D></C></A>`.

Element `<A>` is the root element, and when parsed would return a `Depth` of `0`. Elements `<B>` and `<C>` are contained in `<A>` and are hence a `Depth` value of `1`. Element `<D>` is contained in `<C>`. The `Depth` property value associated with `<D>` (depth of `2`) should, therefore, be one more than the `Depth` property associated with `<C>` (depth of `1`).

❑ **Type** — The type of each node is determined using the `NodeType` property of `XmlReader`. The node returned is of enumeration type, `XmlNodeType`. Permissible node types include `Attribute`, `Element`, and `Whitespace`. (Numerous other node types can also be returned, including `CDATA`, `Comment`, `Document`, `Entity`, and `DocumentType`.)

❑ **Name** — The type of each node is retrieved using the `Name` property of `XmlReader`. The name of the node could be an element name, such as `<ElokuvaTilaus>`, or an attribute name, such as `ElokuvaId`.

❑ **Attribute Count** — The number of attributes associated with a node is retrieved using the `AttributeCount` property of `XmlReader`'s `NodeType`.

❑ **Value** — The value of a node is retrieved using the `Value` property of `XmlReader`. For example, the element node `<Nimi>` contains a value of `Grease`.

Subroutine `ShowXmlNode()` is implemented as follows:

```
Private Sub ShowXmlNode(ByVal reader As XmlReader)

    If reader.Depth > 0 Then
```

```
            For depthCount As Integer = 1 To reader.Depth
                Console.Write(" ")
            Next
        End If


        If reader.NodeType = XmlNodeType.Whitespace Then

            Console.Out.WriteLine("Type: {0} ", reader.NodeType)

        ElseIf reader.NodeType = XmlNodeType.Text Then

            Console.Out.WriteLine("Type: {0}, Value: {1} ", _
                                  reader.NodeType, _
                                  reader.Value)

        Else

            Console.Out.WriteLine("Name: {0}, Type: {1}, " & _
                                  "AttributeCount: {2}, Value: {3} ", _
                                  reader.Name, _
                                  reader.NodeType, _
                                  reader.AttributeCount, _
                                  reader.Value)

        End If

    End Sub
```

Within the `ShowXmlNode()` subroutine, each level of node depth adds two spaces to the output generated:

```
If reader.Depth > 0 Then
    For depthCount As Integer = 1 To reader.Depth
        Console.Write(" ")
    Next
End If
```

You add these spaces in order to make human-readable output (so you can easily determine the depth of each node displayed). For each type of node, `ShowXmlNode()` displays the value of the `NodeType` property. The `ShowXmlNode()` subroutine makes a distinction between nodes of type `Whitespace` and other types of nodes. The reason for this is simple: A node of type `Whitespace` does not contain a name or attribute count. The value of such a node is any combination of white-space characters (space, tab, carriage return, and so on). Therefore, it does not make sense to display the properties if the `NodeType` is `XmlNodeType.WhiteSpace`. Nodes of type `Text` have no name associated with them, so for this type, subroutine `ShowXmlNode` only displays the properties `NodeType` and `Value`. For all other node types, the `Name`, `AttributeCount`, `Value`, and `NodeType` properties are displayed.

For the finalization of this module, add a `Sub Main` as follows:

```
Sub Main(ByVal args() As String)
    ReadMovieXml("..\MovieManage.xml")
End Sub
```

Here's an example construction of the `MovieManage.xml` file:

```xml
<?xml version="1.0" encoding="utf-8" ?>
<MovieOrderDump>

 <FilmOrder_Multiple>
    <multiFilmOrders>
        <FilmOrder>
            <name>Grease</name>
            <filmId>101</filmId>
            <quantity>10</quantity>
        </FilmOrder>
        <FilmOrder>
            <name>Lawrence of Arabia</name>
            <filmId>102</filmId>
            <quantity>10</quantity>
        </FilmOrder>
        <FilmOrder>
            <name>Star Wars</name>
            <filmId>103</filmId>
            <quantity>10</quantity>
        </FilmOrder>
    </multiFilmOrders>
 </FilmOrder_Multiple>

 <PreOrder>
    <FilmOrder>
        <name>Shrek III - Shrek Becomes a Programmer</name>
        <filmId>104</filmId>
        <quantity>10</quantity>
    </FilmOrder>
 </PreOrder>

 <Returns>
    <FilmOrder>
        <name>Star Wars</name>
        <filmId>103</filmId>
        <quantity>2</quantity>
    </FilmOrder>
 </Returns>

</MovieOrderDump>
```

Running this module produces the following output (a partial display, as it would be rather lengthy):

```
Name: xml, Type: XmlDeclaration, AttributeCount: 2, Value: version="1.0"
encoding="utf-8"
Name: version, Type: Attribute, AttributeCount: 2, Value: 1.0
Name: encoding, Type: Attribute, AttributeCount: 2, Value: utf-8
Type: Whitespace
Name: MovieOrderDump, Type: Element, AttributeCount: 0, Value:
 Type: Whitespace
 Name: FilmOrder_Multiple, Type: Element, AttributeCount: 0, Value:
  Type: Whitespace
```

```
Name: multiFilmOrders, Type: Element, AttributeCount: 0, Value:
 Type: Whitespace
 Name: FilmOrder, Type: Element, AttributeCount: 0, Value:
  Type: Whitespace
  Name: name, Type: Element, AttributeCount: 0, Value:
   Type: Text, Value: Grease
```

This example managed to use three methods and five properties of `XmlReader`. The output generated was informative but far from practical. `XmlReader` exposes over 50 methods and properties, which means that we have only scratched the surface of this highly versatile class. The remainder of this section looks at the `XmlReaderSettings` class, introduces a more realistic use of `XmlReader`, and demonstrates how the classes of `System.Xml` handle errors.

The XmlReaderSettings Class

Just like the `XmlWriter` object, the `XmlReader` object requires settings to be applied for instantiation of the object. This means that you can apply settings specifying how the `XmlReader` object behaves when it is reading whatever XML you might have for it. This includes settings for dealing with white space, schemas, and more:

Property	Initial Value	Description
CheckCharacters	True	This property, if set to `True`, performs a character check on the contents of the retrieved object. Legal characters can be found at www.w3.org/TR/ REC-xml#charsets.
CloseOutput	False	Specifies whether the `XmlWriter` should also close the stream or the `System.IO.TextWriter` object
ConformanceLevel	Conformance Level.Document	Allows for the XML to be checked to ensure that it follows certain specified rules. Possible conformance-level settings include `Document`, `Fragment`, and `Auto`.
IgnoreComments	False	Defines whether comments should be ignored or not
IgnoreProcessing Instructions	False	Defines whether processing instructions contained within the XML should be ignored
IgnoreWhitespace	False	Defines whether the `XmlReader` object should ignore all insignificant white space
LineNumberOffset	0	Defines the line number at which the `LineNumber` property starts counting within the XML file
LinePosition Offset	0	Defines the position in the line number at which the `LineNumber` property starts counting within the XML file

Table continues on the next page

Property	Initial Value	Description
NameTable	An empty XmlNameTable object	Enables the XmlReader to work with a specific XmlNameTable object that is used for atomized string comparisons
ProhibitDtd	False	Defines whether the XmlReader should perform a DTD validation
Schemas	An empty XmlSchemaSet object	Enables the XmlReader to work with an instance of the XmlSchemaSet class
ValidationFlags	Validation Flags. AllowXml Attributes and Validation Flags. Process-Identity Constraints	Enables you to apply validation schema settings. Possible values include AllowXmlAttributes, ProcessIdentityConstraints, ProcessInlineSchema, ProcessSchemaLocation, ReportValidationWarnings, and None.
ValidationType	None	Specifies whether the XmlReader will perform validation or type assignment when reading. Possible values include Auto, DTD, None, Schema, and XDR.
XmlResolver		A write-only property that enables you to access external documents

An example of using this setting class to modify the behavior of the XmlReader class is as follows:

```
Dim myXmlSettings As New XmlReaderSettings()
myXmlSettings.IgnoreWhitespace = True
myXmlSettings.IgnoreComments = True

Using readMovieInfo As XmlReader = XmlReader.Create(fileName, myXmlSettings)
   ' Use XmlReader object here.
End Using
```

In this case, the XmlReader object that is created ignores the white space that it encounters as well as any of the XML comments. These settings, once established with the XmlReaderSettings object, are then associated with the XmlReader object through its Create() method.

Traversing XML Using XmlTextReader

An application can easily use XmlReader to traverse a document that is received in a known format. The document can thus be traversed in a deliberate manner. You implemented a class that serialized arrays of movie orders. The next example takes an XML document containing multiple XML documents of that type and traverses them. Each movie order is forwarded to the movie supplier by sending a fax. The document is traversed as follows:

```
Read root element: <MovieOrderDump>
    Process each <FilmOrder_Multiple> element
        Read <multiFilmOrders> element
            Process each <FilmOrder>
                Send fax for each movie order here
```

The basic outline for the program's implementation is to open a file containing the XML document to parse and to traverse it from element to element:

```
Dim myXmlSettings As New XmlReaderSettings()

Using readMovieInfo As XmlReader = XmlReader.Create(fileName, myXmlSettings)
    readMovieInfo.Read()
    readMovieInfo.ReadStartElement("MovieOrderDump")

    Do While (True)
        '******************************************************
        '* Process FilmOrder elements here                    *
        '******************************************************
    Loop

    readMovieInfo.ReadEndElement()   '  </MovieOrderDump>

End Using
```

The preceding code opened the file using the constructor of `XmlReader`, and the `End Using` statement takes care of shutting everything down for you. The code also introduced two methods of the `XmlReader` class:

❑ `ReadStartElement(String)` — This verifies that the current in the stream is an element and that the element's name matches the string passed to method `ReadStartElement()`. If the verification is successful, then the stream is advanced to the next element.

❑ `ReadEndElement()` — This verifies that the current element is an end tab, and if the verification is successful, then the stream is advanced to the next element.

The application knows that an element, `<MovieOrderDump>`, will be found at a specific point in the document. The `ReadStartElement()` method verifies this foreknowledge of the document format. Once all the elements contained in element `<MovieOrderDump>` have been traversed, the stream should point to the end tag `</MovieOrderDump>`. The `ReadEndElement()` method verifies this.

The code that traverses each element of type `<FilmOrder>` similarly uses the `ReadStartElement()` and `ReadEndElement()` methods to indicate the start and end of the `<FilmOrder>` and `<multiFilmOrders>` elements. The code that ultimately parses the list of movie orders and faxes the movie supplier (using the `FranticallyFaxTheMovieSupplier()` subroutine) is as follows:

```
Dim myXmlSettings As New XmlReaderSettings()
```

```
Using readMovieInfo As XmlReader = XmlReader.Create(fileName, myXmlSettings)
      readMovieInfo.Read()
      readMovieInfo.ReadStartElement("MovieOrderDump")

   Do While (True)
       readMovieInfo.ReadStartElement("FilmOrder_Multiple")
       readMovieInfo.ReadStartElement("multiFilmOrders")

       Do While (True)
           readMovieInfo.ReadStartElement("FilmOrder")
           movieName = readMovieInfo.ReadElementString()
           movieId = readMovieInfo.ReadElementString()
           quantity = readMovieInfo.ReadElementString()
           readMovieInfo.ReadEndElement() ' clear </FilmOrder>

           FranticallyFaxTheMovieSupplier(movieName, movieId, quantity)

           ' Should read next FilmOrder node
           ' else quits
           readMovieInfo.Read()

           If ("FilmOrder" <> readMovieInfo.Name) Then
               Exit Do
           End If
       Loop

       readMovieInfo.ReadEndElement() ' clear </multiFilmOrders>
       readMovieInfo.ReadEndElement() ' clear </FilmOrder_Multiple>

       ' Should read next FilmOrder_Multiple node
       ' else you quit
       readMovieInfo.Read() ' clear </MovieOrderDump>

       If ("FilmOrder_Multiple" <> readMovieInfo.Name) Then
           Exit Do
       End If
   Loop

      readMovieInfo.ReadEndElement()  '  </MovieOrderDump>

   End Using
```

Three lines within the preceding code contain a call to the ReadElementString method:

```
movieName = readMovieInfo.ReadElementString()
movieId = readMovieInfo.ReadElementString()
quantity = readMovieInfo.ReadElementString()
```

While parsing the stream, it was known that an element named <name> existed and that this element contained the name of the movie. Rather than parse the start tag, get the value, and parse the end tag, it was easier just to get the data using the ReadElementString() method. This method retrieves the data string associated with an element and advances the stream to the next element. The ReadElementString() method was also used to retrieve the data associated with the XML elements <filmId> and <quantity>.

The output of this example is a fax, not shown here because the point of this example is to demonstrate that it is simpler to traverse a document when its form is known. The format of the document is still verified by `XmlReader` as it is parsed.

The `XmlReader` class also exposes properties that provide more insight into the data contained in the XML document and the state of parsing: `IsEmptyElement`, `EOF`, and `IsStartElement`.

.NET CLR-compliant types are not 100% inline with XML types, so the .NET Framework 2.0 has introduced some new methods in the `XmlReader` that make the process of casting from one of these XML types to .NET types easier.

Using the `ReadElementContentAs()` method, you can easily perform the necessary casting required:

```
Dim username As String = _
    myXmlReader.ReadElementContentAs(GetType(String), DBNull.Value)
Dim myDate As DateTime = _
    myXmlReader.ReadElementContentAs(GetType(DateTime), DBNull.Value)
```

Also available is a whole series of direct casts through new methods such as the following:

- ❏ `ReadElementContentAsBase64()`
- ❏ `ReadElementContentAsBinHex()`
- ❏ `ReadElementContentAsBoolean()`
- ❏ `ReadElementContentAsDateTime()`
- ❏ `ReadElementContentAsDecimal()`
- ❏ `ReadElementContentAsDouble()`
- ❏ `ReadElementContentAsFloat()`
- ❏ `ReadElementContentAsInt()`
- ❏ `ReadElementContentAsLong()`
- ❏ `ReadElementContentAsObject()`
- ❏ `ReadElementContentAsString()`

In addition to these methods, the raw XML associated with the document can also be retrieved, using `ReadInnerXml()` and `ReadOuterXml()`. Again, this only scratches the surface of the `XmlReader` class, a class you will find to be quite rich in functionality.

Handling Exceptions

XML is text and could easily be read using mundane methods such as `Read()` and `ReadLine()`. A key feature of each class that reads and traverses XML is inherent support for error detection and handling. To demonstrate this, consider the following malformed XML document found in the file named `Malformed.xml`:

```
<?xml version="1.0" encoding="IBM437" ?>
<ElokuvaTilaus ElokuvaId="101", Maara="10">
```

```
    <Nimi>Grease</Nimi>
<ElokuvaTilaus>
```

This document may not immediately appear to be malformed. By wrapping a call to the method you developed (movieReadXML), you can see what type of exception is raised when XmlReader detects the malformed XML within this document:

```
Try
    movieReadXML("Malformed.xml")
Catch xmlEx As XmlException
    Console.Error.WriteLine("XML Error: " + xmlEx.ToString())
Catch ex As Exception
    Console.Error.WriteLine("Some other error: " + ex.ToString())
End Try
```

The methods and properties exposed by the XmlReader class raise exceptions of type System.Xml.XmlException. In fact, every class in the System.Xml namespace raises exceptions of type XmlException. Although this is a discussion of errors using an instance of type XmlReader, the concepts reviewed apply to all errors generated by classes found in the System.Xml namespace.

The properties exposed by XmlException include the following:

❑   Data — A set of key/value pairs that enable you to display user-defined information about the exception

❑   HelpLink — The link to the help page that deals with the exception

❑   InnerException — The System.Exception instance indicating what caused the current exception

❑   LineNumber — The number of the line within an XML document where the error occurred

❑   LinePosition — The position within the line specified by LineNumber where the error occurred

❑   Message — The error message that corresponds to the error that occurred. This error took place at the line in the XML document specified by LineNumber and within the line at the position specified by LinePostion.

❑   Source — Provides the name of the application or object that triggered the error

❑   SourceUri — Provides the URI of the element or document in which the error occurred

❑   StackTrace — Provides a string representation of the frames on the call stack when the error was triggered

❑   TargetSite — The method that triggered the error

The error displayed when subroutine movieReadXML processes Malformed.xml is as follows:

```
XML Error: System.Xml.XmlException: The ',' character, hexadecimal value 0x2C,
    cannot begin a name. Line 2, position 49.
```

This indicates there is a comma separating the attributes in element `<FilmOrder>` (`ElokuvaTilaus="101"`, `Maara="10"`). This comma is invalid. Removing the comma and running the code again gives the following output:

```
XML Error: System.Xml.XmlException: This is an unexpected token. Expected
'EndElement'. Line 5, position 27.
```

Again, you can recognize the precise error. In this case, you do not have an end element, `</ElokuvaTilaus>`, but you do have an opening element, `<ElokuvaTilaus>`.

The properties provided by the `XmlException` class (such as `LineNumber`, `LinePosition`, and `Message`) provide a useful level of precision when tracking down errors. The `XmlReader` class also exposes a level of precision with respect to the parsing of the XML document. This precision is exposed by the `XmlReader` through properties such as `LineNumber` and `LinePosition`.

Using the MemoryStream Object

A very useful class that can greatly help you when working with XML is `System.IO.MemoryStream`. Rather than needing a network or disk resource backing the stream (as in `System.Net.Sockets.NetworkStream` and `System.IO.FileStream`), `MemoryStream` backs itself up onto a block of memory. Imagine that you want to generate an XML document and e-mail it. The built-in classes for sending e-mail rely on having a `System.String` containing a block of text for the message body, but if you want to generate an XML document, then you need a stream.

If the document is reasonably sized, then write the document directly to memory and copy that block of memory to the e-mail. This is good from a performance and reliability perspective because you don't have to open a file, write it, rewind it, and read the data back in again. However, you must consider scalability in this situation because if the file is very large, or if you have a great number of smaller files, then you could run out of memory (in which case you have to go the "file" route).

This section describes how to generate an XML document to a `MemoryStream` object, reading the document back out again as a `System.String` value and e-mailing it. What you'll do is create a new class called `EmailStream` that extends `MemoryStream`. This new class contains an extra method called `CloseAndSend()` that, as its name implies, closes the stream and sends the e-mail message.

First create a new console application project called `EmailStream`. The first task is to create a basic `Customer` object that contains a few basic members and can be automatically serialized by .NET through use of the `SerializableAttribute` attribute:

```vb
<Serializable()> Public Class Customer

    ' members...
    Public Id As Integer
    Public FirstName As String
    Public LastName As String
    Public Email As String

End Class
```

The fun part now is the `EmailStream` class itself. This needs access to the `System.Web.Mail` namespace, so you need to add a reference to the `System.Web` assembly. The new class should also extend `System.IO.MemoryStream`, as shown here:

```
Imports System.IO
Imports System.Web.Mail

Public Class EmailStream
    Inherits MemoryStream
```

The first job of `CloseAndSend()` is to start putting together the mail message. This is done by creating a new `System.Web.Mail.MailMessage` object and configuring the sender, recipient, and subject:

```
' CloseAndSend - close the stream and send the email...
Public Sub CloseAndSend(ByVal fromAddress As String, _
                        ByVal toAddress As String, _
                        ByVal subject As String)

    ' Create the new message...
    Dim message As New MailMessage
    message.From = fromAddress
    message.To = toAddress
    message.Subject = subject
```

This method will be called once the XML document has been written to the stream, so you can assume at this point that the stream contains a block of data. To read the data back out again, you have to rewind the stream and use a `System.IO.StreamReader`. Before you do this, however, call `Flush()`. Traditionally, streams have always been buffered — that is, the data is not sent to the final destination (the memory block in this case, but a file in the case of a `FileStream`, and so on) each time the stream is written. Instead, the data is written in (pretty much) a nondeterministic way. Because you need all the data to be written, you call `Flush()` to ensure that all the data has been sent to the destination and that the buffer is empty.

In a way, `EmailStream` is a great example of buffering. All the data is held in a memory "buffer" until you finally send the data on to its destination in a response to an explicit call to this method:

```
' Flush and rewind the stream...

Flush()
Seek(0, SeekOrigin.Begin)
```

Once you've flushed and rewound the stream, you can create a `StreamReader` and dredge all the data out into the `Body` property of the `MailMessage` object:

```
' Read out the data...

Dim reader As New StreamReader(Me)
message.Body = reader.ReadToEnd()
```

After you've done that, close the stream by calling the base class method:

```
' Close the stream...

Close()
```

Finally, send the message:

```
' Send the message...

SmtpMail.Send(message)

End Sub
```

To call this method, you need to add some code to the `Main` method. First create a new `Customer` object and populate it with some test data:

```
Imports System.Xml.Serialization

Module Module1

  Sub Main()

    ' Create a new customer...
    Dim customer As New Customer
    customer.Id = 27
    customer.FirstName = "Bill"
    customer.LastName = "Gates"
    customer.Email = "bill.gates@microsoft.com"
```

After you've done that, you can create a new `EmailStream` object. You then use `XmlSerializer` to write an XML document representing the newly created `Customer` instance to the block of memory that `EmailStream` is backing to:

```
    ' Create a new email stream...
    Dim stream As New EmailStream

    ' Serialize...
    Dim serializer As New XmlSerializer(customer.GetType())
    serializer.Serialize(stream, customer)
```

At this point, the stream will be filled with data, and after all the data has been flushed, the block of memory that `EmailStream` backs on to will contain the complete document. Now you can call `CloseAndSend` to e-mail the document:

```
    ' Send the email...
    stream.CloseAndSend("evjen@yahoo.com", _
      "evjen@yahoo.com", "XML Customer Document")
  End Sub

End Module
```

You probably already have the Microsoft SMTP service properly configured — this service is necessary to send e-mail. You also need to make sure that the e-mail addresses used in your code go to your e-mail address! Run the project and check your e-mail; and you should see something similar to what is shown in Figure 11-2.

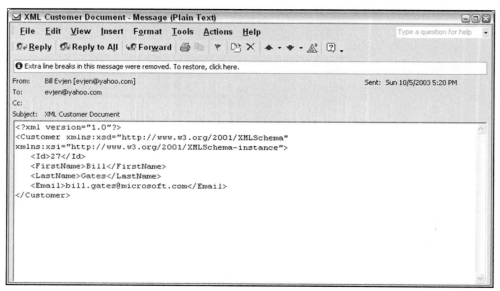

Figure 11-2

Document Object Model (DOM)

The classes of the System.Xml namespace that support the Document Object Model (DOM) interact as illustrated in Figure 11-3.

Figure 11-3

Within this diagram, an XML document is contained in a class named `XmlDocument`. Each node within this document is accessible and managed using `XmlNode`. Nodes can also be accessed and managed using a class specifically designed to process a specific node's type (`XmlElement`, `XmlAttribute`, and so on). XML documents are extracted from `XmlDocument` using a variety of mechanisms exposed through such classes as `XmlWriter`, `TextWriter`, `Stream`, and a file (specified by filename of type `String`). XML documents are consumed by an `XmlDocument` using a variety of load mechanisms exposed through the same classes.

Where a DOM-style parser differs from a stream-style parser is with respect to movement. Using the DOM, the nodes can be traversed forward and backward. Nodes can be added to the document, removed from the document, and updated. However, this flexibility comes at a performance cost. It is faster to read or write XML using a stream-style parser.

The DOM-specific classes exposed by `System.Xml` include the following:

❑ `XmlDocument` — Corresponds to an entire XML document. A document is loaded using the `Load()` method. XML documents are loaded from a file (the filename specified as type `String`), `TextReader`, or `XmlReader`. A document can be loaded using `LoadXml()` in conjunction with a string containing the XML document. The `Save()` method is used to save XML documents. The methods exposed by `XmlDocument` reflect the intricate manipulation of an XML document. For example, the following self-documenting creation methods are implemented by this class: `CreateAttribute()`, `CreateCDataSection()`, `CreateComment()`, `CreateDocumentFragment()`, `CreateDocumentType()`, `CreateElement()`, `CreateEntityReference()`, `CreateNavigator()`, `CreateNode()`, `CreateProcessingInstruction()`, `CreateSignificantWhitespace()`, `CreateTextNode()`, `CreateWhitespace()`, and `CreateXmlDeclaration()`. The elements contained in the document can be retrieved. Other methods support the retrieving, importing, cloning, loading, and writing of nodes.

❑ `XmlNode` — Corresponds to a node within the DOM tree. This class supports datatypes, namespaces, and DTDs. A robust set of methods and properties are provided to create, delete, and replace nodes: `AppendChild()`, `Clone()`, `CloneNode()`, `CreateNavigator()`, `InsertAfter()`, `InsertBefore()`, `Normalize()`, `PrependChild()`, `RemoveAll()`, `RemoveChild()`, `ReplaceChild()`, `SelectNodes()`, `SelectSingleNode()`, `Supports()`, `WriteContentTo()`, and `WriteTo()`. The contents of a node can similarly be traversed in a variety of ways: `FirstChild`, `LastChild`, `NextSibling`, `ParentNode`, and `PreviousSibling`.

❑ `XmlElement` — Corresponds to an element within the DOM tree. The functionality exposed by this class contains a variety of methods used to manipulate an element's attributes: `AppendChild()`, `Clone()`, `CloneNode()`, `CreateNavigator()`, `GetAttribute()`, `GetAttributeNode()`, `GetElementsByTagName()`, `GetNamespaceOfPrefix()`, `GetPrefixOfNamespace()`, `InsertAfter()`, `InsertBefore()`, `Normalize()`, `PrependChild()`, `RemoveAll()`, `RemoveAllAttributes()`, `RemoveAttributeAt()`, `RemoveAttributeNode()`, `RemoveChild()`, `ReplaceChild()`, `SelectNodes()`, `SelectSingleNode()`, `SetAttribute()`, `SetAttributeNode()`, `Supports()`, `WriteContentTo()`, and `WriteTo()`.

❑ `XmlAttribute` — Corresponds to an attribute of an element (`XmlElement`) within the DOM tree. An attribute contains data and lists of subordinate data, so it is a less complicated object than an `XmlNode` or an `XmlElement`. An `XmlAttribute` can retrieve its owner document (property, `OwnerDocument`), retrieve its owner element (property, `OwnerElement`), retrieve its parent

419

node (property, `ParentNode`), and retrieve its name (property, `Name`). The value of an `XmlAttribute` is available via a read-write property named `Value`. The methods available to `XmlAttribute` include `AppendChild()`, `Clone()`, `CloneNode()`, `CreateNavigator()`, `GetNamespaceOfPrefix()`, `GetPrefixOfNamespace()`, `InsertAfter()`, `InsertBefore()`, `Normalize()`, `PrependChild()`, `RemoveAll()`, `RemoveChild()`, `ReplaceChild()`, `SelectNodes()`, `SelectSingleNode()`, `WriteContentTo()`, and `WriteTo()`.

Given the diverse number of methods and properties (and there are many more than those listed here) exposed by `XmlDocument`, `XmlNode`, `XmlElement`, and `XmlAttribute`, it should be clear that any XML 1.0 or 1.1-compliant document can be generated and manipulated using these classes. In comparison to their XML stream counterparts, these classes afford more flexible movement within the XML document and through any editing of XML documents.

A similar comparison could be made between DOM and data serialized and deserialized using XML. Using serialization, the type of node (for example, attribute or element) and the node name are specified at compile time. There is no on-the-fly modification of the XML generated by the serialization process.

Other technologies that generate and consume XML are not as flexible as the DOM. This includes ADO.NET and ADO, which generate XML of a particular form. The default install of SQL Server 2000 does expose a certain amount of flexibility when it comes to the generation (`FOR XML` queries) and consumption of XML (`OPENXML`). SQL Server 2005 has more support for XML and even supports an XML datatype. SQL Server 2005 also expands upon the `FOR XML` query with `FOR XML TYPE`. The choice between using classes within the DOM and a version of SQL Server is a choice between using a language, such as Visual Basic, to manipulate objects or installing SQL Server and performing most of the XML manipulation in SQL.

DOM Traversing Raw XML Elements

The first DOM example loads an XML document into an `XmlDocument` object using a string that contains the actual XML document. This scenario is typical of an application that uses ADO.NET to generate XML, but then uses the objects of the DOM to traverse and manipulate this XML. ADO.NET's `DataSet` object contains the results of ADO.NET data access operations. The `DataSet` class exposes a `GetXml` method that retrieves the underlying XML associated with the `DataSet`. The following code demonstrates how the contents of the `DataSet` are loaded into the `XmlDocument`:

```
Dim xmlDoc As New XmlDocument
Dim ds As New DataSet

' Set up ADO.NET DataSet() here
xmlDoc.LoadXml(ds.GetXml())
```

This example simply traverses each XML element (`XmlNode`) in the document (`XmlDocument`) and displays the data accordingly. The data associated with this example is not retrieved from a `DataSet` but is instead contained in a string, `rawData`, which is initialized as follows:

```
Dim rawData As String = _
    "<multiFilmOrders>" & _
    "  <FilmOrder>" & _
    "    <name>Grease</name>" & _
    "    <filmId>101</filmId>" & _
```

```
"      <quantity>10</quantity>" & _
"   </FilmOrder>" & _
"   <FilmOrder>" & _
"      <name>Lawrence of Arabia</name>" & _
"      <filmId>102</filmId>" & _
"      <quantity>10</quantity>" & _
"   </FilmOrder>" & _
"</multiFilmOrders>"
```

The XML document in `rawData` is a portion of the XML hierarchy associated with a movie order. The basic idea in processing this data is to traverse each `<FilmOrder>` element in order to display the data it contains. Each node corresponding to a `<FilmOrder>` element can be retrieved from your `XmlDocument` using the `GetElementsByTagName()` method (specifying a tag name of `FilmOrder`). The `GetElementsByTagName()` method returns a list of `XmlNode` objects in the form of a collection of type `XmlNodeList`. Using the `For Each` statement to construct this list, the `XmlNodeList` (`movieOrderNodes`) can be traversed as individual `XmlNode` elements (`movieOrderNode`). The code for handling this is as follows:

```
Dim xmlDoc As New XmlDocument
Dim movieOrderNodes As XmlNodeList
Dim movieOrderNode As XmlNode

xmlDoc.LoadXml(rawData)

' Traverse each <FilmOrder>
movieOrderNodes = xmlDoc.GetElementsByTagName("FilmOrder")

For Each movieOrderNode In movieOrderNodes
    '*********************************************************
    ' Process <name>, <filmId> and <quantity> here
    '*********************************************************
Next
```

Each `XmlNode` can then have its contents displayed by traversing the children of this node using the `ChildNodes()` method. This method returns an `XmlNodeList` (`baseDataNodes`) that can be traversed one `XmlNode` list element at a time:

```
Dim baseDataNodes As XmlNodeList
Dim bFirstInRow As Boolean

baseDataNodes = movieOrderNode.ChildNodes
bFirstInRow = True

For Each baseDataNode As XmlNode In baseDataNodes
  If (bFirstInRow) Then
    bFirstInRow = False
  Else
    Console.Out.Write(", ")
  End If
  Console.Out.Write(baseDataNode.Name & ": " & baseDataNode.InnerText)
Next
Console.Out.WriteLine()
```

The bulk of the preceding code retrieves the name of the node using the `Name` property and the `InnerText` property of the node. The `InnerText` property of each `XmlNode` retrieved contains the data associated with the XML elements (nodes) `<name>`, `<filmId>`, and `<quantity>`. The example displays the contents of the XML elements using `Console.Out`. The XML document is displayed as follows:

```
name: Grease, filmId: 101, quantity: 10
name: Lawrence of Arabia, filmId: 102, quantity: 10
```

Other, more practical, methods for using this data could have been implemented, including the following:

❑   The contents could have been directed to an ASP.NET `Response` object, and the data retrieved could have been used to create an HTML table (`<table>` table, `<tr>` row, and `<td>` data) that would be written to the `Response` object.

❑   The data traversed could have been directed to a `ListBox` or `ComboBox` Windows Forms control. This would enable the data returned to be selected as part of a GUI application.

❑   The data could have been edited as part of your application's business rules. For example, you could have used the traversal to verify that the `<filmId>` matched the `<name>`. Something like this could have been done if you really wanted to validate the data entered into the XML document in any manner.

Here is the example in its entirety:

```
Dim rawData As String = _
    "<multiFilmOrders>" & _
    "   <FilmOrder>" & _
    "      <name>Grease</name>" & _
    "      <filmId>101</filmId>" & _
    "      <quantity>10</quantity>" & _
    "   </FilmOrder>" & _
    "   <FilmOrder>" & _
    "      <name>Lawrence of Arabia</name>" & _
    "      <filmId>102</filmId>" & _
    "      <quantity>10</quantity>" & _
    "   </FilmOrder>" & _
    "</multiFilmOrders>"

Dim xmlDoc As New XmlDocument
Dim movieOrderNodes As XmlNodeList
Dim movieOrderNode As XmlNode
Dim baseDataNodes As XmlNodeList
Dim bFirstInRow As Boolean

xmlDoc.LoadXml(rawData)

' Traverse each <FilmOrder>
movieOrderNodes = xmlDoc.GetElementsByTagName("FilmOrder")

For Each movieOrderNode In movieOrderNodes
  baseDataNodes = movieOrderNode.ChildNodes
  bFirstInRow = True
  For Each baseDataNode As XmlNode In baseDataNodes
    If (bFirstInRow) Then
```

```
      bFirstInRow = False
   Else
     Console.Out.Write(", ")
   End If
   Console.Out.Write(baseDataNode.Name & ": " & baseDataNode.InnerText)
  Next
  Console.Out.WriteLine()
Next
```

DOM Traversing XML Attributes

This next example demonstrates how to traverse data contained in attributes and how to update the attributes based on a set of business rules. In this example, the XmlDocument object is populated by retrieving an XML document from a file. After the business rules edit the object, the data is persisted back to the file:

```
Dim xmlDoc As New XmlDocument

xmlDoc.Load("..\MovieSupplierShippingListV2.xml")
'*********************************************
' Business rules process document here
'*********************************************

xmlDoc.Save("..\MovieSupplierShippingListV2.xml")
```

The data contained in the file, MovieSupplierShippingListV2.xml, is a variation of the movie order. You have altered your rigid standard (for the sake of example) so that the data associated with individual movie orders is contained in XML attributes instead of XML elements. An example of this movie order data is as follows:

```
<FilmOrder name="Grease" filmId="101" quantity="10" />
```

You have already seen how to traverse the XML elements associated with a document, so let's assume that you have successfully retrieved the XmlNode associated with the <FilmOrder> element:

```
Dim attributes As XmlAttributeCollection
Dim filmId As Integer
Dim quantity As Integer

attributes = node.Attributes()
For Each attribute As XmlAttribute In attributes
  If 0 = String.Compare(attribute.Name, "filmId") Then
    filmId = attribute.InnerXml
  ElseIf 0 = String.Compare(attribute.Name, "quantity") Then
    quantity = attribute.InnerXml
  End If
Next
```

The preceding code traverses the attributes of an XmlNode by retrieving a list of attributes using the Attributes() method. The value of this method is used to set the attributes' object (datatype, XmlAttributeCollection). The individual XmlAttribute objects (variable, attribute) contained in attributes are traversed using a For Each loop. Within the loop, the contents of the filmId and the quantity attribute are saved for processing by your business rules.

Your business rules execute an algorithm that ensures that the movies in the company's order are provided in the correct quantity. This rule specifies that the movie associated with `filmId=101` must be sent to the customer in batches of six at a time due to packaging. In the event of an invalid quantity, the code for enforcing this business rule keeps removing a single order from the `quantity` value until the number is divisible by six. Then this number is assigned to the `quantity` attribute. The `Value` property of the `XmlAttribute` object is used to set the correct value of the order's quantity. The code performing this business rule is as follows:

```
If filmId = 101 Then
   ' This film comes packaged in batches of six.
   Do Until (quantity / 6) = True
      quantity -= 1
   Loop

   Attributes.ItemOf("quantity").Value = quantity
End If
```

What is elegant about this example is that the list of attributes was traversed using `For Each`. Then `ItemOf` was used to look up a specific attribute that had already been traversed. This would not have been possible by reading an XML stream with an object derived from the XML stream reader class, `XmlReader`.

You can use this code as follows:

```
Sub TraverseAttributes(ByRef node As XmlNode)
    Dim attributes As XmlAttributeCollection
    Dim filmId As Integer
    Dim quantity As Integer

    attributes = node.Attributes()

    For Each attribute As XmlAttribute In attributes
        If 0 = String.Compare(attribute.Name, "filmId") Then
            filmId = attribute.InnerXml
        ElseIf 0 = String.Compare(attribute.Name, "quantity") Then
            quantity = attribute.InnerXml
        End If
    Next

    If filmId = 101 Then
        ' This film comes packaged in batches of six
        Do Until (quantity / 6) = True
            quantity -= 1
        Loop

        Attributes.ItemOf("quantity").Value = quantity
    End If
End Sub


Sub WXReadMovieDOM()
    Dim xmlDoc As New XmlDocument
    Dim movieOrderNodes As XmlNodeList
    xmlDoc.Load("..\MovieSupplierShippingListV2.xml")
```

```
    ' Traverse each <FilmOrder>
    movieOrderNodes = xmlDoc.GetElementsByTagName("FilmOrder")

    For Each movieOrderNode As XmlNode In movieOrderNodes
        TraverseAttributes(movieOrderNode)
    Next

    xmlDoc.Save("..\MovieSupplierShippingListV2.xml")
End Sub
```

XSLT Transformations

XSLT is a language that is used to transform XML documents so that they can be presented visually. You have performed a similar task before. When working with XML serialization, you rewrote the FilmOrder class. This class was used to serialize a movie order object to XML using nodes that contained English-language names. The rewritten version of this class, ElokuvaTilaus, serialized XML nodes containing Finnish names. Source Code Style attributes were used in conjunction with the XmlSerializer class to accomplish this transformation. Two words in this paragraph send chills down the spine of any experienced developer: rewrote and rewritten. The point of an XSL transform is to use an alternate language (XSLT) to transform the XML rather than rewriting the source code, SQL commands, or some other mechanism used to generate XML.

Conceptually, XSLT is straightforward. A file with an .xslt extension describes the changes (transformations) that will be applied to a particular XML file. Once this is completed, an XSLT processor is provided with the source XML file and the XSLT file, and performs the transformation. The System.Xml .Xsl.XslTransform class is such an XSLT processor. A new processor in .NET 2.0 is the XsltCommand object found at SystemXml.Query.XsltCommand. This section looks at using both of these processors.

The XSLT file is itself an XML document, although certain elements within this document are XSLT-specific commands. Dozens of XSLT commands can be used in writing an XSLT file. The first example explores the following XSLT elements (commands):

- ❑ stylesheet — This element indicates the start of the style sheet (XSL) in the XSLT file.

- ❑ template — This element denotes a reusable template for producing specific output. This output is generated using a specific node type within the source document under a specific context. For example, the text <xsl: template match="/"> selects all root notes ("/") for the specific transform template.

- ❑ for-each — This element applies the same template to each node in the specified set. Recall the example class (FilmOrder_Multiple) that could be serialized. This class contained an array of movie orders. Given the XML document generated when a FilmOrder_Multiple is serialized, each movie order serialized could be processed using <xsl:for-each select = "FilmOrder_Multiple/multiFilmOrders/FilmOrder">.

- ❑ value-of — This element retrieves the value of the specified node and inserts it into the document in text form. For example, <xsl:value-of select="name" /> would take the value of the XML element <name> and insert it into the transformed document.

When serialized, the `FilmOrder_Multiple` class generates XML such as the following (where ... indicates where additional `<FilmOrder>` elements may reside):

```
<?xml version="1.0" encoding="you-ascii" ?>
<FilmOrder_Multiple>
    <multiFilmOrders>
        <FilmOrder>
            <name>Grease</name>
            <filmId>101</filmId>
            <quantity>10</quantity>
        </FilmOrder>
        ...
    </multiFilmOrders>
</FilmOrder_Multiple>
```

The preceding XML document is used to generate a report that is viewed by the manager of the movie supplier. This report is in HTML form, so that it can be viewed via the Web. The XSLT elements you previously reviewed (`stylesheet`, `template`, and `for-each`) are the only XSLT elements required to transform the XML document (in which data is stored) into an HTML file (data that can be displayed). An XSLT file `DisplayThatPuppy.xslt` contains the following text, which is used to transform a serialized version, `FilmOrder_Multiple`:

```
<?xml version="1.0" encoding="UTF-8" ?>
<xsl:stylesheet xmlns:xsl="http://www.w3.org/1999/XSL/Transform" version="1.0">
 <xsl:template match="/">
        <HTML>
        <TITLE>What people are ordering</TITLE>
        <BODY>
            <TABLE BORDER="1">
              <TR>
                <TD><B>Film Name</B></TD>
                <TD><B>Film ID</B></TD>
                <TD><B>Quantity</B></TD>
              </TR>
              <xsl:for-each select=
               "FilmOrder_Multiple/multiFilmOrders/FilmOrder">
              <TR>
                 <TD><xsl:value-of select="name" /></TD>
                 <TD><xsl:value-of select="filmId" /></TD>
                 <TD><xsl:value-of select="quantity" /></TD>
              </TR>
              </xsl:for-each>
           </TABLE>
        </BODY>
        </HTML>
   </xsl:template>
</xsl:stylesheet>
```

In the preceding XSLT file, the XSLT elements are marked in bold. These elements perform operations on the source XML file containing a serialized `FilmOrder_Multiple` object and generate the appropriate HTML file. Your file contains a table (marked by the table tag, `<TABLE>`) that contains a set of rows (each row marked by a table row tag, `<TR>`). The columns of the table are contained in table data tags, `<TD>`. The XSLT file contains the header row for the table:

```
<TR>
    <TD><B>Film Name</B></TD>
    <TD><B>Film ID</B></TD>
    <TD><B>Quantity</B></TD>
</TR>
```

Each row containing data (an individual movie order from the serialized object, `FilmOrder_Multiple`) is generated using the XSLT element, `for-each`, to traverse each `<FilmOrder>` element within the source XML document:

```
<xsl:for-each select=
    "FilmOrder_Multiple/multiFilmOrders/FilmOrder">
```

The individual columns of data are generated using the `value-of` XSLT element, in order to query the elements contained within each `<FilmOrder>` element (`<name>`, `<filmId>`, and `<quantity>`):

```
<TR>
    <TD><xsl:value-of select="name" /></TD>
    <TD><xsl:value-of select="filmId" /></TD>
    <TD><xsl:value-of select="quantity" /></TD>
</TR>
```

The code to create a displayable XML file using the `XslTransform` object is as follows:

```
Dim myXslTransform As XslTransform = New XslTransform

Dim destFileName As String = "..\ShowIt.html"

myXslTransform.Load("..\DisplayThatPuppy.xslt")
myXslTransform.Transform("..\FilmOrders.xml", destFileName)

System.Diagnostics.Process.Start(destFileName)
```

This consists of only seven lines of code, with the bulk of the coding taking place in the XSLT file. The previous code snippet created an instance of a `System.Xml.Xsl.XslTransform` object named `myXslTransform`. The `Load()` method of this class is used to load the XSLT file you previously reviewed, `DisplayThatPuppy.xslt`. The `Transform()` method takes a source XML file as the first parameter, which in this case was a file containing a serialized `FilmOrder_Multiple` object. The second parameter is the destination file created by the transform (`ShowIt.html`). The `Start()` method of the `Process` class is used to display the HTML file. This method launches a process that is most suitable for displaying the file provided. Basically, the extension of the file dictates which application will be used to display the file. On a typical Windows machine, the program used to display this file is Internet Explorer, as shown in Figure 11-4.

Figure 11-4

Don't confuse displaying this HTML file with ASP.NET. Displaying an HTML file in this manner takes place on a single machine without the involvement of a Web server. Using ASP.NET is more complex than displaying an HTML page in the default browser.

As demonstrated, the backbone of the `System.Xml.Xsl` namespace is the `XslTransform` class. This class uses XSLT files to transform XML documents. `XslTransform` exposes the following methods and properties:

❑   `XmlResolver` — This get/set property is used to specify a class (abstract base class, `XmlResolver`) that is used to handle external references (import and include elements within the style sheet). These external references are encountered when a document is transformed (the method, `Transform()`, is executed). The `System.Xml` namespace contains a class, `XmlUrlResolver`, which is derived from `XmlResolver`. The `XmlUrlResolver` class resolves the external resource based on a URI.

❑   `Load` — This overloaded method loads an XSLT style sheet to be used in transforming XML documents. It is permissible to specify the XSLT style sheet as a parameter of type `XPathNavigator`, filename of XSLT file (specified as parameter type `String`), `XmlReader`, or `IXPathNavigable`. For each of type of XSLT supported, an overloaded member is provided that allows an `XmlResolver` to also be specified. For example, it is possible to call `Load(String, XmlResolver)` where `String` corresponds to a filename and `XmlResolver` is an object that handles references in the style sheet of type `xsl:import` and `xsl:include`. It would also be permissible to pass in a value of `Nothing` for the second parameter of the `Load()` method (so that no `XmlResolver` would be specified). Note that considerable changes have been made to the parameters that the `Load()` method takes between versions 1.0 and 1.1 of the .NET Framework. Look at the SDK documentation for details on any late-breaking changes that you might encounter when working with the `XslTransform` class.

❑   `Transform` — This overloaded method transforms a specified XML document using the previously specified XSLT style sheet and an `XmlResolver`. The location where the transformed XML is to be output is specified as a parameter to this method. The first parameter of each overloaded method is the XML document to be transformed. This parameter can be represented as an `IXPathNavigable`, XML filename (specified as parameter type `String`), or `XPathNavigator`. Considerable changes have been made to the parameters that the `Transform()` method takes between versions 1.0 and 1.1 of the .NET Framework. Check the SDK documentation for details on any changes that you might encounter when working with the `XslTransform` class.

The most straightforward variant of the `Transform()` method is `Transform(String, String, XmlResolver)`. In this case, a file containing an XML document is specified as the first parameter, a filename that receives the transformed XML document is specified as the second parameter, and the `XmlResolver` is used as the third parameter. This is exactly how the first XSLT example utilized the `Transform` method:

```
myXslTransform.Transform("..\FilmOrders.xml", destFileName)
```

The first parameter to the `Transform` method can also be specified as `IXPathNavigable` or `XPath-Navigator`. Either of these parameter types allows the XML output to be sent to an object of type `Stream`, `TextWriter`, or `XmlWriter`. When these two flavors of input are specified, a parameter containing an object of type `XsltArgumentList` can be specified. An `XsltArgumentList` object contains a list of arguments that are used as input to the transform.

When working with a .NET 2.0 project, it is preferable to use the `XslCompiledTransform` object instead of the `XslTransform` object, because the `XslTransform` object is considered obsolete. When using the new `XslCompiledTransform` object, you construct the file using the following code:

```
Dim myXslCompiledTransform As XslCompiledTransform = New XslCompiledTransform

Dim destFileName As String = "..\ShowIt.html"

myXslCompiledTransform.Load("..\DisplayThatPuppy.xslt")
myXslCompiledTransform.Transform("..\FilmOrders.xml", destFileName)

System.Diagnostics.Process.Start(destFileName)
```

The `XslCompiledTransform` object uses the same `Load()` and `Transform()` methods as the `XslTransform` object from .NET 1.0/1.1. The new `Transform()` method provides the following signatures:

```
XslCompiledTransform.Transform(IXPathNavigable, XmlWriter)
XslCompiledTransform.Transform(IXPathNavigable, XsltArgumentList, XmlWriter)
XslCompiledTransform.Transform(IXPathNavigable, XsltArgumentList, TextWriter)
XslCompiledTransform.Transform(IXPathNavigable, XsltArgumentList, Stream)
XslCompiledTransform.Transform(XmlReader, XmlWriter)
XslCompiledTransform.Transform(XmlReader, XsltArguementList, XmlWriter)
XslCompiledTransform.Transform(XmlReader, XsltArguementList, TextWriter)
XslCompiledTransform.Transform(XmlReader, XsltArguementList, Stream)
XslCompiledTransform.Transform(XmlReader, XsltArguementList, XmlWriter,
    XmlResolver)
XslCompiledTransform.Transform(String, String)
XslCompiledTransform.Transform(String, XmlWriter)
XslCompiledTransform.Transform(String, XsltArguementList, XmlWriter)
XslCompiledTransform.Transform(String, XsltArguementList, TextWriter)
XslCompiledTransform.Transform(String, XsltArguementList, Stream)
```

In this case, `String` is a representation of the `.xslt` file that should be used in the transformation. Here, `String` represents the location of specific files (whether it is source files or output files). Some of the signatures also allow for output to `XmlWriter` objects, streams, and `TextWriter` objects. These can be used by also providing additional arguments using the `XsltArgumentList` object.

The preceding example used the second signature `XslCompiledTransform.Transform(String, String)`, which asked for the source file and the destination file (both string representations of the location of said files):

```
myXslCompiledTransform.Transform("..\FilmOrders.xml", destFileName)
```

XSLT Transforming between XML Standards

The first example used four XSLT elements to transform an XML file into an HTML file. Such an example has merit, but it doesn't demonstrate an important use of XSLT: transforming XML from one standard into another standard. This may involve renaming elements/attributes, excluding elements/attributes, changing datatypes, altering the node hierarchy, and representing elements as attributes, and vice versa.

A case of differing XML standards could easily happen to your software that automates movie orders coming into a supplier. Imagine that the software, including its XML representation of a movie order, is so successful that you sell 100,000 copies. However, just as you're celebrating, a consortium of the largest movie supplier chains announces that they are no longer accepting faxed orders and that they are introducing their own standard for the exchange of movie orders between movie sellers and buyers.

Rather than panic, you simply ship an upgrade that includes an XSLT file. This upgrade (a bit of extra code plus the XSLT file) transforms your XML representation of a movie order into the XML representation dictated by the consortium of movie suppliers. Using an XSLT file enables you to ship the upgrade immediately. If the consortium of movie suppliers revises their XML representation, you are not obliged to change your source code. Instead, you can simply ship the upgraded XSLT file that ensures that each movie order document is compliant.

The specific source code that executes the transform is as follows:

```
Dim myXslCompiledTransform As XslCompiledTransform = New XslCompiledTransform

myXslCompiledTransform.Load("..\ConvertLegacyToNewStandard.xslt")
myXslCompiledTransform.Transform("..\MovieOrdersOriginal.xml",
    "..\MovieOrdersModified.xml")
```

The three lines of code accomplish the following:

1. Create an `XslCompiledTransform` object
2. Use the `Load` method to load an XSLT file (`ConvertLegacyToNewStandard.xslt`)
3. Use the `Transform` method to transform a source XML file (`MovieOrdersOriginal.xml`) into a destination XML file (`MovieOrdersModified.xml`)

Recall that the input XML document (`MovieOrdersOriginal.xml`) does not match the format required by your consortium of movie supplier chains. The content of this source XML file is as follows:

```
<?xml version="1.0" encoding="utf-8" ?>
<FilmOrder_Multiple>
    <multiFilmOrders>
        <FilmOrder>
            <name>Grease</name>
            <filmId>101</filmId>
```

```
            <quantity>10</quantity>
        </FilmOrder>
        ...
    </multiFilmOrders>
</FilmOrder_Multiple>
```

The format exhibited in the preceding XML document does not match the format of the consortium of movie supplier chains. To be accepted by the collective of suppliers, you must transform the document as follows:

❑   Remove element <FilmOrder_Multiple>.

❑   Remove element <multiFilmOrders>.

❑   Rename element <FilmOrder> to <DvdOrder>.

❑   Remove element <name> (the film's name is not to be contained in the document).

❑   Rename element <quantity> to HowMuch and make HowMuch an attribute of <DvdOrder>.

❑   Rename element <filmId> to FilmOrderNumber and make FilmOrderNumber an attribute of <DvdOrder>.

❑   Display attribute HowMuch before attribute FilmOrderNumber.

A great many of the steps performed by the transform could have been achieved using an alternative technology. For example, you could have used Source Code Style attributes with your serialization to generate the correct XML attribute and XML element name. If you had known in advance that a consortium of suppliers was going to develop a standard, you could have written your classes to be serialized based on the standard. The point was that you didn't know and now one standard (your legacy standard) has to be converted into a newly adopted standard of the movie suppliers' consortium. The worst thing you could do would be to change your working code and then force all users working with the application to upgrade. It is vastly simpler to add an extra transformation step to address the new standard.

The XSLT file that facilitates the transform is named ConvertLegacyToNewStandard.xslt. A portion of this file is implemented as follows:

```xml
<?xml version="1.0" encoding="UTF-8" ?>
<xsl:stylesheet version="1.0" xmlns:xsl="http://www.w3.org/1999/XSL/Transform">
  <xsl:template match="FilmOrder">
    <!-- rename <FilmOrder> to <DvdOrder> -->
    <xsl:element name="DvdOrder">
      <!-- Make element 'quantity' attribute HowMuch
           Notice attribute HowMuch comes before attribute FilmOrderNumber -->
      <xsl:attribute name="HowMuch">
        <xsl:value-of select="quantity"></xsl:value-of>
      </xsl:attribute>
      <!-- Make element filmId attribute FilmOrderNumber -->
      <xsl:attribute name="FilmOrderNumber">
        <xsl:value-of select="filmId"></xsl:value-of>
      </xsl:attribute>
    </xsl:element>
    <!-- end of DvdOrder element -->
  </xsl:template>
</xsl:stylesheet>
```

In the previous snippet of XSLT, the following XSLT elements are used to facilitate the transformation:

❑ `<xsl:template match="FilmOrder">` — All operations in this `template` XSLT element take place on the original document's `FilmOrder` node.

❑ `<xsl:element name="DvdOrder">` — The element corresponding to the source document's `FilmOrder` element will be called `DvdOrder` in the destination document.

❑ `<xsl:attribute name="HowMuch">` — An attribute named `HowMuch` will be contained in the previously specified element. The previously specified element is `<DvdOrder>`. This `attribute` XSLT element for `HowMuch` comes before the `attribute` XSLT element for `FilmOrderNumber`. This order was specified as part of your transform to adhere to the new standard.

❑ `<xsl:value-of select='quantity'>` — Retrieve the value of the source document's `<quantity>` element and place it in the destination document. This instance of XSLT element `value-of` provides the value associated with attribute `HowMuch`.

Two new XSLT elements have crept into your vocabulary: `element` and `attribute`. Both of these XSLT elements live up to their names. Specifying the XSLT element named `element` places an element in the destination XML document. Specifying the XSLT element named `attribute` places an attribute in the destination XML document. The XSLT transform found in `ConvertLegacyToNewStandard.xslt` is too long to review here. When reading this file in its entirety, remember that this XSLT file contains inline documentation to specify precisely what aspect of the transformation is being performed at which location in the XSLT document. For example, the following XML code comments indicate what the XSLT element `attribute` is about to do:

```
<!-- Make element 'quantity' attribute HowMuch
        Notice attribute HowMuch comes before attribute FilmOrderNumber -->
<xsl:attribute name="HowMuch">
        <xsl:value-of select='quantity'></xsl:value-of>
</xsl:attribute>
```

The preceding example spanned several pages but contained just three lines of code. This demonstrates that there is more to XML than learning how to use it in Visual Basic and the .NET Framework. Among other things, you also need a good understanding of XSLT, XPath, and XQuery.

Other Classes and Interfaces in System.Xml.Xsl

We just took a good look at XSLT and the `System.Xml.Xsl` namespace, but there is a lot more to it than that. Other classes and interfaces exposed by `System.Xml.Xsl` namespace include the following:

❑ `IXsltContextFunction` — This interface accesses at runtime a given function defined in the XSLT style sheet.

❑ `IXsltContextVariable` — This interface accesses at runtime a given variable defined in the XSLT style sheet.

❑ `XsltArgumentList` — This class contains a list of arguments. These arguments are XSLT parameters or XSLT extension objects. The `XsltArgumentList` object is used in conjunction with the `Transform` method of `XslTransform`.

❑   `XsltContext` — This class contains the state of the XSLT processor. This context information allows XPath expressions to have their various components resolved (functions, parameters, and namespaces).

❑   `XsltException`, `XsltCompileException` — These classes contain the information pertaining to an exception raised while transforming data. `XsltCompileException` is derived from `XsltException`.

ADO.NET

ADO.NET enables Visual Basic applications to generate XML documents and use such documents to update persisted data. ADO.NET natively represents its `DataSet`'s underlying datastore in XML. ADO.NET also enables SQL Server–specific XML support to be accessed. This chapter focuses on those features of ADO.NET that enable the XML generated and consumed to be customized. ADO.NET is covered in detail in Chapter 10.

The `DataSet` properties and methods that are pertinent to XML include `Namespace`, `Prefix`, `GetXml()`, `GetXmlSchema()`, `InferXmlSchema()`, `ReadXml()`, `ReadXmlSchema()`, `WriteXml()`, and `WriteXmlSchema()`. An example of code that uses the `GetXml` method is shown here:

```
Dim adapter As New _
    SqlClient.SqlDataAdapter("SELECT ShipperID, CompanyName, Phone " & _
                "FROM Shippers", _
                "SERVER=localhost;UID=sa;PWD=sa;Database=Northwind;")
Dim ds As New DataSet

adapter.Fill(ds)
Console.Out.WriteLine(ds.GetXml())
```

The preceding code uses the sample `Northwind` database (which comes with SQL Server 2000 and MSDE), retrieving all rows from the `Shippers` table. This table was selected because it contains only three rows of data. The XML returned by `GetXml()` is as follows (where ... signifies that `<Table>` elements were removed for the sake of brevity):

```
<NewDataSet>
  <Table>
    <ShipperID>1</ShipperID>
    <CompanyName>Speedy Express</CompanyName>
    <Phone>(503) 555-9831</Phone>
  </Table>
  ...
</NewDataSet>
```

What you are trying to determine from this XML document is how to customize the XML generated. The more customization you can perform at the ADO.NET level, the less need there will be later. With this in mind, note that the root element is `<NewDataSet>` and that each row of the `DataSet` is returned as an XML element, `<Table>`. The data returned is contained in an XML element named for the column in which the data resides (`<ShipperID>`, `<CompanyName>`, and `<Phone>`, respectively).

The root element, `<NewDataSet>`, is just the default name of the `DataSet`. This name could have been changed when the `DataSet` was constructed by specifying the name as a parameter to the constructor:

```
Dim ds As New DataSet("WeNameTheDataSet")
```

If the previous version of the constructor was executed, then the `<NewDataSet>` element would be renamed `<WeNameTheDataSet>`. After the `DataSet` has been constructed, you can still set the property `DataSetName`, thus changing `<NewDataSet>` to a name such as `<WeNameTheDataSetAgain>`:

```
ds.DataSetName = "WeNameTheDataSetAgain"
```

The `<Table>` element is actually the name of a table in the `DataSet`'s `Tables` property. Programmatically, you can change `<Table>` to `<WeNameTheTable>`:

```
ds.Tables("Table").TableName = "WeNameTheTable"
```

You can customize the names of the data columns returned by modifying the SQL to use alias names. For example, you could retrieve the same data but generate different elements using the following SQL code:

```
SELECT ShipperID As TheID, CompanyName As CName, Phone As TelephoneNumber FROM
Shippers
```

Using the preceding SQL statement, the `<ShipperID>` element would become the `<TheID>` element. The `<CompanyName>` element would become `<CName>`, and `<Phone>` would become `<TelephoneNumber>`. The column names can also be changed programmatically by using the `Columns` property associated with the table in which the column resides. An example of this follows, where the XML element `<TheID>` is changed to `<AnotherNewName>`:

```
ds.Tables("WeNameTheTable").Columns("TheID").ColumnName = "AnotherNewName"
```

This XML could be transformed using `System.Xml.Xsl`. It could be read as a stream (`XmlTextReader`) or written as a stream (`XmlTextWriter`). The XML returned by ADO.NET could even be deserialized and used to create an object or objects using `XmlSerializer`. The point is to recognize what ADO.NET-generated XML looks like. If you know its format, then you can transform it into whatever you like.

ADO.NET and SQL Server 2000's Built-In XML Features

Those interested in fully exploring the XML-specific features of SQL Server should take a look at *Professional SQL Server 2000 Programming* by Robert Vieira (Wrox Press, 2000). However, because the content of that book is not .NET-specific, the next example forms a bridge between *Professional SQL Server 2000 Programming* and the .NET Framework.

Two of the major XML-related features exposed by SQL Server are as follows:

❑ FOR XML — The FOR XML clause of an SQL SELECT statement enables a rowset to be returned as an XML document. The XML document generated by a FOR XML clause is highly customizable with respect to the document hierarchy generated, per-column data transforms, representation of binary data, XML schema generated, and a variety of other XML nuances.

❑   OPENXML — The OPENXML extension to Transact-SQL enables a stored procedure call to manipulate an XML document as a rowset. Subsequently, this rowset can be used to perform a variety of tasks, such as SELECT, INSERT INTO, DELETE, and UPDATE.

SQL Server's support for OPENXML is a matter of calling a stored procedure call. A developer who can execute a stored procedure call using Visual Basic in conjunction with ADO.NET can take full advantage of SQL Server's support for OPENXML. FOR XML queries have a certain caveat when it comes to ADO.NET. To understand this caveat, consider the following FOR XML query:

```
SELECT ShipperID, CompanyName, Phone FROM Shippers FOR XML RAW
```

Using SQL Server's Query Analyzer, this FOR XML RAW query generated the following XML:

```
<row ShipperID="1" CompanyName="Speedy Express" Phone="(314) 555-9831" />
<row ShipperID="2" CompanyName="United Package" Phone="(314) 555-3199" />
<row ShipperID="3" CompanyName="Federal Shipping" Phone="(314) 555-9931" />
```

The same FOR XML RAW query can be executed from ADO.NET as follows:

```
Dim adapter As New _
    SqlDataAdapter("SELECT ShipperID, CompanyName, Phone " & _
                   "FROM Shippers FOR XML RAW", _
                   "SERVER=localhost;UID=sa;PWD=sa;Database=Northwind;")
Dim ds As New DataSet

adapter.Fill(ds)
Console.Out.WriteLine(ds.GetXml())
```

The caveat with respect to a FOR XML query is that all data (the XML text) must be returned via a result set containing a single row and a single column named XML_F52E2B61-18A1-11d1-B105-00805F49916B. The output from the preceding code snippet demonstrates this caveat (where ... represents similar data not shown for reasons of brevity):

```
<NewDataSet>
  <Table>
    <XML_F52E2B61-18A1-11d1-B105-00805F49916B>
      /&lt;row ShipperID="1" CompanyName="Speedy Express"
      Phone="(503) 555-9831"/&gt;
      ...
    </XML_F52E2B61-18A1-11d1-B105-00805F49916B>
  </Table>
</NewDataSet>
```

The value of the single row and single column returned contains what looks like XML, but it contains /< instead of the less-than character, and /> instead of the greater-than character. The symbols < and > cannot appear inside XML data, so they must be entity-encoded — that is, represented as /> and /<. The data returned in element <XML_F52E2B61-18A1-11d1-B105-00805F49916B> is not XML, but data contained in an XML document.

To fully utilize FOR XML queries, the data must be accessible as XML. The solution to this quandary is the ExecuteXmlReader() method of the SQLCommand class. When this method is called, an SQLCommand object assumes that it is executed as a FOR XML query and returns the results of this query as an XmlReader object. An example of this follows:

```
Dim connection As New _
    SqlConnection("SERVER=localhost;UID=sa;PWD=sa;Database=Northwind;")
Dim command As New _
    SqlCommand("SELECT ShipperID, CompanyName, Phone " & _
               "FROM Shippers FOR XML RAW")
Dim memStream As MemoryStream = New MemoryStream
Dim xmlReader As New XmlTextReader(memStream)

connection.Open()
command.Connection = connection
xmlReader = command.ExecuteXmlReader()
' Extract results from XMLReader
```

The XmlReader created in this code is of type XmlTextReader, which derives from XmlReader. The XmlTextReader is backed by a MemoryStream; hence, it is an in-memory stream of XML that can be traversed using the methods and properties exposed by XmlTextReader. Streaming XML generation and retrieval has been discussed earlier.

Using the ExecuteXmlReader() method of the SQLCommand class, it is possible to retrieve the result of FOR XML queries. What makes the FOR XML style of queries so powerful is that it can configure the data retrieved. The three types of FOR XML queries support the following forms of XML customization:

❑ FOR XML RAW — This type of query returns each row of a result set inside an XML element named <row>. The data retrieved is contained as attributes of the <row> element. The attributes are named for the column name or column alias in the FOR XML RAW query.

❑ FOR XML AUTO — By default, this type of query returns each row of a result set inside an XML element named for the table or table alias contained in the FOR XML AUTO query. The data retrieved is contained as attributes of this element. The attributes are named for the column name or column alias in the FOR XML AUTO query. By specifying FOR XML AUTO, ELEMENTS, it is possible to retrieve all data inside elements, rather than inside attributes. All data retrieved must be in attribute or element form. There is no mix-and-match capability.

❑ FOR XML EXPLICIT — This form of the FOR XML query enables the precise XML type of each column returned to be specified. The data associated with a column can be returned as an attribute or an element. Specific XML types, such as CDATA and ID, can be associated with a column returned. Even the level in the XML hierarchy in which data resides can be specified using a FOR XML EXPLICIT query. This style of query is fairly complicated to implement.

FOR XML queries are flexible. Using FOR XML EXPLICIT and the movie rental database, it would be possible to generate any form of XML movie order standard. The decision that needs to be made is where XML configuration takes place. Using Visual Basic, a developer could use XmlTextReader and XmlTextWriter to create any style of XML document. Using the XSLT language and an XSLT file, the same level of configuration can be achieved. SQL Server and, in particular, FOR XML EXPLICIT, enable the same level of XML customization, but this customization takes place at the SQL level and may even be configured to stored procedure calls.

XML and SQL Server 2005

As a representation for data, XML is ideal in that it is a self-describing data format that enables you to provide your datasets as complex datatypes. It also provides order to your data. SQL Server 2005 embraces this direction.

More and more developers are turning to XML as a means of data storage. For instance, Microsoft Office enables documents to be saved and stored as XML documents. As an increasing number of products and solutions turn toward XML as a means of storage, this allows for a separation between the underlying data and the presentation aspect of what is being viewed. XML is also being used as a means of communicating datasets across platforms and the enterprise. The entire XML Web Services story is a result of this new capability. Simply said, XML is a powerful alternative to your data storage solutions.

Just remember that the power of using XML isn't only about storing data as XML somewhere (whether that is XML files or not); it is also about the ability to quickly get at this XML data and to be able to query the data that is retrieved.

SQL Server 2005 makes a big leap toward XML in adding an XML datatype. This enables you to unify the relational aspects of the database and the current desires to work with XML data.

FOR XML has also been expanded from within this latest edition of SQL Server. This includes a new TYPE directive that returns an XML datatype instance. In addition, the NET 2.0 Framework includes a new namespace — System.Data.SqlXml — that enables allows you to easily work with the XML data that comes from SQL Server 2005. The SqlXml object is an XmlReader-derived type. Another addition is the use of the SqlDataReader object's GetXml() method.

XML in ASP.NET 2.0

Most Microsoft-focused Web developers have usually concentrated on either Microsoft SQL Server or Microsoft Access for their data storage needs. Today, however, a considerable amount of data is stored in XML format, so considerable inroads have been made in improving Microsoft's core Web technology to work easily with this format.

The XmlDataSource Server Control

ASP.NET 2.0 introduced a series of data source controls to bridge the gap between your datastores (such as XML) and the data-bound controls at your disposal. These new data controls not only enable you to retrieve data from various datastores, they also enable you to easily manipulate the data (using paging, sorting, editing, and filtering) before the data is bound to an ASP.NET server control.

With XML being as important as it is, a specific data source control has been added to ASP.NET 2.0 just for retrieving and working with XML data. The XmlDataSource control enables you to connect to your XML data and use this data with any of the ASP.NET data-bound controls. Just like the SqlDataSource and the ObjectDataSource controls (which are some of the other data source controls), the XmlDataSource control enables you to not only retrieve data, but also to insert, delete, and update data items. With the world turning more and more to XML data formats, such as Web Services, RSS feeds, and more, this control is a valuable resource for your Web applications.

To show the `XmlDataSource` control in action, first create a simple XML file and include this file in your application. The following code reflects a simple XML file of Russian painters:

```
<?xml version="1.0" encoding="utf-8" ?>
<Artists>
    <Painter name="Vasily Kandinsky">
       <Painting>
           <Title>Composition No. 218</Title>
           <Year>1919</Year>
       </Painting>
    </Painter>
    <Painter name="Pavel Filonov">
       <Painting>
           <Title>Formula of Spring</Title>
           <Year>1929</Year>
       </Painting>
    </Painter>
    <Painter name="Pyotr Konchalovsky">
       <Painting>
           <Title>Sorrento Garden</Title>
           <Year>1924</Year>
       </Painting>
    </Painter>
</Artists>
```

Now that the `Painters.xml` file is in place, the next step is to use an ASP.NET `DataList` control and connect this `DataList` control to an `<asp:XmlDataSource>` control, as shown here:

```
<%@ Page Language="VB"%>

<html xmlns="http://www.w3.org/1999/xhtml" >
<head runat="server">
    <title>XmlDataSource</title>
</head>
<body>
    <form id="form1" runat="server">
        <asp:DataList ID="DataList1" Runat="server" DataSourceID="XmlDataSource1">
            <ItemTemplate>
                <p><b><%# XPath("@name") %></b><br />
                <i><%# XPath("Painting/Title") %></i><br />
                <%# XPath("Painting/Year") %></p>
            </ItemTemplate>
        </asp:DataList>

        <asp:XmlDataSource ID="XmlDataSource1" Runat="server"
         DataFile="~/Painters.xml" XPath="Artists/Painter">
        </asp:XmlDataSource>
    </form>
</body>
</html>
```

This is a simple example, but it shows you the power and ease of using the `XmlDataSource` control. You should pay attention to only two attributes in this example. The first is the `DataFile` attribute. This attribute points to the location of the XML file. Because the file resides in the root directory of the application, it is simply `~/Painters.xml`. The next attribute included in the `XmlDataSource` control is the `XPath` attribute. The `XmlDataSource` control uses XPath for the filtering of XML data. In this case, the `XmlDataSource` control is taking everything within the `<Painter>` set of elements. The value `Artists/Painter` means that the `XmlDataSource` control navigates to the `<Artists>` element and then to the `<Painter>` element within the specified XML file.

The `DataList` control next must specify the `DataSourceID` as the `XmlDataSource` control. In the `<ItemTemplate>` section of the `DataList` control, you can retrieve specific values from the XML file by using XPath commands. The XPath commands filter the data from the XML file. The first value retrieved is an element attribute (`name`) contained in the `<Painter>` element. When you retrieve an attribute of an element, you preface the name of the attribute with an @ symbol. In this case, you simply specify `@name` to get the painter's name. The next two XPath commands go deeper into the XML file and get the specific painting and the year of the painting. Remember to separate nodes with a `/`. When run in the browser, this code produces the results shown in Figure 11-5.

Figure 11-5

Besides working from static XML files like the `Painters.xml` file shown earlier, the `XmlDataSource` file can work from dynamic, URL-accessible XML files. One popular XML format that is pervasive on the Internet today is *blogs*, or *weblogs*. Blogs, or personal diaries, can be viewed either in the browser, through an RSS-aggregator, or just as pure XML.

Looking at my blog in Figure 11-6, you can see the XML it produces directly in the browser. (You can find a lot of blogs to play with for this example at `weblogs.asp.net`. This screen shot uses my blog found at `www.geekswithblogs.net/evjen`).

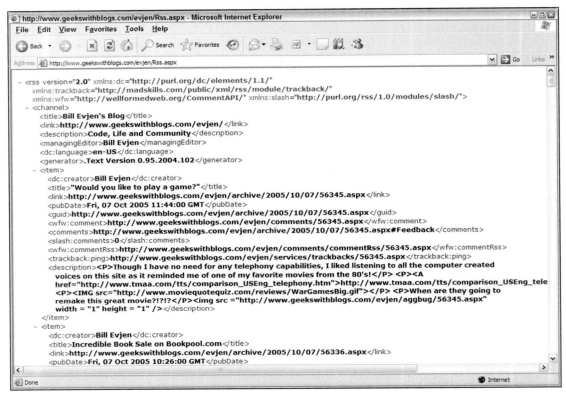

Figure 11-6

Now that you know the location of the XML from the blog, you can use this XML with the XmlDataSource control and display some of the results in a DataList control. The code for this example is shown here:

```
<%@ Page Language="VB"%>

<html xmlns="http://www.w3.org/1999/xhtml" >
<head runat="server">
    <title>XmlDataSource</title>
</head>
<body>
    <form id="form1" runat="server">
        <asp:DataList ID="DataList1" Runat="server" DataSourceID="XmlDataSource1">
            <HeaderTemplate>
                <table border="1" cellpadding="3">
            </HeaderTemplate>
            <ItemTemplate>
                <tr><td><b><%# XPath("title") %></b><br />
                <i><%# XPath("pubDate") %></i><br />
                <%# XPath("description") %></td></tr>
            </ItemTemplate>
            <AlternatingItemTemplate>
                <tr bgcolor="LightGrey"><td><b><%# XPath("title") %></b><br />
```

```
                    <i><%# XPath("pubDate") %></i><br />
                    <%# XPath("description") %></td></tr>
            </AlternatingItemTemplate>
            <FooterTemplate>
                </table>
            </FooterTemplate>
        </asp:DataList>

        <asp:XmlDataSource ID="XmlDataSource1" Runat="server"
         DataFile="http://geekswithblogs.net/evjen/Rss.aspx"
         XPath="rss/channel/item">
         </asp:XmlDataSource>
    </form>
</body>
</html>
```

This example shows that the `DataFile` points to a URL where the XML is retrieved. The `XPath` property filters out all the `<item>` elements from the RSS feed. The `DataList` control creates an HTML table and pulls out specific data elements from the RSS feed, such as the `<title>`, `<pubDate>`, and `<description>` elements.

Running this page in the browser results in something similar to what is shown in Figure 11-7.

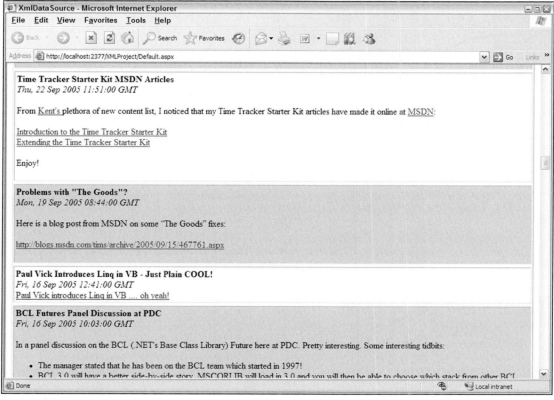

Figure 11-7

441

This approach also works with XML Web Services, even those for which you can pass in parameters using HTTP-GET. You just set up the `DataFile` value in the following manner:

```
DataFile="http://www.someserver.com/GetWeather.asmx/ZipWeather?zipcode=63301"
```

The XmlDataSource Control's Namespace Problem

One big issue with using the `XmlDataSource` control is that when using the XPath capabilities of the control, it is unable to understand namespace-qualified XML. The `XmlDataSource` control chokes on any XML data that contains namespaces, so it is important to yank out any prefixes and namespaces contained in the XML.

To make this a bit easier, the `XmlDataSource` control includes the attribute `TransformFile`. This attribute takes your XSLT transform file, which can be applied to the XML pulled from the `XmlDataSource` control. That means you can use an XSLT file, which will transform your XML in such a way that the prefixes and namespaces are completely removed from the overall XML document. An example of this XSLT document is illustrated in the following example:

```
<?xml version="1.0" encoding="UTF-8"?>
<xsl:stylesheet version="1.0"
 xmlns:xsl="http://www.w3.org/1999/XSL/Transform">
    <xsl:output method="xml" version="1.0" encoding="UTF-8" indent="yes"/>
    <xsl:template match="*">
      <!-- Remove any prefixes -->
      <xsl:element name="{local-name()}">
          <!-- Work through attributes -->
          <xsl:for-each select="@*">
             <!-- Remove any attribute prefixes -->
             <xsl:attribute name="{local-name()}">
                 <xsl:value-of select="."/>
             </xsl:attribute>
          </xsl:for-each>
      <xsl:apply-templates/>
      </xsl:element>
    </xsl:template>
</xsl:stylesheet>
```

Now, with this XSLT document in place within your application, you can use the `XmlDataSource` control to pull XML data and strip that data of any prefixes and namespaces:

```
<asp:XmlDataSource ID="XmlDataSource1" runat="server"
 DataFile="NamespaceFilled.xml" TransformFile="~/RemoveNamespace.xsl"
 XPath="ItemLookupResponse/Items/Item"></asp:XmlDataSource>
```

The Xml Server Control

Since the very beginning of ASP.NET, there has always been a server control called the `Xml` server control. This control performs the simple operation of XSLT transformation upon an XML document. The control is easy to use, as all you do is point to the XML file you wish to transform using the `DocumentSource` attribute, and the XSLT transform file using the `TransformSource` attribute.

To see this in action, use the `Painters.xml` file shown earlier. Create your XSLT transform file, as shown in the following example:

```xml
<?xml version="1.0" encoding="utf-8"?>

<xsl:stylesheet version="1.0"
    xmlns:xsl="http://www.w3.org/1999/XSL/Transform">

  <xsl:template match="/">
      <html>
      <body>
        <h3>List of Painters &amp; Paintings</h3>
        <table border="1">
          <tr bgcolor="LightGrey">
            <th>Name</th>
            <th>Painting</th>
            <th>Year</th>
          </tr>
          <xsl:apply-templates select="//Painter"/>
        </table>
      </body>
      </html>
  </xsl:template>

  <xsl:template match="Painter">
    <tr>
      <td>
        <xsl:value-of select="@name"/>
      </td>
      <td>
        <xsl:value-of select="Painting/Title"/>
      </td>
      <td>
        <xsl:value-of select="Painting/Year"/>
      </td>
    </tr>
  </xsl:template>

</xsl:stylesheet>
```

With the XML document and the XSLT document in place, the final step is to combine the two using the Xml server control provided by ASP.NET:

```aspx
<%@ Page Language="VB" %>

<html xmlns="http://www.w3.org/1999/xhtml" >
<head id="Head1" runat="server">
    <title>XmlDataSource</title>
</head>
<body>
    <form id="form1" runat="server">
        <asp:Xml ID="Xml1" runat="server" DocumentSource="~/Painters.xml"
          TransformSource="~/PaintersTransform.xsl"></asp:Xml>
    </form>
</body>
</html>
```

The result is shown in Figure 11-8.

Figure 11-8

Summary

Ultimately, XML could be the underpinning of electronic commerce, banking transactions, and data exchange of almost every conceivable kind. The beauty of XML is that it isolates data representation from data display. Technologies such as HTML contain data that is tightly bound to its display format. XML does not suffer this limitation, yet at the same time it has the readability of HTML. Accordingly, the XML facilities available to a Visual Basic application are vast, and a large number of XML-related features, classes, and interfaces are exposed by the .NET Framework.

This chapter showed you how to use `System.Xml.Serialization.XmlSerializer` to serialize classes. Source Code Style attributes were introduced in conjunction with serialization. This style of attributes enables the customization of the XML serialized to be extended to the source code associated with a class. What is important to remember about the direction of serialization classes is that a required change in the XML format becomes a change in the underlying source code. Developers should resist the temptation to rewrite the serialized classes in order to conform to some new XML data standard (such as the example movie order format endorsed by your consortium of movie rental establishments). Technologies such as XSLT, exposed via the `System.Xml.Query` namespace, should be examined first as alternatives. This chapter demonstrated how to use XSLT style sheets to transform XML data using the classes found in the `System.Xml.Query` namespace.

The most useful classes and interfaces in the `System.Xml` namespace were reviewed, including those that support document-style XML access: `XmlDocument`, `XmlNode`, `XmlElement`, and `XmlAttribute`. The `System.Xml` namespace also contains classes and interfaces that support stream-style XML access: `XmlReader` and `XmlWriter`.

Finally, you looked at Microsoft's SQL Server 2005 and XQuery, as well as how to use XML with ASP.NET 2.0.

Security in the .NET Framework

This chapter covers the basics of security and cryptography. It begins with a brief discussion of the .NET Framework's security architecture, because this affects all the solutions you may choose to implement.

The .NET Framework provides you with additional tools and functionality with regard to security. You now have the `System.Security.Permissions` namespace, which enables you to control code access permissions along with role-based and identity permissions. Through your code, you can control access to objects programmatically, as well as receive information on the current permissions of objects. This security framework will assist you in determining whether you have permissions to run your code, instead of getting halfway through execution and having to deal with permission-based exceptions. This chapter covers the following:

- ❑ Concepts and definitions
- ❑ · Permissions
- ❑ Roles
- ❑ Principals
- ❑ Code access permissions
- ❑ Role-based permissions
- ❑ Identity permissions
- ❑ Managing permissions
- ❑ Managing policies
- ❑ Cryptography

Cryptography is the cornerstone of the .NET Web Services security model, so the second half of this chapter discusses the basis of cryptography and how to implement it. Specifically, it covers the following:

❑   Hash algorithms

❑   SHA

❑   MD5

❑   Secret key encryption

❑   Public key cryptography standard

❑   Digital signatures

❑   Certification

❑   Secure Sockets Layer communications

Let's begin by looking at some security concepts and definitions.

> **As always, the code for this chapter is available for download from** www.wrox.com, **which you may want in order to follow along.**

Security Concepts and Definitions

The following table describes the different types of security illustrated in this chapter and how they can relate to real-world scenarios:

Security Type	Related Concept in Security.Permissions Namespace or Utility	Purpose
NTFS	None	Allows for detailing of object rights, e.g., locking down of specific files
Security Policies	Caspol.exe utility, PermView.exe utility	Set up overall security policy for a machine or user from an operating system level
Cryptographic	Strong name and assembly, generation, SignCode.exe utility	Use of public key infrastructure and certificates
Programmatic	Groups and permission sets	For use in pieces of code that are being called into. Provides extra security to prevent users of calling code from violating security measures implemented by the program that are not provided for on a machine level.

There are many approaches to providing security on your machines where your shared code is hosted. If multiple shared code applications are on one machine, each piece of shared code can be called from many front-end applications. Each piece of shared code will have its own security requirements for accessing environment variables — such as the registry, the file system, and other items — on the machine that it is running on. From an NTFS perspective, the administrator of your server can only lock down those items on the machine that are not required to be accessed from any piece of shared code running on it. Therefore, some applications will need additional security built in to prevent any calling code from doing things it is not supposed to do.

The machine administrator can further assist the programmers by using the utilities provided with .NET to establish additional machine and/or user policies that programs can implement. Toward that end, the .NET environment provides programmatic security through code access security, role-based security, and identity security. As a final security measure, you can use the cryptographic methods provided to require the use of certificates in order to execute your code.

Security in the .NET infrastructure uses some basic concepts that are discussed here. Code security is managed and accessed in the .NET environment through the use of security policies. Security policies have a relationship that is fundamentally tied to either the machine that the code is running on, or to particular users under whose context the code is running. To this end, any modifications to the policy are done either at the machine level or the user level.

You establish the security policy on a given set of code by associating it with an entity called a *group*. A group is created and managed within each of the machine- and user-based policies. These group classifications are set up so that you can place code into categories. You want to establish new code groups when you are ready to categorize the pieces of code that would run on a machine, and assign the permissions that users will have to access the code. For instance, if you wanted to group all Internet applications and then group all non-Internet applications, you would establish two groups and associate each of your applications with its respective group.

Once you have the code separated into groups, you can define different permission sets for each group. If you wanted to limit your Internet applications' access to the local file system, you could create a permission set that limits that access and associates the Internet application group with the new permission set. By default, the .NET environment provides one code group named `All Code` that is associated with the `FullTrust` permission set.

Permission sets are unique combinations of security configurations that determine what each user with access to a machine can do on that machine. Each set determines what a user has access to — for instance, whether they can read environment variables, the file system, or execute other portions of code. Permission sets are maintained at the machine and user levels through the utility `Caspol.exe`. Through this utility, you can create your own permission sets, though the following seven permission sets that ship with the .NET infrastructure are also useful:

Permission Set	Explanation
FullTrust	Allows full access to all resources; adds assembly to a special list that has FullTrust access
Everything	Allows full access to everything covered by default named permission sets, but differs from FullTrust in that the group is not added to the FullTrust assembly list
Nothing	Denies all access including Execution
Execution	Allows execution-only access
SkipVerification	Allows objects to bypass all security verification
Internet	Grants default rights that are normal for Internet applications
LocalInternet	Grants rights that are not as restricted as Internet, but not full trust

Security that is used within the programming environment also makes use of permission sets. Through code you can control access to files in a file system, environment variables, file dialogs, isolated storage, reflections, registry, sockets, and UI. Isolated storage and virtual file systems are new operating system–level storage locations that can be used by programs and are governed by the machine security policies. These file systems keep a machine safe from file system intrusion by designating a regulated area for file storage. The main access to these items is controlled through code access permissions.

Although many methods that we use in Visual Basic 2005 give an identifiable return value, the only return value we get from security methods is when the method fails. If a security method succeeds, it does not provide a return value. If it fails, then it returns an exception object reflecting the specific error that occurred.

Permissions in the System.Security.Permissions Namespace

The System.Security.Permissions namespace is the namespace used in the code to establish and use permissions to access many things, such as the file system, environment variables, and the registry within your programs. The namespace controls access to both operating system–level objects as well as code objects. In order to use the namespace in your project, you need to include the Imports System.Security.Permissions line with any of your other Imports statements in your project. Using this namespace gives you access to the CodeAccessPermission and PrincipalPermission classes for using role-based permissions and utilizing information supplied by Identity permissions. CodeAccessPermission is the main class that we will use, as it controls access to the operating system–level objects our code needs in order to function. Role-based permissions and Identity permissions grant access to objects based on the identity of the user of the program that is running carries with them (the user context).

In the following table, classes that end with Attribute, such as EnvironmentPermissionAttribute, are classes that enable you to modify the security level at which your code is allowed to interact with each respective object. The attributes that you can specify reflect either `Assert`, `Deny`, or `PermitOnly` permissions.

If permissions are asserted, you have full access to the object, whereas if you have specified `Deny` permissions you are not allowed to access the object through your code. If you have `PermitOnly` access, only objects within your program's already determined scope can be accessed, and you cannot add any more resources beyond that scope. The table also deals with security in regard to software publishers. A *software publisher* is a specific entity that is using a digital signature to identify itself in a Web-based application. The following is a table of the namespace members that apply to Windows Forms programming, with an explanation of each:

Class	Description
CodeAccessSecurityAttribute	Specifies security access to objects such as the registry and file system
EnvironmentPermission	Controls the ability to see and modify system and user environment variables
EnvironmentPermissionAttribute	Allows security actions for environment variables to be added via code
FileDialogPermission	Controls the ability to open files via a file dialog
FileDialogPermissionAttribute	Allows security actions to be added for file dialogs via code
FileIOPermission	Controls the capability to read and write files in the file system
FileIOPermissionAttribute	Allows security actions to be added for file access attempts via code
GacIdentityPermission	Defines the identity permissions for files that come from the global assembly cache (GAC). This is a new class in the .NET Framework 2.0.
GacIdentityPermissionAttribute	Allows security actions to be added for files that originate from the GAC
IsolatedStorageFilePermission	Controls access to a private virtual file system within the isolated storage area of an application
IsolatedStorageFilePermission Attribute	Allows security actions to be added for private virtual file systems via code
IsolatedStoragePermission	Controls access to the isolated storage area of an application
IsolatedStoragePermission Attribute	Allows security actions to be added for the isolated storage area of an application

Table continues on the next page

Class	Description
KeyContainerPermission	Controls access to key containers. This is a new class in the .NET Framework 2.0.
KeyContainerPermissionAccess Entry	Defines the access rights for particular key containers
KeyContainerPermissionAccess EntryCollection	Represents a collection of KeyContainerPermission-AccessEntry objects
KeyContainerPermissionAccess EntryEnumerator	Represents the enumerators for the objects contained in the KeyContainerPermissionAccessEntryCollection object
KeyContainerPermissionAttribute	Allows security actions to be added for key containers
PermissionSetAttribute	Allows security actions to be added for a permission set
PrincipalPermission	Controls the ability to make checks against an active principal
PrincipalPermissionAttribute	Allows for checking against a specific user. Security principals are a user and role combination used to establish security identity.
PublisherIdentityPermission	Allows access based on the identity of a software publisher
PublisherIdentityPermission Attribute	Allows security actions to be added for a software publisher
ReflectionPermission	Controls access to nonpublic members of a given type
ReflectionPermissionAttribute	Allows for security actions to be added for public and nonpublic members of a given type
RegistryPermission	Controls access to registry keys and values
RegistryPermissionAttribute	Allows security actions to be added for registry keys and values
ResourcePermissionBase	Controls the ability to work with the code access security permissions
ResourcePermissionBaseEntry	Allows you to define the smallest part of a code access security permission set
SecurityAttribute	Controls which security attributes are representing code; used to control the security when creating an assembly

Class	Description
SecurityPermission	The set of security permission flags for use by .NET; this collection is used when you want to specify a permission flag in your code
SecurityPermissionAttribute	Allows security actions for the security permission flags
StorePermission	Controls access to stores that contain X509 certificates. This is a new class in the .NET Framework 2.0.
StorePermissionAttribute	Allows security actions to be added for access stores that contain X509 certificates
UIPermission	Controls access to user interfaces and use of the Windows clipboard
UIPermissionAttribute	Allows security actions to be added for UI interfaces and the use of the clipboard

Code Access Permissions

Code access permissions are controlled through the CodeAccessPermission class within the System .Security namespace, and its members make up the majority of the permissions we'll use in our attempt to secure our code and operating environment. The following table describes the class methods available:

Method	Description
Assert	Sets the permission to full access so that the specific resource can be accessed even if the caller hasn't been granted permission to access the resource
Copy	Copies a permission object
Demand	Returns whether or not all callers in the call chain have been granted the permission to access the resource in a given manner
Deny	Denies all callers access to the resource
Equals	Determines whether a given object is the same instance of the current object
FromXml	Establishes a permission set given a specific XML encoding. This parameter is an XML encoding
GetHashCode	Returns a hash code associated with a given object
GetType	Returns the type of a given object

Table continues on the next page

Method	Description
Intersect	Returns the permissions that two permission objects have in common
IsSubsetOf	Returns a result indicating whether the current permission object is a subset of a specified permission
PermitOnly	Specifies that only those resources within this permission object can be accessed even if code has been granted permission to other objects
RevertAll	Reverses all previous `assert`, `deny` or `permit-only` methods
RevertAssert	Reverses all previous assert methods
RevertDeny	Reverses all previous deny methods
RevertPermit-Only	Reverses all previous permit-only methods
ToString	Returns a string representation of the current permission object
ToXml	Creates an XML representation of the current permission object
Union	Creates a permission that is the union of two permission objects

Role-Based Permissions

Role-based permissions are permissions granted based on the user and the role that code is being called with. Users are generally authenticated within the operating system platform and hold a Security Identifier (SID) that is associated within a security context. The SID can further be associated with a role or a group membership that is established within a security context. The .NET role functionality supports those users and roles associated within a security context and has support for generic and custom users and roles through the concept of principals. A *principal* is an object that holds the current caller credentials, which is termed the identity of the user. Principals come in two types: Windows principals and non-Windows principals. Windows-based principal objects are objects that store the Windows SID information regarding the current user context associated with the code that is calling into the module role-based permissions that are being used. Non-Windows principals are principal objects that are created programmatically via a custom login methodology and which are made available to the current thread.

Role-based permissions are not set against objects within your environment like code access permissions. They are instead a permission that is checked within the context of the current user and role that a user is part of. Within the System.Security.Permissions namespace, the concept of the principals and the PrincipalPermission class of objects are used to establish and check permissions. If a programmer passes the user and role information during a call as captured from a custom login, then the PrincipalPermission class can be used to verify this information as well. During the verification, if the user and role information is Null, then permission is granted, regardless of the user and role. The PrincipalPermission class does not grant access to objects, but has methods that determine whether a caller has been given permissions according to the current permission object through the `Demand()` method. If a security exception is generated, then the user does not have sufficient permission.

The following table describes the methods in the `PrincipalPermission` class:

Method	Description
Copy	Copies a permission object
Demand	Returns whether or not all callers in the call chain have been granted the permission to access the resource in a given manner
Equals	Determines whether a given object is the same instance of the current object
FromXml	Establishes a permission set given a specific XML encoding
GetHashCode	Returns a hash code associated with a given object
GetType	Returns the type of a given object
Intersect	Returns the permissions that two permission objects have in common specified in the parameter
IsSubsetOf	Returns a result indicating whether the current permission object is a subset of a specified permission
IsUnrestricted	Returns a result indicating whether the current permission object is unrestricted
ToString	Returns a string representation of the current permission object
ToXml	Creates an XML representation of the current permission object
Union	Creates a permission that is the union of two permission objects

As an example of how you might use these methods, the following code snippet captures the current Windows principal information and displays it on the screen in the form of message box output. Each element of the principal information could be used in a program to validate against, and thus restrict, code execution based on the values in the principal information. This example inserts an `Imports System.Security.Principal` line at the top of the module so you can use the identity and principal objects:

```
Imports System.Security.Principal
Imports System.Security.Permissions

Private Sub RoleBasedPermissions_Click(ByVal sender As System.Object, _
    ByVal e As System.EventArgs) Handles RoleBasedPermissions.Click

    Dim objIdentity As WindowsIdentity = WindowsIdentity.GetCurrent
    Dim objPrincipal As New WindowsPrincipal(objIdentity)
    MessageBox.Show(objPrincipal.Identity.IsAuthenticated.ToString())
```

```
            MessageBox.Show(objIdentity.IsGuest.ToString())
            MessageBox.Show(objIdentity.ToString())
            objIdentity = Nothing
            objPrincipal = Nothing

    End Sub
```

This code illustrates a few of the properties that could be used to validate against when a caller wants to run your code. Sometimes you want to ensure that the caller is an authenticated user, and not someone who bypassed the security of your machine with custom login information. You can achieve that through the following line of code:

```
MessageBox.Show(objPrincipal.Identity.IsAuthenticated.ToString())
```

It outputs in the MessageBox as either True or False depending on whether the user is authenticated or not. Another piece of information to ensure that your caller is not bypassing system security would be to check whether the account is operating as a guest. The following line of code accomplishes that:

```
MessageBox.Show(objIdentity.IsGuest.ToString())
```

IsGuest() returns either True or False, depending on whether the caller is authenticated as a guest. The final MessageBox in the example displays the ToString() value for the identity object. This is a value that tells you what type of identity it is, either a Windows identity or a non-Windows identity. The line of code that executes it is as follows:

```
MessageBox.Show(objIdentity.ToString())
```

The output from the IsString() method is shown in Figure 12-1.

Figure 12-1

Again, the principal and identity objects are used in verifying the identity or aspects of the identity of the caller attempting to execute your code. Based on this information, you can lock down or release certain system resources. You will learn how to lock down and release system resources through the code access permissions examples that follow.

Identity Permissions

Identity permissions are pieces of information, also called *evidence*, by which a piece of code can be identified. Examples of the evidence would be the strong name of the assembly or the digital signature associated with the assembly.

A strong name is a combination of the name of a program, its version number, and its associated cryptographic key and digital signature files.

Identity permissions are granted by the runtime based on information received from the trusted host, or someone who has permission to provide the information. Therefore, they are permissions that you don't specifically request. Identity permissions provide additional information to be used by the runtime when you configure items in the `Caspol.exe` utility. The additional information that the trusted host can supply includes the digital signature, the application directory, or the strong name of the assembly.

Managing Code Access Permissions

This section looks at the most common type of permissions — programmatic access — and how they are used. This example uses a Windows Form with four buttons on it. This Windows Form illustrates the concept previously mentioned — namely, that when a method fails, an exception object is generated, which contains your feedback. Note at this point that in the case of a real-world example, you would be setting up permissions for a calling application. In many instances, you don't want a calling application to be able to access the registry, or you want a calling application to be able to read memory variables, but not change them.

However, in order to demonstrate the syntax of the commands, in the examples that follow we have placed the attempts against the objects we have secured in the same module. We first set up the permission that we want and grant the code the appropriate access level we wish it to be able to utilize. Then we use code that accesses our security object to illustrate the effect our permissions have on the code that accesses the objects. We'll also be tying together many of the concepts discussed so far by way of these examples.

To begin, let's look at an example of trying to access a file in the file system, which illustrates the use of the `FileIOPermission` class in our `Permissions` namespace. In the first example, the file `C:\testsecurity\testing.txt` has been secured at the operating system level so that no one can access it. In order to do this, the system administrator sets the operating system security on the file to no access:

```
Imports System.Security.Principal
Imports System.Security.Permissions
Imports System.IO

Private Sub FileIO_Click(ByVal sender As System.Object, _
    ByVal e As System.EventArgs) Handles FileIO.Click

  Dim oFp As FileIOPermission = New _
    FileIOPermission(FileIOPermissionAccess.Write, "C:\testsecurity\testing.txt")

  oFp.Assert()

  Try
    Dim objWriter As New IO.StreamWriter _
      (File.Open("C:\testsecurity\testing.txt", IO.FileMode.Open))
    objWriter.WriteLine("Hi there!")
    objWriter.Flush()
    objWriter.Close()
    objWriter = Nothing
  Catch objA As System.Exception
    MessageBox.Show(objA.Message)
  End Try

End Sub
```

Let's walk through the code. In this example, we are going to attempt to open a file in the `C:\testsecurity` directory called `testing.txt`. We set the file access permissions within our code so that the method, irrespective of who called it, should be able to get to it with the following lines:

```
Dim oFp As FileIOPermission = New _
    FileIOPermission(FileIOPermissionAccess.Write, "C:\testsecurity\testing.txt")

oFp.Assert()
```

This example used the `Assert()` method, which declares that the resource should be accessible even if the caller has not been granted permission to access the resource. However, in this case, because the file is secured at the operating system level (by the system administrator), we get the error shown in Figure 12-2, which was caught by exception handling.

Figure 12-2

Now let's look at that example again with full operating system rights, but the code permissions set to Deny:

```
Protected Sub btnFileIO_Click(ByVal sender As Object, ByVal e As System.EventArgs)

    Dim oFp As FileIOPermission = New _
        FileIOPermission(FileIOPermissionAccess.Write, _
            "C:\testsecurity\testing.txt")

    oFp.Deny()

    Try
        Dim objWriter As New IO.StreamWriter _
            (File.Open("C:\testsecurity\testing.txt", _
            IO.FileMode.Open))
        objwriter.WriteLine("Hi There!")
        objWriter.Flush()
        objWriter.Close()
        objWriter = Nothing

    Catch objA As System.Exception
        messagebox.Show(objA.Message)

    End Try

End Sub
```

The `Deny()` method denies all callers access to the object, regardless of whether the operating system granted them permission. This is usually a good thing to put into place, as not every method you implement needs full and unfettered access to system resources. This helps prevent accidental security vulnerabilities that your method may expose. With the `Deny()` method, we catch the error shown in Figure 12-3 in the exception handler.

Request for the permission of type 'System.Security.Permissions.FileIOPermission, mscorlib, Version=2.0.3600.0, Culture=neutral, PublicKeyToken=b77a5c561934e089' failed.

OK

Figure 12-3

As you can see, this error differs from the first by reflecting a `System.Security.Permissions .FileIOPermission` failure, as opposed to an OS-level exception.

The following example shows how you would use the `EnvironmentPermission` class of the namespace to look at `EnvironmentVariables`:

```
Protected Sub TestEnvironmentPermissions_Click _
    (ByVal sender As Object, ByVal e As System.EventArgs) _
    Handles TestEnvironmentPermissions.Click

    Dim oEp As EnvironmentPermission = New EnvironmentPermission _
        (EnvironmentPermissionAccess.Read, "Temp")

    Dim sEv As String
    oEp.Assert()

    Try
        sEv = Environment.GetEnvironmentVariable("Temp")
        MessageBox.Show("Assert was a success")
    Catch objA As System.Exception
        MessageBox.Show("Assert failed")
    End Try

    System.Security.CodeAccessPermission.RevertAssert()
    oEp.Deny()

    Try
        sEv = Environment.GetEnvironmentVariable("Temp")
        MessageBox.Show("Deny was a success")
    Catch objA As System.Exception
        MessageBox.Show("Deny failed")
    End Try

    MessageBox.Show(oEp.ToString)

End Sub
```

There is a lot going on in this example, so consider it carefully. We first establish an environment variable permission and use the `Assert()` method to ensure access to the code that follows:

```
Dim oEp As EnvironmentPermission = New EnvironmentPermission _
    (EnvironmentPermissionAccess.Read, "Temp")

Dim sEv As String
oEp.Assert()
```

We then try to read the environment variable into a string. If the string read succeeds, then we then pop up a message box to reflect the success. If the read fails, a message box reflects the failure:

```
Try
    sEv = Environment.GetEnvironmentVariable("Temp")
    MessageBox.Show("Assert was a success")
Catch objA As System.Exception
    MessageBox.Show("Assert failed")
End Try
```

Next, we revoke the assert we previously issued by using the `RevertAssert()` method, and establish `Deny` permissions:

```
System.Security.CodeAccessPermission.RevertAssert()
oEp.Deny()
```

We then try again to read the variable, and write the appropriate result to a message box:

```
Try
    sEv = Environment.GetEnvironmentVariable("Temp")
    MessageBox.Show("Deny failed")
Catch objA As System.Exception
    MessageBox.Show("Deny was a success")
End Try
```

Finally, we write the `ToString()` of the method to another message box. Following is the output of all three message boxes as a result of running this subroutine. The first two message box messages give us the feedback from our `Assert()` and `Deny()` code, followed by the output of our `ToString()` method:

```
Assert was a success

Deny failed

<IPermission class="System.Security.Permissions.EnvironmentPermission, mscorlib,
 Version=2.0.0.0, Culture=neutral, PublicKeyToken=b77a5c561934e089"
 version="1" Read="Temp" />
```

As you can see, the `ToString()` method is an XML representation of the permission object currently in effect. The first and second message boxes that are output reflect the system information of the version of the Visual Basic security environment that was running at the time the button was clicked. The third message box is the environment variable name surrounded by the `Read` tags, which was the permission in effect at the time the `ToString()` method was executed.

Look at one more example of where the permissions would affect you in your program functionality, that of accessing the registry. You would generally access the registry on the computer that was the central server for a component in your Windows Forms application.

When you use the `EventLog` methods to create entries in the machine Event Logs, you access the registry. To illustrate this concept, the following code example denies permissions to the registry:

```
Protected Sub TestRegistryPermissions_Click(ByVal sender As Object, _
                                    ByVal e As System.EventArgs) _
                                    Handles TestRegistryPermissions.Click

    Dim oRp As New _
        RegistryPermission(Security.Permissions.PermissionState.Unrestricted)
    oRp.Deny()

    Dim objLog As New EventLog
    Dim objLogEntryType As EventLogEntryType

    Try
        Throw (New EntryPointNotFoundException)
    Catch objA As System.EntryPointNotFoundException
        Try
            If Not System.Diagnostics.EventLog.SourceExists("Example") Then
                System.Diagnostics.EventLog.CreateEventSource("Example", "System")
            End If

            objLog.Source = "Example"
            objLog.Log = "System"
            objLogEntryType = EventLogEntryType.Information
            objLog.WriteEntry("Error: " & objA.message, objLogEntryType)
        Catch objB As System.Exception
            MessageBox.Show(objB.Message)
        End Try
    End Try

End Sub
```

Walking through the code, you start with setting up the registry permission and setting it to `Deny` access:

```
Dim oRp As New _
    RegistryPermission(Security.Permissions.PermissionState.Unrestricted)
oRp.Deny()
```

Next, you `Throw` an exception on purpose in order to set up writing to an Event Log:

```
Throw (New EntryPointNotFoundException)
```

When the exception is caught, it checks the registry to make sure a specific type of registry entry source is already in existence:

```
If Not System.Diagnostics.EventLog.SourceExists("Example") Then
    System.Diagnostics.EventLog.CreateEventSource("Example", "System")
End If
```

At this point, the code fails with the error message shown in Figure 12-4.

Request for permission of type 'System.Security.Permissions.RegistryPermission' failed.

OK

Figure 12-4

These examples can serve as a good basis for use in developing classes that access the other objects within the scope of the Permissions namespace, such as reflections and UI permissions.

Managing Security Policy

As stated in the introduction to the chapter, two new command-line utilities (Caspol.exe and Permview.exe) help in configuring and viewing security policy at both machine and user levels. When you manage security policy at this level, you are doing so as an administrator of a machine or user policy for a machine that is hosting code that will be called from other front-end applications. Caspol.exe is a command-line utility with many options for configuring your security policies (Caspol stands for Code Access Security Policy). User and machine policy are associated with groups and permission sets. One group is automatically provided, the AllCode group.

The Caspol utility has two categories of commands. The first category listed in the following table is the set of commands that provide feedback on the current security policy:

Command	Short Command	Parameters	Effect
-List	-l	None	This lists the combination of the available groups and permission sets
-ListGroups	-lg	None	This lists only groups
-ListPset	-lp	None	This lists only permission sets
-ListFulltrust	-lf	None	This lists only assemblies that have full trust privileges
-List Description	-ld	None	This lists code group names and descriptions
-Reset	-rs	None	This resets the machine and user policies to the default for .NET. This is handy if a policy creates a condition that is not recoverable. Use this command carefully, as you will lose all changes made to the current policies.

Command	Short Command	Parameters	Effect
`--ResolveGroup`	`-rsg`	Assembly File	This lists what groups are associated with a given assembly file
`--ResolvePerm`	`-rsp`	Assembly File	This lists what permission sets are associated with a given assembly file

This is not the list in its entirety, but some of the more important commands. Now let's look at some examples of output from our previous listed commands. If you wanted to list the groups active on your local machine at the Visual Studio command prompt, you would type the following:

```
Caspol -Machine -ListGroups
```

The output looks similar to that shown in Figure 12-5 (it varies slightly depending on the machine you are working on).

Figure 12-5

Let's look at the output in a bit more detail so that you are aware of some of the other things that are listed besides what was specifically requested. The third line shows that code access security checking is ON. On the following line, the machine is checking for the user's right to execute the `Caspol` utility, as Execution checking is ON. The Policy change prompt is also ON, so if the user executes a `Caspol` command that changes system policy, then a confirmation prompt appears to verify that this is really intentional.

The level is also listed on the screen prior to the requested output, which is detailed at the bottom, listing the groups present on the machine. The policies pertain to two levels: the machine and the user. When changing policy, if the user is not an administrator, then the user policy is affected unless the user specifically applies the policy to the machine through use of the `-machine` switch, as illustrated in the screen shot. If the user is an administrator, then the machine policy is affected unless the user specifically applies the policy to the user level through the use of the `-user` switch.

Let's now look at another request result example. This time we ask for a listing of all of the permission sets on the machine. At the command prompt, you would type the following:

```
Caspol -machine -listpset
```

This would result in output similar to that shown in Figure 12-6. The following output has been shortened for space considerations, but it would contain a listing of all the code explicitly set to execute against the seven permission sets mentioned in the definitions section. In addition, note that the output is an XML representation of a permission object. The listing details the named permission sets and what each one has as active rights. For instance, the fifth permission set is named `LocalIntranet`, while the next lines detail the `Permission` class, an environment permission with read access to the environment variable – USER-NAME. The next class detail is regarding `FileDialogpermissions`, and it lists those as being unrestricted. The output then goes on to detail the effective settings for `IsolatedStorage` and others.

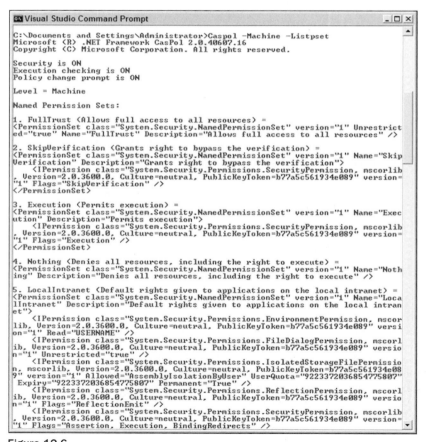

Figure 12-6

Let's now look at the second category of commands that go with the `Caspol` utility, shown in the following table. These are the commands that we will use to actually modify policy:

Command	Short Command	Parameters	Effect
-AddFullTrust	-af	Assembly File Name	Adds a given `Assembly` file to the full trust permission set
-AddGroup	-ag	Parent Label, Membership, Permission Set Name	Adds a code group to the code group hierarchy
-AddPSet	-ap	Permission Set Path, Permission Set Name	Adds a new named permission set to the policy; the permission set should be an XML file
-ChgGroup	-cg	Membership, Permission Set Name	Changes a code group's information
-ChgPset	-cp	File Name, Permission Set Name	Changes a named permission set's information
-Force	-f		This option is not recommended. It forces `Caspol` to accept policy changes even if the change could prevent `Caspol` itself from being executed
-Recover	-r		Recovers policy information from a backup file controlled by the utility
-RemFullTrust	-rf	Assembly File Name	Removes a given `Assembly` file from the full trust permission set
-RemGroup	-rg	Label	Removes a code group
-RemPSet	-rp	Permission Set Name	Removes a permission set. The seven default sets cannot be removed.

As before, this is not a comprehensive list of all the available commands, so consult the MSDN documentation for the complete listing if needed. Let's begin our discussion of these commands with a few more definitions that help clarify the parameters associated with the commands. An assembly file is created within Visual Basic each time you do a build whereby your version is a release version. An assembly needs to have a strong name associated with it in order to be used in your permissions groupings. It gets a strong name from being associated with a digital signature uniquely identifying the assembly. You carry out this association in addition to providing other pieces of evidence to be used with the strong name within the `AssemblyInfo.vb` file of your project.

To do this, open the `AssemblyInfo.vb` file within Visual Studio 2005. This file is automatically created for you by Visual Studio when you create a project. Simply add a new assembly attribute to the list:

```
<Assembly: AssemblyKeyFileAttribute("myKey.snk")>
```

This associates your assembly with an existing originating key file in order for Visual Studio to generate a strong name during the build process. Be sure to place the key file in the project directory, as this is where Visual Studio looks for it during the build process.

During the build, Visual Studio generates the strong name, after which you can add your assembly to your security configuration. Place the executable, `SecurityApp.exe` (your executable will be the name of your project), which was created from the build, into the `C:\testsecurity` directory on the local machine for use with the policy method illustrations.

If you wanted to add your assembly to the `fulltrust` permission set, you would type **Caspol -addfulltrust C:\testsecurity\SecurityApp.exe.**

Figure 12-7 shows the outcome of the command.

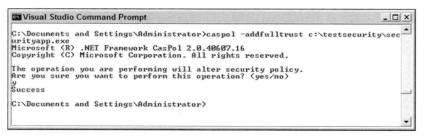

Figure 12-7

As you can see, you are prompted before your command alters your security policy, and then the new application is added to the `fulltrust` assembly list. You can confirm it was added by issuing the following command:

```
Caspol -listfulltrust
```

An excerpt of output from the command that includes the new assembly would look like what is shown in Figure 12-8.

Figure 12-8

This shows the application name, version, and key information associated with the .exe file when the build was performed. Now let's look at the creation and addition of a permission set to the permission sets in the security policy. Permission sets can be created by hand, in any text editor, in an XML format and saved as an .xml file (this example saves it as securityexample.xml). Following is a listing from one such file that was created for this example:

```
<PermissionSet class="System.Security.NamedPermissionSet" version="1">
   <Permission class="System.Security.Permissions.FileIOPermission, mscorlib,
          SN=03689116d3a4ae33" version="1">
     <Read> C:\TestSecurity </Read>
   </Permission>
   <Permission class="System.Security.Permissions.EnvironmentPermission,
          mscorlib, SN=03689116d3a4ae33" version="1">
     <Read> [TEMP] </Read>
   </Permission>
   <Name>SecurityExample</Name>
   <Description>Gives Full File Access</Description>
</PermissionSet>
```

The listing has multiple permissions within the permission set. The listing sets up read file permissions within one set of tags as shown:

```
<Permission class="System.Security.Permissions.FileIOPermission, mscorlib,
            SN=03689116d3a4ae33" version="1">
  <Read> C:\TestSecurity </Read>
</Permission>
```

You then set up read access to the `Temp` environment variable in the second set of permission tags:

```
<Permission class="System.Security.Permissions.EnvironmentPermission,
            mscorlib, SN=03689116d3a4ae33" version="1">
  <Read> [TEMP] </Read>
</Permission>
```

The listing also gives our custom permission set the name of `SecurityExample` with a description:

```
<Name>SecurityExample</Name>
<Description>Gives Full File Access</Description>
```

When you want to add your permission set to your policy, you would type the following command:

```
Caspol -addpset C:\testsecurity\securityexample.xml securityexample
```

The last command issues the `-addpset` flag to indicate that you want to add a permission set, followed by the XML file containing the permission set, followed finally by the name of the permission set. Figure 12-9 shows the outcome of your command.

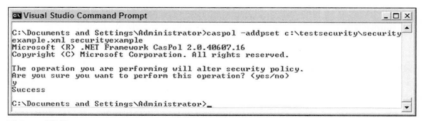

Figure 12-9

You can then list your security permission sets by typing `Caspol -listpset`. Figure 12-10 shows the excerpt of the new security permission set.

As you can see, typing `Caspol -listpset` provides a listing of just the permission sets within your policy. The named permission set `SecurityExample` shows up under the `Named Permission Sets` heading, and its description is listed just after its name.

Once you have a permission set, you can add a group that your assembly object fits into and which enforces the new permission set. You add this group by using the `AddGroup` switch in `Caspol`. The `AddGroup` switch has a couple of parameters that need more explanation. The first parameter is `parent_label`. As shown in Figure 12-11, the `All code` group has a "1" before it. The labels within code groups have a hierarchy that is established when you add groups, so you need to specify what your parent label would be. In this case, because the only one that exists is "1," that is what you designate.

```
Visual Studio Command Prompt                                          _ □ x
n="1" Level="SafePrinting" />
</PermissionSet>

7. securityexample =
<PermissionSet class="System.Security.NamedPermissionSet" version="1" Name="secu
rityexample">
        <IPermission class="System.Security.Permissions.EnvironmentPermission, mscor
lib, Version=2.0.3600.0, Culture=neutral, PublicKeyToken=b77a5c561934e089" versi
on="1" />
        <IPermission class="System.Security.Permissions.FileIOPermission, mscorlib,
Version=2.0.3600.0, Culture=neutral, PublicKeyToken=b77a5c561934e089" version="1
" />
</PermissionSet>

8. Everything (Allows unrestricted access to all resources covered by built-in p
ermissions) =
<PermissionSet class="System.Security.NamedPermissionSet" version="1" Name="Ever
ything" Description="Allows unrestricted access to all resources covered by buil
t-in permissions">
        <IPermission class="System.Security.Permissions.EnvironmentPermission, mscor
lib, Version=2.0.3600.0, Culture=neutral, PublicKeyToken=b77a5c561934e089" versi
on="1" Unrestricted="true" />
        <IPermission class="System.Security.Permissions.FileDialogPermission, mscorl
ib, Version=2.0.3600.0, Culture=neutral, PublicKeyToken=b77a5c561934e089" versio
n="1" Unrestricted="true" />
        <IPermission class="System.Security.Permissions.FileIOPermission, mscorlib,
Version=2.0.3600.0, Culture=neutral, PublicKeyToken=b77a5c561934e089" version="1
" Unrestricted="true" />
        <IPermission class="System.Security.Permissions.IsolatedStorageFilePermissio
n, mscorlib, Version=2.0.3600.0, Culture=neutral, PublicKeyToken=b77a5c561934e08
9" version="1" Unrestricted="true" />
        <IPermission class="System.Security.Permissions.ReflectionPermission, mscorl
ib, Version=2.0.3600.0, Culture=neutral, PublicKeyToken=b77a5c561934e089" versio
n="1" Unrestricted="true" />
        <IPermission class="System.Security.Permissions.RegistryPermission, mscorlib
, Version=2.0.3600.0, Culture=neutral, PublicKeyToken=b77a5c561934e089" version=
"1" Unrestricted="true" />
        <IPermission class="System.Security.Permissions.SecurityPermission, mscorlib
, Version=2.0.3600.0, Culture=neutral, PublicKeyToken=b77a5c561934e089" version=
"1" Flags="Assertion, UnmanagedCode, Execution, ControlThread, ControlEvidence,
ControlPolicy, SerializationFormatter, ControlDomainPolicy, ControlPrincipal, Co
ntrolAppDomain, RemotingConfiguration, Infrastructure, BindingRedirects" />
```

Figure 12-10

Because you designate 1, the new group becomes a child of 1. The second parameter is membership. The membership parameter has a certain list of options that you can add based on the following table. Each option designates a piece of information you are providing about the pieces of code you will add to your group. For instance, you might state that you will only be adding code that has a specific signature with the -Pub option, or only code in a certain application directory with the -AppDir option.

Option	Description
-All	All code
-Pub	Code that has a specific signature on a certificate file
-Strong	Code that has a specific strong name, as designated by a filename, code name, and version
-Zone	Code that fits into the following zones: MyComputer, Intranet, Trusted, Internet, or Untrusted
-Site	Originating on a website
-Hash	Code that has a specific assembly hash
-AppDir	A specific application directory
-SkipVerif	Code that requests the skipverification permission
-URL	Originating at a specific URL
-Custom	Code that requires a custom membership condition

The third parameter to the `AddGroup` command is the permission set name that you want to be associated with your group. The group that we will create will be under parent label 1, and we will designate the `-Zone` parameter as `MyComputer` because the code lives on a local drive. We will also associate the new group with our `SecurityExample` permission set by typing the following command:

```
Caspol -addgroup 1. -Zone MyComputer SecurityExample
```

Output from the command was successful, as shown in Figure 12-11.

Figure 12-12 shows the `-listgroups` command used for listing the new group. You can see that a 1.6 level was added, with the `SecurityExample` permission set attached to all code that fits into the MyComputer Zone. You can verify that the assembly object fits into the MyComputer Zone by using the `resolveperm` command, as shown in Figure 12-13.

The bottom of the figure lists which `ZoneIdentityPermission` the assembly object has been associated with — MyComputer. In addition, each assembly gets a `URLIdentityPermission` specifying the location of the executable.

Figure 12-11

Figure 12-12

Not only do you have the utility that helps with managing security permission sets and groups, you also have a utility that views the security information regarding an assembly, `Permview.exe`. (`Permview` stands for Permissions Viewer.)

`Permview` is not as complex as `Caspol` because its main purpose is to provide a certain type of feedback regarding the security requests of assemblies. In fact, the `Permview` utility only has two switches: one for the output location, and one for declarative security to be included in the output. In order to specify an output location, the switch is `/Output`, and then a file path is appended to the command line after the switch. The `Permview` utility brings up another concept not covered yet: declarative security.

Figure 12-13

Declarative security is displayed in the `Permview` utility with the `/Decl` switch; it is security that a piece of code requests at an assembly level. Because it is at the assembly level, the line that requests the security is at the top of the Visual Basic module, even before your `Imports` statements. You can request one of three levels of security, as described in the following table:

Level	Description
RequestMinimum	Permissions the code must have in order to run
RequestOptional	Permissions that code may use, but could run without
RequestRefused	Permissions that you want to ensure are never granted to the code

Requesting permissions at the assembly level helps ensure that the code will be able to run, and won't get permission-based security exceptions. Because you have users calling your code, the declarative security ensures that the callers have proper security to do all that your code requires; otherwise, a security exception is thrown. The following example shows the syntax for requesting minimum permissions; the code would be placed at the top of our procedure. This example also illustrates syntax described in the table at the beginning of the chapter regarding permissions in the `Security.Permissions` namespace. Moreover, it illustrates the use of a security constant, `SecurityAction.RequestMinimum`, for the type of security you are requesting:

```
<Assembly: SecurityPermissionAttribute(SecurityAction.RequestMinimum)>
```

Once this line is added to the assembly by means of the `AssemblyInfo.vb` file, `Permview` will report on what the assembly requested by listing minimal, optional, and refused permission sets, including the security permission set under the minimal set listing.

Figuring Minimum Permissions Required for Application

Before the .NET Framework 2.0, one of the big requests from developers who were building and deploying applications was the need for clarification regarding which permissions were required for the application to run. This was sometimes a difficult task, as developers would build their applications under Full Trust and then the applications would be deployed to a machine that didn't have those kinds of privileges.

The .NET Framework 2.0 introduces a new tool that can be used to fully understand which permissions your application is going to need in order to run on another machine. This command-line tool, `PermCalc.exe`, does this by emulating the complete path of your assembly and all the permissions that it would require.

To use `PermCalc.exe`, open the Visual Studio command prompt and navigate to the location of the assembly you want to check. `PermCalc.exe` takes the following command structure:

```
PermCalc.exe [Options] <assembly>
```

You can also have `PermCalc.exe` evaluate more than a single assembly:

```
PermCalc.exe [Options] <assembly> <assembly>
```

For example, running the `PermCalc.exe` tool on the `SecurityApp.exe` resulted in the following:

```
Microsoft (R) .NET Framework Permissions Calculator.
Copyright (C) Microsoft Corporation 2003. All rights reserved.

<Assembly Name="C:\Documents and Settings\Administrator\My Documents\Visual
  Studio\Projects\SecurityApp\SecurityApp\obj\Debug\securityapp.exe">
<PermissionSet class="System.Security.PermissionSet"
  version="1">
<IPermission class="System.Security.Permissions.EnvironmentPermission, mscorlib,
  Version=2.0.0.0, Culture=neutral, PublicKeyToken=b77a5c561934e089"
  version="1"
```

```
                 Unrestricted="true"/>
<IPermission class="System.Security.Permissions.FileIOPermission, mscorlib,
 Version=2.0.0.0, Culture=neutral, PublicKeyToken=b77a5c561934e089"
 version="1"
 Unrestricted="true"/>
<IPermission class="System.Security.Permissions.RegistryPermission, mscorlib,
 Version=2.0.0.0, Culture=neutral, PublicKeyToken=b77a5c561934e089"
 version="1"
 Unrestricted="true"/>
<IPermission class="System.Security.Permissions.SecurityPermission, mscorlib,
 Version=2.0.0.0, Culture=neutral, PublicKeyToken=b77a5c561934e089"
 version="1"
 Flags="UnmanagedCode, Execution, ControlEvidence, ControlPrincipal,
 RemotingConfiguration"/>
<IPermission class="System.Net.SocketPermission, System, Version=2.0.0.0,
 Culture=neutral, PublicKeyToken=b77a5c561934e089"
 version="1"
 Unrestricted="true"/>
<IPermission class="System.Diagnostics.PerformanceCounterPermission, System,
 Version=2.0.0.0, Culture=neutral, PublicKeyToken=b77a5c561934e089"
 version="1"
 Unrestricted="true"/>
<IPermission class="System.Net.NetworkInformation.NetworkInformationPermission,
 System, Version=2.0.0.0, Culture=neutral, PublicKeyToken=b77a5c561934e089"
 version="1"
 Access="Read"/>
</PermissionSet>

</Assembly>
```

From this output, you can see the permissions that would be required for the application to run on someone's machine. These results were generated using the following command:

```
PermCalc.exe -under SecurityApp.exe
```

The option -under should be used when you are unsure of the exact permissions, as PermCalc.exe actually overestimates the permissions by default. Using -under forces PermCalc.exe to underestimate the permissions instead.

Using Visual Studio to Figure Minimum Permissions

Looking at the properties of your solution in Visual Studio, note the new Security tab. In the past, one of the problems in testing your application's security and permissioning was that as a developer, you were always forced to develop your programs under Full Trust. This means that you have access to the system's resources in a very open and free manner. This was an issue because the programs that you build typically cannot run under Full Trust and you still have to test the application's abilities to tap into the system's resources in which the program is being run.

The Security tab is a new GUI to the PermCalc.exe tool that enables you to run your applications under different types of zones. Figure 12-14 shows this new page.

Figure 12-14

After checking the Enable ClickOnce Security Settings check box, you can specify whether the application will be running on the client machine under Full Trust or whether the application will only have partial trust status. You can also select the zone in which your application will run. The options include the following:

❑ Local Intranet
❑ Internet
❑ Custom

After selecting the zone type, you can examine all the various permissions that are required by the application in order to run.

Clicking the Calculate Permissions button on the form enables you to do just that (see Figure 12-15). Visual Studio examines the assembly and provides you with information about which permissions for which assemblies would be required to run the application in the zone specified.

Once analyzed, Visual Studio presents information about what is needed from each of the assemblies in order for the application to function, as shown in Figure 12-16.

Figure 12-15

Figure 12-16

What makes this section of the application's property pages even better is that from the text box of assemblies listed, you can highlight selected assemblies and fine-tune their permissions even further — granularizing the permissions the assemblies are allowed to work with. For instance, highlighting the `FileIOPermission` line in the text box and clicking the Properties button enables you to fine-tune how the permissioning around this assembly functions. The Permission Settings dialog that appears is shown in Figure 12-17.

The `FileIOPermission` part of the permission settings enables you to specify the file path that the assembly is allowed to access, as well as the actions that the assembly is allowed to take in the path defined.

The capability to examine assemblies is not only provided through the new command-line tool, `PermCalc.exe`; even Visual Studio joins in and allows for easy management and understanding of your applications.

Figure 12-17

Security Tools

Microsoft provides many security tools in its .NET SDK. Most of these tools are console-based utility applications. These tools can be used to help implement the security processes outlined earlier. They are not described in great detail, though they do deserve a review. Basically, two groups of tools are provided with the SDK:

- ❑ Permissions and assembly management tools
- ❑ Certificate management tools

Permissions and Assembly Management Tools

Program Name	Function
Caspol.exe	Stands for Code Access Security Policy tool. This tool enables you to view and modify security settings.
Signcode.exe	A file signing tool that enables you to digitally sign your executable files
Storeadm.exe	An administrative tool for isolated storage management. Restricts code access to the filing system.
Permcalc.exe	Emulates the complete path of your assembly and all the permissions that it requires. It can also evaluate assemblies and provide information on the permissions an end user would require to run the program. This is a new command-line tool provided by the .NET Framework 2.0.
Permview.exe	Displays an assembly's requested access permissions

Program Name	Function
Peverify.exe	Checks whether the executable file will pass the runtime test for type-safe coding
Secutil.exe	Extracts a public key from a certificate and puts it in a format that is usable in your source code
Sn.exe	Creates assemblies with strong names — that is, a digitally signed namespace and version information

Certificate Management Tools

Program Name	Function
Makecert.exe	Creates an X.509 certificate for testing purposes
Certmgr.exe	Assembles certificates into a CTL (Certificate Trust List). Can also be used for revoking certificates.
Chktrust.exe	Validates a signed file containing data, its PKCS#7 hash, and a X.509 certificate
Cert2spc.exe	Creates an SPC (Software Publisher Certificate) from an X.509 certificate

Exceptions Using the SecurityException Class

In this latest release of the .NET Framework, the SecurityException class has been greatly expanded in order to provide considerably more detailed information on the types of exceptions that are encountered in a security context.

In the past, using the .NET Framework versions 1.0/1.1, the SecurityException class provided very little information in terms of actually telling you what was wrong and why the exception was thrown. Due to this limitation, the .NET Framework 2.0 added a number of new properties to the SecurityException class. The following table details the properties of the SecurityException class:

Properties	Description
Action	Retrieves the security action that caused the exception to occur
Demanded	Returns the permissions, permission sets, or permission set collections that caused the error to occur
DenySetInstance	Returns the denied permissions, permissions sets, or permission set collections that caused the security actions to fail
FailedAssemblyInfo	Returns information about the failed assembly

Table continues on the next page

Properties	Description
FirstPermissionThatFailed	Returns the first permission contained in the permissions set or permission set collection that failed
GrantedSet	Returns the set of permissions that caused the security actions to fail
Method	Returns information about the method connected to the exception
PermissionState	Returns the state of the permission that threw the exception
PermissionType	Returns the type of the permission that threw the exception
PermitOnlySetInstance	Returns a permissions set or permission set collection that is part of the permit-only stack frame if a security action has failed
RefusedSet	Returns the permissions that were refused by the assembly
Url	Returns the URL of the assembly that caused the exception
Zone	Returns the zone of the assembly that caused the exception

Clearly, you can get your hands on a lot of information if a security exception is thrown in your application. For instance, you can use something similar to the following `Catch` section of code to check for security errors:

```
Dim myFile as FileStream

Try
   myFile = My.Computer.FileSystem.GetFileInfo("C:\testingsecurity\testing.txt")
Catch ex As Security.SecurityException
   MessageBox.Show(ex.Method.Name.ToString())
End Try
```

One nice addition to the `SecurityException` class is how Visual Studio so easily works with it. When you encounter a `SecurityException` error while working in the debug mode of your solution, you will see something similar to the warning shown in Figure 12-18 directly in the IDE.

It is also possible to get Visual Studio to provide a detailed view of the error by breaking down the `SecurityException` object in the Locals window of Visual Studio when you catch the error using a `Try-Catch` statement.

Cryptography Basics

Rather than present a general exposition of cryptography, this section is meant to familiarize you with basic techniques required to deal with .NET security and protecting your Web Services through encryption. The three building blocks you need are hashing algorithms, secret key encryption, and an understanding of the Public Key Cryptographic System (PKCS).

Figure 12-18

Hashing algorithms digest long sequences of data into short footprints, the most popular being 64-bit hash keys. The two most popular hashing algorithms are SHA (Secure Hash Algorithm) and MD5 (Message-Digest algorithm 5). These hash keys are used for signing digital documents; in other words, the hash is generated and encrypted using a private key.

Secret key encryption is commonly used to protect data through passwords and pass phrases (long phrases that would be difficult to guess). Secret key encryption is suitable for situations where the encrypted data needs to be accessed by the same person who protected it.

Public Key Cryptography is most widely used in protecting the data through encryption. It is also used for digital signatures. Public Key Cryptography is based on asymmetric keys, which means you always have a pair of keys. One is known to all and is called the *public key*. The other key of the pair is kept secret and is known only to the owner. This is called the *private key*. If you use the public key to encrypt data, it can only be decrypted using the corresponding private key of the key pair, and vice versa.

The public key is known to all, so anyone can decrypt the information. However, the private key is known only to the owner, so this process acts as a digital signature. In other words, if the public key decrypts the message, then you know that the sender was the owner of the private key. As suggested earlier, rather than encrypt the whole document using the private key, a hash algorithm is used to digest the data into a compact form, which is then encrypted using the private key. The result of this process is called the *digital signature* of the digital document.

If the data is encrypted using the public key, then it can then only be decrypted by the corresponding private key, which means that only the owner of the private key will be able to read the unencrypted data. This can be used for encryption purposes. The cryptographic namespace of the .NET Framework is `System.Security.Cryptography`.

Hash Algorithms

Hash algorithms are also called *one-way functions* because of their mathematical property of nonreversibility. The hash algorithms reduce large binary strings into a fixed-length binary byte array. This fixed-length binary array is used for computing digital signatures, as explained earlier.

To verify a piece of information, the hash is recomputed and compared against a previously computed hash value. If both values match, the data has not been altered. The cryptographic hashing algorithms map a large stream of binary data to a much shorter fixed length, so it is theoretically possible for two different documents to have the same hash key.

Although, in theory, it is possible for two documents to have the same MD5 hash key and a different check sum, it is computationally impossible to create a forged document having the same hash key as the original hash value. Take the case of a virus attack on an executable code. In the late 1980s, as a protective measure against accidental or malicious damage to the code integrity, the most sophisticated technique was to create a check sum or a CRC (cyclic redundancy check).

Virus makers drew cunning designs to create viruses that added padding code to the victim's files so that the check sum and CRC remained unchanged in spite of the infection. However, using MD5 hash values, this kind of stealth attack is rendered unfeasible.

Windows Meta Files (WMF) still use check sums in the file header. For example, the .NET Framework class `System.Drawing.Imaging.WmfPlaceableFileHeader` has a read/write property of type `short` called `Checksum`. However, due to ease of computation, this check sum is used as a cheap mode of protection against accidental damage, rather than against malicious attacks.

Here is a simple program to calculate a check sum:

```
' Cryptography/Checksum.vb

Imports System
Imports System.IO

Module Module1
```

This is the entry point for the program. Here, you check to see whether you've received the correct argument from the command line to run the program, and stop the program if you haven't:

```
Public Sub Main(ByVal CmdArgs() As String)
    If (CmdArgs.Length <> 1) Then
        Console.WriteLine("Usage: Checksum <filename>")
        End
    End If
```

First, you open the file for which the check sum is to be computed:

```
Dim fs As FileStream = File.OpenRead(CmdArgs(0))
```

You then compute the check sum, close the file, and then output the result to the screen:

```
        Dim sum As Short = compute(fs)
        fs.Close()

        Console.WriteLine(sum)
    End Sub
```

The following method computes the check sum:

```
        Function compute(ByVal strm As Stream)
            Dim sum As Long = 0
            Dim by As Integer

            strm.Position = 0
            by = strm.ReadByte

            While (by <> -1)
                sum = (((by Mod &HFF) + sum) Mod &HFFFF)
                by = strm.ReadByte
            End While

            Return CType((sum Mod &HFFFF), Short)
        End Function
    End Module
```

Compile this program with the following in the VB compiler (or build and run your application if you are using Visual Studio:

```
vbc Checksum.vb
```

Run it with the following:

```
Checksum <filename>
```

Due to their unsafe nature, check sums and CRCs are sometimes deemed poor cousins of cryptographic hash algorithms. Next you will look into classes provided by the .NET Framework to cater to cryptographic-grade algorithms.

Cryptographic Hash Algorithms

The abstract class `System.Security.Cryptography.HashAlgorithm` represents the concept of cryptographic hash algorithms within the .NET Framework. The framework provides eight classes that extend the `HashAlgorithm` abstract class:

❑   `MD5CryptoServiceProvider` (extends abstract class `MD5`)

❑   `RIPEMD160Managed` (extends abstract class `RIPEMD160`)

- ❑ SHA1CryptoServiceProvider (extends abstract class SHA1)

- ❑ SHA256Managed (extends abstract class SHA256)

- ❑ SHA384Managed (extends abstract class SHA384)

- ❑ SHA512Managed (extends abstract class SHA512)

- ❑ HMACSHA1 (extends abstract class KeyedHashAlgorithm)

- ❑ MACTripleDES (extends abstract class KeyedHashAlgorithm)

The last two classes belong to a class of algorithm called *keyed hash algorithms*. The keyed hashes extend the concept of the cryptographic hash with the use of a shared secret key. This is used for computing the hash of data transported over an unsecured channel.

The following is an example of computing a hash value of a file:

```
' Cryptography/TestKeyHash.vb

Imports System
Imports System.IO
Imports System.Security.Cryptography
Imports System.Text
Imports System.Runtime.Serialization.Formatters

Module Module1
    Public Sub Main(ByVal CmdArgs() As String)
        If (CmdArgs.Length <> 1) Then
            Console.WriteLine("Usage: TestKeyHash <filename>")
            End
        End If
```

The following snippet creates the object instance of the .NET SDK Framework class with a salt (a random secret to confuse a snooper):

```
Dim key() As Byte = Encoding.ASCII.GetBytes("My Secret Key".ToCharArray())
Dim hmac As HMACSHA1 = New HMACSHA1(key)
Dim fs As FileStream = File.OpenRead(CmdArgs(0))
```

The next four lines compute the hash, convert the binary hash into a printable Base64 format, close the file, and then print the Base64 encoded string as the result of hashing to the screen:

```
        Dim hash() As Byte = hmac.ComputeHash(fs)
        Dim b64 As String = Convert.ToBase64String(hash)
        fs.Close()

        Console.WriteLine(b64)
    End Sub
End Module
```

The code can be compiled at the command line using the following:

```
vbc TestKeyHash.vb
```

To execute the code, use the following command at the console prompt:

```
TestKeyHash TestKeyHash.vb
```

This should produce a hashed output:

```
IOEj/D0rOxjEqCD8qHoYm+yWw6I=
```

The previous example uses an instance of the HMACSHA1 class. The output displayed is a Base64 encoding of the binary hash result value. Base64 encoding is widely used in MIME and XML file formats to represent binary data. To recover the binary data from a Base64-encoded string, you could use the following code fragment:

```
Dim orig() As Byte = Convert.FromBase64String(b64)
```

The XML parser, however, does this automatically, as you will see in later examples.

SHA

Secure Hash Algorithm (SHA) is a block cipher that operates on a block size of 64 bits. However, the subsequent enhancements of this algorithm have bigger key values, thus increasing the value range and therefore enhancing the cryptographic utility. Note that the bigger the key value sizes, the longer it takes to compute the hash. Moreover, for relatively smaller data files, smaller hash values are more secure. To put it another way, the hash algorithm's block size should be less than or equal to the size of the data itself.

The hash size for the SHA1 algorithm is 160 bits. The following code shows how to use it, and is similar to the HMACSHA1 code discussed previously:

```
' Cryptography/TestSHA1.vb

Imports System
Imports System.IO
Imports System.Security.Cryptography
Imports System.Text
Imports System.Runtime.Serialization.Formatters

Module Module1
    Public Sub Main(ByVal CmdArgs() As String)
        If (CmdArgs.Length <> 1) Then
            Console.WriteLine("Usage: TestSHA1 <filename>")
            End
        End If
        Dim fs As FileStream = File.OpenRead(CmdArgs(0))

        Dim sha As SHA1 = New SHA1CryptoServiceProvider()
        Dim hash() As Byte = sha.ComputeHash(fs)
        Dim b64 As String = Convert.ToBase64String(hash)
        fs.Close()

        Console.WriteLine(b64)
    End Sub
End Module
```

The .NET Framework provides bigger key size algorithms as well — namely, SHA256, SHA384, and SHA512. The numbers at the end of the name indicate the block size.

The class SHA256Managed extends the abstract class SHA256, which in turn extends the abstract class HashAlgorithm. The Forms Authentication module of ASP.NET security (System.Web.Security.FormsAuthenticationModule) uses SHA1 as one of its valid formats to store and compare user passwords.

MD5

MD5 stands for Message-Digest algorithm 5. It is a cryptographic, one-way hash algorithm. The MD5 algorithm competes well with SHA. MD5 is an improved version of MD4, devised by Ronald Rivest of RSA fame. In fact, FIPS PUB 180-1 states that SHA-1 is based on similar principles to MD4. The salient features of this class of algorithms are as follows:

- ❏ It is computationally unfeasible to forge an MD5 hash digest.
- ❏ MD5 is not based on any mathematical assumption such as the difficulty of factoring large binary integers.
- ❏ MD5 is computationally cheap, and therefore suitable for low latency requirements.
- ❏ It is relatively simple to implement.

MD5 is the de facto standard for hash digest computation, due to the popularity of RSA. The .NET Framework provides an implementation of this algorithm through the class MD5CryptoServiceProvider in the System.Security.Cryptography namespace. This class extends the MD5 abstract class, which in turn extends the abstract class HashAlgorithm. This class shares a common base class with SHA1, so the examples previously discussed can be modified easily to accommodate it:

```
Dim fs As FileStream = File.OpenRead(CmdArgs(0))

Dim md5 As MD5 = New MD5CryptoServiceProvider()
Dim hash() As Byte = md5.ComputeHash(fs)

Dim b64 As String = Convert.ToBase64String(hash)
fs.Close()

Console.WriteLine(b64)
```

RIPEMD-160

Based on MD5, RIPEMD-160 started as a project in Europe called RIPE (RACE Integrity Primitives Evaluation Message Digest) in 1996. By 1997, the design of RIPEMD-160 was finalized. RIPEMD-160 is a 160-bit hash algorithm and is meant to be a replacement for MD4 and MD5.

The .NET Framework 2.0 introduced the RIPEMD160 class to work with this iteration of encryption techniques. The following code demonstrates the use of this class:

```
Dim fs As FileStream = File.OpenRead(CmdArgs(0))

Dim myRIPEMD As New RIPEMD160Managed()
```

```
Dim hash() As Byte = myRIPEMD.ComputeHash(fs)

Dim b64 As String = Convert.ToBase64String(hash)

fs.Close()
Console.WriteLine(b64)
```

Secret Key Encryption

Secret key encryption is widely used to encrypt data files using passwords. The simplest technique is to seed a random number using a password, and then encrypt the files with an XOR operation using this random number generator.

The .NET Framework represents the secret key by an abstract base class SymmetricAlgorithm. Four concrete implementations of different secret key algorithms are provided by default:

- DESCryptoServiceProvider (extends abstract class DES)
- RC2CryptoServiceProvider (extends abstract class RC2)
- RijndaelManaged (extends abstract class Rijndael)
- TripleDESCryptoServiceProvider (extends abstract class TripleDES)

Let's explore the SymmetricAlgorithm design. As indicated by the following example code, two separate methods are provided to access encryption and decryption. Here is a console application program that encrypts and decrypts a file, given a secret key:

```
' Cryptography/SymEnc.vb

Imports System.Security.Cryptography
Imports System.IO
Imports System.Text
Imports System
 Module Module1
    Public Sub Main(ByVal CmdArgs() As String)
        If (CmdArgs.Length <> 4) Then
            UsageAndExit()
        End If
```

The following computes the index of the algorithm that we'll use:

```
Dim algoIndex As Integer = CmdArgs(0)
If (algoIndex < 0 Or algoIndex >= algo.Length) Then
    UsageAndExit()
End If
```

We open the input and output files (the filename represented by CmdArgs(3) is the output file, and CmdArgs(2) is the input file):

```
Dim fin As FileStream = File.OpenRead(CmdArgs(2))
Dim fout As FileStream = File.OpenWrite(CmdArgs(3))
```

We create the symmetric algorithm instance using the .NET Framework class `SymmetricAlgorithm`. This uses the algorithm name indexed by the `CmdArgs(0)` parameter. After this, we set the key parameters and display them onscreen for information:

```
Dim sa As SymmetricAlgorithm = _
    SymmetricAlgorithm.Create(algo(algoIndex))
sa.IV = Convert.FromBase64String(b64IVs(algoIndex))
sa.Key = Convert.FromBase64String(b64Keys(algoIndex))
Console.WriteLine("Key " + CType(sa.Key.Length, String))
Console.WriteLine("IV " + CType(sa.IV.Length, String))
Console.WriteLine("KeySize: " + CType(sa.KeySize, String))
Console.WriteLine("BlockSize: " + CType(sa.BlockSize, String))
Console.WriteLine("Padding: " + CType(sa.Padding, String))
```

At this point, we check which operation is required, and execute the appropriate static method:

```
    If (CmdArgs(1).ToUpper().StartsWith("E")) Then
        Encrypt(sa, fin, fout)
    Else
        Decrypt(sa, fin, fout)
    End If
End Sub
```

Here is where the encryption itself takes place:

```
Public Sub Encrypt(ByVal sa As SymmetricAlgorithm, _
                   ByVal fin As Stream, _
                   ByVal fout As Stream)
    Dim trans As ICryptoTransform = sa.CreateEncryptor()
    Dim buf() As Byte = New Byte(2048) {}
    Dim cs As CryptoStream = _
        New CryptoStream(fout, trans, CryptoStreamMode.Write)
    Dim Len As Integer

    fin.Position = 0
    Len = fin.Read(buf, 0, buf.Length)

    While (Len > 0)
        cs.Write(buf, 0, Len)
        Len = fin.Read(buf, 0, buf.Length)
    End While

    cs.Close()
    fin.Close()
End Sub
```

Here's the decryption method:

```
Public Sub Decrypt(ByVal sa As SymmetricAlgorithm, _
                   ByVal fin As Stream, _
                   ByVal fout As Stream)
    Dim trans As ICryptoTransform = sa.CreateDecryptor()
    Dim buf() As Byte = New Byte(2048) {}
```

```
        Dim cs As CryptoStream = _
            New CryptoStream(fin, trans, CryptoStreamMode.Read)
        Dim Len As Integer

        Len = cs.Read(buf, 0, buf.Length)

        While (Len > 0)
            fout.Write(buf, 0, Len)
            Len = cs.Read(buf, 0, buf.Length)
        End While

        fin.Close()
        fout.Close()
    End Sub
```

This next method prints usage information:

```
    Public Sub UsageAndExit()
        Console.Write("Usage SymEnc <algo index> <D|E> <in> <out> ")
        Console.WriteLine("D =decrypt, E=Encrypt")

        For i As Integer = 0 To (algo.Length - 1)
            Console.WriteLine("Algo index: {0} {1}", i, algo(i))
        Next i
        End
    End Sub
```

The static parameters used for object creation are indexed by CmdArgs(0). How you arrive at these magic numbers is explained shortly:

```
        Dim algo() As String = {"DES", "RC2", "Rijndael", "TripleDES"}
        Dim b64Keys() As String = {"YE32PGCJ/g0=", _
            "vct+rJ09WuUcR61yfxniTQ==", _
            "PHDPqfwE3z25f2UYjwwfwg4XSqxvl8WYmy+2h8t6AUg=", _
            "Q1/1WoraddTH3IXAQUJGDSYDQcYYuOpm"}
        Dim b64IVs() As String = {"onQX8hdHeWQ=", _
            "jgetiyz+pIc=", _
            "pd5mgMMfDI2Gxm/SK15I8A==", _
            "6jpFrUh8FF4="}
    End Module
```

After compilation, this program can encrypt and decrypt using all four of the symmetric key implementations provided by the .NET Framework. The secret keys and their initialization vectors (IVs) have been generated by a simple source code generator, examined shortly.

The following commands encrypt and decrypt files using the DES algorithm. The first command takes a text file, 1.txt, and uses the DES algorithm to create an encrypted file called 2.bin. The next command decrypts this file and stores it in 3.bin:

```
    SymEnc 0 E 1.txt 2.bin
    SymEnc 0 D 2.bin 3.bin
```

The first parameter of the SymEnc program is an index to the string array, which determines the algorithm to be used:

```
Dim algo() As String = {"DES", "RC2", "Rijndael", "TripleDES"}
```

The string defining the algorithm is passed as a parameter to the static Create() method of the abstract class SymmetricAlgorithm. This class has an abstract factory design pattern:

```
Dim sa As SymmetricAlgorithm = SymmetricAlgorithm.Create(algo(algoIndex))
```

To encrypt, we get an instance of the ICryptoTransform interface by calling the CreateEncryptor() method of the SymmetricAlgorithm class extender:

```
Dim trans As ICryptoTransform = sa.CreateEncryptor()
```

Similarly, for decryption, we get an instance of the ICryptoTransform interface by calling the CreateDecryptor() method of the SymmetricAlgorithm class instance:

```
Dim trans As ICryptoTransform = sa.CreateDecryptor()
```

We use the class CryptoStream for both encryption and decryption, but the parameters to the constructor differ. Encryption uses the following code:

```
Dim cs As CryptoStream = New CryptoStream(fout, trans, CryptoStreamMode.Write)
```

Similarly, decryption uses this code:

```
Dim cs As CryptoStream = New CryptoStream(fin, trans, CryptoStreamMode.Read)
```

We call the Read() and Write() methods of the CryptoStream for decryption and encryption, respectively. For generating the keys, we use a simple code generator, as follows:

```
' Cryptography/SymKey.vb

Imports System.Security.Cryptography
Imports System.Text
Imports System.IO
Imports System
Imports Microsoft.VisualBasic.ControlChars

Module Module1
    Public Sub Main(ByVal CmdArgs() As String)
        Dim keyz As StringBuilder = New StringBuilder
        Dim ivz As StringBuilder = New StringBuilder
        keyz.Append("Dim b64Keys() As String = { _" + VbCrLf)
        ivz.Append(VbCrLf + "Dim b64IVs() As String = { _" + VbCrLf )
```

The algorithm names for symmetric keys used by .NET SDK are given the correct index values here:

```
Dim algo() As String = {"DES", "RC2", "Rijndael", "TripleDES"}
```

For each of the algorithms, we generate the keys and IV:

```
Dim comma As String = ", _" + VbCrLf

For i As Integer = 0 To 3
    Dim sa As SymmetricAlgorithm = SymmetricAlgorithm.Create(algo(i))

    sa.GenerateIV()
    sa.GenerateKey()

    Dim Key As String
    Dim IV As String

    Key = Convert.ToBase64String(sa.Key)
    IV = Convert.ToBase64String(sa.IV)
    keyz.AppendFormat(tab + """" + Key + """" + comma)
    ivz.AppendFormat(tab + """" + IV + """" + comma)
    If i = 2 Then comma = " "
Next i
```

Here, we print or emit the source code:

```
        keyz.Append("}")
        ivz.Append("}")
        Console.WriteLine(keyz.ToString())
        Console.WriteLine(ivz.ToString())
    End Sub
End Module
```

The preceding program creates a random key and an initializing vector for each algorithm. This output can be inserted directly into the `SymEnc.vb` program. The simplest way to do this is to type the following:

```
SymKey > keys.txt
```

This redirects the information into a file called `keys.txt`, which you can then use to cut and paste the values into your program. You use the `StringBuilder` class along with the control character `crlf` (carriage return and line feed) to format the text so that it can be inserted directly into your program. You then convert the binary data into Base64 encoding using the public instance method `ToBase64String()` of the class `Convert`. Kerberos, the popular network authentication protocol supported by Windows Server 2003, Windows 2000, and all of the UNIX flavors, uses secret key encryption for implementing security.

PKCS

The Public Key Cryptographic System is a type of asymmetric key encryption. This system uses two keys, one private and the other public. The public key is widely distributed, whereas the private key is kept secret. One cannot derive or deduce the private key by knowing the public key, so the public key can be safely distributed.

The keys are different, yet complementary. That is, if you encrypt data using the public key, then only the owner of the private key can decipher it, and vice versa. This forms the basis of PKCS encryption.

If the private key holder encrypts a piece of data using his or her private key, any person having access to the public key can decrypt it. The public key, as the name suggests, is available publicly. This property of the PKCS is exploited along with a hashing algorithm, such as SHA or MD5, to provide a verifiable digital signature process.

The abstract class `System.Security.Cryptography.AsymmetricAlgorithm` represents this concept in the .NET Framework. Two concrete implementations of this class are provided by default:

❑ `DSACryptoServiceProvider`, which extends the abstract class `DSA`

❑ `RSACryptoServiceProvider`, which extends the abstract class `RSA`

DSA (Digital Signature Algorithm) was specified by NIST (National Institute of Standards and Technology) in January 2000. The original DSA standard, however, was issued by NIST way back in August 1991. DSA cannot be used for encryption and is good only for digital signature. Digital signature is discussed in more detail in the next subsection.

RSA algorithms can also be used for encryption as well as digital signatures. RSA is the de facto standard and has much wider acceptance than DSA. RSA is a tiny bit faster than DSA as well.

The RSA algorithm is named after its three inventors: Rivest, Shamir, and Adleman. It was patented in the United States, but the patent expired in September 2000. RSA can be used for both digital signature and data encryption. It is based on the assumption that large numbers are extremely difficult to factor. The use of RSA for digital signatures is approved within the FIPS PUB 186-2 and is defined in the ANSI X9.31 standard document.

To gain some practical insights into RSA implementation of the .NET Framework, consider the following code (for this to compile, you also have to make a reference to the `System.Security` DLL in your project):

```
' Cryptography/TestRSAKey.vb

Imports System.Security.Cryptography.Xml

Module Module1
    Sub Main()
        Dim RSA As RSAKeyValue = New RSAKeyValue
        Dim str As String = RSA.Key.ToXmlString(True)
        System.Console.WriteLine(str)
    End Sub
End Module
```

This code creates a pair of private and public keys and prints it out at the command line in XML format. To compile the preceding code, simply open a console session, run `corvar.bat` (if necessary), set the .NET SDK paths, and compile the program by typing the following command:

```
TestRSAKey.vb
```

This should produce a file called `TestRSAKey.exe`. Execute this program and redirect the output to a file such as `key.xml`:

```
TestRSAKey > key.xml
```

The file `key.xml` contains all the private and public members of the generated RSA key object. You can open this XML file in Internet Explorer 5.5 or later. If you do so, you will notice that the private member variables are also stored in this file. The binary data representing the large integers is encoded in `Base64` format.

The program listed above uses an `RSAKeyValue` instance to generate a new key pair. The class `RSAKeyValue` is contained in the `System.Security.Cryptography.Xml` namespace. This namespace can be thought of as the XML face of the .NET cryptographic framework. It contains a specialized, lightweight implementation of XML for the purpose of cryptography, and the model allows XML objects to be signed with a digital signature.

The `System.Security.Cryptography.Xml` namespace classes depend upon the classes contained in the `System.Security.Cryptography` namespace for the actual implementation of cryptographic algorithms.

The `key.xml` file, generated by redirecting the output of the Visual Basic test program `TestRSAKey`, contains both private and public keys. However, you need to keep the private key secret while making the public key widely available. Therefore, you need to separate out the public key from the key pair. Here is the program to do it:

```
' Cryptography/TestGetPubKey.vb

Imports System.Text
Imports System.Security.Cryptography
Imports System.IO
Imports System

Module Module1
    Public Sub Main(ByVal CmdArgs() As String)
        If (CmdArgs.Length <> 1) Then
            Console.WriteLine("Usage: TestGetPubKey <key pair xml>")
            End
        End If

        Dim xstr As String = File2String(CmdArgs(0))
```

The following code creates an instance of the RSA implementation and reinitializes the internal variables through the XML formatted string:

```
        Dim rsa As RSACryptoServiceProvider = New RSACryptoServiceProvider()
        rsa.FromXmlString(xstr)

        Dim x As String = rsa.ToXmlString(False)
        Console.WriteLine(x)
    End Sub

    Public Function File2String(ByVal fname As String)
        Dim finfo As FileInfo = New FileInfo(fname)
        Dim buf() As Byte = New Byte(finfo.Length) {}
        Dim fs As FileStream = File.OpenRead(fname)

        fs.Read(buf, 0, buf.Length)
```

```
            Return (New ASCIIEncoding).GetString(buf)
      End Function
End Module
```

This program is logically similar to `TestRSAKey.vb` except that it has to read the key file and pass a different parameter in the `ToXmlString()` method.

The cryptography classes use a lightweight XML implementation, thus avoiding the elaborate ritual of parsing the fully formed generic XML data containing serialized objects. This has another advantage, speed, because it bypasses the DOM parsers. To compile the previous code, type the following:

```
vbc /r:System.Security.dll TestGetPubKey.vb
```

This should produce the file `TestGetPubKey.exe`. Run this file, giving `key.xml` as the name of the input file, and redirect the program's output to `pub.xml`. This file contains an XML formatted public key. The binary data, basically binary large integers, are `Base64` encoded. You may recall that `key.xml` contains both the public and private key pairs, and was generated by redirecting the output of `TestRSAKey.exe`. The following line redirects `key.xml`'s public key to `pub.xml`:

```
TestGetPubKey key.xml > pub.xml
```

The following program tests the encrypt and decrypt feature of the RSA algorithm:

```vb
' Cryptography/TestCrypt.vb

Imports System
Imports System.IO
Imports System.Security.Cryptography
Imports System.Text

Module Module1
    Public Sub Main(ByVal CmdArgs() As String)
        If (CmdArgs.Length <> 4) Then
            Console.WriteLine("Usage: TestCrypt <key xml> <E|D> <in> <out>")
            Console.WriteLine(" E= Encrypt, D= Decrypt (needs private key)")
            End
        End If
```

Here, you read the public or private key into memory:

```vb
Dim xstr As String = File2String(CmdArgs(0))
```

You create an instance of an RSA cryptography service provider and initialize the parameters based on the XML lightweight filename passed in `CmdArgs(0)`:

```vb
Dim RSA As New RSACryptoServiceProvider()
RSA.FromXmlString(xstr)
```

Display the key filename:

```vb
Console.WriteLine("Key File: " + CmdArgs(0))
Dim op As String= "Encrypted"
```

Read the input file and store it into a byte array:

```
Dim info As FileInfo = New FileInfo(CmdArgs(2))
Dim inbuflen As Integer = CType(info.Length, Integer)
Dim inbuf() As Byte = New Byte(inbuflen-1) {}
Dim outbuf() As Byte
Dim fs As FileStream = File.OpenRead(CmdArgs(2))

fs.Read(inbuf, 0, inbuf.Length)
fs.Close()
```

Either encrypt or decrypt depending on the CmdArgs(1) option:

```
If (CmdArgs(1).ToUpper().StartsWith("D")) Then
    op = "Decrypted"
    outbuf = rsa.Decrypt(inbuf, False)
Else
    outbuf = rsa.Encrypt(inbuf, False)
End If
```

Now, write the result in the output buffer into the file and display the result:

```
    fs = File.OpenWrite(CmdArgs(3))
    fs.Write(outbuf, 0, outbuf.Length)
    fs.Close()

    Console.WriteLine(op + " input [" + CmdArgs(2) + "] to output [" _
                    + CmdArgs(3) + "]")
End Sub
```

Here's a helper method to read the filename passed as an argument and convert the content to a string:

```
    Public Function File2String(ByVal fname As String)
        Dim finfo As FileInfo = New FileInfo(fname)
        Dim buf() As Byte = New Byte(finfo.Length) {}
        Dim fs As FileStream = File.OpenRead(fname)

        fs.Read(buf, 0, buf.Length)
        fs.Close()

        Return (New ASCIIEncoding).GetString(buf)
    End Function
End Module
```

This test program encrypts or decrypts a short file depending on the parameters supplied to it. It takes four parameters: the XML formatted private or public key file, option E or D, representing the encrypt or decrypt options, respectively, and input and output filenames.

This program can be compiled with the following command:

```
vbc /r:System.Security.dll TestCrypt.vb
```

The preceding command produces a PE file, `TestCrypt.exe`. To test the encrypt and decrypt functions, create a small plain-text file called `1.txt`. Recall that we also created two other files, `key.xml` and `pub.xml`. The file `key.xml` contains a key pair, and `pub.xml` contains the public key extracted from the file `key.xml`.

To encrypt the plain-text file `plain.txt`, use the following command:

```
TestCrypt pub.xml E 1.txt rsa.bin
```

Note that we have used the public key file to encrypt it. You can type the output on the console, but this won't make any sense because it contains binary data. You could use a binary dump utility to dump out the file's content. If you do this, note that the total number of bytes is 128, compared to the input of 13 bytes. This is because the RSA is a block cipher algorithm and the block size equals the key size, so the output is always in multiples of the block size. You may wish to rerun the preceding examples with larger files to see the resulting encrypted file length.

Now decrypt the file to get back the original text:

```
TestCrypt key.xml D rsa.bin decr.txt
```

The `key.xml` file, which also contains the private key, is used to decrypt because you use the public key to encrypt, and the private key to decrypt. In other words, anyone may send encrypted documents to you if they know your public key, but only you can decrypt such messages. The reverse is true for digital signatures, covered in the next section.

Digital Signature Basics

Digital signature is the encryption of a hash digest (for example, MD5 or SHA-1) of data using a public key. The digital signature can be verified by decrypting the hash digest and comparing it against a hash digest computed from the data by the verifier.

As noted earlier, the private key is known only to the owner, so the owner can sign a digital document by encrypting the hash computed from the document. The public key is known to all, so anyone can verify the signature by recomputing the hash and comparing it against the decrypted value, using the public key of the signer.

The .NET Framework provides DSA and RSA digital signature implementations by default. This section considers only DSA, as RSA was covered in the preceding section. Both of the implementations extend the same base class, so all programs for DSA discussed next work for RSA as well.

First, go through the same motions of producing a key pair and a public key file and then sign and verify the signature:

```
' Cryptography/GenDSAKeys.vb


Imports System
Imports System.Security.Cryptography
Imports VB_Security.FileUtil
```

```
Module Module1
    Public Sub Main(ByVal CmdArgs() As String)
        Dim dsa As DSACryptoServiceProvider = New DSACryptoServiceProvider()
        Dim prv As String = dsa.ToXmlString(True)
        Dim pub As String = dsa.ToXmlString(False)
        Dim fileutil As FileUtil = New FileUtil()

        fileutil.SaveString("dsa-key.xml", prv)
        fileutil.SaveString("dsa-pub.xml", pub)

        Console.WriteLine("Created dsa-key.xml and dsa-pub.xml")
    End Sub
End Module
```

This code generates two XML-formatted files, `dsa-key.xml` and `dsa-pub.xml`, containing private and public keys, respectively. Before you can run this, however, you need to create the `FileUtil` class used to output the two files:

```
' Cryptography/FileUtil.vb

Imports System.IO
Imports System.Text

Public Class FileUtil
    Public Sub SaveString(ByVal fname As String, ByVal data As String)
        SaveBytes(fname, (New ASCIIEncoding).GetBytes(data))
    End Sub

    Public Function LoadString(ByVal fname As String)
        Dim buf() As Byte = LoadBytes(fname)
        Return (New ASCIIEncoding).GetString(buf)
    End Function

    Public Function LoadBytes(ByVal fname As String)
        Dim finfo As FileInfo = New FileInfo(fname)
        Dim length As String = CType(finfo.Length, String)
        Dim buf() As Byte = New Byte(length) {}
        Dim fs As FileStream = File.OpenRead(fname)

        fs.Read(buf, 0, buf.Length)
        fs.Close()

        Return buf
    End Function

    Public Sub SaveBytes(ByVal fname As String, ByVal data() As Byte)
        Dim fs As FileStream = File.OpenWrite(fname)

        fs.SetLength(0)
        fs.Write(data, 0, data.Length)
        fs.Close()
    End Sub
End Class
```

The following code signs the data:

```
' Cryptography/DSASign.vb

Imports System
Imports System.IO
Imports System.Security.Cryptography
Imports System.Text
Imports VB_Security.FileUtil

Module Module1
    Public Sub Main(ByVal CmdArgs() As String)
        If CmdArgs.Length <> 3 Then
            Console.WriteLine("Usage: DSASign <key xml> <data> <sign>")
            End
        End If

        Dim fileutil As FileUtil = New FileUtil()
        Dim xkey As String = fileutil.LoadString(CmdArgs(0))
        Dim fs As FileStream = File.OpenRead(CmdArgs(1))
```

The following two lines of code create the DSA provider instance and reconstruct the private key from the XML format:

```
Dim dsa As DSACryptoServiceProvider = New DSACryptoServiceProvider()
dsa.FromXmlString(xkey)
```

The next line signs the file:

```
        Dim sig() As Byte = dsa.SignData(fs)
        fs.Close()
        fileutil.SaveString(CmdArgs(2), Convert.ToString(sig))
        Console.WriteLine("Signature in {0}} file", CmdArgs(2))
    End Sub
End Module
```

To verify the signature, you can use the following sample code:

```
' Cryptography/DSAVerify.vb

Imports System
Imports System.IO
Imports System.Security.Cryptography
Imports System.Text
Imports VB_Security.FileUtil

Module Module1
    Public Sub Main(ByVal CmdArgs() As String)
        If CmdArgs.Length <> 3 Then
            Console.WriteLine("Usage: DSAVerify <key xml> <data> <sign>")
            End
        End If
```

```
        Dim fileutil As FileUtil = New FileUtil()
        Dim xkey As String = fileutil.LoadString(CmdArgs(0))
        Dim data() As Byte = fileutil.LoadBytes(CmdArgs(1))
        Dim xsig As String = fileutil.LoadString(CmdArgs(2))
        Dim dsa As DSACryptoServiceProvider = New DSACryptoServiceProvider()

        dsa.FromXmlString(xkey)
        Dim xsigAsByte() As Byte = New Byte(xsig) {}

        Dim verify As Boolean
        verify = dsa.VerifyData(data, xsigAsByte)
        Console.WriteLine("Signature Verification is {0}", verify)
    End Sub
End Module
```

The actual verification is done using the highlighted code fragment. The next four commands compile the source files:

```
vbc /target:library FileUtil.vb
vbc /r:FileUtil.dll GenDSAKeys.vb
vbc /r:FileUtil.dll DSASign.vb
vbc /r:FileUtil.dll DSAVerify.vb
```

There are many helper classes within the System.Security.Cryptography and the System.Security.Cryptography.Xml namespaces, and they provide many features to help deal with digital signatures and encryption, and, at times, provide overlapping functionality. Therefore, there is more than one way of doing the same thing.

X.509 Certificates

X.509 is a public key certificate exchange framework. A public key certificate is a digitally signed statement by the owner of a private key, trusted by the verifier (usually a certifying authority), that certifies the validity of the public key of another entity. This creates a trust relationship between two unknown entities. This is an ISO standard specified by the document ISO/IEC 9594-8. X.509 certificates are also used in SSL (Secure Sockets Layer), which is covered in the next section.

There are many certifying authority services available over the Internet. VeriSign (www.verisign.com) is the most popular. This company was also founded by the RSA trio themselves. You can run your own Certificate Authority (CA) service over an intranet using Microsoft Certificate Server.

The Microsoft .NET Framework SDK also provides tools for generating certificates for testing purposes. The following command generates a test certificate:

```
makecert -n CN=Test test.cer
```

You can view it by double-clicking the test.cer file from Windows Explorer. The certificate is shown in Figure 12-19. From the same dialog box, you can also install this certificate on your computer by clicking the Install Certificate button.

Figure 12-19

Three classes dealing with X.509 certificates are provided in the .NET Framework in the namespace `System.Security.Cryptography.X509Certificates`. The following program loads and manipulates the certificate created earlier:

```vb
' Cryptography/LoadCert.vb

Imports System
Imports System.Security.Cryptography.X509Certificates

Module Module1
    Public Sub Main(ByVal CmdArgs() As String)
        If CmdArgs.Length <> 1 Then
            Console.Write("Usage loadCert <cert file>")
            End
        End If

        Dim cert As X509Certificate = _
            X509Certificate.CreateFromCertFile(CmdArgs(0))

        Console.WriteLine("Hash= {0}", cert.GetCertHashString())
        Console.WriteLine("Effective Date= {0}", _
                    cert.GetEffectiveDateString())
        Console.WriteLine("Expire Date= {0}", _
                    cert.GetExpirationDateString())
        Console.WriteLine("Issued By= {0}", cert.Issuer.ToString())
        Console.WriteLine("Issued To= {0}", cert.Subject.ToString())
        Console.WriteLine("Algo= {0}", cert.GetKeyAlgorithm())
```

```
        Console.WriteLine("Pub Key= {0}", cert.GetPublicKeyString())
    End Sub
End Module
```

The static method loads `CreateFromCertFile` (the certificate file) and creates a new instance of the class `X509Certificate`. The next section deals with SSL, which uses X.509 certificates to establish the trust relationship.

Secure Sockets Layer

The SSL (Secure Sockets Layer) protocol provides privacy and reliability between two communicating applications over the Internet. SSL is built over the TCP layer. In January 1999, the IETF (Internet Engineering Task Force) adopted an enhanced version of SSL 3.0 called TLS, which stands for Transport Layer Security. TLS is backwardly compatible with SSL, and is defined in RFC 2246. However, the name SSL was retained due to wide acceptance of this Netscape protocol name.

SSL provides connection-oriented security and has the following four properties:

❑   Connection is private and encryption is valid for the current session only.

❑   Symmetric key cryptography, like DES, is used for encryption. However, the session secret key is exchanged using public key encryption.

❑   Digital certificates are used to verify the identities of the communicating entities.

❑   Secure hash functions, such as SHA and MD5, are used for message authentication code (MAC).

The SSL protocol sets the following goals for itself:

❑   **Cryptographic security** — Uses symmetric key for session and public key for authentication

❑   **Interoperability** — Interpolates OS and programming languages

❑   **Extensibility** — Adds new protocols for encrypting data that are allowed within the SSL framework

❑   **Relative efficiency** — Reduces computation and network activity by using caching techniques

The following is a simplified discussion of the SSL algorithm sequence. Two entities communicating using SSL protocols must have a public-private key pair, optionally with digital certificates validating their respective public keys.

At the beginning of a session, the client and server exchange information to authenticate each other. This ritual of authentication is called the *handshake protocol*. During this, a session ID, the compression method, and the cipher suite to be used are negotiated. If the certificates exist, they are then exchanged. Although certificates are optional, either the client or the server may refuse to continue with the connection and end the session in the absence of a certificate.

After receiving each other's public keys, a set of secret keys based on a randomly generated number is exchanged by encrypting it with each other's public keys. After this, the application data exchange can commence. The application data is encrypted using a secret key, and a signed hash of the data is sent to verify data integrity.

Microsoft implements the SSL client in the .NET Framework classes. However, the server-side SSL can be used by deploying your service through the IIS Web server. The following code fragment can be used to access SSL protected Web servers from the .NET platform:

```
Dim req As WebRequest = WebRequest.Create("https://www.reuters.com")
Dim result As WebResponse = req.GetResponse()
```

Note that the preceding URL starts with `https`, which signals the `WebRequest` class (part of `System.Net`) to use the SSL protocol. Interestingly, the same code is useful for accessing unsecured URLs as well.

The following is a program for accessing a secured URL. It takes care of the minor details, such as encoding:

```
' Cryptography/GetWeb.vb

Imports System
Imports System.IO
Imports System.Net
Imports System.Text

Module Module1
    Public Sub Main(ByVal CmdArgs() As String)
        If CmdArgs.Length <> 1 Then
            Console.WriteLine("Usage: GetWeb URL")
            Console.WriteLine("Example: GetWeb https://www.reuters.com")
            End
        End If
        Dim ms As String
```

You call the `Create()` method (shown in a moment) with a URL and an encoding format:

```
    Try
        ms = Create(CmdArgs(0), "utf-8")
        Console.WriteLine(ms)
    Catch x As Exception
        Console.WriteLine(x.StackTrace)
        Console.WriteLine("Bad URL: {0}", CmdArgs(0))
    End Try
End Sub
```

Next is the `Create()` method. Using the .NET Framework `WebRequest` object, you create an HTTP secured request object and get its response stream:

```
Function Create(ByVal url As String, ByVal encod As String) As String
    Dim req As WebRequest = WebRequest.Create(url)
    Dim result As WebResponse = req.GetResponse()
    Dim ReceiveStream As Stream = result.GetResponseStream()
```

Create an encoding instance from the .NET Framework object, `Encoding`:

```
Dim enc As Encoding = System.Text.Encoding.GetEncoding(encod)
```

Here, you create the stream reader:

```
Dim sr As StreamReader = New StreamReader(ReceiveStream, enc)
```

You read the stream fully — the entire Web page or serialized object is read into the `responseString`:

```
        Dim response As String = sr.ReadToEnd()
        Return response
    End Function
    Dim MaxContentLength As Integer = 16384 ' 16k
End Module
```

The preceding console application gets a secured (SSL) protected URL and displays the content on the console. To compile the code, use the following command:

```
vbc /r:System.dll GetWeb.vb
```

Summary

This chapter covered the basics of security and cryptography. It started with an overview of the security architecture of the .NET Framework and looked at four types of security: NTFS, security policies, cryptographic, and programmatic.

It went on to examine the security tools and functionality that the .NET Framework provides. You examined the `System.Security.Permissions` namespace and learned how you can control code access permissions, role-based permissions, and identity permissions. You also learned how you can manage code access permissions and security policies for your code. Two tools were used — `Caspol.exe` and `Permview.exe` — to help configure and view security at both the machine and user levels.

The second half of the chapter looked at cryptography, both the underlying theory and how it can be applied within your applications. You looked at the different types of cryptographic hash algorithms, including SHA, MD5, Secret Key Encryption, and PKCS. You should also understand how you can use digital certificates (specifically, X.509 certificates) and Secure Socket Layers.

13

Visual Studio 2005

In theory, it's possible to work with Visual Basic without Visual Studio 2005. In practice, however, the two are rather inseparable; without a version of Visual Studio 2005, you're forced to work from the command line to create project files by hand and make calls to the associated compilers and related tools necessary to build your application. Thus, while it is possible and, as shown in Chapter 17, sometimes even necessary, to work outside the Visual Studio 2005 Integrated Development Environment (IDE), Visual Studio 2005 is the preferred environment for developing Visual Basic applications.

With the release of Visual Studio 2005, Microsoft expanded on the different versions of Visual Studio available for use. Unlike the early versions, they've expanded what we'll call the high-end and low-end packages associated with Visual Studio. At the low-cost end, currently free, is Visual Basic 2005 Express Edition. This tool enables you to build desktop applications with Visual Basic only. At the high end, Microsoft offers Visual Studio Team System, available only with a high-cost MSDN subscription, which includes many tools that help improve collaboration between developers.

Of course, the focus of this chapter is how Visual Studio enables you to use Visual Basic to build applications geared toward "better, faster, cheaper" business goals. To this end, we'll be examining features of Visual Studio starting with those in the Core Visual Basic 2005 Express Edition and building up to the full Visual Studio Team Suite. Topics include the following:

- ❏ Versions of Visual Studio
- ❏ Project templates
- ❏ Project properties — application, compilation, debug, etc.
- ❏ Forms as classes
- ❏ Setting form properties
- ❏ IntelliSense, code expansion, and code snippets
- ❏ Selecting a runtime environment

- [ ] Debugging
- [ ] Recording and using macros
- [ ] Class Designer
- [ ] Visual Studio tools for Office
- [ ] Team System — Team Suite Client Tools
- [ ] Team Foundation Server — Team Explorer

This chapter provides an overview of many of the capabilities of Visual Studio 2005, with a brief intro-duction to the features available by using one of the more feature-rich versions of Visual Studio. The goal is to demonstrate how Visual Studio makes you, as a developer, more productive and successful.

Visual Studio 2005 Versions from Express through Team Suite

First we should clarify one thing that's common across all versions of Visual Studio 2005. This version of the IDE was designed to work with version 2.0 of the .NET Framework. Microsoft introduced Visual Studio 2005 with .NET 2.0 and the two items went through development as a single unit. It will be impor-tant to remember that Visual Studio 2005 was optimized for .NET 2.0, as opposed to .NET 1.x or .NET 3.0.

Similar to the way that Visual Studio 2003 was focused on .NET 1.1 and Visual Studio .NET (2002) was focused on .NET 1.0, each version of Visual Studio is optimized for a particular version of .NET. Similarly, even though the title of this book is .NET 3.0, the various versions of Visual Studio 2005 are actually opti-mized for .NET 2.0, and with the exception of unsupported add-ons, don't support the new features of .NET 3.0.

Fortunately, Microsoft chose to keep Visual Basic and ASP.NET unchanged for the .NET 3.0 Framework release. However, when looking at the new .NET 3.0 Framework elements such as Windows Presentation Foundation, Windows Communication Foundation, and Windows Workflow Foundation, these items need to be addressed outside of Visual Studio. Thus, while Visual Studio 2005 is separate from Visual Basic and .NET development, in practical terms the two are tightly coupled.

With those ground rules in place, what versions of Visual Studio 2005 are available and what are the pri-mary differences between them? As already mentioned, Visual Basic 2005 Express is at the bottom tier in terms of price and features. It is accompanied there by Visual Web Developer 2005 Express Edition for those developers who are developing Web applications as opposed to desktop applications. These two tools are separate, but both support developing different types of Visual Basic applications, and coinci-dentally both are free.

In addition, these two development tools ship with two additional components covered briefly here: MSDN Express Edition and SQL Server 2005 Express Edition. MSDN is, of course, the Microsoft Developer Network, which has placed most of its content online. It's the source for not only the core lan-guage documentation for Visual Basic, but also articles on almost every product oriented to developers using Microsoft technology. Full versions of Visual Studio ship with the full MSDN library so that you can access its content locally. However, the Express Edition tools actually ship with a pared-down 200 MB set of documentation files — of course, that's still a lot of documentation.

Similar to the language and Web-based tools, Microsoft has a SQL Server Express Edition package. This package actually has a history, in that it replaces the MSDE database engine that was available with SQL Server 2000. The new SQL Server Express engine provides the core SQL Server 2005 database engine. Unlike MSDE, it also offers a free management application available via separate download from Microsoft.

When you install Visual Studio 2005, including the Express Editions, you are also given an opportunity to install this core database engine. The elements of this engine are freely redistributable, so if you are looking for a set of core database features based on ADO.NET, you can create your application and deploy your SQL Server 2005 Express Edition database without being concerned about licensing. SQL Server is covered in more detail in Chapter 14.

Getting back to the differences in versions, the Express Edition tools provide the core components necessary to create Visual Basic applications (Windows or Web) based on the core IDE. The following table provides a quick summary of what versions are available, including a description of how each extends Visual Studio:

Visual Studio Edition	Description
Visual Basic 2005 Express Edition	This is the core set of functionality required for creating Windows-based applications. Includes the IDE with full local debugging support and support for three project types — Windows Application, Dynamic Link Library, and Console Application. Includes two starter kits, with additional starter kits available for download.
Visual Web Developer 2005 Express Edition	This is the core set of functionality required for building Web applications. It supports both Visual Basic and C# and allows for local debugging of your Web application. Includes a starter kit.
Visual Studio 2005 Standard Edition	Provides a combined development language for the core Visual Studio languages (J#, VB, C# and C++). Adds the Object Modeling tool. Provides combined support for both Windows and Web applications and provides additional support for application deployment. It also provides support for Mobile Application Development, integration with a source control tool, and macros within Visual Studio.
Visual Studio 2005 Professional Edition	Expands on Visual Studio Standard Edition with additional integration to SQL Server and support for XSLTs. Also allows for remote debugging of Web applications.
Visual Studio 2005 Tools for Office	A suite that can be combined with other Visual Studio 2005 products, this package provides support for Office integration with .NET 2.0. It supports only VB and C# but also adds native support for Microsoft Access 2003.

Table continues on the next page

Visual Studio Edition	Description
Visual Studio 2005 Team Edition for*	When Visual Studio 2005 was released, Microsoft provided three specialized versions of Visual Studio 2005 Team Suite, each of which contained everything from the previously mentioned versions (combine Visual Studio 2005 Professional Edition with Visual Studio Tools for Office) plus a subset of the Team Suite client tools. The editions were Team Edition for Architects, Team Edition for Developers, and Team Edition for Testers. Since then, Microsoft has announced a fourth edition, Team Edition for Database Developers. Each edition contains a subset of the full Team Suite of tools, and includes a client license for Microsoft Team Foundation Server. These must be purchased as part of an annual MSDN package.
Visual Studio 2005 Team Suite	The full Team Suite includes all of the core features of Visual Studio 2005 Professional Edition and Visual Studio Tools for Office. It also includes all of the tools from Visual Studio Team Suite — static code analysis, code profiling (performance testing), unit tests (which may be written in Visual Basic), application and deployment graphical design tools, Web and load-testing tools, and a variety of related tools to enhance development. This tool, like the Team Edition versions of Visual Studio, is focused on enabling developers to be productive in a shared collaborative environment. It works best when combined with Microsoft Team Foundation Server for source control and collaboration capabilities.

The Express Edition tools are best described as targeting students and hobbyists, not because you can't create serious applications but because they provide only limited support for a shared development environment. For example, one of the starter kits available for Visual Basic 2005 Express Edition is a sample of integration with Lego's Mindstorms. Again, the Express Tools are oriented toward a developer who works independently, while still providing full access to features of the Visual Basic language, which is why this chapter begins by using this version of the IDE.

Eventually, however, a developer needs additional tools and projects. This is where the full versions of Visual Studio 2005 (Standard and Professional) come in. With an increasing level of support for team development, the more advanced versions add macro support and, more importantly, an Object Modeling tool that is amazing. As discussed later in this chapter, the Object Modeling tool enables you to create a visual representation of the classes in your solution and then convert that representation into code. Moreover, the tool supports what is known as *round-trip engineering*. This means that not only can you use the graphical model to generate code, you can also take a project's source files and regenerate an updated version of the graphical model — that is, edit that model in its graphical format and then update the associated source files.

Visual Studio Tools for Office (VSTO) is targeted primarily at enterprise developers, developers who work in corporate organizations (either as employees or consultant/contractors). This tool provides a way for users of the enterprise editions of Microsoft Office 2003 to extend these office productivity tools with applicationlike features. Many organizations use Microsoft Office for tasks that border on custom applications. This is especially true for Microsoft Excel. VSTO provides project templates based on these Microsoft Office products that enable, for example, a spreadsheet to retrieve its contents from an SQL Server database instead of the local file system. These tools provide the capability not only to manipulate data retrieval and saving, but also to customize the user interface, including direct access to the Task Pane and custom toolbar options within Microsoft Office products.

Visual Studio 2005 Team Suite and the various Team Edition products focus on extending a developer's reach beyond just writing code. These tools are used to examine code for flaws, manage the deployment environment, or define relationships between applications. The suite is focused on tools that support repeatable software processes and best practices. They are geared toward examining source code for hidden flaws that might not cause the code to fail but might hide a hidden security flaw or make it difficult to maintain or deploy the application. More importantly, the suite includes tools for creating unit test tools that can attempt to cause the code to fail, whether through bad input data or heavy load. The Team Suite tools are focused on automating software development best practices for application teams, as opposed to actually writing the application.

Complete coverage of all of Team System warrants a book of its own, especially when you take into account all of the collaborative features introduced by Team Foundation Server and its tight integration with both Team Build and SharePoint Server. Team Foundation Server goes beyond just being a replacement for Visual Source Safe. It is the basis for true process-driven development, and it even includes documentation to help train your organization on two process models supported by Microsoft. The Team System extensions to the Microsoft software development suite are nontrivial, and are discussed in more detail at the end of this chapter.

Creating a Project from a Project Template

While it is possible to create a Visual Basic application working entirely outside of Visual Studio 2005, it is much easier to start from Visual Studio 2005. After you install Visual Studio you are presented with a screen similar to the one shown in Figure 13-1 for Visual Studio 2005 Express Edition. The default behavior is for the IDE to start by displaying this start page in its central section. The start page lists your most recent projects in the upper left corner, some tips for getting started below that, and a headline section below that. You may or may not immediately recognize that this content is essentially HTML text; more important, the right-side content is based on a Web Service call that retrieves and caches articles appropriate for your version of Visual Studio.

The start page looks similar regardless of which version of Visual Studio 2005 you are running. The idea is to provide a generic starting point either to select the application you intend to work on, to quickly receive vital news related to offers, as shown in the figure, or to connect with external resources via the community links.

Once here, the next step is to create your first project. Selecting File ➪ New Project opens the New Project dialog, shown in Figure 13-2. This dialog provides you with a selection of templates customized by application type. One option is to create a Class Library project. Such a project doesn't include a user interface; and instead of creating an assembly with an .EXE file, it creates an assembly with a .DLL file. The difference, of course, is that an .EXE file indicates an executable that can be started by the operating system, whereas a .DLL file represents a library referenced by an application.

> *One of the ongoing challenges with describing the menu options for Visual Studio is that the different versions have slight differences in look and feel too numerous to mention. For example File ➪ New Project in Visual Basic Express becomes File ➪ New ➪ Project in Visual Studio. Thus, your display may vary slightly from what is shown or described here, although we attempt to showcase significant differences.*

Figure 13-1

Figure 13-2

Noteworthy in Figure 13-2 are the starter kits, which are included with Visual Basic 2005 Express Edition. These kits go beyond just the basic files associated with a generic project template and include source files associated with a specific application. You'll also note that the dialog includes a reference to My Templates. This section of the New Project window enables you to install additional templates. For example, the Microsoft site for Visual Basic includes several additional starter kits for Lego Mindstorms, a blackjack game, and others you can install. Additionally, third parties such as Dot Net Nuke provide custom templates associated with their application. Dot Net Nuke is an excellent example of this, and the version 4.4 starter kit package installs three templates in Visual Studio, two in Visual Basic and one in C#.

In order to keep the discussion of project templates in context, Figure 13-3 is an example of the same dialog opened from Visual Studio 2005 Team Suite. In this context, note that not only do you have additional project templates related to Visual Basic, but another pane that groups the templates into project types has been added. Figures 13-2 and 13-3 have different display options selected in the upper-right corner related to the size of the template icons only.

A quick note regarding the New Project dialog: Not all project types are listed within this dialog. If you want to create an ASP.NET 2.0 website, you need to start that process by creating a new website instead of creating a new project. This option is not available to Visual Basic Express users; instead, these users should install the Visual Web Developer 2005 Express Edition, which has a similar user interface (not shown here). Finally, note that Visual Studio 2005 Service Pack 1 added the ASP.NET 1.x application projects back into this dialog, as well as a template for Outlook-based VSTO projects.

Figure 13-3

Expanding the top level of the Visual Basic tree in Figure 13-3 shows that a project type can be further separated into a series of categories:

❏ **Windows** — Projects used to create applications that run on the local computer within the CLR. Because such projects can run on any operating system (OS) hosting the framework, the category "Windows" is something of a misnomer.

❏ **Office** — Visual Studio Tools for Office (VSTO). These are .NET applications that are hosted under Office 2003. Note that templates are provided for Excel and Word only.

❏ **Smart Device** — These are projects that target the .NET Compact Framework. Such applications may run on one or more handheld devices and make use of a different runtime environment from full .NET applications.

❏ **Database** — This template creates a project that supports classes that will run within SQL Server 2005. All versions of SQL Server 2005 (from Express through Enterprise) support the .NET Framework as part of their runtime, and such projects have a unique set of runtime constraints. This is a very different project template from the Database project template provided under Visual Studio 2003 and still available under the Other Project Types option.

❏ **Starter Kits** — The same starter kits shown in the default view for the Visual Basic 2005 Express Edition are available under this section.

❏ **Test** — This section is available only to those using Visual Studio Team Suite. It contains the template for a Visual Basic Unit Test project.

❏ **Web** — With Visual Studio Service Pack 1, the ASP.NET 1.x project file-based Web applications were restored to Visual Studio 2005. ASP.NET eliminated the need for Web applications to use project files; however, some developers found this counterintuitive and Microsoft restored the capability to identify the files of a Web application as part of a project file.

Visual Studio has other categories for projects, and you have access to other development languages and far more project types than this chapter has room for. For now, you can select a Windows Application project template to use as an example project for this chapter.

For this example, use `ProVB.NET` as the project name and then click the OK button. Visual Studio takes over and uses the Windows Application template to create a new Windows Forms project. The project contains a blank form that can be customized, and a variety of other elements that you can explore. Before customizing any code, let's first look at the elements of this new project.

The Solution Explorer

While the solution window both exists and is applicable for Express Edition users, it will never contain more than a single project. Those with a version of Visual Studio above the Express Edition level have the capability to leverage multiple projects in a single solution. A .NET solution can contain projects of any .NET language and can include the database, testing, and installation projects as part of the overall solution. The advantage of combining these projects is that it is easier to debug projects that are in a common solution.

Before discussing these files in detail, let's take a look at the next step, which is to reveal a few additional details about your project. Click the second button on the left in Solution Explorer to display all of the project files, as shown in Figure 13-4. As this image shows, there are many other files that make up your project. Some of these, such as those under the My Project grouping, don't require you to edit them directly. Instead, you can double-click on the My Project entry in the Solution Explorer and open the pages to edit your project settings. You do not need to change any of the default settings for this project, but the next section of this chapter walks you through the various property screens.

The `bin` and `obj` directories shown are used when building your project. The `obj` directory contains the first-pass object files used by the compiler to create your final executable file. The "binary" or compiled version of your application is then placed in the `bin` directory by default. Of course, referring to the Microsoft Intermediate Language (MSIL) code as binary is something of a misnomer, as the actual translation to binary does not occur until runtime when your application is compiled by the Just-In-Time (JIT) compiler. However, Microsoft continues to use the `bin` directory as the default output directory for your project's compilation.

Figure 13-4

Figure 13-4 also shows that the project does not contain an `app.config` file by default. Most experienced ASP.NET developers are familiar with the use of `web.config` files. `App.config` files work on the same principle in that they contain XML, which is used to store project-specific settings such as database connection strings and other application-specific settings. Using a `.config` file instead of having your settings in the Windows registry enables your applications to run side by side with another version of the application without the settings from either version impacting the other. Because each version of your application resides in its own directory, its settings are contained in the directory with it, which enables the different versions to run with unique settings. Before we are done going through the project properties, we will add an `App.Config` file to this project.

Finally, the Solution Explorer includes your actual source file(s). In this case, the `Form1.vb` file is the primary file associated with the default Windows form. You'll be customizing this form shortly, but before looking at that, it seems appropriate to look at some of the settings available by opening your project properties. An easy way to do this is to double-click on the My Project heading shown in Figure 13-4.

My Project Properties

Visual Studio displays a vertically tabbed display for editing your project settings. The My Project display shown in Figure 13-5, which is the view for users of Express Edition, is the same for all versions of Visual Studio. The project properties give you access to several different aspects of your project. Some, such as Signing, Security, and Publish, are covered in later chapters. For now, just note that this display makes it easier to carry out several tasks that once required engineers to work outside the Visual Studio environment.

Notice that you can customize your assembly name from this screen, as well as reset the type of application and object to be referenced when starting your application. However, resetting the type of your application is not recommended. If you start with the wrong application type, it is better to create a new application, due to all the embedded settings in the application template.

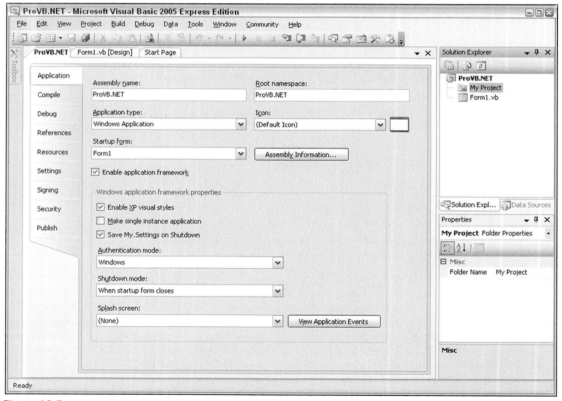

Figure 13-5

In the next section you will look at a button for changing your assembly information, as well as the capability to define a root namespace for your application classes. Namespaces are covered in detail in Chapter 8, and unlike C#, which requires you to explicitly set the namespace in each source file, Visual Basic allows you to define a default.

Assembly Information Screen

Selecting the Assembly Information button from within your My Project window opens the Assembly Information dialog box. Within this dialog, shown in Figure 13-6, it is possible to define file properties, such as your company's name and versioning information, which will be embedded in the operating system's file attributes for your project's output. The frame of the assembly file shows that by default it contains several standard values. This dialog is new to Visual Studio 2005 and replaces the way that engineers were forced to directly edit the XML contained in the `AssemblyInfo.vb` source file associated with an application.

Figure 13-6

Assembly Attributes

The `AssemblyInfo.vb` file contains attribute blocks, which are used to set information about the assembly. Each attribute block has an *assembly modifier,* shown in the following example:

```
<Assembly: AssemblyTitle("")>
```

All the attributes set within this file provide information that is contained within the assembly metadata. These properties are displayed in the Assembly Information dialog, which is opened from the project's properties page (select the Compile tab and then click the Assembly Information button). The attributes contained within the file are summarized in the following table:

Attribute	Description
Title	Sets the name of the assembly, which appears within the file properties of the compiled file as the Description
Description	This attribute is used to provide a textual description of the assembly, which is added to the Comments property for the file.
Company	Sets the name of the company that produced the assembly. The name set here appears within the Version tab of the file properties.
Product	Sets the product name of the resulting assembly. The product name appears within the Version tab of the file properties.
Copyright	The copyright information for the assembly. This value appears on the Version tab of the file properties.
Trademark	Used to assign any trademark information to the assembly. This information appears on the Version tab of the file properties.
Assembly Version	This attribute is used to set the version number of the assembly. Assembly version numbers can be generated, which is the default setting for .NET applications. This is covered in more detail in Chapter 21.
File Version	This attribute is used to set the version number of the executable files. This and other deployment-related settings are covered in more detail in Chapter 21.
COM Visible	This attribute is used to indicate whether this assembly should be registered and made available to COM applications.
Guid	If the assembly is to be exposed as a traditional COM object, then the value of this attribute becomes the ID of the resulting type library.

Not requiring developers to edit these settings directly at the XML level is one of the many ways in which Visual Studio 2005 was designed to enhance developer productivity over Visual Studio 2003.

Compile Settings

The Compile tab (see Figure 13-7) was previously shown in Chapter 2, but that was the version associated with Visual Basic Express Edition. This is one of two screens in the project settings that varies between versions of Visual Studio 2005. Specifically, there are two differences between this screen and the version shown in Chapter 2.

The first difference is at the top of the page, where you can select from Configuration settings. These settings refer to how your project is compiled in Debug or Release mode. Because these versions are only available when working with Visual Studio 2005 Standard or above, the discussion of these build configuration settings is handled later in this chapter in the section entitled "Build Configurations." For Visual Basic Express Edition developers, just recognize that your application always builds in debug mode until you deploy/publish the project, in which case the project is automatically compiled in release mode.

As noted in Chapter 2, Visual Basic 2005 supports the default configuration elements `Option Explicit` and `Option Strict`, which automatically reset several of the settings shown in the dialog. In most cases, it is recommended that you enable both `Option Explicit` and `Option Strict`.

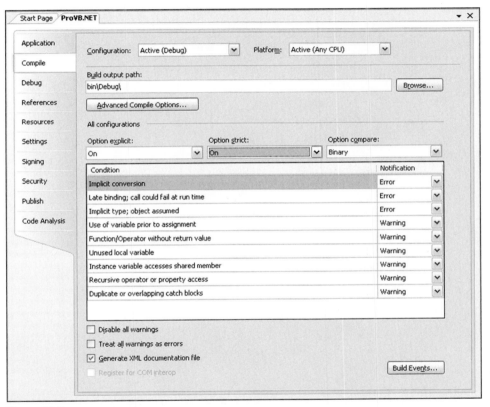

Figure 13-7

Below the grid of individual settings in Figure 13-7 is a series of check boxes. The first two relate to warnings and neither is enabled. They are mutually exclusive, and the first makes warning messages disappear, which is probably a bad idea. The alternative is to treat warnings like errors, which may cause more trouble than it's worth, especially when you consider some of the items that generate warnings. Next, notice that near the bottom of the dialog is an option to generate XML comments for your assembly. These comments are generated based on the XML comments that you enter for each of the classes, methods, and properties in your source file. Unfortunately, these last settings are not available for Visual Basic 2005 Express Edition developers, although creating such comments, as shown later in this chapter, is possible even for Express Edition users.

Debug Properties

The Express Edition of Visual Basic 2005 supports local debugging. This means it supports not only the .NET-related Debug and Trace classes discussed in Chapter 9, but actual breakpoints and the associated interactive debugging available in all versions of Visual Studio. However, as noted, the full versions of Visual Studio provide enhanced debugging options not available in Visual Basic 2005 Express Edition. Figures 13-8 and 13-9 show the project debugger startup options from Visual Basic Express and Visual Studio 2005 Team Suite, respectively. Note that the Express Edition page has only three of the settings that are part of the more expensive version of Visual Studio.

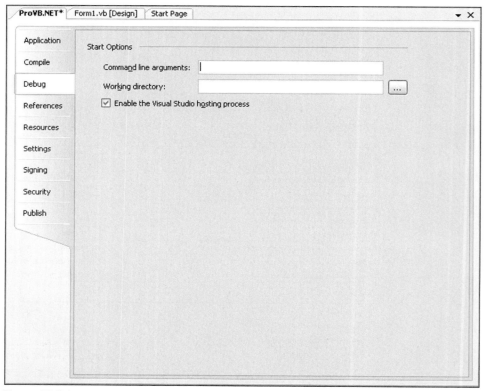

Figure 13-8

As shown in Figure 13-8, Express Edition users have three options related to starting the debugger. The first is to apply command-line arguments to the startup of a given application. This, of course, is most useful for Console applications, but in some cases developers add command-line parameters to GUI applications. The second option is to select a different directory to be used to run the application. Generally, this isn't necessary, but it's desirable in some cases because of path or permission require-ments or having an isolated runtime area.

Figure 13-9

Figure 13-9 shows additional options, beginning with Start Action. The default action shown is actually the only option available to Express users — which is to start the current project. However, Visual Studio 2005 developers have two additional options. The first is to start an external program. In other words, if you are working on a DLL or a user control, then you might want to have that application start, which can then execute your assembly. Doing this is essentially a shortcut from needing to bind to a running process.

Similarly for Web development, you can reference a specific URL to start that Web application. This is often a mixed blessing, as with ASP.NET 2.0 Visual Studio automatically attempts to start an ASP.NET application based on the page you are currently editing. This is a change from ASP.NET 1.x, which allowed you to define a start page. Because ASP.NET 2.0 does not use project files, the new behavior was introduced. In most cases it works just fine, but if you have a Web application requiring authentication, then in most cases it makes more sense to actually place that URL into the debug settings for your application.

The next set of options aligns with those of the Express Edition, except for that third item — Use remote machine. As noted, Visual Studio 2005 provides support for remote debugging, although such debugging is often more trouble than it's worth. Using the Debug and Trace classes and effective error handling, it is generally easier to determine remote errors with existing tools. However, for those rare environments where an application only runs on a central server, and for which developers have the necessary permissions to run the debugger but not a copy of Visual Studio on that server, it is possible to leverage remote debugging.

Finally, as might be expected, users of Visual Studio 2005 who work with multiple languages and are given tools to tightly integrate with SQL Server have additional debuggers. The first of these is support for debugging outside of the CLR — what is known as *unmanaged code*. As a Visual Basic developer, the only time you should be using unmanaged code is when you are referencing legacy COM components. The developers most likely to use this debugger work in C++. The next option turns on support for SQL Server debugging, a potentially useful feature. In short, it's possible, although the steps are not trivial, to have the Visual Studio debugging engine step directly into T-SQL stored procedures so that you can see the interim results as they occur within a complex stored procedure.

References

It's possible to add additional references as part of your project. Similar to the default code files that are created with a new project, each project template has a default set of referenced libraries. Actually, it has a set of imported namespaces and then a subset of the imported namespaces also referenced across the project. This means that while you can easily reference the classes in the referenced namespaces, you still need to fully qualify a reference to, for example, a `System.Collections.Generics.List` class. For Windows Forms applications, the list of default referenced namespaces is fairly short:

Reference	Description
System	Often referred to as the root namespace. All the base datatypes (`String`, `Object`, and so on) are contained within the `System` namespace. This namespace also acts as the root for all other `System` classes.
System.Data	Classes associated with ADO.NET and database access. This namespace is the root for SQL Server, Oracle, and other data access classes.
System.Deployment	Classes used for One Touch Deployment. This namespace is covered in more detail in Chapter 22.
System.Drawing	Provides access to the GDI+ graphics functionality
System.Windows.Forms	Classes used to create traditional Windows-based applications. This namespace is covered in more detail in Chapters 15 and 16.
System.XML	Root namespace for all of the XML classes

To review the details of the imported and referenced namespaces, select the References tab in your My Project display, as shown in Figure 13-10. Note that this tab enables you to check for unused references and even define reference paths. More important, it is from this tab that you select other .NET class libraries and applications, as well as COM components. Selecting the Add drop-down button gives you the option to add a reference to a local DLL or a Web Service.

When referencing DLLs you have three options: reference an assembly from the GAC, reference an assembly based on a file path, or reference another assembly from within your current solution. Each of these options has advantages and disadvantages. The only challenge for assemblies that are in the GAC is that your application is dependent on what is potentially a shared resource. In general, however, for assemblies that are already in the GAC, referencing them is a straightforward, easily maintainable process.

Figure 13-10

Similarly, referencing assemblies that are part of other projects in your solution is straightforward and highly recommended when possible. Because Visual Studio can map updates to these assemblies as they occur during a build of the solution, it's possible for Visual Studio to automatically update the referenced assemblies in your executable project to be the latest build of the referenced DLLs that are part of the same solution. Note that the target needs to be an executable. Visual Studio will automatically update references between DLL projects in a common solution.

This is different from adding a reference to a DLL that is located within a specified directory. When you create a reference via a path specification, Visual Studio can check that path for an updated copy of the reference, but your code is no longer as portable as it would be with a project reference. More important, unless there is a major revision, Visual Studio usually fails to detect the types of changes you are likely to make to that file during the development process. As a result, you'll need to manually update the referenced file in the local directory of the assembly that's referencing it. In general, unless you have only the compiled version of that assembly, it's best to leverage project references versus path-based references.

Resources

In addition to referencing other assemblies, it is quite common for a .NET application to need to reference things such as images, icons, audio, and other files. These files aren't used to provide application logic but are used at runtime to provide support for the look, feel, and even text used to communicate with the application's user. In theory, you can reference a series of images associated with your application by looking for those images based on the installed file path of your application. Doing so, however, places your application's runtime behavior at risk, because a user might choose to replace, copy for profit, or just delete your files.

This is where project references become useful. Instead of placing the raw files onto the operating system alongside your executable, Visual Studio will package these files into your executable so that they are less likely to be lost or damaged. Figure 13-11 shows the Resources tab, which enables you to review and edit all your existing resources within a project, as well as import files for use as resources in your project. It even allows you to create new resources from scratch.

Note one little-known feature of this tab: Using the Add Resource drop-down button and selecting an image (not an existing image but one based on one of the available image types) will create a new image file and automatically open Microsoft Paint (for Express Edition developers); this enables you to actually create the image that will be in the image file. Users of Visual Studio 2005 have additional capabilities not supported by Visual Basic's Express Edition.

For one thing, instead of needing to use Paint, Visual Studio provides a basic image editing tool, so when Visual Studio developers add a new image (not from a file), this editor opens within Visual Studio.

Additionally, within the list of Add Resource items, Visual Studio users can select or create a new icon. Choosing to create a new icon opens Visual Studio's icon editor, which provides a basic set of tools for creating custom icons to use as part of your application. This makes working with .ico files easier in that you don't have to hunt or purchase such files from the Internet and can instead create your own icons. However, images aren't the only resources that you can embed with your executable.

Resources also apply to the fixed text strings that your application uses. By default, people tend to embed this text directly into the source code so that it is easily accessible to the developer. Unfortunately, this leaves the application difficult to localize for use with a second language. The solution is to group all of those text strings together and thus create a resource file containing all of the text strings, which is still part of and easily accessible to the application source code. When the application is converted for use in another language, this list of strings can be converted, making the process of localization easier. Localization is covered further in Chapter 6.

Settings

New support for application settings within .NET 2.0 is a major enhancement that is often overlooked. In .NET 1.x it was possible to create a settings file. As noted earlier in the discussion of the Solution Explorer, the default project template does not create any application settings; accordingly, an App.Config file is not needed and not created. App.Config files are XML files that define any custom application settings that a developer wants to be able to change without needing to recompile the application. Because these settings live in an XML file, they can be modified in between or even during application execution.

One original goal of .NET was to reduce the version conflict that occurs when a component has registered with global settings and two different applications are attempting to reference two different versions of that component. Because the settings were global and stored in the central system registry, the result was a conflict as the different applications each wanted its specific component and related settings.

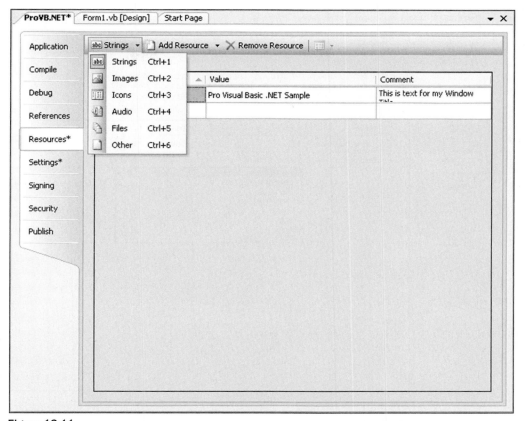

Figure 13-11

.NET provided the capability to place version-specific project references in a local directory with the application, enabling two different applications to reference the appropriate version of that component. However, the second part of the problem was the central application settings. The App.config file provides the same capability, but its goal is allowing for local storage of application settings. Under .NET 1.x, support for application settings was still minimal, as most developers were still looking to the central system registry for this purpose. At the same time, the developer tools associated with settings were also minimal.

Fortunately, under .NET 2.0 this changed dramatically. Visual Basic 2005 provides significant support for application settings, including the Settings tab shown in Figure 13-12. This tab enables Visual Basic developers to identify application settings and automatically create these settings within the App.config file.

Figure 13-12 illustrates several elements related to the application settings capabilities of Visual Basic. The first setting is of type String. Under .NET 1.x, all application settings were seen as strings, and this was considered a weakness. Accordingly, you can see that the second setting, LastLocation, exposes the Type drop-down, illustrating that under Visual Basic 2005 you can create a setting that has a well-defined type.

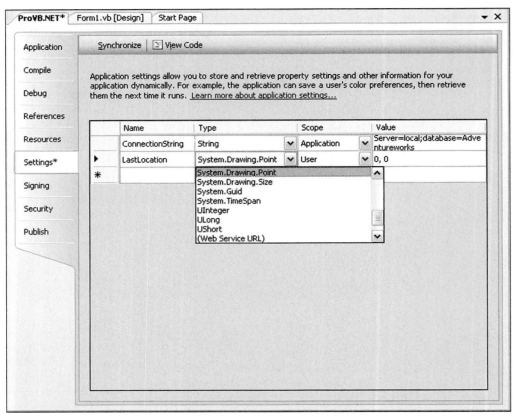

Figure 13-12

However, strongly typed settings are not the most significant set of changes related to application settings. The very next column defines the scope of a setting. There are two possible choices — application wide or user specific. The settings defined with application scope are available to all users of the application. As shown in Figure 13-12, this example creates a sample connection string to store for the application.

The alternative is a user-specific setting. Such settings have a default value; in this case, the last location defaults to 0,0. However, once a user has read that default setting, the application generally will update and save the user-specific value for that setting. As noted by the Last Location setting, each user of this application might close the application after having moved it to a new location on the screen, and the goal of such a setting would be to reopen the application in the same location it was last seen. Thus, the application would update this setting value, and Visual Basic makes it easy to do this, as shown in the following code:

```
My.Settings.LastLocation = Me.Location
My.Settings.Save()
```

That's right — all it takes in Visual Basic 2005 is two lines of code that leverage the My namespace for you to update a user's application setting and save the new value. Meanwhile, let's take a look at what is occurring within the newly generated App.config file. The following XML settings demonstrate how the App.config file defines the setting values that you manipulate from within Visual Studio:

```xml
<?xml version="1.0" encoding="utf-8" ?>
<configuration>
    <configSections>
        <sectionGroup name="applicationSettings" type=
"System.Configuration.ApplicationSettingsGroup, System, Version=2.0.0.0,
Culture=neutral, PublicKeyToken=b77a5c561934e089" >
            <section name="ProVB.NET.My.MySettings" type=
"System.Configuration.ClientSettingsSection, System, Version=2.0.0.0,
Culture=neutral, PublicKeyToken=b77a5c561934e089" requirePermission="false" />
        </sectionGroup>
        <sectionGroup name="userSettings" type=
"System.Configuration.UserSettingsGroup, System, Version=2.0.0.0, Culture=neutral,
PublicKeyToken=b77a5c561934e089" >
            <section name="ProVB.NET.My.MySettings" type=
"System.Configuration.ClientSettingsSection, System, Version=2.0.0.0,
Culture=neutral, PublicKeyToken=b77a5c561934e089"
allowExeDefinition="MachineToLocalUser" requirePermission="false" />
        </sectionGroup>
    </configSections>

    <applicationSettings>
        <ProVB.NET.My.MySettings>
            <setting name="ConnectionString" serializeAs="String">
                <value>Server=local;database=Adventureworks</value>
            </setting>
        </ProVB.NET.My.MySettings>
    </applicationSettings>

    <userSettings>
        <ProVB.NET.My.MySettings>
            <setting name="LastLocation" serializeAs="String">
                <value>0, 0</value>
            </setting>
        </ProVB.NET.My.MySettings>
    </userSettings>
</configuration>
```

As you can see, Visual Studio has automatically generated all the XML needed to define these settings and save the default values. It is possible not only to update application settings with Visual Basic, but also to arrange to encrypt those settings, although this action is outside the scope of what you can do from Visual Studio.

There are additional tabs related to your project's properties, but these are primarily associated with deployment. Therefore, in the interest of getting to some code, let's look at the source files that were generated when you created the ProVB.NET project from the Windows application template.

Project ProVB.NET in Visual Studio

The Form Designer opens by default when a new project is created. If you have closed it, you can easily reopen it by right-clicking Form1.vb in the Solution Explorer and selecting View Designer from the pop-up menu. From this window, you can also bring up the code view for this form. However, Figure 13-13 illustrates the default view you get when your project template completes. On the screen is the design surface upon which you can drag controls from the Toolbox to build your user interface and update properties associated with your form.

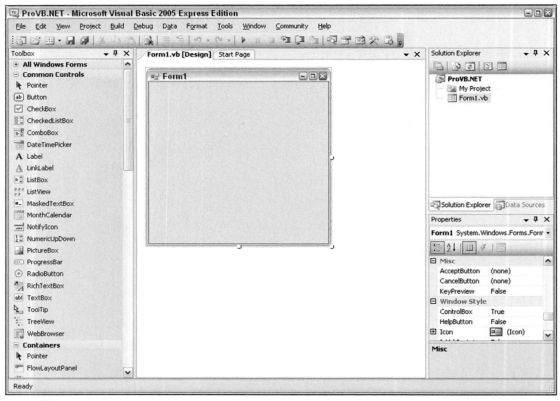

Figure 13-13

The Properties pane, shown in more detail in Figure 13-14, is by default placed in the lower-right corner of the Visual Studio window. Like many of the other windows in the IDE, if you close it, it can be accessed through the View menu. Alternatively, you can use the F4 key to reopen this window. The Properties window is used to set the properties of the currently selected item control in the display.

Each control you place on your form has its own distinct set of properties. For example, in the design view, select your form. You'll see the Properties window adjust to display the properties of Form1, as shown in Figure 13-14. This is the list of properties associated with your form. If you want to limit how small a user can reduce the display area of your form, then you can now define this as a property. For your sample, go to the `Text` property and change the default of Form1 to Professional VB.NET. Once you have accepted the property change, the new value is displayed as the caption of your form. Later in this section, you'll set form properties in code. You'll see that .NET properties are defined within your source file, unlike other environments where properties you edit through the user interface are hidden in some binary or proprietary portion of the project.

Figure 13-14

Now that you've looked at the form's properties, open the code associated with this file by either right-clicking `Form1.vb` in the Solution Explorer and selecting code view, or right-clicking the form in the View Designer and selecting View Code from the pop-up menu.

You can see that the initial display of the form looks very simple. There is no code in the `Form1.vb` file. This is a change from Visual Studio 2003, where you would have a generated section of code in a collapsed region in your source file. Instead, Visual Basic 2005 introduces a capability called *partial classes*. Partial classes are covered in Chapter 3, and Visual Studio leverages them for the code, which is generated as part of the user interface designer.

Visual Studio places all the generated source code for your form in the file `Form1.Designer.vb`. Because the "Designer" portion of this name is a convention that Visual Studio can recognize, it will hide these files by default when you review your project in the Solution Explorer. As noted earlier, by asking Visual Studio to "show all files," you can find these generated files. If you open a "Designer.vb" file, you'll see that quite a bit of custom code is generated by the Visual Studio already in your project.

To do this, go to the toolbar located in the Solution Explorer window and select the Show All Files button. This will change your project display and a small plus sign will appear next to the `Form1.vb` file. Expanding this entry displays the `Form1.Designer.vb` file, which you can open within the IDE. Doing this for Form1.Designer.vb for the ProVB.NET project you created will result in a window similar to the one shown in Figure 13-15.

Note that the contents of this file are generated; for now, don't try to make any changes. Visual Studio automatically regenerates the entire file when a property is changed, so any changes may be lost. The following lines start the declaration for your form in the file `Form1.Designer.vb`:

```
<Global.Microsoft.VisualBasic.CompilerServices.DesignerGenerated()> _
Partial Public Class Form1
    Inherits System.Windows.Forms.Form
```

Figure 13-15

The first line is an attribute that can be ignored. Next is the line that actually declares a new class called `Form1`. Note that in spite of the naming convention used by Visual Studio to hide the generated UI class implementation, the name of your class and the file in which it exists are not tightly coupled. Thus, your form will be referenced in the code as `Form1` unless you modify the name used in the class declaration. Similarly, you can rename the file that contains the class without changing the actual name of the class.

One of the powerful results of forms being implemented as classes is that you can now derive one form from another form. This technique is called *visual inheritance,* although the elements that are actually inherited may not be displayed.

Form Properties Set in Code

As noted earlier, Visual Studio keeps every object's custom property values in the source code. To do this, Visual Studio adds a method to your form class called `InitializeComponent`. As the name suggests, this method handles the initialization of the components contained on the form. A comment before the procedure warns you that the Form Designer modifies the code contained in the procedure, and that you should not modify the code directly. This module is part of the `Form1.Designer.vb` source file, and Visual Studio updates this section as changes are made through the IDE.

```
'NOTE: The following procedure is required by the Windows Form Designer
'It can be modified using the Windows Form Designer.
'Do not modify it using the code editor.
<System.Diagnostics.DebuggerStepThrough()> Private Sub _
        InitializeComponent()
    Me.SuspendLayout()
    '
    'Form1
    '
    Me.AutoScaleDimensions = New System.Drawing.SizeF(6.0!, 13.0!)
    Me.AutoScaleMode = System.Windows.Forms.AutoScaleMode.Font
    Me.ClientSize = New System.Drawing.Size(292, 266)
    Me.Name = "Form1"
    Me.Text = "Professional VB.NET"
    Me.ResumeLayout(False)

End Sub
```

The seven lines of the `InitializeComponent` procedure assign values to the properties of your `Form1` class. All the properties of the form and controls are now set directly in code. When you change the value of a property of the form or a control through the Properties window, an entry is added to `InitializeComponent` that assigns that value to the property. Previously, while examining the Properties window, you set the `Text` property of the form to Professional VB.NET Intro, which caused the following line of code to be added automatically:

```
Me.Text = "Professional VB.NET Intro"
```

The properties of the form class that are set in `InitializeComponent` by default are shown in the following table:

Property	Description
Suspend Layout	This property tells the form to not make updates to what is displayed to the user. It is called so that as each change is made, the form doesn't seem to appear in pieces.
AutoScaleDimensions	Initializes the size of the font used to lay out the form at design time. At runtime, the font that is actually rendered is compared with this property, and the form is scaled accordingly.
AutoScaleMode	Indicates that the form will use fonts that are automatically scaled based on the display characteristics of the runtime environment
ClientSize	Sets the area in which controls can be placed (the client area). It is the size of the form minus the size of the title bar and form borders.
Name	This property is used to set the textual name of the form.
ResumeLayout	Tells the form that it should resume the normal layout and displaying of its contents

Code Regions

Source files in Visual Studio allow you to collapse blocks of code. The idea is that in most cases you can reduce the code seen on screen, and which seems to separate other modules within a given class, by collapsing the code so it isn't visible; this feature is known as *outlining*. For example, if you are comparing the load and save methods and in between you have several other blocks of code, then you can "hide" this code, which isn't part of your current focus.

By default, there is a minus sign next to every method (sub or function). This makes it easy to hide or show code on a method-by-method basis. If the code for a method is hidden, the method declaration is still shown and has a plus sign next to it indicating that the body code is hidden. This feature is very useful when a developer is working on a few key methods in a module and wishes to avoid scrolling through many screens of code that are not relevant to the current task.

It is also possible to hide custom regions of code. The #Region directive is used for this within the IDE, though it has no effect on the actual application. A region of code is demarcated by the #Region directive at the top and the #End Region directive at the end. The #Region directive that is used to begin a region should include a description. The description appears next to the plus sign shown when the code is minimized.

The outlining enhancement was probably inspired by the fact that the Visual Studio designers generate a lot of code when a project is started. Being able to see the underpinnings of your generated UI does make it is easier for the developer to understand what is happening, and possibly to manipulate the process in special cases. However, as you can imagine, it can become problematic; hence the #Region directive, which can be used to organize groups of common code and then visually minimize them.

Visual Studio 2005 developers, but not Express Edition developers, can also control outlining throughout a source file. Outlining can be turned off by selecting Edit ⇨ Outlining ⇨ Stop Outlining from the Visual Studio menu. This menu also contains some other useful functions. A section of code can be temporarily hidden by highlighting it and selecting Edit ⇨ Outlining ⇨ Hide Selection. The selected code will be replaced by an ellipsis with a plus sign next to it, as if you had dynamically identified a region within the source code. Clicking the plus sign displays the code again.

Tabs versus MDI

You may have noticed in Figure 13-15 that the Code View and Form Designer windows open in a tabbed environment. This environment is the default for working with the code windows inside Visual Studio, but you can toggle this setting, which enables you to work with a more traditional MDI-based interface. Such an interface opens each code window within a separate frame instead of anchoring it to the tabbed display of the integrated development environment (IDE).

To change the arrangement that is used between the tabbed and MDI interface, use the Options dialog box (accessible via Tools ⇨ Options); this setting is available as one of the environment settings. You can also force the development environment to use the MDI as opposed to the tabbed interface (for a single session) by using the command-line option /mdi when Visual Studio is started.

Running ProVB.NET

Now that you've reviewed the elements of your generated project, let's test the code before you continue. To run an application from within Visual Studio, there are several options; the first is to click the Start button, which looks like the play button on a tape recorder. Alternatively, you can go to the Debug menu and select Start. Finally, the most common way of launching applications is to press F5.

Once the application starts, you will see an empty form display with the standard control buttons (in the upper-right corner) from which you can control the application. The form name should be Professional VB.NET Intro, which you applied earlier. At this point, the sample doesn't have any custom code to examine, so the next step is to add some simple elements to this application.

Customizing the Text Editor

In addition to being able to customize the overall environment provided by Visual Studio, you can customize several specific elements related to your development environment. Both Visual Studio 2005 and Visual Basic 2005 Express Edition have a rich set of customizations related to a variety of different environment and developer settings. Admittedly, Visual Studio 2005's feature set results in a larger number of available options for editing, but rest assured that the Express Edition contains many more options for editing than most people expect. A good example that's common to both IDEs is the way the Text Editor allows for much more customization. If you've ever had to show code to an audience — for example, in a group code review — the ability to adjust things such as font size and other similar options is great.

To leverage Visual Studio's settings, go to the Tools menu and select Options to open the Options dialog box, shown in Figure 13-16. Within the dialog box, make sure the Show All Settings check box is selected. Next, select the Text Editor folder, and then select the All Languages folder. This section allows you to make changes to the Text Editor, which are applied across every supported development language. Additionally, you can select the Basic folder to make changes that are specific to how the Text Editor will behave when you edit VB source code.

From this dialog box, it is possible to modify the number of spaces that each tab will insert into your source code and to manage several other elements of your editing environment. One little-known but useful capability of the Text Editor is line numbering. Checking the Line numbers check box will cause the editor to number all lines, which provides an easy way to unambiguously reference lines of code.

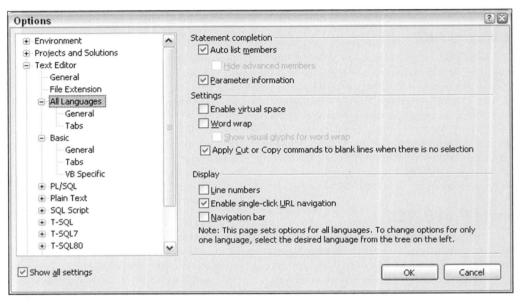

Figure 13-16

A new feature of Visual Studio 2005 is the capability to track your changes as you edit. Enabling the Track Changes setting under the Text Editor options causes Visual Studio to provide a colored indicator in places where you have modified a file. This indicator is a color bar at the left margin of your display. It shows which portions of a source file have been recently edited and whether those changes have been saved to disk.

IntelliSense, Code Expansion, and Code Snippets

One of the reasons Microsoft Visual Studio is one of the most popular development environments is that it has been designed to support developer productivity. That sounds really good, but let's back it up. People who are unfamiliar with Visual Studio might just assume that "productivity" refers to organizing and starting projects. Certainly, as shown with the project templates and project settings discussed so far, this is true, but those features don't speed your development after you've created the project.

This section covers three features that target your productivity while writing code. They are of differing value and are specific to Visual Studio. IntelliSense has always been a popular feature of Microsoft tools and applications. Code Expansion is a new feature with Visual Studio 2005; it enables you to type a keyword, such as "select," and then press the Tab key to automatically insert a generic select-case code block, which you can then customize. Going beyond this, you can use the right mouse button and insert a code snippet at the location of your mouse click. As you can tell, each of these builds on the developer productivity capabilities of Visual Studio.

IntelliSense

IntelliSense has been enhanced in Visual Studio 2005, enabling you to not only work with the methods of a class, but also automatically display the list of possible values associated with an enumerated list of properties when one has been defined. IntelliSense also provides a tooltip-like list of parameter definitions when you are making a method call. You'll see an example of this feature later in this chapter.

Additionally, if you type `Exit` and a space, IntelliSense displays a drop-down list of keywords that could follow `Exit`. Other keywords that have drop-down lists to present available options include `Goto`, `Implements`, `Option`, and `Declare`. IntelliSense generally displays more tooltip information in the environment than before and helps the developer match up pairs of parentheses, braces, and brackets.

Finally, note that IntelliSense is based on your editing context. While editing a file, there may come a point at which you are looking for a specific item to show up in IntelliSense. You repeatedly type slightly different versions but nothing appears. IntelliSense has recognized that you aren't in a method or are outside of the scope of a class, so it has removed those items that are inappropriate for your current location in your source code from the list of items available from IntelliSense.

Code Expansion

Going beyond IntelliSense is Code Expansion. Code Expansion recognizes that certain keywords are consistently associated with other lines of code. At the most basic level, this occurs when you declare a new Function or Sub: Visual Studio automatically inserts the End Sub or End Function line once you press Enter. Essentially, Visual Studio is expanding the declaration line to include its matching end point. However, real code expansion goes beyond this.

With real code expansion, you can type a keyword such as `For`, `ForEach`, `Select`, or any of a number of Visual Basic keywords. If you then use the Tab key, Visual Studio will attempt to recognize that keyword and insert the block of code that you would otherwise need to remember and type yourself. Instead of needing to remember how to format the control values of a `Select` statement, you can just type this first part of the command and then press Tab to get the following code block:

```
Select Case VariableName
    Case 1

    Case 2

    Case Else
End Select
```

Unfortunately, this is one case where just showing you the code isn't enough. That's because the code that is inserted has active regions within it that represent key items you will customize. Thus, Figure 13-17 provides a better representation of what is inserted when you expand the `Select` keyword into a full `Select Case` statement.

When the block is inserted the editor automatically positions your cursor in the first highlighted block — `VariableName`. When you start typing the name of the variable that applies, the editor automatically clears that static VariableName string, which is acting as a placeholder. Once you have entered the variable name you want, you can just press Tab. At that point the editor automatically jumps to the next highlighted item. This capability to insert a block of boilerplate code and have it automatically respond to your customization is a great feature.

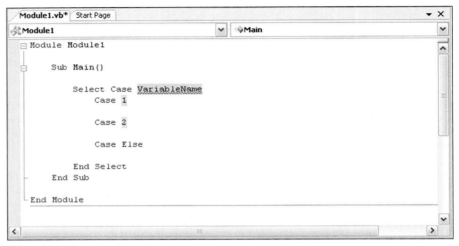

Figure 13-17

Another advantage of the code expansion is that Visual Studio not only enables you to quickly shift between the values that need to be customized, but these values are also linked where appropriate. Another popular, potentially the most popular, code expansion shortcut is the one for creating a new property in a class. If at the class level you type the word "property" followed by Tab, you will find the code shown in Figure 13-18 inserted into your code. On the surface this code is very similar to what you see when you expand the `Select` statement. Note that although you type "property," even the internal value is part of this code expansion.

The difference, however, is that the same value `String` in Figure 13-18 is repeated for the property. The value you see is actually not the default; the default everywhere you see `String` in Figure 13-18 is `Integer`. However, when you change the first such entry from `Integer` to `String`, Visual Studio automatically updates all three locations because it knows they are linked.

Figure 13-18

It is this capability to fully integrate the template supporting the expanded code with the edits you'll need to make that makes code expansion such a valuable tool. Moreover, Visual Studio went one step further and included blocks of code that don't translate to language keywords.

Code Snippets

It is possible, with a click of your mouse, to browse a library of code blocks, which, as with code expansion, you can insert into your source file. However, unlike code expansion, these snippets aren't triggered by a keyword. Instead, you right-click and (as shown in Figure 13-19) select Insert Snippet from the context menu. This starts the selection process for whatever code you want to insert.

The snippet library is installed with Visual Studio 2005 and is fully expandable, as discussed later in this chapter. Snippets are categorized by the function each is focused on. For example, all the code you can reach via code expansion is also available as snippets, but snippets go well beyond that list. There are snippet blocks for XML related actions, for operating system interface code, for items related to Windows Forms, and, of course, a lot of data-access-related blocks. The whole idea is that, unlike code expansion, which enhances the language in a way similar to IntelliSense, code snippets are blocks of code focused on functions developers often write from scratch.

As shown in Figure 13-20, the insertion of a snippet triggers the creation of a placeholder tag and a context window showing the categories of snippets. Each of the folders can contain a combination of snippet files or subdirectories containing still more snippet files. Visual Basic 2005 Express contains a subset of the folders provided with Visual Studio 2005. Visual Studio 2005 includes additional categories not shown in Figure 13-20. In addition, Visual Studio 2005 includes the folder My Code Snippets, to which you can add your own custom snippet files.

Selecting a folder enables you to select from one of its subfolders or a snippet file. Once you select the snippet of interest, Visual Studio inserts the associated code into your source file. Figure 13-21 shows the results of adding an operating system snippet to some sample code. The specific snippet in question is the code within the sub ReviewAppErrors. The selected snippet was Windows Operating System>Event Logs>Read Entries Created by a Particular Application from the Event Log, which isn't included with Visual Basic 2005 Express, although the code is still valid.

Figure 13-19

Figure 13-20

As you can see, this code snippet isn't just a block of code that can be used anywhere. Instead, it is specific to reading the Application Log, and its use in the ReviewAppErrors method is based on the idea that many applications log their errors to the Event Log so that they can be reviewed either locally or from another machine in the local domain. The key, however, is that the snippet has pulled in the necessary class references, many of which might not be familiar to you, and has placed them in context. This speeds not only the time spent typing this code, but also the time spent recalling exactly which classes need to be referenced and which methods need to be called and customized.

Finally, it is also possible to shortcut the menu tree. Specifically, if you know the shortcut for a snippet, you can type that and press Tab to have Visual Studio insert that snippet. For example, typing evReadApp followed by Tab will insert the same snippet shown in Figure 13-21.

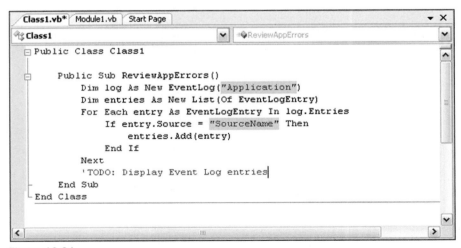

Figure 13-21

Tools such as Code Snippets and especially Code Expansion are even more valuable when you work in multiple languages. Keep in mind, however, that Visual Studio isn't limited to the features that come in the box. It's possible to extend Visual Studio not only with additional controls and project templates, but also with additional editing features.

Additional Components for Visual Studio 2005

You might be interested in adding two additional tools that work with Visual Studio. Even better, both are free. The first is a tool for creating your own Visual Basic snippets. As discussed, snippets can be powerful tools when you need to replicate relatively small but commonly used blocks of code that will be customized. While Visual Studio ships with several such snippets, Microsoft probably hasn't thought of the snippet you want the most.

This is where the first tool comes in: a Snippet Editor for Visual Basic code snippets. This editor doesn't actually live within Visual Studio 2005; it just updates the snippet files you want to use from Visual Studio. Behind the scenes, snippets are actually XML files with embedded text that represents the code used in the snippet. What the Snippet Editor does is read that XML and interpret all of the embedded logic related to things such as replacement blocks. This tool makes it possible for Visual Basic developers to create custom snippets without worrying about the XML formatting details. It is available from MSDN at `http://msdn2.microsoft.com/en-us/vbasic/ms789085.aspx`.

The second tool is a true add-in to Visual Basic 2005. When Microsoft was announcing features for .NET 2.0, it was apparent that Visual Basic and C# had different feature lists. As time went by, the developers in each community started to better understand what these features represented, and in many cases demanded their inclusion. One such feature was native support in C# for refactoring, the ability to modify a variable name to take "i" and call it "loopControl" so that it's more readable. Modifying code to improve the underlying structure, performance, and maintainability is referred to generically as *refactoring*.

Traditionally, such changes might make code more maintainable but were often more risk than reward; as a result they seldom were made. The problem, of course, is that a human tends to miss that one remaining reference to the old version of that method or variable name. More important, it was time-consuming to find all of the correct references. However, the compiler knows where these are, and that's the idea behind automated refactoring; you tell Visual Studio what you want to change and it goes through your code and makes all the necessary changes, using the same rules the compiler uses to compile your code.

This is a great maintenance tool; unfortunately, by the time most Visual Basic developers understood what it implied it was too late for the Visual Basic team to implement a solution in Visual Studio 2005. However, the team did step up, rather than just say, "So sad, too bad." They found a commercial product that actually had more features than what the C# team was developing from scratch. Then they bought a license for every Visual Studio developer, allowing free download of that tool. With it, you can quickly clean up some gnarly, hard-to-read code and turn it into well-structured logic that's much more maintainable. The free version of that tool is available at `www.devexpress.com/Products/NET/IDETools/VBRefactor/`.

Enhancing a Sample Application

To start enhancing the application, you are going to use the control Toolbox. Close the `Form1.designer.vb` file and switch your display to the `Form1.vb [Design]` tab. The Toolbox window is available whenever a form is in Design mode. By default, the Toolbox, shown in Figure 13-22, lives on the left-hand side of Visual Studio as a tab. When you click this tab, the control window expands and you can then drag controls onto your form. Alternatively, if you have closed the Toolbox tab, you can go to the View menu and select Toolbox.

If you haven't set up the Toolbox to be permanently visible, it will slide out of the way and disappear whenever focus is moved away from it. This helps maximize the available screen real estate. If you don't like this feature and want the Toolbox to be permanently visible, just click the pushpin icon on the Toolbox's title bar.

The Toolbox contains literally dozens of standard controls, and these controls have been categorized so it's easier to find them. Figure 13-22 shows the result of dragging a Button control from the Toolbox and depositing it in the location where you want it on the form. The result is a new button displaying the text "Button1." Adding another button would trigger the default naming and text of Button2.

Figure 13-22

Before customizing the first control added to this form, take a closer look at the Visual Studio Toolbox. An expanded view is shown in Figure 13-23. The tools are broken out by category, but this list of categories isn't static. Visual Studio 2005 Standard and above editions enable you to create your own custom controls. When you create such controls, the IDE will — after they have been compiled — automatically add them to the display, when you are working in the same solution as the controls. These would be local references to controls that become available within the current solution.

Additionally, depending on whether you are working on a Web or a Windows Forms application, your list of controls in the Toolbox will vary. Windows Forms has a set of controls that leverages the power of the Windows operating system. Web applications, conversely, tend to have controls oriented to working in a disconnected environment.

It's also possible to have third-party controls to your environment. Such controls can be registered with Visual Studio and are then displayed within every project you work on. The ASP.NET 2.0 AJAX controls are a good example of controls that can be added to your environment. Controls can add their own categories to the Toolbox so that they are grouped together and therefore easy to find.

Figure 13-23

Return to the button you've dragged onto the form; it's ready to go in all respects. However, Visual Studio has no way of knowing how you want to customize it. Start by going to the Properties window and changing its text property to "Hello World." You can then change the button's (Name) property to ButtonHelloWorld. Having made these changes, double-click the button in the display view. Double-clicking tells Visual Studio that you want to add an event handler to this control, and by default Visual Studio adds an On_Click event handler for buttons. The IDE then shifts the display to the code view so that you can customize this handler (see Figure 13-24).

While the event handler can be added through the designer, it's also possible to add event handlers from the code view. After you double-click the button, Visual Studio will transfer you to the code view and display your new event handler. Notice that in code view there are drop-down boxes on the top of the edit window. The boxes indicate the current object on the left — in this case, your new button; and the current method on the right — in this case, the click-event handler. You can add new handlers for other events on your button or form using these drop-down lists.

The drop-down box on the left-hand side lists the objects for which event handlers can be added. The drop-down box on the right-hand side lists all the events for the selected object. For now, you have created a new handler for your button's click event, and it's time to look at customizing the code associated with this event.

Customizing the Code

With the code window open to the newly added event handler for the "Hello World" button, you can start to customize this handler. Note that adding a control and event handler involves elements of generated code. Visual Studio adds code to the Form1.Designer.vb file. These changes occur in addition to the default method implementation you see in the editable portion of your source code.

Adding XML Comments

One of the new features of Visual Studio 2005 is the ability to create XML comments for Visual Basic. XML comments are a much more powerful feature than you probably realize, because they are also recognized by Visual Studio for use in IntelliSense. To add a new XML comment to your handler, go to the line before the handler and type three single quotation marks: ' ' '. This triggers Visual Studio to replace your single quotation marks with the following block of comments. You can trigger these comments in front of any method, class, or property in your code:

```
''' <summary>
'''
''' </summary>
''' <param name="sender"></param>
''' <param name="e"></param>
''' <remarks></remarks>
```

Note that Visual Studio has provided a template that offers a place to include a summary of what this method does. It also provides placeholders to describe each parameter that is part of this method. Not only are the comments entered in these sections available within the source code, when it's compiled you'll also find an XML file in the project directory summarizing all your XML comments that can be used to generate documentation and help files for the said source code. By the way, if you refactor a method and add new parameters, the XML comments also support IntelliSense for the XML tags that represent your parameters.

Customizing the Event Handler

Now customize the code for the button handler, as this method doesn't actually do anything by default. Add a command to open a message box and show the "Hello World" message. Use the `System.Windows.Forms.MessageBox` class. Fortunately, because that namespace is automatically imported into every source file in your project, thanks to your project references, you can reference the `MessageBox.Show` method directly. The `Show` method has several different parameters, and as shown in Figure 13-24, not only does the IDE provide a tooltip for the list of parameters, it also provides help on the appropriate value for individual parameters.

Figure 13-24

The completed call to MessageBox.Show should look similar to the following code block. Note that the underscore character is used to continue the command across multiple lines. Also note that unlike previous versions of Visual Basic, where parentheses were sometimes unnecessary, in .NET the syntax best practice is to use parentheses for every method call:

```
MessageBox.Show("Hello World", _
               "Hello World Message Box", _
               MessageBoxButtons.OK, _
               MessageBoxIcon.Information)
```

Once you have entered this line of code, you may notice a squiggly line underneath some portion of your text. This occurs when there is an error in the line you have typed. In previous versions of Visual

Basic, the development environment would interrupt your progress with a dialog box, but with .NET, the IDE works more like the latest version of Word. Instead of interrupting your progress, it highlights the problem and allows you to continue working on your code. This is a feature of Visual Basic that isn't available in other .NET languages such as C#. Visual Basic is constantly reviewing your code to ensure that it will compile; and when it encounters a problem it immediately notifies you of the location without interrupting your work.

Reviewing the Code

Now that you have created a simple Windows application, let's review the elements of the code that have been added by the IDE. Following is the entire Form1.Designer.vb source listing. Highlighted in this listing are the lines of code that have changed since the original template was used to generate this project:

```
<Global.Microsoft.VisualBasic.CompilerServices.DesignerGenerated()> _
Partial Public Class Form1
    Inherits System.Windows.Forms.Form

    'Form overrides dispose to clean up the component list.
    <System.Diagnostics.DebuggerNonUserCode()> _
    Protected Overloads Overrides Sub Dispose(ByVal disposing As Boolean)

        If disposing AndAlso components IsNot Nothing Then
                components.Dispose()
        End If
        MyBase.Dispose(disposing)
    End Sub

    'Required by the Windows Form Designer
    Private components As System.ComponentModel.Icontainer
    'NOTE: The following procedure is required by the Windows Form Designer
    'It can be modified using the Windows Form Designer.
    'Do not modify it using the code editor.
    <System.Diagnostics.DebuggerStepThrough()> _
    Private Sub InitializeComponent()
        Me. ButtonHelloWorld = New System.Windows.Forms.Button()
        Me.SuspendLayout()
        '
        'ButtonHelloWorld
        '
        Me.ButtonHelloWorld.Location = New System.Drawing.Point(112, 112)
        Me.ButtonHelloWorld.Name = "ButtonHelloWorld"
        Me.ButtonHelloWorld.Size = New System.Drawing.Size(75, 23)
        Me.ButtonHelloWorld.TabIndex = 0
        Me.ButtonHelloWorld.Text = "Hello World"
        '
        'Form1
        '
        Me.AutoScaleDimensions = New System.Drawing.SizeF(6.0!, 13.0!)
        Me.AutoScaleMode = System.Windows.Forms.AutoScaleMode.Font    Me.ClientSize =
New System.Drawing.Size(292, 273)
        Me.Controls.Add(Me.ButtonHelloWorld)
```

```
    Me.Name = "Form1"
     Me.Text = "Professional VB.NET"
     Me.ResumeLayout(False)
   End Sub
   Friend WithEvents ButtonHelloWorld As System.Windows.Forms.Button
 End Class
```

After the class declaration in the generated file, the first change made to the code is the addition of a new variable to represent the new button:

```
Friend WithEvents ButtonHelloWorld As System.Windows.Forms.Button
```

When any type of control is added to the form, a new variable is added to the form class. Controls are represented by variables; and, just as form properties are set in code, form controls are added in code. The Button class in the System.Windows.Forms namespace implements the button control on the Toolbox. Each control added to a form has a class that implements the functionality of the control. For the standard controls, these classes are usually found in the System.Windows.Forms namespace. The WithEvents keyword has been used in the declaration of the new variable so that it can respond to events raised by the button.

The bulk of the code changes are in the InitializeComponent procedure. Eight lines of code have been added to help set up and display the button control. The first addition to the procedure is a line that creates a new instance of the Button class and assigns it to the button variable:

```
Me.ButtonHelloWorld = New System.Windows.Forms.Button()
```

Before a button is added to the form, the form's layout engine must be paused. This is done using the next line of code:

```
Me.SuspendLayout()
```

The next four lines of code set the properties of the button. The Location property of the Button class sets the location of the top-left corner of the button within the form:

```
Me.ButtonHelloWorld.Location = New System.Drawing.Point(112, 112)
```

The location of a control is expressed in terms of a Point structure. Next, the Name property of the button is set:

```
Me.ButtonHelloWorld.Name = "ButtonHelloWorld"
```

The Name property acts in exactly the same way as it did for the form, setting the textual name of the button. The Name property has no effect on how the button is displayed on the form; it is used to recognize the button's context within the source code. The next two lines of code assign values to the TabIndex and Text properties of the button:

```
Me.ButtonHelloWorld.TabIndex = 0
Me.ButtonHelloWorld.Text = "Hello World"
```

The `TabIndex` property of the button is used to set the order in which the control is selected when a user cycles through the controls on the form using the Tab key. The higher the number, the later the control gains focus. Each control should have a unique number for its `TabIndex` property. The `Text` property of a button sets the text that appears on the button.

Once the properties of the button have been set, it needs to be added to the form. This is accomplished with the next line of code:

```
Me.Controls.Add(Me.ButtonHelloWorld)
```

The `System.Windows.Forms.Form` class (from which your `Form1` class is derived) has a property called `Controls` that keeps track of all of the child controls of the form. Whenever you add a control to a form in the designer, a line similar to the preceding one is added automatically to the form's initialization process.

Finally, near the bottom of the initialization logic is the final code change. The form is given permission to resume the layout logic:

```
Me.ResumeLayout(False)
```

In addition to the code that has been generated in the `Form1.Designer.vb` source file, you have created code that lives in the `Form1.vb` source file:

```
Imports System.Windows.Forms
Public Class Form1
    ''' <summary>
    '''
    ''' </summary>
    ''' <param name="sender"></param>
    ''' <param name="e"></param>
    ''' <remarks></remarks>
    Private Sub ButtonHelloWorld_Click (ByVal sender As System.Object, _
                          ByVal e As System.EventArgs) _
                          Handles ButtonHelloWorld.Click
        MessageBox.Show("Hello World", _
                    "Hello World Message Box", _
                    MessageBoxButtons.OK, _
                    MessageBoxIcon.Information)
    End Sub
End Class
```

This code reflects the event handler added for the button. The code contained in the handler was already covered, with the exception of the naming convention for event handlers. Event handlers have a naming convention similar to that in previous versions of Visual Basic: the control name is followed by an underscore and then the event name. The event itself may also have a standard set of parameters. At this point, you can test the application, but let's first review your build options.

Building Applications

For this example, it is best just to build your sample application using the Debug build configuration. The first step is to ensure that Debug is selected as the active configuration in the Configuration drop-down list box discussed in the previous section. Visual Studio provides an entire Build menu with the various options available for building an application. There are essentially two options for building applications:

❑ **Build** — This option uses the currently active build configuration to build the project or solution, depending upon what is available.

❑ **Publish** — For Visual Basic developers this option starts the process of doing a release build, but note that it also ties in with the deployment of your application, in that you are asked to provide an URL where the application will be published.

The Build menu supports building for either the current project or the entire solution. Thus, you can choose to build only a single project in your solution or all of the projects that have been defined as part of the current configuration. Of course, anytime you choose to test-run your application, the compiler will automatically perform a compilation check to ensure that you run the most recent version of your code.

You can either select Build from the menu or use the Ctrl+Shift+B keyboard combination to initiate a build. When you build your application, the Output window along the bottom edge of the development environment will open. As shown in Figure 13-25, it displays status messages associated with the build process. This window indicates your success in building your application. Once your application has been built successfully, you will find the executable file located in the targeted directory. By default, for .NET applications this is the \bin subdirectory of your project directory.

If you encounter any problems building your application, Visual Studio provides a separate window to help track them. If an error occurs, the Task List window will open as a tabbed window in the same region occupied by the Output window shown in Figure 13-25. Each error triggers a separate item in the Task List; if you double-click an error, Visual Studio automatically repositions you on the line with the error. Once your application has been built successfully, you can run it.

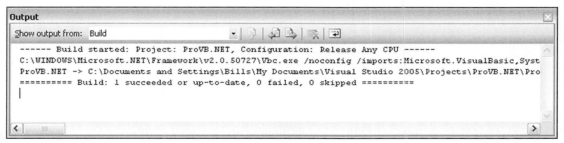

Figure 13-25

Running an Application in the Debugger

As discussed earlier, there are several ways to start your application. Starting the application launches a series of events. First, Visual Studio looks for any modified files and saves those files automatically. It then verifies the build status of your solution and rebuilds any project that does not have an updated binary, including dependencies. Finally, it initiates a separate process space and starts your application with the Visual Studio debugger attached to that process.

When your application is running, the look and feel of Visual Studio's IDE changes, with different windows and button bars becoming visible. While your solution and code remain visible, the IDE displays additional windows such as the Call Stack, Locals, and Watch windows (see the bottom section of Figure 13-26). Note that not all of these windows are available to users of Visual Studio Express Edition. These windows are used by the debugger for reviewing the current value of variables within your code.

Figure 13-26

At this point, the debugger doesn't really play much of a role in running your application. The power of the Visual Studio debugger is its interactive debugging. To demonstrate this, with your application running, select Visual Studio as the active window. Change your display to the Form1.vb code view (not design view) and click in the border alongside the line of code you added to open a message box when the "Hello World" button is clicked. Doing this creates a breakpoint on the selected line (refer to Figure 13-26). Return to your application and then click the "Hello World" button. Visual Studio takes the active focus and within your code window, and the line with your breakpoint is now selected.

Breakpoints

You are seeing a breakpoint in action. The key to working with Visual Studio is to recognize the value of the debugger. It is, in fact, more important than any of the developer productivity features of Visual Studio. Once you are on this breakpoint you have control of every aspect of your running code. For example, move your mouse and hover over the parameter sender and you can see a reference to this object. More important, you see a small plus sign on the right-hand side, which if clicked expands the pop-up showing details about the properties of this object. You can do this for any local variable. Windows such as Locals and Autos display similar information on your variables, and you can use these to update those properties while the application is running.

Once at this breakpoint, you can control your application by leveraging the Debug toolbar. This toolbar comes with several options for managing the flow of your application. On the left is a run button and a stop button and a button that may remind you of a carriage return. That return arrow button restarts your application. The toolbar has three buttons that show arrows in relation to a series of lines. These are Step-In, Step-Over, and Step-Out, respectively.

Step-In tells the debugger to attempt to walk to whatever line of code is first within the next method or property you call. Keep in mind that if you pass a property value as a parameter to a method, the first such line of code is in the Get method of the parameter. Once there, you may want to step out. Stepping out of a method tells the debugger to execute the code in the current method and return you to the line that called this method. Thus, you could step out of the property and then step in again to get into the method you are actually interested in debugging.

Of course, sometimes you don't want to step into a method; this is where the Step-Over button comes in. It enables you to call whatever method(s) are on the current line and step to the next sequential line of code in the method you are currently debugging. Each of the buttons shown on the debugging toolbar in Figure 13-25 has an accompanying shortcut key for experienced developers who want to move quickly through a series of breakpoints.

However, breakpoints go beyond what you can do with them at runtime. Visual Basic 2005 Express Edition does not support the advanced properties of breakpoints, but Visual Studio provides additional properties for working with them. As shown in Figure 13-27, it's also possible to add specific properties to your breakpoints. The context menu shows several possible options. You can disable breakpoints that you don't currently want to stop your application flow. You can also move a breakpoint, although it's usually easier to just click and delete the current location, and then click and create a new breakpoint at the new location.

More important, it's possible to specify that a given breakpoint should only execute if a certain value is defined (or undefined). In other words, you can make hitting a given breakpoint conditional, and a pop-up window enables you to define this condition. Similarly, if you've ever wanted to stop on the thirty-seventh iteration of a loop, you know the pain of repeatedly stopping at a breakpoint inside a loop. Visual Studio allows you to specify that a given breakpoint should only stop your application after some specified number of hits.

The next option is one of the more interesting options if you need to carry out a debug session in a live environment. It's possible to create a breakpoint on the debug version of code and then add a filter that ensures you are the only user to stop on that breakpoint. This means that if you are in an environment where multiple people are working against the same executable, you can add a breakpoint that won't interfere with the other users of the applications.

Similarly, instead of just stopping at a breakpoint, you can also tell the breakpoint to execute some other code, possibly even a Visual Studio macro, when a given breakpoint is reached. These actions are some-what limited and are not frequently used, but in some situations this capability can be used to your advantage.

Figure 13-27

Note that breakpoints are saved when a solution is saved by the IDE. There is also a Breakpoints window, which provides a common location for managing breakpoints that you may have set across several different source files.

Other Debug-Related Windows

As noted earlier, when you run an application in Debug mode, Visual Studio .NET 2003 opens a series of windows related to debugging. Each of these windows provides a view of a limited set of the overall environment in which your application is running. From these windows, it is possible to find things such as the list of calls (stack) used to get to the current line of code or the present value of all the variables currently available. Visual Studio has a powerful debugger that is fully supported with IntelliSense, and these windows extend the debugger.

Output

Recall that the build process puts progress messages in this window. Similarly, your program can also place messages in it. Several options for accessing this window are discussed in later chapters, but at the simplest level the `Console` object echoes its output to this window during a debug session. For example, the following line of code can be added to your sample application:

```
Console.WriteLine("This is printed in the Output Window")
```

This line of code will cause the string `This is printed in the Output Window` to appear in the Output window when your application is running. You can verify this by adding this line in front of the command to open the message box. Then, run your application and have the debugger stop on the line where the message box is opened. Examining the contents of the Output window, you will find that your string is displayed.

Anything written to the Output window is shown only while running a program from the environment. During execution of the compiled module, no Output window is present, so nothing can be written to it. This is the basic concept behind other objects such as the `Debug` and `Trace` objects, which are covered in more detail in Chapter 9.

Call Stack

The Call Stack window lists the procedures that are currently calling other procedures and waiting for their return. The call stack represents the path through your code that has led to the currently executing command. This can be a valuable tool when you are trying to determine what code is executing a line of code that you didn't expect to execute.

Locals

The Locals window is used to monitor the value of all variables that are currently in scope. This is a fairly self-explanatory window that shows a list of the current local variables and next to each item the value of the variable. As in previous versions of Visual Studio, this display supports the examination of the contents of objects and arrays via a tree-control interface. It also supports the editing of those values, so if you want to change a string from empty to what you thought it would be, just to see what else might be broken, then feel free to do so from here.

Watch Windows

There are four Watch windows, called Watch 1 to Watch 4. Each window can hold a set of variables or expressions for which you want to monitor the value. It is also possible to modify the value of a variable from within a Watch window. The display can be set to show variable values in decimal or hexadecimal format. To add a variable to a Watch window, right-click the variable in the Code Editor and then select Add Watch from the pop-up menu.

Immediate Window

The Immediate window, as its name implies, allows you to evaluate expressions. This window becomes available while you are in Debug mode. This is a powerful window, one which can save or ruin a debug session. For example, using the sample from earlier in this chapter, you can start the application and press the button to stop on the breakpoint. Go to the Immediate Window, and enter **?Button1.Text = "Click Me"** and press return. You should get a response of false as the Immediate window evaluates this statement.

Notice the preceding **?**, which tells the debugger to evaluate your statement, rather than execute it. Repeat the preceding but omit the question mark: **Button1.Text = "Click Me"**. Press F5 or click the Run button to return control to your application, and notice the caption on your button. From the Immediate window you have updated this value. This window can be very useful if you are working in Debug mode and need to modify a value that is part of a running application.

Autos

Finally, as the chapter prepares to transition to features that are only available in Visual Studio and not Visual Basic 2005 Express, there is the Autos window. The Autos window displays variables used in the statement currently being executed and the statement just before it. These variables are identified and listed for you automatically, hence the window's name. This window shows more than just your local variables. For example, if you are in Debug mode on the line to open the MessageBox in the ProVB.NET sample, then the MessageBox constants referenced on this line are shown in this window. This window enables you to see the content of every variable involved in the currently executing command. As with the Locals window, you can edit the value of a variable during a debug session. However, this window is in fact specific to Visual Studio and not available to users of Visual Basic 2005 Express.

Useful Features of Visual Studio 2005

The focus of most of this chapter has been on creating a simple application, working in either Visual Basic 2005 Express Edition or Visual Studio 2005. It's now time to leave the set of features supported by the Express Edition and look at some features that are available only to Visual Studio developers. These features include, but are not limited to, the following items, beginning with features available to all Visual Studio 2005 developers.

When Visual Studio 2005 is started, you configure your custom IDE profile. Unlike previous versions of .NET, whereby you selected a set of preferences that you would then use for all your development, Visual Studio 2005 allows you to select either a language-specific or task-specific profile and then change that profile whenever you desire.

Configuration settings are managed through the Tools ⇨ Import and Export Settings menu option. This menu option opens a simple wizard, which first saves your current settings and then allows you to select an alternate set of settings. By default, Visual Studio ships with settings for Visual Basic, Web Development, and C#, to name a few, but by exporting your settings you can create and share your own custom settings files.

The Visual Studio settings file is an XML file that enables you to capture all your Visual Studio configuration settings. This might sound trivial, but it's not. This feature allows for standardization of Visual Studio across different team members. The advantages of a team sharing settings go beyond just a common look and feel.

Build Configurations

Prior to .NET, a Visual Basic project had only one set of properties. There was no way to have one set of properties for a debug build and a separate set for a release build. As a result, you had to manually change any environment-specific properties before you built the application. This has changed with the introduction of *build configurations,* which enable you to have different sets of project properties for debug and release builds. Visual Studio does not limit you to only two build configurations. It's possible to create additional custom configurations. The properties that can be set for a project have been split into two groups: those that are independent of build configuration and therefore apply to all build configurations, and those that apply only to the active build configuration. For example, the Project Name and Project Location properties are the same irrespective of what build configuration is active, whereas the code optimization options vary, depending on the active build configuration. This isn't a new concept, and it has been available to Visual C++ developers for some time, but .NET was the first time it was available for VB developers.

Currently, under Visual Studio 2005, the default settings for developers who choose to customize Visual Studio 2005 based on Visual Basic settings do not include the two build configuration settings in the project property pages. By default, Visual Basic applications are built in Debug mode until they are deployed. This enables the Visual Basic developer to be unaware of the build configuration settings. However, if a project's build type is changed, then the VB developer is by default unaware and unable to change the setting.

To display these settings in Visual Studio, select Tools ➪ Options. On the Options dialog, select the Projects and Solutions tree item; and on the settings for projects and solutions, select the "Show advanced build configurations" check box. This will update the user interface to properly display the build configurations, even though your other settings reflect those of a Visual Basic development environment.

The advantage of multiple configurations is that it's possible to turn off optimization while an application is in development and add symbolic debug information that helps locate and identify errors. When you are ready to ship the application, you can switch to the release configuration and create an executable that is optimized for production.

At the top of Figure 13-28 is a drop-down list box labeled Configuration. Typically, four options are listed in this box — the currently selected configuration, Active; the Debug and Release options; and a final option, All Configurations. When changes are made on this screen, they are applied only to the selected configuration(s). Thus, on the one hand, when Release is selected, any changes are applied only to the settings for the Release build. If, on the other hand, All Configurations is selected, then any changes made are applied to all of the configurations, Debug, and Release. Similarly, if Active is selected, then in the background the changes are made to the underlying configuration that is currently active.

Alongside this is a Platform drop-down. Typically, you should not change this setting; its purpose is to allow you to optimize the generation of your MSIL for a specific processor. For example, 32-bit processors have different optimization than 64-bit AMD processors, which differ from Intel's 64-bit Itanium processors. While the .NET CLR allows you to abstract these differences, Visual Studio allows you to target a specific platform.

The window below the two drop-downs displays the individual properties that are dependent on the active build configuration. The first such setting is the location where your project's binary files will be sent. Notice that VB now defaults to separate `bin/debug` and `bin/release` directories, so you can keep separate copies of your executables. Below this is the `Advanced` button, which opens a window containing some low-level compiler optimizations. In most cases, you won't need to change these settings, but they are available for those working with low-level components.

Figure 13-28

Below these settings is the All Configurations section. This label is somewhat misleading; it would be better if it said "All of the available configuration settings." Of course, that's a bit long, but the point is that while these settings can be different for each configuration, the grid contains all of the primary configuration settings.

All of these settings are project-specific, but when working with a solution it is possible to have more than one project in the same solution. While you are forced to manage these settings independently for each project, there is another form of project configuration related to multiple projects. You are most likely to use this when working with integrated Setup projects, where you might want to build only the Setup project when you are working on a release build.

To customize which projects are included in each build configuration, you need the Configuration Manager for the solution. Projects are assigned to build configurations through the Configuration Manager. If, and only if, your solution has multiple projects, then it is possible to open the Configuration Manager from the Build menu by selecting Configuration Manager. Alternatively, the Configuration Manager can be opened using the drop-down list box to the right of the Run button on the Visual Studio toolbar. The active configuration drop-down box contains the following options: Debug, Release, and Configuration Manager. The first two default options are the currently available configurations. Selecting the bottom option, Configuration Manager, opens the dialog box shown in Figure 13-29.

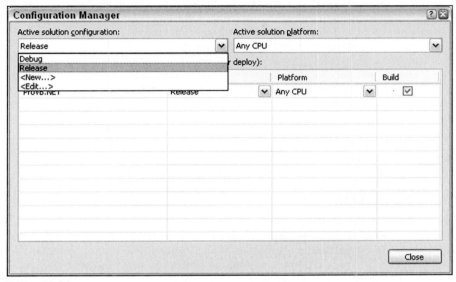

Figure 13-29

The Configuration Manager contains an entry for each project in the current solution. It is possible to include a project or exclude it from the selected configuration by clearing the check box in the column of the grid labeled Build. This is a valuable capability when a solution has multiple projects so that time isn't wasted waiting while a project that isn't being worked on is recompiled. The build configuration is commonly used when a Setup project is added to a solution. The normal plan is to rebuild only the Setup package when a release version of the actual application project is created. Note that regardless of the build configuration, it's possible to build any assembly by right-clicking that project and selecting the Build option from the pop-up menu.

The Task List

The Task List is a great productivity tool that tracks not only errors but also pending changes and additions. It's also a good way for the Visual Studio environment to communicate information that the developer needs to know, such as any current errors. The Task List is displayed by selecting Task List from the View menu. The Task List has two views, Comments and User Tasks, and it displays either group of tasks based on the selection in the drop-down box that is part of this window.

The Comment option is used for tasks embedded in code comments. This is done by creating a standard comment with the apostrophe and then starting the comment with the Visual Studio keyword TODO. The keyword can be followed with any text that describes what needs to be done. Once entered, the text of these comments shows up in the Task List. Note that users can create their own comment tokens in the options for Visual Studio via `Tools` ➪ Options ➪ Environment ➪ Task List. Other predefined keywords include `HACK` and `UNDONE`.

Besides helping developers track these pending coding issues as tasks, leveraging comments embedded in code results in another benefit. Just as with errors, clicking a task in the Task List causes the Code Editor to jump right to the location of the task without hunting through the code for it. Also of note, though we are not going to delve into it, the Task List is integrated with Team Foundation Server if you are using this for your collaboration and source control.

The second type of tasks are user tasks. These may not be related to a specific item within a single file. Examples are tasks associated with resolving a bug, or a new feature. It is possible to enter tasks into the Task List manually. Within the Task List is an image button showing a red checkmark. Pressing this button creates a new task in the Task List and enables you to edit the description of your new task.

In previous versions of Visual Studio, the Task List window was used to display compilation errors, but under Visual Studio 2005 the Error List became a separate window.

The Command Window

The Command window can be opened from the Other Windows section of the View menu. When opened, the window displays a > prompt. This is a command prompt at which you can execute commands — specifically, Visual Studio commands. While Visual Studio is designed to be a GUI environment with limited shortcuts, the Command window allows you to type — with the assistance of IntelliSense — the specific command you want.

The Command window can be used to access Visual Studio menu options and commands by typing them instead of selecting them in the menu structure. For example, type **File.AddNewProject** and press Enter — the dialog box to add a new project will appear. Similarly, if you type **Debug.Start,** you initiate the same build and start actions that you would from the Visual Studio UI.

The Server Explorer

As development has become more server-centric, developers have a greater need to discover and manipulate services on the network. The Server Explorer is a feature in Visual Studio that makes this easier. Visual Interdev started in this direction with a Server Object section in the Interdev toolbox. The Server Explorer in Visual Studio is more sophisticated in that it enables you to explore and even alter your application's database or your local registry values. With the assistance of an SQL Database project template (part of the Other Project types), it's possible to fully explore and alter an SQL Server database. You can define the tables, stored procedures, and other database objects as you might have previously done with the SQL Enterprise Manager.

You open the Server Explorer in much the same way you open the control Toolbox. When you hover over or click the Server Explorer's tab, the window expands from the left-hand side of the IDE. Once it is open, you will see a display similar to the one shown in Figure 13-30. Note that this display has two top-level entries. The first, Data Connections, is the starting point for setting up and configuring the database connection. You can right-click on this and define the SQL Server connection settings that will be used in your application to connect to the database. The Server Explorer is a window from the Data

Source window that opens in the same location. The Data Source window provides a way to manage and view project-specific database connections such as those used in data binding.

The second top-level entry, Servers, focuses on other server data that may be of interest to you and your application. When you expand the list of available servers (refer to Figure 13-30), you will see that you have access to several server resources. The Server Explorer even provides the capability to stop and restart services on the server. Notice the wide variety of server resources that are available for inspection or use in the project. Having the Server Explorer available means you don't have to go to an outside resource to find, for example, what message queues are available.

Figure 13-30

By default, you have access to the resources on your local machine; but if you are in a domain, it is possible to add other machines, such as your Web server, to your display. The Add Server option enables you to select and inspect a new server. To explore the Event Logs and registry of a server, you need to add this server to your display. Use the add server button in the button bar to open the dialog and identify the server to which you would like to connect. Once the connection is made, you can explore the properties of that server.

Recording and Using Macros in Visual Studio 2005

Visual Studio macros are part of the environment and are available to any language. Macro options are accessible from the Tools ⇨ Macros menu, as shown in Figure 13-31. The concept of macros is simple: Record a series of keystrokes and/or menu actions, and then play them back by pressing a certain keystroke combination.

For example, suppose that one particular function call with a complex set of arguments is constantly being called on in code, and the function call usually looks the same except for minor variations in the arguments. The keystrokes to code the function call could be recorded and played back as necessary, which would insert code to call the function, which could then be modified as necessary.

551

Figure 13-31

Macros can be far more complex than this, containing logic as well as keystrokes. The macro capabilities of Visual Studio are so comprehensive that macros have their own IDE (accessed via Tools ➪ Macros ➪ Macros IDE).

Macros can also be developed from scratch in this environment, but more commonly they are recorded using the Record Temporary Macro option on the Macros menu and then renamed and modified in the development environment. Here is an example of recording and modifying a macro:

1. Start a new Windows Application project.

2. In the new project, add a button to `Form1`, which was created with the project.

3. Double-click the button to get to its `Click` event routine.

4. Select Tool_Macros_Record Temporary Macro. A small toolbar will appear on top of the IDE with a button to control the recording of a macro (Pause, Stop, and Cancel).

5. Press the Enter key, and then type the following line of code:

```
Console.WriteLine("Macro test")
```

6. Press the Enter key again.

7. In the small toolbar, press the Stop button.

8. Select Tools ➪ Macros ➪ Macro Explorer. The Macro Explorer will appear (in the location normally occupied by the Solution Explorer), with the new macro in it. You can name the macro anything you like.

9. Right-click the macro and select Edit to get to the Macro Editor. You will see the following code in your macro:

```
DTE.ActiveDocument.Selection.NewLine()
DTE.ActiveDocument.Selection.Text = "Console.WriteLine(""Macro test"")"
DTE.ActiveDocument.Selection.NewLine()
```

The code that appears in Step 9 may vary, depending on how you typed in the line. If you made a mistake and backspaced, for example, those actions will have their own corresponding lines of code. As a result, after you record a macro, it is often worthwhile to examine the code and remove any unnecessary lines.

The code in a macro recorded this way is just standard VB code, and it can be modified as desired. However, there are some restrictions on what you can do inside the macro IDE. For example, you cannot refer to the namespace for setting up database connections, because this might constitute a security violation.

To run a macro, you can just double-click it in the Macro Explorer or select Tools ➪ Macros ➪ Run Macro. You can also assign a keystroke to a macro in the Keyboard dialog box in the Tools ➪ Options ➪ Environment folder.

One final note on macros is that they essentially enable you to generate code that can then be transferred to a Visual Studio Add-In project. An Add-In project is a project designed to extend the properties of Visual Studio. To create a new Add-In project, open the New Project dialog and select Other Project Types — Extensibility. You can then create a Visual Studio Add-In project. Such a project enables you to essentially share your macro as a new feature of Visual Studio. For example, if Visual Studio 2005 doesn't provide a standard way to get formatted comments, you might create an add-in that enables you to automatically generate your comment template so you wouldn't need to retype it repeatedly.

Class Diagrams

One of the new features of Visual Studio 2005 is the capability to generate class diagrams. A *class diagram* is a graphical representation of the objects that are part of your application. By right-clicking on your project in the Solution Explorer, you can select View Class Diagram from the context menu. Alternatively, you can choose to Add a New item to your project. In the same window where you can add a new class you have the option to add a new class diagram. The class diagram uses a ".cd" file extension for its source files. It is a graphical display, as shown in Figure 13-32.

Adding such a file to your project creates a dynamically updated representation of your project's classes. As shown in Figure 13-32, the current class structures for even a simple project are immediately represented when you create the diagram. It is possible to add one class diagram per subdirectory in your project. The class diagram graphically displays the relationships between objects — for example, when one object contains another object or even object inheritance. The diagram itself is a living, breathing document in the sense that when you change your source code the diagram is also updated. The diagram isn't something you create at the start of your project and then allow to become out of date as your actual implementation changes the class relationships.

Figure 13-32

More importantly, you can at any time open up the class diagram, make changes to one or more of your existing objects, or create new objects and define their relationship to your existing objects, and when done Visual Studio will automatically update your existing source files and create new source files as necessary for the newly defined objects.

As shown in Figure 13-32, the class diagram files (*.cd) open in the same main display area used for the Visual Studio UI designer and viewing code. They are, however, a graphical design surface that behaves more like Visio than the User Interface designer. Individual objects can be compressed or have their property and method details exposed. Additionally, items such as the relationships between classes can be shown graphically instead of being represented as properties.

In addition to the editing surface, when working with the Class Designer a second window is displayed. As shown in Figure 13-32, the Class Details window is generally located in the same space as your Output, Tasks, and other windows. The Class Details window provides detailed information about each of the properties and methods of the classes you are working with in the Class Designer. You can add and edit methods, properties, fields, and even events associated with your classes. While you can't write code from this window, you can update parameter lists and property types. The Class Diagram tool is an excellent tool for reviewing your application structure.

Team System

The focus of this chapter has been on how you, as a Visual Basic developer, can leverage Visual Studio 2005. At the top end of Visual Studio 2005 is the full Team Suite, and just below that are the various Team Editions. These are part of the umbrella of products referred to as *Team System*. In order to reduce confusion, this section takes a brief look at the tools from Team Suite that are part of the Visual Studio 2005 Team Edition for Software Developers. These tools are focused less on languages and developing code than on managing development and the development of applications.

Architecturally, Team System has two main elements: the server-side components, which operate under Team Foundation Server, and the Client Components, which are grouped under the Team Suite umbrella. Team Foundation Server (TFS) is in a sense the replacement for Visual Source Safe (VSS). However, thinking of it only in those terms is a bit like thinking of the modern automobile as the replacement for the horse and carriage. Understandably, the focus of TFS is on server-side components, but TFS includes a client installation package. This package ships with the server, but includes add-ins to Visual Studio as well as Visual Studio Tools for Office documents that you need in order to work with the server products.

Team Suite is a set of components that are integrated with and ship with Visual Studio 2005. These components were initially categorized into three roles: Architects, Developers, and Testers. Team Suite consolidates the tools appropriate for all these roles in a single product. Since its original release, Microsoft has announced and started offering technology previews for database developers. These tools are also available to users of Team Suite. The underlying concept is that each role needs certain tools in order to better carry out the associated daily tasks, and in some cases these tools overlap between roles.

While having a single product that incorporates all these tools is nice, the cost can become an issue. Thus, Microsoft introduced the idea of Team Editions. To better manage the cost to the developer, these would provide the same server components access to all of the roles, but on the client side they would include only the tools appropriate for a specific role. Thus, from the standpoint of TFS and the server components of Team Suite, there are no differences between Team Suite and a Team Edition. The only differences exist in the tools provided as part of the client's version of Visual Studio.

Team Foundation Server (TFS)

The server components of Team System are not directly integrated into Visual Studio 2005, but it is appropriate to mention a couple of key attributes of TFS that extend it beyond VSS. Similar to VSS, the primary role most developers see for TFS is that of source control. This is the ability to ensure that if multiple people are working on the same project and with the same set of source files, then no two of them can make changes to the same file at the same time.

Actually, that's a bit of an oversimplification. The default mode for TFS is to allow those two people to work on the same file, and then have the second person attempting to save changes merge his or her changes with the previously saved changes. The point of this is to ensure that developers check files in and out of source control so that they don't overwrite or lose each other's changes. In terms of its features and usability compared with VSS, TFS is much more capable of supporting remote team members. A project that literally takes hours to download remotely from VSS can download in a few minutes from TFS.

However, that covers just the source control features, and as mentioned previously TFS goes well beyond source control. The most obvious way is that TFS approaches project development from the role of the project manager. It doesn't consider a Visual Studio project file to represent the definition of a project. Instead, it recognizes that a project is based on a customer or contract relationship and may be made up of several seemingly unrelated projects in Visual Studio. Thus, when you define a project you create an area where all of the projects and solutions and their associated source files can be stored.

As part of the creation process you select a process template — and there are third-party templates available — and create a SharePoint website based on that template. The SharePoint website becomes the central point of collaboration for the project's team. In addition to hosting the documentation associated with your selected software development process, this site acts as a central location for task lists, requirements, Microsoft Project files, and other materials related to your project. In essence, TFS leverages SharePoint to add a group collaboration element to your projects.

As important as this is, an even more important capability TFS supports is that of a build lab. TFS provides another optional product called *Team Build,* which leverages the Visual Studio build engine to enable you to schedule automated builds. This isn't just a simple scheduling service; the Team Build engine not only retrieves and compiles your application files, it also sends update notices recognizing the status of the build, and can be instructed to automatically leverage some of the Team Suite tools such as Code Analysis and Unit Testing. The capability to automate your builds and deploy them on a daily basis to a test environment encourages processes that focus on product quality and mirror industry best practices.

Finally, TFS ships with the Team Explorer. This is a Visual Studio add-in on steroids. It includes not only new menu items for Visual Studio, but also a new window similar in concept to the Solution Explorer but that instead provides access to your TFS projects. It also provides a series of windows in Visual Studio related to source control, and others related to Tasks. TFS is in many ways the single most important tool in the Team System product line, even though it doesn't truly exist within Visual Studio.

Team Editions

While TFS is available to all users of one of the versions of Team System, on the client side there are several different editions. As noted, Team Suite contains everything, but what about the role-based editions? There are currently three versions of the Team Edition packages: Team Edition for Architects, Team Edition for Software Developers, and Team Edition for Software Testers. These packages are described in detail on Microsoft's website, but here is a thumbnail review of the contents of each.

Team Edition for Architects isn't just focused on software architects. This edition contains tools oriented to the interaction of different applications, and the interaction between physical servers and the components that will be installed on those servers. The architect tools essentially work at a level above the Class Designer. These tools enable you to define applications that can then become Visual Studio projects. The designers support designating the security requirements for deploying these applications and allow the architect to compare the requirements of a given application with the settings on a physical server. The goal is to enable an architect to determine quickly whether a new application will work when it is actually deployed into production, and to understand how different applications will interact.

Team Edition for Software Developers is an excellent subset of tools for developers. The details of this edition are the focus for the following sections in this chapter. In short, the Developers edition provides tools to analyze the quality of your source code, to test an application's performance in relation to the system resources it consumes, and to create automated unit tests. This last feature is in many ways the most important feature for improving your code quality.

Team Edition for Software Testers doesn't focus on documenting how an application should work so much as on coding and automating tests. It has all of the same unit testing capabilities of the Developers edition but includes additional test tools for Web applications and for load testing Web applications. It also includes some basic tools for documenting and defining tests; but just as with Team Build, the focus is on being able to create and customize automated tests.

Team Edition for Developers

This set of tools, which has been integrated with Visual Studio, is focused on the needs of the application developer. Unlike the Architect tools, those for developers are to a large extent taken from existing, free tools. However, unlike those tools, the Team Suite versions have been fully integrated with Visual Studio and TFS. Don't let the fact that many of these tools are based on freely available tools fool you; many modifications and improvements have been made.

Code Analysis

Code analysis, or static code analysis, is a tool for reviewing your source code — although that's not quite how it works. The basic paradigm reflects the fact that there are certain common best practices when writing code, and that once you have documented these best practices it is possible to write a tool that looks at source code and determines whether these practices have been followed. Visual Studio's static code analysis is incorporated into your project settings for Windows Forms–based projects, as shown in Figure 13-33. For Web applications, there isn't a project file to hold the project settings, so it is possible to configure and run static code analysis from the website menu in Visual Studio.

However, the tool doesn't actually look at your source code. Instead, it uses reflection; and once your project has been compiled, it queries the MSIL code your project generates. While this may seem surprising, remember that this tool is looking for several best practices, which may be implemented in different ways in your source code but will always compile in a standard manner.

Figure 13-33

As shown in Figure 13-33, even when you have the code analysis tools available, they are by default not enabled for your project. This is because enabling code analysis significantly extends your compile time. In most cases you'll want to enable these settings for a build or two, and then disable the checks for most of your debug builds. As you can see, to enable analysis you merely check the Enable Code Analysis check box.

Once you have enabled the code analysis checks, you also have the option to define exactly which rules you want to apply. Figure 13-33 illustrates that the checks are divided into different categories of rules, with a corresponding status for each category. The status shown in this configuration screen describes what should happen if you fail to pass one of these rules in a given category. It is not an indicator of the current state of your code.

Instead, this status represents what should be reported as part of your compilation results when you have enabled code analysis. Note that each of the categories can be enabled or disabled as part of your code analysis. It is then possible to expand the display to list the rules in each category. This enables you to have some rule violations act as compilation errors instead of warnings. You can also enable or disable having the analyzer check individual rules. Outside of the scope of this chapter is the capability to actually identify within your source code those items that may be flagged by the code analyzer but that are valid exceptions to the rule being checked.

Performance Tools

Performance checks are something every developer talks about wanting. Visual Studio provides *dynamic code analysis,* or performance, tools for your application. These tools are available from the Tools menu, shown in Figure 13-34. The performance tools provide two runtime environments to measure the performance of your application: Sampling and Instrumented. Note that if you are working within a virtual PC, then you need to use the instrumented version of the performance tools.

Sampling for performance testing is a non-intrusive method of checking your application performance. Essentially, Visual Studio starts your application normally, but behind the scenes it is interfaced into the system performance counters. As your application runs, the performance monitoring engine captures the system performance, and when your application completes it provides reports describing that performance. Details about what your application was actually doing to cause a behavior isn't available, but you can get a realistic feel of the impact on the system.

Instrumentation, conversely, is an intrusive form of performance monitoring. Choosing to make an instrumentation run the performance tools triggers the addition of special MSIL commands into your compiled executable. These calls are placed at the start and finish of methods and properties within your executable. Then, as your code executes, the performance engine can gauge how long it takes for specific calls within your application to execute.

Keep in mind that both methods of performance testing affect the underlying performance of the application. It is true that running a performance monitor of any type has built-in overhead that affects your application. However, the goal of performance testing isn't to know the exact timing marks of your application, but rather to identify areas that deviate significantly from the norm, and, more important, to establish a baseline from which you can track any significant changes as code is modified.

Figure 13-34

Unit Tests

Automated unit tests are arguably the most important of the tools provided to the developer as part of Team Edition. To create a new Unit Test, go to the Test menu in Visual Studio and select New Test. This opens the Add New Test dialog, shown in Figure 13-35.

Note that the dialog shown in Figure 13-35 isn't from Visual Studio 2005 Team Edition for Software Developers. It is from Visual Studio 2005 Team Suite, the difference being several more project templates, representing the full suite of templates available to a Software Tester. Developers will normally only see the Unit Test and Unit Test Wizard templates available in this screen. Given this, developers should work with the Unit Test Wizard to generate new tests. This wizard walks you through the process of generating a new test project.

Once you have completed the final step in the wizard to define your test project, you are presented with the screen shown in Figure 13-36. This screen shows each of your project's classes, and expands into the methods and properties available in that class. Note that the screen shown is based on the ProVB.NET sample application, which consists of a single form. Displayed are several inherited methods in addition to the custom methods on the form. In fact, the custom methods are not shown in the figure. This screen enables you to review those properties and methods that are part of the My namespace. Specifically, you can run tests against the settings and resources that you expect will be included in your project.

Figure 13-35

Figure 13-36

What's missing is any type of review of the actual UI elements that a user of your application would interact with. The unit test engine that ships with Team System does not support actual UI testing; it is focused on testing methods that exist in your code. However, the purpose of this screen is to enable Visual Studio to generate the source code associated with testing your application. Clicking the OK button triggers the generation of these tests, which will be grouped in a new test project. Because the project name shown in Figure 13-36 wasn't customized, you'll see the newly generated project in Figure 13-37.

The creation of a Unit Test project is not a trivial event. Even though it occurs as quickly as any other project template, the results are significant. First, notice in the Solution Explorer shown in Figure 13-37 that another project has been added to the ProVB.NET solution. This new test project includes a documentation file, AuthoringTests.txt, with tips and instructions for writing unit tests. In addition, this screen shows a subset of the contents of the Form1Test.vb source file. It is opened to some of the comments accompanying the methods stubs to implement the tests for your selected methods.

Figure 13-37

Unit tests present a unique challenge — because you are writing test code, they are an expensive feature to initially implement. Therefore, even though automated unit tests are valuable, organizations often have trouble committing to their development. Nonetheless, a well-written set of tests more than pays for itself. How do you estimate that cost? As a rule of thumb, consider estimating as much time for writing tests as you expect to spend writing the code to be tested.

Summary

In this chapter, you have taken a dive into the versions and features of Visual Studio. This chapter has helped you to explore the new Visual Studio IDE and demonstrated how powerful the features of the IDE are, even in the freely available Visual Basic 2005 Express Edition. Following are some of the key points covered in this chapter:

❑   How to create projects and the different project templates available

❑   Code regions and how you can use them to conceal code

❑   Versions of Visual Studio 2005

❑   The properties and settings of your Visual Studio 2005 projects

❑   Running an application in Debug mode and working with breakpoints

❑   Building configurations and modifying the build configuration of your project

❑   The Class Designer

❑   Team System: Team Foundation Server and Team Suite

❑   Tools in Visual Studio 2005 Team Edition for Software Developers

❑   Automated unit tests

You've seen that Visual Studio 2005 is highly customizable and comes in a variety of flavors. Numerous windows can be hidden, docked, or undocked. They can be layered in tabs and moved within the IDE. Visual Studio contains many tools, including some that extend its core capabilities. Keep in mind that whether you are using Visual Basic 2005 Express Edition or Visual Studio 2005 Team Suite, the core elements associated with compiling your application are the same.

Working with SQL Server

While most of the relationship between a developer and an SQL Server relates to querying or saving data, SQL Server 2005 created a new way of working with databases. SQL Server 2005 added integration with the .NET Framework. This provided two main benefits. First, you can use Visual Basic to create elements in the database, such as user-defined types, stored procedures, and functions. These objects may work alone or in concert with the normal Transact-SQL objects. Second, you can expose Web Services from your databases, enabling .NET and other client applications to execute code on the database.

Transact-SQL (T-SQL), while a well-featured language, lacks a number of features that are common in general-purpose languages such as Visual Basic. VB includes better support for looping and conditional statements than T-SQL. In addition, the .NET Framework is available for use with Visual Basic, meaning you have access to tools for network access, string handling, mathematical processing, internationalization, and more. If your stored procedures need access to features such as these, then it may be beneficial to look at using VB, not T-SQL.

This chapter describes how and, possibly more important, why you can use Visual Basic to create these objects in SQL Server 2005. It covers how you can adapt existing data access code to run within the database, and leverage the common language runtime. Finally, the chapter describes the new capability of hosting Web Services within SQL Server, and how you can create these Web Services using Visual Basic.

CLR Integration in SQL Server 2005

As the Developer Division within Microsoft worked on .NET Framework 2.0 and Visual Basic 2005, other teams within SQL Server were working on the new version of SQL Server. The SQL teams wanted to leverage the Framework. However, at the time, the ability to host the .NET Framework was limited. The two groups worked together to better identify hosting APIs, with the result that they were able to integrate the common language runtime into SQL Server 2005. This integration means that developers can use Visual Basic code within the context of SQL Server. It is no longer true that success as a DBA is dependent on knowing T-SQL. In addition, it is no longer necessary for the data access code to be written outside the database. The benefit to both groups is more flexibility in choosing a development language, and more capabilities for your database programming.

CLR integration is disabled by default on SQL Server 2005. This is a safety measure, as most users do not need the features it provides. By not enabling it, there's one less avenue for attack by hackers. In order to enable creating SQL objects using Visual Basic, you need to enable the integration. This is done by executing the SQL statement that follows in a query window in the SQL Management Console. Note that this is not a decision that should be taken lightly. Enabling any feature means that hackers also have the feature available to them, so enabling a feature as powerful as CLR integration means that if compromised, then your server can become a dangerous tool. Here is the code:

```
sp_configure 'clr enabled', 1
GO
RECONFIGURE
GO
```

Now that you've been scared away from enabling CLR integration, it is an incredibly useful tool in some circumstances. T-SQL, for all of its power, is a relatively limited language compared with Visual Basic. It lacks many of the conditional or looping constructs that developers are used to, such as the `with` statement. In addition, debugging has traditionally been fairly weak with T-SQL. Finally, the ability to use external libraries in T-SQL is limited. You can get around these limits by using Visual Basic to replace T-SQL when appropriate.

Deciding between T-SQL and Visual Basic

Once you have enabled CLR integration with your database, your next set of decisions revolves around when to use T-SQL and the native services of SQL Server versus when to use Visual Basic and the .NET Framework. Your final choice should be based on the needs of the application, rather than because a technology is new or interesting. The following table outlines some of the common scenarios for building applications with SQL Server:

Scenario	T-SQL	Visual Basic
User-defined types	Generally should be the first, if not only, choice	Can be used if you will need to integrate with other managed code, or if the UDT will need to provide additional methods. Also a good idea if the UDT will be shared with external VB code.
Functions and stored procedures	Use when the code is to process data in bulk, or with little procedural code.	Use if the code requires extensive procedural processing or calculations, or if you need access to external libraries, such as the .NET Framework

Scenario	T-SQL	Visual Basic
Extended stored procedures	Typically the main method used to provide new functionality to SQL Server. For example, the xp_send-mail procedure enables sending e-mail from T-SQL. Generally, extended stored procedures should be avoided in favor of creating the procedures in managed code. This is partly due to the complexity involved in creating secure extended procedures, but mostly because they will be removed from a future version of SQL Server.	Use if you need access to external code or libraries, such as the .NET Framework. Depending on your needs, the code may be limited to working within the context of SQL Server, or it may access external resources, such as network services. The benefits of better memory management and security make VB a better choice for creating these extended stored procedures.
Code location	T-SQL code can only exist within SQL Server. This enables optimizations of queries.	VB code may exist either within SQL Server or on the client. This may mean that you can typically take code from the client and adapt it for running within SQL Server. The code would then execute closer to the data, generally increasing performance. In addition, the hardware running SQL Server is typically more efficient than the average desktop, resulting in code that executes faster.
Web Services	T-SQL supports the creation of Web Services to make any function or stored procedure available via SOAP.	Functions and stored procedures written in VB may be exposed as Web Services from SQL Server. The better support for XML handling and procedural logic may mean that it is easier to create these Web Services in Visual Basic.
XML handling	T-SQL has been extended to provide some capability in reading and writing XML. These extensions only provide the capability to work with the XML as a whole, however.	Provides excellent XML handling, both for working with the document as a whole and via streaming APIs. Generally, if you need to do a lot of XML handling, using Visual Basic will make your life a lot easier.

Creating User-defined Types

One feature of SQL Server that does not usually get the attention it deserves is the capability to create user-defined types (UDTs). These enable the developer to define new types that may be used in columns, functions, stored procedures, and so on. They can make database development easier by applying specific constraints to values, or by identifying the intent of a column. For example, when presented with a table containing a column of type varchar(11), you may still be unsure as to the purpose of the value, but if that column is instead of type `ssn`, you would recognize this (if you are in the United States) as a social security number.

With SQL Server 2005, you can create UDTs using Visual Basic. In addition to the normal benefits of user-defined types, UDTs written in VB have an additional benefit — they may also provide functionality in the form of methods. This means that you can essentially extend the functionality of your database by providing these methods.

UDTs written using Visual Basic are implemented as structures or classes. Because Visual Studio defaults to creating UDTs as structures, this will be assumed here, but keep in mind that you can also create them as classes. The properties or fields of the structure become the subtypes of the UDT. Public methods are also accessible, just as they would be in a VB application.

In addition to the normal code used when writing structures, you must also implement other items to make your UDT work with SQL Server. First, your structure should have the attribute `Microsoft .SqlServer.Server.SqlUserDefinedType`. This attribute identifies the structure as being a SQL Server UDT. In addition, marking the class with the `Serializable` attribute is highly recommended. The `SqlUserDefinedType` attribute has a number of parameters that provide information affecting how SQL Server works with the type. These parameters are described in the following table:

Parameter	Value	Description
Format	Native or UserDefined	Identifies the serialization format. If you use `Native` (the default when you create your UDT with Visual Studio), it uses the SQL Server serialization model. If you set it to `UserDefined`, you must also implement `Microsoft.SqlServer.Server.IBinarySerialize`. This interface includes methods for reading and writing your data type. Generally, using `Native` is safe enough, unless your datatype requires special handling to avoid saving it incorrectly. For example, if you were storing a media stream, you would likely set that as `UserDefined` to avoid writing the stream incorrectly.
IsByteOrdered	Boolean	True if the data is stored in byte order, false if it is stored using some other. If this is true, you can use the default comparison operators with the type, as well as use it as a primary key. If it is possible to define one instance of this UDT as being larger than another, then `IsByteOrdered` is likely true. If it is not, such as with a latitude value, then `IsByteOrdered` is false.
IsFixedLength	Boolean	This should be set to true if all instances of this type are the same size. If the UDT includes only fixed-size elements, such as int, double, or char(20), then this is true. If it includes variable-sized elements, such as varchar(50) or text, then it should be false. This is a marker to enable optimizations by the SQL Server query processor.

Parameter	Value	Description
ValidationMethodName	String	Name of a method to be used to validate the data in the UDT. This method is used when loading the UDT, and should return true if the data is valid.
MaxByteSize	Integer, with a maximum of 8000	Defines the maximum size of the UDT, in bytes

In addition to this attribute, each user-defined type also needs to implement the shared method `Parse`, and the instance method `ToString`. These methods enable conversion between your new datatype and the interim format, `SqlString`. Finally, while not a requirement, you should also implement `INullable` in your structure. This interface requires the addition of the `IsNull` property. This enables your UDT to deal with null values, either stored in the database or passed from the client.

> *If you are using Visual Studio to create your UDTs, it's best to create and debug all of your UDTs before you begin to use them, especially if you need to use them in any table columns. This is because VB drops all of the objects you create in a SQL Server project when deploying your project. If you have any tables that use any user-defined types, you will be unable to drop the UDT and therefore deploy the changes you've made. If you need to make changes, you may receive an error similar to "Cannot drop type 'Location' because it is currently in use." This error causes the deploy step of your project to fail. If this happens, change the column type or temporarily drop the table. You can then redeploy the UDT as needed. Don't forget to change the column back or re-create the table.*

While you can write code that will integrate with SQL Server using any DLL, Visual Studio provides the SQL Server Project (see Figure 14-1). This project type generates a DLL, but also connects the DLL to the database.

Figure 14-1

When you create a new SQL Server Project, Visual Studio prompts you to identify the database that will host the DLL. At this point, you can either select an existing database connection or create a new one. Visual Studio also asks if you want to enable SQL/CLR debugging on the connection. Typically, you will want to enable this on development servers. However, keep in mind that when debugging, the server is limited to the single connection. Once the project is created, you can add the various database types via the Project menu. Deploying the project loads the created DLL into the database. You can confirm that it is loaded by looking at the Assemblies folder in the Server Explorer (see Figure 14-2).

Figure 14-2

The following code example shows a simple `Location` user-defined type written in Visual Basic. This type identifies a geographic location. We will use it throughout the remainder of the chapter to track the location of customers and stores. The `Location` type has two main properties, `Latitude` and `Longitude`. Create this file by selecting New User-defined Type from the Project menu. Here is the code:

```
Imports System
Imports System.Data
Imports System.Data.SqlClient
Imports System.Data.SqlTypes
Imports Microsoft.SqlServer.Server

<Serializable()> _
<Microsoft.SqlServer.Server.SqlUserDefinedType(Format.Native)> _
Public Structure Location
    Implements INullable

    Public ReadOnly Property IsNull() As Boolean Implements INullable.IsNull
        Get
```

```vb
            If Me.Latitude = Double.NaN OrElse Me.Longitude = Double.NaN Then
                _isNull = True
            Else
                _isNull = False
            End If

            Return _isNull
        End Get
    End Property

    Public Shared ReadOnly Property Null As Location
        Get
            Dim result As Location = New Location
            result._isNull = True
            result.Latitude = Double.NaN
            result.Longitude = Double.NaN
            Return result
        End Get
    End Property

    Public Overrides Function ToString() As String
        Return String.Format("{0}, {1}", Latitude, Longitude)
    End Function

    Public Shared Function Parse(ByVal s As SqlString) As Location
        If s.IsNull Then
            Return Null
        End If

        Dim result As Location = New Location
        Dim temp() As String = s.Value.Split(CChar(","))
        If (temp.Length > 1) Then
            result.Latitude = Double.Parse(temp(0))
            result.Longitude = Double.Parse(temp(1))
        End If
        Return result
    End Function

    Public Function Distance(ByVal loc As Location) As Double
        Dim result As Double
        Dim temp As Double
        Dim deltaLat As Double
        Dim deltaLong As Double
        Const EARTH_RADIUS As Integer = 6378    'kilometers
        Dim lat1 As Double
        Dim lat2 As Double
        Dim long1 As Double
        Dim long2 As Double

        'convert to radians
        lat1 = Me.Latitude * Math.PI / 180
        long1 = Me.Longitude * Math.PI / 180
        lat2 = loc.Latitude * Math.PI / 180
        long2 = loc.Longitude * Math.PI / 180
```

```
            'formula from http://mathforum.org/library/drmath/view/51711.html
            deltaLong = long2 - long1
            deltaLat = lat2 - lat1
            temp = (Math.Sin(deltaLat / 2)) ^ 2 + _
                Math.Cos(lat1) * Math.Cos(lat2) * (Math.Sin(deltaLong / 2)) ^ 2
            temp = 2 * Math.Atan2(Math.Sqrt(temp), Math.Sqrt(1 - temp))
            result = EARTH_RADIUS * temp

            Return result
        End Function
```

```
        Private _lat As Double
        Private _long As Double
        Private _isNull As Boolean
        Public Property Latitude() As Double
            Get
                Return _lat
            End Get
            Set(ByVal value As Double)
                _lat = value
            End Set
        End Property
        Public Property Longitude() As Double
            Get
                Return _long
            End Get
            Set(ByVal value As Double)
                _long = value
            End Set
        End Property
    End Structure
```

In addition to the `Latitude` and `Longitude` properties, the `Location` type also defines a `Distance` method. This is used to identify the distance between two locations. It uses the formula for calculating the distance between two points on a sphere to calculate the distance. This formula is better described at the "Ask Dr. Math" forum. As the Earth is not a perfect sphere, this calculation should only be considered an estimate, but it is close enough for our needs.

Now that you have created the `Location` type, you can use it in the definition of a table. This example creates part of an e-commerce application to demonstrate the use of `Location` and other SQL Server features.

Imagine if you will that you are creating an application for an online store that also has brick and mortar locations. When a customer orders a product, you must obviously ship it from some location. Major online sellers likely have large warehouses that they can use to fulfill these orders. However, they are generally limited to shipping from these warehouses. Other companies also have physical stores that stock many of the items available for order. Wouldn't it make sense that if one of those stores has stock and is closer to the customer, then you would use the stock in the store to fulfill the order from the website? It would save on shipping costs, and it would get the product to the customer faster. This would save you money, and lead to happier customers who are more likely to order from you again. This hypothetical scenario would likely be called into play many times throughout the day; therefore, moving it to a stored procedure would be useful to improve performance. The calculations would be closer to the data, and the database server itself could perform optimizations on it if needed.

Open the database using SQL Management Studio or the Server Explorer in Visual Studio. Create a table called Stores. This table will be used to track the physical store locations. See Figure 14-3 for the layout of this table. Note that the new `Location` datatype should appear at the bottom of the list of datatypes; it is not inserted in alphabetical order.

Column Name	Data Type	Allow Nulls
id	int	☐
Name	nvarchar(50)	☐
Street	nvarchar(512)	☐
City	nvarchar(50)	☐
State	char(2)	☐
Zip	varchar(50)	☑
GeoLocation	Location	☑
		☐

Figure 14-3

The `id` column is defined as an identity column, and is the primary key. Don't bother adding any data to the table yet, unless you know the appropriate latitude and longitude for each location. We'll create a function for calculating the location in a moment.

In addition to the Stores table, create two other tables, one for products (see Figure 14-4), and the other to track the stock (see Figure 14-5) available in each store.

Column Name	Data Type	Allow Nulls
id	int	☐
Name	nvarchar(50)	☐
Price	money	☐
		☐

Figure 14-4

As with the Stores table, the id column is an identity field. The Name field will represent the name of the product, and Price will reflect the unit price of each item. A typical product table would likely have other columns as well; this table has been kept as simple as possible for this example.

Column Name	Data Type	Allow Nulls
StoreID	int	☐
ProductID	int	☐
Quantity	int	☐
		☐

Figure 14-5

The Stock table will provide the connection between the Stores and Products tables. It uses the combination of the two primary keys as its key. This means that each combination of store and product will have a single entry, with the quantity of the product per store.

Now that the tables are in place for the sample, we'll turn our attention to creating a way to determine the location, using a SQL Server function written in Visual Basic.

Creating Functions

Functions are a feature of SQL Server enabling a simple calculation that returns either a scalar value or a table of values. These functions differ from stored procedures in that they are typically used to perform some calculation or action, rather than specifically acting on a table. You can create functions in either T-SQL or Visual Basic.

When creating functions with Visual Basic, you define a class with one or more methods. Methods that you want to make available as SQL Server functions should be marked with the `Microsoft.SqlServer.Server.SqlFunctionAttribute` attribute. SQL Server will then register the methods, and they may be used in your database. The `SqlFunction` attribute takes a number of optional parameters, shown in the following table:

Parameter	Value	Description
DataAccess	Either `DataAccessKind.None` or `DataAccessKind.Read`	Set to `DataAccessKind.Read` if the function will access data stored in the database.
SystemDataAccess	Either `SystemDataAccessKind.None` or `SystemDataAccessKind.Read`	Set to `SystemDataAccessKind.Read` if the function will access data in the system tables of the database.
FillRowMethodName	String	The name of the method that will return each row of data. This is only used if the function returns tabular data.
IsDeterministic	Boolean	Set to true if the function is deterministic — that is, if it will always produce the same result, given the same input and database output. (A random function would obviously not be deterministic). The default is false.
IsPrecise	Boolean	Set to true if the function does not use any floating point calculations. The default is false.
TableDefinition	String	Provides the table definition of the return value. Only needed if the function returns tabular data.

By default, SQL Server 2005 loads Visual Basic objects into a safe environment. This means that they cannot call external code or resources. In addition, Code Access Security (CAS) limits access to some aspects of the .NET Framework. You can change this behavior by explicitly setting the permission level under which the code will run. The following table outlines the available permission levels:

Permission Level	Safe	External	Unsafe
Code access	Limited to code running within SQL Server context	Ability to access external resources	Unlimited
Framework access	Limited	Limited	Unlimited
Verifiability	Yes	Yes	No
Native code	No	No	Yes

Use the minimum permission level needed to get your code to run. Typically, this means you need only the Safe level. This permission level provides access to the libraries providing data access, XML handling, mathematical calculations, and other commonly needed capabilities.

If you need access to other network resources, such as the capability to call out to external Web Services or SMTP servers, enable the External permission level. This also provides all the capabilities provided by the Safe permission level.

You should only enable the Unsafe permission level in the rarest of occasions, when you need access to native code. Code running within this permission level provides full access to any code available to it, so it may represent a security hole for your application.

If you attempt to deploy a VB DLL that requires external access, you will receive this lengthy — but not entirely helpful — error message:

```
CREATE ASSEMBLY for assembly 'FooStore' failed because assembly 'FooStore' is not
authorized for PERMISSION_SET = EXTERNAL_ACCESS. The assembly is authorized when
either of the following is true: the database owner (DBO) has EXTERNAL ACCESS
ASSEMBLY permission and the database has the TRUSTWORTHY database property on; or
the assembly is signed with a certificate or an asymmetric key that has a
corresponding login with EXTERNAL ACCESS ASSEMBLY permission.
```

The error message provides the steps required to enable external access. At this point, you have two options:

❑ Provide the External Access Assembly permission to the user account associated with the database owner. You should not do this unless the second option is not possible. This creates a dangerous security hole in your database. It would mean that any Visual Basic code running on the server would have external access permissions, and complete access to the database.

❑ Sign the assembly and create an account that uses this signature. Then provide the External Access Assembly permission to that account. This is the preferred method for enabling safe external access by a Visual Basic assembly. By signing your assembly and giving the assembly (and the user id associated with the signature) permission, you are limiting the amount of code that can access other servers.

The following steps outline how to provide external access permissions to a VB assembly using Visual Studio. First, set the permission level to External (see Figure 14-6) and provide a name for the owner of the assembly. This is done using the database page of the project's property pages.

Figure 14-6

Once you have enabled external access for your Visual Basic code, you need to sign your assembly. Sign the assembly on the Signing tab of the properties dialog (see Figure 14-7). Use an existing key file or create a new one.

Once you have signed and built the assembly, the next steps are to create a key in the database based on the signature of the assembly and create a user who will be associated with the key. This is done using a T-SQL query. Run the following query in SQL Management Studio:

```
USE master
GO
CREATE ASYMMETRIC KEY FooStoreKey
   FROM EXECUTABLE FILE = 'C:\FooStore.dll'
GO

CREATE LOGIN FooUser
   FROM ASYMMETRIC KEY FooStoreKey
GRANT EXTERNAL ACCESS ASSEMBLY TO FooUser
GO
```

Figure 14-7

Creating a new asymmetric key must be done from the master database. The DLL listed in the FROM EXECUTABLE FILE clause should be the DLL you just created in Visual Basic; adjust the path in the SQL statement to match the location of your DLL. Once the key is created, you can create a new login based on this key, and provide that user with external access. You should also add that login to the database and give it permission to access the desired objects.

Now that the assembly can access external sites, you are ready to begin coding the function that will convert the addresses to latitude and longitude (that is, geocode the address). Numerous companies sell databases or services that provide this capability, but Yahoo! has a free Web Service that geocodes addresses (see the Resources section at the end of this chapter for the URL). It can be called up to 5,000 times a day, more than enough for this sample (but probably not enough for a real store).

The Geocode service is accessed by sending a GET request to http://api.local.yahoo.com/ MapsService/V1/geocode with the following parameters:

Parameter	Description
appid	(Required) The unique string used to identify each application using the service. Note that this parameter name is case sensitive. For testing purposes, you can use YahooDemo (used by the Yahoo samples themselves). However, your own applications should have unique application IDs, which you can register at `http://api.search.yahoo.com/webservices/register_application`.
street	(Optional) The street address you are searching for. This should be URL-encoded. That is, spaces should be replaced with + characters, and high ASCII or characters such as <, /, >, etc., should be replaced with their equivalent using '%##' notation.
city	(Optional) The city for the location you are searching for. This should be URL-encoded, although this is really only necessary when the city name contains spaces or high ASCII characters.
state	(Optional) The U.S. state (if applicable) you are searching for. Either the two-letter abbreviation or full name (URL-encoded) will work.
zip	(Optional) The U.S. zip code (if applicable) you are searching for. This can be in either 5-digit or 5+4-digit format.
location	(Optional) A free-form field of address information containing the URL-encoded and comma-delimited request. This provides an easier method for querying, rather than setting the individual values listed above, e.g., location=1600+Pennsylvania+Avenue+NW,+Washington,+DC

The following code shows the full source for the fnGetLocation function:

```
Imports System
Imports System.Data
Imports System.Data.SqlClient
Imports System.Data.SqlTypes
Imports Microsoft.SqlServer.Server
Imports System.Xml
Imports System.Text

Partial Public Class UserDefinedFunctions

    'Replace YahooDemo with your key
    Private Const YAHOO_APP_KEY As String = "YahooDemo"
    Private Const BASE_URL As String = _
        "http://api.local.yahoo.com/MapsService/V1/geocode"

    <Microsoft.SqlServer.Server.SqlFunction()> _
    Public Shared Function fnGetLocation(ByVal street As SqlString, _
        ByVal city As SqlString, _
        ByVal state As SqlString, _
        ByVal zip As SqlString) As Location

        Dim result As New Location
```

```
Dim query As New StringBuilder

'uses Yahoo geocoder to geocode the location
'limited to 5000 calls/day

'construct URL
' URL should look like:
'    http://api.local.yahoo.com/MapsService/V1/geocode?
'        appid=YahooDemo&street=701+First+Street&city=Sunnyvale&state=CA

query.AppendFormat("{0}?appid={1}", BASE_URL, YAHOO_APP_KEY)
If Not street.IsNull Then
    query.AppendFormat("&street={0}", street)
End If
If Not city.IsNull Then
    query.AppendFormat("&city={0}", city)
End If
If Not state.IsNull Then
    query.AppendFormat("&state={0}", state)
End If
If Not zip.IsNull Then
    query.AppendFormat("&zip={0}", zip)
End If
'Debug.Print(query.ToString())

'send request
Using r As XmlReader = XmlReader.Create(query.ToString())
    'parse output
    While r.Read
        If r.IsStartElement("Latitude") Then
            ' longitude directly follows latitude in the result xml
            result.Latitude = Double.Parse(r.ReadElementString)
            result.Longitude = Double.Parse(r.ReadElementString)
            Exit While
        End If
    End While
End Using

        Return result
    End Function
End Class
```

Most of the code in the preceding sample is used to create the appropriate URL to create the query. The query should look as follows:

```
http://api.local.yahoo.com/MapsService/V1/geocode?appid=YahooDemo&street=701+
First+Street&city=Sunnyvale&state=CA&country=USA
```

While the YahooDemo appid will work for testing, there is a good chance that it will not work at times. As the query is limited to 5,000 requests for each appid, if too many people call the geocoder in one day, the request will fail. Therefore, you should request your own appid for testing, and replace the preceding appid with your own. You can request your own appid at the following Web page:

```
http://api.search.yahoo.com/webservices/register_application
```

You probably noticed that the preceding code uses a `StringBuilder` *to construct the query. Why not simply concatenate strings to create the query? There are a number of reasons, but the most important is performance. As strings in Visual Basic are immutable, concatenation requires the creation of new strings each time. For example, the simple expression* `Dim s As String = "Hello" & "world"` *actually requires three strings, two of which are immediately discarded. The* `StringBuilder` *class has been built to avoid this repeated creation and disposal of objects, and the resulting code has much better performance than what you could achieve with simple concatenation.*

Once the query is constructed, an `XmlReader` is used to execute the query. The resulting XML from a call to Yahoo!'s geocoder looks like the following:

```
<?xml version="1.0" ?>
<ResultSet xmlns:xsi="http://www.w3.org/2001/XMLSchema-instance"
    xmlns="urn:yahoo:maps"
    xsi:schemaLocation="urn:yahoo:maps
      http://api.local.yahoo.com/MapsService/V1/GeocodeResponse.xsd">
  <Result precision="address"
      warning="The exact location could not be found,
        here is the closest match: 701 First Ave, Sunnyvale, CA 94089">
    <Latitude>37.416384</Latitude>
    <Longitude>-122.024853</Longitude>
    <Address>701 FIRST AVE</Address>
    <City>SUNNYVALE</City>
    <State>CA</State>
    <Zip>94089-1019</Zip>
    <Country>US</Country>
  </Result>
</ResultSet>
<!-- ws02.search.scd.yahoo.com uncompressed/chunked Mon Dec  4 16:33:28 PST 2006
-->
```

While you could load all of this into an `XmlDocument` for processing, the `XmlReader` is generally faster. In addition, because all that is really needed are the two values for latitude and longitude, using the `XmlReader` enables the code to extract these two values quickly, and without the overhead of loading all the other data. The `XmlReader` class implements `IDisposable`, so ensure the correct handling and disposal of the class either by setting the object to nothing in a `Try...Finally` block or by employing the `Using` statement:

```
Using r As XmlReader = XmlReader.Create(query.ToString())
    'parse output
    While r.Read
        If r.IsStartElement("Latitude") Then
            ' longitude directly follows latitude in the result xml
            result.Latitude = Double.Parse(r.ReadElementString)
            result.Longitude = Double.Parse(r.ReadElementString)
            Exit While
        End If
    End While
End Using
```

As shown in Chapter 11, you create the `XmlReader` using the shared `Create` method. This method has a number of overridden versions. In this case, the string version of the URL is used to create the

`XmlReader`. The code then loops through the resulting XML until the start element for the `Latitude` element is found. As we know, the two values are next to each other; the code may then access them and stop reading. Figure 14-8 shows testing this new function in SQL Server Management Studio.

Figure 14-8

Using the User-defined Function

Even though the `fnGetLocation` function is written in Visual Basic, you can still use this function from T-SQL. This means that you can use either VB or T-SQL for a given SQL Server object, whichever is better suited to the scenario. The following code shows the procedure used to insert new stores. This procedure is written in T-SQL, but it calls the function written in Visual Basic. Alternately, you could create an insert trigger that calls the function to determine the location of the store. Here is the procedure code:

```
CREATE PROCEDURE dbo.procInsertStore
(
    @name nvarchar(50),
    @street nvarchar(512),
    @city nvarchar(50),
    @state char(2),
```

```
  @zip varchar(50)
)
AS
  /* need to populate location */
  DECLARE @loc AS Location;

  SET @loc = dbo.fnGetLocation(@street, @city, @state, @zip);

  INSERT INTO Stores (Name, Street, City, State, Zip, GeoLocation)
      OUTPUT INSERTED.id
  VALUES (@name, @street, @city, @state, @zip, @loc);


  RETURN @@IDENTITY
```

The stored procedure uses the function and user-defined type just as it would use the same objects written in T-SQL. Before storing the store data, it calls the Web Service to determine the latitude and longitude of the location, and then stores the data in the table.

Now you can add data to the three tables. Add a few stores (see Figure 14-9) using the stored procedure. The actual data is not that important, but having multiple stores relatively close to one another will be useful later.

id	Name	Street	City	State	Zip	GeoLocation
1	Store #50	357 108th Ave NE	Bellevue	WA	NULL	47.613399, -122.196403
2	Store #63	15703 NE 56th Ave	Redmond	WA	NULL	47.658031, -122.130822
3	Store #11	611 Broadway	New York	NY	10012	40.725712, -73.996735
4	Store #23	23 W 60th St	New York	NY	10010	40.769261, -73.982669
5	Store #34	340 W North Ave	Chicago	IL		41.911237, -87.638002
6	Store #26	2550 N Clark St	Chicago	IL	NULL	41.928468, -87.642395
*	NULL NULL	NULL	NULL	NULL	NULL	NULL

Figure 14-9

Similarly, add a number of items to the Products table (see Figure 14-10). Again, the data itself is not important, only that you have a variety of items from which to choose.

id	Name	Price
1	Widget	3.5000
2	Doodad	12.9900
3	Thingie	4.9500
4	Whatchamacallit	52.9800
5	Macguffin	99.9900
*	NULL	NULL	NULL

Figure 14-10

Finally, add the data to the Stock table (see Figure 14-11). There should be a single entry for each combination of store and product. Make certain that you have a variety of quantities on hand for testing.

StoreID	ProductID	Quantity
1	1	0
1	2	0
1	3	0
1	4	4
1	5	2
2	1	0
2	2	2
2	3	0
2	4	0
2	5	1
3	1	1
3	2	4
3	3	2
3	4	4
3	5	2
4	1	0
4	2	2
4	3	3
4	4	0
4	5	1
5	1	4
5	2	0
5	3	1
5	4	2

Figure 14-11

Now that you have some data to work with, and a function for determining the latitude and longitude of any address, you're ready to examine how to create a stored procedure in Visual Basic to locate the nearest store with available stock to the customer.

Creating Stored Procedures

A feature that has received a great deal of fanfare with SQL Server 2005 is the capability to create stored procedures in Visual Basic 2005 (or rather, in any .NET language). This feature supplements the long-standing use of T-SQL as the language for stored procedures. At the same time, it raises more questions: When should you use T-SQL, and when should you use Visual Basic? Is Visual Basic suitable for all stored procedures?

As with most questions of this type, the answer is a resounding, "It depends." T-SQL is a powerful language for dealing with sets of information, which are groups of items you can define using some criteria (i.e., the result of a SELECT statement). Visual Basic lacks any real functionality for dealing with sets, at least until LINQ is released. This provides us with at least some of the answers to the questions posed above.

T-SQL is the better choice when you must deal with a set of data. It is a great language for doing bulk changes to a list of items, or for rapidly finding all items that match some criterion — for example, to change the area codes of some of the phone numbers stored, or to find all the customers who have purchased more than 10 items in the last 30 days. Doing the same tasks using VB would lead to long looping tests that would need to walk through all the items stored.

Just as with user-defined types and functions, you identify methods as being stored procedures with an attribute. In the case of stored procedures, this is `Microsoft.SqlServer.Server.SqlProcedure-Attribute`. This attribute is basically a marker attribute; there are no additional parameters that have any dramatic effect on the behavior of the code.

When creating a stored procedure in Visual Basic, keep a few considerations in mind. First, and likely most important, is the context. You are no longer running as a separate piece of code, but within SQL Server. Tasks that require long processing mean that whatever resources you are using will be unavailable to other code. This could cause your database to become less responsive, leading to more slowdowns. Therefore, always remain conscious of the resources you are using, and the amount of time you lock them.

The second major change when creating stored procedures in VB is the connection to the data. When writing standalone VB code that accesses data, you need to create a connection to a class that implements `IDbConnection` — frequently, `SqlConnection` or `OleDbConnection`. The connection string used identifies the database, user id, and so on. However, in a stored procedure, you are running within the context of SQL Server itself, so most of this information is superfluous. This makes connecting to the datasource much easier:

```
Using connection As New SqlConnection("context connection=true")
...'work with the data here
End Using
```

The connection string is now reduced to the equivalent of "right where the code is running." The user id, database and other parameters are implied by the context in which the code is running.

Once you have connected to the database, the rest of the code is basically the same as you are used to performing with other ADO.NET code. This means that migrating code that accesses SQL Server to run as a stored procedure is fairly easy: change the connection string used to connect to the database, and add the `SqlProcedure` attribute.

Returning Data from a Stored Procedure

Once you have performed whatever manipulation is required to get your data, you obviously need to send it back to the user. With normal ADO.NET, you would create a `DataSet` or `SqlDataReader` and use the methods and properties of the class to extract the data. However, the data access code running within a stored procedure is running in the context of SQL Server, and the stored procedure must behave in the same way as other stored procedures. Therefore, you must change your code slightly to accommodate this behavior.

When returning data using ADO.NET, you typically have a few options. The first option depends on whether you need to return a single value or one or more rows of data.

Returning a Single Value

If you are returning a single value from the stored procedure, create your stored procedure as a subroutine. The data you return should be a ByRef parameter of the subroutine. Finally, you need to mark this parameter as an out-parameter using the System.Runtime.InteropServices.Out attribute. For example, if you were attempting to create a stored procedure that returned the total value of all the items available at a selected store, you would create it similar to the procedure shown here:

```
Imports System
Imports System.Data
Imports System.Data.SqlClient
Imports System.Data.SqlTypes
Imports Microsoft.SqlServer.Server
Imports System.Runtime.InteropServices


Partial Public Class StoredProcedures
    <Microsoft.SqlServer.Server.SqlProcedure()> _
    Public Shared Sub procGetStoreInventoryValue(ByVal storeID As Int32, _
        <Out()> ByRef totalValue As Single)

        Dim query As String = "SELECT SUM(Products.Price * Stock.Quantity) " & _
            "FROM Products INNER JOIN Stock ON " & _
            "Products.id = Stock.ProductID " & _
            "WHERE Stock.StoreID = @storeID"
        Using conn As New SqlConnection("context connection = true")
            conn.Open()
            Using cmd As New SqlCommand(query, conn)
                cmd.Parameters.Add("@storeID", SqlDbType.Int).Value = storeID
                totalValue = CSng(cmd.ExecuteScalar())
            End Using
        End Using
    End Sub
End Class
```

As this stored procedure doesn't really do any processing of the data, or mathematical calculations, it would probably be best created using T-SQL.

The procedure is fairly basic: It uses the current connection to execute a block of SQL, and returns the value from that SQL. As before, the SqlConnection and SqlCommand values are created using the new Using statement. This ensures that they are disposed of, freeing the memory used, when the code block is completed.

Just as when working with ByRef parameters in other code, any changes made to the variable within the procedure are reflected outside the method. The Out attribute extends this to identify the parameter as a value that needs to be marshaled out of the application. It is needed to change the behavior of the ByRef variable. Normally, the ByRef variable is an In/Out value. You must have it at least available when you make the call. By marking it with the Out attribute, you mark it as not having this requirement.

Returning Multiple Values

Things become slightly more complex if you want to return one or more rows of data. In a sense, your code needs to replicate the data transfer that would normally occur when a stored procedure is executed within SQL Server. The data must somehow be transferred to the TDS (tabular data stream). How do you create this TDS? Fortunately, SQL Server 2005 provides you with a way: via the `SqlPipe` class. The `SqlContext` class provides access to the `SqlPipe` class via its `Pipe` property. The `SqlPipe` class has a number of methods that may be used to return data back to the code that called the stored procedure.

Method	Description
ExecuteAndSend	Takes a `SqlCommand`, executes it, and returns the result. This is the most efficient of the methods that may be used to return data, as it does not need to generate any memory structures.
Send(SqlDataReader)	Takes a `SqlDataReader` and streams out the resulting data to the client. This is slightly slower than the preceding method, but recommended if you need to perform any processing on the data before returning.
Send(SqlDataRecord)	Returns a single row of data to the client. This is a useful method if you are generating the data and only need to return a single row.
Send(String)	Returns a message to the client. This is not the same as a scalar string value, however. Instead, this is intended for sending informational messages to the client. The information sent back may be retrieved using the `InfoMessage` event of the `SqlConnection`.
SendResultsStart	Used to mark the beginning of a multi-row block of data. This method takes a `SqlDataRecord` that is used to identify the columns that will be sent with subsequent `SendResultsRow` calls. This method is most useful when you must construct multiple rows of data before returning to the client.
SendResultsRow	Used to send a `SqlDataRecord` back to the client. You must already have called `SendResultsStart` using a matching `SqlDataRecord`, or an exception will occur.
SendResultsEnd	Marks the end of the transmission of a multi-row block of data. This can only be called after first calling `SendResultsStart`, and likely one or more calls to `SendResultsRow`. If you fail to call this method, then any other attempts to use the `SqlPipe` will cause an exception.

If all you want to do is execute a block of SQL and return the resulting data, then use the `ExecuteAndSend` method. (Actually, in this case, you should likely be using T-SQL, but there may be cases that justify doing this in VB). This method avoids the overhead involved in creating any memory structures to hold the data in an intermediate form. Instead, it streams the data just as it would if the procedure were written in T-SQL.

The next most commonly used method for returning data is the version of the `Send` method that takes a `SqlDataReader`. With this method, your code can return a block of data pointed at by a `SqlDataReader`.

This method, as well as the version of Send that takes a SqlDataRecord, is commonly used when some processing of the data is needed before returning. They do require that some memory structures be created, so they are not as fast at returning data as the ExecuteAndSend method.

The version of Send taking a SqlDataRecord object can be a handy method for constructing and returning a single row of data (or more when using SendResultsRow).

The SqlDataRecord class is new with the Microsoft.SqlServer.Server namespace, and represents a single row of data. Why a new datatype instead of just leveraging DataSet? The creators needed an object that was capable of being converted into the tabular data stream format used by SQL Server. There are two ways to return a SqlDataRecord. If only a single row of data needs to be returned, you use the Send(SqlDataRecord) method. If multiple records will be returned, then you use SendResultsStart, SendResultsRow, and SendResultsEnd (see below). In each case, you are responsible for creating and populating the values for each column in the SqlDataRecord.

Columns within a SqlDataRecord are defined using the SqlMetaData class. Each column requires the definition of an instance of a separate SqlMetaData object, with the constructor of SqlDataRecord taking an param array of these objects. Each SqlMetaData object defines the type, size, and maximum length (if appropriate) of the data for the column. The following code shows the creation of a SqlDataRecord with four columns:

```
Dim rec As SqlDataRecord
rec = New SqlDataRecord( _
    new SqlMetaData("col1", SqlDbType.Int), _
    new SqlMetaData("col2", SqlDbType.VarChar, 25), _
    new SqlMetaData("col3", SqlDbType.Float), _
    new SqlMetaData("col4", SqlDbType.Text, 512))
```

You can retrieve data from each of the columns in two ways: You can use the GetValue method, which returns the value stored in the nth column of the SqlDataRecord as an Object. Alternately, you can return the data as a particular datatype using one of the many GetXXX methods, where XXX is the type required. For example, to return the value stored in the second column above as a string, you would use GetString(1). Similarly, there are SetValue and SetXXX methods for setting the value of each column. Once you have created your SqlDataRecord and populated its values, you return it to the client by passing it to the Send method of the SqlPipe, as in the following code:

```
rec.SetInt32(0, 42)
rec.SetString(1, "Some string")
rec.SetFloat(2, 3.14)
rec.SetString(3, "Some longer string")

SqlContext.Pipe.Send(rec)
```

The version of the Send method that takes a string is slightly different from the other two variants. Rather than return data, the intent of the Send(String) version is to return information to the calling application — the equivalent of the T-SQL print statement. You can receive this data by adding a handler to the InfoMessage event of the SqlConnection.

The final three methods of the SqlPipe used for returning multiple rows of data are used together. SendResultsStart marks the beginning of a set of rows, SendResultsRow is used to send each row, and SendResultsEnd marks the end of the set of rows.

In addition to marking the start of the block of data, SendResultsStart is used to define the structure of the returned data. This is done by using a SqlDataRecord instance. Once you have called SendResultsStart, the only valid methods of SqlPipe that you can use are SendResultsRow and SendResultsEnd. Calling any other method results in an exception. The records you send back with each call of SendResultsRow should match the structure defined in the SendResultsStart method. In fact, to conserve server resources, it is a good idea to use the same SqlDataRecord instance for all of these calls. If you create a new SqlDataRecord with each row, you are wasting memory, as each of these objects will be marked for garbage collection. The basic process for using these three methods would work as follows:

```
Dim rec As New SqlDataRecord(cols)
SqlContext.Pipe.SendResultsStart(rec)
For I As Integer = 1 To 10
    'populate the record
    rec.SetInt32(0, I)
    rec.SetString(1, "Row #" & I.ToString())
    rec.SetFloat(2, I * Math.PI)
    rec.SetString(3, "Information about row #" & I.ToString())
    SqlContext.Pipe.SendResultsRow(rec)
Next
SqlContext.Pipe.SendResultsEnd()
```

The following code shows the complete class, containing the stored procedure for determining the nearest store with available stock:

```
Imports System
Imports System.Data
Imports System.Data.SqlClient
Imports System.Data.SqlTypes
Imports Microsoft.SqlServer.Server
Imports System.Collections.Generic

Partial Public Class StoredProcedures
    <Microsoft.SqlServer.Server.SqlProcedure()> _
    Public Shared Sub procGetClosestStoreWithStock(ByVal street As SqlString, _
        ByVal city As SqlString, _
        ByVal state As SqlString, _
        ByVal zip As SqlString, _
        ByVal productID As SqlInt32, _
        ByVal quantity As SqlInt32)

        Dim loc As Location
        Dim query As String = "SELECT id, Name, Street, City, " & _
            "State, Zip, GeoLocation " & _
            "FROM Stores INNER JOIN Stock on Stores.id = Stock.StoreId " & _
            "WHERE Stock.ProductID = @productID " & _
            "AND Stock.Quantity > @quantity " & _
            "ORDER BY Stock.Quantity DESC"
        Dim dr As SqlDataReader
        Dim result As SqlDataRecord = Nothing

        'get location of requested address
        loc = UserDefinedFunctions.fnGetLocation(street, city, state, zip)
```

```
        Using connection As New SqlConnection("context connection=true")
            connection.Open()
            'pipe is used to return data to the user
            Dim pipe As SqlPipe = SqlContext.Pipe
            'get stores with stock
            Using cmd As New SqlCommand(query, connection)
                With cmd.Parameters
                    .Add("@productID", SqlDbType.Int).Value = productID
                    .Add("@quantity", SqlDbType.Int).Value = quantity
                End With

                dr = cmd.ExecuteReader()

                'find the closest store
                Dim distance As Double
                Dim smallest As Double = Double.MaxValue
                Dim storeLoc As Location
                Dim rowData(6) As Object
                While (dr.Read)
                    dr.GetSqlValues(rowData)
                    storeLoc = DirectCast(rowData(6), Location)
                    distance = loc.Distance(storeLoc)
                    If distance < smallest Then
                        result = CopyRow(rowData)
                        smallest = distance
                    End If
                End While

                pipe.Send(result)
            End Using
        End Using

    End Sub

    Private Shared Function CopyRow(ByVal data() As Object) As SqlDataRecord
        Dim result As SqlDataRecord
        Dim cols As New List(Of SqlMetaData)

        'set up columns
        cols.Add(New SqlMetaData("id", SqlDbType.Int))
        cols.Add(New SqlMetaData("Name", SqlDbType.NVarChar, 50))
        cols.Add(New SqlMetaData("Street", SqlDbType.NVarChar, 512))
        cols.Add(New SqlMetaData("City", SqlDbType.NVarChar, 50))
        cols.Add(New SqlMetaData("State", SqlDbType.Char, 2))
        cols.Add(New SqlMetaData("Zip", SqlDbType.VarChar, 50))
        result = New SqlDataRecord(cols.ToArray())

        'copy data from row to record
        result.SetSqlInt32(0, DirectCast(data(0), SqlInt32))
        result.SetSqlString(1, DirectCast(data(1), SqlString))
        result.SetSqlString(2, DirectCast(data(2), SqlString))
        result.SetSqlString(3, DirectCast(data(3), SqlString))
        result.SetSqlString(4, DirectCast(data(4), SqlString))
        result.SetSqlString(5, DirectCast(data(5), SqlString))
```

```
        Return result
    End Function
End Class
```

There are three basic steps to the stored procedure. First, it needs to determine the location of the inputted address. Next, it needs to find stores with available stock — that is, with stock greater than the requested amount. Finally, it needs to find the store on that list that is closest to the inputted address.

Getting the location of the address is probably the easiest step, as the `fnGetLocation` function already exists. Rather than needing to create and use a `SqlConnection`, however, because the function is a shared method of the `UserDefinedFunctions` class, you can use it directly from your code. This shows another benefit of the way that the VB-SQL interaction was designed. The code is the same that you would have used in a system written completely in VB, but in this case it's actually calling a SQL Server scalar function.

Obtaining the list of stores with stock is a matter of creating a `SqlCommand` and using it to create a `SqlDataReader`. Again, this is basically the same as in any other VB application. The difference here is that the code will execute within SQL Server. Therefore, the `SqlConnection` is defined using the connection string `"context connection = true"`.

The final step in the stored procedure — finding the nearest store — requires some mathematical calculations (within the `Location.Distance` method). While the previous two steps could have been performed easily in straight T-SQL, it is this step that would have been the most awkward to perform using that language. The code loops through each row in the list of stores with available stock. Because all of the values from each row are needed, the `GetSqlValues` method copies the current row to an array of `Object` values. Within this array is the `GeoLocation` column, a value that can be cast to a `Location` object. Once this is done, the `Distance` method may be used to determine the distance between the input address and the store's address. Once the minimum distance has been determined, the `Send(SqlDataRecord)` method of the `SqlPipe` class is used to write the data to the output stream, returning it to the calling function.

The `CopyRow` function is used to create the `SqlDataRecord` to return. The first step in creating a `SqlDataRecord` is defining the columns of data. The constructor for the `SqlDataRecord` requires an array of `SqlMetaData` objects that define each column. The preceding code uses the `List` generic collection to make defining this array easier. Once the columns are defined, the data returned from the `GetValues` method is used to populate the columns of the new `SqlDataRecord`.

Exposing Web Services from SQL Server

One additional new feature of SQL Server 2005 was the addition of support for exposing Web Services directly from the server. Doing this means that there is no requirement for IIS on the server, as the requests are received and processed by SQL Server. You define what ports will be used to host the Web Service. The structure of the Web Service is defined based on the parameters and return data of the function or stored procedure you use as the source of the Web Service.

Exposing Web Services directly from SQL Server 2005 is only supported on the Standard and above editions. SQL Server Express does not support creating Web Services in this manner.

When you are architecting a scenario and planning on exposing Web Services from SQL Server, keep in mind at least one important question: Why? As in, why do you think you need to expose this database functionality outside of the SQL Server? It's not a trivial question. It means that you plan on hanging data off of the server, possibly for public access. On the surface, it's a dangerous scenario not to be taken lightly. Most of the scenarios in which it makes sense to provide Web Services directly from a SQL Server involve systems entirely behind a firewall, where Web Services are used as the conduit between departments.

The following code example shows the basic syntax of the CREATE ENDPOINT command. Although both AS HTTP and AS TCP are shown, only one can occur per create endpoint command:

```
CREATE ENDPOINT endPointName [ AUTHORIZATION login ]
STATE = { STARTED | STOPPED | DISABLED }
AS HTTP (
  PATH = 'url',
  AUTHENTICATION =( { BASIC | DIGEST | INTEGRATED | NTLM | KERBEROS } [ ,...n ] ),
  PORTS = ( { CLEAR | SSL} [ ... n ] )
  [ SITE = {'*' | '+' | 'webSite' },]
  [, CLEAR_PORT = clearPort ]
  [, SSL_PORT = SSLPort ]
  [, AUTH_REALM = { 'realm' | NONE } ]
  [, DEFAULT_LOGON_DOMAIN = { 'domain' | NONE } ]
  [, COMPRESSION = { ENABLED | DISABLED } ]
  )
AS TCP (
  LISTENER_PORT = listenerPort
  [ , LISTENER_IP = ALL | (<4-part-ip> | <ip_address_v6> ) ]
  )
FOR SOAP(
  [ { WEBMETHOD [ 'namespace' .] 'method_alias'
    (   NAME = 'database.owner.name'
      [ , SCHEMA = { NONE | STANDARD | DEFAULT } ]
      [ , FORMAT = { ALL_RESULTS | ROWSETS_ONLY } ]
    )
  } [ ,...n ] ]
  [   BATCHES = { ENABLED | DISABLED } ]
  [ , WSDL = { NONE | DEFAULT | 'sp_name' } ]
  [ , SESSIONS = { ENABLED | DISABLED } ]
  [ , LOGIN_TYPE = { MIXED | WINDOWS } ]
  [ , SESSION_TIMEOUT = timeoutInterval | NEVER ]
  [ , DATABASE = { 'database_name' | DEFAULT }
  [ , NAMESPACE = { 'namespace' | DEFAULT } ]
  [ , SCHEMA = { NONE | STANDARD } ]
  [ , CHARACTER_SET = { SQL | XML }]
  [ , HEADER_LIMIT = int ]
  )
```

Consider the following main points when creating an endpoint:

❑   **What stored procedure or function (or UDF) will you be exposing?** This is identified in the WebMethod clause. There may be multiple Web methods exposed from a single endpoint. Each will have a separate `WebMethod` parameter listing. This parameter identifies the database object you will expose, and allows you to give it a new name.

❑ **What authentication will clients need to use?** Typically, if your clients are part of the same network, then you use integrated or NTLM authentication. If clients are coming across the Internet or from non-Windows, then you may want to use Kerberos, digest, or basic authentication.

❑ **What network port will the service use?** The basic options when creating an HTTP endpoint are CLEAR (using HTTP, typically on port 80) or SSL (using HTTPS, typically on port 443). Generally, you should use SSL when the data transmitted requires security and you are using public networks. Note that Internet Information Services (IIS) and other Web servers also use these ports. If you have both IIS and SQL Server on the same machine, alternate ports (using CLEAR_PORT or SSL_PORT) for your HTTP endpoints. When creating TCP endpoints, select a LISTENER_PORT that is unused on your server. HTTP allows for the broadest reach and number of possible clients, while TCP allows for better performance. If you are making the Web Service available over the Internet, you would generally use HTTP and TCP within the firewall, where you can control the number and type of clients.

To continue our example, you can make the `procGetClosestStoreWithStock` procedure available as a Web Service using the following code:

```
CREATE ENDPOINT store_endpoint
  STATE = STARTED
AS
HTTP(
  PATH = '/fooStore',
  AUTHENTICATION = (INTEGRATED),
  PORTS = (CLEAR),
  CLEAR_PORT = 8888,
  SITE = 'localhost'
  )
FOR
SOAP(
  WEBMETHOD 'GetNearestStore' (name = 'fooStore.dbo.procGetClosestStoreWithStock'),
  WSDL = DEFAULT,
  SCHEMA = STANDARD,
  DATABASE = 'fooStore', NAMESPACE = 'http://fooStore.com/webmethods'
  );
```

Endpoints are created within the master database, as they are part of the larger SQL Server system, and not stored within each database. The endpoint defined in the preceding code creates a SOAP wrapper around the `procGetClosestStoreWithStock` stored procedure, making it available as `GetNearestStore`. Integrated security is used, which means that any users would need network credentials on the SQL Server. If this service were available over the Internet, you might use Digest or Basic instead. Because the server is also running IIS, the port for the service was moved to 8888. Once the service is created, you can create clients based on the WSDL of the service.

Accessing the Web Service

SQL Server makes some of the work easier when hosting Web Services. The WSDL for the service is automatically generated. Many SOAP tools, such as Visual Studio, enable the creation of wrapper classes by using the WSDL for the service.

The WSDL for a SQL Server Web Service may be a little daunting when you first see it, as it's quite lengthy. This is primarily because the WSDL includes definitions for the various SQL Server datatypes as well as for the Web Services you create. Figure 14-12 shows part of the WSDL, the part created for the procGetClosestStoreWithStock procedure.

Figure 14-12

As you can see from the WSDL, two main structures are defined: GetNearestStore and GetNearestStoreResponse. The GetNearestStore document is what is sent to the Web Service. It includes definitions of each of the columns sent, along with the expected datatypes and sizes.

GetNearestStoreResponse is the return document. In the preceding sample, you can see that it is of type SqlResultStream. This type, also defined in the WSDL, is the tabular data stream returned from SQL Server. It consists of the return value from the stored procedure and any result sets of data. This will be converted to an Object array by the SOAP wrapper classes. You can then convert these data blocks to other types.

Whenever you create a Web Service, it's helpful to create a simple test form that can be used to test the service. Add a new Windows Forms project to the solution (or create a new Project/Solution). Select the Add Web Reference command from the Solution Explorer, and select the FooStore service (see Figure 14-13).

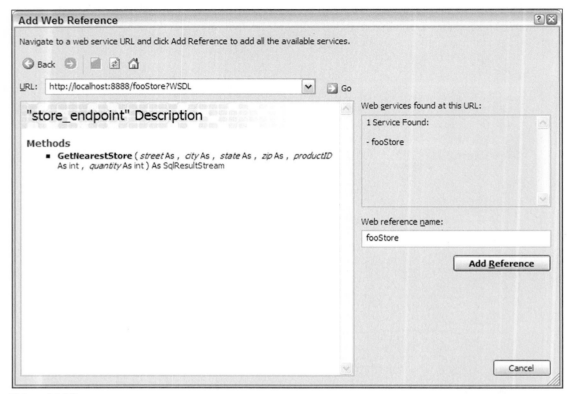

Figure 14-13

Once you have the connection to the Web Service, you're ready to begin laying out the fields of the test form. Most of the fields are TextBox controls, with the exception of the Product ComboBox and the DataGridView on the bottom. The following table describes the properties set on the controls:

Control	Property	Value
TextBox	Name	StreetField
TextBox	Name	CityField
TextBox	Name	StateField
	MaxLength	2
TextBox	Name	ZipField
	MaxLength	11

Control	Property	Value
ComboBox	Name	ProductList
TextBox	Name	QuantityField
Button	Name	GetNearestStoreButton
	Text	&Get Nearest Store
DataGridView	Name	ResultGrid
	AllowUserToAddRows	False
	AllowUserToDeleteRows	False
	ReadOnly	True

Organize the controls on the form in any way you find aesthetically pleasing. Figure 14-14 shows one option.

Figure 14-14

The code for the test form is as follows:

```
Imports System.Data
Imports System.Data.SqlClient

Public Class MainForm


    Private Sub GetNearestStoreButton_Click(ByVal sender As System.Object, _
        ByVal e As System.EventArgs) Handles GetNearestStoreButton.Click
        Using svc As New fooStore.store_endpoint
            Dim result() As Object
            Dim data As New DataSet

            result = svc.GetNearestStore(Me.StreetField.Text, _
                Me.CityField.Text, _
                Me.StateField.Text, _
                Me.ZipField.Text, _
                CInt(Me.ProductList.SelectedValue), _
                CInt(Me.QuantityField.Text))

            If result IsNot Nothing Then
                data = DirectCast(result(0), DataSet)
                Me.ResultGrid.DataSource = data.Tables(0)
            End If
        End Using
    End Sub

    Private Sub MainForm_Load(ByVal sender As System.Object, _
        ByVal e As System.EventArgs) Handles MyBase.Load
        Dim ds As New DataSet
        Using conn As New SqlConnection(My.Settings.FooStoreConnectionString)
            Using da As New SqlDataAdapter("SELECT id, Name FROM PRODUCTS", conn)
                da.Fill(ds)
                With Me.ProductList
                    .DataSource = ds.Tables(0)
                    .ValueMember = "id"
                    .DisplayMember = "Name"
                End With
            End Using
        End Using
    End Sub
End Class
```

The test form consists of two methods. The Load method is used to retrieve the data that populates the product drop-down. The call to the Web Service takes place in the Button click event. This method calls the Web Service wrapper, passing in the values entered on the form. Recall that the Web Service returns two result sets: the data and the return value.

Run the test application. Enter an address close to one of the stores, and select a product and quantity you know to be available. Click the Get Nearest Store button. After a brief delay, the store's address should appear (see Figure 14-15). Try again with a larger quantity or different product so that another store is returned. Depending on the stock available at each of the store locations, the nearest store may not be all that near.

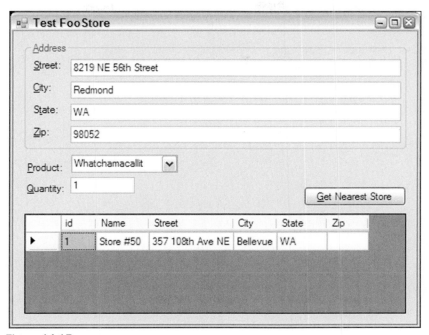

Figure 14-15

Summary

For all the great features included in SQL Server 2005, one of the most useful for the Visual Basic developer is the capability to move your code into the database. By integrating the common language runtime (CLR) with SQL Server, developers now have a choice when creating data access code between T-SQL and VB. While the implications of having your database run VB code can be a little unnerving, the benefits you receive in terms of flexibility and power may be just what you need in some applications. Visual Basic provides a number of tools that are not normally available when working with T-SQL, such as access to the classes of the .NET Framework. While you should only use VB in stored procedures and other database structures when it is appropriate, in those situations you can dramatically improve the scalability, performance, and functionality of your database applications.

Resources

❏ SQL Server Developer Center (`http://msdn.microsoft.com/sql`)
Main developer resource for information on the features of SQL Server

❏ Ask Dr. Math (`http://mathforum.org/library/drmath/`)
A great resource for mathematical algorithms

❏ Yahoo Developer Center (`http://developer.yahoo.com/dotnet/`)
Information on accessing Yahoo! services using Visual Basic

Windows Forms

Windows Forms is the part of the .NET Framework base classes used to create user interfaces for local applications, often called Win32 clients. It is dramatically improved over the forms and controls available in pre-.NET versions of Visual Basic. Although some familiar controls have been retired, no significant functionality has been lost, and a lot of new capabilities have been added.

Windows Forms uses the version number of the related .NET Framework. Thus, the version in Visual Basic 2005 is Windows Forms 2.0. That version number is retained even for .NET Framework version 3.0, because no changes were made to Windows Forms in that version. This chapter sometimes refers to the version number to emphasize differences from the versions included in Visual Basic 2002 and 2003. Those versions are Windows Forms 1.0 and 1.1, respectively.

After explaining why Windows Forms is an important user interface option for .NET applications, this chapter starts its technical content by summarizing the changes in Windows Forms 2.0. This enables those with some experience in previous versions of Windows Forms to quickly identify key changes.

Then the chapter looks at forms, controls, and their behaviors, with emphasis on those elements that are most important for routine application development. Windows Forms is one of the larger namespaces in .NET, so a complete discussion is beyond the scope of this chapter. Instead, this chapter highlights those things developers need to know first.

Chapter 16 includes more advanced treatment of certain aspects of Windows Forms. After gaining a basic understanding of the key capabilities in this chapter, you'll be ready to go on to the more advanced concepts in that chapter.

The Importance of Windows Forms

As discussed in Chapter 1, "smart client" applications are becoming more prevalent under .NET. There are certain application scenarios in which a responsive, intelligent UI is preferred over a less capable browser-based UI. This makes Windows Forms an important part of the .NET Framework. Windows Forms can be used both for local applications and applications that are "Internet-enabled" by using Web Services to access and manage data on remote Internet servers.

It's also more practical in .NET-based systems to support both browser-based and smart-client user interfaces in the same system. Middle-tier components can easily be designed to work with both, so it's not an "either or" choice — Windows Forms interfaces may be mixed with browser-based Web Forms interfaces.

Changes in Windows Forms Version 2.0

If you have already used Windows Forms 1.0 or 1.1, much of the material in this chapter will be familiar to you. To help you quickly focus on the new capabilities in Windows Forms 2.0, here is a summary of changes and additions.

Changes in Existing Controls

Changes to existing controls in Windows Forms 2.0 are minor, but are helpful additions of functionality. Some changes apply to all controls because they are part of the base `Control` class in Windows Forms 2.0. Other changes apply only to specific controls.

Smart Tags

Many controls in Windows Forms 2.0 display a small triangle or glyph toward the top, right side of the control when highlighted in the visual designer. This is a new feature called a *smart tag*. If you click this glyph, you get a pop-up dialog with common operations for the control. Many of the features that you access through the property box can also be accessed through the smart tag. In general, this chapter uses the Properties window for manipulation of properties, but you should be aware of the smart tag short-cut for commonly used features.

AutoCompletion in Text Boxes and Combo Boxes

Text boxes and combo boxes get new properties for autocompletion of text entries. This capability could be added manually or with third-party controls in previous versions, but is now built in. The `AutoCompleteMode` property controls how autocompletion works in the control, while the `AutoCompleteSource` and `AutoCompleteCustomSource` properties tell the control where to get entries for autocompletion.

An example of autocompletion in action is shown later, in the section entitled "Advanced Capabilities for Data Entry."

New Properties for All Controls

The base `Control` class, which is a base class for all Windows Forms controls, has several new properties in Windows Forms 2.0. Because all controls inherit from this class, all Windows Forms controls gain these new properties and the new functionality that goes along with them.

Two of the new properties, Padding and Margin, are most useful when used in conjunction with some new controls, TableLayoutPanel and FlowLayoutPanel. Those two properties are discussed later in the chapter. The other new properties are discussed here. They include MaximumSize, MinimumSize, and UseWaitCursor.

MaximumSize and MinimumSize Properties

The MaximumSize and MinimumSize properties specify the maximum and minimum height and width of a control. Forms had these properties in Windows Forms 1.0 and 1.1, but now all controls have them.

If the maximum height and width are both set to the default value of 0, then there is no maximum. Similarly, if the minimum height and width are set to zero, then there is no minimum. The form or control can be any size.

If these properties are set to anything else, the settings become limits on the size of the control. For example, if the MaximumSize height and width are both set to 100, then the control cannot be bigger than 100×100 pixels. The visual designer will not make the control any larger on the form design surface. Attempting to set the height or width of the control in code at runtime to a value greater than 100 will cause it to be set to 100 instead.

The MaximumSize and MinimumSize properties can be reset at runtime to enable sizing of the controls outside the limits imposed at design time. However, the properties have a return type of Size, so resetting either property requires creating a Size structure. For example, you can reset the MinimumSize property for a button named Button1 with the following line of code:

```
Button1.MinimumSize = New Size(20, 20)
```

This sets the new minimum width and height to 20 pixels.

The Size structure has members for Height and Width. Those can be used to fetch the current minimum or maximum sizes for either height or width. For example, to find the current minimum height for Button1, the following line of code would be used:

```
Dim n As Integer = Button1.MinimumSize.Height
```

UseWaitCursor Property

Windows Forms interfaces can make use of threading or asynchronous requests to allow tasks to execute in the background. When a control is waiting for some asynchronous request to finish, it is helpful to indicate that to the user by changing the mouse cursor when the mouse is inside the control. Normally, the cursor used is the familiar hourglass, which is called the WaitCursor in Windows Forms.

For any control, setting the UseWaitCursor property to True causes the cursor to change to the hourglass (or whatever is being used for the WaitCursor) while the mouse is positioned inside the control. This allows a control to visually indicate that it is waiting for something. The typical usage is to set UseWaitCursor to True when an asynchronous process is begun and then set it back to False when the process is finished and the control is ready for normal operation again.

New Controls

Windows Forms 2.0 includes a number of new controls. Some are brand-new controls that offer completely new functionality. Others are replacements for existing controls, offering additional functionality.

WebBrowser Control

Even smart client applications often need to display HTML or browse websites. Windows Forms 1.0 or 1.1 did not include a true Windows Forms control for browsing. The legacy ActiveX browsing control built into Windows could be used via interoperability, but this had drawbacks for deployment and versioning.

The legacy ActiveX control is still the ultimate foundation for browsing capability, but Windows Forms 2.0 includes an intelligent Windows Forms wrapper that makes it much easier to use and deploy the control.

MaskedTextbox control

Windows Forms 1.0 offered replacements for almost all of the controls available in Visual Basic 6, but one notable exception was the MaskedEdit control. In Windows Forms 1.0 and 1.1, masked edit capabilities were available only through third-party controls or by doing your own custom development.

That omission has now been rectified. The MaskedTextbox control resembles the old MaskedEdit control in functionality. It allows a mask for input and a variety of useful properties to control user interaction with the control. More information on this control is available in the section "Advanced Capabilities for Data Entry."

TableLayoutPanel and FlowLayoutPanel Controls

Browser-based user interfaces are good at dynamically arranging controls at runtime, because browser windows can be different sizes for different users. Forms-based interfaces have traditionally lacked such capabilities. Dynamic positioning can be done in forms, but it requires writing a lot of sizing and positioning logic.

Two new controls in Windows Forms 2.0 mimic layout capabilities in a browser, offering better options for dynamic positioning of controls: FlowLayoutPanel and the TableLayoutPanel. Both are containers than can automatically reposition controls that are placed in them, based on the current space available in the container.

An example illustrating usage of both controls is included in the section "Dynamic Sizing and Positioning of Controls."

Replacements for Older Windows Forms Controls

The Toolbar, MainMenu, ContextMenu, and StatusBar controls in Windows Forms 1.0 and 1.1 offered basic functionality, and these controls are still available in Windows Forms 2.0, but in most cases you won't want to use these controls because there are new replacements with significantly enhanced capabilities. Because the old versions are still available, the new versions have different names. The table that follows summarizes these replacements:

Old Control	New Control	Most Important New Capabilities
Toolbar	ToolStrip	Allows many new types of controls on the toolbar. Supports *rafting*, which enables the toolbar to be detached by the user and float over the application. Allows users to add or remove buttons or other toolbar elements. Includes new cosmetics, allowing toolbars to look like those in Office 2003.
MainMenu	MenuStrip	Both new menu controls inherit from ToolStrip, which allows new cosmetics and more flexible placement.
ContextMenu	ContextMenuStrip	
StatusBar	StatusStrip	Inherits from ToolStrip, which allows new cosmetics and makes it easier to embed other controls in a status bar.
Splitter	SplitContainer	Less difficult to set up

The old versions no longer show up by default in the Toolbox. If you want to use them in new projects, you must add them to the Toolbox by right-clicking on the Windows Forms Toolbox tab, selecting Choose Items, and placing a check mark on the older control that you want added to the Toolbox. However, you'll probably only want to use the older controls for compatibility with older projects, using the improved versions for new development.

These controls are covered in more detail, including examples, in the sections "Toolbars and the New ToolStrip Control," "Menus," and "Dynamic Sizing and Positioning of Controls."

Default Instances of Forms

In VB6 and earlier, a form named Form1 could be shown by merely including the following line:

```
Form1.Show
```

This capability was not available in Visual Basic 2002 and 2003. Instead, a form was treated like any other class, and had to be instantiated before use. Typical code to show a form in Windows Forms 1.0 and 1.1 looked like this:

```
Dim f As New Form1()
f.Show
```

This technique is still recommended because it fits object-oriented conventions. However, the first form returns to Visual Basic 2005, with the minor change of parentheses at the end of the call:

```
Form1.Show()
```

Showing a form without instancing it, as in the first form above, is referred to as using the default instance of the form. That default instance is available from anywhere in a project containing a form. There is only one default instance, and any reference to it will bring up the same underlying instance of the form.

Another way to get to the default instance of a form is through the new My namespace. The following line has exactly the same effect of showing the default instance of a form:

```
My.Forms.Form1.Show()
```

The System.Windows.Forms Namespace

You've already seen how namespaces are used to organize related classes in the .NET Framework. The main namespace used for Windows Forms classes is System.Windows.Forms. The classes in this namespace are contained in the System.Windows.Forms.dll assembly.

If you choose a Windows application project or Windows Control Library project in VS.NET, a reference to System.Windows.Forms.dll is added by default. In some other cases, such as creating a library that will work with controls, you need to add that reference manually. (You can see more about creating controls in Windows Forms in Chapter 16.)

Using Forms

A form is just a special kind of class in Windows Forms. A class becomes a form based on inheritance. A form must have the System.Windows.Forms class in its inheritance tree, which causes the form to have the behavior and object interface a form requires.

The previous section on changes in Windows Forms 2.0 mentioned that forms can be used by referring to a default instance. However, the preferred technique is to treat a form like any other class, which means creating an instance of the form and using the instance. Typical code would look like this:

```
Dim f As New Form1
f.Show()
```

There is one circumstance in which loading a form the same way as a class instance yields undesirable results. Let's cover that next.

Showing Forms via Sub Main

When a form is instanced via the technique just described, it is referenced by an object variable, which establishes an object reference to the instance. References are covered in detail in Chapter 2.

References can go away as object variables go out of scope or are set to other references or to `Nothing`. When all object references to a form are gone, the form is disposed of and therefore vanishes. This is particularly apparent if you want to start your application with a `Sub Main`, and then show your first form inside `Sub Main`. You might think this would work:

```
' This code will not work in VB 2005!!
Sub Main()

    ' Do start up work here
    ' After start up work finished, show the main form...
    Dim f As New Form1
    f.Show()

End Sub
```

What happens if you try this, however, is that `Form1` briefly appears and then immediately vanishes, and the application quits. That's because the object variable f went out of scope, and it was the only reference to the form that was shown. Therefore, the form was destroyed because it had no references pointing to it.

To get around this behavior, you could use the default instance as the startup form, but there's a better way that stays within good object-oriented conventions. Replace the line that shows the form, as shown in the following code:

```
' This code will work fine in VB 2005
Sub Main()

    ' Do start up work here
    Dim f As New Form1
    Application.Run(f)

End Sub
```

Now `Sub Main` will transfer control to the form, and the form won't vanish when `Sub Main` ends.

Setting the Startup Form

Instead of using `Sub Main` as your application entry point, you can also define a startup form, which is the form that will be loaded first when your application begins. To define the startup form, you need to open the Properties dialog box for the project and set the Startup form setting. Do this using the Project ⇨ Properties menu. You can also invoke the window by right-clicking the project name in Solution Explorer and selecting Properties from the context menu. The Properties dialog for a Windows application is shown in Figure 15-1.

If the Properties menu item doesn't appear under your Project menu, open the Solution Explorer (Ctrl+Alt+L), highlight the project name (it will be in bold font), and then try again.

Figure 15-1

Startup Location

Often, you'll want a form to be centered on the screen when it first appears. VB.NET does this automatically for you when you set the StartPosition property. The following table shows the settings and their meanings:

StartPosition Value	Effect
Manual	Show the form positioned at the values defined by the form's Location property
CenterScreen	Show the form centered on the screen
WindowsDefaultLocation	Show the form at the window's default location
WindowsDefaultBounds	Show the form at the window's default location, with the window's default bounding size
CenterParent	Show the form centered in its owner

Form Borders

Forms have a number of border options in Windows Forms. The `FormBorderStyle` property is used to set the border option, and the options can affect the way a form can be manipulated by the user. The options available for `FormBorderStyle` include the following:

- ❑ `None` — No border, and the user cannot resize the form
- ❑ `FixedSingle` — Single 3-D border, and the user cannot resize the form
- ❑ `Fixed3D` — 3-D border, and the user cannot resize the form
- ❑ `FixedDialog` — Dialog-box-style border, and the user cannot resize the form
- ❑ `Sizeable` — Same as `FixedSingle`, except that the user can resize the form
- ❑ `FixedToolWindow` — Single border, and the user cannot resize the form
- ❑ `SizeableToolWindow` — Single border, and the user can resize the form

Each of these has a different effect on the buttons that appear in the title bar of the form. For details, check the help topic for the `FormBorderStyle` property.

Always on Top — The TopMost Property

Some forms need to remain visible at all times, even when they do not have the focus. Examples are floating toolbars and tutorial windows. In Windows Forms, forms have a property called `TopMost`. Set it to `True` to have a form overlay other forms even when it does not have the focus.

Note that a form with `TopMost` set to `True` is on top of all applications, not just the hosting application. If you need a form to only be on top of other forms in the application, this capability is provided by an owned form.

Owned Forms

As with the `TopMost` property, an owned form floats above the application, but it does not interfere with using the application. An example is a search-and-replace box. However, an owned form is not on top of all forms, just the form that is its owner.

When a form is owned by another form, it is minimized and closed with the owner form. Owned forms are never displayed behind their owner form, but they do not prevent their owner form from gaining the focus and being used. However, if you want to click on the area covered by an owned form, the owned form has to be moved out of the way first.

A form can only have one "owner" at a time. If a form that is already owned by `Form1` is added to the owned forms collection for `Form2`, then the form is no longer owned by `Form1`.

There are two ways to make a form owned by another form. It can be done in the owner form or in the owned form.

AddOwnedForm() Method

In the owner form, another form can be made owned with the `AddOwnedForm()` method. Here is code to make an instance of `Form2` become owned by `Form1`. This code would reside somewhere in `Form1` and would typically be placed just before the line that shows the instance of `Form2` to the screen:

```
Dim frm As New Form2
Me.AddOwnedForm(frm)
```

Owner Property

The relationship can also be set up in the owned form. This is done with the `Owner` property of the form. Here is a method that would work inside `Form2` to make it owned by a form that is passed in as an argument to the function:

```
Public Sub MakeMeOwned(frmOwner As Form)
    Me.Owner = frmOwner
End Sub
```

Because this technique requires a reference to the owner inside the owned form, it is not used as often as using the `AddOwnedForm()` method in the `Owner` form.

OwnedForms Collection

The owner form can access its collection of owned forms with the `OwnedForms` property. Here is code to loop through the forms owned by a form:

```
Dim frmOwnedForm As Form
For Each frmOwnedForm In Me.OwnedForms
  Console.WriteLine(frmOwnedForm.Text)
Next
```

The owner form can remove an owned form with the `RemoveOwnedForm` property. This could be done in a loop like the previous one, with code like the following:

```
Dim frmOwnedForm As Form
For Each frmOwnedForm In Me.OwnedForms
  Console.WriteLine(frmOwnedForm.Text)
  Me.RemoveOwnedForm(frmOwnedForm)
Next
```

This loop would cause an owner form to stop owning all of its slaved forms. Note that those deslaved forms would not be unloaded, they would simply no longer be owned.

Making Forms Transparent and Translucent

Windows Forms offers advanced capabilities to make forms translucent, or parts of a form transparent. You can even change the entire shape of a form.

The Opacity Property

The `Opacity` property measures how opaque or transparent a form is. A value of 0 percent makes the form fully transparent. A value of 100 percent makes the form fully visible. Any value greater than 0 and less than 100 makes the form partially visible, as if it were a ghost. Note that an opacity value of 0 percent disables the capability to click the form.

Very low levels of opacity, in the range of 1 or 2 percent, make the form effectively invisible, but still allow the form to be clickable. This means that the `Opacity` property has the potential to create mischievous applications that sit in front of other applications and "steal" their mouse clicks and other events.

Percentage values are used to set the opacity in the Properties window. However, if you want to set the `Opacity` *property in code, you must use values between 0 and 1 instead, with 0 being equivalent to 0 percent and 1 being equivalent to 100 percent.*

Tool and dialog windows that should not completely obscure their background are one example of a usage for `Opacity`. Setting expiration for a "free trial" by gradually fading out the application's user interface is another.

The following block of code shows how to fade a form out and back in when the user clicks a button named `Button1`. You may have to adjust the `Step` value of the array, depending on your computer's performance:

```
Private Sub Button1_Click(ByVal sender As System.Object, _
                     ByVal e As System.EventArgs) _
                     Handles Button1.Click
    Dim i As Double
    For i = -1 To 1 Step 0.005
      ' Note - opacity is a value from 0.0 to 1.0 in code
      ' Absolute value is used to keep us in that range
      Me.Opacity = System.Math.Abs(i)
      Me.Refresh
    Next i
End Sub
```

The TransparencyKey Property

Instead of making an entire form translucent or transparent, the `TransparencyKey` property enables you to specify a color that will become transparent on the form. This enables you to make some sections of a form transparent, while other sections are unchanged.

For example, if `TransparencyKey` is set to a red color and some areas of the form are that exact shade of red, then they will be transparent. Whatever is behind the form shows through in those areas; and if you click in one of those areas, you are actually clicking the object behind the form.

`TransparencyKey` can be used to create irregularly shaped "skin" forms. A form can have its `BackgroundImage` property set with an image, and by just painting a part of the image with the `TransparencyKey` color, you can make parts of the form disappear.

The Region Property

Another way to gain the capability of "skins" is by using the `Region` property of a form. The `Region` property allows a shape for a form to be encoded as a "graphics path," thereby changing the shape from the default rectangle to another shape. A path can contain line segments between points, curves and arcs, and outlines of letters, in any combination.

The following example changes the shape of a form to an arrow. Create a new Windows application. Set the FormBorderStyle property of Form1 to None. Then place the following code in the Load event for Form1:

```
Dim PointArray(6) As Point
PointArray(0) = New Point(0, 40)
PointArray(1) = New Point(200, 40)
PointArray(2) = New Point(200, 0)
PointArray(3) = New Point(250, 100)
PointArray(4) = New Point(200, 200)
PointArray(5) = New Point(200, 160)
PointArray(6) = New Point(0, 160)
Dim myGraphicsPath As _
System.Drawing.Drawing2D.GraphicsPath = _
        New System.Drawing.Drawing2D.GraphicsPath

myGraphicsPath.AddPolygon(PointArray)
Me.Region = New Region(myGraphicsPath)
```

When the program is run, Form1 will appear in the shape of a right-pointing arrow. If you lay out the points in the array, you will see that they have become the vertices of the arrow.

Visual Inheritance

By inheriting from System.Windows.Forms.Form, any class automatically gets all the properties, methods, and events that a form based on Windows Forms is supposed to have. However, a class does not have to inherit directly from the System.Windows.Forms.Form class to become a Windows form. It can become a form by inheriting from another form, which itself inherits from System.Windows.Forms.Form. In this way, controls originally placed on one form can be directly inherited by a second form. Not only is the design of the original form inherited, but also any code associated with these controls (the processing logic behind an Add New button, for example). This means that you can create a base form with processing logic required in a number of forms, and then create other forms that inherit the base controls and functionality.

VB 2005 provides an Inheritance Picker tool to aid in this process. Note, however, that a form must be compiled into either an .exe or .dll file before it can be used by the Inheritance Picker. Once that is done, the addition of a form that inherits from another form in the project can be achieved by selecting Project ➪ Add Windows Form and then choosing the template type of Inherited Form in the resulting dialog.

Scrollable Forms

Some applications need fields that will fit on a single screen. While you could split the data entry into multiple screens, an alternative is a scrollable form.

You can set your forms to automatically have scrollbars when they are sized smaller than the child controls they contain. To do that, set the AutoScroll property of your form to True. When you run your program, resize the form to make it smaller than the controls require and presto — instant scrolling.

You cannot have both `Autoscroll` and `IsMdiContainer` set to `True` at the same time. MDI containers have their own scrolling functionality. If you set `Autoscroll` to `True` for an MDI container, the `IsMdiContainer` property will be set to `False`, and the form will therefore cease to be an MDI container.

MDI Forms

MDI (Multiple Document Interface) forms are forms that are created to hold other forms. The MDI form is often referred to as the *parent*, and the forms displayed within the MDI parent are often called *children*. Figure 15-2 shows a typical MDI parent with several children displayed within it.

Figure 15-2

Creating an MDI Parent Form

In Windows Forms, a regular form is converted to an MDI parent form by setting the `IsMDIContainer` property of the form to `True`. This is normally done in the Properties window at design time.

A form can also be made into an MDI parent at runtime by setting the `IsMDIContainer` property to `True` in code. However, the design of an MDI form is usually rather different from that of a normal form, so this approach is not often needed.

Differences in MDI Parent Forms between VB6 and VB 2005

In VB6, an MDI parent form can only contain controls that have a property called `Align`, which is similar to the `Dock` property in Windows Forms. These controls, such as a `PictureBox`, can then contain other controls.

In Windows Forms, an MDI parent can contain any control that a regular form can contain. Buttons, labels, and the like can be placed directly on the MDI surface. Such controls will appear in front of any MDI child forms that are displayed in the MDI client area.

It is still possible to use controls such as `PictureBoxes` to hold other controls on a Windows Forms MDI parent. These controls can be docked to the side of the MDI form with the `Dock` property, which is discussed in the section "Dynamic Sizing and Positioning of Controls."

MDI Child Forms

In Windows Forms, a form becomes an MDI child at runtime by setting the form's MDIParent property to point to an MDI parent form. This makes it possible to use a form as either a standalone form or an MDI child in different circumstances. In fact, the MDIParent property cannot be set at design time — it must be set at runtime to make a form an MDI child. (Note that this is completely different from VB6, where it was necessary to make a form an MDI child at design time.)

Any number of MDI child forms can be displayed in the MDI parent client area. The currently active child form can be determined with the ActiveForm property of the MDI parent form.

An MDI Example in VB 2005

To see these changes to MDI forms in action, you can do the following step-by-step exercise. It shows the basics of creating an MDI parent and making it display an MDI child form:

1. Create a new Windows application. It will have an empty form named Form1. Change both the name of the form and the form's Text property to MDIParentForm.

2. In the Properties window, set the IsMDIContainer property for MDIParentForm to True. This designates the form as an MDI container for child windows. (Setting this property also causes the form to have a different default background color.)

3. From the Toolbox, drag a MenuStrip control to the form. Create a top-level menu item called File with submenu items called New MDI Child and Quit. Also create a top-level menu item called Window. The File ➪ New MDI Child menu option will create and show new MDI child forms at runtime, and the Window menu will keep track of the open MDI child windows.

4. In the Component Tray at the bottom of the form, click the MenuStrip item and select Properties. In the Properties window, set the MDIWindowListItem property to WindowToolStripMenuItem. This enables the Window menu to maintain a list of open MDI child windows, with a check mark next to the active child window.

5. Create an MDI child form to use as a template for multiple instances. To do so, select Project ➪ Add Windows Form and click the Add button in the Add New Item dialog box. That will result in a new blank form named Form2. Place any controls you like on the form. As an alternative, you can reuse any of the forms created in previous exercises in this chapter.

6. Now go back to MDIParentForm. In the menu editing bar, double-click the New MDI Child option under File. The Code Editor will appear, with the cursor in the event routine for that menu option. Place the following code in the event:

```
Protected Sub NewMdiChildToolStripMenuItem _Click(ByVal sender As Object,
                          ByVal e As System.EventArgs)

    ' This line may change if you are using a form with a different name.
    Dim NewMDIChild As New Form2()
    'Set the Parent Form of the Child window.
    NewMDIChild.MDIParent = Me
    'Display the new form.
    NewMDIChild.Show()
End Sub
```

7. In the menu editing bar for MDIParentForm, double-click the Quit option under File. The Code Editor will appear, with the cursor in the event routine for that menu option. Place the following code in the event:

```
Protected Sub QuitToolStripMenuItem_Click(ByVal sender As Object, _
                         ByVal e As System.EventArgs)
    End
End Sub
```

8. Now run and test the program. Use the File ➪ New MDI Child option to create several child forms. Note how the Window menu option automatically lists them with the active one checked and allows you to activate a different one.

Arranging Child Windows

MDI parent forms have a method called LayoutMDI that will automatically arrange child forms in the familiar cascade or tile layout. For the preceding example, add a menu item to your Windows menu called Tile Vertical and insert the following code into the menu item's Click event to handle it:

```
Me.LayoutMdi(MDILayout.TileVertical)
```

To see an example of the rearrangement, suppose that the MDI form in Figure 15-2 is rearranged with the MDILayout.TileVertical option. It would then look similar to the image in Figure 15-3.

Figure 15-3

Dialog Forms

In VB6 and earlier, forms were shown with the Show method, and this technique is still used in Windows Forms. In both VB6 and VB 2005, the Show method by default displays modeless forms, which are forms that allow the user to click off them onto another form in the application.

Applications also sometimes need forms that retain control until their operation is finished. That is, you can't click off such a form onto another form. Such a form is called a *modal* form.

In VB6, showing a modal form required using a special parameter on the Show method. Showing a form modally is done differently in Windows Forms, with the ShowDialog() method. Here is code for showing a modal dialog in Windows Forms:

```
Dim frmDialogForm As New DialogForm
frmDialogForm.ShowDialog()
```

DialogResult

It is common when showing a dialog form to need to get information about what action the user selected. This was often done with a custom property in VB6, but Windows Forms has a built-in property for that purpose. When a form is shown with the ShowDialog() method, the form has a property called DialogResult to indicate its state.

The DialogResult property can take the following enumerated results:

- ❑ DialogResult.Abort
- ❑ DialogResult.Cancel
- ❑ DialogResult.Ignore
- ❑ DialogResult.No
- ❑ DialogResult.None
- ❑ DialogResult.OK
- ❑ DialogResult.Retry
- ❑ DialogResult.Yes

When the DialogResult property is set, the dialog is hidden as a byproduct. That is, setting the DialogResult property causes an implicit call to the Hide method of the dialog form, so that control is released back to the form that called the dialog.

The DialogResult property of a dialog box can be set in two ways. The most common way is to associate a DialogResult value with a button. Then, when the button is pressed, the associated value is automatically placed in the DialogResult property of the form.

To set the DialogResult value associated with a button, the DialogResult property of the button is used. If this property is set for the button, it is unnecessary to set the DialogResult in code when the button is pressed. Here is an example that uses this technique.

In Visual Studio 2005, start a new VB Windows application. On the automatic blank form that comes up (named Form1), place a single button and set its Text property to Dialog.

Now add a new Windows Form by selecting Project ➪ Add Windows Form and name it DialogForm.vb. Place two buttons on DialogForm and set the following properties for the buttons:

Property	Value for First Button	Value for Second Button
Name	OKButton	CancelButton
Text	OK	Cancel
DialogResult	OK	Cancel

Do not put any code in `DialogForm` at all. The form should look like the one shown in Figure 15-4.

Figure15-4

On the first form, `Form1`, place the following code in the `Click` event for `Button1`:

```
Private Sub Button1_Click(ByVal sender As System.Object, _
    ByVal e As System.EventArgs) Handles Button1.Click
    Dim frmDialogForm As New DialogForm()
    frmDialogForm.ShowDialog()

    ' You're back from the dialog - check user action.
    Select Case frmDialogForm.DialogResult
      Case DialogResult.OK
        MsgBox("The user pressed OK")
      Case DialogResult.Cancel
        MsgBox("The user pressed cancel")
    End Select
    frmDialogForm = Nothing
End Sub
```

Run and test the code. When a button is pressed on the dialog form, a message box should be displayed (by the calling form) indicating the button that was pressed.

The second way to set the `DialogResult` property of the form is in code. In a `Button_Click` event, or anywhere else in the dialog form, a line like the following can be used to set the `DialogResult` property for the form and simultaneously hide the dialog form, returning control to the calling form:

```
Me.DialogResult = DialogResult.Ignore
```

This particular line sets the dialog result to `DialogResult.Ignore`, but setting the dialog result to any of the permitted values also hides the dialog form.

Forms at Runtime

The life cycle of a form is like that of all objects. It is created and later destroyed. Forms have a visual component, so they use system resources, such as handles. These are created and destroyed at interim stages within the lifetime of the form. Forms can be created and will hold state as a class, but will not appear until they are activated. Likewise, closing a form doesn't destroy its state.

The following table summarizes the states of a form's existence, how you get the form to that state, the events that occur when the form enters a state, and a brief description of each:

Code	Events Fired	Description
MyForm = New Form1	Load	The form's New() method will be called (as will InitializeComponent).
MyForm.Show() or	HandleCreated	Use Show() for modeless display.
MyForm.ShowDialog()	Load	Use ShowDialog() for modal display.
	VisibleChanged	The HandleCreated event only fires the first time the form is shown or after it has previously been closed.
	Activated	
MyForm.Activate()	Activated	A form can be activated when it is visible but does not have the focus.
MyForm.Hide()	Deactivate	Hides the form (sets the Visible property to False)
	VisibleChanged	
MyForm.Close()	Deactivate	Closes the form and calls Dispose to release the window's resources
	Closing	During the Closing event, you can set the CancelEventArgs.Cancel property to True to abort the close.
	Closed	
	VisibleChanged	
	HandleDestroyed	Also called when the user closes the form using the control box or X button
	Disposed	The Deactivate event will only fire if the form is currently active.
		Note: There is no longer an Unload event. Use the Closing or Closed event instead.
MyForm.Dispose()	None	Use the Close() method to finish using your form.
MyForm = Nothing	None	Releasing the reference to the form flags it for garbage collection. The garbage collector calls the form's Finalize() method.

Controls

The controls included in Windows Forms provide basic functionality for a wide range of applications. The controls in Windows Forms 2.0 are very similar to those in previous versions of Windows Forms, but there are some significant differences to the controls in VB6. This section covers the features that all controls use (such as docking) and summarizes the standard controls available to you. Important changes from pre-.NET versions of Visual Basic (VB6 and earlier) are briefly mentioned.

Control Tab Order

The VS2005 design environment enables you to set the tab order of the controls on a form simply by clicking them in sequence. To activate the feature, open a form in the designer and select View ⇨ Tab Order. This will result in a small number in the upper-left corner of each control on your form, representing the tab index of that control.

To set the values, simply click on each control in the sequence you want the tab flow to operate. The screen shot in Figure 15-5 shows a simple form with the tab order feature enabled.

Figure 15-5

In Windows Forms 2.0, it is possible to have two or more controls with the same tab index value. At runtime, Visual Basic will break the tie by using the z-order of the controls. The control that is highest in the z-order receives the focus first. The z-order is a ranking number that determines which controls are in front of or behind other controls. (The term comes from the z-axis, which is an axis perpendicular to the traditional x- and y-axes.) The z-order can be changed by right-clicking the control and selecting Bring to Front.

Dynamic Sizing and Positioning of Controls

Windows Forms 2.0 includes a variety of ways to allow user interfaces to be dynamic. Controls can be set to automatically stretch and reposition themselves as a form is resized. Controls can also be dynamically arranged inside some special container controls intended for that purpose. This section covers all these ways of allowing dynamic sizing and positioning of controls.

Docking

Docking refers to gluing a control to the edge of a parent control. Good examples of docked controls are menu bars and status bars, which are typically docked to the top and bottom of a form, respectively. All visual controls have a `Dock` property.

To work through an example, create a new Windows application and place a `Textbox` on a form. Set the `Text` property of the `TextBox` to `I'm Getting Docked`. The result when you show the form should look something like Figure 15-6.

Figure 15-6

Suppose that you need to glue this `TextBox` to the top of the form. To do this, view the `Dock` property of the label. If you pull it down, you'll see a small graphic like the one shown in Figure 15-7.

Figure 15-7

Simply click the top section of the graphic to stick the label to the top of the form. The other sections give you other effects. (A status bar would use the bottom section, for example. Clicking the box in the middle causes the control to fill the form.) The `TextBox` control will immediately "stick" to the top of your form. When you run your program and stretch the window sideways, you'll see the effect shown in Figure 15-8.

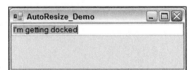

Figure 15-8

> If you attempt to dock multiple controls to the same edge, Windows Forms must decide how to break the tie. Precedence is given to controls in reverse z-order. In other words, the control that is furthest back in the z-order will be the first control next to the edge. If you dock two controls to the same edge and want to switch them, then right-click the control you want docked first and select Send to Back.

If you want a gap between the edge of your form and the docked controls, set the `DockPadding` property of the parent control. You can set a different value for each of the four directions (`Left`, `Right`, `Top`, `Bottom`). You can also set all four properties to the same value using the `All` setting.

Anchoring

Anchoring is similar to docking except that you can specifically define the distance that each edge of your control will maintain from the edges of a parent. To see it in action, add a button to the form in the docking example. The result should look like Figure 15-9.

Figure 15-9

Dropping down the Anchor property of the button gives you the graphic shown in Figure 15-10.

Figure 15-10

The four rectangles surrounding the center box enable you to toggle the anchor settings of the control. Figure 15-10 shows the default anchor setting of Top, Left for all controls.

When the setting is on (dark gray), the edge of the control maintains its starting distance from the edge of the parent as the parent is resized. If you set the anchor to two opposing edges (such as the left and right edges), the control stretches to accommodate this, as shown in Figure 15-11.

Figure 15-11

One of the most common uses of anchoring is to set the Anchor property for buttons in the lower-right portion of a form. Setting the Anchor property of a button to Bottom, Right causes the button to maintain a constant distance to the bottom-right corner of the form.

You can also set the Anchor property in code. The most common scenario for this would be for a control created on-the-fly. To set the Anchor property in code, you must add together the anchor styles for all the sides to which you need to anchor. For example, setting the Anchor property to Bottom, Left would require a line of code like this:

```
MyControl.Anchor = Ctype(AnchorStyles.Bottom + AnchorStyles.Right, AnchorStyles)
```

Sizable Containers

Previous versions of Windows Forms used the `Splitter` control to allow resizing of containers. This control is still available in Windows Forms 2.0, but does not appear by default in the Toolbox. In its place is a replacement control, `SplitContainer`, that provides the same functionality with less work on your part.

A single `SplitContainer` acts much like two panels with an appropriately inserted `Splitter`. You can think of it as a panel with two sections, with the divider between the sections movable so that the relative sizes of the sections can be changed by a user.

To use a `SplitContainer`, simply drop it on a form, resize it, and position the draggable divider to the appropriate point. If you want the divider to be horizontal instead of vertical, you change the `Orientation` property. Then you can place controls in each subpanel in any way you like. It is common to insert a control such as a TreeView or ListBox, and then dock it to its respective subpanel. This makes such contained controls resizable by the user. A typical example of a `SplitContainer` in action is shown in Figure 15-12.

Figure 15-12

The cursor in Figure 15-12 shows that the mouse is hovering over the divider, allowing repositioning of the divider by dragging the mouse. A `SplitContainer` may be nested inside another `SplitContainer`. This enables you to build forms in which several parts are resizable relative to each other.

FlowLayoutPanel Control

The summary of new features mentioned a new control for Windows Forms 2.0 called the `FlowLayout-Panel` control. This control allows dynamic layout of controls contained within the `FlowLayoutPanel`, based on the size of the `FlowLayoutPanel`.

`FlowLayoutPanel` works conceptually much like a simple HTML page shown in a browser. The controls that are placed in the `FlowLayoutPanel` are positioned in sequence horizontally until there's not enough space for the next control, which then wraps further down for another row of controls. The following walkthrough demonstrates this capability.

Start a new Windows application project. On the blank `Form1` included in the new project, place a `FlowLayoutPanel` control toward the top of the form, and make it a bit less wide than the width of the form. Set the `Anchor` property for the `FlowLayoutPanel` to `Top`, `Left`, and `Right`. Set the `BorderStyle` property for the `FlowLayoutPanel` to `FixedSingle` so it's easy to see.

Place three `Button` controls in the `FlowLayoutPanel`, keeping their default sizes. The form you create should look like the one shown in Figure 15-13.

Figure 15-13

Run the application. The initial layout will be similar to the design-time layout. However, if you resize the form to about two thirds of its original width, the layout of the buttons changes. Because there is no longer enough room for them to be arranged side by side, the arrangement automatically switches. Figure 15-14 shows the form in three configurations: first with its original width, then narrower so that only two buttons fit in the `FlowLayoutPanel`, and finally so narrow that the buttons are all stacked in the `FlowLayoutPanel`.

Figure 15-14

Note that no logic of any kind was added to the form — the `FlowLayoutPanel` handles the repositioning of the buttons automatically. In fact, any position information you set for the button controls is ignored if they are placed in a `FlowLayoutPanel`.

Padding and Margin Properties

To assist in positioning controls in the `FlowLayoutPanel`, all controls have a new property called `Margin`. There are settings for `Margin.Left`, `Margin.Right`, `Margin.Top`, and `Margin.Bottom`. These settings determine how much space is reserved around a control when calculating its automatic position in a `FlowLayoutPanel`.

You can see the `Margin` property in action by changing the `Margin` property for one or more of the buttons in the previous example. If you change all the `Margin` settings for the first `Button` to 10 pixels, for example, and run the application, the form will look like the one shown in Figure 15-15.

The first button now has a 10-pixel separation from all the other controls in the `FlowLayoutPanel`, as well as a 10-pixel separation from the edges of the `FlowLayoutPanel` itself.

Figure 15-15

The `Padding` property is for the `FlowLayoutPanel` or other container control. When a control is embedded into a `FlowLayoutPanel`, the `Padding.Left`, `Padding.Right`, `Padding.Top`, and `Padding.Bottom` properties of the `FlowLayoutPanel` determine how far away from the inside edge of the container to position the control.

You can see the `Padding` property in action by changing the `Padding` property for the `FlowLayout-Panel` in the previous example. If you set all `Padding` settings to 20 pixels, and reset the `Margin` property for the first `Button` back to the default, then the form will look like Figure 15-16 in the visual designer.

Figure 15-16

Notice that all the controls in the `FlowLayoutPanel` are now at least 20 pixels from the edges.

The `Padding` property is also applicable to other container controls, if the contained controls have their `Dock` property set. If the settings for `Padding` are not zero, a docked control will be offset from the edge of the container by the amount specified by the `Padding` property.

TableLayoutPanel Control

The other new control for dynamic layout is the `TableLayoutPanel`. This control consists of a table of rows and columns, resulting in a rectangular array of cells. You can place one control in each cell. However, that control can itself be a container, such as a `Panel` or `FlowLayoutPanel`.

The dimensions of the columns and rows can be controlled by setting some key properties. For columns, set the number of columns with the `ColumnCount` property, and then control each individual column with the `ColumnStyles` collection. When you click on the button for the `ColumnStyles` collection, you'll get a designer window that enables you to set two key properties for each column — `SizeType` and `Width`.

`SizeType` can be set to one of the following enumerations:

❑   `Absolute` — Sets the column width to a fixed size in pixels

❑   `AutoSize` — Indicates that the size of the column should be managed by the `TableLayoutPanel`, which allocates width to the column depending on the widest control contained in the column

❑   `Percent` — Sets the percentage of the `TableLayoutPanel` to use for the width of the column

The `Width` property is only applicable if you do not choose a `SizeType` of `AutoSize`. It sets either the number of pixels for the width of the column (if the `SizeType` is `Absolute`) or the percentage width for the column (if the `SizeType` is set to `Percent`).

Similarly, for rows, there is a `RowCount` property to set the number of rows, and a `RowStyles` collection to manage the size of the rows. Each row in `RowStyles` has a `SizeType`, which works the same way as `SizeType` does for `Columns` except that it manages the height of the row instead of the width of a column. The `Height` property is used for rows instead of a `Width` property, but it works in a corresponding way. `Height` is either the number of pixels (if `SizeType` is `Absolute`) or a percentage of the height of the `TableLayoutPanel` (if `SizeType` is `Percent`). If `SizeType` is `AutoSize`, then a row is sized to the height of the tallest control in the row.

An advanced UI layout technique is to first create a `TableLayoutPanel`, and then embed a `FlowLayoutPanel` in some of the cells of the `TableLayoutPanel`. This allows several controls to be contained in a cell and repositioned as the size of the cell changes.

A step-by-step example of using a TableLayoutPanel, with an embedded FlowLayoutPanel, is included in the next chapter in the section "Creating a Composite UserControl."

Panel and GroupBox Container Controls

Of course, not all applications need the dynamic layout of the containers just discussed. Windows Forms includes two controls that are static containers, in which the positions and layout of the contained controls are not adjusted at all.

In VB6, the `Frame` control was used for this purpose. However, Windows Forms has two such containers, with minor differences between them: the `GroupBox` control and the `Panel` control.

These two are similar in the following ways:

❑   They can serve as a container for other controls.

❑   If they are hidden or moved, then the action affects all the controls in the container.

The `GroupBox` control is the one that most closely resembles an old VB6 `Frame` control visually. It acts much like a VB6 `Frame` control too, with one significant exception: There is no way to remove its border. It always has a border, and it can have a title, if needed. The border is always set the same way. Figure 15-17 shows a form with a `GroupBox` control containing three `RadioButtons`.

Figure 15-17

The Panel control has three major differences from GroupBox:

❑ It has options for displaying its border in the BorderStyle property, with a default of no border.

❑ It has the capability to scroll if its AutoScroll property is set to True.

❑ It cannot set a title or caption.

Figure 15-18 shows a form containing a Panel control with its BorderStyle property set to FixedSingle, with scrolling turned on by setting AutoScroll to True, and with a CheckedListBox that is too big to display all at once (which forces the Panel to show a scrollbar).

Figure 15-18

Extender Providers

There is a new family of components in Windows Forms that can only be used in association with visual controls. These components are known as *extender providers*. They work with the Visual Studio IDE to cause new properties to appear in the Properties window for controls on the form.

Extender providers have no visible manifestation except in conjunction with other controls, so they appear in the component tray. The three extender providers available with Windows Forms 2.0 are the HelpProvider, the ToolTip, and the ErrorProvider. All three work in basically the same way. Each extender provider implements the properties that are "attached" to other controls. The best way to see how this works is to go through an example, so let's do that with a ToolTip component.

ToolTip

The ToolTip is the simplest of the built-in extender providers. It adds just one property to each control, named ToolTip on ToolTip1 (assuming the ToolTip control has the default name of ToolTip1). This property works very much the same way the ToolTipText property works in VB6, and in fact replaces it.

To see this in action, create a Windows Forms application. On the blank `Form1` that is created for the project, place a couple of buttons. Take a look at the Properties window for `Button1`. Notice that it does not have a `ToolTip` property of any kind.

Drag over the `ToolTip` control, which will be placed in the component tray. Go back to the Properties window for `Button1`. A property named `ToolTip on ToolTip1` is now present. Set any string value you like for this property.

Run the project and hover the mouse pointer over `Button1`. You will see a tooltip containing the string value you entered for the `ToolTip on ToolTip1` property.

Other properties of the `ToolTip` component enable you to control other characteristics of the tooltip, such as the initial delay before the tooltip appears.

New in Windows Forms 2.0 is the capability to change the shape of tooltips to a "balloon." This is done by setting the `IsBalloon` property of the `Tooltip` component to `True`. Instead of a hovering rectangular tooltip, the tooltip has a rounded rectangular outline with a pointer to the control it is associated with, not unlike the dialog balloons in a comic strip. Figure 15-19 shows an example.

Figure 15-19

HelpProvider

The `HelpProvider` enables controls to have associated context-sensitive help available by pressing F1. When a `HelpProvider` is added to a form, all controls on the form get these new properties, which show up in the controls' Properties window.

Property	Usage
HelpString on HelpProvider1	Provides a pop-up tooltip for the control when F1 is pressed while the control has the focus. If the `HelpKeyword` and `HelpNavigator` properties (see later) are set to provide a valid reference to a help file, then the `HelpString` value is ignored in favor of the information in the help file.
HelpKeyword on HelpProvider1	Provides a keyword or other index to use in a help file for context-sensitive help for this control. The `HelpProvider1` control has a property that indicates the help file to use. This replaces the `HelpContextID` property in VB6.
HelpNavigator on HelpProvider1	Contains an enumerated value that determines how the value in `HelpKeyword` is used to refer to the help file. There are several possible values for displaying such elements as a topic, an index, or a table of contents in the help file.
ShowHelp on HelpProvider1	Determines whether the `HelpProvider` control is active for this control

Filling in the `HelpString` property immediately causes the control to provide tooltip help when F1 is pressed while the control has the focus. The `HelpProvider` control has a property to point to a help file (either an HTML help file or a Win32 help file), and the help topic in the `HelpTopic` property points to a topic in this file.

ErrorProvider

The `ErrorProvider` component presents a simple, visual way to indicate to a user that a control on a form has an error associated with it. The added property for controls on the form when an `ErrorProvider` is used is called `Error on ErrorProvider1` (assuming the `ErrorProvider` has the default name of `ErrorProvider1`). Setting this property to a string value causes the error icon to appear next to a control, and for the text to appear in a tooltip if the mouse hovers over the error icon.

Figure 15-20 shows a screen with several text boxes, and an error icon next to one (with a tooltip). The error icon and tooltip are displayed and managed by an `ErrorProvider`.

Figure 15-20

The `ErrorProvider` component's default icon is a red circle with an exclamation point. When the `Error` property for the text box is set, the icon blinks for a few moments, and hovering over the icon causes the tooltip to appear. Writing your own code to set the `Error` property is explained in the section "Working with Extender Providers in Code."

Properties of Extender Providers

In addition to providing other controls with properties, extender providers also have properties of their own. For example, the `ErrorProvider` has a property named `BlinkStyle`. When it is set to `NeverBlink`, the blinking of the icon is stopped for all controls that are affected by the `ErrorProvider`.

Other properties of the `ErrorProvider` enable you to change things such as the icon used and where the icon appears in relation to the field containing the error. For instance, you might want the icon to appear on the left side of a field instead of the default right side. You can also have multiple error providers on your form. For example, you may wish to give users a warning, rather than an error. A second error provider with a yellow icon could be used to provide this feature.

Working with Extender Providers in Code

Setting the `Error` property in the previous example can be done with the Properties window, but this is not very useful for on-the-fly error management. However, setting the `Error` property in code is not done with typical property syntax. By convention, extender providers have a method for each extended property they need to set, and the arguments for the method include the associated control and the property setting. To set the `Error` property in the previous example, the following code was used:

```
ErrorProvider1.SetError(txtName, "You must provide a location!")
```

The name of the method to set a property is the word Set prefixed to the name of the property. This line of code shows that the Error property is set with the SetError method of the ErrorProvider.

There is a corresponding method to get the value of the property, and it is named with Get prefixed to the name of the property. To determine the current Error property setting for txtName, you would use the following line:

```
sError = ErrorProvider1.GetError(txtName)
```

Similar syntax is used to manipulate any of the properties managed by an extender provider. The discussion of the tooltip provider earlier mentioned setting the tooltip property in the Properties window. To set that same property in code, the syntax would be as follows:

```
ToolTip1.SetToolTip(Button1, "New tooltip for Button1")
```

Advanced Capabilities for Data Entry

New for Windows Forms 2.0 are a couple of advanced capabilities for data entry. Textbox and Combobox controls now have autocompletion capabilities, and a new MaskedTextbox allows entry of formatted input such as phone numbers.

Autocompletion

Responsive user interfaces help users accomplish their purposes, thereby making them more productive. One classic way to do this is with *autocompletion*.

An example of autocompletion is IntelliSense in Visual Studio. Using IntelliSense, the user only has to type in a few letters, and Visual Studio presents a list of probable entries matching those letters. If the desired entry is found, the user only needs to select it, rather than type the entire entry.

Autocompletion is available in Windows Forms 2.0 with text boxes and combo boxes. Both use a set of properties to control how autocompletion works and from where the list of entries available to the user comes.

To see autocompletion in action, create a Windows application project. Drag a Textbox from the toolbox onto the blank Form1 created for the project. Set the AutoCompleteMode for the text box to Suggest in the Properties window. Then set the AutoCompleteSource to CustomSource. Finally, click the button in the setting window for AutoCompleteCustomSource. You'll see a window for adding entries that is very similar to the window for entering items for a list box or combo box.

Enter the following items into the dialog:

```
Holder
Holland
Hollis
Holloway
Holly
Holstein
Holt
```

Start the project and type **Hol** into the text box. As soon as you start typing, a drop-down will appear that contains entries matching what you've typed, including all seven elements in the list. If you then type another 1, the list will decrease to four elements that begin with Holl. If you then type an o, the list will contain only the entry Holloway.

The AutoCompleteMode has two other modes. The Append mode does not automatically present a drop-down, but instead appends the rest of the closest matching entry to the text in the Textbox or ComboBox, and highlights the untyped characters. This allows the closest matching entry to be placed in the text area without the user explicitly selecting an entry.

The SuggestAppend mode combines Suggest and Append. The current best match is displayed in the text area, and the drop-down with other possibilities is automatically displayed. This mode is the one most like IntelliSense.

You can also set the list of items to be included in the autocompletion list at runtime, which is the most common usage scenario. A list of items from a database table would typically be loaded for autocompletion. Here is typical code to create a list of items and attach the list to a combo box:

```
Dim nReturn As Integer
nReturn = autoCompleteStringCollection1.Add("Holder")
nReturn = autoCompleteStringCollection1.Add("Holland")
nReturn = autoCompleteStringCollection1.Add("Hollis")
nReturn = autoCompleteStringCollection1.Add("Holloway")
ComboBox1.AutoCompleteCustomSource = autoCompleteStringCollection1
```

For this sample to work properly, the Combobox control's AutoCompleteSource property must be set to CustomSource.

Several built-in lists are available to use for autocompletion. Instead of setting AutoCompleteSource to CustomSource, you can set it to sources such as files in the file system, or URLs recently used in Internet Explorer. See the documentation for AutoCompleteSource for additional options; or, if you are using AutoCompleteSource in code, IntelliSense will show the options available.

MaskedTextbox Control

The new features summary discussed the addition of a MaskedTextbox control, which fills in for the old VB6 MaskedEdit control. If you have used MaskedEdit in VB6, the MaskedTextbox will feel quite familiar.

After dragging a MaskedTextbox control to a form, you typically want to first set the mask associated with the control. You can do this in the Properties window by selecting the Mask property, but you can also click the smart tag (right-pointing arrow) on the right side of the MaskedTextbox. In either case, you can either construct a mask manually or select one of the commonly used masks from a list.

If you need to create your own mask, you need to design it based on a set of formatting characters:

Mask Character	Description
#	Digit placeholder
.	Decimal placeholder. The actual character used is the one specified as the decimal placeholder in your international settings. This character is treated as a literal for masking purposes.
,	Thousands separator. The actual character used is the one specified as the thousands separator in your international settings. This character is treated as a literal for masking purposes.
:	Time separator. The actual character used is the one specified as the time separator in your international settings. This character is treated as a literal for masking purposes.
/	Date separator. The actual character used is the one specified as the date separator in your international settings. This character is treated as a literal for masking purposes.
\	Treat the next character in the mask string as a literal. This allows you to include the #, &, A, and ? characters in the mask. This character is treated as a literal for masking purposes.
&	Character placeholder. Valid values for this placeholder are ANSI characters in the following ranges: 32–126 and 128–255.
>	Converts all the characters that follow to uppercase
<	Converts all the characters that follow to lowercase
A	Alphanumeric character placeholder (entry required). For example: a–z, A–Z, or 0–9.
a	Alphanumeric character placeholder (entry optional)
9	Digit placeholder (entry optional). For example: 0–9.
C	Character or space placeholder (entry optional). This operates exactly like the & placeholder and ensures compatibility with Microsoft Access.
?	Letter placeholder. For example: a–z or A–Z.
Literal	All other symbols are displayed as literals — that is, as themselves.

Literal characters are simply inserted automatically by the MaskedTextbox control. If you have literal characters for the parentheses in a phone number, for example, the user need not type these in order for them to show up in the text area of the control.

As an example of a mask, suppose that you have an account number that must consist of exactly two uppercase letters and five digits. You could construct a mask of >??00000. The first character forces all letters to uppercase. The two question marks specify two required alphabetic characters, and the five zeros specify five required digits.

Once you have set the Mask for the MaskedTextbox, all entries into the control will be coerced to the Mask pattern. Keystrokes that don't conform will be thrown away.

Validating Data Entry

Most controls that you place on a form require that its content be validated in some way. A text box might require a numeric value only or simply require that the user provide any value and not leave it blank.

The ErrorProvider component discussed earlier makes this task significantly easier than it was in previous versions. To illustrate the use of an ErrorProvider in data validation, create a new Windows application project and change the Text property for the blank Form1 to Data Validation Demo. Then place two text boxes on the form that will hold a user ID and password, as shown in Figure 15-21.

Figure 15-21

Name the first text box UserNameTextBox and name the second text box PasswordTextBox. Drag an ErrorProvider onto the form, which will cause it to appear in the component tray. In the next section, you'll add the code that simply verifies that the user has filled in both text boxes and gives a visual indication, via the ErrorProvider, if either of the fields has been left blank.

The Validating Event

The Validating event fires when your control begins its validation. It is here that you need to place the code that validates your control, and set a visual indication for the error. Insert the following code to see this in action:

```
Private Sub UserNameTextBox_Validating(ByVal sender As Object, _
                        ByVal e As System.ComponentModel.CancelEventArgs) _
                        Handles UserNameTextBox.Validating
    If userNameTextbox.Text = "" Then
        ErrorProvider1.SetError(UserNameTextBox, "User Name cannot be blank")
    Else
        ErrorProvider1.SetError(UserNameTextBox, "")
    End If
End Sub
Private Sub PasswordTextBox_Validating(ByVal sender As Object, _
                        ByVal e As System.ComponentModel.CancelEventArgs) _
```

```
                              Handles PasswordTextBox.Validating
        If passwordTextbox.Text = "" Then
            ErrorProvider1.SetError(PasswordTextBox, "Password cannot be blank")
        Else
            ErrorProvider1.SetError(PasswordTextBox, "")
        End If
    End Sub
```

Run the program and then tab between the controls without entering any text to get the error message. You'll see an icon blink next to each of the text box controls; and if you hover over an error icon, you'll see the appropriate error message.

There is also a `Validated` event that fires after a control's `Validating` event. It can be used, for example, to do a final check after other events have manipulated the contents of the control.

The CausesValidation Property

The `CausesValidation` property determines whether the control will participate in the validation events on the form. A control with a `CausesValidation` setting of `True` (it is `True` by default) has two effects:

❑   The control's `Validating`/`Validated` events fire when appropriate.

❑   The control triggers the `Validating`/`Validated` events for other controls.

It is important to understand that the validation events fire for a control not when the focus is lost but when the focus shifts to a control that has a `CausesValidation` value of `True`.

To see this effect, set the `CausesValidation` property of the password text box in your application to `False` (be sure to leave it `True` for the user ID and OK button). When you run the program, tab off the user ID text box and again to the OK button. Notice that it isn't until the focus reaches the OK button that the validating event of the user ID text box fires. Also notice that the validating event of the Password field never fires.

Ultimately, if you determine that the control is not valid, you need to specify what happens. That may include setting the focus to the control that needs attention (as well as indicating the error with an `ErrorProvider`).

Toolbars and the New ToolStrip Control

As mentioned in the summary of new features in Windows Forms 2.0, the `ToolStrip` control replaces the `Toolbar` control from Windows Forms 1.0 and 1.1. `ToolStrip` has many improvements. It supports movement to sides of a form other than the place where it was laid out, and you have much more flexibility in placing items on the toolbar. It also integrates better with the IDE to assist in creating toolbars and manipulating the many settings available.

The `ToolStrip` does not sit alone on a form. When a `ToolStrip` is dragged onto a form, the container that actually sits on the form is called a `RaftingContainer`. This container handles the positioning so that the toolbar created by a `ToolStrip` can be dragged to other parts of the form.

The `ToolStrip` sits inside the `RaftingContainer` and is the container for toolbar elements. It handles the sizing of the toolbar, movement of toolbar elements, and other general toolbar functions.

The items on the toolbar must be from a set of controls specially designed to serve as toolbar items. All of these items inherit from the `ToolStripItem` base class. The controls available for toolbar items are as follows:

Control	Description
ToolStripButton	Replicates the functionality of a regular `Button` for a toolbar
ToolStripLabel	Replicates the functionality of a regular `Label` for a toolbar
ToolStripSeparator	A visual toolbar element that displays a vertical bar to separate other groups of elements (no user interaction)
ToolStripComboBox	Replicates the functionality of a regular `ComboBox` for a toolbar. This item must be contained within a `ToolStripControlHost` (see below).
ToolStripTextBox	Replicates the functionality of a regular `TextBox` for a toolbar. This item must be contained within a `ToolStripControlHost` (see below).
ToolStripControlHost	A hosting container for other controls that reside on a `ToolStrip`. It can host any of the following controls: `ToolStripComboBox`, `ToolStripTextBox`, other Windows Forms controls, or user controls.
ToolStripDropDownItem	A hosting container for toolbar elements that feature drop-down functionality. Can host a `ToolStripMenuItem`, a `ToolStripSplitButton`, or a `ToolStripDropDownButton`.
ToolStripDropDownButton	A button that supports drop-down functionality. Clicking the button shows a list of options, and the user must then click the one desired. This item is used when the user needs to select from a group of options, none of which is used a large majority of the time.
ToolStripSplitButton	A combination of a regular button and a drop-down button. This item is often used when there is a frequently used option to click, but you also need to offer the user other options that are less frequently used.
ToolStripMenuItem	A selectable option displayed on a menu or context menu. This item is typically used with the menu controls that inherit from the `ToolStrip`, discussed later in this chapter in the section "Menus."

Note that almost any control can be hosted on a toolbar using the `ToolStripControlHost`. However, for buttons, text boxes, labels, and combo boxes, it is much easier to use the `ToolStrip` version instead of the standard version.

Creating a ToolStrip and Adding Toolbar Elements

Try an example to see how to build a toolbar using the `ToolStrip` control. Create a new Windows application. Add a `ToolStrip` control to the blank `Form1` that is included with the new project. Make the form about twice its default width so that you have plenty of room to see the `ToolStrip` as you work on it.

The `ToolStrip` is positioned at the top of the form by default. It does not contain any elements, although if you highlight the `ToolStrip` control in the component tray, a "menu designer" will appear in the `ToolStrip`.

The easiest way to add multiple elements to the `ToolStrip` is to use the designer dialog for the `ToolStrip`. Highlight the `ToolStrip` in the component tray and click the button in the Properties window for the `Items` property. You'll see a designer dialog like the one shown in Figure 15-22.

Figure 15-22

The drop-down in the upper-left corner contains the different types of items that can be placed on the toolbar. The names in the drop-down are the same as the ones in the table of controls except that the "Toolstrip" prefix is not present. Add one each of the following types, with the setting specified:

- ❏ `Button` — Set the `Text` property to `Go`. Set the Display property to `Text`.
- ❏ `ComboBox` — Leave the `Text` property blank. Set `DropDownStyle` to `DropDownList`. Open the Items dialog and add the names of some colors.
- ❏ `SplitButton` — Set the `Text` property to `Options`. Set the Display property to `Text`.
- ❏ `TextBox` — Leave the `Text` property blank.

Click OK. The `ToolStrip` will look like the one shown in Figure 15-23.

Figure 15-23

You can now handle events on any of these toolbar elements the same way you would any other controls. You can double-click to get a `Click` event routine or access the event routines through the dropdowns in the Code Editor.

To make the `Toolstrip` more dynamic, it must be embedded in a `ToolStripContainer`. You can do that manually by dragging one over and putting the `Toolstrip` in it, but the easy way to do it is to click the smart tag on the `Toolstrip` and then select Embed in `ToolStripContainer`. This causes a `ToolStripContainer` to appear on your form. Set the `Dock` property for the `ToolStripContainer` to `Fill` and it will provide a surface for the `Toolstrip` that includes all four edges of the form.

Run your program. Using the mouse, grab the dotted handle on the far left edge of the toolbar. If you drag this to the right, the toolbar will be repositioned. If you drag it to other positions on the form, then the entire toolbar will dock to different edges of the form.

Allowing the User to Move Toolbar Elements

By default, the `AllowItemReorder` property of the `ToolStrip` is set to `False`. If you change that to `True`, then the elements on the toolbar can be moved around in relation to one another (reordered) at runtime.

Change the `AllowItemReorder` property to `True` for the `ToolStrip` and run your program again. Hold down the Alt key and drag elements on the toolbar around. They will assume new positions on the toolbar when you drop them.

Creating a Standard Set of Toolbar Elements

If you need a toolbar that has the typical visual elements for cut, copy, paste, and so on, it is not necessary to create the elements. The designer will do it for you.

Create a new form in your project and drag a `Toolstrip` onto it. As before, it will be positioned at the top and will not contain any elements.

With the `Toolstrip` highlighted in the component tray, click the `Item` property. Below the properties in the Properties window, a link named Insert Standard Items will appear. Click that link; elements will be inserted into the `Toolstrip`, making it look like the one in Figure 15-24.

Figure 15-24

Menus

Menus are added to a form in VB.NET 2005 by dragging controls called `MenuStrip` or `ContextMenuStrip` onto your form. `MenuStrip` implements a standard Windows-style menu at the top of the form. `ContextMenuStrip` allows a pop-up menu with a right mouse button click.

These controls are actually subclasses of the `ToolStrip`, so much of the information you learned earlier in this chapter about working with the `ToolStrip` also applies to the `MenuStrip` and `ContextMenuStrip`. When dragged onto the form, these controls appear in the component tray just as the `ToolStrip` does, and you access the designer for these controls the same way you do for the `ToolStrip`. However, because these are menus, the most common way of adding items is to type items directly into the menu designer that appears when the control is highlighted.

The menu designer is extremely intuitive — the menu appears on your form just as it would at runtime, and you simply fill in the menu items you need. Each item can be renamed, and each can have a `Click` event associated with it.

Adding Standard Items to a Menu

If your form's menu needs to have the standard top-level options (File, Edit, and so on) and the typical options under these items, then you can have all these typical options inserted for you automatically.

To see this capability in action, drag a `MenuStrip` to a form and then click the smart tag (the right arrow at the right edge) for the `MenuStrip` to bring up the designer dialog. Click the link at the bottom of the dialog that says Insert Standard Items.

Icons and Checkmarks for Menu Items

Each menu item has an `Image` property. Setting this property to an image causes the image to appear on the left side of the text for the menu option. You can see this property in use by looking at the standard items inserted in the preceding example. The File ➪ Save option has an icon of a diskette, which is produced by setting the image property of that item.

Items can also have check marks beside them. This is done by changing the `Checked` property of the item to `True`. You can do this at design time or runtime, enabling you to manipulate the check marks on menus as necessary.

Context Menus

To implement a context menu for a form or any control on a form, drag a `ContextMenuStrip` to the form and add the menu items. Items are added and changed the same way as they are with the `MenuStrip`.

To hook a context menu to a control, set the control's `ContextMenuStrip` property to the `ContextMenuStrip` menu control you want to use. Then, when your program runs and you right-click in the control, the context menu will pop up.

Dynamically Manipulating Menus at Runtime

Menus can be adjusted at runtime using code. Context menus, for instance, may need to vary depending on the state of your form. The following walkthrough shows how to add a new menu item to a context menu and how to clear the menu items.

Create a new Windows application. On the blank Form1 for the project, drag over a MenuStrip control. Using the menu designer, type in a top-level menu option of File. Under that option, type in options for Open and Save.

Now place a button on the form. Double-click the button to get its Click event, and place the following code into the event:

```
Dim NewItem As New ToolStripMenuItem
NewItem.Text = "Save As"
' Set any other properties of the menu item you like.

FileToolStripMenuItem.DropDownItems.Add(NewItem)
AddHandler NewItem.Click, _
    AddressOf Me.NewMenuItem_Click
```

Add the event handler referenced in this code at the bottom of the form's code:

```
Private Sub NewMenuItem_Click(ByVal sender As System.Object, _
                              ByVal e As System.EventArgs)
   MessageBox.Show("New menu item clicked!")
End Sub
```

If you now run the program and look at the menu, it will only have File and Save options. Clicking the button will cause a new Save As item to be added to the menu, and it will be hooked to the event routine called NewMenuItem_Click.

Common Dialogs

Windows Forms provides you with seven common dialog controls. Each is a control that opens a predefined form that is identical to the one used by the operating system.

These dialogs cannot be shown modeless. They have a ShowDialog method to show them modally. That method returns one of the standard DialogResult values, as discussed in the section "Dialogs" earlier in this chapter.

OpenFileDialog and SaveFileDialog

These two controls open the standard dialog control that allows a user to select files on the system. They are quite similar except for the buttons and labels that appear on the actual dialog box when it is shown to the user. Each prompts the user for a file on the system by allowing the user to browse the files and folders available.

Use the following properties to set up the dialog boxes:

Property	Comments
InitialDirectory	Defines the initial location that is displayed when the dialog opens. For example, OpenFileDialog1.InitialDirectory = "C:\Program Files"
Filter	String that defines the Files of Type list. Separate items using the pipe character. Items are entered in pairs; the first of each pair is the description of the file type, and the second half is the file wildcard. For example: OpenFileDialog1.Filter = "All Files$|*.* |Text Files|*.txt|Rich Text Files|*.rtf"
FilterIndex	Integer that specifies the default filter item to use when the dialog box opens. For example, with the preceding filter used, default to text files as follows: OpenFileDialog1.FilterIndex = 2
RestoreDirectory	Boolean value that, when True, forces the system's default directory to be restored to the location it was in when the dialog box was first opened. This is False by default.
Filename	Holds the full name of the file that the user selected, including the path
ShowDialog()	Displays the dialog

The following code opens the standard dialog box, asking the user to select a file that currently exists on the system, and simply displays the choice in a message box upon return:

```
OpenFileDialog1.InitialDirectory = "C:\"
OpenFileDialog1.Filter = "Text files|*.txt|All files|*.*"
OpenFileDialog1.FilterIndex = 1
OpenFileDialog1.RestoreDirectory = True
If OpenFileDialog1.ShowDialog() = Windows.Forms.DialogResult.OK Then
    MessageBox.Show("You selected """ & OpenFileDialog1.FileName & """")
End If
```

ColorDialog Control

As the name implies, this control gives the user a dialog box from which to select a color. Use the following properties to set up the dialog boxes as follows:

```
ColorDialog1.Color = TextBox1.BackColor
ColorDialog1.AllowFullOpen = True
If ColorDialog1.ShowDialog()= Windows.Forms.DialogResult.OK Then
    TextBox1.BackColor = ColorDialog1.Color
End If
```

Property	Comments
Color	The System.Drawing.Color that the user selected. You can also use this to set the initial color selected when the user opens the dialog.
AllowFullOpen	Boolean value that, when True, allows the user to select any color. If False, the user is restricted to the set of default colors.
ShowDialog()	Displays the dialog

FontDialog Control

This control displays the standard dialog box, allowing a user to select a font. Use the following properties to set up the dialog boxes:

Property	Comments
Font	The System.Drawing.Font that the user selected. Also used to set the initial font.
ShowEffects	Boolean value that, when True, makes the dialog box display the text effects options of underline and strikeout.
ShowColor	Boolean value that, when True, makes the dialog box display the combo box of the font colors. The ShowEffects property must be True for this to have an effect.
FixedPitchOnly	Boolean value that, when True, limits the list of font options to only those that have a fixed pitch (such as Courier or Lucida console).
ShowDialog()	Displays the dialog

Using these properties looks like this:

```
FontDialog1.Font = TextBox1.Font
FontDialog1.ShowColor = True
FontDialog1.ShowEffects = True
FontDialog1.FixedPitchOnly = False
If FontDialog1.ShowDialog()= Windows.Forms.DialogResult.OK Then
    TextBox1.Font = FontDialog1.Font
End If
```

Printer Dialog Controls

There are three more common dialog controls: PrintDialog, PrintPreviewDialog, and PageSetup-Dialog. They can all be used to control the output of a file to the printer, and you can use these in conjunction with the PrintDocument component to run and control print jobs.

Drag and Drop

Implementing a drag-and-drop operation in the .NET Framework is accomplished by a short sequence of events. Typically, it begins in a MouseDown event of one control, and always ends with the DragDrop event of another.

To demonstrate the process, begin with a new Windows application. Add two list boxes to your form, and add three items to the first using the Items Property Designer. This application allows you to drag the items from one list box into the other.

The first step in making drag and drop work is specifying whether or not a control will accept a drop. By default, all controls reject such an act and do not respond to any attempt by the user to drop something onto them. In this case, set the AllowDrop property of the second list box (the one without the items added) to True.

The next item of business is to invoke the drag-and-drop operation. This is typically done in the MouseDown event of the control containing the data you want to drag (although you're not restricted to it). The DoDragDrop method is used to start the operation. This method defines the data that will be dragged and the type of dragging that will be allowed. Here, you'll drag the text of the selected list box item, and permit both a move and a copy of the data to occur.

Switch over to the code window of your form and add the following code to the MouseDown event of ListBox1:

```
Private Sub ListBox1_MouseDown(ByVal sender As Object, _
                        ByVal e As System.Windows.Forms.MouseEventArgs) _
                        Handles ListBox1.MouseDown
    Dim DragDropResult As DragDropEffects
    If e.Button = MouseButtons.Left Then
        DragDropResult = ListBox1.DoDragDrop( _
                    ListBox1.Items(ListBox1.SelectedIndex), _
                    DragDropEffects.Move Or DragDropEffects.Copy)
        ' Leave some room here to check the result of the operation
        ' (You'll fill it in next).
    End If
End Sub
```

Notice the comment about leaving room to check the result of the operation. You'll fill that in shortly. For now, calling the DoDragDrop method has gotten you started.

The next step involves the recipient of the data — in your case, ListBox2. Two events here are important to monitor — DragEnter and DragDrop.

As you can guess by the name, the DragEnter event occurs when the user first moves over the recipient control. The DragEnter event has a parameter of type DragEventArgs that contains an Effect property and a KeyState property.

The Effect property enables you to set the display of the drop icon for the user to indicate whether a move or a copy occurs when the mouse button is released. The KeyState property enables you to determine the state of the Ctrl, Alt, and Shift keys. It is a Windows standard that when both a move or a copy can occur, a user is to indicate the copy action by holding down the Ctrl key. Therefore, in this event, you check the `KeyState` property and use it to determine how to set the `Effect` property.

Add the following code to the `DragEnter` event of `ListBox2`:

```
Private Sub ListBox2_DragEnter(ByVal sender As Object, _
                               ByVal e As DragEventArgs) _
                               Handles ListBox2.DragOver
    If e.KeyState = 9 Then ' Control key
        e.Effect = DragDropEffects.Copy
    Else
        e.Effect = DragDropEffects.Move
    End If
End Sub
```

Note that you can also use the `DragOver` event if you want, but it will fire continuously as the mouse moves over the target control. In this situation, you only need to trap the initial entry of the mouse into the control.

The final step in the operation occurs when the user lets go of the mouse button to drop the data at its destination. This is captured by the `DragDrop` event. The parameter contains a property holding the data that is being dragged. It's now a simple process of placing it into the recipient control as follows:

```
Private Sub ListBox2_DragDrop(ByVal sender As Object, _
                              ByVal e As System.Windows.Forms.DragEventArgs) _
                              Handles ListBox2.DragDrop
    ListBox2.Items.Add(e.Data.GetData(DataFormats.Text))
End Sub
```

One last step: You can't forget to manipulate `ListBox1` if the drag and drop was a move. Here's where you'll fill in the hole you left in the `MouseDown` event of `ListBox1`. Once the `DragDrop` has occurred, the initial call that invoked the procedure returns a result indicating what ultimately happened. Go back to the `ListBox1_MouseDown` event and enhance it to remove the item from `Listbox1` if it was moved (and not simply copied):

```
Private Sub ListBox1_MouseDown(ByVal sender As Object, _
              ByVal e As System.Windows.Forms.MouseEventArgs) _
              Handles ListBox1.MouseDown
    Dim DragDropResult As DragDropEffects

    If e.Button = MouseButtons.Left Then
        DragDropResult = ListBox1.DoDragDrop( _
                    ListBox1.Items(ListBox1.SelectedIndex), _
                    DragDropEffects.Move Or DragDropEffects.Copy)
        ' If operation is a move (and not a copy), then remove then
        ' remove the item from the first list box.
        If DragDropResult = DragDropEffects.Move Then
          ListBox1.Items.RemoveAt(ListBox1.SelectedIndex)
        End If
    End If
End Sub
```

When you're done, run your application and drag the items from Listbox1 into Listbox2. Try a copy by holding down the Ctrl key when you do it. The screen shot in Figure 15-25 shows the result after Item1 has been moved and Item3 has been copied a few times.

Figure 15-25

Summary of Standard Windows.Forms Controls

Windows Forms, of course, contains most of the controls that you are accustomed to using in pre-.NET versions of Visual Basic. This section lists the basic controls that are generally quite intuitive and don't warrant a full example to explain. Where appropriate, the important differences from pre-.NET versions of Visual Basic are stated.

- ❑ Button

  - ❑ Known as CommandButton in VB6 and earlier
  - ❑ Now uses the Text property instead of Caption
  - ❑ Can now display both an icon and text simultaneously. The image is set using the Image property (instead of Picture). The image position can be set using the ImageAlign property (left, right, center, and so on).
  - ❑ Text on the button can be aligned using the TextAlign property.
  - ❑ Can now have different appearances using the FlatStyle property
  - ❑ No longer has the Default and Cancel properties. These are now managed by the form itself using the AcceptButton and CancelButton properties.

- ❑ CheckBox

  - ❑ Now uses the Text property instead of Caption
  - ❑ Can now appear as a toggle button using the Appearance property
  - ❑ Check box and text can now be positioned within the defined area using the CheckAlign and TextAlign properties.
  - ❑ Uses the CheckState property instead of Value
  - ❑ Has a FlatStyle property controlling the appearance of the check box

- ❑ CheckedListBox

  - ❑ A list box that has check boxes beside each item (see Listbox)

639

❑ ComboBox

- ❑ As with the new ListBox control, can now hold a collection of objects instead of an array of strings (see ListBox).

- ❑ Now has a MaxDropDownItems property that specifies how many items to display when the list opens

❑ DateTimePicker

- ❑ Formerly known as a DTPicker

❑ DomainUpDown

- ❑ A simple one-line version of a list box

- ❑ Can hold a collection of objects and will display the ToString() result of an item in the collection

- ❑ Can wrap around the list to give a continuous scrolling effect using the Wrap property

❑ HScrollBar

- ❑ Unchanged

❑ ImageList

- ❑ Same as previous versions, but with an improved window for managing the images within the list. The MaskColor property is now TransparentColor.

❑ Label

- ❑ Essentially the same as previous versions

- ❑ Caption is now Text

- ❑ Can now display an image and text

- ❑ The TextAlign property is especially useful. The text of a label beside a text box in VB6 would always be a few pixels higher than the text in the text box. Now, by setting the label's TextAlign property so that the vertical alignment is Middle, this problem is solved.

- ❑ Can now specify whether a mnemonic should be interpreted (if UseMnemonic is True, then the first ampersand (&) in the Text property specifies underlining the following character and having it react to the Alt key shortcut, placing the focus on the next control in the tab order that can hold focus, such as a text box).

❑ LinkLabel

- ❑ Identical to a label, but behaves like a hyperlink with extra properties such as LinkBehavior (for example, HoverUnderline), LinkColor, and ActiveLinkColor

❑ ListBox

- ❑ A list box can now hold a collection of objects, instead of an array of strings. Use the DisplayMember property to specify what property of the objects to display in the list, and the ValueMember property to specify what property of the objects to use as the values of the list items. (This is similar to the ItemData array from previous versions.) For example, a combo box could store a collection of employee objects, and display to the user the `Name` property of each, as well as retrieve the `EmployeeId` as the value of the item currently selected.

- ❑ Can no longer be set to display check boxes using a `Style` property. Use the `CheckedListBox` control instead.

❑ `ListView`

- ❑ Same functionality as the VB6 version but with an improved Property Editor that enables you to define the list view item collection and its sub-items at design time
- ❑ Sub-items can have their own font display properties.
- ❑ New `HeaderStyle` property instead of `HideColumnHeaders`

❑ `MonthCalendar`

- ❑ Formerly known as `MonthView`

❑ `NotifyIcon`

- ❑ Gives a form an icon in the system tray
- ❑ Tooltip of the icon is set by the `Text` property of the control
- ❑ Pop-up menus are set using a `ContextMenu` control (see the "Menus" section earlier in chapter).

❑ `NumericUpDown`

- ❑ A single-line text box that displays a number and up/down buttons that increment/decrement the number when clicked

❑ `PictureBox`

- ❑ `Image` property defines the graphic to display instead of `Picture`
- ❑ Use the `SizeMode` property to autostretch or center the picture.

❑ `ProgressBar`

- ❑ Now has a `Step()` method that automatically increments the value of the progress bar by the amount defined in the `Step` property

❑ `RadioButton`

- ❑ Formerly known as `OptionButton`
- ❑ Use the `Checked` property to specify value (formerly `Value`).
- ❑ Use `CheckAlign` and `TextAlign` to specify where the radio button and text appear in relation to the area of the control.

❑ `RichTextBox`

- ❑ Essentially the same control as before with a few new properties such as `ZoomFactor`, `WordWrap`, `DetectURLs`, and `AutoWordSelection`
- ❑ Use the `Lines()` array to get or set specific individual lines of text of the control.

❑ TabControl

    ❑ Formerly known as the `TabStrip` control

    ❑ Now has a `TabPages` collection of `TabPage` objects. A `TabPage` object is a subclass of the `Panel` control specialized for use in the `TabControl`.

    ❑ Uses the `Appearance` property to display the tabs as buttons, if desired (formerly the `Style` property of the `TabStrip` control)

❑ TextBox

    ❑ Now has a `CharacterCasing` property that can automatically adjust the text entered into uppercase or lowercase

    ❑ `ReadOnly` property now used to prevent the text from being edited. This used to be the `Locked` property. (The `Locked` property now determines whether the control can be moved or resized.)

    ❑ Now has `Cut`, `Copy`, `Paste`, `Undo`, and `ClearUndo` methods

❑ Timer

    ❑ This is essentially unchanged from previous versions.

    ❑ The timer is now disabled by default.

    ❑ You cannot set the interval to zero to disable it.

❑ TrackBar

    ❑ Formerly known as the `Slider` control, it is essentially unchanged.

❑ TreeView

    ❑ Same functionality as in VB6 but with a new Node Tree Editor that allows you to visually design the tree

❑ VScrollBar

    ❑ Unchanged

Retired Controls

The following list outlines the controls from VB6 that you won't find in Windows Forms and how to reproduce their functionality:

❑ Spinner

    ❑ Use the `DomainUpDown` or `NumericUpDown` control.

❑ Line and Shape

    ❑ Windows Forms has no `Line` or `Shape` control, nor any immediate equivalent. A "cheap" way of reproducing a horizontal or vertical line is to use a label control. Set its background color to that of the line you want, and then either the `Size.Height` or `Size.Width` value to 1.

❑   Diagonal lines and shapes must be drawn using GDI+ graphics methods.

❑   `DirListBox`, `FileListBox`, `DriveListBox`

❑   You would typically use these controls to create a file system browser similar to Windows Explorer. Windows Forms has no equivalent controls. You can use the `OpenFileDialog` and `SaveFileDialog` (see the previous section) to meet your needs in most circumstances.

❑   `Image`

❑   Use the `PictureBox` control.

Working Without Control Arrays

Control arrays, a feature of VB6 and earlier versions, are not present in Windows Forms 2.0. They were needed for two capabilities:

❑   To have a single method handle the events of multiple controls

❑   To dynamically add new controls to your form at runtime

Both of these capabilities can be accomplished in Windows Forms, but the techniques used are different.

To have a single method handle multiple controls, you must arrange for those controls' events to be attached to the method. You can do that with multiple controls specified in a `Handles` clause, or by using `AddHandler` for each control.

There is no `Index` property as in old-style control arrays in VB6. Instead, simply use the `Sender` parameter of the event handler to determine which control originated the event.

A simple example is helpful to see how to set this up. Create a new Windows application and set the `Text` property of the blank `Form1` to `Add Dynamic Control Demo`. Then add two buttons to the form, as shown in Figure 15-26.

Figure 15-26

Double-click `Button1` to switch over to the code that handles the `Button1.Click` event. To make this method respond to the `Button2.Click` event as well, simply add the `Button2.Click` event handler to the end of the `Handles` list, and then add some simple code to display a message box indicating what button triggered the event:

```
' Note the change in the method name from Button1_Click. Since
' two objects are hooked up, it's a good idea to avoid having the
' method specifically named to a single object.
```

```
Private Sub Button_Click(ByVal sender As System.Object, _
                ByVal e As System.EventArgs) _
        Handles Button1.Click, Button2.Click
    Dim buttonClicked As Button
    buttonClicked = CType(sender, Button)
    ' Tell the world what button was clicked
    MessageBox.Show("You clicked " & buttonClicked.Text)
End Sub
```

Run the program and click the two buttons. Each one will trigger the event and display a message box with the appropriate text from the button that was clicked.

Now enhance the program to add a third button dynamically at runtime. Add another button to your form that will trigger the addition of Button3, as shown in Figure 15-27.

Figure 15-27

Name the new button AddNewButton and add the following code to handle its Click event:

```
Private Sub AddNewButton_Click(ByVal sender As System.Object, _
                ByVal e As System.EventArgs) _
                Handles addNewButton.Click

    Dim newButton As Button

    ' Create the new control
    newButton = New Button()

    ' Set it up on the form
    newButton.Location = New System.Drawing.Point(184, 12)
    newButton.Size = New System.Drawing.Size(75, 23)
    newButton.Text = "Button3"

    ' Add it to the form's controls collection
    Me.Controls.Add(newButton)

    ' Hook up the event handler.
    AddHandler newButton.Click, AddressOf Me.Button_Click
End  Sub
```

When the AddNewButton button is clicked, the code creates a new button, sets its size and position, and then does two essential things. First, it adds the button to the form's controls collection, and second, it connects the Click event of the button to the method that handles it.

With this done, run the program and click the addNewButton button. Button3 will appear. Then, simply click Button3 to prove that the click event is being handled. You should get the result shown in Figure 15-28.

Figure 15-28

Other Handy Programming Tips

Here are some other handy programming tips for using Windows Forms:

❑   **Switch the focus to a control** — Use the .Focus() method. To set the focus to TextBox1, for example, use the following code:

```
TextBox1.Focus()
```

❑   **Quickly determine the container control or parent form** — With the use of group boxes and panels, controls are often contained many times. You can now use the FindForm method to immediately get a reference to the form. Use the GetContainerControl method to access the immediate parent of a control.

❑   **Traversing the tab order** — Use the GetNextControl method of any control to get a reference to the next control on the form in the tab order.

❑   **Convert client coordinates to screen coordinates (and back)** — Want to know where a control is in screen coordinates? Use the PointToScreen method. Convert back using the PointToClient method.

❑   **Change the z-order of controls at runtime** — Controls now have both BringToFront and SendToBack methods.

❑   **Locate the mouse pointer** — The control class now exposes a MousePosition property that returns the location of the mouse in screen coordinates.

❑   **Managing child control** — Container controls, such as a group box or panel, can use the HasChildren property and Controls collection to determine the existence of, and direct references to, child controls, respectively.

❑   **Maximize, minimize, restore a form** — Use the form's WindowState property.

Summary

The new features and improvements to Windows Forms simplify development of rich client and smart client interfaces, and allow new capabilities that user interface designers did not have in pre-.NET versions of Visual Basic. Coupled with the easy deployment of .NET applications, we are in the midst of a resurgence in forms-based programs.

Becoming a capable Windows Forms developer requires becoming familiar with the controls that are available, and their properties, events, and methods. This takes time. If you are coming from the VB6 world, much of your expertise will continue to be useful with Windows Forms. This chapter has highlighted the most important differences you need to know about. If you are less familiar with form-based interfaces, you can expend a fair amount of time using the reference documentation to find the control capabilities you need.

Many professional Windows Forms developers need to go beyond just creating forms and laying out controls. Complex applications often also require creation of new controls or enhancement of built-in controls. The capabilities for doing this were limited in earlier versions of Visual Basic, but are much more impressive in VB 2005. Accordingly, the next chapter discusses how to create and modify Windows Forms controls, along with some additional advanced Windows Forms topics.

16

Windows Forms
Advanced Features

The previous chapter discussed the basics of Windows Forms 2.0. These capabilities are sufficient for straightforward user interfaces for systems written in VB 2005, along with the built-in capabilities of forms and controls available in Windows Forms 2.0.

However, as applications become larger and more complex, it becomes more important to use the advanced capabilities of the .NET environment to better structure the application. Poorly structured large systems tend to have redundant code. Repeated code patterns end up being used (in slightly different variations) in many, many places in an application, which has many bad side effects—longer development time, less reliability, more difficult debugging and testing, and tougher maintenance.

Examples of needs that often result in repeated code include making sure that fields are entered by the user, that the fields are formatted correctly, and that `null` fields in the database are handled correctly. Proper object-oriented design can encapsulate such functionality, making it unnecessary to use repeated code.

In VB6 and earlier systems, the techniques available to reduce redundant code were limited. You could write functions to be accessed from various places, for example, and you could write `UserControls` to encapsulate some functionality.

Your options in Visual Basic 2005 are much broader. Using the full object-oriented capabilities of the .NET environment, plus additional capabilities specific to Windows Forms programming, you can componentize your logic, allowing the same code to be used in numerous places in your application.

This chapter discusses techniques for componentizing code in Windows Forms applications. It is assumed that you have already read Chapters 3 and 4 on inheritance and other object-oriented techniques available in .NET before working with this chapter.

Packaging Logic in Visual Controls

As shown in the last chapter, Windows Forms user interfaces are based on using controls. A control is simply a special type of .NET class (just as forms are). As a fully object-oriented programming environment, VB 2005 gives you the capability to inherit and extend classes, and controls are no exception. Therefore, it is possible to create new controls that go beyond what the built-in controls can do.

There are four primary sources of controls for use on Windows Forms interfaces:

❑   Controls packaged with the .NET Framework (referred to in this chapter as built-in controls)

❑   Existing ActiveX controls that are imported into Windows Forms (these are briefly discussed in Chapter 23)

❑   Third-party .NET-based controls from a software vendor

❑   Custom controls that are created for a specific purpose in a particular project or organization

If you are able to build your application with controls from the first three categories, so much the better. Using prewritten functionality that serves the purpose is generally a good idea. However, this chapter assumes you need to go beyond such prepackaged functionality.

If you are primarily familiar with versions of Visual Basic before the .NET era (VB6 and earlier), you know that the only technique available then for such packaging was UserControls. While UserControls is also available in Windows Forms (and is much improved), this is only one of several techniques available for writing visual controls.

Custom Controls in Windows Forms

There are three basic techniques for the creation of custom Windows Forms controls in .NET, corresponding to three different starting points. This range of options offers the flexibility to choose a technique that allows an appropriate balance between simplicity and flexibility:

❑   You can inherit from an existing control.

❑   You can build a composite control (using the UserControl class as your starting point).

❑   You can write a control from scratch (using the very simple Control class as your starting point).

These are in rough order of complexity, from simplest to most complex. Let's look at each one with a view to understanding the scenarios in which each one is useful.

Inherit from an Existing Control

The simplest technique starts with a complete Windows Forms control that is already developed. A new class is created that inherits the existing control. This new class has all the functionality of the base class from which it inherits, and the new logic can be added to create additional functionality in this new class or, indeed, to override functionality from the parent (when permitted).

Here are some typical examples where it might make sense to extend an existing Windows Forms control:

- ❑ A text box used for entry of American-style dates
- ❑ A self-loading list box, combo box, or data grid
- ❑ A `Combobox` that had a mechanism to be reset to an unselected state
- ❑ A `NumericUpDown` control that generates a special event when it reaches 80 percent of its maximum allowed value

Each of these scenarios starts with an existing control that simply needs some additional functionality. The more often such functionality is needed in your project, the more sense it makes to package it in a custom control. If a text box that needs special validation or editing will be used in only one place, it probably doesn't make sense to create an inherited control. In that case, simply adding some logic in the form where the control is used to handle the control's events and manipulating the control's properties and methods are probably sufficient.

Build a Composite Control

In some cases, a single existing control does not furnish the needed functionality, but a combination of two or more existing controls does. Here are some typical examples:

- ❑ A set of buttons with related logic that are always used together (such as Save, Delete, and Cancel buttons on a file maintenance form)
- ❑ A set of text boxes to hold a name, address, and phone number, with the combined information formatted and validated in a particular way
- ❑ A set of option buttons with a single property exposed as the chosen option

As with inherited controls, composite controls are only appropriate for situations that require the same functionality in multiple places. If the functionality is only needed once, then simply placing the relevant controls on the form and including appropriate logic right in the form is usually better.

Composite controls are the closest relative to VB6 `UserControls`, and because of that they are sometimes referred to as `UserControls`. In fact, the base class used to create composite controls is the `UserControl` class in Windows Forms.

Write a Control from Scratch

If a control needs to have special functionality not related to any existing control, then it can be written from scratch to draw its own visual interface and implement its own logic. This option requires more work, but it enables you to do just about anything that is possible within .NET and Windows Forms, including very sophisticated drawing of a user interface.

To write a control from scratch, it is necessary to inherit from the `Control` class, which provides basic functionality such as properties for colors and size. With this basic functionality already built in, your required development tasks include adding any specific properties and methods needed for this control, writing rendering logic that will paint the control to the screen, and handling mouse and keyboard input to the control.

Inheriting from an Existing Control

With this background on the options for creating custom controls, the next step is to look in depth at the procedures used for their development. First up is creating a custom control by inheriting from an existing control and extending it with new functionality. This is the simplest method for the creation of new controls, and the best way to introduce generic techniques that apply to all new controls.

After looking at the general steps needed to create a custom control via inheritance, an example illustrates the details. It is important to understand that many of the techniques described for working with a control created through inheritance also apply to the other ways that a control can be created. Whether inheriting from the `Control` class, the `UserControl` class, or from an existing control, a control is a .NET class. Creating properties, methods, and events, and coordinating these members with the Visual Studio designers, is done in a similar fashion, regardless of the starting point.

Overview of the Process

Here are the general stages involved in creating a custom control via inheritance from an existing control. This is not a step-by-step recipe, just an overview. An example follows that goes into more detail on specific steps, but those steps follow these following stages:

1. Create or open a Windows Control Library project and add a new Custom Control to the project. The class that is created will inherit from the `System.Windows.Forms.Control` base class. The line that specifies the inherited class must be changed to inherit from the control that is being used as the starting point.

2. The class file then gets new logic added as necessary to add new functionality. Then the project is compiled with a `Build` operation in order to create a DLL containing the new control's code.

3. The control is now ready to be used. It can be placed in the Windows Forms Toolbox with the Choose Items option in Visual Studio 2005. From that point forward, it can be dragged onto forms like any other control.

Stage 2, of course, is where the effort lies. New logic for the custom control may include new properties, methods, and events. It may also include intercepting events for the base control and taking special actions as necessary. These tasks are done with standard .NET coding techniques.

Several coding techniques are specific to developing Windows Forms controls, such as the use of particular .NET attributes. While our example includes adding routine properties and events, we will focus on these special techniques for programming controls.

Writing Code for an Inherited Control

This section discusses how to place new logic in an inherited control, with special emphasis on techniques that go beyond basic object orientation. A detailed example using the techniques follows this section.

Creating a Property for a Custom Control

Creating a property for a custom control is just like creating a property for any other class. It is necessary to write a property procedure, and to store the value for the property somewhere, most often in a module-level variable, which is often called a *backing field*.

Properties typically need a default value — that is, a value the property takes on automatically when a control is instantiated. Typically, this means setting the backing field that holds the property value to some initial value. That can be done when the backing field is declared, or it can be done in the constructor for the control.

Here's the code for a typical simple property for a custom control:

```
Dim _nMaxItemsSelected As Integer = 10
Public Property MaxItemsSelected() As Integer
  Get
    Return _nMaxItemsSelected
  End Get
  Set(ByVal Value As Integer)
    If Value < 0 Then
      Throw New ArgumentException("Property value cannot be negative")
    Else
      _nMaxItemsSelected = Value
    End If
  End Set
End Property
```

Once a property is created for a control, it automatically shows up in the Properties window for the control. However, you can use some additional capabilities to make the property work better with the designers and the Properties window in Visual Studio.

Coordinating with the Visual Studio IDE

Controls are normally dragged onto a visual design surface, which is managed by the Visual Studio IDE. For your control to work effectively with the IDE, it must be able to tell the IDE the *default value* of its properties. The IDE needs the default value of a property for two important capabilities:

❑ To reset the value of the property (done when a user right-clicks the property in the Properties window and selects Reset)

❑ To decide whether to set the property in designer-generated code. A property that is at its default value does not need to be explicitly set in the designer-generated code.

There are two ways for your control to work with the IDE to accomplish these tasks. For properties that take simple values, such as integers, Booleans, floating-point numbers, or strings, .NET provides an attribute. For properties that take complex types, such as structures, enumerated types, or object references, two methods need to be implemented.

Attributes

You can learn more about attributes in Chapter 5, but a short summary of important points is included here. Attributes reside in namespaces, just as components do. The attributes used in this chapter are in the System.ComponentModel namespace. To use attributes, the project must have a reference to the assembly containing the namespace for the attributes. For System.ComponentModel, that's no problem — the project automatically has the reference.

However, the project will not automatically have an Imports for that namespace. Attributes could be referred to with a full type name, but that's a bit clumsy. To make it easy to refer to the attributes in code, put the following line at the beginning of all modules that will need to use the attributes discussed in this chapter:

```
Imports System.ComponentModel
```

That way, an attribute can be referred to with just its name. For example, the DefaultValue attribute, discussed in detail below, can be declared like this:

```
< DefaultValue(4)> Public Property MyProperty() As Integer
```

All the examples in this chapter assume that the Imports *statement has been placed at the top of the class, so all attributes are referenced by their short name. If you get a compile error on an attribute, it's likely that you've omitted that line.*

An attribute for a property must be on the same line of code as the property declaration. Of course, line continuation characters can be used so that an attribute is on a separate physical line but still on the same logical line in the program. For example, the last example could also be written as

```
< DefaultValue(4)> _
Public Property MyProperty() As Integer
```

Setting a Default Value with an Attribute

The .NET Framework contains many attributes. Most are used to tag classes, properties, and methods with metadata — that is, information that some other entity, such as a compiler or the Visual Studio IDE, might need to know.

For example, the DefaultValue attribute tells the Visual Studio IDE the default value of a property. Let's change the preceding code for a simple property to include a DefaultValue attribute. Here are the first few lines, showing the change to the property declaration that applies the attribute:

```
Dim mnMaxItemsSelected As Integer = 10
 <DefaultValue(10)> Public Property MaxItemsSelected() As Integer
   Get
     Return mnMaxItemsSelected
 ...
```

Including the DefaultValue attribute allows the Properties window to reset the value of the property back to the default value. That is, if you right-click the property in the Properties window and select Reset from the pop-up context menu, the value of the property returns to 10 from any other value to which it happens to be set.

Another effect of the attribute can be seen in the code generated by the visual designer. If the preceding property is set to any value that is not the default, a line of code appears in the designer-generated code to set the property value. This is called *serializing* the property.

That is, if the value of MaxItemsSelected is set to 5, then a line of code something like this appears in the designer-generated code:

```
MyControl.MaxItemsSelected = 5
```

If the property has the default value of 10 (because it was never changed, or because it was reset to 10), then the line to set the property value is not present in the designer-generated code. That is, the property does not need to be serialized in code if the value is at the default.

To see serialized code, you need to look in the partial class that holds the Windows Forms designer-generated code. This partial class is not visible in the Solution Explorer by default. To see it, you need to press the Show All Files button in the Solution Explorer.

Alternate Techniques for Working with the IDE

The last sample property returned an `Integer`. Some custom properties return more complex types, such as structures, enumerated types, or object references. These properties cannot use a simple `DefaultValue` attribute to take care of resetting and serializing the property. An alternate technique is needed.

For complex types, designers check to see whether a property needs to be serialized by using a method on the control containing the property. The method returns a Boolean value that indicates whether a property needs to be serialized (`True` if it does, `False` if it does not).

For the following examples, suppose a control has a property named `MyColor`, which is of type `Color`. The `Color` type is a structure in Windows Forms, so the normal `DefaultValue` attribute can't be used with it. Further suppose the backing variable for the property is named `_MyColor`.

In this case, the method to check serialization would be called `ShouldSerializeMyColor`. It would typically look something like the following code:

```
Public Function ShouldSerializeMyColor() As Color
  If Color.Equals(_MyColor, Color.Red) Then
    Return False
  Else
    Return True
  End If
End Function
```

This is a good example of why a `DefaultValue` attribute can't work for all types. There is no equality operator for the `Color` type, so you have to write appropriate code to perform the check to see whether the current value of the `MyColor` property is the default. In this case, that's done with the `Equals` method of the `Color` type.

If a property in a custom control does not have a related `ShouldSerializeXXX` method or a `DefaultValue` attribute, then the property is always serialized. Code for setting the property's value will always be included by the designer in the generated code for a form, so it's a good idea to always include either a `ShouldSerializeXXX` method or a `DefaultValue` attribute for every new property created for a control.

Providing a Reset Method for a Control Property

The `ShouldSerialize` method only takes care of telling the IDE whether to serialize the property value. Properties that require a `ShouldSerialize` method also need a way to reset a property's value to the default. This is done by providing a special reset method. In the case of the `MyColor` property, the reset method is named `ResetMyColor`. It would look something like the following:

```
Public Sub ResetMyColor()
  _MyColor = Color.Red
End Sub
```

Other Useful Attributes

`DefaultValue` is not the only attribute that is useful for properties. The `Description` attribute is also one that should be used consistently. It contains a text description of the property, and that description shows up at the bottom of the Properties windows when a property is selected. To include a `Description` attribute, the declaration of the preceding property would appear as follows:

```
<DefaultValue(100), _
Description("This is a pithy description of my property")> _
Public Property MyProperty() As Integer
```

Such a property will look like Figure 16-1 when highlighted in the Properties window.

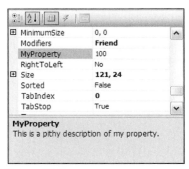

Figure 16-1

Another attribute you will sometimes need is the `Browsable` attribute. As mentioned earlier, a new property appears in the Properties window automatically. In some cases, you may need to create a property for a control that you do not want to show up in the Properties window. In that case, you use a `Browsable` attribute set to `False`. Here is code similar to the last one, making a property nonbrowsable in the Properties window:

```
<Browsable(False)> _
Public Property MyProperty() As Integer
```

One additional attribute you may want to use regularly is the `Category` attribute. Properties can be grouped by category in the Properties window by pressing a button at the top of the window. Standard categories include Behavior, Appearance, etc. You can have your property appear in any of those categories, or you can make up a new category of your own. To assign a category to a property, use code like this:

```
<Category("Appearance")> _
Public Property MyProperty() As Integer
```

There are other attributes for control properties that are useful in specific circumstances. If you understand how the common ones discussed here are used, then you can investigate additional attributes for other purposes in the documentation.

Defining a Custom Event for the Inherited Control

Events in .NET are covered in Chapters 2 and 3. In summary, for controls, the process for creating and handling an event includes these steps:

❑ Declare the event in the control. The event can have any arguments that are appropriate, but it cannot have named arguments, optional arguments, or arguments that are `ParamArrays`. Though it is not required, normally you will want to follow the same convention as events in the .NET Framework, which means an event declaration similar to this:

```
Public Event MyEvent(ByVal sender As Object, e As EventArgs)
```

❑ Elsewhere in the control's code, implement code to raise the event. The location and circumstances of this code vary depending on the nature of the event, but a typical line that raises the preceding event looks like the following code:

```
RaiseEvent MyEvent(Me, New EventArgs)
```

❑ The form that contains the control can now handle the event. The process for doing that is the same as handling an event for a built-in control.

As the preceding example shows, the standard convention in .NET is to use two arguments for an event — Sender, which is the object raising the event, and e, which is an object of type EventArgs or a type that inherits from EventArgs. This is not a requirement of the syntax (you can actually use any arguments you like when you declare your event), but it's a consistent convention throughout the .NET Framework, so it is used in this chapter. It is suggested that you follow this convention as well, because it will make your controls consistent with the built-in controls in their operation.

The following example illustrates the concepts discussed. In this example, you create a new control that contains a custom property and a custom event. The property uses several of the attributes discussed.

A CheckedListBox Limiting Number of Selected Items

This example inherits the built-in CheckedListBox control and extends its functionality. If you are not familiar with this control, it works just like a normal ListBox control except that selected items are indicated with a check in a check box at the front of the item, rather than by highlighting the item.

To extend the functionality of this control, the example includes the creation of a property called MaxItemsToSelect. This property holds a maximum value for the number of items that a user can select. The event that fires when a user checks an item is then monitored to determine whether the maximum has already been reached.

If selection of another item would exceed the maximum number, then the selection is prevented, and an event is fired to let the consumer form know that the user has tried to exceed the maximum limit. The code that handles the event in the form can then do whatever is appropriate. In this case, a message box is used to tell the user that no more items can be selected.

The `DefaultValue`, `Description`, and `Category` attributes are placed on the `MaxItemsToSelect` property to coordinate with the IDE.

Here is the step-by-step construction of our example:

1. Start a new Windows Control Library project in Visual Studio. Give it the name `MyControls`. In the Solution Explorer, select the `UserControl1.vb` file, right-click it, and delete it.

2. Select Project ⇨ Add New Item, and select the item template called Custom Control. Name the item `LimitedCheckedListBox`.

3. Click the button in the Solution Explorer to show all files for the project. Bring up the file `LimitedCheckedListBox.Designer.vb`, which is found by clicking the plus sign next to `LimitedCheckedListBox.vb`.

4. At the top of the `LimitedCheckedListbox.Designer.vb` code, look for the line that reads `Inherits System.Windows.Forms.Control`.

5. Change that line to read `Inherits System.Windows.Forms.CheckedListbox`.

6. Add the following declarations at the top of the code (before the line declaring the class):

```
Imports System.ComponentModel
```

This enables you to utilize the attributes required from the `System.ComponentModel` namespace.

7. The code for `LimitedCheckedListBox.vb` will contain an event for painting the control. Since you are not doing a control that draws its own surface, delete that event. (It won't hurt to leave it, but you don't need it.)

8. Now begin adding code specifically for this control. First, you need to implement the `MaxItemsToSelect` property. A module-level variable is needed to hold the property's value, so insert this line just under the class declaration line:

```
Private _nMaxItemsToSelect As Integer = 4
```

9. Now create the code for the property itself. Insert the following code into the class just above the line that says `End Class`:

```
<DefaultValue(4), Category("Behavior"), _
Description("The maximum number of items allowed to be checked")> _
Public Property MaxItemsToSelect() As Integer
  Get
    Return _nMaxItemsToSelect
  End Get
  Set(ByVal Value As Integer)
    If Value < 0 Then
      Throw New ArgumentException("Property value cannot be negative")
    Else
      _nMaxItemsToSelect = Value
```

```
      End If
   End Set
End Property
```

This code sets the default value of the `MaxItemsToSelect` property to 4, and sets a description for the property to be shown in the Properties window when the property is selected there. It also specifies that the property should appear in the Behavior category when properties in the Properties window are sorted by category.

10.   Declare the event that will be fired when a user selects too many items. The event will be named `MaxItemsExceeded`. Just under the code for Step 9, insert the following line:

```
Public Event MaxItemsExceeded(Sender As Object, e As EventArgs)
```

11.   Insert code into the event routine that fires when the user clicks on an item. For the `CheckedListBox` base class, this is called the `ItemCheck` property. Open the left-hand drop-down box in the code window and select the option `LimitedCheckedListBox` Events. Then, select the `ItemCheck` event in the right-hand drop-down box of the code window. The following code will be inserted to handle the `ItemCheck` event:

```
Private Sub LimitedCheckedListBox_ItemCheck(ByVal sender As Object, _
        ByVal e As System.Windows.Forms.ItemCheckEventArgs) _
        Handles MyBase.ItemCheck

End Sub
```

12.   The following code should be added to the `ItemCheck` event to monitor it for too many items:

```
Private Sub LimitedCheckedListBox_ItemCheck(ByVal sender As Object, _
        ByVal e As System.Windows.Forms.ItemCheckEventArgs) _
        Handles MyBase.ItemCheck
If (Me.CheckedItems.Count >= _nMaxItemsToSelect) _
   And (e.NewValue = CheckState.Checked) Then
   RaiseEvent MaxItemsExceeded(Me, New EventArgs)
   e.NewValue = CheckState.Unchecked
End If
End Sub
```

13.   Build the project to create a DLL containing the `LimitedCheckedListBox` control.

14.   Add a new Windows Application project to the solution (using the File ⇨ Add Project ⇨ New Project menu) to test the control. Name the new project anything you like. Right-click the project in the Solution Explorer, and select Set as Startup Project in the pop-up menu. This will cause your Windows application to run when you press F5 in Visual Studio.

15.   Scroll to the top of the controls in the Toolbox. The `LimitedCheckedListBox` control should be there.

16.   The Windows Application will have a `Form1` that was created automatically. Drag a `LimitedCheckedListBox` control onto `Form1`, just as you would a normal list box. Change the `CheckOnClick` event for the `LimitedCheckedListBox` to `True` (to make testing easier). This property was inherited from the base `CheckedListBox` control.

17. In the `Items` property of the `LimitedCheckedListBox`, click the button to add some items. Insert the following list of colors: Red, Yellow, Green, Brown, Blue, Pink, and Black. At this point, your Windows Application Project should have a `Form1` that looks something like Figure 16-2.

Figure 16-2

18. Bring up the code window for `Form1`. In the left-hand drop-down box above the code window, select `LimitedCheckedListBox1` to get to its events. Then, in the right-hand drop-down box, select the `MaxItemsExceeded` event. The empty event will look like the following code:

```
Private Sub LimitedCheckedListBox1_MaxItemsExceeded( _
          ByVal sender As System.Object, e As System.EventArgs) _
          Handles LimitedCheckedListBox1.MaxItemsExceeded

    End Sub
```

19. Insert the following code to handle the event:

```
MsgBox("You are attempting to select more than " & _
      LimitedCheckedListBox1.MaxItemsToSelect & _
      " items. You must uncheck some other item " & _
      " before checking this one.")
```

20. Start the Windows Application project. Check and uncheck various items in the list box to verify that the control works as intended. You should get a message box whenever you attempt to check more than four items. (Four items is the default maximum, and it was not changed.) If you uncheck some items, then you can check items again until the maximum is once again exceeded. When finished, close the form to stop execution.

21. If you want to check the serialization of the code, look at the designer-generated code in the partial class for `Form1` (named `LimitedCheckedListBox.Designer.vb`), and examine the properties for `LimitedCheckedListBox1`. Note how there is no line of code that sets `MaxSelectedItems`. Remember that if you don't see the partial class in the Solution Explorer, then you'll need to press the Show All button at the top of the Solution Explorer.

22. Go back to the Design mode for `Form1` and select `LimitedCheckedListBox1`. In the Properties window, change the `MaxSelectedItems` property to 3.

23. Return to the partial class and look again at the code that declares the properties for `LimitedCheckedListBox1`. Note that there is now a line of code that sets `MaxSelectedItems` to the value of 3.

24. Go back to the Design mode for `Form1` and select `LimitedCheckedListBox1`. In the Properties window, right-click the `MaxSelectedItems` property. In the pop-up menu, select Reset. The property will change back to a value of `4`, and the line of code that sets the property that you looked at in the last step will be gone.

These last few steps showed that the `DefaultValue` attribute is working as it should.

The Control and UserControl Base Classes

In the earlier example, a new control was created by inheriting from an existing control. As is standard with inheritance, this means the new control began with all the functionality of the control from which it inherited. Then new functionality was added.

This chapter didn't discuss the base class for this new control (`CheckedListBox`) because you probably already understand a lot about the properties, methods, events, and behavior of that class. However, you are not likely to be as familiar with the base classes used for the other techniques for control creation, so it's appropriate to discuss them now.

Two generic base classes are used as a starting point to create a control. It is helpful to understand something about the structure of these classes to see when the use of each is appropriate.

> *The classes discussed in this chapter are all in the* `System.Windows.Forms` *namespace. There are similarly named classes for some of these in the* `System.Web.UI` *namespace (which is used for Web Forms), but these classes should not be confused with anything discussed in this chapter.*

The Control Class

The `Control` class is contained within the `System.Windows.Forms` namespace and contains base functionality to define a rectangle on the screen, provide a handle for it, and process routine operating system messages. This enables the class to perform such functions as handling user input through the keyboard and mouse. The `Control` class serves as the base class for any component that needs a visual representation on a Win32-type graphical interface. Besides built-in controls and custom controls that inherit from the `Control` class, the `Form` class also ultimately derives from the `Control` class.

In addition to these low-level windowing capabilities, the `Control` class also includes such visually related properties as `Font`, `ForeColor`, `BackColor`, and `BackGroundImage`. The `Control` class also has properties that are used to manage layout of the control on a form, such as docking and anchoring.

> *The* `Control` *class does not contain any logic to paint to the screen except to paint a background color or show a background image. While it does offer access to the keyboard and mouse, it does not contain any actual input processing logic except for the ability to generate standard control events such as* `Click` *and* `KeyPress`. *The developer of a custom control based on the* `Control` *class must provide all of the functions for the control beyond the basic capabilities provided by the* `Control` *class.*

A standard set of events is also furnished by the `Control` class, including events for clicking the control (`Click`, `DoubleClick`), for keystroke handling (`KeyUp`, `KeyPress`, `KeyDown`), for mouse handling (`MouseUp`, `MouseHover`, `MouseDown`, etc.), and drag-and-drop operations (`DragEnter`, `DragOver`,

DragLeave, DragDrop). Also included are standard events for managing focus and validation in the control (GotFocus, Validating, Validated). See the help files on the Control class for details on these events and a comprehensive list.

The UserControl Class

The built-in functionality of the Control class is a great starting point for controls that will be built from scratch, with their own display and keyboard handling logic. However, the Control class has limited capability for use as a container for other controls.

That means that composite controls do not typically use the Control class as a starting point. Composite controls combine two or more existing controls, so the starting point must be able to manage contained controls. The class that meets this requirement is the UserControl class. Because it ultimately derives from the Control class, it has all of the properties, methods, and events discussed earlier for that class.

However, the UserControl class does not derive directly from the Control class. It derives from the ContainerControl class, which, in turn, derives from the ScrollableControl class.

As the name suggests, the ScrollableControl class adds support for scrolling the client area of the control's window. Almost all the members implemented by this class relate to scrolling. They include AutoScroll, which turns scrolling on or off, and controlling properties such as AutoScrollPosition, which gets or sets the position within the scrollable area.

The ContainerControl class derives from ScrollableControl and adds the capability to support and manage child controls. It manages the focus and the capability to tab from control to control. It includes properties such as ActiveControl to point to the control with the focus, and Validate, which validates the most recently changed control that has not had its validation event fired.

Neither ScrollableControl nor ContainerControl are usually inherited from directly; they add functionality that is needed by their more commonly used child classes: Form and UserControl.

The UserControl class can contain other child controls, but the interface of UserControl does not automatically expose these child controls in any way. Instead, the interface of UserControl is designed to present a single, unified interface to outside clients such as forms or container controls. Any object interface that is needed to access the child controls must be specifically implemented in your custom control. The following example demonstrates this.

A Composite UserControl

Our earlier example showed inheriting an existing control, which was the first of the three techniques for creating custom controls. The next step up in complexity and flexibility is to combine more than one existing control to become a new control. This is similar to the process of creating a UserControl in VB6, but it is easier to do in Windows Forms.

The main steps in the process of creating a UserControl are as follows:

❑ Start a new Windows Control Library project, and assign names to the project and the class representing the control.

❏ The project will contain a design surface that looks a lot like a form. You can drag controls onto this surface just as you would a form. Writing code that works with the controls, such as event routines, is done the same way as with a form, but with a few extra considerations that don't apply to most forms. In particular, it is important to handle resizing when the UserControl is resized. This can be done by using the Anchor and Dock properties of the constituent controls, or you can create resize logic that repositions and resizes the controls on your UserControl when it is resized on the form containing it. Another option is to use FlowLayoutPanel and/or TableLayoutPanel controls to do automatic layout.

❏ Create properties of the UserControl to expose functionality to a form that will use it. This typically means creating a property to load information into and get information out of the control. Sometimes properties to handle cosmetic elements are also necessary.

❏ Build the control and use it in a Windows application exactly as you did for the inherited controls discussed earlier.

There is a key difference between this type of development and inheriting a control, as shown in the preceding examples. A UserControl will not by default expose the properties of the controls it contains. It exposes the properties of the UserControl class plus any custom properties that you give it. If you want properties for contained controls to be exposed, you must explicitly create logic to expose them.

Creating a Composite UserControl

To demonstrate the process of creating a composite UserControl, the next exercise builds one that is similar to what is shown in Figure 16-3. The control is named ListSelector.

Figure 16-3

This type of layout is common in wizards and other user interfaces that require selection from a long list of items. The control has one list box holding a list of items that can be chosen (on the left), and another list box containing the items chosen so far (on the right). Buttons enable items to be moved back and forth.

Loading this control means loading items into the left list box, which we will call SourceListBox. Getting selected items back out involves exposing the items that are selected in the right list box, named TargetListBox.

The buttons in the middle that transfer elements back and forth are called AddButton, AddAllButton, RemoveButton, and ClearButton, from top to bottom, respectively.

There are several ways to handle this kind of interface element in detail. A production-level version would have the following characteristics:

❑ Buttons would gray out (disable) when they are not appropriate. For example, btnAdd would not be enabled unless an item were selected in lstSource.

❑ Items could be dragged and dropped between the two list boxes.

❑ Items could be selected and moved with a double-click.

Such a production-type version contains too much code to discuss in this chapter. For simplicity, the exercise has the following limitations:

❑ Buttons do not gray out when they should be unavailable.

❑ Drag-and-drop is not supported. (Implementation of drag-and-drop was discussed in Chapter 15, if you are interested in adding it to the example.)

❑ No double-clicking is supported.

This leaves the following general tasks to make the control work, and these tasks are detailed in the step-by-step exercise that follows:

❑ Create a UserControl and name it ListSelector.

❑ Add the list boxes and buttons to the ListSelector design surface, using a TableLayoutPanel and a FlowLayoutPanel to control layout when the control is resized.

❑ Add logic to transfer elements back and forth between the list boxes when buttons are pressed. (More than one item may be selected for an operation, so several items may need to be transferred when a button is pressed.)

❑ Expose properties to enable the control to be loaded, and for selected items to be fetched by the form that contains the control.

Resizing the Control

As shown in Figure 16-3, there are three main areas of the control — the two Listbox controls and a vertical strip between them that holds the buttons. As the control is resized, these areas need to also be appropriately resized.

If the ListSelector control gets too small, there won't be enough room for the buttons and the list boxes to display properly, so it needs to have a minimum size. That's enforced by setting the MinimumSize property for the UserControl in the designer. The MinimumSize property is inherited from the Control class (as discussed in the previous chapter).

The rest of the resizing is handled by using a TableLayoutPanel that contains three columns, one for each of the three areas. That is, the first column of the TableLayoutPanel will hold SourceListBox, the second column will hold the buttons, and the third column will hold `TargetListBox`. The capabilities of the `TableLayoutPanel` enable the middle column to be a fixed size, and the left and right columns to share all remaining width.

The middle column could contain a standard `Panel` in the middle column to hold the buttons, but it's a bit easier to use a `FlowLayoutPanel` because it will automatically stack the buttons.

Exposing Properties of Contained Controls

Most of the controls contained in the composite control in this exercise do not need to expose their interfaces to the form that will use the composite control. The buttons, for example, are completely private to the `ListSelector` — none of their properties or methods need to be exposed.

The easiest way to load up the control is to expose the `Items` property of the source list box. Similarly, the easiest way to allow access to the selected items is to expose the `Items` property of the target list box. The `Items` property exposes the entire collection of items in a list box, and can be used to add, clear, or examine items. No other properties of the list boxes need to be exposed.

The exercise also includes a `Clear` method that clears both list boxes simultaneously. This allows the control to be easily flushed and reused by a form that consumes it.

Stepping through the Example

Here is the step-by-step procedure to build our composite `UserControl`:

1. Start a new Windows Control Library project. Name it `ListSelector`.

2. Right-click on the `UserControl1.vb` module that is generated for the project and select Rename. Change the name of the module to `ListSelector.vb`. This automatically changes the name of your class to `ListSelector`.

3. Go to the design surface for the control. Increase the size of the control to about 300 × 200. Then drag a `TableLayoutPanel` onto the control, and set the `Dock` property of the `TableLayoutPanel` to `Fill`.

4. Click the smart tag (the triangular glyph in the upper-right corner) of the `TableLayoutPanel`. A menu will appear. Select Edit Rows and Columns.

5. Highlight Column2 and click the Insert button. The `TableLayoutPanel` will now have three columns. In the new column just inserted (the new Column2), the width will be set to an absolute size of 20 pixels. Change that width to 100 pixels. The dialog containing your column settings should now look like Figure 16-4.

6. Click the Show drop-down menu in the upper-left corner and select Rows. Press the Delete button to delete a row because you need only one row in the control. Click OK. The design surface for the control should now look similar to Figure 16-5.

Figure 16-4

Figure 16-5

7. Drag a Listbox into the first cell and another one into the third cell. Drag a FlowLayoutPanel into the middle cell. For all three of these, set the Dock property to Fill.

8. Drag four buttons into the FlowLayoutPanel in the middle. At this point your control should look like Figure 16-6.

Figure 16-6

9. Change the names and properties of these controls as shown in the following table:

Original Name	New Name	Properties to Set for Control
Listbox1	SourceListBox	
Listbox2	TargetListBox	
Button1 Size.Width = 90	AddButton	Text = "Add >"
Button2 Size.Width = 90	AddAllButton	Text = "Add All >>"
Button3 Margin.Top = 20 Size.Width = 90	RemoveButton	Text = "< Remove"
Button4 Size.Width = 90	ClearButton	Text = "<< Clear"

10. In the Properties window, click the drop-down at the top and select ListSelector so that the properties for the UserControl itself appear in the Properties window. Set the MinimumSize height and width to 200 pixels each.

11. Create the public properties and methods of the composite control. In this case, you need the following members:

Member	Purpose
Clear method	Clears both list boxes of their items
SourceItems property	Exposes the items collection for the source list box
SelectedItems property	Exposes the items collection for the target list box

The code for these properties and methods is as follows:

```
<Browsable(False)> _
Public ReadOnly Property SourceItems() As ListBox.ObjectCollection
    Get
         Return SourceListBox.Items
    End Get
End Property

<Browsable(False)> _
Public ReadOnly Property SelectedItems() As ListBox.ObjectCollection
    Get
         Return TargetListBox.Items
    End Get
End Property

Public Sub Clear()
    SourceListBox.Items.Clear()
    TargetListBox.Items.Clear()
End Sub
```

12. Put logic in the class to transfer items back and forth between the list boxes and clear the target list box when ClearButton is pressed. This logic manipulates the collections of items in the list boxes, and is fairly brief. You need one helper function to check whether an item is already in a list box before adding it (to avoid duplicates). Here are the click events for each of the buttons, with the helper function at the top:

```
Private Function ItemInListBox(ByVal ListBoxToCheck As ListBox, _
                               ByVal ItemToCheck As Object) As Boolean
    Dim bFound As Boolean = False
    For Each Item As Object In ListBoxToCheck.Items
        If Item Is ItemToCheck Then
            bFound = True
            Exit For
        End If
    Next
    Return bFound
End Function

Private Sub AddButton_Click(ByVal sender As System.Object, _
```

```
                                    ByVal e As System.EventArgs) _
                                Handles AddButton.Click
        For Each SelectedItem As Object In SourceListBox.SelectedItems
            If Not ItemInListBox(TargetListBox, SelectedItem) Then
                TargetListBox.Items.Add(SelectedItem)
            End If
        Next
    End Sub

    Private Sub AddAllButton_Click(ByVal sender As System.Object, _
                                ByVal e As System.EventArgs) _
                                Handles AddAllButton.Click
        For Each SelectedItem As Object In SourceListBox.Items
            If Not ItemInListBox(TargetListBox, SelectedItem) Then
                TargetListBox.Items.Add(SelectedItem)
            End If
        Next
    End Sub

    ' For both the following operations, we have to go through the
    ' collection in reverse because we are removing items.

    Private Sub RemoveButton_Click(ByVal sender As System.Object, _
                                ByVal e As System.EventArgs) _
                                Handles RemoveButton.Click
        For iIndex As Integer = TargetListBox.SelectedItems.Count - 1 To 0 Step -1
            TargetListBox.Items.Remove(TargetListBox.SelectedItems(iIndex))
        Next iIndex
    End Sub

    Private Sub ClearButton_Click(ByVal sender As System.Object, _
                                ByVal e As System.EventArgs) _
                                Handles ClearButton.Click
        For iIndex As Integer = TargetListBox.Items.Count - 1 To 0 Step -1
            TargetListBox.Items.Remove(TargetListBox.Items(iIndex))
        Next iIndex
    End Sub
```

The logic in the Click events for RemoveButton and ClearButton needs a bit of explanation. Because items are being removed from the collection, it is necessary to go through the collection in reverse. Otherwise, the removal of items will confuse the looping enumeration and a runtime error will be generated.

13. Build the control. Then create a Windows Application project to test it in. You can drag the control from the top of the Toolbox, add items in code (via the Add method of the SourceItems collection), resize, and so on. When the project is run, the buttons can be used to transfer items back and forth between the list boxes, and the items in the target list box can be read with the SelectedItems property.

Keep in mind that you can also use the techniques for inherited controls in composite controls, too. You can create custom events, apply attributes to properties, and create ShouldSerialize and Reset methods to make properties work better with the designer. (That wasn't necessary here because our two properties were ReadOnly.)

Building a Control from Scratch

If your custom control needs to draw its own interface, you should use the `Control` class as your starting point. Such a control gets a fair amount of base functionality from the `Control` class. A partial list of properties and methods of the `Control` class was included earlier in the chapter. These properties arrange for the control to automatically have visual elements such as background and foreground colors, fonts, window size, and so on.

However, such a control does not automatically use any of that information to actually display anything (except for a `BackgroundImage`, if that property is set). A control derived from the `Control` class must implement its own logic for painting the control's visual representation. In all but the most trivial examples, such a control also needs to implement its own properties and methods to gain the functionality it needs.

The techniques used in the earlier example for default values and the `ShouldSerialize` and `Reset` methods all work fine with the controls created from the `Control` class, so that capability is not discussed again. Instead, this section focuses on the capability that is very different in the `Control` class — the logic to paint the control to the screen.

Painting a Custom Control with GDI+

The base functionality used to paint visual elements for a custom control is in the part of .NET called GDI+. A complete explanation of GDI+ is too complex for this chapter, but an overview of some of the main concepts is needed.

What Is GDI+?

GDI+ is an updated version of the old GDI (Graphics Device Interface) functions provided by the Windows API. GDI+ provides a new API for graphics functions, which then takes advantage of the Windows graphics library.

The System.Drawing Namespace

The GDI+ functionality can be found in the `System.Drawing` namespace and its subnamespaces. Some of the classes and members in this namespace will look familiar if you have used the Win32 GDI functions. Classes are available for such items as pens, brushes, and rectangles. Naturally, the `System.Drawing` namespace makes these capabilities much easier to use than the equivalent API functions.

With the `System.Drawing` namespace, you can manipulate bitmaps and use various structures for dealing with graphics such as `Point`, `Size`, `Color`, and `Rectangle`. In addition, there are a number of classes for use in drawing logic. The first three such classes you need to understand represent the surface on which drawing takes place, and the objects used to draw lines and fill shapes:

❑ `Graphics` — Represents the surface on which drawing is done. Contains methods to draw items to the surface, including lines, curves, ellipses, text and so on.

❑ `Pen` — Used for drawing line-based objects

❑ `Brush` — Used for filling shapes (includes its subclasses)

The `System.Drawing` namespace includes many other classes and some subsidiary namespaces. Let's look at the `Graphics` class in a bit more detail.

The System.Drawing.Graphics Class

Many of the important drawing functions are members of the `System.Drawing.Graphics` class. Methods such as `DrawArc`, `FillRectangle`, `DrawEllipse`, and `DrawIcon` have self-evident actions. More than 40 methods provide drawing-related functions in the class.

Many drawing members require one or more points as arguments. A point is a structure in the `System.Drawing` namespace. It has X and Y values for horizontal and vertical positions, respectively. When a variable number of points are needed, an array of points may be used as an argument. The next example uses points.

The `System.Drawing.Graphics` class cannot be directly instantiated. That is, you can't just enter code like the following to get an instance of the `Graphics` class:

```
Dim grfGraphics As New System.Drawing.Graphics() ' This does not work!!
```

This doesn't work because the constructor for the class is not public. It is only supposed to be manipulated by objects that can set the `Graphics` class up for themselves. There are several ways to get a reference to a `Graphics` class, but the one most commonly used in the creation of Windows controls is to get one out of the arguments in a `Paint` event. That technique is used in a later example. For now, to understand the capabilities of GDI+ a little better, let's do a quick example on a standard Windows Form.

Using GDI+ Capabilities in a Windows Form

Here is an example of a form that uses the `System.Drawing.Graphics` class to draw some graphic elements on the form surface. The example code runs in the `Paint` event for the form, and draws an ellipse, an icon (which it gets from the form itself), and two triangles: one in outline and one filled.

Start a Windows Application project in VB 2005. On the `Form1` that is automatically created for the project, place the following code in the `Paint` event for the form:

```
' Need a pen for the drawing. We'll make it violet.
Dim penDrawingPen As New _
        System.Drawing.Pen(System.Drawing.Color.BlueViolet)

' Draw an ellipse and an icon on the form
e.Graphics.DrawEllipse(penDrawingPen, 30, 100, 30, 60)
e.Graphics.DrawIcon(Me.Icon, 90, 20)

' Draw a triangle on the form.
' First have to define an array of points.
Dim pntPoint(2) As System.Drawing.Point

pntPoint(0).X = 150
pntPoint(0).Y = 100

pntPoint(1).X = 150
pntPoint(1).Y = 150
```

```
pntPoint(2).X = 50
pntPoint(2).Y = 70

e.Graphics.DrawPolygon(penDrawingPen, pntPoint)

' Do a filled triangle.
' First need a brush to specify how it is filled.
Dim bshBrush As System.Drawing.Brush
bshBrush = New SolidBrush(Color.Blue)

' Now relocate the points for the triangle.
' We'll just move it 100 pixels to the right.
pntPoint(0).X += 100
pntPoint(1).X += 100
pntPoint(2).X += 100
e.Graphics.FillPolygon(bshBrush, pntPoint)
```

Start the program. When it comes up, the form will look something like Figure 16-7.

Figure 16-7

To apply GDI+ to control creation, you create a custom control that displays a "traffic light," with red, yellow, and green signals that can be displayed via a property of the control. GDI+ classes will be used to draw the traffic light graphics in the control.

Start a new project in VB 2005 of the Windows Control Library type and name it TrafficLight. The created module has a class in it named UserControl1. We want a different type of control class, so you need to get rid of this one. Right-click on this module in the Solution Explorer and select Delete.

Next, right-click on the project and select Add New Item. Select the item type of Custom Control and name it TrafficLight.vb.

As with the other examples in this chapter, it is necessary to include the Imports statement for the namespace containing the attribute you will use. This line should go at the very top of the code module for TrafficLight.vb:

```
Imports System.ComponentModel
```

The `TrafficLight` control needs to know which "light" to display. The control can be in three states: red, yellow, and green. An enumerated type will be used for these states. Add the following code just below the previous code:

```
Public Enum TrafficLightStatus
    statusRed = 1
    statusYellow = 2
    statusGreen = 3
End Enum
```

The example also needs a module-level variable and a property procedure to support changing and retaining the state of the light. The property is named `Status`.

To handle the `Status` property, first place a declaration directly under the last enumeration declaration that creates a module-level variable to hold the current status:

```
Private mStatus As TrafficLightStatus = TrafficLightStatus.statusGreen
```

Then, insert the following property procedure in the class to create the `Status` property:

```
<Description("Status (color) of the traffic light")> _
Public Property Status() As TrafficLightStatus
    Get
        Status = mStatus
    End Get
    Set(ByVal Value As TrafficLightStatus)
        If mStatus <> Value Then
            mStatus = Value
            Me.Invalidate()
        End If
    End Set
End Property
```

The `Invalidate` method of the control is used when the `Status` property changes, and it forces a redraw of the control. Ideally, this type of logic should be placed in all of the events that affect the rendering of the control.

Now add procedures to make the property serialize and reset properly:

```
Public Function ShouldSerializeStatus() As Boolean
    If mStatus = TrafficLightStatus.statusGreen Then
        Return False
    Else
        Return True
    End If
End Function

Public Sub ResetStatus()
    Me.Status = TrafficLightStatus.statusGreen
End Sub
```

Place code to do painting of the control, to draw the "traffic light" when the control repaints. We will use code similar to that used previously. The code generated for the new custom control will already have a blank `OnPaint` method inserted. You just need to insert the following highlighted code into that event, below the comment line that says `Add your custom paint code here`:

```
Protected Overrides Sub OnPaint(ByVal pe As _
                          System.Windows.Forms.PaintEventArgs)
    MyBase.OnPaint(pe)

    'Add your custom paint code here
    Dim grfGraphics As System.Drawing.Graphics
    grfGraphics = pe.Graphics

    ' Need a pen for the drawing the outline. We'll make it black.
    Dim penDrawingPen As New _
        System.Drawing.Pen(System.Drawing.Color.Black)

    ' Draw the outline of the traffic light on the control.
    ' First have to define an array of points.
    Dim pntPoint(3) As System.Drawing.Point

    pntPoint(0).X = 0
    pntPoint(0).Y = 0

    pntPoint(1).X = Me.Size.Width - 2
    pntPoint(1).Y = 0

    pntPoint(2).X = Me.Size.Width - 2
    pntPoint(2).Y = Me.Size.Height - 2

    pntPoint(3).X = 0
    pntPoint(3).Y = Me.Size.Height - 2

    grfGraphics.DrawPolygon(penDrawingPen, pntPoint)

    ' Now ready to draw the circle for the "light"
    Dim nCirclePositionX As Integer
    Dim nCirclePositionY As Integer
    Dim nCircleDiameter As Integer
    Dim nCircleColor As Color

    nCirclePositionX = Me.Size.Width * 0.02
    nCircleDiameter = Me.Size.Height * 0.3
    Select Case Me.Status
        Case TrafficLightStatus.statusRed
            nCircleColor = Color.OrangeRed
            nCirclePositionY = Me.Size.Height * 0.01
        Case TrafficLightStatus.statusYellow
            nCircleColor = Color.Yellow
            nCirclePositionY = Me.Size.Height * 0.34
        Case TrafficLightStatus.statusGreen
            nCircleColor = Color.LightGreen
            nCirclePositionY = Me.Size.Height * 0.67
```

```
        End Select

        Dim bshBrush As System.Drawing.Brush
        bshBrush = New SolidBrush(nCircleColor)
        ' Draw the circle for the signal light
         grfGraphics.FillEllipse(bshBrush, nCirclePositionX, _
                  nCirclePositionY, nCircleDiameter, nCircleDiameter)
    End Sub
```

Build the control library by selecting Build from the Build menu. This will create a DLL in the /bin directory where the control library solution is saved.

Then, start a new Windows Application project. Drag a TrafficLight control from the top of the Toolbox onto the form in the Windows Application project. Notice that its property window includes a Status property. Set that to statusYellow. Note that the rendering on the control on the form's design surface changes to reflect this new status. Change the background color of the TrafficLight control to a darker gray to improve its contrast. (The BackColor property for TrafficLight was inherited from the Control class.)

At the top of the code for the form, place the following line to make the enumerated value for the traffic light's status available:

```
    Imports TrafficLight.TrafficLight
```

Add three buttons (named btnRed, btnYellow, and btnGreen) to the form to make the traffic light control display as red, yellow, and green. The logic for the buttons looks something like the following:

```
    Private Sub btnRed_Click(ByVal sender As System.Object, _
                  ByVal e As System.EventArgs) Handles btnRed.Click
        TrafficLight1.Status = TrafficLightStatus.statusRed
    End Sub

    Private Sub btnYellow_Click(ByVal sender As System.Object, _
                  ByVal e As System.EventArgs) Handles btnYellow.Click
        TrafficLight1.Status = TrafficLightStatus.statusYellow
    End Sub

    Private Sub btnGreen_Click(ByVal sender As System.Object, _
                  ByVal e As System.EventArgs) Handles btnGreen.Click
        TrafficLight1.Status = TrafficLightStatus.statusGreen
    End Sub
```

In the Solution Explorer, right-click your test Windows Application, and select Set as Startup Project. Then press F5 to run. When your test form comes up, you can change the "signal" on the traffic light by pressing the buttons. Figure 16-8 shows a sample screen.

Of course, you can't see the color in a black-and-white screen shot, but as you might expect from its position, the circle is yellow. The "red light" displays at the top of the control, and the "green light" displays at the bottom. These positions are all calculated in the Paint event logic, depending on the value of the Status property.

Figure 16-8

For a complete example, it would be desirable for the control to allow the user to change the Status by clicking on a different part of the "traffic light." That means including logic to examine mouse clicks, calculate whether they are in a given area, and change the Status property if appropriate. In the code available for download for this book, the TrafficLight example includes such functionality.

Attaching an Icon for the Toolbox

By default, the icon that appears in the Toolbox next to your control's name is a gear-shaped icon. However, you can use an attribute on the class declaration that defines your control to specify a different icon to place in the Toolbox. The attribute needed is the ToolboxBitmap attribute. It can be used in several ways.

If the icon you want to use is already defined for another control, then you can have your control get the icon out of the existing control. Suppose, for example, you want to use the icon for a Textbox as the icon for your TrafficLight control. In that case, the line that declares the class

```
Public Class TrafficLight
```

should be changed to add the attribute as follows:

```
<ToolboxBitmap(GetType(System.Windows.Forms.TextBox))> _
Public Class TrafficLight
```

You can also use an icon that resides in a graphic file. Several of these are included with Visual Studio in a zip file installed in the Common7\VS2005ImageLibrary subdirectory of the VS.NET directory (which is usually under Program Files on your main system drive). Or, you can define your own icons in the Paint accessory of Windows by defining an image size of 16 × 16 pixels and then painting the icon.

In either case, you'll want your icon to be part of the assembly containing your control. Add your icon to the project that contains your control, and set its Build Action property to Embedded Resource. Then the ToolboxBitmap attribute is used to refer to the icon in the assembly, as shown here:

```
<ToolboxBitmap(GetType(TrafficLight), "MyIcon.bmp")> _
Public Class TrafficLight
```

This overload of the ToolboxBitmap attribute first takes a Type object, which indicates the location of the assembly containing the type. The second argument specifies the resource within that assembly to use.

After adding the attribute, just rebuild the control to incorporate the icon in the control's DLL. Note that you must remove the control from the Toolbox and re-add it to see the changed icon. Also note that the icon won't show up for the automatic Toolbox entry for the control at the top of the Toolbox — it is only used when the control is placed in the Toolbox via the Choose Items option.

Embedding Controls in Other Controls

Another technique that is valuable for creating custom controls is to embed other controls. In a sense, the `UserControl` does this. However, when a `UserControl` is used as the base class, by default it only exposes the properties of the `UserControl` class. Instead, you may want to use a control such as `Textbox` or `Grid` as the starting point, but embed a `Button` in the `Textbox` or `Grid` to obtain some new functionality.

The embedding technique relies on the fact that in Windows Forms, all controls can be containers for other controls. Visual Basic developers are familiar with the idea that `Panels` and `GroupBoxes` can be containers, but in fact a `TextBox` or a `Grid` can also be a container of other controls.

This technique is best presented with an example. The standard `ComboBox` control does not have a way for the user to reset to a "no selection" state. Once an item is selected, setting to that state requires code that sets the `SelectedIndex` to -1.

This exercise creates a `ComboBox` that has a button to reset the selection state back to "no selection." That enables the user to access that capability directly. Now that you have done several controls in examples, rather than proceed step by step, we'll just show the code for such a `ComboBox` and discuss how the code works:

```
Public Class SpecialComboBox
    Inherits ComboBox

    Dim WithEvents btnEmbeddedButton As Button

    Public Sub New()

        Me.DropDownStyle = ComboBoxStyle.DropDownList

        ' Fix up the embedded button.
        btnEmbeddedButton = New Button
        btnEmbeddedButton.Width = SystemInformation.VerticalScrollBarWidth
        btnEmbeddedButton.Top = 0
        btnEmbeddedButton.Height = Me.Height - 4
        btnEmbeddedButton.BackColor = SystemColors.Control
        btnEmbeddedButton.FlatStyle = FlatStyle.Popup
        btnEmbeddedButton.Text = "t"
        Dim fSpecial As New Font("Wingdings 3", Me.Font.Size - 1)
        btnEmbeddedButton.Font = fSpecial

        btnEmbeddedButton.Left = Me.Width - btnEmbeddedButton.Width - _
            SystemInformation.VerticalScrollBarWidth

        Me.Controls.Add(btnEmbeddedButton)
```

```
        btnEmbeddedButton.Anchor = CType(AnchorStyles.Right _
            Or AnchorStyles.Top Or AnchorStyles.Bottom, AnchorStyles)
        btnEmbeddedButton.BringToFront()

    End Sub

    Private Sub btnEmbeddedButton_Click(ByVal sender As Object, _
            ByVal e As System.EventArgs) Handles btnEmbeddedButton.Click
        Me.SelectedIndex = -1
        Me.Focus
    End Sub

    Private Sub BillysComboBox_DropDownStyleChanged(ByVal sender As Object, _
            ByVal e As System.EventArgs) Handles MyBase.DropDownStyleChanged
        If Me.DropDownStyle <> ComboBoxStyle.DropDownList Then
            Me.DropDownStyle = ComboBoxStyle.DropDownList
            Throw New _
                InvalidOperationException("DropDownStyle must be DropDownList")
        End If
    End Sub
End Class
```

As in the first example in the chapter, this example inherits from a built-in control. Thus, it immediately gets all the capabilities of the standard ComboBox. All you need to add is the capability to reset the selected state.

To do that, you need a button for the user to press. The class declares the button as a private object named btnEmbeddedButton. Then, in the constructor for the class, the button is instantiated, and its properties are set as necessary. The size and position of the button need to be calculated. This is done using the size of the ComboBox and a special system parameter called SystemInformation.VerticalScrollBarWidth. This parameter is chosen because it is also used to calculate the size of the button used to drop down a combo box. Thus, your new embedded button will be the same width as the button that the regular ComboBox displays for dropping down the list.

Of course, you need to display something in the new button to indicate its purpose. For simplicity, the preceding code displays a lowercase "t" using the WingDings 3 font (which all Windows systems should have installed). This causes a left-pointing triangle to appear, as shown in Figure 16-9, which is a screen shot of the control in use.

Figure 16-9

The button is then added to the Controls collection of the ComboBox. You may be surprised to learn that a ComboBox even has a Controls collection for embedded controls, but all controls in Windows Forms have one.

Finally, the `Anchor` property of the new button is set to maintain the position if the `SpecialComboBox` is resized by its consumer.

Besides the constructor, only a couple of small routines are needed. The `click` event for the button must be handled, and in it the `SelectedIndex` must be set to `-1`. In addition, because this functionality is only for combo boxes with a style of `DropDownList`, the `DropDownStyleChanged` event of the `ComboBox` must be trapped, and the style prevented from being set to anything else.

Summary

This chapter discussed how to create custom controls in VB.NET, and illustrated how much easier it is to do this compared with previous versions of Visual Basic. The advent of full inheritance capabilities in VB.NET means that it is a lot easier for developers to utilize functionality simply by inheriting from the namespaces built into the .NET Framework. It is probably best to start by overriding these existing controls in order to learn the basics of creating properties and coordinating them with the designer, building controls and testing them, and so on. These techniques can then be extended by the creation of composite controls, as illustrated by the examples within the chapter.

You have learned how to create controls in the following ways:

❑   By inheriting from another control

❑   By building a composite control

❑   By writing a control from scratch, based on the `Control` class (although this takes more work than the other two methods)

In the course of writing a control from scratch, it was necessary to discuss the basics of GDI+, but if you are going to do extensive work with GDI+, you will need to seek out additional resources to aid in that effort.

The key concept that you should take away from this chapter is that Windows Forms controls are a great way both to package functionality that will be reused across many forms and to create more dynamic, responsive user interfaces much more quickly with much less code.

17

Windows Presentation Foundation

Windows Presentation Foundation (WPF) — previously known as Avalon — is the next generation for user interfaces, and it's a key architectural component in the .NET 3.0 Framework. This chapter introduces you to the WPF programming model and discusses key elements you'll need to know in working with WPF. Rest assured you will be creating applications that leverage the features of WPF in the future. It may not happen until after the release of developer productivity tools supporting it, but eventually it will replace the many and varied user interface models that currently exist.

The libraries that make up WPF were released in conjunction with the release of Windows Vista — not the commercial and much-publicized public release of Vista in January 2007, but rather the initial release of Vista to enterprise partners in November of 2006. The libraries shipped with Vista and coincidentally with Microsoft Office 2007, but what you may or may not notice is the lack of development tools at the same time. Microsoft has managed to follow a software deployment pattern that's proved successful for many large application environments: first release a library that introduces new features, and then build and release the tools and software that can truly leverage the classes in the new library.

The result of ordering these items is a little like following the ready-aim-fire model (vs. ready-fire-aim). First, Microsoft looked into its market and systems and found a major need. It prepared a design to solve this need and readied a solution. Next, it took aim at making sure the solution (WPF) would stand up, and at stabilizing that solution so it could have a valid target for the need created by the solution. That target is the tools needed to productively leverage these new libraries, and Microsoft can now aim these tools at a fixed target, the released library, as opposed to a moving target.

In the past, as we saw with .NET 2.0 and the release of Visual Studio 2005, having both a tool suite and the libraries it supports changing at the same time caused some difficulties. Anyone can tell you it's much easier to hit a fixed target than a moving one. Aiming at a moving target for .NET 2.0

resulted in delivery challenges — which in retrospect were probably costly even to a world-class development organization such as Microsoft. However, with .NET 3.0, the libraries are available now, even as Microsoft continues to build not only enhancements to its current development suite — Visual Studio — but also a new suite of development tools, the Expressions suite.

This chapter takes you through several key areas, including the following:

- ❏ What, where, why, how — WPF strategy
- ❏ WPF elements and compatibility
- ❏ Creating a WPF application
- ❏ Introduction to XAML
- ❏ Visual Studio integration
- ❏ Expression suite of tools

Keep in mind that, like all the new capabilities being introduced with .NET 3.0, WPF is still at an early stage, on what is sometimes called the "bleeding edge" of technology. There are fewer examples of working with this technology; and the tools, where they exist, are still in beta. This means that if you try to leverage the technology now, you run the risk of having that decision come back to bite you when you hit a wall.

Additionally, the knowledge required to work with this technology is still more advanced; you'll see that we work from the command line for several of the examples, and you need to understand some of the underpinnings of Visual Studio 2005 and how it compiles your Visual Basic applications. Eventually, this will all be hidden under the automated processes of Visual Studio, but for now be prepared to delve deeply into this technology. Accordingly, it's appropriate for you to understand why WPF is going to be such a big deal as we move forward.

What, Where, Why, How — WPF Strategy

When .NET was released, most people realized that in terms of application development a paradigm shift was occurring. The release of WPF is the first step in yet another paradigm shift, this one focused on how user interfaces are designed and implemented. Therefore, it's appropriate to take a little time to look at not just where the user interface models are coming from, but where they are going. This understanding is part of how WPF fits in and explains not only why you'll want WPF in the future, but also how you can start leveraging it today.

The original user interfaces were punch cards for input and hard copy text for output. OK, maybe that's going a little too far back. Instead, let's jump ahead to the part of the user interface's resume that applies to where we're going today. The 1980s through 1990s saw several computer and software manufacturers introduce the graphical user interface (GUI). These GUI environments, while implemented differently on different platforms, became a part of the operating system. For Windows, this is the User32.dll and its companion UI classes. The original Visual Basic 1.0 was designed to enable developers to interact in a simple manner with these files, unlike C++, which referenced the raw User32 interfaces for everything.

Over time, Visual Basic's simple drag-and-drop approach to creating the forms users would access as part of an application in that GUI environment helped make it the most popular development language.

Over time, however, the paradigm started to shift, and applications began migrating to the Web. The Web introduced its own way of creating forms, one that used HTML. The HTML model is more declarative. For example, the HTML page declares it wants a Textbox, but it's up to the browser to interpret and provide the code that handles the actual object. This model is also supported on Windows and by Microsoft both in Internet Explorer (the parsing engine) and in ASP.NET.

This brings up the next example, .NET and Windows Forms. When .NET was introduced it shipped with two user-interface implementations, ASP.NET's HTML-based UI and the desktop-centric Windows Forms. It's important to realize that Windows Forms isn't based on the same code that User32 windows are, even though the programming model whereby the designer adds the code to a portion of the application's source is similar. The managed environment represents both the second and third programming models for developing user interfaces under Windows. Of course, other platforms include still other GUI models, but these three GUI models represent the ones Microsoft must now support.

Thus, Microsoft is left repeating many user-interface controls with three distinct implementations, a pain that Microsoft feels. After all, when .NET 1.0 was released, one of the main complaints about migrating applications from Win32 to Windows Forms was the lack of available controls. Since then, Microsoft continuously finds itself updating a rendering engine used within Internet Explorer (and other tools) for the UI elements of HTML, and a totally unrelated rendering engine used for .NET Windows Forms, keeping the Win32 in place.

However, the real challenge for Microsoft mirrors your challenge. For developers, the pain starts with the fact that a user interface can't be transported seamlessly between a Web-based version of an application and a local desktop version of the same application, or across platforms. For example, Microsoft can't design a UI for Outlook and reuse it for Outlook Web Access (OWA). Instead, it needs a different team of developers with different skills to create the OWA interface, and have you seen a remotely downloadable Windows Forms-based OWA application?

Let's face it, there hasn't been much economic incentive to create both a Windows Forms-based and ASP.NET-based user interface for the same application. Until doing such a task is almost painless, people will continue to select an environment and build their application targeting that model. Thus, while there are several options for creating a user interface, they all represent "either-or" decisions.

This is where the WPF model comes in. Based more on the HTML model, WPF is a declarative way of designing interfaces. The idea is that you can use a declarative model to design your user interface and then compile or include that definition with either a desktop or Web or even another operating system version of your application. WPF uses XML to declare the user-interface elements, relying on a standard known as the *eXtensible Application Markup Language (XAML)*. This standard is pronounced "zamel" (rhymes with camel). It enables you to layer elements and include things such as colors and nondistinct shapes.

XAML goes well beyond what you normally expect to find in an HTML UI, yet at the same time the format should feel somewhat familiar to those who know HTML and/or XML. As for the implementation of code to interpret XAML UI declarations, Microsoft introduced the components that make up WPF. Having this code ship with Microsoft's new Vista operating system and available as part of .NET 3.0 for existing operating systems will begin to make XAML interfaces the standard across desktops, the Web, and even handheld devices. It's also important to note that XAML's underlying class implementation differs from the model used for previous GUI implementations.

Raster Graphics and Vector Graphics

Currently, when you create a Windows Forms control you decide how large, in pixels, that button should be. A similar action is taken with regard to HTML forms, where you can specify either a size in pixels or a percentage of the screen. In both cases, the computer simply lays out a square or rounded square based on a flat set of pixels. It does the same with other images you use, working with what are known as *raster graphics*. Raster graphics are a collection of points on the surface of a screen that represent an image.

The alternative form of graphics is known as *vector graphics*. A vector is a line with a point of origin that continues forward in space from that point of origin. Vector graphics aren't based on a collection of points, but rather on a series of vectors. A plane representing the surface of your screen is placed in the path of these vectors, which define a set of points, and that is what you see on your screen. Vector graphics provide much better and more realistic image manipulation. Note that while you can incorporate a raster image with vector graphics, since you can place the raster image in your virtual plane, the reverse isn't feasible.

WPF is the first forms-based engine that relies on this vector-based model. The good news is that you can create user interfaces that truly look fantastic. The bad news is that you need to account for the fact that computing a series of vectors and the plane that intersects those vectors requires more CPU or Graphical Processing Unit (GPU) cycles. Thus, just as you've heard with the Vista UI, all WPF user interfaces require a bit more computing horsepower. Another appeal of the WPF model is that the graphical capabilities, which are built around the Direct-X model, provide a much more appealing user interface.

Most of this chapter focuses on the underlying XAML that's used to define your WPF applications. Fortunately, WPF resolves the pain developers feel, even if it isn't a near-term solution to the support of multiple UI models that causes Microsoft pain. Microsoft will, of course, need to support all its previous GUI models in addition to WPF for the foreseeable future. However, Microsoft is motivated by the same advantages the rest of us can leverage — better graphics and the idea that a single application can have a UI that runs in multiple environments. This is a major factor in Microsoft's future as it focuses on things like Office Live. As developers, we can also start to leverage WPF and possibly even start to think about using WPF/E — WPF Everywhere — the standard for supporting handheld devices. We can create application user interfaces that operate both within a Web browser and on the local device — desktop, laptop, handheld, and so on — outside the Web browser.

Installing and Configuring WPF to Build Applications

Regardless of your operating system, you need to install software in order to build a WPF application. As noted, WPF was released with Vista; those intrepid developers, who in the early days were working on a beta and eventually a release version of Vista, had WPF available in their environment. However, if you were (or are) running the Windows XP operating system, then — just as with every other version of .NET — you need to add WPF to your operating system. In the past, with things such as .NET 1.x and 2.0, you usually did this by installing Visual Studio, which included not only the base runtime libraries but also several debug-related libraries.

Unfortunately, there isn't currently a complete package that includes WPF. Instead, you need to install the new runtime package and then supplement that manually with some low-level tools in order to work with those libraries. The first package you need is the full .NET 3.0 runtime package available on MSDN. To reiterate, if you are running Windows Vista, then the runtime for .NET 3.0 is already installed. Windows 2003 Server and Windows XP developers need to go to MSDN and download the freely available runtime libraries for .NET 3.0, which are available under the .NET Framework Home section of MSDN. As of this writing, you need to install the "release" version of this package and not one of the beta or "release candidate" versions, which are still available.

You can verify your installation by looking in your `<System Root>\Microsoft.NET\Framework` folder for a folder labeled `V3.0`. Within this folder you'll find a WPF directory containing the library files that you will reference in your WPF applications. Of course, your references will be to a set of namespaces contained in those library files, but those are the actual files you will be referencing. Even so, this doesn't mean you are ready to start building WPF applications.

Regardless of your operating system, you need a second software package in order to build a WPF application. The Windows Vista SDK (Software Development Kit) is a collection of libraries, tools, and upgrades that you need in order to build a WPF application. Similar to the .NET 3.0, this package contains released software. However, while it does make some additional tools available and provide some optional link libraries to Visual Studio 2005, the SDK does not upgrade Visual Studio 2005 to enable you to build WPF and other .NET 3.0 applications. These tools make it possible to build WPF applications from the command line, which is where this chapter starts.

Later in this chapter, the Visual Studio 2005 Extensions for WPF/WCF are covered. However, this is a Community Technology Preview, and will not be updated to a release product. Thus, depending on your work environment, you may find that the corporate or government IT department you work for is not interested in having you install this software. Similarly, Visual Studio "Orcas," the next version of Visual Studio, is in beta, and will target the next version of .NET, tentatively known as .NET 3.5. It is also covered later in this chapter; however, for now let's examine the low-level details of WPF.

Creating a WPF Application

This example creates a simple "Hello World" application that will act as the basis for our larger projects. Rather than get too technical about the elements of a WPF application, let's start with just a simple XAML declaration of a main window titled "Hello World." The sample application consists of two files: an XAML source file named `App.xaml` and a Visual Basic project file named `provb_net.vbproj`.

The XAML shown in the following section declares a new `Application` and associates the appropriate XML namespace to describe the document contents. It then declares an `Application.MainWindow` and assigns the string "Hello World" to the `Title` property of that window. The XAML also declares that the window should be visible. The first thing to notice is that there isn't a line of code in this XAML file, just a few declarations:

```
<Application
    xmlns="http://schemas.microsoft.com/winfx/2006/xaml/presentation">
    <Application.MainWindow>
        <Window Title='Hello World' Visibility='Visible' />
    </Application.MainWindow>
</Application>
```

The next step is running this declared application. In this case, you need to compile the application. You could run the Visual Basic compiler from the command line by typing `vbc`, but that requires a lot of path-dependent statements in order to pull together the libraries. Instead, use the MSBuild engine that ships with Visual Studio 2005. You still need to put together the references, but they go into an MSProject file instead of just being on the command line. Thus, you can invoke MSBuild and have it work out the details and reuse the majority of your typing. You're still working at the command line, but you aren't typing complex parameter lists in order to compile.

There isn't space in this chapter to cover all of the details of the MSBuild engine. For more complete coverage, check on MSDN in the MSBuild Reference section. However, take a minute to review a few of the primary elements that you'll need in order to create a build. The following table lists a few of the top-level XML nodes, with a brief description of the role each plays in the build process:

Project File Nodes	Description
PropertyGroup	This section contains a series of tags that describe what is being compiled, such as whether you are compiling an executable or library, what the name of the compiled file should be, whether it is a debug or release version, etc.
ItemGroup	This section has two roles. The first is to provide a list of references. You'll recognize these items based on the fact that XML nodes within this section are of type Reference. The Reference nodes name the namespaces that are being referenced by your application. The second use of the ItemGroup node is to define the list of source files that are part of a project. The section(s) contain the complete list of source files, so if you open an existing project file you'll find that many files hidden by Visual Studio are listed in the project file.
Import	The Import node is essentially a node that lists other projects to import. To MSBuild, constructs such as C# and VB don't really exist; instead, MSBuild looks for a project that contains all the standard references for such a language. It then imports this generic project, which provides not only the necessary reference files, but also a reference task to execute the appropriate compiler.

Before you start typing this file, let's cheat. Take an existing .vbproj file and open it for editing. This is not a completely trivial task, but for this example you'll mostly be deleting items. Start by reducing the number of PropertyGroups to 1. Then review the items in this property group and keep only the items in the following example. As you can see, this is a much shorter list of items. Then, delete the ItemGroup declarations, keeping one for the references and a second for the project files:

```
<Project DefaultTargets="Build"
                    xmlns="http://schemas.microsoft.com/developer/msbuild/2003">
  <PropertyGroup>
    <Configuration>Debug</Configuration>
    <Platform>AnyCPU</Platform>
    <RootNamespace>ProVB_NET</RootNamespace>
    <AssemblyName>ProVB_Net</AssemblyName>
    <OutputType>winexe</OutputType>
    <OutputPath>.\bin\Debug\</OutputPath>
  </PropertyGroup>
  <ItemGroup>
```

```
      <Reference Include="System" />
      <Reference Include="WindowsBase" />
      <Reference Include="PresentationCore" />
      <Reference Include="PresentationFramework" />
   </ItemGroup>
   <ItemGroup>
      <ApplicationDefinition Include="App.xaml" />
   </ItemGroup>

   <Import Project="$(MSBuildBinPath)\Microsoft.VisualBasic.targets" />
   <Import Project="$(MSBuildBinPath)\Microsoft.WinFX.targets" />
</Project>
```

Continuing to reference the sample MSBuild project file, note that it has only four project references. The first, System, should be familiar to you as a .NET developer. However, the other three all reference WPF namespaces. These files contain the code that implements the elements of the WPF you have declared in your XAML file. You need to add these references to the file you copied.

The second item group contains the list of files in your application. In this case, there is only a single file named App.xaml, which contains the XAML code shown earlier. This section includes additional file references as you make more complex projects, but for this simple example it only has that one entry.

Finally, there are two Import references in the preceding sample. The first of these should already be present in the file you've copied. It's the reference to the Visual Basic targets project. For now, even though you don't have any Visual Basic code in your example, leave that, because you will be adding Visual Basic code to the project in future examples. To this you need to add a second target — WPF. WinFx was the working name for .NET 3.0 prior to release. Accordingly, this name is still preserved behind the scenes; the Microsoft.WinFx.targets project contains the logic associated with building WPF, and other .NET 3.0, project types.

The next step is to execute your project. Executing the build engine is done from the command line. Open a command window and modify your directory to be your project directory. At the command prompt, add the following:

```
   msbuild ProVB_Net.vbproj
```

The preceding triggers Visual Studio's build engine and builds your executable. If there are any errors, they are displayed within the command window. If you don't have any errors, then you should be able to navigate down to the subdirectory identified in your project file \bin\debug and find your new executable provb net.exe. Running this executable produces the window shown in Figure 17-1.

Figure 17-1

At this point, you may be wondering why, if the Visual Studio build engine is building your WPF application, was it stated earlier that Visual Studio 2005 isn't compatible with your WPF project? The answer is that while the Vista SDK updates provide the target files and associated compilers necessary for your WPF application, it doesn't update Visual Studio 2005 to be able to work with your WPF project within the Visual Studio graphical user environment. Thus, while you can compile .NET 3.0 applications, Visual Studio 2005 doesn't really contain the logic that would enable you to edit these projects and their associated source files.

XAML

The example doesn't have much purpose yet, but it makes it easier to keep the discussion of XAML in context. The next step is to take a more detailed look at just what XAML is and how it relates to WPF. XAML is a markup-based protocol. Similar to SOAP and several other XML-based formats, the XAML specification describes a potentially open standard for describing user-interface elements. WPF is Microsoft's implementation of this standard. Currently, XAML isn't an open standard and it's unknown whether XAML will ever be a true open standard. However, the .NET 3.0 implementation, which separates the definition of the XAML elements from the implementation of WPF, means that this is still a possibility for XAML.

Regardless of whether XAML ever actually becomes an open standard, Microsoft has implemented WPF across two XML namespaces. One namespace is focused on the definition of XAML, and the second is focused on WPF's implementation of the XAML specification. Looking back at the "Hello World" sample presented earlier, the `App.xaml` file contains the following namespace declaration:

```
xmlns="http://schemas.microsoft.com/winfx/2006/xaml/presentation"
```

The preceding line is similar to an `Imports` statement for XML in that it indicates a set of nodes and keywords that will be used within the associated XML file. In this case, the `winfx/2006/xaml/presentation` namespace contains the definition of WPF — not the definition of XAML keywords, but rather the definition of WPF, which is why you see statements such as `Application.Window` in that XML. The classes contained in the presentation namespace are the .NET implementation of WPF. The XAML file contains declarations referencing these classes, either as part of the XAML standard or as part of WPF. To start working with commands and controls that are part of the XAML standard, a second namespace reference is needed:

```
xmlns:x=http://schemas.microsoft.com/winfx/2006/xaml
```

This second reference is used throughout most XAML files to declare the actual XAML language standard. By convention, it is aliased as `x:`. For those of you who may not have done much ASP.NET development, this means that within the XAML you'll see things like `x:Class`, `x:Code`, and other similar nodes. These are the actual XAML declarations; and they are, as you might guess, a subset of what is in WPF. What is important to remember is that the XAML namespace can be and is used for things other than just WPF. As you'll see in Chapter 25, Workflow Foundation (WF) is based on XAML; it has its own `/workflows` namespace.

XAML Namespace

XAML is defined as a language consisting of a collection of elements, attributes, and related objects. These objects are referenced from the XAML namespace, which by convention precedes each class with an "`x:`". WPF extends and maps these declarative structures back into .NET, using specific classes that are part of the .NET 3.0 `System.Windows` namespace.

Before getting to the syntax, take a look at the three categories of XML statement you will find within the XAML namespace: attribute, markup extension, and XAML directive. Each is a separate category of language element.

Within XML, attributes refer to named properties that are associated with a given XML node. Thus, the XML node "object" might have several attributes such as ID, Name, Text, etc., that are associated with it. These attributes in XML live within the definition of the XML node. They are not contained within the XML node but its definition, as shown below:

```
<object id="myObject"></object>
```

Within XAML, the list of attributes includes those in the following table. Be aware that the term "object" in the following snippets can be replaced with one of several WPF objects, including `Application`, `Window`, `Button`, `Brush`, and so on:

XAML Attributes	Description
x:Class	Used to reference the root class for an XAML document. Each document can be associated with a single root object. An example of using this attribute is `<object x:Class="class"> </object>`
x:ClassModifier	Modifies the class definition for a given XAML document. Specifically, it enables you to indicate that a given class doesn't provide a public interface. Public is the default. `<object x:Class="class" x:ClassModifier="Friend"> </object>`
x:FieldModifier	Unlike classes, which are by default public, fields within objects are by default assigned with the modifier `Friend`. If you have added an object within XAML that you want available to other classes (within your code behind), then the `FieldModifier` needs to declare this field with the modifier of `Friend`. This property can only be used with objects that also have the `x:Name` attribute shown here: `<object x:Name="LoginWindow" x:FieldModifier="Public"></object>`
x:Key	Some objects, such as the `Dictionary` object and other collection objects, allow items to be indexed via a key. Such a key must be named, and this attribute is used to provide a unique key name. Note that most XAML applications leverage a resource dictionary, which is a common use of this attribute. Keys need to be unique within the scope of the object to which they are applicable. `<object.Resources>` `<SolidColorBrush x:Key="string"/>` `</object.Resources>`

Table continues on the next page

XAML Attributes	Description
x:Name	Similar to a key, but used more for the naming of objects within the scope of an application. Such objects are not public by default, but typically represent the controls and related user-interface objects used by your application. `<object x:Name="LoginWindow"></object>`

x:Shared	This actually maps to what Visual Basic users understand the keyword `Shared` to mean. By default, if your application requests an object from your XAML resources, then you will get the same instance of the requested resource. You can use this property such that each time a given object is requested, a new instance of that object is created.
	`<ResourceDictionary>`
	`    <object x:shared="false"/>`
	`</ResourceDictionary>`

x:Subclass	This attribute can be used in conjunction with an x:Class declaration. It essentially allows your XAML to inherit from another class; however, as a Visual Basic user you won't use this attribute because you can do this in a much more natural manner in the code-behind-source file associated with your class.
	`<object x:Class="class"`
	`x:Subclass="namespace.subclass"></object>`

x:TypeArguments	This attribute enables you to create a collection of x:Type markup extensions. This collection acts as the parameters to the constructor for a generic class to ensure that the associated types are defined with the constructor. This attribute must be used with a class declaration, and the associated class must be a generic.
	`<object x:class="PageFunction"`
	`x:TypeArguments="{x:Type=type1}">`
	`</object>`

Notice that none of the preceding attributes are actually referenced as a node within XML. Instead, they modify the properties associated with a node. Thus, the attributes are modifiers, as opposed to the next category of elements: markup extensions. As implied by the word extensible in the name Extensible XML, one of the features of this model is that the format allows for the definition of extensions. These extensions expand on the base elements associated with that markup definition. XAML includes a limited number of such extensions. Unlike an attribute, a markup extension can be used to create an XML node or a collection of XML attributes. When used to create a node, the markup extension allows for the definition of property values within this node. When used to allow for the creation of a collection of attributes, it can be recognized by the surrounding curly braces, as shown in the preceding TypeArguments definition. Markup extensions for XAML are shown in the following table:

XAML Markup Extension	Description

x:Array	Used to provide support for arrays. The array declaration allows for the assignment of a datatype, to support strong typing and the inclusion of a series of elements. An example of this code is:
	
	``xml
	<x:Array Type="object">
	    <myObject1/>
	    <myObject2/>
	</x:Array>
	``

x:Null	Nothing in Visual Basic, but the extension is implemented based on the C#/C++ keyword of null. Will set an object property to null, which may or may not be the default state when that object property is created. x:Null has no additional modifiers and is typically implemented as a node, as opposed to an attribute, as it references the value of its parent node.
	
	``xml
	<object><object.property>
	    <x:Null/>
	</object.property></object>
	``

x:Static	Supports the reference of constant values, shared properties of objects, and enumeration values. Similar to an attribute, it is most commonly used as an attribute with the format: X:static "{namespace.class}" This extension is used to gain access to common values that are defaults for your application — for example, to the system colors used by the operating system.
	
	``xml
	<object Background="{x:Static
	SystemColors.ControlBrush}"></object>
	``

x:Type	As previously introduced with the x:Typename attribute, the x:Type extension allows for the specification of a type when creating an object that is a generic. However, it has a second use: the specification of a property type. Thus, if you create an object that has properties, the x:Type extension is used to specify the type associated with that property.
	
	``xml
	<object><object.property>
	    <x:Type TypeName="namespace.class"/>
	</object.property></object>
	``

Don't let that last extension confuse you; there are two ways that markup extensions are used — either as attributes contained within curly braces or as nodes that may contain their own attributes and properties. Some, such as x:Static, always appear as attributes; others, such as x:Null and x:Array, always appear as nodes; and of course x:Type can be found in either location. Up until now, all the XAML language elements have been used to operate within the definition of XML. That is, they define attributes and nodes, and as long as you understand the definition of the keyword you can understand the data it references.

XAML Directive	Description
x:Code	Enables you to embed Visual Basic code directly into your XAML file. However, although you can do it, you shouldn't: It's considered a very poor coding practice not only because it isolates code outside of a code-behind file, but also because such code makes the XAML dependent on a language for compilation, and is isolated and more difficult to debug and maintain. However, you may come across such an element. In general, it is considered best to further nest any embedded code within an x:Code block within a CDATA block as shown in the following sample, so that the XAML parsing engine doesn't attempt to parse the code. Thus, a code block will look similar to this: ```<object><x:Code> <![CDATA[// code instructions, usually enclosed by CDATA... Sub MyMethod() End Sub]]></x:Code></object>```
x:XData	The second item you might want to embed within your XAML document that isn't standard XAML is another XML document. You might want to display an e-mail message or a Word document that has been converted to XML, and of course you might want this data to be within your XAML document. The key point is that you don't want this additional XML to accidentally use the same tag information associated with your XAML. Thus, you need to provide an x:XData directive containing your root data node, which contains your custom data. Note that in most cases the "object'" node in this sample will be a System.Windows.Data.XMLDataProvider as opposed to a Window or some other object. A sample of this is shown here: ```<object><x:XData> <dataItems xmlns="yourNamespace"> ... </dataItems> <elementDataRoot></x:XData></object>```

As you can see, the scope of the XML definition for what you're going to see within a XAML file is not that complex. You're probably wondering where all the controls, windows, and even the application object that we've already seen in action are. These items, while defined as part of the WPF implementation, are not part of the core XAML language definition. They are the WPF extensions, and the reason why you added a second namespace reference to the Presentation folder. Everything else you see in XAML that falls into this second category is also available for reference from your .NET application, so let's take a look at the integration of XAML and Visual Basic.

Application Code

In the first "Hello World," you'll recall that the XAML file began by creating an instance of an `Application` object. In this instance, the `Application` object was declared in the XAML file. The `Application` object is required for all WPF applications. Just as with your Visual Basic Windows Forms code, the `Application` object represents the application to the CLR. It is this object that represents the base reference for things such as garbage collection, and it is registered as the primary process. Because the `Application` object is implemented as an object in the `System.Windows` namespace, it supports properties, methods, and events just like any other class.

In fact, it is possible to do much of your WPF programming from within accompanying class files that may or may not contain the references to the `Application` class, but let's start by defining how XAML can be integrated with code. After all, at some point you probably expect to start seeing some Visual Basic code again. The "Hello World" sample was a pure XAML application. In most cases, as a Visual Basic developer, you'll start with a Visual Basic application. Because Visual Basic provides the underlying application object, you won't define this object. Instead, you'll create `Window` and `Page` objects that are referenced by your built-in Visual Basic `Application` object.

Even in XAML it is best practice to separate the `Window` object(s) that will be in your application from the `Application` object, so let's quickly take care of that: Instead of having an empty window, let's create a window with a button in it, and a code-behind file with an event handler for the click button. Begin with the updated application file:

```
<Application
    xmlns="http://schemas.microsoft.com/winfx/2006/xaml/presentation"
    StartupUri="MainWindow.xaml">
</Application>
```

As you can see, this file has gotten much smaller. In fact, in most cases when you create a new WPF application from one of the tools, you'll find that this file isn't used at all; instead, you can leverage the `Application` object created within your .NET code. Moving on, let's look at the new `MainWindow.xaml` source file that defines the main window with a single button:

```
<Window x:Class="MainWindow"
    xmlns="http://schemas.microsoft.com/winfx/2006/xaml/presentation"
    xmlns:x="http://schemas.microsoft.com/winfx/2006/xaml"
    Title="Hello from VB" Height="233" Width="308">
    <Grid>
        <Button Margin="100,85,100,85" Name="ButtonHello" Click="VBButtonClick">
        Say Hello?</Button>
    </Grid>
</Window>
```

The preceding code should look similar to what you saw in the original application code, but several items have been added. For starters, this XAML references the XAML namespace in addition to the WPF namespace. It also defines a default size for the application window of 233 × 308 pixels, and the very first line where the window is declared includes an `x:Class` reference (discussed later in relation to the code-behind). As for a height of 233, as you'll see when we discuss the Cider designer, the border on the top and bottom of a typical window takes up 33 pixels, thus leaving 200 for the display area. Similarly, the left and right borders take up an additional eight pixels from the width, leaving a 300-pixel display area.

Within the window the first control is a grid. Why the grid? By default, if that grid weren't present, there would be no way to reference specific points within the window. The window just defines a blank area, and if you placed a button within the window the button would fill the entire window. That isn't the desired behavior, so a grid is layered on top of the window. Then, notice that the button defines an attribute of `Margin`. `Margin` is a property on the WPF class, and the points it defines are used to specify where the borders for the button should be displayed. In this case, the button should start 100 pixels from the left and 100 pixels from the right margin, respectively. In addition, the top of the button should start 85 pixels from the top and 85 pixels from the bottom of the display area.

This isn't the only way to manage the display of elements within a window, but it is one of the more precise ways. Conversely, the parameters included act more like a button that is bound to the four borders of the window; resize this sample window and watch the button's size change. It's far better to use only a distance from the top and a distance from the bottom in the `Margin` property and provide a height and width for the button. You'll look at control layout again later in this chapter.

In addition to the `Margin` property, note that the button has a `Name` property that defines an event handler for the `Click` event. The name of the event handler's procedure is `VBButtonClick`, and that procedure will be found in the remainder of the partial class definition for the main window. As noted earlier, the XAML file's first line includes a class attribute. The class attribute is actually a reference to a partial class. The remainder of the class definition should be defined in your new code-behind file (named `MainWindow.xaml.vb` by convention). The `Partial Public Class MainWindow` should be defined as shown in the following code block:

```
Partial Public Class MainWindow
    Inherits System.Windows.Window

    Public Sub New()
        InitializeComponent()
    End Sub

    Public Sub VBButtonClick(ByVal sender As Object, _
            ByVal e As System.Windows.RoutedEventArgs)
        ButtonHello.Content = "Hello VB'er"
        System.Windows.MessageBox.Show("Hello VB'er")
    End Sub

End Class
```

You may recall from Chapter 15 that the libraries for Windows Forms are located in the `System.Windows.Forms` namespace. This namespace is implemented in `System.Windows.Forms.dll` and is the parent namespace for things such as Forms controls. The WPF, on the other hand, is located in the `System.Windows` namespace directly. It is implemented in the `System.PresentationUI.dll` and contains the implementation for the WPF classes. Most of these classes mirror what you'll find for Windows Forms, but they have been implemented based on WPF requirements.

In the preceding code snippet the `MainWindow` class is inheriting from the `Window` object defined in the `System.Windows` namespace. It then implements a default constructor, which includes a call to `InitializeComponent()`. This is a required call when creating a code-behind file for a WPF XAML. The second method is the event handler added to handle the `click` event for the button on the form. Note that by default this `click` event does not need a `Handles` clause as part of its declaration.

After that, you'll note that it relies on a `System.Windows` parameter for routed events. However, it is the code within the handler that is of interest. Notice that the code references the `ButtonHello` declared in the XAML for this window. There is no other file where this button is defined or instantiated. The integration of XAML and Visual Basic allows you to reference this declared object from the XAML file. Of more concern to most developers, however, is the property being referenced, `Content`. One of the changes that occurred with Windows Forms was that controls such as buttons had `Text` properties that were consistently used for the display text. However, under WPF, the `Text` property no longer exists — as shown momentarily — and instead you reference the `Content` property.

Why the change in properties? Under Windows Forms, if you wanted to display an image on a button, then you needed either a special property or a special button. WPF recognized that there wasn't any reason the button's display couldn't adapt to handle an `Object`. This had two implications, especially given how this was implemented. The first implication was that an object would potentially come with its own style of output. While some of these, such as text or images, could be coded, in reality there's no way to know all the possible objects.

This leads to the second implication, related to the fact that the object assigned as "content" for the button might completely obscure the button. This resulted in the idea that controls could be layered. The content of one control would sit "on top" of the control that hosted it. This is the behavior you already see implemented in our example. At the back of the display are the window and its frame; layered atop the window is the display grid; atop the grid is the button — and we could continue from there.

In short, an object such as a button doesn't need to know how the content of custom objects will be displayed; it simply has to notify the object that it needs to be displayed. The preceding is a simplification, but it does reflect the core idea of how the WPF interacts between various controls. The resulting interaction model is much more robust because controls are not "contained," but rather are layered.

Getting back to the preceding code-behind logic, the second statement in the example makes a call to a WPF message box to display a simple message. The goal here is twofold: to demonstrate that the WPF is a complete departure from Windows Forms and to illustrate that, where possible, you'll find familiar structures. In general, this handler is a simple example of how, from Visual Basic, you can still interact with the XAML form and the user interface. It's just that under WPF you now reference a different set of .NET libraries. At this point, you should compile and run this simple example.

However, before attempting to compile the new application using MSBuild, a few updates to the project file are in order. The good news is that these updates are limited to a few lines. Essentially, you simply need to include the new `MainWindow` files into the list of files associated with the project. This change is shown in the following XML snippet:

```
<Project DefaultTargets="Build"
xmlns="http://schemas.microsoft.com/developer/msbuild/2003">
...
  <ItemGroup>
    <Page Include="MainWindow.xaml" />
    <Compile Include="MainWindow.xaml.vb" />
      <ApplicationDefinition Include="App.xaml" />
  </ItemGroup>
...
</Project>
```

Notice that the order of the files in the include file does not matter, but what type of action is associated with each does. The new XAML file is listed as a Page, while the Visual Basic source file associated with it is tagged as needing compilation. The MSBuild engine simply passes this list of files to the targets defined in the project file, and the targets each recognize the appropriate file types. The Visual Basic target recognizes the Compile tag and builds the MSIL from the .vb file(s). Then the WinFx engine recognizes the Page and ApplicationDefinition tags and builds the remainder of the executable, combining the MSIL from the Visual Basic compilation with the window definitions to create the .exe file, which is your application. Figure 17-2 illustrates a test run of the application, showing the main window before the button is pressed and the message box after the button is pressed. The dotted line within the button indicates that this is the default button, a visual indicator that appears in the main window after the button is pressed.

Figure 17-2

The preceding example provides a more reasonable base framework from which to work as we move forward. As some of the key elements of WPF are described, this basic application framework will act as a basis. Let's start by discussing what controls are available and how they can be manipulated.

Controls

As noted under WPF, there is an entirely different set of libraries for developing applications. However, aside from the fact that these controls exist in a different library, to a large extent how you interact with them from Visual Basic is the same. The control has a set of properties. The XAML file may assign these values in the declarative format of XML, but you can still reference the same properties on the instances of the objects that the framework creates.

Thus, in the preceding example you saw that just as with existing .NET applications, controls are assigned a name, also known as an id, and that from the application code it is possible to address a control based on this name. Once the control is referenced, it is possible to update properties and retrieve values. Additionally, it is possible to create controls programmatically and add them to an existing window's control set. Thus, everything you've done in the past both with Windows Forms and ASP.NET is still possible. On the surface, the WPF controls have more in common with existing programming models than might at first seem apparent.

Having uttered that heresy against this new paradigm, it's time to examine what is meant by a paradigm shift with the XAML model. As noted, it starts with the fact that your controls are no longer "contained," but rather are layered. This may sound like a minor change, but the implications are significant. The `button` class provides an excellent example of how this change impacts how controls are approached in WPF. Under previous UI models, an object had a container of some sort. For example, a panel could contain other controls of certain types, but not necessarily all types. A button's content was generally text unless you had a button configured for images, but you couldn't really find a button configured to contain, say, a drop-down list box, unless you wrote custom display implementation.

By moving to a more layered approach, you can create a single control that handles text, images, and other controls. The technique chosen to accomplish that was for those controls that support layering to include a *content presenter control*. Thus, the button has a layer of generic button code — background color, border, size, and so on — which is managed within the display for the button. Then the button has a content presenter, which takes whatever was placed into the button's `content` property and calls the presentation logic for that control. This enables most controls to contain other controls.

As for the specific controls available in WPF, let's start with a couple of the bottom-layer elements. The one seen thus far in this chapter is the `Window` control. As demonstrated in the first "Hello World" example, a window includes a frame and a title in addition to its content area. You might want to then apply a layout grid or a panel — for example a stack panel — within this content area. However, you could also take a different tack and place a `Page` control within this window. A `Page` control is, of course, the base UI element for a Web application, so it becomes easy to see how this paradigm of the content area can support the layering of two different user-interface implementations. When the application is running on a local computer, it can encapsulate the pages in a `Window` control; and when hosted in a browser, it can simply use those same pages without the window layer.

However, the preceding paragraph also mentions other controls called *panels*. `Panel` is an abstract base class, and there are different types of panels. Stack panels are a form of panel control. The purpose of a stack panel is to align a set of controls into a single column (horizontal or vertical). There are several panel implementations, including the canvas and grid. When you start working with WPF, among the items you'll need to understand are the different types of panels, as you will want to leverage the unique characteristics of different panels for consistent behavior.

Aside from standard user interface controls, the WPF contains all of the controls such as Tabs, Toolbars, ToolTips, TextBoxes, Drop Downs, Validation, and so on that you can find in every other Windows-based user-interface model. Going through a list of all the possible controls would take up too much space and not provide all that much value. Instead, let's take a quick look outside the controls. It should also be noted that the WPF namespace consists of several graphics, ink, and even data and data-bound controls.

Resources

For most applications there comes a point where you want to include one or more resources with your application. A resource can be anything, including a static string, an image, and a graphics element. Because the final example in this chapter looks at an image resource, this section uses a graphical element as a resource.

As noted earlier in the introduction to XAML syntax, the definition for `x:Key` included the label `object.Resources`. The implication is that objects of different types can include resources. The scope of a resource, then, is defined by the scope of the object with which it is associated. For a resource that will span your application, you can in fact define that resource within your application XAML. Resources that are to be available within a given window are defined in the XAML file for that window. The following XAML demonstrates adding a resource to the application file of the sample application created earlier:

```
<Application
    xmlns="http://schemas.microsoft.com/winfx/2006/xaml/presentation"
    xmlns:x="http://schemas.microsoft.com/winfx/2006/xaml"
    StartupUri="MainWindow.xaml">
    <Application.Resources>
        <SolidColorBrush x:Key='greenbrush' Color='Green' />
    </Application.Resources>
</Application>
```

A `SolidColorBrush` is one of several graphical devices that can be used to fill in an area with color or create graphics within your application display. In this case, the resource in question is creating a green brush. Notice that it is assigned an `x:Key` value that, as far as XAML is concerned, is the identity and name of this resource. Once this has been assigned, objects within your XAML can reference this resource and apply it to an object or property. To illustrate this, the following XAML code shows a reference of this brush to change the background color of the button Hello, which is part of the `MainWindow.xaml` file:

```
<Grid>
    <Button Margin="100,85,100,85" Background="{StaticResource greenbrush}"
Name="ButtonHello" Click="VBButtonClick">
        Say Hello?</Button>
</Grid>
```

This resource could, of course, be referenced by several different resources, but if you want to slightly adjust the background color of dozens of resources, having to place that resource reference into each of your objects isn't the most efficient way of implementing that solution. After all, each time someone edited your source file in any way, that person would need to be aware of the requirement to add this resource as the background color. Fortunately, one of the other concepts XAML borrows from the Web-based idea of style sheets enables you to define a *style statement*, which is then applied to all objects of the same type.

Styles

Styles essentially leverage the concept of resources but instead of having a resource that objects reference with a style, you are referencing objects of a common type and assigning a property to those objects. In short, styles provide a mechanism for you to apply a theme across an application. If another developer later adds new elements to your application, the styles are automatically applied.

Styles are defined like resources; in fact, they are defined within the same XML area in which resources are defined. By defining a style at the application level, the style can be applied across all of the windows in the application. For example, take the resource defined earlier and use it instead to help create a style. Note that in this case the XAML references the resource previously defined. This is a best practice, as in most cases you will be defining a different style resource for each object type.

```
<Application
    xmlns="http://schemas.microsoft.com/winfx/2006/xaml/presentation"
    xmlns:x="http://schemas.microsoft.com/winfx/2006/xaml"
    StartupUri="MainWindow.xaml">
    <Application.Resources>
```

```
        <SolidColorBrush x:Key='greenbrush' Color='Green' />
      <Style x:Key='{x:Type Button}' TargetType='{x:Type Button}'>
        <Setter Property='Background' Value='{StaticResource greenbrush}' />
      </Style>
      </Application.Resources>
  </Application>
```

To have these styles use the same value, you would define a common resource and apply it to each of your styles, which are then applied to all of the objects of the appropriate type. When handling resources, it was necessary to apply the resource to the object property you wanted to target. The style encapsulates this same behavior in a single location. Notice that the key is assigned to all objects of the type Button. The preceding example works great if you want all the buttons to have this style, but what if you only want certain buttons to have this theme?

In that case, you can revert to something closer to the resource model. Instead of using a key based on the object type, you would use a custom key and then apply that key to certain objects of the associated type. The associated type for a style is defined in the TargetType attribute of your style definition.

Layout

Recall how the button you defined was essentially bound to the four borders of your application window. This was because of the limited amount of layout information available at that point. WPF supports a very robust model for control layout, which it achieves by leveraging the ability to layer controls, and by providing a set of controls directly related to layout. Combined with the ability to define a reasonable set of layout information for each control, what you wind up with is an adaptable environment that can at the extreme provide unique behavior.

So how does the process work? Within each control are the basic elements associated with the sizing of that control. As with past versions of Windows Forms, you have the concept of height and width and the four limitations: MaxHeight, MaxWidth, MinHeight, and MinWidth. Most developers tend to rely on setting the height and width of controls and forget about the rest.

However, that's more of a style behavior and isn't really our focus. More important is the concept of layered controls. What happens when you layer an image on top of the button? The first thing to recognize is that if a control is layered on top of another control, then its display boundaries are limited by the underlying control boundaries. However, depending on the control, the control that is layered on top of it may change the boundaries of the underlying control. The example shown in the next section makes use of this layout behavior using an image.

Finally, as noted in our example earlier, the layering of images allows for the definition of different panels. WPF provides a series of different "panel" controls that are used to provide a framework for control layout. The grid is probably the one most familiar to .NET Windows Forms developers because it maps most closely to the default behavior of Windows Forms — in fact, the Visual Studio 2005 Windows Forms Designer actually displays a grid on your form if you request it.

However, the grid isn't the only control that inherits from panel. Others include StackPanel, Canvas, DockPanel, ToolBar and Tab-related controls. Each of these provides unique layout behavior. Because these are available as controls and because you can nest controls, you can combine these different layout paradigms within different sections of a single form, which enables you to group controls and achieve common layout behavior of related controls.

Visual Studio Integration

The first reaction of most developers is, "How do I know what controls are available from this library, and, more importantly, how do I know what properties are the correct properties on these controls?" Because the majority of WPF applications show all the controls in XAML files, it almost seems like magic. However, in reality you can use Visual Basic to expose all of those classes from within Visual Studio. As part of the process for beta testing .NET Framework 3.0, Microsoft released a series of Visual Studio 2005 packages to extend the reach of Visual Studio 2005. The last of these packages was released in November 2006; and while it is not release quality, it provides an environment in which you can better visualize and test your XAML applications.

Keep in mind that if you are in an environment where you cannot use pre-release software, then you may have a challenge getting permission to install this package. However, available on MSDN are the "Visual Studio 2005 extensions for .NET Framework 3.0 (WCF & WPF), November 2006 CTP." This package provides support for WPF and for the Windows Communication Format. Omitted from this package is the Windows Workflow Foundation. The extensions for Workflow are in a separate package, which you can choose to install or not. The extension packages for Visual Studio all require that you have already installed .NET 3.0 and the Vista SDK described earlier in this chapter.

Finally, a quick note on why we are demonstrating with this set of tools on Windows XP. Currently, Visual Studio 2005 on Vista is at times inconsistent. The Service Pack 1 package for Visual Studio 2005 that has been released targets Windows XP, not Vista. Therefore, to reduce inconsistencies, Windows XP was chosen for these examples. Also note that "Orcas," the code name for the next version of Visual Studio — which will provide native support for WPF and all of the .NET 3.0 Framework features — is in beta. Orcas will provide a complete implementation of the WPF designer code named "Cider." Trying to leverage that environment would have introduced a consistency problem. Between now and the release of Visual Studio Orcas, the extensions to Visual Studio 2005 are not going to change. Visual Studio Orcas, however, will go through several different Community Technology Preview releases and is likely to undergo significant changes. Using Visual Studio 2005 provides a more consistent interface that will remain consistent throughout the Visual Studio Orcas development cycle.

Shown in Figure 17-3 is the new project screen from Visual Studio 2005 after the Visual Studio Extensions for .NET Framework 3.0 have been installed. It contains a new category for .NET Framework 3.0. Within this category are four standard project types, three of which are related to WPF. The first is for creating a Windows application, which is the one you can choose to follow in this simple example; it shows some of the current tool capabilities and limitations.

Just as with other Visual Studio 2005 templates, after you have selected the template and had Visual Studio create your template, you are presented with your project in Visual Studio 2005. Unlike a pure Visual Basic project, however, in place of the default forms you'll find an `App.xaml` and `Window1.xaml` as your project contents. Additionally, this is a good time to compare the project settings that are created by Visual Studio 2005 with those of the manually created sample `.vbproj file` used earlier in this chapter. The easiest way to do this is to right-click your project name in Visual Studio 2005 Solution Explorer and then choose to "unload" the project. The project contents will collapse and the project names will be grayed out and labeled as unavailable, as shown in Figure 17-4.

Once you have unloaded the project, right-click it; now the option to load the project file into the Visual Studio editor is available. Loading the project file into the editor provides a display similar to the one shown in Figure 17-4, and allows you to directly edit and access the project file's settings.

Figure 17-3

Figure 17-4

Now that you've had a chance to review the contents of the project file, go ahead and reload the contents of the project. Figure 17-5 shows one default solution in the Solution Explorer. It indicates that `Window1.xaml` has been opened for editing and displays the graphical UI editing surface. There is quite a bit to discuss in this image, so let's work from left to right, top to bottom.

On the far left side is the Toolbox. The XAML Toolbox looks and behaves similarly to the standard Windows Forms Toolbox discussed in Chapter 13. However, this Toolbox contains the controls supported by XAML. The controls displayed in the figure do not constitute the complete list of available controls, but it does illustrate the fact that the WPF offers a feature-rich set of controls. The controls can be dragged and dropped onto the design surface; in fact, drag and drop a button onto the form and resize it as shown in the display. The caption of the button will be Show Image. You'll find that the design surface has new guides to help position your control; pay attention to these lines, as they also imply that a control is bound to that border of the window.

Take the time to set the `Margin` property for your new button to bind it to the top and left borders at a space of around 18 pixels. Next, set the button to a height of 30 and a width of 100. Don't declare an event handler for the `click` event. This example uses an alternative method for defining the event handler that bypasses the XAML declaration file.

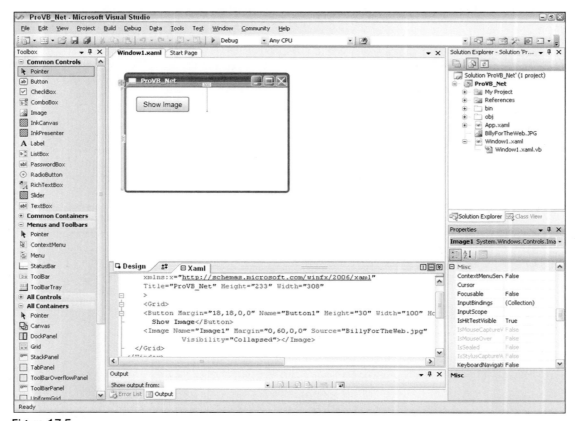

Figure 17-5

As for the design surface, you probably recognize at once the `ProVB_Net` graphical portion of that design, and on first glance you might think that the tab labeled XAML is actually a separate window. However, it is in fact part of the design surface even though it contains the XAML declarations that describe your window. As you move your cursor's focus from the upper half of the design window to the lower half, Visual Studio automatically reinterprets and updates your display. If you type in some invalid design information, then the graphical portion of the display will stop displaying your user interface until you correct your syntax in the XAML.

More interesting is the small square between the Design and XAML tabs in Figure 17-5. This small square currently highlighted enables you to swap the display of these two panels so that when you are focused on working with the XAML statements you can do so in a larger display area. Then, when you are focused on using the Windows designer, you can have that portion of the display dominate your working area.

Note that the system requirements of the Extension for .NET Framework 2.0 indicate that it is compatible with Visual Basic 2005 Express Edition. However, be forewarned — what the system requirements allow, the release notes take away. While the package can be installed with Visual Basic Express Edition, there is a key exclusion to the supported capabilities — namely, the Visual Designer. Installing it with one of the Express Editions is not a recommended configuration. Note that this specifically refers to the designer support shown in Figure 17-5.

Getting back to our example: In addition to adding the button, let's also add a simple image control to the display. You'll position the control-display area to be located below the button and allow it to stretch with the other three borders. The result is some XAML code that looks similar to the following:

```
<Image Name="Image1" Margin="0,60,0,0" Source="BillyForTheWeb.jpg" Visible="Collapsed">
</Image>
```

The preceding line references a local copy of an image file. This file needs to be added to the project and reside in the project directory, as it's referenced locally. The expectation is that, when the application is compiled, the executable will contain an embedded version of this image resource. If you compile this same statement using MSBuild, then everything builds as expected, and the resulting application works almost as expected. You may find that the image doesn't appear as expected when the application is run and the event handler described below is called. The challenge is that the image file (which is part of the application) needs to have the property to include this as a resource set. The build action must not be Embedded Resource; it must be resource. If it isn't, then the image won't be compiled correctly for the XAML reference.

The next step is to go to the code view for your application. This brings up a second minor issue. If you right-click within the designer, you aren't offered the opportunity to switch to code view for your XAML file. Fortunately, you can move to the Solution Explorer on the far right side and go to the code view by right-clicking on the file there. Note that if you can't find that context menu option for some reason (beta software has its moments), then use the button at the top of the Solution Explorer to display all files, after which you'll see the `window1.xaml.vb` file and can double-click on it to open it for editing.

At this point, build your application. The reason for this is that once you've compiled your XAML code, Visual Studio can then provide IntelliSense capabilities on the properties of your XAML objects. This limitation is likely to disappear in the next version of Visual Studio, but for now it is just a minor annoyance. Once you have built the XAML, you can reference Image1 and Button1 and get a better sense of what properties are available on each.

For now, add the code shown here to your source file:

```
Public Sub VBButtonClick(ByVal sender As Object, _
    ByVal e As System.Windows.RoutedEventArgs) _
    Handles Button1.Click
  Button1.Content = "Hello Billy"
  Image1.Visibility = Windows.Visibility.Visible
End Sub
```

This code adds a handler for Button1 (since you haven't renamed the default control names in this example). However, in this case you can leverage the traditional Visual Basic-style `Handles` keyword. Thus, instead of having a handler in the XAML, the handler is placed in Visual Basic. From an existing application this model probably most closely matches the way you could move an existing handler to the XAML model. It also enables you to see within your application code which methods are in fact event handlers.

At this point, go ahead and compile and run your application. First, check whether the button handler is working. When the button is pressed, the text on the button should change and the image that was collapsed (and essentially invisible) should become visible. If only the button text changes, then the odds are good that there is a problem with the image resource you attempted to include. Otherwise, if you are using the sample code available from the Wrox website, then you should see the screen and image shown in Figure 17-6.

As you move the borders on this display, the image maintains the proper aspect. Behind the scenes, even though the `Image` control has been defined to have a margin of zero from each of the window borders, the image still wants to maintain its aspect. WPF allows this behavior to controls, as discussed earlier in the layout discussion. The image is given the borders of the control on which it is layered, and then the image determines its display size within those limitations. Finally, both the image and the control on which it is layered are displayed.

Figure 17-6

While WPF is still not fully supported by the tool suite, it does provide a quick and easy way for you to start becoming familiar with this new application development paradigm for user interfaces. You can start designing and planning the next versions of your applications to use these new controls, and by the time the tools release, you will be ready to leverage them for the production version of your application.

Keep in mind that this single chapter hasn't covered all the new features you can potentially leverage with WPF — that would require an entire book. Instead, you should now have an understanding of the base principals of the WPF programming model and how it integrates with Visual Basic.

Orcas

Orcas is the code name for the version of Visual Studio that will follow Visual Studio 2005. This development environment will include the new WPF designer environment code-named *Cider* as well as several other enhancements. This tool is currently available in beta, and if you are planning to work with .NET 3.0 features, it is recommended that you participate in this beta program. Visual Studio Orcas will incorporate changes beyond those discussed in this chapter, including new data access strategies and other new features such as Language-Integrated Query (LINQ). LINQ is a new way of accessing both SQL and XML data without needing specialized query languages such as T-SQL and XQuery. This well-publicized feature is outside the scope of this book, but be aware that it will change how you work with much of your application data.

Expression Suite of Tools

In addition to a new version of Visual Studio, with an updated forms designer, Microsoft is also working on a new set of design tools. Called the *Expression Suite*, it consists of four different graphic design tools. These tools focus on creating vector-based graphics (vs. raster), which can then be incorporated into your WPF display. The tools are not in any way integrated with development languages such as C# or Visual Basic, and as such aren't a focus of this book. If you want to create a hyped-up graphical interface, then you'll want to take a look at these tools for help in designing the complex graphics that you can then use within your WPF display.

Summary

This material focused on the WPF libraries that were released in 2006. Still to come, as noted, are things such as Orcas and WPF/E. WPF/E is the concept discussed in the beginning of the chapter — namely, that the WPF and XAML declarations can be supported not only across application models (desktop, web, etc.) but across devices and operating systems. WPF/E is still in its infancy but it has the potential to continue the UI paradigm shift beyond Windows. Other important concepts you should take away from this chapter include the following:

- ❑ XAML is a declarative standard for defining your user interface.

- ❑ WPF-based applications leverage traditional programming languages such as Visual Basic.

- ❑ WPF separates the UI creator from the business logic developer.

- ❑ WPF has been released — unlike the tools for automating the production of WPF applications.

- ❑ Now is the time to start becoming familiar with XAML-based user interface programming; the tools aren't fully ready, but you have a solid baseline from which to work.

- ❑ The new Expression design suite will expand on the creativity of design.

This chapter has focused on the WPF libraries within the context of building new applications. The question that is likely still echoing in your head is, what about my existing applications? Chapter 18 continues working with the WPF libraries, but looks at how to leverage WPF elements in an existing application.

18

Integrating WPF with Windows Forms

Windows Presentation Foundation (WPF) was introduced in the last chapter as Microsoft's next-generation solution to graphical user-interface development. In terms of user interfaces, the transition to this new model will be similar in significance and paradigm shift to the shift from COM-based Visual Basic to Visual Basic .NET. In other words, the paradigms and syntax familiar to developers of Windows applications are changing, and most of the changes are not backwardly compatible. Currently, there are no plans for an automated migration from any existing user-interface paradigm, forms, or Web, to the new WPF format.

Yes, again you will need to transition existing application source code to a new technology paradigm. Perhaps not this year or next, but at some point the WPF paradigm will be used to update the look and feel of existing applications. How will this transition compare to the last major .NET-related transition — the one from COM? Whereas Visual Studio includes a tool to aid in migrating code from the COM-based world to .NET, there will not be a migration tool provided to transition existing user interfaces to WPF. You might consider this to be a good thing, considering the history of the current migration tools. However, Microsoft is providing libraries that enable user-interface developers to integrate these two interface models. In the long run, this integration will probably go the way of COM-Interop, which is to say it will be available but carry such a stigma that people will only use it when absolutely necessary.

This chapter takes you through several key areas of Windows Forms Integration, including the following:

- ❏   Forms integration — Crossbow
- ❏   Using WPF controls in Windows Forms
- ❏   Using Windows Forms controls in WPF
- ❏   Interop limitations

This is a fairly short list, but you might want to consider reviewing some of the Interop limitations. After all, nothing clarifies some of the differences between the capabilities of these two user-interface platforms quite like a look at the limitations when they are viewed together. Just as with COM-Interop, the key for this tool is to help you, the developer, transition your application from Windows Forms to WPF over time, while working with time and budget constraints that all developers face and potentially waiting on the availability of a control that isn't available in the .NET 3.0 version of WPF.

Forms Integration — Crossbow

Crossbow was the code name for the project to provide a library that enables WPF applications to host Windows Forms controls and vice versa. The Crossbow project's focus was to provide a .NET library that developers could leverage; what it created was the `WindowsFormsIntegration` library. `WindowFormsIntegration.dll` supports the `Windows.Forms.Integration` namespace. This namespace provides the tools necessary for using WPF and Windows Forms in a single application. At the core of this namespace are the two classes `ElementHost` and `WindowsFormHost`. These two classes provide for interoperability in the WPF and the Windows Forms environment, respectively.

The place to start, then, is with the location of this library. Its installation location isn't where I expected, with the .NET 3.0 libraries. Instead, when you install the .NET 3.0 Framework, this library is placed with some other libraries into a directory under Program Files. The full path is: `C:\Program Files\ Reference Assemblies\Microsoft\Framework\v3.0\WindowsFormsIntegration.dll`.

The next step in looking at this library is to review a list of the classes and the delegate that make up the `Windows.Forms.Integration` namespace:

Class	Description
ChildChangedEventArgs	This class is used when passing event arguments to the `ChildChanged` event. This event occurs on both the `WindowsFormsHost` and `ElementHost` classes when the content of the `Child` property is changed.
ElementHost	This is the core class for embedding WPF controls within Windows Forms. Using the `Child` property, you identify the top-level object (probably some type of panel) that will be hosted, and via this object define an area that will be controlled by that object. The object referenced by the host can contain other controls, but the host references only this one.
IntegrationExceptionEventArgs	This is the base class for the Integration and Property Mapping exception classes. It provides the common implementation used by these classes.
LayoutExceptionEventArgs	This class enables you to return information related to a Layout error within a host class to the hosting environment, Windows Forms, or WPF.

Class	Description
PropertyMap	A property on each of the host classes. It provides a way for a Windows Form to tell a nested ElementHost that the size of the containing form has changed. It works the same for WPF applications hosting a WindowsFormHost control and it supports most control properties.
PropertyMappingExceptionEventArgs	Similar to the layout exception class, this enables a hosted control to return information related to an exception to the hosting environment.
WindowsFormsHost	This is the primary control when a WPF application wants to host Windows Forms controls. Similar to the ElementHost, the actual WIndowsFormsHost object contains only a single child — typically a user control. This control can then contain an array of controls, but it is this class which acts as the virtual Windows Form that is referencing the user control.
PropertyTranslator	This is the only delegate in this namespace. It is used within your Visual Basic code to enable you to translate properties from a WindowsFormsHost control to a WPF Element Host control (and vice versa). Essentially, you provide it with the property to be updated and the value to update that property with, and this method passes that value across the boundary from one UI model to the other. It works in conjunction with the PropertyMap class.

These classes enable your application to host controls within its display area. As noted, when you add the appropriate host class to your display area, it contains a control. This element contains only a single control in order to allow the integration library to assign this control the display area allocated to the host. Thus, when you assign a control to a WindowsFormsHost, behind the scenes the Margin, Docking, AutoSizing, and Location properties of the WindowsFormsHost control are automatically applied to the Child control. These properties are then controlled via the host for your outermost control.

You might still want to control the layout characteristics of elements within the control hosted by the WPF, but you should think of the top-level control, which is the child, as being controlled by the host object. Similarly, the ElementHost control automatically controls the display characteristics associated, including the following properties: Height, Width, Margin, HorizontalAlignment, and VerticalAlignment. In both cases, the host control acts as the virtual display area for the hosted control, and you should manage that display area via the host control, not the child it contains. Even though both controls are targeted at area controls such as user controls and panels, their purpose is to access controls and features across the UI display models.

Hosting WPF Controls in Windows Forms

Enabling you to host WPF controls within your existing Windows Forms–based applications is key to giving you an opportunity to introduce new functionality that requires the capabilities of WPF without forcing you to entirely rewrite your application. This way, even as you work on upgrading an existing application to WPF, you aren't forced to take on a single large project. As for the integration itself, it isn't page- or window-based, although you can introduce new WPF windows to an existing application. The integration is focused on enabling you to incorporate new controls into your existing application.

Accordingly, the model is based around the idea that you can encapsulate the functionality of a new WPF control as a user control. This has a couple of key advantages, the first being that if you've been working with .NET, you are already familiar with user controls and how they function. Once again, the paradigms of previous user-interface models appear and are reused within WPF. The second big advantage to having this modeled around user controls is that as more of your application moves to WPF, you don't have to rewrite the user controls you create today when later they are used within a pure WPF environment.

At some point you'll move the user control outside of the integration `ElementHost` control that will host it in Windows Forms. However, the underlying control can remain unchanged. To demonstrate integration, it is assumed that you have downloaded and installed the package Visual Studio 2005 Extensions for .NET Framework 3.0 (WCF & WPF), November 2006 CTP, and its prerequisites, as described in Chapter 17. This package updates Visual Studio 2005 and, as illustrated in Figure 17-3 from that chapter, provides three new templates for creating WPF projects. The one you need for Windows Forms Integration is the Windows Control Library.

However, the first step is to open Visual Studio 2005 and go to the New Project dialog. From here, select the Windows category of Templates and create a new Windows Forms application. For example purposes you can name this `ProVBWinForm_Interop`. As discussed in Chapter 13, Visual Studio uses the template to create a new Windows Forms project. At this point, using the File menu, add a second project to your solution.

This time, select the .NET Framework 3.0 category, and instead of creating a new application create a new Custom Control Library (WPF). For demonstration purposes, use the name `InteropControlLibrary`. When you are done, the Visual Studio Solution Explorer will look similar to what is shown in Figure 18-1. The next step is to add the customization to the newly created WPF library, after which the Windows Form application will be updated to reference the integration library and the new WPF control.

The first step in customization is to add a splitter to the control's surface area. You may find that your newly created control has no actual display area. That's because the control is designed to automatically adapt to display controls placed on it. For this example, edit the XAML for your control and add `Height` and `Width` attributes to the user control. You can use a height of 281 pixels and a width of 230 characters. Note that instead of assigning a size to the user control, you could assign a fixed size to the grid with the same results.

Now divide this grid. By selecting the display area for your control, you'll find that if you move your mouse over the left edge, small horizontal and vertical windows appear around the control. As you move your mouse up and down within this display area, a horizontal line and a positional arrow appear.

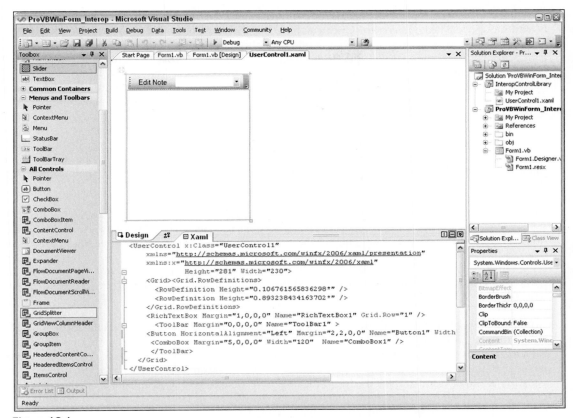

Figure 18-1

On either side of the point representing your mouse are numbers in the small vertical window; these represent the number of pixels in the display above and below your cursor, respectively. By clicking in that window you create a Grid.RowDefinition:

```
<Grid.RowDefinitions>
    <RowDefinition Height="0.106761565836298*" />
    <RowDefinition Height="0.893238434163702*" />
</Grid.RowDefinitions>
```

The preceding lines of XAML demonstrate the type of addition to the Grid control definition you should see. Looking at the generated XAML, note that each of the two defined rows represent a percentage of the screen. Thus, as the screen resizes these areas will both increase in height. You can change this default behavior by changing the Height attribute of the row definitions. Instead of using a percentage, you could in fact use an integer value representing a number of pixels; and if only one of the two rows is assigned this Height attribute, then the remaining row automatically expands to fill the remaining display area. The Grid.RowDefinition settings create the boundary between the toolbar and the main display area for the user control shown in Figure 18-1.

The goal is to create a control that has the appearance of a toolbar, with a button and drop-down list box sitting above a text edit control. Once you have the grid row positioned in the upper quarter of the control's display area, drag a `RichTextBox` into the bottom portion of the display area. You can give it a set of zero or near-zero margins, and delete any `Height` and `Width` properties for this control. This will bind the control to the borders of its display area. For this example, the control's definition should include the statement `Grid.Row="1"`. Because the grid contains two rows, and because the rows are viewed as a zero-based array of display panes, this places the control in the second pane; without this definition, as you'll see with the toolbar, items are associated with `Grid.Row` zero.

The next step is to add a new `ToolBar` control to the display. Similar to the way in which you just added a `RichTextBox` control to the lower pane, now add a `ToolBar` control to the upper window. Again edit the `Margin` settings, making the `ToolBar` fill the entire display area. Next, drag a `Button` control from the toolbox into the display area of the `ToolBar`.

Unfortunately, the default behavior of the designer doesn't currently layer this `Button` within the `ToolBar`, so edit the XAML again. In this case, remove the closing slash "/" from the `ToolBar` declaration and then add a separate closing tag for the `ToolBar`. Place this closing tag on the line below your newly added `Button` control. Then edit the margin settings for the button so that you bind the display within the toolbar and fill the vertical area of the toolbar. To better manage the size of the `Button`, add a `Width` property set to a value such as 75. In addition, change the display value of the text for the button to `Edit Note`.

Add a `ComboBox` to the display next to the button. If, when you drag and drop it on the form, it isn't automatically placed on the toolbar, move the default definition of the `ComboBox` within the definition of the toolbar. Edit the `Margin` settings, but in this case the first value isn't the distance in pixels from the left edge of the display area; instead, it is the number of pixels from the control to the left. Thus, a number such as 5 indicates that the left edge of the `ComboBox` should be placed 5 pixels from the right edge of the `Edit Note` button. In order to finish defining the display of the `ComboBox`, set its remaining margin settings to 0 and assign it a default width of 120 pixels.

The preceding steps define the simple control shown in Figure 18-1; the complete XAML is shown in the following code block. This completes the definition of your sample WPF control library, so compile your application to ensure there aren't any pending errors.

```
<UserControl x:Class="UserControl1"
    xmlns="http://schemas.microsoft.com/winfx/2006/xaml/presentation"
    xmlns:x="http://schemas.microsoft.com/winfx/2006/xaml"
            Height="281" Width="230">
    <Grid><Grid.RowDefinitions>
      <RowDefinition Height="0.106761565836298*" />
      <RowDefinition Height="0.893238434163702*" />
    </Grid.RowDefinitions>
    <RichTextBox Margin="1,0,0,0" Name="RichTextBox1" Grid.Row="1" />
      <ToolBar Margin="0,0,0,0" Name="ToolBar1" >
    <Button HorizontalAlignment="Left" Margin="2,0,0,0" Name="Button1"
Width="75">Edit Note</Button>
      <ComboBox Margin="5,0,0,0" Width="120"  Name="ComboBox1" />
      </ToolBar>
  </Grid>
</UserControl>
```

The next step is to customize the Windows Forms application. Begin by adding the three required references that enable you to embed this control. The first is the `Windows.Forms.Integration` library, the second is the .NET 3.0 `PresentationCore` library, and the last is the `InteropControlLibrary`. As shown earlier, you can access the project properties for your Windows Forms project (in the References tab).

Choose to add references, and in the list of available .NET libraries you'll find `PresentationCore.dll` available as a reference. Other presentation libraries are also available from this screen, and you can choose to add these to your project as well.

Using the Browse button, navigate to `C:\Program Files\Reference Assemblies\Microsoft\Framework\v3.0` and add the `WindowsFormsIntegration.dll` assembly to your project. Finally, switch to the project's References tab and add a reference to your local project.

Now go to the design view for the `Form1.vb` file that was created by the Windows Forms template when you created this project. Extend the default size of the design surface with the size of your control in mind. Make sure that the form has enough height to place a command `Button` below the WPF user control, and drag and drop a button onto your form. This demonstration isn't going to customize this button or its events, but it does simplify the next step.

Looking through the Toolbox, you will probably find that the `ElementHost` control associated with the interface library isn't available. The solution is to add it directly into `Forms1.Designer.vb`. To access this form, use the Solution Explorer to display all files. Then, looking below `Form1.vb`, you'll find the design file. Double-click to open the file and you'll see the generated partial class definition associated with your form. The next code block contains the bottom half of this file:

```
'NOTE: The following procedure is required by the Windows Form Designer
'It can be modified using the Windows Form Designer.
'Do not modify it using the code editor.
<System.Diagnostics.DebuggerStepThrough()> _
Private Sub InitializeComponent()
    Me.Button1 = New System.Windows.Forms.Button
    Me.ElementHost1 = New System.Windows.Forms.Integration.ElementHost
    Me.SuspendLayout()
    '
    'Button1
    '
    Me.Button1.Location = New System.Drawing.Point(96, 238)
    Me.Button1.Name = "Button1"
    Me.Button1.Size = New System.Drawing.Size(75, 23)
    Me.Button1.TabIndex = 0
    Me.Button1.Text = "Button1"
    Me.Button1.UseVisualStyleBackColor = True
    '
    'ElementHost1
    '
    Me.ElementHost1.Location = New System.Drawing.Point(0, 0)
    Me.ElementHost1.Name = "ElementHost1"
    Me.ElementHost1.Size = New System.Drawing.Size(300, 230)
    Me.ElementHost1.TabIndex = 1
    Me.ElementHost1.BackColor = System.Drawing.SystemColors.Control
    '
```

```
'Form1
'
Me.AutoScaleDimensions = New System.Drawing.SizeF(6.0!, 13.0!)
Me.AutoScaleMode = System.Windows.Forms.AutoScaleMode.Font
Me.ClientSize = New System.Drawing.Size(292, 273)
Me.Controls.Add(Me.Button1)
Me.Controls.Add(Me.ElementHost1)
Me.Name = "Form1"
Me.Text = "Form1"
Me.ResumeLayout(False)

End Sub
Friend WithEvents Button1 As System.Windows.Forms.Button
Private WithEvents ElementHost1 As System.Windows.Forms.Integration.ElementHost
End Class
```

At this point, disregard the note included in this file and edit the file to add the ElementHost control to your form. Working from top to bottom in this file, the first step is to add a new instance of the ElementHost control:

```
Me.ElementHost1 = New System.Windows.Forms.Integration.ElementHost
```

This line assigns an instance of an ElementHost control to the variable ElementHost1, which you will define later in this process. The next step is to copy the information associated with the Button that was added in order to define the characteristics of your newly added control. The definition of the button's properties provides a template, which you can then customize to define the properties for the host control:

```
'
'ElementHost1
'
Me.ElementHost1.Location = New System.Drawing.Point(0, 0)
Me.ElementHost1.Name = "ElementHost1"
Me.ElementHost1.Size = New System.Drawing.Size(300, 230)
Me.ElementHost1.TabIndex = 1
Me.ElementHost1.BackColor = System.Drawing.SystemColors.Control
```

As shown, the location of the control can be placed in the upper-left corner of the display; the name of the control is assigned to match the variable name; and the size is set large enough to encapsulate your entire WPF control's display area. The TabIndex is optional and in this case can be set to 1, which leaves only the back color. Note that instead of the property defined for the button, here the property being referenced is BackColor. In the preceding sample code, it is set to match the default background color of the form, but if you want to highlight the bounds of your ElementHost control you can easily set this to a different color. The next step is to add your new control instance to the array of controls contained on the form:

```
Me.Controls.Add(Me.ElementHost1)
```

This adds your instance of the ElementHost control to the control array referenced by the Windows Form. The final step is to add the declaration of the ElementHost1 variable. This is placed along with the declaration of your button control at the bottom of the file. This declaration needs to include the

`WithEvents` modifier, as you want your application to be able to raise and respond to events associated with the contents of the host control:

```
Private WithEvents ElementHost1 As System.Windows.Forms.Integration.ElementHost
```

Note that we haven't yet added an instance of the actual WPF control that you actually want to embed in your application. The reason for this has to do with the properties that `ElementHost` currently exposes in Visual Studio 2005. If you save your changes to `Form1.Designer.vb` and switch to design view for Form1, your display should look similar to the one shown in Figure 18-2. Note the expanded Properties pane. This is currently set to display/edit the properties for `ElementHost1`.

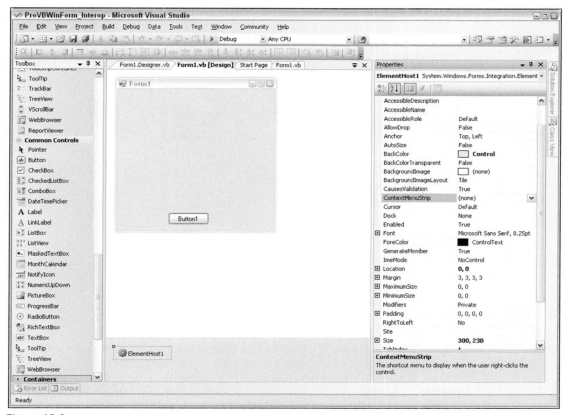

Figure 18-2

This list of properties looks similar to the lists available for other Windows Forms controls. You can modify the color settings of the host control and generally customize its layout details. Visual Studio automatically regenerates the `Form1.Designer.vb` file. The problem is that the `Child` property of the `ElementHost` control is not in this list. This is a problem because if you do attempt to place a reference to that property into the designer-generated code, then whenever anyone changes one of these properties in the designer, Visual Studio won't regenerate that code block because it doesn't recognize that property.

The result is that with this version of the WPF extensions for Visual Studio, you need to assign the `Child` property in the `Load` event of the form. Thus, double-click on the surface of your form and have Visual Studio generate the `Form1_Load` event handler. To this event handler add the line of code that instantiates an instance of your `InteropControlLibrary UserControl1` object as the `Child` control for your `Element Host` control:

```
Public Class Form1

    Private Sub Form1_Load(ByVal sender As Object, ByVal e As System.EventArgs)
Handles Me.Load
        Me.ElementHost1.Child = New InteropControlLibrary.UserControl1()
    End Sub
End Class
```

With the preceding code in place, it's time to build and run your application. When you review the design display, note that your embedded WPF control does not display in design view because it is not loaded. However, after building and running your control you should see a display similar to the one shown in Figure 18-3.

Figure 18-3

This illustrates how you can create a new WPF component that can be incorporated into an existing Windows Forms application. Therefore, you can start the process of migrating your application to WPF while still focusing the majority of your available resources on adding new capabilities to your existing application. Migration means you are not forced to attempt to spend the majority of your cycles rewriting your existing interface. Instead, you can integrate these two display methodologies. The preceding example demonstrates one way of working with a WPF control within a Windows Forms application.

Other methods for carrying out the same tasks, including adding WPF controls within the context of the same project, are also possible. Defining WPF controls within a Windows Forms project reduces your ability to migrate your control into a larger WPF model, and requires that you edit the project file to instruct MSBuild to include the WPF targets. Editing your MSBuild file is demonstrated in Chapter 17 if you choose to approach WPF integration using this method. However, because at some point you may have migrated all but just a few key complex controls, you may find that instead you want to host these Windows Forms controls within a WPF page or window. Using the method demonstrated in this chapter makes that transition easy, as you'll just be hosting Windows Forms controls in WPF.

Hosting Windows Forms Controls in WPF

In the case of WPF hosting Windows Forms controls, you might choose to do this if you have an existing application that relies on certain controls that have not yet been implemented in WPF. For example, the following list of controls are not supported in WPF in .NET 3.0:

BindingNavigator	ColorDialog	DataGridView
DateTimePicker	ErrorProvider	FolderBrowserDialog
FontDialog	HelpProvider	ImageList
LinkLable	MaskedTextBox	MonthCalendar
NotifyIcon	PageSetupDialog	PrintDocument
PrintPreviewDialog	PropertyGrid	

In addition to this list of controls that aren't directly supported, still other controls may behave differently in this release. For example, the ComboBox control in WPF doesn't provide built-in support for AutoComplete. In other cases, such as the HelpProvider (F1 Help), a control isn't supported because the WPF provides an alternative implementation. Even if you have an application in which the existing user interface takes advantage of one of the preceding control's features, it is understandable that you might be interested in integrating your existing investment in the next version of your application.

As noted, this isn't an ideal scenario, and it's likely that with the next release of Visual Studio and its companion .NET upgrade, tentatively named .NET 3.5, the control you need will be available. However, in this initial WPF release there is a real possibility that if you have heavily leveraged a DataGridView control, you will want to reuse your existing control as opposed to attempting to design a custom replacement.

To walk through this process, create a new WPF Windows Application called WPFInterop. This process is described in Chapter 17, so once you have that application, go straight back to the File menu and use the Add option to add a second project to this solution. This time, pick a Windows Control Library called EmbeddedControl. Again, Visual Studio will execute the template to create a new project. At this point you will have access to a new control called UserControl1. Go to the designer for this new user control and add a Button and a DataGridView control to the design surface, as shown in Figure 18- 4.

Figure 18-4 shows one way to arrange these controls. For the purposes of this demonstration, these controls are static so you can add the columns shown in the grid manually through Visual Studio. Resize the grid to fit within the display area of your user control. This demonstration focuses on display characteristics, so there is no need to edit the default code-behind or provide an action for the click event of the button.

Having created a new UserControl1, build the project so that the EmbeddedControl has been compiled, and then close this window. The next step is to update your WPF project with the appropriate references. Three references need to be added. From the Project Settings window, select the References tab. Add a reference to the .NET assembly System.Windows.Forms. Then, using the Browse button, navigate to the Reference Assemblies directory mentioned earlier in this chapter. Go to the .NET 3.0 folder to add a reference to WindowsFormIntegration.dll. Finally, add a new project reference to the EmbeddedControl project. After adding all three references, close the Project Settings window and recompile the project.

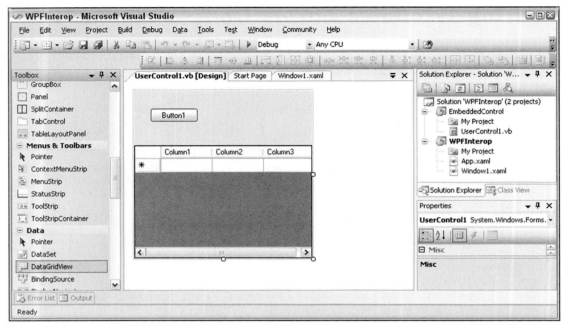

Figure 18-4

Having created a new user control and added the references, open the `Window1.xaml` file that's created with this template. In that XAML file you'll see the "Window" declaration. This declaration in Visual Studio imports two namespaces, as discussed in Chapter 17. You need to add two additional references. The first is for the Windows Forms namespace, which you should alias "wf." In the code block that follows, this namespace references `System.Windows.Forms` and includes a second attribute, `assembly`, that references the name of the assembly file:

```
<Window x:Class="Window1"
    xmlns="http://schemas.microsoft.com/winfx/2006/xaml/presentation"
    xmlns:x="http://schemas.microsoft.com/winfx/2006/xaml"
    xmlns:wf ="clr-namespace:System.Windows.Forms;assembly=System.Windows.Forms"
    xmlns:uc ="clr-namespace:EmbeddedControl;assembly=EmbeddedControl"
  Title="WPFInterop" Height="300" Width="300">
```

The second imported namespace is used to reference your `EmbeddedControl` project. In this case, alias this namespace as "uc." This reference to your local project follows the same format as the reference to the `System.Windows.Forms` namespace. The full reference is shown in the preceding code block.

After adding these references, switch to design view and add a button to the upper-right corner of the display. This button will illustrate the fact that although WPF and Windows Forms share the same control, the display of that control is very different. After adding this control, return to the XAML view within Visual Studio (see Figure 18-5). Add the following lines to the default grid after the declaration of the button control:

```
<WindowsFormsHost Margin="0,90,0,0">
  <uc:UserControl1 x:Name="ButtonGrid"></uc:UserControl1>
</WindowsFormsHost>
```

These three lines declare a new `WindowsFormsHost` control and place it 90 pixels below the top edge of your grid. The remaining sides of the control are bound to your window's borders. Within this `WindowsFormsHost` control is an instance of `UserControl1` named `ButtonGrid`.

Until you switch from the XAML window back to your display, you probably won't see that the Visual Studio designer has a problem interpreting this XAML. As shown in Figure 18-5, the design window now shows a very useful "Whoops!" screen. This doesn't mean that your application won't compile and run, but that the designer can't interpret it.

Figure 18-5

In case you have a compilation problem or are uncertain of the contents of the XAML file shown in Figure 18-5, the full `Window1.xaml` file is shown in the following code block:

```
<Window x:Class="Window1"
    xmlns="http://schemas.microsoft.com/winfx/2006/xaml/presentation"
    xmlns:x="http://schemas.microsoft.com/winfx/2006/xaml"
    xmlns:wf ="clr-namespace:System.Windows.Forms;assembly=System.Windows.Forms"
    xmlns:uc ="clr-namespace:EmbeddedControl;assembly=EmbeddedControl"
  Title="WPFInterop" Height="300" Width="300">
    <Grid>
        <Button Height="23" HorizontalAlignment="Left" Margin="29,43,0,0"
Name="Button1" VerticalAlignment="Top" Width="75">Button</Button>
        <WindowsFormsHost Margin="0,90,0,0">
            <uc:UserControl1 x:Name="ButtonGrid"></uc:UserControl1>
        </WindowsFormsHost>
    </Grid>
</Window>
```

At this point you can run the application. You should see the results shown in Figure 18-6.

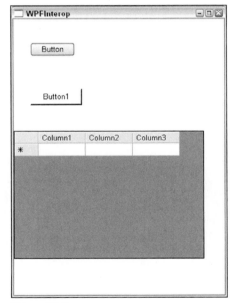

Figure 18-6

The first item that should jump out at you is that the `EmbeddedControl` has lost the Windows XP visual styling. Referring back to Figure 18-6, you can confirm that this styling was present in the designer for this control. However, the integration library has limitations, much like those found in the new design tools you are using in Visual Studio 2005. To resolve this issue, go to the code-behind file for your

`Window1.xaml` file, `Window1.xaml.vb`. Within the `New` method, either before or after the call to `InitializeComponent()`, add the following line of code:

```
System.Windows.Forms.Application.EnableVisualStyles()
```

Rerun the application. The visual styling is now correct. However, you should also be able to see that the way WPF and Windows Forms renders this style on a similar control is still different. Thus, you'll want to ensure that you minimize the number of similar controls you reference on different sides of the host boundary. In this case, you simply needed to manually reset the display settings for your control to indicate that it should use the XP styling; however, this visual provides an excellent introduction to the next topic.

Integration Limitations

The challenge with integration is that these two display models don't operate under the same set of paradigms. The thing to remember, then, is that when you are working with encapsulating a control, that control — be it WPF or Windows Forms — will be affected by the environment in which it is hosted. For example, if you host a WPF control inside a Windows Forms application, then the ability to control low-level graphical display characteristics such as opacity or background is driven by the rules for Windows Forms. Unlike WPF, which layers control characteristics supporting the display of a control at a layer below the current control, Windows Forms controls are contained; when the control doesn't paint a background on your WPF control, the display may see that region as not painted and use a black background instead. Note that setting the `Transparency` property is supported when hosting WPF controls on a Windows Form. You can play with the background color used for the `ElementHost` control earlier in this chapter to get a feel for this issue.

Recognizing that the host control is often limited by the underlying environment containing it is a good guide for predicting limitations. Although sometimes the actual characteristics of the parent application framework might come as a surprise, as you gain more experience with WPF you'll be able to predict where issues are likely to exist. For example, you can create both window- and page-based WPF applications, but these applications work on a different model, as `page`-based WPF application windows are stateless. To support this stateless nature, the `WindowsFormsHost` control fully refreshes the contained control each time the `page` is refreshed — losing any user input that you might expect to remain within a Windows control.

Another issue can arise with the advanced scaling capabilities of WPF. While Windows Forms controls are scalable, Windows Forms doesn't support the concept of scaling down to 0 and then restoring properly.

Similarly, be aware of the message loop, current control focus, and property mapping of hosted controls. The host controls support passing messages to the controls they contain, but across the application the ordering of messages may not occur in the expected order. Similarly, when a `WindowsFormsHost` control has passed focus to a contained control and then the form is minimized, the host control may lose track of which control within its `Child` has that focus. As a result, even though the unseen host has the current focus within your WPF application, there is no visible control with that focus. Finally, there are additional potential issues with property mapping other than the background issue described earlier, so you need to watch the behavior of these controls carefully.

The preceding list is not a complete list of potential issues you may encounter when attempting to integrate these two distinct user-interface implementations. One final warning is that you can't nest host controls. Both Windows Forms and WPF can contain multiple-host controls within a given window, but each of these host controls must be separate and of the same type. Thus, you can't create a WPF application that will host a `WindowsFormsHost` control in such a way that a portion of that control contains an `ElementHost` control. In other words, controls hosted in one environment can't host controls that are part of the environment hosting them. If you're integrating controls, try to minimize the number of user controls or panels containing the host controls so that you don't accidentally attempt to nest the embedded host controls in another layer of integration.

Summary

This chapter extended the coverage of WPF with regard to how you can make your Windows Forms applications work with WPF controls. It introduced the `WindowsFormsIntegration` library and the capability to have WPF and Windows Forms components provide elements of an application user interface. Similar to other transitional libraries, the focus is on supporting business needs and not on complete support for the features of Windows Forms within the WPF environment. Key points from this chapter include the following:

❑ It is possible to start a migration to a WPF-based application interface using the `Windows-FormsIntegration` library and the `ElementHost` class.

❑ Such an interface enables you to embed enhanced image processing into an existing Windows Forms application.

❑ Using the `WindowsFormsHost` class enables you to embed a complex business or third-party control that you are not ready to replace within a WPF application.

❑ Using the Interoperability library can support key business-driven components, but it may impact the visual appeal of your user interface.

While this chapter introduced the new integration library, you may have noticed that this isn't being advertised as the greatest feature. This isn't because the feature didn't require significant effort to create or wasn't well designed. This library is an excellent resource — in the limited area for which it was designed: to support your transition from Windows Forms to WPF. Using this library across one or two releases of your application as you migrate to a WPF-based user interface is an excellent way to manage complexity, but always remember that you want to fully commit to the WPF-based paradigms, which means moving beyond this library.

Finally, if you do have the opportunity to create a complete new user interface and can avoid the added complexity associated with working with this integration class, then you should.

19

Working with ASP.NET 2.0

The evolution of ASP.NET continues! The progression from Active Server Pages 3.0 to ASP.NET 1.0 was revolutionary, to say the least, and we are here to tell you that the evolution from ASP.NET 1.0/1.1 to ASP.NET 2.0 is just as exciting and dramatic.

The introduction of ASP.NET 1.0/1.1 changed the Web programming model; but ASP.NET 2.0 is just as revolutionary in the way it increases productivity. The primary goal of ASP.NET 2.0 is to enable you to build powerful, secure, and dynamic applications using the least possible amount of code. Although this book covers the new features provided by ASP.NET 2.0, it also covers most of what the ASP.NET technology offers.

The Goals of ASP.NET 2.0

ASP.NET 2.0 is a major release of the product and an integral part of the .NET Framework 2.0. This release of ASP.NET heralds a new wave of development that should eliminate any of the remaining barriers to adopting this new way of coding Web applications.

When the ASP.NET team started working on ASP.NET 2.0, it had specific goals to achieve. These goals focused around developer productivity, administration and management, as well as performance and scalability. These goals are achieved with this milestone product release.

Developer Productivity

Much of the focus of ASP.NET 2.0 is on productivity. Huge productivity gains were made with the release of ASP.NET 1.*x* — could it be possible to expand further on those gains?

One goal the development team had for ASP.NET 2.0 was to eliminate much of the tedious coding that ASP.NET originally required and to make common ASP.NET tasks easier. The team developing ASP.NET 2.0 had the goal of reducing by two-thirds the number of lines of code required for an ASP.NET application. It succeeded; you will be amazed at how quickly you can create your applications in ASP.NET 2.0.

Administration and Management

The initial release of ASP.NET focused on the developer, and little thought was given to the people who had to administer and manage all the ASP.NET applications that were built and deployed. Instead of working with consoles and wizards as they did in the past, administrators and managers of these new applications now had to work with unfamiliar XML configuration files such as `machine.config` and `web.config`.

To remedy this situation, ASP.NET 2.0 now includes a Microsoft Management Console (MMC) snap-in that enables Web application administrators to edit configuration settings easily on-the-fly through IIS.

Performance and Scalability

One of the goals for ASP.NET 2.0 set by the Microsoft team was to provide the world's fastest Web application server. This book addresses a number of performance enhancements available in ASP.NET 2.0.

One of the most exciting performance enhancements is the new caching capability aimed at exploiting Microsoft's SQL Server. ASP.NET 2.0 now includes a feature called *SQL cache invalidation*. Before ASP.NET 2.0, it was possible to cache the results that came from SQL Server and to update the cache based on a time interval — for example, every 15 seconds or so. This meant that the end user might see stale data if the result set changed sometime during that 15-second interval.

In some cases, this time interval result set is unacceptable. In an ideal situation, the result set stored in the cache is destroyed if any underlying change occurs in the source from which the result set is retrieved — in this case, SQL Server. With ASP.NET 2.0, you can make this happen with the use of SQL cache invalidation. When the result set from SQL Server changes, the output cache is triggered to change, and the end user always sees the latest result set. The data presented is never stale.

Other big areas of change in ASP.NET are performance and scalability. ASP.NET 2.0 now provides 64-bit support, which means you can now run your ASP.NET applications on 64-bit Intel or AMD processors. In addition, because ASP.NET 2.0 is fully backwardly compatible with ASP.NET 1.0 and 1.1, you can now take any former ASP.NET application, recompile it on the .NET Framework 2.0, and run it on a 64-bit processor.

New Compilation System

In ASP.NET 2.0, code is constructed and compiled in a new way. Compilation in ASP.NET 1.0 was always a tricky scenario. With ASP.NET 1.0, you could build an application's code-behind files using ASP.NET and Visual Studio, deploy it, and then watch as the `.aspx` files were compiled page by page as each page was requested. If you made any changes to the code-behind file in ASP.NET 1.0, it was not reflected in your application until the entire application was rebuilt. That meant that the same page-by-page request had to be done again before the entire application was recompiled.

Everything regarding how ASP.NET 1.0 worked with classes and compilation changed with the release of ASP.NET 2.0. The mechanics of the new compilation system actually begin with how a page is structured. In ASP.NET 1.0, you constructed your pages either by using the code-behind model or by placing all the server code inline between `<script>` tags on your `.aspx` page. Most pages were constructed using the code-behind model because this was the default when using Visual Studio .NET 2002 or 2003. It was quite difficult to create your page using the inline style in these IDEs. If you did, you were deprived of the use of IntelliSense, which can be quite the lifesaver when working with the tremendously large collection of classes that the .NET Framework offers.

ASP.NET 2.0 offers a new code-behind model because the .NET Framework 2.0 offers the capability to work with *partial classes* (also called *partial types*). Upon compilation, the separate files are combined into a single offering. This gives you much cleaner code-behind pages. The code that was part of the Web Form Designer Generated section of your classes is separated from the code-behind classes that you create yourself. Contrast this with the ASP.NET 1.0 .aspx file's need to derive from its own code-behind file to represent a single logical page.

ASP.NET 2.0 applications can include an \App_Code directory in which you place your class's source. Any class placed here is dynamically compiled and reflected in the application. Unlike ASP.NET 1.0, you do not use a separate build process when you make changes. This enables a "just save and hit" deployment model like the one in classic ASP 3.0. Visual Studio Web Developer also automatically provides IntelliSense for any objects that are placed in the \App_Code directory, whether you are working with the code-behind model or are coding inline.

ASP.NET 2.0 also provides you with tools that enable you to precompile your ASP.NET applications — both .aspx pages and code behind — so that no page within your application has latency when it is retrieved for the first time. This is also a great way to discover any errors in the pages without invoking every page. Precompiling your ASP.NET 2.0 applications is as simple as using aspnet_compiler.exe and employing some of the available flags. As you precompile your entire application, you receive error notifications if any errors are found anywhere within it. Precompilation also enables you to deliver only the created assembly to the deployment server, thereby protecting your code from snooping, unwanted changes, and tampering after deployment.

Health Monitoring for Your ASP.NET Applications

The built-in health-monitoring capabilities are new and rather significant features designed to make it easier to manage a deployed ASP.NET application. Health monitoring provides what the term implies — the capability to monitor the health and performance of your deployed ASP.NET applications.

ASP.NET health monitoring is built around various health-monitoring events (which are referred to as *Web events*) occurring in your application. Using the new health monitoring system enables you to perform event logging for Web events such as failed logins, application starts and stops, or any unhandled exceptions. The event logging can occur in more than one place, so you can log to the Event Log or even back to a database. In addition to performing this disk-based logging, you can also use the system to e-mail health-monitoring information.

Besides working with specific events in your application, you can use the health-monitoring system to take health snapshots of a running application. As with most systems built into ASP.NET 2.0, you can extend the health-monitoring system and create your own events for recording application information.

Reading and Writing Configuration Settings

Using the WebConfigurationManager class, you have the capability to read and write to the server or application configuration files. This means that you can write and read settings in the machine.config or the web.config files that your application uses.

The capability to read and write to configuration files is not limited to working with the local machine in which your application resides. You can also perform these operations on remote servers and applications.

Of course, a GUI way exists for performing these read or change operations on the configuration files at your disposal. Most exciting, however, is that the built-in GUI tools that provide this functionality (such as the new ASP.NET MMC snap-in) use the WebConfigurationManager class that is also available for building custom administration tools.

Localization

ASP.NET 2.0 improves upon previous versions by making it easier to localize applications. In addition to using Visual Studio, you can create resource files (.resx) that enable you to dynamically change the pages you create based upon the culture settings of the requester.

ASP.NET 2.0 also provides the capability to provide resources application-wide or just to particular pages in your application through the use of two new application folders — App_GlobalResources and App_LocalResources.

The items defined in any .resx files you create are then accessible directly in the ASP.NET server controls or programmatically, using expressions such as the following:

```
<%= Resources.Resource.Question %>
```

This new system is straightforward and simple to implement.

New Objects for Accessing Data

One of the more code-intensive tasks in ASP.NET 1.0 was the retrieval of data. In many cases, this meant working with a number of objects. If you have been working with ASP.NET for a while, you know that it is an involved process to display data from a Microsoft SQL Server table within a DataGrid server control. For instance, you first had to create a number of new objects, including a SqlConnection object followed by a SqlCommand object. When those objects were in place, you then created a SqlDataReader to populate your DataGrid by binding the result to the DataGrid. In the end, a table appeared containing the contents of the data you were retrieving (such as the Customers table from the Northwind database).

ASP.NET 2.0 eliminates this intensive procedure with the introduction of a new set of objects that work specifically with data access and retrieval. These new data controls are so easy to use that you access and retrieve data to populate your ASP.NET server controls without writing any code. Even better, this new functionality is not limited to Microsoft's SQL Server. In fact, several data source server controls are at your disposal, and you can create your own. In addition to the SqlDataSource server control, ASP.NET 2.0 introduces the AccessDataSource, XmlDataSource, ObjectDataSource, and SiteMapDataSource server controls.

New Server Controls

So far, you have seen a number of new server controls that you can use when building your ASP.NET 2.0 pages. For example, the preceding section described the new data source server controls that you can use to access different kinds of datastores. You also saw the use of the new GridView server control, which is an enhanced version of the previous DataGrid control used in ASP.NET 1.0.

ASP.NET 2.0 provides more than 50 additional new server controls! In fact, so many new server controls have been introduced that the next IDE for building ASP.NET applications, Visual Studio 2005, had to reorganize the Toolbox in which all the server controls are stored. They are now separated into categories, unlike the list used in Visual Studio .NET or the ASP.NET Web Matrix. The new Visual Studio 2005 Toolbox is shown in Figure 19-1.

Figure 19-1

A New IDE for Building ASP.NET 2.0 Pages

With ASP.NET 1.0/1.1, you can build your ASP.NET application using Notepad, Visual Studio .NET 2002 and 2003, as well as the hobbyist-focused ASP.NET Web Matrix. ASP.NET 2.0 adds another IDE to the Visual Studio family — Visual Studio 2005. Visual Studio 2005 offers some dramatic enhancements that completely change the way in which you build your ASP.NET applications.

One rather dramatic change to the IDE is that Visual Studio 2005 builds applications using a *file-based system*, not the project-based system used by Visual Studio .NET. When using Visual Studio .NET in the past, you had to create new projects (for example, an ASP.NET Web Application project). This process created a number of project files in your application in addition to the `Default.aspx` page. Because everything was based on a singular project, it was very difficult to develop applications in a team environment.

Conversely, Web projects in Visual Studio 2005 are based on a file-system approach. No project files are included in your project, which makes it easy for multiple developers to work on a single application without bumping into each other. Other changes are those to the compilation system discussed earlier. You can now build your ASP.NET pages using the inline model or the new code-behind model. Either way, you have full IntelliSense capabilities. This, in itself, is powerful and innovative. Figure 19-2 shows IntelliSense running from an ASP.NET page that is being built using the inline model.

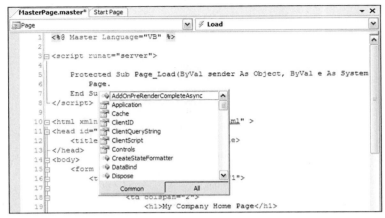

Figure 19-2

Another feature of Visual Studio 2005 borrowed from the ASP.NET Web Matrix is that you do not need IIS on your development machine. Visual Studio 2005 has a built-in Web server that enables you to launch pages from any folder in your system with relative ease.

Building ASP.NET Applications

If you are new to ASP.NET and building your first set of applications in ASP.NET 2.0, you may be amazed by all the wonderful new server controls it provides. You may marvel at how it enables you to work with data more effectively using the new data providers, and you may be impressed at how easily you can build in security and personalization.

The outstanding capabilities of ASP.NET 2.0 do not end there, however. This section looks at many exciting additions that facilitate working with ASP.NET pages and applications. One of the first steps you, as the developer, should take when starting a project is to become familiar with the foundation you are building on and the options available for customizing that foundation.

Application Location Options

With ASP.NET 2.0, you have the option — using Visual Studio 2005 — to create an application with a virtual directory mapped to IIS, or a standalone application outside the confines of IIS. Whereas Visual Studio .NET forced developers to use IIS for all Web applications, Visual Studio 2005 (and Visual Web Developer Express Edition, for that matter) includes a built-in Web server that you can use for development, much like the one used in the past with the ASP.NET Web Matrix.

> This built-in Web server was previously presented to developers as a code sample called Cassini. In fact, the code for this mini Web server is freely downloadable from the ASP.NET team website found at www.asp.net.

The Built-In Web Server

By default, Visual Studio 2005 builds applications without the use of IIS. You can see this when you select New Web Site in the IDE. By default, the location provided for your application is `C:\Documents and Settings\[user]\My Documents\Visual Studio 2005\WebSites` (shown in Figure 19-3). It is not `C:\Inetpub\wwwroot\` as it would have been in Visual Studio .NET 2003/2002. By default, any site that you build and host inside `C:\Documents and Settings\[user]\My Documents\Visual Studio 2005\WebSites` (or any other folder you create) uses the built-in Web server that is part of Visual Studio 2005. If you use the built-in Web server from Visual Studio 2005, you are not locked into the `Websites` folder; you can create any folder you want in your system.

To change from this default, you have a handful of options. Click the Browse button in the New Web Site dialog. This brings up the Choose Location dialog, shown in Figure 19-4.

Figure 19-3

Figure 19-4

If you continue to use the built-in Web server that Visual Studio 2005 provides, you can choose a new location for your Web application from this dialog. To do so, select a new folder and save your `.aspx` pages and any other associated files to this directory. When using Visual Studio 2005, you can run your application completely from this location. This new way of working with the ASP.NET pages you create is ideal if you don't have access to a Web server, as it enables you to build applications that don't reside on a machine with IIS. This means you can develop ASP.NET applications on operating systems such as Windows XP Home Edition.

IIS

From the Choose Location dialog, you can also change where your application is saved and which type of Web server your application employs. To use IIS (as you probably did when you used Visual Studio .NET 2003/2002), click the Local IIS button. This changes the text area to show you a list of all the virtual application roots on your machine.

To create a new virtual root for your application, highlight Default Web Site. Two accessible buttons appear at the top of the dialog (see Figure 19-5). Looking from left to right, the first button in the upper-right corner of the dialog is for creating a new Web application — or a virtual root. This button is shown as a globe inside a box. The second button enables you to create virtual directories for any of the virtual roots you create. The third button is a delete button, which enables you to delete any selected virtual directories or virtual roots on the server.

Figure 19-5

After you have created the virtual directory you want, click Open. Visual Studio 2005 then goes through the standard process to create your application. But now, instead of depending on the built-in Web server from ASP.NET 2.0, your application will use IIS. When you invoke your application, the URL now consists of something like `http://localhost/myweb/default.aspx`, which means it is using IIS.

FTP

Not only can you decide on the type of Web server for your Web application when you create it using the Choose Location dialog, you can also decide where to locate your application. The previous options built applications that resided on your local server. The FTP option enables you to actually store and even code your applications while they reside on a server somewhere else in your enterprise — or on the other side of the planet. You can also use the FTP capabilities to work on different locations within the same server. This new built-in capability provides a wide range of possible options and represents a major enhancement to the IDE. Previously difficult to accomplish, this task is now quite simple, as illustrated in Figure 19-6.

Figure 19-6

To create your application on a remote server using FTP, simply provide the server name, the port to use, and the directory — as well as any required credentials. If the correct information is provided, then Visual Studio 2005 reaches out to the remote server and creates the appropriate files for the start of your application, just as if it were doing the job locally. From this point on, you can open your project and connect to the remote server using FTP.

Web Site Requiring FrontPage Extensions

The last option in the Choose Location dialog is the Remote Site option (see Figure 19-7). Clicking this button provides a dialog that enables you to connect to a remote or local server that utilizes FrontPage Extensions.

Figure 19-7

The ASP.NET Page Structure Options

ASP.NET 2.0 provides two paths for structuring the code of your ASP.NET pages. The first path utilizes the code-inline model. This model should be familiar to classic ASP 2.0/3.0 developers because all the code is contained within a single `.aspx` page. The second path uses ASP.NET's code-behind model, which allows for code separation of the page's business logic from its presentation logic. In this model, the presentation logic for the page is stored in an `.aspx` page, whereas the logic piece is stored in a separate class file: `.aspx.vb` or `.aspx.cs`.

One of the major complaints about Visual Studio .NET 2002 and 2003 is that it forces you to use the code-behind model when developing your ASP.NET pages because it doesn't understand the code-inline model. The code-behind model in ASP.NET was introduced as a new way to separate the presentation code and business logic. The following example (called Example 1 because it's referred to again later) shows a typical `.aspx` page generated using Visual Studio .NET 2002 or 2003:

```
<%@ Page Language="vb" AutoEventWireup="false" Codebehind="WebForm1.aspx.vb"
    Inherits="WebApplication.WebForm1"%>
<!DOCTYPE HTML PUBLIC "-//W3C//DTD HTML 4.0 Transitional//EN">
<HTML>
 <HEAD>
    <title>WebForm1</title>
    <meta name="GENERATOR" content="Microsoft Visual Studio .NET 7.1">
    <meta name="CODE_LANGUAGE" content="Visual Basic .NET 7.1">
    <meta name="vs_defaultClientScript" content="JavaScript">
    <meta name="vs_targetSchema"
      content="http://schemas.microsoft.com/intellisense/ie5">
 </HEAD>
 <body>
```

```
        <form id="Form1" method="post" runat="server">
           <P>What is your name?<br>
           <asp:TextBox id="TextBox1" runat="server"></asp:TextBox><BR>
           <asp:Button id="Button1" runat="server" Text="Submit"></asp:Button></P>
           <P><asp:Label id="Label1" runat="server"></asp:Label></P>
        </form>
    </body>
</HTML>
```

The code-behind file created within Visual Studio .NET 2002/2003 for the `.aspx` page is shown in the next example (Example 2, for future reference):

```
Public Class WebForm1
    Inherits System.Web.UI.Page

#Region " Web Form Designer Generated Code "

    'This call is required by the Web Form Designer.
    <System.Diagnostics.DebuggerStepThrough()> Private Sub InitializeComponent()

    End Sub
    Protected WithEvents TextBox1 As System.Web.UI.WebControls.TextBox
    Protected WithEvents Button1 As System.Web.UI.WebControls.Button
    Protected WithEvents Label1 As System.Web.UI.WebControls.Label

    'NOTE: The following placeholder declaration is required by the Web Form
       Designer.
    'Do not delete or move it.
    Private designerPlaceholderDeclaration As System.Object

    Private Sub Page_Init(ByVal sender As System.Object, ByVal e As
       System.EventArgs) Handles MyBase.Init
        'CODEGEN: This method call is required by the Web Form Designer
        'Do not modify it using the code editor.
        InitializeComponent()
    End Sub

#End Region

    Private Sub Page_Load(ByVal sender As System.Object, ByVal e As
       System.EventArgs) Handles MyBase.Load
        'Put user code to initialize the page here
    End Sub

    Private Sub Button1_Click(ByVal sender As System.Object, ByVal e As
       System.EventArgs) Handles Button1.Click
        Label1.Text = "Hello " & TextBox1.Text
    End Sub
End Class
```

This code-behind page from ASP.NET 1.0/1.1 shows that a lot of the code that developers never have to deal with is hidden in the `#Region` section of the page. Because ASP.NET 2.0 is built on top of .NET 2.0, it can now take advantage of the new .NET Framework capability of partial classes. Partial classes enable you to separate your classes into multiple class files, which are then combined into a single class when the application is compiled. Because ASP.NET 2.0 combines all this page code for you behind the scenes when the application is compiled, the code-behind files you work with in ASP.NET 2.0 are simpler in appearance and the model is easier to use. You are presented with only the pieces of the class that you need.

Inline Coding

With the .NET Framework 1.0/1.1, developers went out of their way (and outside Visual Studio .NET) to build their ASP.NET pages inline, avoiding the code-behind model that was so heavily promoted by Microsoft and others. Visual Studio 2005 (as well as Visual Web Developer 2005 Express Edition) enables you to build your pages easily using this coding style. To build an ASP.NET page inline instead of using the code-behind model, you simply select the page type from the Add New Item dialog and make sure that the Place Code in Separate File check box is unchecked. You can access this dialog by right-clicking the project or the solution in the Solution Explorer and selecting Add New Item (see Figure 19-8).

Figure 19-8

In fact, many page types have options for both inline and code-behind styles. The following table shows your inline options when selecting files from this dialog:

File Options Using Inline Coding	File Created
Web Form	`.aspx` file
Master Page	`.master` file
Web User Control	`.ascx` file
Web Service	`.asmx` file

By using the Web Form option with a few controls, you get a page that encapsulates not only the presentation logic, but the business logic as well:

```
<%@ Page Language="VB" %>

<!DOCTYPE html PUBLIC "-//W3C//DTD XHTML 1.1//EN"
 "http://www.w3.org/TR/xhtml11/DTD/xhtml11.dtd">

<script runat="server">
    Protected Sub Button1_Click(ByVal sender As Object, _
       ByVal e As System.EventArgs)

        Label1.Text = "Hello " & Textbox1.Text
    End Sub
</script>

<html xmlns="http://www.w3.org/1999/xhtml" >
<head runat="server">
    <title>Simple Page</title>
</head>
<body>
    <form runat="server">
        What is your name?<br />
        <asp:Textbox ID="Textbox1" Runat="server"></asp:Textbox><br />
        <asp:Button ID="Button1" Runat="server" Text="Submit"
         OnClick="Button1_Click" />
        <p><asp:Label ID="Label1" Runat="server"></asp:Label></p>
    </form>
</body>
</html>
```

From this example, you can see that all the business logic is encapsulated between `<script>` tags. The greatest advantage of the inline model is that the business logic and the presentation logic are contained within the same file. Some developers find that having everything in a single viewable instance makes working with the ASP.NET page easier. In addition, Visual Studio 2005 now provides IntelliSense when working with the inline coding model and ASP.NET 2.0. In the past, this capability did not exist. Visual Studio forced you to use the code-behind model; and even if you rigged it so your pages were using the inline model, you lost all IntelliSense capabilities.

New Code-Behind Model

The other option for constructing your ASP.NET 2.0 pages is to build your files using the new code-behind model. We say *new* because, even though the idea of the code-behind model is the same as it was in previous versions of ASP.NET, the code-behind model used in ASP.NET 2.0 is quite different.

To create a new page in your ASP.NET solution that uses the code-behind model, select the page type you want from the New File dialog. To build a page that uses the code-behind model, you first select the page in the Add New Item dialog and make sure the Place Code in Separate File check box is checked. The following table shows you the options for pages that use the code-behind model:

File Options Using Code-Behind	File Created
Web Form	`.aspx` file `.aspx.vb` or `.aspx.cs` file
Master Page	`.master` file `.master.vb` or `.master.cs` file
Web User Control	`.ascx` file `.ascx.vb` or `.ascx.cs` file
Web Service	`.asmx` file `.vb` or `.cs` file

The idea of using the code-behind model is to separate the business logic and presentation logic into separate files. This makes it easier to work with your pages, especially if you are working in a team environment where visual designers work on the UI of the page and coders work on the business logic that sits behind the presentation pieces. In the earlier code labeled Examples 1 and 2, you saw how pages using the code-behind model in ASP.NET 1.0/1.1 were constructed. To see the difference in ASP.NET 2.0, take a look at how its code-behind pages are constructed in the following two examples, the first for the presentation piece and the second for the code-behind piece:

```
<%@ Page Language="VB" AutoEventWireup="false" CodeFile="Default.aspx.vb"
    Inherits="_Default" %>

<!DOCTYPE html PUBLIC "-//W3C//DTD XHTML 1.1//EN"
 "http://www.w3.org/TR/xhtml11/DTD/xhtml11.dtd">

<html xmlns="http://www.w3.org/1999/xhtml" >
<head runat="server">
    <title>Simple Page</title>
</head>
<body>
    <form runat="server">
        What is your name?<br />
        <asp:Textbox ID="Textbox1" Runat="server"></asp:Textbox><br />
        <asp:Button ID="Button1" Runat="server" Text="Submit"
         OnClick="Button1_Click" />
        <p><asp:Label ID="Label1" Runat="server"></asp:Label></p>
    </form>
</body>
</html>
```

Code-behind example:

```
Partial Class _Default
    Inherits System.Web.UI.Page

    Protected Sub Button1_Click(ByVal sender As Object, _
        ByVal e As System.EventArgs) Handles Button1.Click

        Label1.Text = "Hello " & TextBox1.Text
    End Sub
End Class
```

The `.aspx` page using this new ASP.NET 2.0 code-behind model has some attributes in the `Page` directive that are different from those you are familiar with from previous versions of ASP.NET. The first is the `CodeFile` attribute. This new attribute in the `Page` directive is meant to point to the code-behind page that is used with this presentation page. In this case, the value assigned is `Default.aspx.vb`. The second attribute needed is the `Inherits` attribute. This attribute was available in previous versions of ASP.NET, but was infrequently used. This attribute specifies the name of the class that is bound to the page when the page is compiled. The directives are simple enough in ASP.NET 2.0. Take another look at the preceding code-behind page.

The new code-behind page is rather simple in appearance because of the partial class capabilities that .NET 2.0 provides. You can see that the class created in the code-behind file uses partial classes, employing the new `Partial` keyword in Visual Basic 2005. This enables you to simply place the methods that you need in your `Page` class. In this case, you have a button-click event and nothing else.

ASP.NET 2.0 Page Directives

ASP.NET directives are part of every ASP.NET page. You can control the behavior of your ASP.NET pages by using these directives. Here is an example of the `Page` directive:

```
<%@ Page Language="VB" AutoEventWireup="false" CodeFile="Default.aspx.vb"
    Inherits="_Default" %>
```

Eleven directives are at your disposal in your ASP.NET pages or user controls. You use these directives in your applications whether the page uses the code-behind model or the inline coding model.

Basically, these directives are commands that the compiler uses when the page is compiled. Directives are simple to incorporate into your pages. A directive is written in the following format:

```
<%@ [Directive] [Attribute=Value] %>
```

A directive is opened with `<%@` and closed with `%>`. It is best to put these directives at the top of your pages or controls because this is traditionally where developers expect to see them (although the page still compiles if the directives are located elsewhere. Of course, you can also add more than a single attribute to your directive statements, as shown here:

```
<%@ [Directive] [Attribute=Value] [Attribute=Value] %>
```

The following table describes the directives at your disposal in ASP.NET 2.0:

Directive	Description
Assembly	Links an assembly to the page or user control to which it is associated
Control	Page directive meant for use with user controls (.ascx)
Implements	Implements a specified .NET Framework interface
Import	Imports specified namespaces into the page or user control
Master	Enables you to specify a master page — specific attributes and values to use when the page parses or compiles. This directive can be used only with master pages (.master).
MasterType	Associates a class name to a page in order to get at strongly typed references or members contained within the specified master page
OutputCache	Controls the output caching policies of a page or user control
Page	Enables you to define page-specific attributes and values to use when the page parses or compiles. This directive can be used only with ASP.NET pages (.aspx).
PreviousPageType	Enables an ASP.NET page to work with a postback from another page in the application
Reference	Links a page or user control to the current page or user control
Register	Associates aliases with namespaces and class names for notation in custom server control syntax

ASP.NET Page Events

ASP.NET developers consistently work with various events in their server-side code. Many of the events that they work with pertain to specific server controls. For instance, if you want to initiate some action when the end user clicks a button on your Web page, you create a button-click event in your server-side code, as shown in the following example:

```
Protected Sub Button1_Click(sender As Object, e As EventArgs) Handles Button1.Click
    Label1.Text = TextBox1.Text
End Sub
```

In addition to the server controls, developers also want to initiate actions at specific moments when the ASP.NET page is being either created or destroyed. The ASP.NET page itself has always had a number of events for these instances. Following is a list of all the page events you could use in ASP.NET 1.0/1.1:

❏ AbortTransaction

❏ CommitTransaction

❏ DataBinding

❏ Disposed

❏ Error

❏ Init

❏ Load

❏ PreRender

❏ Unload

One popular page event from this list is Load, which is used in VB as shown in the following (called Example 4 for later reference):

```vb
Protected Sub Page_Load(ByVal sender As Object, ByVal e As System.EventArgs)
    Handles Me.Load

    Response.Write("This is the Page_Load event")
End Sub
```

Besides the page events just shown, ASP.NET 2.0 adds the following new events:

❏ InitComplete: Indicates that initialization of the page is completed

❏ LoadComplete: Indicates that the page has been completely loaded into memory

❏ PreInit: Indicates the moment immediately before a page is initialized

❏ PreLoad: Indicates the moment before a page has been loaded into memory

❏ PreRenderComplete: Indicates the moment directly before a page has been rendered in the browser

You construct these new page events just as you did the previously shown page events. For example, you use the PreInit event as follows:

```vb
<script runat="server" language="vb">
    Protected Sub Page_PreInit(ByVal sender As Object, ByVal e As System.EventArgs)
        Page.Theme = Request.QueryString("ThemeChange")
    End Sub
</script>
```

If you create an ASP.NET 2.0 page and turn on tracing, you can see the order in which the main page events are initiated:

1. PreInit

2.   `Init`

3.   `InitComplete`

4.   `PreLoad`

5.   `Load`

6.   `LoadComplete`

7.   `PreRender`

8.   `PreRenderComplete`

9.   `Unload`

With the addition of these new options, you can now work with the page and the controls on the page at many different points in the page-compilation process.

ASP.NET Application Folders

When you create ASP.NET applications, ASP.NET 2.0 uses a file-based approach. You can add as many files and folders as you want within your application without recompiling each and every time a new file is added to the overall solution. ASP.NET 2.0 includes the capability to automatically precompile your ASP.NET applications dynamically.

ASP.NET 1.0/1.1 compiled everything in your solution into a DLL. This isn't necessary with ASP.NET 2.0 because applications have a defined folder structure. Using the ASP.NET 2.0 defined folders, you can have your code automatically compiled for you, your application themes accessible throughout your application, and your globalization resources available whenever you need them. The following sections look at each of these defined folders.

\App_Code Folder

The `\App_Code` folder is meant to store your classes, `.wsdl` files, and typed datasets. Any of these items stored in this folder are then automatically available to all the pages within your solution. The nice thing about the `\App_Code` folder is that when you place something inside it, Visual Studio 2005 automatically detects this and compiles it if it is a class (such as a `.vb` file), automatically creates your XML Web service proxy class (from the `.wsdl` file), or automatically creates a typed dataset for you from your `.xsd` files. After the files are automatically compiled, these items are then immediately available to any of your ASP.NET pages in the same solution. Let's look at how to employ a simple class in your solution using the `\App_Code` folder.

Create an `\App_Code` folder by right-clicking the solution and choosing Add ASP.NET Folder ⇨ App_Code. Note that Visual Studio 2005 treats this folder differently than the other folders in your solution. The `\App_Code` folder appears in a different color (gray), with a document pictured next to the folder icon (see Figure 19-9).

Figure 19-9

After the `\App_Code` folder is in place, right-click the folder and select Add New Item. The Add New Item dialog that appears offers only a few options for the types of files that you can place within this folder, including a Class file, a Text file, a DataSet, a Report, and a Class Diagram if you are using Visual Studio 2005. Visual Web Developer 2005 Express Edition offers only the Class file, Text file, and DataSet file. For the first example, select the file of type Class and name the class `Calculator.vb`. The following code shows how the `Calculator` class should appear:

```vb
Imports Microsoft.VisualBasic

Public Class Calculator
    Public Function Add(ByVal a As Integer, ByVal b As Integer) As Integer
        Return (a + b)
    End Function
End Class
```

Simply save this file, and it is now available to use in any pages in your solution. To see this in action, create a simple `.aspx` page that has just a single `Label` server control. The following example shows the code to place within the `Page_Load` event to make this new class available:

```vb
<%@ Page Language="VB" %>

<!DOCTYPE html PUBLIC "-//W3C//DTD XHTML 1.1//EN"
 "http://www.w3.org/TR/xhtml11/DTD/xhtml11.dtd">

<script runat="server">
    Protected Sub Page_Load(ByVal sender As Object, ByVal e As System.EventArgs)
        Dim myCalc As New Calculator
        Label1.Text = myCalc.Add(12, 12)
    End Sub
</script>
```

When you run this `.aspx` page, note that it utilizes the `Calculator` class without any problem, with no need to compile the class before use. In fact, right after saving the `Calculator` class in your solution or moving the class to the `\App_Code` folder, you also immediately receive IntelliSense capability on the methods that the class exposes (as illustrated in Figure 19-10).

Figure 19-10

To see how Visual Studio 2005 works with the \App_Code folder, open the Calculator class again in the IDE and add a Subtract() method. Your class should now appear as shown here:

```
Imports Microsoft.VisualBasic

Public Class Calculator
    Public Function Add(ByVal a As Integer, ByVal b As Integer) As Integer
        Return (a + b)
    End Function

    Public Function Subtract(ByVal a As Integer, ByVal b As Integer) As Integer
        Return (a - b)
    End Function
End Class
```

After you add the Subtract() method to the Calculator class, save the file and go back to your .aspx page. Note that the class has been recompiled by the IDE, and the new method is now available to your page (see Figure 19-11). You see this directly in IntelliSense.

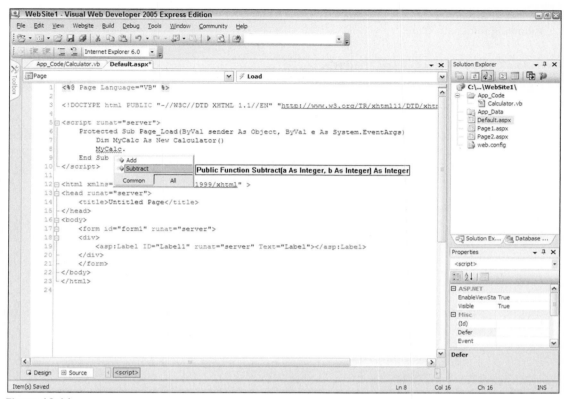

Figure 19-11

Everything placed in the \App_Code folder is compiled into a single assembly. The class files placed within the \App_Code folder are not required to use a specific language. For example, even if all the pages of the solution are written in Visual Basic 2005, the Calculator class in the \App_Code folder of the solution can be built in C# (Calculator.cs).

Because all the classes contained in this folder are built into a single assembly, you *cannot* have classes of different languages sitting in the root \App_Code folder, as in the following example:

```
\App_Code
    Calculator.cs
    AdvancedMath.vb
```

Having two classes made up of different languages in the \App_Code folder (as shown here) causes an error to be thrown. It is impossible for the assigned compiler to work with two different languages. Therefore, in order to be able to work with multiple languages in your \App_Code folder, you must make some changes to the folder structure and the web.config file.

First, add two new subfolders to the `\App_Code` folder: a `\VB` folder and a `\CS` folder. This gives you the following folder structure:

```
\App_Code
    \VB
        Add.vb
    \CS
        Subtract.cs
```

This still will not correctly compile these class files into separate assemblies, at least not until you make some additions to the `web.config` file. Most likely, you don't have a `web.config` file in your solution at the moment, so add one through the Solution Explorer. After it is added, change the `<compilation>` node so that it is structured as shown here:

```
<compilation>
    <codeSubDirectories>
        <add directoryName="VB"></add>
        <add directoryName="CS"></add>
    </codeSubDirectories>
</compilation>
```

Now that this is in place in your `web.config` file, you can work with each of the classes in your ASP.NET pages. In addition, any C# class placed in the `CS` folder is now automatically compiled just like any of the classes placed in the `VB` folder. Because you can add these directories in the `web.config` file, you are not required to name them `VB` and `CS`; you can use whatever names you want.

\App_Data Folder

The `\App_Data` folder holds the datastores used by the application. It is a good spot to centrally store all the datastores your application might use. The `\App_Data` folder can contain Microsoft SQL Express files (`.mdf` files), Microsoft Access files (`.mdb` files), XML files, and more.

The user account utilized by your application has read and write access to any of the files contained within the `\App_Data` folder. By default, this is the ASPNET account. Another reason to store all your data files in this folder is that much of the ASP.NET system — from the membership and role management systems to the GUI tools such as the ASP.NET MMC snap-in and ASP.NET Web Site Administration Tool — is built to work with the `\App_Data` folder.

\App_Themes Folder

Themes are a new way of providing a common look-and-feel to your site across every page. You implement a theme by using a `.skin` file, CSS files, and images used by the server controls of your site. All these elements can make a *theme*, which is then stored in the `\App_Themes` folder of your solution. By storing these elements within the `\App_Themes` folder, you ensure that all the pages within the solution can take advantage of the theme and easily apply its elements to the controls and markup of the page.

\App_GlobalResources Folder

Resource files are string tables that can serve as data dictionaries for your applications when they require changes to content based on things such as changes in culture. You can add Assembly Resource files (`.resx`) to the `\App_GlobalResources` folder, and they are dynamically compiled and made part of the solution for use by all your `.aspx` pages in the application. When using ASP.NET 1.0/1.1, you had to use the `resgen.exe` tool and compile your resource files to a `.dll` or `.exe` for use within your solution. Now it is considerably easier to deal with resource files in ASP.NET 2.0. Simply place your application-wide resources in this folder to make them instantly accessible.

\App_LocalResources

Even if you are not interested in constructing applicationwide resources using the `\App_GlobalResources` folder, you may want resources that can be used for a single `.aspx` page. You can do this very simply by using the `\App_LocalResources` folder.

Add page-specific resource files to the `\App_LocalResources` folder by constructing the name of the `.resx` file in the following manner:

- ❑ `Default.aspx.resx`
- ❑ `Default.aspx.fi.resx`
- ❑ `Default.aspx.ja.resx`
- ❑ `Default.aspx.en-gb.resx`

Now, the resource declarations used on the `Default.aspx` page are retrieved from the appropriate file in the `\App_LocalResources` folder. By default, the `Default.aspx.resx` resource file is used if another match is not found. If the client is using a culture specification of `fi-FI` (Finnish), however, the `Default.aspx.fi.resx` file is used instead.

\App_WebReferences

The `\App_WebReferences` folder is a new name for the `Web References` folder used in previous versions of ASP.NET. Using the `\App_WebReferences` folder, you have automatic access to the remote Web Services referenced from your application.

\App_Browsers

The `\App_Browsers` folder holds `.browser` files, which are XML files used to identify the browsers making requests to the application and understand the capabilities of these browsers. You can find a list of globally accessible `.browser` files at `C:\Windows\Microsoft.NET\Framework\v2.0.50727\CONFIG\Browsers`. In addition, if you want to change any part of these default browser definition files, just copy the appropriate `.browser` file from the `Browsers` folder to your application's `\App_Browsers` folder and change the definition.

Global.asax

When you add a new item to your ASP.NET application, you get the Add New Item dialog. From here, you can add a Global Application Class to your applications. This adds a `Global.asax` file. This file is used by the application to hold application-level events, objects, and variables — all of which are accessible application-wide. Active Server Pages developers had something similar with the `Global.asa` file.

Your ASP.NET applications can have only a single `Global.asax` file, which supports a number of items. When it is created, you are given the following template:

```
<%@ Application Language="VB" %>

<script runat="server">

    Sub Application_Start(ByVal sender As Object, ByVal e As EventArgs)
        ' Code that runs on application startup
    End Sub

    Sub Application_End(ByVal sender As Object, ByVal e As EventArgs)
        ' Code that runs on application shutdown
    End Sub

    Sub Application_Error(ByVal sender As Object, ByVal e As EventArgs)
        ' Code that runs when an unhandled error occurs
    End Sub

    Sub Session_Start(ByVal sender As Object, ByVal e As EventArgs)
        ' Code that runs when a new session is started
    End Sub

    Sub Session_End(ByVal sender As Object, ByVal e As EventArgs)
        ' Code that runs when a session ends.
        ' Note: The Session_End event is raised only when the sessionstate mode
        ' is set to InProc in the Web.config file. If session mode is
        ' set to StateServer
        ' or SQLServer, the event is not raised.
    End Sub

</script>
```

Just as you can work with page-level events in your `.aspx` pages, you can work with overall application events from the `Global.asax` file. In addition to the events listed in this code example, the following list details some of the events you can structure inside this file:

❑ `Application_Start`: Called when the application receives its very first request. It is an ideal spot in your application to assign any application-level variables or state that must be maintained across all users.

❑ `Session_Start`: Similar to the `Application_Start` event except that this event is fired when an individual user accesses the application for the first time. For instance, the `Application_Start` event fires once when the first request comes in, which gets the application going, but the `Session_Start` is invoked for each end user who requests something from the application for the first time.

❑ `Application_BeginRequest`: Although it is not listed in the preceding template provided by Visual Studio 2005, the `Application BeginRequest` event is triggered before each and every request that comes its way. This means that when a request comes into the server, before this

744

request is processed, the `Application_BeginRequest` is triggered and dealt with before any processing of the request occurs.

❑   `Application_AuthenticateRequest`: This is triggered for each request and enables you to set up custom authentications for a request.

❑   `Application_Error`: Triggered when an error is thrown anywhere in the application by any user of the application. This is an ideal spot to provide application-wide error handling or an event recording the errors to the server's Event Logs.

❑   `Session_End`: When running in `InProc` mode, this event is triggered when an end user leaves the application.

❑   `Application_End`: Triggered when the application comes to an end. This is an event that most ASP.NET developers won't often use because ASP.NET does such a good job of closing and cleaning up any objects that are left around.

In addition to the global application events that the `Global.asax` file provides access to, you can also use the following directives in this file, just as you can with other ASP.NET pages:

❑   `@Application`

❑   `@Assembly`

❑   `@Import`

These directives perform in the same way when they are used with other ASP.NET page types. An example of using the `Global.asax` file is shown in the next code example. It demonstrates how to log when the ASP.NET application domain shuts down. When this happens, the ASP.NET application abruptly comes to an end, so place any logging code in the `Application_End` method of the `Global.asax` file:

```vb
<%@ Application Language="VB" %>
<%@ Import Namespace="System.Reflection" %>
<%@ Import Namespace="System.Diagnostics" %>

<script runat="server">

    Sub Application_End(ByVal sender As Object, ByVal e As EventArgs)
        Dim MyRuntime As HttpRuntime = _
            GetType(System.Web.HttpRuntime).InvokeMember("_theRuntime", _
            BindingFlags.NonPublic Or BindingFlags.Static Or _
            BindingFlags.GetField, _
            Nothing, Nothing, Nothing)

        If (MyRuntime Is Nothing) Then
            Return
        End If

        Dim shutDownMessage As String = _
            CType(MyRuntime.GetType().InvokeMember("_shutDownMessage", _
            BindingFlags.NonPublic Or BindingFlags.Instance Or _
            BindingFlags.GetField, _
            Nothing, MyRuntime, Nothing), System.String)

        Dim shutDownStack As String = _
```

```
            CType(MyRuntime.GetType().InvokeMember("_shutDownStack", _
            BindingFlags.NonPublic Or BindingFlags.Instance Or
            BindingFlags.GetField, _
            Nothing, MyRuntime, Nothing), System.String)

        If (Not EventLog.SourceExists(".NET Runtime")) Then
            EventLog.CreateEventSource(".NET Runtime", "Application")
        End If

        Dim logEntry As EventLog = New EventLog()
        logEntry.Source = ".NET Runtime"
        logEntry.WriteEntry(String.Format(_
            "shutDownMessage={0}\r\n\r\n_shutDownStack={1}", _
            shutDownMessage, shutDownStack), EventLogEntryType.Error)
    End Sub

</script>
```

With this code in place in your `Global.asax` file, start your ASP.NET application. Next, do something to cause the application to restart. For example you could make a change to the `web.config` file while the application is running. This triggers the `Application_End` event, resulting in the addition to the Event Log shown in Figure 19-12.

Figure 19-12

ASP.NET Server Controls

In the past, one of the difficulties in working with classic ASP was that you were completely in charge of the entire HTML output from the browser by virtue of the server-side code you wrote. Although this might seem ideal, it created a problem because each browser interpreted the HTML given to it in a slightly different manner.

The two main browsers at the time were Internet Explorer and Netscape Navigator. This meant that not only did developers have to be cognizant of the browser type to which they were outputting HTML, they also had to take into account which versions of those particular browsers might be making a request to their application. Some developers resolved the issue by creating two separate applications. When an end user made an initial request to the application, the code made a browser check to see what browser type made the request. Then, the ASP page redirected the request: down one path for an IE user or down another path for a Netscape user.

Because requests came from so many different versions of the same browser, developers often designed for the lowest possible version that might be used to visit the site. Everyone loses when the lowest common denominator is used as the target. This technique ensures that the page is rendered properly in most browsers making a request, but it also forces developers to dumb down their applications. If applications are built for the lowest common denominator, developers can't take advantage of some of the more advanced features offered by newer browser versions.

ASP.NET server controls overcome these obstacles. When using the server controls provided by ASP.NET, you are not specifying the HTML to be output from your server-side code. Rather, you are specifying the functionality you want to see in the browser, letting the ASP.NET determine the output to be sent to the browser.

When a request comes in, ASP.NET examines the request to see which browser type is making the request, as well as the version of the browser, and then it produces HTML output specific to that browser. This process is accomplished by processing a User Agent header retrieved from the HTTP Request to *sniff* the browser. This means that you can now build for the best browsers out there without worrying about whether features will work in the different browsers making requests to your applications. Because of the previously described capabilities, these controls are often referred to as *smart controls*.

Types of Server Controls

ASP.NET provides two distinct types of server controls — HTML server controls and Web server controls. Each type of control is quite different; and as you work with ASP.NET, you will see that much of the focus is on the Web server controls. This doesn't mean that HTML server controls have no value. They do provide you with many capabilities — some that Web server controls do not.

You might be asking yourself which is the better control type to use. It really depends on what you are trying to achieve. HTML server controls map to specific HTML elements. You can place an `HtmlTable` server control on your ASP.NET page that works dynamically with a `<table>` element. On the other hand, Web server controls map to specific functionality that you want on your ASP.NET pages. This means an `<asp:Panel>` control might use a `<table>` or an `<IFrame>` element — it really depends on the capability of the requesting browser.

The following table summarizes some advice on when to use HTML server controls and when to use Web server controls:

Control Type	Use This Control Type...
HTML Server	When converting traditional ASP 3.0 Web pages to ASP.NET Web pages and speed of completion is a concern. It is a lot easier to change your HTML elements to HTML server controls than it is to change them to Web server controls. When you prefer a more HTML-type programming model. When you want to explicitly control the code that is generated for the browser.
Web Server	When you require a richer set of functionality to perform complicated page requirements. When you are developing Web pages that will be viewed by a multitude of browser types and that require different code based upon these types. When you prefer a more Visual Basic–type programming model that is based on the use of controls and control properties.

Of course, some developers like to separate certain controls from the rest and place them in their own categories. For instance, you may see references to the following types of controls:

❑ **List controls:** Enable data to be bound to them for display purposes of some kind

❑ **Rich controls:** Controls, such as the Calendar control, that display richer content and capabilities than other controls

❑ **Validation controls:** Controls that interact with other form controls to validate the data that they contain

❑ **Mobile controls:** Specific to output to devices such as mobile phones, PDAs, and more

❑ **User controls:** Not really controls, but page templates that you can work with as you would a control on your ASP.NET page

❑ **Custom controls:** Controls that you build yourself and use in the same manner as the supplied ASP.NET server controls that come with the default install of ASP.NET 2.0

When you are deciding between HTML server controls and Web server controls, remember that no hard-and-fast rules exist about which type to use. You might find yourself working with one control type more than another, but certain features are available in one control type that might not be available in the other. If you are trying to accomplish a specific task and don't see a solution with the control type you are using, another control type may very well hold the answer. Keep in mind that you can mix and match these control types. Nothing prevents you from using both HTML server controls and Web server controls on the same page or within the same application.

Building with Server Controls

You have a couple of ways to use server controls to construct your ASP.NET pages. You can use tools that are specifically designed to work with ASP.NET 2.0 that enable you to visually drag and drop controls onto a design surface and manipulate the behavior of the control, or you can work with server controls directly through code input.

Working with Server Controls on a Design Surface

Visual Studio 2005 enables you to visually create an ASP.NET page by dragging and dropping visual controls onto a design surface. You can get to this visual design option by clicking the Design tab at the bottom of the IDE when viewing your ASP.NET page. In this view, you also can place the cursor on the page in the location where you want the control to appear and then double-click the control you want in the Toolbox window of Visual Studio. Unlike previous versions of Visual Studio, Visual Studio 2005 does a really good job of not touching your code when switching between the Design and Source tabs.

In the Design view of your page, you can highlight a control and the properties for the control appear in the Properties window. For example, Figure 19-13 shows a Button control selected, with its properties displayed in the Properties window on the right.

Figure 19-13

Changing the properties in the window changes the appearance or behavior of the highlighted control. Because all controls inherit from a specific base class (`WebControl`), you can highlight multiple controls at the same time and change the base properties of all the controls at once by holding down the Ctrl key as you make your control selections.

Coding Server Controls

You also can work from the code page directly. Because many developers prefer this, it is the default when you first create your ASP.NET page. Hand-coding your own ASP.NET pages may seem to be a slower approach than simply dragging and dropping controls onto a design surface, but it isn't as slow as you might think. You get plenty of assistance in coding your applications from Visual Studio 2005. As you start typing in Visual Studio, the IntelliSense features kick in and help you with code autocompletion. Figure 19-14, for example, shows an IntelliSense drop-down list of possible code completion statements that appeared as the code was typed.

Figure 19-14

The IntelliSense focus is on the most commonly used attribute or statement for the control or piece of code that you are working with. Using IntelliSense effectively as you work is a great way to code with speed.

As with Design view, the Source view of your page enables you to drag and drop controls from the Toolbox onto the code page itself. For example, dragging and dropping a `TextBox` control onto the code page produces the same results as dropping it on the design page:

```
<asp:TextBox ID="TextBox1" Runat="server"></asp:TextBox>
```

You can also highlight a control in Source view or simply place your cursor in the code statement of the control, and the Properties window displays the properties of the control. You can apply properties directly in the Properties window of Visual Studio, and these properties are dynamically added to the code of your control.

Working with Server Control Events

ASP.NET uses more of a traditional Visual Basic event model than classic ASP. Instead of working with interpreted code, you are actually coding an event-based structure for your pages. Classic ASP used an interpreted model: When the server processed the Web page, the code of the page was interpreted line by line in a linear fashion whereby the only "event" implied was the page loading. This meant that occurrences you wanted to initiated early in the process were placed at the top of the page.

Today, ASP.NET uses an event-driven model. Items or coding tasks are initiated only when a particular event occurs. A common event in the ASP.NET programming model is `Page_Load`, shown here:

```
Protected Sub Page_Load(ByVal sender As Object, ByVal e As System.EventArgs)
    ' Code actions here
End Sub
```

Not only can you work with the overall page — as well as its properties and methods at particular moments in time through page events — you can also work with the server controls contained on the page through particular control events. For example, one common event for a button on a form is `Button_Click`, illustrated here:

```
Protected Sub Button1_Click(ByVal sender As Object, ByVal e As System.EventArgs)
    ' Code actions here
End Sub
```

The event shown here is fired only when the end user actually clicks the button on the form that has an `OnClick` attribute value of `Button1_Click`. Therefore, not only does the event handler exist in the server-side code of the ASP.NET page, but that handler is also hooked up using the `OnClick` property of the server control in the associated ASP.NET page markup, as illustrated in the following code:

```
<asp:Button ID="Button1" Runat="server" Text="Button" OnClick="Button1_Click" />
```

How do you fire these events for server controls? You have a couple of ways to go about it. The first way is to pull up your ASP.NET page in Design view and double-click the control for which you want to create a server-side event. For instance, double-clicking a `Button` server control in Design view creates the structure of the `Button1_Click` event within your server-side code, whether the code is in a code-behind file or inline. This creates a stub handler for that server control's most popular event.

That said, be aware that a considerable number of additional events are available to the `Button` control that you cannot access by double-clicking the control. To access them, pull up the page that contains the server-side code, select the control from the first drop-down list at the top of the IDE, and then choose the particular event you want for that control in the second drop-down list. Figure 19-15 shows the event drop-down list displayed. You might, for example, want to work with the `Button` control's `PreRender` event, rather than its `Click` event. The handler for the event you choose is placed in your server-side code.

Figure 19-15

The second way is to create server-side events for your server controls from the Properties window of Visual Studio. This works only from Design view of the page. In Design view, highlight the server control that you want to work with. The properties for the control will appear in the Properties window, along with an icon menu. One of the icons, the Events icon, is represented by a lightning bolt within the IDE.

Clicking the Events icon pulls up a list of events available for the control. Simply double-click one of the events to get that event structure created in your server-side code. After you have an event structure in place, you can program specific actions you want to occur when the event is fired.

Manipulating Pages and Server Controls with JavaScript

Developers generally like to include some of their own custom JavaScript functions in their ASP.NET pages. You have a couple of ways to do this. The first is to apply JavaScript directly to the controls on your ASP.NET pages. For example, the following simple `Label` server control displays the current date and time:

```
Protected Sub Page_Load(ByVal sender As Object, ByVal e As System.EventArgs)
    TextBox1.Text = DateTime.Now.ToString()
End Sub
```

This little bit of code displays the current date and time on the page of the end user. The problem is that the date and time displayed are correct for the Web server that generated the page. If the user is in the Pacific time zone (PST) and the Web server is in the Eastern time zone (EST), the page won't be correct for that viewer. If you want the time to be correct for anyone visiting the site, regardless of where they reside in the world, then you can employ JavaScript to work with the `TextBox` control:

```
<%@ Page Language="VB" %>

<html xmlns="http://www.w3.org/1999/xhtml" >
<head runat="server">
    <title>Using JavaScript</title>
</head>
<body onload="javascript:document.forms[0]['TextBox1'].value=Date();">
    <form id="form1" runat="server">
    <div>
        <asp:TextBox ID="TextBox1" Runat="server" Width="300"></asp:TextBox>
    </div>
    </form>
</body>
</html>
```

In this example, even though you are using a standard `TextBox` server control from the Web server control family, you can access this control using JavaScript that is planted in the `onload` attribute of the `<body>` element. The value of the `onload` attribute actually points to the specific server control via an anonymous function by using the value of the `ID` attribute from the server control: `TextBox1`. You can get at other server controls on your page by employing the same methods. This bit of code produces a text box with the current date and time inside of it.

ASP.NET uses the new `Page.ClientScript` property to register and place JavaScript functions on your ASP.NET pages. Three of these methods are reviewed here. Other methods and properties are available through the `ClientScript` object (which references an instance of `System.Web.UI.ClientScriptManager`), but these are the most useful ones. You can find the rest in the SDK documentation.

The `Page.RegisterStartupScript` and `Page.RegisterClientScriptBlock` methods from the .NET Framework 1.0/1.1 are now considered obsolete. Both of these options for registering scripts required a key/script set of parameters. Because two separate methods were involved, key name collisions were very likely. The `Page.ClientScript` property is meant to bring all the script registrations under one umbrella, making your code less error prone.

Using Page.ClientScript.RegisterClientScriptBlock

The `RegisterClientScriptBlock` method enables you to place a JavaScript function at the top of the page. This means that the script is in place for the startup of the page in the browser. Its use is shown here:

```
<%@ Page Language="VB" %>

<script runat="server">
    Protected Sub Page_Load(ByVal sender As Object, ByVal e As System.EventArgs)
      Dim myScript As String = "function AlertHello() { alert('Hello ASP.NET'); }"
        Page.ClientScript.RegisterClientScriptBlock(Me.GetType(), "MyScript", _
          myScript, True)
    End Sub
</script>

<html xmlns="http://www.w3.org/1999/xhtml" >
<head runat="server">
    <title>Adding JavaScript</title>
</head>
<body>
    <form id="form1" runat="server">
    <div>
        <asp:Button ID="Button1" Runat="server" Text="Button"
        OnClientClick="AlertHello()" />
    </div>
    </form>
</body>
</html>
```

You create the JavaScript function `AlertHello()` as a string called `myScript`. Then, using the `Page.ClientScript.RegisterClientScriptBlock` method, you program the script to be placed on the page. The two possible constructions of the `RegisterClientScriptBlock` method are as follows:

❑   `RegisterClientScriptBlock` (*type, key, script*)

❑   `RegisterClientScriptBlock` (*type, key, script, script tag specification*)

The preceding example specifies the type as `Me.GetType()`, the key, the script to include, and then a `Boolean` value setting of `True` so that .NET places the script on the ASP.NET page with `<script>` tags automatically. When running the page, you can view the source code for the page to see the results:

```
<html xmlns="http://www.w3.org/1999/xhtml" >
<head><title>
    Adding JavaScript
</title></head>
<body>
    <form method="post" action="JavaScriptPage.aspx" id="form1">
<div>
<input type="hidden" name="__VIEWSTATE"
 value="/wEPDwUKMTY3NzE5MjIyMGRkiyYSRMg+bcXi9DiawYlbxndiTDo=" />
```

```
    </div>

    <script type="text/javascript">
    <!--
    function AlertHello() { alert('Hello ASP.NET'); }// -->
    </script>

        <div>
            <input type="submit" name="Button1" value="Button" onclick="AlertHello();"
             id="Button1" />
        </div>
        </form>
    </body>
    </html>
```

From this, you can see that the script specified was indeed included on the ASP.NET page before the page code. Not only were the `<script>` tags included, but the proper comment tags were added around the script (so older browsers will not break).

Using Page.ClientScript.RegisterStartupScript

The `RegisterStartupScript` method is similar to the `RegisterClientScriptBlock` method. The big difference is that the `RegisterStartupScript` places the script at the bottom of the ASP.NET page instead of at the top. In fact, the `RegisterStartupScript` method even takes the same constructors as the `RegisterClientScriptBlock` method:

❑   `RegisterStartupScript` (*type, key, script*)

❑   `RegisterStartupScript` (*type, key, script, script tag specification*)

What difference does it make where the script is registered on the page? A lot, actually! If you have a bit of JavaScript that is working with one of the controls on your page, in most cases you want to use the `RegisterStartupScript` method instead of `RegisterClientScriptBlock`. For example, you would use the following code to create a page that includes a simple `<asp:TextBox>` control that contains a default value of `Hello ASP.NET`:

```
<asp:TextBox ID="TextBox1" Runat="server">Hello ASP.NET</asp:TextBox>
```

Then use the `RegisterClientScriptBlock` method to place a script on the page that utilizes the value in the `TextBox1` control:

```
Protected Sub Page_Load(ByVal sender As Object, ByVal e As System.EventArgs)
    Dim myScript As String = "alert(document.forms[0]['TextBox1'].value);"
    Page.ClientScript.RegisterClientScriptBlock(Me.GetType(), "myKey", myScript, _
        True)
End Sub
```

Running this page results in the JavaScript error shown in Figure 19-16.

Figure 19-16

The error occurs because the JavaScript function fired before the text box was even placed on the screen. Therefore, the JavaScript function did not find `TextBox1`, which caused an error to be thrown by the page. Now try the `RegisterStartupScript` method shown here:

```
Protected Sub Page_Load(ByVal sender As Object, ByVal e As System.EventArgs)
    Dim myScript As String = "alert(document.forms[0]['TextBox1'].value);"
    Page.ClientScript.RegisterStartupScript(Me.GetType(), "myKey", myScript, _
        True)
End Sub
```

This approach puts the JavaScript function at the bottom of the ASP.NET page, so when the JavaScript actually starts, it finds the `TextBox1` element and works as planned, as shown in Figure 19-17.

Figure 19-17

Using Page.ClientScript.RegisterClientScriptInclude

The final method is `RegisterClientScriptInclude`. Many developers place their JavaScript inside a `.js` file, which is considered a best practice because it makes it very easy to make global JavaScript changes to the application. You can register the script files on your ASP.NET pages through the use of the `RegisterClientScriptInclude` method, shown here:

```
Dim myScript As String = "myJavaScriptCode.js"
Page.ClientScript.RegisterClientScriptInclude("myKey", myScript)
```

This creates the following construction on the ASP.NET page:

```
<script src="myJavaScriptCode.js" type="text/javascript"></script>
```

Summary

This chapter covered a lot of ground. It discussed some of the issues concerning ASP.NET applications as a whole and the options you have when building and deploying these new applications. With the help of Visual Studio 2005, you now have options regarding which Web server to use when building your application and whether to work locally or remotely through the new built-in FTP capabilities.

ASP.NET 2.0 and Visual Studio 2005 make it easy to build your pages using an inline coding model or a new and better code-behind model that is simpler to use and easier to deploy. You also learned about the new cross-posting capabilities and the new fixed folders that ASP.NET 2.0 has incorporated to make your life easier. These folders make their resources available dynamically with no work on your part. Finally, you saw some of the outstanding new compilation options that you have at your disposal. The next chapter examines some of the more advanced systems available to you in ASP.NET 2.0.

ASP.NET 2.0 Advanced Features

ASP.NET is an exciting technology. It enables the creation and delivery of remotely generated applications (Web applications) accessible via a simple browser — a container that many are rather familiar with. The purpose of Web-based applications (in our case, ASP.NET applications) is to deliver only a single instance of the application to the end user over HTTP. This means that the end users viewing your application will always have the latest and greatest version at their disposal. Because of this, many companies today are looking at ASP.NET to not only deliver the company's website, but also to deliver some of their latest applications for their employees, partners, and customers.

The last chapter took a look at some of the basics of ASP.NET 2.0. This chapter continues on that path and shows you some additional and exciting technologies that you'll find in ASP.NET 2.0, including master pages, configuration, data access, and more.

This chapter touches upon many topics, as ASP.NET has become a rather large offering with many possibilities and capabilities. Sit back, pull up that keyboard, and enjoy!

Applications and Pages

The previous chapter took a look at the structure of ASP.NET pages and their life cycle. There's quite a bit you can do with the applications and pages in ASP.NET to change how they behave or how you compile and deliver them. This section looks at some of these possibilities.

Cross-Page Posting

The way in which Active Server Pages 2.0/3.0 (also called *classic ASP*) worked was that values from forms were usually posted to other pages. These pages were typically steps in a process that the end user worked through. With the introduction of ASP.NET, pages in this environment posted back results to themselves in a step called a *postback*. One of the most frequent requests of Web developers in the ASP.NET world has been the capability to do postbacks, not only to the page from which the values originated, but also to other pages within the application. This feature has been provided with the release of ASP.NET 2.0.

Cross-page posting (as it is referred to) is an easy functionality to achieve now. It gives you the capability to post page values from one page (Page1.aspx) to an entirely different page (Page2.aspx). Normally, when posting to the same page (as with ASP.NET 1.0/1.1), you could capture the postback in a postback event, as shown here:

```
If Page.IsPostBack Then
    ' do work here
End If
```

Now take a look at Page1.aspx and see how you accomplish cross-page posting with ASP.NET 2.0:

```
<%@ Page Language="VB" %>

<script runat="server">
    Protected Sub Button1_Click(ByVal sender As Object, _
        ByVal e As System.EventArgs)

        Label1.Text = "Your name is: " & TextBox1.Text & "<br>" & _
            "Your appointment is on: " & Calendar1.SelectedDate.ToLongDateString()
    End Sub
</script>

<html xmlns="http://www.w3.org/1999/xhtml" >
<head runat="server">
    <title>Cross-Page Posting</title>
</head>
<body>
    <form id="form1" runat="server">
    <div>
        What is your name?<br />
        <asp:TextBox ID="TextBox1" runat="server"></asp:TextBox>
        <br />
        <br />
        When is your appointment?<br />
        <asp:Calendar ID="Calendar1" runat="server">
        </asp:Calendar><br />
        <asp:Button ID="Button1" OnClick="Button1_Click" runat="server"
         Text="Do a PostBack to this Page" />
        <br />
        <br />
        <asp:Button ID="Button2" runat="server"
         Text="Do a PostBack to Another Page" PostBackUrl="~/Page2.aspx" />
        <br />
        <br />
        <asp:Label ID="Label1" runat="server"></asp:Label>
    </div>
    </form>
</body>
</html>
```

With `Page1.aspx`, there is nothing really different about this page — except for the `Button2` server control. This page contains a new attribute, which you will find with the `Button`, `ImageButton`, and `LinkButton` controls — the `PostBackUrl` attribute. The value of this attribute points to the location of the file that this page should post to. In this case, the `PostBackUrl` attribute states that this page should post to `Page2.aspx`. This is the only thing needed on the `Page1.aspx` to cause it to post back to another page. As for `Button1`, you can see that this is a simple button that will cause the page to post back to itself. This is nothing; this was the case even in ASP.NET 1.x. You can see the event handler for this postback in the `OnClick` attribute within the `Button1` control. Pressing this button causes the page to post back to itself and to populate the `Label1` control at the bottom of the page.

Clicking on the second button, though, will post to the second page, which is shown here:

```
<%@ Page Language="VB" %>

<script runat="server">
    Protected Sub Page_Load(ByVal sender As Object, ByVal e As System.EventArgs)
        Dim pp_TextBox1 As TextBox
        Dim pp_Calendar1 As Calendar

        pp_TextBox1 = CType(PreviousPage.FindControl("TextBox1"), TextBox)
        pp_Calendar1 = CType(PreviousPage.FindControl("Calendar1"), Calendar)

        Label1.Text = "Your name is: " & pp_TextBox1.Text & "<br>" & _
            "Your appointment is on: " & _
            pp_Calendar1.SelectedDate.ToLongDateString()
    End Sub
</script>

<html xmlns="http://www.w3.org/1999/xhtml" >
<head runat="server">
    <title>Second Page</title>
</head>
<body>
    <form id="form1" runat="server">
    <div>
        <asp:Label ID="Label1" runat="server"></asp:Label>
    </div>
    </form>
</body>
</html>
```

In this page, the first step is the creation in the `Page_Load` event of instances of both the `TextBox` and `Calendar` controls. From here, these instances are populated with the values of these controls on the previous page (`Page1.aspx`) by using the `PreviousPage.FindControl()` method. The `String` value assigned to the `FindControl` method is the `ID` value of the ASP.NET server control from the originating page (in our case, `TextBox1` and `Calendar1`). Once you have assigned the values to these control instances, you can then start working with the new controls and their values as if they were posted from the same page.

You can also expose the server controls and other items as properties from Page1.aspx, as illustrated in this partial code sample:

```
<%@ Page Language="VB" %>

<script runat="server">
    Public ReadOnly Property pp_TextBox1() As TextBox
        Get
            Return TextBox1
        End Get
    End Property

    Public ReadOnly Property pp_Calendar1() As Calendar
        Get
            Return Calendar1
        End Get
    End Property

    Protected Sub Button1_Click(ByVal sender As Object, _
        ByVal e As System.EventArgs)

        Label1.Text = "Your name is: " & TextBox1.Text & "<br>" & _
            "Your appointment is on: " & Calendar1.SelectedDate.ToLongDateString()
    End Sub
</script>
```

Once you have exposed the properties you want from Page1.aspx, you can easily get at these properties in the cross-page postback by using the new PreviousPageType page directive, as shown in the following example:

```
<%@ Page Language="VB" %>
<%@ PreviousPageType VirtualPath="~/Page1.aspx" %>

<script runat="server">
    Protected Sub Page_Load(ByVal sender As Object, ByVal e As System.EventArgs)
        Label1.Text = "Your name is: " & PreviousPage.pp_TextBox1.Text & "<br>" & _
            "Your appointment is on: " & _
            PreviousPage.pp_Calendar1.SelectedDate.ToLongDateString()
    End Sub
</script>
```

After your properties are on Page1.aspx, you can access them easily by strongly typing the PreviousPage property on Page2.aspx by using the PreviousPageType directive. The PreviousPageType directive specifies the page from which the post will come. Using this directive enables you to specifically point at Page1.aspx. This is done using the VirtualPath attribute of the PreviousPageType directive. The VirtualPath attribute takes a String whose value is the location of the directing page.

Once this association has been made, you can then use the PreviousPage property, and you will see that the pp_TextBox1 and pp_Calendar1 properties that were created on Page1.aspx are now present in Visual Studio 2005's IntelliSense (see Figure 20-1). Working with the PreviousPage property is a bit easier and is less error prone than using weak typing.

Figure 20-1

One thing to guard against is a browser hitting a page that is expecting information from a cross-page post; this action causes errors if the information the second page is expecting isn't there. You always had to guard against pages that were looking for postback information — even when dealing with ASP.NET pages (1.0/1.1) that performed postbacks to themselves. With standard pages that aren't cross-page posting, you could protect your code from this postback behavior through the use of the `Page.IsPostBack` property, as shown here:

```
If Page.IsPostBack Then
    ' code here
End If
```

When cross-page posting, use the `Page.IsCrossPagePostBack` property:

```
<%@ Page Language="VB" %>
<%@ PreviousPageType VirtualPath="~/Page1.aspx" %>

<script runat="server">
    Protected Sub Page_Load(ByVal sender As Object, ByVal e As System.EventArgs)
        If PreviousPage.IsCrossPagePostBack Then
            Label1.Text = "Your name is: " & PreviousPage.pp_TextBox1.Text & "<br>" & _
                "Your appointment is on: " & _
                PreviousPage.pp_Calendar1.SelectedDate.ToLongDateString()
        Else
```

```
            Response.Redirect("Page1.aspx")
        End If
    End Sub
</script>
```

In this example, if someone hits this page without going to Page1.aspx first to get cross-posted to Page2.aspx, then the request will be checked to determine whether the request is a cross-post. If it is (checked using the Page.IsCrossPagePostBack property), then the code is run; otherwise, the request is redirected to Page1.aspx.

ASP.NET Compilation

With ASP.NET. you can observe this compilation process and how it works when you hit one of the ASP.NET pages you have built for the first time. You'll notice that it takes a few seconds for the page to be generated. When an ASP.NET page is referenced in the browser for the first time, the request is passed to the ASP.NET parser that creates the class file in the language of the page. It is passed to the parser based on the file's extension (.aspx) because ASP.NET realizes that this file extension type is meant for its handling and processing. After the class file has been created, it is compiled into a DLL and then written to the disk of the Web server. At this point, the DLL is instantiated and processed, and an output is generated for the initial requester of the ASP.NET page. This process is detailed in Figure 20-2.

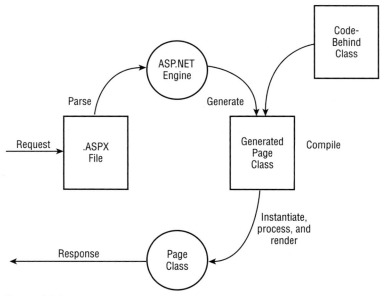

Figure 20-2

On the next request, great things happen. Instead of going through the entire process again for the second and subsequent requests, the request simply causes an instantiation of the already created DLL, which sends out a response to the requester (see Figure 20-3).

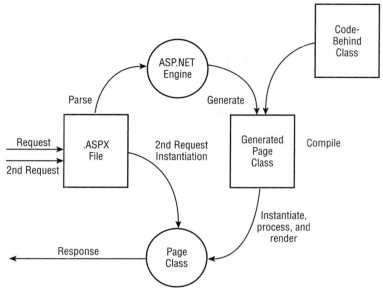

Figure 20-3

Previously, because of the mechanics of this process, if you made changes to your .aspx code-behind pages, it was necessary to recompile your application. This was quite a pain if you had a larger site and didn't want your end users to experience the extreme lag that occurs when an .aspx page is referenced for the first time after compilation. Many developers, consequently, began to develop their own tools that automatically hit every single page within the application to remove this first-time lag hit from the end user's browsing experience.

ASP.NET 2.0 offers a few ways to precompile your entire application with a single command that you can issue through a command line. One type of compilation is referred to as *in-place precompilation*. In order to precompile your entire ASP.NET application, you must use the aspnet_compiler.exe tool that comes with ASP.NET 2.0. To do so, open the Command Prompt window and navigate to C:\Windows\Microsoft.NET\Framework\v2.0.xxxxx\. Once there, you can work with the aspnet_compiler tool. You can also access this tool directly by pulling up the Visual Studio 2005 Command Prompt window. Choose Start ➪ All Programs ➪ Microsoft Visual Studio 2005 ➪ Visual Studio Tools ➪ Visual Studio 2005 Command Prompt.

After you get the command prompt, use the aspnet_compiler.exe tool to perform an in-place pre-compilation using the following command:

```
aspnet_compiler -p "C:\Inetpub\wwwroot\WROX" -v none
```

In the example just shown, -v is a command for the virtual path of the application — which is provided by using /WROX. The next command is -p, which points to the physical path of the application. In this case, it is C:\Websites\WROX. Finally, the last bit, C:\Wrox, is the location of the compiler output. The following table describes the possible commands for the aspnet_compiler.exe tool:

Command	Description
-m	Specifies the full IIS metabase path of the application. If you use the -m command, you cannot use the -v or -p command.
-v	Specifies the virtual path of the application to be compiled. If you also use the -p command, the physical path is used to find the location of the application.
-p	Specifies the physical path of the application to be compiled. If this is not specified, the IIS metabase is used to find the application.
[targetDir]	Specifies the target directory in which the compiled files should be placed. If this is not specified, the output files are placed in the application directory.

After compiling the application, you can go to C:\Wrox to see the output. Here, you see all the files and file structures that were in the original application, but if you look at the content of one of the files, the file is simply a placeholder. In the actual file is the following comment:

```
This is a marker file generated by the precompilation tool
and should not be deleted!
```

In fact, you find a Code.dll file in the bin folder where all the page code is located. Because it is in a DLL file, it provides great code obfuscation as well. From here on, all you do is move these files to another server using FTP or Windows Explorer, and you can run the entire Web application from these files. When you have an update to the application, you simply provide a new set of compiled files. Sample output is displayed in Figure 20-4.

Figure 20-4

Note that this compilation process doesn't compile *every* type of Web file. In fact, it compiles only the ASP.NET-specific file types, omitting from the compilation process the following types of files:

❑   HTML files

❑   XML files

❑   XSD files

❑   web.config files

❑   Text files

You can't do much to get around this, except in the case of the HTML files and the text files. For these file types, just change the file extension of these file types to .aspx; they are then compiled into the Code.dll like all the other ASP.NET files.

Master Pages

Many Web applications are built so that each page of the application has some similarities. For instance, there may be a common header that is used on every page of your application. Similarly, there may be other common page elements, including navigation sections, advertisements, footers, and more. It really isn't common to have each of your Web pages have its own unique look and feel. Most people are looking for uniformity in their applications in order to give end users what works, through a multi-paged application.

What is needed for these types of applications is a way to provide a template that can be used by your pages — a sort of visual inheritance (such as you can achieve with Windows Forms). With a feature in ASP.NET 2.0 called *master pages*, you can employ visual inheritance in your Web applications.

The use of master pages means that you are working with a template file (the master page), which has a .master extension. Once a .master page is created, you can then take a *content page*, with an .aspx extension, and create an association between the two files. Doing this enables ASP.NET to take these two files and combine them into a single Web page to display in a browser, as illustrated in Figure 20-5.

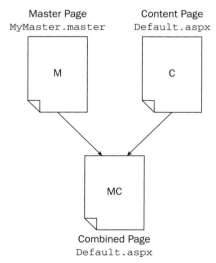

Figure 20-5

The following sections describe how you make this work. First, you need to create the master page.

Creating a Master Page

The first step is to create a template that will end up being your master page. You can build a master page using any text editor (such as Notepad), but it is far easier to use Visual Studio 2005 or Visual Web Developer, as shown here.

Start within the Solution Explorer. Right-click on the solution and select Add New Item. In the Add New Item dialog you will find the option to add a master page to the solution, as shown in Figure 20-6.

Figure 20-6

Your master page options are quite similar to those when working with a standard `.aspx` page. You can create master pages to be inline or you can have master pages that utilize the code-behind model. If you wish to use the code-behind model, make sure that you have the "Place code in separate file" check box checked in the dialog — otherwise, leave it blank. Creating an inline master page produces a single `.master` file. Using the code-behind model produces a `.master` file in addition to a `.master.vb` or `.master.cs` file.

A master page should be built so that it contains one or more content regions that are utilized by the content pages. The following master page example (named `Wrox.master`) contains two of these content areas:

```
<%@ Master Language="VB" %>

<!DOCTYPE html PUBLIC "-//W3C//DTD XHTML 1.1//EN"
 "http://www.w3.org/TR/xhtml11/DTD/xhtml11.dtd">

<script runat="server">

</script>
```

```
<html xmlns="http://www.w3.org/1999/xhtml" >
<head runat="server">
    <title>Wrox</title>
</head>
<body>
    <form id="form1" runat="server">
    <div>
        <table cellpadding="3" border="1">
            <tr bgcolor="silver">
                <td colspan="2"><h1>The Wrox Company Homepage</h1></td>
            </tr>
            <tr>
                <td>
                    <asp:ContentPlaceHolder ID="ContentPlaceHolder1"
                     runat="server">
                    </asp:ContentPlaceHolder>
                </td>
                <td>
                    <asp:ContentPlaceHolder ID="ContentPlaceHolder2"
                     runat="server">
                    </asp:ContentPlaceHolder>
                </td>
            </tr>
            <tr>
                <td colspan="2">Copyright 2006 - Wrox</td>
            </tr>
        </table>
    </div>
    </form>
</body>
</html>
```

The first thing to notice is the `<% Master %>` directive at the top of the page instead of the standard `<% Page %>` directive. This specifies that this is a master page and cannot be generated without a content page associated with it. It isn't a page that you can pull up in the browser. In this case, the `Master` directive simply uses the `Language` attribute and nothing more, but it has a number of other attributes at its disposal to fine-tune the behavior of the page.

The idea is to code the master page as you would any other `.aspx` page. This master page contains a simple table and two areas that are meant for the content pages. These areas are defined with the use of the `ContentPlaceHolder` server control. This page contains two such controls. It is *only* in these two specified areas where content pages will be allowed to interject content into the dynamically created page (as shown shortly).

The nice thing about working with master pages is that you aren't limited to working with them in the Code view of the IDE; Visual Studio 2005 also enables you to work with them in Design view as well, as shown in Figure 20-7.

In this view, you can work with the master page by simply dragging and dropping controls onto the design surface, just as you would with any typical .aspx page.

Figure 20-7

Creating the Content Page

Now that there is a master page in your project that you can utilize, the next step is to create a content page that does just that. Right-click on the solution from within the Solution Explorer of Visual Studio 2005 and select Add New Item. This time, though, you are going to add a typical Web Form to the project. However, before you click the Add button, be sure to check the "Select a Master Page" check box in the dialog. This informs VS 2005 that you are going to be building a content page that will be associated with a master page. Doing this pulls up a new dialog, which enables you to select a master page to associate with this new file, as shown in Figure 20-8.

In this case, if you have been following along with the example, you should only have a single master page available in the dialog, though it is possible to have as many different master pages as you wish in a single project. Select the Wrox.master page and press the OK button.

The page created will have only a single line of code to it:

```
<%@ Page Language="VB" MasterPageFile="~/Wrox.master" Title="Untitled Page" %>
```

This file is quite a bit different from a typical .aspx page. First, there is none of the default HTML code, script tags, and DOCTYPE declarations that are the norm. Second, note the addition of the MasterPageFile attribute in the Page directive. This new attribute makes the association to the master page that will be used for this content page. In this case, it is the Wrox.master file created earlier.

Figure 20-8

Though there isn't much to show while in the Source view of Visual Studio when looking at a content page, the real power of master pages can be seen when you switch to the Design view of the same page (see Figure 20-9).

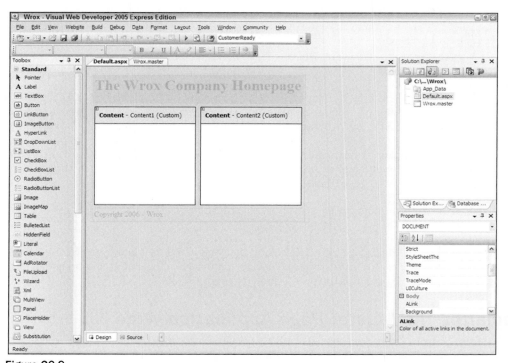

Figure 20-9

This view shows you the entire template and the two content areas that this content page is allowed to deal with. All the grayed-out areas are off-limits and do not allow for any changes from the content page, while the available areas allow you to deal with any type of content you wish. For instance, not only can you place raw text in these content areas, you can also add anything that you would normally place into a typical .aspx page. For an example, create a simple form in one of the content areas and place an image in the other. This code is shown here:

```
<%@ Page Language="VB" MasterPageFile="~/Wrox.master" Title="My Content Page" %>

<script runat="server">
 Protected Sub Button1_Click(ByVal sender As Object, ByVal e As System.EventArgs)
    Label1.Text = "Hello " & Textbox1.Text
 End Sub
</script>

<asp:Content ID="Content1" ContentPlaceHolderID="ContentPlaceHolder1"
 runat="server">
   <b>Enter in your name:<br />
   <asp:TextBox ID="TextBox1" runat="server"></asp:TextBox>
   <asp:Button ID="Button1" runat="server" Text="Submit" OnClick="Button1_Click" />
   <br />
   <br />
   <asp:Label ID="Label1" runat="server"></asp:Label>
   </b>
</asp:Content>

<asp:Content ID="Content2" ContentPlaceHolderID="ContentPlaceHolder2"
 runat="server">
    <asp:Image ID="Image1" runat="server" ImageUrl="wrox_logo.gif" />
</asp:Content>
```

Even from this simple example you can see the differences between a content page and a regular .aspx page. Most important, this page doesn't contain any <form> element or any of the <html> structure that you would normally see in a typical Web form. All of this content is instead stored inside the master page itself.

This content page contains two Content server controls. Each of these Content server controls maps to a specific <asp:ContentPlaceHolder> control from the master page. This association is made through the use of the ContentPlaceHolderID attribute of the Content control:

```
<asp:Content ID="Content1" ContentPlaceHolderID="ContentPlaceHolder1"
 runat="Server"> ... </asp:Content>
```

Just as with typical .aspx pages, you can create any event handlers you may need for your content page. This particular example uses a button-click event for when the end user submits the form. Running this example produces the results shown in Figure 20-10.

Declaring the Master Page Application-Wide

As shown in the examples thus far, we have been declaring the master page from the content page through the use of the MasterPageFile attribute of the Page directive:

```
<%@ Page Language="VB" MasterPageFile="~/Wrox.master" Title="My Content Page" %>
```

Figure 20-10

You can apply this attribute to each of your content pages or you can make this declaration in the web.config file of your application, as shown here:

```
<configuration>
    <system.web>
        <pages masterPageFile="~/Wrox.master"></pages>
    </system.web>
</configuration>
```

From the <pages> node in the web.config file, you declare that all your content pages will use a specific master page through the use of the masterPageFile attribute. Doing this means that your content pages can simply use the following Page directive construction:

```
<%@ Page Language="VB" Title="My Content Page" %>
```

The nice thing about making the master page declaration in the web.config file is you don't have to make this declaration on any of your solution's content pages; if you later decide to change the template and associate all the content pages to a brand-new master page, you can change every content page instantaneously in one spot.

Doing this has no effect on the regular .aspx pages in your solution. They will still function as normal. Moreover, if you have a content page that you wish to associate with a different master page other than the one specified in the web.config file, then you simply use the MasterPageFile attribute in the Page directive of the page. This will override any declaration that you may have in the web.config file.

Providing Default Content in Your Master Page

Earlier, you saw how to use a basic ContentPlaceHolder control. In addition to using it as shown, you can also create ContentPlaceHolder controls that contain default content:

```
<asp:ContentPlaceHolder ID="ContentPlaceHolder1" runat="server">
    Here is some default content!
</asp:ContentPlaceHolder>
```

For default content, you can again use whatever you want, including any other ASP.NET server controls. A content page that uses a master page containing one of these ContentPlaceHolder controls can then either override the default content — by just specifying content (which overrides the original content declared in the master page) — or keep the default content contained in the control.

Data-Driven Applications

ASP.NET 2.0 provides some unique data-access server controls that make it easy for you to get at the data you need. As data for your applications finds itself in more and more types of datastores, it can sometimes be a nightmare to figure out how to get at and aggregate these information sets onto a Web page in a simple and logical manner. ASP.NET data source controls are meant to work with a specific type of datastore by connecting to the datastore and performing operations such as inserts, updates, and deletes — all on your behalf. The following table details the new data source controls at your disposal:

Data Source Control	Description
SqlDataSource	Enables you to work with any SQL-based database, such as Microsoft SQL Server or even Oracle
AccessDataSource	Enables you to work with a Microsoft Access file (.mbd)
ObjectDataSource	Enables you to work with a business object or a Visual Studio 2005 data component
XmlDataSource	Enables you to work with the information from an XML file or even a dynamic XML source (for example, an RSS feed)
SiteMapDataSource	Enables you to work with the hierarchical data represented in the site map file (.sitemap)

ASP.NET itself provides a number of server controls that you can use for data-binding purposes. That means you can use these data source controls as the underlying data systems for a series of controls with very little work on your part. These data-bound controls in ASP.NET include the following:

- ❏ `<asp:GridView>`
- ❏ `<asp:DataGrid>`
- ❏ `<asp:DetailsView>`
- ❏ `<asp:TreeView>`
- ❏ `<asp:Menu>`
- ❏ `<asp:DataList>`
- ❏ `<asp:Repeater>`
- ❏ `<asp:DropDownList>`
- ❏ `<asp:BulletedList>`
- ❏ `<asp:CheckBoxList>`
- ❏ `<asp:RadioButtonList>`
- ❏ `<asp:ListBox>`
- ❏ `<asp:AdRotator>`

The newest and most sought-after control in this group is the GridView control. This control was introduced in ASP.NET 2.0 and makes the DataGrid control more or less obsolete. The GridView control enables paging, sorting, and editing with very little work on your part. The next section looks at using the GridView control with SQL Server and taking advantage of these advanced features.

Using the GridView and SqlDataSource Controls

For an example of using these two controls together to display some information, let's turn to Visual Studio 2005. Start a new page and drag and drop a `GridView` control onto the design surface of the page. Pulling up the smart tag for the control on the design surface, you can click the Auto Format link to give your `GridView` control a better look and feel, rather than the default provided.

Next, drag and drop an `SqlDataSource` control onto the design surface. This control is a middle-tier component, so it appears as a gray box on the design surface. The first step is to configure the `SqlDataSource` control to work with the data you want from your Microsoft SQL Server instance (see Figure 20-11).

Figure 20-11

Working through the configuration process for the `SqlDataSource` control, you must choose your data connection and then indicate whether you want to store this connection in the `web.config` file (shown in Figure 20-12). This is highly advisable.

Figure 20-12

Within this configuration process you also choose the table you're going to work with, and test out the queries that the wizard will generate. For this example, choose the Customers table and select every row by checking the * check box, as shown in Figure 20-13.

Figure 20-13

After working through the configuration process, you will notice that your web.config file has changed to include the connection string:

```
<configuration>
```

```
<connectionStrings>
    <add name="NorthwindConnectionString"
    connectionString="Server=.;Integrated Security=True;Database=Northwind"
    providerName="System.Data.SqlClient" />
</connectionStrings>
```

```
<system.web>
    ...
    </system.web>
</configuration>
```

Once you have configured the SqlDataSource control, the next step is to tie the GridView control to this SqlDataSource control instance. This can be done through the GridView control's smart tag, as shown in Figure 20-14. You can also enable paging and sorting for the control in the same form.

Figure 20-14

The code generated by the wizard (it is also how you would code it yourself) is shown here:

```
<%@ Page Language="VB" %>

<script runat="server">

</script>

<html xmlns="http://www.w3.org/1999/xhtml" >
<head runat="server">
    <title>GridView Example</title>
</head>
<body>
    <form id="form1" runat="server">
    <div>
        <asp:GridView ID="GridView1" runat="server" BorderWidth="1px"
         BackColor="White" GridLines="Vertical"
         CellPadding="3" BorderStyle="Solid" BorderColor="#999999"
         ForeColor="Black" DataSourceID="SqlDataSource1"
         DataKeyNames="CustomerID" AutoGenerateColumns="False" AllowPaging="True"
         AllowSorting="True">
            <FooterStyle BackColor="#CCCCCC"></FooterStyle>
            <PagerStyle ForeColor="Black" HorizontalAlign="Center"
             BackColor="#999999"></PagerStyle>
            <HeaderStyle ForeColor="White" Font-Bold="True"
             BackColor="Black"></HeaderStyle>
            <AlternatingRowStyle BackColor="#CCCCCC"></AlternatingRowStyle>
            <Columns>
                <asp:BoundField ReadOnly="True" HeaderText="CustomerID"
                 DataField="CustomerID"
                 SortExpression="CustomerID"></asp:BoundField>
                <asp:BoundField HeaderText="CompanyName" DataField="CompanyName"
                 SortExpression="CompanyName"></asp:BoundField>
                <asp:BoundField HeaderText="ContactName" DataField="ContactName"
                 SortExpression="ContactName"></asp:BoundField>
                <asp:BoundField HeaderText="ContactTitle" DataField="ContactTitle"
                 SortExpression="ContactTitle"></asp:BoundField>
                <asp:BoundField HeaderText="Address" DataField="Address"
                 SortExpression="Address"></asp:BoundField>
                <asp:BoundField HeaderText="City" DataField="City"
                 SortExpression="City"></asp:BoundField>
                <asp:BoundField HeaderText="Region" DataField="Region"
                 SortExpression="Region"></asp:BoundField>
                <asp:BoundField HeaderText="PostalCode" DataField="PostalCode"
                 SortExpression="PostalCode"></asp:BoundField>
                <asp:BoundField HeaderText="Country" DataField="Country"
                 SortExpression="Country"></asp:BoundField>
                <asp:BoundField HeaderText="Phone" DataField="Phone"
                 SortExpression="Phone"></asp:BoundField>
                <asp:BoundField HeaderText="Fax" DataField="Fax"
                 SortExpression="Fax"></asp:BoundField>
            </Columns>
            <SelectedRowStyle ForeColor="White" Font-Bold="True"
             BackColor="#000099"></SelectedRowStyle>
        </asp:GridView>
```

```
        <asp:SqlDataSource ID="SqlDataSource1" runat="server"
         SelectCommand="SELECT * FROM [Customers]"
         ConnectionString="<%$ ConnectionStrings:NorthwindConnectionString %>">
        </asp:SqlDataSource>
      </div>
    </form>
  </body>
</html>
```

First consider the SqlDataSource control. This control has some important attributes to pay attention to. The first is the SelectCommand attribute. This is the SQL query that you will be using. In this case, it is a Select * From [Customers] query (meaning you are grabbing everything from the Customers table of the Northwind database). The second attribute to pay attention to is the ConnectionString attribute. The interesting aspect of this attribute is the use of <%$ ConnectionStrings:NorthwindConnectionString %> to get at the connection string. This value points at the settings placed inside the web.config file for those who don't want to hard-code their connection strings directly in the code of their pages. If you did want to do this, you would use something similar to the following construction:

```
ConnectionString="Server=(local);Trusted_Connection=True;Integrated Security=SSPI;
    Persist Security Info=True;Database=Northwind"
```

Looking now to the GridView control, you can see how easy it is to add the capability to perform paging and sorting capabilities to the control. It is simply a matter of adding the attributes AllowPaging and AllowSorting to the control and setting their values to True (they are set to False by default):

```
<asp:GridView ID="GridView1" runat="server" BorderWidth="1px"
 BackColor="White" GridLines="Vertical"
 CellPadding="3" BorderStyle="Solid" BorderColor="#999999"
 ForeColor="Black" DataSourceID="SqlDataSource1"
 DataKeyNames="CustomerID" AutoGenerateColumns="False" AllowPaging="True"
 AllowSorting="True">
    <!-- Inner content removed for clarity -->
</asp:GridView>
```

Each of the columns from the Customers table of the Northwind database is defined in the control through the use of the <asp:BoundField> control, a subcontrol of the GridView control. The BoundField control enables you to specify the header text of the column through the use of the HeaderText attribute. The DataField attribute actually ties the values that are displayed in this column to a particular value coming from the Customers table, and the SortExpression attribute should use the same values for sorting — unless you are sorting on a different value than what is being displayed.

In the end, your page should look similar to what is shown in Figure 20-15.

Allowing Editing and Deleting of Records with GridView

Now let's expand upon the previous example by allowing for the editing and deleting of records that are displayed in the GridView. If you are using the Visual Studio 2005 SqlDataSource Configuration Wizard to accomplish these tasks, then you need to take some extra steps beyond what was shown in the previous GridView example.

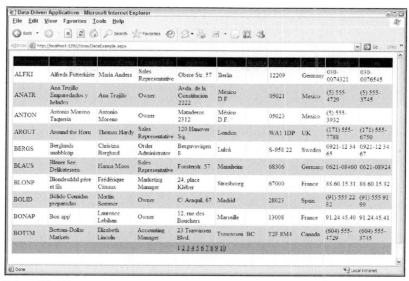

Figure 20-15

Go back to the `SqlDataSource` control on the design surface of your Web page and pull up the control's smart tag. Select the Configure Data Source option to reconfigure the `SqlDataSource` control to enable the editing and deletion of data from the Customers table of the Northwind database.

When you come to the screen in the Configure Select Statement dialog (see Figure 20-16), click the Advanced button.

Figure 20-16

This will pull up the Advanced SQL Generation Options dialog, shown in Figure 20-17.

Figure 20-17

As shown in this dialog, select the Generate Insert, Update, and Delete statements check box. This will construct the `SqlDataSource` control to not only handle the simple Select query, but also the Update and Delete queries. Press OK and then work through the rest of the wizard.

Return to the `GridView` control's smart tag and select the Refresh Schema. You will also find check boxes in the smart tag now for editing and deleting rows of data. Make sure both of these check boxes are checked, as shown in Figure 20-18.

Figure 20-18

Now look at what changed in the code. First, the `SqlDataSource` control has changed to allow for the updating and deletion of data:

```
<asp:SqlDataSource ID="SqlDataSource1" runat="server"
 SelectCommand="SELECT * FROM [Customers]"
 ConnectionString="<%$ ConnectionStrings:AppConnectionString1 %>"
 DeleteCommand="DELETE FROM [Customers] WHERE [CustomerID] = @original_CustomerID"
 InsertCommand="INSERT INTO [Customers] ([CustomerID], [CompanyName],
    [ContactName], [ContactTitle], [Address], [City], [Region], [PostalCode],
    [Country], [Phone], [Fax]) VALUES (@CustomerID, @CompanyName, @ContactName,
    @ContactTitle, @Address, @City, @Region, @PostalCode, @Country, @Phone, @Fax)"
 UpdateCommand="UPDATE [Customers] SET [CompanyName] = @CompanyName, [ContactName]
    = @ContactName, [ContactTitle] = @ContactTitle, [Address] = @Address, [City] =
    @City, [Region] = @Region, [PostalCode] = @PostalCode, [Country] = @Country,
```

```
            [Phone] = @Phone, [Fax] = @Fax WHERE [CustomerID] = @original_CustomerID">
                <DeleteParameters>
                    <asp:Parameter Type="String" Name="CustomerID"></asp:Parameter>
                </DeleteParameters>
                <UpdateParameters>
                    <asp:Parameter Type="String" Name="CompanyName"></asp:Parameter>
                    <asp:Parameter Type="String" Name="ContactName"></asp:Parameter>
                    <asp:Parameter Type="String" Name="ContactTitle"></asp:Parameter>
                    <asp:Parameter Type="String" Name="Address"></asp:Parameter>
                    <asp:Parameter Type="String" Name="City"></asp:Parameter>
                    <asp:Parameter Type="String" Name="Region"></asp:Parameter>
                    <asp:Parameter Type="String" Name="PostalCode"></asp:Parameter>
                    <asp:Parameter Type="String" Name="Country"></asp:Parameter>
                    <asp:Parameter Type="String" Name="Phone"></asp:Parameter>
                    <asp:Parameter Type="String" Name="Fax"></asp:Parameter>
                    <asp:Parameter Type="String" Name="CustomerID"></asp:Parameter>
                </UpdateParameters>
                <InsertParameters>
                    <asp:Parameter Type="String" Name="CustomerID"></asp:Parameter>
                    <asp:Parameter Type="String" Name="CompanyName"></asp:Parameter>
                    <asp:Parameter Type="String" Name="ContactName"></asp:Parameter>
                    <asp:Parameter Type="String" Name="ContactTitle"></asp:Parameter>
                    <asp:Parameter Type="String" Name="Address"></asp:Parameter>
                    <asp:Parameter Type="String" Name="City"></asp:Parameter>
                    <asp:Parameter Type="String" Name="Region"></asp:Parameter>
                    <asp:Parameter Type="String" Name="PostalCode"></asp:Parameter>
                    <asp:Parameter Type="String" Name="Country"></asp:Parameter>
                    <asp:Parameter Type="String" Name="Phone"></asp:Parameter>
                    <asp:Parameter Type="String" Name="Fax"></asp:Parameter>
                </InsertParameters>
    </asp:SqlDataSource>
```

Second, other queries have been added to the control. Using the `DeleteCommand`, `InsertCommand`, and `UpdateCommand` attributes of the `SqlDataSource` control, these functions can now be performed just as `Select` queries were enabled through the use of the `SelectCommand` attribute. As you can see in the queries, a lot of parameters are defined within them. These parameters are then assigned through the `<DeleteParameters>`, `<UpdateParameters>`, and `<InsertParameters>` elements. Within each of these subsections, the actual parameters are defined through the use of the `<asp:Parameter>` control, where you also assign the datatype of the parameter (through the use of the `Type` attribute) and the name of the parameter.

Besides these changes to the `SqlDataSource` control, only one small change has been made to the `GridView` control:

```
<Columns>
    <asp:CommandField ShowDeleteButton="True"
     ShowEditButton="True"></asp:CommandField>
    <asp:BoundField ReadOnly="True" HeaderText="CustomerID" DataField="CustomerID"
     SortExpression="CustomerID"></asp:BoundField>
    <asp:BoundField HeaderText="CompanyName" DataField="CompanyName"
     SortExpression="CompanyName"></asp:BoundField>
    <asp:BoundField HeaderText="ContactName" DataField="ContactName"
```

```
      SortExpression="ContactName"></asp:BoundField>
    <asp:BoundField HeaderText="ContactTitle" DataField="ContactTitle"
      SortExpression="ContactTitle"></asp:BoundField>
    <asp:BoundField HeaderText="Address" DataField="Address"
      SortExpression="Address"></asp:BoundField>
    <asp:BoundField HeaderText="City" DataField="City"
      SortExpression="City"></asp:BoundField>
    <asp:BoundField HeaderText="Region" DataField="Region"
      SortExpression="Region"></asp:BoundField>
    <asp:BoundField HeaderText="PostalCode" DataField="PostalCode"
      SortExpression="PostalCode"></asp:BoundField>
    <asp:BoundField HeaderText="Country" DataField="Country"
      SortExpression="Country"></asp:BoundField>
    <asp:BoundField HeaderText="Phone" DataField="Phone"
      SortExpression="Phone"></asp:BoundField>
    <asp:BoundField HeaderText="Fax" DataField="Fax"
      SortExpression="Fax"></asp:BoundField>
</Columns>
```

The only change needed for the GridView control is the addition of a new column from which editing and deleting commands can be initiated. This is done with the `<asp:CommandField>` control. From this control, you can see that we also enabled the Edit and Delete buttons through a Boolean value. Once built and run, your new page will look like the one shown in Figure 20-19.

Figure 20-19

Don't Stop There!

Due to limited space, this chapter can only present one example, but it is important to realize that many other `DataSource` controls are at your disposal. The `ObjectDataSource` control is rather powerful for those who wish to enforce a strict *n*-tier model and separate the data retrieval logic into an object that the `GridView` and other data-bound controls can work with. The `XmlDataSource` control is one control that you will most likely find yourself using a lot, as more and more data is being stored as XML, including dynamic data (such as Web logs via RSS). These `DataSource` controls are fine-tuned for the type of data-stores for which they are targeted, so you will find a lot of benefit in exploring their capabilities in detail.

Navigation

People rarely build Web applications that are made up of just a single page instance. Instead, applications are usually made up of multiple pages that are all related to each other in some fashion. Some applications have a workflow through which end users can work from page to page, while other applications have a navigation structure that allows for free roaming throughout the pages. Sometimes the navigation structure of a site gets complex, and managing this complexity can become rather cumbersome.

ASP.NET 2.0 includes a way of managing the navigational structure of your Web applications. Using this system, you first define your navigational structure through an XML file that can then be bound to a couple of different server controls focused on navigation.

This makes it rather easy when you have to introduce changes to the structure of your navigation or make name changes to pages contained within this structure. Instead of going from page to page throughout your entire application, changing titles or page destinations, you can now make these changes in one place — an XML file — and the changes are instantaneously reflected throughout your application.

The first step in working with the ASP.NET navigation system is to reflect your navigational structure in the `web.sitemap` file, the XML file that will contain the complete site structure. For instance, suppose you want the following site structure:

```
Home
        Books
        Magazines
                U.S. Magazines
                European Magazines
```

This site structure has three levels to it, with multiple items in the lowest level. You can reflect this in the `web.sitemap` file as follows:

```
<?xml version="1.0" encoding="utf-8" ?>
<siteMap xmlns="http://schemas.microsoft.com/AspNet/SiteMap-File-1.0" >
    <siteMapNode url="default.aspx" title="Home" description="The site homepage">
        <siteMapNode url="books.aspx" title="Books"
         description="Books from our catalog" />
        <siteMapNode url="magazines.aspx" title="Magazines"
         description="Magazines from our catalog">
          <siteMapNode url="magazines_us.aspx" title="U.S. Magazines"
```

```
                description="Magazines from the U.S." />
            <siteMapNode url="magazines_eur.aspx" title="European Magazines"
            description="Magazines from Europe" />
        </siteMapNode>
    </siteMapNode>
</siteMap>
```

To create a `web.sitemap` file in Visual Studio 2005, go to the Add New Items dialog and select the Site Map option. You can place the preceding content in this file. To move a level down in the hierarchy, nest `<siteMapNode>` elements within other `<siteMapNode>` elements. A `<siteMapNode>` element can contain several different attributes, as defined in the following table:

Attribute	Description
Title	The `title` attribute provides a textual description of the link. The `String` value used here is the text used for the link.
Description	The `description` attribute not only reminds you what the link is for, it is also used for the `ToolTip` attribute on the link. The `ToolTip` attribute is the yellow box that shows up next to the link when the end user hovers the cursor over the link for a couple of seconds.
Url	The `url` attribute describes where the file is located in the solution. If the file is in the root directory, then simply use the filename, such as `default.aspx`. If the file is located in a subfolder, be sure to include the folders in the `String` value used for this attribute, e.g., `MySubFolder/MyFile.aspx`.
Roles	If ASP.NET security trimming is enabled, you can use the `roles` attribute to define which roles are allowed to view and click the provided link in the navigation.

Using the SiteMapPath Server Control

One of the available server controls that works with a `web.sitemap` file is the `SiteMapPath` control. This control provides a popular structure found on many Internet websites. Sometimes called *breadcrumb navigation*, this feature is simple to implement in ASP.NET.

To see an example of this control at work, let's create a page that would be at the bottom of the site map structure. Within the project that contains your `web.sitemap` file, create an ASP.NET page named `magazines_us.aspx`. On this page, simply drag and drop a `SiteMapPath` control onto the page. You will find this control under the Navigation section in the Visual Studio Toolbox. This control's code looks as follows:

```
<asp:SiteMapPath ID="SiteMapPath1" runat="server"></asp:SiteMapPath>
```

What else do you need to do to get this control to work? Well, nothing! Simply build and run the page to see the results shown in Figure 20-20.

Figure 20-20

The `SiteMapPath` control defines the end user's place in the application's site structure. It shows the current page the user is on (U.S. Magazines) as well as the two pages above it in the hierarchy.

The `SiteMapPath` control requires no `DataSource` control, as it automatically binds itself to any `.sitemap` file it finds in the project, and nothing is required on your part to make this happen. The `SiteMapPath`'s smart tag enables you to customize the control's appearance too, so you can produce other results, as shown in Figure 20-21.

Figure 20-21

The code for this version of the `SiteMapPath` control is as follows:

```
<asp:SiteMapPath ID="SiteMapPath1" runat="server" PathSeparator=" : "
 Font-Names="Verdana" Font-Size="0.8em">
   <PathSeparatorStyle Font-Bold="True" ForeColor="#507CD1"></PathSeparatorStyle>
   <CurrentNodeStyle ForeColor="#333333"></CurrentNodeStyle>
   <NodeStyle Font-Bold="True" ForeColor="#284E98"></NodeStyle>
   <RootNodeStyle Font-Bold="True" ForeColor="#507CD1"></RootNodeStyle>
</asp:SiteMapPath>
```

This example illustrates that a lot of style elements and attributes can be used with the `SiteMapPath` control. Many options at your disposal enable you to create breadcrumb navigation that is unique.

Menu Server Control

Another navigation control enables end users of your application to navigate throughout the pages based upon information stored within the `web.sitemap` file. The `Menu` server control produces a compact navigation system that pops up sub-options when the user hovers the mouse over an option. The result of the `Menu` server control when bound to the site map is shown in Figure 20-22.

Figure 20-22

To build this, you must be working off of the web.sitemap file created earlier. After the web.sitemap file is in place, place a Menu server control on the page, along with a SiteMapDataSource control:

```
<asp:Menu ID="Menu1" runat="server" DataSourceID="SiteMapDataSource1">
</asp:Menu>
<asp:SiteMapDataSource ID="SiteMapDataSource1" runat="server" />
```

The SiteMapDataSource control automatically works with the application's web.sitemap file. In addition to the SiteMapDataSource control, the other item included is the Menu server control, which uses the typical ID and Runat attributes, in addition to the DataSourceID attribute, to connect this control with what is retrieved from the SiteMapDataSource control.

Like the other controls provided by ASP.NET, you can easily modify the look and feel of this control. By clicking the Auto Format link in the control's smart tag, you can give the control the "classic" look and feel. This setting produces the result shown in Figure 20-23.

Figure 20-23

As with the other controls, a lot of sub-elements contribute to the changing look of the control's style:

```
<asp:Menu ID="Menu1" runat="server" DataSourceID="SiteMapDataSource1"
 Font-Names="Verdana" Font-Size="0.8em" BackColor="#B5C7DE" ForeColor="#284E98"
 StaticSubMenuIndent="10px" DynamicHorizontalOffset="2">
    <StaticSelectedStyle BackColor="#507CD1"></StaticSelectedStyle>
    <StaticMenuItemStyle HorizontalPadding="5"
     VerticalPadding="2"></StaticMenuItemStyle>
    <DynamicMenuStyle BackColor="#B5C7DE"></DynamicMenuStyle>
    <DynamicSelectedStyle BackColor="#507CD1"></DynamicSelectedStyle>
```

```
        <DynamicMenuItemStyle HorizontalPadding="5"
         VerticalPadding="2"></DynamicMenuItemStyle>
        <DynamicHoverStyle ForeColor="White" Font-Bold="True"
         BackColor="#284E98"></DynamicHoverStyle>
        <StaticHoverStyle ForeColor="White" Font-Bold="True"
         BackColor="#284E98"></StaticHoverStyle>
    </asp:Menu>
```

The TreeView Server Control

The last navigation server control to look at is the `TreeView` control. This control enables you to render a hierarchy of data. The `TreeView` control is not only meant for displaying what is contained within the `.sitemap` file; you can also use this control to represent other forms of hierarchical data, such as data that you might store in a standard XML file.

You may have encountered a similar `TreeView` control in .NET when using the IE Web controls, which also contained a `TreeView` control. That previous `TreeView` control was limited to working only in Microsoft's Internet Explorer, whereas the new `TreeView` control works in a wide variety of browsers.

The `TreeView` control is similar to the `Menu` control in that it won't bind automatically to the `web.sitemap` file, but instead requires an underlying `DataSource` control. The code for displaying the contents of the `.sitemap` file is shown in the following example:

```
    <asp:TreeView ID="TreeView1" runat="server" DataSourceID="SiteMapDataSource1">
    </asp:TreeView>
    <asp:SiteMapDataSource ID="SiteMapDataSource1" runat="server" />
```

As with the `Menu` control example, a `SiteMapDataSource` is needed. After a basic `SiteMapDataSource` control is in place, position a `TreeView` control on the page and set the `DataSourceId` property to `SiteMapDataSource1`. This simple construction produces the result shown in Figure 20-24.

Figure 20-24

Remember that by using the Auto Format link from the control's smart tag, you can format the `TreeView` control in a wide variety of ways.

The `TreeView` isn't meant only for site maps; as mentioned, it can build upon any underlying hierarchical data set. For instance, you can display a hierarchical data structure from a standard XML file just as easily. Suppose you have the following XML file:

```
<?xml version="1.0" encoding="utf-8" ?>
<Hardware>
    <Item Category="Motherboards">
        <Option Choice="Asus" />
        <Option Choice="Abit" />
    </Item>
    <Item Category="Memory">
        <Option Choice="128mb" />
        <Option Choice="256mb" />
        <Option Choice="512mb" />
    </Item>
    <Item Category="Hard Drives">
        <Option Choice="40GB" />
        <Option Choice="80GB" />
        <Option Choice="100GB" />
    </Item>
    <Item Category="Drives">
        <Option Choice="CD" />
        <Option Choice="DVD" />
        <Option Choice="DVD Burner" />
    </Item>
</Hardware>
```

It's obvious that this XML file is not meant for site navigation, but for options from which end user can make selections. As stated, the `TreeView` control is quite extensible. For example, the following code creates a page that uses the preceding XML file:

```
<%@ Page Language="VB" %>

<script runat="server">
    Protected Sub Button1_Click(ByVal sender As Object, _
        ByVal e As System.EventArgs)

        If TreeView1.CheckedNodes.Count > 0 Then
            Label1.Text = "We are sending you information on:<p>"

            For Each node As TreeNode In TreeView1.CheckedNodes
                Label1.Text += node.Text & " " & node.Parent.Text & "<br>"
            Next
        Else
            label1.Text = "You didn't select anything. Sorry!"
        End If
    End Sub
</script>

<html xmlns="http://www.w3.org/1999/xhtml" >
<head runat="server">
    <title>The TreeView Control</title>
</head>
```

```
<body>
    <form id="form1" runat="server">
    <div>
        Please select the following items that you are interesting in:
        <br />
        <br />
        <asp:TreeView ID="TreeView1" runat="server"
         DataSourceID="XmlDataSource1" ShowLines="True">
            <DataBindings>
                <asp:TreeNodeBinding TextField="Category"
                 DataMember="Item"></asp:TreeNodeBinding>
                <asp:TreeNodeBinding ShowCheckBox="True" TextField="Choice"
                 DataMember="Option"></asp:TreeNodeBinding>
            </DataBindings>
        </asp:TreeView> <br />
        <br />
        <asp:Button ID="Button1" runat="server"
         Text="Submit Choices" OnClick="Button1_Click" />
        <br />
        <br />
        <asp:Label ID="Label1" runat="server"></asp:Label>
        <asp:XmlDataSource ID="XmlDataSource1" runat="server"
         DataFile="~/Hardware.xml">
        </asp:XmlDataSource>
    </div>
    </form>
</body>
</html>
```

This example uses an XmlDataSource control instead of the SiteMapDataSource control. The XmlDataSource control associates itself with the XML file shown earlier (Hardware.xml) through the use of the DataFile attribute.

The TreeView control then binds itself to the XmlDataSource control through the use of the DataSourceID attribute, which here is pointed to XmlDataSource1. Another interesting addition in the root TreeView node is the ShowLines attribute, set to True. This feature of the TreeView causes every node in the hierarchy to show its connection to its parent node through a visual line.

When working with XML files, which can basically be of any construction, you must bind the nodes of the TreeView control to specific values that come from the XML file. This is done through the use of the <DataBindings> element. This element encapsulates one or more TreeNodeBinding objects. Two of the more important available properties of a TreeNodeBinding object are DataMember and TextField. The DataMember property points to the name of the XML element that the TreeView control should look for. The TextField property specifies the XML attribute of that particular XML element. If you do this correctly with the use of the <DataBindings> construct, you get the result shown in Figure 20-25.

In the button click event from our example, you can see how easy it is to iterate through each of the checked nodes from the TreeView selection by creating instances of TreeNode objects. These selections are made from one of the TreeNodeBinding objects, which sets the ShowCheckBox property to True.

Figure 20-25

Membership and Role Management

ASP.NET contains a built-in membership and role management system that can be initiated either through code or the ASP.NET Web Site Administration Tool. This is an ideal system for authenticating users to access a page or even your entire site. This management system not only provides a new API suite for managing users, but also provides you with some server controls that interact with this API.

As the first step in setting up your site's security and the user roles, open the ASP.NET Web Site Administration Tool. You can launch this tool through a button in the Visual Studio 2005 Solution Explorer or by clicking Website ⇨ ASP.NET Configuration in the Visual Studio menu. When the tool opens in the document window, click the Security tab, shown in Figure 20-26.

Click the link to start the Security Setup Wizard, shown in Figure 20-27.

The wizard first asks whether your application will be available on the public Internet or hosted on an intranet. If you select Internet, then your website will be enabled with Forms Authentication. If you select Intranet, then your site will be configured to work with Windows Integrated Authentication. For our example, select the Internet option.

Figure 20-26

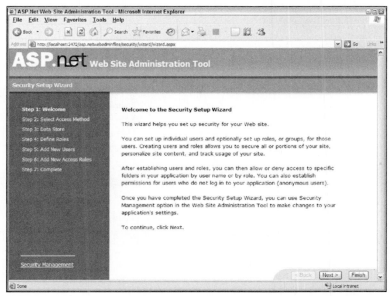

Figure 20-27

Working through the wizard, you are also asked whether you are going to work with role management. Enable role management by checking the appropriate check box and add a role titled `Manager`. After this step, you can actually enter users into the system. Fill out information for each user you want in the system, as shown in Figure 20-28.

The next step is to create the access rules for your site. You can pick specific folders and apply the rules for the folder. In this example, anyone in the `Manager` role would have access to the site, while anonymous users would be denied access. This is shown in Figure 20-29.

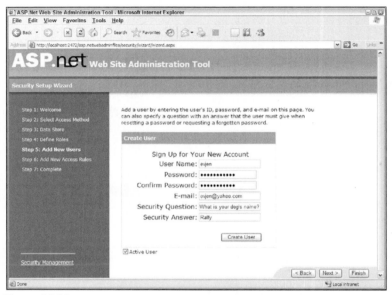

Figure 20-28

Figure 20-29

Click the Finish button to exit the wizard. If you refresh the Solution Explorer in Visual Studio, a new datastore (an SQL Server Express Edition `.mdf` file) appears in the `App_Data` folder. This is where all of the user and role information is stored. Note that you can configure both of the systems (the membership and role management systems) to work with other datastores besides these SQL Express data files. For example, you can configure these systems to work with a full-blown version of Microsoft's SQL Server. Notice in the Solution Explorer that if you didn't already have a web.config file, you have one now. The contents added to the web.config file includes the following:

```
<?xml version="1.0" encoding="utf-8"?>
<configuration>
    <system.web>
        <authorization>
            <allow roles="Manager" />
            <deny users="?" />
        </authorization>
        <roleManager enabled="true" />
        <authentication mode="Forms" />
    </system.web>
</configuration>
```

This shows all the settings that were enabled. The <authorization> section allows for users who are in the role of Manager, and denies all anonymous users (defined with a question mark). The <roleManager> element turns on the role management system, while the <authentication> element turns on forms authentication. Now, let's utilize these configurations.

Create a login page, as everyone will access any page in this application as an anonymous user first. The login page enables people to enter their credentials in order to be authorized in the Manager role created earlier.

ASP.NET includes a slew of controls that make working with the membership and role management systems easier. On the login page (Login.aspx), place a simple Login server control:

```
<asp:Login ID="Login1" runat="server"></asp:Login>
```

The nice thing here is that you have to do absolutely nothing to tie this Login control to the .mdf database created earlier through the wizard. Now access another page in the application (other than the Login.aspx page) and start up that page. This example started up Default.aspx (which only contains a simple text statement), but looking at Figure 20-30 you can see from the URL specified in the browser that I was redirected to Login.aspx because I wasn't yet authenticated.

Figure 20-30

The `Login.aspx` page enables me to enter my credentials, which then authorize me in the `Manager` role. Pressing the `Login` button causes the browser to redirect me to the appropriate page. I am now authenticated and authorized for the site!

Personalization

Many Web applications have features that allow for personalization of some kind. This might be as simple as greeting the users by name, or it might deal with more advanced issues such as content placement. Whatever the case, personalization techniques have always been tricky. Developers have used anything from cookies, sessions, or database entries to control the personalization that users can perform on their pages.

ASP.NET 2.0 includes an easy to use and configure personalization system. It is as simple as making entries in the `web.config` file to get the personalization system started. Like the membership and role management systems, the personalization system also uses an underlying datastore. The next example continues to work with the SQL Server Express Edition .mdb file.

This example creates two properties, `FirstName` and `LastName`, both of type `String`. First, alter the `web.config` file. The changed `web.config` file is shown here:

```
<?xml version="1.0"?>
<configuration>
   <system.web>
      <profile>
         <properties>
            <add name="FirstName" type="System.String" />
            <add name="LastName" type="System.String" />
         </properties>
      </profile>
   </system.web>
</configuration>
```

Now that the profile properties we're going to store for each user are configured in the `web.config` file, the next step is to build a simple ASP.NET page that utilizes these property settings. Create a simple page that contains two `TextBox` controls that ask end users for their first and last names. We will then input the values collected into the personalization engine via a button `click` event. The code for this page is as follows:

```
<%@ Page Language="VB" %>

<script runat="server">
   Protected Sub Button1_Click(ByVal sender As Object, _
      ByVal e As System.EventArgs)

      Profile.FirstName = TextBox1.Text
      Profile.LastName = TextBox1.Text

      Label1.Text = "First name: " & Profile.FirstName & _
         "<br>Last name: " & Profile.LastName
```

```
        End Sub
</script>

<html xmlns="http://www.w3.org/1999/xhtml" >
<head runat="server">
    <title>Welcome Page</title>
</head>
<body>
    <form id="form1" runat="server">
    <div>
        First name:<br />
        <asp:TextBox ID="TextBox1" runat="server"></asp:TextBox>
        <br />
        Last name:<br />
        <asp:TextBox ID="TextBox2" runat="server"></asp:TextBox>
        <br />
        <asp:Button ID="Button1" runat="server" Text="Submit Information"
         OnClick="Button1_Click" />
        <br />
        <br />
        <asp:Label ID="Label1" runat="server"></asp:Label>
    </div>
    </form>
</body>
</html>
```

When this page is posted back to itself, the values placed into the two text boxes are placed into the personalization engine and associated with this particular user through the use of the `Profile` object. When working with the `Profile` object in Visual Studio, note that the custom properties you created are provided to you through IntelliSense. Once stored in the personalization engine, they are then available to you on any page within the application through the use of the same `Profile` object.

Configuring ASP.NET

Configuring ASP.NET has been greatly enhanced in this release. Instead of working purely with various XML configuration files to manage how ASP.NET works and performs, you can now use an MMC ASP.NET Snap-In. To access this ASP.NET configuration tool, open IIS (5.0 or 6.0) and expand the Web Sites folder. This folder shows a list of all the websites configured to work with IIS. Remember that not all your websites are configured to work in this manner. It is also possible that you built your Web application to make use of the ASP.NET built-in Web server.

After you find the application you are looking for in the Web Sites folder, right-click that application and select Properties from the list. This brings up the MMC console. Click the far-right ASP.NET tab to get the results shown in Figure 20-31.

Selecting one of the application folders also enables you to edit the `web.config` file from the MMC snap-in; selecting Properties for the default website (the root node) enables you to edit the `machine.config` file as well.

Figure 20-31

In addition to being able to edit the ASP.NET features shown in Figure 20-31, the ASP.NET tab also includes an Edit Configuration button that provides a tremendous number of modification capabilities to use in the `web.config` file. When you click this button, you are provided with a multi-tabbed GUI, ASP.NET Configuration Settings (see Figure 20-32).

Figure 20-32

Working with the ASP.NET Provider Model

When ASP.NET 2.0 was being developed, plenty of requests for new capabilities came into the ASP.NET team. Users wanted to be able to store sessions by means other than the three methods — `InProc`, `StateServer`, and `SQLServer`. One such request was for a provider that could store sessions in an Oracle database. This might seem like a logical thing to add to ASP.NET in the days of ASP.NET 1.1, but if the team added a provider for Oracle, they would soon get requests to add even more providers for other databases and data storage methods. For this reason, instead of building providers for every possible scenario, the developers designed a provider model that enabled them to add any providers they wished. Thus was born the new provider model found in ASP.NET 2.0.

ASP.NET 2.0 introduced a lot of new systems that require state storage of some kind. In addition, instead of recording state in a fragile mode (the way sessions are stored by default), many of these new systems require their state to be stored in more concrete datastores such as databases or XML files. This also enables a longer-lived state for the users visiting an application — something else that is required by these new systems.

The systems found in ASP.NET 2.0 that require advanced state management include the following:

❑   Membership

❑   Role management

❑   Site navigation

❑   Personalization

❑   Health-monitoring Web events

❑   Web parts personalization

❑   Configuration file protection

The membership system enables ASP.NET to work from a user store of some kind to create, delete, or edit application users. Because it is apparent that developers want to work with an unlimited amount of different datastores for their user store, they need a means to change the underlying user store for their ASP.NET applications easily. The provider model found in ASP.NET 2.0 is the answer.

Out of the box, ASP.NET 2.0 provides two membership providers that enable you to store user information: the SQL Server and the Active Directory membership providers (found at `System.Web.Security.SqlMembershipProvider` and `System.Web.Security.ActiveDirectoryMembershipProvider`, respectively). In fact, for each of the systems (as well as for some of the ASP.NET 1.*x* systems), a series of providers is available to alter the way the state of that system is recorded. Figure 20-33 illustrates these providers.

As shown in the diagram, ASP.NET provides a large number of providers out of the box. Some systems have only a single provider (such as the profile system, which includes only a provider to connect to SQL Server), whereas other systems include multiple providers (such as the WebEvents provider, which includes six separate providers). The next section describes how to set up SQL Server to work with a number of the providers presented in this chapter. You can use SQL Server 7.0, 2000, or 2005 for the back-end datastore for many of the providers presented (although not all of them). After this explanation is an overview of the available providers built into ASP.NET 2.0.

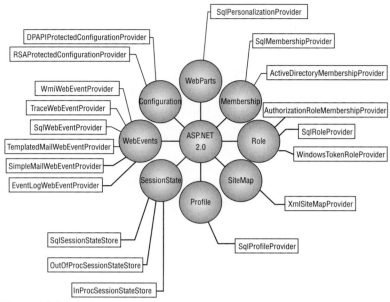

Figure 20-33

Working with Microsoft SQL Server 7.0, 2000, or 2005

Quite a number of providers work with SQL Server. For instance, the membership, role management, personalization, and other systems work easily with SQL Server. However, all these systems work with the new Microsoft SQL Server Express Edition file (.mdf) by default instead of with one of the full-blown versions of SQL Server, such as SQL Server 7.0, SQL Server 2000, or SQL Server 2005.

To work with either Microsoft SQL Server 7.0, 2000, or 2005, you must set up the database using the aspnet_regsql.exe tool. Working with aspnet_regsql.exe creates the necessary tables, roles, stored procedures, and other items needed by the providers. To access this tool, open the Visual Studio 2005 Command Prompt by selecting Start ➪ All Programs ➪ Visual Studio 2005 ➪ Visual Studio Tools ➪ Visual Studio 2005 Command Prompt. This gives you access to the ASP.NET SQL Server Setup Wizard. The ASP.NET SQL Server Setup Wizard is an easy to use tool that facilitates setup of SQL Server to work with many of the systems built into ASP.NET 2.0, such as the membership, role management, and personalization systems. The Setup Wizard provides two ways for you to set up the database: using a command-line tool or using a GUI tool.

The ASP.NET SQL Server Setup Wizard Command-Line Tool

The command-line version of the Setup Wizard gives developers optimal control over how the database is created. Working from the command line using this tool is not difficult, so don't be intimidated by it.

You can get at the actual tool, aspnet_regsql.exe, from the Visual Studio Command Prompt if you have Visual Studio 2005. At the command prompt, type **aspnet regsql.exe -?** to get a list of all the command-line options at your disposal for working with this tool.

The following table describes some of the available options for setting up your SQL Server instance to work with the personalization framework:

Command Option	Description
-?	Displays a list of available option commands
-W	Uses the Wizard mode. This uses the default installation if no other parameters are used.
-S <server>	Specifies the SQL Server instance to work with
-U <login>	Specifies the username for logging in to SQL Server. If you use this, then you also use the -P command.
-P <password>	Specifies the password to use for logging in to SQL Server. If you use this, then you also use the -U command.
-E	Provides instructions to use the current Windows credentials for authentication
-C	Specifies the connection string for connecting to SQL Server. If you use this, you don't need to use the -U and -P commands because they are specified in the connection string itself.
-A all	Adds support for all the available SQL Server operations provided by ASP.NET 2.0, including membership, role management, profiles, site counters, and page/control personalization
-A p	Adds support for working with profiles
_R all	Removes support for all the available SQL Server operations that have been previously installed. These include membership, role management, profiles, site counters, and page/control personalization.
-R p	Removes support for the profile capability from SQL Server
-d <database>	Specifies the database name to use with the application services. If you don't specify a database name, then aspnetdb is used.
/sqlexportonly <filename>	Instead of modifying an instance of a SQL Server database, use this command in conjunction with the other commands to generate a SQL script that adds or removes the features specified. This command creates the scripts in a file that has the name specified in the command.

To modify SQL Server to work with the personalization provider using this command-line tool, you enter a command such as the following:

```
aspnet_regsql.exe -A all -E
```

After you enter the preceding command, the command-line tool creates the features required by all the available ASP.NET 2.0 systems. The results are shown in the tool itself, as illustrated in Figure 20-34.

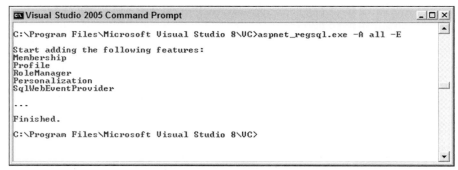

Figure 20-34

When this action is completed, you can see that a new database, aspnetdb, has been created in the SQL Server Enterprise Manager of Microsoft SQL Server 2000 (the database used for this example). You now have the appropriate tables for working with all the ASP.NET 2.0 systems that are able to work with SQL Server (see Figure 20-35).

Figure 20-35

One advantage of using the command-line tool, rather than the GUI-based version of the ASP.NET SQL Server Setup Wizard, is that you can install in the database just the features you're interested in working with, instead of installing everything (as the GUI-based version does). For instance, if you want only the membership system to interact with SQL Server 2000 — not any of the other systems (such as role management and personalization) — then you can configure the setup so that only the tables, roles, stored procedures, and other items required by the membership system are established in the database. To set up the database for the membership system only, use the following on the command line:

```
aspnet_regsql.exe –A m –E
```

The ASP.NET SQL Server Setup Wizard GUI Tool

Instead of working with the tool through the command line, you can also work with a GUI version of the same wizard. To get at the GUI version, type the following at the Visual Studio command prompt:

```
aspnet_regsql.exe
```

At this point, the ASP.NET SQL Server Setup Wizard welcome screen appears, as shown in Figure 20-36.

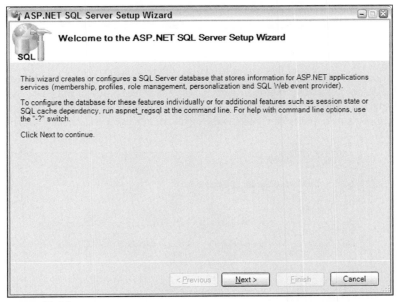

Figure 20-36

Clicking the Next button gives you a new screen that offers two options: one to install management features into SQL Server and the other to remove them (see Figure 20-37).

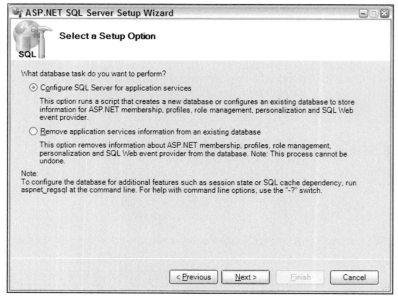

Figure 20-37

From here, choose "Configure SQL Server for application services" and click Next. The third screen (see Figure 20-38) asks for the login credentials to SQL Server and the name of the database to perform the operations. The Database option is `<default>` — meaning the wizard creates a database called `aspnetdb`. If you want to choose a different folder, such as the application's database, choose the appropriate option.

Figure 20-38

After you have made your server and database selections, click Next. The screen shown in Figure 20-39 asks you to confirm your settings. If everything looks correct, click the Next button — otherwise, click Previous and correct your settings.

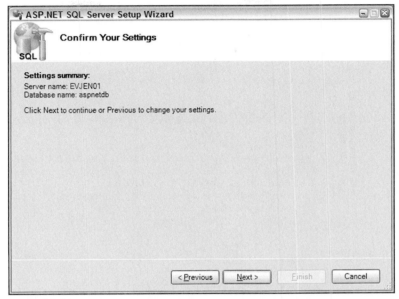

Figure 20-39

When this is complete, you get a notification that everything was set up correctly.

Connecting Your Default Provider to a New SQL Server Instance

After you set up the full-blown Microsoft SQL Server to work with the various systems provided by ASP.NET 2.0, you create a connection string to the database in your `machine.config.comments` or `web.config` file, as shown in the following code:

```
<configuration>

    <connectionStrings>
        <add name="LocalSql2000Server"
          connectionString="data source=127.0.0.1;Integrated Security=SSPI" />
    </connectionStrings>

</configuration>
```

You may want to change the values provided if you are working with a remote instance of SQL Server, rather than an instance that resides on the same server as the application. Changing this value in the `machine.config` file changes how each ASP.NET application uses this provider. Applying this setting in the `web.config` file causes only the local application to work with this instance.

After the connection string is set up, look further in the `<providers>` area of the section you are going to work with. For instance, if you are using the membership provider, you want to work with the `<membership>` element in the configuration file. The settings to change SQL Server are shown here:

```
<configuration>

  <connectionStrings>
    <add name="LocalSql2000Server"
      connectionString="data source=127.0.0.1;Integrated Security=SSPI" />
  </connectionStrings>

  <system.web>

          <membership defaultProvider="AspNetSql2000MembershipProvider">
            <providers>
                <add name="AspNetSql2000MembershipProvider"
                    type="System.Web.Security.SqlMembershipProvider,
                        System.Web, Version=2.0.0.0, Culture=neutral,
                        PublicKeyToken=b03f5f7f11d50a3a"
                    connectionStringName="LocalSql2000Server"
                    enablePasswordRetrieval="false"
                    enablePasswordReset="true"
                    requiresQuestionAndAnswer="true"
                    applicationName="/"
                    requiresUniqueEmail="false"
                    passwordFormat="Hashed"
                    maxInvalidPasswordAttempts="5"
                    minRequiredPasswordLength="7"
                    minRequiredNonalphanumericCharacters="1"
                    passwordAttemptWindow="10"
                    passwordStrengthRegularExpression="" />
            </providers>
        </membership>

  </system.web>

</configuration>
```

With these changes in place, the SQL Server 2000 instance is now one of the providers available for use with your applications. The name of this instance is `AspNetSql2000MembershipProvider`. You can see that this instance also uses the connection string of `LocalSql2000Server`, which was defined earlier.

Pay attention to some important attribute declarations in the preceding configuration code. For example, the provider used by the membership system is defined via the `defaultProvider` attribute found in the main `<membership>` node. Using this attribute, you can specify whether the provider is one of the built-in providers or whether it is a custom provider that you have built yourself or received from a third party. With the code in place, the membership provider now works with Microsoft SQL Server 2000 (as shown in this example) instead of the Microsoft SQL Server Express Edition files.

Summary

This chapter and the previous chapter offered a whirlwind tour of ASP.NET 2.0 and some of the application features that you can provide to the projects you develop. ASP.NET is highly focused on the area of developer productivity, and works very hard at providing you access to the features and functions that most websites need to employ today. This chapter covered the following ASP.NET technologies:

- ❑ Cross-page posting
- ❑ ASP.NET compilation techniques
- ❑ Master pages
- ❑ The datasource controls
- ❑ The new navigation system and some of the navigation server controls
- ❑ Membership and role management

A nice aspect of the features presented is that you can either utilize the wizards that are built into the underlying technology or simply avoid these wizards and employ the technologies yourself. Either way is fine. Another useful aspect of the technologies introduced is that they all allow for a huge amount of customization. You can alter the behavior and output of these technologies to achieve exactly what you are looking for. If you want to dig deeper into ASP.NET, be sure to take a look at *Professional ASP.NET 2.0 Special Edition* (Wiley, 2006).

21

Assemblies

By now, you've probably developed some programs in .NET, so you've seen the modules produced by the .NET compilers, which have file extensions of .dll or .exe. Most .NET modules are DLLs, including class libraries and those that serve as code-behind for ASP.NET. Windows applications, console applications, and Windows Services are examples of .NET modules that are executables and thus have an extension of .exe.

These .NET-compiled modules, both DLLs and EXEs, are referred to as *assemblies*. Assemblies are the unit of deployment in .NET, containing both compiled code and metadata that is needed by the .NET common language runtime (CLR) to run the code. Metadata includes information such as the code's identity and version, dependencies on other assemblies, and a list of types and resources exposed by the assembly.

Basic development in .NET doesn't require you to know any more than that. However, as your applications become more complex, and as you begin considering such issues as deployment and maintenance of your code, you need to understand more about assemblies. This chapter addresses that need, including the following:

❑   What assemblies are and how they are used

❑   The general structure of an assembly

❑   How assemblies can be versioned

❑   The global application cache (GAC), including how and when to use it

❑   How assemblies are located and loaded by the CLR

After you are familiar with these essentials, Chapter 22 uses this information to discuss deployment in depth.

Assemblies

The assembly is used by the CLR as the smallest unit for the following:

- Deployment
- Version control
- Security
- Type grouping
- Code reuse

An assembly must contain a manifest, which tells the CLR what else is in the assembly. The other elements can be any of the following three categories:

- Type metadata
- Microsoft Intermediate Language (MSIL) code
- Resources

An assembly can be just one file. Figure 21-1 details the contents of a single-file assembly.

Alternatively, the structure can be split across multiple files, as shown in Figure 21-2. This is just one example of a multiple-file assembly configuration.

Figure 21-1

Figure 21-2

An assembly can only have one manifest section across all the files that make up the assembly. There is nothing stopping you, however, from having a resource section (or any of the other sections of type `Metadata` and MSIL code) in each of the files that make up an assembly.

The Manifest

The manifest is the part of the assembly that contains a list of the other elements contained in the assembly and basic identification information for the assembly. The manifest contains the largest part of the information that enables the assembly to be self-describing. Elements listed in the manifest are placed in appropriate sections. The manifest includes the sections displayed in Figure 21-3. These sections are covered later in the chapter.

To look at the manifest for a particular assembly, you can use the IL Disassembler (`Ildasm.exe`), which is part of the .NET Framework SDK. For version 3.0 of the framework, the SDK is combined with the Windows SDK, downloadable from Microsoft's website. Because Visual Studio 2005 only includes version 2.0 of the .NET Framework, you need to download and install the SDK for .NET Framework 3.0 as a separate operation from installing Visual Studio. Most downloads for .NET are available at `www.microsoft.com/net`, and there is a link on that page for .NET Framework 3.0. As of this writing, the download page for .NET Framework 3.0 also has a link to download the SDK.

After the SDK is installed, `Ildasm.exe` is available in the SDK's `bin` directory. If you install to the default location, which is normally the Program Files directory on the C: drive, then the path for that directory is `C:\Program Files\Microsoft SDKs\Windows\v6.0\bin`. You can start `Ildasm.exe` by navigating to that directory and double-clicking on `Ildasm.exe`. The version of `Ildasm.exe` in the SDK for .NET Framework 3.0 can examine earlier versions of .NET assemblies, and in fact the following example is one of the system assemblies installed with .NET Framework 2.0.

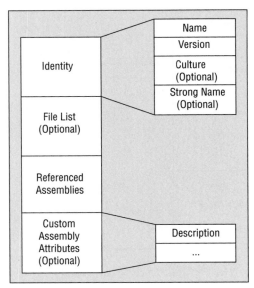

Figure 21-3

When `Ildasm.exe` loads, you can browse for an assembly to view by selecting File ⇨ Open. Once an assembly has been loaded into `Ildasm.exe`, it disassembles the metadata contained within the assembly and presents you with a tree view layout of the data. Initially, the tree view shows only top-level elements, as illustrated in Figure 21-4.

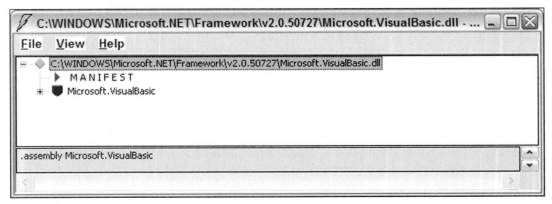

Figure 21-4

The full path of the assembly you are viewing represents the root node. The first node below the root is called MANIFEST, and as you've probably guessed it contains all the information about the assembly's manifest. If you double-click this node, a new window is displayed with the information contained within the manifest. The manifest for a complex assembly can be rather long. For our example, three sections of a manifest are shown in Figures 21-5, 21-6, and 21-7. Figure 21-5 shows the top of the manifest, which contains the external references needed by this assembly, including both Windows libraries and other .NET assemblies on which this assembly depends.

Figure 21-5

Figure 21-6 shows a portion of the manifest further down, containing the beginning of the section for this particular assembly, which begins listing the metadata about the assembly in the form of attributes.

Figure 21-6

Figure 21-7 shows the identity section of the manifest, discussed next.

Figure 21-7

The Identity Section

The identity section of the manifest is used to uniquely identify a particular assembly. This section contains some standard information, such as the version number, and may also contain some optional elements, such as a strong name for the assembly (discussed next). There are certain restrictions on the information that must appear in the identity section, depending on the type of assembly. Assemblies come in two types: application-private and shared (differences between the two types are covered shortly).

The identity section of an assembly can be found by looking for the `.assembly` (without a following `extern`) directive in the Manifest window of `Ildasm.exe`. In Figure 21-6, the line that denotes the beginning of the identity section is as follows:

```
.assembly Microsoft.VisualBasic
```

The identity section can contain a number of subsections. Every assembly has a name that is declared as part of the `.assembly` directive; in the case of the last line, you can see the assembly is called `Microsoft.VisualBasic`. The name of the assembly is very important, because this is what the CLR uses to locate the actual file that contains the assembly. The extension `.dll` is appended to the assembly name to indicate the name of the file that contains the assembly manifest.

The Version Number

The identity section must also contain an entry that describes what version of the assembly it is. A version number for an assembly is presented by the `.ver` directive in `Ildasm.exe`, and by looking through the output you can see that the `Microsoft.VisualBasic` assembly has a version number of 8:0:0:0, as indicated by the following entry in the `.assembly` section:

```
.ver 8:0:0:0
```

A version number contains four parts:

```
Major : Minor : Build : Revision
```

Assemblies that have the same name but different version numbers are treated as completely different assemblies. If you have an assembly on your machine that has a version number of 1.5.2.3 and another version of the same assembly with a version number of 1.6.0.1, then the CLR treats them as different assemblies. The version number of an assembly is part of what is used to define dependencies between assemblies.

Strong Names

The identity section can also contain an optional *strong name*. The strong name is not a name per se, but a public key that has been generated by the author of the assembly to uniquely identify it. A strong name is used to ensure that your assembly has a unique signature compared to other assemblies that may have the same name. Strong names were introduced to combat DLL hell by providing an unambiguous way to differentiate among assemblies.

A strong name is based on public-private key encryption and creates a unique identity for your assembly. The public key is stored in the identity section of the manifest. A signature of the file containing the assembly's manifest is created and stored in the resulting PE file. The .NET Framework uses these two signatures when resolving type references to ensure that the correct assembly is loaded at runtime. A strong name is indicated in the manifest by the .publickey directive in the .assembly section.

Signing an Assembly with a Strong Name

As mentioned above, applying a strong name to an assembly is based on public-private key encryption. The public and private keys are related, and a set is called a public-private *key pair*. Applying a strong name to an assembly is usually called *signing* the assembly with the strong name.

You can create a key pair with the sn.exe utility. At the Visual Studio command prompt, enter the following command:

```
sn -k pairname.snk
```

You should replace "pairname" with an appropriate name, often the name of your product or system. The same key pair can be used to apply a strong name to all the assemblies in your system.

Once you have a key pair, you need to add it to any projects in Visual Studio that need to generate a strong named assembly. To do that, just select Project ➪ Add Existing Item, and browse to the key pair.

The final step is to change the module AssemblyInfo.vb to apply the strong name. AssemblyInfo.vb was automatically created when your project was created, and is under the My Project area in Solution Explorer. If you can't see a plus sign to expand My Project, press the Show All Files button at the top of Solution Explorer.

In AssemblyInfo.vb, insert a line that looks like this:

```
<Assembly: AssemblyKeyFile("pairname.snk")>
```

Again, you should replace "pairname" with the name you actually used for the key pair file earlier. The next time your project is built, the resulting assembly will have a strong name, generated by using the key pair you have indicated.

You can also sign an assembly with a strong name by compiling at the command line. This might be the case if you want to sign the assembly outside of Visual Studio. A typical command line to compile and sign a Visual Basic assembly looks like this:

```
vbc
/reference:Microsoft.VisualBasic.dll
/reference:System.Windows.Forms.dll
/target:library
/keyfile:c:\mykeys\keypair.snk
/out:MyAssembly.dll
/rootnamespace:MyAssembly
*.vb
```

The separate elements of the command line have been placed on different lines for ease of reading, but they should all be on the same line in actual use. The preceding is just a template. You would need to change the /reference options to include any references needed by your assembly. You would also need to specify the correct file path for your own key pair file (.snk file) and apply your assembly and root namespace names.

Finally, strong names can be applied with a technique called *delay signing*. That's beyond the scope of this chapter, but the Visual Studio help files include step-by-step instructions. Delayed signing is helpful when assemblies need to be properly strong-named during development (so that any problems with strong names are detected at that point), but it is undesirable for all the developers to have a copy of the key pair that will be used for signing the final compiled version of the assembly.

The Culture

The final part of an assembly's identity is its *culture*, which is optional. Cultures are used to define the country/language for which the assembly is targeted.

The combination of name, strong name, version number, and culture is used by the CLR to enforce version dependencies. For example, you could create one version of your assembly targeted at English users, another for German users, another for Finnish users, and so on.

Cultures can be general, as in the case of English, or more specific, as in the case of US-English. Cultures are represented by a string that can have two parts to it: primary and secondary (optional). The culture for English is en, and the culture for US-English is en-us. See Chapter 6 for more about cultures in .NET.

If a culture is not indicated in the assembly, then it is assumed that the assembly can be used for any culture. Such an assembly is said to be *culture neutral*.

A culture can be assigned to an assembly by including the attribute AssemblyCulture from the System.Reflection namespace in your assembly's code (usually within the AssemblyInfo.vb file):

```
<Assembly: AssemblyCulture("en")>
```

The culture of an assembly is represented in the manifest by the `.locale` directive in the `.assembly` section:

```
.locale = (65 00 6E 00 00 00)                          // e.n...
```

Referenced Assemblies

It was mentioned earlier that the first section of the manifest contains referenced assemblies. An assembly reference is indicated in the manifest with the `.assembly extern` directive (refer to Figure 21-5).

The first piece of information included is the name of the referenced assembly. Figure 21-5 shows a reference to the `mscorlib` assembly. This name is used to determine the name of the file that contains the actual assembly. The CLR takes the name of the assembly reference and appends `.dll`. For example, in the last example, the CLR will look for a file called `mscorlib.dll`. The assembly `mscorlib` is a special assembly in .NET that contains all the definitions of the base types used in .NET, and is referenced by all assemblies.

The .publickeytoken Directive

If the assembly being referenced contains a strong name, then a hash of the public key of the referenced assembly is stored as part of the record to the external reference. This hash is stored in the manifest using the `.publickeytoken` directive as part of the `.assembly extern` section. The assembly reference shown in Figure 21-5 contains a hash of the strong name of the `mscorlib` assembly. The stored hash of the strong name is compared at runtime to a hash of the strong name (`.publickey`) contained within the referenced assembly to help ensure that the correct assembly is loaded. The value of the `.publickeytoken` is computed by taking the lower 8 bytes of a hash (SHA1) of the strong name of the referenced assemblies.

The .Ver Directive

The version of the assembly being referenced is also stored in the manifest. This version information is used with the rest of the information stored about a reference to ensure that the correct assembly is loaded (this is discussed later). If an application references version 1.1.0.0 of an assembly, it will not load version 2.1.0.0 of the assembly unless a version policy (also discussed later) exists to indicate otherwise. The version of the referenced assembly is stored in the manifest using the `.ver` directive as part of a `.assembly extern` section.

The .Locale Directive

If an assembly that is being referenced has a culture, then the culture information is also stored in the external assembly reference section using the `.locale` directive. The combination of name, strong name (if it exists), version number, and culture are what make up a unique version of an assembly.

Assemblies and Deployment

The information in the manifest enables reliable determination of the identity and version of an assembly. This is the basis for the deployment options available in .NET, and for the side-by-side execution of assemblies that helps .NET overcome DLL hell. This section looks at these issues in detail.

Application-Private Assemblies

It was mentioned earlier that assemblies can be of two types. The first is an application-private assembly. As the name implies, this type of assembly is used by one application only and is not shared. This is the default style of assembly in .NET and is the main mechanism by which an application can be independent of changes to the system.

Application-private assemblies are deployed into the application's own directory. Because application-private assemblies are not shared, they do not need a strong name. This means that, at a minimum, they only need to have a name and version number in the identity section of the manifest. Because the assemblies are private to the application, the application does not perform version checks on the assemblies, as the application developer has control over the assemblies that are deployed to the application directory. If strong names exist, however, the CLR will verify that they match.

If all the assemblies that an application uses are application-private and the CLR is already installed on the target machine, then deployment is quite simple. Chapter 22 discusses this implication in more detail.

Shared Assemblies

The second type of assembly is the shared assembly. As the name suggests, this type of assembly can be shared among several different applications that reside on the same server. This type of assembly should only be used when it is important to share assemblies among many applications. For example, a Windows Forms control purchased as part of a package may be used in many of your applications, and thus it is better to install a shared version of the assembly rather than copies of it for each application. The .NET Framework assemblies themselves are also examples of shared assemblies.

Certain requirements are placed upon shared assemblies. The assembly needs to have a globally unique name, which is not a requirement of application-private assemblies. As mentioned earlier, a strong name is used to create a globally unique name for an assembly. As the assembly is shared, all references to the shared assembly are checked to ensure that the correct version is being used by an application.

Shared assemblies are stored in the global assembly cache (GAC), which is usually located in the `assembly` folder in the `Windows` directory (for example, in Windows XP, `C:\Windows\Assembly`). However, it's not enough to just copy an assembly into that directory. The process for placing an assembly in the GAC is similar in concept to registering a COM DLL. That process is discussed in detail later.

No other changes to the code of the assembly are necessary to differentiate it from that of an application-private assembly. In fact, just because an assembly has a strong name does not mean that it has to be deployed as a shared assembly; it could just as easily be deployed in the application directory as an application-private assembly.

Installing a shared assembly into the GAC requires administrator rights on the machine. This is another factor complicating deployment of shared assemblies. Because of the extra effort involved in the creation and deployment of shared assemblies, you should avoid this type of assembly unless you really need it.

The Global Assembly Cache (GAC)

Each computer that has the .NET runtime installed has a GAC. However, assemblies in the GAC are always stored in the same folder, no matter which version of .NET you have. The folder is a subfolder of your main Windows folder, and it is named `Assembly`. If you have multiple versions of the .NET Framework, assemblies in the GAC for all of them are stored in this directory.

As previously noted, a strong name is required for an assembly placed in that GAC. That strong name is used to identify a particular assembly. However, another piece of metadata is also used for verification of an assembly. When an assembly is created, a hash of the assembly is placed in the metadata. If an assembly is changed (with a binary editor, for example), the hash of the assembly will no longer match the hash in the metadata. The metadata hash is checked against the actual hash when an assembly is placed in the GAC with the `gacutil.exe` utility (described later). If the two hash codes do not match, the installation cannot be completed.

The strong name is also used when an application resolves a reference to an external assembly. It checks whether the public key stored in the assembly is equal to the hash of the public key stored as part of the reference in the application. If the two do not match, then the application knows that the external assembly has not been created by the original author of the assembly.

You can view the assemblies contained within the GAC by navigating to the directory using the Windows Explorer.

The `gacutil.exe` utility that ships with .NET is used to add and remove assemblies from the GAC. To add an assembly into the GAC using the `gacutil.exe` tool, use the following command line:

```
gacutil.exe /i myassembly.dll
```

Recall that the assembly being loaded must have a strong name.

To remove an assembly, use the `/u` option, like this:

```
gacutil.exe /u myassembly.dll
```

`gacutil.exe` has a number of other options. You can examine them and see examples of their usage by typing in the following command:

```
gacutil.exe /?
```

Versioning Issues

In COM, versioning of DLLs had some significant limitations. For example, a different DLL with the same nominal version number could be indistinguishable from the one desired.

.NET's versioning scheme was specifically designed to alleviate the problems of COM. The major capabilities of .NET that solve versioning issues are as follows:

- ❑ Application isolation
- ❑ Side-by-side execution
- ❑ Self-describing components

Application Isolation

For an application to be isolated it should be self-contained and independent. This means that the application should rely on its own dependencies for ActiveX controls, components, or files, and not have those files shared with other applications. The option of having application isolation is essential for a good solution to versioning problems.

If an application is isolated, components are owned, managed by, and used by the parent application alone. If a component is used by another application, even if it is the same version, the other application must have its own copy. This ensures that each application can install and uninstall dependencies and not interfere with other applications.

> **Does this sound familiar? This is what most early Windows and DOS applications did until COM required registration of DLLs in the registry and placement of shared DLLs in the system directory. The wheel surely does turn!**

The .NET Framework enables application isolation by allowing developers to create application-private assemblies. These are in the application's own directory, and if another application needs the same assembly, it can be duplicated in that application's directory.

This means that each application is independent from the other. This isolation works best for many scenarios. It is sometimes referred to as a *zero-impact deployment* because by either installing or uninstalling such an application there is no chance of causing problems for any other application.

Side-by-Side Execution

Side-by-side execution occurs when multiple versions of the same assembly can run at the same time. Side-by-side execution is performed by the CLR. Components that are to execute side-by-side must be installed within the application directory or a subdirectory of it.

With application assemblies, versioning is not much of an issue. The interfaces are dynamically resolved by the CLR. You can replace an application assembly with a different version, and the CLR will load it and make it work with the other assemblies in the application, as long as the new version does not have any interface incompatibilities. The new version may even have elements of the interface that are new and that don't exist in the old version (new properties or methods). As long as the existing class interface elements used by the other application assemblies are unchanged, the new version will work fine. In the discussion of exactly how the CLR locates a referenced assembly, which follows, you'll learn more about how this works.

Self-Describing

In the earlier section on the manifest, the self-describing nature of .NET assemblies was mentioned. The term "self-describing" means that all the information the CLR needs to know to load and execute an assembly is inside the assembly itself.

Self-describing components are essential to .NET's side-by-side execution. Once the extra version is known by the CLR to be needed, everything else about the assembly needed to run side-by-side is in the assembly itself. Each application can get its own version of an assembly, and all the work to coordinate the versions in memory is performed transparently by the CLR.

Versioning becomes more important with shared assemblies. Without good coordination of versions, .NET applications with shared assemblies are subject to some of the same problems as COM applications. In particular, if a new version of a shared assembly is placed in the GAC, there must be a means to control which applications get which version of a shared assembly. This is accomplished with a *versioning policy*.

Version Policies

As discussed earlier, a version number includes four parts: major, minor, build, and revision. The version number is used as part of the identity of the assembly. When a new version of a shared assembly is created and placed in the GAC, any of these parts can change. Which ones change affects how the CLR views compatibility for the new assembly.

When the version number of a component only changes according to its build and revision parts, it is compatible. This is often referred to as *Quick Fix Engineering (QFE)*. It's only necessary to place the new assembly in the GAC, and it will automatically be considered compatible with applications that were created to use the older version that had different numbers for the build and revision.

If either the major or minor build number changes, however, compatibility is not assumed by the CLR. In that case, there are manual ways to indicate compatibility if necessary, and these are covered later in this section.

When an application comes across a type that is implemented in an external reference, the CLR has to determine what version of the referenced assembly to load. What steps does the CLR go through to ensure that the correct version of an assembly is loaded? To answer this question, you need to look at version policies and how they affect what version of an assembly is loaded.

The Default Versioning Policy

Let's start by looking at the default versioning policy. This policy is what is followed in the absence of any configuration files on the machine that modify the versioning policy. The runtime default behavior is to consult the manifest for the name of the referenced assembly and the version of the assembly to use.

If the referenced assembly does not contain a strong name, then it is assumed that the referenced assembly is application-private and is located in the application's directory. The CLR takes the name of the referenced assembly and appends `.dll` to create the filename that contains the referenced assembly's manifest. The CLR then searches in the application's directory for the filename; if it's found, it uses the version indicated, even if the version number is different from the one specified in the manifest. Therefore, the version numbers of application-private assemblies are not checked, because the application developer, in theory, has control over which assemblies are deployed to the application's directory. If the file cannot be found, the CLR raises a `System.IO.FileNotFoundException`.

Automatic Quick Fix Engineering Policy

If the referenced assembly contains a strong name, then the process by which an assembly is loaded is different:

1. The three different types of assembly configuration files (discussed later) are consulted, if they exist, to see whether they contain any settings that will modify which version of the assembly the CLR should load.

2. The CLR then checks whether the assembly has been requested and loaded in a previous call. If it has, it uses the loaded assembly.

3. If the assembly is not already loaded, then the GAC is queried for a match. If a match is found, it is used by the application.

4. If any of the configuration files contains a codebase (discussed later) entry for the assembly, then the assembly is looked for in the location specified. If the assembly cannot be found in the location specified in the codebase, a TypeLoadException is raised to the application.

5. If there are no configuration files or if there are no codebase entries for the assembly, then the CLR probes for the assembly starting in the application's base directory.

6. If the assembly still isn't found, then the CLR asks the Windows Installer service if it has the assembly in question. If it does, then the assembly is installed and the application uses it. This is a feature called *on-demand installation*.

If the assembly hasn't been found by the end of this entire process, then a TypeLoadException is raised.

Although a referenced assembly contains a strong name, this does not mean that it has to be deployed into the GAC. This enables application developers to install a version with the application that is known to work. The GAC is consulted to see whether it contains a version of an assembly with a higher build.revision number to enable administrators to deploy an updated assembly without having to reinstall or rebuild the application. This is known as the *Automatic Quick Fix Engineering Policy*.

Configuration Files

The default versioning policy described earlier may not be the most appropriate policy for your requirements. Fortunately, you can modify this policy through the use of XML configuration files to meet your specific needs. Two types of configuration files can hold versioning information:

❑ The first is an *application configuration file,* and it is created in the application directory. As the name implies, this configuration file applies to a single application only. You need to create the application configuration file in the application directory with the same name as the application filename, appending .config. For example, suppose that you have a Windows Forms application called HelloWorld.exe installed in the C:\HelloWorld directory. The application configuration file would be C:\HelloWorld\HelloWorld.exe.config.

❑ The second type of configuration file is called the *machine configuration file*. It is named machine.config and can be found in the C:\Windows\Microsoft.NET\Framework\ v2.0.xxxx\ CONFIG directory. The machine.config file overrides any other configuration files on a machine and can be thought of as containing global settings.

The main purpose of the configuration file is to provide binding-related information to the developer or administrator who wishes to override the default policy handling of the CLR.

Specifically, the configuration file, as it's written in XML, has a root node named `<configuration>`, and it must have the end node of `</configuration>` present to be syntactically correct. The configuration file is divided into specific types of nodes that represent different areas of control. These areas are as follows:

- Startup
- Runtime
- Remoting
- Crypto
- Class API
- Security

Although all of these areas are important, this chapter covers only the first two. All of the settings discussed can be added to the application configuration file. Some of the settings (these are pointed out) can also be added to the machine configuration file. If a setting in the application configuration file conflicts with one in the machine configuration file, then the setting in the machine configuration is used. When we talk about assembly references in the following discussion of configuration settings, we are talking exclusively about *shared assemblies* (which implies that the assemblies have a strong name, as assemblies in the GAC are required to have one).

Startup Settings

The `<startup>` node of the application and machine configuration files has a `<requiredRuntime>` node that specifies the runtime version required by the application. This is because different versions of the CLR can run on a machine side by side. The following example shows how you would specify the version of the .NET runtime inside the configuration file:

```
<configuration>
  <startup>
    <requiredRuntime version ="2.0.xxxx" safemode ="true"/>
  </startup>
</configuration>
```

Runtime Settings

The runtime node, which is written as `<runtime>` (not to be confused with `<requiredRuntime>`), specifies the settings that manage how the CLR handles garbage collection and versions of assemblies. With these settings, you can specify which version of an assembly the application requires, or redirect it to another version entirely.

Loading a Particular Version of an Assembly

The application and machine configuration files can be used to ensure that a particular version of an assembly is loaded. You can indicate whether this version should be loaded all the time or only to replace a specific version of the assembly. This functionality is supported through the use of the

`<assemblyIdentity>` and `<bindingRedirect>` elements in the configuration file, as shown in the following example:

```
<configuration>
  <runtime>
    <assemblyBinding xmlns="urn:schemas-microsoft-com:asm.v1">
      <dependentAssembly>
        <assemblyIdentity name="AssemblyName"
                          publickeytoken="b77a5c561934e089"
                          culture="en-us"/>
          <bindingRedirect oldVersion="*"
                          newVersion="2.0.50.0"/>
      </dependentAssembly>
    </assemblyBindings>
  </runtime>
</configuration>
```

The `<assemblyBinding>` node is used to declare settings for the locations of assemblies and redirections via the `<dependentAssembly>` node and the `<probing>` node (which you will look at shortly).

In the last example, when the CLR resolves the reference to the assembly named `AssemblyName`, it loads version 2.0.50.0 instead of the version that appears in the manifest. If you want to load only version 2.0.50.0 of the assembly when a specific version is referenced, then you can replace the value of the `oldVersion` attribute with the version number that you would like to replace (for example, 1.5.0.0). The `publickeytoken` attribute is used to store the hash of the strong name of the assembly to replace. This ensures that the correct assembly is identified. The same is true of the `culture` attribute.

Defining the Location of an Assembly

The location of an assembly can also be defined in both the application and machine configuration files. You can use the `<codeBase>` element to inform the CLR of the location of an assembly. This enables you to distribute an application and have the externally referenced assemblies downloaded the first time they are used (on-demand downloading):

```
<configuration>
  <runtime>
    <assemblyBinding xmlns="urn:schemas-microsoft-com:asm.v1">
      <dependentAssembly>
        <assemblyIdentity name="AssemblyName"
                          publickeytoken="b77a5c561934e089"
                          culture="en-us"/>
        <codeBase version="2.0.50.0"
                  href="http://www.wrox.com/AssemblyName.dll/>
      </dependentAssembly>
    </assemblyBindings>
  </runtime>
</configuration>
```

You can see from this example that whenever a reference to version 2.0.50.0 of the assembly `AssemblyName` is resolved (and the assembly isn't already on the user's computer), the CLR will try to load the assembly from the location defined in the `href` attribute. The location defined in the `href` attribute is a standard URL and can be used to locate a file across the Internet or locally.

If the assembly cannot be found or the details in the manifest of the assembly defined in the `href` attribute do not match those defined in the configuration file, the loading of the assembly will fail and you will receive a `TypeLoadException`. If the version of the assembly in the preceding example is actually 2.0.60.0, then the assembly will load because the version number is only different by build and revision number.

Providing the Search Path

The final use of configuration files to look at is that of providing the search path for use when locating assemblies in the application's directory. This setting only applies to the application configuration file. By default, the CLR will search for an assembly only in the application's base directory — it will not look in any subdirectories. You can modify this behavior by using the `<probing>` element in an application configuration file, as shown in the following example:

```
<configuration>
  <runtime>
    <assemblyBinding xmlns="urn:schemas-microsoft-com:asm.v1">
      <probing privatePath="regional"/>
    </assemblyBinding>
  </runtime>
</configuration>
```

The `privatePath` attribute can contain a list of directories relative to the application's directory (separated by a semicolon) that you would like the CLR to search in when trying to locate an assembly. The `privatePath` attribute cannot contain an absolute pathname.

As part of an assembly reference being resolved, the CLR checks in the application's base directory for it. If it cannot find it, then it looks through, in order, all the subdirectories specified in the `privatePath` variable, as well as looking for a subdirectory with the same name as the assembly. If the assembly being resolved is called `AssemblyName`, then the CLR also checks for the assembly in a subdirectory called `AssemblyName`, if it exists.

This isn't the end of the story, though. If the referenced assembly being resolved contains a culture setting, then the CLR also checks for culture-specific subdirectories in each of the directories it searches in. For example, if the CLR is trying to resolve a reference to an assembly named `AssemblyName` with a culture of `en` and a `privatePath` equal to that in the last example, and the application being run has a home directory of `C:\ExampleApp`, then the CLR will look in the following directories (in the order shown):

- ❑ `C:\ExampleApp`
- ❑ `C:\ExampleApp\en`
- ❑ `C:\ExampleApp\en\AssemblyName`
- ❑ `C:\ExampleApp\regional\en`
- ❑ `C:\ExampleApp\regional\en\AssemblyName`

As you can see, the CLR can probe quite a number of directories to locate an assembly. When an external assembly is resolved by the CLR, it consults the configuration files first to determine whether it needs to modify the process by which it resolves an assembly. As discussed, you can modify the resolution process to suit your needs.

Dynamic Loading of Assemblies

The preceding discussion about locating and loading assemblies refers to assemblies that are known at compile time through the application's references. There is an alternative method of locating and loading an assembly that is useful for certain scenarios.

In this technique, the location of the assembly is supplied by the application, using a URL or filename. The normal rules for locating the assembly do not apply — only the location specified by the application is used.

The location is just a string variable, so it may come from a configuration file or database. In fact, the assembly to be loaded may be newly created, and perhaps did not even exist when the original application was compiled. Because the information to load the assembly can be passed into the application on-the-fly at runtime, this type of assembly loading is called *dynamic loading*.

The Assembly Class

References to assemblies, and operations to be performed on assemblies in code, are mostly contained in a .NET Framework class called the `Assembly` class. It is part of the `System.Reflection` namespace. In the code examples that follow, assume that the following `Imports` statement is at the top of the code module:

```
Imports System.Reflection
```

The `Assembly` class has a shared method called `LoadFrom`, which takes a URL or filename and returns a reference to the assembly at that location. Here's a code example of `LoadFrom` in action, getting an assembly reference from a URL:

```
Dim asmDynamic As [Assembly]
asmDynamic = [Assembly].LoadFrom("http://www.dotnetmasters.com/loancalc2.dll")
```

The brackets around `Assembly` are needed because it is a reserved keyword in Visual Basic. The brackets indicate that the word applies to the `Assembly` class, and the keyword is not being used.

After these lines are executed, the code contains a reference to the assembly at the given location. That enables other operations on the assembly to take place. One such operation is getting a reference to a particular type (which could be a class, structure, or enumeration) in the assembly. The reference to a type is needed to instantiate the type when an assembly is loaded dynamically. The `GetType` method of the `Assembly` class is used to get the reference, using a string that represents the identification of the type. The identification consists of the full namespace path that uniquely identifies the type within the current application.

For example, suppose that you wanted to get an instance of a certain form that was in the assembly, with a namespace path of `MyProject.Form1`. The following line of code would get a reference to the type for that form:

```
Dim typMyForm As Type = formAsm.GetType("MyProject.Form1")
```

The type reference can then be used to generate an instance of the type. To do this you need another class in `System.Reflection` called the `Activator` class. This class has a shared method called

`CreateInstance`, which takes a type reference and returns an instance of that type. (If you are familiar with Active Server Pages and older versions of Visual Basic, `CreateInstance` is functionally similar to the `CreateObject` function in those environments.) You could, therefore, get an instance of the form with these lines:

```
Dim objForm As Object
objForm = Activator.CreateInstance(typeMyForm)
```

`CreateInstance` always returns a generic object. That means it may be necessary to coerce the returned reference to a particular type to gain access to the type's interface. For example, assuming that you knew the object was actually a Windows Form, you could coerce the preceding instance into the type of `System.Windows.Forms.Form` and then do normal operations that are available on a form:

```
Dim FormToShow As Form = CType(objForm, System.Windows.Forms.Form)
FormToShow.MdiParent = Me
FormToShow.Show()
```

At this point, the form will operate normally. It will behave no differently from a form that was in a referenced assembly (except for potential code access security limitations, as discussed in Chapter 12).

If the newly loaded form needs to load other classes in the dynamic assembly, nothing special needs to be done. For example, suppose that the form just shown needs to load an instance of another form, named `Form2`, that resides in the same dynamically loaded assembly. The standard code to instantiate a form will work fine. The CLR will automatically load the `Form2` type because it already has a reference to the assembly containing `Form2`.

Furthermore, suppose that the dynamically loaded form needs to instantiate a class from another DLL that is not referenced by the application. For example, suppose that the form needs to create an instance of a `Customer` object, and the `Customer` class is in a different DLL. As long as that DLL is in the same folder as the dynamically loaded DLL, the CLR will automatically locate and load the second DLL.

Dynamic Loading Example

To see dynamic loading in action, do the following step-by-step example:

1. Open a new Windows Application in Visual Studio. Name it DynamicLoading. On the blank `Form1` that appears, drag a `Button` from the Toolbox, and set its `Text` property to `Load`.

2. Double-click the Load button to get to its `Click` event in the Code Editor. Then go to the top of the code module and insert the following `Imports` statement:

```
Imports System.Reflection
```

3. Insert the following code into the button's `Click` event:

```
Dim sLocation As String = "C:\Deploy\DynamicForms.dll"
If My.Computer.FileSystem.FileExists(sLocation) Then

    Dim sType As String = "DynamicForms.Form1"
    Dim DynamicAssembly As [Assembly] = _
            [Assembly].LoadFrom(sLocation)
    Dim DynamicType As Type = DynamicAssembly.GetType(sType)
```

```
        Dim DynamicObject As Object
        DynamicObject = Activator.CreateInstance(DynamicType)

        ' We know it's a form - cast to form type
        Dim FormToShow As Form = CType(DynamicObject, Form)
        FormToShow.Show()
    Else
        MsgBox("Unable to load assembly " & sLocation & _
                " because the file does not exist")

    End If
```

4. Run the program and click the Load button. You should get a message box with the message "Unable to load assembly C:\Deploy\DynamicForms.dll because the form does not exist." *Leave this program running while you carry out the next few steps.*

5. Start another, separate Visual Studio instance, and create a new Windows Application project named DynamicForms. On the blank Form1 that appears, drag over a few controls. It doesn't really matter what controls you drag onto Form1. The version that can be downloaded for the book includes some labels, buttons, and text boxes.

6. In the properties for DynamicForms, change the Application type. In the drop-down for Application type, select Class Library.

7. Build the DynamicForms project by selecting Build ⇨ Build DynamicForms from the Visual Studio menu. This will place a file named `DynamicForms.dll` in the project's `\bin\Debug` directory (or the `\bin\Release` directory if you happen to have the Release configuration set in Visual Studio).

8. Create a directory named `C:\Deploy` and copy the `DynamicForms.dll` file to that directory.

9. Return to the running program DynamicLoading. Click the Load button again. This time, it should load the assembly from the DLL you just copied and launch an instance of Form1 from the DynamicForms project.

Notice that the `DynamicForms.dll` was created and compiled after the `DynamicLoading.exe` project that loaded it. It is not necessary to recompile or even restart `DynamicLoading.exe` to load a new assembly dynamically, as long as `DynamicLoading.exe` knows the location of the assembly and the type to be loaded from it.

Putting Assemblies to Work

The previous code examples include hard-coded strings for the location of the assembly and the identification of the type. There are uses for such a technique, such as certain types of Internet deployment of an application. However, when using dynamic loading, it is common for these values to be obtained from outside the code. For example, a database table or an XML-based configuration file can be used to store the information.

This enables you to add new capabilities to an application on-the-fly. A new assembly with new functionality can be written, and then the location of the assembly and the identity of the type to load from the assembly can be added to the configuration file or database table.

Unlike application assemblies automatically located by the CLR, which must be in the application's directory or a subdirectory of it, dynamically loaded assemblies can be anywhere the application knows how to get to. Possibilities include the following:

❑ A website

❑ A directory on the local machine

❑ A directory on a shared network machine

The security privileges available to code vary, depending on where the assembly was loaded from. Code loaded from a URL via HTTP, as shown earlier, has a very restricted set of privileges by default compared to code loaded from a local directory. Chapter 12 has details on code access security, default security policies, and how default policies can be changed.

Summary

Assemblies are the basic unit of deployment and versioning in .NET. Simple applications can be written and installed without knowing much about assemblies. More complex applications require an in-depth understanding of the structure of assemblies, the metadata they contain, and how assemblies are located and loaded by the CLR.

You have looked at how the identity of an assembly is used to allow multiple versions of an assembly to be installed on a machine and run side by side. This chapter explained how an assembly is versioned, the process by which the CLR resolves an external assembly reference, and how you can modify this process through the use of configuration files.

You also looked at how an assembly stores information such as version number, strong name, and culture about any external assemblies that it references, information checked at runtime to ensure that the correct version of the assembly is referenced. You learned how you can use versioning policies to override this in the case of a buggy assembly. The assembly is the single biggest aid in reducing the errors that can occur due to DLL hell, and in helping with deployment.

The chapter also discussed the capability to load an assembly dynamically, based on a location that is derived at runtime. This capability is useful for some special deployment scenarios, such as simple Internet deployment. Understanding all these elements helps you understand how to structure an application, when and how to use shared assemblies, and the deployment implications of your choices for assemblies.

Simple applications are usually created with no strong names or shared assemblies, and all assemblies for the application are deployed to the application directory. Versioning issues are rare as long as class interfaces are consistent.

Complex applications may require shared assemblies to be placed in the GAC, which means that those assemblies must have strong names, and you must control your version numbers. You also need to understand your options for allowing an application to load a version of an assembly other than the one it would load by default, or for loading assemblies dynamically using an application-specific technique to determine the assembly's location. This chapter has covered the basics for all of these needs.

22

Deployment

One of the significant advantages of .NET over its predecessor, COM, is dramatically improved deployment. NET offers a host of deployment options that were not available for older, COM-based software. These options completely change the economics of deployment. The changes are so important that they can even alter the preferred architecture for a system written in .NET.

Deployment encompasses many activities required to place an application into a production environment. Setting up databases, placing software in appropriate directories on servers, and configuring options for a particular installation are some of the actions that fall under the deployment category. Deployment also includes handling of changes and upgrades to the application.

This chapter discusses the major deployment options for .NET applications. The previous chapter on assemblies should be considered a prerequisite for this chapter, as assemblies are the basic unit of deployment.

First you'll look at some of the problems that can occur when you deploy applications, along with a number of terms that are used when talking about application deployment. Next is a look at how .NET addresses many of these deployment issues. The remainder of the chapter covers the following:

❑   Creating deployment projects in Visual Studio 2005, which enable initial installation of applications

❑   Deployment of the .NET Framework itself on systems where it does not already reside

❑   Updating applications on servers, including components and ASP.NET applications

❑   Installing and updating Windows Forms applications on client machines with ClickOnce, Microsoft's proprietary deployment technology

Deployment in .NET is a huge topic, which can't be adequately covered in one chapter. What this chapter should give you is an understanding of, a basic knowledge of, and the desire to learn more about the options available to you.

Application Deployment

In the context of this chapter, *application deployment* includes two principal functions:

❑ The process of taking an application, packaging it up, and installing it on another machine

❑ The process of updating an application that has already been installed with new or changed functionality

Deployment can, in some cases, also include placing the .NET Framework itself on a particular machine. This chapter assumes that the .NET Framework is installed on any machines in question. During the discussion of creating deployment projects, you will learn what to do if the .NET Framework is not available on a system.

Why Deployment Is Easier in .NET

Pre-.NET applications for Microsoft Windows were typically based on a technology called *COM*. While COM had many interesting benefits as a development platform, its most significant weakness was deployment. All components in a COM environment had to be *registered*, which means that they had a record embedded in the local machine's registry to assist in identifying and locating the component.

COM components also had inflexible versioning capabilities, resulting in the possibility that two versions, both needed by applications, could not simultaneously be available on the same machine. The versioning requirements of COM led to a condition colloquially referred to as *DLL hell*.

As covered in the previous chapter, assemblies in .NET are self-describing. All the information needed to execute an assembly is normally contained in the assembly itself. There is no need to place any information in the Windows registry. If the CLR can find an assembly needed by an application (the process of location is discussed in Chapter 21), then the assembly can be run.

The previous chapter also discussed side-by-side execution of .NET assemblies. Multiple versions of an assembly can be executed by .NET, even if they have exactly the same interface and nominal version number. The implication for deployment is that each application can deploy the assemblies it needs and be assured that there will be no conflict with the assemblies needed by other applications.

These .NET capabilities provide a range of deployment possibilities, from simple to complex. Let's start by looking at the simplest method of deployment, which harkens back to the days of DOS-XCOPY deployment.

XCOPY Deployment

The term *XCOPY deployment* was coined to describe an ideal deployment scenario. Its name derives from the DOS xcopy command. With XCOPY deployment, all you have to do to deploy an application is copy the directory (including all child directories) to the computer on which you would like to run the program.

XCOPY deployment was not available for older COM-based software because a COM component had to be registered on the machine. Because no registration is needed in .NET, and because the .NET CLR always looks in an application's directory for necessary assemblies, copying assemblies into the application directory is quite sufficient.

XCOPY deployment is fine for very simple applications, but most business applications require other dependencies (such as databases and message queues) to be created on the new computer. .NET cannot help with those, so applications that have them need more sophisticated deployment.

Using the Windows Installer

The *Windows Installer* service is available on all operating systems that support .NET Framework 3.0. It was specifically created for installation of applications onto a Windows system.

The Windows Installer service uses a file called a *Windows Installer package file* to install an application. Such files have an extension of .msi, which is an acronym derived from "Microsoft Installer." The files that make up a product can be packaged inside the .msi file, or externally in a number of cabinet files.

When users request that a particular application be installed, they can just double-click the .msi file. The Windows Installer service reads the file and determines what needs to be done (such as which files need to be copied and where they need to be copied to) to install the application. All the installation rules are implemented centrally by the service and do not need to be distributed as part of a setup executable. The Windows Installer package file contains a list of actions (such as *copy file mfc40.dll to the Windows system folder*) and what rules need to be applied to these actions.

The Windows Installer service also has a rollback method to handle failed installations. If the installation fails for some reason, the Windows Installer service will rollback the computer to its original state. You can manually create a Windows Installer package file using the Windows Installer SDK tools. However, it's much easier to use Visual Studio. Several templates in VS 2005 create projects that output .msi files, as discussed in detail in the section "Visual Studio Deployment Projects."

ClickOnce Deployment

An alternative to Windows Installer for Windows Forms applications is *ClickOnce*. This deployment technology was first included in Visual Studio 2005. Creating ClickOnce deployments is simpler than creating .msi files, but the most important ClickOnce advantage is that it is designed to deploy over the Internet. ClickOnce is discussed in the section "Internet Deployment of Windows Applications."

Visual Studio Deployment Projects

Visual Studio 2005 provides a set of project templates that can be used to help package your application and deploy it. Most of these templates use Windows Installer technology.

Project Templates

Before looking at the project templates, you should understand the difference between setup and deployment. *Setup* is the process that you use to package your application. *Deployment* is the process of installing an application on another machine, usually through a setup application/process.

The five project templates available within Visual Studio 2005 can be created by the same means as any other project type, by using the New Project dialog box, as shown in Figure 22-1.

Figure 22-1

As shown in Figure 22-1, you need to select the Other Project Types node and then the Setup and Deployment Projects node from the tree view of project types on the left side of the dialog box. Of the six available project templates, there are five actual project templates:

- ❑ CAB Project
- ❑ Merge Module Project
- ❑ Setup Project
- ❑ Web Setup Project
- ❑ Smart Device CAB Project

Also included is a wizard (called the Setup Wizard) that can be used to help create any of the project templates listed (except the Smart Device CAB Project).

The CAB Project Template

The CAB Project template is used to create a *cabinet file*. A cabinet file (.cab) can contain any number of files. It is often used to package a set of related components in an application.

Controls hosted within Internet Explorer are often packaged into a cabinet file, and a reference is added to the file in the Web page that uses the control. When Internet Explorer encounters this reference, it confirms that the control isn't already installed on the user's computer, at which point it downloads the cabinet file, extracts the control, and installs it to a protected part of the user's computer. You can compress cabinet files to reduce their size, thereby reducing the time it takes to download them.

The Merge Module Project Template

The Merge Module Project template is used to create a *merge module,* which is similar to a cabinet file in that it can be used to package a group of files. The difference is that a merge module file (.msm) cannot be used by itself to install the files that it contains. The merge module file created by this project template can only be used within another setup project.

Merge modules were introduced as part of the Microsoft Windows Installer technology to enable a set of files to be packaged into an easy to use file that could be reused and shared between Windows Installer–based setup programs. The idea is to package all the files and any other resources (for example, registry entries, bitmaps, and so on) that are dependent on each other into the merge module.

This type of project can be very useful for packaging a component and all its dependencies. The resulting merge file can then be used in the setup program of each application that uses the component. This allows applications such as Crystal Reports to have a prepackaged deployment set that can be integrated into the deployment of other applications.

The Setup Project Template

The Setup Project template is used to create a standard Windows Installer setup for an application, which is normally installed in the Program Files directory of a user's computer.

The Web Setup Project Template

The Web Setup Project template is used to create a Windows Installer setup program that can be used to install a project into a virtual directory of a Web server. It is intended to be used to create a setup program for a Web application, which may contain ASP.NET Web Forms or Web Services.

The Smart Device CAB Project Template

The Smart Device CAB Project template is used to create a CAB file for an application that runs on a device containing the .NET Compact Framework, such as a PocketPC device. Such applications are often referred to as *mobile applications,* and they have many capabilities and limitations that do not apply to other .NET-based applications. This book does not discuss mobile applications, so this template type is not discussed here.

The Setup Wizard

You can use the Setup Wizard to help guide you through the creation of any of the previous setup and deployment project templates except the Smart Device CAB template.

Creating a Deployment Project

A deployment project can be created in exactly the same way as any other project in Visual Studio 2005. The deployment project can be standalone or part of a solution that contains other projects.

To illustrate a typical deployment project, this section presents a simple walk-through of one of the most commonly used templates for a deployment project — the Setup Project, which is used to deploy a Windows application.

Walk-through

You first need to create an application that will serve as the desktop application you want to deploy. Create a new project, and choose Windows Application from the list of available Visual Basic project templates. Name the project "SampleForDeployment," and don't add any code to it.

Next, add a new project to the solution and choose Setup Project from the list of available Setup and Deployment Project templates. You will now have a Visual Studio solution containing two projects.

When created, the deployment project does not contain any files. It has a folder called `Detected Dependencies`, which is discussed later. You need to add the executable file from your Windows application SampleForDeployment to the deployment project.

You add files to a setup deployment project using the Add function, which is available in two places. You can select the deployment project in Solution Explorer and use the Add option from the Project menu, or you can right-click the setup project file in Solution Explorer and choose Add from the pop-up menu. Both these methods enable you to choose from one of four options:

❏　If you select File from the submenu, you are presented with a dialog box from which you can browse for and select a particular file to add to the setup project. Use this method when a file needed by the application is not the output from another project within the solution.

❏　The Merge Module option enables you to include a merge module in the deployment project. Third-party vendors can supply merge modules or you can create your own with Visual Studio.

❏　The Assembly option can be used to select a .NET component (assembly) to be included in the deployment project.

❏　If the deployment project is part of a solution (as in this walk-through), you can select Project ↔ Add ↔ Project Output. This enables you to add the output from any of the projects in the solution to the setup project.

You want to add the output of the Windows application project to the setup project. Select the Project Output menu item to bring up the dialog box shown in Figure 22-2.

The Add Project Output Group dialog box is split into several parts:

❏　The combo box at the top contains a list of the names of all the nondeployment projects in the current solution. In your case, there is only one project — SampleForDeployment.

❏　Below the combo box is a list box containing all the possible outputs from the selected project. You are interested in the Primary output, so make sure that this is selected. The different types of output are summarized in the following table.

❏　Below the list of possible outputs is a combo box that enables you to select the configuration to use for the selected project. Select the (Active) option, because this uses whatever configuration is in effect when the project is built.

Click OK to return to the solution.

Figure 22-2

Project Output	Description
Primary output	The primary output of a project is the resulting DLL or EXE that is produced by building the particular project.
Localized resources	The localized resource of a project is a DLL that contains only resources. The resources within the DLL are specific to a culture or locale. This is often called a *satellite DLL*.
Debug Symbols	When the particular project in question is compiled, a special file is created that contains special debugging information about the project. These are called *debug symbols*. The debug symbols for a project have the same name as the primary output but with an extension of .pdb. The debug symbols provide information to a debugger when an application is being run through it.
Content Files	ASP.NET Web applications have content files that are part of the website, such as HTML files, images files, and so forth. This option allows inclusion of such content as part of a deployment.
Source Files	This includes all the source files for the selected project, including the project file. The solution file is *not* included.
Documentation Files	Source code for a project may contain comments that are formatted so that documentation in an XML format can automatically be produced. This option accesses those XML documentation files.
XML Serialization Assemblies	A project may contain XML schemas. If so, assemblies can be generated that contain classes based on those schemas. This option includes those assemblies.

Now, not only has the output from the Windows application been added to the setup project, but the DetectedDependencies folder also contains an entry.

Whenever you add a .NET component to this deployment project, its dependencies are added to this folder. The dependencies of the dependencies are also added and so on until all the required files have been added. The files listed in the DetectedDependencies folder are included in the resulting setup and, by default, are installed into the application's directory as application-private assemblies. This default behavior helps reduce the possible effects of DLL hell by making the application use its own copies of dependent files.

If you do not want a particular dependency file to be included in the resulting setup, you can exclude it by right-clicking the particular entry under DetectedDependencies and selecting Exclude from the pop-up menu. For example, you may decide that you want to exclude a detected dependency from the setup of an application because you know that the dependency is already installed on the target computer. The dependency will then have the familiar, small "circle and slash" icon before its name to indicate that it has been excluded.

> *Dependencies can also be excluded by selecting the particular dependency and using the Properties window to set the Exclude property to True. The listed dependencies are refreshed whenever a .NET file is added to or removed from the setup project, taking into account any files that have already been excluded.*

You can select an item in the setup project in Solution Explorer and that particular item's properties will be displayed in the Properties window. There are too many properties to discuss them all. Instead, we will take a look at the properties from the root setup node and each of the two different project items. Before we start the discussion, make sure that the root setup node is selected, and take some time to browse the list of available properties.

The root setup node represents the output from this deployment project type: a Windows Installer package (.msi). Therefore, the Properties window contains properties that affect the resulting .msi that is produced.

Important Properties of the Root Setup Node

The ProductName property is used to set the text name of the product that this Windows Installer package is installing. By default, it is set to the name of the setup project (in this case, Setup1). The value of this property is used throughout the steps of the resulting setup. For instance, it is used for the text of the title bar when the resulting .msi file is run. The property is used along with the Manufacturer property to construct the default installation directory:

```
C:\ProgramFiles\<Manufacturer>\<ProductName>
```

The ProductName property is also used by the Add/Remove Programs control panel applet (see Figure 22-3) to show that the application is installed.

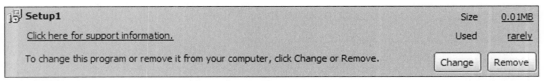

Figure 22-3

As shown in Figure 22-3, you can click a link to get support information about the selected application. That link yields a dialog similar to the one shown in Figure 22-4.

Figure 22-4

The information in this dialog is derived from several properties of the setup project:

Support Information	Related Properties	Description
Publisher	Manufacturer	The Manufacturer property is used to help create the default installation directory for the project and display of the manufacturer of the application within the Windows Installer package.
Version	ManufacturerUrl	This property is used in conjunction with the Manufacturer property to make a hyperlink for the Publisher part of the support information. If a value is entered, the name of the publisher will be underlined, providing a clickable link to visit the publisher's website.
	Version	This is the version number of the Windows Installer package. It can be changed to match the version number of the application that the package installs, but this has to be done manually.
Contact	Author	This property is used to hold the name of the company/person that created the Windows Installer package. By default, this has the same value as the Manufacturer property.
Support Information	SupportPhone	This property can be used to provide a support telephone number for the application.
	SupportUrl	This property can be used to provide a URL for the product's support website. The value of this property is represented as a hyperlink in the support information window.
Comments	Description	This property can be used to include any information that you would like to appear in the support information window. For instance, it could be used to detail the opening hours of your support department.

You may need to set several additional properties of the root node. The `AddRemoveProgramsIcon` property enables you to set the icon that appears in the Add/Remove Programs control panel applet. The default of (None) means that the default icon will be used. You can select an icon with the (Browse) option. The icon can be a standalone icon file or you can select an executable or DLL that contains an icon you want to use.

The `Title` property is used to set the textual title of the application installed. By default, this property has the same name as the setup project. The remaining properties for the root setup node are for various advanced options, and are not discussed in this walk-through.

Properties of the Primary Output Project Item

Earlier, you added the primary output from the SampleForDeployment Windows application to your deployment project. It should now appear as an item in that project. Primary Output project items also have several important properties that you should know about, including the following:

Property	Description
Condition	This enables you to enter a condition that will be evaluated when the installation is run. If the condition evaluates to `True`, then the file will be installed; if the condition evaluates to `False`, then the file won't be installed. If you only wanted a particular file to be installed and the installation was being run on Microsoft Windows 2000 or better, you could enter the following for the condition: `VersionNT >= 5`.
Dependencies	Selecting this property displays a window that shows all the dependencies of the selected project output.
Exclude	Use this property to indicate whether you want the project output to be excluded from the resulting Windows Installer package.
Folder	This property enables you to select the target folder for the project outputs.
KeyOutput	This property expands to provide information about the main file that makes up the project output. In your case, it will show information for the `WindowsApplication.exe` file.
Outputs	Selecting this property displays a window listing all the files that are part of the project output, including where these files are located on the development machine.
Permanent	This property is used to indicate whether the files that make up the project output should be removed when the application is uninstalled (`False`) or left behind (`True`). It is advisable to remove all files installed by an application when the application is uninstalled. Therefore, this property should be set to `False`, which it is the default.
ReadOnly	This property is used to set the read-only file attribute of all the files that make up the project output. As the name suggests, this makes the file read-only on the target machine.

Property	Description
Register	This property enables you to instruct the Windows Installer to register the files contained within the project output as COM objects. This only applies to projects (for example, the Class Library project template) that have been compiled with the Register for COM Interop project property set.
Vital	This property is used to indicate that the files contained within the project output are vital to the installation — if the installation of these files fails, then the installation as a whole should fail. The default value is True.

Properties of the Detected Dependency Items

Items that reside in the DetectedDependencies folder have some of the preceding properties, and they also have some read-only properties that provide you with detailed information about the item. This chapter does not include a detailed discussion of those informational properties.

This has been a brief look at the Setup Project template. It uses all the project defaults and provides a standard set of steps to users when they run the Windows Installer package. Of course, a real application needs more than a single application file and its dependencies. The setup project can be customized extensively to meet those additional needs.

Besides adding more files to the deployment project, you may need to create shortcuts, directories, registry entries, and so on. These customizations and more can be accomplished using the set of built-in editors, covered in the section "Modifying the Deployment Project."

Creating a Deployment Project for an ASP.NET Web Application

Another commonly used deployment scenario is that of a Web application that has been created using the ASP.NET Web Application Project template. Typically, the Web application is developed on a development Web server, and you need to create a deployment project to transfer the finished application to a production Web server.

For this scenario, the template to use is the Web Setup Project template. There is one major difference between this template and the previous Setup Project template: The Web Setup Project, by default, deploys the application to a virtual directory of the Web server on which the setup is run, whereas a Setup Project deploys the application to the Program Files folder on the target machine by default.

There are substantial similarities in producing a deployment project for this scenario and producing a Windows application deployment project as shown in the walk-through. They both produce a Windows Installer package and have the same set of project properties discussed earlier in the walk-through.

As in the previous walk-through, you need to add the output of the Web application to the deployment project. This is accomplished in pretty much the same way as the previous walk-through: by right-clicking on a Web setup project and selecting Add ⇨ Project Output. There is one key difference. When you add the project representing the website, the only option you have for the type of files to add is Content Files, which encompasses the files that make up the website.

A typical resulting project will look similar to Figure 22-5.

Figure 22-5

As before, if you build such a project, the result in an .msi file, which can be used in this case to deploy a website.

Modifying the Deployment Project

The previous walk-through created a default Windows Installer package for a particular project template. You didn't customize the steps or actions that were performed when the package was run. What if you want to add a step to the installation process that displays a ReadMe file to the user? Or what if you need to create registry entries on the installation computer?

This section focuses on additional capabilities for deployment projects. Most of these capabilities are accessed by using a series of "editors" for changing parts of the deployment project. Six editors are available for customizing a Windows Installer–based deployment project:

❑ File System Editor

❑ Registry Editor

❑ File Types Editor

❑ User Interface Editor

❑ Custom Actions Editor

❑ Launch Conditions Editor

The editors are accessible through the View ➪ Editor menu option or by using the corresponding buttons at the top of Solution Explorer.

You can also modify the resulting Windows Installer package through the project's Properties window. This section offers a brief look at each of the six editors and the project properties, and shows how they can be used to modify the resulting Windows Installer package. You will use the project created in the Windows application walk-through in this section.

Project Properties

The first step you take in customizing the Windows Installer package is to use the project properties. The project's Property Pages dialog box is accessed by right-clicking the root of the setup project in Solution Explorer and selecting Properties from the pop-up menu. You can also select the Properties item from the Project menu when the setup project is the active project. Both of these methods bring up the project's Property Pages dialog box, illustrated in Figure 22-6.

Figure 22-6

The Build Page

The only page on the properties dialog is the Build page. The options on that page can be used to affect the way that the resulting Windows Installer package is built.

As with most other projects in VS 2005, you can create different build configurations. You use the Configuration combo box to select the build configuration for which you want to alter properties. In Figure 22-6, the properties for the currently active build configuration, Debug, are being modified. The button labeled Configuration Manager allows you to add, remove, and edit the build configurations for this project.

The Output file name field can be used to modify where the resulting Windows Installer package (.msi) file will be created. You can modify the filename and path directly or you can browse for a location.

Package Files

The next setting, Package files, enables you to specify how the files that make up the installation are packaged. The following table describes the possible settings:

Package	Description
As loose uncompressed files	When you build the project, the files that are to be included as part of the installation are copied to the same directory as the resulting Windows Installer package (`.msi`) file. As mentioned earlier, this directory can be set using the Output file name setting.
In setup file	When the project is built, the files that are to be included as part of the installation are packaged in the resulting Windows Installer package file. When you use this method, you only have one file to distribute. This is the default setting.
In cabinet file(s)	With this option, when the project is built, the files that are to be included as part of the installation are packaged into a number of cabinet files.

Prerequisites

Prerequisites are standard components that may be needed to install or run the application, but are not a part of the application. There are several of these, as shown in Figure 22-7, which is the dialog that is displayed when the Prerequisites button is pressed.

The .NET Framework is checked by default. You should only uncheck it if you are sure that all the machines upon which your application will be installed already have the Framework installed.

Figure 22-7

If the box for any of these prerequisites is checked, the resulting installation package will automatically check for the presence of that prerequisite and install it if required. If you are installing from a CD or network share, it is common for the packages that install these prerequisites to be placed in the same location as your installation package. The default settings assume that this is true and install the prerequisites from that location.

However, you can specify a different location for packages that install prerequisites. You can select the "Download prerequisites from the following location:" option at the bottom of the dialog and then specify the URL at which the packages will be located. Alternatively, you can select "Download prerequisites from the component vendor's web site," which uses the installation URL from the previous dialog (refer to Figure 22-6).

.NET 3.0 applications can only be installed on Windows XP or later. Windows Installer 2.0 is available on all those operating systems, so it is unnecessary to have the Windows Installer 2.0 prerequisite.

Compression

You also have the option to modify the compression used when packaging the files that are to be contained within the installation program. The three options (Optimized for speed, Optimized for size, and None) are self-explanatory and are not covered in this book. The default is Optimized for speed.

Setting the Cabinet File Size

If you want to package the files in cabinet files, then you have the option to specify the size of those resulting cabinet file(s):

❑   You can let the resulting cabinet file be of unlimited size. What this effectively means is that all the files will be packaged into one big cabinet file. The resulting size of the cabinet file will also be dependent on the compression method selected.

❑   If you are installing from floppy disks or CDs, creating one large cabinet file may not be appropriate. In this case, you can specify the maximum size of the resulting cabinet file(s). If you select this option, you need to fill in the maximum size that a cabinet file can be (in KB). If all the files that need to be contained within this installation exceed this size, then multiple cabinet files will be created.

The File System Editor

The File System Editor is automatically displayed for you in VS 2005's document window when you first create the setup project. You can also access this editor and the other editors that are available via the View ➪ Editor menu option in the VS 2005 IDE. The File System Editor is used to manage all the file system aspects of the installation:

❑   Creating folders on the user's machine

❑   Adding files to the folders defined

❑   Creating shortcuts

Basically, this is the editor that you use to define what files need to be installed and where they are installed on the user's machine. The File System Editor is split into two panes in the document window, as shown in Figure 22-8.

Figure 22-8

The left pane shows a list of the folders that have been created automatically for the project. When you select a folder in the left pane, two things happen: First, the right pane of the editor displays a list of the files that are to be installed into the selected folder; and second, the Properties window changes to show you the properties of the currently selected folder.

Adding Items to a Folder

To add an item that needs to be installed to a folder, you can either right-click the folder in the left pane and choose Add from the pop-up menu or select the required folder and right-click in the right pane and again choose Add from the pop-up menu. You will be presented with four options, three of which were discussed earlier in the walk-through:

❏   Project output

❏   File

❏   Assembly

The fourth option (Folder) enables you to add a subfolder to the currently selected folder. This subfolder then becomes a standard folder that can be used to add files. If you add any .NET components or executables, the dependencies of these components are also added to the installation automatically.

Adding Special Folders

When you create a new deployment project, a set of standard folders is created for you (listed in the desktop application section). If the folders created do not match your requirements, then you can also use the File System Editor to add special folders. To add a special folder, right-click anywhere in the left pane (other than on a folder). You will be presented with a pop-up menu that has one item: Add Special Folder. This menu item expands to show you a list of folders that you can add to the installation (folders already added to the project are grayed out).

You can choose from several system folders, summarized in the following table:

Name	Description	Windows Installer Property
Common Files folder	Files (nonsystem) shared by multiple applications are usually installed to this folder.	[CommonFilesFolder]
Common Files folder (64-bit)	Same as Common Files folder, but for 64-bit systems	[CommonFiles64Folder]
Fonts folder	This folder is used to contain all the fonts that are installed on the computer. If your application used a specific font, then you want to install it into this folder.	[FontsFolder]
Program Files folder	Most applications are installed in a directory below the Program Files folder. This acts as root directory for installed applications.	[ProgramFilesFolder]
Program Files folder (64-bit)	Same as Program Files folder, but for 64-bit systems	[ProgramFiles64Folder]
System folder	This folder is used to store shared system files. The folder typically holds files that are part of the OS.	[SystemFolder]
System folder (64-bit)	Same as System folder, but for 64-bit systems.	[System64Folder]
User's Application Data folder	This folder is used to store data, on a per-application basis, that is specific to a user.	[CommonAppDataFolder]
User's Desktop folder	This folder represents the user's desktop. It can be used to create and display an application shortcut, which users can click to start your application.	[DesktopFolder]
User's Favorites folder	This folder is used as a central place to store links to the user's favorite websites, documents, folders, and so on.	[FavoritesFolder]

Table continues on the next page

Name	Description	Windows Installer Property
User's Personal Data folder	This is where a user stores important files. It is normally referred to as My Documents.	[PersonalFolder]
User's Programs Menu	This is where shortcuts are created to applications that appear on the user's Program menu. This is an ideal place to create a shortcut to your application.	[ProgramMenuFolder]
User's Send To Menu	This folder stores all the user's "Send To" shortcuts. A Send To shortcut is displayed when you right-click a file in the Windows Explorer and choose Send To. The Send To shortcut usually invokes an application by passing in the pathname of the files from which it was invoked.	[SendToFolder]
User's Start Menu	This folder can be used to add items to the user's Start menu. This is not often used.	[StartMenuFolder]
User's Startup folder	This folder is used to start applications whenever the user logs in to the computer. If you want your application to start every time the user logs in, then you can add a shortcut to your application in this folder.	[StartupFolder]
User's Template folder	This folder contains templates specific to the logged-in user. Templates are usually used by applications such as Microsoft Office 2000.	[TemplateFolder]
Windows folder	The Windows root folder. This is where the OS is installed.	[WindowsFolder]
Global Assembly Cache folder	This folder is used to store all the shared assemblies on the user's computer.	

If none of the built-in folders match your requirements, you can create your own custom folder. Right-click in the left pane of the File Editor and choose Custom Folder from the pop-up menu.

The new folder is created in the left pane of the editor. The name of the folder is in edit mode, so type in the name and press Enter. The folder will now be selected, and the Properties window will have changed to show the properties of the new folder. The properties of a folder are summarized in the following table:

Property	Description
(Name)	This is the name of the selected folder. The Name property is used within the setup project as the means by which you select a folder.
AlwaysCreate	This property is used to indicate whether this folder should be created on installation even if it's empty (True). If the value is False and there are no files to be installed into the folder, then the folder will not be created. The default is False.
Condition	This enables you to enter a condition that will be evaluated when the installation is run. If the condition evaluates to True, then the folder will be created; if the condition evaluates to False, then the folder won't be created.
DefaultLocation	This is where you define where the folder is going to be created on the target machine. You can enter a literal folder name (such as C:\Temp), use a Windows Installer property, or use a combination of the two. A Windows Installer property contains information that is filled in when the installer is run. In the last table of special folders is a column called Windows Installer property. The property defined in this table is filled in with the actual location of the special folder at runtime. Therefore, if you enter [WindowsFolder] as the text for this property, the folder created represents the Windows special folder.
Property	This property is used to define a Windows Installer property that can be used to override the DefaultLocation property of the folder when the installation is run.
Transitive	This property indicates whether the condition specified in the Condition property is reevaluated on subsequent (re)installs. If the value is True, then the condition is checked on each additional run of the installation. A value of False causes the condition to be run only the first time the installation is run on the computer. The default value is False.

Suppose you name your folder "Wrox Press" and set the DefaultLocation property for your folder to [FavoritesFolder]\Wrox Press. You could now add some shortcuts to this folder using the technique described in the following section. When the installation is run, a new folder is added to the user's favorite folder called Wrox Press, and those shortcuts will be placed in it.

Creating Shortcuts

The first step in creating a shortcut is to locate the file that is to be the target of the shortcut. Select the target file and right-click it. The pop-up menu that appears includes an option to create a shortcut to the selected file, which will be created in the same folder. Select this option.

To add the shortcut to the user's desktop, you need to move this shortcut to the folder that represents the user's desktop. Likewise, you could move this shortcut to the folder that represents the user's Programs menu. Cut and paste the new shortcut to the User's Desktop folder in the left pane of the editor. The shortcut will be added to the user's desktop when the installation is run. You will probably want to rename the shortcut, which can be easily done via the Rename option of the pop-up menu.

You have only taken a brief look at the File System Editor. There are many additional capabilities you can explore.

The Registry Editor

The next editor that you are going to look at is the Registry Editor, which can be used for the following:

❏   Create registry keys

❏   Create values for registry keys

❏   Import a registry file

Like the File System Editor, the Registry Editor is split into two panes, as illustrated in Figure 22-9.

Figure 22-9

The left pane of the editor represents the registry keys on the target computer. When you select a registry key, two things happen: the right pane of the editor is updated to show the values that are to be created under the selected registry key, and if the registry key selected is not a root key in the left pane, the Properties window will be updated with a set of properties for this registry key.

When you create a new deployment project, a set of registry keys will be created for you that correspond to the standard base registry keys of Windows. Notice in Figure 22-9 that there is a key defined with a name of [Manufacturer]. When the installation is run, this is replaced with the value of the Manufacturer property described earlier in the chapter. [Manufacturer] is a property of the installation and can be used elsewhere within the installation. Several of these properties are defined that can be used in much the same way (consult the "Property Reference" topic in the MSDN documentation for a full list).

Adding a Value to a Registry Key

Before adding a value, you must select the registry key that is going to hold the value (or create it). There are several ways to add the registry value:

❏   Right-click the registry key and use the resulting pop-up menu.

❑　Right-click in the right-hand pane and use the resulting pop-up menu.

❑　Use the Action menu.

For illustrational purposes here, select one of the Software registry keys. The Action menu will contain one item, New, which contains a number of submenu items:

❑　Key

❑　String value

❑　Environment string value

❑　Binary value

❑　DWORD value

Using this menu, you can create a new registry key below the currently selected key (via Key), or you can create a value for the currently selected registry key using one of the four Value types: String, Environment String, Binary, and DWORD.

For example, suppose you need to create a registry entry that informs the application whether or not to run in the debug mode. The registry value must be applicable to a particular user, must be called `Debug`, and must contain the text `True` or `False`.

The first step is to select the following registry key in the left pane of the editor:

    HKEY_CURRENT_USER\Software [Manufacturer].

The registry key `HKEY>\_CURRENT>\_USER` is used to store registry settings that apply to the currently logged-in user.

Create a value that is applicable to only this application and not all applications created by you. To do so, create a new registry key below the `HKEY>\_CURRENT>\_USER\ Software\[Manufacturer]` key that is specific to this product (select the Action ⇨ New@ ⇨ Key menu item).

When the key is created, the key name will be editable, so give it a name of `[ProductName]` and press Enter. This creates a key that is given the name of the product contained within this Windows Installer package. The `ProductName` property of the setup was discussed earlier in this chapter.

Now that you have created the correct registry key, the next step is to create the actual registry value. Make sure that your new registry key is selected, and choose String Value from the Action ⇨ New menu and give the new value a name of Debug.

Once the value has been created, you can set a default value for it in its Properties window, in this case `False`. When the Windows Installer package is run in the Debug registry, the value will be created. If a value already exists in the registry, the Windows Installer package will overwrite the existing value with that defined in the Registry Editor.

You can move most keys and values in the Registry Editor around by using cut and paste or simply by dragging and dropping the required item.

The alternative to creating registry entries during installation is to have your application create registry entries the first time they are needed. However, note one significant difference from registry keys created with a Windows Installer package. The uninstall corresponding to a Windows Installer installation automatically removes any registry keys created during the install. If the registry entries are created by the application instead, then the uninstall has no way of knowing that these registry entries should be removed.

Importing Registry Files

If you already have a registry file that contains the registry settings that you would like to be created, then you can import the file into the Registry Editor. To import a registry file, you need to make sure the root node (Registry on Target Machine) is selected in the left pane of the editor. You can then use the Import item of the Action menu to select the registry file to import.

> *Registry manipulation should be used with extreme caution. Windows relies heavily on the registry, and you can cause yourself a great number of problems if you delete, overwrite, or change registry values and keys without knowing the full consequences of the action.*

If you want to create the registry entries that are required to create file associations, then you can use the editor covered next.

The File Types Editor

The File Types Editor can be used to create the required registry entries to establish a *file association* for the application being installed. A file association is simply a link between a particular file extension and a particular application. For example, the file extension `.doc` is normally associated with Microsoft WordPad or Microsoft Word.

When you create a file association, not only do you create a link between the file extension and the application, but you also define a set of actions that can be performed from the context menu of the file with the associated extension. For example, if you right-click a document with an extension of `.doc`, you get a context menu that can contain any number of actions — for example, Open and Print. The action in bold (Open, by default) is the default action to be called when you double-click the file, so in the example, double-clicking a Word document will start Microsoft Word and load the selected document.

Let's walk through the creation of a file extension for the application. Suppose that the application uses a file extension of `.set` and the file is to be opened in the application when it is double-clicked. Start the File Types editor, which contains a single pane. In a new deployment project, this pane will only contain a root node called "File Types on Target Machine."

To add a new file type, you need to make sure the root element is selected in the editor. You can then choose Add File Type from the Action menu, or right-click on the root node and select Add File Type. Give the new file type the name "Example File Type."

Next, you must set the extension and application for this file type. Use the Properties window (shown in Figure 22-10). Enter `.set` as the value for the `Extensions` property.

To associate an application with this file type, you need to use the `Command` property. The ellipsis button for this property presents you with a dialog box in which you can select an executable file contained within any of the folders defined in the File System Editor. In this case, you select `Primary Output from WindowsApplication (active)` from the `Application Folder` as the value for `Command`.

Figure 22-10

When this new file type was first created, a default action was added for you called &Open — select it. Now take a look at the Properties window again. Notice the Arguments property: You can use this to add command-line arguments to the application defined in the last step. In the case of the default action that has been added for you, the arguments are "%1", where the value "%1" will be replaced by the file-name that invoked the action. You can add your own hard-coded arguments (such as /d). An action is set to be the default by right-clicking it and selecting Set as Default from the pop-up menu.

The User Interface Editor

The User Interface Editor, shown in Figure 22-11, is used to manage the interface that is shown during the installation of the application. The editor enables you to define the dialog boxes that are displayed to the user and in what order they are shown.

Figure 22-11

The editor uses a tree view with two root nodes: Install and Administrative Install. Below each of these nodes are three nodes that represent the stages of installation: Start, Progress, and End. Each of the three stages can contain a number of dialog boxes that are displayed to the user when the resulting Windows Installer package is run. A default set of dialog boxes is predefined when you create the deployment project. The default dialog boxes that are present depend on the type of deployment project: Setup Project or Web Setup Project. Figure 22-11 shows the dialog boxes that were added by default to a Setup Project. However, if you are creating a Web Setup Project, the Installation Folder dialog box will be replaced by an Installation Address dialog box.

Using Figure 22-11, the following section discusses the two modes in which the installer can be run, and the three stages of the installation.

Installation Modes

The installation can run in two modes, which correspond to the two root nodes of the editor: Install and Administrative Install. These distinguish between an end user installing the application and a system administrator performing a network setup.

> To use the Administrative Install mode of the resulting Windows Installer package, you can use `msiexec.exe` with a command-line parameter, e.g.,
>
> ```
> msiexec.exe /a <PACKAGE>.msi
> ```

Install mode is most frequently used and is what you will use in this example. As mentioned earlier, the steps the installation goes through can be split into three stages and are represented as subnodes of the parent installation mode.

The Start Stage

The Start stage is the first stage of the installation. It contains the dialog boxes that are displayed to the user before the actual installation of the files begins. The Start stage should be used to gather any information from the user that may affect what is installed and where it is installed.

This stage is commonly used to ask the user to select the base installation folder for the application and to indicate what parts of the system should be installed. Another common task at this stage is to ask users their name and organization. At the end of this stage, the Windows Installer service determines how much disk space is required on the target machine and confirms that this amount of space is available. If the space is not available, then the user receives an error and the installation ends.

The Progress Stage

The Progress stage is the second stage of the installer and is where the actual installation of the files occurs. There isn't usually any user interaction in this stage of installation. Typically, one dialog box indicates the current progress of the installation, which is calculated automatically.

The End Stage

Once the actual installation of the files has finished, the installer moves into the End stage. The most common use of this stage is to inform the user that the installation has been completed successfully. It is often used to provide the option of running the application immediately or to view any release notes.

Customizing the Order of Dialog Boxes

The order in which the dialog boxes appear within the tree view determines the order in which they are presented to the user during an installation. Dialog boxes cannot be moved between different stages.

The order of the dialog boxes can be changed by dragging the respective dialog boxes to the position in which you want them to appear. You can also move a particular dialog box up or down in the order by right-clicking the dialog box and selecting either Move Up or Move Down.

Adding Dialog Boxes

A set of predefined dialog boxes has been added to the project for you, allowing for actions such as prompting a user for a registration code. If these do not match your requirements, you can add or remove dialog boxes in any of the stages.

When adding a dialog box, you have the option to use a built-in dialog box or import one. To illustrate how to add a dialog box, consider an example that adds a dialog box to display a ReadMe file to the user of Windows Installer package. The ReadMe file needs to be displayed before the actual installation of the files occurs.

The first step is to choose the mode in which the dialog box is to be shown: Install or Administrative Install. This example uses the Install mode. Next, you need to determine the stage at which the dialog box is to be shown. In the example, you want to display the ReadMe file to the user before the actual installation of the files occurs, which means that you have to show the ReadMe file in the Start stage. Make sure the Start node is selected below the Install parent node.

You are now ready to add the dialog box. Using the Action menu again, select the Add Dialog menu item, which displays the Add Dialog dialog box (see Figure 22-12), where you can choose from the built-in dialog boxes.

Figure 22-12

As shown in Figure 22-12, there are a number of built-in dialog boxes to choose from. Each dialog box has a short description that appears at the bottom of the window to inform you of its intended function. In this case, you want to use the Read Me dialog box, so select it and click OK.

New dialog boxes are always added as the last dialog box in the stage to which they are added, so move it into the correct position. In this case, you want the Read Me dialog box to be shown immediately after the Welcome dialog box, so drag and drop it into position.

Properties of the Dialog Boxes

Like most other project items in Visual Studio, dialog boxes have a set of properties that you can change to suit your needs using the Properties window. When a dialog box is selected, you will notice that the Properties window varies according to the properties of the selected dialog box. The properties that appear depend on the dialog box selected. Details of all the properties of the built-in dialog boxes can be found by looking at the "Properties of the User Interface Editor" topic in the MSDN documentation.

The Custom Actions Editor

The Custom Actions Editor (see Figure 22-13) is used for fairly advanced installations. It enables you to define actions that are to be performed due to one of the following installation events: Install, Commit, Rollback, and Uninstall. For example, you can use this editor to define an action that creates a new database when the installation is committed.

Figure 22-13

The custom actions that are added using this editor can be Windows script-based, compiled executables, or DLLs.

Load this editor by right-clicking on the Setup1 project and selecting View ➪ Custom Actions. The editor uses a tree view to represent the information. The four nodes in the tree view represent each of the four installation events to which you can add custom actions, as shown in Figure 22-13.

As with the User Interface Editor, the order in which the actions appear determines the order in which they are run, and this can be modified simply by dragging and dropping the actions or by using the context menus of the actions to move them up or down.

Adding a Custom Action

To add a custom action, you must select the node of the event into which you want to install the action. You can then use the Action menu to select the executable, DLL, or script that implements the custom action. The four actions that are defined in the editor are described in the following table:

Event	Description
Install	The actions defined for this event are run when the installation of the files has finished, but before the installation has been committed.
Commit	The actions defined for this event are run when the installation has been committed and has therefore been successful.
Rollback	The actions defined for this event are run when the installation fails and rolls back the machine to the state it was in before the install was started.
Uninstall	The actions defined for this event are run when the application is being uninstalled from the machine.

Suppose you wanted to start your application as soon as the installation is completed successfully. Use the following process to accomplish this.

First, decide when the action must occur. Using the preceding table, you can see that the Commit event is run when the installation has been successful. Make sure that this node is selected in the editor. You are now ready to add the actual action you would like to happen when the Commit event is called. Using the Action menu again, select the Add Custom Action menu item, which displays a dialog box that you can use to navigate to and select a file (.exe, .dll, or windows script) from any that are included in the File System Editor. In this example, select Primary output from WindowsApplication (Active), which is contained within the Application folder.

As with most items in the editors, the new custom action has a number of properties. The following table describes some of the ones you are most likely to need:

Property	Description
(Name)	This is the name given to the selected custom action.
Arguments	This property enables you to pass command-line arguments into the executable that makes up the custom action. This only applies to custom actions that are implemented in executable files (.exe). By default, the first argument passed in indicates what event caused the action to run. It can have the following values: /Install /Commit /Rollback /Uninstall
Condition	This enables you to enter a condition that will be evaluated before the custom action is run. If the condition evaluates to True, then the custom action will run; if the condition evaluates to False, then the custom action will not run.

Table continues on the next page

Property	Description
CustomActionData	This property enables you to pass additional information to the custom action.
InstallerClass	If the custom action is implemented by an Installer class in the selected component, then this property must be set to True. If not, then it must be set to False. (consult the MSDN documentation for more information on the Installer class, which is used to create special installers for such .NET applications as Windows Services. The Installer class is located in the System.Configuration.Install namespace)

Set the InstallClass property to equal False, because your application does not contain an installer class.

That's it. When you run the Windows Installer package and the installation is successful, the application automatically starts. The custom action that you implemented earlier is very simple, but custom actions can be used to accomplish any customized installation actions that you could want. Take some time to play around with what can be accomplished using custom actions. For instance, try creating a custom action that writes a short file into the Application directory.

The Launch Conditions Editor

The Launch Conditions Editor can be used to define a number of conditions for the target machine that must be met before the installation will run. For example, if your application relies on the fact that the user has Microsoft Word 2000 installed on his or her machine in order to run your application, you can define a launch condition that checks this.

You can define a number of searches that can be performed to help create launch conditions:

❑ File search

❑ Registry search

❑ Windows Installer search

As with the Custom Actions Editor, the Launch Conditions Editor (shown in Figure 22-14) uses a tree view to display the information contained within it. The example shows a Custom Actions Editor that has had an item added. The steps for adding that item are covered later.

Figure 22-14

There are two root nodes. The first (Search Target Machine) is used to display the searches that have been defined. The second (Launch Conditions) contains a list of the conditions that will be evaluated when the Windows Installer package is run on the target machine.

As with many of the other editors, the order in which the items appear below these two nodes determines the order in which the searches are run and the order in which the conditions are evaluated. If you wish, you can modify the order of the items in the same manner as previous editors.

The searches are run and then the conditions are evaluated as soon as the Windows Installer package is run, before any dialog boxes are shown to the user.

Let's look at an example of adding a file search and launch condition to a setup project. For argument's sake, let's say that you want to ensure that your users have Microsoft Word 2003 installed on their machine before they are allowed to run the installation for your application.

Adding a File Search

To add a file search, you begin by searching for the Microsoft Word 2003 executable.

Making sure the Search Target Machine node is currently selected in the editor, add a new file search by selecting the Add File Search item from the Action menu. The new item should be given a meaningful name, so enter **Word2003Search**. The result is shown in Figure 22-14.

Modifying the File Search Properties

Like most items contained within the editors mentioned in this chapter, the new file search item has a set of properties that you can modify using the Properties window. The properties of the file search item determine the criteria that are used when searching for the file. Most of the properties are self-explanatory and have been covered in previous sections, so they are not covered in this chapter.

In this example, you need to search for the Microsoft Word 2003 executable, which means that a number of these properties need to be modified to match your own search criteria.

The first property that requires modification is `FileName`. In this case, you need to search for the Microsoft Word 2003 executable, so enter `winword.exe` as the value for this property. Previous versions of Microsoft Word used the same filename.

There is no need to search for the file from the root of the hard drive. The `Folder` property can be used to define the starting folder for the search. By default, the value is `[SystemFolder]`, which indicates that the search will start from the Windows `system` folder. There are a number of these built-in values; if you are interested, you can see what these folders correspond to in the "Adding Special Folders" section.

In this example, you do not want to search the Windows `system` folder because Microsoft Word is usually installed in the `Program Files` folder. Set the value of the `Folder` property to `[ProgramFilesFolder]` to indicate that this should be your starting folder.

When the search starts, it only searches the folder specified in the `Folder` property, as indicated by the default value (0) of the `Depth` property. The `Depth` property is used to specify how many levels of subfolders the search will look in from the starting folder specified for the file in question.

Note some performance issues relating to the Depth property. If a search is performed for a file that is very deep in the file system hierarchy, it can take a long time to find the file. Therefore, wherever possible, use a combination of the Folder and Depth properties to decrease the possible search range. The file that you are searching for in your example will probably be at a depth of greater than 1, so change the value to 3.

There may be different versions of the file that you are searching for on a user's machine. You can use the remaining properties to specify a set of requirements for the file that must be met for it to be found — for example, minimum version number or minimum file size.

You are searching for the existence of Microsoft Word 2003; this means you need to define the minimum version of the file that you want to find. To search for the correct version of winword.exe, enter 11.0.0.0 as the value for the MinVersion property. This ensures that the user has Microsoft Word 2003 or later installed and not an earlier version.

To use the results of the file search, there must be a name for the results. This name is assigned to a Windows Installer property, and is normally used to create a launch condition later. The Property property is where this name is specified.

For this example, enter **WORDEXISTS** as the value for the Property property. If the file search is successful, the full path to the found file will be assigned to this Windows Installer property; otherwise, it will be left blank. At this point, the Properties window should look as shown in Figure 22-15.

Figure 22-15

Creating a Launch Condition

A file search alone is pretty useless. The second step of the process of ensuring that the user has Microsoft Word 2003 installed is creating a launch condition that uses the results of the file search.

Make sure that the Launch Conditions node is selected in the editor, and add a new launch condition to the project by selecting Add Launch Condition from the Action menu. You need to give this new item a meaningful name; in this case (see Figure 22-16), give it the name Word2003Exists.

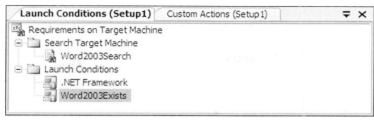

Figure 22-16

This new item has a number of properties to modify. The first property you will change is called `Message`, and it is used to set the text of the message box that appears if this condition is not met. Enter any meaningful description that explains why the installation cannot continue.

The next property that you need to change is called `Condition`, and it is used to define a valid deployment condition that is to be evaluated when the installation runs. The deployment condition entered must evaluate to `True` or `False`. When the installer is run, the condition is evaluated; if the result of the condition is `False`, then the message defined is displayed to the user and the installation stops.

For this example, you need to enter a condition that takes into account whether the `winword.exe` file was found. You can use the Windows Installer property defined earlier (`WORDEXISTS`) as part of the condition. Because the property is empty if the file was not found, and nonempty if the file was found, you can perform a simple test to determine whether the property is empty to create the condition. Enter `WORDEXISTS <> ""` as the value for the `Condition` property.

It is hoped that the preceding discussion of this search enables you to use the other searches and create your own launch conditions. That completes our brief look at the editors you can use to modify the resulting Windows Installer package to suit your needs. Although this has been only a brief overview of the functionality of the editors, they are extremely powerful, and worth investment of your time for further investigation.

Building

The final step is to build the deployment or setup project you have created. There is no difference between how you build a Visual Basic .NET application and a deployment/setup project. If the project is the only project contained within the solution, then you can just use the Build item from the Build menu, which causes the project to be built. As with the other projects, you are informed of what is happening during the build through the Output window.

The deployment/setup project can also be built as part of a multiproject solution. If the Build Solution item is chosen from the Build menu, then all the projects in the solution are built. Any deployment or setup projects are built last. This ensures that if they contain the output from another project in the solution, they get the latest build of that project.

Internet Deployment of Windows Applications

The earlier discussions of creating an installation package for your application presumed that you were able to transfer the MSI file to each machine that needed installation, either electronically or via some storage medium such as a CD-ROM. This works well for installations within an organization and can work acceptably for initial installation from CD-ROMs on distributed systems.

However, the availability of the Internet has raised the bar for acceptable deployment of Windows-based client applications. Perhaps the most important advantage of browser-based applications has been their ease of deployment for the user. For Windows Forms applications to be cost-competitive with browser-based applications, low-cost deployment over the Internet is needed.

Fortunately, there are several ways to get low-cost deployment over the Internet, including the following:

❑   "No-touch" deployment

❑   Deployment with ClickOnce, a capability added to Visual Studio 2005

❑   Components or libraries that contain deployment capabilities, such as the Application Updater Application Block

Different deployment techniques are suitable for different applications. This section looks at each technique and discusses how it works and what kinds of applications it is suitable for use with.

No-Touch Deployment

Built into all versions of the .NET Framework is the capability to run applications from a Web server instead of from the local machine. There are two ways to do this, depending on how the application is launched.

First, an application EXE that exists on a Web server can be launched via a standard HTML hyperlink. An application named `MyApp.exe` that is located at `www.mycompany.com/apps` can be launched with the following HTML in a Web page:

```
<a href="http://www.mycompany.com/apps/MyApp.exe">Launch MyApp</a>
```

When the hyperlink is clicked on a system with the .NET Framework installed, Internet Explorer transfers control to the .NET Framework to launch the program. The framework then tries to load the EXE assembly, which does not yet exist on the client. At that point, the assembly is automatically fetched from the deployment Web server and placed on the local client machine. It resides on the client machine in an area called the *application download cache*, which is a special directory on the system managed by the .NET. Framework.

If the EXE tries to load a class from another application assembly (typically a DLL), then that assembly is assumed to be in the same directory on the Web server as the EXE. The application assembly is also transferred to the application download cache and loaded for use.

This process continues for any other application assemblies that are needed. The application is said to *trickle-feed* to the client system.

Automatic Updating

Whenever an assembly in the application download cache is needed, the .NET Framework automatically checks for a new version in the appropriate directory on the Web server. Thus, the application can be updated for all client machines by simply placing an assembly on the Web server.

Using a Launch Application

One drawback of this technique for deploying the application is that it can only be launched from a Web page or other means of accessing a URL (such as a shortcut or the Start ⇨ Run dialog).

To get around this limitation, you can get a similar deployment capability by using a small launching application that uses dynamic loading to start the main application. Dynamic loading was discussed in the previous chapter. In this case, the location for the assembly used in dynamic loading will be the URL of the assembly on the Web server.

An application that uses this technique still gets all the trickle feeding and auto-update features of an application launched straight from a URL.

Limitations of No-Touch Deployment

No-touch deployment is useful for simple applications, but has some serious drawbacks for more complex applications:

❑ An active Internet connection is required to run the application — no offline capability is available.

❑ Only assemblies can be deployed via no-touch deployment — application files such as configuration files cannot be included.

❑ Applications deployed via no-touch deployment are subject to code-access security limitations, as discussed in Chapter 12.

❑ No-touch deployment has no capability to deploy any prerequisites for the application or any COM components that it may need.

Given the limitations of no-touch deployment, Microsoft has added an alternative to the .NET Framework 2.0 called *ClickOnce*. It is essentially a complete replacement for no-touch deployment. Thus, while no-touch deployment is still supported in .NET Framework 2.0, it is no longer recommended for use, and is not discussed further.

ClickOnce Deployment

A more advanced form of Internet and network deployment uses a new technology in .NET Framework 2.0 called ClickOnce. It is intended to overcome the limitations of no-touch deployment and to provide a robust, easy-to-implement deployment option for a wide range of applications.

ClickOnce has several advantages over alternatives such as no-touch deployment, including the following:

❑ **Updating from a Web server with user control** — No-touch deployment only allows completely automatic updating from the Web server. ClickOnce can be configured for completely automatic updates from a Web server, but it can also be set up to allow more control by the user over when the application is installed and uninstalled.

❑ **Offline Access** — Applications deployed with ClickOnce can be configured to run in an offline condition too. Applications that can be run offline have a shortcut installed on the Start menu.

ClickOnce also has advantages over applications installed with Windows Installer. These include auto-updating of the application from the deployment server, and installation of the application by users who are not administrators. (Windows Installer applications require the active user to be an administrator of the local machine. ClickOnce applications can be installed by users with reduced permissions.)

ClickOnce deployment can be performed from a Web server, a network share, or read-only media such as a CD-ROM or DVD-ROM. The following discussion assumes you are using a Web server for deployment, but you can substitute a network share if you do not have access to a Web server.

> **ClickOnce does not require the .NET Framework 2.0 or 3.0 to be installed on the Web server you use for ClickOnce deployment. However, it does require that the Web server understand how to handle files with extensions** .application **and** .manifest. **The configuration for these extensions is done automatically if the .NET Framework is installed on the Web server. However, on servers that do not contain the framework, you will probably have to do the configuration manually.**
>
> **Each extension that a Web server can handle must be associated with an option called a** *MIME type* **that tells the Web server how to handle that file extension when serving a file. The MIME type for each extension used by ClickOnce should be set to** application/x-ms-application. **If you do not know how to configure MIME types for your Web server, ask a network administrator or other professional who can.**

Configuring an Application for ClickOnce

For a simple case, no special work is needed to prepare a typical Windows application to be deployed via ClickOnce. Unlike the deployment options discussed earlier, it is not necessary to add additional projects to the solution. If you use standard options in ClickOnce, it is also unnecessary to add any custom logic to your application. All the work to enable ClickOnce deployment for an application can be performed by selecting options in the IDE.

It is possible to control the ClickOnce deployment by writing your own custom logic controlling the ClickOnce deployment processes. However, that capability is beyond the scope of this book and is not discussed here. Instead, this chapter covers basic configuration of ClickOnce and common options that do not require you to write any code.

Online vs. Locally Installed Applications

Applications installed via ClickOnce are one of two types:

❑ **Online applications**, which can only be accessed by the user when the system has a connection to the website used to deploy the application

❑ **Offline applications**, which can also be used when there is no connection available

Online applications must be launched with a URL (Uniform Resource Locator), a standard filename, or a UNC (Universal Naming Convention) filename. This may be done in various ways, such as clicking a link in a Web page, typing a URL into the Address text box of a browser, typing a filename into the Address text box of Windows Explorer, or selecting a shortcut on the local machine that contains the

URL or filename. However, ClickOnce does not automatically add any such mechanisms to a user's machine to access the application. That is up to you.

Offline applications can also be launched with a URL or UNC, and are always launched that way the first time. The differences are as follows:

❑ When ClickOnce does the initial installation of the application on the user's machine, by default it places a shortcut to the application on the user's Start ➪ Programs menu.

❑ The application can be started from the shortcut, and will run with no connection to the original location used for installation. Of course, any functionality of the application that depends on a network or Internet connection will be affected if the system is not online. It is your responsibility to build the application in such a way that it functions properly when offline.

Deploying an Online Application

A walk-through of deployment for a simple Windows application will demonstrate the basics of ClickOnce. This first walk-through deploys an online application to a Web server, which is one of the simpler user scenarios for ClickOnce.

First, create a simple Windows Application in Visual Studio, and name it SimpleApp. On the blank Form1 that is created as part of the application, place a single button.

To enable ClickOnce deployment, access the Build menu and select the Publish SimpleApp option. The ClickOnce publishing wizard will appear. The first screen in the wizard is shown in Figure 22-17.

Figure 22-17

The location will default to a local Web server, but as discussed earlier, deployment can be done to a network share or even a local directory. Change the location if the default is not appropriate for your circumstances. Once you've verified the location to publish, click Next.

Select one of the two types of ClickOnce applications discussed earlier. Because this example is for an online application, click the second option to make the application only available online (see Figure 22-18).

Figure 22-18

Click Next to see a summary of your selection, and then click Finish. The ClickOnce deployment process will begin. A new item called `SimpleApp_TemporaryKey.pfx` will be added to your project, a complete build will be done, a new virtual directory will be created for the application on the Web server, and the files needed to deploy the application will be copied to that virtual directory. (The new item is discussed in the section "Signing the Manifest.")

When the process is complete, a Web page will be generated that contains the link needed to deploy the application. The Web page will have a Run button that activates the link. If you click this button, the application will be deployed by ClickOnce. (You may wish to view the source for this Web page to obtain the HTML needed to launch the application from your own Web pages.)

First, the prerequisites for the application are verified. In this case, that just means the .NET Framework. Next, a Security Warning dialog is displayed, asking whether it is acceptable to run the application, as shown in Figure 22-19. You can run the application by clicking Run, or click Cancel, which aborts the process. Click the Run button, and after a short delay you will see the application's form appear.

Figure 22-19

If you now make any changes to the SimpleApp application, you must publish the application again to make the changes available via ClickOnce. You can do that by stepping through the publishing wizard once again. More about automatic updating of ClickOnce applications is discussed later in the section "The Update Process."

Deploying an Offline Application

In the second screen of the publishing wizard, if you select the first option, then the installation process has some differences:

❑   The Web page that ClickOnce generates to test the deployment will have an Install button instead of a Run button.

❑   When the button is pressed, a shortcut to the application is added to the user's Start ⇨ Programs menu. The shortcut will be in the program folder named for the company name that was entered when Visual Studio was installed.

❑   The application is launched at the end of the install process, as it was with an online app, but future launches can be accomplished with the same URL or via the shortcut in the Start menu.

Files and Directories Produced by ClickOnce

The virtual directory used by ClickOnce to deploy your application contains a number of files for different aspects of the deployment. Figure 22-20 shows what the directory for SimpleApp looks like after ClickOnce has finished copying all needed files.

The virtual directory contains a folder for the first version of SimpleApp, which by default is version 1.0.0.0. It also contains the Web page that is displayed after ClickOnce finishes, named publish.htm.

The next file is setup.exe. This is an executable that does not need the .NET Framework to run. It is used during the ClickOnce process for all the activities that must take place before the application is launched, including activities such as checking for the presence of the .NET Framework. It is discussed further in the section "The Bootstrapper."

Figure 22-20

The next file is `SimpleApp.application`. The ".application" extension is specific to ClickOnce, and indicates a special file called a *manifest*. This is an XML-based file that contains all the information needed to deploy the application, such as what files are needed and what options have been chosen. There is also a file named `SimpleApp_1_0_0_0.application`, which is the manifest specifically associated with version 1.0.0.0.

Each version of the application has its own manifest, and the one named `SimpleApp.application` (with no embedded version number) is typically the currently active one. (Thus, the link to the application does not need to change when the version number changes.) Other files associated with a version are in the folder for that version.

Signing the Manifest

Because the manifest controls the update process, it is essential that ClickOnce be assured that the manifest is valid. This is done by signing the manifest, using a public-private key pair. As long as a third party does not have the key pair, that party cannot "spoof" a manifest, preventing any malicious interference in the ClickOnce deployment process.

A key pair is automatically generated when you publish with ClickOnce. However, you can supply your own key pair if you like. Options for signing the application are discussed in the section "ClickOnce Configuration Options."

Note that your application assemblies do not need to be signed for them to be used in a ClickOnce deployment. Only the manifest needs to be signed. The manifest contains hash codes of all the assemblies involved, and those hash codes are checked before assemblies are used. This prevents malicious third parties from inserting their own versions of your assemblies.

The Update Process

By default, all ClickOnce applications check for updates each time the application is launched. This is done by getting the current version of the manifest and checking whether any changes have been made since the last time the application was launched. This process is automatic, so there's nothing you need to do to make it happen, but it's helpful for you to understand the steps that are taken.

For an online application, when a change is detected, it is immediately applied by downloading any changed files. Then the application is launched. In spirit, this is similar to a browser-based application, because the user does not have any option to use an older version.

For an application available offline, when changes are detected, the user is asked if the update should be made. The user can choose to decline the update. There is a configuration option that enables you to specify a minimum version number, which can force a user to accept an update. We will look at ClickOnce configuration options later.

If an update is made for an offline application, then the previous version is kept. The user then has the capability to rollback to that version using the Add/Remove Programs option in the Control Panel. Users can also uninstall the ClickOnce-deployed application from that same location.

Only one older version is kept. If there are older versions, they are removed when a new version is installed, so that the only versions available at any point in time are the current version and the one immediately before it. If a rollback is made to the immediately preceding version, it cannot be rolled back any further to earlier versions.

You can control the update process by including code in your application that detects when changes have been made, and apply the changes as necessary. As previously mentioned, this chapter does not cover writing such logic. There are samples available in the MSDN documentation for this capability.

ClickOnce Configuration Options

In Visual Studio 2005, the properties for a Windows Application project now include several pages that affect ClickOnce. (You can get to the properties for a project by right-clicking on it in the Solution Explorer and selecting Properties.)

The Signing tab page includes options for signing the ClickOnce manifest. There are buttons to select a particular certificate from a store or a file, or to generate a new test certification for signing. This page also contains an option to sign the assembly that is compiled from the project, but as mentioned above, this is not necessary for ClickOnce to operate.

The Security tab page controls options relating to the code access security permissions needed by the application to run. Because the application is being deployed from a source off of the local machine, if you use ClickOnce, then code access security limitations are in effect, as described in Chapter 12. A typical example of the Security tab page is shown in Figure 22-21.

Using the options on the Security tab page, you can calculate the permissions needed by the application, using the button labeled Calculate Permissions. You can also arrange to test your application against a particular set of permissions. To do that, change the default option "This is a full trust application" to the option immediately below it, labeled "This is a partial trust application." Then select the zone from which the application will be installed. When the application is run by Visual Studio, permission for that zone will be enforced.

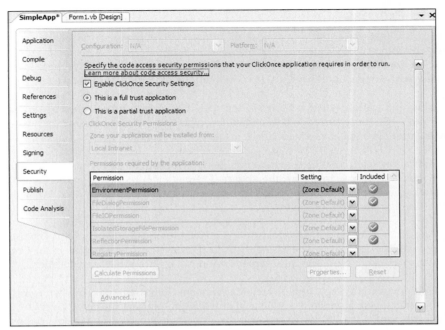

Figure 22-21

All of the other ClickOnce configuration options are on the tab page labeled Publish, shown in Figure 22-22.

Figure 22-22

You can set many options with the Publish page, but here are some of the most important:

Property/Option	Purpose	Where to set it on the page
Publish Location	Specifies the virtual directory, network directory, or local directory to which the application will be published by ClickOnce	Text box labeled Publishing Location. (Note that this can also be set in the first screen of the Publish Wizard.)
Installation URL	Specifies the location from which your application will be deployed by users. By default, this is the same as the Publish Location, but may be set to be elsewhere.	Textbox labeled Installation URL.
Install Mode	Selects the online only vs. offline mode for the application.	Option buttons under Install Mode and Settings. (Note that this can also be set in the second screen of the Publish Wizard.)
Publish Version	Sets the version of the application for publishing purposes. ClickOnce requires version changes to properly auto-update the application.	The text boxes under Publish Version. If the check box under those boxes is checked, the publish version will be automatically incremented each time the application is published.
Prerequisites	Specifies the software that must be installed before your application can itself be installed, including elements such as the .NET Framework	The Prerequisites button brings up a dialog box that allows standard prerequisites to be checked. The .NET Framework is checked by default. The dialog also allows you to specify the location for downloading prerequisites. See the section "The Bootstrapper" for more information on prerequisites.
Miscellaneous options	Options for various purposes such as the product name	The Options button brings up a dialog box that allows these options to be set.
Updates	Options that control the update process, including when the application updates (before or after it starts), the minimum version number required, and so on	These options are only available for applications that can run offline. The Updates button brings up a dialog box controlling these options.

The Bootstrapper

Because applications deployed by ClickOnce are a part of the .NET Framework, the .NET Framework must be available on the user's machine before your application can be installed and run. In addition, your application may require other items such as a database or COM component to be installed.

To provide for such needs, ClickOnce includes a "bootstrapper" that runs as the first step in the ClickOnce process. The bootstrapper is not a .NET program, so it can run on systems that do not yet have the .NET Framework installed. The bootstrapper is contained in a program called Setup.exe, which is included by ClickOnce as part of the publishing process.

When setup.exe runs, it checks for the prerequisites needed by the application, as specified in the Prerequisites options just discussed. If needed, these options are then downloaded and installed. Only when the user's system contains installed prerequisites does ClickOnce attempt to install and run your Windows application. The MSDN documentation includes more details on configuring and using the ClickOnce bootstrapper.

Manual Editing of ClickOnce Manifests

Sometimes an application manifest created by ClickOnce needs to be manually changed. For example, if the application contains dynamically loaded .NET DLLs (as discussed in the previous chapter), then such DLLs are not automatically included in a ClickOnce manifest.

In creating a manifest for an installation, ClickOnce relies on the compile-time references for the application being deployed. It places any application assemblies that have compile-time references into the manifest.

However, dynamically loaded assemblies do not have a compile-time reference. That means ClickOnce can't put them in the manifest automatically. If you have dynamically loaded assemblies in your Windows Forms application, then you must add them to the manifest manually.

ClickOnce includes a tool for manual editing of the manifest. Called MAGE.exe, it can be started from the Visual Studio 2005 command prompt. It offers a UI to open a manifest and perform various manual operations upon it. Figure 22-23 shows what it looks like after a manifest is opened and the page for manipulating files in the manifest is selected.

MAGE.exe can also be used from the command line, so you can create batch files or Powershell scripts to automate insertion of files in a ClickOnce manifest. A complete discussion of using MAGE.exe is beyond the scope of this chapter, but the help files for MAGE.exe are extensive, and you can find MSDN samples showing its use.

Rolling Back or Uninstalling ClickOnce Applications

In addition to deploying an application for use, ClickOnce also creates the capability to uninstall or rollback applications that are deployed with the offline option. Such applications will have an entry in the Add/Remove Programs section of the Control Panel. That entry offers an uninstall option, and if a rollback version is present, then an option to rollback the last update is available.

Only one level of rollback is available. If multiple updates have been done, the user can only rollback to the most recent one before the current one. Once a rollback is done, no further rollback is possible until another update has been deployed.

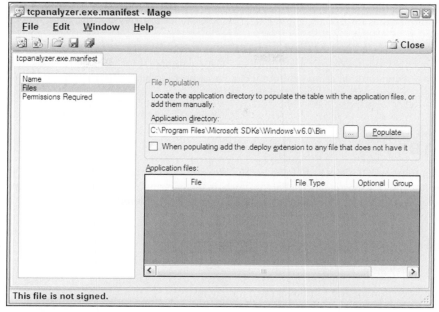

Figure 22-23

ClickOnce vs. Other Deployment Technologies

ClickOnce is a complete replacement for no-touch deployment. However, there are other deployment scenarios for which ClickOnce may not be the ideal solution. For example, ClickOnce can only deploy a per-user installation; it cannot install an application once to be used by all users on the system.

ClickOnce may be used in combination with technologies such as the Windows Installer. If you create .msi files, as discussed earlier in the chapter, you may include them as part of ClickOnce's bootstrapper process. This is an advanced technique not discussed in this book, but you can learn more about this capability in the MSDN documentation.

For cases in which ClickOnce is not appropriate, you may wish to use more customized deployment technologies. These are discussed next.

Custom Deployment Options

If an application needs deployment capabilities not covered by the technologies discussed so far, it may be necessary to use alternative technologies, or even develop them yourself. For example, you can create a deployment function that checks via a Web service to see when updating needs to take place and that uses FTP to transfer files from a Web server to a client machine.

Updater Application Block

Rather than start from scratch on such deployment/installation technology, you can look at starting points such as the Updater Application Block. Created by Microsoft's Patterns and Practices Group, the

Updater Application Block can be downloaded from Microsoft's website. It includes manifest-based checking of modules for updating and background transfer of new modules using the same transfer technology as Windows Update.

You can use the Updater Application Block as is, or customize it for your own needs. For example, you could create a version that allows different classes of users to have different update strategies, so that new updates go out to a select group of users first.

Summary

An application must be deployed to be useful. How an individual application should be deployed depends heavily on circumstances. Factors such as the geographic distribution of the application, its complexity, and how often it will be updated must be considered when choosing an appropriate strategy.

The main possibilities for deployment are as follows:

- ❏ XCOPY deployment
- ❏ Installation via the Windows Installer
- ❏ No-touch deployment
- ❏ ClickOnce deployment
- ❏ Deployment with other technologies such as the Application Updater Block

This chapter has covered each of these, with some discussion of their applicability. It will be helpful for you to understand all of these options to make appropriate decisions for the deployment of individual applications.

On the one hand, simple utilities, for example, might be best installed by simply copying files. On the other hand, standalone applications that have many dependencies on COM-based components will more often use Windows Installer technology. Applications that depend on Web services for data will often be best deployed with ClickOnce. Corporate applications with special needs for security during installation, or that need to install an application once for multiple users, may be better off using the Application Updater Block.

It's also helpful to understand that these options are not mutually exclusive. You may have an application with COM dependencies that needs to use an .msi file for an initial install, but then gets the rest of the application and future updates via ClickOnce or the Application Updater Block. Whatever your application, the plethora of application deployment technologies available for .NET-based applications means you should be able to find an option or combination that suits your needs.

Working with Classic COM and Interfaces

However much we try, we just can't ignore the vast body of technology surrounding Microsoft's Component Object Model, or COM. Over the years, this model has been the cornerstone of so much Microsoft-related development that we have to take a long, hard look at how we are going to integrate all that technology into the new world of .NET.

This chapter begins by taking a brief backward glance at COM, and then compares it with the way that components interact in .NET. It also takes a look at the tools Microsoft provides to help link the two together. Having looked at the theory, you then try it out by building a few example applications. First you take a legacy basic COM object and run it from a Visual Basic 2005 program. Then you repeat the trick with a full-blown ActiveX control. Finally, you run some Visual Basic code in the guise of a COM object.

> More information on how to make COM and VB6 code interoperate with the .NET platform can be found in *Professional Visual Basic Interoperability: COM and VB6 to .NET* (Wiley, 2002).

As all that is done, try to remember one thing: COM is, to a large extent, where .NET came from. In addition, with all the time and resources that have been invested in this technology, it is important to consider the best ways to both maintain these investments and integrate them into new investments being made.

Understanding COM

Before looking into the COM-.NET interoperability story, it's important to understand COM's main concepts. This section doesn't attempt to do more than skim the surface, however. While the basic concepts are fundamentally simple, the underlying technology is anything but simple. Some of the most impenetrable books on software ever written have COM as their subject, and we have no wish to add to these.

COM was Microsoft's first full-blown attempt at creating a language-independent standard for programming. The idea was that interfaces between components would be defined according to a binary standard. This means that you could, for the first time, invoke a VB component from a VC++ application, and vice versa. It would also be possible to invoke a component in another process or even on another machine, via Distributed COM (DCOM). You won't be looking at out-of-process servers here, however, because the vast majority of components developed to date are in-process. To a large extent, DCOM was fatally compromised by bandwidth, deployment, and firewall problems and never achieved a high level of acceptance.

A COM component implements one or more *interfaces,* some of which are standards provided by the system, and some of which are custom interfaces defined by the component developer. An interface defines the various methods that an application may invoke. Once specified, an interface definition is supposed to be inviolate, so that even when the underlying code changes, applications that use the interface don't need to be rebuilt. If the component developers find that they have left something out, then they should define a new interface containing the extra functionality in addition to that in the original interface. This has, in fact, happened with a number of standard Microsoft interfaces. For example, the `IClassFactory2` interface extends the `IClassFactory` interface by adding features for managing the creation of licensed objects.

The key to getting applications and components to work together is *binding.* COM offers two forms of binding, early and late:

❑   In *early binding,* the application uses a *type library* at compile time to work out how to link in to the methods in the component's interfaces. A type library can exist as a separate file, with the extension `.tlb`, or as part of the DLL containing the component code.

❑   In *late binding,* no connection is made between the application and its components at compile time. Instead, the COM runtime searches through the component for the location of the required method when the application is actually run. This has two main disadvantages: it's slower and it's unreliable. If a programming error is made (for example, the wrong method is called, or the right method with the wrong number of arguments), then it isn't caught at compile time.

When a type library is not explicitly referred to, there are two ways to identify a COM component, by *class ID,* which is actually a GUID, and by *ProgID,* which is a string and looks something like `"MyProject.MyComponent"`. These are all cross-referenced in the registry. In fact, COM makes extensive use of the registry to maintain links between applications, their components, and their interfaces. All experienced COM programmers know their way around the registry blindfolded.

VB6 has a lot of COM features embedded into it, to the extent that many VB6 programmers aren't even aware that they are developing COM components. For instance, if you create a DLL containing an instance of a VB6 class, then you have in fact created a COM object without even asking for one. The relative ease of this process is demonstrated in this chapter.

There are clearly similarities between COM and .NET, so to a large extent, all you have to do to make them work together is put a wrapper around a COM object to turn it into an assembly, and vice versa.

COM and .NET in Practice

It's time to get serious and see if all this seamless integration really works. To do this, we have to simulate a legacy situation. Suppose your enterprise depends on a particular COM object that was written for you a long time ago by staff who are no longer in the organization. All you know about the component is that the code within it works perfectly and you need to employ it for your .NET application.

You have one, possibly two, options in this case. If you have the source code of the COM component (which is not always the case) and you have sufficient time (or, to put it another way, money), you can upgrade the object to .NET and continue to maintain it under Visual Studio 2005. For the purist, this is the ideal solution for going forward. However, maintaining the source as it exists under Visual Studio isn't really a viable option. Visual Studio does offer an upgrade path, but it doesn't cope well with COM objects using interfaces specified as abstract classes.

If upgrading the object to a .NET component isn't an option for you, all you really can do is include the DLL as it stands as a COM object, register it on the server containing the .NET Framework, and use the .NET interoperability tools to integrate the two technologies. This is the path that this chapter takes for the example.

Therefore, what you need for this example is a genuine legacy COM object. This chapter uses a genuine legacy VB6 component to integrate within a .NET application. For the next section, this chapter steps back in time and uses VB6 for the classic component required. If you aren't very interested in VB6, then feel free to skip this section. In any case, the DLL created is available as part of the code download from this book.

A Legacy Component

For the legacy component, imagine that you have some kind of analytics engine that requires a number of calculations. Because of the highly complex nature of these calculations, their development has been given to specialists, while the user interface for the application has been given to some UI specialists. A COM interface has been specified to which all calculations must conform. This interface has the name IMegaCalc and has the following methods:

Method	Description
Sub AddInput(InputValue as Double)	Adds the input value to the calculation
Sub DoCalculation( )	Performs the calculation
Function GetOutput( ) as Double	Gets the output from the calculation
Sub Reset( )	Resets the calculation for the next time

Step 1: Defining the Interface

When building any component, the first thing you have to do is define your interface. In VB6, the way to do this is to create an abstract class — that is, one without any implementation. Therefore, create an ActiveX DLL project called MegaCalculator. You do this by creating a new project and then changing its name to `MegaCalculator` by means of the Project ➪ Project1 Properties dialog box. Then, create a class called `IMegaCalc`. This is what the code should looking like:

```
Option Explicit

Public Sub AddInput(InputValue As Double)
End Sub

Public Sub DoCalculation()
End Sub

Public Function GetOutput() As Double
End Function

Public Sub Reset()
End Sub
```

From the main menu, select File ➪ Make MegaCalculator.dll to define and register the interface.

Step 2: Implementing the Component

For the purposes of this demonstration, the actual calculation that you're going to perform is fairly mundane: In fact, the component is going to calculate the mean of a series of numbers. Create another ActiveX DLL project called `MeanCalculator`. Add a reference to the type library for the interface that you're going to implement by selecting the `MegaCalculator` DLL via the References dialog box that appears when you select Project ➪ References.

Having done that, go ahead and write the code for the mean calculation. You do this in a class called `MeanCalc`:

```
Option Explicit

Implements IMegaCalc

Dim mintValue As Integer
Dim mdblValues() As Double
Dim mdblMean As Double

Private Sub Class_Initialize()
  IMegaCalc_Reset
End Sub

Private Sub IMegaCalc_AddInput(InputValue As Double)
  mintValue = mintValue + 1
  ReDim Preserve mdblValues(mintValue)
  mdblValues(mintValue) = InputValue
End Sub

Private Sub IMegaCalc_DoCalculation()
  Dim iValue As Integer
  mdblMean = 0#
  If (mintValue = 0) Then Exit Sub

  For iValue = 1 To mintValue
```

```
      mdblMean = mdblMean + mdblValues(iValue)
   Next iValue

   mdblMean = mdblMean / mintValue
End Sub

Private Function IMegaCalc_GetOutput() As Double
   IMegaCalc_GetOutput = mdblMean
End Function

Private Sub IMegaCalc_Reset()
   mintValue = 0
End Sub
```

As before, you select File ⇨ Make MeanCalculator.dll to build and register the component. It has a default interface called MeanCalc (which contains no methods, and is thus invisible to the naked eye), plus an implementation of IMegaCalc.

Step 3: Registering the Legacy Component

If you have made it this far, then you should now have your legacy component. When developing your new .NET application on the same machine, you don't need to do anything more because your component is already registered by the build process. However, if you're working on an entirely new machine, you need to register it there. To do that, open a command window and register it with the following command using regsvr32.exe found at C:\Windows\system32:

```
regsvr32 MeanCalculator.dll
```

From there, you should then see the result shown in Figure 23-1.

Figure 23-1

Because MeanCalculator implements an interface from MegaCalculator, you have to repeat the trick with that DLL:

```
regsvr32 MegaCalculator.dll
```

That action should yield the results shown in Figure 23-2. You're now ready to use your classic component from a .NET application.

Figure 23-2

The .NET Application

For the .NET application used in this chapter, you only need to instantiate an instance of the `MeanCalc` object and get it to work out a mean calculation for you. In order to accomplish this task, create a .NET Windows Application project in Visual Basic called `CalcApp`. Laid out, the form looks like what is shown in Figure 23-3.

Figure 23-3

The two text boxes are called `txtInput` and `txtOutput`, respectively; the second one is not enabled for user input. The three command buttons are `btnAdd`, `btnCalculate`, and `btnReset`, respectively.

Referencing the Legacy COM Component from .NET

Before you dive into writing the code behind the buttons on the form, you first need to make your new application aware of the `MeanCalculator` component. Add a reference to the component via the Project ➪ Add Reference menu item. This brings up the Add Reference dialog box, which contains five tabs: .NET, COM, Projects, Browse, and Recent. From the COM tab, select `MeanCalculator` and `MegaCalculator` in turn (see Figure 23-4).

Press the OK button after you highlight both of the required components. Note that in the list of references in the Solution Explorer, you can now see the `MeanCalculator` and `MegaCalculator` components. This view is presented in Figure 23-5.

Figure 23-4

Figure 23-5

Inside the .NET Application

Now that you have successfully referenced the components in the .NET application, you can go ahead and finish coding the application, using the functionality provided via the COM components. To start making use of the new capabilities provided from the COM component, add a global variable (mobjMean) to the code that will hold a reference to an instance of the mean calculation component, as shown here:

```
Public Class Form1

    Dim mobjMean As MeanCalculator.MeanCalc
```

Next, create a Form1_Load event to which you will add the following instruction, which creates the component you're going to use:

```
Private Sub Form1_Load(ByVal sender As Object, _
    ByVal e As System.EventArgs) Handles Me.Load

    mobjMean = New MeanCalculator.MeanCalc()

End Sub
```

Finally, you need to add the code behind the buttons on the form. First, working with the Add button, add the following code that calls the COM component:

```
Private Sub btnAdd_Click(ByVal sender As Object, _
                         ByVal e As System.EventArgs) _
                         Handles btnAdd.Click

    mobjMean.AddInput(CDbl(txtInput.Text))

End Sub
```

Here, you're adding whatever is in the input text box into the list of numbers for the calculation. Next, here's the code-behind for the `Calculate` button:

```
Private Sub btnCalculate_Click(ByVal sender As Object, _
                               ByVal e As System.EventArgs) _
                               Handles btnCalculate.Click

    mobjMean.DoCalculation()
    txtOutput.Text = mobjMean.GetOutput()

End Sub
```

This performs the calculation, retrieves the answer, and puts it into the output text box — all of this from the COM component. Finally, the code behind the `Reset` button simply resets the calculation:

```
Private Sub btnReset_Click(ByVal sender As Object, _
            ByVal e As System.EventArgs) Handles btnReset.Click

    mobjMean.Reset()

End Sub
```

Trying It All Out

Of course, the proof of the pudding is in the eating, so let's see what happens when you run your application. Compile and run the application and place one value in the first text box, for example, − 2, and click the Add button on the form. Next, enter another value, for example, − 3, and click the Add button again. When you click Calculate, you'll get the mean of the two values (2.5 in this case), as shown in Figure 23-6.

Figure 23-6

Using TlbImp Directly

In the preceding example, there's actually quite a lot going on under the covers. Every time you import a COM DLL into Visual Studio, it creates a *default interop assembly*, which is basically a .NET assembly that acts as a wrapper for the COM object. If you're doing this a lot, it might be better to do the wrapping once and for all, and then let your application developers import the resulting .NET assembly instead. Let's see how you might accomplish this task.

The process that creates the default interop assembly on behalf of Visual Studio is called `TlbImp.exe`. The name stands for *Type Library Import*, and that's pretty much what it does. It's included in the .NET Framework SDK, and you might find it convenient to extend the `PATH` environment variable to include the `\bin` directory of the .NET Framework SDK.

`TlbImp` takes a COM DLL as its input and generates a .NET assembly DLL as its output. By default, the .NET assembly has the same name as the type library, which will — in the case of VB6 components — always be the same as the COM DLL. This means you have to explicitly specify a different output file. You do this by using the `/out:` switch. If you want to see what's going on at each step in the process, then you should also specify the `/verbose` flag:

```
tlbimp MegaCalculator.dll /out:MegaCalculatorNet.dll /verbose
```

For this example, start with `MegaCalculator`, because `MeanCalculator` has a reference to `MegaCalculator`. If you start with `MeanCalculator`, you get an error indicating that there is a reference to `MegaCalculator` and that `TlbImp` will not be able to overwrite the `MegaCalculator.dll`. The way to get around this is to start with `MegaCalculator` by giving `TlbImp` the command, as shown previously. Once this is accomplished, `TlbImp` will inform you of the success or failure in creating a .NET assembly of the name `MegaCalculatorNet.dll`.

Now that you have `MegaCalculatorNet.dll` in place, you can work with `MeanCalculator` and make sure that the reference now points to the new `MegaCalculatorNet.dll`. You can accomplish this by using the following command:

```
tlbimp MeanCalculator.dll /out:MeanCalculatorNet.dll
    reference:MegaCalculatorNet.dll /verbose
```

The result of this command is shown in Figure 23-7.

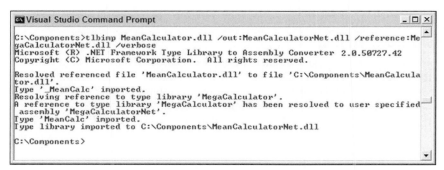

Figure 23-7

Notice that `TlbImp` has encountered a reference to another COM type library, `MegaCalculator`, and it has very kindly in turn imported `MegaCalculatorNet` instead. Having converted your COM DLLs into .NET assemblies, you can now reference them in an application as you would any other .NET DLL.

Late Binding

You've seen that you can successfully do early binding on COM components within a .NET application, but what if you want to do late binding instead? What if you don't have access to a type library at application development time? Can you still make use of the COM component? Does the .NET equivalent of late binding even exist?

The answer is that, yes, it does, but, no, it's not as transparent as with VB6. Let's take a look at what one used to do in VB6. If you wanted to do early binding, you would do this:

```
Dim myObj As MyObj
Set myObj = New MyObj

MyObj.MyMethod (...)
```

For late binding, it would look like this instead:

```
Dim myObj As Object
Set myObj = CreateObject ("MyLibrary.MyObject")
MyObj.MyMethod (...)
```

There's actually an enormous amount of activity going on under the covers here; if you're interested in looking into this further, try *Building N-Tier Applications with COM and Visual Basic 6.0* by Ash Rofail and Tony Martin (Wiley, 1999).

An Example for Late Binding

For the sample being built in this chapter, let's extend the calculator to a more generic framework that can feed inputs into a number of different calculation modules, rather than just the fixed one it currently implements. For this example, you'll keep a table in memory of calculation ProgIDs and present the user with a combo box to select the correct one.

The Sample COM Object

The first problem you encounter with late binding is that you can only late bind to the default interface, which in this case is `MeanCalculator.MeanCalc`, not `MeanCalculator.IMegaCalc`. Therefore, you need to redevelop your COM object as a standalone library, with no references to other interfaces.

As before, you'll build a DLL under the VB6 IDE, copy it over to your .NET environment, and reregister it there. You'll call this new VB6 DLL `MeanCalculator2.dll`, and the code in the class (called `MeanCalc`) should look as follows:

```
Option Explicit

Dim mintValue As Integer
Dim mdblValues() As Double
Dim mdblMean As Double

Private Sub Class_Initialize()
  Reset
End Sub

Public Sub AddInput(InputValue As Double)
```

```
      mintValue = mintValue + 1
      ReDim Preserve mdblValues(mintValue)
      mdblValues(mintValue) = InputValue
  End Sub

  Public Sub DoCalculation()
    Dim iValue As Integer
    mdblMean = 0#

    If (mintValue = 0) Then Exit Sub

    For iValue = 1 To mintVal
      mdblMean = mdblMean + mdblValues(iValue)
    Next iValue

    mdblMean = mdblMean / mintValue
  End Sub

  Public Function GetOutput() As Double
    GetOutput = mdblMean
  End Function

  Public Sub Reset()
    mintValue = 0
  End Sub
```

As before, move this across to your .NET server and register it using `RegSvr32`.

The Calculation Framework

For your generic calculation framework, you'll create a new application in Visual Basic 2005 called `CalcFrame`. You'll basically use the same dialog box as last time, but with an extra combo box at the top of the form. This new layout is illustrated in Figure 23-8.

The new combo box is called `cmbCalculation`. For this to work, you also need to disable the controls `txtInput`, `btnAdd`, `btnCalculate`, and `btnReset`, until you know whether the selected calculation is valid. Begin your application by importing the `Reflection` namespace; you need this for handing the application's late binding:

```
Imports System.Reflection
```

Figure 23-8

Once the form is in place, add a few member variables to the code of your application:

```
Public Class Form1
    Inherits System.Windows.Forms.Form
    Private mstrObjects() As String
    Private mnObject As Integer
    Private mtypCalc As Type
    Private mobjcalc As Object
```

From there, add a few new lines to Form1_Load:

```
Private Sub Form1_Load(ByVal sender As Object, _
    ByVal e As System.EventArgs) Handles Me.Load

    mnObject = 0
    AddObject("Mean", "MeanCalculator2.MeanCalc")
    AddObject("StdDev", "StddevCalculator.StddevCalc")

    If (mnObject > 0) Then
        cmbCalculation.SelectedIndex = 0
    End If
End Sub
```

What you're doing here is building a list of calculations. Once finished, you select the first one in the list. Let's take a look at that subroutine AddObject:

```
Private Sub AddObject(ByVal strName As String, ByVal strObject As String)
    cmbCalculation.Items.Add(strName)
    mnObject = mnObject + 1
    ReDim Preserve mstrObjects(mnObject)
    mstrObjects(mnObject - 1) = strObject
End Sub
```

The preceding code segment adds the calculation name to the combo box, and its ProgID to an array of strings. Neither of these is sorted, so you get a one-to-one mapping between them. Check out what happens when you select a calculation via the combo box:

```
Private Sub cmbCalculation_SelectedIndexChanged(ByVal sender As Object, _
                                    ByVal e As System.EventArgs) _
                        Handles cmbCalculation.SelectedIndexChanged
    Dim intIndex As Integer
    Dim bEnabled As Boolean

    intIndex = cmbCalculation.SelectedIndex
    mtypCalc = Type.GetTypeFromProgID(mstrObjects(intIndex))

    If (mtypCalc Is Nothing) Then
        mobjcalc = Nothing
        bEnabled = False
    Else
        mobjcalc = Activator.CreateInstance(mtypCalc)
        bEnabled = True
    End If
```

```
        txtInput.Enabled = bEnabled
        btnAdd.Enabled = bEnabled
        btnCalculate.Enabled = bEnabled
        btnReset.Enabled = bEnabled
    End Sub
```

There are two key calls in this example. The first is to `Type.GetTypeFromProgID`. This takes the incoming `ProgID` string and converts it to a `Type` object. This process either succeeds or fails; if it fails, you disable all controls and let the user try again. If it succeeds, however, you create an instance of the object described by the type. You do this in the call to the static method `Activator.CreateInstance()`.

For this example, assume that your user has selected a calculation that you can successfully instantiate. What next? The user enters a number and clicks the Add button on the form:

```
Private Sub btnAdd_Click(ByVal sender As Object, _
    ByVal e As System.EventArgs) Handles btnAdd.Click

        Dim objArgs() As [Object] = {CDbl(txtInput.Text)}
        mtypCalc.InvokeMember("AddInput", BindingFlags.InvokeMethod, _
            Nothing, mobjcalc, objArgs)

    End Sub
```

The important call here is to the `InvokeMember()` method. Let's take a closer look at what is going on. Five parameters are passed into the `InvokeMember()` method:

❑   The first parameter is the name of the method that you want to call: `AddInput` in this case. Therefore, instead of going directly to the location of the routine in memory, you ask the .NET runtime to find it for you.

❑   The value from the `BindingFlags` enumeration tells it to invoke a method.

❑   The next parameter provides language-specific binding information, which isn't needed in this case.

❑   The fourth parameter is a reference to the COM object itself (the one you instantiated using `Activator.CreateInstance`).

❑   Finally, the fifth parameter is an array of objects representing the arguments for the method. In this case, there's only one argument, the input value.

Something very similar to this is going on underneath VB6 late binding, except that here it's exposed in all its horror. In some ways, that's not a bad thing, because it should bring it home that late binding is something to avoid if possible. Anyway, let's carry on and complete the program. Here are the remaining event handlers for the other buttons:

```
Private Sub btnCalculate_Click(ByVal sender As Object, _
        ByVal e As System.EventArgs) Handles btnCalculate.Click

    Dim objResult As Object
    mtypCalc.InvokeMember("DoCalculation", BindingFlags.InvokeMethod, _
                    Nothing, mobjcalc, Nothing)
    objResult = mtypCalc.InvokeMember("GetOutput", _
                BindingFlags.InvokeMethod, Nothing, mobjcalc, Nothing)
```

```
        txtOutput.Text = objResult

    End Sub

    Private Sub btnReset_Click(ByVal sender As Object, _
                ByVal e As System.EventArgs) Handles btnReset.Click

        mtypCalc.InvokeMember("Reset", BindingFlags.InvokeMethod, _
            Nothing, mobjcalc, Nothing)

    End Sub
```

Running the Calculation Framework

Let's quickly complete the job by running the application. Figure 23-9 shows what happens when you select the nonexistent calculation StdDev.

Figure 23-9

As shown in the screen shot, the input fields have been disabled, as desired. Figure 23-10 shows what happens when you repeat the earlier calculation using Mean. This time, the input fields are enabled, and the calculation can be carried out as before.

Figure 23-10

One final word about late binding. You took care to ensure that you checked whether the object was successfully instantiated. In a real-life application, you also need ensure that the method invocations were successful and that all exceptions were caught — you don't have the luxury of having the compiler find all your bugs for you.

ActiveX Controls

Let's move on from basic COM objects to ActiveX controls. You're going to do pretty much the same you did with the basic COM component (apart from late binding, which has no relevance to ActiveX controls) — build a legacy control using VB6 and then import it into your .NET Visual Basic project.

The Legacy ActiveX Control

For your legacy ActiveX control, you are going to build a simple buttonlike object that is capable of interpreting a mouse click and can be one of two colors according to its state. To accomplish this task, you will take a second foray into VB6, so if you don't have VB6 handy, feel free to skip the next section, download the OCX file, and pick it up when you start developing your .NET application.

Step 1: Creating the Control

This time, within the VB6 IDE, you need to create an ActiveX Control project. For this example, call the project `Magic`, and the control class `MagicButton`, to reflect its remarkable powers. From the Toolbox, select a `Shape` control and place it on the `UserControl` form that VB6 provides for you. Rename the shape provided on the form to `shpButton`, and change its properties as follows:

Property	Value
FillStyle	0 — Solid
Shape	4 — Rounded Rectangle
FillColor	Gray (&H00808080&)

Add a label on top of the `Shape` control and rename it to `lblText`. Change this control's properties to the following:

Property	Value
BackStyle	0 — Solid 0Transparent
Alignment	2Center

Switch to the code view of the `MagicButton` component. Within the code presented, add two properties called `Caption` and `State`, and an event called `Click()`, as well as code to handle the initialization of the properties and persisting them, to ensure that the shape resizes correctly and that the label is centered. You also need to handle mouse clicks within the code. The final code of the `MagicButton` class should look as follows:

```
Option Explicit

Public Event Click()

Dim mintState As Integer
```

```
Public Property Get Caption() As String
  Caption = lblText.Caption
End Property

Public Property Let Caption(ByVal vNewValue As String)
  lblText.Caption = vNewValue
  PropertyChanged ("Caption")
End Property

Public Property Get State() As Integer
  State = mintState
End Property

Public Property Let State(ByVal vNewValue As Integer)
  mintState = vNewValue
  PropertyChanged ("State")

  If (State = 0) Then
    shpButton.FillColor = &HFFFFFF&
  Else
    shpButton.FillColor = &H808080&
  End If
End Property

Private Sub UserControl_InitProperties()
  Caption = Extender.Name
  State = 1
End Sub

Private Sub UserControl_ReadProperties(PropBag As PropertyBag)
  Caption = PropBag.ReadProperty("Caption", Extender.Name)
  State = PropBag.ReadProperty("State", 1)
End Sub

Private Sub UserControl_WriteProperties(PropBag As PropertyBag)
  PropBag.WriteProperty "Caption", lblText.Caption
  PropBag.WriteProperty "State", mintState
End Sub

Private Sub UserControl_Resize()
  shpButton.Move 0, 0, ScaleWidth, ScaleHeight
  lblText.Move 0, (ScaleHeight - lblText.Height) / 2, ScaleWidth
End Sub

Private Sub lblText_Click()
  RaiseEvent Click
End Sub

Private Sub UserControl_MouseUp(Button As Integer, Shift As Integer, _
                                X As Single, Y As Single)
  RaiseEvent Click
End Sub
```

If you build this, you'll get an ActiveX control called `Magic.ocx`.

888

Step 2: Registering Your Legacy Control

You now have your legacy control. As before, if you're developing your new .NET application on the same machine, then you don't need to do anything more, because your control will already be registered by the build process. However, if you're working on an entirely new machine, you need to register it there. As before, open a command window and register it as follows:

```
regsvr32 Magic.ocx
```

Having done that, you're ready to build your .NET application.

A .NET Application, Again

This .NET application is even more straightforward than the last one. All you're going to do this time is display a button that changes color whenever the user clicks it. To begin, create a .NET Windows Application project in Visual Basic called ButtonApp. Before you start to develop it, however, extend the Toolbox to incorporate your new control by selecting Tools ⇨ Choose Toolbox Items. Figure 23-11 shows the resulting dialog.

Figure 23-11

When you click the OK button, you can see that your magic button class is now available to you in the Toolbox (see Figure 23-12). Add the Magic.MagicButton control to your form, as shown in Figure 23-13, by checking the box next to the control name. Note that references to AxMagic and Magic are added to the project in the Solution Explorer window within the References folder, as shown in Figure 23-14.

Figure 23-12

Figure 23-13

Figure 23-14

All you need to do now is initialize the `Caption` property to `ON`, change the `Text` of the form to `Button Application`, and code up a handler for the mouse `Click` event:

```
Private Sub AxMagicButton1_ClickEvent(ByVal sender As Object, _
        ByVal e As System.EventArgs) Handles AxMagicButton1.ClickEvent

    AxMagicButton1.CtlState = CType(1 - AxMagicButton1.CtlState, Short)
    If (AxMagicButton1.CtlState = 0) Then
        AxMagicButton1.Caption = "OFF"
    Else
        AxMagicButton1.Caption = "ON"
    End If

End Sub
```

Note something slightly peculiar happening here. In the course of importing the control into .NET, the variable State mutated into CtlState. This is because there is already a class in the AxHost namespace called State, which is used to encapsulate the persisted state of an ActiveX control.

Trying It All Out, Again

What happens when you run this application? Notice the control in the ON position, as presented in Figure 23-15. If you click the control, it changes to the OFF position, as shown in Figure 23-16.

Figure 23-15

Figure 23-16

Using .NET Components in the COM World

So far, this chapter has established, through a couple of examples, that you can use your COM legacy components within any of your .NET-based applications. You don't have to throw everything out *quite* yet. It's now time to consider the opposite question: Can you run .NET components in the COM world?

Why on earth would you want to run .NET components in the COM world? It's not immediately obvious, in fact, because migration to .NET would almost certainly be application-led in most cases, rather than component-led. However, it's possible (just) to imagine a situation in which a particularly large application remains not based on .NET, while component development moves over to .NET. Let's assume that that's the case for the next section. The technology's quite cool, anyway.

A .NET Component

Let's take a look at the .NET component. Here, you'll implement an exact copy of the functionality created earlier with the `MegaCalculator` and `MeanCalculator` components, except you will use Visual Basic rather than VB6.

Begin by creating a Class Library project called `MegaCalculator2`. Here is the entire code of the interface for the class library:

```
Public Interface IMegaCalc

   Sub AddInput(ByVal InputValue As Double)

   Sub DoCalculation()
   Function GetResult() As Double
   Sub Reset()

End Interface
```

Now create another Class Library project called `MeanCalculator3`. This will contain a class called `MeanCalc` that is going to implement the `IMegaCalc` interface, in a precise analog of the `MeanCalc` in your original VB6 `MeanCalculator` project. As before, you need to add a reference to `MegaCalculator2` first, although this time it will be a true .NET Framework reference, and you'll have to browse for it (see Figure 23-17).

Figure 23-17

This is what the code looks like:

```
Public Class MeanCalc
   Implements MegaCalculator2.IMegaCalc

   Dim mintValue As Integer
   Dim mdblValues() As Double
   Dim mdblMean As Double

   Public Sub AddInput(ByVal InputValue As Double) _
```

```
          Implements MegaCalculator2.IMegaCalc.AddInput
      mintValue = mintValue + 1
      ReDim Preserve mdblValues(mintValue)
      mdblValues(mintValue - 1) = InputValue
   End Sub

   Public Sub DoCalculation()_
          Implements MegaCalculator2.IMegaCalc.DoCalculation
      Dim iValue As Integer

      mdblMean = 0

      If (mintValue = 0) Then Exit Sub

      For iValue = 0 To mintValue - 1 Step 1
         mdblMean = mdblMean + mdblValues(iValue)
      Next iValue

      mdblMean = mdblMean / iValue
   End Sub

   Public Function GetResult() As Double Implements _
                MegaCalculator2.IMegaCalc.GetResult
      GetResult = mdblMean
   End Function

   Public Sub Reset() Implements MegaCalculator2.IMegaCalc.Reset
      mintValue = 0
   End Sub

   Public Sub New()
      Reset()
   End Sub

End Class
```

This is all quite similar to the VB6 version, apart from the way in which `Implements` is used. After this is all in place, build the assembly. Now we come to the interesting part: How do you register the resulting assembly so that a COM-enabled application can make use of it?

RegAsm

The tool provided with the .NET Framework SDK to register assemblies for use by COM is called `RegAsm`. This tool is very simple to use. If all you're interested in is late binding, then you simply run it as presented in Figure 23-18.

The only challenge with `RegAsm` is finding the thing. It's usually found lurking in `C:\Windows\ Microsoft.NET\Framework\<version>`, where `<version>` is the current .NET Framework version number. You might find it useful to add this to your path in the system environment. You can also use the Visual Studio command prompt to directly access this tool.

However, there's probably even less reason for late binding to an exported .NET component than there is for early binding, so we'll move on to look at early binding. For this, you need a type library, so add another parameter, `/tlb` (see Figure 23-19).

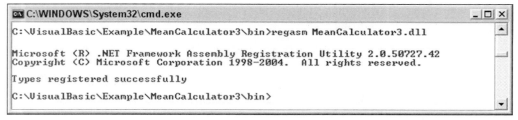

Figure 23-18

Figure 23-19

If you now take a look in the target directory, not only do you have the original MeanCalculator3
.dll, but you've also acquired a copy of the MegaCalculator2.dll and two type libraries:
MeanCalculator3.tlb and MegaCalculator2.tlb. You need both of these, so it was good of RegAsm
to provide them for you. You need the MegaCalculator2 type library for the same reason that .NET
needed the MegaCalculator assembly: because it contains the definition of the IMegaCalc interface
that MeanCalculator is using.

Testing with a VB6 Application

Turning the tables again, build a VB6 application to see whether this is really going to work. Copy the
type libraries over to your pre-.NET machine (if that's where VB6 is running) and create a Standard EXE
project in VB6. Call this project CalcApp2. Within this project, you need to create references to the two
new type libraries, so go to the References dialog box, browse to find them, and select them, as shown in
Figure 23-20.

Figure 23-20

Figure 23-21

At this point, you have everything you need to create the application. Create it as you did for the Visual Basic CalcApp (see Figure 23-21). As before, the text boxes are txtInput and txtOutput, respectively, and the command buttons are btnAdd, btnCalculate, and btnReset. Here's the code behind it:

```
Option Explicit

Dim mobjCalc As MeanCalculator3.MeanCalc
Dim mobjMega As MegaCalculator2.IMegaCalc

Private Sub btnAdd_Click()
  mobjMega.AddInput (txtInput.Text)
End Sub

Private Sub btnCalculate_Click()
  mobjMega.DoCalculation
  txtOutput.Text = mobjMega.GetResult
End Sub

Private Sub btnReset_Click()
  mobjMega.Reset
End Sub

Private Sub Form_Load()
  Set mobjCalc = New MeanCalculator3.MeanCalc
  Set mobjMega = mobjCalc
End Sub
```

Notice that this time you have to explicitly get hold of a reference to the interface IMegaCalc. The default interface of the component, MeanCalc, is entirely empty.

Make the executable via the File ⇨ Make CalcApp2.exe menu item, and then move it back to your .NET machine (unless, of course, you're already there). Run it up and see what happens (see Figure 23-22).

Figure 23-22

Well, that's not *quite* what you expected. What's happened here? In COM, the location of the DLL containing the component is available via the registry. In .NET, the assembly always has to be in either the current directory or the global assembly. All the registry is doing for you here is converting a COM reference to a .NET one; it's not finding the .NET one for you.

But this is pretty easy to sort out. To resolve this problem, move the two assemblies, `MegaCalculator3` and `MeanCalculator2`, to your current directory and try again (see Figure 23-23).

That's better. You've established that in the unlikely event of having to run .NET from a COM-oriented application, Microsoft has provided you with the tools necessary to do the job.

Figure 23-23

TlbExp

In fact, Microsoft provides you with not one, but *two* alternative tools. The other one is `TlbExp`, which, as its name suggests, is the counterpart of `TlbImp`. Figure 23-24 shows how you can use `TlbExp` to achieve the same result as `RegAsm` in the previous section.

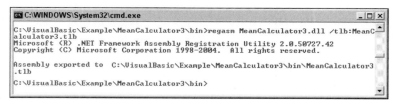

Figure 23-24

Summary

COM isn't going to go away for quite some time, so .NET applications have to interoperate with COM, and they have to do it well. By the end of this chapter, you have achieved several things:

❑ You managed to make a .NET application early bind to a COM component, using the import features available in Visual Basic.

❑ You looked at the underlying tool, `Tlbimp`.

❑ You managed to make it late bind as well, although it wasn't a pleasant experience.

❑ You incorporated an ActiveX control into a .NET user interface, again using the features of Visual Basic.

❑ You looked at using `Regasm` and `TlbExp` to export type libraries from .NET assemblies, in order to enable VB6 applications to use .NET assemblies as if they were COM components.

24

Threading

One of the results of the move from 16-bit to 32-bit computing was the ability to write code that made use of threads, but although Visual C++ developers have been able to use threads for some time, Visual Basic developers haven't had a truly reliable way to do so, until now. Previous techniques involved accessing the threading functionality available to Visual C++ developers. Although this worked, actually developing multithreaded code without adequate debugger support in the Visual Basic environment was nothing short of a nightmare.

For most developers, the primary motivation for multithreading is the ability to perform long-running tasks in the background, while still providing the user with an interactive interface. Another common scenario is when building server-side code that can perform multiple long-running tasks at the same time. In that case, each task can be run on a separate thread, enabling all the tasks to run in parallel.

This chapter introduces you to the various objects in the .NET Framework that enable any .NET language to be used to develop multithreaded applications.

What Is a Thread?

The term *thread* is short for *thread of execution*. When your program is running, the CPU is actually running a sequence of processor instructions, one after another. You can think of these sequential instructions as forming a thread that is being executed by the CPU. A thread is, in effect, a pointer to the currently executing instruction in the sequence of instructions that make up the application. This pointer starts at the top of the program and moves through each line, branching and looping when it comes across decisions and loops. When the program is no longer needed, the pointer steps outside of the program code and the program is effectively stopped.

Most applications have only one thread, so they are only executing one sequence of instructions. Some applications have more than one thread, so they can simultaneously execute more than one sequence of instructions. It is important to realize that each CPU in your computer can only execute one thread at a time, with the exception of hyperthreaded processors that essentially contain multiple CPUs inside a single CPU. If you only have one CPU, then your computer can execute only one thread at a time. Even when an application has several threads, only one can run at a time in this case. If your computer has two or more CPUs, then each CPU will run a different thread at the same time. In this case, more than one thread in your application may run at the same time, each on a different CPU.

Of course, when you have a computer with only one CPU, on which several programs can be actively running at the same time, the statements in the previous paragraph fly in the face of visual evidence. Yet it is true that only one thread can execute at a time on a single-CPU machine. What you *perceive* to be simultaneously running applications is really an illusion created by the Windows operating system through a technique called *preemptive multithreading*, which is discussed later in the chapter.

All applications have at least one thread — otherwise, they couldn't do any work, as there would be no pointer to the thread of execution. The principle of a thread is that it enables your program to perform multiple actions, potentially at the same time. Each sequence of instructions is executed independently of other threads.

The classic example of *multithreaded* functionality is Microsoft Word's spell checker. When the program starts, the execution pointer begins at the top of the program and eventually gets itself into a position where you're able to start writing code. However, at some point Word starts another thread and creates another execution pointer. As you type, this new thread examines the text and flags any spelling errors as you go, underlining them with a red oval (see Figure 24-1).

The principle of a thread is that it allows your program to perform multiple actions, potentially at the same tiiiiiime. Each sequence of instructions is executed independently of other threads.

Figure 24-1

Every application has one primary thread. This thread serves as the main process thread through the application. Imagine you have an application that starts up, loads a file from disk, performs some processing on the data in the file, writes a new file, and then quits. Functionally, it might look like Figure 24-2.

This simple application needs only a single thread. When the program is told to run, Windows creates a new process and creates the *primary thread*. To understand more about exactly what it is that a thread does, you need to understand how Windows and the computer's processor deal with different processes.

Processes, AppDomains, and Threads

Windows is capable of keeping many programs in memory at once and allowing the user to switch between them. Windows can also run programs in the background, possibly under different user identities. The capability to run many programs at once is called *multitasking*.

Each of these programs that your computer keeps in memory runs in a single *process*. A process is an isolated region of memory that contains a program's code and data. All programs run within a process, and code running in one process cannot access the memory within any other process. This prevents one program from interfering with any other program.

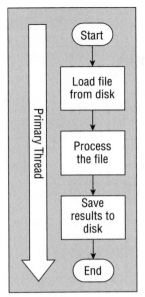

Figure 24-2

The process is started when the program starts and exists for as long as the program is running. When a process is started, Windows sets up an isolated memory area for the program and loads the program's code into that area of memory. It then starts the main thread for the process, pointing it at the first instruction in the program. From that point, the thread runs the sequence of instructions defined by the program.

Windows supports *multithreading*, so the main thread might execute instructions that create more threads within the same process. These other threads run within the same memory space as the main thread — all sharing the same memory. Threads within a process are not isolated from each other. One thread in a process can tamper with data being used by other threads in that same process. However, a thread in one process cannot tamper with data being used by threads in any other processes on the computer.

At this point, you should understand that Windows loads program code into a process and executes that code on one or more threads. The .NET Framework adds another concept to the mix: the *AppDomain*. An AppDomain is very much like a process in concept. Each AppDomain is an isolated region of memory, and code running in one AppDomain cannot access the memory of another AppDomain.

The .NET Framework introduced the AppDomain to make it possible to run multiple, isolated programs within the same Windows process. It turns out to be relatively expensive to create a Windows process in terms of time and memory. It is much cheaper to create a new AppDomain within an existing process.

Remember that Windows has no concept of an AppDomain; it only understands the concept of a process. The only way to get *any* code to run under Windows is to load it into a process. This means that each .NET AppDomain exists within a process. The result is that all .NET code runs within an AppDomain *and* within a Windows process (see Figure 24-3).

Figure 24-3

In most cases, a Windows process contains one AppDomain, which contains your program's code. The main thread of the process executes your program's instructions. The result is that the existence of the AppDomain is largely invisible to your program.

In some cases, most notably ASP.NET, a Windows process will contain multiple AppDomains, each with a separate program loaded (see Figure 24-4).

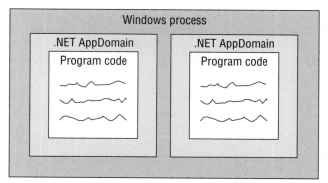

Figure 24-4

ASP.NET uses this technique to isolate Web applications from each other without having to start an expensive new Windows process for each virtual root on the server.

Note that AppDomains do not change the relationship between a process and threads. Each process has a main thread and may have other threads. Therefore, even in the ASP.NET process, with multiple AppDomains, there is only one main thread. Of course, ASP.NET creates other threads, so multiple Web applications can execute simultaneously, but there's only a single main thread in the entire process.

Thread Scheduling

Earlier in the chapter it was noted that visual evidence suggests that multiple programs, and thus multiple threads, execute simultaneously, even on a single-CPU computer. Again, this is an illusion created by the operating system, through the use of a concept called *time slicing* or *time sharing*.

In reality, only one thread runs on each CPU at a time, with the exception of hyperthreaded processors, which are essentially multiple CPUs in one. In a single-CPU machine, this means that only one thread is ever executing at any one time. To provide the illusion that many things are happening at the same time, the operating system never lets any one thread run for very long, giving other threads a chance to get a bit of work done as well. As a result, it *appears* that the computer is executing several threads at the same time.

The length of time each thread is allowed to run is called a *quantum*. Although a quantum can vary, it is typically around 20 milliseconds. Once a thread has run for its quantum, the OS stops the thread and allows another thread to run. When that thread reaches its quantum, yet another thread is allowed to run, and so on. A thread can also give up the CPU before it reaches its quantum. This happens frequently, as most I/O operations and numerous other interactions with the Windows operating system cause a thread to give up the CPU.

Because the length of time each thread can run is so short, it's never noticeable that threads are being started and stopped. This is the same concept animators use when creating cartoons or other animated media. As long as the changes happen faster than you can perceive them, you have the illusion of motion, or, in this case, simultaneous execution of code.

The technology used by Windows is called *preemptive multitasking*. It is preemptive because no thread is ever allowed to run beyond its quantum. The operating system always intervenes and allows other threads to run. This ensures that no single thread can consume all the processing power on the machine to the detriment of other threads.

It also means that you can never be sure when your thread will be interrupted and another thread allowed to run. This is the primary source of the complexity of multithreading, as it can cause race conditions when two threads access the same memory. If you attempt to solve a race condition with a lock, it can cause deadlock conditions when two threads attempt to access the same lock. You'll learn more about these concepts later. For now, understand that writing multithreaded code can be exceedingly difficult.

The entity that executes code in Windows is the thread. This means that the operating system is primarily focused on scheduling threads to keep the CPU or CPUs busy at all times. The operating system does not schedule either processes or AppDomains. Processes and AppDomains are merely regions of memory that contain your code — threads are what execute the code.

Threads have priorities, and Windows always allows higher priority threads to run before lower priority threads. In fact, if a higher priority thread is ready to run, Windows will cut short a lower priority thread's quantum to allow the higher priority thread to execute sooner. The result is that Windows has a bias towards threads of higher priority.

Setting thread priorities can be useful in situations where you have a process that requires a lot of processor muscle, but it doesn't matter how long the process takes to do its work. Setting a program's thread to a low priority allows that program to run continuously with little impact on other programs, so if you need to use Word or Outlook or another application, Windows gives more processor time to these applications and less time to the low-priority program. This enables the computer to work smoothly and efficiently for the user, letting the low-priority program only use otherwise wasted CPU power.

Threads may also voluntarily suspend themselves before their quantum is complete. This happens frequently — for example, when a thread attempts to read data from a file. It takes significant time for the I/O subsystem to locate the file and start retrieving the data. You can't have the CPU sitting idle during that time, especially when other threads could be running. Instead, the thread enters a wait state to indicate that it is waiting for an external event. The Windows scheduler immediately locates and runs the next ready thread, keeping the CPU busy while the first thread waits for its data.

Windows also automatically suspends and resumes threads depending on its perceived processing needs, the various priority settings, and so on. Suppose you're running one AppDomain containing two threads. If you can somehow mark the second thread as dormant (in other words, tell Windows that it has nothing to do), there's no need for Windows to allocate time to it. Effectively, the first thread receive 100 percent of the processor horsepower available to that process. When a thread is marked as dormant, it's said to be in a *wait state*.

Windows is particularly good at managing processes and threads. It's a core part of Windows' functionality, so its developers have spent a lot of time ensuring that it's super-efficient and as bug-free as software can be. This means that creating and spinning up threads is very easy to do and happens very quickly. In addition, threads only take up a small amount of system resources. However, there is a caveat you should be aware of.

The activity of stopping one thread and starting another is called *context switching*. This switching happens relatively quickly, but only if you're careful with the number of threads you create. Remember that this happens for each active thread at the end of each quantum (if not before) — so after at most 20 milliseconds. If you spin up too many threads, the operating system spends all its time switching between different threads, perhaps even getting to a point where the code in the thread doesn't get a chance to run because as soon as you've started the thread it's time for it to stop again.

Creating thousands of threads is not the right solution. What you need is a balance between the number of threads that your application requires and the number of threads that Windows can handle. There's no magic number or right answer to the question of how many threads you should create. Just be aware of context switching and experiment a little.

Consider the Microsoft Word spell check example. The thread that performs the spell check is around all the time. Imagine you have a blank document containing no text. At this point, the spell check thread is in a wait state. If you type a single word into the document and then pause, Word will pass that word over to the thread and signal it to start working. The thread uses its own slice of the processor power to examine the word. If it finds something wrong with it, then it tells the primary thread that a spelling problem was found and that the user needs to be alerted. At this point, the spell check thread drops back into a wait state until more text is entered into the document. Word doesn't spin up the thread whenever it needs to perform a check — rather, the thread runs all the time, but if it has nothing to do, it drops into this efficient wait state. (You'll learn about how the thread starts again later.)

Again, this is an oversimplification. Word actually "wakes up" the thread at various times, but the principle is sound — the thread is given work to do, it reports the results, and then it starts waiting for the next chunk of work to do. So why is all this important? If you plan to author multithreaded applications, you need to understand how the operating system will be scheduling your threads, as well as the threads of all other processes on the system. Most important, you need to recognize that your thread can be interrupted at any time so that another thread can run.

Thread Safety and Thread Affinity

Most of the .NET Framework base class library is not *thread safe*. Thread-safe code is code that can be called by multiple threads at the same time without negative side effects. If code is not thread-safe, then calling that code from multiple threads at the same time can result in unpredictable and undesirable side effects, potentially even crashing your application. When dealing with objects that are not thread safe, you must ensure that multiple threads never simultaneously interact with the same object.

For example, suppose you have a `ListBox` control (or any other control) on a Windows Form and you start updating that control with data from multiple threads. You'll find that your results are undependable. Sometimes you'll see all your data in order, but other times it will be out of order, and other times some data will be missing. This is because Windows Forms controls are not thread safe and don't behave properly when used by multiple threads at the same time.

To determine whether any specific method in the .NET Base Class Library is thread safe, refer to the online help. If no mention of threading appears in association with the method, then the method is *not* thread safe.

The Windows Forms subset of the .NET Framework is not only not thread safe, it also has *thread affinity*. Thread affinity means that objects created by a thread can only be used by that thread. Other threads should never interact with those objects. In the case of Windows Forms, this means that you must ensure that multiple threads never interact with Windows Forms objects (such as forms and controls). This is important because when you're creating interactive multithreaded applications, you must ensure that only the thread that created a form interacts directly with that form.

As you'll see, Windows Forms includes technology by which a background thread can safely make method calls on forms and controls by transferring the method call to the thread that owns the form.

When to Use Threads

If we regard computer programs as being either application software or service software, we find there are different motivators for each one. Application software uses threads primarily to deliver a better user experience. Common examples are as follows:

❑   **Microsoft Word** — Background spell checker

❑   **Microsoft Word** — Background printing

❑   **Microsoft Outlook** — Background sending and receiving of e-mail

❑   **Microsoft Excel** — Background recalculation

You can see that in all of these cases, threads are used to do "something in the background." This provides a better user experience. For example, you can still edit a Word document while Word is spooling another document to the printer. Similarly, you can still read e-mails while Outlook is sending your new e-mail. As an application developer, you should use threads to enhance the user experience. At some point during the application startup, code running in the primary thread will have spun up another thread to be used for spell checking. As part of the "allow user to edit the document" process, you give the spell checker thread some words to check. This thread separation means that the user can continue to type, even though spell checking is still taking place.

Service software uses threads to both deliver scalability and improve the service offered. For example, imagine you have a Web server that receives six incoming connections simultaneously. That server needs to service each of the requests in parallel; otherwise, the sixth thread would have to wait for you to finish threads one through five before it even got started. Figure 24-5 shows how IIS might handle incoming requests.

Figure 24-5

The primary motivation for multiple threads in a service like this is to keep the CPU busy servicing user requests even when other user requests are blocked waiting for data or other events. If you have six user requests, the odds are high that some or all of them will read from files or databases and thus will spend many milliseconds in wait states. While some of the user requests are in wait states, other user requests need CPU time and can be scheduled to run. The result is higher scalability because the CPU, I/O, and other subsystems of the computer are kept as busy as possible at all times.

Designing a Background Task

The specific goals and requirements for background processing in an interactive application are quite different from a server application. By interactive application, I am talking about Windows Forms or Console applications. While a Web application might be somewhat interactive, in fact all your code runs on the server, and so Web applications are server applications when it comes to threading.

Interactive Applications

In the case of interactive applications (typically Windows Forms applications), your design must center on having the background thread do useful work, but also interact appropriately (and safely) with the thread managing the UI. After all, you typically want to let the user know when the background process starts, stops, and does interesting things over its life. The following list summarizes the basic requirements for the background thread:

❏   Indicate that the background task has started

❏   Provide periodic status or progress information

❏   Indicate that the background task has completed

❏   Enable the user to request that the background task be canceled

While every application is different, these four requirements are typical for background threads in an interactive application.

As noted earlier, most of the .NET Framework is not thread safe, and Windows Forms is even more restrictive by having thread affinity. You want your background task to be able to notify the user when it starts, stops, and provides progress information. The fact that Windows Forms has thread affinity complicates this, because your background thread can never directly interact with Windows Forms objects. Fortunately, Windows Forms provides a formalized mechanism by which code in a background thread can send messages to the UI thread so that the UI thread can update the display for the user.

This is done through the use of the `BackgroundWorker` control, which is found in the Components tab of the Toolbox. The purpose of the `BackgroundWorker` control is to start, monitor, and control the execution of background tasks. The control makes it easy for code on the application's primary thread to start a task on a background thread. It also makes it easy for the code running on the background thread to notify the primary thread of progress and completion. Finally, it provides a mechanism by which the primary thread can request that the background task be canceled, and for the background thread to notify the primary thread when it has completed the cancellation.

All this is done in a way that safely transfers control between the primary thread (which can update the UI) and the background thread (which cannot update the UI).

Server Applications

In the case of server programs, your design should center on the background thread being as efficient as possible. Server resources are precious, so the quicker the task can complete, the fewer resources you'll consume over time. Interactivity with a UI isn't a concern, as your code is running on a server, detached from any UI. The key to success in server coding is to avoid or minimize locking, thus maximizing throughput because your code is never stopped by a lock.

For example, Microsoft went to great pains to design and refine ASP.NET to minimize the number of locks required from the time a user request hits the server to the time an ASPX page's code is running. Once the page code is running, no locking occurs, so the page code can just run, top to bottom, as fast and efficiently as possible.

Avoiding locking means avoiding shared resources or data. This is the dominant design goal for server code — to design programs to avoid scenarios in which multiple threads need access to the same variables or other resources. Anytime multiple threads may access the same resource, you need to implement locking to prevent the threads from colliding with each other. We'll discuss locking later in the chapter, as sometimes it is simply unavoidable.

Implementing Threading

At this point you should have a basic understanding of threads and how they relate to the process and AppDomain concepts. You should also realize that for interactive applications, multithreading is not a way to improve performance, but rather a way to improve the end user experience by providing the illusion that the computer is executing more code simultaneously. In the case of server-side code, multithreading enables higher scalability by enabling Windows to better utilize the CPU along with other subsystems such as I/O.

A Quick Tour

When a background thread is created, it points to a method or procedure that will be executed by the thread. Remember that a thread is just a pointer to the current instruction in a sequence of instructions to be executed. In all cases, the first instruction in this sequence is the start of a method or procedure.

When using the `BackgroundWorker` control, this method is always the control's `DoWork` event handler. Keep in mind that this method can't be a function. There is no mechanism by which a method running on one thread can return a result directly to code running on another thread. This means that anytime you design a background task, you should start by creating a `Sub` in which you write the code to run on the background thread.

In addition, because the goals for interactive applications and server programs are different, your designs for implementing threading in these two environments are different. This means that the way you design and code the background task will vary.

By way of explanation, let's work with a simple method that calculates prime numbers. This implementation is naïve, and can take quite a lot of time when run against larger numbers, so it makes for a useful example of a long-running background task. Do the following:

1. Create a new Windows Forms Application project named `Threading`.
2. Add two `Button` controls, a `ListBox` and a `ProgressBar` control to `Form1`.
3. Add a `BackgroundWorker` control to `Form1`.
4. Set its `WorkerReportsProgress` and `WorkerSupportsCancellation` properties to `True`.
5. Add the following to the form's code:

```
Public Class Form1

#Region " Shared data "

  Private mMin As Integer
  Private mMax As Integer
  Private mResults As New List(Of Integer)
```

```vbnet
#End Region

#Region " Primary thread methods "

  Private Sub btnStart_Click(ByVal sender As System.Object, _
    ByVal e As System.EventArgs) Handles btnStart.Click

    ProgressBar1.Value = 0
    ListBox1.Items.Clear()
    mMin = 1
    mMax = 10000
    BackgroundWorker1.RunWorkerAsync()

  End Sub


  Private Sub btnCancel_Click(ByVal sender As System.Object, _
    ByVal e As System.EventArgs) Handles btnCancel.Click

    BackgroundWorker1.CancelAsync()

  End Sub


  Private Sub BackgroundWorker1_ProgressChanged( _
    ByVal sender As Object, ByVal e As _
    System.ComponentModel.ProgressChangedEventArgs) _
    Handles BackgroundWorker1.ProgressChanged

    ProgressBar1.Value = e.ProgressPercentage

  End Sub

  Private Sub BackgroundWorker1_RunWorkerCompleted( _
    ByVal sender As Object, ByVal e As _
    System.ComponentModel.RunWorkerCompletedEventArgs) _
    Handles BackgroundWorker1.RunWorkerCompleted

    For Each item As String In mResults
      ListBox1.Items.Add(item)
    Next

  End Sub

#End Region

#Region " Background thread methods "

  Private Sub BackgroundWorker1_DoWork(ByVal sender As Object, _
    ByVal e As System.ComponentModel.DoWorkEventArgs) _
    Handles BackgroundWorker1.DoWork

    mResults.Clear()
```

```vbnet
      For count As Integer = mMin To mMax Step 2
        Dim isPrime As Boolean = True

        For x As Integer = 1 To CInt(count / 2)
          For y As Integer = 1 To x
            If x * y = count Then
              ' the number is not prime
              isPrime = False
              Exit For
            End If
          Next
          ' short-circuit the check
          If Not isPrime Then Exit For
        Next

        If isPrime Then
          mResults.Add(count)
        End If

        Me.BackgroundWorker1.ReportProgress( _
          CInt((count - mMin) / (mMax - mMin) * 100))

        If Me.BackgroundWorker1.CancellationPending Then
          Exit Sub
        End If

      Next

    End Sub

#End Region

End Class
```

The `BackgroundWorker1_DoWork()` method implements the code to find the prime numbers. This method is automatically run on a background thread by the `BackgroundWorker1` control. Notice that the method is a `Sub`, so it returns no value. Instead, it stores its results in a variable — in this case, a `List(Of Integer)`. The idea is that once the background task is complete, you can do something useful with the results.

When `btnStart` is clicked, the `BackgroundWorker` control is told to start the background task. In order to initialize any data values before launching the background thread, the `mMin` and `mMax` variables are set before the task is started.

Of course, you want to display the results of the background task. Fortunately, the `BackgroundWorker` control raises an event when the task is complete. In this event handler you can safely copy the values from the `List(Of Integer)` into the `ListBox` for display to the user.

Similarly, the `BackgroundWorker` control raises an event to indicate progress as the task runs. Notice that the `DoWork()` method periodically calls the `ReportProgress()` method. When this method is called, the progress is transferred from the background thread to the primary thread via the `ProgressChanged` event.

Finally, you may have the need to cancel a long-running task. It is never wise to directly terminate a background task. Instead, you should send a request to the background task asking it to stop running. This enables the task to cleanly stop running so it can close any resources it might be using and shut down properly.

To send the cancel request, call the `BackgroundWorker` control's `CancelAsync()` method. This sets the control's `CancellationPending` property to `True`. Notice how this value is periodically checked by the `DoWork()` method; and if it is `True`, you exit the method, effectively canceling the task.

Running the code now demonstrates that the UI remains entirely responsive while the background task is running, and the results are displayed when available.

Threading Options

Now that we've explored the basics of threading in an interactive application, let's look at the various threading options at our disposal. The .NET Framework offers two ways to implement multithreading. Regardless of which approach you use, you must specify the method or procedure that the thread will execute when it starts.

First, you can use the thread pool provided by the .NET Framework. The thread pool is a managed pool of threads that can be reused over the life of your application. Threads are created in the pool on an as-needed basis, and idle threads in the pool are reused, thus keeping the number of threads created by your application to a minimum. This is important because threads are an expensive operating system resource.

> **The thread pool should be your first choice in most multithreading scenarios.**

Many built-in .NET Framework features already use the thread pool. In fact, you've already used it, because the `BackgroundWorker` control runs its background tasks on a thread from the thread pool. In addition, anytime you do an asynchronous read from a file, URL, or TCP socket, the thread pool is used on your behalf; and anytime you implement a remoting listener, a website, or a Web Service, the thread pool is used. Because the .NET Framework itself relies on the thread pool, it is an optimal choice for most multithreading requirements.

Second, you can create your own thread object. This can be a good approach if you have a single, long-running background task in your application. It is also useful if you need fine-grained control over the background thread. Examples of such control include setting the thread priority or suspending and resuming the thread's execution.

Using the Thread Pool

The .NET Framework provides a thread pool in the `System.Threading` namespace. This thread pool is self-managing. It creates threads on demand and, if possible, reuses idle threads that already exist in the pool.

The thread pool won't create an unlimited number of threads. In fact, it creates at most 25 threads per CPU in the system. If you assign more work requests to the pool than it can handle with these threads, your work requests are queued until a thread becomes available. This is typically a good feature, as it helps ensure that your application won't overload the operating system with too many threads.

There are five primary ways to use the thread pool: through the `BackgroundWorker` control, by calling `BeginXYZ()` methods, via `Delegates`, manually via the `ThreadPool.QueueUserWorkItem()` method, or by using a `System.Timers.Timer` control. Of the five, the easiest is to use the `BackgroundWorker` control.

Using the BackgroundWorker Control

The previous quick tour of threading explored the `BackgroundWorker` control, which enables you to easily start a task on a background thread, monitor that task's progress, and be notified when it is complete. It also enables you to request that the background task cancel itself. All this is done in a safe manner, with control transferred from the primary thread to the background thread and back again without you having to worry about the details.

Using BeginXYZ() Methods

Many of the .NET Framework objects support both synchronous and asynchronous invocation. For instance, you can read from a TCP socket by using the `Read()` method or the `BeginRead()` method. The `Read()` method is synchronous, so you're blocked until the data is read.

The `BeginRead()` method is asynchronous, so you are not blocked. Instead, the read operation occurs on a background thread in the thread pool. You provide the address of a method that is called automatically when the read operation is complete. This *callback* method is invoked by the background thread, so your code also ends up running on the background thread in the thread pool.

Behind the scenes, this behavior is all driven by delegates. Rather than explore TCP sockets or some other specific subset of the .NET Framework class library, let's move on and discuss the underlying technology itself.

Using Delegates

A *delegate* is a strongly typed pointer to a function or method. Delegates are the underlying technology used to implement events within Visual Basic, and they can be used directly to invoke a method, given just a pointer to that method.

Delegates can be used to launch a background task on a thread in the thread pool. They can also transfer a method call from a background thread to the UI thread. The `BackgroundWorker` control uses this technology behind the scenes on your behalf, but you can use delegates directly as well.

To use delegates, your worker code must be in a method, and you must define a delegate for that method. The delegate is a pointer for the method, so it must have the same method signature as the method itself:

```
Private Delegate Sub TaskDelegate(ByVal min As Integer, ByVal max As Integer)

Private Sub FindPrimesViaDelegate(ByVal min As Integer, ByVal max As Integer)

    mResults.Clear()
```

```
        For count As Integer = min To max Step 2
          Dim isPrime As Boolean = True

          For x As Integer = 1 To CInt(count / 2)
            For y As Integer = 1 To x
              If x * y = count Then
                ' the number is not prime
                isPrime = False
                Exit For
              End If
            Next
            ' short-circuit the check
            If Not isPrime Then Exit For
          Next

          If isPrime Then
            mResults.Add(count)
          End If

        Next
      End Sub
```

Running background tasks via delegates enables you to pass strongly typed parameters to the background task, thus clarifying and simplifying your code. Now that you have a worker method and corresponding delegate, you can add a new button and write code in its `click` event handler to use it to run `FindPrimes` on a background thread:

```
    Private Sub btnDelegate_Click(ByVal sender As System.Object)
          ByVal e As System.EventArgs) Handles btnDelegate.Click
      ' run the task
      Dim worker As New TaskDelegate(AddressOf FindPrimesViaDelegate)
      worker.BeginInvoke(1, 10000, AddressOf TaskComplete, Nothing)
    End Sub
```

First, you create an instance of the delegate, setting it up to point to the `FindPrimesViaDelegate()` method. Next, you call `BeginInvoke()` on the delegate to invoke the method.

The `BeginInvoke()` method is the key here. `BeginInvoke()` is an example of the `BeginXYZ()` methods discussed earlier; and as you'll recall, they automatically run the method on a background thread in the thread pool. This is true for `BeginInvoke()` as well, meaning that `FindPrimes` are run in the background and the UI thread is not blocked, so it can continue to interact with the user.

Notice all the parameters passed to `BeginInvoke`. The first two correspond to the parameters defined on the delegate — the `min` and `max` values that should be passed to `FindPrimes`. The next parameter is the address of a method that is automatically invoked when the background thread is complete. The final parameter (to which you've passed `Nothing`) is a mechanism by which you can pass a value from your UI thread to the method that is invoked when the background task is complete.

This means that you need to implement the `TaskComplete()` method. This method is invoked when the background task is complete. It runs on the background thread, not on the UI thread, so remember that this method can't interact with any Windows Forms objects. Instead, it will contain the code to invoke an `UpdateDisplay()` method on the UI thread via the form's `BeginInvoke()` method:

```
Private Sub TaskComplete(ByVal ar As IAsyncResult)

  Dim update As New UpdateDisplayDelegate(AddressOf UpdateDisplay)
  Me.BeginInvoke(update)

End Sub

Private Delegate Sub UpdateDisplayDelegate()

Private Sub UpdateDisplay()

  For Each item As String In mResults
    ListBox1.Items.Add(item)
  Next

End Sub
```

Notice how a delegate is used to invoke the `UpdateDisplay()` method as well, thus illustrating how delegates can be used with a `Form` object's `BeginInvoke()` method to transfer control back to the primary thread. The same technique could be used to allow the background task to notify the primary thread of progress as the task runs.

Now when you run the application, you'll have a responsive UI, with the `FindPrimesViaDelegate()` method running in the background within the thread pool.

Manually Queuing Work

The final option for using the thread pool is to manually queue items for the thread pool to process. This is done by calling `ThreadPool.QueueUserWorkItem()`. This is a `Shared` method on the `ThreadPool` class that directly places a method into the thread pool to be executed on a background thread.

This technique doesn't allow you to pass arbitrary parameters to the worker method. Instead, it requires that the `worker` method accept a single parameter of type `Object`, through which you can pass an arbitrary value. You can use this to pass multiple values by declaring a class with all your parameter types. Add the following class *inside* the `Form1` class:

```
Private Class params
  Public min As Integer
  Public max As Integer

  Public Sub New(ByVal min As Integer, ByVal max As Integer)
    Me.min = min
    Me.max = max
  End Sub

End Class
```

Then you can make `FindPrimes` accept this value as an `Object`:

```
Private Sub FindPrimesInPool(ByVal state As Object)
  Dim params As params = DirectCast(state, params)
  mResults.Clear()

  For count As Integer = params.min To params.max Step 2
    Dim isPrime As Boolean = True

    For x As Integer = 1 To CInt(count / 2)
      For y As Integer = 1 To x
        If x * y = count Then
          ' the number is not prime
          isPrime = False
          Exit For
        End If
      Next
      ' short-circuit the check
      If Not isPrime Then Exit For
    Next

    If isPrime Then
      mResults.Add(count)
    End If

  Next

  Dim update As New UpdateDisplayDelegate(AddressOf UpdateDisplay)
  Me.BeginInvoke(update)

End Sub
```

This is basically the same method used with delegates, but it accepts an object parameter, rather than the strongly typed parameters. Notice that the method uses a delegate to invoke the `UpdateDisplay` method on the UI thread when the task is complete. When you manually put a task on the thread pool, there is no automatic callback to a method when the task is complete, so you must do the callback in the worker method itself.

Now you can manually queue the worker method to run in the thread pool within the `Click` event handler:

```
Private Sub btnPool_Click(ByVal sender As System.Object, _
      ByVal e As System.EventArgs) Handles btnPool.Click

  ' run the task
  System.Threading.ThreadPool.QueueUserWorkItem( _
    AddressOf FindPrimesInPool, New params(1, 10000))
End Sub
```

The `QueueUserWorkItem()` method accepts the address of the worker method — in this case, `FindPrimes`. This worker method must accept a single parameter of type `Object` or you'll get a compile error here.

The second parameter to `QueueUserWorkItem()` is the object to be passed to the worker method when it is invoked on the background thread. In this case, you're passing a new instance of the `params` class defined earlier. This enables you to pass your parameter values to `FindPrimes`.

When you run this code, you'll again find that you have a responsive UI, with `FindPrimes` running on a background thread in the thread pool.

Using System.Timers.Timer

Beyond `BeginXYZ()` methods, delegates, and manually queuing work items, there are various other ways to get your code running in the thread pool. One of the most common is through the use of a special `Timer` control. The `Elapsed` event of this control is raised on a background thread in the thread pool.

This is different from the `System.Windows.Forms.Timer` control, where the `Tick` event is raised on the UI thread. The difference is very important to understand, because you can't directly interact with Windows Forms objects from background threads. Code running in the `Elapsed` event of a `System.Timers.Timer` control must be treated like any other code running on a background thread.

The exception to this is if you set the `SynchronizingObject` property on the control to a Windows Forms object such as a `Form` or a `Control`. In this case, the `Elapsed` event is raised on the appropriate UI thread, rather than on a thread in the thread pool. The result is basically the same as using `System.Windows.Forms.Timer` instead.

Manually Creating a Thread

Thus far, we've been working with the .NET thread pool. You can also manually create and control background threads through code. To manually create a thread, you need to create and start a `Thread` object. This looks something like the following:

```
' run the task
Dim worker As New Thread(AddressOf FindPrimes)
worker.Start()
```

While this seems like the obvious way to do multithreading, the thread pool is typically the preferred approach. This is because there is a cost to creating and destroying threads, and the thread pool helps avoid that cost by reusing threads when possible. When you manually create a thread as shown here, you must pay the cost of creating the thread each time or implement your own scheme to reuse the threads you create.

However, manual creation of threads can be useful. The thread pool is designed to be used for background tasks that run for a while and then complete, thus allowing the background thread to be reused for subsequent background tasks. If you need to run a background task for the entire duration of your application, the thread pool is not ideal, because that thread would never become available for reuse. In such a case, you're better off creating the background thread manually.

An example of this is the aforementioned spell checker in Word, which runs as long as you're editing a document. Running such a task on the thread pool would make little sense, as the task will run as long as the application, so instead it should be run on a manually created thread, leaving the thread pool available for shorter running tasks.

The other primary reason for manual creation of threads is when you want to be able to interact with the `Thread` object as it is running. You can use various methods on the `Thread` object to interact with and control the background thread. These are described in the following table:

Method	Description
Abort	Stops the thread. This is not recommended, as no cleanup occurs. This is not a graceful shutdown of the thread.
ApartmentState	Sets the COM apartment type used by this thread — important if you're using COM `interop` in the background task
Join	Blocks your current thread until the background thread is complete
Priority	Enables you to raise or lower the priority of the background thread so Windows will schedule it to get more or less CPU time relative to other threads
Sleep	Causes the thread to be suspended for a specified period of time
Suspend	Suspends a thread — temporarily stopping it without terminating the thread
Resume	Restarts a suspended thread

Many other methods are available on the `Thread` object as well; consult the online help for more details. You can use these methods to control the behavior and lifetime of the background thread, which can be useful in advanced threading scenarios.

Shared Data

In most multithreading scenarios, you have data in your main thread that needs to be used by the background task on the background thread. Likewise, the background task typically generates data that is needed by the main thread. These are examples of *shared data*, or data that is used by multiple threads.

Remember that multithreading means you have multiple threads within the same process, and in .NET within the same AppDomain. Because memory within an AppDomain is common across all threads in that AppDomain, it is very easy for multiple threads to access the same objects or variables within your application.

For example, in our original prime example, the background task needed the `min` and `max` values from the main thread, and all the implementations have used a `List(Of Integer)` to transfer results back to the main thread when the task was complete. These are examples of shared data. Note that we didn't do anything special to make the data shared — the variables were shared by default.

When you're writing multithreaded code, the trickiest issue is managing access to shared data within your AppDomain. You don't, for example, want two threads writing to the same piece of memory at the same time. Equally, you don't want a group of threads reading memory that another thread is in the process of changing. This management of memory access is called *synchronization*. It's properly managing synchronization that makes writing multithreaded code difficult.

When multiple threads want to simultaneously access a common bit of shared data, use synchronization to control things. This is typically done by blocking all but one thread, so only one thread can access the shared data. All other threads are put into a wait state by using a blocking operation of some sort. Once the nonblocked thread is done using the shared data, it releases the block, allowing another thread to resume processing and to use the shared data.

The process of releasing the block is often called an *event*. When we say "event," we are *not* talking about a Visual Basic event. Although the naming convention is unfortunate, the principle is the same — something happens and we react to it. In this case, the nonblocked thread causes an event, which releases some other thread so it can access the shared data.

Although blocking can be used to control the execution of threads, it's primarily used to control access to resources, including memory. This is the basic idea behind synchronization — if you need something, you block until you can access it.

Synchronization is expensive and can be complex. It is expensive because it stops one or more threads from running while another thread uses the shared data. The whole point of having multiple threads is to do more than one thing at a time, and if you're constantly blocking all but one thread, then you lose this benefit.

It can be complex because there are many ways to implement synchronization. Each technique is appropriate for a certain class of synchronization problem, and using the wrong one in the wrong place increases the cost of synchronization.

It is also quite possible to create *deadlocks*, whereby two or more threads end up *permanently* blocked. You've undoubtedly seen examples of this. Pretty much anytime a Windows application totally locks up and must be stopped by the Task Manager, you are seeing an example of poor multithreading implementation. The fact that this happens even in otherwise high-quality commercial applications (such as Microsoft Outlook) is confirmation that synchronization can be very hard to get right.

Avoid Sharing Data

Because synchronization has so many downsides in terms of performance and complexity, the best thing you can do is avoid or minimize its use. If at all possible, design your multithreaded applications to avoid reliance on shared data, and to maintain tight control over the use of any shared data that is required.

Typically, some shared data is unavoidable, so the question becomes how to manage that shared data to avoid or minimize synchronization. Two primary schemes are used for this purpose.

Transferring Data Copies

The first approach is to avoid sharing of data by always passing references to the data between threads. If you also ensure that neither thread uses the same reference, then each thread has its own copy of the data, and no thread needs access to data being used by any other threads.

This is exactly what you did in the prime example where you started the background task via a delegate:

```
Dim worker As New TaskDelegate(AddressOf FindPrimesViaDelegate)
worker.BeginInvoke(1, 10000, AddressOf TaskComplete, Nothing)
```

The `min` and `max` values are passed as `ByVal` parameters, meaning they are copied and provided to the `indPrimes()` method. No synchronization is required here because the background thread never tries to access the values from the main thread. We passed copies of the values a different way when we manually started the task in the thread pool:

```
System.Threading.ThreadPool.QueueUserWorkItem( _
    AddressOf FindPrimesInPool, New params(1, 10000))
```

In this case, we created a `params` object into which we put the `min` and `max` values. Again, those values were copied before they were used by the background thread. The `FindPrimesInPool()` method never attempted to access any parameter data being used by the main thread.

Transferring Data Ownership

What we've done so far works great for variables that are *value types*, such as `Integer`, and *immutable* objects, such as `String`. It won't work for *reference types*, such as a regular object, because reference types are never passed by value, only by reference.

To use reference types, we need to change our approach. Rather than return a copy of the data, we'll return a reference to the object containing the data. Then we'll make sure that the background task stops using *that* object, and starts using a new object. As long as different threads aren't simultaneously using the same objects, there's no conflict.

You can enhance the prime application to provide the prime numbers to the UI thread as it finds them, rather than in a batch at the end of the process. To see how this works, we'll alter the original code based on the `BackgroundWorker` control. That is the easiest, and typically the best, way to start a background task, so we'll use it as a base implementation.

The first thing to do is to alter the `DoWork()` method so it periodically returns results. Rather than use the shared `mResults` variable, we'll use a local `List(Of Integer)` variable to store the results. Each time we have enough results to report, we'll return that `List(Of Integer)` to the UI thread, and create a new `List(Of Integer)` for the next batch of values. This way, we're never sharing the same object between two threads. The required changes are highlighted:

```
Private Sub BackgroundWorker1_DoWork(ByVal sender As Object, _
    ByVal e As System.ComponentModel.DoWorkEventArgs) _
    Handles BackgroundWorker1.DoWork

    'mResults.Clear()
    Dim results As New List(Of Integer)

    For count As Integer = mMin To mMax Step 2
        Dim isPrime As Boolean = True

        For x As Integer = 1 To CInt(count / 2)
            For y As Integer = 1 To x
                If x * y = count Then
                    ' the number is not prime
                    isPrime = False
                    Exit For
                End If
            Next
```

```
      ' short-circuit the check
      If Not isPrime Then Exit For
    Next

    If isPrime Then
      'mResults.Add(count)
      results.Add(count)
      If results.Count >= 10 Then
        BackgroundWorker1.ReportProgress( _
          CInt((count - mMin) / (mMax - mMin) * 100), results)
        results = New List(Of Integer)
      End If
    End If

    BackgroundWorker1.ReportProgress( _
      CInt((count - mMin) / (mMax - mMin) * 100))

    If BackgroundWorker1.CancellationPending Then
      Exit Sub
    End If

  Next

  BackgroundWorker1.ReportProgress(100, results)

End Sub
```

The results are now placed into a local `List(Of Integer)`. Anytime the list has 10 values, we return it to the primary thread by calling the `BackgroundWorker` control's `ReportProgress()` method, passing the `List(Of Integer)` as a parameter.

The important thing here is to then immediately create a new `List(Of Integer)` for use in the `DoWorker()` method. This ensures that the background thread is never trying to interact with the same `List(Of Integer)` object as the UI thread.

Now that the `DoWork()` method is returning results, alter the code on the primary thread to use those results:

```
  Private Sub BackgroundWorker1_ProgressChanged( _
    ByVal sender As Object, _
    ByVal e As System.ComponentModel.ProgressChangedEventArgs) _
    Handles BackgroundWorker1.ProgressChanged


    ProgressBar1.Value = e.ProgressPercentage
    If e.UserState IsNot Nothing Then
      For Each item As String In CType(e.UserState, List(Of Integer))
        ListBox1.Items.Add(item)
      Next
    End If

  End Sub
```

Anytime the `ProgressChanged` event is raised, the code checks to see whether the background task provided a state object. If it did provide a state object, then you cast it to a `List(Of Integer)` and update the UI to display the values in the object.

At this point, you no longer need the `RunWorkerCompleted()` method, so it can be removed or commented out. If you run the code at this point, not only is the UI continually responsive, but the results from the background task are displayed as they are discovered, rather than in a batch at the end of the process. As you run the application, resize and move the form while the prime numbers are being found. Although the *displaying* of the data may be slowed down as you interact with the form (because the UI thread can only do so much work), the *generation* of the data continues independently in the background and is not blocked by the UI thread's work.

When you rely on transferring data ownership, you ensure that only one thread can access the data at any given time by ensuring that the background task never uses an object once it returns it to the primary thread.

Sharing Data with Synchronization

So far, you've seen ways to avoid the sharing of data, but sometimes you'll have a requirement for data sharing, in which case you'll be faced with the complex world of synchronization.

As discussed earlier, incorrect implementation of synchronization can cause performance issues, deadlocks, and application crashes. Success is dependent on serious attention to detail. Problems may not manifest in testing, but when they happen in production they are often catastrophic. You can't *test* to ensure proper implementation; you must prove it in the same way mathematicians prove mathematical truths — by careful logical analysis of all possibilities.

Built-in Synchronization Support

Some objects in the .NET Framework have built-in support for synchronization, so you don't need to write it yourself. In particular, most of the collection-oriented classes have optional support for synchronization, including `Queue`, `Stack`, `Hashtable`, `ArrayList`, and more.

Rather than transfer ownership of `List(Of Integer)` objects from the background thread to the UI thread as shown in the last example, you can use the synchronization provided by the `ArrayList` object to help mediate between the two threads.

To use a synchronized `ArrayList`, you need to change from the `List(Of Integer)` to an `ArrayList`. Additionally, the `ArrayList` must be created a special way:

```
Private Sub BackgroundWorker1_DoWork(ByVal sender As Object, _
  ByVal e As System.ComponentModel.DoWorkEventArgs) _
  Handles BackgroundWorker1.DoWork

  'mResults.Clear()
  'Dim results As New List(Of Integer)
  Dim results As ArrayList = ArrayList.Synchronized(New ArrayList)
```

What you're doing here is creating a normal `ArrayList`, and then having the `ArrayList` class "wrap" it with a synchronized wrapper. The result is a thread-safe `ArrayList` object that automatically prevents multiple threads from interacting with the data in invalid ways.

Now that the `ArrayList` is synchronized, you don't need to create a new one each time you return the values to the primary thread. Comment out the following line in the `DoWork()` method:

```
If results.Count >= 10 Then
  BackgroundWorker1.ReportProgress( _
    CInt((count - mMin) / (mMax - mMin) * 100), results)
  'results = New List(Of Integer)
End If
```

Finally, update the code on the primary thread to properly display the data from the `ArrayList`:

```
Private Sub BackgroundWorker1_ProgressChanged( _
  ByVal sender As Object, _
  ByVal e As System.ComponentModel.ProgressChangedEventArgs) _
  Handles BackgroundWorker1.ProgressChanged


  ProgressBar1.Value = e.ProgressPercentage
  If e.UserState IsNot Nothing Then
    Dim result As ArrayList = CType(e.UserState, ArrayList)
    For index As Integer = ListBox1.Items.Count To result.Count - 1
      ListBox1.Items.Add(result(index))
    Next
  End If

End Sub
```

Because the entire list is accessible at all times, you need only copy the new values to the `ListBox`, rather than loop through the entire list. This works out well anyway, because the `For Each` statement isn't thread safe even with a synchronized collection. To use the `For Each` statement, you'd need to enclose the entire loop inside a `SyncLock` block:

```
Dim result As ArrayList = CType(e.UserState, ArrayList)
SyncLock result.SyncRoot
  For Each item As String in result
    ListBox1.Items.Add(item)
  Next
End SyncLock
```

The `SyncLock` statement in Visual Basic is used to provide an exclusive lock on an object. Here it is being used to get an exclusive lock on the `ArrayList` object's `SyncRoot`. This means all the code within the `SyncLock` block can be sure that it is the only code interacting with the contents of the `ArrayList`. No other threads can access the data while your code is in this block.

Synchronization Objects

While many collection objects optionally provide support for synchronization, most objects in the .NET Framework or in third-party libraries are not thread safe. To safely share these objects and classes in a multithreaded environment, you must manually implement synchronization.

To manually implement synchronization, you must rely on help from the Windows operating system. The .NET Framework includes classes that wrap the underlying Windows operating system concepts, however, so you don't need to call Windows directly. Instead, you use the .NET Framework synchronization objects.

Synchronization objects have their own special terminology. Most of these objects can be acquired and released. In other cases, you wait on an object until it is signaled.

For objects that can be acquired, the idea is that when you have the object, you have a lock. Any other threads trying to acquire the object are blocked until you release the object. These types of synchronization objects are like a hot potato — only one thread has it at a time and other threads are waiting for it. No thread should hold onto such an object any longer than necessary, as that slows down the whole system.

The other class of objects comprises those that wait on the object — which means your thread is blocked. Some other thread will signal your object, which releases you (to become unblocked). Many threads can be waiting on the same object, and when the object is signaled, all the blocked threads are released. This is basically the exact opposite of an acquire/release type object. The following table lists the primary synchronization objects in the .NET Framework:

Object	Model	Description
AutoResetEvent	Wait/Signal	Allows a thread to release other threads that are waiting on the object
Interlocked	N/A	Allows multiple threads to safely increment and decrement values that are stored in variables accessible to all the threads
ManualResetEvent	Wait/Signal	Allows a thread to release other threads that are waiting on the object
Monitor	Acquire/Release	Defines an exclusive application-level lock whereby only one thread can hold the lock at any given time
Mutex	Acquire/Release	Defines an exclusive systemwide lock whereby only one thread can hold the lock at any given time
ReaderWriterLock	Acquire/Release	Defines a lock whereby many threads can read data, but exclusive access is provided to one thread for writing data

Exclusive Locks and the SyncLock Statement

Perhaps the easiest type of synchronization to understand and implement is an *exclusive lock*. When one thread holds an exclusive lock, no other thread can obtain that lock. Any other thread attempting to obtain the lock is blocked until the lock becomes available.

There are two primary technologies for exclusive locking: the monitor and mutex objects. The monitor object allows a thread in a process to block other threads in the same process. The mutex object allows a thread in any process to block threads in the same process or in other processes. Because a mutex has systemwide scope, it is a more expensive object to use and should only be used when cross-process locking is required.

Visual Basic includes the SyncLock statement, which is a shortcut to access a monitor object. While it is possible to directly create and use a System.Threading.Monitor object, it is far simpler to just use the SyncLock statement (briefly mentioned in the ArrayList object discussion), so that is what we'll do here.

Exclusive locks can be used to protect shared data so only one thread at a time can access the data. They can also be used to ensure that only one thread at a time can run a specific bit of code. This exclusive bit of code is called a *critical section*. While critical sections are an important concept in computer science, it is far more common to use exclusive locks to protect shared data, and that's what this chapter focuses on.

You can use an exclusive lock to lock virtually any shared data. For example, you can change your code to use the SyncLock statement instead of a synchronized ArrayList. Change the declaration of the ArrayList in the DoWork method so it is global to the form and no longer synchronized:

```
Private results As New ArrayList
```

This means you're responsible for managing all synchronization yourself. First, in the DoWork method, protect all access to the results variable:

```
If isPrime Then
    Dim numberOfResults As Integer
    SyncLock results.SyncRoot
       results.Add(count)
       numberOfResults = results.Count
    End SyncLock
    If numberofresults >= 10 Then
       BackgroundWorker1.ReportProgress( _
          CInt((count - mMin) / (mMax - mMin) * 100), results)
    End If
End If
```

Notice how the code has changed so both the Add() and Count() method calls are contained within a SyncLock block. This ensures that no other thread can be interacting with the ArrayList while you make these calls. The SyncLock statement acts against an object — in this case, results.SyncRoot.

> *The trick to making this work is to ensure that all code throughout the application wraps any access to* results *within the* SyncLock *statement. If any code doesn't follow this protocol, then there will be conflicts between threads!*

Because SyncLock acts against a specific object, you can have many active SyncLock statements, each working against a different object:

```
SyncLock obj1
   ' blocks against obj1
End SyncLock

SyncLock obj2
   ' blocks against obj2
End SyncLock
```

Note that neither obj1 nor obj2 is altered or affected by this at all. The only thing you're saying here is that while you're within a SyncLock obj1 code block, any other thread attempting to execute a SyncLock obj1 statement will be blocked until you've executed the End SyncLock statement.

Next, change the UI update code in the ProgressChanged method:

```
ProgressBar1.Value = e.ProgressPercentage
If e.UserState IsNot Nothing Then
  Dim result As ArrayList = CType(e.UserState, ArrayList)
  SyncLock result
    For index As Integer = ListBox1.Items.Count To result.Count - 1
      ListBox1.Items.Add(result(index))
    Next
  End SyncLock
End If
```

Again, notice how the interaction with the ArrayList is contained within a SyncLock block. While this version of the code will operate just fine, it is very slow. In fact, you can pretty much stall out the whole processing by continually moving or resizing the window while it runs. This is because the UI thread is blocking the background thread via the SyncLock call, and if the UI thread is totally busy moving or resizing the window, then the background thread can be entirely blocked during that time as well.

Reader–Writer Locks

While exclusive locks are an easy way to protect shared data, they are not always the most efficient. Your application will often contain some code that is updating shared data, and other code that is only reading from shared data. Some applications do a great deal of data reading, and only periodic data changes.

Because reading data doesn't change anything, there's nothing wrong with having multiple threads read data at the same time, as long as you can ensure that no threads are *updating* data while you're trying to read. In addition, you typically only want one thread updating at a time.

What we have then is a scenario in which we want to allow many concurrent readers, but if the data is to be changed, then one thread must temporarily gain exclusive access to the shared memory. This is the purpose behind the ReaderWriterLock object.

Using a ReaderWriterLock, you can request either a read lock or a write lock. If you obtain a read lock, you can safely read the data. Other threads can simultaneously obtain read locks and safely read the data.

Before you can update data, you must obtain a write lock. When you request a write lock, any other threads requesting either a read or write lock are blocked. If any outstanding read or write locks are in progress, you'll be blocked until they are released. Once there are no outstanding locks (read or write), you'll be granted the write lock. No other locks are granted until you release the write lock, so your write lock is an exclusive lock.

Once you release the write lock, any pending requests for other locks are granted, allowing either another single writer to access the data or multiple readers to simultaneously access the data. You can adapt the sample code to use a System.Threading.ReaderWriterLock object. Start by using the code that was just created based on the `SyncLock` statement with a `Queue` object as shared data. First, create an instance of the `ReaderWriterLock` in a formwide variable:

```
' lock object
Private mRWLock As New System.Threading.ReaderWriterLock
```

Because a `ReaderWriterLock` is just an object, you can have many lock objects in an application if needed. You could use each lock object to protect different bits of shared data. Then you can change the `DoWork` method to make use of this object instead of the `SyncLock` statement:

```
If isPrime Then
  Dim numberOfResults As Integer
  mRWLock.AcquireWriterLock(100)
  Try
     results.Add(count)
  Finally
     mRWLock.ReleaseWriterLock()
  End Try
  mRWLock.AcquireReaderLock(100)
  Try
     numberOfResults = results.Count
  Finally
     mRWLock.ReleaseReaderLock()
  End Try
  If numberOfResults >= 10 Then
    BackgroundWorker1.ReportProgress( _
      CInt((count - mMin) / (mMax - mMin) * 100), results)
  End If
End If
```

Before you write or alter the data in the `ArrayList`, you need to acquire a writer lock. Before reading any data from the `ArrayList`, you need to acquire a reader lock.

If any thread holds a reader lock, attempts to get a writer lock are blocked. When any thread requests a writer lock, any *other* requests for a reader lock are blocked until after that thread gets (and releases) its writer lock. In addition, if any thread has a writer lock, other threads requesting a reader (or writer) lock are blocked until that writer lock is released.

The result is that there can be only one writer, and while the writer is active, there are no readers. However, if no writer is active, then there can be many concurrent reader threads running at the same time.

Note that all work done while a lock is held is contained within a `Try..Finally` block. This ensures that the lock is released regardless of any exceptions you might encounter.

> It is critical to always release locks you're holding. Failure to do so may cause your application to become unstable and crash or lock up unexpectedly.

Failure to release a lock will almost certainly block other threads, possibly forever — causing a deadlock situation. The alternate fate is that the other threads will request a lock and time out, throwing an exception and causing the application to fail. Either way, if you don't release your locks, you'll cause application failure.

Now, update the code in the `ProgressChanged` method:

```
ProgressBar1.Value = e.ProgressPercentage
If e.UserState IsNot Nothing Then
   Dim result As ArrayList = CType(e.UserState, ArrayList)
   mRWLock.AcquireReaderLock(100)
   Try
      For index As Integer = ListBox1.Items.Count To result.Count - 1
         ListBox1.Items.Add(result(index))
      Next
   Finally
      mRWLock.ReleaseReaderLock()
   End Try
End If
```

Again, before reading from `results`, you get a reader lock, releasing it in a `Finally` block once you're done. This code will run a bit smoother than the previous implementation, but the UI thread can be kept busy with resizing or moving the window, thus causing it to hold the reader lock and preventing the background thread from running, as it won't be able to acquire a writer lock.

AutoReset Events

Both the `Monitor` (`SyncLock`) and `ReaderWriterLock` objects follow the acquire/release model, whereby threads are blocked until they can acquire control of the appropriate lock.

You can flip the paradigm by using the `AutoResetEvent` and `ManualResetEvent` objects. With these objects, threads voluntarily wait on the event object. While waiting, they are blocked and do no work. When another thread signals (raises) the event, any threads waiting on the event object are released and do work.

You can signal an event object by calling the object's `Set()` method. To wait on an event object, a thread calls that object's `WaitOne()` method. This method blocks the thread until the event object is signaled (the event is raised).

Event objects can be in one of two states: signaled or not signaled. When an event object is signaled, threads waiting on the object are released. If a thread calls `WaitOne()` on an event object that is signaled, then the thread isn't blocked and continues running. However, if a thread calls `WaitOne()` on an event object that is not signaled, then the thread is blocked until some other thread calls that object's `Set()` method, thus signaling the event.

`AutoResetEvent` objects automatically reset themselves to the not signaled state as soon as any thread calls the `WaitOne()` method. In other words, if an `AutoResetEvent` is not signaled and a thread calls `WaitOne()`, then that thread will be blocked. Another thread can then call the `Set` method, thus signaling the event. This both releases the waiting thread and immediately resets the `AutoResetEvent` object to its not signaled state.

You can use an `AutoResetEvent` object to coordinate the use of shared data between threads. Change the `ReaderWriterLock` declaration to declare an `AutoResetEvent` instead:

```
Dim mWait As New System.Threading.AutoResetEvent(False)
```

By passing `False` to the constructor, you're telling the event object to start out in its not signaled state. Were you to pass `True`, it would start out in the signaled state, and the first thread to call `WaitOne` would *not* be blocked, but would trigger the event object to automatically reset its state to not signaled.

Next, you can update `DoWork()` to use the event object. In order to ensure that both the primary and background threads don't simultaneously access the `ArrayList` object, use the `AutoResetEvent` object to block the background thread until the UI thread is done with the `ArrayList`:

```
If isPrime Then
  Dim numberOfResults As Integer
  results.Add(count)
  numberOfResults = results.Count
  If numberOfResults >= 10 Then
    BackgroundWorker1.ReportProgress( _
      CInt((count - mMin) / (mMax - mMin) * 100), results)
    mWait.WaitOne()
  End If
End If
```

This code is much simpler than using the `ReaderWriterLock`. In this case, the background thread assumes it has exclusive access to the `ArrayList` until the `ReportProgress` method is called to invoke the primary thread to update the UI. When that occurs, the background thread calls the `WaitOne` method so it is blocked until released by the primary thread.

In the UI update code, change the code to release the background thread:

```
ProgressBar1.Value = e.ProgressPercentage
If e.UserState IsNot Nothing Then
  Dim result As ArrayList = CType(e.UserState, ArrayList)
  For index As Integer = ListBox1.Items.Count To result.Count - 1
    ListBox1.Items.Add(result(index))
  Next
  mWait.Set()
End If
```

This is done by calling the `Set()` method on the `AutoResetEvent` object, thus setting it to its signaled state. This releases the background thread so it can continue to work. Notice that the `Set` method isn't called until after the primary thread is completely done working with the `ArrayList` object.

As with the previous examples, if you continually move or resize the form, then the UI thread becomes so busy it won't ever release the background thread.

ManualReset Events

A `ManualResetEvent` object is very similar to the `AutoResetEvent` just used. The difference is that with a `ManualResetEvent` object you're in total control over whether the event object is set to its signaled or not signaled state. The state of the event object is never altered automatically.

This means you can manually call the `Reset` method, rather than rely on it to occur automatically. The result is that you have more control over the process and can potentially gain some efficiency.

To see how this works, change the declaration to create a `ManualResetEvent`:

```
' wait object
Dim mWait As New System.Threading.ManualResetEvent(True)
```

Notice that you're constructing it with a `True` parameter. This means that the object will initially be in its signaled state. Until it is reset to a nonsignaled state, `WaitOne()` calls won't block on this object.

Change the `DoWork()` method as follows:

```
        If isPrime Then
          mWait.WaitOne()
          Dim numberOfResults As Integer
          results.Add(count)
          numberOfResults = results.Count
          If numberOfResults >= 10 Then
            mWait.Reset()
            BackgroundWorker1.ReportProgress( _
              CInt((count - mMin) / (mMax - mMin) * 100), results)
          End If
        End If
```

This is quite different from the previous code. Before interacting with the `ArrayList` object, the code calls `WaitOne()`. This causes it to block if the primary thread is active. Remember that initially the lock object is signaled, so the `WaitOne()` call will *not* block.

Then, before transferring control to the primary thread to update the UI, you call `mWait.Reset()`. The `Reset` event sets the lock object to its nonsignaled state. Until its `Set()` method is called, any `WaitOne()` methods will block. No changes are required to the UI update code. It already calls the `Set()` method when it is done interacting with the `ArrayList`.

The result is that the background thread can continue to search for prime numbers while the UI is being updated. The only time the background thread will block is if it finds a prime number before the UI is done with its update process.

Summary

This chapter took a fairly involved look at the subject of threading in .NET and demonstrated the rich set of threading functionality now available to Visual Basic developers.

Proper implementation of multithreaded code is very difficult, and proving that multithreaded code will always run as expected requires careful code walk-throughs, as it can't be proven through testing. Due to this, it is best to avoid the use of multithreading when possible.

However, multithreading can be a useful way to run lengthy tasks in the background while continuing to provide the user with an interactive experience. When using multithreading, try to avoid using shared data, and instead relay data between the UI and background threads using messaging techniques, as shown in this chapter.

If you must share data between multiple threads, be sure to use appropriate synchronization primitives to ensure that only one thread interacts with the data at any given time. Be aware of the performance implications of using synchronization objects, and design carefully to avoid deadlocks.

Threading can be useful in specialized situations, and its use should be limited whenever possible.

25

Windows Workflow Foundation

While Windows Communication Foundation and Windows Presentation Foundation enjoy much of the attention, the .NET Framework 3.0 also comes with another "Foundation": Windows Workflow Foundation (usually abbreviated WF). WF can be a powerful tool in developing applications, as it provides a standard means of adding workflow to an application. Workflow refers to the steps involved in an application. Most business applications contain one or more workflows, such as the approval steps in an expense-tracking application, or the steps involved in paying for a cart full of items at an online store. Normally, a workflow is created in code, and is inextricably bound to the application. WF enables developers to graphically build the workflow, keeping it logically separated from the code itself. It also enables the workflow to change as the needs of the business change. These workflows may be as complex as needed, and may integrate human processes or Web Services.

This chapter looks at how you can take advantage of WF in your applications: how you can add and edit workflows, how you can integrate workflows into an existing business process, and how the graphical tools used to build workflows with Visual Studio can help you communicate with business users and avoid errors caused by mistakes in the workflow.

Workflow in Applications

Just what is workflow? It's a very heavily used word, and many developers use it in multiple contexts. For our purposes, it is the description of the steps involved in some process performed at least partially by a computer. Workflows are common in many types of business applications. For example, if you were building an application for tracking employee expense reports, the workflow might look something like the following:

1. The employee completes a form and submits it into the system.

2.   The employee prints the expense report form, attaches original invoices, and sends it to accounting for a permanent record.

3.   The system examines the data in the expense report:

   a.   Depending on the rules defined by the company, it may be automatically approved, require management approval, or require investigation by the accounting department. Some of the rules that may come into play would likely be the expense types, the amount of each expense, how the expense was paid, and so on.

   b.   Copies of the expense report are e-mailed if additional approval is required.

   c.   If approved, the expense report continues in the workflow; otherwise, it is returned to the submitting employee for correction (or to complain to the employee's manager).

4.   Expense report values are recorded in the accounting system.

5.   A check is printed and sent to the happy employee. This step may be delayed if the originals have not been received. Alternatively, the company may delay future expense reimbursement requests.

The steps in a workflow may be carried out by a human or computer; they may require custom code or calculations, or may need to integrate with an external application. Building workflows into an application is frequently a difficult process. Unless developers completely understand the process (and they rarely do), identifying the true workflow used for a process requires interviewing multiple people at one or more companies. This often results in conflicting descriptions of the steps involved, or of the actions required at each step, requiring someone to decide on the actual intent.

Even after the exact workflow has been defined, it frequently changes. This may be due to some new legal requirements, a company merger, or even (frequently) the whims of management. In traditional applications, this would likely mean that a developer would have to change the code for one or more steps of the process, ideally without introducing any new bugs into the system. In short, developing workflow applications using traditional tools can be a difficult process. WF makes building and maintaining these workflows easier by abstracting away the logic of the workflow, and by providing several of the common services required.

Building Workflows

The actual workflow files in WF are XML files written in a version of XAML. This is the same XAML used to describe Windows Presentation Foundation (WPF) files. (See Chapter 17 for more details on WPF). They describe the actions to perform within the workflow, and the relationship between those actions. You can create a workflow using only a text editor, but Visual Studio makes creating these workflows much easier. It provides a graphical designer that enables developers to visually design the workflow, creating the XAML in the background.

```
<RuleDefinitions xmlns="http://schemas.microsoft.com/winfx/2006/xaml/workflow">
  <RuleDefinitions.Conditions>
    <RuleExpressionCondition Name="TranslationCallWorked">
      <RuleExpressionCondition.Expression>
        <ns0:CodeBinaryOperatorExpression Operator="ValueEquality"
```

```
            xmlns:ns0="clr-namespace:System.CodeDom;Assembly=System, Version=2.0.0.0,
            Culture=neutral, PublicKeyToken=b77a5c561934e089">
            <ns0:CodeBinaryOperatorExpression.Left>
              <ns0:CodeBinaryOperatorExpression Operator="ValueEquality">
                <ns0:CodeBinaryOperatorExpression.Left>
                  <ns0:CodeMethodInvokeExpression>
                    <ns0:CodeMethodInvokeExpression.Parameters>
                      <ns0:CodeFieldReferenceExpression
                        FieldName="OutputTextProperty">
                        <ns0:CodeFieldReferenceExpression.TargetObject>
                          <ns0:CodeTypeReferenceExpression
                            Type="TranslateActivity.TranslateActivity" />
                        </ns0:CodeFieldReferenceExpression.TargetObject>
                      </ns0:CodeFieldReferenceExpression>
                    </ns0:CodeMethodInvokeExpression.Parameters>
                    <ns0:CodeMethodInvokeExpression.Method>
                      <ns0:CodeMethodReferenceExpression MethodName="GetValue">
                        <ns0:CodeMethodReferenceExpression.TargetObject>
                          <ns0:CodeThisReferenceExpression />
                        </ns0:CodeMethodReferenceExpression.TargetObject>
                      </ns0:CodeMethodReferenceExpression>
                    </ns0:CodeMethodInvokeExpression.Method>
                  </ns0:CodeMethodInvokeExpression>
                </ns0:CodeBinaryOperatorExpression.Left>
                <ns0:CodeBinaryOperatorExpression.Right>
                  <ns0:CodePrimitiveExpression />
                </ns0:CodeBinaryOperatorExpression.Right>
              </ns0:CodeBinaryOperatorExpression>
            </ns0:CodeBinaryOperatorExpression.Left>
            <ns0:CodeBinaryOperatorExpression.Right>
              <ns0:CodePrimitiveExpression>
                <ns0:CodePrimitiveExpression.Value>
                  <ns1:Boolean xmlns:ns1="clr-namespace:System;Assembly=mscorlib,
                    Version=2.0.0.0, Culture=neutral,
                    PublicKeyToken=b77a5c561934e089">false</ns1:Boolean>
                </ns0:CodePrimitiveExpression.Value>
              </ns0:CodePrimitiveExpression>
            </ns0:CodeBinaryOperatorExpression.Right>
          </ns0:CodeBinaryOperatorExpression>
        </RuleExpressionCondition.Expression>
      </RuleExpressionCondition>
    </RuleDefinitions.Conditions>
  </RuleDefinitions>
```

The workflow is composed of a number of rule definitions. Each definition includes activities, conditions, and expressions. Activities are the steps involved in the workflow. They are executed based on the workflow's design and the conditions included. Controlling the behavior of the workflow are conditions, which are evaluated and may result in code running. Finally, expressions describe the individual tests used as part of the conditions. For example, each side of an equality condition would be expressions. When building the workflow by hand, you are responsible for creating the markup. Fortunately, Visual Studio writes it as you design your workflow.

Adding Workflow with Windows Workflow Foundation

Windows Workflow Foundation is composed of a number of components that work together with your application to carry out the desired workflow. Six main components make up any WF application:

❑ **Host process** — This is the executable that will host the workflow. Typically, this is your application, and is usually a Windows Form, ASP.NET, or Windows service application. The workflow is hosted and runs within this process. All normal rules of application design apply here: If another application needs to communicate with the workflow, then you need to use Web Services or remoting to communicate between the two applications.

❑ **WF runtime services** — Windows Workflow Foundation provides several essential services to your application. Most notable, of course, is the capability to execute workflows. This service is responsible for loading, scheduling, and executing your workflows within the context of the host process. In addition to this service, WF provides services for persistence and tracking. The persistence service enables saving the state of a workflow as needed. Because a workflow may take a long time to complete, having multiple workflows in process can use a lot of the memory of the computer. The persistence services enable the workflow to be saved for later use. When there is more to complete, the workflow can be reactivated and continue, even after weeks of inactivity. The tracking services enable the developer to monitor the state of the workflows. This is particularly useful when you might have multiple workflows active at any given time (such as in a shopping checkout workflow). The tracking services enable the creation of applications to monitor the health of your workflow applications.

❑ **Workflow runtime engine** — The runtime engine is responsible for executing each workflow instance. It runs in-process within the host process. Each engine may execute multiple workflow instances simultaneously, and multiple engines may be running concurrently within the same host process.

❑ **Workflow** — The workflow is the list of steps required to carry out an action. It may be created graphically using a tool such as Visual Studio, or manually. Each workflow is composed of one or more activities, and may consist of workflow markup and/or code. Multiple instances of a workflow may be active at any given moment in an application.

❑ **Activity library** — The activity library is a collection of the standard actions used to create workflows. There are several different types of activities. Some are used to communicate with outside processes, while others affect the flow of a workflow.

❑ **Custom activities** — In addition to the standard activities that exist within the activity library, developers can create custom activities. This may be to support a particular application you need to integrate with WF, or as a simplification of a complex composite activity. Creating custom activities is done mostly through attributes and inheritance.

Figure 25-1 shows how the main components of WF fit together.

Windows Workflow Foundation supports two main styles of creating workflows: *sequential* and *state machine*. Sequential workflows (see Figure 25-2) are the classic flowchart style of process. They begin when some action initiates the workflow, such as the submission of an expense report or a user decision to check out a shopping cart. The workflow then continues stepwise through the activities until it comes to the end. There may be branching or looping, but generally the flow moves down the workflow. Sequential workflows are best when a set series of steps are needed for the workflow.

Figure 25-1

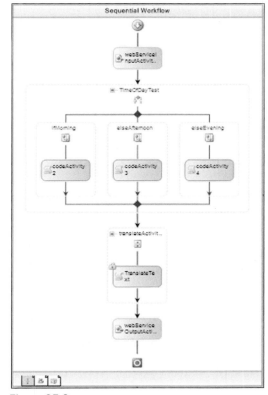

Figure 25-2

State machine workflows (see Figure 25-3) are less linear than sequential workflows. They are typically used when the data moves through a series of steps toward completion. At each step, the state of the application has a particular value. Transitions move the state between steps. One example of a state machine workflow that most people are familiar with (unfortunately) is voice mail. Most voice-mail systems are collections of states, represented by a menu. You move between the states by pressing the keys of your phone. State machine workflows can be useful when the process you are modeling is not necessarily linear. There may still be some required steps, but generally the flow may iterate between the steps for some time before completion.

A good way to identify a candidate for a state machine workflow is determining whether the process is defined in terms of modes. For example, a shopping site is a classic example of a state machine. The user is either in browse mode or cart view mode. Selecting checkout would likely initiate a sequential workflow, as the steps in that process are more easily described in a linear fashion.

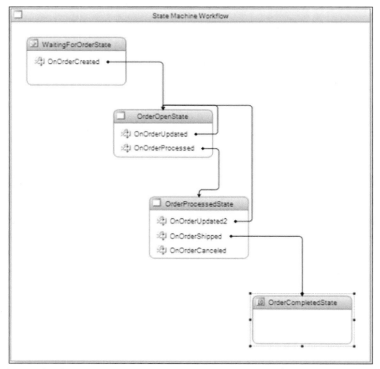

Figure 25-3

A Simple Workflow

As with any other programming endeavor, the best way to understand WF is to create a simple workflow and extend it with additional steps. Start Visual Studio and create a new Sequential Workflow Console Application (see Figure 25-4) called HelloWorkflow.

Figure 25-4

This project creates two files: a module that includes the Main for the application and the workflow. The sequential workflow begins life with only two steps: start and finish, as shown in Figure 25-5. You build the workflow by adding steps between these two.

Figure 25-5

To begin, drag a Code activity between the start and finish markers. Note the red exclamation mark on the new activity in the diagram (shown without color in Figure 25-6). WF makes heavy use of these tips to help you identify the next step in the process.

Sequential Workflow

codeActivity
1

Property 'ExecuteCode' is not set.

Figure 25-6

Click the code tip and select the menu item Property 'ExecuteCode' is not set. This will bring up the Properties window for the Code activity. Enter **SayGreetings** and press Enter. This brings up the code window for the activity. Add the following code:

```
Private Sub SayGreetings(ByVal sender As System.Object, _
    ByVal e As System.EventArgs)
      Console.WriteLine("Hello world, from workflow")
      Console.WriteLine("Press enter to continue")
      Console.ReadLine()
End Sub
```

Notice that coding the action for the activity is the same as any other event. Run the project to see the console window (see Figure 25-7), along with the message you should be expecting.

While trivial, the project makes a useful test bed for experimenting with the various activities. Add an IfElse activity before the Code activity. IfElse activities are one of the main ways to add logic and control of flow to your workflows. They have a condition property that determines when each half of the flow will be executed. The condition may be code that executes or a declarative rule. For this example, declarative rules are enough. You create these rules in the Rule Condition Editor (see Figure 25-8). To display the Rule Condition Editor, select `Declarative Rule Condition` for the `Condition` property of the `ifElseBranchActivity` component. Once you have selected `Declarative Rule Condition`, you can click the ellipsis to display the dialog.

Figure 25-7

Figure 25-8

Clicking New brings up the Rule Condition Editor (see Figure 25-9). This enables you to create simple expressions that will be used by the IfElse activity to determine flow.

Figure 25-9

Set the rule on the If half of the IfElse activity to determine whether the current time is before noon:

```
System.DateTime.Now.TimeOfDay.Hours < 12
```

Right-click on the activity and select Add Branch to create a third branch to the IfElse activity. Set the condition for this one as you did for the first activity, but use 18 for the value to check for hours.

Add Code activities to each of the three sections of the diagram (see Figure 25-10). You will use these activities to affect the message that is displayed. Assign the properties as follows:

Activity	Property	Value
codeActivity2	ExecuteCode	SetMessageMorning
codeActivity3	ExecuteCode	SetMessageAfternoon
codeActivity4	ExecuteCode	SetMessageEvening

Finally, change the code in the workflow to the following (note that this replaces the SayGreetings method created earlier):

```
Public class Workflow1
    Inherits SequentialWorkflowActivity

    Private Message As String
    Private Sub SayGreetings(ByVal sender As System.Object, _
```

```
          ByVal e As System.EventArgs)
          Console.WriteLine(Message & ", from workflow")
          Console.WriteLine("Press enter to continue")
          Console.ReadLine()
    End Sub

    Private Sub SetMessageMorning(ByVal sender As System.Object, _
      ByVal e As System.EventArgs)
          Message = "Good morning"
    End Sub
    Private Sub SetMessageAfternoon(ByVal sender As System.Object, _
      ByVal e As System.EventArgs)
          Message = "Good afternoon"
    End Sub
    Private Sub SetMessageNight(ByVal sender As System.Object, _
      ByVal e As System.EventArgs)
          Message = "Good night"
    End Sub
End Class
```

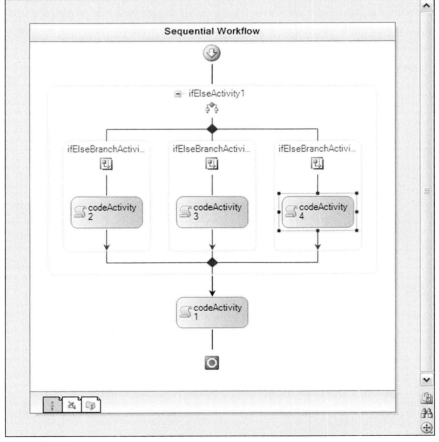

Figure 25-10

Each of the three `SetMessage` methods changes the greeting as appropriate. The final greeting is displayed in the `SayGreetings` method. Run the project again. You should be greeted appropriately for the time of day.

While this workflow is probably overkill to generate a simple message, the example does show many of the common steps in defining a workflow. Workflows are composed of multiple activities. Many activities can in turn be composed of other activities. Activities may use declarative properties, or code may be executed as needed.

Standard Activities

The standard WF activities can be divided into five major categories:

❏ **Activities that communicate with external code** — These activities are either called by external code to initiate a workflow or are used to call to external code as part of a workflow.

❏ **Control of flow activities** — These activities are the equivalent of Visual Basic's `If` statement or `While` loop. They enable the workflow to branch or repeat as needed to carry out a step.

❏ **Scope activities** — These activities group a number of other activities together into some logical element. This is usually done to mark a number of activities that participate in a transaction.

❏ **State activities** — These activities are used exclusively in state machine workflows. They represent the state of the process involved as part of the overall state machine.

❏ **Action activities** — These activities perform some action as part of the overall workflow.

In order for a workflow to begin, there must be some way for external code to initiate it. In addition, a workflow would be limited if there were no way for the workflow to execute external code and/or Web Services. The standard activities that are used to communicate with external code include the following:

Activity	Description
CallExternalMethod	As the name implies, this activity calls an external method. The activity requires two properties. The first identifies an interface shared by the workflow and the external code. The second identifies the method on that interface that will be called. If the method requires additional parameters, then they appear on the property grid after setting the other two properties. This method is frequently used in combination with the HandleExternalEvent activity. This activity executes the external method synchronously, so be cautious when calling external methods that will take a long time to execute.
HandleExternalEvent	Receives a trigger from an external block of code. This is a commonly used activity to initiate a workflow when the workflow is running in the context of a Windows Forms or ASP.NET application. As with the CallExternalMethod activity, it requires at least two properties. The first identifies a shared interface and the second identifies the event on that interface that will be received.

Activity	Description
InvokeWebService	Calls an external Web Service. You assign a WSDL file to the activity and it generates a proxy class for the Web Service. You must also identify the method on that class that will be called. The SessionId property is used to identify the session that will be used for the requests. All requests with the same SessionId value share the session. If the SessionId is blank, then this activity creates a new session per request.
InvokeWorkflow	Calls another workflow. This is a useful activity for chaining multiple workflows together, reducing the complexity of each workflow. The external workflow must complete before the current workflow continues.
WebServiceInput	Receives an incoming Web Service request. You must publish the workflow containing this activity for it to work. You publish the workflow by selecting Publish as Web Service from the Project menu. This generates a new Web Service project that includes the output from the workflow project as well as an ASMX file that serves as the address for the workflow.
WebServiceOutput	Produces the output for a Web Service request. This activity is used in partnership with the WebServiceInput activity.
WebServiceFault	Triggers a Web Service error. This is used in partnership with the WebServiceInput activity to signal an error with the Web Service call.

All programming languages need some form of control of flow to regulate the applications. Visual Basic includes language elements such as If..Else, Do..While, For..Next, and Select Case to perform these actions. WF includes a number of activities to perform similar actions, although the options are more limited:

Activity	Description
IfElse	Provides for executing two or more different workflow paths based on the status of a condition. The condition may be code or an expression. This is a commonly used activity to branch a workflow.
Listen	Provides for executing two or more different workflow paths based on an event. The path chosen is selected by the first event that occurs. This is a useful activity to use to monitor a class that could generate multiple events (such as a class that could either approve or reject a request).
Policy	Provides for executing multiple rules. Each rule is a condition with some resulting action. This activity provides a way to group multiple related rules into a single activity.

Table continues on the next page

Activity	Description
Replicator	Enables the workflow to create multiple instances of an activity for processing. The resulting child activities may run serially or in parallel. This is an excellent way to divide a large task: For example, you could have the Replicator activity create multiple child activities that are responsible for mailing a newsletter to a large list. The child activities could run in parallel, dividing the list into smaller groups for faster processing.
While	Loops the workflow until a condition has been met. The condition may be the result of code or an expression. This is typically used to receive multiple input values or to process multiple requests, such as a batch job.

Several composite activities may cooperate to complete a single logical action by grouping other activities:

Activity	Description
CompensatableSequence	Similar to the Sequence activity (see below), this activity differs in that it supports "undoing" the child activities. You can think of this in terms of a transaction: If one child activity fails, then the completed activities must be undone. The CompensatableSequence activity includes handles that enable the developer to perform this correction.
ConditionedActivityGroup	Includes a number of child activities that are run based on a condition. All child activities will execute until some defined condition occurs. This provides a means of grouping a number of related activities into a single activity.
EventDriven	Responds to an external event to initiate a set of activities. This is similar to the HandleExternalEvent activity, but the events are internal to the workflow. This activity is commonly used in a state-machine workflow to move between the states.
FaultHandler	Enables handling an error within a workflow. You use the FaultHandler activity to either correct or report the error gracefully. For example, a timeout may occur, triggering a fault condition in the workflow. This handler would contain other activities that are responsible for an alternate method of processing the item.
Parallel	Contains a series of child activities that run concurrently. You should only use this if the child activities either do not affect the data or the order of change is not important.
Sequence	Contains a series of child activities that run in order. This is the default model for an workflow. Each child activity must complete before the next one begins.

State activities represent the current state of the data and process for the workflow. They are only used within state-machine workflows:

Activity	Description
State	Represents the current state of the workflow. For example, in a workflow driving a voice-mail system, the state would represent the current menu that the client is on.
StateFinalization	Provides an activity to handle the actions needed as a given state is completed. This would provide a place to record the user's selection or to free up resources used by the state.
StateInitialization	Provides an activity to handle the actions needed before the given state is entered. This would enable the creation of any data or code needed to prepare for the state functioning.

The final group of activities are those that perform some action. You already saw this activity type in the form of the Code activity. These activities are the cornerstone of any workflow. The standard activities in this group include the following:

Activity	Description
Code	Enables custom Visual Basic code to be performed at a stage in the workflow. You can use these wherever you need to perform some action not done by another activity. Whenever you use one of these — especially if you use the same type of code frequently — you should consider moving the code into a custom activity.
Compensate	Enables custom code to undo a previous action. This is typically done if an error occurs within the workflow.
Delay	Pauses the flow of the workflow. This is typically used to schedule some event. For example, you might have a workflow that is responsible for printing a daily report. The Delay activity could be used to schedule this printout so that it is ready as the workers come in to read it. You can either set the delay explicitly by setting the `TimeoutDuration` property or set it via code using the event identified in the `InitializeTimeoutDuration` property.
Suspend	Temporarily stops the workflow. This is usually due to some extraordinary event that you would want an administrator or developer to correct. The workflow will continue to receive requests, but not complete them past the Suspend activity. The administrator may then resume the workflow to complete processing.
Terminate	Ends the workflow immediately. This should only be done in extreme situations such as when the workflow is not capable of any further processing (e.g., it has lost the connection to a database or other needed resource).
Throw	Creates an exception that can be caught by the code hosting the workflow. This provides a means of propagating an error from the workflow to the containing code.

Building Custom Activities

In addition to the standard activity library, WF supports extensibility through the creation of custom activities. Creating custom activities is a matter of creating a new class that inherits from `Activity` (or one of the existing child classes). Several available attributes enable the customization of the activity and how it appears when you use it in your workflows.

Creating custom activities is the primary means of extending WF. You might use custom activities to simplify a complex workflow, grouping a number of common activities into a single new activity. Alternatively, custom activities can create a workflow that is easier to understand, using terms that are more familiar to the developers and business experts. Finally, custom activities can be used to support software used within the business, such as activities to communicate with a CRM or ERP system.

To see the steps required for creating a custom activity, the next exercise creates a simple activity that wraps the Google translation service. Create a new project using the Workflow Activity Library template. This project will create a DLL that contains the activities you create. Name the project `TranslationActivity`. It will include a single custom activity initially. This activity inherits from `SequenceActivity`, so it might include multiple child activities. You can change this as needed, but it's a good enough default for most activities. Drag a Code activity onto the designer. This activity does the actual translation work. Alternately, you could change the top-level class to inherit from `Activity` and override the `Execute` method to perform the translation. Name the new activity `TranslateActivity`.

Because the new activity will be used to convert between a number of set language pairs, create an enumeration containing the valid options. This enumeration can be expanded as new options become available. You can either add this enumeration to a new class file or add it to the bottom of the current module (after the `End Class` statement):

```
Public Enum TranslationOptions As Integer
    EnglishToFrench
    EnglishToSpanish
    EnglishToGerman
    EnglishToItalian
    EnglishToRussian
    EnglishToChinese
    FrenchToEnglish
    SpanishToEnglish
    GermanToEnglish
    ItalianToEnglish
    RussianToEnglish
    ChineseToEnglish
End Enum
```

The new activity has three properties: the input text, a language pair that defines the source and target languages, and the output text (the latter being a read-only property). You can create properties normally in an activity, but it is beneficial to create them so that they participate in the workflow and are available to other activities. In order to do this, use the following pattern to describe your properties:

```
Public Shared SomeProperty As DependencyProperty = _
    DependencyProperty.Register("PropertyName", _
    GetType(ReturnType), _
    GetType(ClassName))
```

```
        Public Property PropertyName () As ReturnType
        Get
            Return CType(MyBase.GetValue(SomeProperty), _
                ReturnType)
        End Get
        Set(ByVal value As ReturnType)
            MyBase.SetValue(SomeProperty, value)
        End Set
    End Property
```

The initial shared field of type DependencyProperty identifies the field that will be used to communicate with other activities. DependencyProperty is a common type used in WPF programming, enabling easier communication between nested types. The Public property enables the more common use of the property. Notice that it stores the data in the shared property between all instances of the type.

As described, there are three properties in the translation activity:

```
Public Shared InputTextProperty As DependencyProperty = _
    DependencyProperty.Register("InputText", _
    GetType(System.String), _
    GetType(TranslateActivity))
Public Shared TranslationTypeProperty As DependencyProperty = _
    DependencyProperty.Register("TranslationType", _
    GetType(TranslationOptions), _
    GetType(TranslateActivity))
Public Shared OutputTextProperty As DependencyProperty = _
    DependencyProperty.Register("OutputText", _
    GetType(System.String), _
    GetType(TranslateActivity))

<DesignerSerializationVisibilityAttribute(DesignerSerializationVisibility.Visible)> _
    <BrowsableAttribute(True)> _
    <DescriptionAttribute("Text to be translated")> _
    Public Property InputText() As String
    Get
        Return CStr(MyBase.GetValue(InputTextProperty))
    End Get
    Set(ByVal value As String)
        MyBase.SetValue(InputTextProperty, value)
    End Set
End Property

<DesignerSerializationVisibilityAttribute(DesignerSerializationVisibility.Visible)> _
<BrowsableAttribute(False)> _
<DescriptionAttribute("Translated text")> _
Public ReadOnly Property OutputText() As String
    Get
        Return CStr(MyBase.GetValue(OutputTextProperty))
    End Get
End Property

<DesignerSerializationVisibilityAttribute(DesignerSerializationVisibility.Visible)> _
<BrowsableAttribute(True)> _
```

```
    <DescriptionAttribute("Language pair to use for the translation")> _
    Public Property TranslationType() As TranslationOptions
        Get
            Return CType(MyBase.GetValue(TranslationTypeProperty), TranslationOptions)
        End Get
        Set(ByVal value As TranslationOptions)
            MyBase.SetValue(TranslationTypeProperty, value)
        End Set
    End Property
```

Attributes are added to the properties to enable communication with the designer. The core translation method is assigned to the `ExecuteCode` property of the Code activity. It calls the Google translation service and extracts the result from the returned HTML:

```
Private Const SERVICE_URL As String = "http://translate.google.com/translate_t"

Private Sub Translate(ByVal sender As System.Object, _
    ByVal e As System.EventArgs)
    'uses Google's translation service to translate text
    '
    Dim req As String = _
        String.Format("hl=en&ie=UTF8&text={0}&langpair={1}", _
        Encode(Me.InputText), _
        BuildLanguageClause(Me.TranslationType))
    Dim client As New Net.WebClient
    Dim resp As String

    Try
        resp = client.UploadString(SERVICE_URL, req)
        If Not String.IsNullOrEmpty(resp) Then
            MyBase.SetValue(OutputTextProperty, _
                Decode(ExtractText(resp)))
        End If
    Catch ex As Exception
        Console.WriteLine("Error translating text: " & ex.Message)

    End Try

End Sub
```

A typical request to the Google translation service is performed using the service's Web page, available at `www.google.com/translate_t`. However, you can make the same type of request the Web page would, and parse the resulting HTML to extract the returned text. The request is made using a POST, to enable sending large blocks of text. For safety, the text is URL encoded using the `HttpUtility` class.

The routines used by the `Translate` method are as follows:

```
Private _langOptions As New List(Of String)()

Public Sub New()

    ' This call is required by the Windows Form Designer.
    InitializeComponent()
```

```vb
        ' Add any initialization after the InitializeComponent() call.
        _langOptions.Add("en|fr")
        _langOptions.Add("en|es")
        _langOptions.Add("en|de")
        _langOptions.Add("en|it")
        _langOptions.Add("en|zn-CH")
        _langOptions.Add("en|ru")
        _langOptions.Add("fr|en")
        _langOptions.Add("es|en")
        _langOptions.Add("de|en")
        _langOptions.Add("it|en")
        _langOptions.Add("ru|en")
        _langOptions.Add("zn-CH|en")

    End Sub

    Private Sub Translate(ByVal sender As System.Object, _
        ByVal e As System.EventArgs)
        'uses Google's translation service to translate text
        '
        Dim req As String = _
            String.Format("hl=en&ie=UTF8&text={0}&langpair={1}", _
            Encode(Me.InputText), _
            BuildLanguageClause(Me.TranslationType))
        Dim client As New Net.WebClient
        Dim resp As String

        Try
            resp = client.UploadString(SERVICE_URL, req)
            If Not String.IsNullOrEmpty(resp) Then
                MyBase.SetValue(OutputTextProperty, _
                    Decode(ExtractText(resp)))
            End If
        Catch ex As Exception
            Console.WriteLine("Error translating text: " & ex.Message)

        End Try

    End Sub

    Private Function Encode(ByVal value As String) As String
        Return Web.HttpUtility.UrlEncode(value)
    End Function
    Private Function Decode(ByVal value As String) As String
        Return Web.HttpUtility.HtmlDecode(value)
    End Function

    Private Function BuildLanguageClause( _
        ByVal languages As TranslationOptions) As String

        Dim result As String = String.Empty
        result = _langOptions.Item(languages)
        Return result
    End Function
```

```
Private Function ExtractText(ByVal value As String) As String
    Dim result As String = String.Empty
    Dim r As RegularExpressions.Regex
    Dim m As RegularExpressions.Match

    r = New RegularExpressions.Regex("<div?[^>]*>(?<result>[^<]*)</div", _
        RegularExpressions.RegexOptions.IgnoreCase Or _
        RegularExpressions.RegexOptions.Multiline Or _
        RegularExpressions.RegexOptions.IgnorePatternWhitespace)
    m = r.Match(value)
    If m IsNot Nothing Then
        result = m.Groups.Item("result").Value
    End If

    Return result
End Function
```

The _langOptions list is used to track the strings needed by the various language pairs. This is used by the BuildLanguageClause method to write the appropriate pair to the posted data. The order of the items in the TranslationOptions enumeration matches the order in which items are added to the list, so the BuildLanguageOptions method simply does a lookup into the list.

The ExtractText function uses a regular expression to extract the translated text. The translated text appears in a <div> tag within the resulting HTML. Fortunately, it is the only <div>, although you could modify the regular expression to look for a div with the id of result_box.

```
<div id=result_box dir=ltr>Bonne chance, Mandrin. Je pense que ceci pourrait juste
fonctionner </div>
```

The resulting activity can now be compiled and included in other workflows. Just as with custom controls, you can add this DLL to the Toolbox using the Choose Toolbox Items dialog after it has been compiled. If the Workflow Activity project is in the same solution as the workflow, it will be automatically added to the Toolbox after it has been compiled. Figure 25-11 shows the Translate activity added to the earlier example.

Recall that the Message field was used to store the message you wanted the workflow to generate. This is the text you want to translate. Click the ellipsis button on the InputText property in the property grid to bring up the Bind property dialog (see Figure 25-12). This enables you to visually connect the Message field to the input of the TranslateActivity.

The last change to the workflow is to update the text you output. Change the code for the SayGreetings method to display the OutputText of the TranslateActivity, as shown here:

```
Private Sub SayGreetings(ByVal sender As System.Object, _
    ByVal e As System.EventArgs)
    Console.WriteLine(Me.translateActivity1.OutputText & ", from workflow")
    Console.WriteLine("Press enter to continue")
    Console.ReadLine()
End Sub
```

Figure 25-11

Figure 25-12

Select the `TranslationType` and run the test project. Depending on the time of day and the language selected, you should see something similar to Figure 25-13.

Figure 25-13

Using Workflows with Other Applications

Workflows are not typically standalone applications, or run as part of a `Console` application, although this is an excellent way to develop them initially. Usually, workflows are created to work within some larger application, so you need to integrate your workflow with the rest of your application, whether it is a Windows Forms application or ASP.NET.

Using Workflow Foundation with Windows Forms

When combining WF with Windows Forms, there are three main points of contact: hosting (and starting) the workflow, setting parameters for the workflow, and getting data out of the workflow.

Recall that the workflow runs within a host process. This process may be the Windows Forms process itself or an external one. If the Windows Forms process is hosting the workflow, then the workflow only exists as long as the application is running. The alternative is a workflow hosted within a Windows Service or another Windows Forms application. In this case, your application needs to use some form of inter-process communication to communicate with the workflow. Typically, this would take the form of remoting between the two applications. Either way, the application that hosts the workflow needs to initialize the WF runtime, load the workflow, and start it. In addition, the workflow host may initialize event handlers for the events that the WF runtime will throw. The following code shows an example of hosting the WF runtime and loading a workflow:

```
Imports System.Workflow.Activities
```

```
Imports System.Workflow.ComponentModel
Imports System.Workflow.Runtime

Public Class MainForm

    Private WithEvents wr As WorkflowRuntime
    Private wf As WorkflowInstance

    Private Sub StartButton_Click(ByVal sender As System.Object, _
        ByVal e As System.EventArgs) Handles StartButton.Click

        If wr Is Nothing Then
            wr = New WorkflowRuntime()
            wr.StartRuntime()
        End If

        'load a new instance of the workflow
        wf = wr.CreateWorkflow(GetType(TranslatedWorkflowDLL.SimpleWorkflow))
        'Start the workflow
        wf.Start()

    End Sub

    Private Sub MainForm_FormClosing(ByVal sender As Object, _
        ByVal e As System.Windows.Forms.FormClosingEventArgs) _
        Handles Me.FormClosing

        If (wr IsNot Nothing) Then
            If (wr.IsStarted) Then
                wr.StopRuntime()
            End If
        End If
    End Sub
End Sub
```

In addition to the this, you have to load references to the three Workflow DLLs, and to the assembly that holds the workflow you want to create. Notice that you must create and start the WF runtime before you can load and start workflows. While the preceding code only creates a single instance of a workflow, you can create multiple instances from a single application. Stopping the runtime is not absolutely necessary, but gives you better control when the resources used by the WF runtime are freed.

The second step in working with WF and Windows Forms is providing parameters to the workflow. This is done by supplying a `Dictionary` when you create the workflow. The items in the `Dictionary` should match the public properties of the workflow. This changes the code used to create the workflow in the preceding sample as follows:

```
'load a new instance of the workflow
Dim parms As New Dictionary(Of String, Object)
parms.Add("Message", Me.MessageField.Text)
wf = wr.CreateWorkflow(GetType(TranslatedWorkflowDLL.SimpleWorkflow), parms)
```

By using a `Dictionary` with an `Object` value, any type of data can be supplied to the workflow. This provides flexibility in terms of the number and type of parameters you supply to the workflow, including changing the parameters over time.

The final step when working with WF and Windows Forms is retrieving data from the workflow. This is slightly more difficult than it may first seem because the workflow runs on a separate thread from the Windows Forms code. Therefore, the workflow can't directly access the controls on a form, and vice versa. The communication between the two is best performed by having the workflow generate events. The following code receives the `WorkflowCompleted` event and updates the `ListBox` on the form:

```
Private Sub wr_WorkflowCompleted(ByVal sender As Object, _
    ByVal e As System.Workflow.Runtime.WorkflowCompletedEventArgs) _
    Handles wr.WorkflowCompleted

    If Me. EventList.InvokeRequired Then
        Me. EventList.Invoke(New EventHandler(Of WorkflowCompletedEventArgs)( _
            AddressOf Me.wr_WorkflowCompleted), _
            New Object() {sender, e})
    Else
        Me.EventList.Items.Add("Translation: " & _
            e.OutputParameters("Message").ToString())
    End If

End Sub
```

Recall that the workflow runtime is actually running on a separate thread. Therefore, any attempts to access the `EventList` directly throw an exception. The first time through this code, the `InvokeRequired` property of the `EventList` is true. This means that the running code is executing on a separate thread. In this case, the code invokes a new instance of the event, passing in copies of the sender and `EventArgs`. This has the side effect of marshalling the data across to the thread containing the form. In this case, `InvokeRequired` is false, and you can retrieve the data from the workflow. Figure 25-14 shows the result.

Figure 25-14

Using Workflow Foundation with ASP.NET

Combining ASP.NET with Windows Workflow Foundation raises many of the same issues involved in using WF with other technologies. That is, you still need to host the services and the runtime of WF within the host process under which ASP.NET runs. However, developing solutions using ASP.NET offers more features and requires more decisions than other solutions. In particular, it is possible to publish workflows as ASP.NET Web Services. Hosting workflows within ASP.NET solutions is similar to hosting workflows with Windows Forms, with a difference being that an ASP.NET solution might actually be supporting multiple concurrent users. This means that you must be more aware of where the runtime is created and how instances are created and freed.

You can host a workflow as a Web Service if it has one or more `WebServiceInput` activities. This activity represents a SOAP endpoint. The `WebServiceInput` activity needs two properties set: `InterfaceType` and `MethodName`. Communication between the client code and the Web Service is achieved via a shared interface. This interface is the value needed for the `InterfaceType` property. It represents the contract between the client code and the `WebServiceInput` activity. The `MethodName` identifies the method on the interface that will initiate the Web Service call. The first `WebServiceInput` activity should have the `IsActivating` property set to true. In addition to the `WebServiceInput` activity, the workflow should also include a `WebServiceOutput` if the method includes a return value. Including a `WebServiceFault` activity is also useful if you need to return an error to the client code. If the Web Service has parameters or return values, these may be mapped to the properties of the workflow using the Bind property dialog (refer to Figure 25-12).

Once you have built the workflow including these activities (see Figure 25-15), you must publish it as a Web Service. This adds an additional ASP.NET Web Service project to the solution. The wizard creates the ASMX file that wraps the workflow and adds the required settings to the `web.config` file. The ASMX wrapper does nothing but delegate to the workflow class.

```
<%@WebService Class="TranslatedWorkflowDLL.SimpleWorkflow_WebService" %>
```

Figure 25-15

The additional settings in the configuration file add a new section for configuring the
WorkflowRuntime and load the workflow HTTP handler that translates the incoming request:

```
<?xml version="1.0"?>
<configuration>
  <configSections>
    <section name="WorkflowRuntime"
      type="System.Workflow.Runtime.Configuration.WorkflowRuntimeSection,
      System.Workflow.Runtime, Version=3.0.00000.0, Culture=neutral,
      PublicKeyToken=31bf3856ad364e35"/>
  </configSections>
  <WorkflowRuntime Name="WorkflowServiceContainer">
    <Services>
    <add type="System.Workflow.Runtime.Hosting.ManualWorkflowSchedulerService,
        System.Workflow.Runtime, Version=3.0.0.0, Culture=neutral,
        PublicKeyToken=31bf3856ad364e35"/>
    <add
      type="System.Workflow.Runtime.Hosting.DefaultWorkflowCommitWorkBatchService,
        System.Workflow.Runtime, Version=3.0.0.0, Culture=neutral,
        PublicKeyToken=31bf3856ad364e35"/>
    </Services>
  </WorkflowRuntime>
  <appSettings/>
  <connectionStrings/>
  <system.web>
    <httpModules>
      <add type="System.Workflow.Runtime.Hosting.WorkflowWebHostingModule,
        System.Workflow.Runtime, Version=3.0.0.0, Culture=neutral,
        PublicKeyToken=31bf3856ad364e35" name="WorkflowHost"/>
    </httpModules>
  </system.web>
</configuration>
```

The resulting Web Service works just like any other created by Visual studio: You can access it in a
browser to receive a test form (Figure 25-16), request the WSDL, and access it using Web Service clients.

Figure 25-16

Beyond Web Services, ASP.NET applications can also host and access regular workflows. When hosting workflows in ASP.NET, you must be aware of the fact that your application may be accessed by many concurrent users, so you must also be aware of when you create the runtime instance. In addition, remember that each workflow instance can use a good deal of memory. Therefore, limit the creation of workflows to when they are needed and free them quickly when they are no longer needed.

As you will probably want a single workflow runtime instance supporting all of your workflows, the best place to create the workflow runtime is when the application first starts. You can do this in the application's `Start` event in the `global.asax` file:

```
Sub Application_Start(ByVal sender As Object, ByVal e As EventArgs)
    Dim wfRun As New System.Workflow.Runtime.WorkflowRuntime
    Dim wfSked As _
      New System.Workflow.Runtime.Hosting.ManualWorkflowSchedulerService

    wfRun.AddService(wfSked)
    wfRun.StartRuntime()
    Application.Item("WorkflowRuntime") = wfRun
End Sub
```

This ensures that the same runtime is available to all sessions. In addition, free up the resources used by the runtime when the application ends:

```
Sub Application_End(ByVal sender As Object, ByVal e As EventArgs)
    Dim wfRun As System.Workflow.Runtime.WorkflowRuntime
    wfRun = CType(Application.Item("WorkflowRuntime"), _
        System.Workflow.Runtime.WorkflowRuntime)
    wfRun.StopRuntime()

End Sub
```

Running a workflow instance is now a matter of retrieving the runtime instance and using it to execute the workflow. This leads to another issue related to the way Web pages are handled. Recall that the workflow typically runs asynchronously. This could mean that the workflow instance continues to run in the background after the Web page has returned. Therefore, you must run the workflow instance synchronously, so that it completes before returning data to the Web page:

```
Dim wfRun As WorkflowRuntime
wfRun = CType(Application.Item("WorkflowRuntime"), WorkflowRuntime)

Dim wfSked As ManualWorkflowSchedulerService
wfSked = wfRun.GetService(GetType(ManualWorkflowSchedulerService))

Dim wfInst As WorkflowInstance
wfInst = wfRun.CreateWorkflow(GetType(SimpleWorkflow))
wfInst.Start()

wfSked.RunWorkflow(wfInst.InstanceId)
```

The preceding code extracts the workflow runtime from the `Application` storage. It then retrieves the workflow scheduling service that was associated with the runtime as part of the `Application_Start` event handler. This scheduling service executes the workflows synchronously. This ensures that the entire workflow runs before the Web page is returned. The runtime is also used to create a new instance of the workflow desired, which is then started and associated with the scheduler. You could provide parameters to the workflow just as you did with the Windows Forms sample, by creating a `Dictionary` and populating it with the properties. This `Dictionary` would then be provided as a second parameter on the `CreateWorkflow` call. Similarly, you could retrieve the result of the workflow using the `Output-Parameters` property in the `Completed` event handler for the workflow, just as you did with Windows Forms.

Summary

While Windows Workflow Foundation does not have the visual glitz of WPF or the broad reach of WCF, it is a highly useful addition to the .NET Framework 3.0. Most business applications have some need for workflow, and having a standard means of creating this workflow ensures that the workflow is fully featured and accurately reflects business needs. As WF is readily available with the .NET Framework, developers no longer need to recreate a core business rules engine with each application. WF is extensible, so developers can take advantage of it in their applications, without being limited to the designed features.

As with the other components of the .NET Framework, WF integrates well into other applications, including Windows Forms and ASP.NET applications. It provides the means to extract the frequently complex workflow from those applications, and to graphically design the workflow. This graphical representation can be used to communicate the process with business users, increasing the chance that the workflow is represented correctly. Finally, as the business needs change, it is a simple process to update the workflow, without requiring changes to the core application.

Resources

While Windows Workflow Foundation is a relatively new component of the .NET Framework, you can already find useful websites for information:

❑ Microsoft .NET Framework 3.0 Community (`http://wf.netfx3.com`).
The main community site for WF and the other frameworks added with .NET Framework 3.0. This site has a number of useful samples, custom activities, and forums available.

❑ WF on MSDN (`http://msdn.microsoft.com/workflow`).
Articles, documentation, and more assistance on the main MSDN site.

26

XML Web Services

This chapter begins with a short history of multi-tier architecture and network operating systems, a discussion of the early days of the network-as-the-computer, and a discussion of where system architecture is heading today. (The reason for this diversion is to understand the rationale behind Web Services.)

Next, this chapter looks at a sample Web Service, and walks through making it accessible to the Internet as well as accessing it from a client application — both with the Visual Studio IDE and using command-line tools. From there, the chapter moves on to a key feature of Web Services, the *Service Repository*, *Discovery*, and *Universal Description, Discovery, and Integration (UDDI)* features that enable remote programmers to correctly access Web Services.

Finally, the chapter delves into more in-depth topics during the discussion of the four namespaces found in the .NET Framework class library (`System.Web.Services`, `System.Web.Description`, `System.Web.Services.Discovery`, and `System.Web.Services.Protocols`) that deal with Web Services and how to utilize them with Visual Basic 2005. Moving on, the chapter discusses topics such as security, transactions, and the downsides of any distributed architecture (including any downsides associated with the Web Services model), followed by a short discussion of where you go from here and how you get there.

Introduction to Web Services

A Web Service is a means of exposing application logic or data via standard protocols such as XML, or, more specifically, SOAP (Simple Object Access Protocol). A Web Service comprises one or more functions, packaged together for use in a common framework throughout a network. This idea is illustrated in Figure 26-1, where Web Services provide access to information through standard Internet protocols, such as HTTP. By using a Web Services Description Language (WSDL) contract, consumers of the Web Service can learn about the structure of the data the Web Service provides, as well as all the details about how to actually consume it. A WSDL is a description of the remote interface offered from the Web Service.

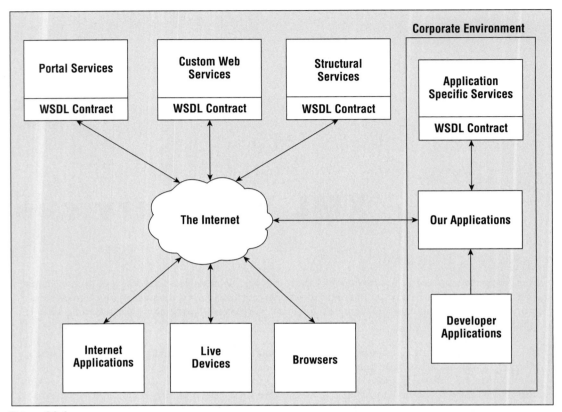

Figure 26-1

This simple concept provides for a very wide variety of potential uses by developers of Internet and intranet applications alike, as presented in Figure 26-1. Today, in many cases, the Web Services model is the heart of the next generation of systems architecture because they are all of the following:

❑ **Architecturally neutral** — Web services don't depend on a proprietary wire format, schema description, or discovery standard.

❑ **Ubiquitous** — Any service that supports the associated Web Service standards can support the service.

❑ **Simple** — Creating Web Services is easy, quick, and can be free. The data schema is human readable. Any programming language can participate.

❑ **Interoperable** — Because the Web Services all conform to the same standards, they can all speak to one another.

In basic terms, a Web Service is an object with an XML document describing all of the methods, properties, and events sitting between the code and the caller. Any body of code written in just about any programming language can be described with this XML document, and any application that understands XML (or SOAP) over the assigned protocol (such as HTTP) can access the object. That's because the parameters you type after the function name are passed via XML to the Web Service, and because SOAP is an open standard.

Microsoft has put a wrapper around all of the XML schemas that support Web Services (including SOAP and WSDL), so they end up looking like .NET or COM objects. The following sections look at how the world views a Web Service, and how Microsoft views Web Services.

Early Architectural Designs

An understanding of the history of the search for a decent *remote method invocation (RMI)* protocol is imperative to an understanding of why Web Services are so important. Each of the RMI systems created before the current Web Services model solved a particular set of problems, and you will see how current Web Services represent the next stage in the evolution of these cross-platform boundaries to solve the problems that former technologies tried to address.

The Network Angle

Throughout the history of computing, networking operations were largely handled by the operating system. UNIX, the networking host of early computing, featured a body of shell operations that provided remarkable user control over network operations. Personal computing was slower to catch up: Microsoft and Apple software didn't inherently support networking protocols until the mid-1990s. Third-party add-ons by Novell and Banyan were available earlier, but they were only an adjunct to the operating system. The concept of the network being the computer didn't fully infiltrate the development community until the expansion of the World Wide Web.

Application Development

Let's break away from networking for a minute and look at how application development progressed through this time. Early time-sharing operating systems enabled several people to use the same application with its built-in data. These single-tier systems didn't allow for growth in the system's size, and data redundancy became the standard, with nightly batch jobs to synchronize the data becoming commonplace through the 1970s and early '80s.

Eventually, the opportunity presented by networks became the overriding factor in systems development, and enterprise network developers began offering the loosely termed *Object Request Brokers (ORBs)* on their systems: Microsoft's *Transaction Server (MTS)*, *Common Object Request Broker Architecture (CORBA)*, and the like. These ORBs allowed for the separation of the user interface from the business logic using tightly coupled method pooling. This three-tier architecture brings you to the present in development terms, so let's step back and let networking catch up.

Merging the Two with the Web

The HTTP protocol was born in 1990. There had been several other information delivery protocols before, such as Gopher, but what made HTTP different were the extensibility of the related language, HTML, and the flexibility of the transport layer, TCP/IP. Suddenly, movement of many formats of data was possible in a stateless, distributed way. Software-as-a-service was born.

Over the next decade, low-level protocols supported by network systems and the Internet became a staple in applications, with SMTP and FTP providing file and information transfer among distributed servers. *Remote procedure calls (RPC)* took things to the next level, but they were platform specific, with UNIX implementations in CORBA and Microsoft's Distributed COM (DCOM) leading the pack.

Enterprise development took a clue from the emerging technologies in wide area network (WAN) networking and personal computing, and development for these large-scale business systems began to mature. As usage of networks grew, developers began to solve problems of scalability, reliability, and adaptability, with the traditional flat-format programming model. Multitier development began to spread the data, processing, and user interface of applications over several machines connected by local area networks (LANs).

This made applications more scalable and reliable by accommodating growth and providing redundancy. Gradually, vendor compliance and the Java programming language provided adaptability, enabling applications to run in a variety of circumstances on a variety of platforms.

However, there was a dichotomy between the capabilities of the network and the features of the programming environment. Specifically, after the introduction of XML, there still existed no "killer app" using its power. XML is a subset of Standard Generalized Markup Language (SGML), an international standard that describes the relationship between a document's content and its structure. It enables developers to create their own tags for hierarchical data transport in an HTML-like format. With HTTP as a transport and SOAP as a protocol, still needed was an interoperable, ubiquitous, simple, broadly supported system for the execution of business logic throughout the world of Internet application development.

The Foundations of Web Services

The hunt began with a look at the existing protocols. As had been the case for years, the Microsoft versus Sun Alliance debate was heating up among RPC programmers. CORBA versus DCOM was a source of continuing argument for developers using those platforms for distributed object development. After Sun added Remote Method Invocation to Java with Java-RMI, there were three distributed object protocols that fit none of the requirements.

Because DCOM and RMI are manufacturer-specific, it makes sense to start with those. CORBA is centrally managed by the Object Management Group, so it is a special case and should be considered separately.

RMI and DCOM provide distributed object invocation for their respective platforms — extremely important in this era of distributed networks. Both accommodate enterprisewide reuse of existing functionality, which dramatically reduces cost and time-to-market. Both provide encapsulated object methodology, preventing changes to one set of business logic from affecting another. Finally, similar to ORB-managed objects, maintenance and client weight are reduced by the simple fact that applications using distributed objects are by nature multitier.

DCOM

DCOM's best feature is the fact that it is based on COM, surely one of the most prevalent desktop object models in use today. COM components are shielded from one another, and calls between them are so well defined by the OS-specific languages that there is practically no overhead to the methods. Each

COM object is instantiated in its own space, with the necessary security and protocol providers. If an object in one process needs to call an object in another process, COM handles the exchange by intercepting the call and forwarding it through one of the network protocols.

When you use DCOM, all you are doing is making the wire a bit longer. With Windows NT4, Microsoft added the TCP/IP protocol to the COM network architecture and essentially made DCOM Internet-savvy. Aside from the setup on the client and server, the interobject calls are transparent to the client, and even to the programmer.

Any Microsoft programmer can tell you, though, that DCOM has its problems. First, there is a customer wire transport function, so most firewalls do not allow DCOM calls to get through, even though they are by nature quite benign. There is no way to query DCOM about the methods and properties available, unless you have the opportunity to get the source code or request the remote component locally. In addition, there is no standard data transfer protocol (though that is less of a problem because DCOM is mostly for Microsoft networks).

Remote Method Invocation in Java

RMI is Sun's answer to DCOM. Java relies on a really neat, but very proprietary, protocol called *Java Object Serialization*, which protects objects marshaled as a stream. The client and server both need to be constructed in Java for this to work, but it further simplifies RMI because Java doesn't care whether the serialization takes place on one machine or across a continent. Similarly to DCOM, RMI enables the object developer to define an interface for remote access to certain methods.

CORBA

CORBA uses Internet Inter-ORB Protocol to provide remote method invocation. It is remarkably similar to Java Object Serialization in this regard. Because it is only a specification, though, it is supported by a number of languages on diverse operating systems. With CORBA, the ORB does all the work, such as finding the pointer to the parent, instantiating it so that it can receive remote requests, carrying messages back and forth, and disputing arbitration and garbage collecting. The CORBA objects use specially designed sub-ORB objects called *basic* or *portable object adapters* to communicate with remote ORBs, giving developers more leeway in code reuse.

At first sight, it seems CORBA is your ace in the hole. There is only one problem — it doesn't really work that way. CORBA suffers from the same problem Web Browsers do — poor implementations of the standards, which causes lack of interoperability between ORBs. With IE and Netscape, minor differences in the way the pages display is written off as cosmetic. When there is a problem with the CORBA standard, however, it is a *real* problem. Not only are looks affected, but also network interactions, as if there were 15 different implementations of HTTP.

The Problems

The principal problem of the DCOM/CORBA/RMI methods is the complexity of the implementation. The transfer protocol of each of these is based on manufacturers' standards, generally preventing interoperability. In essence, the left hand has to know what the right hand is doing. This prevents a company using DCOM from communicating with a company using CORBA, emphasizing platform as a reason for doing business with one another.

First, there's the problem of wire format. Each of these three methods uses an OS-specific wire format that encompasses information supplied only by the operating system in question. The problem with this is that two diverse machines cannot usually share information. The benefit is security: Because the client and server can make assumptions about the availability of functionality, data security can be managed with API calls to the operating system.

The second problem is the number of issues associated with describing the format of the protocol. Apart from the actual transport layer, there must be a schema or layout for the data that moves back and forth. Each of the three contemporary protocols makes numerous assumptions between the client and server. DCOM, for instance, provides ADO/RDS for data transport, whereas RMI has JDBC. While we can endlessly argue the benefits of one over the other, we can at least agree that they don't play well together.

The third problem is knowing where to find broadly available services, even within your own network. We've all faced the problem of having to call up the COM+ MMC panel so that we could remember how to spell this component or that method. When the method is resident on a server ten buildings away and you don't have access to the MMC console, the next step is digging through the text documentation, if there is any.

The Other Players

On a path to providing these services, we stumble across a few other technologies. While *Java applets* and Microsoft's *client-side ActiveX* technically aren't distributed object invocations, they do provide distributed computing and provide important lessons. Fortunately, we can describe both in the same section because they are largely the same, with different operating systems as their backbone.

Applets and client-side ActiveX are both attempts to use the HTTP protocol to send thick clients to the end user. In circumstances where a user can provide a platform previously prepared to maintain a thicker-than-HTML client base to a precompiled binary, the ActiveX and Applet protocols pass small applications to the end user, usually running a Web browser. These applications are still managed by their servers, at least loosely, and usually provide custom data transmission, utilizing the power of the client to manage the information distributed, as well as display it.

This concept was taken to the extreme with *Distributed Applet-Based Massively Parallel Processing*, a strategy that used the power of the Internet to complete processor-intense tasks such as 3-D rendering or massive economic models with a small application installed on the user's computer. If you view the Internet as a massive collection of parallel processors, sitting mostly unused, you have the right idea. An example of this type of processing is provided by United Devices (www.ud.com).

In short, HTTP can provide distributed computing. The problem is that the tightly coupled connection between the client and server has to go, given the nature of today's large enterprises. The HTTP angle did show developers that using an industry-recognized transport method solved problem number one, wire format. Using HTTP meant that regardless of the network, the object could communicate. The client still had to know a lot about the service being sent, but the network didn't.

The goal? *Distributed Object Invocation Meets the World Wide Web.* The problems are wire format, protocol, and discovery. The solution is a standards-based, loosely coupled method invocation protocol with a huge catalog. Microsoft, IBM, and Ariba set out in 1999 to create just that, and generated the RFC for Web Services.

What All the Foundations Missed

You may notice that in reviewing the majority of the earlier services there has been little mention of language. This is because it was a problem overlooked by the foundations. Even RMI didn't recognize the reality that you can't make everyone use the same language, even a great language.

HTTP — A Language-Independent Protocol

What we need is a language-independent protocol that accommodates a standard wire transfer, protocol language, and catalog service. Java with Remote Scripting and ActiveX taught us that HTTP is the wire transfer of choice. Why? What does HTTP do that is so great? First, it is simple. The header added to a communication by HTTP is straightforward enough that power users can type it at a command prompt if they have to. Second, it doesn't require a special data protocol; it just uses ASCII text. Another reason is that HTTP traffic can easily get through firewalls (port 80 is usually open). Finally, it is extensible. Additional headers can be added to the HTTP header for application-specific needs, and any intermediary software can just ignore it.

XML — Cross-Language Data Markup

Now that we have a standard wire transfer protocol that we know works, we need a language and a transport mechanism. Existing languages don't really have data description functions, aside from the data management object models such as ADO. XML fits the bill because it is self-describing. There's no need for the left hand to know what the right hand is doing. An XML file transported over HTTP doesn't need to know the answering system's network protocol or its data description language. The concepts behind XML are so light and open that everyone can agree to support them. In fact, almost everyone has. XML has become the ASCII of the Web.

XML is important to Web Services because it provides a universal format for information to be passed from system to system. We knew that, but Web Services actually uses XML as the object invocation layer, changing the input and output to tightly formatted XML, making it platform and language independent.

SOAP — The Transfer You Need

Enter Simple Object Access Protocol (SOAP), which uses HTTP to package essentially one-way messages from service to service in such a way that business logic can interpolate a request/response pair. In order for your Web page to get an example, a SOAP request would look something like this:

```
POST /Directory HTTP/1.1
Host: Ldap.companyname.com
Content-Type: text/xml; charset="utf-8"
Content-Length: 33
SOAPAction: "Some-URI"\vs

<SOAP-ENV:Envelope
 xmlns:SOAP-ENV="http://schemas.xmlsoap.org/soap/envelope/"
 SOAP-ENV:encodingStyle="http://schemas.xmlsoap.org/soap/encoding/">
 <SOAP-ENV:Body>
   <m:FindPerson xmlns:m="Some-URI">
     <NAME>Gates</NAME>
   </m: FindPerson>
 </SOAP-ENV:Body>
</SOAP-ENV:Envelope>
```

This is an HTTP page request, just like one you'd see for an HTML page except that the `Content-Type` specifies XML, and there is the addition of the `SOAPAction` header. SOAP has made use of the two most powerful parts of HTTP: content neutrality and extensibility. Here is the response statement from the server:

```
HTTP/1.1 200 OK
Content-Type: text/xml;
charset="utf-8"
Content-Length: 66

<SOAP-ENV:Envelope
 xmlns:SOAP-ENV="http://schemas.xmlsoap.org/soap/envelope/"
 SOAP-ENV:encodingStyle="http://schemas.xmlsoap.org/soap/encoding/"/>
  <SOAP-ENV:Body>
    <m:FindPersonResponse xmlns:m="Some-URI">
     <DIRECTORY>Employees
     <PERSON>
        <NAME>Bill Gates</NAME>
        <FUNCTION>Architect
           <TYPE>Web Services</TYPE>
        </FUNCTION>
        <CONTACT>
           <PHONE TYPE=CELL>123-456-7890</PHONE>
           <PHONE TYPE=HOME>555-111-2222</PHONE>
        </CONTACT>
     </PERSON>
     </DIRECTORY>
    </m: FindPersonResponse >
  </SOAP-ENV:Body>
</SOAP-ENV:Envelope>
```

SOAP enables you to send the XML files back and forth among remote methods. It is similar to XML-RPC, a protocol developed by Dave Winer in parallel with the SOAP protocol. Both protocols provide similar structures, but it is the official SOAP protocol that is used by Visual Basic and the entire .NET platform.

SOAP isn't specific to .NET, either. The SOAP Toolkit is another set of tools that Microsoft's Web Services Team provides free of charge. It contains a wonderful WSDL editor, retrofit objects for Windows 2000 and Windows NT4 servers, and more. You can find it at `http://msdn.microsoft.com/webservices`.

Web Services Description Language

A Web Services Description Language (WSDL) document is a set of definitions that is utilized to describe the interface of any of your Web Services. Six elements are defined and used by the SOAP protocol: `types`, `message`, `portType`, `binding`, `port`, and `service`. Essentially adding another layer of abstraction, the purpose of WSDL is to isolate remote method invocations from their wire transport and data definition language. Once again, it is a specification, not a language, so it is much easier to get companies to agree to its use.

Because WSDL is just a set of descriptions in XML, it is not so much a protocol as a grammar. Following is the sample service contract for the `HelloWorld` Web Service you'll be building shortly. You can see this file by visiting `http://localhost/HelloWorldExample/Service.asmx?WSDL` using your Web browser after you create the examples:

```xml
<?xml version="1.0" encoding="utf-8" ?>
<wsdl:definitions xmlns:soap="http://schemas.xmlsoap.org/wsdl/soap/"
 xmlns:tm="http://microsoft.com/wsdl/mime/textMatching/"
 xmlns:soapenc="http://schemas.xmlsoap.org/soap/encoding/"
 xmlns:mime="http://schemas.xmlsoap.org/wsdl/mime/"
 xmlns:tns="http://localhost/webservice" xmlns:s="http://www.w3.org/2001/XMLSchema"
 xmlns:soap12="http://schemas.xmlsoap.org/wsdl/soap12/"
 xmlns:http="http://schemas.xmlsoap.org/wsdl/http/"
 targetNamespace="http://localhost/webservice"
 xmlns:wsdl="http://schemas.xmlsoap.org/wsdl/">
    <wsdl:types>
        <s:schema elementFormDefault="qualified"
         targetNamespace="http://localhost/webservice">
            <s:element name="HelloWorld">
                <s:complexType />
            </s:element>
            <s:element name="HelloWorldResponse">
                <s:complexType>
                    <s:sequence>
                        <s:element minOccurs="0" maxOccurs="1" name="HelloWorldResult"
                         type="s:string" />
                    </s:sequence>
                </s:complexType>
            </s:element>
        </s:schema>
    </wsdl:types>
    <wsdl:message name="HelloWorldSoapIn">
        <wsdl:part name="parameters" element="tns:HelloWorld" />
    </wsdl:message>
    <wsdl:message name="HelloWorldSoapOut">
        <wsdl:part name="parameters" element="tns:HelloWorldResponse" />
    </wsdl:message>
    <wsdl:portType name="WebServiceSoap">
        <wsdl:operation name="HelloWorld">
            <wsdl:input message="tns:HelloWorldSoapIn" />
            <wsdl:output message="tns:HelloWorldSoapOut" />
        </wsdl:operation>
    </wsdl:portType>
    <wsdl:binding name="WebServiceSoap" type="tns:WebServiceSoap">
        <wsdl:documentation>
            <wsi:Claim conformsTo="http://ws-i.org/profiles/basic/1.0"
             xmlns:wsi="http://ws-i.org/schemas/conformanceClaim/" />
        </wsdl:documentation>
        <soap:binding transport="http://schemas.xmlsoap.org/soap/http"
         style="document" />
        <wsdl:operation name="HelloWorld">
            <soap:operation soapAction="http://localhost/webservice/HelloWorld"
             style="document" />
            <wsdl:input>
                <soap:body use="literal" />
            </wsdl:input>
```

```
            <wsdl:output>
                <soap:body use="literal" />
            </wsdl:output>
        </wsdl:operation>
    </wsdl:binding>
    <wsdl:binding name="WebServiceSoap12" type="tns:WebServiceSoap">
        <soap12:binding transport="http://schemas.xmlsoap.org/soap/http"
          style="document" />
        <wsdl:operation name="HelloWorld">
            <soap12:operation soapAction="http://localhost/webservice/HelloWorld"
              style="document" />
            <wsdl:input>
                <soap12:body use="literal" />
            </wsdl:input>
            <wsdl:output>
                <soap12:body use="literal" />
            </wsdl:output>
        </wsdl:operation>
    </wsdl:binding>
    <wsdl:service name="WebService">
        <wsdl:port name="WebServiceSoap" binding="tns:WebServiceSoap">
            <soap:address location="http://localhost:40718/Reuters/WebService.asmx" />
        </wsdl:port>
        <wsdl:port name="WebServiceSoap12" binding="tns:WebServiceSoap12">
            <soap12:address
              location="http://localhost:40718/Reuters/WebService.asmx" />
        </wsdl:port>
    </wsdl:service>
</wsdl:definitions>
```

This is what makes it all work. Notice that each of the inputs and outputs of the `HelloWorldResponse` function is defined as an element in the schema. The .NET Framework uses this to build library files that understand how best to format the outgoing requests, so no matter what operating system develops the WSDL, as long as it is well formed according to the WSDL specification, any type of application (it doesn't necessarily need to be a .NET application) can consume it with a simple SOAP request.

In fact, IIS with the .NET Framework is set up to use the WSDL document in order to provide a great auto-generated user interface for developers and consumers to check out and test Web Services. After removing the `?wsdl` from the preceding URL, you'll see a very nicely formatted documentation screen for the service. Click the function name and you'll get the screen shown in Figure 26-2. This is all dynamically generated based upon the contents of the WSDL document, which is itself dynamically generated by .NET.

The WSDL document can also be expanded in order to define your own descriptions. You can use the `Description` property of both the `WebService()` and `WebMethod()` attributes to provide more details for this .NET-generated test page for your XML Web Services.

Building a Web Service

Building Web Services with Visual Studio 2005 is *incredibly* easy. Microsoft has made it a cakewalk to put together a new Web Service application and expose methods off that Web Service.

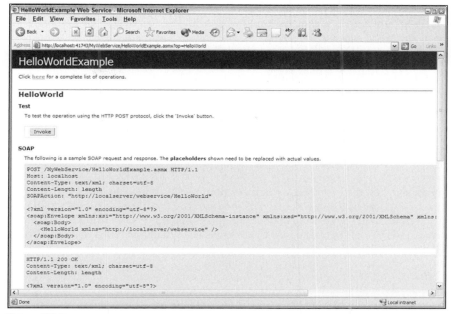

Figure 26-2

To get started, create an ASP.NET Web Service application. Find this option by clicking File ⇨ New ⇨ Web Site in Visual Studio. From there, Visual Studio will ask you for the location of the Web server. Enter this as `C:\Documents and Settings\Bill\My Documents\Visual Studio 2005\WebSites\ HelloWordExample`.

Unlike an ASP.NET Web Application project, Visual Studio creates an `.asmx` file, rather than an `.aspx` file. The `.asmx` file extension is short for Active Server Methods, derived from the fact that it contains methods that will be exposed through the Web Service.

By default, Visual Studio creates the Web Service using the code-behind model for the Web Service page. In addition to the `.asmx` file, Visual Studio also creates a `Service.vb` file and places this file in the `App_Code` folder of the project.

Open the `Service.asmx` file in Visual Studio. It contains only the `WebService` page directive, as shown here:

```
<%@ WebService Language="VB" CodeBehind="~/App_Code/Service.vb"
    Class="Service" %>
```

You use the `@WebService` directive instead of the `@Page` directive. The simple `WebService` directive has only four possible attributes:

❑   `Class` — Required. It specifies the class used to define the methods and datatypes visible to the XML Web Service clients.

❏   CodeBehind — Required only when you are working with an XML Web Service file using the code-behind model. It enables you to work with Web Services in two separate and more manageable pieces instead of a single file. The CodeBehind attribute takes a string value that represents the physical location of the second piece of the Web Service — the class file containing all the Web Service logic. In ASP.NET 2.0, it is best to place the code-behind files in the App_Code folder, starting with the default Web Service created by Visual Studio when you initially opened the Web Service project.

❏   Debug — Optional. It takes a setting of either True or False. If the Debug attribute is set to True, the XML Web Service is compiled with debug symbols in place; setting the value to False ensures that the Web Service is compiled without the debug symbols in place.

❏   Language — Required. It specifies the language used for the Web Service.

Instead of focusing on the Service.asmx page, double-click on the Service.vb file to open the file in the document window of Visual Studio. With the Service.vb file in the document window, notice that the single method on the page is decorated with the <WebMethod()> attribute. This attribute (System.Web.Services.WebMethodAttribute) is used to tell ASP.NET to expose this particular method through the Web Service.

Directly after the WebServiceBinding attribute, place the WebService attribute in code to define a custom namespace, which the industry recommends you always provide. The value of the namespace can be whatever you see fit; it doesn't have to be an actual URL, just a unique identifier:

```
Imports System.Web
Imports System.Web.Services
Imports System.Web.Services.Protocols

<WebService(Namespace:="http://localhost/HelloWorldExample")> _
<WebServiceBinding(ConformsTo:=WsiProfiles.BasicProfile1_1)> _
<Global.Microsoft.VisualBasic.CompilerServices.DesignerGenerated()> _
Public Class Service
    Inherits System.Web.Services.WebService

    <WebMethod()> _
    Public Function HelloWorld() As String
        Return "Hello World"
    End Function

End Class
```

Now add a new method called GoodbyeWorld, without a WebMethod attribute:

```
Public Function GoodbyeWorld() As String
  Return "Goodbye World"
End Function
```

Run the project. Visual Studio will open the Service.asmx file. By default, Web Services display a test interface (see Figure 26-3) that enables you to see which methods are available and execute them.

Figure 26-3

Notice that only the `HelloWorld()` method is displayed. This is the only method decorated with the `WebMethod` attribute; and hence the reason why `GoodbyeWorld()` and all of the inherited methods on the `Service` class were not displayed. Clicking the link enables you to invoke the method, as shown in Figure 26-4.

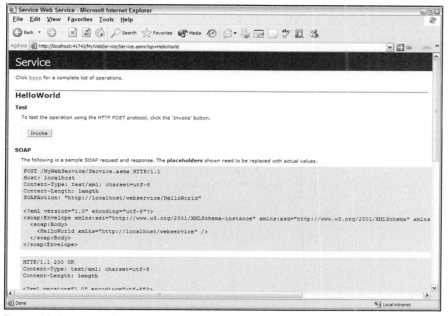

Figure 26-4

If you do this, the URL `http://localhost:#####/HelloWorldExample/Service.asmx/HelloWorld?` is requested, which happens to be the URL for this specific method (running with the built-in Web Server provided with Visual Studio). You'll then see the payload of the SOAP document directly in the browser, which contains the results of the call, as illustrated in Figure 26-5.

Figure 26-5

That's pretty much all there is to Web Services from an implementation perspective when working with the .NET Framework. The .NET Framework deals with all of the plumbing (SOAP, WSDL, and so on) discussed in the first part of this chapter on your behalf, so you only have to add properly decorated methods to the service.

A Realistic Example

Although the previous example was very easy to implement, it doesn't demonstrate a real-world application of Web Services. Let's take a look at a more realistic example by building a Web Service that sends out a richer set of data from a database instead. For this example, imagine that a third-party provider hosts the site. The SQL server is behind a firewall, and the IIS server is in a demilitarized zone — a safe, though exposed, network position, as shown in Figure 26-6.

To get the data from your site to the remote site, you need to call a Web Service on the remote Web server from your intranet. The SOAP envelope is sent via HTTP, so the firewall allows it to pass through, and ADO.NET on the IIS server handles the actual database manipulation. The remote firewall allows database calls only from the IIS server, and the data is updated safely because of the security.

In real life, the method GetEmployees() would be local to your intranet server, and the database file would be a SQL server on a second server. Across the Internet, as shown in Figure 26-6, the Web Service would be on an IIS server sitting outside the network firewall. The DLL that actually provides the data functions would be on an application server inside the firewall, and the database would again be on a separate server.

For this application, though, you need to create a Web Service that exposes some of the Contact table, as well as some of the Employee table, from the sample AdventureWorks database, across the intranet, that will later be consumed by a Web application. Keep in mind that Web Services not only expose simple values, but also a richer data set of values such as entire tables from a datastore (for example, SQL Server).

Start this example by first creating a new Web Service project in Visual Studio called WebService1.

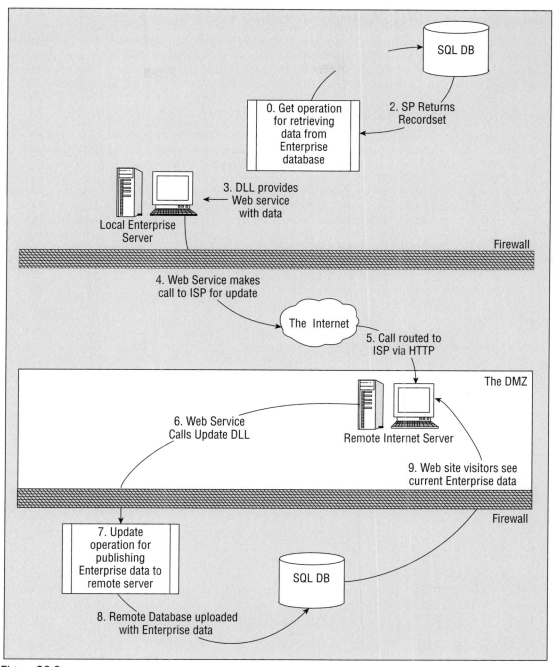

SQL DB

0. Get operation for retrieving data from Enterprise database

2. SP Returns Recordset

3. DLL provides Web service with data

Local Enterprise Server

Firewall

4. Web Service makes call to ISP for update

The Internet

5. Call routed to ISP via HTTP

The DMZ

6. Web Service Calls Update DLL

Remote Internet Server

9. Web site visitors see current Enterprise data

Firewall

7. Update operation for publishing Enterprise data to remote server

SQL DB

8. Remote Database uploaded with Enterprise data

Figure 26-6

Using Visual Studio 2005 to Build Web Services

The Visual Studio 2005 IDE shows a marked improvement from the add-ins provided for Visual Studio 6 in the SOAP Toolkit. For instance, Web Services are shown as references on a project, rather than in a separate dialog box. The discovery process, discussed later, is used to its fullest, providing much more information to the developer. In short, it is nearly as easy to consume a Web Service with Visual Basic as it is to use DLLs.

Producing a Typed DataSet

For simplicity, you'll use Visual Studio to first create a typed `DataSet`, which will be returned from the `WebMethod` that you later produce. This IDE enables you to quickly and easily create the needed data access without having to dig through a lot of ADO.NET code.

Right-click the `WebService1` project in the Solution Explorer and select Add New Item. From the provided menu of file options, select `DataSet`. Change the name of this file to `MyDataComponent.xsd`. This creates an already strongly typed `DataSet` on-the-fly. In addition, Visual Studio requests to place this file in the `App_Code` folder of your solution. Confirm this request, because having it in the `App_Code` folder allows for programmatic access to the `DataSet` (see Figure 26-7).

Figure 26-7

Once created, the `MyDataComponent.xsd` file opens itself in Visual Studio. This file appears as a blue screen in the document window, with a single `DataTable` on its design surface. Along with the file, the TableAdapter Configuration Wizard also opens, as shown in Figure 26-8.

The first step in the TableAdapter Configuration Wizard is establishing a data connection. If a connection is not already in place, create one by clicking the New Connection button. Using this dialog, make a new connection to the sample `AdventureWorks_Data.mdf` database, which is a SQL Server Express Edition database file. You can find this and other SQL Server 2005 samples online on the MSDN website (`http://msdn.microsoft.com`) under the title of SQL Server 2005 Samples and Sample Databases (July 2006).

Once the connection is in place, you can move the database file to your project and store the connection in the `web.config` file. Choosing both of these actions will copy the `AdventureWorks_Data.mdf` database file to the `App_Data` folder in your project, and the connection to this database file will now be named and placed within the `web.config` file of your ASP.NET Web Service project.

```
<connectionStrings>
   <add name="AdventureWorks_DataConnectionString"
    connectionString="Data Source=.\SQLEXPRESS;AttachDbFilename=|DataDirectory|
       \AdventureWorks_Data.mdf;Integrated Security=True;Connect Timeout=30;
       User Instance=True"
    providerName="System.Data.SqlClient" />
</connectionStrings>
```

Figure 26-8

Once the connection to the datastore is established, click the Next button. In the dialog that appears, pick the command type that you want to work with. Typically, the options are working with either direct SQL commands, existing stored procedures, or stored procedures that you can create directly in the wizard. For this example, choose the first option: Use SQL Statements.

The next page in the wizard asks for the query that you want to use to load the table data. Input the following:

```
SELECT HumanResources.Employee.EmployeeID, HumanResources.Employee.Title,
    HumanResources.Employee.Gender,
    HumanResources.Employee.HireDate, Person.Contact.Title AS EXPR1,
    Person.Contact.FirstName, Person.Contact.MiddleName,
    Person.Contact.LastName, Person.Contact.EmailAddress, Person.Contact.Phone
FROM Person.Contact INNER JOIN
    HumanResources.Employee ON Person.Contact.ContactID =
        HumanResources.Employee.ContactID
```

Clicking the Next button results in a page from which you can select the methods that the wizard will generate (as shown in Figure 26-9). These are the methods used in your Web Service to load data into data sets for transmission. In this case, the `Fill()` and `GetData()` methods are specified with the first two options in the dialog. In some cases, you might want to also select the last check box, which creates the additional `Insert()`, `Update()`, and `Delete()` methods that you might want to later expose via a Web Service. When you are done, click the Next button again to proceed to the next step in the TableAdapter Configuration Wizard.

Figure 26-9

Figure 26-10 shows the last page of the wizard. This final page just shows the results of all the actions taken in the preceding steps.

Figure 26-10

After clicking the Finish button, note that the design surface of the `MyDataComponent.xsd` file changes to reflect the data that comes from the two tables of the `AdventureWorks` database (see Figure 26-11).

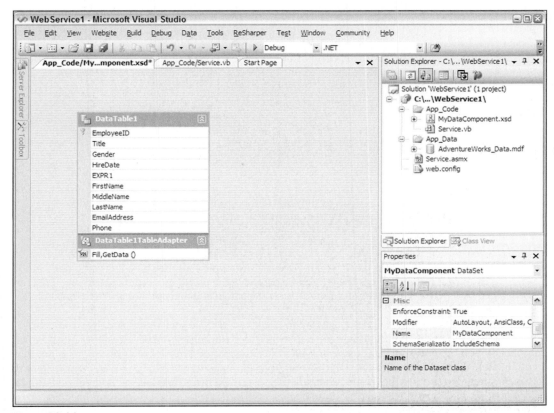

Figure 26-11

At this point, your typed data set is now in place and ready for use by the Web Service. Looking at the results on the design surface of the `.xsd` file, you can see that indeed the typed `MyDataComponent` data set is in place and contains a single `DataTable` called `DataTable1`. In addition to this there is also a `DataTable1TableAdapter` object with `Fill()` and `GetData()` methods in place.

Building the Service

Right-click `Service.asmx` from within Solution Explorer in Visual Studio and select View Code. Rename the `HelloWorld()` function to `GetEmployees()`. From here, simply retrieve data from the `DataTable1TableAdapter` that was created when you created the `.xsd` file earlier:

```
Imports System.Web
Imports System.Web.Services
Imports System.Web.Services.Protocols
```

```
<WebService(Namespace:="http://www.lipperweb.com/namespace")> _
<WebServiceBinding(ConformsTo:=WsiProfiles.BasicProfile1_1)> _
<Global.Microsoft.VisualBasic.CompilerServices.DesignerGenerated()> _
Public Class Service
    Inherits System.Web.Services.WebService

    <WebMethod()> _
    Public Function GetEmployees() As MyDataComponent.DataTable1DataTable
        Dim da As New MyDataComponentTableAdapters.DataTable1TableAdapter
        Dim ds As New MyDataComponent.DataTable1DataTable

        da.Fill(ds)

        Return ds
    End Function
End Class
```

Right-click the `Service.asmx` file in Solution Explorer and select View in Browser. If there are no errors, a simple screen listing `GetEmployees` as the sole method of the service appears. Click the Service Description line. You'll get a screen like the one shown earlier in Figure 26-2.

Consuming the Service

Although the Web Service is in place, you really have seen only half the story. Exposing data and logic as SOAP to disparate systems across the enterprise or across the world is a simple task using .NET, and particularly ASP.NET. The other half of the story is the actual consumption of an XML Web Service into another application.

It is important to understand that you are not limited to consuming Web Services only into ASP.NET applications, as shown shortly. Consuming Web Services into other types of applications is not that difficult; in fact, it is rather similar to how you would consume them using ASP.NET. Remember that the Web Services you come across can be consumed in Window Forms, Windows Presentation Foundation applications, mobile applications, other databases, and more. You can even consume Web Services with other Web Services, resulting in a single Web Service made up of what is basically an aggregate of other Web Services.

For this consuming application, provide a Web application called WSEmployees by creating a new ASP.NET Web Site project with that name. For this example, create this new project within your current solution: Right-click on the WebService1 solution and select Add ➪ New Web Site from the menu. Once complete, your solution will now contain a project called WebService1 and another called WSEmployees. The first step to take within your WSEmployees project is to create a Web reference to the remote XML Web Service that was created in the WebService1 project.

Adding a Web Reference

The only bit of magic here is the adding of a Web reference to the project using the Visual Studio IDE. As described later, you are really creating a proxy based upon the WSDL file of the service and referencing the proxy in the project, but the IDE makes this all quite simple.

To create the proxy needed by the consuming application, right-click the WSCustomers project in the Solution Explorer and select Add Web Reference from the list of options. In this form, enter the WSDL file of the Web Service to which you want to make a reference. If the Web Service is a .NET Web Service (with an .asmx file extension), simply input the URL of the .asmx file and nothing more because the wizard automatically adds ?wsdl at the end of the input. If you are referencing a Java Web Service, then place the URL for the .wsdl file in this wizard. In most cases, you would simply enter the URL of the service you are interested in consuming in the address bar of the Add Web Reference dialog. For this example, click the "Web Services found at this URL" link. The dialog box should appear as shown in Figure 26-12.

Figure 26-12

The service description page you see when you build your service appears in the left pane of the wizard, with .NET-specific information in the right. Click the Add Reference button at the right of the window to add this reference to your project. The service appears in a new folder within the Solution Explorer called Web References, as shown in Figure 26-13.

In making the reference, you can see that the .wsdl file was copied over, as well as the typed DataSet, MyDataComponent. The power of this Web Services model is that it can work with the GetEmployees() method as if it were now local to your machine, when in fact it is hosted in an entirely different application.

Figure 26-13

Building the Consumer

The COM architecture continually promised "one line of code" to generate great results. Web Services live up to the promise, minus the declarations. Now the only thing left to do is call the referenced Web Service and pass the generated `DataTable` that comes from the `DataSet`. Compared to the scores of lines of XML needed to pass the `DataSet` in the existing Microsoft technologies, this is a breeze.

The first step to consuming an `.aspx` page is simply to make a reference to the proxy that Visual Studio created and then call the `GetEmployees()` WebMethod through this instantiated object. The results pulled from the `GetEmployees()` method are then displayed in a `GridView` control, which is placed on a Web form.

You have a couple of ways to achieve this. The first method is to use an `ObjectDataSource` control, which does the work of invoking the `GetEmployees()` WebMethod and then displaying the results in the `GridView` control. (The second method, discussed a bit later, is to manually write the required code.) To work through this example, drop a `GridView` and an `ObjectDataSource` server control onto the design surface of the Web Form. Open the smart tag of the `ObjectDataSource` control and select Configure Data Source. You are then presented with the Configure Data Source Wizard.

In the first page of this wizard, uncheck the Show Only Data Components check box and select `local-host.Service` from the drop-down list. Click the Next button to choose the SELECT method for that `ObjectDataSource` control to use (shown in Figure 26-14).

Figure 26-14

From the drop-down list on this page of the wizard, select `GetEmployees()`, `returns` `DataTable1DataTable` and click Finish to progress to the next step of binding the `GridView` control to the returned `DataTable` from this `ObjectDataSource` control.

Now, turn your attention to the `GridView` control. In configuring this control, open the control's smart tag. From the drop-down list, select `ObjectDataSource1` as the data source control for this control. Note that once you do this, the `GridView` control expands to include all the appropriate columns from the result set you specified earlier from the `AdventureWorks` database.

Now, in the same smart tag, enable paging by selecting the appropriate check boxes. The code generated by Visual Studio is shown here:

```
<%@ Page Language="VB" AutoEventWireup="false" CodeFile="Default.aspx.vb"
    Inherits="_Default" %>

<!DOCTYPE html PUBLIC "-//W3C//DTD XHTML 1.0 Transitional//EN"
  "http://www.w3.org/TR/xhtml1/DTD/xhtml1-transitional.dtd">

<html xmlns="http://www.w3.org/1999/xhtml" >
<head runat="server">
    <title>Consuming Application</title>
</head>
<body>
```

```
<form id="form1" runat="server">
<div>
    <asp:GridView ID="GridView1" runat="server" AllowPaging="True"
     AutoGenerateColumns="False"
     DataKeyNames="EmployeeID" DataSourceID="ObjectDataSource1">
        <Columns>
            <asp:BoundField DataField="EmployeeID" HeaderText="EmployeeID"
             InsertVisible="False"
             ReadOnly="True" SortExpression="EmployeeID" />
            <asp:BoundField DataField="Title" HeaderText="Title"
             SortExpression="Title" />
            <asp:BoundField DataField="Gender" HeaderText="Gender"
             SortExpression="Gender" />
            <asp:BoundField DataField="HireDate" HeaderText="HireDate"
             SortExpression="HireDate" />
            <asp:BoundField DataField="EXPR1" HeaderText="EXPR1"
             SortExpression="EXPR1" />
            <asp:BoundField DataField="FirstName" HeaderText="FirstName"
             SortExpression="FirstName" />
            <asp:BoundField DataField="MiddleName" HeaderText="MiddleName"
             SortExpression="MiddleName" />
            <asp:BoundField DataField="LastName" HeaderText="LastName"
             SortExpression="LastName" />
            <asp:BoundField DataField="EmailAddress" HeaderText="EmailAddress"
             SortExpression="EmailAddress" />
            <asp:BoundField DataField="Phone" HeaderText="Phone"
             SortExpression="Phone" />
        </Columns>
    </asp:GridView>
    <asp:ObjectDataSource ID="ObjectDataSource1" runat="server"
     SelectMethod="GetEmployees"
     TypeName="localhost.Service"></asp:ObjectDataSource>
</div>
</form>
</body>
</html>
```

Once the page is complete, build and run it. That's it. There is now a table in the Web form with all the data from a remote SQL Server Express Edition file that can be paged — and you didn't have to write *any* code to achieve this functionality! The page results are shown in Figure 26-15.

Now consider doing the same thing but instead spending a little time writing some code. This is a good move because it offers more control over the situation (if desired), and it teaches you more about what is going on.

Create a page that includes only a GridView server control. From here, you get at the data that comes from the Web Service in the Page_Load event. This is illustrated in the following example:

```
<%@ Page Language="VB" %>

<script runat="server">
    Sub Page_Load(ByVal sender As Object, ByVal e As System.EventArgs)
```

```
        Dim ws As New localhost.Service

        GridView1.DataSource = ws.GetEmployees()
        GridView1.DataBind()
    End Sub
</script>

<html xmlns="http://www.w3.org/1999/xhtml" >
<head runat="server">
    <title>Consuming Application</title>
</head>
<body>
    <form id="form1" runat="server">
    <div>
        <asp:GridView ID="GridView1" Runat="server"
         AllowPaging="True" AllowSorting="True">
        </asp:GridView>
    </div>
    </form>
</body>
</html>
```

EmployeeID	Title	Gender	HireDate	EXPR1	FirstName	MiddleName	LastName	EmailAddress	Phone
1	Production Technician - WC60	M	7/31/1996 12:00:00 AM		Guy	R	Gilbert	guy1@adventure-works.com	320-555-0195
2	Marketing Assistant	M	2/26/1997 12:00:00 AM		Kevin	F	Brown	kevin0@adventure-works.com	150-555-0189
3	Engineering Manager	M	12/12/1997 12:00:00 AM		Roberto		Tamburello	roberto0@adventure-works.com	212-555-0187
4	Senior Tool Designer	M	1/5/1998 12:00:00 AM		Rob		Walters	rob0@adventure-works.com	612-555-0100
5	Tool Designer	M	1/11/1998 12:00:00 AM		Thierry	B	D'Hers	thierry0@adventure-works.com	168-555-0183
6	Marketing Manager	M	1/20/1998 12:00:00 AM		David	M	Bradley	david0@adventure-works.com	913-555-0172
7	Production Supervisor - WC60	F	1/26/1998 12:00:00 AM		JoLynn	M	Dobney	jolynn0@adventure-works.com	903-555-0145
8	Production Technician - WC10	F	2/6/1998 12:00:00 AM		Ruth	Ann	Ellerbrock	ruth0@adventure-works.com	145-555-0130
9	Design Engineer	F	2/6/1998 12:00:00 AM	Ms.	Gail	A	Erickson	gail0@adventure-works.com	849-555-0139
10	Production Technician - WC10	M	2/7/1998 12:00:00 AM		Barry	K	Johnson	barry0@adventure-works.com	206-555-0180

1 2 3 4 5 6 7 8 9 10 ...

Figure 26-15

The first line of code contained in the `Page_Load` event instantiates the proxy object that was created for you. The next line assigns the `DataSource` property of the `GridView` server control to the result set from the `GetEmployees()` WebMethod call. Finally, close everything by calling the `DataBind()` method of the `GridView` control. By compiling and running the XML Web Service, you can retrieve from the database the view of the Employees table that you created earlier from the `AdventureWorks` database. A returned dataset contains a wealth of information, including the following:

❑   An XSD definition of the XML contained in the `DataSet`

❑   The employee information from the Employees table of the AdventureWorks database

On the consumption side, consumers of this XML Web Service can easily use the XSD definition and the XML contained within the `DataTable` within their own applications. If consumers are then consuming this `DataTable` into .NET applications, they can easily bind this data to a `GridView` and use it within their applications with minimal lines of code.

Overloading WebMethods

In the object-oriented world of .NET, it is quite possible to use method overloading in the code you develop. A true object-oriented language has support for *polymorphism*, of which method overloading is a part. Method overloading enables you to have multiple methods that use the same name but have different signatures. With method overloading, one method can be called, but the call is routed to the appropriate method based on the full signature of the request. An example of standard method overloading is illustrated in the following code listing:

```
Public Function HelloWorld() As String
    Return "Hello"
End Function

Public Function HelloWorld(ByVal FirstName As String) As String
    Return "Hello " & FirstName
End Function
```

In this example, both methods have the same name, `HelloWorld`. Which one is called when you invoke `HelloWorld` depends on the signature you pass to the method. For instance, you might provide the following:

```
Label1.Text = HelloWorld()
```

This yields a result of just `Hello`. However, you might invoke the `HelloWorld()` method using the following signature:

```
Label1.Text = HelloWorld("Bill Evjen")
```

This returns a result of `Hello Bill Evjen`. As you can see, method overloading is a great feature that can be effectively utilized by your ASP.NET applications — but how do you go about overloading `WebMethods`?

If you have already tried to overload any of your WebMethods, you probably got the following error when you pulled up the Web Service in the browser:

```
Both System.String HelloWorld(System.String) and System.String HelloWorld() use the
message name 'HelloWorld'. Use the MessageName property of the WebMethod custom
attribute to specify unique message names for the methods.
```

As this error states, the extra step you have to take to overload WebMethods is to use the MessageName property. The following bit of code shows how:

```
<WebMethod(MessageName:="HelloWorld")> _
Public Function HelloWorld() As String
    Return "Hello"
End Function

<WebMethod(MessageName:="HelloWorldWithFirstName")> _
Public Function HelloWorld(ByVal FirstName As String) As String
    Return "Hello " & FirstName
End Function
```

In addition to adding the MessageName property of the WebMethod attribute, you have to disable your Web Service's adherence to the WS-I Basic Profile 1.0 specification — which it wouldn't be doing if you perform WebMethod overloading with your Web Services. You can disable conformance to the WS-I Basic Profile specification in a couple of ways. The first way is to add the <WebServiceBinding> attribute to your code, as illustrated here:

```
<WebServiceBinding(ConformsTo := WsiProfiles.None)> _
Public Class MyOverloadingExample
    ' Code here
End Class
```

The other option is to turn off the WS-I Basic Profile 1.0 capability in the web.config file, as shown in the following bit of code:

```
<configuration>
  <system.web>
    <webServices>
      <conformanceWarnings>
        <remove name="BasicProfile1_1" />
      </conformanceWarnings>
    </webServices>
  </system.web>
</configuration>
```

After you have enabled your Web Service to overload WebMethods, you can see both WebMethods defined by their MessageName value properties when you pull up the Web Service's interface test page in the browser (see Figure 26-16).

Figure 26-16

Although the names of the WebMethods are distinct (based on the MessageName property values you assigned in your code through the Web Service's test page), when the developer consuming the Web Service makes a Web reference to your Web Service, he or she sees only a single method name available (in this example, HelloWorld). This is shown in the IntelliSense of Visual Studio 2005 in the application consuming these methods (see Figure 26-17).

```vb
<%@ Page Language="VB" %>

<!DOCTYPE html PUBLIC "-//W3C//DTD XHTML 1.1//EN" "http://www.w3.org/TR/xhtml1

<script runat="server">
    Sub Page_Load(ByVal sender As Object, ByVal e As System.EventArgs)
        Dim ws As New WroxOverloading.Overloading()
        ws.HelloWorld(
    End       ▲ 2 of 2 ▼  HelloWorld (FirstName As String) As String
</script>

<html xmlns="http://www.w3.org/1999/xhtml" >
<head runat="server">
    <title>Overloading WebMethods</title>
</head>
<body>
    <form id="form1" runat="server">
    <div>
        <asp:Label ID="Label1" Runat="server" Text="Label"></asp:Label>

    </div>
    </form>
</body>
</html>
```

Figure 26-17

In the yellow box that pops up to guide developers on the signature structure, two options are available — one is an empty signature, and the other requires a single string.

Caching Web Service Responses

Caching is an important feature in almost every application that you build with .NET. Although many features in the .NET Framework provide different vehicles for caching, a feature of Web Services in .NET enables you to cache the SOAP response sent to any of the service's consumers.

First, by way of review, remember that caching is the capability to maintain an in-memory store where data, objects, and various items are stored for reuse. This feature increases the responsiveness of the applications you build and manage. Sometimes, returning cached results can greatly affect performance.

XML Web Services use an attribute to control caching of SOAP responses — the CacheDuration property. The following bit of code shows its use:

```
<WebMethod(CacheDuration:=60)> _
Public Function GetServerTime() As String
    Return DateTime.Now.ToLongTimeString()
End Function
```

As you can see, CacheDuration is used within the WebMethod attribute much like the Description and Name properties. CacheDuration takes an Integer value that is equal to the number of seconds during which the SOAP response is cached.

When the first request comes in, the SOAP response is cached by the server, and the consumer gets the same timestamp in the SOAP response for the next minute. After that minute is up, the stored cache is discarded, and a new response is generated and stored in the cache again for servicing all other requests for the next minute.

Among the many benefits of caching your SOAP responses, you will find that your application's performance is greatly improved when you have a response that is repeatedly re-created without any change.

SOAP Headers

One of the more common forms of extending the capabilities of SOAP messages is to add metadata of the request to the SOAP message itself. The metadata is usually added to a section of the SOAP envelope called the *SOAP header*. Figure 26-18 shows the structure of a SOAP message.

```
Soap Envelope

Soap Header

Soap Body
```

Figure 26-18

The entire SOAP message is referred to as a *SOAP envelope*. Contained within the SOAP message is the *SOAP body* — a piece of the SOAP message that you have been working with in every example thus far. It is a required element of the SOAP message.

The one optional component of the SOAP message is the SOAP header. It is the part of the SOAP message in which you can place any metadata about the overall SOAP request instead of incorporating it in the signature of any of your WebMethods. It is important to keep metadata separate from the actual request.

What kind of information does it contain? It could include a lot of things. One of the more common items placed in the SOAP header is any authentication/authorization functionality required to consume your Web Service or to get at specific pieces of logic or data. Usernames and passwords are good examples of what you might include inside the SOAP headers of your messages.

Building a Web Service with SOAP Headers

You can build upon the sample HelloWorld Web service presented in the default .asmx page when it is first pulled up in Visual Studio. Name the new .asmx file HelloSoapHeader.asmx. First, add a class that is an object representing what is to be placed in the SOAP header by the client, as shown in the following example:

```
Public Class HelloHeader
    Inherits System.Web.Services.Protocols.SoapHeader

    Public Username As String
    Public Password As String
End Class
```

The class, representing a SOAP header object, has to inherit from the SoapHeader class from System.Web.Services.Protocols.SoapHeader. The SoapHeader class serializes the payload of the <soap:header> element into XML for you. In this example, the SOAP header requires two elements — a username and a password, both of type String. The names you create in this class are those used for the sub-elements of the SOAP header construction, so it is important to name them descriptively.

The following code shows the Web Service class that instantiates an instance of the HelloHeader class:

```
<WebService(Namespace:="http://www.wrox.com/helloworld")> _
<WebServiceBinding(ConformsTo:=WsiProfiles.BasicProfile1_1, _
  EmitConformanceClaims:=True)> _
Public Class HelloSoapHeader
    Inherits System.Web.Services.WebService

    Public myHeader As HelloHeader

    <WebMethod(), SoapHeader("myHeader")> _
    Public Function HelloWorld() As String
        If (myHeader Is Nothing) Then
            Return "Hello World"
        Else
            Return "Hello " & myHeader.Username & ". " & _
                "<br>Your password is: " & myHeader.Password
```

```
        End If
    End Function

End Class
```

The Web Service, `HelloSoapHeader`, has a single `WebMethod` — `HelloWorld`. Within the Web Service class, but outside of the `WebMethod` itself, create an instance of the `SoapHeader` class:

```
Public myHeader As HelloHeader
```

Now that you have an instance of the `HelloHeader` class that you created earlier called `myHeader`, you can use that instantiation in your `WebMethod`. Because Web Services can contain any number of `WebMethod`s, it is not necessary for all `WebMethod`s to use an instantiated SOAP header. You specify whether a `WebMethod` uses a particular instantiation of a SOAP header class by placing the `SoapHeader` attribute before the `WebMethod` declaration:

```
<WebMethod(), SoapHeader("myHeader")> _
Public Function HelloWorld() As String
    ' Code here
End Function
```

Here, the `SoapHeader` attribute takes a `string` value of the name of the instantiated `SoapHeader` class — in this case, `myHeader`.

The `WebMethod` actually makes use of the `myHeader` object. If the `myHeader` object is not found (meaning the client did not send a SOAP header with the constructed SOAP message), a simple "`Hello World`" is returned. However, if values are provided in the SOAP header of the SOAP request, those values are used in the returned `string` value.

Consuming a Web Service Using SOAP Headers

It isn't difficult to build an ASP.NET application that makes a SOAP request to a Web Service using SOAP headers. As with the Web Services that don't include SOAP headers, you make a Web reference to the remote Web Service directly in Visual Studio.

For the ASP.NET page, create a simple page with a single `Label` control. The output of the Web Service is placed in this control. Following is the code for the ASP.NET page:

```
<%@ Page Language="VB" %>

<script runat="server">
    Protected Sub Page_Load(ByVal sender As Object, ByVal e As System.EventArgs)
        Dim ws As New localhost.HelloSoapHeader()
        Dim wsHeader As New localhost.HelloHeader()

        wsHeader.Username = "Bill Evjen"
        wsHeader.Password = "Bubbles"
        ws.HelloHeaderValue = wsHeader

        Label1.Text = ws.HelloWorld()
    End Sub
```

```
    </script>

    <html xmlns="http://www.w3.org/1999/xhtml" >
    <head runat="server">
        <title>Working with SOAP headers</title>
    </head>
    <body>
        <form id="form1" runat="server">
        <div>
            <asp:Label ID="Label1" Runat="server"></asp:Label>
        </div>
        </form>
    </body>
    </html>
```

Two objects are instantiated. The first is the actual Web Service, HelloSoapHeader. The second, which is instantiated as wsHeader, is the SoapHeader object. After both of these objects are instantiated and before making the SOAP request in the application, you construct the SOAP header. This is as easy as assigning values to the Username and Password properties of the wsHeader object. After these proper-ties are assigned, you associate the wsHeader object to the ws object through the use of the HelloHeaderValue property. After you have made the association between the constructed SOAP header object and the actual WebMethod object (ws), you can make a SOAP request, just as you would normally do:

```
    Label1.Text = ws.HelloWorld()
```

Running the page produces the result shown in Figure 26-19.

Figure 26-19

Note that the SOAP request reveals that the SOAP header was indeed constructed into the overall SOAP message, as shown in the following SOAP request:

```
    <?xml version="1.0" encoding="utf-8" ?>
    <soap:Envelope xmlns:soap="http://schemas.xmlsoap.org/soap/envelope/"
     xmlns:xsi="http://www.w3.org/2001/XMLSchema-instance"
     xmlns:xsd="http://www.w3.org/2001/XMLSchema">
```

```
    <soap:Header>
      <HelloHeader xmlns="http://www.wrox.com/helloworld/">
        <Username>Bill Evjen</Username>
        <Password>Bubbles</Password>
      </HelloHeader>
    </soap:Header>
    <soap:Body>
      <HelloWorld xmlns="http://www.wrox.com/helloworld/" />
    </soap:Body>
</soap:Envelope>
```

This returns the SOAP response shown here:

```
<?xml version="1.0" encoding="utf-8" ?>
<soap:Envelope xmlns:soap="http://schemas.xmlsoap.org/soap/envelope/"
 xmlns:xsi="http://www.w3.org/2001/XMLSchema-instance"
 xmlns:xsd="http://www.w3.org/2001/XMLSchema">
    <soap:Body>
      <HelloWorldResponse xmlns="http://www.wrox.com/helloworld/">
        <HelloWorldResult>Hello Bill Evjen. Your password is:
          Bubbles</HelloWorldResult>
      </HelloWorldResponse>
    </soap:Body>
</soap:Envelope>
```

Requesting Web Services Using SOAP 1.2

Most Web Services use SOAP version 1.1 for the construction of their messages. However, SOAP 1.2 became a W3C Recommendation in June 2003 (see www.w3.org/TR/soap12-part1/). The nice thing about XML Web Services in the .NET Framework 2.0 platform is that they are capable of communicating in both the 1.1 and 1.2 versions of SOAP.

In an ASP.NET application that is consuming a Web Service, you can control whether the SOAP request is constructed as a SOAP 1.1 message or a 1.2 message. The next example changes the previous example to use SOAP 1.2 instead of the default setting of SOAP 1.1:

```
<%@ Page Language="VB" %>

<script runat="server">
    Protected Sub Page_Load(ByVal sender As Object, ByVal e As System.EventArgs)
        Dim ws As New localhost.HelloSoapHeader()
        Dim wsHeader As New localhost.HelloHeader()

        wsHeader.Username = "Bill Evjen"
        wsHeader.Password = "Bubbles"
        ws.HelloHeaderValue = wsHeader

        ws.SoapVersion = System.Web.Services.Protocols.SoapProtocolVersion.Soap12

        Label1.Text = ws.HelloWorld()
    End Sub
</script>
```

This example first provides an instantiation of the Web Service object and uses the new `SoapVersion` property. The property takes a value of `System.Web.Services.Protocols.SoapProtocolVersion.Soap12` to work with SOAP 1.2 specifically. With this bit of code in place, the SOAP request takes the structure shown here:

```xml
<?xml version="1.0" encoding="utf-8"?>
<soap:Envelope xmlns:soap="http://www.w3.org/2003/05/soap-envelope"
 xmlns:xsi="http://www.w3.org/2001/XMLSchema-instance"
 xmlns:xsd="http://www.w3.org/2001/XMLSchema">
    <soap:Header>
        <HelloHeader xmlns="http://www.wrox.com/helloworld/">
            <Username>Bill Evjen</Username>
            <Password>Bubbles</Password>
        </HelloHeader>
    </soap:Header>
    <soap:Body>
        <HelloWorld xmlns="http://www.wrox.com/helloworld/" />
    </soap:Body>
</soap:Envelope>
```

One difference between the two examples is the `xmlns:soap` namespace that is used. The difference actually resides in the HTTP header. Comparing the SOAP 1.1 and SOAP 1.2 messages, you can see a difference in the `Content-Type` attribute. In addition, the SOAP 1.2 HTTP header does not use the `soapaction` attribute because this is now combined with the `Content-Type` attribute.

You can turn off either SOAP 1.1 or SOAP 1.2 capabilities with the Web Services that you build by making the proper settings in the `web.config` file, as illustrated here in this snippet of configuration code:

```xml
<configuration xmlns="http://schemas.microsoft.com/.NetConfiguration/v2.0">
    <system.web>
        <webServices>
            <protocols>
                <remove name="HttpSoap"/> <!-- Removes SOAP 1.1 abilities -->
                <remove name="HttpSoap1.2"/> <!-- Removes SOAP 1.2 abilities -->
            </protocols>
        </webServices>
    </system.web>
</configuration>
```

Visual Basic and System.Web.Services

The SOAP Toolkit provides a number of wizards to navigate most of the obstacle course required to set up a Web Service, but the .NET Framework class library provides the abstract classes. The `System.Web.Services` namespace provides four classes and three other namespaces that enable programmatic exposure of methods to the Web.

System.Web.Services Namespace

The `System.Web.Services` namespace includes the following component classes:

❑   WebService

❏   WebMethodAttribute

❏   WebServiceAttribute

❏   WebServicesBindingAttribute

The WebService class is the base class from which all the ASP.NET services are derived, and it includes access to the public properties for Application, Context, Server, Session, Site, and User. ASP programmers will recognize these objects from the ASP namespace. Web Services can access the IIS object model from the WebService class, including application-level variables:

```
Imports System.Web
Imports System.Web.Services
Imports System.Web.Services.Protocols

<WebService(Namespace:="http://www.lipperweb.com/namespace")> _
<WebServiceBinding(ConformsTo:=WsiProfiles.BasicProfile1_1)> _
Public Class Util
    Inherits System.Web.Services.WebService

   <WebMethod(Description:="Application Hit Counter", EnableSession:=False)> _
   Public Function HitCounter() As String

      Dim HitCounter As Integer

      If (Application("HitCounter") Is DBNull.Value) Then
         Application("HitCounter") = 1
      Else
         Application("HitCounter") = Application("HitCounter") + 1
      End If

      HitCounter = Application("HitCounter")

      Return HitCounter

   End Function

End Class
```

WebService is an optional base class, used only if access to ASP.NET objects is desired. The WebMethodAttribute class, however, is a necessity if the class needs to be available over the Web.

The WebServiceAttribute class is similar to the WebMethodAttribute class in that it enables the addition of the description string to an entire class, rather than method by method. We recommend adding it before the previous class declaration:

```
<WebService(Description:="Common Server Variables")> _
Public Class ServerVariables
    Inherits System.Web.Services.WebService
```

Instead of using WSDL in the contract to describe these services, the System.Web.Services namespace provides programmatic access to these properties. IIS Service Discovery uses these descriptions when queried. This way, you have removed the necessity to struggle with myriad protocols surrounding Service Contract Language and SOAP.

System.Web.Services.Description Namespace

The `System.Web.Services.Description` namespace provides a host of classes that provide total management of the WSDL descriptions for your Web Service. This object manages every element in the WSDL schema as a class property.

For example, the preceding discussion on the benefits of WSDL description mentioned the benefits of being able to query a Web Service about its methods and parameters. The `System.Web.Services.Description` namespace provides methods for the discovery of methods and parameters, gathering the information from the service contract and providing it to the object model in Visual Basic code.

When working on the HTTP GET protocol (as opposed to SOAP, for instance), simply pass in the required `sEmail` parameter through the use of a `querystring`. You can find details about this in the Web Service's WSDL description. In the successive `<wsdl:message>` sections, you find all parameter info for all three protocols, including HTTP GET (if enabled via the `web.config` file):

```
<wsdl:message name="IsValidEmailHttpGetIn">
    <wsdl:part name="sEmail" type="s:string" />
</wsdl:message>
<wsdl:message name="IsValidEmailHttpGetOut">
    <wsdl:part name="Body" element="tns:boolean" />
</wsdl:message>
```

Invoking this Web Service using HTTP GET, use the following construct:

```
http://localserver/Validate.asmx?sEmail=evjen@yahoo.com
```

Note that HTTP GET is disabled by default because it is deemed a security risk. If you wish to enable HTTP GET for your XML Web Services, then configure it for this in the `web.config` file of your Web Service solution, as shown here:

```
<configuration>
   <system.web>
      <webServices>
         <protocols>
            <add name="HttpGet"/>
         </protocols>
      </webServices>
   </system.web>
</configuration>
```

System.Web.Services.Discovery Namespace

The `System.Web.Services.Discovery` namespace provides access to all of the wonderful features of the `.disco` files on a dynamic basis. Because Microsoft is currently trying to integrate Web Services as a remoting protocol and is not pushing the public service side as much, you don't see the use of `.disco` files as often in the Microsoft side of things. Your business partner might be using them, though, so this namespace proves useful. For instance, you can access the `DiscoveryDocument` using the `Discovery` class:

```
Imports System.Web.Services.Discovery
```

```
ReadOnly Property DiscoveryDocument(strURL As String) As DiscoveryDocument
    Get
        DiscoveryDocument = DiscoveryClientProtocol.Discover(strURL)
    End Get
End Property
```

Like the `System.Web.Services.Description` namespace, the `System.Web.Services.Discovery` namespace provides many tools to build a `.disco` document on-the-fly.

System.Web.Services.Protocols Namespace

All of the wire service problems solved with HTTP and SOAP are handled in the `System.Web.Services.Protocols` namespace. When handling references to classes also referenced in other Web Service namespaces, the `System.Web.Services.Protocols` namespace proves to be a handy tool. The objects referenced by the `System.Web.Services.Protocols` namespace include the following (among others):

❑   Cookies per RFC 2019

❑   HTML forms

❑   HTTP request and response

❑   MIME

❑   Server

❑   SOAP, including `SoapException`, the only error-handling mechanism

❑   URIs and URLs

❑   XML

The `System.Web.Services.Protocols` namespace is particularly handy for managing the connection type by a client. A consumer of a Web Service can use the HTTP GET or HTTP POST protocol to call a service, as well as the HTTP SOAP protocol. Microsoft's .NET initiative focuses on SOAP as the ultimate means of connecting disparate data sources. The `System.Web.Services.Protocols.SoapDocumentMethodAttribute` class enables developers to set special attributes of a public method for when a client calls it using SOAP:

```
Imports System.Web
Imports System.Web.Services
Imports System.Web.Services.Protocols

<WebService(Namespace:="http://www.lipperweb.com/namespace")> _
<WebServiceBinding(ConformsTo:=WsiProfiles.BasicProfile1_1)> _
Public Class Util
    Inherits System.Web.Services.WebService

  <SoapDocumentMethod(Action:="http://MySoapMethod.org/Sample", _
    RequestNamespace:="http://MyNamespace.org/Request", _
    RequestElementName:="GetUserNameRequest", _
    ResponseNamespace:="http://MyNamespace.org/Response", _
    ResponseElementName:="GetUserNameResponse")> _
```

```
    WebMethod(Description:="Obtains the User Name")> _
    Public Function GetUserName()
        '...
    End Function

End Class
```

Architecting with Web Services

Web Services impart two remarkable benefits to users — one rather obvious, the other less so. First, they replace common binary RPC formats, such as DCOM, CORBA, and RMI. Because these use a proprietary communication protocol, they are significantly less architecturally flexible than Web Services. As devices utilize more and more of the Internet, platform neutrality will be a great advantage.

Less obvious but more important, Web Services will be used to transfer structured business communications in a secure manner, potentially ending the hold that sterling has on the Electronic Data Interchange (EDI) market. HTTPS with 128-bit SSL can provide the security necessary for intracompany information transfer. Furthermore, Microsoft has recently (as of this writing) released Web Services Enhancements 3.0 (WSE), as well as the Windows Communication Foundation (WCF), which enables you to easily use WS-Security and other advanced protocols to apply credentials, encryption, and digital signing to your SOAP messages in an easy and straightforward manner.

Why Web Services?

So, why Web Services? Well, they are remarkably easy to deploy with Visual Basic. The key to remoting with Web Services is the WSDL contract — written in the dense WSDL protocol you saw earlier. IIS 5.0, 6.0, and 7.0 does that in conjunction with the .NET Framework, analyzing the VB code and dynamically generating the WSDL code for the contract.

In addition, Web Services are inherently cross-platform, even when created with Microsoft products. Yes, you've heard this before, but so far this seems to be true. The standard XML schemas are centrally managed, and IBM mostly built the WSDL specification, so Microsoft seems to have toed the line on this one.

Finally, they best represent where the Internet is heading — toward an architecturally neutral collection of devices, rather than millions of PCs surfing the World Wide Web. Encapsulating code so that you can simply and easily allow cell phones to use your logic is a major boon to developers, even if they don't know it yet.

How This All Fits Together

Note that Web Services are not a feature of the .NET Framework per se. In fact, Web Services run fine on Windows NT4 SP6, with the SOAP Toolkit installed. You can do most anything you are doing here with VB6 and IIS 4.0.

However, the .NET Framework encapsulates the Web Service protocol into objects. It is now an integrated part of the strategy, rather than an add-on. If you are currently working in a VB6 environment, take a look at the SOAP Toolkit (downloadable from MSDN at `http://msdn.microsoft.com/`

webservices), and understand that the services you build are available not only to different flavors of Windows, but also to IBM and Sun platforms.

The goal of Web Services is to provide a loosely coupled, ubiquitous, universal information exchange format. Toward that end, SOAP is not the only mechanism for communicating with Web Services — the HTTP GET and HTTP POST protocols are also supported by the .NET Framework. Response is via HTTP, just like normal RPCs with SOAP. This enables legacy Web applications to make use of Web Services without the benefit of the .NET Framework.

State Management for XML Web Services

The Internet is *stateless* by nature. Many of the techniques used for managing state in ASP.NET Web applications are the same techniques you can use within the XML Web Services built on the .NET platform. Remember that XML Web Services are part of the ASP.NET model, and both application types have the same objects at their disposal.

Therefore, just like an ASP.NET application, XML Web Services can also use the `Application` object or the `Session` object. These sessions can also be run in the same process as the XML Web Service application itself — out of process, using the .NET `StateServer`, or by storing all the sessions within SQL Server.

To use sessions within XML Web Services built on the .NET platform, you must turn on this capability within the `WebMethod` attribute by using the `EnableSession` property. By default, the `EnableSession` property is set to `False`, so to use the `HTTPSessionState` object, set this property to `True`, as shown here:

```
Imports System.Web
Imports System.Web.Services
Imports System.Web.Services.Protocols

<WebService(Namespace:="http://www.lipperweb.com/namespace")> _
<WebServiceBinding(ConformsTo:=WsiProfiles.BasicProfile1_1)> _
Public Class Service
    Inherits System.Web.Services.WebService

   <WebMethod(EnableSession:=True)> _
   Public Function SessionCounter() As Integer
      If Session("Counter") Is Nothing Then
         Session("Counter") = 1
      Else
         Session("Counter") = CInt(Session("Counter")) + 1
      End If

      Return CInt(Session("Counter"))
   End Function

End Class
```

The `EnableSession` property goes directly in the parentheses of the `WebMethod` declaration. This property takes a Boolean value and needs to be set to `True` in order to work with the `Session` object.

Security in Web Services

Opening up a procedure call to remoting makes applications vulnerable to accidents, poor end-user implementation, and crackers. Any application design needs to include some level of security. Web Services demand the inclusion of security.

Security problems with Web Services fall into two categories — interception and unauthorized use. SOAP messages intercepted by crackers potentially expose private information, such as account numbers and passwords, to the public. Unauthorized use at best costs money and at worst wreaks havoc within a system.

Very few of the concepts discussed here are things we would like to see in the hands of those wearing the black hats. Even the simple validation service handles e-mail addresses — a valuable commodity in this world of "opt in" spamming. If you add social security or account numbers to the service, then this becomes even more of a concern. Fortunately, the wire transport of choice — HTTPS — provides a 128-bit solution.

In addition, as mentioned earlier, by using Microsoft's Web Services Enhancements (WSE) and the Windows Communication Foundation capabilities, you now can easily apply security standards such as WS-Security to your SOAP messages.

The Secure Sockets Layer

The Secure Sockets Layer, or SSL, is a protocol consumed by HTTP in the transfer of Internet data from the Web server to the browser. On the Web, the process works like this:

1. The user calls a secure Web document, and a unique public key is generated for the client browser, using the server's root certificate.
2. A message encrypted with the server's public key is sent from the browser.
3. The server can decrypt the message using its private key.

The protocol in the URI represents how HTTP would appear if it were changed to HTTPS:

```
<address uri="https://aspx.securedomains.com/evjen/Validate.asmx" />
```

The service would then make an SSL call to the server. Remember that SSL is significantly slower than HTTP, so you will suffer a performance hit. Given the sensitivity of much of the information passing over Web Services, it is probably worth the slowdown.

Directory-Level Security

You also have the option to code security into your applications. This solves different problems from SSL, and, in fact, you may wish to combine the two services for a complete security solution.

Unauthorized access is a potential problem for any remote system, but even more so for Web Services. The open architecture of the system provides crackers with all the information they need to plan an attack. Fortunately, simplicity is often the best defense. Using the NT security options already on the server is the best way to defend against unauthorized users.

You can use NTFS permissions for individual directories within an application and require users to provide a valid username and password combination if they wish to access the service.

> *Web Service security is a large area to cover. For more information, refer to the documentation included with the .NET Framework SDK.*

The best approach to security is to use SSL and directory-level security together. It is slow, and at times inconvenient, but this is a small price to pay for the heightened level of security. Though this is different from the traditional role-based COM+ security, it is still very effective for running information across the wire.

Other Types of Security

The Windows platform also provides for other forms of security. For instance, the Windows CryptoAPI supplies access to most of the commonly used encryption algorithms — aside from the protocols used in the Secure Sockets Layer. Digital certificates (sort of a personal form of SSL `ServerCertificates`) are now rapidly becoming a powerful force in security.

The Downside

There is a downside to any distributed architecture. We've covered most of them in this chapter and suggested workarounds — security, state, speed, and connectivity. Let's go over them once more to ensure that Web Services are the way to go.

Security

The key to the issue and solution of security problems is the management of client expectations. If Web Services are built securely to begin with, then you won't face situations that draw concern or scrutiny. Consider the security of everything you write. It's fairly easy, and the payoff is great.

State

State is less of a problem in a distributed architecture because in Windows DNA, Microsoft has been saying for years that *n*-tier statefulness has to go. Most developers are used to the idea, but if you aren't, then you need to get on the boat with the rest of us. Architect your solutions to be loosely coupled. That's what Web Services are designed to do.

Transactions

Web Services are not made for transactional systems. If the Web server at `MyCompany.com` was to access a database at UPS, for example, and the connection dropped in the middle, the lock on the database would remain without giving the network system at UPS a chance to solve the problem. Web Services are by nature loosely coupled. They are not designed for tight transactional integration.

A common use of Web Services, communication between differing systems, prompted a number of technology architects to design several XML transaction protocols, such as 2PC. These packages provide the two systems with an understanding that the network link will remain stable.

Speed and Connectivity

Speed and connectivity are going to be a continuing problem until we have the ubiquitous bandwidth George Gilder talks about in his book *Telecosm* (Free Press, 2000). Right now, the majority of Internet devices that could really benefit from Web Services — cell phones, PDAs, and the like — are stuck at the paltry 14,000-bits per second currently supported by most wireless providers.

For application development, this is a concern because when the router goes down, the application goes down. Right now, intranets continue to function when the ISP drops the ISDN. With Web Services running the links to customers and suppliers, that ISDN line becomes the company lifeline. Redundancy of connections and a firm partnership with your service provider are the only solution.

Where We Go from Here

The cell phone is a listening device. It listens for a call to its network address from the cell network. When it receives one, it follows some logic to handle the call. Sound familiar? This works just like the RPC architecture and will be the format for a new host of devices that listen for Web Service calls over the G3 wireless network.

The first lines of the W3C XML group's charter state the following:

> "Today, the principal use of the World Wide Web is for interactive access to documents and applications. In almost all cases, such access is by human users, typically working through web browsers, audio players, or other interactive front-end systems. The Web can grow significantly in power and scope if it is extended to support communication between applications, from one program to another."

New business communication will be via XML and Web Services, rather than EDI and VANs. Micropayment may actually become a reality. Scores of promises that the Internet has made since its inception can be fulfilled with Web Services and XML. It won't stop there, though. The power of listening devices will bring Web Services development into user-to-user markets from business-to-business ones.

It sounds far-fetched, but it is hoped that you can see how the power of Web Services on .NET could make this possible. SOAP isn't just about replacing the RPC architecture already out there. It is a fundamentally different way to think about the network as the platform.

Summary

This chapter looked at the need for an architecturally neutral, ubiquitous, easy-to-use, and interoperable system to replace DCOM, RMI, and CORBA. It discussed how Web Services fill the gaps successfully because HTTP is used as the language-independent protocol, XML is its language (in WSDL) and transport mechanism, and SOAP enables you to package messages for sending over HTTP.

The chapter also described how to create and consume Web Services programmatically using Visual Basic, and discussed the abstract classes provided by the .NET Framework class library to set up and work with Web Services. In particular, it looked at the `WebService`, `WebServiceAttribute`, `WebMethodAttribute`, and `WebServiceBindingAttribute` component classes of the `System.Web.Services` namespace, in addition to the `System.Web.Services.Description`, `System.Web.Services.Discovery`, and `System.Web.Services.Protocols` namespaces.

Finally, it outlined some of the downsides to using any distributed architecture (Web Services included), but it finished with an optimistic note on where Web Services might take us in the future.

27

Remoting

Remoting is the .NET technology that enables code in one application domain (`AppDomain`) to call into the methods and properties of objects running in another application domain. A major use of remoting is in the classic *n*-tier desktop approach, where presentation code on the desktop needs to access objects running on a server somewhere on the network. Another primary use for remoting is when code in ASP.NET Web Forms or Web Services needs to call objects running on an application server somewhere else on the network. In short, remoting is the technology to use when your *n*-tier code needs to talk to the business or data tier running on an application server.

Remoting is conceptually somewhat similar to Web Services. Both remoting and Web Services are TCP/IP-based technologies that allow communication between different machines over an IP network. This means that they both pass through firewalls, and they both provide stateless and connectionless communication between machines. These two technologies share a lot of the same principles.

> It is important to recognize that Microsoft has merged the functionality of remoting, Web Services, enterprise services, and MSMQ (Microsoft Message Queue) into the Windows Communication Foundation (WCF) — the next generation of the technologies. You can find more information on WCF in Chapter 30.

When working with XML Web Services, the biggest problem with SOAP is that it is not lightweight. It's designed with maximum platform interoperability in mind, which puts certain limits on how data can be transferred. For example, imagine that platform A stores integer variables as a 4-byte block of memory, with the lowest-value byte appearing first. Now imagine that platform B also uses a 4-byte block of memory, but this time the highest-value byte appears first. The encoding of the value is different. Without some form of conversion, if you copy that block of bytes from platform A to platform B, then the platforms won't agree on what the number actually is. In this scenario, one platform thinks it has the number 4, whereas the other thinks that the number is actually `536870912`.

SOAP gets around this problem by representing numbers (and everything else) as strings of ASCII characters — since ASCII is a text-encoding standard that most platforms can understand. However, this means that the native binary representations of the numbers have to be converted to text each time the SOAP document has to be constructed. In addition, the values themselves have to be packaged in something that you can read (with a little bit of effort). This leads to two problems: massive bloat (a 4-byte value starts taking hundreds of bytes to store) and wasted CPU cycles used in converting from native encoding to text encoding and back again.

You can live with all these problems if you only want to run your Web Service on, say, Windows 2000, and have it accessed through a client running on a cell phone. SOAP is designed to do this kind of thing. However, if you have a Windows XP desktop application that wants to use objects hosted on a Windows 2000 server (using the same platform), the bloated network traffic and wastage in terms of conversion is sub-optimal at best and ridiculous at worst.

Remoting lets you enjoy the same power of Web Services but without the downside. If you want, you can connect directly to the server over TCP and send binary data without having to do any conversions. If one Windows computer has a 4-byte block of memory holding a 32-bit integer value, you can safely copy the bit pattern to another Windows computer and both will agree on the number. In effect, network traffic sanity is restored and processor time isn't wasted doing conversions.

Remoting Overview

It's important to understand several basics about remoting, including the basic terms and related objects, which are covered in the following sections.

Basic Terminology

A normal object is not accessible via remoting. By default, .NET objects are only accessible to other code running within the same .NET `AppDomain`.

A *remote object* is an object that's been made available over remoting by inheriting from `System.MarshalByRefObject`. These objects are often also called `MBROs`. Remote objects are the same kinds of objects that you build normally, but they inherit from `MarshalByRefObject` and you must register them with the `Remoting` subsystem to make them available to clients. They are anchored to the machine and `AppDomain` where they were created, and you communicate with them over the network. The wonderful aspect of this situation is that the client is working with a proxy object, instantiated by the client, that allows programmatic access to the remote object just as if it were in the same process as your client application, even though it actually resides in a completely separate process — even on a completely separate machine.

A *serializable object* is an object that's been made available over remoting by marking the class with the `<Serializable()>` attribute. These objects move from machine to machine or `AppDomain` to `AppDomain`. They are not attached to any particular location, so they are unanchored objects. A common example of a serializable object is the `DataSet`, which can be returned from a server to a client across the network. The `DataSet` physically moves from server to client via the serialization technology in the .NET Framework.

A *remoting host* is a server application that configures remoting to listen for client requests. Remoting runs within the host process, using the memory and threads of the host process to handle any client requests. The most common remoting host is IIS. You can create custom remoting hosts, which are typically created as a Windows Service, so they can run even when no user is logged in to the server. It is also possible to have any .NET application be a remoting host, which enables you to emulate ActiveX EXE behaviors to some degree. This last technique is most commonly used when creating peer-to-peer-style applications.

A *channel* is a way of communicating between two machines. In order for two separate application processes to communicate with each other, a *transport channel* is opened between the processes. A transport channel is a combination of underlying technologies required to open a network connection and use a particular protocol to send the bytes to the receiving application. .NET includes two channels: TCP and HTTP. A channel works with a stream of data and creates an object based upon the transport protocol. The TCP channel is a lightweight channel designed for transporting binary data between two computers. (The TCP channel is different from the TCP protocol that HTTP also uses.) It works using sockets, discussed in much more detail in Chapter 29. TCP is better suited for an intranet environment because an intranet sits behind a firewall, and TCP does not always cross firewalls easily. Using TCP also means that a *binary formatter* is used by default, which actually reduces the size of the object being transported. Having smaller packages to transport allows for better and faster network communications.

HTTP, as you already know, is the protocol that Web servers use. The HTTP channel hosted in IIS is the recommended approach by Microsoft. HTTP is a firewall-friendly transport because HTTP traffic generally flows directly through firewalls over port 80 (which is generally open on most computers).

After a channel is established through a specific port, a *formatter object* is needed to initiate the serialization or deserialization of the object. A formatter object serializes or marshals an object's data into a format in which it can be transferred down the channel. In order for an object to move through the channel from one process to another, the formatter must take the object that you are sending and serialize it into the network stream. Out of the box, you have two formatter objects: `BinaryFormatter` and `SoapFormatter`. The `BinaryFormatter` is more efficient and is recommended. The `SoapFormatter` is not recommended and may be discontinued in future versions of the .NET Framework.

A *message* is a communication between the client and server. It holds the information about the remote object and the method or property that's being invoked, as well as any parameters.

A *proxy* is used on the client side to call into the remote object. To use remoting, you don't typically have to worry about creating the proxy — .NET can do it for you. However, there's a slightly confusing split between something called a *transparent proxy* and a *real proxy*. A transparent proxy is so called because "you can't see it." When you request a remote object, a transparent proxy is what you get. It looks like the remote object (that is, it has the same properties and methods as the original). This means that your client code can use the remote object or a local copy of the object without your having to make any changes and without your knowing there is any difference. The transparent proxy defers the calls to the real proxy. The real proxy is what actually constructs the message, sends it to the server, and waits for the response. You can think of the transparent proxy as a "fake" object that contains the same methods and properties that the real object contains.

The real proxy is effectively a set of helper functions that manages the communications. You don't use the real proxy directly; instead, the transparent proxy calls into the real proxy on your behalf.

A *message sink* is an "interceptor object." Before messages go into the channel, these are used to do some further processing on them, perhaps to attach more data, to reformat data before it is sent, for route debugging information, or to perform security checking. On the client side, you have an *envoy sink*. On the server side, you have a *server context sink* and an *object context sink*. In typical use, you can ignore these.

Message sinks are a pretty advanced topic and allow for some powerful extensions to the remoting model. It is not recommended that you create custom sinks, channels, or formatters, so they are not covered in this book. Creating them is not recommended because they will not transfer directly to WCF, the next generation of the technology from Microsoft. If you do opt to create your own custom sink, formatter, or channel, expect to rewrite it from scratch when you upgrade to WCF.

Figures 27-1 and 27-2 show how these concepts fit together.

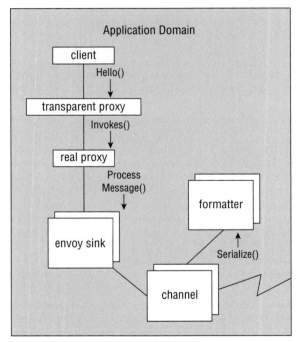

Figure 27-1

Figure 27-1 shows how a client calls the Hello() method of a transparent proxy object. The transparent proxy looks just like the real object, so the client doesn't even realize that remoting is involved. The transparent proxy then invokes the real proxy, which converts the method call into a generic remoting message.

This message is sent through any messaging sinks configured on the client. These messaging sinks may transform the message in various ways, including adding encryption or compressing the data. The message is then serialized by the formatter object. The result is a byte stream that is sent to the server by using the channel configured for use on the client.

Figure 27-2 shows how the server handles the message. The message comes into the server via a channel. The message is then deserialized by the formatter object and run through any messaging sinks configured on the server. These messaging sinks typically mirror those on the client, unencrypting or decompressing the data as appropriate.

Finally, the message is decoded by the object context sink, which uses the information in the message to invoke the method on the actual object. The object itself has no idea that it was invoked via remoting, as the method call was merely relayed from the client.

Figure 27-2

SingleCall, Singleton, and Activated Objects

In remoting, objects are divided into three camps: wellknown objects, *client-activated* objects, and serializable objects.

❑ The wellknown objects run on the server and perform a service for the remote application, such as *give me a list of all the customers* or *create an invoice*. They can be configured to act similarly to a Web Service or to use what's called a *singleton pattern* (which is discussed shortly).

❑ Client-activated (Activated) objects are created for each client and maintain state on the server over time. In many ways, these objects act similarly to COM objects you may have accessed via DCOM in the past.

❑ Serializable objects can move from machine to machine as needed. For instance, a serializable object can be created on the server (by a wellknown or Activated object), and then returned to a client. When the object is returned to the client, it is physically copied *to the client machine*, where it can be used by client code.

The following table summarizes the types of object:

Type	Calling Semantics	Key Attributes
SingleCall (wellknown)	An object is created for each client method call made to the server.	Stateless, per-method lifetime, atomic methods, no threading issues, anchored to AppDomain where created.
Singleton (wellknown)	One object exists on the server and is used to handle all method calls from all clients.	Stateful, long-lived, shared instance, thread synchronization required, anchored to AppDomain where created.
Activated	The client creates Activated objects on the server. The client can create many such objects. Activated objects are available only to the client that created the object.	Stateful, long-lived, per-client instances, threading issues only if client is multithreaded, anchored to AppDomain where created.
Serializable	The object is automatically copied from machine to machine when it is passed as a parameter or returned as the result of a function.	Stateful, long-lived, no threading issues, non-anchored (moves across network automatically).

SingleCall Objects

SingleCall objects act much like typical Web Service objects. Each time a client calls a method on a SingleCall object, an object is created specifically to handle that method call. Once the method call is complete, the object is not reused and is garbage collected by the .NET runtime.

SingleCall objects also work the way a JIT (just-in-time) Activated object does in COM+, and match the way most people use MTS or COM+ objects. In those environments, good developers typically create a server-side object, make a method call, and then release the object.

These objects must inherit from System.MarshalByRefObject, so they are MBROs. This means that they always run in the AppDomain and Windows process where they are created. If they are created on a server in a host process, that is where they live and run. Clients interact with them across the network.

The most commonly used type of service object in remoting is the SingleCall object. Not only do these objects provide semantics similar to Web Services, MTS, and COM+, but they also provide the simplest programming model.

Because an object is created for each method call, these objects are inherently stateless. Even if an object tried to keep state between calls, it would fail because the object is destroyed after each method is complete. This helps ensure that no method call can be affected by previous method calls or contaminate subsequent method calls.

Each method call runs on its own thread (from the .NET thread pool, as discussed in Chapter 24). However, because each method call also gets its very own object, there's typically no contention between threads, so you don't need to worry about writing synchronization or locking code in your SingleCall code.

Technically, it is possible to encounter synchronization issues if there are shared stateful objects on the server. It requires substantial work to create and access such shared objects and is not covered in this book. Typically, this type of model is not used, so threading is a non-issue with SingleCall *objects.*

Because of their automatic isolation, statelessness, and threading simplicity, SingleCall objects are the preferred technology for creation of server code in remoting.

Singleton Objects

Singleton objects are quite different from SingleCall objects. Only one Singleton object exists at a time, and it may exist for a long time and maintain state. All client method calls from all users are routed to this one Singleton object. This means that all clients have equal, shared access to any state maintained by the Singleton object.

These objects must inherit from System.MarshalByRefObject, so they are MBROs. This means that they always run in the AppDomain and Windows process where they are created. If they are created on a server in a host process, that is where they live and run. Clients interact with them across the network.

As with the SingleCall scenario, all method calls are run on threads from the .NET thread pool, which means multiple simultaneous method calls can be running on different threads at the same time. As discussed in Chapter 24, this can be complex, as you have to write multithreaded synchronization code to ensure that these threads don't collide as they interact with your Singleton object.

Singleton objects have a potentially unpredictable life span. When the first client makes the first method call to the object, it is created. From that point forward, it remains in memory for an indeterminate period of time. As long as it remains in memory, all method calls from all the clients are handled by this one object. However, if the object is idle for a long time, remoting may release it to conserve resources. In addition, some remoting hosts may recycle their AppDomain objects, which automatically causes the destruction of all your objects. Therefore, you can never be certain that the data stored in memory in the object will remain available over time. This means that any long-term state data must be written to a persistent store like a database.

Due to the complexity of shared memory, thread synchronization, and dealing with object lifetime issues, Singleton objects are more complex to design and code than SingleCall objects. While they can be useful in specialized scenarios, they aren't as widely used as SingleCall objects.

Activated Objects

Client-activated (or Activated) objects are different from both SingleCall and Singleton objects. Activated objects are created by a client application, and they remain in memory on the server over time. They are associated with just that one client, so they are not shared between clients. They are stateful objects, meaning they can maintain data in memory during their lifetime.

These objects must inherit from System.MarshalByRefObject, so they are MBROs. This means that they always run in the AppDomain and Windows process where they are created. If they are created on a server in a host process, that is where they live and run. Clients interact with them across the network.

A client can create multiple Activated objects on the server. The objects remain on the server until the client releases the objects or the server Appdomain is reset (which can happen with some types of remoting host). If the client doesn't contact the server for several minutes, then the server assumes the client abandoned the objects and it releases them.

`Activated` objects typically don't have any threading issues. The only way multiple threads will run in the same Activated object is if the client is multithreaded, and multiple client threads simultaneously make method calls to the same server-side Activated object. If this is the case in your application, then you'll have to deal with shared data and synchronization issues, discussed in Chapter 24.

While long-lived, stateful, per-client objects can be useful in some specialized scenarios, they are not commonly used in most client/server or *n*-tier application environments. Storing per-client state in an object on the server reduces the scalability and fault tolerance of a system.

Serializable Objects

While `SingleCall`, `Singleton`, and `Activated` objects are always anchored to the `Appdomain`, Windows process, and machine where they are created, this is not the case with `Serializable` objects.

`Serializable` objects can move from machine to machine as needed. The classic example of this is the ADO.NET `DataSet`, which can be returned as a result of a function on a server. The `DataSet` physically moves to the client machine, where it can be used by client code. When the client wants to update the `DataSet`, it simply passes the object to the server as a parameter, causing the `DataSet` to physically move to the server machine.

These objects *do not* inherit from `System.MarshalByRefObject`. Instead, they are decorated with the `<Serializable()>` attribute and may optionally implement the `ISerializable` interface. The following is a very basic implementation of a `<Serializable()>` object:

```
<Serializable()> _
Public Class Customer
  Private mName As String = ""

  Public Property Name() As String
    Get
      Return mName
    End Get
    Set(ByVal value As String)
      mName = value
    End Set

  Public Sub Load()
    ' Load data here.
  End Sub
End Class
```

`<Serializable()>` objects are not anchored to the `Appdomain` or Windows process where they were created. The remoting subsystem automatically serializes these objects' data and transfers it across the network to another machine. On that other machine, a new instance of the objects is created and loaded with the data, effectively cloning the objects across the network.

When working with serializable objects, it's typically a good idea to use a `SingleCall` object on the server to create the `Serializable` object and call any server-side methods (such as those to load the object with data from a database). The `SingleCall` object then returns the serializable object to the client as a function result so the client can interact with the object. The `SingleCall` object's method might look like this:

```
Public Function GetCustomer(ByVal ID As Integer) As Customer
```

```
    Dim cust As New Customer()
    cust.Load(ID)
    Return cust

End Function
```

The client code might look like this:

```
Dim cust As Customer

cust = myService.GetCustomer(123)
TextBox1.Text = cust.Name()
```

Note that both server and client code have direct, local access to the `Customer` object because it is automatically copied from the server to the client as a result of the `GetCustomer()` method call.

`Serializable` objects can be very useful in many client/server scenarios, especially if the application is created using object-oriented application design principles.

Implementing Remoting

When you implement an application using remoting, there are three key components to the application:

Client	The application calling the server
Server Library	The DLL containing the objects to be called by the client
Host	The application running on the server that hosts remoting and the Server Library

Basically, you create your server-side objects in a Visual Basic class library project. Then, you expose the classes in that DLL from your server-side remoting host application. With the objects exposed on the server, you can then create client applications that call the objects in the Server Library DLL. You might also have some other optional components to support various scenarios:

Interface	A DLL containing interfaces that are implemented by the objects in the Server Library
Proxy	A DLL containing generated proxy code based on the objects in the Server Library
Shared Library	A DLL containing serializable objects that must be available to both the Server Library and the client

Each of these is discussed in detail as it is used later in the chapter. For now, it's time to get into some code and see how remoting works.

A Simple Example

To begin, you will create a simple remoting application that consists of a library DLL containing the server-side code, a remoting host application, and a client to call the library DLL on the server.

Keep in mind that both the host and the client need access to the type information that describes the classes in the library DLL. The type information includes the name of the classes in the DLL and the methods exposed by those classes.

The host needs the information because it will be exposing the library DLL to clients via remoting. The client needs the information in order to know which objects to create and what methods are available on those objects.

You know that the library DLL will be on the server, so it is easy enough for the host application to just reference the DLL to get the type information. The client is a bit trickier though, as the library DLL won't necessarily be on the client machine. You have three options for getting the type information to the client:

Reference the library DLL	This is the simplest approach, as the client just references the DLL directly and therefore has all the type information. The drawback is that the DLL must be installed on the client along with the client application.
Use an interface DLL	This approach is more complex. The classes in the library DLL must implement formal interfaces as defined in this interface DLL. The client can then reference just the interface DLL, so the library DLL doesn't need to be installed on the client machine. The way the client invokes the server is different when using interfaces.
Generate a proxy DLL	This approach is of moderate complexity. The server must expose the objects via HTTP, so you can run the soapsuds.exe command-line utility. The utility creates an assembly containing the type information for the library DLL classes exposed by the server. The client then references this proxy assembly, rather than the library DLL.

You'll implement all three options in this chapter, starting with the simplest — referencing the library DLL directly from the client application.

Library DLL

To begin, create the library DLL. This is just a regular Class Library project, so open Visual Studio .NET (Visual Studio) and create a new class library named SimpleLibrary. Remove Class1.vb and add a new class named Calculator. Because you're creating a well-known remoting object, it must inherit from MarshalByRefObject:

```
Public Class Calculator
   Inherits MarshalByRefObject
End Class
```

That's really all there is to it. At this point, the Calculator class is ready to be exposed from a server via remoting. Of course, you need to add some methods that clients can call.

Any and all `Public` methods written in the `Calculator` class are available to clients. How you design the methods depends entirely on whether you plan to expose this class as `SingleCall`, `Singleton`, or `Activated`. For `SingleCall`, you know that an instance of `Calculator` will be created for *each method call*, so there's absolutely no point in using any class-level variables. After all, they'll be destroyed along with the object when each method call is complete.

Nor can you have the client call a sequence of methods on your object. Each method call gets its own object, and is entirely isolated from any previous or subsequent method calls. In short, each method must stand alone.

For illustration purposes, you need to prove that the server-side code is running in a different process from the client code. The easiest way to prove this is to return the `thread ID` where the code is running. You can compare this `thread ID` to the `thread ID` of the client process. If they are different, then you can be sure that the server-side code really is running on the server (or at least in another process on your machine).

Add the following method:

```
Public Function GetThreadID() As Integer

    Return Threading.Thread.CurrentThread.ManagedThreadId

End Function
```

You can add other `Public` methods as well if you'd like:

```
Public Function Add(ByVal a As Integer, ByVal b As Integer) As Integer

    Return a + b

End Function
```

Because this is a calculator class, it seems appropriate that it should do some calculations. At this point, you have a simple but functional `Calculator` class. Build the solution to create the DLL. Your remoting host application will use this DLL to provide the calculator functionality to clients.

Host Application

With the server-side library complete, you can create a remoting host. It is recommended that you use IIS as a remoting host, but it is possible to create a custom host as well. You'll use IIS later in the chapter, but for now let's see how you can create a custom host in a `Console` Application for testing.

> *Most custom hosts are created as a Windows Service so the host can run on the server even when no user is logged into the machine. However, for testing purposes, a console application is easier to create and run.*

The advantage to a custom host is that you can host a remoting server on any machine that supports the .NET Framework. This includes Windows 98 and later. If you use IIS as a host, you can only host on Windows 2000 and later, which is a bit more restrictive.

The drawback to a custom host is that it isn't as robust and capable as IIS — at least, not without a lot of work. For this chapter's example, you won't attempt to make your host as powerful as IIS. You'll just stick with the basic process of creating a custom host.

Setting Up the Project

Create a new solution in Visual Studio, with a console application named `SimpleServer`. The remoting host will be interacting with remoting, so reference the appropriate framework DLL. Use the `Add Reference` dialog box to add a reference to `System.Runtime.Remoting,` as shown in Figure 27-3.

Figure 27-3

Then, in `Module1`, import the appropriate namespace:

```
Imports System.Runtime.Remoting
```

At this point, you can configure and use remoting, but before you do that, you need access to the DLL containing the classes you plan to expose via remoting — in this case, `SimpleLibrary.dll`.

Referencing the Library DLL

There are two ways to configure remoting: via a configuration file or via code. If you opt for the configuration file approach, then the only requirement is that `SimpleLibrary.dll` be in the same directory as your host application. You don't even need to reference `SimpleLibrary.dll` from the host. If you opt to configure remoting via code, then your host must reference `SimpleLibrary.dll`.

Even if you go with the configuration file approach, referencing `SimpleLibrary.dll` from the host project enables Visual Studio to automatically keep the DLL updated in your project directory, and any setup project you might create will automatically include `SimpleLibrary.dll`. In general, it is a good idea to reference the library DLL from the host, and that's what you'll do here.

Add a reference to `SimpleLibrary.dll` by clicking the Browse button in the Add References dialog box and navigating to the `SimpleLibrary\bin\Release` directory, as shown in Figure 27-4. Note that if you are running in debug mode, then you will find the DLL in the `Debug` folder, rather than the `Release` folder.

Figure 27-4

All that remains now is to configure remoting.

Configuring Remoting

The typical way to do this is with a configuration file. Open the `app.config` file (add this file to your project if it isn't already present) in the `SimpleServer` project. In this `config` file you'll add a section to configure remoting. Remember that XML is case sensitive, so the slightest typo here will prevent remoting from being properly configured:

```xml
<?xml version="1.0" encoding="utf-8" ?>
<configuration>
  <system.runtime.remoting>
    <application>
      <!-- The following section defines the classes you're
           exposing to clients from this host. -->
      <service>
        <wellknown mode="SingleCall"
             objectUri="Calculator.rem"
             type="SimpleLibrary.Calculator, SimpleLibrary" />
      </service>

      <channels>
        <channel ref="tcp" port="49341" />
      </channels>

    </application>
  </system.runtime.remoting>
</configuration>
```

Notice that all configuration is within the `<system.runtime.remoting>` element, and then within an `<application>` element. The real work happens first inside the `<service>` element. The `<service>` element tells remoting that you're configuring server-side components. It is within this block that you define the classes you want to make available to clients. You can define both `wellknown` and `Activated` classes here. In this case, you're defining a `wellknown` class:

```
<wellknown mode="SingleCall"
    objectUri="Calculator.rem"
    type="SimpleLibrary.Calculator, SimpleLibrary" />
```

The mode will be either `SingleCall` or `Singleton`, as discussed earlier in the chapter.

The `objectUri` is the "end part" of the URL that clients will use to reach your server. You'll revisit this in a moment, but the following shows basically how it fits (depending on whether you're using the TCP or HTTP protocol):

```
tcp://localhost:49341/Calculator.rem
```

or

```
http://localhost:49341/Calculator.rem
```

The `.rem` extension on the `objectUri` is important. It indicates that remoting should handle the client request, and is used by the networking infrastructure to route the request to the right location. You can optionally use the `.soap` extension to get the same result. The `.rem` and `.soap` extensions are totally equivalent.

Finally, the type defines the full type name and assembly where the actual class can be found. Remoting uses this information to dynamically load the assembly and create the object when requested by a client. You can have many `<wellknown>` blocks here to expose all the server-side classes you want to make available to clients.

The other key configuration block is where you specify which remoting channel (protocol) you want to use. You can choose between the TCP and HTTP channels:

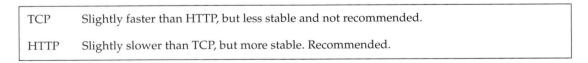

TCP	Slightly faster than HTTP, but less stable and not recommended.
HTTP	Slightly slower than TCP, but more stable. Recommended.

Since you'll look at the HTTP channel later, you're using the TCP channel now. Either way, you need to specify the IP port number on which you'll be listening for client requests. When choosing a port for a server, you should keep the following port ranges in mind:

❑ **0–1023** — Well-known ports reserved for specific applications such as Web servers, mail servers, and so on

❑ **1024–49151** — Registered ports that are reserved for various widely used protocols such as DirectPlay

❑   **49152–65535** — Intended for dynamic or private use, such as for applications that might be performing remoting with .NET

You set remoting to use a TCP channel, listening on port 49341:

```
<channels>
  <channel ref="tcp" port="49341" />
</channels>
```

With the `.config` file created, the only thing remaining is to tell remoting to configure itself based on this information. To do this, add the following code to `Sub Main`:

```
Sub Main()
  RemotingConfiguration.Configure( _
    AppDomain.CurrentDomain.SetupInformation.ConfigurationFile, True)
  Console.Write("Press <enter> to exit")
  Console.Read()
End Sub
```

The `Console.Write` and `Console.Read` statements ensure that the application remains running until you are ready for it to terminate. The line that actually configures remoting is as follows:

```
RemotingConfiguration.Configure( _
  AppDomain.CurrentDomain.SetupInformation.ConfigurationFile)
```

You are calling the `Configure` method, which tells remoting to read a `.config` file and process the `<system.runtime.remoting>` element in that file. You want it to use your application configuration file, so you pass that path as a parameter. Fortunately, you can get the path from your `AppDomain` object, so you don't have to hard-code the filename.

Configuring Remoting via Code

Your other option is to configure the remoting host via code. To do this you'd write different code in `Sub Main`:

```
Sub Main()

  RemotingConfiguration.RegisterWellKnownServiceType( _
    GetType(SimpleLibrary.Calculator), _
    "Calculator.rem", _
    WellKnownObjectMode.SingleCall)

  System.Runtime.Remoting.Channels.ChannelServices.RegisterChannel( _
    New System.Runtime.Remoting.Channels.Tcp.TcpServerChannel(49341), True)
  Console.Write("Press <enter> to exit")
  Console.Read()
End Sub
```

Here, you're providing the exact same information as you did in the `.config` file, only via code. You call `RegisterWellKnownServiceType`, passing the mode, `objectUri`, and type data, just as you did in the `.config` file. Then, you call `RegisterChannel`, passing a new instance of the `TcpServerChannel` configured to use the port you chose earlier.

The result is the same as using the `.config` file. Most server applications use a `.config` file to configure remoting because it enables you to change things such as the channel and port without having to recompile the host application.

Build the solution. At this point your host is ready to run. Open a Command Prompt window, navigate to the `bin` directory, and run `SimpleServer.exe`.

The Client Application

The final piece of the puzzle is creating a client application that calls the server.

Setting Up the Project

This example creates a new Visual Studio solution with a Windows Application named `SimpleClient`. As discussed earlier, the client needs access to the type information for the classes it wants to call on the server. The easiest way to get this type information is to have it reference `SimpleLibrary.dll`. Because you'll be configuring remoting, you also need to reference the remoting DLL. Then import the remoting namespace in `Form1`:

```
Imports System.Runtime.Remoting
```

Now you can write code to interact with the `Calculator` class. Add controls to the form as shown in Figure 27-5.

Figure 27-5

Name the controls as follows (in order): `ConfigureButton`, `CodeConfigureButton`, `LocalThreadButton`, `LocalThread`, `RemoteThreadButton`, `RemoteThread`. First, write the code to get the `thread ID` values for each object:

```
Private Sub LocalThreadButton_Click( _
  ByVal sender As System.Object, ByVal e As System.EventArgs) _
  Handles LocalThreadButton.Click

  LocalThread.Text = CStr(Threading.Thread.CurrentThread.ManagedThreadId)

End Sub

Private Sub RemoteThreadButton_Click( _
    ByVal sender As System.Object, ByVal e As System.EventArgs) _
    Handles RemoteThreadButton.Click

 Dim calc As New SimpleLibrary.Calculator
```

```
    RemoteThread.Text = CStr(calc.GetThreadID)

  End Sub
```

Displaying the thread ID of the local process is easily accomplished. More interesting, though, is that your code to interact with the `Calculator` class doesn't look special in any way. Where's the remoting code?

Using the concept of *location transparency,* it is possible to write "normal" code that interacts with an object whether it is running locally or remotely. This is an important and desirable trait for distributed technologies, and remoting supports the concept. Looking at the preceding code, you can't tell whether the `Calculator` object is local or remoting; its location is transparent.

All that remains is to configure remoting so that it knows that the `Calculator` object should, in fact, be created remotely. As with the server, you can configure clients either via a `config` file or through code.

Before you configure remoting, keep in mind that if remoting is not configured before the first usage of `SimpleLibrary.Calculator`, then the `Calculator` object will be created locally. If that happens, then configuring remoting won't help, and you'll never create remote `Calculator` objects.

To prevent this from happening, make sure you can't interact with the class until after remoting is configured. Typically, this is done by configuring remoting as the application starts up, either in `Sub Main` or in the first form's `Load` event, but in this case you're going to configure remoting behind some buttons, so a different approach is required.

In `Form_Load`, add the following code:

```
  Private Sub Form1_Load( _
    ByVal sender As System.Object, ByVal e As System.EventArgs) _
    Handles MyBase.Load

    RemoteThreadButton.Enabled = False

  End Sub
```

This prevents you from requesting the remote thread. You won't enable this button until after remoting has been configured either through the `config` file or code.

Configuring Remoting

To configure remoting via a `config` file, you first need to add a `config` file to the project. Select Project ➪ Add New Item to add an Application Configuration file. Be sure to keep the default name of `App.config`. In this file, add the following code:

```
<?xml version="1.0" encoding="utf-8" ?>
<configuration>
  <system.runtime.remoting>
    <application>
      <!-- The following section defines the classes you're
           getting from the remote host. -->
      <client>
```

```
        <wellknown mode="SingleCall"
              type="SimpleLibrary.Calculator, SimpleLibrary"
              url="tcp://localhost:49341/Calculator.rem" />
        </client>
      </application>
    </system.runtime.remoting>
  </configuration>
```

In this case, you're using the `<client>` element, telling remoting that you're configuring a client. Within the `<client>` block, you define the classes that should be run on a remote server, both `wellknown` and `Activated`. In this case you have a `wellknown` class:

```
<wellknown
        type="SimpleLibrary.Calculator, SimpleLibrary"
        url="tcp://localhost:49341/Calculator.rem" />
```

On the client, you only need to provide remoting with two bits of information: the class and assembly that should be run remotely. This is done with the `type` attribute, which specifies the full type name and assembly name for the class, just as you did on the server. You also need to provide the full URL for the class on the server.

You defined this URL when you created the server, though it might not have been clear at the time. When you defined the class for remoting on the server, you specified an `objectUri` value (`Calculator.rem`). You also specified the channel (TCP) and port (49341) on which the server will listen for client requests. Combined with the server name itself, you have a URL:

```
tcp://localhost:49341/Calculator.rem
```

The channel is `tcp://`, the server name is `localhost` (or whatever the server name might be), the port is `49341`, and the object's URI is `Calculator.rem`. This is the unique address of your `SimpleLibrary.Calculator` class on the remote server.

As with the server configuration, you might have multiple elements in the `.config` file, one for each server-side object you wish to use. These can be a mix of `<wellknown>` and `<activated>` elements. With the configuration set up, you just need to tell remoting to read the file. You do this behind the `ConfigureButton` control:

```
Private Sub ConfigureButton_Click( _
  ByVal sender As System.Object, ByVal e As System.EventArgs) _
  Handles ConfigureButton.Click

  RemotingConfiguration.Configure( _
    AppDomain.CurrentDomain.SetupInformation.ConfigurationFile, True)

  ConfigureButton.Enabled = False
  CodeConfigureButton.Enabled = False
  RemoteThreadButton.Enabled = True

End Sub
```

Once remoting is configured in an application, you can't configure it again, so you're disabling the two configuration buttons. You're also enabling the button to retrieve the remote thread ID. Now that remoting has been configured, it is safe to interact with `SimpleLibrary.Calculator`. The line of code that configures remoting is the same as it was in the server:

```
RemotingConfiguration.Configure( _
  AppDomain.CurrentDomain.SetupInformation.ConfigurationFile)
```

Again, you're telling remoting to read your application configuration file to find the `<system.run-time.remoting>` element and process it.

Configuring Remoting via Code

Another option for configuring remoting is to do it via code. You must provide the same information in your code as you did in the `.config` file. Put this behind the `CodeConfigureButton` control:

```
Private Sub CodeConfigureButton_Click( _
  ByVal sender As System.Object, ByVal e As System.EventArgs) _
  Handles CodeConfigureButton.Click
  RemotingConfiguration.RegisterWellKnownClientType( _
    GetType(SimpleLibrary.Calculator), "tcp://localhost:49341/Calculator.rem")

  ConfigureButton.Enabled = False
  CodeConfigureButton.Enabled = False
  RemoteThreadButton.Enabled = True

End Sub
```

The `RegisterWellKnownClientType` method requires that you specify the type of the class to be run remotely — in this case, `SimpleLibrary.Calculator`. You also need to provide the URL for the class on the remote server, just as you did in the `.config` file.

Regardless of whether you do the configuration via code or the `.config` file, the result is that the .NET runtime now knows that any attempt to create a `SimpleLibrary.Calculator` object should be routed through remoting, so the object will be created on the server.

Compile and run the application. Try configuring remoting both ways. In both cases, you should discover that the local thread ID and the remote thread ID are different, proving that the Calculator code is running on the server, not locally in the Windows application (see Figure 27-6).

Figure 27-6

Of course, your specific thread ID values will vary from those shown here. The important point is that they are different from each other, establishing that the local code and remote code are running in different places.

Using IIS as a Remoting Host

You've seen how to create a very basic custom host. In most production environments, however, such a basic host isn't directly useful. You typically need to create a Windows Service, add management and logging facilities, implement security, and so forth. Alternately, you could just use IIS as the host and get all those things automatically. It is often better to use IIS as a remoting host than to try to create your own.

Creating the Host

Using IIS as a host is a straightforward exercise. First, create a Web project by creating a new solution in Visual Studio with an Empty Web Site named SimpleHost, as shown in Figure 27-7.

Figure 27-7

When you click OK, Visual Studio will properly create and configure the virtual root on your server. The next task is to ensure that the SimpleLibrary.dll is in the bin directory under the virtual root. You could copy the DLL there by hand, but it is often easier to simply add a reference to the DLL from the website. This enables Visual Studio to automatically copy the DLL to the right location, and it has the added benefit that if you create a deployment project, the DLL is automatically included as part of the setup.

Add a reference to SimpleLibrary.dll using the Add References dialog box, as you did previously in the SimpleServer and SimpleClient projects. This way, Visual Studio will ensure that the DLL is available as needed.

All that remains now is to configure remoting. The only thing you need to do within an IIS host is add the `<system.runtime.remoting>` section to the `web.config` file. Remoting is automatically configured based on `web.config` by ASP.NET.

Select Project ⇨ Add New Item to add a Web Configuration file. Be sure to use the default name of `web.config`. This adds a `web.config` file to the project with a series of default settings. You may opt to change some of these settings for your environment. In particular, these settings enable you to control security options and so forth.

More important, add the remoting configuration to the file:

```xml
<?xml version="1.0" encoding="utf-8" ?>
<configuration>
  <system.runtime.remoting>
    <application>
      <!-- The following section defines the classes you're
           exposing to clients from this host. -->
      <service>
        <wellknown mode="SingleCall"
            objectUri="Calculator.rem"
            type="SimpleLibrary.Calculator, SimpleLibrary" />
      </service>

    </application>
  </system.runtime.remoting>
```

An IIS host can only support the HTTP channel. In addition, the port on which the host listens is defined by IIS, not by your configuration file. Therefore, all you need to do here is define the classes you want to expose to clients. Do this within the `<service>` element, just like with a custom host. Again, you use a `<wellknown>` element to define your class:

```xml
<wellknown mode="SingleCall"
      objectUri="Calculator.rem"
      type="SimpleLibrary.Calculator, SimpleLibrary" />
```

The `<wellknown>` element shown here is the exact same definition used with the custom host, and you'll get the same result. The primary difference between your custom host and the IIS host is that IIS cannot use the TCP channel; it only uses the HTTP channel. This means that the URL for your server-side class is different:

```
http://localhost/SimpleHost/Calculator.rem
```

The channel defines the protocol, which is `http://`. The server name is `localhost` (or whatever your server name might be). The virtual root within IIS is `SimpleHost`, named just as it is with any Web project. Finally, the `objectUri` value for your class (`Calculator.rem`) rounds out the URL.

Again, the `.rem` extension is important. This extension (or the equivalent `.soap` extension) tells IIS to route the client request to ASP.NET, and it tells ASP.NET to route the request to remoting so it can be properly handled by invoking your `Calculator` class.

At this point, the remoting host is done and ready to go. It is using the HTTP protocol, so you can test it with the browser by navigating to the following URL:

```
http://localhost/SimpleHost/Calculator.rem?wsdl
```

This should return an XML description of the host service and all the classes exposed from the host.

Updating the Client Application

With a new host set up, you can change the client application to use this IIS host instead of the custom host. To do so, change the URL for the object when you configure remoting. If you're using the .config file to configure remoting, you make the following change:

```
<?xml version="1.0" encoding="utf-8" ?>
<configuration>
  <system.runtime.remoting>
    <application>
      <!- the following section defines the classes you're
          getting from the remote host ->
      <client>
        <wellknown
              type="SimpleLibrary.Calculator, SimpleLibrary"
              url="http://localhost/SimpleHost/Calculator.rem" />
      </client>
    </application>
  </system.runtime.remoting>
</configuration>
```

After making this change to App.config, be sure to rebuild the project so Visual Studio copies the new .config file to the bin directory and renames it to SimpleClient.exe.config.

When configuring remoting via code, change the code as follows:

```
Private Sub CodeConfigureButton_Click( _
   ByVal sender As System.Object, ByVal e As System.EventArgs) _
   Handles CodeConfigureButton.Click

   RemotingConfiguration.RegisterWellKnownClientType( _
     GetType(SimpleLibrary.Calculator), _
     "http://localhost/SimpleHost/Calculator.rem")
   ConfigureButton.Enabled = False
   CodeConfigureButton.Enabled = False
   RemoteThreadButton.Enabled = True

End Sub
```

In either case, you're simply changing the URL, so remoting now routes your calls to the IIS host instead of your custom host.

Using the Binary Formatter in IIS

One thing to note about using IIS as a host is that it always uses the HTTP channel. The HTTP channel defaults to using the SoapFormatter instead of the BinaryFormatter to encode the data sent across the network. While SOAP is a fine format, it is extremely verbose. The `BinaryFormatter` generates about one-third the number of bytes as the `SoapFormatter` to send the same data.

As stated, the `SoapFormatter` class is the default formatter when using an HTTP channel with .NET remoting, and this class serializes any objects that it receives into a SOAP 1.1–compliant text format. The HTTP channel uses the `SoapFormatter` to serialize the objects that it sends through the channel. After the object is received and serialized into XML, this formatter also adds any appropriate SOAP headers to the message before it is sent through the channel.

Besides the `SoapFormatter`, the `BinaryFormatter` class is typically used when sending an object through a TCP network protocol. When objects are sent using the `BinaryFormatter`, these objects are more compact and therefore require less network utilization.

For production code, it's good practice to use the `BinaryFormatter` to reduce the amount of data sent across the network and to improve performance. The formatter is controlled by the client, so you need to update the client configuration of remoting.

You can change the `.config` file as follows:

```xml
<?xml version="1.0" encoding="utf-8" ?>
<configuration>
  <system.runtime.remoting>
    <application>
      <!- the following section defines the classes you're
           getting from the remote host ->
      <client>
        <wellknown
            type="SimpleLibrary.Calculator, SimpleLibrary"
            url="http://localhost/SimpleHost/Calculator.rem" />
      </client>
  <!-- use the binary formatter over the
       http channel ->
  <channels>
    <channel ref="http">
     <clientProviders>
       <formatter ref="binary" />
     </clientProviders>
    </channel>
  </channels>
    </application>
  </system.runtime.remoting>
</configuration>
```

The highlighted XML configures remoting, so when it initializes the HTTP channel, it does so with a `BinaryFormatter` instead of the default `SoapFormatter`. To do the equivalent to the XML configuration in code, you import a couple of namespaces into `Form1`:

```vb
Imports System.Runtime.Remoting.Channels
Imports System.Runtime.Remoting.Channels.Http
```

This also requires that the `SimpleClient` project reference the `System.Runtime.Remoting.dll` assembly. Do this using the Add References dialog as you did earlier in the `SimpleLibrary` project. Next, add the following when configuring remoting:

```
Private Sub CodeConfigureButton_Click( _
    ByVal sender As System.Object, ByVal e As System.EventArgs) _
    Handles CodeConfigureButton.Click

    RemotingConfiguration.RegisterWellKnownClientType( _
        GetType(SimpleLibrary.Calculator), _
        "http://localhost/SimpleHost/Calculator.rem")

    ' Use the binary formatter with the
    ' HTTP channel.
    Dim clientFormatter As New BinaryClientFormatterSinkProvider
    Dim channel As New HttpChannel(Nothing, clientFormatter, Nothing)
    ChannelServices.RegisterChannel(channel)
    ConfigureButton.Enabled = False
    CodeConfigureButton.Enabled = False
    RemoteThreadButton.Enabled = True

End Sub
```

As with the `.config` file approach, you're specifically creating the `HttpChannel` object, specifying that it should use a `BinaryFormatter`, rather than the default.

At this point, you've explored the basic use of remoting. You've created a library DLL, a client that uses the library DLL, and two different types of remoting hosts, so the library DLL can run on the server.

There are many other facets of remoting to explore, more than what fits into this single chapter. The rest of the chapter explores some of the more common features that you might encounter or use in your applications. You'll have to take them pretty fast, but the complete code for each is available in the code download for the book.

Using Activator.GetObject

In your simple client you configured remoting so that all attempts to use `SimpleLibrary.Calculator` were automatically routed to a specific server via remoting. If you want more control and flexibility, you can take a different approach by using the `System.Activator` class. The full code for this example is in the `ActivatorClient` project.

Instead of configuring remoting to always know where to find the remote class, you can specify it as you create the remote object. Because you won't be configuring remoting, you don't need a reference to `System.Runtime.Remoting.dll`, nor do you need any of the remoting configuration code you had in the client to this point.

Simply replace the use of the `New` keyword with a call to `Activator.GetObject`. To use the custom host, you'd use the following code to retrieve the remote thread ID:

```
Private Sub RemoteThreadButton_Click( _
    ByVal sender As System.Object, ByVal e As System.EventArgs) _
```

```
    Handles RemoteThreadButton.Click

    Dim calc As SimpleLibrary.Calculator

    calc = CType(Activator.GetObject( _
      GetType(SimpleLibrary.Calculator), _
      "tcp://localhost:49341/Calculator.rem"), _
      SimpleLibrary.Calculator)
    RemoteThread.Text = CStr(calc.GetThreadID)

  End Sub
```

For this to work, the `SimpleServer` application must be running before the `RemoteThread` button is clicked. The `Activator.GetObject` method accepts the type of object to create (`SimpleLibrary.Calculator`) and the URL where the object can be found. To use the IIS host, you'd change the URL as follows:

```
    calc = CType(Activator.GetObject( _
      GetType(SimpleLibrary.Calculator), _

      "http://localhost/SimpleHost/Calculator.rem"), _
      SimpleLibrary.Calculator)
```

With this approach you lose location transparency, as it is obvious that you're using a remote object; but you gain explicit control over where the remote object is created. This can be useful when you want to programmatically control the URL on a per-call basis.

Interface-Based Design

One drawback to the simple implementation used thus far is that the library DLL (`SimpleLibrary.dll`) must be installed on the client machine. Sometimes this isn't desirable because you don't want clients to have access to the server-side code. There are two solutions to this problem: using an interface DLL or using a generated proxy.

Interface DLL

To use this approach, you create a new DLL that contains interface definitions for your server-side classes and their methods. For instance, in the `SimpleInterface` project, you have this interface defined:

```
    Public Interface  ICalculator
      Function GetThreadID() As Integer
      Function Add(ByVal a As Integer, ByVal b As Integer) As Integer
    End Interface
```

This interface defines the methods on your `Calculator` class. You need to update the `Calculator` class to implement this interface. The `SimpleLibrary` project must reference the `SimpleInterface` DLL; then you can do the following in your `Calculator` class:

```
    Public Class Calculator
      Inherits MarshalByRefObject
```

```
   Implements SimpleInterface.ICalculator
   Public Function GetThreadID() As Integer _
      Implements SimpleInterface.ICalculator.GetThreadID

     Return AppDomain.GetCurrentThreadId

   End Function

   Public Function Add(ByVal a As Integer, ByVal b As Integer) As Integer _
      Implements SimpleInterface.ICalculator.Add

        Return a + b

   End Function

End Class
```

At this point, the `SimpleLibrary.Calculator` class can be invoked either directly or via the `ICalculator` interface. Be sure to rebuild the custom and IIS host projects so that the new `SimpleLibrary` and `SimpleInterface` DLLs are both copies to the host directories. Note that because `SimpleLibrary.Calculator` is still available natively, your existing client applications (`SimpleClient` and `ActivatorClient`) will continue to run just fine.

Updating the Client Application

The `InterfaceClient` project only references `SimpleInterface.dll`, not `SimpleLibrary.dll`, so the client machine doesn't need to install `SimpleLibrary.dll` for the client to run, meaning the client has no access to the actual server-side code.

Because you don't have access to the types in `SimpleLibrary`, you can't use them in your code. The only types you can use come from `SimpleInterface`. This means that your code to retrieve the remote thread ID is a bit different. To use the custom host, do the following:

```
Private Sub RemoteThreadButton_Click( _
   ByVal sender As System.Object, ByVal e As System.EventArgs) _
   Handles RemoteThreadButton.Click

   Dim calc As SimpleInterface.ICalculator

   calc = CType(Activator.GetObject( _
     GetType(SimpleInterface.ICalculator), _
     "tcp://localhost:49341/Calculator.rem"), _
     SimpleInterface.ICalculator)

   RemoteThread.Text = CStr(calc.GetThreadID)

End Sub
```

Note that the `calc` variable is now declared as type `ICalculator`, rather than `Calculator`. In addition, you're using `Activator.GetType`. This is required when using interfaces because you can't use the `New` keyword at all. You can't do the following:

```
calc = New SimpleInterface.ICalculator()
```

The result is a compiler error because it isn't possible to create an instance of an interface. Therefore, you can't just configure remoting and use location transparency; you must use `Activator.GetObject` to have remoting create an instance of the object on the server.

Remoting knows how and where to create the object based on the URL you provide. It then converts the object to the right type (`SimpleInterface.ICalculator`) based on the type you provide in the `GetObject` call. If the remote object doesn't implement this interface, then you'll get a runtime exception.

Using Generated Proxies

Another way to create a client that doesn't reference the library DLL is to use the `soapsuds.exe` command-line utility to create a proxy assembly for the service and the classes it exposes. This proxy assembly is then referenced by the client application, giving the client access to the server type information so that it can interact with the server objects.

Proxy DLL

To create the proxy DLL, run the `soapsuds.exe` utility with the following command line:

```
> soapsuds -url:http://localhost/SimpleHost/Calculator.rem?wsdl -oa:SimpleProxy.dll
```

Note that you're going against the IIS host here because it uses the HTTP protocol. This won't work against your current custom host, as the `soapsuds.exe` utility doesn't understand the `tcp://` prefix. To use this against a custom host, you'd have to make sure the custom host used the HTTP protocol.

Creating the Client Application

The code download includes a `ProxyClient` project. This is a Windows application that references only `SimpleProxy.dll`. There is no reference to `SimpleLibrary.dll` or `SimpleInterface.dll` — this client relies entirely on the generated proxy assembly to interact with the server.

The best part of this is that the generated proxy contains the same namespace and class names as the service on the server. In other words, it appears that you are working with `SimpleLibrary.Calculator`, because the proxy is set up with that same namespace and class name. To get the remote thread ID, write the following code:

```
Private Sub RemoteThreadButton_Click( _
  ByVal sender As System.Object, ByVal e As System.EventArgs) _
  Handles RemoteThreadButton.Click

    Dim calc As New SimpleLibrary.Calculator()
    RemoteThread.Text = CStr(calc.GetThreadID)

  End Sub
```

This is the same code used in the original simple example. You've come full circle at this point, but now the client application doesn't directly reference your library DLL.

Summary

Remoting is a powerful technology that provides many of the capabilities of Web Services and DCOM, plus some new capabilities of its own. Using remoting, you can create both Windows and Web applications that interact with objects on an application server across the network.

On the server you can create `SingleCall`, `Singleton`, and `Activated` objects. These three object types provide a great deal of flexibility in terms of *n*-tier application design and should be able to meet almost any need. `SingleCall` gives you behavior similar to Web Services or typical COM+ objects. `Activated` gives you objects that act similar to COM objects exposed via DCOM. `Singleton` objects are unique to remoting and enable all your clients to share a single stateful object on the server.

You can also create `Serializable` objects, which can move from machine to machine as needed. Using this type of object enables you to easily move data and business logic from server to client and back again. This technology is particularly exciting for object-oriented development in a distributed environment.

In this chapter, you created a library DLL and exposed it to clients from both a custom and IIS remoting host. You then created client applications to use your server-side code by referencing the library DLL directly, using an interface DLL and using the `soapsuds.exe` utility to create a proxy DLL. These techniques apply not only to `SingleCall` objects but also to `Singleton` and `Activated` objects, so you should have a good grounding in the techniques available for using remoting in your environment.

28

Enterprise Services

Chapter 23 explored the vast hinterland of legacy software known as COM. This chapter looks at "what COM did next" and how it fits into the world of .NET, in the form of *.NET Enterprise Services*. You would be forgiven for thinking that Enterprise Services is yet another version of legacy software, except that much of it hasn't been around for long enough to be considered legacy. However, there is more to it than that. The features made available by Enterprise Services are still very valuable today for creating scalable, distributed applications.

To understand Enterprise Services, go back in time to around 1997 when a number of technologies began to emerge from Microsoft, including *Microsoft Transaction Server (MTS), Microsoft Message Queuing (MSMQ),* and *Microsoft Clustering Services.* The aim of these developments was to bring something that had previously been esoteric, specialized, and generally mainframe-based within the scope of standard PC technology, putting these technologies in the hands of developers.

Handling transactions involved a considerable extension to the NT/COM runtime. It also involved the introduction of several new standard COM interfaces, some to be used or implemented by transactional components and some to be used or implemented by the underlying resource managers, such as SQL Server. These additions, along with some other innovations relating to areas such as asynchronous COM, came to be known as *COM +.*

This chapter explores the .NET Enterprise Services. In particular, it looks at transaction processing and queued components using the classes of the `System.EnterpriseServices` and `System.Transactions` namespaces. This is an enormous subject that could easily fill a whole book by itself, so this chapter only scratches the surface of it. However, by the end of the chapter, you will understand how all the pieces fit together. Let's begin by looking at what transactions are, and how they fit into Visual Basic 2005.

> You can find more information about transactions in .NET in *Professional VB.NET Transactions* (Wiley, 2002).

Transactions

A *transaction* is one or more linked units of processing placed together as a single unit of work, which either succeeds or fails. If the unit of work succeeds, all work is then committed. If the unit fails, then every item of processing is rolled back and the process is returned to its original state.

The standard transaction example involves transferring money from account A to account B. The money must either end up in account B (and nowhere else), or — if something goes wrong — stay in account A (and go nowhere else). This avoids the very undesirable case in which we have taken money from account A but haven't put it in account B.

The ACID Test

Transaction theory starts with *ACID*. According to the ACID theory, all transactions should have the following properties:

- **Atomicity** — A transaction is *atomic*; that is, everything is treated as one unit. However many different components the transaction involves, and however many different method calls on those components there are, the system treats it as a single operation that either entirely succeeds or entirely fails. If it fails, then the system is left in the state it was in before the transaction was attempted.

- *Consistency* — All changes are done in a consistent manner. The system goes from one valid state to another.

- *Isolation* — Transactions that are going on at the same time are isolated from each other. If transaction A changes the system from state 1 to state 2, transaction B will see the system in either state 1 or 2, but not some half-baked state in between the two.

- *Durability* — If a transaction has been committed, the effect is permanent, even if the system fails.

Let's illustrate this with a concrete example. Imagine that, having spent a happy afternoon browsing in your favorite bookstore, you decide to shell out some of your hard-earned dollars for a copy of, yes, *Professional VB 2005 with .NET 3.0* (wise choice). You take the copy to the checkout, and exchange a bit of cash for the book. A transaction is going on here: You pay money and the store provides you with a book.

There are only two reasonable outcomes either you get the book and the store gets its money or you don't get the book and the store doesn't get its money. If, for example, there is insufficient credit on your card, then you'll leave the shop without the book. In that case, the transaction doesn't happen. The only way for the transaction to complete is both for you to get the book and the store to get its money. This is the principle of atomicity.

If the store provides you with a copy of some other book instead, then you would reasonably feel that you ended up with an outcome that was neither anticipated nor desirable. This would be a violation of the principle of consistency.

Now imagine that there is one copy of the book in the store, and another potential buyer of that book has gone up to the cashier next to you. As far as the person at the other cashier is concerned, your respective transactions are isolated from each other (even though you are competing for the same resource). Either your transaction succeeds or the other person's does. What definitely *doesn't* happen is that the bookstore decides to exert the wisdom of Solomon and give you half each.

Now suppose you take the book home and the bookstore calls you to ask if they can have the book back. Apparently, an important customer (well, far more important than you, anyway) needs a copy. You would find this a tad unreasonable, and a violation of the principle of durability.

At this point, it's worth considering what implications all this is likely to have on the underlying components. How can you ensure that all of the changes in the system can be unwound if the transaction is aborted at some point? Perhaps you're in the middle of updating dozens of database files and something goes wrong.

There are three aspects to rescuing this situation with transactions:

❑ Knowledge that something has gone wrong

❑ Knowledge to perform the recovery

❑ Coordination of the recovery process

The middle part of the process is handled by the resource managers themselves; the likes of SQL Server and Oracle are fully equipped to deal with transactions and rollback (even if the resource manager in question is restarted partway through a transaction), so you don't need to worry about any of that. The last part of the process, coordination, is handled by the .NET runtime (or at least the Enterprise Services part of it). The first part, knowing that something is wrong, is shared between the components themselves and the .NET runtime. This isn't at all unusual: Sometimes a component can detect that something has gone wrong itself and signal that recovery is necessary, while on other occasions it may not be able to do so, because it has crashed.

Later, you will see how all this works as you build a transactional application.

Transactional Components

What components are actually managed by Enterprise Services? What purpose do they serve? To answer that, you need to consider what a typical real-world *n*-tier application looks like. The bottom tier is the persistent datastore, typically an industry-standard database such as SQL Server or Oracle. However, there are other possible datastores, including the file system. These are termed *resource managers* because they manage resources. The software here is concerned with maintaining the integrity of the application's data and providing rapid and efficient access to it. The top tier is the user interface. This is a completely different specialization, and the software here is concerned with presenting a smooth, easy-to-follow front end to the end user. This layer shouldn't actually do any data manipulation at all, apart from whatever formatting is necessary to meet each user's presentational needs. The interesting stuff is in the tiers in between — in particular, the business logic. In the .NET/COM+ transactional model, the software elements that implement this are components running under the control of the Enterprise Services runtime.

Typically, these components are called into being to perform some sort of transaction and then, to all intents and purposes, disappear again. For example, a component might be called into play to transfer information from one database to another in such a way that the information was either in one database or the other, but not both. This component might have a number of different methods, each of which did a different kind of transfer. However, each method call would carry out a complete transfer:

```
Public Sub TransferSomething()
   TakeSomethingFromA
   AddSomethingToB
End Sub
```

Crucially, this means that most transaction components have no concept of *state*; there are no properties that hold values between method calls. You can see the reason for this if you imagine what would happen if you had a number of instances of the preceding components all vying for the attention of the database. If instance one of the control started the transfer, remembering the state or current values of A and B just after instance two had done the same, you could end up with the state being different between the two instances. This would violate the isolation of the transaction. Persistence is left to the outside tiers in this model. This takes a little bit of getting used to at first, because it runs counter to everything that you learned in Object-orientation 101 classes, so take a minute or two to consider what you're actually gaining from this.

The business logic is the area of the system that requires all the transactional management. Anything that happens here needs to be monitored and controlled to ensure that all the ACID requirements are met. The neatest way to do this in a component-oriented framework is to develop the business logic as components that are required to implement a standard interface. The transaction management framework can then use this interface to monitor and control how the logic is implemented from a transactional point of view. The transaction interface is a means for the business logic elements to talk to the transaction framework and for the transaction framework to talk back to the logic elements.

So what's all this about not having state? Well, if you maintain state inside your components, then you immediately have a scaling problem. The middle tiers of your application are now seriously resource-hungry. If you want an analogy from another area of software, consider why the Internet scales so well: because HTTP is a stateless protocol. Every HTTP request stands in isolation, so no resources are tied up in maintaining any form of session. It's the same with transactional components.

This is not to say that you can't ever maintain state inside your transactional components. You can, but it's not recommended, and the examples in this chapter don't illustrate it.

An Example of Transactions

For our transaction example, we're going to build a simple business-logic component that transfers data from one bank account (Wrox's, in fact) to another one. Wrox's bank account will be represented by a row in one database, while the other will be represented by a row in another one.

Before beginning, note one important point: You can't have transactions without any resource managers. It's very tempting to think that you can experiment with transactional component services without actually involving, say, a database, because (as you shall see) none of the methods in the transactional classes makes any explicit references to one. However, if you do try to do this, then you will find that your transactions don't actually trouble the system's statistics. Fortunately, you don't need to lay out your hard-earned cash for a copy of SQL Server (nice though that is), because Visual Studio 2005 comes with a lightweight (but fully functional) copy of SQL Server, which goes under the name of *SQL Server 2005*

Express Edition, or more simply *SQL Express*. In addition, SQL Express is available separately, so you can even work with databases if you use Visual Basic Express.

Creating the Databases

First, set up the databases. Check whether the Server Explorer tab is visible in Visual Studio 2005 (see Figure 28-1). If not, open it by selecting View ➪ Server Explorer. Create a new database in the Data Connections tree.

Figure 28-1

Next, right-click Data Connections and select New Database from the menu. Alternately, you can click the icon that looks like a plus sign over a can with a plug (not quite the universal symbol for a database, but it will have to do). A new dialog box appears (see Figure 28-2).

Figure 28-2

Enter the database name (BankOfWrox) and select Use Windows Authentication. After clicking OK, you are prompted to create the database if it doesn't exist. You should now see BankOfWrox in the list of data connections (see Figure 28-3).

Set up the database. If you open up the new node, you should see a number of other nodes, including Tables. Right-click this and then select New Table from the menu. Another dialog box should appear (see Figure 28-4). Create two columns, Name and Amount, as shown. Make sure that Name is set up to be the primary key. When you click the close box, you'll be asked if you want to save the changes to Table1. Select Yes, and another dialog box will appear (see Figure 28-5).

Figure 28-3

Figure 28-4

Figure 28-5

Use the name Accounts for the table. You should now see a child node called Accounts below Tables in the tree. That completes the creation of BankOfWrox. Repeat the process for BankOfMe. The structure is exactly the same (although it doesn't need to be for the purposes of this example). Don't forget to set Name as the primary key. We could have created these two as separate rows in the same database, but it doesn't really simulate the scenario where Enterprise Services is intended (inter-application communication).

Populating Your Databases

The next thing to do is populate the databases. If you right-click over Accounts for either database and select Show Table Data from Table from the menu, you will see a grid that enables you to add rows and initialize the values of their columns (see Figure 28-6).

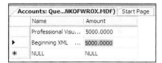

Figure 28-6

Enter two accounts in `BankOfWrox` — Professional Visual Basic 2005 and Beginning XML — and allocate $5,000 to each. Now repeat the process for `BankOfMe`, setting up one account, `Me`, with $0 in it (so you're either (a) broke or (b) wise enough not to leave any cash lying around in this sort of account).

The Business Logic

The next step is to create the transactional component to support the business logic. Create a new Class Library project called `Transactions`. Then, add a reference to `System.EnterpriseServices` (see Figure 28-7).

Figure 28-7

This reference is needed because in order to come under the control of the Enterprise Services runtime, the component must inherit from the `System.EnterpriseServices.ServicedComponent` class:

```vb
Imports System.EnterpriseServices
Imports System.Configuration
Imports System.Data.SqlClient

<Assembly: ApplicationName("WroxTransactions")>
<Assembly: ApplicationAccessControl(True)>
Public Class BankTransactions
    Inherits ServicedComponent
```

Here's the main function in the component, `TransferMoney`:

```
Public Sub TransferMoney(ByVal amount As Decimal, _
    ByVal sourceBank As String, _
    ByVal sourceAccount As String, _
    ByVal destinationBank As String, _
    ByVal destinationAccount As String)

    Try
        Withdraw(sourceBank, sourceAccount, amount)
        Try
            Deposit(destinationBank, destinationAccount, amount)
        Catch ex As Exception
            'deposit failed
            Throw New _
              ApplicationException("Error transfering money, deposit failed.", _
              ex)
        End Try

        'both operations succeeded
        ContextUtil.SetComplete()
    Catch ex As Exception
        'withdraw failed
        Throw New _
          ApplicationException("Error transfering money, withdrawal failed.", _
          ex)
    End Try
End Sub
```

Ignoring for the moment the references to `ContextUtil`, you can see that we have effectively divided up the logic into two halves: the half that takes money from the Wrox account (represented by the private function `Withdraw`), and the half that adds it to your account (represented by the private function `Deposit`). For the function to complete successfully, each of the two halves must complete successfully.

So what does `ContextUtil` do? The `ContextUtil` class represents the context of the transaction. Within that context are basically two bits that control the behavior of the transaction from the point of view of each participant: the *consistent* bit and the *done* bit. The done bit determines whether or not the transaction is finished, so that resources can be reused. The consistent bit determines whether or not the transaction was successful from the point of view of the participant. This is established during the first phase of the two-phase commit process. In complex distributed transactions involving more than one participant, the overall consistency and doneness are voted on, so that a transaction is only consistent or done when everyone agrees that it is. If a transaction completes in an inconsistent state, it is not allowed to proceed to the second phase of the commit.

In this case, there is only a single participant, but the principle remains the same. We can determine the overall outcome by setting these two bits, which is done via `SetComplete` and `SetAbort`, which are static methods in the `ContextUtil` class. Both of these set the done bit to `True`. `SetComplete` also sets the consistent bit to `True`, whereas `SetAbort` sets the consistent bit to `False`. In this example, `SetComplete` is only set if both halves of the transaction are successful.

The First Half of the Transaction

Now it's time to see what's going on in the two halves of the transaction itself. The component is responsible for reading and writing to the two databases, so it needs two connection strings. You could hard-code these into the component, but a better solution is to use the new My Settings feature to include them. Double-click My Project in the Solution Explorer and navigate to the Settings tab. Add the two connection strings using the names `BankOfWrox` and `BankOfMe`, as shown in Figure 28-8.

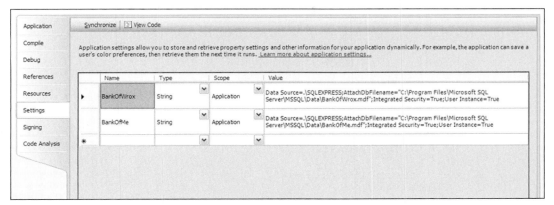

Figure 28-8

1. Here's the function that removes money from the Wrox account:

```
Private Sub Withdraw(ByVal bank As String, _
  ByVal account As String, _
  ByVal amount As Decimal)
```

2. Establish a connection to the database, and retrieve the current account balance from it:

```
Dim ConnectionString As String
Dim SQL As String
Dim conn As SqlConnection = Nothing
Dim cmdCurrent As SqlCommand
Dim currentValue As Decimal
Dim cmdUpdate As SqlCommand

ConnectionString = My.Settings.Item(bank).ToString
SQL = String.Format("SELECT Amount FROM Accounts WHERE Name = '{0}'", _
  account)
```

3. The call to `ExecuteScalar` retrieves a single value from the database — in this case, the amount for the requested account. Note that we have started an exception handler with the `Try` keyword. We'll finish the `Try` block in a moment:

```
Try
        conn = New SqlConnection(ConnectionString)
        conn.Open()

        cmdCurrent = New SqlCommand(SQL, conn)
        currentValue = CDec(cmdCurrent.ExecuteScalar())
```

4. Note the current balance and determine whether you can afford to transfer the amount asked for. If not, raise an `Exception`:

```
'check for overdrafts
        If amount > currentValue Then
            Throw New ArgumentException("Attempt to overdraft account")
        End If
```

5. Otherwise, subtract the amount, and update the table accordingly:

```
'otherwise, we're good to withdraw
        SQL = _
            String.Format("UPDATE Accounts SET Amount = {0} WHERE Name = '{1}'", _
            currentValue - amount, account)
        cmdUpdate = New SqlCommand(SQL, conn)
        cmdUpdate.ExecuteNonQuery()
```

6. Close the exception handler and the database:

```
Catch ex As Exception
        Throw New DataException("Error withdrawing", ex)
    Finally
        If Not conn Is Nothing Then
            conn.Close()
        End If
    End Try
End Sub
```

The Second Half of the Transaction

The second half of the transaction is similar, except that the failure conditions are slightly different. First, we stipulate that we don't want any transfer of less than $50. Second, we've inserted a bug such that an attempt to transfer a negative amount will cause a divide by zero. (You'll see why we added this rather bizarre act of sabotage in a moment.) Here's the code:

```
Private Sub Deposit(ByVal bank As String, _
  ByVal account As String, _
  ByVal amount As Decimal)

    Dim ConnectionString As String
    Dim SQL As String
    Dim conn As SqlConnection = Nothing
    Dim cmdCurrent As SqlCommand
    Dim currentValue As Decimal
    Dim cmdUpdate As SqlCommand

    ConnectionString = My.Settings.Item(bank).ToString
    SQL = String.Format("SELECT Amount FROM Accounts WHERE Name = '{0}'", _
      account)

    If amount < 0 Then
        amount = amount / 0
    ElseIf amount < 50 Then
        Throw New ArgumentException("Value of deposit must be greater than $50")
    Else
```

```
     Try
          conn = New SqlConnection(ConnectionString)
          conn.Open()

          'get the current value
          cmdCurrent = New SqlCommand(SQL, conn)
          currentValue = CDec(cmdCurrent.ExecuteScalar())

          SQL = _
            String.Format("UPDATE Accounts SET Amount = {0} WHERE Name = '{1}'", _
            currentValue + amount, account)

          cmdUpdate = New SqlCommand(SQL, conn)
          cmdUpdate.ExecuteNonQuery()
     Finally
          If Not conn Is Nothing Then
               conn.Close()
          End If
     End Try
  End If

End Sub
```

The business logic component is complete. Let's see how you can bring it under the control of Enterprise Services. First, of course, you need to build your DLL in VS.NET.

Why did we add the divide by zero error? This gives you a chance to see what happens to the transaction when an exception occurs in your code. The transaction will automatically fail and rollback, which means that your data will still be in a good state at the end.

Registering Your Component

Because the Enterprise Services infrastructure is COM-oriented, you need to expose the .NET component as a COM component, and register it with Component Services. Component Services handles all transaction coordination; that is, Component Services tracks any changes and restores the data should the transaction fail. First, some changes to the component are needed to enable this COM interaction. Prepare to take a trip down memory lane.

All COM components must have a GUID (Global Unique Identifier) that uniquely identifies it to the COM infrastructure. This was done for you in Visual Basic 6.0, but with .NET it requires you to add a value. In addition, your component needs an attribute to make it visible to COM. You can set both of these in the Assembly Information dialog. Double-click My Project in the Solution Explorer. On the Application page, click Assembly Information. There should already be a Guid assigned to your component. Check off Make Assembly COM-Visible. This makes all of the Public types accessible to COM. (see Figure 28-9)

You should also update the Assembly Version fields as you make changes to the component.

> *Chapter 21 contains more information about strong names and assemblies.*

The problem is that the assembly is a private assembly. In order to make it available to the transaction framework, it needs to be a shared assembly. To do this, give the assembly a *cryptographically strong name*, generally referred to as its *strong name*.

Figure 28-9

Cryptographically strong means that the name has been signed with the private key of a dual key pair. This isn't the place to go into a long discussion on dual-key cryptography, but essentially a pair of keys is generated, one public and one private. If something is encrypted using the private key, it can only be decrypted using the public key from that pair, and vice versa. It is therefore an excellent tool for preventing tampering with information. If, for example, the name of an assembly were to be encrypted using the private key of a pair, then the recipient of a new version of that assembly could verify the origin of that new version, and be confident that it was not a rogue version from some other source. This is because only the original creator of the assembly retains access to its private key.

Giving the Assembly a Strong Name

You now have to make sure that your assembly uses the strong name. You can create a new strong name file, or assign an existing strong name file on the Signing tab of the Project Designer dialog (see Figure 28-10).

Figure 28-10

Registering with Component Services

Once you've built the DLL again, you can run `RegSvcs` to register the DLL with Component Services (see Figure 28-11).

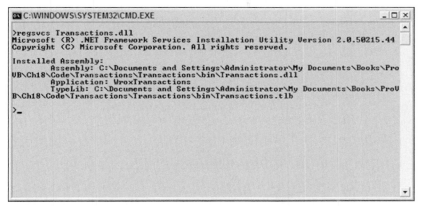

Figure 28-11

`RegSvcs` does a few things at this point. It creates a COM Type Library for the DLL. This enables it to communicate with COM. In addition, it creates a COM+ application for the component.

The Component Services Console

The *Component Services Console* is the control interface for Component Services. This is an MMC snap-in, which you can find (on Windows 2000 and XP) by selecting Control Panel ➪ Administrative Tools ➪ Component Services. If you open it, you'll see something like what is shown in Figure 28-12.

Figure 28-12

You should be able to find the sample under COM+ Applications. A COM+ application is a set of related COM+ components that have been packaged together. RegSvcs creates a new application for every component that it registers. If you want to bundle together a series of components from separate DLLs, you can do this, but you can only do it by creating a new application via the Component Services Console (try right-clicking COM+ Applications and then selecting New). We'll explore the console a little more as we go on.

Now you need a test application. Second, and more important, you need to tell Component Services that you're interested in transactions.

A Test Application

Deal with the first problem right away by creating a Windows Application project called TestTransactions and a very simple form (see Figure 28-13).

Figure 28-13

The text field is called TransferField and the command button is called TransferButton. In order to access the transactional component, add references to a couple of DLLs. First, add a reference to the transactional component DLL itself. You'll need to browse for this, as it isn't currently in the global assembly cache. Second, in order to access the objects in this DLL, you also need to make the application aware of the System.EnterpriseServices assembly, so add a reference to that as well. Having done that, it's time to import Transactions into the application:

```
Imports Transactions
```

Here's the code behind the TransferButton button:

```
Private Sub TransferButton_Click(ByVal sender As System.Object, _
  ByVal e As System.EventArgs) Handles TransferButton.Click
    Dim txn As New BankTransactions
    Try
        txn.TransferMoney(CDec(Me.TransferField.Text), _
          "BankOfWrox", "Professional Visual Basic 2005", _
          "BankOfMe", "Me")
        MessageBox.Show(String.Format("{0:C} transfered from {1} to {2}", _
            CDec(Me.TransferField.Text), "BankOfWrox", "BankOfMe"), _
            "Transfer Succeeded", _
            MessageBoxButtons.OK, _
            MessageBoxIcon.Information)
```

```
        Catch ex As Exception
            MessageBox.Show(ex.Message, "Transfer failed", _
              MessageBoxButtons.OK, _
              MessageBoxIcon.Error)

        End Try

    End Sub
```

The Transaction Attribute

Now it's time to tell Component Services how the component should enter a transaction. There are two ways of doing this: via the Component Services Console or via an attribute in code. To do it via the Component Services Console, open the Explorer tree to locate the `Transactions` component (as shown in Figure 28-14).

Figure 28-14

Select one of the available options; you'll learn what these all mean in a moment. It's a little tiresome to require the system manager to do this every time, especially if you already know that your component is always going to have the same transaction characteristics. An alternative mechanism is available: You can explicitly set up an attribute in the code for your component.

Attributes are items of declarative information that can be attached to the elements of code, such as classes, methods, data members, and properties. Anything that uses these can query their values at runtime. One such attribute is called `TransactionAttribute`, which, unsurprisingly, is used for specifying the transaction characteristics of a component class. The value of this attribute is taken from an enumeration called `TransactionOption`. Both `TransactionAttribute` and `TransactionOption` are found within the `System.EnterpriseServices` namespace. The enumeration can take the following values:

Value	Description
Disabled	Ignore any transaction in the current context. This is the default.
NotSupported	Create the component in a context with no governing transaction.
Required	Share a transaction if one exists; create a new transaction if necessary.
RequiresNew	Create the component with a new transaction, regardless of the state of the current context .
Supported	Share a transaction if one exists. If it doesn't, create the component.

The available values are exactly the same as the ones shown in the `Transaction` tab. This case is a standalone transaction, so either `RequiresNew` or `Required` are equally valid.

Before changing the component, deregister the current version to avoid any confusion (see Figure 28-15).

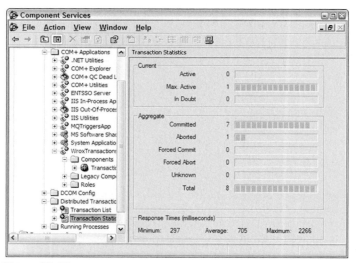

Figure 28-15

Now go back to the `Transactions` project and make the change:

```
<Assembly: ApplicationName("WroxTransactions")>
<Assembly: ApplicationAccessControl(True)>
<Transaction(TransactionOption.RequiresNew)> _

Public Class BankTransactions
    Inherits ServicedComponent
```

Having made the change, rebuild `Transactions` and then reregister it as before. Now run the test application. Enter 1000 and click the Confirm button. You might be able to see the number of current active transactions briefly go from none to one (depending on your computer, this may be too fast to see), followed by the number of committed transactions and the total both going up by one. Great, you've implemented your first transaction. If you check the two databases, the amount in `BankOfWrox`'s Professional Visual Basic account has been reduced to $4,000, whereas Jon's account in `BankOfMe` has been increased by $1,000.

Invalid Data

What happens if you enter a value that you know is invalid? There are two options here: either try to transfer more money than there is in the Professional Visual Basic account, or try to transfer less than the "approved limit." Run the application again and try to transfer $10. As expected, the transaction will fail, and no changes will be made to the accounts. Professional Visual Basic still has $4,000, and your account still has $1,000. This isn't too much of a big deal, because the invalid condition is spotted before any database manipulation is carried out. If you look at the transaction statistics, the number of *aborted* transactions has been incremented this time.

Now try to transfer $10,000. This time, the first part of the transaction is successful, but the *second* part fails. Again the number of aborted transactions is incremented, but what's happened to the database? Well, fortunately for everyone concerned, there is still $4,000 in the Professional Visual Basic account, and still $1,000 in your account. The *entire* transaction has failed.

When Something Goes Wrong

Recall that bit of mindless vandalism that we did to the `Deposit` function so that it would divide by zero if we entered a negative value? Here's where we get to try it out. Run the application again, and try to transfer $-1. You should receive an error message. It was halfway through a transaction, but never mind, because when you look at the transaction statistics, the aborted count has gone up by one. More important, if you check the databases, the Pro VB account *still* has $4,000, and the other account still has $1,000, so you're protected against software failures as well.

Other Aspects of Transactions

Several other topics relate to transactions, such as Just-In-Time activation and object pooling.

Just-In-Time

Creating and deleting components takes time. Instead of discarding the component when finished with it, why not keep it around in case another instance is required? The mechanism by which this is done is called *Just-In-Time* (JIT) *activation*, and it's set by default for all automatic transactional components (it's unset by default for all other COM+ components, however). This is another reason why holding state is undesirable within components — it limits the ability to share components.

All good transactional components are entirely stateless, but real life dictates differently. For example, you might want to maintain a link to your database, one that would be expensive to set up every time. The JIT mechanism provides a couple of methods that you can override in the `ServicedComponent` class in this case.

The method that is invoked when a JIT component is activated is called `Activate`, and the component that is invoked when it is deactivated is called, unsurprisingly, `Deactivate`. In `Activate` and `Deactivate` you put the things that you would normally put in your constructor and deconstructor. JIT can also be activated by adding the `JustInTimeActivation` attribute to any class within `ServicedComponent`.

Object Pooling

You can, if you want, take this a stage further and maintain a pool of objects already constructed and prepared to be activated whenever required. When the object is no longer required (that is, it's deactivated), it is returned to the pool until the next time it is required. By retaining objects, you don't have to continually create them anew, which in turn reduces the performance costs of your application. You can use the `ObjectPooling` attribute within your class to determine how the pool is to operate:

```
<Transaction(TransactionOption.RequiresNew), _
 ObjectPooling(MinPoolSize:=5, MaxPoolSize:=20, _
                      CreationTimeOut:=30)> _
Public Class BankTransactions
```

Queued Components

The traditional component programming model is very much a *synchronous* one. Put simply, you invoke a method and you get a result. Unfortunately, very many real-world problems are inherently *asynchronous*. You can't always wait for a response to your request before moving on to the next task. The real-world analogy here is the difference between phoning someone and sending an e-mail. Phoning is a synchronous process. Either the phone is answered (a successful transaction) or it isn't (or you've called a wrong number, another form of unsuccessful transaction). E-mailing someone is asynchronous; you have no control over how long the e-mail takes to arrive, or when the person will actually look at it. Therefore, in order to tackle everything that the real world throws at us, we need an asynchronous component model for those scenarios where it is appropriate.

Why only some scenarios? The synchronous model is quite simple to manage, because the three possible outcomes of a request are quite straightforward to handle. First, the request can be successful. Second, the software can crash. Finally, the software can simply not respond at all, in which case it times out. However, when dealing with asynchronous requests, expect all manner of unusual conditions. For example, the target system may not currently be operational, so you have to make a decision regarding how long to wait before it comes back up again. Each outstanding request takes up system resources, so they need to be managed carefully; you need to be able to determine when the response comes back; you need to make certain that the recipient only receives a given message once, and so on. We are, in fact, dealing with a different infrastructure than MTS here, an infrastructure to handle reliable messaging. Microsoft's product to tackle this type of problem is Microsoft Message Queue (MSMQ).

The idea behind reliable messaging is that once you have asked the system to send a message to a given target, you can effectively stop worrying about it. The system handles storing and forwarding of messages to their target, and handles retries and timeouts, ensuring it is received only once, and returning messages to the dead letter queue if all else fails. MSMQ is, in fact, a whole technology in itself, and can seem quite complex. However, Enterprise Services provides a handy, simple abstraction called *queued components*.

Queued components take the sometimes gnarly aspects of working with MSMQ and make them easier to work with than the raw queue handling. Instead, you have the concepts of recorders, listeners, and players. Recorders create messages that are put on a queue. Eventually, a listener receives the message. This could happen immediately or it could take weeks if the two components are disconnected. Finally, the player does whatever the message requests. Naturally, this places some restrictions on the kind of component that can be used. For example, you can't have any output arguments or return values. If you have either of these, the values can't be set until the action is complete, removing the benefit of the asynchronous aspects of the call. However, there are some cool things that you can do, explored in the next section.

> In order to run the queued components examples, MSMQ is needed, which comes with Windows 2000 and XP. However, you need to install it separately using the Add Windows Components dialog.

An Example of Queued Components

This example creates a very simple logging component that takes a string as its input and writes it out to a sequential file, as well as outputs it in a message box. For the purposes of a simple example, the client and the server are on the same machine; in a production scenario they would be separate. The benefit of using queued components here is that the logging doesn't slow down the main process.

Create a Class Library project called `Reporter`. As usual, add a reference to the `System.EnterpriseServices` namespace. First define an interface:

```
Imports System.IO
Imports System.EnterpriseServices
Public Interface IReporter
   Sub Log(ByVal message As String)
End Interface
```

Notice that the `Log` method follows the requirements listed previously. There is no return value, and all parameters are input only. We need to separate out the interface from the implementation because the implementation, residing on the server, is going to be sitting on another machine somewhere. The client isn't the slightest bit interested in the details of this; all it needs to know is how to interface to it.

Take a look at the actual implementation. As with the transactional component, we inherit from `ServicedComponent`, and implement the interface just defined. However, notice the `<InterfaceQueuing()>` attribute that indicates to the component services runtime that the interface can be queued (we did the same for the interface):

```
<InterfaceQueuing(Interface:="IReporter")> Public Class Reporter
   Inherits ServicedComponent
   Implements IReporter
```

In the logging method, simply output a message box, open a `StreamWriter` component to append to the log file, and then close it:

```
Sub Log(ByVal message As String) Implements IReporter.Log
    MsgBox(strText)
    Using writer As StreamWriter = _
        New StreamWriter("c:\account.log", True)
            writer.WriteLine(String.Format("{0}: {1}", _
              DateTime.Now, message))
            writer.Close()
        End Using
    End Sub
End Class
```

That's it for the code for the component. To enable queuing, click the Show All Files button on the Solution Explorer to see the hidden files for the project. Open the My Project item and then open the `AssemblyInfo.vb` file. Ensure that it has these attributes:

```
'Enterprise Services attributes
<Assembly: EnterpriseServices.ApplicationAccessControl(False, _
    Authentication:=EnterpriseServices.AuthenticationOption.None)>
<Assembly: EnterpriseServices.ApplicationQueuing(Enabled:=True, _
    QueueListenerEnabled:=True)>
<Assembly: EnterpriseServices.ApplicationName("WroxQueue")>
```

Next, ensure that queuing is correctly enabled for this component. The next line is a special line to enable message queuing to work correctly in a workgroup environment, by switching off authentication. If we didn't do this, we would need to set up an entire domain structure. (In a production scenario, that's exactly what you would use, so you would need to remove this line.) Finally, ensure that the component runs as a server, rather than as a library. This was optional in the case of transactional components, but it's mandatory for queued components. You'll soon see why. In addition, you should add a strong name file to your project, as you did with the `Transactions` component.

Consoles Again

It's time to build your component. Once built, register it using `RegSvcs` just as you did with the `Transactions` component. Take a look at the Component Services Console to see how it's going. Also, look again more closely at Figure 28-16. That looks fine, but there's one other console to check out: the *Computer Management Console*. Access this either from the system console or by right-clicking the My Computer icon and selecting Manage from the menu. Tucked away at the bottom is the relevant part. Open Services and Applications to find it. Component Services has set up some queues for us. There are five queues feeding into the main one, so the infrastructure is ready. Keep in mind that all this would be running on the server machine in a production scenario, not the client.

Building the Client

The problem is that all the code you've written in this project is built on top of the MSMQ infrastructure, which is, inevitably, a COM infrastructure. Worse, the current tasks involve *marshaling* COM objects into a stream suitable for inserting into a queued message. For the purposes of this discussion, think of marshaling as intelligently serializing the contents of a method invocation on an interface. We do this in such a way that they can then be deserialized at the other end and turned into a successful invocation of the same method in a remote implementation of the interface. We get COM to do this for us by constructing a *moniker*, which is basically an intelligent name.

Figure 28-16

Begin by creating a Windows Application project called `TestReporter`. Add a reference to the `Reporter` component in the usual manner. Figure 28-17 shows the form.

Figure 28-17

The text box is called `MessageField`, and the button is called `SendButton`. Here's the code:

```
Imports System.Runtime.InteropServices
Public Class MainForm
  Inherits System.Windows.Forms.Form
  Private Sub SendButton_Click(ByVal sender As System.Object, _
```

```
                              ByVal e As System.EventArgs) _
                              Handles SendButton.Click
```

Here's the crucial section. Note the references to the interface and how the object is instantiated:

```
        Dim logger As Queues.IReporter

        Try
            logger = CType(Marshal.BindToMoniker("queue:/new:Queues.Reporter"), _
                Queues.IReporter)
```

Here's the queued call:

```
    logger.Log(Me.MessageField.Text)
```

Finally, release the reference to the underlying COM object:

```
            Marshal.ReleaseComObject(logger)
            MessageBox.Show("Message sent")

        Catch ex As Exception
            MessageBox.Show(ex.Message, "Error sending message")
        End Try
```

It's not pretty, but you only have to do it once to use it repeatedly.

Queuing Invocations

Now try using this application to put a message onto the queue. Run it up and enter a suitable message, such as "Hello everyone" (see Figure 28-18).

Figure 28-18

We've definitely created a message, so that represents our invocation. If we were able to read it, we would see the message you typed in earlier embedded somewhere in it. (Unfortunately, the console only allows us to inspect the start of the message, but we can see the name of the component in there.) Why hasn't anything happened? We haven't actually started our server. Recall that our component has to run as a server. This is why. The server has to sit there all the time, serving the incoming queue. Therefore, go to the Component Services Console, right-click Reporter, select Start from the menu, and you're off. Lo and behold, there's the message box (see Figure 28-19).

Figure 28-19

Now that the message has been delivered, return to the Component Services Console. Right-clicking over the message queue and selecting Refresh confirms that the message has indeed been removed from the queue. Look in `account.log` and notice that it has been updated as well. Now, running the application results in the message boxes popping up right away.

Transactions with Queued Components

Why were you instructed to call that file `account.log`? MSMQ, like SQL Server, is a resource manager, and it can take part in transactions. At first, this is a little counterintuitive because how on earth can anything as asynchronous as MSMQ have anything to do with transactions? The point is that it is *reliable*. Anything you put into a queue is guaranteed to come out the other end. If we take the transaction to the point at which a message is securely in the queue, we definitely have something that can participate. What happens at the other end of the queue is an entirely separate transaction. Of course, if something goes wrong there, you may need to look at setting up a compensating transaction coming back the other way to trigger some kind of rollback.

For the final example, then, we're going to take our original transactional component and add in a queued element, so that not only does the transfer of money take place, but that fact is also logged to a remote file. Use exactly the same queued component as last time, which is why we called the file `account.log`.

Begin by making a clone of `TestTransactions` called `TestQueuedTransactions`. Add a reference to `Queues` and an `Imports` statement:

```
Imports System.Runtime.InteropServices
```

You also need a new private subroutine:

```
Private Shared Sub LogTransaction(ByVal amount As Decimal, _
    ByVal sourceBank As String, ByVal sourceAccount As String, _
    ByVal destinationBank As String, ByVal destinationAccount As String)
```

```
        Dim logger As Queues.IReporter

        Try
            logger = CType(Marshal.BindToMoniker("queue:/new:Queues.Reporter"), _
                Queues.IReporter)

            logger.Log(String.Format("{0:c} transfered from {1}:{2} to {3}:{4}", _
                amount, _
                sourceBank, sourceAccount, _
                destinationBank, destinationAccount))

            Marshal.ReleaseComObject(logger)
            MessageBox.Show("Message sent")

        Catch ex As Exception
            MessageBox.Show(ex.Message, "Error sending message")
        End Try
    End Sub
```

This may look similar to the previous queued component example application. Finally, add a call to this subroutine in the `Button_Click` event handler:

```
    Private Sub TransferButton_Click(ByVal sender As System.Object, _
        ByVal e As System.EventArgs) Handles TransferButton.Click
        Dim txn As New Transactions.BankTransactions
        Try
            txn.TransferMoney(CDec(Me.TransferField.Text), _
                "BankOfWrox", "Professional VB", _
                "BankOfMe", "Me")
            LogTransaction(CDec(Me.TransferField.Text), _
                "BankOfWrox", "Professional VB", _
                "BankOfMe", "Me")

            MessageBox.Show(String.Format("{0:C} transfered from {1} to {2}", _
                CDec(Me.TransferField.Text), "BankOfWrox", "BankOfMe"), _
                "Transfer Succeeded", _
                MessageBoxButtons.OK, _
                MessageBoxIcon.Information)

        Catch ex As Exception
            MessageBox.Show(ex.Message, "Transfer failed", _
                MessageBoxButtons.OK, _
                MessageBoxIcon.Error)

        End Try
    End Sub
```

Here, we're including a queued component in our transaction. It's been deliberately placed at the beginning to determine whether it genuinely takes part in the two-phase committal. If the transaction fails, you shouldn't see any messages come through

You also need to make a small change to the `Reporter` component, but you need to shut it down via the Component Services Console first. The change is very simple. To ensure that the queued component takes part in the transaction it must be marked with the `Transaction` attribute:

```
<InterfaceQueuing(Interface:="Reporter.IReporter"), _
Transaction(TransactionOption.Required)> _
Public Class Reporter
```

If you now transfer $1,000, we see the usual "Transfer complete" message box, and if you start up the `Reporter` component, you also see the message box from our queued component (see Figure 28-20).

Figure 28-20

If you try it again, you see the queued message coming through first, so you know it's OK for valid transfers. What happens if you try to transfer $100? As we know from the earlier example, this will fail, and indeed, we see the "Transfer failed" message box from the main component, but not a peep out of the queued component.

Transactions and System.Transactions

While the classes within `System.EnterpriseServices` make working with transactions easier, they are not the only way to define transactions with VB. Visual Basic 2005 includes a new set of classes: those within the `System.Transactions` namespace. As the name implies, these classes make it easier to define and work with transactions in your code. You may well ask at this point, "Why do we need two sets of classes that work with transactions?" As with many such questions, there are a couple of answers, each of which provides part of the answer.

The classes of `System.Transaction`, particularly the `Transaction` class itself, abstract the code from the resource managers participating in the transaction. While this is similar to the goal of the COM+ model described earlier, it is subtly different. The classes of Enterprise Services worked with the Distributed Transaction Coordinator (MSDTC), which in turn worked with the participating resource managers. The `Transaction` class does not need to work with the MSDTC and can coordinate multiple resource managers itself.

The classes of `System.Transaction` provide the means of creating your own resource managers. These resource managers may then participate in transactions. At first, you may balk at this prospect, wondering how you could write something that manages all the details of a transactional datastore. Aren't the details enormous? Fortunately, the classes make it easy to enlist in a transaction and report on your results.

Creating Transactions

`System.Transaction` supports two means of working with transactions: *implicit* and *explicit*. With implicit transactions, you define a boundary for the transaction. Any resource managers you use within this boundary become part of the transaction. That is, if you have defined a boundary and then call a database such as SQL Server, the actions performed on the database are part of the transaction. Explicit transactions, as you may have guessed, mean that you explicitly commit or rollback the transaction as needed.

Using the implicit model can greatly simplify the code involved in a transaction. For example, the TransferMoney method used in the preceding sample could be rewritten to use an implicit transaction:

```
Public Sub TransferMoney(ByVal amount As Decimal, _
  ByVal sourceBank As String, _
  ByVal sourceAccount As String, _
  ByVal destinationBank As String, _
  ByVal destinationAccount As String)

    Using scope As New TransactionScope
        Withdraw(sourceBank, sourceAccount, amount)
        Deposit(destinationBank, destinationAccount, amount)
    End Using
End Sub
```

The Using clause wraps the two methods within an implicit transaction. All resource managers that recognize transactions participate in this transaction. The Using clause guarantees that the TransactionScope object is disposed of when the transaction is complete.

Using explicit transactions requires a bit more code, but provides greater control over the transaction. You can use either the Transaction or the CommittableTransaction class to wrap transactions in this model. CommittableTransaction is a child class of Transaction, and adds the capability to commit a transaction, as the name implies.

Using a CommittableTransaction in the bank sample changes the TransferMoney method as follows:

```
Public Sub TransferMoney(ByVal amount As Decimal, _
    ByVal sourceBank As String, _
    ByVal sourceAccount As String, _
    ByVal destinationBank As String, _
    ByVal destinationAccount As String)

    Using txn As New CommittableTransaction
        Withdraw(sourceBank, sourceAccount, amount, txn)
        Deposit(destinationBank, destinationAccount, amount, txn)
    End Using
End Sub
```

Notice that the Withdraw and Deposit methods now have an additional parameter to receive the transaction. These additions enable the two methods to vote on the transaction:

```
Private Sub Deposit(ByVal bank As String, _
  ByVal account As String, _
  ByVal amount As Decimal, _
```

```
        ByVal txn As CommittableTransaction)

    Dim ConnectionString As String
    Dim SQL As String
    Dim cmdCurrent As SqlCommand
    Dim currentValue As Decimal
    Dim cmdUpdate As SqlCommand


    ConnectionString = My.Settings.Item(bank).ToString
    SQL = String.Format("SELECT Amount FROM Accounts WHERE Name = '{0}'", _
        account)

    If amount < 0 Then
        amount = amount / 0
    ElseIf amount < 50 Then
        Throw New ArgumentException("Value of deposit must be greater than 50")
    Else
        Using conn As New SqlConnection(ConnectionString)
            Try
                conn.Open()
                'join the transaction
                conn.EnlistTransaction(txn)
                'get the current value
                cmdCurrent = New SqlCommand(SQL, conn)
                currentValue = CDec(cmdCurrent.ExecuteScalar())

                SQL = String.Format("UPDATE Accounts SET Amount = " _
                    "{0} WHERE Name = '{1}'", _
                    currentValue + amount, account)

                cmdUpdate = New SqlCommand(SQL, conn)
                cmdUpdate.ExecuteNonQuery()
                txn.Commit()
            Catch ex As Exception
                'deal with transaction here
                txn.Rollback()
                Throw New DataException("Error depositing", ex)
            End Try
        End Using
    End If

End Sub
```

The principal change here is that the SQL connection must be enlisted in the transaction using the `EnlistTransaction` (or `EnlistDistributedTransaction`) method. Once it is a part of the transaction, it can then use the transaction methods to commit or rollback each part of the transaction.

Using the `TransactionScope` and Transaction classes can greatly decrease the amount of effort involved in creating and working with transactions in your applications. Generally, using implicit transactions using `TransactionScope` is easier, less error prone, and should be your first choice.

Creating Resource Managers

In addition to using the classes in `System.Transactions` for managing transactions, you can also use them to define your own resource managers. These resource managers can then participate in transactions with databases, MSDTC, message queues, and more. There are three basic steps in defining a resource manager:

1. Create an enlistment class. This class is used to track the resource manager's participation in the transaction. That is, this is the class that will vote on whether the transaction should complete or be rolled back. This class should implement the `IEnlistmentNotification` interface.

2. Enlist the new enlistment class in the transaction. There are two main ways the class may participate in the transaction: EnlistDurable and EnlistVolatile. You use EnlistDurable is if your resource manager stores data permanently, such as in a file or database. EnlistVolatile is used if your resource manager stores its information in memory or in some other nonrecoverable location.

3. Implement the methods of the IEnlistmentNotification interface to react to the states of the transaction. The IEnlistmentNotification interface provides four methods: `Prepare`, `Commit`, `Rollback`, and `InDoubt`. `Commit` and `Rollback` are self-explanatory, used at these two phases of the transaction. `Prepare` is called before `Commit`, to determine whether it is possible to commit the transaction. Finally, `InDoubt` is called if the transaction is questionable. This can happen if the transaction coordinator has lost track of one of the resource managers.

Why would you define your own resource managers and not simply use an existing one such as SQL Server? You might need to store data in another database that does not directly participate in transactions. Alternately, you may want to enable a normally nontransactional component with transactional behavior. For example, the cache in ASP.NET does not support adding items to the cache using transactions. You could create a resource manager that wraps the ASP.NET cache and adds support for commit and rollback of entries. This might be part of a system in which you want to use the cache as an in-memory datastore. While this would work without the transactions, adding transactional support would ensure that if the database write fails for any reason, then the entry could be rolled back out of the cache.

Summary

This chapter looked at creating applications using the classes of `System.EnterpriseServices` and `System.Transactions`. We first examined transactions, and their importance in maintaining data correctness when multiple simultaneous changes may affect your data. Properly applied, transactions can ensure that even with multiple users editing data, your database always reflects the correct data. We also looked at asynchronous processing using MSMQ and queued components. Many scenarios, such as logging or other "background" processes, are better handled using asynchronous code. Queued components make building these asynchronous handlers much easier.

There are many other aspects of Enterprise Services that we haven't looked at, including role-based security, object constructors, and more. It is definitely worth investing in a book such as *Professional VB.NET Transactions* by Matthew Bortniker and James Conrad (Wiley, 2002) for more details on these features.

In addition to creating transactions with the Enterprise Services classes, Visual Basic 2005 adds the `System.Transactions` namespace. This namespace provides even more ways of implementing transactions in your code. Beyond their use in creating transactions, they can also be used to create your own resource managers: datastores that can participate in transactions.

29

Network Programming

Just as it is difficult to live your life without talking with people, your applications also need to communicate, perhaps with other programs or perhaps with hardware devices. As shown throughout this book, you can use a variety of techniques to have your program communicate, including .NET Remoting, Web Services, and Enterprise Services. This chapter looks at yet another way to communicate: using the basic protocols that the Internet and many networks have been built on. You will learn how the classes in System.Net can provide a variety of techniques for communicating with existing applications such as Web or FTP servers, and how you can use them to create your own communication applications.

Before you start writing applications using these classes, however, it would be good to get some background on how networks are bolted together, and how machines and applications are identified.

Protocols, Addresses, and Ports

No discussion of a network is complete without a huge number of acronyms, seemingly random numbers, and the idea of a protocol. For example, the World Wide Web runs using a protocol called HTTP, or HyperText Transfer Protocol. Similarly, there is File Transfer Protocol (FTP), Network News Transfer Protocol (NNTP), and Gopher, also a protocol. Each application you run on a network communicates with another program using a defined protocol. The protocol is simply the expected messages each program sends the other, in the order they should be sent. For a real-world example, if you want to go see a movie with a friend, a simplified conversation could look like this:

```
You: Dials phone
Friend: Hears phone ringing, answers phone, "Hello"
You: "Hello. Want to go see 'Freddie and Jason Escape from New York, part 6?'"
Friend: "No, I saw that one already. What about 'Star Warthogs?'"
You: "OK, 9:30 showing downtown?"
Friend: "Yes"
You: "Later"
Friend: "See you," hangs up
```

Apart from a bad taste in movies, you can see a basic protocol here. Someone initiates a communication channel. The recipient accepts the channel and signals the start of the communication. The initial caller then sends a series of messages to which the recipient replies, either to signify they have been received or as either a positive or negative response. Finally, one of the messages indicates the end of the communication channel, and the two disconnect.

Similarly, network applications have their own protocols defined by the application writer. For example, sending an e-mail using SMTP (Simple Mail Transfer Protocol) could look like this:

```
220 schroedinger Microsoft ESMTP MAIL Service, Version: 6.0.2600.2180 ready at
Wed, 6 Oct 2004 15:58:28 -0700
HELLO
250 schroedinger Hello [127.0.0.1]
FOO
500 5.3.3 Unrecognized command
MAIL FROM: me
250 2.1.0 me@schroedinger....Sender OK
RCPT TO: him
250 2.1.5 him@schroedinger
DATA
354 Start mail input; end with <CRLF>.<CRLF>
subject: Testing SMTP

Hello World, via mail.
.
250 2.6.0 <SCHROEDINGERKaq65r500000001@schroedinger> Queued mail for delivery
QUIT
221 2.0.0 schroedinger Service closing transmission channel


Connection to host lost.
```

In this case, lines beginning with numbers are coming from the server, while the items in uppercase (and the message itself) were sent from the client. If the client sends an invalid message (as in the `"FOO"` message in the preceding code example), it receives a gentle rebuff from the server, whereas correct messages receive an `"OK"` or `"Go on"` reply. Traditionally, for SMTP and many other protocols, the reply is a three-digit number (see the following table) identifying the response (the text after the number, such as `"2.1.0 me@schroedinger...Sender OK,"` isn't really needed). The return values for the services generally fall into one of five ranges. Each range identifies a certain family of responses:

Range	Description
100–199	Message is good, but the server is still working on the request
200–299	Message is good, and the server has completed acting on the request
300–399	Message is good, but the server needs more information to work on the request
400–499	Message is good, but the server could not act on the request. You may try the request again to see if it works in the future
500–599	The server could not act on the request. Either the message was bad or an error occurred. It likely won't work next time.

Other protocols use this technique as well (leading to the infamous HTTP 404 error for "Page not found"), but they don't have to. Having a good reference is key to your success, and the best reference for existing protocols is the Request for Comments (RFC) for the protocol. These are the definitions that are used by protocol authors to create their implementation of the standard. Many of these RFCs are available online at the IETF (www.ietf.org) and the World Wide Web Consortium (www.w3.org).

Addresses and Names

The next important topic necessary to a thorough understanding of network programming is the relationship between the names and addresses of each of the computers involved. Each form of network communication (such as TCP/IP networks such as the Internet) has its own way of mapping the name of a computer (or host) to an address. The reason for this is simple: Computers deal with numbers better than text, and humans can remember text better than numbers (generally). Therefore, while you may have named your computer something clever like "l33t_#4x0R," applications and other computers know it by its IP (Internet Protocol) address. This address is a 32-bit value, usually written in four parts (each part is a byte that is a number from 0 to 255), such as 192.168.1.39. This is the standard the Internet has operated on for many years. However, because only about four billion unique addresses can be generated using this method, another standard, IPv6, has been proposed. It is called IPv6 because it is the sixth recommendation in the series (the older 32-bit addresses are often called IPv4 to differentiate them from this new standard). With IPv6, a 128-bit address is used, leading to a maximum number of about 3×10^{28} unique addresses — more than enough for every Internet-enabled toaster.

This IP (whether IPv4 or IPv6) address must uniquely identify each host on a network (actually subnetwork, as you'll see shortly). If not, messages cannot be routed to their destination properly, and chaos ensues. The matter gets more complicated when another 32-bit number, the *subnet mask*, is brought into the picture. This is a value that is masked (using a Boolean AND operation) over the address to identify the subnetwork of the network that the computer is on. All addresses on the same subnetwork must be unique. Two subnetworks may have the same address, however, as long as the subnet mask is different between the two.

Many common subnetworks use the value 255.255.255.0 for the subnet mask. When this is applied to the network address (see below), only the last address is considered significant. Therefore, the subnetwork can only include 254 unique addresses (0 and 255 are used for other purposes).

```
Network address:      192.168. 1.107
Subnet Mask:          255.255.255. 0
Result:               192.168. 1. 0
```

Because computers and humans use two different means of identifying computers, there must obviously be some way for the two to be related. The term for this process is *name resolution*. In the case of the Internet, a common means of name resolution is yet another protocol, the *Domain Naming System (DNS)*. A computer, when faced with an unknown text-based name, sends a message to the closest DNS server. It then determines whether it knows the IP address of that host. If it does, then it passes it back to the requester. If not, then it asks another DNS server. This process continues until either the IP address is found or you run out of DNS servers. Once the IP address is found, all the servers (and the original computer) store that number for a while in case they are asked again.

Keeping in mind the problems that can ensue during name resolution can often solve many development problems. For example, if you are having difficulty communicating with a computer that should be responding, then it may be because your computer simply can't resolve the name of the remote computer. Try using the IP address instead. This removes any name-resolution problems from the equation, and may allow you to continue developing while someone else fixes the name-resolution problem.

Ports: They're Not Just for Ships

As the previous sections described, each computer or host on a network is uniquely identified by an address. How does your computer determine which running applications, possibly of many, are meant to receive a given message arriving on the network? This is determined by the port the message is targeted at. The port is another number, in this case an integer value from 1 to 32,767. The unique combination of address and port identifies the target application.

For example, assume you currently have a Web server (IIS) running, as well as an SMTP server, and a few browser windows open. If a network message comes in, how does the operating system "know" which of these applications should receive the packet? Each of the applications (either client or server) that may receive a message is assigned a unique port number. In the case of servers, this is typically a fixed number, whereas client applications, such as your Web browser, are assigned a random available port.

To make communication with servers easier, they typically use a well-known assigned port. In the case of Web servers, this is port 80, while SMTP servers use port 25. You can see a list of common servers and their ports in the file `%windows%\system32\drivers\etc\services`.

If you're writing a server application, you can either use these common port numbers (and you should if you're attempting to write a common type of server) or choose your own. If you're writing a new type of server, choose a port that has not been assigned to another server; choosing a port higher than 1024 should prevent any conflicts, as these are not assigned. When writing a client application, it isn't usually necessary to assign a port, as a dynamic port is assigned to the client for communication with a server.

> *Ports below 1024 should be considered secure ports, and applications that use them should have administrative access.*

Firewalls: Can't Live with Them, Can't Live without Them

Many people have a love/hate relationship with firewalls. While they are invaluable in today's network, sometimes it would be nice if they got out of the way. A firewall is a piece of hardware or software that monitors network traffic, either incoming, outgoing, or both. They can be configured to allow only particular ports or applications to transmit information beyond the firewall. They protect against hackers or viruses that may attempt to connect to open ports, leveraging them to their own ends. They protect against spyware applications that may attempt to communicate from your machine.

They also "protect" against any network programming you may attempt to do. You must invariably cooperate with your network administrators, working within their guidelines for network access. If they make only certain ports available, then your applications should use only those ports. Alternately, you may be able to get them to configure the firewalls involved to permit the ports needed by your applications. Thankfully, creating network messages is a bit easier with Visual Basic 2005. The following sections demonstrate how.

The System.Net Namespace

Most of the functionality used when writing network applications is contained within the System.Net and System.Net.Sockets namespaces. The main classes in these namespaces that this chapter covers are as follows:

- ❑ WebRequest and WebResponse, and their subclasses, including the new FtpWebRequest
- ❑ WebClient, the simplified WebRequest for common scenarios
- ❑ HttpListener, the new capability to create your own Web server

Additional classes, methods, properties, and events have been added to the System.Net *and* System.Net.Sockets *namespaces in the .NET Framework 2.0. See the updated reference for these namespaces at* http://msdn2.microsoft.com/library/system.net.aspx *as of this writing.*

Web Requests (and Responses)

When most people think of network programming these days, they're really thinking of communication via a Web server or client, so it shouldn't be surprising that a set of classes is needed for this communication. In this case, it is the abstract WebRequest class and the associated WebResponse. These two classes represent the concept of a request/response communication with a Web server or similar server. As these are abstract classes, that is, MustInherit classes, they cannot be created by themselves. Instead, you create the subclasses of WebRequest that are optimized for specific types of communication.

The most important properties and methods of the WebRequest class are described in the following table:

Member	Description
Create	Method used to create a specific type of WebRequest. This method uses the URL (either as a string or as an Uri class) passed to identify and create a subclass of WebRequest.
GetRequestStream	Method that allows access to the outgoing request. This enables you to include additional information, such as POST data, to the request before sending.
GetResponse	Method used to perform the request and retrieve the corresponding WebResponse
Credentials	Property that enables you to set the user ID and password for the request if they are needed to perform the request
Headers	Property that enables you to change or add to the headers for the request
Method	Property used to identify the action for the request, such as GET or POST. The list of available methods is specific to each type of server.
Proxy	Property that enables you to identify a proxy server for the communication if needed. Note that you generally don't need to set this property, as Visual Basic 2005 detects the settings for Internet Explorer and uses them by default.
Timeout	Property that enables you to define the time permitted for the request before you "give up" on the server

Each subclass of WebRequest supports these methods, providing a very consistent programming model for communication with a variety of server types. The basic model for working with any of the subclasses of WebRequest can be written in the following pseudocode:

```
Declare variables as either WebRequest and WebResponse, or the specific child classes
Create the variable based on the URL
Make any changes to the Request object you may need
Use the GetResponse method to retrieve the response from the server
Get the Stream from the WebResponse
Do something with the Stream
```

If you decide to change the protocol (for example, from HTTP to a file-based protocol), the only thing that needs to change is the URL used to retrieve the object.

Working with FileWebRequest and HttpWebRequest

The first two types of WebRequest that became available were FileWebRequest and HttpWebRequest. FileWebRequest is used less frequently; it represents a request to a local file, using the "file://" URL format. You may have seen this type of request if you attempted to open a local file using your Web browser, such as Internet Explorer, Firefox, or Navigator. Generally, however, the subclass most developers will use is HttpWebRequest. This class enables you to make HTTP requests to a Web server without requiring a browser. This could enable you to communicate with a Web server, or, using the time-honored tradition of *screen scraping*, to retrieve data available on the Web.

One hurdle many developers encounter when first working with HttpWebRequest is that there is no available constructor. Instead, you must use the WebRequest.Create method (or the Create method of your desired subclass) to create new instances of any of the subclasses. This method uses the URL requested to create the appropriate subtype of WebRequest. For example, this would create a new HttpWebRequest:

```
Dim req As HttpWebRequest = WebRequest.Create("http://msdn.microsoft.com")
```

Note that if you have Option Strict turned on (and you should), the preceding code produces an error. Instead, you should explicitly cast the return value of Create to the desired type:

```
Dim req As HttpWebRequest = _
   DirectCast(WebRequest.Create("http://msdn.microsoft.com"), _
   System.Net.HttpWebRequest)
```

Putting It Together

In order to demonstrate how to use WebRequest/WebResponse, the following example shows how to wrap a Web call into a Visual Basic class. In this case, we'll wrap Google's define: keyword, which enables you to retrieve a set of definitions for a word (for example, http://www.google.com/search?q=define%3A+isbn), and then use that in a sample application (see Figure 29-1.)

1. Create a new Windows application. The example project is named DefinePad.

2. Add a new class to the project. This will hold the actual WebRequest code. Call it GoogleClient.

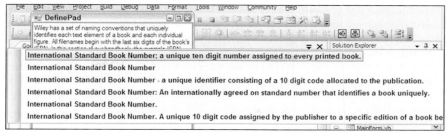

Figure 29-1

3. Add a reference to the `System.Web.DLL`, as you will need access to some of its functionality later.

4. In the `GoogleClient.vb` file, add `Imports` statements to make the coding a little briefer:

```
Imports System.IO
Imports System.Net
Imports System.Web
Imports System.Collections.Generic
```

5. The main function in `GoogleClient` is a `Define` function that returns an array of strings. Each string will be one definition returned by Google:

```
Public Function Define(ByVal word As String) As String()
    Dim req As HttpWebRequest = Nothing
    Dim resp As HttpWebResponse
    Dim query As String
    Dim result As New List(Of String)

    query = "http://www.google.com/search?q=define%3A" & _
      HttpUtility.UrlEncode(word)

    Try
        req = DirectCast(WebRequest.Create(query), HttpWebRequest)
        With req
            .Method = "GET"
            resp = req.GetResponse
            If resp.StatusCode = HttpStatusCode.OK Then
                ParseResponse(resp.GetResponseStream, result)
            Else
                MessageBox.Show("Error calling definition service")
            End If
        End With
    Catch ex As Exception

    End Try

    Return result.ToArray()

End Function
```

6. The first task is to guarantee that no invalid characters appear in the query string when you send the request, such as a space, accented character, or other non-ASCII character. The `System.Web.HttpUtility` class has a number of handy shared methods for encoding strings, including the `UrlEncode` method. This replaces characters with a safe representation of the character that looks like `%value`, where the value is the Unicode code for the character. For example, in the definition of the preceding query variable, the `%3A` is actually the colon character (":") that has been encoded. Anytime you retrieve a URL based on user input, encode it because there is no guarantee the resulting URL is safe to send.

7. Once the query is ready, create the `WebRequest`. As the URL is for an HTTP resource, an `HttpWebRequest` is created. While the default method for `WebRequest` is a `GET`, it's still good practice to set it. You'll create the `ParseResponse` method shortly to process the stream returned from the server.

8. Also noteworthy in this piece of code is the return value for this method, and how it is created. In order to return arrays of a specific type (rather than return actual collections from a method), you must either know the actual size to initialize the array or use the new `List` generic type or the older `ArrayList`. These classes behave like the Visual Basic 6.0 `Collection` class, which enables you to add items, and it grows as needed. They also have a handy method that allows you to convert the array into an array of any type; you can see this in the return statement. The `ArrayList` requires you to do a bit more work. If you want to use an `ArrayList` for this method, then you must identify the type of array you'd like to return. The resulting return statement would look like this using an `ArrayList`:

```
Return result.ToArray(GetType(String))
```

9. The `ProcessRequest` method parses the stream returned from the server and converts it into an array of items. Note that this is slightly simplified: In a real application, you would likely want to return an array of objects, where each object provides access to the definition and the URL of the site providing it:

```
Private Sub ParseResponse(ByVal input As System.IO.Stream, _
  ByRef output As List(Of String))
        'definitions are in a block beginning with <p>Definitions for...
        'then are marked with <li> tags
        'yes, I should use Regular Expressions for this
        'this format will also likely change in the future.
        Dim reader As New StreamReader(input)
        Dim work As String = reader.ReadToEnd
        Dim blockStart As String = "<p>Definitions of"
        Dim pos As Integer = work.IndexOf(blockStart)
        Dim posEnd As Integer
        Dim temp As String

    Do
        pos = work.IndexOf("<li>", pos + 1)
        If pos > 0 Then
            posEnd = work.IndexOf("<br>", pos)
            temp = work.Substring(pos + 4, posEnd - pos - 4)
            output.Add(ParseDefinition(temp))
            pos = posEnd + 1
        End If
```

```
        Loop While pos > 0

End Sub
```

10. The code is fairly simple, using the time-honored tradition of *screen scraping* — processing the HTML of a page to find the section you need and then removing the HTML to produce the result.

11. The last part of the `GoogleClient` class is the `ParseDefinition` method that cleans up the definition, removing the link and other HTML tags:

```
Private Function ParseDefinition(ByVal input As String) As String
    Dim result As String = ""
        Dim lineBreak As Integer

        lineBreak = input.IndexOf("<br>")
        If lineBreak > 0 Then
            result = input.Substring(0, input.IndexOf("<br>"))
        Else
            result = input
        End If
        Return result.Trim
End Function
```

12. Now, with class in hand, you can create a client to use it. In this case, you'll create a simple text editor that adds the capability to retrieve definitions for words. Go back to the `Form` created for the application, and add controls as shown in Figure 29-2.

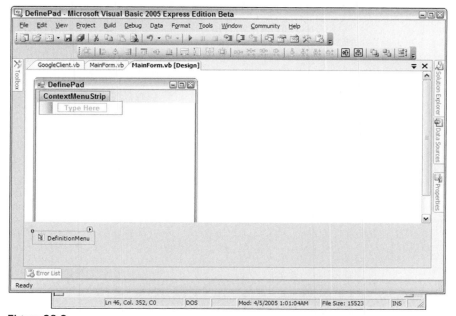

Figure 29-2

13. The user interface for `DefinePad` is simple: a `TextBox` and a `ContextMenuStrip`.

Control	Property	Value
TextBox	Name	TextField
	Multiline	True
	Dock	Fill
	ContextMenuStrip	DefinitionMenu
ContextMenuStrip	Name	DefinitionMenu

14. The only code in the `Form` is for the `Opening` event of the `ContextMenuStrip`. Here, you add the definitions to the menu. Add the following code to the handler for the `Opening` event:

```
Private Sub DefinitionMenu_Opening(ByVal sender As Object, _
  ByVal e As System.ComponentModel.CancelEventArgs) _
  Handles DefinitionMenu.Opening
    Dim svc As New GoogleClient
    Dim definitions() As String
    Dim definitionCount As Integer

    DefinitionMenu.Items.Clear()

    Try
        'define the currently selected word
        If TextField.SelectionLength > 0 Then
            definitions = svc.Define(TextField.SelectedText)

            'build context menu of returned definitions
            definitionCount = definitions.Length
            If definitionCount > 6 Then
                definitionCount = 6
            ElseIf definitionCount = 0 Then
                'we can't do anymore, so exit
                Dim item As New ToolStripButton
                item.Text = "Sorry, no definitions available"
                DefinitionMenu.Items.Add(item)
                Exit Sub
            End If

            For i As Integer = 1 To definitionCount
                Dim item As New ToolStripButton
                item.Text = definitions(i)
                DefinitionMenu.Items.Add(item)
            Next
        End If

    Catch ex As Exception
        MessageBox.Show(ex.Message, "Error getting definitions", _
            MessageBoxButtons.OK, MessageBoxIcon.Error)
```

```
        End Try
    End Sub
```

15. The bulk of the code in this event is to limit the number of items displayed in the menu. The actual functional part of the routine is the call to the `Define` method of the `GoogleClient`. If you trace through the code as you run, you'll see the `WebRequest` generated, the call made, and the resulting response stream parsed into the individual items as desired. Finally, you can use the returned list to create a set of menu items (that don't actually do anything), and display the "menu." Clicking on any definition closes the menu.

16. To test the application, run it. Type or copy some text into the text box, select a word, and right-click on it. After a brief pause, you should see the definitions for the word (see Figure 29-3 for definitions of "developer").

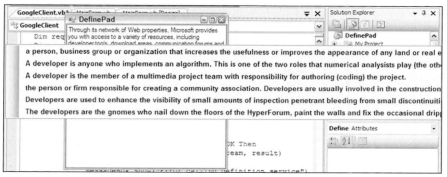

Figure 29-3

While they are not as "sexy" as Web Services, using this technique (`WebRequest`, screen scraping of the resulting HTML) can provide your applications with access to a great deal of the functionality of the Internet.

Working with FtpWebRequest

One of the new sets of classes added to the `System.Net` namespace in Visual Basic 2005 is another type of Web request — the `FtpWebRequest`. This class, and the related `FtpWebResponse`, is used to communicate with FTP servers. While the `HttpWebRequest/Response` can be used for simple file uploading and retrieving, the `FtpWebRequest` adds the capability to browse or create directories, delete files, and more. The following table describes some of the added functionality in the `FtpWebRequest`:

Member	Description
Abort	Used when performing an asynchronous operation. This command terminates the current operation.

Table continues on the next page

Member	Description
Abort	Used when performing an asynchronous operation. This command terminates the current operation.
Binary	A Boolean value that determines whether the data transfer should be treated as binary or text. Set to true when you are transferring a binary file, and text otherwise.
Method	While not new, the behavior of this method is quite important with the `FtpWebRequest` as it defines the action to perform. See the section below on `WebRequestMethods.Ftp` that defines the possible values.
Passive	Boolean value that determines how the client and server should communicate. If this is set to true, the server does not initiate communication back to the client. Instead, it waits until the client initiates the communication. This is typically needed when communicating through a firewall that might not allow the server to open a connection to the client machine.

WebRequestMethods.Ftp

As described above, the actual request made by the `FtpWebRequest` is identified by the `Method` property. This is a string property that can be set to any value recognized by your FTP server, but you will often want to set it to one of the values in the `WebRequestMethods.Ftp` structure:

Field	Description
AppendFile	Adds content to an existing file
DeleteFile	Deletes a file from the server (if you have permission)
DownloadFile	Retrieves a file from the FTP server
GetDateTimeStamp	Gets the date and time the file was last modified
GetFileSize	Gets the size of the file on the FTP server
ListDirectory	Gets the file and directory names for a directory on the FTP server. The data returned is a list of the files, each on a line (that is, separated by CRLF characters). This method doesn't provide an easy way to determine which of the items returned are directories or files.
ListDirectoryDetails	Gets the file and directory information for a directory on the FTP server. This method returns a good deal of information about each item, including attributes, permissions, date of last modification, and size. Just as with the `ListDirectory` method, each file's (or directory's) information is on a single line.
MakeDirectory	Creates a directory on the server

Field	Description
PrintWorkingDirectory	Gets the current path on the FTP server
RemoveDirectory	Removes a directory from the server (if you have permission)
UploadFile	Uploads a file to the FTP server
UploadFileWithUniqueName	Similar to UploadFile, but this method ensures that the new file has a unique filename. This is great when you allow the user to upload files but don't want possible name collisions to happen, or if you don't really care what name the file is (e.g., when the file contents just need processing but not saving).

Creating an FTP Client

In order to demonstrate using the FtpWebRequest, the next section covers how to create a simple FTP server browser. The application will enable you to connect to a server, browse the available files, and download files (see Figure 29-4.)

Figure 29-4

Even though this application is a Windows Forms application, we separate the FTP handling to a class for use in other applications:

1. Create a new Windows application called FTP Browser.

2. Before creating the user interface, define the class that will provide the functionality. Add a new class to the project called `FtpClient.vb`. This class will be used to create wrapper functionality to make working with `FtpWebRequest` easier. First, add the `Imports` statements for later use:

```
Imports System.IO
Imports System.Net
Imports System.Text
Imports System.Collections.Generic
```

3. Add two properties to the class. This is for the user ID and password that will be used by the `FtpClient`:

```
Private _user As String
Private _pwd As String

Public Property UserId() As String
    Get
        Return _user
    End Get
    Set(ByVal value As String)
        _user = value
    End Set
End Property

Public Property Password() As String
    Get
        Return _pwd
    End Get
    Set(ByVal value As String)
        _pwd = value
    End Set
End Property
```

4. The Form will use two methods, `GetDirectories` and `GetFiles`. These two methods are basically the same:

```
Public Function GetDirectories(ByVal url As String) As String()
    'line should look like:
    'dr-xr-xr-x    1 owner       group
    ' 0 Nov 25   2002 bussys"
    ' if the first character is a 'd', it's a directory
    Return GetDirectoryEntries(url, "d")
End Function

Public Function GetFiles(ByVal url As String) As String()
    'line should look like:
    '-r-xr-xr-x    1 owner       group
    ' 1715 May 20   1996 readme.txt
    ' if the first character is a '-', it's a file
    Return GetDirectoryEntries(url, "-")
End Function
```

5. Obviously, both `GetDirectories` and `GetFiles` simply return the result of another helper routine, `GetDirectoryEntries`. The only difference between the information returned for a file and a directory is that directories have the directory attribute set to d, whereas files have a blank (–) in that position:

```
Private Function GetDirectoryEntries(ByVal url As String, _
    ByVal directoryAttribute As String) As String()

    Dim result As New List(Of String)
    Dim str As Stream = Nothing
    Dim temp As String
    Dim words() As String
    Dim splitChars() As Char = {' 'c}

    DoFtpRequest(url, _
        WebRequestMethods.Ftp.ListDirectoryDetails, _
        False, str)
    Try
        Using reader As StreamReader = New StreamReader(str)
            Do
                temp = reader.ReadLine

                If temp <> Nothing Then
                    'split into component parts
                    words = temp.Split(splitChars, _
                        StringSplitOptions.RemoveEmptyEntries)
                    If words(0).StartsWith(directoryAttribute) Then
                        result.Add(words(8))
                    End If
                End If
            Loop While temp <> Nothing
        End Using
    Catch ex As Exception
        MessageBox.Show(ex.Message, "Error getting files from " & url)
    End Try

    Return result.ToArray()

End Function
```

6. The `GetDirectoryEntries` method uses another helper method you'll create shortly to execute the `WebRequestMethods.Ftp.ListDirectoryDetails` method on the FTP server. This method returns the resulting response stream in the `str` parameter. The code then loops through the returned content. Each of the directory entries appears on a separate line, so `ReadLine` is perfect here. The line is split on spaces, and then added to the return value if it has the desired value for the first character (that represents it if it's a directory or a file).

7. The `GetDirectoryEntries` method calls a helper method that does the actual `FtpWebRequest`. This method returns the resulting stream by way of a `ByRef` parameter:

```
Private Function DoFtpRequest(ByVal url As String, _
    ByVal method As String, ByVal useBinary As Boolean, _
    ByRef data As Stream) As FtpStatusCode
```

```
         Dim result As FtpStatusCode


         Dim req As FtpWebRequest
         Dim resp As FtpWebResponse
         Dim creds As New NetworkCredential(UserId, Password)

         req = DirectCast(WebRequest.Create(url), FtpWebRequest)

         With req
             .Credentials = creds
             .UseBinary = useBinary
             .UsePassive = True
             .KeepAlive = True

             'make initial connection
             .Method = method
             resp = .GetResponse()

             data = resp.GetResponseStream
             result = resp.StatusCode

         End With

         Return result
     End Function
```

The appropriate type of WebRequest is created, the properties are set, and the final request is sent.

8. With the class created, we can move our attention back to the user interface. Return to the Form and add MenuStrip and SplitContainer controls. You can leave the names and other properties of these controls at their defaults. Create three items under the File menu: Connect, Download, and Exit. You may also want to add an ImageList control, and populate it with appropriate graphics for open and closed folders. The following table lists the properties set on the ImageList in the sample project:

Property	Value
TransparentColor	Transparent
Images – open	Used the OpenFold.ico graphic from the Visual Studio 2005 Image Library (located in the icons\Win9x directory)
Images – closed	Used the ClsdFold.ico graphic from the Visual Studio 2005 Image Library (located in the icons\Win9x directory)

9. Add a TreeView control to the left side of the SplitContainer, and a ListView to the right side. Set the properties as shown in the following tables:

TreeView

Property	Value
Name	DirectoryTree
Dock	Fill
PathSeparator	/
ImageList	The name of your `ImageList` control
SelectedImageKey	The open image's name
ImageKey	The closed image's name

ListView

Property	Value
Name	FileList
Dock	Fill
MultiSelect	False
View	List

10. Open the code view for the form and add a few private variables to the `Form` class:

```
Private ftp As New FtpClient
Private baseUrl As String
Private downloadPath As String
```

11. Next, add a handler for the `Form_Load` event; this will initialize the `TreeView` and `FtpClient` objects:

```
Private Sub MainForm_Load(ByVal sender As Object, _
   ByVal e As System.EventArgs) Handles Me.Load
      'initialize form
      With Me.DirectoryTree
         .Nodes.Add("/")
      End With
      'initialize ftp client
      With ftp
         .UserId = My.Settings.user
         .Password = My.Settings.email
      End With
      downloadPath = My.Settings.downloadPath

End Sub
```

12. Notice the calls to My.Settings when initializing the FtpClient. The Settings collection is available to the My object when you have created settings values in the My Project dialog. Open the Solution Explorer and double-click My Project. Select the Settings tab and add the three values (see Figure 29-5).

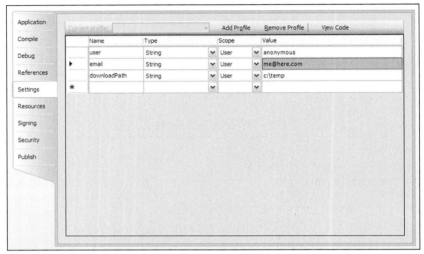

Figure 29-5

13. Now return to adding the code to the form. Enable connecting to the FTP server and retrieving the initial list of directories to add to the TreeView. Add this to the Connect menu item:

```
Private Sub ConnectToolStripMenuItem_Click(ByVal sender As System.Object, _
  ByVal e As System.EventArgs) Handles ConnectToolStripMenuItem.Click
    'makes a new connection to an FTP server

    baseUrl = InputBox("Enter FTP site to open", "FTP Browser", _
      "ftp://ftp.microsoft.com")
    Me.DirectoryTree.Nodes.Clear()
    'add the base node
    Me.DirectoryTree.Nodes.Add(baseUrl)
    AddNodes(Me.DirectoryTree.Nodes(0), baseUrl)

End Sub
```

14. The event prompts the user for the address of the FTP server to connect with, and then adds it to the TreeView via a helper subroutine, AddNodes:

```
Private Sub AddNodes(ByVal parent As TreeNode, ByVal url As String)
    Dim dirs() As String

    Me.Cursor = Cursors.WaitCursor

    dirs = ftp.GetDirectories(url)
    For Each dir As String In dirs
```

```
            With parent.Nodes.Add(dir)
                .Nodes.Add("NoNodeHere", "empty")
            End With
        Next

        Me.Cursor = Cursors.Default
    End Sub
```

15. The `AddNodes` method retrieves the list of directories for the selected URL. In this, the first call for an FTP server, it retrieves the root directory. Later, the same method is used to retrieve subdirectories by requesting a URL containing the full path. Notice the addition of a fake node to each of the directories (the `"NoNodeHere"` item). This ensures that each of the added directories has the plus symbol next to it in the `TreeView`, implying that there is content below it. We will remove the empty node later when we request the actual subdirectories.

16. Initially, each of the directories is empty except for the `"NoNodeHere"` item. You can use the presence of this node to determine whether you need to request subdirectories. If it still exists, call `AddNodes` when the user attempts to expand the `TreeView` node:

```
Private Sub DirectoryTree_BeforeExpand(ByVal sender As Object, _
  ByVal e As System.Windows.Forms.TreeViewCancelEventArgs) _
  Handles DirectoryTree.BeforeExpand
    Dim thisNode As TreeNode

    thisNode = e.Node
    If thisNode.Nodes.ContainsKey("NoNodeHere") Then
        'we haven't retrieved this nodes children yet
        'remove the empty node
        thisNode.Nodes("NoNodeHere").Remove()
        'get the real children now
        AddNodes(thisNode, baseUrl + thisNode.FullPath)
    End If

End Sub
```

17. If `"NoNodeHere"` still exists, remove it, and then call the `AddNodes` method again, passing this node and its path. This calls the FTP server again, retrieving the child directories of the selected directory. You perform this before the node is expanded, so before the user can see the `"NoNodeHere"` node. If the subdirectories have already been requested, then the `"NoNodeHere"` node won't be in the `TreeView` anymore, and so the code to call the FTP server won't be called again.

18. After the node has been expanded, it is selected. Now retrieve the list of files in that directory to display in the `ListView` control:

```
Private Sub DirectoryTree_AfterSelect(ByVal sender As System.Object, _
  ByVal e As System.Windows.Forms.TreeViewEventArgs) _
  Handles DirectoryTree.AfterSelect
    Dim thisNode As TreeNode
    Dim files() As String

    thisNode = e.Node

    'we don't want to do this for the root node
```

```
    If thisNode.Text <> "/" Then
        'get files for this directory
        Me.Cursor = Cursors.WaitCursor
        'clear the current list
        Me.FileList.Items.Clear()
        files = ftp.GetFiles(baseUrl + thisNode.FullPath)
        For Each fil As String In files
            Me.FileList.Items.Add(fil)
        Next

        Me.Cursor = Cursors.Default
    End If
End Sub
```

This code is fairly simple. First, the `ListView` is cleared of existing files. Then, the `FtpClient` is called, retrieving the list of files in the selected directory. These are then added to the `ListView`.

19. You should now be able to run the application and browse an FTP server (see Figure 29-6). Note that because we haven't added any credentials, only anonymous FTP servers can be browsed. If you want to connect to FTP servers that require authentication, set UserId and Password as appropriate, or query them from the user.

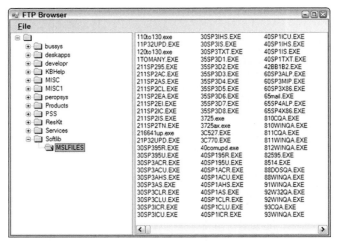

Figure 29-6

20. For a few finishing touches, we'll set the Download menu item to be usable only if a file is selected, and add the code for the Exit menu item. Set the initial value for Enabled to false for the Download menu item, and add the following code to the handler for the `ListView`'s `SelectedIndexChanged` event:

```
Private Sub FileList_SelectedIndexChanged(ByVal sender As System.Object, _
    ByVal e As System.EventArgs) Handles FileList.SelectedIndexChanged
    Me.DownloadToolStripMenuItem.Enabled = _
        CBool(Me.FileList.SelectedItems.Count)
End Sub
```

21. When there is a selected item, the Count will be > 0, which converts to True. If 0 items are selected, then this will be False.

22. The code for the Exit menu item is simple enough:

```
Private Sub ExitToolStripMenuItem_Click(ByVal sender As System.Object, _
    ByVal e As System.EventArgs) Handles ExitToolStripMenuItem.Click
      Me.Close()
End Sub
```

23. Finally, add the code for the Download menu item:

```
Private Sub DownloadToolStripMenuItem_Click(ByVal sender As Object, _
    ByVal e As System.EventArgs) Handles DownloadToolStripMenuItem.Click
      'download currently selected file (but only if something is selected)

      ftp.DownloadFile(baseUrl & _
        Me.DirectoryTree.SelectedNode.FullPath & _
        "/" & Me.FileList.SelectedItems(0).Text, _
        downloadPath & Me.FileList.SelectedItems(0).Text)
End Sub
```

24. Obviously, we need to add the `DownloadFile` method to the `FtpClient` class. Here's the code:

```
Public Sub DownloadFile(ByVal url As String, _
    ByVal destination As String)
      Dim str As Stream = Nothing

      DoFtpRequest(url, _
          WebRequestMethods.Ftp.DownloadFile, _
          True, _
          str)

      Using reader As StreamReader = New StreamReader(str)
          Using writer As StreamWriter = _
            New StreamWriter(File.OpenWrite(destination))
              writer.Write(reader.ReadToEnd)
          End Using
      End Using

End Sub
```

Note the repeat use of the `DoFtpRequest` method. However, this time, we pass `True` for the binary, just in case the file we're transferring is not a text-based file. Using the new `Using` block, we create a new `StreamReader` around the output stream of the response, and a new `StreamWriter` to a local output file. By using the `Using` block, we guarantee that the associated readers, writers, and streams will all be closed when we're done using them. The `Using` block is functionally identical to the following .NET Framework 1.1 code:

```
Dim reader As StreamReader
Try
    reader = New StreamReader(str)
    ...
Finally
```

```
      reader.Flush()
      reader.Close()
      reader = Nothing
   End Try
```

Now you can test out the new download code. Run the application again, connect to an FTP server, select a file, and then select Download from the File menu. You should see the newly created file appear in your download directory (see Figure 29-7).

Figure 29-7

While creating a full-blown FTP client would be a fair bit more work, it is hoped that you can see how the functionality of the FtpWebRequest and FtpWebResponse classes makes communicating with an FTP server much easier than before, not to mention writing the core functionality yourself using sockets.

Simplifying Common Web Requests with WebClient

When I first saw a demo of WebRequest *in early 2000, I was delighted. Here was the capability to easily access Internet resources waiting for me to play with. However, one of the other attendees of the demo asked, "Why is that so difficult? You need to do so much to get it to work." The next time I saw the same* WebRequest *demo, the presenter concluded with, "For those of you doing the common scenarios, we have an even easier way." He then went on to show us how to use* System.Net.WebClient.

For those times when you just want to send a GET or POST request and download a file or the resulting data, you can forget about WebRequest/WebResponse. WebClient abstracts away all of the little details of making Web requests, and makes it amazingly easy to grab data from the Web. The important methods and properties of the `WebClient` class are described in the following table:

Member	Description
DownloadData	Returns a Byte array of data from the server. This is essentially the same as if you had called the Read method on the stream returned from GetResponse?Stream. You could then save this to a binary file, or convert to text using an appropriate encoding. However, see DownloadFile and DownloadString for two easier ways of performing these tasks.
DownloadFile	Retrieves a file from the server and saves it locally
DownloadString	Returns a block of text from the server
OpenRead	Returns a stream providing data from the server. This is essentially the same stream returned from the call to GetResponseStream.
OpenWrite	Returns a stream you can use to write to the server. This is essentially the same as creating a WebRequest and writing to the GetResponse stream.
UploadData	Sends a Byte array of data to the server. See UploadFile, UploadString, and UploadValues for easier ways of performing this task.
UploadFile	Sends a local file to the server for processing
UploadString	POSTs a string to the server. This is very handy when you are simulating HTML form input.
UploadValues	Sends a set of name/value pairs to the server. This is similar to the format used by QueryString values, and this method is quite useful for simulating HTML input.
BaseAddress	The base URL the WebClient will access — for example: http://www .example.com.
Credentials	Credentials that will be used when performing any request. You can create a new NetworkCredential to use this, or alternately, set the UseDefaultCredentials property to true to use the credentials the user has logged in with.
Headers	Collection of headers that will be used for the request
Proxy	Overrides the proxy settings from Internet Explorer if set. By default, you should never need to set this property, as the normal proxy settings are chosen by default.
QueryString	Collection of name/value pairs that will be sent with the request. This represents the values after the '?' on a request.
ResponseHeaders	Collection of headers returned by the server after the request is completed

All of the `DownloadX` and `UploadX` methods also support an asynchronous version of the method, called `DownloadXAsync`, such as `DownloadFileAsync` or `UploadValuesAsync`. These methods perform the actual request on a background thread, and fire an event when the task is completed. If your application has some form of user interface, such as a Form, you should generally use these methods to keep your application responsive.

As `WebClient` uses the `WebRequest` classes to actually perform its magic, it can greatly simplify network coding. For example, just replace the code used in the `WebRequest` sample created earlier.

Before:

```
Public Function Define(ByVal word As String) As String()
    Dim req As HttpWebRequest = Nothing
    Dim resp As HttpWebResponse
    Dim query As String
    Dim result As New List(Of String)

    query = "http://www.google.com/search?q=define%3A" & _
      HttpUtility.UrlEncode(word)

    Try
        req = DirectCast(WebRequest.Create(query), HttpWebRequest)
        With req
            .Method = "GET"
            resp = req.GetResponse
            If resp.StatusCode = HttpStatusCode.OK Then
                ParseResponse(resp.GetResponseStream, result)
            Else
                MessageBox.Show("Error calling definition service")
            End If
        End With
    Catch ex As Exception

    End Try

    Return result.ToArray()

End Function
```

After:

```
Public Function Define(ByVal word As String) As String()
    Dim client As New WebClient
    Dim query As String
    Dim result As New List(Of String)

    query = "http://www.google.com/search?q=define%3A" & _
      HttpUtility.UrlEncode(word)

    Try
        result = ParseResponse(client.DownloadString(query))
    Catch ex As Exception
```

```
        End Try

        Return result.ToArray()

    End Function
```

`WebClient` avoids all of the stream handling required for `WebRequest`, but you should still know how `WebRequest` operates, as this knowledge is directly applicable to `WebClient`.

Creating Your Own Web Server with HttpListener

One feature of the .NET Framework 2.0 that got me extremely excited was the new `HttpListener` class (and related classes). This class enables you to very easily create your own Web server. While it likely wouldn't be a replacement for IIS, it can enable you to add Web server functionality to other applications. For example, rather than use remoting or MSMQ to create a communication channel between two applications, why not use HTTP? Each instance could host its own little Web server, and then you could use `HttpWebRequest` or `WebClient` to communicate between them. Alternately, many applications and hardware devices now provide a built-in Web application, enabling you to configure the device or application via a Web browser.

> *The fine print: The `HttpListener` class relies on the new `Http.sys` functionality built into IIS 6.0, so you must be using an operating system that includes `http.sys` as a systemwide HTTP service. Only Windows Server 2003, Windows XP SP2, and Vista (and future versions of the operating system) include this functionality — yet another reason to upgrade, and to install Service Packs. Future operating systems should all provide this functionality.*

`HttpListener` works by registering one or more *prefixes* with `http.sys`. Once this is done, any requests intercepted by the HTTP subsystem are passed on to the registered listener. An `HttpListenerContext` object is created and passed to your listener. This context contains properties for the `Request` and `Response` objects, just as the `Context` object in ASP.NET does. Again, similar to Web applications, you read the request from the `Request` property, and write the response to the `Response` property. Closing the response sends the resulting page to the user's browser. The following table describes the important members of `HttpListener`:

Member	Description
Abort	Shuts down the server without finishing any existing requests
Close	Shuts down the server after finishing handling any existing requests
Start	Starts the listener receiving requests
Stop	Stops the listener from receiving requests
IsListening	Property that determines whether the listener is currently receiving requests
Prefixes	Collection of the types of requests that this listener will respond to. These are the "left-hand side" of the URL, such as "http://localhost:8080/" or "http://serverName:1234/vrootName/". Note that you must end the prefix in a slash or you will receive a runtime error. If you have IIS installed on the same server, you can use port 80, as long as a vroot with the same name is not already defined by IIS.

Creating Your Web Server

To demonstrate using `HttpListener`, this example creates a Windows Service to host its functionality. This could simulate a management or monitoring interface to a Windows Service that would enable authenticated individuals to use the Windows Service remotely or to get other information out of it. Here are the steps:

1. Create a new Windows Service application called MiniServer. The server won't do much on its own, but it will host an `HttpListener`.

2. From the Components section of the Toolbox, add a `BackgroundWorker` component named BackgroundWork. The other properties can remain at their defaults. This BackgroundWorker will be used to process HTTP requests on a background thread, simplifying the handling of the threads.

3. Switch to code view for the service. Add the `Imports` statements you need to the top of the file:

```
Imports System.Net
Imports System.IO
Imports System.Web
Imports System.Text
```

4. Add the private members to the class. In addition, add a constant to identify the port number the service will use for listening. Select a port that currently isn't in use on your computer. The example uses 9090:

```
Private listener As New HttpListener()
Private theService As String

Private Const PORT As Integer = 9090
```

5. In the `OnStart` method, set up the list of prefixes to which the server will respond. This can be as simple as adding a port address to the URL, or include specific vroots. The sample includes examples of each:

```
Protected Overrides Sub OnStart(ByVal args() As String)
    Dim machineName As String

    machineName = System.Environment.MachineName
    theService = HttpUtility.UrlEncode(Me.ServiceName)

    Me.EventLog.WriteEntry("Service Name: " & Me.ServiceName)

    With listener
        .Prefixes.Add(String.Format("http://{0}:{1}/", _
          "localhost", PORT.ToString))
        .Prefixes.Add(String.Format("http://{0}:{1}/", _
          machineName, PORT.ToString))
        .Prefixes.Add(String.Format("http://{0}/{1}/", _
          "localhost", theService))
        .Prefixes.Add(String.Format("http://{0}/{1}/", _
          machineName, theService))
        .Start()
```

```
        End With
        'start up the background thread
        Me.BackgroundWork.RunWorkerAsync()

End Sub
```

In this case, the server will respond to a prefix in any of the formats (the sample computer is called Tantalus):

```
http://localhost:9090/
http://tantalus:9090/
http://localhost/sampleservice/
http://tantalus/sampleservice/
```

> There is one important point to keep in mind as you add prefixes: They must end in a slash (/) character. If not, you will get a runtime error when the listener attempts to add that prefix.

If you already have a Web server listening on port 80, such as IIS, do not include the last two prefixes. Only a single application can listen to each port, so this service will not be able to start if the other service is already monitoring port 80.

After initializing the `Prefixes` collection, calling the `Start` method binds the listener to the appropriate ports and vroots and starts it accepting requests. However, we don't want to actually receive the requests in the `OnStart` handler. Remember that the service doesn't actually start until after this method has completed, so having a lot of processing in the `OnStart` will actually prevent the service from completing. Therefore, we use another of the new features of Visual Basic 2005, the `BackgroundWorker` component, to handle the requests. Call its `RunWorkerAsync` method to start the background task (in our case, the `HttpListener`).

6. The `OnStop` method will serve to shut down the `HttpListener`:

```
Protected Overrides Sub OnStop()
    With listener
        .Stop()
        .Close()
    End With
End Sub
```

7. The background task performed by the `BackgroundWorker` component can be any process that you don't want to interfere with the normal application's processing. If this were a Windows Forms application, then having a long-running loop or other process running might prevent the application from drawing or responding to the user's requests. Beyond that, you can do anything you want in the background task, with one exception: Because a Windows Forms application works in a single foreground task, one can't directly access the controls on the Form from the background task. Instead, if the background task must change properties on the controls, it should fire events. The controls can then subscribe to those events, where you can access the properties. In this Windows Service, it has no such user interface, so that problem is avoided.

The actual work you want the `BackgroundWorker` to perform is in the `DoWork` event handler:

```
Private Sub BackgroundWork_DoWork(ByVal sender As System.Object, _
  ByVal e As System.ComponentModel.DoWorkEventArgs) Handles BackgroundWork.DoWork
    Dim context As HttpListenerContext
    Dim path As String
    Dim defaultPage As String

    'this is where we actually process requests
    While listener.IsListening
        context = listener.GetContext
        path = context.Request.Url.AbsolutePath.ToLower

        'strip out the serviceName if you're using the URL format:
        'http://server/servicename/path
        If path.StartsWith("/" & theService.ToLower) Then
            path = path.Substring(theService.Length + 1)
        End If
        Me.EventLog.WriteEntry("Received request for " & path)


        Select Case path
            Case "/"
                'this would probably be a resource
                defaultPage = "Available pages<ul>" & _
                    "<li><a href='/time'>Current server time</a></li>" & _
                    "<li><a href='/date'>Current date</a></li>" & _
                    "<li><a href='/random'>Random number</a></li></ul>"
            Case "/time"
                SendPage(context.Response, DateTime.Now.ToLongTimeString)
            Case "/date"
                SendPage(context.Response, DateTime.Now.ToLongDateString)
            Case "/random"
                SendPage(context.Response, New Random().Next.ToString)
            Case Else
                'if we don't understand the request, send a 404
                context.Response.StatusCode = 404
        End Select

    End While
End Sub
```

Our background task performs its work in a loop as long as the `HttpListener` is actively listening. Every developer knows that performing a set of tasks in a (relatively) tight loop is dangerous, possibly leading to computer or application lockup. However, the `BackgroundWorker` performs this on another thread, leaving our application responsive.

For this application, we first get access to the context for the listener. The context groups together one client's set of communication with our listener. Similar to the `HttpContext` in ASP.NET, the `HttpListenerContext` provides access to the `HttpListenerRequest` and `HttpListenerResponse` objects, so the first step in handling a request should always be to get this context. Next, the code uses a very simple means of determining the request URL. In a more full-featured implementation, this could be more complex, separating any query values from the path requested, and so on. For this sample, the listener only responds to three main paths — /time, /date, and /random — to receive the current (server) time or date, or a random Integer value. If the user requests anything else, we return a 404.

8. The SendPage subroutine simply writes out a basic HTML page, and the value determined:

```
Private Sub SendPage(ByVal response As HttpListenerResponse, _
  ByVal message As String)
    Dim sb As New StringBuilder

    'build string
    With sb
        .Append("<html><body>")
        .AppendFormat("<h3>{0}</h3>", message)
        .Append("</body></html>")
    End With

    Me.EventLog.WriteEntry(sb.ToString)

    'set up content headers
    With response
        .ContentType = "text/html"
        .ContentEncoding = Encoding.UTF8
        .ContentLength64 = sb.ToString.Length
        Me.EventLog.WriteEntry(sb.ToString.Length.ToString)

        Try
            Using writer As New StreamWriter(.OutputStream)
                With writer
                    .Write(sb.ToString)
                    .Flush()
                End With
            End Using

        Catch ex As Exception
            Me.EventLog.WriteEntry(ex.Message, EventLogEntryType.Error)
        Finally
            'close the response to end
            .Close()
        End Try
    End With
End Sub
```

There shouldn't be anything surprising in this code. Using a StringBuilder, a response is built. Then the content is written back to the browser (see Figure 29-8) using a StreamWriter that is created on top of the Response.OutputStream. Remember to close the Response, or the request will never close until it times out.

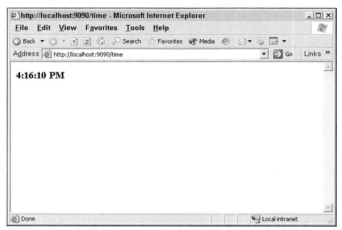

Figure 29-8

9. Before you can test your Windows Service, however, it must be installed. On the Properties window for the actual service, click Add Installer (see Figure 29-9). This adds a new file to the project called `ProjectInstaller.vb`, and adds two components to the file, `ServiceInstaller1` and `ServiceProcessInstaller1`. You can either keep these names or change them as you desire. In addition, set the properties as shown in the following table:

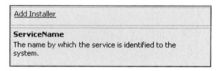

Figure 29-9

Component	Property	Value
ServiceInstaller1	Description	Sample Service from Wrox Professional Visual Basic 2005
	DisplayName	Sample Service
	ServiceName	SampleService
ServiceProcessInstaller1	Account	LocalSystem

Most of these properties only affect the display values for the Windows Service, but the `Account` property of the `ServiceProcessInstaller` deserves special mention. Windows Services run on behalf of the user, so they can actually run under another user account. By setting the `Account` property to `LocalSystem`, you are setting the resulting Windows Service to run under the local system account. This account has a lot of access to the system, so you may want to instead use an account with more limited rights; however, you would have to create this account separately.

10. Build the Windows service. Unfortunately, if you attempt to run the service directly from Visual Basic, you will get an error message (see Figure 29-10).

Figure 29-10

A Windows Service can only run if it has been installed into the system, a task performed using a command-line utility `InstallUtil.exe`. Open the Visual Studio Command Prompt and navigate to the directory where you have built `MiniServer.exe`. Run `installutil miniserver.exe`, and with any luck you'll be greeted with a success message (see Figure 29-11). Note that if you are running Windows Vista, then you need to run the Visual Studio Command Prompt as an administrator. You can do this by right-clicking on the Visual Studio 2005 Command Prompt icon and selecting `Run As Administrator`.

Figure 29-11

11. Start your new service. Open the Services application from Start ➪ All Programs ➪ Administrative Tools. Find the Sample Service in the list (see Figure 29-12) and click Start. You should now be able to request one of the items the service is listening to, such as `http://localhost:9090/time` (see Figure 29-13).

Figure 29-12

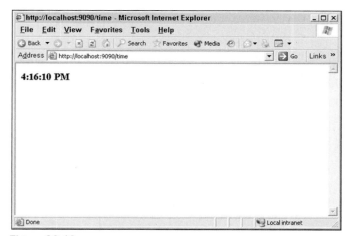

Figure 29-13

To confirm that all of the prefixes work, request one of the values using the vroot, rather than using the port (see Figure 29-14).

Figure 29-14

The `HttpListener` adds yet another powerful way for your applications to communicate. It enables you to extend the reach of your applications to Web browser clients, without requiring the additional administrative and management overhead of IIS.

Summary

Programming directly to the network provides a great deal of power and flexibility. Of course, all of that power and flexibility comes at a cost. Many of the services provided by higher-level technologies, such as Web Services or remoting, aren't available, and must often be re-created. However, in those situations where you must communicate with an existing application, or when you need the ultimate in control and speed, using the classes in `System.Net` makes life easier than it would be otherwise.

This chapter looked at many of the classes that expose network programming. You've seen how to make Web requests without a browser, so you can use the data on the Internet in your applications; you've seen how you can leverage the bare sockets layer to write your own communication protocols; and you've seen some of the new classes in Visual Basic 2005 for creating FTP clients and Web servers.

Windows Communication
Foundation (WCF)

Until now, building components that were required to communicate a message from one point to another was not always the simplest of tasks. This was because there was more than one technology in Microsoft's belt that you could have used for such an action.

For instance, you could have used ASP.NET Web Services, Web Service Enhancements 3.0 (WSE), MSMQ, Enterprise Services, .NET Remoting, and even the System.Messaging namespace. Each one of these technologies has pros and cons associated with it. ASP.NET Web Services (also known as *ASMX Web Services*) provided the capability to easily build interoperable Web Services. The WSE enabled you to easily build services that took advantage of some of the WS-* message protocols. MSMQ enabled the queuing of messages, making it easy to work with solutions that were only intermittently connected. Enterprise Services, provided as a successor to COM+, offered an easy means to build distributed applications. .NET Remoting was a fast way to move messages from one .NET application to another. And this is only the Microsoft world — it doesn't include all the options available in other environments, such as the Java world.

With these options for a Microsoft developer alone, it can be tough to decide what path to take with the applications you're trying to build. With this problem in mind, Microsoft has brought forth the Windows Communication Foundation (WCF).

WCF is a new framework for building service-oriented applications. Microsoft wanted to provide its developers with a framework that would provide the fastest means to getting a proper service-oriented architecture up and running. Using the WCF, you will be able to take advantage of all of the items that made the aforementioned distribution technologies powerful. WCF is the answer and the successor to all these other message distribution technologies.

WCF is a new component of the .NET Framework 3.0. Therefore, to work through the examples of this chapter, you need the .NET Framework 3.0 installed on your machine.

The Larger Move to SOA

Looking at what WCF provides, you will find that it is part of a larger move that organizations are making to the much talked about *service-oriented architecture,* or *SOA.* An SOA is a message-based service architecture that is vendor agnostic. This means you have the capability to distribute messages across a system, and the messages are interoperable with other systems that would otherwise be considered incompatible with the provider system.

Looking back, you can see the gradual progression to the service-oriented architecture model. In the 1980s, the revolutions arrived amid the concept of everything being an object. When object-oriented programming came on the scene, it was enthusiastically accepted as the proper means to represent entities within a programming model. The 1990s took that one step further, and the component-oriented model was born. This enabled objects to be encapsulated in a tightly coupled manner. It was only recently that the industry turned to a service-oriented architecture, once developers and architects needed to take components and have them distributed to other points in an organization, to their partners, or to their customers. This distribution system needed to have the means to transfer messages between machines that were generally incompatible with one another. In addition, the messages had to include the ability to express the metadata about how a system should handle a message.

If you ask 10 people what an SOA is, you'll probably get 11 different answers, but there are some common principles that are considered to be foundations of a service-oriented architecture:

❑ **Boundaries are explicit** — Any datastore, logic, or entity uses an interface to expose its data or capabilities. The interface provides the means to hide the behaviors within the service, and the interface front-end enables you to change this behavior as required without affecting downstream consumers.

❑ **Services are autonomous** — All the services are updated or versioned independently of one another. This means that you do not upgrade a system in its entirety; instead, each component of these systems is an individual entity within itself and can move forward without waiting for other components to progress forward. Note that with this type of model, once you publish an interface, that interface must remain unchanged. Interface changes require new interfaces (versioned, of course).

❑ **Services are based upon contracts, schemas, and policies** — All services developed require a contract regarding what is required to consume items from the interface (usually done through a WSDL document). Along with a contract, schemas are required to define the items passed in as parameters or delivered through the service (using XSD schemas). Finally, policies define any capabilities or requirements of the service.

❑ **Service compatibility that is based upon policy** — The final principle enables services to define policies (decided at runtime) that are required to consume the service. These policies are usually expressed through WS-Policy.

If your own organization is considering establishing an SOA, the WCF is a framework that works on these principles and makes it relatively simple to implement. The next section looks at what the WCF offers. Then you can dive into building your first WCF service.

WCF Overview

As stated, the Windows Communication Foundation is a means to build distributed applications in a Microsoft environment. Though the distributed application is built upon that environment, this doesn't mean that the consumers are required to be Microsoft clients or to take any Microsoft component or technology to accomplish the task of consumption. On the other hand, building WCF services means you are also building services that abide by the principles set forth in the aforementioned SOA discussion and that these services are vendor agnostic — thus, they are able to be consumed by almost anyone.

WCF is built upon the .NET Framework 3.0, which also includes the Windows Presentation Foundation and the Windows Workflow Foundation. Because it is part of the .NET Framework, as a developer you are able to use Visual Studio 2005 to build WCF services. Being able to build your services in Visual Studio just as you build any other .NET-based application also means that you can take advantage of the various integrated development systems offered via the IDE, such as debugging, Visual Studio's outstanding IntelliSense capabilities, refactoring, and more.

Note that because this is a .NET Framework 3.0 component, you are actually limited to the operating systems in which you can run a WCF service. While the other Microsoft distribution technologies previously mentioned in this chapter really do not have too many limitations on the Microsoft operating systems in which they can run, a .NET Framework 3.0 application can only run on Windows XP SP2, Windows Vista, or the upcoming Windows Server "Longhorn."

Capabilities of WCF

The WCF framework provides you with the capability to build all kinds of distributed applications. You can build Web Services just as you could previously in earlier .NET Framework releases. This means that your services will support SOAP, and therefore will be compatible with older .NET technologies, older Microsoft technologies, and even non-Microsoft technologies (such as any Java-based consumers).

WCF is not about pure SOAP over a wire, but you can work with an Infoset, and create a binary representation of your SOAP message that can then be sent along your choice of protocol. This is for folks who are concerned about the performance of their services and have traditionally turned to .NET Remoting for this binary-based distribution system.

The WCF framework can also work with a message through its life cycle, meaning that WCF can deal with transactions like those of the Enterprise Services mentioned earlier. Along with distributed transactions, WCF can deal with the queuing of messages, and it allows for the intermittent connected nature that an application or process might have to deal with.

When you need to get messages from one point to another, the WCF is the big gun in your arsenal to get the job accomplished. For instance, most developers might be thinking of using the WCF primarily to communicate ASP.NET Web Service-like messages (SOAP) from one disparate system to another, but you can use the WCF for much more than this. For instance, WCF can be used to communicate messages to components contained on the same machine on which the WCF service is running. This means you can use the WCF to communicate with components contained in different processes on the same machine. You can also use the WCF to communicate with components on another machine — even if that machine is not a Microsoft-based machine.

Probably the biggest and most exciting part of the WCF model is that it enables you to develop a service once and then expose that service via multiple endpoints (even endpoints on entirely different protocols) via simple configuration changes.

Working with the WS-* Protocols

There hasn't been a larger set of WS-* specifications that any other Microsoft distribution technology can work with but that WCF cannot. WCF understands a framework of WS-* specifications, and these specifications can be enabled to allow for defined ways of dealing with security, reliability, and transactions. For this capability, many previous developers turned to the WSE. Figure 30-1 shows the architectural stack on which the WCF relies.

Figure 30-1

WCF can make use of these specifications if the developer wishes. Messages, as defined by the Messaging layer, rely on SOAP (sent as open text or in a binary format). The other advanced WS-* specifications make heavy use of the SOAP header, thereby enabling messages to be self-contained and not have any real reliance on the transport protocol to provide items such as security, reliability, or any other capability beyond the simple transmission of the message itself. *Message Transmission Optimization Mechanism (MTOM)* is a new capability to replace *Direct Internet Message Encapsulation (DIME)* as a means to transmit binary objects along with a SOAP message. An example binary object would be a JPEG image that you want to expose through a WCF service.

The Metadata section enables you to define your interface. When you build a service that you want to include in your application, you need to determine which parameters the service requires in order for the consumption process to work. In addition, after you pass the parameters to the service, you need to know what is returned so you can properly use the passed information within your own application. Without this information, using the service would prove rather difficult. Just as there are standard ways to represent the message itself with technologies such as SOAP, there is an industry standard for getting a description of a service that you are attempting to consume. The WCF framework makes use of the *Web Services Description Language (WSDL)* to describe the service. WSDL is a language that uses XML to describe a service and define the format of the messages a service understands. The other item the WCF provides from the Metadata layer is WS-Policy. This specification provides consumers with an understanding of what is actually required to consume a service.

The Security part of WCF enables you to work with WS-Security. Before WS-Security came along, the initial lack of a security model in Web Services kept many companies from massively adopting them companywide and moving onto a service-oriented architecture. WS-Security, developed by Microsoft, IBM, and VeriSign, addresses the main areas that are required to keep messages secure — credential exchange, message integrity, and message confidentiality.

WS-Security enables two entities to exchange their security credentials from within the message itself (actually from the SOAP header of the message). The great thing about WS-Security is that it doesn't require a specific type of credential set to be used. Instead, it allows any type of credentials to be used. In addition, because it is possible to send messages through multiple routers and, in effect, bounce messages from here to there before they reach their final destination, you want to ensure that the messages are not tampered with in transport. As messages move from one SOAP router to another, these SOAP nodes can make additions to or subtractions from the messages. If such SOAP nodes were to get into the hands of malicious parties, the integrity of the messages could be compromised. This is where WS-Security comes into play. The other area WS-Security helps with is when you need to have WS-Security encrypt all or part of your SOAP messages. When your messages are zipping across the virtual world, there is a chance that they might be intercepted and opened for viewing by parties who should not be looking at their contents. That's why it's often beneficial to somehow scramble the contents of the message. When it reaches the intended receiver, the application can then use your encryption key and unscramble the message to read the contents.

WS-SecureConversation works to establish a connection that enables entities to exchange multiple messages and maintain their established security arrangements. WS-Trust, conversely, works in conjunction with WS-Security and allows for the issuance of security tokens and a way in which entities can exchange these tokens. This specification also deals with establishing trust relationships between two entities.

WS-ReliableMessaging allows for reliable end-to-end communications of messages to ensure that they are delivered.

The Transactions section allows for the use of WS-Coordination and WS-AtomicTransaction. WS-Coordination is there for the purposes of addressing the description of the relationships that multiple services have to one another. As companies start developing a multitude of services within their enterprise, they realize that many of the services developed have a relationship with one another, and that's where WS-Coordination comes into play. This specification is meant to be expanded by other specifications that will further define particular coordination types.

WS-AtomicTransaction uses WS-Coordination and WS-Security to allow for the definition of a service transaction process. An atomic transaction is a way of creating a transaction process that works on an all-or-nothing basis. These transactions are meant to be short-lived, so when you use them you are locking data resources and holding onto physical resources such as connections, threads, and memory.

The important part of this discussion is that you have a whole slew of WS-* specifications at your disposal. The nice thing in working with WCF is that you really don't have to be aware that these specifications are even there — you can access the capabilities these specifications offer through programmatic or declarative programming.

Building a WCF Service

Building a WCF service is not hard to accomplish. If you are working from a .NET Framework 2.0 environment, you need to install the .NET Framework 3.0.

You can find out where to download the .NET Framework 3.0 from Microsoft's .NET Framework portal at http://msdn.microsoft.com/netframework/.

From there, to build WCF services directly in Visual Studio 2005, you need to install the Visual Studio 2005 extensions for .NET Framework 3.0 (WCF and WPF). Download these Visual Studio extensions if you're using Visual Studio 2005. At the end of 2007, Microsoft should release the next version of Visual Studio, which will include these extensions by default. Installing the extensions into Visual Studio 2005 will add a WCF project to your IDE. This view of the project from the New Project dialog is presented in Figure 30-2.

Figure 30-2

When you build a WCF project in this manner, the idea is that you build a traditional class library that is compiled down to a DLL that can then be added to another project. The separation of code and projects is a powerful division on larger projects. That said, though, you can also just as easily build a WCF service directly in your .NET project, whether that is a console application or a Windows Forms application. The approach taken for the examples in this chapter show you how to build a WCF service that is hosted in a console application. Keep in mind that for the services you actually build and deploy, it is usually better to build them directly as a WCF Service Library project and use the created DLL in your projects or in IIS itself.

Before we jump into building a WCF service, first consider what makes up a service built upon the WCF framework.

What Makes a WCF Service

When looking at a WCF service, it is important to realize that it is made up of three parts: the service, one or more endpoints, and an environment in which to host the service.

A service is a class that is written in one of the .NET-compliant languages. The class can contain one or more methods that are exposed through the WCF service. A service can have one or more endpoints. An endpoint is used to communicate through the service to the client.

Endpoints themselves are also made up of three parts. These parts are usually defined by Microsoft as the ABC of WCF. Each letter of WCF means something in particular in the WCF model. Similarly,

❏ "A" is for address

❏ "B" is for binding

❏ "C" is for contract

Basically, you can think of this as follows: "A" is the *where*, "B" is the *how*, and "C" is the *what*. Finally, a hosting environment is where the service is contained. This constitutes an application domain and process. All three of these elements (the service, the endpoints, and the hosting environment) are put together to create a WCF service offering, as depicted in Figure 30-3.

Figure 30-3

The next step is to create a basic service using the WCF framework.

Creating Your First WCF Service

To build your service, prior to hosting it, two main steps need to occur. The first is to create a service contract, followed by a step to create a data contract. The service contract is really a class with the methods that you want to expose from the WCF service. The data contract is a class that specifies the structure you want to expose from the interface.

Once you have a service class in place, you can host it almost anywhere you want. This example shows you how to host the WCF service inside a console application. Therefore, first create a new console application project called VbWCF_Service1.

To create a WCF service, you need to make a reference to the System.ServiceModel.dll. To do this, right-click on the console application project in the Solution Explorer and select Add Reference from the provided menu. In the .NET tab of the Add Reference dialog, shown in Figure 30-4, is the .NET Framework 3.0 version of the System.ServiceModel.dll (though it has a runtime version v2.0.50727).

Figure 30-4

Note that we are only going to host the WCF service from the console application. The WCF service is something that you would normally build as its own entity, such as the WCF Class Library project, and then include the created DLL into your host, such as the console application.

This example first demonstrates how to build the WCF service. The next step is the requirements that need to be put into place for the service to be hosted in the console application.

Creating the Interface

To create your service you need a service contract. The service contract is the interface of the service. This consists of all the methods exposed as well as the input and output parameters that are required to invoke the methods. To accomplish this task, create a class file in your project called Calculator.vb. The interface you need to create is presented here:

```
Imports System
Imports System.ServiceModel
```

```
<ServiceContract()> _
Public Interface ICalculator
    <OperationContract()> _
    Function Add(ByVal a As Integer, ByVal b As Integer) As Integer

    <OperationContract()> _
    Function Subtract(ByVal a As Integer, ByVal b As Integer) As Integer

    <OperationContract()> _
    Function Multiply(ByVal a As Integer, ByVal b As Integer) As Integer

    <OperationContract()> _
    Function Divide(ByVal a As Integer, ByVal b As Integer) As Integer
End Interface

Public Class Calculator

End Class
```

This is pretty much the normal interface definition you would expect, but with a couple of new attributes included. To gain access to these required attributes, you need to make a reference to the `System.ServiceModel` namespace. This will give you access to the `<ServiceContract()>` and `<OperationContract()>` attributes.

The `<ServiceContract()>` attribute is used to define the class or interface as the service class, and it needs to precede the opening declaration of the class or interface. In this case, the example in the preceding code is based upon an interface:

```
<ServiceContract()> _
Public Interface ICalculator

    ' Code removed for clarity

End Interface
Within the interface, four methods are defined. Each of these methods are going to
be exposed through the WCF service as part of the service contract, and for this
reason, they are all required to have the <OperationContract()> attribute applied
to them.
    <OperationContract()> _
    Function Add(ByVal a As Integer, ByVal b As Integer) As Integer
```

Utilizing the Interface

The next step is to create a class that implements the interface. Not only is the new class implementing the interface defined, it is also implementing the service contract. You can add this class to the same `Calculator.vb` file. The following code illustrates the implementation of this interface:

```
Imports System
Imports System.ServiceModel

<ServiceContract()> _
Public Interface ICalculator
    <OperationContract()> _
```

```vb
        Function Add(ByVal a As Integer, ByVal b As Integer) As Integer

        <OperationContract()> _
        Function Subtract(ByVal a As Integer, ByVal b As Integer) As Integer

        <OperationContract()> _
        Function Multiply(ByVal a As Integer, ByVal b As Integer) As Integer

        <OperationContract()> _
        Function Divide(ByVal a As Integer, ByVal b As Integer) As Integer
    End Interface

Public Class Calculator
    Implements ICalculator

    Public Function Add(ByVal a As Integer, ByVal b As Integer) As Integer _
        Implements ICalculator.Add

        Return (a + b)
    End Function

    Public Function Subtract(ByVal a As Integer, ByVal b As Integer) As Integer _
        Implements ICalculator.Subtract

        Return (a - b)
    End Function

    Public Function Multiply(ByVal a As Integer, ByVal b As Integer) As Integer _
        Implements ICalculator.Multiply

        Return (a * b)
    End Function

    Public Function Divide(ByVal a As Integer, ByVal b As Integer) As Integer _
        Implements ICalculator.Divide

        Return (a / b)
    End Function
End Class
```

From these new additions, you can see that nothing is done differently with the Calculator class than what you might do otherwise. It is a simple class that implements the ICalculator interface and provides implementations of the Add(), Subtract(), Multiply(), and Divide() methods.

With the interface and the class available, you now have your WCF service built and ready to go. The next step is to get the service hosted. Note that this is a simple service. One of the simplicities of the service is that it only exposes simple types, rather than a complex type. This enables you to build only a service contract and not have to deal with the construction of a data contract. The construction of data contracts is presented later in this chapter.

Hosting the WCF Service in a Console Application

The next step is to take the service just developed and host it in some type of application process. You have many available hosting options, including the following:

- Console applications
- Windows Forms applications
- Windows Presentation Foundation applications
- Managed Windows Services
- Internet Information Services (IIS) 5.1
- Internet Information Services (IIS) 6.0
- Internet Information Services (IIS) 7.0 and the Windows Activation Service (WAS)

As stated earlier, this example hosts the service in a simple console application. There are a couple of ways to activate hosting — either through the direct coding of the hosting behaviors or through declarative programming (usually done via the configuration file).

For this example, the console application will define the host through coding the behaviors of the host environment directly. Following is the code for the console application, through the `Module1.vb` file (this block is referred to later in the chapter as the console-application code example):

```vb
Imports System
Imports System.ServiceModel
Imports System.ServiceModel.Description

Module Module1

    Sub Main()
        Using serviceHost As ServiceHost = New ServiceHost(GetType(Calculator))
            Dim ntb As NetTcpBinding = New NetTcpBinding(SecurityMode.None)
            serviceHost.AddServiceEndpoint(GetType(ICalculator), ntb, _
                New Uri("net.tcp://192.168.1.102:8080/Calculator/"))

            Dim smb As New ServiceMetadataBehavior()
            smb.HttpGetEnabled = True
            smb.HttpGetUrl = New Uri("http://localhost:8000/docs")

            serviceHost.Description.Behaviors.Add(smb)

            serviceHost.Open()

            Console.WriteLine("Press the <ENTER> key to close the host.")
            Console.ReadLine()
        End Using
    End Sub

End Module
```

A couple of things are going on in this file. First, to gain access to working with any of the WCF framework pieces, you need a reference to the `System.ServiceModel` and the `System.ServiceModel.Description` namespaces in the file. The `System.ServiceModel` gives you access to defining things like the endpoints that you need to create, while the `System.ServiceModel.Description` namespace reference gives you access to defining things like the WSDL file.

Remember that creating endpoints uses the ABC model (address, binding, and contract). The address part here is `net.tcp://192.168.1.102:8080/Calculator`. The binding is a TCP binding — `NetTcpBinding` — while the contract part is the `ICalculator` interface.

> *The 192.168.1.102 IP address is specific to my machine; you should use your own IP address for the example. You can get your IP address by typing* `ipconfig` *at a command prompt.*

Many different bindings are available to you when coding WCF services. In this case, this example makes use of the `NetTcpBinding`. The full list available is as follows:

❑   `System.ServiceModel.BasicHttpBinding`

❑   `System.ServiceModel.Channels.CustomBinding`

❑   `System.ServiceModel.MsmqBindingBase`

❑   `System.ServiceModel.NetNamedPipeBinding`

❑   `System.ServiceModel.NetPeerTcpBinding`

❑   `System.ServiceModel.NetTcpBinding`

❑   `System.ServiceModel.WSDualHttpBinding`

❑   `System.ServiceModel.WSHttpBindingBase`

Clearly, several bindings are available to you. In the preceding example, the `NetTcpBinding` class is the named pipe being used. This means that the service being built will be delivered over TCP.

In the first step of the example, for console-application code, a `ServiceHost` is established:

```
Using serviceHost As ServiceHost = New ServiceHost(GetType(Calculator))

    ' Code removed for clarity

End Using
```

By working with the `Using` keyword, when the `End Using` statement is encountered, the `ServiceHost` object is destroyed. In the creation of the host, the `Calculator` type is assigned. From there, the endpoint is established. In this case, a `NetTcpBinding` object is created with a security setting of `None` through the command `SecurityMode.None`:

```
Dim ntb As NetTcpBinding = New NetTcpBinding(SecurityMode.None)
```

This means that no security is applied to the message. The other options include `Message`, `Transport`, and `TransportWithMessageCredential`. The `Message` option signifies that the security credentials will be included in the message itself (in the SOAP header, for instance), while the `Transport` option signifies that the transport protocol will take care of the security implementation. The last option, `TransportWithMessageCredential`, means that the message contains some security credentials along with the transport protocol working for the same cause.

Once the `NetTcpBinding` object is in place, the next step is to finalize the endpoint creation. This is done through the use of the `ServiceHost` object's `AddServiceEndpoint()` method:

```
serviceHost.AddServiceEndpoint(GetType(ICalculator), ntb, _
            New Uri("net.tcp://192.168.1.102:8080/Calculator/"))
```

From this, you can see that the entire ABC statement is used in the creation of the endpoint, although not necessarily in ABC order; in fact, the first item defined is actually the "C" — the contract. This is done through the `GetType(ICalculator)` setting. The "B" is next (the binding) with the reference to the `NetTcpBinding` object. Then, finally, the "A" is defined through an instantiation of a `Uri` object pointing to `net.tcp://192.168.1.102:8080/Calculator/`.

The next step is a process to bring forth the WSDL document so that it can be viewed by the developer consuming this service:

```
Dim smb As New ServiceMetadataBehavior()
smb.HttpGetEnabled = True
smb.HttpGetUrl = New Uri("http://localhost:8000/docs")

serviceHost.Description.Behaviors.Add(smb)
```

This bit of code is the reason the `System.ServiceModel.Description` namespace is imported into the file at the beginning. Here, a `ServiceMetadataBehavior` object is created, the object's `HttpGetEnabled` property is set to `True`, and the `HttpGetUrl` property is provided an address of `http://localhost:8000/docs`. The documents can be located at any location of your choosing.

Once the `ServiceMetadataBehavior` object is created as you wish, the next step is associate this object to the `ServiceHost` through the `serviceHost.Description.Behaviors.Add()` method.

After all of these items are defined, you only need to open the `ServiceHost` for business, using the `serviceHost.Open()` method. The console application is kept alive through the use of a `Console.ReadLine()` method call, which waits for the end user to press the Enter key before shutting down the application. You want the `Console.ReadLine()` command there because you want to keep the host open.

Compiling and running this application produces the results illustrated in Figure 30-5.

Reviewing the WSDL Document

The preceding console-application code provides an instantiation of the `ServiceMetadataBehavior` object and defines a `Uri` object for it as well. You can simply type in that address to get at the WSDL file for the service you just built. Therefore, calling `http://localhost:8000/docs` provides the WSDL file shown in Figure 30-6.

Figure 30-5

Figure 30-6

With this WSDL file, you can now consume the service it defines through TCP. Note the following element at the bottom of the document:

```
<wsdl:service name="Calculator">
    <wsdl:port name="NetTcpBinding_ICalculator"
     binding="tns:NetTcpBinding_ICalculator">
        <soap12:address location="net.tcp://192.168.1.102:8080/Calculator/" />
        <wsa10:EndpointReference>
            <wsa10:Address>net.tcp://192.168.1.102:8080/Calculator/</wsa10:Address>
        </wsa10:EndpointReference>
    </wsdl:port>
</wsdl:service>
```

This element in the XML document indicates that in order to consume the service, the end user needs to use SOAP 1.2 over TCP. This is presented through the use of the `<soap12:address>` element in the document. The `<wsa10:EndpointReference>` is a WS-Addressing endpoint definition.

Using this simple WSDL document, you can now build a consumer that makes use of this interface.

Building the WCF Consumer

Now that a TCP service is out there, which you built using the WCF framework, the next step is to build a consumer application that uses the simple `Calculator` service. The consumer sends its request via TCP using SOAP. Using TCP means that the consumption can actually occur with a binary encoding of the SOAP message on the wire, substantially decreasing the size of the payload being transmitted.

This section describes how to consume this service. The first step is to open Visual Studio 2005 and create a new Windows Forms application. Though we are using a Windows Forms application, you can make this consumer call through any other application type within .NET as well.

Call the new Windows Forms application `WCF_Consumer`. This application will consume the `Calculator` service, so it should be laid out as shown in Figure 30-7.

Figure 30-7

Adding a Service Reference

Once you have laid out this form, make a reference to the new WCF service. You do this in a manner quite similar to how it is done with XML Web Service references. Right-click on the solution name from the Solution Explorer in Visual Studio and select Add Service Reference from the dialog. This capability to add a service reference is new to .NET 3.0 — previously, you only had the Add Reference and Add Web Reference options.

Once you have selected Add Service Reference, you are presented with the dialog shown in Figure 30-8.

Figure 30-8

The Add Service Reference dialog asks you for two things: the Service URI (basically a pointer to the WSDL file) and the name you want to give to the reference. The name you provide the reference is the name that will be used for the instantiated object that enables you to interact with the service.

Referring to Figure 30-8, you can see that the name provided to the Service URI setting is `http://localhost:8000/docs`. Remember that this is the location you defined earlier when you built the service. This URI was defined in code directly in the service:

```
Dim smb As New ServiceMetadataBehavior()
smb.HttpGetEnabled = True
smb.HttpGetUrl = New Uri("http://localhost:8000/docs")

serviceHost.Description.Behaviors.Add(smb)
```

Press the OK button in the Add Service Reference dialog. This adds to your project a Service References folder containing some proxy files, as shown in Figure 30-9.

Indeed, the Service References folder is added and two files are contained within this folder: `CalculatorService.map` and `CalculatorService.vb`. The other important addition to note is the `System.ServiceModel` reference, made for you in the References folder. This reference was not there before you made reference to the service through the Add Service Reference dialog.

Figure 30-9

Reviewing the Reference

Looking at the `CalculatorService.map` file, you can see that it is a simple XML file that provides some information about where the WSDL file is located, as well as the location of the service:

```
<?xml version="1.0" encoding="utf-8"?>
<ServiceReference>
    <ProxyGenerationParameters
        ServiceReferenceUri="http://localhost:8000/docs"
        Name="CalculatorService"
        NotifyPropertyChange="True"
        UseObservableCollection="False">
    </ProxyGenerationParameters>
    <EndPoints>
        <EndPoint

    Address="net.tcp://192.168.1.102:8080/Calculator/"

    BindingConfiguration="NetTcpBinding_ICalculator"
            Contract="CalculatorService.ICalculator"
            >
        </EndPoint>
    </EndPoints>
</ServiceReference>
```

This file provides the capability to later update the reference to the service if needed, due to a change in the service interface. You can see this capability by right-clicking on the `CalculatorService.map` file; an Update Service Reference option appears in the provided menu.

The other file, `CalculatorService.vb`, is your proxy to interact with the service. This file is presented here:

```vb
Option Strict Off
Option Explicit On

Namespace CalculatorService

    <System.CodeDom.Compiler.GeneratedCodeAttribute("System.ServiceModel", _
        "3.0.0.0"), _
    System.ServiceModel.ServiceContractAttribute( _
        ConfigurationName:="CalculatorService.ICalculator")> _
    Public Interface ICalculator
        <System.ServiceModel.OperationContractAttribute( _
        Action:="http://tempuri.org/ICalculator/Add", _
        ReplyAction:="http://tempuri.org/ICalculator/AddResponse")> _
        Function Add(ByVal a As Integer, ByVal b As Integer) As Integer

        <System.ServiceModel.OperationContractAttribute( _
        Action:="http://tempuri.org/ICalculator/Subtract", _
        ReplyAction:="http://tempuri.org/ICalculator/SubtractResponse")> _
        Function Subtract(ByVal a As Integer, ByVal b As Integer) As Integer

        <System.ServiceModel.OperationContractAttribute( _
        Action:="http://tempuri.org/ICalculator/Multiply", _
        ReplyAction:="http://tempuri.org/ICalculator/MultiplyResponse")> _
        Function Multiply(ByVal a As Integer, ByVal b As Integer) As Integer

        <System.ServiceModel.OperationContractAttribute( _
        Action:="http://tempuri.org/ICalculator/Divide", _
        ReplyAction:="http://tempuri.org/ICalculator/DivideResponse")> _
        Function Divide(ByVal a As Integer, ByVal b As Integer) As Integer
    End Interface

    <System.CodeDom.Compiler.GeneratedCodeAttribute( _
     "System.ServiceModel", "3.0.0.0")> _
    Public Interface ICalculatorChannel
        Inherits CalculatorService.ICalculator, System.ServiceModel.IClientChannel
    End Interface

    <System.Diagnostics.DebuggerStepThroughAttribute(), _
     System.CodeDom.Compiler.GeneratedCodeAttribute("System.ServiceModel", _
     "3.0.0.0")> _
    Partial Public Class CalculatorClient
        Inherits System.ServiceModel.ClientBase(Of CalculatorService.ICalculator)
        Implements CalculatorService.ICalculator

        Public Sub New()
            MyBase.New
        End Sub

        Public Sub New(ByVal endpointConfigurationName As String)
```

```
                MyBase.New(endpointConfigurationName)
            End Sub

            Public Sub New(ByVal endpointConfigurationName As String, _
                ByVal remoteAddress As String)
                MyBase.New(endpointConfigurationName, remoteAddress)
            End Sub

            Public Sub New(ByVal endpointConfigurationName As String, _
                ByVal remoteAddress As System.ServiceModel.EndpointAddress)
                MyBase.New(endpointConfigurationName, remoteAddress)
            End Sub

            Public Sub New(ByVal binding As System.ServiceModel.Channels.Binding, _
                ByVal remoteAddress As System.ServiceModel.EndpointAddress)
                MyBase.New(binding, remoteAddress)
            End Sub

            Public Function Add(ByVal a As Integer, ByVal b As Integer) As Integer _
                Implements CalculatorService.ICalculator.Add
                Return MyBase.Channel.Add(a, b)
            End Function

            Public Function Subtract(ByVal a As Integer, ByVal b As Integer) _
                As Integer Implements CalculatorService.ICalculator.Subtract
                Return MyBase.Channel.Subtract(a, b)
            End Function

            Public Function Multiply(ByVal a As Integer, ByVal b As Integer) _
                As Integer Implements CalculatorService.ICalculator.Multiply
                Return MyBase.Channel.Multiply(a, b)
            End Function

            Public Function Divide(ByVal a As Integer, ByVal b As Integer) _
                As Integer Implements CalculatorService.ICalculator.Divide
                Return MyBase.Channel.Divide(a, b)
            End Function
        End Class
    End Namespace
```

Here, an interface is defining the four methods and the implementing class `CalculatorClient`, which contains the functions that in turn call the service built earlier in the chapter.

Configuration File Changes

Another addition to your project is the `app.config` file. After the service reference is made, the `app.config` file contains several .NET 3.0 configuration settings. These configuration settings were automatically added by the Visual Studio WCF extensions. The new `app.config` file is presented in the following code block:

```
<?xml version="1.0" encoding="utf-8" ?>
<configuration>
    <system.diagnostics>
        <sources>
```

```
            <!-- This section defines the logging configuration for
                 My.Application.Log -->
            <source name="DefaultSource" switchName="DefaultSwitch">
                <listeners>
                    <add name="FileLog"/>
                    <!-- Uncomment the below section to write to the
                         Application Event Log -->
                    <!--<add name="EventLog"/>-->
                </listeners>
            </source>
        </sources>
        <switches>
            <add name="DefaultSwitch" value="Information" />
        </switches>
        <sharedListeners>
            <add name="FileLog"
                 type="Microsoft.VisualBasic.Logging.FileLogTraceListener,
                     Microsoft.VisualBasic, Version=8.0.0.0, Culture=neutral,
                     PublicKeyToken=b03f5f7f11d50a3a, processorArchitecture=MSIL"
                 initializeData="FileLogWriter"/>
            <!-- Uncomment the below section and replace APPLICATION_NAME
                 with the name of your application to write to the
                 Application Event Log -->
            <!--<add name="EventLog"
                 type="System.Diagnostics.EventLogTraceListener"
                 initializeData="APPLICATION_NAME"/> -->
        </sharedListeners>
    </system.diagnostics>
    <system.serviceModel>
        <bindings>
            <netTcpBinding>
                <binding name="NetTcpBinding_ICalculator" closeTimeout="00:01:00"
                    openTimeout="00:01:00" receiveTimeout="00:10:00"
                    sendTimeout="00:01:00"
                    transactionFlow="false" transferMode="Buffered"
                    transactionProtocol="OleTransactions"
                    hostNameComparisonMode="StrongWildcard" listenBacklog="10"
                    maxBufferPoolSize="524288" maxBufferSize="65536"
                    maxConnections="10"
                    maxReceivedMessageSize="65536">
                    <readerQuotas maxDepth="32" maxStringContentLength="8192"
                        maxArrayLength="16384"
                        maxBytesPerRead="4096" maxNameTableCharCount="16384" />
                    <reliableSession ordered="true" inactivityTimeout="00:10:00"
                        enabled="false" />
                    <security mode="None">
                        <transport clientCredentialType="Windows"
                         protectionLevel="EncryptAndSign" />
                        <message clientCredentialType="Windows" />
                    </security>
                </binding>
            </netTcpBinding>
        </bindings>
        <client>
            <endpoint address="net.tcp://192.168.1.102:8080/Calculator/"
```

```
                        binding="netTcpBinding"
                        bindingConfiguration="NetTcpBinding_ICalculator"
                        contract="CalculatorService.ICalculator"
                        name="NetTcpBinding_ICalculator" />
            </client>
        </system.serviceModel>
    </configuration>
```

The important part of this configuration document is the `<client>` element. This element contains a child element called `<endpoint>` that defines the *where* and *how* of the service consumption process.

The `<endpoint>` element provides the address of the service — `net.tcp://192.168.1.102:8080/Calculator` — and it specifies which binding of the available WCF bindings should be used. In this case, the `netTcpBinding` is the required binding. Even though you are using an established binding from the WCF framework, from the client side you can customize how this binding behaves. The settings that define the behavior of the binding are specified using the `bindingConfiguration` attribute of the `<endpoint>` element. In this case, the value provided to the `bindingConfiguration` attribute is `NetTcpBinding_ICalculator`, which is a reference to the `<binding>` element contained within the `<netTcpBinding>` element:

```
<binding name="NetTcpBinding_ICalculator" closeTimeout="00:01:00"
 openTimeout="00:01:00" receiveTimeout="00:10:00"
 sendTimeout="00:01:00"
 transactionFlow="false" transferMode="Buffered"
 transactionProtocol="OleTransactions"
 hostNameComparisonMode="StrongWildcard" listenBacklog="10"
 maxBufferPoolSize="524288" maxBufferSize="65536"
 maxConnections="10"
 maxReceivedMessageSize="65536">
    <readerQuotas maxDepth="32" maxStringContentLength="8192"
     maxArrayLength="16384"
     maxBytesPerRead="4096" maxNameTableCharCount="16384" />
    <reliableSession ordered="true" inactivityTimeout="00:10:00"
     enabled="false" />
    <security mode="None">
        <transport clientCredentialType="Windows"
         protectionLevel="EncryptAndSign" />
        <message clientCredentialType="Windows" />
    </security>
</binding>
```

As demonstrated, the new Visual Studio 2005 extensions for WCF do make the consumption of these services fairly trivial. The next step is to code the consumption of the service interface to the GUI that was created as one of the first steps.

Writing the Consumption Code

The code to consume the interface is quite minimal. End users will select the radio button of the operation that they are interested in performing. The default radio button selected is Add. The end user places a number in each of the two text boxes provided and clicks the Calculate button to call the service to perform the designated operation on the provided numbers. Here is the code for the form:

```
Public Class Form1

    Private Sub Button1_Click(ByVal sender As System.Object, _
        ByVal e As System.EventArgs) Handles Button1.Click

        Dim result As Integer
        Dim svc As New CalculatorService.CalculatorClient()

        svc.Open()

        If RadioButton1.Checked = True Then
            result = svc.Add(Integer.Parse(TextBox1.Text), _
                Integer.Parse(TextBox2.Text))
        ElseIf RadioButton2.Checked = True Then
            result = svc.Subtract(Integer.Parse(TextBox1.Text), _
                Integer.Parse(TextBox2.Text))
        ElseIf RadioButton3.Checked = True Then
            result = svc.Multiply(Integer.Parse(TextBox1.Text), _
                Integer.Parse(TextBox2.Text))
        ElseIf RadioButton4.Checked = True Then
            result = svc.Divide(Integer.Parse(TextBox1.Text), _
                Integer.Parse(TextBox2.Text))
        End If

        svc.Close()

        Label1.Text = result.ToString()
    End Sub
End Class
```

This is quite similar to what is done when working with Web references from the XML Web Services world. First is an instantiation of the proxy class, as shown with the creation of the svc object:

```
Dim svc As New CalculatorService.CalculatorClient()
```

Working with the ws object now, the IntelliSense options provide you with the appropriate Add(), Subtract(), Multiply(), and Divide() methods. Running this application provides results similar to those presented in Figure 30-10.

Figure 30-10

In this case, the `Add()` method is invoked from the service when the form's Calculate button is pressed. If you add some kind of TCP trace on your machine, you will see results similar to the following:

```
00000000  0B 06 92 01 55 2A 68 74   74 70 3A 2F 2F 74 65 6D   ....U*ht tp://tem
00000010  70 75 72 69 2E 6F 72 67   2F 49 43 61 6C 63 75 6C   puri.org /ICalcul
00000020  61 74 6F 72 2F 41 64 64   52 65 73 70 6F 6E 73 65   ator/Add Response
00000030  0B 41 64 64 52 65 73 70   6F 6E 73 65 13 68 74 74   .AddResp onse.htt
00000040  70 3A 2F 2F 74 65 6D 70   75 72 69 2E 6F 72 67 2F   p://temp uri.org/
00000050  09 41 64 64 52 65 73 75   6C 74 56 02 0B 01 73 04   .AddResu ltV...s.
00000060  0B 01 61 06 56 08 44 0A   1E 00 82 AB 01 44 12 AD   ..a.V.D. .....D..
00000070  A1 8F 9D 89 5A B0 FF 45   A1 D5 29 A9 F4 57 2B A3   ....Z..E ..)..W+.
00000080  44 0C 1E 00 82 AB 14 01   56 0E 42 03 0A 05 42 07   D....... V.B...B.
00000090  8B 00 01 01 01 01                                   ......
```

The response will return something such as the following:

```
00000000  00 01 00 01 02 02 28 6E   65 74 2E 74 63 70 3A 2F   ......(n et.tcp:/
00000010  2F 31 39 32 2E 31 36 38   2E 31 2E 31 30 32 3A 38   /192.168 .1.102:8
00000020  30 38 30 2F 43 61 6C 63   75 6C 61 74 6F 72 2F 03   080/Calc ulator/.
00000030  08 0C 06 B0 01 68 22 68   74 74 70 3A 2F 2F 74 65   .....h"h ttp://te
00000040  6D 70 75 72 69 2E 6F 72   67 2F 49 43 61 6C 63 75   mpuri.or g/ICalcu
00000050  6C 61 74 6F 72 2F 41 64   64 28 6E 65 74 2E 74 63   lator/Ad d(net.tc
00000060  70 3A 2F 2F 31 39 32 2E   31 36 38 2E 31 2E 31 30   p://192. 168.1.10
00000070  32 3A 38 30 38 30 2F 43   61 6C 63 75 6C 61 74 6F   2:8080/C alculato
00000080  72 2F 03 41 64 64 13 68   74 74 70 3A 2F 2F 74 65   r/.Add.h ttp://te
00000090  6D 70 75 72 69 2E 6F 72   67 2F 01 61 62 56 02      mpuri.or g/.a.bV.
000000A0  0B 01 73 04 0B 01 61 06   56 08 44 0A 1E 00 82 AB   ..s...a. V.D.....
000000B0  01 44 1A AD A1 8F 9D 89   5A B0 FF 45 A1 D5 29 A9   .D...... Z..E..).
000000C0  F4 57 2B A3 44 2C 44 2A   AB 14 01 44 0C 1E 00 82   .W+.D,D* ...D....
000000D0  AB 03 01 56 0E 42 05 0A   07 42 09 89 17 42 0B 8B   ...V.B.. .B...B..
000000E0  E9 00 01 01 01                                      .....
```

As before, the requests and responses are sent over TCP as binary, dramatically decreasing the size of the payload for large messages. This is something that .NET Remoting was used for prior to the release of the WCF framework. This concludes the short tutorial demonstrating how to build your own WCF service using the TCP protocol and consume this service directly into a .NET Windows Forms application.

Working with Data Contracts

When building the WCF services so far, the data contract that was defined depended upon simple types or primitive datatypes. In the case of the earlier WCF service, a .NET type of `Integer` was exposed, which in turn was mapped to an XSD type of `int`. You might not have seen the input and output types actually defined in the WSDL document that was provided via the WCF-generated one, but they are there. These types are actually exposed through an imported `.xsd` document (a dynamic document). This bit of the WSDL document is presented here:

```
<wsdl:types>
   <xsd:schema targetNamespace="http://tempuri.org/Imports">
   <xsd:import schemaLocation="http://localhost:8000/docs?xsd=xsd0"
    namespace="http://tempuri.org/" />
   <xsd:import schemaLocation="http://localhost:8000/docs?xsd=xsd1"
```

```
            namespace="http://schemas.microsoft.com/2003/10/Serialization/" />
        </xsd:schema>
    </wsdl:types>
```

Typing in the XSD location of `http://localhost:8000/docs?xsd=xsd0` gives you the input and output parameters of the service. For instance, looking at the definition of the `Add()` method, you will see the following bit of code:

```
<xs:element name="Add">
    <xs:complexType>
        <xs:sequence>
            <xs:element minOccurs="0" name="a" type="xs:int" />
            <xs:element minOccurs="0" name="b" type="xs:int" />
        </xs:sequence>
    </xs:complexType>
</xs:element>
<xs:element name="AddResponse">
    <xs:complexType>
        <xs:sequence>
            <xs:element minOccurs="0" name="AddResult" type="xs:int" />
        </xs:sequence>
    </xs:complexType>
</xs:element>
```

This bit of XML code indicates that there are two required input parameters (a and b) that are of type `int`; in return, the consumer gets an element called `<AddResult>`, which contains a value of type `int`.

As a builder of this WCF service, you didn't have to build the data contract, mainly because this service used simple types. When using complex types, you have to create a data contract in addition to your service contract.

Building a Service with a Data Contract

For an example of working with data contracts, create a new WCF service (again within a Console Application project) called `WCF_WithDataContract`. In this case, you still need an interface that defines your service contract, and then another class that implements that interface. In addition to these items, you also need another class that defines the data contract.

Like the service contract, which makes use of the `<ServiceContract()>` and the `<OperationContract()>` attributes, the data contract uses the `<DataContract()>` and `<DataMember()>` attributes. To gain access to these attributes, you have to make a reference to the `System.Runtime.Serialization` namespace in your project and import this namespace into the file.

The full WCF definition is presented here:

```
Imports System
Imports System.ServiceModel
Imports System.Runtime.Serialization

<DataContract()> _
Public Class Customer
```

```
        <DataMember()> _
        Public FirstName As String

        <DataMember()> _
        Public LastName As String
    End Class

    <ServiceContract()> _
    Public Interface IHelloCustomer
        <OperationContract()> _
        Function HelloFirstName(ByVal cust As Customer) As String

        <OperationContract()> _
        Function HelloFullName(ByVal cust As Customer) As String
    End Interface

    Public Class HelloCustomer
        Implements IHelloCustomer

        Public Function HelloFirstName(ByVal cust As Customer) As String _
            Implements IHelloCustomer.HelloFirstName
                Return "Hello " & cust.FirstName
        End Function

        Public Function HelloFullName(ByVal cust As Customer) As String _
            Implements IHelloCustomer.HelloFullName
                Return "Hello " & cust.FirstName & " " & cust.LastName
        End Function
    End Class
```

Here, you can see that the `System.Runtime.Serialization` namespace is also imported, and the first class in the file is the data contract of the service. This class, the `Customer` class, has two members: `FirstName` and `LastName`. Both of these properties are of type `String`. You specify a class as a data contract through the use of the `<DataContract()>` attribute:

```
<DataContract()> _
Public Class Customer

    ' Code removed for clarity

End Class
```

Now, any of the properties contained in the class are also part of the data contract through the use of the `<DataMember()>` attribute:

```
<DataContract()> _
Public Class Customer
    <DataMember()> _
    Public FirstName As String

    <DataMember()> _
    Public LastName As String
End Class
```

Finally, the `Customer` object is used in the interface as well as the class that implements the `IHelloCustomer` interface.

Building the Host

The next step is the same as before: Change the `Module1.vb` file so that it becomes the host of the WCF service you just built. This task is illustrated in the following example:

```vb
Imports System
Imports System.ServiceModel
Imports System.ServiceModel.Description

Module Module1

    Sub Main()
        Using serviceHost As ServiceHost = New ServiceHost(GetType(HelloCustomer))
            Dim ntb As NetTcpBinding = New NetTcpBinding(SecurityMode.None)
            serviceHost.AddServiceEndpoint(GetType(IHelloCustomer), ntb, _
                New Uri("net.tcp://192.168.1.102:8080/HelloCustomer/"))

            Dim smb As New ServiceMetadataBehavior()
            smb.HttpGetEnabled = True
            smb.HttpGetUrl = New Uri("http://localhost:8000/docs")

            serviceHost.Description.Behaviors.Add(smb)

            serviceHost.Open()

            Console.WriteLine("Press the <ENTER> key to close the host.")
            Console.ReadLine()
        End Using
    End Sub

End Module
```

This host uses the `IHelloCustomer` interface and builds an endpoint at `net.tcp://192.168.1.102:8080/HelloCustomer`. Next, let's look at consuming this service from another console application.

Building the Consumer

Now that the service is running and in place, the next step is to build the consumer. To begin, build a new console application from Visual Studio 2005 and call the project `HelloWorldConsumer`. Again, right-click on the solution and select Add Service Reference from the options provided in the menu.

From the Add Service Reference dialog, add `http://localhost:8000/docs` as the service URI and `HelloCustomerService` as the service reference name, as shown in Figure 30-11.

Add Service Reference

Enter the service URI and reference name and click OK to add all the available services.

Service URI:

http://localhost:8000/docs   Browse ...

Service reference name:

HelloCustomerService

OK   Cancel

Figure 30-11

This will add the changes to the references and the `app.config` file just as before, enabling you to consume the service. The following code shows what is required:

```
Module Module1

    Sub Main()
        Dim svc As New HelloCustomerService.HelloCustomerClient()
        Dim cust As New HelloCustomerService.Customer()

        Dim result As String

        svc.Open()

        Console.WriteLine("What is your first name?")
        cust.FirstName = Console.ReadLine()

        Console.WriteLine("What is your last name?")
        cust.LastName = Console.ReadLine()

        result = svc.HelloFullName(cust)

        svc.Close()

        Console.WriteLine(result)
        Console.ReadLine()
    End Sub

End Module
```

As a consumer, once you make the reference, you will notice that the service reference doesn't just provide a `HelloCustomerClient` object; you will also find the `Customer` object that was defined through the service's data contract.

Therefore, the preceding code block just instantiates both of these objects and builds the `Customer` object before it is passed into the `HelloFullName()` method provided by the service. Running this bit of code will return the results shown in Figure 30-12.

```
file:///C:/Users/Bill/AppData/Local/Temporary Projects/HelloCustomerConsumer/bin/Debug/Hell...
What is your first name?
Bill
What is your last name?
Evjen
Hello Bill Evjen
```

Figure 30-12

Looking at WSDL and the Schema for HelloCustomerService

When you make a reference to the `HelloCustomer` service, looking at the WSDL you will find the following XSD imports:

```
<wsdl:types>
   <xsd:schema targetNamespace="http://tempuri.org/Imports">
      <xsd:import schemaLocation="http://localhost:8000/docs?xsd=xsd0"
       namespace="http://tempuri.org/" />
      <xsd:import schemaLocation="http://localhost:8000/docs?xsd=xsd1"
       namespace="http://schemas.microsoft.com/2003/10/Serialization/" />
      <xsd:import schemaLocation="http://localhost:8000/docs?xsd=xsd2"
       namespace="http://schemas.datacontract.org/2004/07/WCF_WithDataContract" />
   </xsd:schema>
</wsdl:types>
```

`http://localhost:8000/docs?xsd=xsd2` provides the details on your `Customer` object. The code from this file is shown here:

```
<?xml version="1.0" encoding="utf-8" ?>
<xs:schema elementFormDefault="qualified"
 targetNamespace="http://schemas.datacontract.org/2004/07/WCF_WithDataContract"
 xmlns:xs="http://www.w3.org/2001/XMLSchema"
```

```
xmlns:tns="http://schemas.datacontract.org/2004/07/WCF_WithDataContract">
  <xs:complexType name="Customer">
    <xs:sequence>
      <xs:element minOccurs="0" name="FirstName"
      nillable="true" type="xs:string" />
      <xs:element minOccurs="0" name="LastName"
      nillable="true" type="xs:string" />
    </xs:sequence>
  </xs:complexType>
  <xs:element name="Customer" nillable="true" type="tns:Customer" />
</xs:schema>
```

This is an XSD description of the `Customer` object. Making a reference to the WSDL that includes the XSD description of the `Customer` object causes the auto-generated proxy class to create the following class as part of the proxy:

```
<System.CodeDom.Compiler.GeneratedCodeAttribute("System.Runtime.Serialization", _
  "3.0.0.0"), _
  System.Runtime.Serialization.DataContractAttribute( _
  [Namespace]:="http://schemas.datacontract.org/2004/07/WCF_WithDataContract"), _
    System.SerializableAttribute()> _
  Partial Public Class Customer
      Inherits Object
      Implements System.Runtime.Serialization.IExtensibleDataObject

      <System.NonSerializedAttribute()> _
      Private extensionDataField As _
        System.Runtime.Serialization.ExtensionDataObject

      <System.Runtime.Serialization.OptionalFieldAttribute()> _
      Private FirstNameField As String

      <System.Runtime.Serialization.OptionalFieldAttribute()> _
      Private LastNameField As String

      Public Property ExtensionData() As _
        System.Runtime.Serialization.ExtensionDataObject Implements _
          System.Runtime.Serialization.IExtensibleDataObject.ExtensionData
        Get
            Return Me.extensionDataField
        End Get
        Set
            Me.extensionDataField = value
        End Set
      End Property

      <System.Runtime.Serialization.DataMemberAttribute()> _
      Public Property FirstName() As String
        Get
            Return Me.FirstNameField
        End Get
        Set
            Me.FirstNameField = value
        End Set
```

```
            End Property

        <System.Runtime.Serialization.DataMemberAttribute()>  _
        Public Property LastName() As String
            Get
                Return Me.LastNameField
            End Get
            Set
                Me.LastNameField = value
            End Set
        End Property
    End Class
```

Using this model, you can easily build your services with your own defined types.

Namespaces

Note that the services built in the chapter have no defined namespaces. If you looked at the WSDL files that were produced, you would see that the namespace provided is `http://tempuri.org`. Obviously, you don't want to go live with this default namespace. Instead, you need to define your own namespace.

To accomplish this task, the interface's `<ServiceContract()>` attribute enables you to set the namespace, as shown here:

```
<ServiceContract(Namespace:="http://www.lipperweb.com/ns/")> _
Public Interface IHelloCustomer
    <OperationContract()> _
    Function HelloFirstName(ByVal cust As Customer) As String

    <OperationContract()> _
    Function HelloFullName(ByVal cust As Customer) As String
End Interface
```

Here, the `<ServiceContract()>` attribute uses the `Namespace` property to provide a namespace.

Touching on Security

The WCF framework offers a multitude of different WS-* specifications that you can take advantage of in your services without really needing to know how to code for those specifications, as the framework takes care of this for you on your behalf.

To see an example of this, consider the `VbWCF_Service1` solution from the console-application code earlier in this chapter. Take that code and modify it to add a requirement that the service makes use of WS-Security and that the client can only consume the service using WS-Security by supplying their Windows credentials as the user context. The code for this modified service is provided here:

```
Imports System
Imports System.ServiceModel
```

```vb
Imports System.ServiceModel.Description

Module Module1

    Sub Main()
        Using serviceHost As ServiceHost = New ServiceHost(GetType(Calculator))
            Dim ntb As NetTcpBinding = New NetTcpBinding(SecurityMode.Message)
            ntb.Security.Message.ClientCredentialType = _
                MessageCredentialType.Windows
            serviceHost.AddServiceEndpoint(GetType(ICalculator), ntb, _
                New Uri("net.tcp://192.168.1.102:8080/Calculator/"))

            Dim smb As New ServiceMetadataBehavior()
            smb.HttpGetEnabled = True
            smb.HttpGetUrl = New Uri("http://localhost:8000/docs")

            serviceHost.Description.Behaviors.Add(smb)

            serviceHost.Open()

            Console.WriteLine("Press the <ENTER> key to close the host.")
            Console.ReadLine()
        End Using
    End Sub

End Module
```

Instead of the `SecurityMode.None` property, you can also use the `SecurityMode.Message` property. This forces the SOAP message to include a WS-Security header. The next line of code specifies that the credential type that the service needs to make use of is a Windows credential, set with the `MessageCredentialType.Windows` property.

Making a client reference to this service gives you a different `app.config` file than what you had before. Here is the `<system.serviceModel>` element of the `app.config` file:

```xml
<system.serviceModel>
    <bindings>
        <netTcpBinding>
            <binding name="NetTcpBinding_ICalculator" closeTimeout="00:01:00"
              openTimeout="00:01:00" receiveTimeout="00:10:00" sendTimeout="00:01:00"
              transactionFlow="false" transferMode="Buffered"
              transactionProtocol="OleTransactions"
              hostNameComparisonMode="StrongWildcard" listenBacklog="10"
              maxBufferPoolSize="524288" maxBufferSize="65536" maxConnections="10"
              maxReceivedMessageSize="65536" >
                <readerQuotas maxDepth="32" maxStringContentLength="8192"
                  maxArrayLength="16384"
                  maxBytesPerRead="4096" maxNameTableCharCount="16384" />
                <reliableSession ordered="true" inactivityTimeout="00:10:00"
                  enabled="false" />
                <security mode="Message">
                    <transport clientCredentialType="Windows"
                      protectionLevel="EncryptAndSign" />
```

```
                      <message clientCredentialType="Windows" />
              </security>
           </binding>
         </netTcpBinding>
      </bindings>
      <client>
         <endpoint address="net.tcp://192.168.1.102:8080/Calculator/"
          binding="netTcpBinding" bindingConfiguration="NetTcpBinding_ICalculator"
          contract="CalculatorService.ICalculator" name="NetTcpBinding_ICalculator">
            <identity>
                <userPrincipalName value="Bill-PC\Bill" />
            </identity>
         </endpoint>
      </client>
   </system.serviceModel>
```

Note that the `<security>` element defines the client credential type as a Windows credential set and that the credentials provided in the WS-Security SOAP header need to be encrypted and signed.

From the `<client>` element, you have a user principal defined as the credentials provided in the request. Now when the request and response occur, you will find a WS-Security header, which is present in the SOAP header of the message.

Summary

This chapter took a look at one of the newest capabilities provided to the Visual Basic world. VB 2005 using the .NET Framework 3.0 is a great combination for building advanced services that take ASP.NET Web Services, .NET Remoting, Enterprise Services, and MSMQ to the next level.

Though not exhaustive, this chapter broadly outlined the basics of the framework. As you start to dig deeper in the technology, you will find capabilities that are strong and extensible.

31

Windows Services

Modern, multitasking operating systems often need to run applications that operate in the background and that are independent of the user who is logged in. From Windows NT to Windows Vista, such applications are called *Windows Services* (formerly known as NT Services). The tasks carried out by Windows Services are typically long running and have little or no direct interaction with a user (so they don't usually have user interfaces). Such applications may be started when the computer is booted and often continue to run until the computer is shut down.

This chapter covers the following:

❑   The characteristics of a Windows Service

❑   How to interact with a Windows Service using Visual Studio 2005 and the management applets in the Windows Control Panel

❑   How to create, install, and communicate with a Windows Service using Visual Basic

❑   How to debug a Windows Service from within Visual Studio 2005

As VB6 did not offer direct support for the creation of Windows Services, you might be unfamiliar with such applications. To help you understand the variety of such applications, this chapter examines some scenarios for which a Windows Service application is a good solution.

Example Windows Services

Microsoft SQL Server, Exchange Server, Internet Information Server (IIS), and antivirus software all use Windows Services to perform tasks in response to events that occur on the system overall. Only a background service, or Windows Service, that runs no matter which user is logged in, could perform such operations. For example, consider these potential Windows Services:

❑   **A file watcher** — Suppose you are running an FTP server that enables users to place files in a particular directory. You could use a Windows Service to monitor and process files within that directory as they arrive. The service runs in the background and detects when files are changed or added within the directory, and then extracts information from these files in order to process orders, or update address and billing information. You'll see an example of such a Windows Service later in this chapter.

❑ **An automated stock price reporter** — You could build a system that extracts stock prices from a Web Service or website and then e-mails the information to users. You could set thresholds so that an e-mail is only sent out if the stock price reaches a certain price. This Windows Service can be automated to extract the information every 10 minutes, every 10 seconds, or whatever. Because a Windows Service can contain any logic that does not require a user interface, you have a lot of flexibility in constructing such applications.

❑ **Microsoft Transaction Server (MTS)** — This (part of COM+ Services in Windows 2000 and later) is an object broker that manages instances of components. It is used regularly by professional developers. This service runs constantly in the background and manages components as soon as the computer is booted, just like IIS or Exchange Server.

Characteristics of a Windows Service

To properly design and develop a Windows Service, it's important to understand how it differs from a typical Windows program. Here are the most important characteristics of a Windows Service:

❑ A Windows Service can start before a user logs on. The system maintains a list of Windows Services, which be set to start at boot time. Services can also be installed such that they require a manual startup and will not start at bootup.

❑ A Windows Service can run under a different account from that of the current user. Most Windows Services provide functionality that needs to be running all the time, and some load before a user logs on, so they cannot depend on a user being logged on to run.

❑ A Windows Service has its own process. It does not run in the process of a program communicating with it (Chapter 27 has more information on processes).

❑ A Windows Service typically has no user interface. This is because the service may be running under a different account from that of the current user, or the service may start at bootup, which means that the calls to put up a user interface might fail because they are out of context (it is possible to create a Windows Service with a user interface, but Visual Basic 2005 cannot be used to do it; you'll learn why later).

❑ A Windows Service requires a special installation procedure; just clicking on a compiled EXE won't run it. The program must run in a special context in the operating system, and a specific installation process is required to do the configuration necessary for a Windows Service to be run in this special context.

❑ A Windows Service works with a *Service Control Manager* (discussed shortly). The Service Control Manager is required to provide an interface to the Windows Service. External programs that want to communicate with a Windows Service (for example, to start or stop the service) must go through the Service Control Manager. The Service Control Manager is an operating-system-level program, but it has a user interface that can be used to start and stop services, and this interface can be accessed through the Computer Management section of the Control Panel.

Interacting with Windows Services

You can view the services that are used on your computer by opening the Service Control Manager user interface. To do so in Windows 2000, select Administrative Tools ⇨ Services in the Control Panel. In Windows XP Professional, select Start ⇨ All Programs ⇨ Administrative Tools ⇨ Services. Using the Service Control Manager, a service can be set to automatically start when the system is booted, or a service can be started manually. Services can also be stopped or paused. The list of services contained in the Service Control Manager includes the current state for each service. Figure 31-1 shows the Service Control Manager in Windows XP.

Figure 31-1

The Status column indicates the current state of the service. If this column is blank, the service has not been started since the last time the computer was booted. Other possible values for Status are Started, Stopped, and Paused. You can access additional settings and details concerning a service by double-clicking it.

When a service is started, it automatically logs into the system using either a user or system account:

❑   The user account is a regular NT account that allows the program to interact with the system — in essence, the service impersonates a user.

❑   The system account is not associated with a particular user.

The Service Control Manager shown in Figure 31-1 is part of the operating system (OS), which is what supports Windows Services; it is not a part of the .NET Framework. Any service run by the OS is exposed through the Service Control Manager, no matter how the service was created or installed. You can also interact with Windows Services via the Server Explorer in Visual Studio 2005. You'll see this technique later.

Creating a Windows Service

Prior to the release of the .NET Framework, most Windows Services were created with C++. Third-party toolkits were available to enable Windows Services to be created in VB6 and earlier, but deployment problems and threading issues meant that few developers took this route.

In .NET, the functionality needed to interface to the operating system is wrapped up in the .NET Framework classes, so any .NET-compliant language can now be used to create a Windows Service.

The .NET Framework Classes for Windows Services

Several base classes are needed to create a Windows Service:

❑ `System.ServiceProcess.ServiceBase` — Provides the base class for the Windows Service. The class that contains the logic that will run in the service inherits from `ServiceBase`. A single executable can contain more than one service, but each service in the executable is a separate class that inherits from `ServiceBase`.

❑ `System.Configuration.Install.Installer` — This is a generic class that performs the installation chores for a variety of components. One class in a Windows Service process must inherit and extend `Installer` in order to provide the interface necessary to install the service under the various Windows operating systems.

Each class that inherits from `Installer` needs to contain an instance of each of these classes:

❑ `System.ServiceProcess.ServiceProcessInstaller` — This class contains the information needed to install a .NET executable that contains Windows Services (that is, an executable that contains classes that inherit from `ServiceBase`). The .NET installation utility for Windows Services (`InstallUtil.exe`, discussed later) calls this class to get the information it needs to perform the installation.

❑ `System.ServiceProcess.ServiceInstaller` — This class also interacts with the `InstallUtil.exe` installation program. Whereas `ServiceProcessInstaller` contains information needed to install the executable as a whole, `ServiceInstaller` contains information on a specific service in the executable. If an executable contains more than one service, an instance of `ServiceInstaller` is needed for each one.

For most Windows Services you develop, you can let Visual Studio 2005 take care of `Installer`, `ServiceProcessInstaller`, and `ServiceInstaller`. You'll just need to set a few properties. The class you should thoroughly understand is `ServiceBase`, as this is the class that contains the functionality of a Windows Service and therefore must inherit from it.

The ServiceBase Class

`ServiceBase` contains several useful properties and methods, but initially it's more important to understand the events of `ServiceBase`. Most of these events are fired by the Service Control Manager when the state of the service is changed. The most important events are as follows:

Event	How and When the Event is Used
OnStart	Occurs when the service is started. This is where the initialization logic for a service is usually placed.
OnStop	Occurs when the service is stopped. Cleanup and shutdown logic is generally placed here.
OnPause	Occurs when the service is paused. Any logic required to suspend operations during a pause goes here.
OnContinue	Occurs when a service continues after being paused
OnShutdown	Occurs when the operating system is being shut down
OnSessionChange	Occurs when a change event is received from a Terminal Session service. This method was new in .NET Framework 2.0.
OnPowerEvent	Occurs when the system's power management software causes a change in the power status of the system. Usually used to change the behavior of a service when a system is going in or out of a "suspended" power mode. This is more frequent with end users who are working on laptops.
OnCustomCommand	Occurs when an external program has told the Service Control Manager that it wishes to send a command to the service. The operation of this event is covered in "Communicating with the Service."

The events used most frequently are `OnStart`, `OnStop`, and `OnCustomCommand`. The `OnStart` and `OnStop` events are used in almost every Windows Service written in Visual Basic, and the `OnCustomCommand` is used if any special configuration of the service needs to be done while the service is running.

All of these are `Protected` events, so they are only available to classes that inherit from `ServiceBase`. Because of the restricted context in which it runs, a Windows Service component that inherits from `ServiceBase` often lacks a public interface. While you can add public properties and methods to such a component, they are of limited use because outside programs cannot obtain an object reference to running a Windows Service component.

To be active as a Windows Service, an instance of `ServiceBase` must be started via the shared `Run` method of the `ServiceBase` class. However, normally you don't have to write code to do this because the template code generated by Visual Studio 2005 places the correct code in the `Main` subroutine of the project for you.

The most commonly used property of `ServiceBase` is the `AutoLog` property. This `Boolean` property is set to `True` by default. If `True`, then the Windows Service automatically logs the `Start`, `Stop`, `Pause`, and `Continue` events to an Event Log. The Event Log used is the Application Event Log and the Source in the log entries is taken from the name of Windows Service. This automatic event logging is stopped by setting the `AutoLog` property to `False`.

The following File Watcher example goes into more detail about the automatic logging capabilities in a Windows Service, and about Event Logs in general.

Installation-Oriented Classes

The `Installer`, `ServiceProcessInstaller`, and `ServiceInstaller` classes are quite simple to build and use if you are employing Visual Studio 2005. After you create your Windows Service project, Visual Studio 2005 will create a class file called `Service1.vb` for you. To add the `Installer`, `ServiceProcessInstaller`, and `ServiceInstaller` classes to your project, simply right-click the design surface of this `ServiceBase` class, `Service1.vb`, and select Add Installer. This creates the code framework necessary to use them.

The `Installer` class (named `ProjectInstaller.vb` by default in a Windows Service project) generally needs no interaction at all — it is ready to use when created by Visual Studio 2005. However, it may be appropriate to change some properties of the `ServiceProcessInstaller` and `ServiceInstaller` classes. You can do this by simply highlighting these objects on the design surface and changing their properties directly in the Properties window of Visual Studio 2005. The properties that are typically modified for `ServiceProcessInstaller` include the following:

- ❑ `Account` — This specifies the type of account under which the entire service application will run. Different settings give the services in the application different levels of privilege on the local system. We'll use the highest level of privilege, `LocalSystem`, for most of the examples in this chapter in order to keep it simple. If this property is set to `User` (which is the default), then you must supply a username and password, and that user's account is used to determine privileges for the service. If there is any possibility that a service could access system resources that should be "out of bounds," then using the `User` setting to restrict privileges is a good idea. Besides `LocalSystem` and `User`, other possible settings for the `Account` property include `NetworkService` and `LocalService`.

- ❑ `Username` — If `Account` is set to `User`, then this property specifies the user account to use in determining the privileges the system will have and how it interacts with other computers on the network. If this property is left blank, then it is requested when the service is installed.

- ❑ **Password** — This property determines the password to access the user account specified in the `Username` property. If the password is left blank, then it is requested when the service is installed.

- ❑ **HelpText** — Information about the service that will be displayed in certain installation options

If the `Account` property is set to `User`, then it is good practice to set up a special user account for the service, rather than rely on some existing account intended for a live user. The special account can be set up with exactly the appropriate privileges for the service. This way, it isn't as vulnerable to having its password or its privileges inadvertently changed in a way that would cause problems in running the service.

For the `ServiceInstaller` class, the properties you might change include the following:

❑ **DisplayName** — The name of the service displayed in the Service Manager or the Server Explorer can be different from the class name and the executable name if desired, though it's better to make this name the same as the class name for the service.

❑ **StartType** — This specifies how the service is started. The default is `Manual`, which means you must start the service yourself, as it won't start automatically after the system boots. If you want the service to always start when the system starts, change this property to `Automatic`. The Service Manager can be used to override the `StartType` setting.

❑ **ServiceName** — The name of the service that this `ServiceInstaller` handles during installation. If you changed the class name of the service after using the Add Installer option, you would need to change this property to correspond to the new name for the service.

`ServiceProcessInstaller` and `ServiceInstaller` are used as necessary during the installation process, so there is no need to understand or manipulate the methods of these.

Multiple Services within One Executable

It is possible to place more than one class that inherits from `ServiceBase` in a single Windows Service executable. Each such class then allows for a separate service that can be started, stopped, and so on, independently of the other services in the executable.

If a Windows Service executable contains more than one service, then it must contain one `Service-Installer` for each service. Each `ServiceInstaller` is configured with the information used for its associated service, such as the displayed name and the start type (automatic or manual). However, the executable still needs only one `ServiceProcessInstaller`, which works for all the services in the executable. It is configured with the account information that is used for all the services in the executable.

The ServiceController Class

Another important .NET Framework class used with Windows Services is `System.ServiceProcess.ServiceController`. This class is not used when constructing a service. It is used by external applications to communicate with a running service, allowing operations such as starting and stopping the service. The `ServiceController` class is described in detail in "Communicating with the Service."

Other Types of Windows Services

The `ServiceBase` and `ServiceController` classes can be used to create typical Windows Services that work with high-level system resources such as the file system or performance counters. However, some Windows Services need to interact at a deeper level. For example, a service may work at the kernel level, fulfilling functions such as that of a device driver.

Presently, the .NET Framework classes for Windows Services cannot be used to create such lower-level services, which rules out both VB and C# as tools to create them. C++ is typically the tool of choice for these types of services. If the .NET version of C++ is used, the code for such services would typically run in unmanaged mode.

Another type of service that cannot be created with the .NET Framework classes is one that interacts with the Windows desktop. Again, C++ is the preferred tool for such services.

You'll look at the types of services that *are* possible during the discussion of the `ServiceType` property of the `ServiceController` class, in "Communicating with the Service."

Creating a Windows Service in Visual Basic

Now it's time to create and use a Windows Service with Visual Basic, using the previously discussed .NET Framework classes. These tasks are demonstrated later in a detailed example. Here is a high-level description of the necessary tasks:

1. Create a new project of the type Windows Service. By default, the service will be in a module named `Service1.vb`, but it can be renamed, like any other .NET module. (The class that is automatically placed in `Service1.vb` is named `Service1` by default, and it inherits from `ServiceBase`.)

2. Place any logic needed to run when the service is started in the `OnStart` event of the service class. You can find the code listing for the `Service1.vb` file by double-clicking this file's design surface.

3. Add any additional logic that the service needs to carry out its operation. Logic can be placed in the class for the service, or in any other class module in the project. Such logic is typically called via some event that is generated by the operating system and passed to the service, such as a file changing in a directory, or a timer tick.

4. Add an installer to the project. This module provides the interface to the Windows operating system to install the module as a Windows Service. The installer is a class that inherits from `System.Configuration.Install.Installer`, and it contains instances of the `ServiceProcessInstaller` and `ServiceInstaller` classes.

5. Set the properties of the installer modules as necessary. The most common settings needed are the account under which the service will run and the name the service will display in the Service Control Manager.

6. Build the project. This results in an EXE file. For example, if the service were named `WindowsService1`, then the executable file would be named `WindowsService1.exe`.

7. Install the Windows Service with a command-line utility named `InstallUtil.exe`. (As previously mentioned, a service cannot be started by just running the EXE file.)

8. Start the Windows Service with the Service Control Manager (available via the Control Panel ➪ Administrative Tools folder in Windows 2000, or the Start ➪ All Programs ➪ Administrative Tools folder in Windows XP) or with the Server Explorer in Visual Studio 2005.

   You can also start a service from the command console if the proper paths to .NET are set. The command is "NET START *<servicename>*". Note that the *<servicename>* used in this command is the name of the service, not the name of the executable in which the service resides. Depending on the configuration of your system, a service started with any of the aforementioned methods will sometimes fail with an error message that says the service did not start in a timely fashion. This may be because the .NET libraries and other initialization tasks did not finish fast enough to suit the Service Control Manager. If this happens, attempt to start the service again; it usually succeeds the second time.

Steps 2 through 5 can be done in a different order. It doesn't matter whether the installer is added and configured before or after the logic that does the processing for the service is added.

At this point, a service is installed and running. The Service Manager or the Server Explorer can stop the service, or it will be automatically stopped when the system is shut down. The command to stop the service in a command console is "NET STOP <*servicename*>".

The service does not automatically start the next time the system is booted unless it is configured for that. This can be done by setting the StartType property for the service to Automatic when developing the service or it can be done in the Service Manager. Right-clicking the service in the Service Manager provides access to this capability.

This process is superficially similar to doing most other Visual Basic projects. There are a few important differences, however:

❑ You cannot debug the project in the environment as you normally would any other Visual Basic program. The service must be installed and started before it can be debugged. It is also necessary to attach to the process for the service to do debugging. Details about this are included in "Debugging the Service."

❑ Even though the result of the development is an EXE, you should not include any message boxes or other visual elements in the code. The Windows Service executable is more like a component library in that sense, and should not have a visual interface. If you include visual elements such as message boxes, the results can vary. In some cases, the UI code will have no effect. In others cases, the service may hang when attempting to write to the user interface.

❑ Finally, be especially careful to handle all errors within the program. The program is not running in a user context, so a runtime error has no place to report itself visually. Handle all errors with structured exception handling, and use an Event Log or other offline means to record and communicate runtime errors.

Creating a Counter Monitor Service

To illustrate the outlined steps, the following example creates a simple service that checks the value of a performance counter, and when the value of the counter exceeds a certain value, the service beeps every three seconds. This is a good example for stepping through the process of creating, installing, and starting a Windows Service. It contains very little logic, and you can easily tell when it is working.

In the first phase of the example, you create a service that always beeps. Then, in the second phase, you add logic to monitor the performance counter and only beep when the counter exceeds a specific value:

1. Start a new Windows Service project using Visual Studio 2005. Name the project CounterMonitor.

2. In the Solution Explorer, rename `Service1.vb` to `CounterMonitor.vb`.

3. Click the design surface for `CounterMonitor.vb`. In the Properties window, change the `ServiceName` property from `Service1` to `CounterMonitor` (the `Name` property changes the name of the class on which the service is based, while the `ServiceName` property changes the name of the service as known to the Service Control Manager).

4. Right-click the project for the service and select Properties. You will then be presented with the CounterMonitor Property Pages as one of the paged tabs directly in Visual Studio. From the Application tab, set the Application Type drop-down list to Windows Service if necessary (it should already be set to this) and from the drop-down list named Startup Object, make sure `CounterMonitor` is selected (see Figure 31-2).

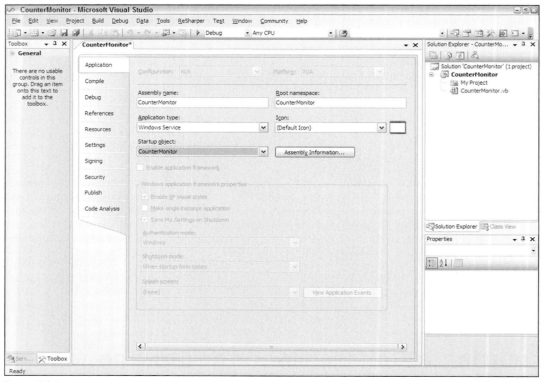

Figure 31-2

5. Go back to the `CounterMonitor.vb` file's design view and open the Visual Studio 2005 Toolbox. Open the Components (not the Windows Forms) node in the Toolbox. Drag a `Timer` control from the Toolbox onto the `CounterMonitor` design surface. It will appear on the design surface with the name `Timer1`. It is very important that you grab the correct Timer object from the Toolbox. Visual Studio 2005 does not have the Timer object for this example in the Toolbox, whereas earlier versions of Visual Studio did. To ensure you have the correct Timer object, right-click on the Toolbox and select Choose Items from the menu. In the .NET Framework Components tab of the Choose Toolbox Items dialog, scroll down until you see a couple of

Timer objects. In the list are a couple of Timer objects from the System.Windows.Forms namespace, but you want to instead choose the Timer object that is part of the System.Timers namespace. This is the Timer object that you want to work with for the rest of this example.

6. In the Properties window for Timer1, change the Interval property to a value of 3000 (that's 3,000 milliseconds, which causes the timer to fire every three seconds).

7. Go to the code for CounterMonitor.vb. Inside the OnStart event handler (which is already created for you in the code), enter the following:

```
Timer1.Enabled = True
```

8. In the OnStop event for the class, enter the following:

```
Timer1.Enabled = False
```

9. Create an Elapsed event for the timer by highlighting Timer1 in the left-hand drop-down box at the top of the code editor window. Then, select the Elapsed event in the right-hand drop-down box from the code view of the file.

10. In the Elapsed event, place the following line of code:

```
Beep()
```

11. Now add an installer to the project. Go back to the design surface for CounterMonitor and right-click it. Select Add Installer. A new file called ProjectInstaller1.vb is created and added to the project. The ProjectInstaller1.vb file will have two components added to its design surface, ServiceProcessInstaller1 and ServiceInstaller1, as shown in Figure 31-3.

Figure 31-3

12. On the ProjectInstaller.vb design surface, highlight the ServiceProcessInstaller1 control. In its Properties window, change the Account property to LocalSystem.

13. Highlight the ServiceInstaller1 control. In its Properties window, type in CounterMonitor as the value of the DisplayName property.

14. Now build the project by right-clicking on the solution and selecting Build from the menu. An EXE named CounterMonitor.exe will be created for the service.

Installing the Service

Now you are ready to install the service. The utility for doing this, InstallUtil.exe, must be run from a command line. It is located in the .NET utilities directory, found at C:\WINNT\Microsoft.NET\ Framework\v2.0.50727 on Windows 2000 and NT systems, or C:\Windows\Microsoft.NET\ Framework\v2.0.50727 on Windows XP and Windows 2003.

You can easily access this utility (and all the other .NET utilities in that directory) using an option from the Programs menu that is installed with Visual Studio 2005. Choose Microsoft Visual Studio 2005 ⇨ Visual Studio Tools ⇨ Visual Studio 2005 Command Prompt. In the command window that appears, change to the directory that contains `CounterMonitor.exe`. By default, when using Visual Studio 2005, you'll find this executable at `C:\Documents and Settings\[ user ]\My Documents\Visual Studio\Projects\CounterMonitor\Projects\CounterMonitor\CounterMonitor\obj\Debug`. Once found, run the following command:

```
InstallUtil CounterMonitor.exe
```

Check the messages generated by `InstallUtil.exe` to ensure that the installation of the service was successful. The utility generates several lines of information; if successful, the last two lines are as follows:

```
The Commit phase completed successfully.

The transacted install has completed.
```

If these two lines do not appear, you need to read all the information generated by the utility to find out why the install did not work. Reasons might include a bad pathname for the executable, or trying to install the service again when it is already installed (it must be uninstalled before it can be reinstalled), as described later.

Starting the Service

Later in this chapter, you will create your own "control panel" screen to start and stop the service. For now, to test the new Windows Service, you will use the Server Explorer in Visual Studio 2005. Open the Server Explorer in Visual Studio 2005 and expand the Services node. The resulting screen is shown in Figure 31-4.

Figure 31-4

If the `CounterMonitor` service does not appear in the list, the installation was unsuccessful. Try the installation again and check the error messages. Right-click the `CounterMonitor` service. Select the Start menu option. You will hear the service beep every three seconds. You can stop the service by right-clicking it again and selecting the Stop menu option.

You can also use the Service Control Manager built into Windows to start the `CounterMonitor` service, shown in Figure 31-5.

Figure 31-5

Start `CounterMonitor` by right-clicking it and selecting Start or by clicking the Start link. As before, you will hear your computer beep every three seconds. Stop the service by right-clicking `CounterMonitor` and selecting Stop or by clicking the Stop link. Note that if you already started the service via the Server Explorer (as described earlier), then it will be in a Started state when you access the Service Control Manager program.

Uninstalling the Service

Uninstalling the service is very similar to installing it. The service must be in a stopped state before it can be uninstalled, but the uninstall operation will attempt to stop the service if it is running. The uninstall operation is done in the same command window (with the Visual Studio 2005 Command Prompt) as the install operation, and the command used is the same as the one for installation, except that the option /u is included just before name of the service. Remember that you need to navigate to `C:\Documents and Settings\[ user ]\My Documents\Visual Studio\Projects\ CounterMonitor\Projects\CounterMonitor\CounterMonitor\obj\Debug` to run this ommand:

```
InstallUtil.exe /u CounterMonitor.exe
```

You can tell that the uninstall was successful if the information displayed by the utility contains the following line:

```
Service CounterMonitor was successfully removed from the system.
```

If the uninstall is unsuccessful, read the rest of the information to find out why. Besides typing in the wrong pathname, another common reason for failure is trying to uninstall a service that is in a running state and could not be stopped in a timely fashion.

Once you have uninstalled `CounterMonitor`, it will no longer show up in the list of available services to start and stop (at least, after a refresh it won't).

> A Windows Service must be uninstalled and reinstalled every time you make changes to it. You should uninstall `CounterMonitor` now because we're about to add new capabilities to it.

Monitoring a Performance Counter

Performance counters are a system-level function of Windows. They are used to track usage of system resources. Performance counters can be expressed as counts (number of times a Web page was hit), or percentages (how much disk space is left), or other types of information. Many counters are automatically maintained by the operating system, but applications can create and manage their own performance counters.

To demonstrate how services can interact with system-level functionality, you will add to the `CounterMonitor` the capability to monitor a particular performance counter, and only beep when the performance counter exceeds a certain value.

Performance counters can be monitored by a user with the Performance Monitor. A variety of performance counters are built into the operating system, providing access to information such as the number of threads currently active on the system, or the number of documents in a print queue. Any of these, and any custom performance counters, can be graphed in the Performance Monitor.

Creating a Performance Counter

This example creates a performance counter named `ServiceCounter`. Then you will change `CounterMonitor` to check that counter and only beep when its value is over 5. To test it, you will also create a small Windows Forms application that increments and decrements the counter.

Performance counters are typically accessed in Visual Studio 2005 through the Server Explorer tab. To see the available performance counters, open Server Explorer, which looks like the screen shown in Figure 31-6.

To see the categories of performance counters, click the plus sign next to the Performance Counters option in the Server Explorer. Several dozen categories will be shown. You can look at the counters in any particular category by clicking the plus sign next to the category.

Figure 31-6

You can also create new categories and new counters. For this example, you need to create a new category for the counter called `Service Counters`. To do that, right-click the Performance Counters option in the Server Explorer and select the Create New Category option. In the resulting Performance Counter Builder dialog box (shown in Figure 31-7), enter the name of the category as `Service Counters`, and create a new counter by clicking the New button and entering `TestCounter` for the name. Once that is complete, click the OK button. Visual Studio 2005 will then create a new category called `Service Counters` that contains a single performance counter called `TestCounter`.

Figure 31-7

Integrating the Counter into the Service

Using a performance counter in the `CounterMonitor` service you created earlier is straightforward. Open the `CounterMonitor` project and go to the design surface for `CounterMonitor`. Then open the Server Explorer so that it shows the `TestCounter` performance counter you created. Click `TestCounter` from within the Server Explorer and drag it onto the `CounterMonitor.vb` design surface.

A new visual control named `PerformanceCounter1` will appear on the page's design surface, ready for use. Change the logic in the `Elapsed` event for `Timer1` as shown here:

```
If PerformanceCounter1.RawValue > mnMaxValue Then
    Beep()
End If
```

The `RawValue` property being used in this code fetches the unformatted value of the counter. For counters that track whole numbers (such as the number of times a Web page is hit), the `RawValue` property is normally used to get the value of the counter for testing or display. Some other types of counters use a `NextValue` method to get a formatted value. See the `CounterType` property of the `PerformanceCounter` class for more information on the types of performance counters available.

Next, put this statement in the code module just under the first line of the `CounterMonitor` class:

```
Dim mnMaxValue As Integer = 5
```

This creates the `mnMaxValue` as a `Private` variable. Now build the service again, install it as before, and start the service. It should not beep at this point because the value in the performance counter is zero. You can leave the counter running, because you will now create a program to change the value in the performance counter, thereby making the service begin beeping.

Changing the Value in the Performance Counter

To manipulate the performance counter, we will build a small forms-based application. Close the `CounterMonitor` solution in Visual Studio and start a new Windows Application Project named `CounterTest`. Place two buttons on `Form1` and change their properties as shown in the following table:

Name	Text
BtnIncrement	Increment Counter
BtnDecrement	Decrement Counter

Then, open the Server Explorer and drag the `TestCounter` performance counter onto the form itself, just as you did earlier with the `CounterMonitor` project. As with all nonvisible components from the Toolbox, the counter will appear in the component tray (just under the form), rather than on the form's design surface.

The `PerformanceCounter1` control for `CounterTest` needs one property change. Set the `ReadOnly` property of the control to `False`. This enables the application to manipulate the counter. (This change was unnecessary for the `CounterMonitor` Windows Service project because that project only reads the value of the performance counter and does not change it.)

Now double-click `btnIncrement` to get to its click event. Place the following code in the event:

```
PerformanceCounter1.Increment()
```

Double-click the `btnDecrement` to get to its click event. Place the following code in the event:

```
PerformanceCounter1.Decrement()
```

Build and run the program and click the Increment button six times. If the `CounterMonitor` service is running, on the sixth click it will begin beeping because the value in the counter has exceeded five. Then click the Decrement button a couple of times, and the beeping will stop.

If you want to monitor the current value of the counter, select Control Panel ⇨ Administrative Tools ⇨ Performance. This program, the Performance Monitor, enables the value of counters to be graphed. To add a counter for display, click the New Counter Set button, right-click the right-hand portion of the Performance Monitor, and add a counter in the dialog box that pops up. Change the Performance Object drop-down list to `Service Counters` and add the `TestCounter` performance counter to the list. When completed, press the Close button. The counter that you created will be monitored by the dialog box. You can use the help for this program for more details on displaying counters in the Performance Monitor.

Communicating with the Service

Up to this point, you've learned how to do the following:

- ❑   Create a Windows Service using Visual Basic.
- ❑   Start and stop a service with the Server Explorer in Visual Studio 2005 or the Service Control Manager in the Control Panel.
- ❑   Make a service work with a system-level function such as a performance counter.

If these procedures are sufficient to start, stop, and check on the service through the Server Explorer or Service Control Manager, and there is no need to do any other communication with the service, then this is all you need. However, it is often helpful to create a specialized application to manipulate your service. This application will typically be able to start and stop a service, and check on its status. The application may also need to communicate with the service to change its configuration. Such an application is often referred to as a *control panel* for the service, even though it does not necessarily reside in the operating system's Control Panel. A commonly used example of such an application is the SQL Server Service Manager, whose icon appears in the tray on the taskbar (normally in the lower right section of the screen) if you have SQL Server installed.

Such an application needs a way to communicate with the service. The .NET Framework base class that is used for such communication is the `ServiceController` class. It is in the `System.ServiceProcess` namespace. You need to add a reference to `System.ServiceProcess.dll` (which contains this namespace) before a project can use the `ServiceController` class.

The `ServiceController` class provides an interface to the Service Control Manager, which coordinates all communication with Windows Services. However, you don't have to know anything about the Service Control Manager to use the `ServiceController` class. You just manipulate the properties and methods of the `ServiceController` class, and any necessary communication with the Service Control Manager is accomplished on your behalf behind the scenes.

It's a good idea to use exactly *one* instance of the `ServiceController` class for each service you are controlling. Multiple instances of `ServiceController` that are communicating with the same service can have timing conflicts. Typically, that means using a module-level object variable to hold the reference to the active `ServiceController`, and instantiating the `ServiceController` during the initialization logic for the application. The following example uses this technique.

The ServiceController Class

The constructor for the `ServiceController` requires the name of the Windows Service with which it will be communicating. This is the same name that was placed in the `ServiceName` property of the class that defined the service. You'll see how to instantiate the `ServiceController` class shortly.

The `ServiceController` class has several members that are useful in manipulating services. Here are the most important methods, followed by another table of the most important properties:

Method	Purpose
Start	A method to start the service
Stop	A method to stop the service
Refresh	A method to make sure the `ServiceController` object contains the latest state of the service (needed because the service might be manipulated from another program)
ExecuteCommand	A method used to send a custom command to the service. This method is covered later in the section "Custom Commands."

Here are the most important properties:

Property	Purpose
CanStop	A property indicating whether the service can be stopped
ServiceName	A property containing the name of the associated service

Property	Purpose
Status	An enumerated property that indicates whether a service is stopped, started, in the process of being started, and so on. The ToString method on this property is useful for getting the status in a string form for text messages. The possible values of the enumeration are as follows: ContinuePending — The service is attempting to continue. Paused — The service is paused. PausePending — The service is attempting to go into a paused state. Running — The service is running. StartPending — The service is starting. Stopped — The service is not running. StopPending — The service is stopping.
ServiceType	A property that indicates the type of service. The result is an enumerated value. The enumerations are as follows: Win32OwnProcess — The service uses its own process (this is the default for a service created in .NET). Win32ShareProcess — The service shares a process with another service (this advanced capability is not covered here). Adapter, FileSystemDriver, InteractiveProcess, KernelDriver, RecognizerDriver — These are low-level service types that cannot be created with Visual Basic because the ServiceBase class does not support them. However, the value of the ServiceType property may still have these values for services created with other tools.

Integrating a ServiceController into the Example

To manipulate the service, we'll enhance the CounterTest program created earlier. Here are step-by-step instructions to do that:

1. Add three new buttons to the CounterTest form, with the following names and text labels:

Name	Text
BtnCheckStatus	Check Status
BtnStartService	Start Service
BtnStopService	Stop Service

2. Add a reference to the DLL that contains the `ServiceController` class: Select Project ➪ Add Reference. On the .NET tab, highlight the `System.ServiceProcess.dll` option and press OK.

3. Add this line at the top of the code for `Form1`:

```
Imports System.ServiceProcess
```

4. As discussed, the project needs only one instance of the `ServiceController` class. Create a module-level object reference to a `ServiceController` class by adding the following line of code within the `Form1` class:

```
Dim myController As ServiceController
```

5. Create a `Form Load` event in `Form1`, and place the following line of code in it to instantiate the `ServiceController` class:

```
myController = New ServiceController("CounterMonitor")
```

You now have a `ServiceController` class named `myController` that you can use to manipulate the `CounterMonitor` Windows Service. In the click event for `btnCheckStatus`, place the following code:

```
Dim sStatus As String
myController.Refresh()
sStatus = myController.Status.ToString

MsgBox(myController.ServiceName & " is in state: " & sStatus)
```

In the click event for `btnStartService`, place this code:

```
Try
    myController.Start()
Catch exp As Exception
    MsgBox("Could not start service or the service is already running")
End Try
```

In the `click` event for `btnStopService`, place this code:

```
If myController.CanStop Then
    myController.Stop()
Else
    MsgBox("Service cannot be stopped or the service is already stopped")
End If
```

Run and test the program. The service may already be running because of one of your previous tests. Make sure the performance counter is high enough to make the service beep, and then test starting and stopping the service.

More About ServiceController

`ServiceController` classes can be created for *any* Windows Service, not just those created in .NET. For example, you could instantiate a `ServiceController` class that was associated with the Windows Service for Internet Information Server (IIS) and use it to start, pause, and stop IIS. The code would look just like the code used earlier for the application that controlled the `CounterMonitor` service. The only difference is that the name of the service would need to be changed in the line that instantiates the `ServiceController` (Step 5).

Keep in mind that the `ServiceController` is not communicating directly with the service. It is working through the Service Control Manager. That means the requests from the Service Controller to start, stop, or pause a service do not behave synchronously. As soon as the `ServiceController` has passed the request to the `ServicesControlManager`, it continues to execute its own code without waiting for the Service Control Manager to pass on the request, or for the service to act on the request.

Custom Commands

Some services need additional operations besides starting and stopping. For example, for the `CounterMonitor` Windows Service, you might want to set the threshold value of the performance counter that causes the service to begin beeping, or you might want to change the interval between beeps.

With most components, you would implement such functionality through a public interface. That is, you would put public properties and methods on the component. However, you cannot do this with a Windows Service because it has no public interface that you can access from outside the service.

To deal with this need, the interface for a Windows Service contains a special event called `OnCustomCommand`. The event arguments include a numeric code that can serve as a command sent to the Windows Service. The code can be any number in the range 128 to 255. (The numbers under 128 are reserved for use by the operating system.)

To fire the event and send a custom command to a service, the `ExecuteCommand` method of the `ServiceController` is used. The `ExecuteCommand` method takes the numeric code that needs to be sent to the service as a parameter. When this method is accessed, the `ServiceController` class tells the Service Control Manager to fire the `OnCustomCommand` event in the service, and to pass it the numeric code.

The next example demonstrates this process in action. Suppose you want to be able to change the interval between beeps for the `CounterMonitor` service. You cannot directly send the beep interval that you want, but you can pick various values of the interval, and associate a custom command numeric code with each.

Suppose you want to be able to set intervals of 1 second, 3 seconds (the default), or 10 seconds. You could set up the following correspondence:

Custom Command Numeric Code	Beep Interval
201	One second (1,000 milliseconds)
203	Three seconds (3,000 milliseconds)
210	Ten seconds (10,000 milliseconds)

Those correspondences in the table are completely arbitrary. You could use any codes between 128 and 255 to associate with the beep intervals. These were chosen because they are easy to remember.

First, you need to change the CounterMonitor service so that it is able to accept the custom commands for the beep interval. To do that, first make sure the CounterMonitor service is uninstalled from any previous installs. Then open the Visual Studio 2005 project for the CounterMonitor service.

Create an OnCustomCommand event in the service: Open the code window for CounterMonitor.vb and type **Protected Overrides OnCustomCommand**. By this point, IntelliSense will kick in and you can press the Tab key to autocomplete the shell event. Notice how it only accepts a single Integer as a parameter:

```
Protected Overrides Sub OnCustomCommand(ByVal command As Integer)

End Sub
```

In the OnCustomCommand event, place the following code:

```
Timer1.Enabled = False
Select Case command
    Case 201
        Timer1.Interval = 1000
    Case 203
        Timer1.Interval = 3000
    Case 210
        Timer1.Interval = 10000
End Select
Timer1.Enabled = True
```

Build the countermonitor service, reinstall it, and start it.

Now you can enhance the CounterTest application created earlier to set the interval. To allow the user to pick the interval, you will use radio buttons. On the CounterTest program Form1 (which currently contains five buttons), place three radio buttons. Set their text labels as follows:

```
RadioButton1 - 1 second
RadioButton2 - 3 seconds
RadioButton3 - 10 seconds
```

Place a button directly under these option buttons. Name it btnSetInterval and set its text to Set Interval. In the click event for this button, place the following code:

```
Dim nIntervalCommand As Integer = 203
If RadioButton1.Checked Then
    nIntervalCommand = 201
End If
If RadioButton2.Checked Then
    nIntervalCommand = 203
End If
If RadioButton3.Checked Then
    nIntervalCommand = 210
End If
myController.ExecuteCommand(nIntervalCommand)
```

At this point, `Form1` should look something like the screen shown in Figure 31-8.

Figure 31-8

Start the `CounterTest` control program and test the capability to change the beep interval. Make sure the performance counter is high enough that the `CounterMonitor` service beeps, and remember that every time you stop and restart the service, it resets the beep interval to three seconds.

Passing Strings to a Service

Because the `OnCustomCommand` event only takes numeric codes as input parameters, you cannot directly pass strings to the service. For example, if you wanted to reconfigure a directory name for a service, you could not just send the directory name over. Instead, it would be necessary to place the information to be passed to the service in a file in some known location on disk. Then a custom command for the service could instruct it to look at the standard file location and read the information in the file. What the service did with the contents of the file would, of course, be customized for the service.

Creating a File Watcher

Now let's step through another example to illustrate what a Windows Service can do and how to construct one. We will build a service that monitors a particular directory and reacts when a new or changed file is placed in the directory. The example Windows Service application waits for those files, extracts information from them, and then logs an event to a system log to record the file change.

As before, create a Windows Service from the built-in template named Windows Service in the New Project screen. Name the new project `FileWatcherService` and click OK. This creates a new service class called `Service1.vb`. Rename this to `FileWatcherService.vb`. Right-click the design surface, select Properties, and set the `ServiceName` property to `FileWatcherService`.

As in the first example, set the application type to Windows Service and reset the project's start object to `FileWatcherService`. All of this is illustrated earlier in this chapter.

Writing Events Using an Eventlog

The way to ensure that the service is doing its job is by having it write events to a system Event Log. Event Logs are available under the Windows operating system. As with many other system-level features, the use of Event Logs is simplified in .NET because a .NET Framework base class does most of the work for you.

There are three Event Logs on the system: Application, Security, and System. Normally, your applications should only write to the Application log. A property of a log entry called Source identifies the application writing the message. This property does not have to be the same as the executable name of the application, but is often given that name to make it easy to identify the source of the message.

You can look at the events in the Event Log by using the Event Viewer. Select Control Panel ⇨ Administrative Tools ⇨ Event Viewer on Windows 2000, and Start ⇨ All Programs ⇨ Administrative Tools ⇨ Event Viewer on Windows XP. The following example uses the Event Viewer to ensure that the service is generating events.

It was mentioned earlier in the chapter that the AutoLog property of the ServiceBase class determines whether the service automatically writes events to the Application log. The AutoLog property instructs the service to use the Application Event Log to report command failures, as well as information for OnStart, OnStop, OnPause, and OnContinue events on the service. What is actually logged to the Event Log is an entry indicating whether the service started successfully and stopped successfully, and any errors that might have occurred. If you look in the Application Event Log now, these events are logged for the CounterMonitor Windows Service that you created and ran earlier in the chapter.

You can turn off the Event Log reporting by setting the AutoLog property to False in the Properties window for the service, but we will leave it set to True for our example. That means some events will be logged automatically (without us including any code for them). Then, we add some code to our service to log additional events not covered by the AutoLog property. First, though, we need to implement a file monitoring control into the project.

Creating a FileSystemWatcher

For performance reasons, you should do all of your work on a separate thread to your main application thread. You want to leave your main application free to accept any requests from the user or the operating system. You can do this by using some of the different components that create their own threads when they are launched. The Timer component and the FileSystemWatcher component are two examples. When the Timer component fires its Elapsed event, a thread is spawned and any code placed within that event will work on that newly created thread. The same thing happens when the events for the FileSystemWatcher component fire.

You can learn more about threading in .NET in Chapter 24.

The FileSystemWatcher Component

The FileSystemWatcher component is used to monitor a particular directory. The component implements Created, Changed, Deleted, and Renamed events, which are fired when files are placed in the directory, changed, deleted, or renamed, respectively.

The operation that takes place when one of these events is fired is up to the application developer. Most often, logic is included to read and process the new or changed files. However, we are just going to write a message to a log file.

To implement the component in the project, drag and drop a `FileSystemWatcher` control from the Components tab of the Toolbox onto the designer surface of `FileWatcherService.vb`. This control is automatically called `FileSystemWatcher1`.

The EnableRaisingEvents Property

The `FileSystemWatcher` control should not generate any events until the service is initialized and ready to handle them. To prevent this, set the `EnableRaisingEvents` property to `False`. This prevents the control from firing any events. We will enable it during the `OnStart` event in the service. These events fired by the `FileSystemWatcher` are controlled using the `NotifyFilter` property, discussed later.

The Path Property

Next, the path that we want to monitor is the `TEMP` directory on the `C:` drive, so set the `Path` property to `C:\TEMP` (be sure to confirm that there is a `TEMP` directory on your `C:` drive). Of course, this path can be changed to monitor any directory depending on your system, including any network or removable drives.

The NotifyFilter Property

We only want to monitor when a file is freshly created or the last modified value of a file has changed. To do this, set the `NotifyFilter` property to `FileName, LastWrite`. We could also watch for other changes such as attributes, security, size, and directory name changes as well, just by changing the `NotifyFilter` property. Note that you specify multiple changes to monitor by including a list of changes separated by commas.

The Filter Property

The types of files that we will look for are text files, so set the `Filter` property to `.txt`. Note that if you were going to watch for all file types, then the value of the `Filter` property would be set to `*.*`.

The IncludeSubdirectories Property

If you wanted to watch subdirectories, you would set the `IncludeSubdirectories` property to `True`. This example leaves it as `False`, which is the default value. Figure 31-9 shows how you should have the properties set.

Figure 31-9

Adding FileSystemWatcher Code to OnStart and OnStop

Now that some properties are set, let's add some code to the OnStart event. You want to start the FileSystemWatcher1 component so it will start triggering events when files are created or copied into the directory you're monitoring, so set the EnableRaisingEvents property to True:

```
Protected Overrides Sub OnStart(ByVal args() As String)
    ' Start monitoring for files
    FileSystemWatcher1.EnableRaisingEvents = True
End Sub
```

Once the file monitoring properties are initialized, you are ready to start the monitoring. When the service stops, you need to stop the file monitoring process. Add this code to the OnStop event:

```
Protected Overrides Sub OnStop()
    ' Stop monitoring for files
    FileSystemWatcher1.EnableRaisingEvents = False
End Sub
```

The EventLog Component

Now you are ready to place an EventLog component in the service to facilitate logging of events. Drag and drop an EventLog control from the Components tab of the Toolbox onto the designer surface of FileWatcherService.vb. This control is automatically called EventLog1.

Set the Log property for Eventlog1 to Application, and set the Source property to FileWatcherService.

The Created Event

Next, we will place some logic in the Created event of the FileSystemWatcher component to log when a file has been created. This event fires when a file has been placed or created in the directory that we are monitoring. It fires because the last modified information on the file has changed.

Select FileSystemWatcher1 from the Class Name drop-down list and select Created from the Method Name drop-down list. The Created event will be added to your code. Add code to the Created event as follows:

```
Public Sub FileSystemWatcher1_Created(ByVal sender As Object, _
        ByVal e As System.IO.FileSystemEventArgs) _
        Handles FileSystemWatcher1.Created
    Dim sMessage As String
    sMessage = "File created in directory - file name is " + e.Name
    EventLog1.WriteEntry(sMessage)
End Sub
```

Notice that the event argument's object (the object named "e" in the event parameters) includes a property called Name. This property holds the name of the file that generated the event.

At this point, you could add the other events for FileSystemWatcher (Changed, Deleted, Renamed) in a similar way and create corresponding log messages for those events. To keep the example simple, we'll just do the Created event in this service.

You need to add an `Installer` class to this project to install the application. This is done as it was in the `CounterMonitor` example, by right-clicking the design surface for the service and selecting Add Installer or by clicking the Add Installer link in the Properties window of Visual Studio 2005. Don't forget to change the `Account` property to `LocalSystem`, or set it to `User` and fill in the `Username` and `Password` properties.

As before, you must install the service using `InstallUtil.exe`. Then, start it with the Server Explorer or the Service Manager. Upon successful compilation of these steps, you will get a message logged for any file with a `.txt` extension that you copy or create in the monitored directory. After dropping some sample text files into the monitored directory, you can use the Event Viewer to ensure that the events are present.

Figure 31-10 shows the Event Viewer with several example messages created by the service. If you right-click one of the events for `FileWatcherService`, you'll see a detail screen. Notice that the message corresponds to the Event Log message we constructed in the `Created` event of the `FileSystemWatcher` control in the service, as shown in Figure 31-11.

Figure 31-10

Debugging the Service

Because a service must be run from within the context of the Service Control Manager, rather than from within Visual Studio 2005, debugging a service is not as straightforward as debugging other Visual Studio 2005 application types. To debug a service, you must start the service and then attach a debugger to the process in which it is running. You can then debug the application using all of the standard debugging functionality of Visual Studio 2005.

> **Don't attach to a process unless you know what the process is and understand the consequences of attaching to and possibly killing that process.**

Figure 31-11

To avoid going through this extra effort, you may want to test out most of the code in your service in a standard Windows Forms application. This test-bed application can have the same components (`FileSystemWatchers`, `EventLogs`, `Timers`, and so on) as the Windows Service, and thus will be able to run the same logic in events. Once you have checked out the logic in this context, you can just copy and paste it into a Windows Service application.

However, sometimes the service itself needs to be debugged directly, so it's important to understand how to attach to the service's process and do direct debugging. You can only debug a service when it's running. When you attach the debugger to the service, you are interrupting it. The service is suspended for a short period while you attach to it. It is also interrupted when you place breakpoints and step through your code.

Attaching to the service's process enables you to debug most, but not all, of the service's code. For instance, because the service has already been started, you cannot debug the code in the service's `OnStart` method this way, or the code in the `Main` method that is used to load the service. To debug the `OnStart` event or any of the Visual Studio 2005 designer code, you have to add a dummy service and start that service first. In the dummy service, you would create an instance of the service that you want to debug. You can place some code in a `Timer` object and create the new instance of the object that you want to debug after 30 seconds or so. Allow enough time to attach to the debugger before the new instance is created. Meanwhile, place breakpoints in your startup code to debug those events, if desired.

Follow these steps to debug a service:

1. Install the service.

2. Start the service, either from the Service Control Manager, from Server Explorer, or from code.

3. In Visual Studio 2005, load the solution for the service. Then select Attach to Process from the Debug menu. The Attach to Process dialog box appears (see Figure 31-12).

4. For a Windows Service, the desired process to attach to is not a foreground process; be sure to check the check box next to the "Show processes from all users" option.

5. In the Available Processes section, click the process indicated by the executable name for the service, and then click Attach.

Figure 31-12

6. You can now debug your process. Place a breakpoint in the code for the service at the place you want to debug. Cause the code in the service to execute (by placing a file in a monitored directory, for example).

7. When finished, select Stop Debugging from the Debug menu.

Let's go through an actual scenario, using our earlier CounterMonitor example. Bring up both the CounterMonitor project and the CounterTest project in separate instances of the Visual Studio 2005 IDE. Make sure that the CounterMonitor service has been started. It is best if you hear it beeping — that way you know it is working. If necessary, increment the performance counter to make it beep.

In the CounterMonitor project, select Debug ⇨ Processes; you'll get a dialog box that shows a list of the foreground processes on the system. Check the box next to "Show system processes." This will expand the list of processes, and one of the processes in the list will be `CounterMonitor.exe`. Highlight it and click Attach.

You'll then get a dialog box asking you what program types you are interested in debugging. Because we are working solely within .NET, check the box next to Common Language Runtime and leave the rest unchecked. Press the OK button, and then press the Close button on the Processes dialog box. You are now attached to the process running `CounterMonitor` in the background.

Place a breakpoint on the first line of the `OnCustomCommand` event:

```
Timer1.Enabled = False
```

Now you are ready to check debugging. Bring up the `CounterTest` program and start it. Press one of the radio buttons to change the beep interval. You will hear the beeping stop because `CounterMonitor.exe` has entered debugging mode. Switch back to the `CounterMonitor` project. The cursor will be on the breakpoint line in `OnCustomCommand`. You can use the normal commands at this point to step through the code.

Summary

This chapter presented a general overview of what a Windows Service is and how to create one with Visual Basic. The techniques in this chapter can be used for many different types of background service. A few examples are as follows:

❑ Automatically moving statistical files from a database server to a Web server

❑ Pushing general files across computers and platforms

❑ A watchdog timer to ensure that a connection is always available

❑ An application to move and process FTP files, or indeed files received from any source

While Visual Basic cannot be used to create every type of Windows Service, it is effective at creating many of the most useful ones. The .NET Framework classes for Windows Services make this creation relatively straightforward. The designers generate much of the routine code needed, and you, as a developer, can concentrate on the code that is specific to your particular Windows Service.

Visual Basic and the Internet

In today's network-centric world, it's very likely that applications will need to work with other computers over a private network, the Internet, or both. This chapter details how to do the following:

❏ Download resources from the Web

❏ Design your own communication protocols

❏ Reuse Internet Explorer in your applications

Downloading Internet Resources

Downloading content from the Web is very easy, so you'll throw together a basic application before getting into some meatier topics. This application downloads HTML from a Web page and displays it in a text box. Later, you'll learn how you can display HTML properly by hosting Internet Explorer (IE) directly using the new `WebBrowser` control in Windows Forms applications, but for now you'll just use plain text.

In order to download a Web page, you need to be able to identity the remote page that you wish to download, make a request of the Web server that can provide that page, listen for the response, and download the data for the resource.

The relevant classes for this example are `System.Uri`, `System.Net.WebRequest`, `System.Net.HttpWebRequest,` and `System.Net.HttpWebResponse`:

❏ `System.Uri` is a useful general-purpose class for expressing a *Uniform Resource Identifier (URI)*. A *Uniform Resource Locator (URL)* is a type of URI (although in reality the terms are so confused that they are often used interchangeably). A URI, however, is "more than" a URL, which is why this .NET class is `Uri` and not `Url`. `System`. You'll find that Uri has many properties for decoding a URI. For example, if you had a string like `www.pretendcompany.com:8080/ myser-vices/myservice.asmx?WSDL`, you could use the `Port` property to extract the port number, the `Query` property to extract the query string, and so on.

❑ A `WebRequest` expresses some kind of Internet resource, whether it is located on the LAN or WAN. (A better name for this class would be `NetRequest`, as the classes aren't specifically related to the Web protocol.)

❑ Protocol-specific descendants of `WebRequest` carry out the actual request: `HttpWebRequest` expresses an HTTP download and `FileWebRequest` expresses a file download — for example, `file://c:/MyFile.txt`.

❑ An `HttpWebResponse` is returned once a connection to the Web server has been made and the resource is available to download.

There are another two major classes related to working with the Internet in the .NET Framework: `System.Net.WebClient` and `System.Net.WebProxy`. `WebClient`, the latter being a helper class that wraps the request and response classes previously mentioned.

Because this is a professional-level book, this example shows you what to do behind the scenes — in effect, re-engineer what `WebClient` can do. You'll look at `WebProxy` later, which enables you to explicitly define a proxy server to use for Internet communications.

Let's use these classes to build an application. Create a new Windows application, create a new form, and add controls to it as shown in Figure 32-1.

Figure 32-1

The control names are `textUrl`, `buttonGo`, and `textData`. The `Anchor` properties of the controls are set so that the form resizes properly. The `textUrl` should be set to Top, Left, Right. Set `buttonGo` to Top, Right, and set `textData` to Top, Left, Bottom, Right.

Add these namespace import declarations to the form's code:

```
Imports System.IO
Imports System.Net
Imports System.Text
```

To keep the code simple, you'll include all the functionality into the `Click` handler of `buttonGo`. Ideally, you want to break the code in the handler out to a separate method. This enriches the interface of the object and promotes good reuse.

The first thing you do here is create a new `System.Uri` based on the URL that the user enters into the text box:

```
Private Sub buttonGo_Click(ByVal sender As System.Object, _
  ByVal e As System.EventArgs) Handles buttonGo.Click

    Dim uri As New Uri(textUrl.Text)
```

Then, illustrate some of the useful properties of `System.Uri`:

```
Dim builder As New StringBuilder()
builder.Append("AbsolutePath: " & uri.AbsolutePath & VbCrLf)
builder.Append("AbsoluteUri: " & uri.AbsoluteUri & VbCrLf)
builder.Append("Host: " & uri.Host & VbCrLf)
builder.Append("HostNameType: " & uri.HostNameType.ToString() & _
                VbCrLf)
builder.Append("LocalPath: " & uri.LocalPath & VbCrLf)
builder.Append("PathAndQuery: " & uri.PathAndQuery & VbCrLf)
builder.Append("Port: " & uri.Port & VbCrLf)
builder.Append("Query: " & uri.Query & VbCrLf)
builder.Append("Scheme: " & uri.Scheme)

MessageBox.Show(builder.ToString())
```

The shared `Create` method of `System.Net.WebRequest` is used to create the actual object that you can use to download the Web resource. Note that you don't create an instance of `HttpWebRequest`; you're working with a return object of type `WebRequest`. However, you'll actually be given an `HttpWebRequest` object, and `WebRequest` chooses the most appropriate class to return based on the URI. This enables you to build your own handlers for different network resources that can be used by consumers who simply supply an appropriate URL.

To make the request and get the response back from the server (so ultimately you can access the data), you call the `GetResponse` method of `WebRequest`. In this case, you'll get an `HttpWebResponse` object — again, it's up to the implementation of the `WebRequest`-derived object, in this case `HttpWebRequest`, to return an object of the most suitable type.

If the request is not OK, you'll get an exception (which for the sake of simplicity you won't bother processing). If the request is OK, you can get the length and type of the response using properties of the `WebResponse` object:

```
Dim request As WebRequest = WebRequest.Create(uri)
Dim response As WebResponse = request.GetResponse()
builder = New StringBuilder()
builder.Append("Request type: " & request.GetType().ToString() & VbCrLf)
builder.Append("Response type: " & response.GetType().ToString() & VbCrLf)
builder.Append("Content length: " & response.ContentLength & _
        " bytes" & VbCrLf)
```

```
builder.Append("Content type: " & response.ContentType & VbCrLf)

MessageBox.Show(builder.ToString())
```

It just remains for you to download the information. You can do this through a stream (`WebResponse` objects return a stream by overriding `GetResponseStream`); moreover, you can use a `System.IO.StreamReader` to download the whole lot in a single call by calling the `ReadToEnd` method. This method only downloads text, so if you want to download binary data you have to use the methods on the `Stream` object directly, or use a `System.IO.BinaryReader`.

```
Dim stream As Stream = response.GetResponseStream()
Dim reader As New StreamReader(stream)
Dim data As String = reader.ReadToEnd()

reader.Close()
stream.Close()

textData.Text = data
End Sub
```

If you run the application, enter a URL of `www.reuters.com`, and click Go, you'll see debugging information about the URL, as shown in Figure 32-2.

Figure 32-2

This is a simple URL. The application tells you that the scheme is `http` and the host name type is `Dns`. If you enter an IP into the URL to be requested, rather than a host name, then this type will come back as `IPv4`. This tells you where the host name came from; in this case, it's a general Internet host name. Next, the application provides information about the response (see Figure 32-3).

Figure 32-3

The response data itself is shown in Figure 32-4.

Figure 32-4

Perhaps the most important exception to be aware of when using these classes is the `System.Net.WebException` exception. If anything goes wrong on the `WebRequest.GetResponse` call, this exception is thrown. Among other things, this exception provides access to the `WebResponse` object through the `Response` property. The `StatusCode` property of `WebResponse` tells you what actually happened through the `HttpStatusCode` enumeration. For example, `HttpStatusCode.NotFound` is the equivalent of the HTTP 404 status code.

Sockets

There may be times when you need to transfer data across a network (either a private network or the Internet) but the existing techniques and protocols don't exactly suit your needs. For example, you can't download resources using the techniques discussed at the start of this chapter, and you can't use Web services (as described in Chapter 26) or remoting (as described in Chapter 27). When this happens, the best course of action is to roll your own protocol using *sockets*.

TCP/IP, and therefore, the Internet itself, is based on sockets. The principle is simple: Establish a port at one end and allow clients to "plug in" to that port from the other end. Once the connection is made, applications can send and receive data through a stream. For example, HTTP nearly always operates on port 80, so a Web server opens a socket on port 80 and waits for incoming connections (Web browsers, unless told otherwise, attempt to connect to port 80 in order to make a request of that Web server).

In .NET, sockets are implemented in the `System.Net.Sockets` namespace and use classes from `System.Net` and `System.IO` to get the stream classes. Although working with sockets can be a little tricky outside of .NET, the framework includes some superb classes that enable you to open a socket for inbound connections (`System.Net.TcpListener`) and for communication between two open sockets (`System.Net.TcpClient`). These two classes, in combination with some threading shenanigans, enable you build your own protocol through which you can send any data you like. With your own protocol, you have ultimate control over the communication.

To demonstrate these techniques, you're going to build Wrox Messenger, a very basic instant messenger application similar to MSN Messenger.

Building the Application

You'll wrap all the functionality of your application into a single Windows application, which will act as both a server that waits for inbound connections and a client that has established outbound connections.

Create a new project called WroxMessenger. Change the title of Form1 to Wrox Messenger and add a TextBox control called textConnectTo and a Button control called buttonConnect. The form should appear as shown in Figure 32-5.

Figure 32-5

You'll learn more about this in greater detail later, but for now it's very important that all of your UI code runs in the same thread, and that the thread is actually the main application that creates and runs Form1.

To keep track of what's happening, you'll add a field to Form1 that enables you to store the ID of the startup thread and report that ID on the caption. This helps provide a context for the thread/UI issues discussed later. You'll also need some namespace imports and a constant specifying the ID of the default port. Add this code to Form1:

```
Imports System.Net
Imports System.Net.Sockets
Imports System.Threading

Public Class Form1

    Private Shared _mainThreadId As Integer
    Public Const ServicePort As Integer = 10101
```

Next, create a New() method for Form1 (Form1.vb) and add this code to the constructor that populates the field and changes the caption:

```
Public Sub New()

    ' This call is required by the Windows Form Designer.
    InitializeComponent()

    ' Add any initialization after the InitializeComponent() call.
    _mainThreadId = System.Threading.Thread.CurrentThread.GetHashCode()

    Text &= "-" & _mainThreadId.ToString()
End Sub
```

Note that you can get to the Form1.vb file's New() method by using Visual Studio and selecting Form1 and New in the uppermost drop-downs in the document window. This causes the Form1.vb file's New() method to be created on your behalf.

To listen for incoming connections, you'll create a separate class called `Listener`. This class uses an instance of `System.Net.Sockets.TcpListener` to wait for incoming connections. Specifically, it opens a TCP port that *any* client can connect to — sockets are not platform-specific. Although connections are always made on a specific, known port, the actual communication takes place on a port of the TCP/IP subsystem's choosing, which means you can support many inbound connections at once, despite the fact that each of them connects to the same port. Sockets are an open standard available on pretty much any platform you can think of. For example, if you publish the specification for your protocol, then developers working on Linux can connect to your Wrox Messenger service.

When you detect an inbound connection, you'll be given a `System.Net.Sockets.TcpClient` object. This is your gateway to the remote client. To send and receive data, you need to get hold of a `System.Net.NetworkStream` object (returned through a call to `GetStream` on `TcpClient`), which returns a stream that you can use.

Create a new class called `Listener`. This thread needs members to hold an instance of a `System.Threading.Thread` object, and a reference back to the `Form1` class that is the main form in the application. Not covered here is how to spin up and down threads, or synchronization. (Refer back to Chapter 24 if you need more information about that.)

Here's the basic code for the `Listener` class:

```
Imports System.Net.Sockets
Imports System.Threading

Public Class Listener

  Private _main As Form1
  Private _listener As TcpListener
  Private _thread As Thread

  Public Sub New(ByVal main As Form1)
    _main = main
  End Sub

  Public Sub SpinUp()

    ' create and start the new thread...
    _thread = New Thread(AddressOf ThreadEntryPoint)
    _thread.Start()
  End Sub
End Class
```

The obvious missing method here is `ThreadEntryPoint()`. This is where you need to create the socket and wait for inbound connections. When you get them, you'll be given a `TcpClient` object, which you pass back to `Form1`, where the conversation window can be created. You would create this method in the `Listener.vb` class file.

To create the socket, create an instance of `TcpListener` and give it a port. In your application, the port you're going to use is `10101`. This port should be free on your computer, but if the debugger breaks on an exception when you instantiate `TcpListener` or call `Start()`, try another port. Once you have done that and called `Start()` to configure the object to listen for connections, you drop into an infinite loop and call `AcceptTcpClient()`. This method blocks until the socket is closed or a connection becomes available. If you get `Nothing` back, either the socket is closed or there's a problem, so you drop out of the thread. If you get something back, then you pass the `TcpClient` over to `Form1` through a call to the (not yet built) `ReceiveInboundConnection()` method:

```
' ThreadEntryPoint...
Protected Sub ThreadEntryPoint()

    ' Create a socket...
    _listener = New TcpListener(Form1.ServicePort)
    _listener.Start()

    ' Loop infinitely, waiting for connections.
    Do While True

        ' Get a connection...
        Dim client As TcpClient = _listener.AcceptTcpClient()
        If client Is Nothing Then
            Exit Do
        End If
        ' Process it...
        _main.ReceiveInboundConnection(client)
    Loop
End Sub
```

It's in the `ReceiveInboundConnection()` method that you'll create the Conversation form that the user can use to send messages.

Creating Conversation Windows

When building Windows Forms applications that support threading, there's always the possibility of running into a problem with the Windows messaging subsystem. This is a very old part of Windows that powers the Windows user interface (the idea has been around since version 1.0 of the platform, although the implementation on modern Windows versions is far removed from the original).

Even those who are not familiar with old-school Windows programming, such as MFC, Win32, or even Win16 development, should be familiar with events. When you move a mouse over a form, you get `MouseMove()` events. When you close a form, you get a `Closed()` event. There's a mapping between these events and the messages that Windows passes around to support the actual display of the windows. For example, whenever you receive a `MouseMove()` event, a message called `WM_MOUSEMOVE` is sent to the window, by Windows, in response to the mouse driver. In .NET, and other Rapid Application Development (RAD) environments such as VB and Delphi, this message is converted into an event that you can write code against.

Although this is getting way off the topic — you know how to build Windows Forms applications by now and don't need the details of messages such as `WM_NCHITTEST` or `WM_PAINT` — it has an important implication. In effect, Windows creates a message queue for each thread into which it posts the messages that the thread's windows have to work with. This queue is looped on a virtually constant basis, and the messages are distributed to the appropriate window (remember that small controls like buttons and text boxes are also windows). In .NET, these messages are turned into events, but unless the message queue is looped the messages don't get through.

Suppose Windows needs to paint a window. It posts a `WM_PAINT` message to the queue. A message loop implemented on the main thread of the process containing the window detects the message and dispatches it on to the appropriate window where it is processed. Now suppose that the queue isn't looped. The message is never picked up and the window is never painted.

In a Windows application, a single thread is usually responsible for message dispatch. This thread is typically (but not necessarily) the main application thread — the one that's created when the process is first created. If you create windows in a different thread, then that new thread has to support the message dispatch loop so that messages destined for the windows get through. However, with `Listener`, you have no code for processing the message loop and there's little point in writing any because the next time you call `AcceptTcpClient()` you're going to block and everything will stop working.

The trick then is to create the windows only in the main application thread, which is the thread that created `Form1` and is processing the messages for all the windows created in this thread. You can pass calls from one thread to the other by calling the `Invoke()` method of `Form1`.

This is where things start to get complicated. There is an awful lot of code to write to get to a point where you can see that the socket connection has been established and get conversation windows to appear. Here's what you need to do:

❑ Create a new Conversation form. This form needs controls for displaying the total content of the conversation, plus a `TextBox` control for adding new messages.

❑ The Conversation window needs to be able to send and receive messages through its own thread.

❑ `Form1` needs to be able to initiate new connections. This will be done in a separate thread that is managed by the thread pool. When the connection has been established, a new Conversation window needs to be created and configured.

❑ `Form1` also needs to receive inbound connections. When it gets one of these, a new Conversation must be created and configured.

Let's look at these challenges one at a time.

Creating the Conversation Form

The simplest place to start is to build the new Conversation form, which needs three `TextBox` controls (`textUsername`, `textMessages`, and `textMessage`) and a `Button` control (`buttonSend`), as shown in Figure 32-6.

Figure 32-6

This class requires a number of fields and an enumeration. It needs fields to hold the username of the user (which you'll default to Evjen), the underlying TcpClient, and the NetworkStream returned by that client. The enumeration indicates the direction of the connection (which will help you when debugging):

```
Imports System.Net
Imports System.Net.Sockets
Imports System.Text
Imports System.Threading
Imports System.Runtime.Serialization.Formatters.Binary

Public Class Conversation

    Private _username As String = "Evjen"
    Private _client As TcpClient
    Private _stream As NetworkStream
    Private _direction As ConversationDirection

    Public Enum ConversationDirection As Integer
        Inbound = 0
        Outbound = 1
    End Enum
```

We won't look into the issues surrounding establishing a thread for exchanging messages at this stage, but we will look at implementing the ConfigureClient() method. This method eventually does more work than this, but for now it sets a couple of fields and calls UpdateCaption():

```
Public Sub ConfigureClient(ByVal client As TcpClient, _
            ByVal direction As ConversationDirection)
    ' Set it up...
    _client = client
    _direction = direction

    ' Update the window...
    UpdateCaption()
End Sub

Protected Sub UpdateCaption()

    ' Set the text.
    Dim builder As New StringBuilder(_username)
    builder.Append(" - ")
    builder.Append(_direction.ToString())
    builder.Append(" - ")
    builder.Append(Thread.CurrentThread.GetHashCode())
    builder.Append(" - ")

    If Not _client Is Nothing Then
        builder.Append("Connected")
    Else
        builder.Append("Not connected")
    End If

    Text = builder.ToString()
End Sub
```

One debugging issue to deal with is that if you're connecting to a conversation on the same machine, then you need a way to change the name of the user sending each message; otherwise, things get confusing. That's what the topmost `TextBox` control is for. In the constructor, set the text for the `textUsername.Text` property:

```
Public Sub New()

    ' This call is required by the Windows Form Designer.
    InitializeComponent()

    ' Add any initialization after the InitializeComponent() call.
    textUsername.Text = _username
End Sub
```

On the `TextChanged` event for this control, update the caption and the internal _username field:

```
Private Sub textUsername_TextChanged(ByVal sender As System.Object, _
                ByVal e As System.EventArgs) _
                Handles textUsername.TextChanged

    _username = textUsername.Text
    UpdateCaption()
End Sub
```

Initiating Connections

`Form1` needs to be able to both initiate connections and receive inbound connections — the application is both a client and a server. You've already created some of the server portion by creating `Listener`; now you'll look at the client side.

The general rule when working with sockets is that anytime you send anything over the wire, you must perform the actual communication in a separate thread. Virtually all calls to send and receive do so in a blocking manner; that is, they block until data is received, block until all data is sent, and so on.

If threads are used well, the UI will keep running as normal, irrespective of the problems that may occur during transmitting and receiving. This is why in the `InitiateConnection()` method on `Form1`, you defer processing to another method called `InitiateConnectionThreadEntryPoint()`, which is called from a new thread:

```
Public Sub InitiateConnection()
    InitiateConnection(textConnectTo.Text)
End Sub

Public Sub InitiateConnection(ByVal hostName As String)

    ' Give it to the threadpool to do...
    ThreadPool.QueueUserWorkItem(AddressOf _
    Me.InitiateConnectionThreadEntryPoint, hostName)
End Sub

Private Sub buttonConnect_Click(ByVal sender As System.Object, _
            ByVal e As System.EventArgs) _
```

```
                    Handles buttonConnect.Click

        InitiateConnection()
    End Sub
```

Inside the thread, you try to convert the host name that you're given into an IP address (`localhost` is used as the host name in the demonstration, but it could be the name of a machine on the local network or a host name on the Internet). This is done through the shared `GetHostEntry()` method on `System.Net.Dns` and returns a `System.Net.IPHostEntry` object. As a host name can point to multiple IP addresses, you'll just use the first one that you're given. You take this address expressed as an IP (for example, `192.168.0.4`) and combine it with the port number to get a new `System.Net.IPEndPoint`. Then, you create a new `TcpClient` from this `IPEndPoint` and try to connect.

If at any time an exception is thrown (which can happen because the name couldn't be resolved or the connection could not be established), you pass the exception to `HandleInitiateConnectionException`. If it succeeds, you pass it to `ProcessOutboundConnection`. Both of these methods will be implemented shortly:

```
    Private Sub InitiateConnectionThreadEntryPoint(ByVal state As Object)

        Try
            ' Get the host name...
            Dim hostName As String = CStr(state)

            ' Resolve...
            Dim hostEntry As IPHostEntry = Dns.GetHostEntry(hostName)
            If Not hostEntry Is Nothing Then

                ' Create an end point for the first address.
                Dim endPoint As New IPEndPoint(hostEntry.AddressList(0), ServicePort)

                ' Create a TCP client...
                Dim client As New TcpClient()
                client.Connect(endPoint)

                ' Create the connection window...
                ProcessOutboundConnection(client)
            Else
                Throw New ApplicationException("Host '" & hostName & _
                    "' could not be resolved.")
            End If
        Catch ex As Exception
            HandleInitiateConnectionException(ex)
        End Try
    End Sub
```

When it comes to `HandleInitiateConnectionException`, you start to see the inter-thread UI problems that were mentioned earlier. When there is a problem with the exception, you need to tell the user, which means you need to move the exception from the thread-pool-managed thread into the main application thread. The principle for this is the same; you need to create a delegate and call that delegate through the `Invoke()` method of the form. This method does all the hard work in marshaling the call across to the other thread.

Here's what the delegates look like. They have the same parameters of the calls themselves. As a naming convention, it's a good idea to use the same name as the method and tack the word `Delegate` on the end:

```
Public Class Form1

    Private Shared _mainThreadId As Integer
    ' delegates...
    Protected Delegate Sub HandleInitiateConnectionExceptionDelegate( _
                                        ByVal ex As Exception)
```

In the constructor for `Form1`, you capture the thread caller's thread ID and store it in `_mainThreadId`. Here's a method that compares the captured ID with the ID of the current thread:

```
Public Shared Function IsMainThread() As Boolean
    If Thread.CurrentThread.GetHashCode() = _mainThreadId Then
        Return True
    Else
        Return False
    End If
End Function
```

The first thing you do at the top of `HandleInitiateConnectionException` is check the thread ID. If it doesn't match, then you create the delegate and call it. Notice how you set the delegate to call back into the same method because the second time it's called you would have moved to the main thread; therefore, `IsMainThread()` returns `True`, and you can process the exception properly:

```
Protected Sub HandleInitiateConnectionException(ByVal ex As Exception)

    ' main thread?
    If IsMainThread() = False Then

        ' Create and call...
        Dim args(0) As Object
        args(0) = ex
        Invoke(New HandleInitiateConnectionExceptionDelegate(AddressOf _
            HandleInitiateConnectionException), args)

        ' return
        Return
    End If

    ' Show it.
    MessageBox.Show(ex.GetType().ToString() & ":" & ex.Message)
End Sub
```

The result is that when the call comes in from the thread-pool-managed thread, `IsMainThread()` returns `False`, and the delegate is created and called. When the method is entered again as a result of the delegate call, `IsMainThread()` returns `True` and you see the message box.

When it comes to `ProcessOutboundConnection()`, you have to again jump into the main UI thread. However, the magic behind this method is implemented in a separate method called

`ProcessConnection()`, which can handle either inbound or outbound connections. Here's the
delegate:

```
Public Class Form1

    Private Shared _mainThreadId As Integer
    Private _listener As Listener

    Protected Delegate Sub ProcessConnectionDelegate(ByVal client As _
        TcpClient, ByVal direction As Conversation.ConversationDirection)
    Protected Delegate Sub HandleInitiateConnectionExceptionDelegate(ByVal _
        ex As Exception)
```

Here's the method itself, which creates the new Conversation form and calls the `ConfigureClient()`
method:

```
Protected Sub ProcessConnection(ByVal client As TcpClient, _
    ByVal direction As Conversation.ConversationDirection)

    ' Do you have to move to another thread?
    If IsMainThread() = False Then

        ' Create and call...
        Dim args(1) As Object
        args(0) = client
        args(1) = direction
        Invoke(New ProcessConnectionDelegate(AddressOf ProcessConnection), args)

        Return
    End If

    ' Create the conversation window...
    Dim conversation As New Conversation()
    conversation.Show()
    conversation.ConfigureClient(client, direction)
End Sub
```

Of course, `ProcessOutboundConnection()` needs to defer to `ProcessConnection()`:

```
Public Sub ProcessOutboundConnection(ByVal client As TcpClient)
    ProcessConnection(client, Conversation.ConversationDirection.Outbound)
End Sub
```

Now that you can connect to something on the client side, let's look at how to receive connections (on
the server side).

Receiving Inbound Connections

You've already built `Listener`, but you haven't created an instance of it or spun up its thread to wait for
incoming connections. To do this, you need a field in `Form1` to hold an instance of the object. You also
need to tweak the constructor. Here's the field:

```
Public Class Form1
```

```
      Private _mainThreadId As Integer
      Private _listener As Listener
```

Here is the new code that needs to be added to the constructor:

```
Public Sub New()

    ' This call is required by the Windows Form Designer.
    InitializeComponent()

    ' Add any initialization after the InitializeComponent() call.
    _mainThreadId = System.Threading.Thread.CurrentThread.GetHashCode()

    Text &= "-" & _mainThreadId.ToString()

    ' listener...
    _listener = New Listener(Me)
    _listener.SpinUp()
End Sub
```

When inbound connections are received, you get a new `TcpClient` object. This is passed back to `Form1` through the `ReceiveInboundConnection()` method. This method, like `ProcessOutboundConnection()`, defers to `ProcessConnection()`. Because `ProcessConnection()` already handles the issue of moving the call to the main application thread, `ReceiveInboundConnection()` looks like this:

```
Public Sub ReceiveInboundConnection(ByVal client As TcpClient)
    ProcessConnection(client, Conversation.ConversationDirection.Inbound)
End Sub
```

If you run the project now, you should be able to click the Connect button and see two windows — Inbound and Outbound (see Figure 32-7).

Figure 32-7

If you close all three windows, the application keeps running because you haven't written code to close down the listener thread, and having an open thread like this keeps the application open. Select Debug ⇨ Stop Debugging in Visual Studio to close the application down by killing all running threads.

By clicking the Connect button you're calling `InitiateConnection()`. This spins up a new thread in the pool that resolves the given host name (`localhost`) into an IP address. This IP address, in combination with a port number, is then used in the creation of a `TcpClient` object. If the connection can be made, then `ProcessOutboundConnection()` is called, which results in the first of the conversation windows being created and marked as "outbound."

This example is somewhat artificial, as the two instances of Wrox Messenger should be running on separate computers. On the remote computer (if you're connecting to `localhost`, this will be the same computer), a connection is received through the `AcceptTcpClient()` method of `TcpListener`. This results in a call to `ReceiveInboundConnection()`, which in turn results in the creation of the second conversation window, this time marked as "inbound."

Sending Messages

The next step is to work out how to exchange messages between the two conversation windows. You already have a `TcpClient` in each case so all you have to do is squirt binary data down the wire on one side and pick it up at the other end. The two conversation windows act as both client and server, so both need to be able to send and receive.

There are three problems to solve:

❑ You need to establish one thread to send data and another thread to receive data.

❑ Data sent and received needs to be reported back to the user so that he or she can follow the conversation.

❑ The data that you want to send has to be converted into a wire-ready format, which in .NET terms usually means serialization.

The power of sockets enables you to define whatever protocol you like for data transmission. If you wanted to build your own SMTP server, you could implement the (publicly available) specifications, set up a listener to wait for connections on port 25 (the standard port for SMTP), wait for data to come in, process it, and return responses as appropriate.

It's best to work in this way when building protocols. Unless there are very strong reasons for not doing so, make your server as open as possible: Do not tie it to a specific platform. This is the way that things are done on the Internet. To an extent, things like Web Services should negate the need to build your own protocols; as you go forward, you will rely instead on the "remote object available to local client" paradigm.

Now it's time to consider the idea of using the serialization features of .NET to transmit data across the network. After all, you've already seen this in action with Web Services and remoting. You can take an object in .NET, use serialization to convert it to a string of bytes, and expose that string down to a Web Service consumer, to a remoting client, or even to a file.

Chapter 27 discussed the `BinaryFormatter` and `SoapFormatter` classes. You could use either of those classes, or create your own custom formatter, to convert data for transmission and reception. In this case, you're going to create a new class called `Message` and use `BinaryFormatter` to crunch it down into a wire-ready format and convert it back again for processing.

This approach isn't ideal from the perspective of interoperability, because the actual protocol used is lost in the implementation of the .NET Framework, rather than being under your absolute control.

If you want to build an open protocol, this is *not* the best way to do it. Unfortunately, the best way is beyond the scope of this book, but a good place to start is to look at existing protocols and standards and model any protocol on their approach. `BinaryFormatter` is quick and dirty, which is why you're going to use it.

The Message Class

The `Message` class contains two fields, _username and _message, which form the entirety of the data that you want to transmit. The code for this class follows; note how the `Serializable` attribute is applied to it so that `BinaryFormatter` can change it into a wire-ready form. You're also providing a new implementation of `ToString`:

```
Imports System.Text

<Serializable()> Public Class Message

    Private _username As String
    Private _message As String

    Public Sub New(ByVal name As String)
        _username = name
    End Sub

    Public Sub New(ByVal name As String, ByVal message As String)
        _username = name
        _message = message
    End Sub

    Public Overrides Function ToString() As String
        Dim builder As New StringBuilder(_username)
        builder.Append(" says:")
        builder.Append(ControlChars.CrLf)
        builder.Append(_message)
        builder.Append(ControlChars.CrLf)

        Return builder.ToString()
    End Function

End Class
```

Now all you have to do is spin up two threads, one for transmission and one for reception, updating the display. You need two threads per *conversation,* so if you have 10 conversations open, you need 20 threads plus the main UI thread, plus the thread running `TcpListener`.

Receiving messages is easy. When calling `Deserialize()` on `BinaryFormatter`, you give it the stream returned to you from `TcpClient`. If there's no data, then this blocks. If there is data, then it's decoded into a `Message` object that you can display. If you have multiple messages coming down the pipe, then `BinaryFormatter` keeps processing them until the pipe is empty. Here's the method for this, which should be added to `Conversation`. Remember that you haven't implemented `ShowMessage()` yet:

```
Protected Sub ReceiveThreadEntryPoint()

    ' Create a formatter...
    Dim formatter As New BinaryFormatter()

    ' Loop
    Do While True
        ' Receive...
        Dim message As Message = formatter.Deserialize(_stream)

        If message Is Nothing Then
            Exit Do
        End If

        ' Show it...
        ShowMessage(message)
    Loop
End Sub
```

Transmitting messages is a bit more complex. You want a queue (managed by a `System.Collections.Queue`) of outgoing messages. Every second, you'll examine the state of the queue. If you find any messages, you use `BinaryFormatter` to transmit them. Because you'll be accessing this queue from multiple threads, you use a `System.Threading.ReaderWriterLock` to control access. To minimize the amount of time you spend inside locked code, you quickly transfer the contents of the shared queue into a private queue that you can process at your leisure. This enables the client to continue to add messages to the queue through the UI, even though existing messages are being sent by the transmit thread.

First, add these members to `Conversation`:

```
Public Class Conversation

    Private _username As String = "Evjen"
    Private _client As TcpClient
    Private _stream As NetworkStream
    Private _direction As ConversationDirection
    Private _receiveThread As Thread
    Private _transmitThread As Thread
    Private _transmitQueue As New Queue()
    Private _transmitLock As New ReaderWriterLock()
```

Now, add this method again to `Conversation`:

```
Protected Sub TransmitThreadEntryPoint()

    ' Create a formatter...
    Dim formatter As New BinaryFormatter()
    Dim workQueue As New Queue()
```

```
    ' Loop
    Do While True

        ' Wait for the signal...
        Thread.Sleep(1000)

        ' Go through the queue...
        _transmitLock.AcquireWriterLock(-1)
        Dim message As Message
        workQueue.Clear()

        For Each message In _transmitQueue
            workQueue.Enqueue(message)
        Next

        _transmitQueue.Clear()
        _transmitLock.ReleaseWriterLock()

        ' Loop the outbound messages...
        For Each message In workQueue

            ' Send it...
            formatter.Serialize(_stream, message)

        Next

    Loop

End Sub
```

When you want to send a message, you call one version of the `SendMessage()` method. Here are all of the implementations, and the `Click` handler for `buttonSend`:

```
Private Sub buttonSend_Click(ByVal sender As System.Object, _
    ByVal e As System.EventArgs) Handles buttonSend.Click

    SendMessage(textMessage.Text)
End Sub

Public Sub SendMessage(ByVal message As String)
    SendMessage(_username, message)
End Sub

Public Sub SendMessage(ByVal username As String, ByVal message As String)
    SendMessage(New Message(username, message))
End Sub

Public Sub SendMessage(ByVal message As Message)
    ' Queue it
    _transmitLock.AcquireWriterLock(-1)
    _transmitQueue.Enqueue(message)
    _transmitLock.ReleaseWriterLock()
```

```
      ' Show it...
      ShowMessage(message)
End Sub
```

ShowMessage() is responsible for updating textMessages so that the conversation remains up to date (notice how you add the message both when you send it and when you receive it so that both parties have an up-to-date thread). This is a UI feature, so it is good practice to pass it over to the main application thread for processing. Although the call in response to the button click comes off the main application thread, the one from inside ReceiveThreadEntryPoint() does not. Here's what the delegate looks like:

```
Public Class Conversation

    ' members...
    Private _username As String = "Evjen"
    Private _client As TcpClient
    Private _stream As NetworkStream
    Private _direction As ConversationDirection
    Private _receiveThread As Thread
    Private _transmitThread As Thread
    Private _transmitQueue As New Queue()
    Private _transmitLock As New ReaderWriterLock()

    Public Delegate Sub ShowMessageDelegate(ByVal message As Message)
```

Here's the method implementation:

```
Public Sub ShowMessage(ByVal message As Message)
    ' Thread?
    If Form1.IsMainThread() = False Then

        ' Run...
        Dim args(0) As Object
        args(0) = message
        Invoke(New ShowMessageDelegate(AddressOf ShowMessage), args)

        ' Return...
        Return
    End If

    ' Show it...
    textMessages.Text &= message.ToString()
End Sub
```

All that remains now is to spin up the threads. This should be done from within ConfigureClient(). Before the threads are spun up, you need to get hold of the stream and store it in the private _stream field. After that, you create new Thread objects as normal:

```
Public Sub ConfigureClient(ByVal client As TcpClient, _
        ByVal direction As ConversationDirection)

    ' Set it up...
```

```
    _client = client
    _direction = direction

    ' Update the window...
    UpdateCaption()
    ' Get the stream...
    _stream = _client.GetStream()

    ' Spin up the threads...
    _transmitThread = New Thread(AddressOf TransmitThreadEntryPoint)
    _transmitThread.Start()
    _receiveThread = New Thread(AddressOf ReceiveThreadEntryPoint)
    _receiveThread.Start()
End Sub
```

At this point, you should be able to connect and exchange messages, as shown in Figure 32-8.

Figure 32-8

Note that the screen shots show the username of the inbound connection as Tuija. This was done with the textUsername text box so that you can follow which half of the conversation comes from where.

Shutting Down the Application

You've yet to solve the problem of neatly closing the application, or, in fact, dealing with one person in the conversation closing down his or her window, indicating a wish to end the conversation. When the process ends (whether neatly or forcefully), Windows automatically mops up any open connections and frees up the port for other processes.

Suppose you have two computers, one window per computer, as you would in a production environment. When you close your window, you're indicating that you want to end the conversation. You need to close the socket and spin down the transmission and reception threads. At the other end, you should be able to detect that the socket has been closed, spin down the threads, and tell the user that the other user has terminated the conversation.

This all hinges on being able to detect when the socket has been closed. Unfortunately, Microsoft has made this very hard, thanks to the design of the `TcpClient` class. `TcpClient` effectively encapsulates a `System.Net.Sockets.Socket` class, providing methods for helping to manage the connection lifetime and communication streams. However, `TcpClient` does not have a method or property that answers the question, "Am I still connected?" Therefore, you need get hold of the `Socket` object that `TcpClient` is wrapping and then you can use its `Connected` property to find out if the connection has been closed.

`TcpClient` does support a property called `Client` that returns a `Socket`, but this property is protected, meaning you can only access it by inheriting a new class from `TcpClient`. There is another way, though: You can use reflection to get at the property and call it without having to inherit a new class.

Microsoft claims that this is a legitimate technique, even though it appears to violate every rule in the book about encapsulation. Reflection is designed not only for finding out which types are available, and learning which methods and properties each type supports, but also for invoking those methods and properties whether they're protected or public. Therefore, in `Conversation`, you need to store the socket:

```
Public Class Conversation

    Private _username As String = "Evjen"
    Private _client As TcpClient
    Private _socket As Socket
```

In `ConfigureClient()`, you need to use `Reflection` to peek into the `Type` object for `TcpClient` and dig out the `Client` property. Once you have a `System.Reflection.PropertyInfo` for this property, you can retrieve its value by using the `GetValue()` method. Don't forget to import the `System.Reflection` namespace:

```
Public Sub ConfigureClient(ByVal client As TcpClient, _
            ByVal direction As ConversationDirection)

    ' Set it up...
    _client = client
    _direction = direction

    ' Update the window...
    UpdateCaption()

    ' Get the stream...
    _stream = _client.GetStream()
    ' Get the socket through reflection...
    Dim propertyInfo As PropertyInfo = _
        _client.GetType().GetProperty("Client", _
        BindingFlags.Instance Or BindingFlags.Public)

    If Not propertyInfo Is Nothing Then
        _socket = propertyInfo.GetValue(_client, Nothing)
    Else
        Throw New Exception("Couldn't retrieve Client property from TcpClient")
    End If
    ' Spin up the threads...
    _transmitThread = New Thread(AddressOf TransmitThreadEntryPoint)
```

```
    _transmitThread.Start()
    _receiveThread = New Thread(AddressOf ReceiveThreadEntryPoint)
    _receiveThread.Start()
End Sub
```

Applications are able to check the state of the socket either by detecting when an error occurs because you've tried to send data over a closed socket or by actually checking whether the socket is connected. If you either don't have a `Socket` available in `socket` (that is, it is `Nothing`), or if you have one and it tells you you're disconnected, you give the user some feedback and exit the loop. By exiting the loop, you effectively exit the thread, which is a neat way of quitting the thread. Notice as well that you might not have a window at this point (you might be the one who closed the conversation by closing the window), so you wrap the UI call in a `Try Catch` (the other side will see a `<disconnect>` message):

```
Protected Sub TransmitThreadEntryPoint()
    ' Create a formatter...
    Dim formatter As New BinaryFormatter()
    Dim workQueue As New Queue()
    ' name...
    Thread.CurrentThread.Name = "Tx-" & _direction.ToString()
    ' Loop...
    Do While True
        ' Wait for the signal...
        Thread.Sleep(1000)
        ' Disconnected?
        If _socket Is Nothing OrElse _socket.Connected = False Then
            Try
                ShowMessage(New Message("Debug", "<disconnect>"))
            Catch
            End Try
            Exit Do
        End If
        ' Go through the queue...
```

`ReceiveThreadEntryPoint()` also needs some massaging. When the socket is closed, the stream is no longer valid and so `BinaryFormatter.Deserialize()` throws an exception. Likewise, you quit the loop and therefore neatly quit the thread:

```
Protected Sub ReceiveThreadEntryPoint()
    ' Create a formatter...
    Dim formatter As New BinaryFormatter()

    ' Loop...
    Do While True

        ' Receive...
        Dim message As Message = Nothing
        Try
            message = formatter.Deserialize(_stream)
        Catch
        End Try

        If message Is Nothing Then
            Exit Do
```

```
            End If
            ' Show it...
            ShowMessage(message)
        Loop
    End Sub
```

How do you deal with actually closing the socket? You tweak the `Dispose()` method of the form itself (you can find this method in the Windows-generated code section of the file), and if you have a `_socket` object you close it:

```
Protected Overloads Overrides Sub Dispose(ByVal disposing As Boolean)
    If disposing Then
        If Not (components Is Nothing) Then
            components.Dispose()
        End If
    End If

    ' Close the socket...
    If Not _socket Is Nothing Then
        _socket.Close()
        _socket = Nothing
    End If

    MyBase.Dispose(disposing)
End Sub
```

Now you'll be able to start a conversation; and if one of the windows is closed, `<disconnect>` will appear in the other, as shown in Figure 32-9. In the background, the four threads (one transmit, one receive per window) will spin down properly.

Figure 32-9

The application itself still won't close properly, even if you close all the windows, because you need to stop the `Listener` when `Form1` closes. To do so, make `Listener` implement `IDisposable`:

```
Public Class Listener
    Implements IDisposable

    Public Sub Dispose() Implements System.IDisposable.Dispose
```

```
    ' Stop it...
    Finalize()
    GC.SuppressFinalize(Me)

End Sub

Protected Overrides Sub Finalize()

    ' Stop the listener...
    If Not _listener Is Nothing Then
        _listener.Stop()
        _listener = Nothing
    End If

    ' Stop the thread...
    If Not _thread Is Nothing Then
        _thread.Join()
        _thread = Nothing
    End If

    ' Call up...
    MyBase.Finalize()

End Sub
```

Now all that remains is to call `Dispose()` from within `Form1`. A good place to do this is in the `Closed` event handler:

```
Protected Overrides Sub OnClosed(ByVal e As System.EventArgs)
    If Not _listener Is Nothing Then
        _listener.Dispose()
        _listener = Nothing
    End If
End Sub
```

After the code is compiled again, the application can be closed.

Using Internet Explorer in Your Applications

A common requirement of modern applications is to display HTML files and other files commonly used with Internet applications. Although the .NET Framework has considerable support for common image formats (such as GIF, JPEG, and PNG), working with HTML used to be a touch trickier in versions 1.0 and 1.1 of the .NET Framework. Life was made considerably easier with the inclusion of the `WebBrowser` control in the .NET Framework 2.0.

> **For information on how to accomplish this task using the .NET Framework 1.0 or 1.1, please review the second and third editions of this book.**

You don't want to have to write your own HTML parser, so using this control to display HTML pages is, in most cases, your only option. Microsoft's Internet Explorer was implemented as a standalone component comprising a parser and a renderer, all packaged up in a neat COM object. The WebBrowser control "simply" utilizes this COM object. There's nothing to stop you from using this COM object directly in your own applications, but it's considerably easier to use the newer control for hosting Web pages in your applications.

Yes, a COM object. There is no managed version of Internet Explorer for use with .NET. Considering that writing an HTML parser is extremely hard, and writing a renderer is extremely hard, it's easy to conclude that it's much easier to use interop to get to Internet Explorer in the .NET applications than to have Microsoft try to rewrite a managed version of it just for .NET. Maybe we will see "Internet Explorer .NET" within the next year or two, but for now you do have to use interop.

Windows Forms and HTML — No Problem!

These sections demonstrate how to build a mini-browser application. Sometimes you might want to display HTML pages without giving users UI widgets such as a toolbar or the capability to enter their own URLs. You might also want to use the control in a nonvisual manner. For example, using the WebBrowser control, you can retrieve Web pages and then print the results without ever needing to display the contents. Let's start, though, by first creating a simple form that contains only a TextBox and a WebBrowser control.

Allowing Simple Web Browsing in Your Windows Application

The first step is to create a new Windows Forms application called MiniBrowser. On the default form, place a single TextBox control and the new WebBrowser control, as shown in Figure 32-10.

Figure 32-10

The idea is that when the end user presses the Enter key (Return key), the URL entered in the text box will be the HTML page that is retrieved and displayed in the WebBrowser control. To accomplish this task, use the following code for your form:

```
Public Class Form1

    Private Sub TextBox1_KeyPress(ByVal sender As Object, _
        ByVal e As System.Windows.Forms.KeyPressEventArgs) Handles TextBox1.KeyPress

        If e.KeyChar = Chr(13) Then
            WebBrowser1.Navigate(TextBox1.Text)
        End If

    End Sub

End Class
```

For this simple example, you check the key presses that are made in the TextBox1 control, and if the key press is a specific one — the Enter key — then you use the WebBrowser control's Navigate() method to navigate to the requested page. The Navigate() method can take a single String value, which represents the location of the Web page to retrieve. The example shown in Figure 32-11 shows the Wrox website.

Figure 32-11

Launching Internet Explorer from Your Windows Application

Sometimes, the goal is not to host a browser inside the application but instead to allow the user to find the website in a typical Web browser. For an example of this task, create a Windows Form that has a LinkLabel control on it. For instance, you can have a form that has a LinkLabel control on it that simply states, "Visit your company website!"

Once this control is in place, use the following code to launch the company's website in an independent browser, as opposed to directly in the form of your application:

```
Public Class Form1

    Private Sub LinkLabel1_LinkClicked(ByVal sender As System.Object, _
        ByVal e As System.Windows.Forms.LinkLabelLinkClickedEventArgs) Handles _
        LinkLabel1.LinkClicked

        Dim wb As New WebBrowser
        wb.Navigate("http://www.wrox.com", True)

    End Sub

End Class
```

In this example, when the LinkLabel control is clicked by the user, a new instance of the WebBrowser class is created. Then, using the WebBrowser's Navigate() method, the code specifies the location of the Web page as well as a Boolean value that specifics whether this end point should be opened within the Windows Form application (a False value) or from within an independent browser (a True value). By default, this is set to False. With the preceding construct, when the end user clicks on the link found in the Windows application, a browser instance is instantiated and the Wrox website is immediately launched.

Updating URLs and Page Titles

Note that when working with the MiniBrowser example in which the WebBrowser control is directly in the form, when you click the links, the text in the TextBox1 control is not updated. You can fix this by listening for events coming off the WebBrowser control and adding handlers to the control.

It's easy to update the form's title with the HTML page's title. Create a DocumentTitleChanged event and update the form's Text property:

```
Private Sub WebBrowser1_DocumentTitleChanged(ByVal sender As Object, _
    ByVal e As System.EventArgs) Handles WebBrowser1.DocumentTitleChanged

    Me.Text = WebBrowser1.DocumentTitle.ToString()

End Sub
```

In this case, when the WebBrowser control notices that the page title has changed (due to changing the page viewed), the DocumentTitleChanged event will fire. In this case, you change the Form's Text property (its title) to the title of the page being viewed using the DocumentTitle property of the WebBrowser control.

Next, update the text string that appears in the Form's text box, based on the complete URL of the page being viewed. To do this, you can use the WebBrowser control's Navigated event:

```
Private Sub WebBrowser1_Navigated(ByVal sender As Object, _
    ByVal e As System.Windows.Forms.WebBrowserNavigatedEventArgs) Handles _
    WebBrowser1.Navigated
```

```
        TextBox1.Text = WebBrowser1.Url.ToString()

End Sub
```

In this case, when the requested page is finished being downloaded in the WebBrowser control, the Navigated event is fired. You simply update the Text value of the TextBox1 control to be the URL of the page. This means that once a page is loaded in the WebBrowser control's HTML container, if the URL changes in this process, then the new URL will be shown in the text box. For example, if you employ these steps and navigate to the Wrox website (www.wrox.com), page's URL will immediately change to http://www.wrox.com/WileyCDA/. This process also means that if the end user clicks on one of the links contained within the HTML view, then the URL of the newly requested page will also be shown in the text box.

Now, if you run the application with the preceding changes put into place, the form title and address bar will work as they do in Microsoft's Internet Explorer, as demonstrated in Figure 32-12.

Figure 32-12

Creating a Toolbar

For this exercise, you'll add a simple toolbar to the top of the control that gives you the usual features you'd expect from a Web browser — that is, Back, Forward, Stop, Refresh, and Home.

Rather than use the ToolBar control, you'll add a set of button controls at the top of the control where you currently have the address bar. Add five buttons to the top of the control, as illustrated in Figure 32-13.

I've changed the text on the buttons to indicate their function. Of course, you can use a screen capture utility to "borrow" button images from IE and use those. The buttons should be named buttonBack, buttonForward, buttonStop, buttonRefresh, and buttonHome. To get the resizing to work properly, make sure that you set the Anchor property of the three buttons on the right to Top, Right.

Figure 32-13

On startup, `buttonBack`, `buttonForward`, and `buttonStop` should be disabled because there is no point to the buttons if there is no initial page loaded. You will later tell the `WebBrowser` control when to enable and disable the Back and Forward buttons, depending on where the user is in the page stack. In addition, when a page is being loaded, you need to enable the Stop button — but you also need to disable the Stop button once the page has finished being loaded.

First, though, you'll add the functionality behind the buttons. The `WebBrowser` class itself has all the methods you need, so this is all very straightforward:

```
Public Class Form1
    Private Sub Form1_Load(ByVal sender As System.Object, _
     ByVal e As System.EventArgs) Handles MyBase.Load
        buttonBack.Enabled = False
        buttonForward.Enabled = False
        buttonStop.Enabled = False
    End Sub

    Private Sub buttonBack_Click(ByVal sender As System.Object, _
     ByVal e As System.EventArgs) Handles buttonBack.Click
        WebBrowser1.GoBack()
        TextBox1.Text = WebBrowser1.Url.ToString()
    End Sub

    Private Sub buttonForward_Click(ByVal sender As System.Object, _
     ByVal e As System.EventArgs) Handles buttonForward.Click
        WebBrowser1.GoForward()
        TextBox1.Text = WebBrowser1.Url.ToString()
    End Sub

    Private Sub buttonStop_Click(ByVal sender As System.Object, _
     ByVal e As System.EventArgs) Handles buttonStop.Click
        WebBrowser1.Stop()
    End Sub
```

```
      Private Sub buttonRefresh_Click(ByVal sender As System.Object, _
       ByVal e As System.EventArgs) Handles buttonRefresh.Click
          WebBrowser1.Refresh()
      End Sub

      Private Sub buttonHome_Click(ByVal sender As System.Object, _
       ByVal e As System.EventArgs) Handles buttonHome.Click
          WebBrowser1.GoHome()
          TextBox1.Text = WebBrowser1.Url.ToString()
      End Sub

      Private Sub buttonSubmit_Click(ByVal sender As System.Object, _
       ByVal e As System.EventArgs) Handles buttonSubmit.Click
          WebBrowser1.Navigate(TextBox1.Text)
      End Sub

      Private Sub WebBrowser1_CanGoBackChanged(ByVal sender As Object, _
       ByVal e As System.EventArgs) Handles WebBrowser1.CanGoBackChanged
          If WebBrowser1.CanGoBack = True Then
              buttonBack.Enabled = True
          Else
              buttonBack.Enabled = False
          End If
      End Sub

      Private Sub WebBrowser1_CanGoForwardChanged(ByVal sender As Object, _
       ByVal e As System.EventArgs) Handles WebBrowser1.CanGoForwardChanged
          If WebBrowser1.CanGoForward = True Then
              buttonForward.Enabled = True
          Else
              buttonForward.Enabled = False
          End If
      End Sub

      Private Sub WebBrowser1_Navigated(ByVal sender As Object, _
       ByVal e As System.Windows.Forms.WebBrowserNavigatedEventArgs) Handles _
      WebBrowser1.Navigated
          TextBox1.Text = WebBrowser1.Url.ToString()
          Me.Text = WebBrowser1.DocumentTitle.ToString()
      End Sub

      Private Sub WebBrowser1_Navigating(ByVal sender As Object, _
       ByVal e As System.Windows.Forms.WebBrowserNavigatingEventArgs) Handles _
      WebBrowser1.Navigating
          buttonStop.Enabled = True
      End Sub

      Private Sub WebBrowser1_DocumentCompleted(ByVal sender As Object, _
       ByVal e As System.Windows.Forms.WebBrowserDocumentCompletedEventArgs) _
       Handles WebBrowser1.DocumentCompleted
          buttonStop.Enabled = False
      End Sub

End Class
```

Several different activities are occurring in this example, as there are so many options for the end user when using this `MiniBrowser` application. First, for each of the button `Click` events, there is a specific `WebBrowser` class method assigned as the action to initiate. For instance, for the Back button on the form, you simply use the Web Browser control's `GoBack()` method. The same is true for the other buttons — for the Forward button you have the `GoForward()` method, and for the other buttons you have methods such as `Stop()`, `Refresh()`, and `GoHome()`. This makes it simple and straightforward to create a toolbar that provides actions similar to those of Microsoft's Internet Explorer.

When the form is first loaded, the `Form1_Load` event disables the appropriate buttons. From there, users can enter a URL in the text box and click the Submit button to have the application retrieve the desired page.

To manage the enabling and disabling of the buttons, you have to key in a couple of events. As mentioned before, whenever downloading begins you need to enable Stop. For this, you simply add an event handler for the `Navigating` event to enable the Stop button:

```
Private Sub WebBrowser1_Navigating(ByVal sender As Object, _
 ByVal e As System.Windows.Forms.WebBrowserNavigatingEventArgs) Handles _
WebBrowser1.Navigating
    buttonStop.Enabled = True
End Sub
```

Next, the Stop button is again disabled when the document has finished loading:

```
Private Sub WebBrowser1_DocumentCompleted(ByVal sender As Object, _
 ByVal e As System.Windows.Forms.WebBrowserDocumentCompletedEventArgs) _
 Handles WebBrowser1.DocumentCompleted
    buttonStop.Enabled = False
End Sub
```

Enabling and disabling the appropriate Back and Forward buttons depends on the ability to go backward or forward in the page stack. This is achieved by using both the `CanGoForwardChanged` and the `CanGoBackChanged` events:

```
Private Sub WebBrowser1_CanGoBackChanged(ByVal sender As Object, _
 ByVal e As System.EventArgs) Handles WebBrowser1.CanGoBackChanged
    If WebBrowser1.CanGoBack = True Then
       buttonBack.Enabled = True
    Else
       buttonBack.Enabled = False
    End If
End Sub

Private Sub WebBrowser1_CanGoForwardChanged(ByVal sender As Object, _
 ByVal e As System.EventArgs) Handles WebBrowser1.CanGoForwardChanged
    If WebBrowser1.CanGoForward = True Then
       buttonForward.Enabled = True
    Else
       buttonForward.Enabled = False
    End If
End Sub
```

Run the project now, visit a Web page, and click through a few links. You should also be able to use the toolbar to enhance your browsing experience. The end product is shown in Figure 32-14.

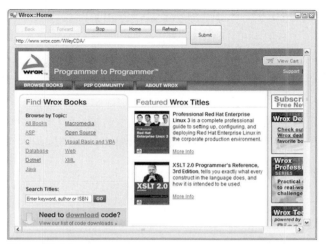

Figure 32-14

Showing Documents Using the WebBrowser Control

You are not limited to using just Web pages within the `WebBrowser` control. In fact, you can allow the end user to view many different types of documents. So far, you have seen how to use the `WebBrowser` control to access documents that have been purely accessible by defining a URL, but the `WebBrowser` control also enables you to use an absolute path and define end points to files such as Word documents, Excel documents, PDFs, and more.

For instance, suppose you are using the following code snippet:

```
WebBrowser1.Navigate("C:\Financial Report.doc")
```

This would open the Word document in your application. Not only would the document appear in the `WebBrowser` control, but the Word toolbar would also be present, as shown in Figure 32-15.

Figure 32-15

In Figure 32-16, the `WebBrowser` control shows an Adobe PDF file.

Figure 32-16

In addition to simply opening specific documents in the control, users can also drag and drop documents onto the `WebBrowser` control's surface, and the document dropped will automatically be opened within the control. To turn off this capability (which is enabled by default), set the `WebBrowser` control's `AllowWebBrowserDrop` property to `False`.

Printing Using the WebBrowser Control

Not only can users use the `WebBrowser` control to view pages and documents, they can also use the control to send these pages and documents to the printer for printing. To print the page or document being viewed in the control, simply use the following construct:

```
WebBrowser1.Print()
```

As before, it is possible to print the page or document without viewing it by using the `WebBrowser` class to load an HTML document and print it without even displaying the loaded document, as shown here:

```
Dim wb As new WebBrowser
wb.Navigate("http://www.wrox.com")
wb.Print()
```

Summary

This chapter began by examining just how easy it is to download resources from a Web server using classes built into the .NET Framework. `System.Uri` enables you to express a URI, and `System.Net.WebRequest`, in combination with `System.Net.HttpWebRequest` and `System.Net.HttpWebResponse`, enables you to physically get hold of the data.

This chapter also described how you can build your own network protocol by using sockets, implemented in the `System.Net.Sockets` namespace. You looked at how `TcpListener` and `TcpClient` make it relatively easy to work with sockets, and you spent a lot of time working with threads and the various UI challenges that such work poses in order to make the application as usable as possible.

Finally, you learned how you can use the new `WebBrowser` control in your own Windows Form application to work with HTML and other documents.

The Visual Basic Compiler

When the .NET Framework was first introduced, one nice addition for the Visual Basic developer was the inclusion of a standalone language compiler. This meant you weren't required to have the Visual Studio .NET 2002 IDE in order to build Visual Basic applications. In fact, you could take the .NET Framework from the Microsoft website (for free), and build Web applications, classes, modules, and more simply using a text editor such as Notepad. You could then take the completed files and compile them using the Visual Basic compiler.

The Visual Basic compiler is included along with the default .NET Framework install. The name of the compiler is vbc.exe and it can be found at

```
C:\WINDOWS\Microsoft.NET\Framework\v2.0.[version]\vbc.exe
```

The vbc.exe.config File

In addition to the vbc.exe file, there is a vbc.exe.config file in the directory as well. This XML file is used to specify the versions of the .NET Framework the compiler should build applications for. Now that there are three versions of the .NET Framework available for our applications to work with, it is important to understand how this configuration file actually works.

With the .NET Framework 2.0 installed, you will find the vbc.exe.config file with the following construction:

```
<?xml version ="1.0"?>
<configuration>
    <startup>
        <supportedRuntime version="v2.0.50727" safemode="true"/>
        <requiredRuntime version="v2.0.50727" safemode="true"/>
    </startup>
</configuration>
```

This `.config` file is basically a typical .NET Framework configuration file with the default `<configuration>` root element included. Nested within the `<configuration>` element, you need to place a `<startup>` element. This is the only child element that is possible in the `vbc.exe`'s configuration file.

Nested within the `<startup>` element, you can use two possible elements: `<supportedRuntime>` and `<requiredRuntime>`.

The `<requiredRuntime>` element really is only needed if your application is going to run on the .NET Framework 1.0 (the very first iteration of the .NET Framework). If your application is going to run from the .NET Framework 1.0, then you build the `vbc.exe.config` file as such:

```
<?xml version ="1.0"?>
<configuration>
    <startup>
        <requiredRuntime version="v1.0.3705" safemode="true"/>
    </startup>
</configuration>
```

Currently, working with three different versions of the .NET Framework, you may wish to compile your applications using the Visual Basic compiler so that they work with multiple versions of the framework. To do this, you could use the `<supportedRuntime>` element:

```
<?xml version ="1.0"?>
<configuration>
    <startup>
        <supportedRuntime version="v2.0.50727" safemode="true"/>
        <supportedRuntime version="v1.1.4322" safemode="true"/>
    </startup>
</configuration>
```

This construction states that the application should first try to run on version 2.0.50727 of the .NET Framework, and if this version of the .NET Framework is not found, then the next preferred version of the framework that the compiled object should work with is version 1.1.4322. When working in this kind of construction, you need to order the framework versions in the XML file so that the most preferred version of the framework you want to utilize is the uppermost element, and the least preferred version of the framework is the last in the node list.

The `<supportedRuntime>` element is meant for .NET Framework versions 1.1 and later. If you are going to utilize the .NET Framework version 1.0, then you should use the `<requiredRuntime>` element.

The `<supportedRuntime>` element contains two possible attributes: `version` and `safemode`. Both attributes are optional. The attribute `version` enables you to specify the specific version you want your application to run against, while `safemode` specifies whether the registry should be searched for the particular framework version. The `safemode` attribute takes a `Boolean` value, and the default value is `false`, meaning the framework version will not be checked.

Simple Steps to Compilation

To show how the Visual Basic compiler works in the simplest manner, let's begin by looking at how to compile a single-class file:

1. Create a module called `MyModule.vb`. We'll keep the module simple, as this example is meant to show you how to compile the items using the `vbc.exe` compiler:

```
Module Module1

    Sub Main()
        Console.WriteLine("Howdy there")
        Console.ReadLine()
    End Sub

End Module
```

2. Once your file is in place, it is then time to use the Visual Basic compiler. If you do have Visual Studio 2005 on the computer, you can open the Visual Studio Command Prompt (found at Start ➪ All Programs ➪ Microsoft Visual Studio 2005 ➪ Visual Studio Tools ➪ Visual Studio Command Prompt). Once open, just navigate to the location of the file and then run the compiler against the file (shown shortly).

3. In most cases, you are probably going to be using the Visual Basic compiler on computers that do not have Visual Studio on them. In those cases, copy and paste the `vbc.exe`, `vbc.exe.config`, and `vbc.rsp` files to the folder where the class file you wish to compile is located. Then you can open a command prompt by selecting Run from the Start menu and typing **cmd** in the text box.

   Another option is to add the compiler to the path itself. This is done by typing the following at the command prompt:

```
path %path%;C:\WINDOWS\Microsoft.NET\Framework\v2.0.50727
```

   Now you can work with the compilation normally and the `vbc.exe` compiler will be found upon compilation.

4. Once the command prompt is open, navigate to the folder that contains both the Visual Basic compiler and the class file that needs compiling. From this location, type the following command at the command prompt:

```
vbc.exe MyModule.vb
```

Items can be compiled in many ways using the Visual Basic compiler, but this is the simplest way to compile this module. This command compiles the .vb file so that it can be utilized by your applications. Running the preceding command produces the following:

```
C:\CoolStuff>vbc.exe MyModule.vb
Microsoft (R) Visual Basic .NET Compiler version 8.0.50727.16
for Microsoft (R) .NET Framework version 2.0.50727.16
Copyright (C) Microsoft Corporation 1987-2003. All rights reserved.
```

What does this operation actually do? Well, in this case, it has created an .exe file for you in the same directory as the `MyModule.vb` file. Looking there, you will find `MyModule.exe` ready to run.

The Visual Basic compiler has a number of options that enable you to dictate what sorts of actions the compiler will take with the compilation process. These flags will be defined soon, but you can specify additional settings by using a forward slash followed by the name of the option and the setting assigned to the option. For instance, if you were going to add a reference to `Microsoft.VisualBasic.dll` along with the compilation, you would construct your compiler command as follows:

```
vbc.exe MyModule.vb /reference:Microsoft.VisualBasic.dll
```

Compiler Output

This section takes a comprehensive look at all the options available for the Visual Basic compiler. To see the full list, type the following command:

```
vbc.exe /?
```

/nologo

This option causes the compiler to perform its compilation without producing the compiler information set shown in previous examples. This is really only useful if you are invoking the compiler in your application, showing the results coming from the compiler to the end user of your application, and if you have no desire to show this information to the user in the result set.

/utf8output

By default, when you use the Visual Basic command-line compiler, it will not do the compilation using UTF-8 encoding. In fact, the Visual Studio 2005 IDE will not even allow this to occur, but using `/utf8output` in the command-line compiler overrides this behavior.

/verbose

Adding this command causes the compiler to output a complete list of what it is doing, including the assemblies that are being loaded and the errors that it receives in the compilation process. Use it as follows:

```
vbc.exe MyModule.vb /reference:Microsoft.VisualBasic.dll /verbose
```

This would produce results such as the following (abbreviated to show small examples of the result output, as it is rather lengthy):

```
Adding assembly reference 'C:\WINDOWS\Microsoft.NET\Framework\v2.0.50727\System.
Data.dll'
```

In addition:

```
Adding import 'System'
Adding import 'Microsoft.VisualBasic'
Adding file 'C:\MyModule.vb'
Adding assembly reference 'C:\WINDOWS\Microsoft.NET\Framework\v2.0.50727\Microso
ft.VisualBasic.dll'
Compiling...
```

Then the compiler starts loading assemblies:

```
Loading C:\WINDOWS\Microsoft.NET\Framework\v2.0.50727\mscorlib.dll.
```

```
Loading C:\WINDOWS\Microsoft.NET\Framework\v2.0.50727\Microsoft.VisualBasic.dll.
```

Until it finishes:

```
Building C:\MyModule.vb.
Building 17d14f5c-a337-4978-8281-53493378c1071.vb.
Compilation successful
```

Optimization

The following sections discuss the optimization features available.

/filealign

Not typically used by most developers, the /filealign setting enables you to specify the alignment of sections, or blocks of contiguous memory, in your output file. It uses the following construction:

```
vbc.exe MyModule.vb /filealign:2048
```

The number assigned is the byte size of the file produced, and valid values include 512, 1024, 2048, 4096, 8192, and 16384.

/optimize

If you go to your project's property page (found by right-clicking on the project in the Visual Studio Solution Explorer), you will see a page for compilation settings. From this page, you can make all sorts of compilation optimizations. To keep your command-line compiler from ignoring these instructions, set the /optimize flag in your compilation instructions:

```
vbc.exe MyModule.vb /optimize
```

By default, optimizations are turned off.

Output files

The following sections explain the output files.

/doc

By default, the compiler does not produce the XML documentation file upon compilation. This new feature of Visual Basic 2005 enables developers to put structured comments in their code that can then be turned into an XML document for easy viewing (along with a style sheet). Including the /doc option causes the compiler to create this documentation. Structure your command as follows if you want to produce this XML documentation file:

```
vbc.exe MyModule.vb /doc
```

You can also specify the name of the XML file as follows:

```
vbc.exe MyModule.vb /doc:MyModuleXmlFile.xml
```

/netcf

This option can't be executed from Visual Studio 2005 itself, but you can use this flag from the Visual Basic command-line compiler. Using /netcf causes the compiler to build your application so that the result is targeted for the .NET Compact Framework, not to the full .NET Framework itself. To accomplish this, use the following construct:

```
vbc.exe MyModule.vb /netcf
```

/out

Using the /out option enables you to change the name and extension of the file that was produced from the compilation. By default, it is the name of the file that contains the Main() procedure or the first source code file in a DLL. To modify this yourself instead of using the defaults, you could use something similar to the following:

```
vbc.exe MyModule.vb /out:MyReallyCoolModule.exe
```

/target

This setting enables you to specify what exactly is output from the compilation process. There are four options: an EXE, a DLL, a module, or a Windows program:

/target:exe — Produces an executable console application. This is the default if no /target option is specified.

/target:library — Produces a dynamic link library (also known as a DLL)

/target:module — Produces a module

/target:winexe — Produces a Windows program

You can also use a short form of this by just using /t:exe, /t:library, /t:module, or /t:winexe.

.NET Assemblies

The following sections detail the .NET assemblies for use.

/addmodule

This option isn't available to Visual Studio 2005, but is possible when using the Visual Basic compiler. Using /addmodule enables you to add a .netmodule file to the resulting output of the compiler. For this, you would use something similar to the following construction:

```
vbc.exe MyModule.vb /addmodule:MyOtherModule.netmodule
```

/delaysign

This compiler option needs to be used in conjunction with the /key or /keycontainer option, which deals with the signing of your assembly. When used with the /delaysign option, the compiler will create a space for the digital signature that is later used to sign the assembly instead of actually signing the assembly at that point. You would use this option in the following manner:

```
vbc.exe MyModule.vb /key:myKey1.sn /delaysign
```

/imports

A commonly used compiler option, the /imports option enables you to import namespaces into the compilation process:

```
vbc.exe MyModule.vb /imports:System
```

Add multiple namespaces by separating them with a comma:

```
vbc.exe MyModule.vb /imports:System, System.Data
```

/keycontainer

This command causes the compiler to create a sharable component and places a public key into the component's assembly manifest while signing the assembly with a private key. Use this option as follows:

```
vbc.exe MyModule.vb /keycontainer:myKey1
```

If your key container that contains the key has a name that includes a space, then you have to place quotes around the value as shown here:

```
vbc.exe MyModule.vb /keycontainer:"my Key1"
```

/keyfile

Similar to the /keycontainer option, the /key option causes the compiler to place a public key into the component's assembly manifest while signing the assembly with a private key. Use this as follows:

```
vbc.exe MyModule.vb /key:myKey1.sn
```

If your key has a name that includes a space, then you must place quotes around the value as shown here:

```
vbc.exe MyModule.vb /key:"my Key1.sn"
```

/libpath

When making references to other assemblies while using the /reference compiler option (mentioned next), you will not always have these referenced assemblies in the same location as the object being compiled. You can use the /libpath option to specify the location of the referenced assemblies, as illustrated here:

```
vbc.exe MyModule.vb /reference:MyAssembly.dll /libpath:c:\Reuters\bin
```

If you want the compiler to search for the referenced DLLs in more than one location, then specify the multiple locations using the /libpath option by separating the locations with a comma:

```
vbc.exe MyModule.vb /reference:MyAssembly.dll /libpath:c:\Reuters\bin, c:\
```

This command means that the compiler will look for the `MyAssembly.dll` in both the `C:\Reuters\bin` directory and the root directory found at `C:\`.

/reference

The `/reference` option enables you to make references to other assemblies in the compilation process. Use it as follows:

```
vbc.exe MyModule.vb /reference:MyAssembly.dll
```

You can also shorten the command option by using just `/r`:

```
vbc.exe MyModule.vb /r:MyAssembly.dll
```

You can make a reference to multiple assemblies by separating them with a comma:

```
vbc.exe MyModule.vb /reference:MyAssembly.dll, MyOtherAssembly.dll
```

Debugging and Error-Checking

The following sections address the many features available for error-checking and debugging.

/bugreport

This option creates a file that is a full report of the compilation process. The `/bugreport` option creates this file, which contains your code and version information on the computer's operating system, as well as the compiler itself. Use this option in the following manner:

```
vbc.exe MyModule.vb /bugreport:bugsy.txt
```

/debug

By default, the Visual Basic compiler will not build objects with attached debugging information included in the generated object. Using the `/debug` option causes the compiler to place this information in the created output file. The use of this option is shown here:

```
vbc.exe MyModule.vb /debug
```

/nowarn

The `/nowarn` option actually suppresses the compiler from throwing any warnings. There are a couple of ways to use this option. The first option is to simply use `/nowarn` without any associated values:

```
vbc.exe MyModule.vb /nowarn
```

Instead of suppressing all the warnings that can come from the compiler, the other option at your disposal is to specify the exact warnings you wish the compiler to suppress, as shown here:

```
vbc.exe MyModule.vb /nowarn:42016
```

In this case, you are telling the compiler not to throw any warnings when it encounters a 42016 error (an implicit conversion warning error). To interject more than one warning code, separate the warning codes with a comma as illustrated here:

```
vbc.exe MyModule.vb /nowarn:42016, 42024
```

You can find a list of available warnings by searching for "Configuring Warnings in Visual Basic" in the MSDN documentation.

/quiet

Like some of the other compiler options, the `/quiet` option is only available to the command-line compiler and is not available when compiling your applications using Visual Studio. The `/quiet` option removes some of the error notifications from the error text output that is typically generated. Normally, when the compiler encounters an error that disallows further compilation, the error notification includes the line of code in the file where the error occurred. The line of code that is presented has a squiggly line underneath the exact bit of code where the error occurred. Using the `/quiet` option causes the compiler to show only the notification line, leaving the code line out of the output. This might be desirable in some situations.

/removeintchecks

By default, the Visual Basic compiler checks all your integer calculations for any possible errors. Possible errors include division by zero or overflow situations. Using the `/removeintchecks` causes the compiler to not look for these kinds of errors in the code of the files being compiled. You would use this option as follows:

```
vbc.exe MyModule.vb /removeintchecks
```

/warnaserror

In addition to finding and reporting errors, the compiler can also encounter situations that are only considered warnings. Even though warnings are encountered, the compilation process will still continue. Using the `/warnaserror` option in the compilation process causes the compiler to treat all warnings as errors. Use this option as shown here:

```
vbc.exe MyModule.vb /warnaserror
```

You might not want each warning to cause an error to be thrown, but instead only specific warnings. For these occasions, you can state the warning ID number that you want to look out for, as shown here:

```
vbc.exe MyModule.vb /warnaserror:42016
```

You can also check for multiple warnings by separating the warning ID numbers with commas:

```
vbc.exe MyModule.vb /warnaserror:42016, 42024
```

Help

The following sections address the compiler's help features.

/?

When you don't have this book for reference, you can use the Visual Basic compiler for a list of options by using the /? option, as shown here:

```
vbc.exe /?
```

This causes the entire list of options and their definitions to be displayed in the command window.

/help

The /help option is the same as the /? option. Both of these options produce the same result. The /help option produces a list of options that can be used with the compiler.

Language

The following sections detail the language options.

/optionexplicit

Always a good idea, using /optionexplicit causes the compiler to check whether any variables in the code are used before they are even declared (yes, this is possible and very bad practice). When variables are found before they are even declared, the compiler throws an error. By default, the compiler does not check the code using the option explicit option. Using this option is shown in the following example:

```
vbc.exe MyModule.vb /optionexplicit
```

/optionstrict

It's also a good idea to use the /optionstrict option in the compilation process. Using this option causes the compiler to check whether you are making any improper type conversions in your code. Widening type conversions are allowed, but when you start performing narrowing type conversions, using this option will cause an error to be thrown by the compiler. By default, the compiler does not look for these types of errors with your type conversions. Use this as shown here:

```
vbc.exe MyModule.vb /optionstrict
```

/optioncompare

By default, the Visual Basic compiler compares strings using a binary comparison. If you wish the string comparisons to use a text comparison, then use the following construction:

```
vbc.exe MyModule.vb /optioncompare:text
```

Preprocessor: /define

The /define option enables you to define conditional compiler constants for the compilation process. This is quite similar to using the #Const directive in your code. Here is an example:

```
vbc.exe MyModule.vb /define:Version="4.11"
```

You can also place definitions for multiple constants, as shown here:

```
vbc.exe MyModule.vb /define:Version="4.11", DebugMode=False
```

For multiple constants, just separate the constants with commas.

Resources

The following sections elaborate on the resources in the compiler.

/linkresource

Instead of embedding resources directly in the generated output file (such as with the /resource option), the /linkresource enables you to create the connection between your resulted objects and the resources that they require. You would use this option in the following manner:

```
vbc.exe MyModule.vb /linkresource=MyResourceFile.res
```

You can then specify if the resource file is supposed to be public or private in the assembly manifest. By default, the resource file is referenced as public. Here is an example of its use:

```
vbc.exe MyModule.vb /linkresource=MyResourceFile.res, private
```

You can shorten the /linkresource option to just /linkres.

/resource

The /resource option enables you to reference managed resource objects. The referenced resource is then embedded in the assembly. You would do this in the following manner:

```
vbc.exe MyModule.vb /resource=MyResourceFile.res
```

Like the /linkresource option, you can specify whether the reference to the resource should be made either public or private. This is done in the following way (the default is public):

```
vbc.exe MyModule.vb /resource=MyResourceFile.res, private
```

You can shorten the /resource option to just /res.

/win32icon

Use this option to embed an .ico file (an image that is actually the application's icon) in the produced file, as shown in the following example:

```
vbc.exe MyModule.vb /win32icon:MyIcon.ico
```

/win32resource

This option enables you to embed a Win32 resource file into the produced file. Use as shown in the following example:

```
vbc.exe MyModule.vb /win32resource=MyResourceFile.res
```

Miscellaneous Features

The rest of this chapter covers some of the more random but very useful features in the compiler. For example, one great feature of the Visual Basic compiler is the use of *response files*. If you have a compilation that you frequently perform, or one that is rather lengthy, you can instead create an .rsp file (the response file), a simple text file containing all the compilation instructions needed for the compilation process. Here is an example .rsp file:

```
# This is a comment
/target:exe
/out:MyCoolModule.exe
/linkresource=MyResourceFile.res
MyModule.vb
SomeOtherClassFile.vb
```

If you save this as MyResponseFile.res, then you can use it as shown in the following example:

```
vbc.exe @MyResponseFile.rsp
```

You can also specify multiple response files:

```
vbc.exe @MyResponseFile.rsp @MyOtherResponseFile.rsp
```

/baseaddress

When creating a DLL using the /target:library option, you can assign the base address of the DLL. By default, this is done for you by the compiler, but if you wish to make this assignment yourself you can. To accomplish this, you would use something similar to the following:

```
vbc.exe MyClass.vb /target:library /baseaddress:0x11110000
```

All base addresses are specified as hexadecimal numbers.

/codepage

By default, the compiler expects all the files to be using an ANSI, Unicode, or UTF-8 code page. Using the compiler's /codepage option, you can specify the code page that the compiler should actually be using. Setting it to one of the defaults is shown here:

```
vbc.exe MyClass.vb /codepage:1252
```

1252 is used for American English and most European languages, although setting it to Japanese Kanji would be just as simple:

```
vbc.exe MyClass.vb /codepage:932
```

/main

Using the /main option, you can point the compiler to the class or module that contains the SubMain procedure. Use as follows:

```
vbc.exe MyClass.vb /main:MyClass.vb
```

/noconfig

By default, the Visual Basic compiler uses the vbc.rsp resource file in the compilation process. Using the /noconfig option tells the compiler to avoid using this file in the compilation process, as shown here:

```
vbc.exe MyClass.vb /noconfig
```

/recurse

The /recurse option tells the compiler to compile all the specified files within a specified directory. Also included will be all child directories of the directory specified. Here is one example of using /recurse:

```
vbc.exe /target:library /out:MyComponent.dll /recurse:MyApplication\Classes\*.vb
```

This command takes all of the .vb files from the MyApplication/Classes directory and creates a DLL called MyComponent.dll.

/rootnamespace

Use this option to specify the namespace to use for compilation:

```
vbc.exe MyClass.vb /rootnamespace:Reuters
```

/sdkpath

This option enables you to specify the location of mscorlib.dll and Microsoft.VisualBasic.dll if they are located someplace other than the default location. This setting is really meant to be used with the /netcf option, described earlier, and is used as follows:

```
vbc.exe /sdkpath:"C:\Program Files\Microsoft Visual Studio 8
    \CompactFrameworkSDK\v1.0.5000\Windows CE" MyModule.vb
```

Looking at the vbc.rsp File

As stated earlier, the vbc.rsp file is there for the compiler's sake. When a compilation is being done, the Visual Basic compiler uses the vbc.rsp file for each compilation (unless you specify the /noconfig option). Inside this .rsp file is a list of compiler commands:

```
# This file contains command-line options that the VB
# command-line compiler (VBC) will process as part
# of every compilation, unless the "/noconfig" option
# is specified.

# Reference the common Framework libraries
/r:Accessibility.dll
/r:Microsoft.Vsa.dll
/r:System.Configuration.Install.dll
/r:System.Data.dll
/r:System.Design.dll
/r:System.DirectoryServices.dll
/r:System.dll
```

```
/r:System.Drawing.Design.dll
/r:System.Drawing.dll
/r:System.EnterpriseServices.dll
/r:System.Management.dll
/r:System.Messaging.dll
/r:System.Runtime.Remoting.dll
/r:System.Runtime.Serialization.Formatters.Soap.dll
/r:System.Security.dll
/r:System.ServiceProcess.dll
/r:System.Web.dll
/r:System.Web.Mobile.dll
/r:System.Web.RegularExpressions.dll
/r:System.Web.Services.dll
/r:System.Windows.Forms.Dll
/r:System.XML.dll

# Import System and Microsoft.VisualBasic
/imports:System
/imports:Microsoft.VisualBasic
```

These commands are the references and imports that are done for each item that you compile using this command-line compiler. You can feel free to play with this file as you choose. If you want to add your own references, then add them to the list and save the file. From then on, every compilation that you make will include the new reference(s). As you get into using the Visual Basic command-line compiler, you will see a lot of power in using .rsp files — even the default Visual Basic one.

Visual Basic Resources

On the Web

The MSDN Visual Basic Developer Center   msdn.microsoft.com/vbasic

Blog — Visual Basic Information   blogs.msdn.com/visualbasicinfo

Blogs of the Microsoft VB team   blogs.msdn.com/vbteam

Blog — Visual Basic FAQs   blogs.msdn.com/vbfaq

The Microsoft Windows Forms site   www.windowsforms.net

The Microsoft ASP.NET site   www.asp.net

VB City   www.vbcity.com

GotDotNet   www.gotdotnet.com

VB.NET Forums   www.vbdotnetforums.com

vbAccelerator.com   www.vbaccelerator.com

DotNetJunkies   www.dotnetjunkies.com

4 Guys from Rolla   www.4guysfromrolla.com

123ASPX   www.123aspx.com

Microsoft Newsgroups   msdn.microsoft.com/newsgroups

Microsoft Developer Centers	`msdn.microsoft.com/developercenters`
VBRun: Microsoft's Visual Basic 6.0 site	`msdn.microsoft.com/VBRun`
.NET Framework 3.0 community site	`www.netfx3.com`
MSDN Forums on VB	`forums.microsoft.com/MSDN/` `default.aspx?ForumGroupID=10&SiteID=1`
CodePlex	`www.codeplex.com`

Books

Professional ASP.NET 2.0 Special Edition (ISBN: 978-0470041789)

Wrox's Visual Basic 2005 Express Edition Starter Kit (ISBN: 0764595733)

ASP.NET 2.0 Website Programming: Problem Design Solution (ISBN: 0764584642)

Beginning VB.NET Databases (ISBN: 0764568000)

Beginning Visual Basic 2005 Databases (ISBN: 076458994X)

Beginning ASP.NET 2.0 (ISBN: 0764588508)

Author Blogs

| Bill Evjen | `www.geekswithblogs.net/evjen` |
| Bill Sheldon | `http://blogs.interknowlogy.com/billsheldon` |

Index